# Chilton's power accessories manual

; / 1975 ed. /

A american cars
from 1968 to 1975

**President**   William A. Barbour
**Executive Vice President**   K. Robert Brink
**Vice President and General Manager**   William D. Byrne
**Editor-In-Chief**   Paul A. Murphy, S.A.E.
**Managing Editor**   John H. Weise, S.A.E.
**Assistant Managing Editor**   Peter J. Meyer, S.A.E.
**Technical Consultants**   Gerard V. Haddon
                           Miles Schofield
                           Edward K. Shea, S.A.E.
**National Sales Manager**   Albert M. Kushnerick
**Service Editors**   John M. Baxter
                     Arthur I. Birney
                     Robert J. Brown
                     Stephen J. Davis, S.A.E.
                     Kerry A. Freeman
                     Martin J. Gunther
                     Martin W. Kane
                     Richard F. Matiza
                     Leo A. Mealey
                     John G. Mohan
                     Ronald L. Sessions
                     N. Banks Spence, Jr.

**CHILTON BOOK COMPANY** Chilton Way, Radnor, PA 19089, U.S.A.

# TABLE OF CONTENTS

# INDEX

# INDEX

## American Motors

# POWER WINDOWS

## General Description

The master control switch uses buss plates to carry current between terminals of the front and rear switches. These buss plates are separated with insulating paper and furnish both ground and voltage. The black wires at the master control switch ground are near the power window circuit breaker located on the instrument panel.

The motors employ two hot wires in order that the direction of window travel may be determined by the polarity of the power supply. The entire system is de-energized unless the ignition switch is on. A 20 amp circuit breaker mounted near the ash receiver protects the entire system.

## Electrical Tests

### Master Switch

1. Remove the escutcheon and housing. Turn on the ignition switch.
2. Leaving the switch attached to the terminal plate, separate the two terminal plate halves to expose the ends of the wire terminals.
3. Connect one test lamp lead to a black wire and the other to the blue terminal. Repeat the test with the other black wire.
4. If the bulb does not light when connected to one or both of the black wires, remove the terminal and connect it to a good chassis ground. If this procedure causes the lamp to light, there is an open spot in the black wire between the switch terminal and the ground terminal.
5. If the bulb does not light when one side is grounded as in the step above, there is an open circuit in the blue wire to the switch or in a circuit breaker. Remove the blue lead at the breaker and connect the test lamp to the breaker terminal and to ground.
6. If the bulb does not light, connect the ungrounded terminal to the brown feed wire on the circuit breaker. If the bulb now lights, the breaker is defective.

### Circuit Breaker Test

1. Remove the yellow wire from the circuit breaker and connect

# POWER WINDOWS TROUBLESHOOTING CHART

| Condition | Possible Cause |
|---|---|
| None of the windows operate | Battery charge inadequate<br>Poor battery terminal connections<br>Circuit breaker inoperative<br>Short or open in main power feed wiring<br>Malfunctioning relay (if applicable)<br>Inoperative master switch<br>Loose wires in main power feed |
| One window does not operate (Neither master nor door control switch will activate it) | Faulty wiring to or from motor<br>Faulty motor<br>Faulty coupling or transmission between motor and window<br>Binding window |
| One window responds only to one of the control switches (One switch activates it, but the other does not) | Faulty switch<br>Faulty feed wire |
| Window operates sluggishly | Binding in window run or transmission<br>Frayed insulation or improper ground<br>Faulty motor |
| Window operates only in one direction | Faulty switch (May be checked by operating window with both master switch and door switch. If the problem exists at only one switch, that switch is faulty)<br>Faulty wiring |
| Window operates intermittently | Faulty wiring (loose connections)<br>Faulty circuit breakers<br>Faulty switch |

a test lamp between the yellow wire and chassis ground.
2. Turn the ignition switch to the 'ON' position. If the test lamp fails to light, there is an open circuit or the ignition switch is defective.
3. Connect the yellow wire to the circuit breaker.
4. Remove the blue wire from the circuit breaker and connect a test lamp between the blue wire and chassis ground. If the lamp lights, the circuit breaker is alright. If the lamp fails to light, replace the circuit breaker.

### Wiring Harness

1. Turn on ignition switch and master control lockout button.
2. Remove the switch escutcheon and housing. Leaving the switch attached to the terminal plate, separate the two terminal plate halves to expose the ends of the wire terminals.
3. Connect the test lamp between the green and white wire terminals.

4. Operate the master switch up and down for that particular window. If the bulb lights with the switch in both directions, the green and white wires between the switch and the master switch are good, and the section of the master switch involved in the test is good.
5. Connect the lamp between the terminal fed by the blue wire with a tracer wire and a ground. If the bulb lights, there is continuity in that wire.

### Individual Switch and Motor

1. Disconnect the orange and yellow motor leads and connect the orange lead to the green lead and the yellow lead to the white lead.
2. Operate the master switch. Operation of the motor indicates that the individual switch is defective. If the motor does not operate, the trim panel should be removed and the motor connections and leads should be checked.

# American Motors

## Control and Safety Switch Test

1. Remove the safety switch escutcheon and housing.
2. Expose the wire terminal ends by releasing the barbed retainer hooks and separating the halfs of the terminal plate.
3. Turn the ignition switch to the on position.
4. Connect one lead of a test light to a black terminal and the other end to the blue terminal.
5. Repeat this procedure with the other black wire in the master switch. If the bulb does not light, disconnect the lead to the test lamp on the black wire terminal and connect it to a chassis ground. If in doing this the bulb lights an open exists between the master switch and the ground terminal on the dash.
6. If the bulb still does not light the circuit breaker is bad or there is an open in the blue wire from the circuit breaker to the master switch.

## ADJUSTMENTS

### Front and Rear Door 1968-73

#### Sedan and Station Wagon

1. Loosen the attaching bolts and move the regulator arm slide channel up or down as necessary to align the window in the channels. Retighten the attaching screws.
2. Loosen the lower stop attaching bolts and lower the window until the top is just at the level of the belt line.

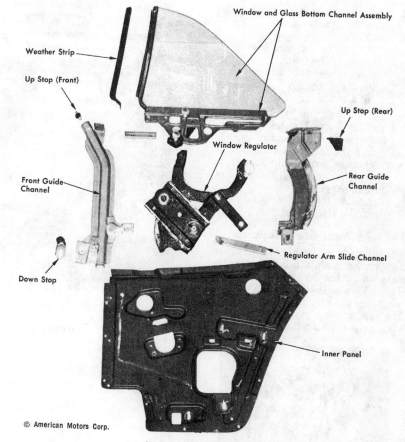

© American Motors Corp.

*Javelin Quarter Window Assembly*

3. Move the lower stop upward as far as it will go and tighten the attaching bolts.
4. On front doors, loosen the mounting screws for the adjustable bracket at the bottom of the front division channel. Position the division channel so the window will operate without binding and tighten the mounting screw.

### 1968-73
#### Hardtop and Convertible

1. Raise the window. If the top front corner of the glass is not aligned with the top rear corner of the division bar channel, loosen the regulator arm slide channel attaching screws.
2. Lower the window two inches. Lower the adjustable end of the regulator arm slide channel until the window aligns properly. Tighten the adjusting screws to 45 in. lbs.
3. Adjust the lower division channel adjusting bracket in or out as necessary to eliminate binding of the window and tighten the adjusting screws.

### 1974-75 Sedan and Station Wagon— Except Matador Coupe

1. Remove the door trim panel and the paper water dam.

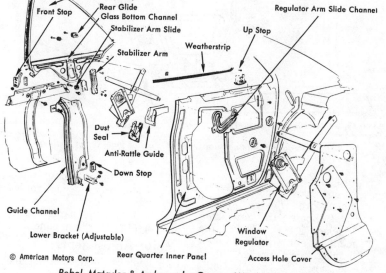

© American Motors Corp.

*Rebel, Matador & Ambassador Quarter Window Assembly*

## American Motors

2. Loosen the screws retaining the regulator guide channel.
3. a. Move the channel up to position the forward corner of glass to the front.
   b. Move the channel down to position the forward corner of glass to the rear.
4. Loosen the front channel retaining screws and move the channel either to the front or rear to obtain the correct position.
5. Tighten all retaining screws to the proper torque. (Refer to the torque chart.)
6. Reinstall the paper water dam and door trim panel.

### 1974-75 Matador Coupe

It is important that the proper relationship be maintained between the glass and latex weather seal. There should be a uniform ¼ inch overlap on the front and top contact areas. The rear contact area should be parallel to the rear weather seal.

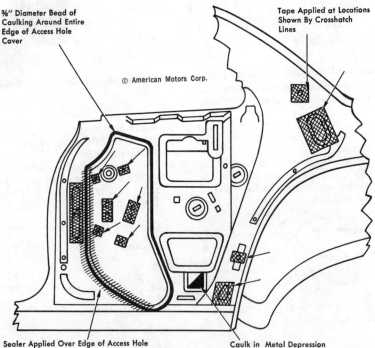

© American Motors Corp.

Glass Bottom Channel Adjusting Screw

Upper Guide Channel Support Attaching Screw

Quarter Window Rear Guide Channel

Rear Glass Bottom Frame Adjusting Screw

Lower Guide Channel Support Screw

*Hornet Hardtop Quarter Window Assembly*

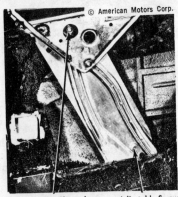

© American Motors Corp.

Upper Guide Channel Attaching Screw

Adjustable Screw

*Hornet Guide Channel Support Screws*

### Minor Adjustments

1. Check the alignment of the weather seal retainer.
2. Remove the door trim panel and paper water dam.
3. a. *Front or Rear Adjustment.* Loosen the upper guide plate-to-plate screws. Move the glass to align the position and tighten the screws.
   b. *Tilt In or Out Adjustment.* Loosen the two lower guide screws. Move the glass in or out to obtain the aligned position.
   c. *Upward Travel Adjustment.* Loosen the front and rear up-stop bracket screws. Move the bracket until proper alignment is obtained. Tighten the screws to the

⅜″ Diameter Bead of Caulking Around Entire Edge of Access Hole Cover

Tape Applied at Locations Shown By Crosshatch Lines

© American Motors Corp.

Sealer Applied Over Edge of Access Hole Cover as Shown by Diagonal Lines

Caulk in Metal Depression

*Rebel, Matador & Ambassador Quarter Window Inner Panel Sealing*

proper torque. (Refer to torque chart.)
   d. *Downward Travel Adjustment.* Loosen the down-stop bracket screw. Move the ment is obtained. Tighten bracket until proper align-the screw to specifications. (Refer to torque chart.)

4. Adjust the retaining brackets to eliminate rattle and for ease of operation.
5. Reinstall the paper water dam and the door trim panel.

### Major Adjustments

1. Remove the door trim panel and the paper water dam.

2. Loosen all the adjusting screws so free movement of the glass is obtained.

3. With the door closed and working from the interior of the car, move the glass to correct relationship between weather seal and glass.

4. Tighten all the adjusting screws to the proper specifications. (Refer to torque chart.)

5. Check the glass for the correct operation. (See minor adjustments for correction.)

6. Install the paper water dam and the door trim panel.

## Quarter Window

### Rambler American Hardtop

1. Pull back the water dam paper. Loosen the window stop attaching screws.

2. Raise the quarter window until it is within 3/16 in. of the glass frame.

3. Raise the stop until it contacts the lower glass frame and tighten the stop mounts to 45 in. lbs. If this admustment corrects operational problems, it is not necessary to continue.

4. Remove the rear seat cushion, seat back, trim panel, water dam paper, and lower inner panel inspection plate.

5. Loosen the stop attaching screws and the regulator attaching screws.

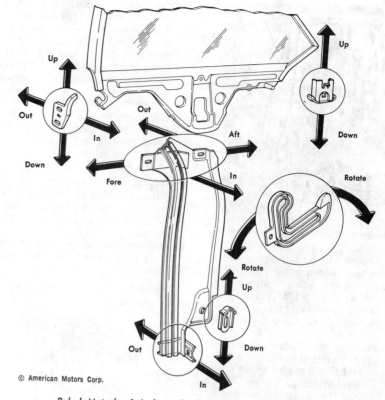

© American Motors Corp.

*Rebel, Matador & Ambassador Quarter Window Adjustments*

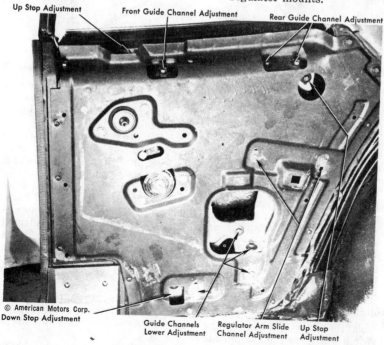

© American Motors Corp.

*Javelin Quarter Window Adjustments*

6. Adjust the window regulator vertically upward or downward until the window will travel upward just high enough to seal properly. Then tighten the four regulator mounts.

7. Loosen the guide channel support attaching screws and move the guide channel forward or backward as necessary to assure an efficient seal with the door window. Then tighten the attaching screws.

8. Adjust the rear guide in a similar manner to ensure proper alignment with the roof rail.

9. Raise the window all the way. Position the rear stop upward until it is against the lower edge of the glass frame and tighten the mounts to 45 in. lbs.

10. Loosen the glass bottom channel adjusting screw and adjust the adjustable roller to ensure alignment of the top of the glass with the roof rail. Retighten the screw.

11. Loosen the jam nut on the lower guide channel support and adjust the adjusting screw for ease of window operation and alignment of the window at the beltline. Retighten the nut.

12. Reinstall the lower inner panel inspection plate, water dam paper, trim panel, seat back, and seat cushion.

### Rebel, Ambassador

1. Remove the rear seat cushion and seat back, the trim panel, and water dam paper.

## American Motors

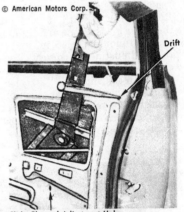

*Quarter Window Regulator Removal*

2. Loosen all the adjusting screws or nuts shown in the illustration.
3. Adjust the guide channel in or out as required to permit free travel up and down with the adjusting stud. Then tighten the jam nut.
4. Position the window forward or aft as required to ensure a proper seal. Tighten the upper guide channel attaching screws.
5. Adjust the attaching bracket at the bottom of the guide channel to permit a good seal with the roof rail. Tighten the adjusting screws.
6. Adjust the regulator arm slide channel adjustment for vertical alignment with the front door window. Tighten the adjusting screw.
7. Adjust the front and up stops so the window, when fully raised, seals properly with the door window and is parallel with the rear of the door window at the front. Tighten the stop mounting screws.
8. Lower the window and adjust the down stop so it cannot be lowered below the top edge of the inner and outer quarter panels.
9. Replace the water dam paper and trim panel and the seat cushion and back.

### Javelin

1. Remove the rear seat cushion and seat back and the trim panel and water dam paper. Loosen all the adjusting nuts and screws shown in the illustration.
2. Adjust the guide channels in or out and fore and aft for free travel of the window (in-out adjustment is provided via a shoul-

der bolt). Tighten the appropriate screws and the jam nut.
3. Tilt the window top to the front or rear until the front edge is parallel with the rear edge of the front door window and tighten the regulator arm slide channel adjusting bolt.
4. Adjust the two upper stops so the window will just reach a fully closed position with the front parallel to the rear of the front door window. Tighten the stop mounts.
5. Adjust the lower stop so the window will lower just until the top edge reaches the top edges of the inner and outer quarter panels.
6. Replace the water dam paper, trim panel, rear seat back, and cushion.

Terminal Plate      Barbed Retainer Hooks

© American Motors Corp.

**Releasing Barbed Clip**

*Removing Switch from Terminal Plate*

### Door Switch

#### Removal

1. Turn off the ignition switch. Remove the two retaining screws and the escutcheon.
2. Remove the switch housing retaining screws. Pull the assembly out far enough so that the back of the assembly is accessible.
3. Release the barbed portion of the retainer clips with a screwdriver and carefully pry the terminal plate from the switch assembly.
4. Use a sharp instrument to depress the retainer clips, going in through the holes in the switch housing.

#### Installation

1. Hold the clips in place on the switch and slide the switch into the housing until there is an

audible "click" indicating proper seating.
2. Reinstall the terminal plate onto the switch assembly.
3. Force the wiring back in under the switch and put the switch housing in place. Install the retainer screws.
4. Replace the escutcheon and install the retaining screws.

## Door Window Regulator

### Front

#### Removal

1. Disconnect the battery. Remove the arm rest, remote control handle, and window regulator control switch escutcheon.
2. Remove the door lock button and remove the trim panel as described above. Carefully pry the water dam paper away from the inner panel.

© American Motors Corp.

                Drift

Slide Channel Adjustment Hole

*Front Door Window Regulator Removal*

3. Raise the window all the way and insert a drift into the hole in the inner panel to hold the glass assembly in the up position.
4. Remove the two lower slide channel screws and the four regulator mounting bolts. Disconnect the motor wiring.
5. Move the regulator first toward the front of the car and then toward the rear in order to disengage the regulator arms from the glass bottom channels. Pull the regulator from the door through the opening.

#### Installation

1. Place the regulator inside the door and engage the regulator arms with the glass bottom channels.
2. Install the lower slide channel

# American Motors

screws and the four regulator mounting bolts. Connect the motor wiring.

3. Remove the drift from the window mechanism.
4. Reinstall the water dam paper, door lock button, and trim panel.
5. Replace the armrest, remote control handle, and window regulator control escutcheon. Connect the battery.

## Rear

### Removal

1. Disconnect the battery. Remove the arm rest and ash tray.
2. Remove the remote control handle and the regulator control handle and the regulator control switch escutcheon.
3. Remove the door lock button and the trim panel. Carefully pry the water dam paper away from the inner panel.
4. Raise the window all the way. Insert a drift into the hole in the inner panel to hold the glass up during removal of the regulator. (See illustration)
5. Disconnect the motor wiring connector. Remove the two lower slide channel screws.
6. Remove the four regulator mounting bolts and then remove the regulator by moving it forward and then rearward to disengage the regulator arms from the glass bottom channels.

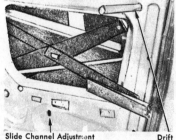

© American Motors Corp.

Slide Channel Adjustment          Drift

*Rear Door Window Regulator Removal*

### Installation

1. Put the regulator in place, engaging the regulator arms with the glass bottom channels. Install the four moutning bolts.
2. Install the lower slide channel screws and reconnect the motor wiring.
3. Remove the drift that is holding the window up.
4. Reinstall the water dam paper, trim panel, and lock button.
5. Replace the remote control handle, the control switch escutch-

eon, the arm rest, and the ash tray. Connect the battery.

## Rear Window Regulator
## 2 Door
### 1968-69

### Removal

1. Remove the rear seat cushion, seat back, arm rest, window switch escutcheon, trim panel, and water dam paper.
2. Remove the stop bracket and replace it in reverse position so it will contact the bottom of the stop stud rather than the top. Position the stop so it will hold the window up all the way and tighten the mounting screws.
3. Note or mark the exact location of the regulator arm slide channel, and then remove it.
4. Remove the regulator attaching bolts.
5. Remove the rear quarter access hole cover plate.
6. Disengage the regulator arms from the glass bottom channel, and pull the regulator out through the access hole.

### Installation

1. The unit should be washed in a solvent and dried with compressed air. Apply a high temperature white lithium grease to the gear teeth, spring, and glass bottom channel slide.
2. Position the regulator and install the regulator arms.
3. Install the access hole cover plate. Position the regulator on the plate and install the mounting bolts.
4. Install the regulator arm slide channel, engaging it with the regulator arm roller. Attach it to the rear quarter inner panel in precisely its original position.
5. Remove the upper stop and reinstall it in the normal position. Adjust it so the window will rise just far enough to seal properly at the front.
6. Install the water dam paper, trim panel, arm rest, seat back, and seat cushion.
7. Adjust the window as specified in the appropriate section if disturbing the position of the regulator arm slide channel has caused operational problems.

### 1970-75

### Removal

1. Remove the armrest from the side to be worked on. Remove the seat cushion.

2. Remove the switch escutcheon, trim panel, and water dam paper.
3. Prop the glass all the way up with an appropriate object.
4. Remove the window switch and wire from the inner panel.
5. Remove the regulator screws and the regulator mounting panel screws.
6. Slide the regulator arm to the rear to disengage the guide.
7. Disconnect the motor wiring and remove the regulator.

### Installation

1. Wash the regulator with a cleaning solvent and dry it with compressed air. Apply a high temperature white lithium grease to the gear teeth and spring and to the glass bottom slide.
2. Install the regulator arm guide to the glass bottom channel.
3. Install the regulator mounting panel but do not install its screws.
4. Mount the regulator to the panel and then install the panel sheet metal attaching screws.
5. Connect the motor to the harness and install the operating switch.
6. Remove the glass support. Install the water dam paper, trim panel, and switch escutcheon.
7. Install the armrest and switch escutcheon.

## Regulator Motor

### Removal

1. Remove window regulator as previously described.
2. Remove the two mounting nuts and pull the motor away from the regulator.

### Installation

1. Align the flat sides of the coupling and transmission shaft.
2. When alignment permits the shaft to slide into the coupling, push the two together, position the motor, and install the mounting nuts.

## Regulator Transmission

### Removal

NOTE: *Follow instructions precisely to ensure proper retention of regulator spring tension. Otherwise, injury may result.*

1. Remove the window regulator from the door.
2. Drill a hole in the mounting bracket through one of the holes in the sector gear. Install a bolt and nut to securely fasten the

## American Motors

sector gear in place. Remove the regulator motor from the drive unit.

3. Insert a screw driver blade into the motor coupling and turn the shaft until all tension on the transmission is relieved.

4. Remove the three mounting bolts and remove the transmission.

### Installation

1. Position the transmission, engaging it with the sector gear.
2. Install the mounting bolts.
3. Remove the safety bolt.

## Chrysler Corporation

### GENERAL INFORMATION

The window lift motors are of the permanent magnet type. A black wire grounds the motors through the master switch and connects with the body at the left cowl panel.

### CIRCUIT BREAKER TEST

Test for voltage at inlet and outlet terminals of the circuit breaker. If voltage exists at the inlet but not at the outlet, replace the breaker.

### SWITCH TEST

1. Remove the switch from the trim panel. This requires sliding a thin blade behind the switch housing at front and rear to depress the retaining clips on 1968 and 1969 models.
2. Separate the multiple terminal block from the main body of the switch.
3. Connect a test lamp between the black and tan terminals. The lamp should light. If not, check both leads for continuity as in step 4.
4. Procure two jumper wires. Connect one between the tan lead and the "up" or "down" terminal, depending upon which way the glass can move. Connect the other jumper between the other "up" or "down" terminal and a ground.
5. If this causes the motor to run, reinstall the switch body on the multiple connector. Operate the switch. If the motor does not run, replace the switch.

### MOTOR TEST

Connect the leads of a test battery to the motor terminals. Repeat the test with the terminals reversed. If the motor operates in both directions it is good. If the motor does not respond at all, remove it and bench test it in case binding of the mechanism is the problem. If it operated in one direction but not in the other, it is faulty and should be replaced.

### TROUBLESHOOTING CHART

| Condition | Possible Cause |
| --- | --- |
| None of the windows operate | Battery charge inadequate<br>Poor battery terminal connections<br>Circuit breaker inoperative<br>Short or open in main power feed wiring<br>Malfunctioning relay (if applicable)<br>Inoperative master switch<br>Loose wires in main power feed |
| One window does not operate (Neither master nor door control switch will activate it) | Faulty wiring to or from motor<br>Faulty motor<br>Faulty coupling or transmission between motor and window<br>Binding window |
| One window responds only to one of the control switches (One switch activates it, but the other does not) | Faulty switch<br>Faulty feed wire |
| Window operates sluggishly | Binding in window run or transmission<br>Frayed insulation or improper ground<br>Faulty motor |
| Window operates only in one direction | Faulty switch (May be checked by operating window with both master switch and door switch. If the problem exists at only one switch, that switch is faulty)<br>Faulty wiring |
| Window operates intermittently | Faulty wiring (loose connections)<br>Faulty circuit breakers<br>Faulty switch |

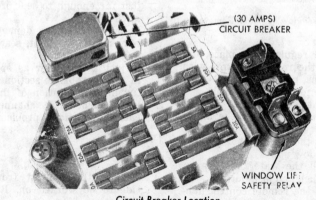

Circuit Breaker Location

(30 AMPS) CIRCUIT BREAKER

WINDOW LIFT SAFETY RELAY

# Chrysler Corporation

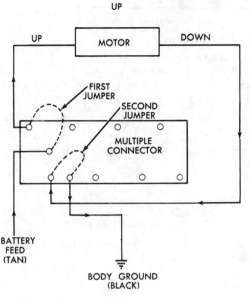
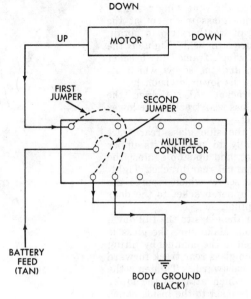

*Testing Electrical Switch*

## FRONT WINDOW ADJUSTMENTS

### Two Door Hardtop Ventless Glass—Front

#### 1974 Imperial, Chrysler, Fury, Monaco

1. Raise the glass ½ inch from the full up position.
2. Loosen the trim support bracket, glass attaching nuts, and glass guide retaining nuts.
3. Adjust the glass forward and rearward to seal against the "A" pillar by positioning the glass in the lift channel bracket slots.
4. Tilt the glass forward and rearward to make the top edge parallel with the roof rail seal. Tighten the nuts on the glass lift channel bracket.
5. Move the guide retainer in and out to position and seal the glass properly against the roof rail seal. Tighten the guide retainer nuts.
6. Adjust the trim support bracket to allow the up stop hooks to engage in the trim support bracket slots (against the plastic liner). Position the glass stabilizers against the glass and tighten the screws.

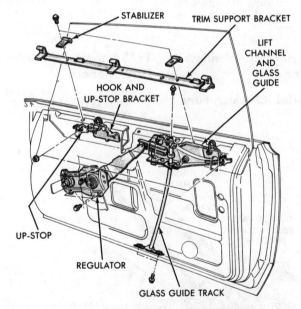

*1974 Imperial, Chrysler, Fury & Monaco*
*Two Door Hardtop Front Door Regulator Assembly*

7. Run the glass up against the roof rail, position the up stops and tighten the nuts.

### Four Door Hardtop— Vented Glass

#### 1974 Imperial, Chrysler, Fury, Monaco

#### 1975 Imperial, Chrysler, Gran Fury, Monaco

1. Loosen all the threaded fasteners which secure the adjustable parts.

2. Raise the glass to the full up position.
3. Position the vent wing assembly vertically against the roof rail weatherstrip. Tilt the assembly forward against the "A" post weatherstrip to obtain an adequate seal. Tighten the nut and washer on the T-bolt and spacer, the screw and washer through the sleeve to the cage nut, division bar lower bracket attachment screw and the vent wing frame lower bracket to inside panel attaching screw.

# Chrysler Corporation

4. Position the vent wing assembly and side glass in or out at the roof rail weatherstrip to obtain an adequate seal. Tighten the vent wing frame to bracket screw, and the screw which attaches the lower division bar to the bracket. Also tighten the side glass rear track to the lower bracket.

5. Move the side glass rear tract vertically to position its upper bracket, and up-stop against the lift channel rear bracket. Tighten the screw which secures the track upper bracket to the door latch pillar.

6. Lower the glass to the full down position. Make sure the glass is engaged in the channel by tilting the side glass rear track forward and backward. Tighten the screw which attaches the lower track bracket to the inside panel.

7. Move the belt mounted glass stabilizer outward to contact the glass. Tighten the stabilizer retaining screw.

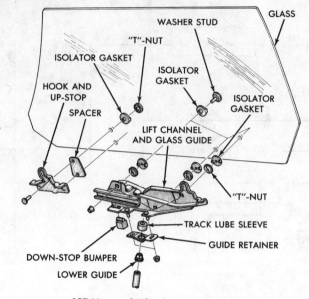

*1974 Imperial, Chrysler, Fury & Monaco*
*Two Door Hardtop Front Door Glass Assembly*

## Four Door Hardtop—Ventless Glass—Front

### 1974 Imperial, Chrysler, Fury, Monaco

### 1975 Imperial, Chrysler, Gran Fury, Monaco

1. Raise the glass about 1/8 inch from the roof rail weather seal.
2. Adjust the pivot guide until the top of the glass is parallel to the weather seal. Tighten the pivot guide mounting nuts.
3. Raise the glass to contact the roof rail weather seal.
4. Adjust the rear track on its

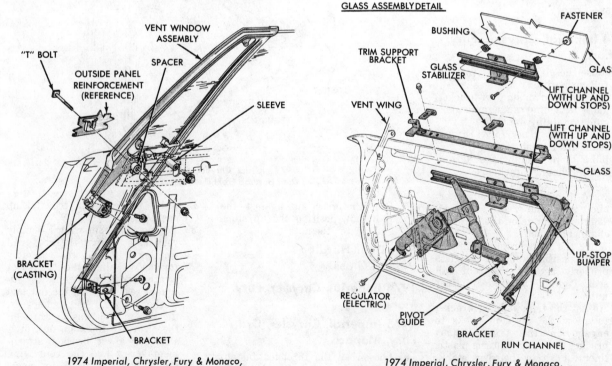

*1974 Imperial, Chrysler, Fury & Monaco,*
*1975 Imperial, Chrysler, Gran Fury & Monaco*
*Four Door Hardtop Front Door Vent Assembly*

*1974 Imperial, Chrysler, Fury & Monaco,*
*1975 Imperial, Chrysler, Gran Fury & Monaco*
*Four Door Hardtop Front Door (Vented) Regulator Assembly*

# Chrysler Corporation

upper bracket so that the forward edge of the glass contacts the "A" pillar seal.

5. Position the glass upper inner edge against the roof rail weatherstrip to attain an adequate seal. Tighten the front and rear track upper bracket retaining screws and the lower bracket retaining nut.

6. Slide the glass up-stops down in the adjustment slots until they firmly contact the upper edge of the glass lift channel. Tighten the attaching nuts.

7. Check the operation of the window by running it up and down and make sure when the glass is at the full up position that it seals properly at the roof "A" pillar. If it doesn't adjust the up-stops or pivot channel.

## Four Door Sedan and Station Wagon—Vented Glass—Front

### 1974 Imperial, Chrysler, Fury, Monaco

### 1975 Imperial, Chrysler, Gran Fury, Monaco

1. Loosen all the threaded fasteners which secure the adjustable parts.

2. Position the vent wing assembly full up vertically in the door frame. Tighten the attaching screws to the upper door frame.

3. Tighten the screw and washer through the sleeve to the cage nut in the belt line/division bar area and division bar to the lower bracket and bracket to the inside panel attaching screw and washer assemblies.

4. Tighten the side glass rear track upper bracket attachment to the door latch pillar attachment (screw and washer).

5. Lower the glass to its full down position. Tilt the rear track fore or aft at its lower bracket to inside the panel attachment (screw and washer) to ensure the rear edge of the glass is engaged in the channel (make parallel to division bar). Adjust the lower end of the track inboard or outboard on its bracket (screw and washer attachment) so it matches the front edge of the glass in the division bar. Tighten these two fasteners.

6. Cycle the glass full up and down. If binding occurs or the glass fails to properly enter the upper door frame, check the po-

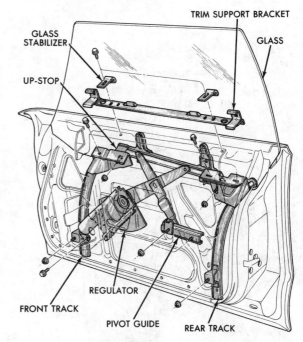

1974 Imperial, Chrysler, Fury & Monaco,
1975 Imperial, Chrysler, Gran Fury & Monaco
Four Door Hardtop Front Door (Ventless) Regulator Assembly

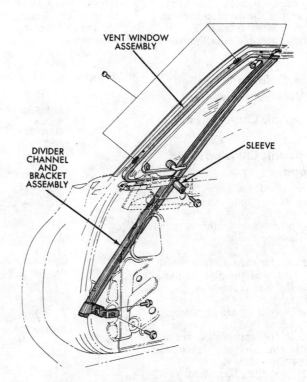

1974 Imperial, Chrysler, Fury & Monaco,
1975 Imperial, Chrysler, Gran Fury & Monaco
Four Door Sedan & Station Wagon Front Door Vent Assembly

# Chrysler Corporation

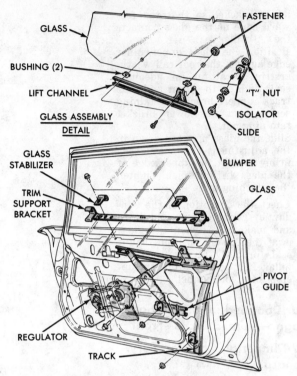

1974 Imperial, Chrysler, Fury & Monaco,
1975 Imperial, Chrysler, Gran Fury & Monaco
*Four Door Sedan & Station Wagon Front
Door (Vented) Regulator Assembly*

1974 Imperial, Chrysler, Fury & Monaco,
1975 Imperial, Chrysler, Gran Fury & Monaco
*Four Door Sedan & Station Wagon Front
Door (Ventless) Regulator Assembly*

sition of the bottom of the rear track and of the division bar (on their brackets) inboard or outboard for possible misalignment. Readjust as required.

## Four Door Sedan and Station Wagon Ventless Glass—Front

### 1974 Imperial, Chrysler, Fury, Monaco

### 1975 Imperial, Chrysler, Gran Fury, Monaco

1. Loosen all of the threaded fasteners which secure the adjustable parts.
2. Raise the glass to around 1/8 inch from the door frame.
3. Adjust the pivot guide to move the glass forward or rearward until the top of the glass is parallel to the door frame.
4. Raise the glass to the full up position. Move the glass forward or rearward so that it is properly seated in the upper glass frame by adjusting the rear track on its upper bracket.
5. Verify that the glass stabilizers are down in place between the glass and trim bracket and support. Position the glass and sta-

bilizers outboard at the belt until the outside of the glass contacts the lower lip of the outside belt weather seal and the inside of the glass contacts the stabilizer. Tighten the stabilizer screws.
6. Tighten the screws that retain

the rear track upper bracket and also tighten the lower bracket retaining nut.

7. Check out the window operation by running the glass up and down.

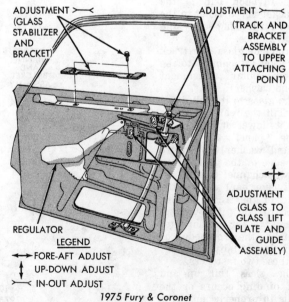

LEGEND
→ FORE-AFT ADJUST
↕ UP-DOWN ADJUST
>—< IN-OUT ADJUST

1975 Fury & Coronet
*Four Door Sedan & Station Wagon Front Door Glass Adjustment*

# Chrysler Corporation

### Four Door Sedan and Station Wagon—Front

### 1975 Fury and Coronet

1. Loosen all the threaded fasteners which secure the adjustable parts.
2. Run the glass all the way up. This will allow the glass to seat in the upper door frame.
3. Access holes in the inner panel permits the use of a lifting tool against the plate and channel assembly to assist in raising the glass to the proper position.
4. Tighten the screws that retain the top of the track.
5. Tighten the screws that retain the bottom of the track.
6. Tighten the glass to the plate and channel assembly attaching nuts.
7. Position the trim support and stabilizer assembly so that the stabilizers contact the glass, tighten the retaining screws.

### Two Door Hardtop, Special and Sedan—Front

### 1974 Satellite and Charger

1. Raise the glass so that a gap of about 1/8 inch occurs between the top of the glass and the roof seal.
2. Move the pivot bracket up or down and set the glass upper edge parallel to the weatherstrip at the roof rail.
3. Move the glass fore or aft to set

the glass to the "A" post weatherstrip.
4. Tighten the front and rear glass track upper bracket screws at the belt line.
5. Tighten the pivot bracket screws.
6. Adjust the up-stop brackets against glass up-stop posts and tighten the bracket screws.
7. Move the bottom of the front track to provide an effective glass to weatherstrip seal at the roof rail.
8. Secure the front track by tightening the retaining nut at the lower bracket.
9. Run the glass approximately 2/3 way down.
10. Tighten the glass rear track assembly lower bracket nut.
11. Position the belt mounted glass stabilizers against the glass and tighten the screws.

### Four Door Sedan and Station Wagon—Front

### 1974 Satellite, Coronet and Charger

### 1975 Charger, Cordoba, Fury and Coronet

1. Run the glass all the way up. This will allow the glass to seat in the upper door frame.
2. Adjust the front and rear tracks in and out, as required. Tighten the track bottom fasteners.
3. Adjust the front track fore and

aft as required. Tighten the track upper bracket fasteners.
4. Adjust the pivot guide to provide proper glass horizontal adjustment. Tighten the pivot guide screws.
5. Position the glass stabilizer brackets against the glass and tighten the retainer screws.

### Two Door Hardtop and Special—Front

### 1975 Imperial, Chrysler, Gran Fury, Monaco

1. Raise glass to the full UP position.
2. Loosen the trim support bracket, the glass lift channel to glass attaching nuts and the glass guide retainer nuts.
3. Adjust the trim support bracket to allow the up-stop hooks to engage in the trim support bracket slots (against plastic liner). Position the glass stabilizers against the glass and tighten the screws.
4. Adjust the glass fore or aft to seal against the "A" pillar by positioning the glass in the lift channel bracket slots.
5. Tilt the glass fore or aft to make the top edge parallel with the roof rail seal. Tighten the nuts on the glass lift channel bracket.
6. Position the glass so it seals against the roof seal by moving the guide retainer in and out. Tighten the guide retainer nuts.

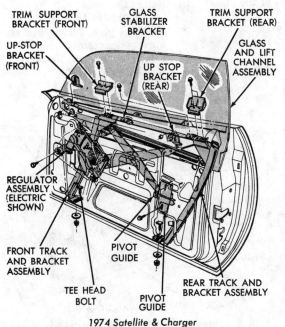

1974 Satellite & Charger
Two Door Hardtop Front Door Regulator Assembly

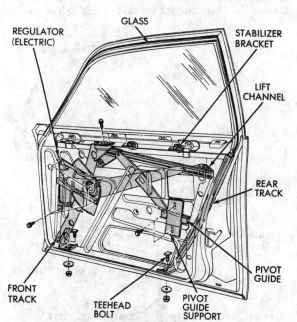

1974 Satellite, Coronet & Charger, 1975 Charger, Cordoba & Coronet
Four Door Sedan Front Door Regulator Assembly

# Chrysler Corporation

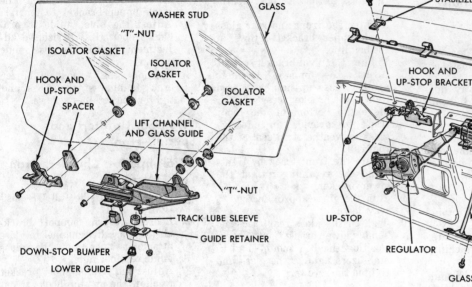

**1975 Imperial, Chrysler, Gran Fury & Monaco**
*Two Door Hardtop & Special Front Door Regulator Assembly*

**1975 Imperial, Chrysler, Gran Fury & Monaco**
*Two Door Hardtop Front Door Glass Assembly*

7. Position the upstops down to contact the plate and front upstops bracket.

## Two Door Sedan, Special and Hardtop—Front

### 1975 Fury, Coronet, Charger and Cordoba

1. Loosen the plate and channel assembly to glass nuts and lower the guide retainer nuts.
2. Loosen the trim support bracket and stabilizer screws and upstop nuts.
3. Raise the glass to the UP position.
4. Move the beltline trim support bracket outboard so that the plastic liners engage the upstop hooks on the plate and channel assembly, and that the stabilizers contact the glass and the glass contacts the lower lip of the outer belt weatherstrip.
5. Tighten the attaching screws.
6. Align the front edge of the glass to the "A" post and parallel to the roof rail weatherseal retainer along the top edge of the glass by moving the glass on the plate and channel assembly fore or aft, or by tilting. Tighten the nuts.

## Two Door Hardtop Ventless Glass—Front

### 1969-73 Imperial, Chrysler, Fury, Polara, and Monaco

1. Raise the glass all the way, loosen all adjustments.
2. Move the glass forward or rearward as necessary to ensure a proper seal with the belt line weatherstrip. Tighten the glass

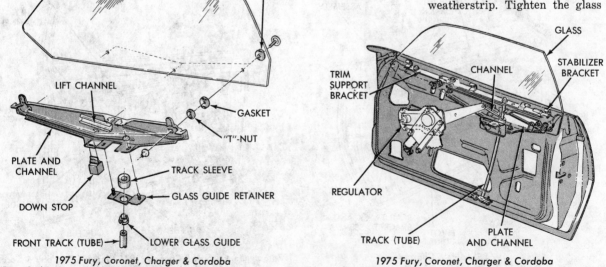

**1975 Fury, Coronet, Charger & Cordoba**
*Two Door Sedan Special & Hardtop Front Door Plate & Channel Assembly*

**1975 Fury, Coronet, Charger & Cordoba**
*Two Door Sedan, Special & Hardtop Front Door Glass Assembly*

# Chrysler Corporation

track upper bracket at the belt line.

3. Move the pivot bracket forward or rearward and adjust the glass so it is parallel with the locating bead of the primary sealing lip. Tighten the pivot bracket and support screw assemblies.

4. Move the front up-stop down until it rests against the bumper on the glass. Tighten the up-stop bracket screw on the front track.

5. Move the rear channel up-stop down against the stop in the rear frame.

6. Tighten the rear channel and bracket upper attaching screw.

7. Move the bottom of the front track so as to create an effective glass to weatherstrip secondary seal. Tighten the glass track to lower bracket screw.

8. Tighten the glass track lower bracket and retainer to the inner panel nut assembly.

9. Run the glass 2/3 of the way down. Tighten the rear channel bracket lower attaching nut.

10. Lower the glass until the top edge is even with or slightly below the belt line of the outer door panel. Avoid letting the glass drop below the weatherstrip. Position the stop on the regulator plate against the stop on the sector. Tighten the regulator plate stop locknut.

11. Tighten items 18 through 25.

## Four Door Hardtop With Ventilator—Front

## 1971-73 Plymouth, Chrysler, Imperial, Polara and Monaco

## Two Door Hardtop, Convertible and Four Door Hardtop With Ventilator—Front

## 1969-70 Chrysler, Imperial, Fury, Polara, and Monaco

1. Lower the glass all the way. Loosen the vent wing screw located on the face of the hinge at the belt line.

2. Align the vent wing with the A post and roof rail weatherstrip and then move it fore and aft until it seals with the weatherstrip. Raise the glass all the way. Set the top edge of the glass parallel with the bead on the roof rail weatherstrip. Secure the vent wing screw at the rear belt attachment.

3. Loosen the vent wing screw on the hinge at the belt line. Raise the glass all the way. Set the top of the glass so it is parallel with the bead on the roof rail weatherstrip. Secure the vent wing screw at the rear belt attachment.

4. Run the glass 1/3 of the way down. Loosen the rear run channel upper attaching screw and adjust the rear run channel upper attachment so the glass will lightly touch the outer weatherstrip and the up-stop bracket on the rear channel when fully raised. Tighten the rear run channel upper attaching screw.

5. Loosen the locknut on the vent wing leg adjusting stud and the screws necessary for adjusting the position of the leg. Raise the glass all the way. Back out the stud until the shoulder of the leg bottoms against the door panel reinforcement and the glass edge and roof rail weatherstrip are parallel.

6. Force the leg outward until there is a secondary seal between the glass and roof rail weatherstrip. Tighten the locknut and the screws involved in the adjustment.

7. Loosen the rear channel upper bracket screw assembly. Position the up-stop located on the rear channel down against the plastic bumper located on the glass. Tighten the adjusting screw.

8. Loosen the rear channel lower attaching nut. Lower the glass about 3/4 of the way. Tighten the nut.

9. Loosen the stop lock nut on the regulator plate. Lower the glass just until the top is even with or slightly below the door outer panel belt line. Avoid permitting the glass to drop below the belt line. Position the regulator plate stop against the stop on the sector. Secure the locknut.

## Hardtop Ventless Glass—Front

## 1971-73 Satellite, Coronet, and Charger

1. Raise the glass all the way. Loosen all adjustments, move the glass forward or backward as necessary to mate the glass with the beltline weatherstrip. Tighten the glass track upper bracket at the belt line.

2. Move the pivot bracket up or down as necessary for parallelism of the glass with the weatherstrip. Tighten the pivot bracket adjustments.

3. Adjust the up stops so the glass will just rise far enough to seal properly, and tighten the up stop adjustments.

4. Move the bottom of the front track in or out as required to ensure a proper seal with the weatherstrip secondary seal. Tighten the glass track lower mounting screw and retainer mounting nut.

5. Lower the glass about 2/3 of the way. Tighten the rear run channel lower bracket attaching nut.

6. Lower the glass just until the top edge is even with the belt line. Position the stop on the regulator plate so it contacts the stop on the sector and tighten the locknut.

## Sedan and Station Wagon Ventless Glass—Front

## 1971-73 Satellite, Coronet and Charger

1. Raise the window all the way.

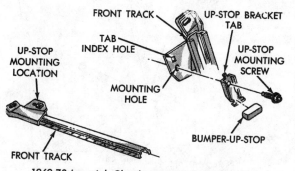

*1969-73 Imperial, Chrysler, Fury, Polara & Monaco*
*Two Door Front Door Window Adjustments*

# Chrysler Corporation

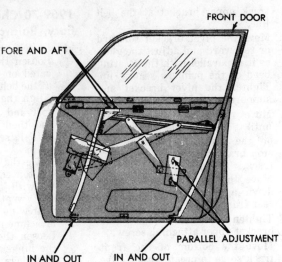

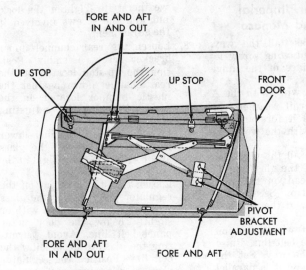

*1971-73 Satellite, Coronet & Charger Hardtop*
*Front Door Window Adjustments*

*1971-73 Satellite, Coronet & Charger Sedan & Wagon*
*Front Door Window Adjustments*

2. Loosen the front track upper attachment and both front and rear track lower attachments.

3. Adjust the front and rear tracks at their lower ends forward and backward and in and out for proper sealing of the window.

4. Tighten the lower track attaching screws. Tighten the front track upper attachment.

5. Loosen the two screws on the pivot bracket, adjust the window until the top edge is parallel with the weatherseal at the top of the door, and tighten the adjustments.

### 1970-73 Barracuda and Challenger

1. Raise the window all the way. Loosen the screw at the belt line on the upper end of the front track.

2. Align the front edge of the glass with the A pillar and the top with the roof rail weatherstrip. Tighten the upper front track attaching screw.

3. Loosen the screws attaching the bottoms of the front and rear tracks. Push the bottom of the front track outboard until the glass contacts the weatherstrip. Allow the rear track to follow on its own. Secure the front and rear track attaching screws.

4. If alignment with the A pillar and roof rail are not correct, adjust the regulator idler arm pivot bracket up or down as necessary.

5. Loosen the up-stop bracket attaching screws, force the brackets downward until the stops rest firmly against the plastic up stops and tighten the bracket attaching screws.

### 1968-70 Belvedere Sedan
### 1969 Satellite Sedan
### 1968-70 Coronet and Charger

1. Open the door and lower the window so the top of the glass is even with the belt line.

2. Move the rear run retainer so it touches the rear edge of the glass and tighten the mounting nut.

3. Position the stop on the regulator so it rests against the stop on the sector and tighten the mount.

### Hardtop and Convertible—Front
### 1970 Belvedere
### 1969 Satellite
### 1969-70 Coronet and Charger

1. Open the door and lower the glass 1/3 of the way. Loosen all adjustments.

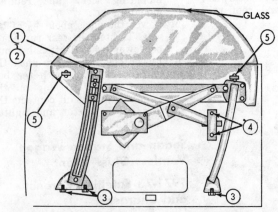

*1970-73 Barracuda & Challenger Door Window Adjustments*

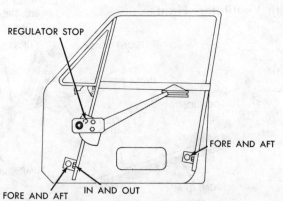

*1968-70 Belvedere Sedan, 1969 Satellite Sedan & 1968-70 Coronet and Charger Front Door Window Adjustments*

# Chrysler Corporation

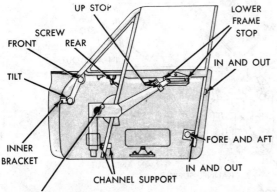

1970 Belvedere, 1969 Satellite & 1969-70 Coronet and Charger
Hardtop and Convertible Door Window Adjustments

1969-70 Imperial, Chrysler, Fury, Polara & Monaco
Sedan and Wagon Front Door Window Adjustments

2. Adjust the rear run channel upper attachment so as to center the window between the inner and outer belt line weatherstrips and tighten the attaching nut.

3. Close the door, raise the window in order to seat the top of the glass and front of the vent wing with the roof rail weatherstrip. Tighten the vent wing belt line screws and nut on the front leg of the vent wing and the vent wing bracket nuts on the inside panel.

4. Position the up stop against the regulator arm and tighten the mount.

5. Tighten the vent wing division channel support screw and the division channel to lower support screw.

6. Open the door, lower the window ½ way and tighten the rear track lower screw. Tighten the screw which attaches the glass run support to the glass run.

7. Lower the window until the top of the glass is even with the belt line outer panel.

8. Position the regulator stop down against the regulator sector and tighten the stop mount.

9. Position the stop located on the lower glass frame against the bumper and tighten its mount.

## Four Door Sedan and Station Wagon—Front

### 1969-70 Fury, Chrysler, Imperial, Polara and Monaco

1. Lower the glass until it is about ⅔ of the way down. Loosen all adjustments shown in the illustration.

2. Tighten the screw which attaches the vent wing lower adjusting rod to the inner panel.

3. Lower the glass until the top is even with the top of the door outer panel. Position the stop on the regulator plate so it rests against the stop on the sector and tighten the locknut. Tighten 6 and 7.

## Sedan—Front

### 1968 Fury, Polara, Monaco, Chrysler and Imperial

1. Open the door and lower the window about halfway. Loosen the glass run retaining screw at the lower end of the run and adjust the position of the run for freedom of movement of the glass. Tighten the screw.

2. Lower the window until the top is just flush with the belt line. Going through the major access hole, loosen the retaining screw for the down stop, lower the stop until it contacts the bumper, and tighten the mounting screw.

## Hardtop and Convertible—Front

### 1968 Fury, Chrysler, Polara, and Monaco

1. Open the door and position the window about ⅔ of the way up.

2. Loosen the rear run upper attaching screw and tilt the run

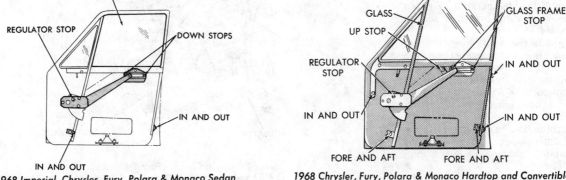

1968 Imperial, Chrysler, Fury, Polara & Monaco Sedan
Front Door Window Adjustments

1968 Chrysler, Fury, Polara & Monaco Hardtop and Convertible
Front Door Window Adjustments

# Chrysler Corporation

in and out until the window is centered between the inner and outer weatherstrips. Retighten the screw.

3. Close the door. Loosen the vent wing belt line attaching screws. Raise the window all the way, and tighten the attaching screws.
4. Adjust the vent wing leg so that the boss of the adjusting stud is against the support and the top of the vent wing and the top of the vent wing is against the roof rail weatherstrip.
5. Adjust the position of the up stop so it is down against the regulator arm.
6. Adjust the lower division bar attachment at the bottom to allow alignment with the glass.
7. With the door open, run the glass half way down. Adjust the rear lower track attachment so the rear track is in alignment with the glass.
8. Lower the glass until the top is even with the belt line. Using the major access hole for access, adjust the position of the lower frame stop so it is against the bumper.

## Hardtop and Convertible—Front

### 1968 Belvedere, Charger and Coronet

1. Open the door and lower the window $\frac{1}{3}$ of the way. Loosen all adjustments.
2. Adjust the rear run channel upper attachment until the window is centered between inner and outer beltline weatherstrips. Tighten the adjusting nut.
3. Loosen the vent wing belt line screws and the nut on the front leg of the vent wing. Close the door and raise the window until it seats with the roof rail weatherstrip and the front of the vent wing contacts the forward portion of the weatherstrip. Tighten the vent wing belt line screws and nut.
4. Tighten the vent wing bracket attaching nuts located on the inside front panel of the door.
5. Adjust the position of the up stop so it is against the regulator arm. Tighten the adjusting screw.
6. Tighten the vent wing division channel support screw and the division channel to lower support screw.
7. Open the door and lower the window $\frac{1}{2}$ of the way. Tighten

the rear track lower screw.
8. Tighten the glass run channel support screw.
9. Lower the window until the top is even with the belt line. Position the regulator stop against the regulator sector stop.
10. Position the glass lower frame stop against the bumper and tighten the mount.

## REAR WINDOW ADJUSTMENTS

### Four Door Hardtop—Rear

### 1974 Imperial, Chrysler, Fury, Monaco

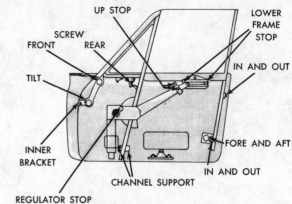

1968 Belvedere, Coronet & Charger Hardtop and Convertible Front Door Window Adjustments

## 1975 Imperial, Chrysler, Gran Fury, Monaco

1. Loosen all of the threaded fasteners before adjustments are made.
2. Raise the glass up until a gap of about $\frac{1}{8}$ inch exists between the top of the glass and the roof rail weather seal.
3. Adjust the pivot guide (position glass in sideview rotation) until the top of the glass is parallel to the weather seal. Tighten the pivot guide retaining nuts.
4. Raise the glass to contact the roof rail weather seal. Adjust the front glass track on its upper bracket (position glass fore or aft) so that the glass contacts

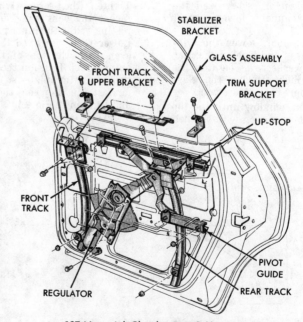

1974 Imperial, Chrysler, Fury & Monaco, 1975 Imperial, Chrysler, Gran Fury & Monaco Four Door Hardtop Rear Door Regulator Assembly

# Chrysler Corporation

the rear edge of the front door glass when it is in the full up position.

5. Position the glass outboard at the belt until the outside of the glass contacts the lower lip of the outside belt weather seal. Holding the glass in this position, adjust the belt-mounted stabilizer bracket outboard so that the rubber stabilizer surfaces contact the glass inside surface. (This adjustment should be for contact only—excessive stabilizer drag causes high window effort.) Tighten the stabilizer attaching screws.

6. Position the glass upper (inboard) edge against the roof rail weatherstrip to attain an adequate seal. Tighten the track upper brackets to the inside panel retaining screws. (Two places for each track). Tighten the track upper brackets to the inside panel retaining screws. (Two places for each track.) Tighten the lower track to inside panel attaching nuts. (One place per track).

7. Adjust the front and rear upstops down against the glass lift channel and bracket assembly. Tighten the up-stop retaining nuts.

8. Operate the regulator through one cycle (glass down and up) to check effort, interferences, and glass "scissor" (fore or aft)

or "cross over" (inboard or outboard) on the front glass rear edge. Perform a similar one cycle test on the front door to confirm rear door glass adjustment when it is in the full up position.

## Four Door Sedan and Station Wagon—Rear

### 1974 Imperial, Chrysler, Fury and Monaco

### 1975 Imperial, Chrysler, Gran Fury, Monaco

1. Loosen the pivot guide nut attachments to the inside panel.
2. Raise the glass until a gap of about 1/8 inch occurs between the top of the glass and the glass run at the top of the door frame.
3. Adjust the pivot guide (tilt glass fore or aft) until the top of the glass is parallel to the frame. Tighten the retaining nuts on the pivot guide.
4. Operate the regulator through one cycle (glass down and up) to check any effort or interferences. Readjust as required.

## Four Door Sedan and Station Wagon—Rear

### 1974 Satellite, Coronet and Charger

1. Raise the glass to nearly full UP so there is a gap of about 1/8 inch between top edge of glass and glass run in top of door frame.
2. Loosen the pivot guide attaching screws to allow the top edge of the glass to be adjusted parallel to frame.
3. Adjust the glass to the DOWN position by adjusting the sector stop on the regulator mounting plate with the glass in the full down position, taking care not to allow the glass to drop below belt weatherstrip during adjustment.
4. Tighten the fasteners.

## Four Door Hardtop—Rear

### 1971-73 Plymouth

### 1969-73 Chrysler, Imperial, Polara, and Monaco

### 1969 Fury

1. Raise the window all the way. Loosen all adjustments.
2. Line up the upper front frame of the glass so it is parallel to the upper rear edge of the door glass frame. Tighten the front track panel reinforcement screw.
3. Lift the bottom edge of the track panel until the front frame of the rear glass is parallel with the rear frame of the front glass. Tighten the center and rear floating screws in the cage nuts.

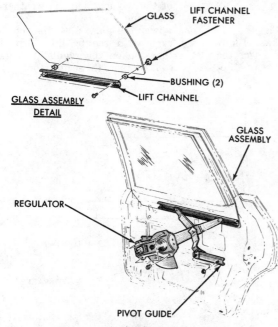

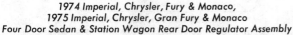

*1974 Imperial, Chrysler, Fury & Monaco,*
*1975 Imperial, Chrysler, Gran Fury & Monaco*
**Four Door Sedan & Station Wagon Rear Door Regulator Assembly**

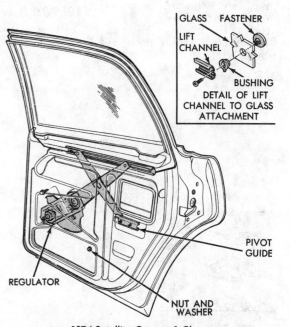

*1974 Satellite, Coronet & Charger*
**Four Door Sedan & Station Wagon Rear Door Regulator Assembly**

# Chrysler Corporation

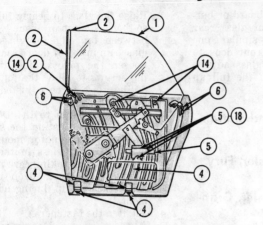

1969-73 Imperial, Chrysler, Polara & Monaco, 1969 Fury, 1971-73 Plymouth Hardtop Rear Door Window Adjustments

1971-73 Satellite, Coronet & Charger Sedan and Wagon Rear Door Window Adjustments

4. Force the bottom of the track panel in or out as necessary to ensure a good seal with the roof weatherstrip. Tighten the adjusting bracket to track panel screws. Tighten the adjusting bracket nut, which is accessible from underneath the door. Tighten the track panel upper attaching screws.

5. Adjust the pivot bracket so the appropriate edges of the upper front corner of the glass are parallel with the front and rear glass frames and the roof rail weatherstrip. Tighten the pivot bracket screws.

6. Adjust the up stops by positioning them downward against the up stops on the glass.

7. Tighten the screws on hinge and lock faces. and callouts 14 through 18.

## Sedan and Station Wagon— Rear

### 1971-73 Satellite, Coronet and Charger

1. Raise the glass all the way.
2. Loosen the pivot channel attaching screws and allow the glass to seat properly in the door frame. Retorque the pivot channel attaching screws.

## Sedan—Rear

### 1969-70 Coronet and Charger

### 1969 Satellite

### 1969-70 Belvedere

1. Loosen the division channel lower bracket screw and lower the window about half way. Re-

torque the screw.
2. Lower the window just until the top is level with the belt line.
3. Adjust the regulator stop so it contacts the sector stop.

## Sedan and Station Wagon— Rear

### 1968-70 Fury, Chrysler, Imperial, Polara, and Monaco

1. Raise the window until it is about 1/8 in. below the door frame. Adjust the pivot bracket for parallelism between the top of the window and the weatherstripping.
2. Lower the glass until the top is even with the beltline. Adjust the stop on the regulator plate so it contacts the sector stop.

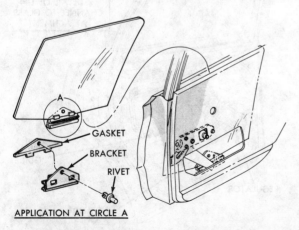

A

— GASKET

— BRACKET

— RIVET

APPLICATION AT CIRCLE A

1969-70 Coronet & Charger, 1969 Satellite, 1969-70 Belvedere Sedan Rear Door Window Adjustments

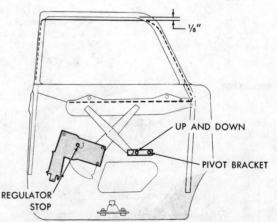

1/8"

UP AND DOWN

PIVOT BRACKET

REGULATOR STOP

1968-70 Imperial, Chrysler, Fury, Polara & Monaco Sedan and Wagon Rear Door Window Adjustments

# Chrysler Corporation

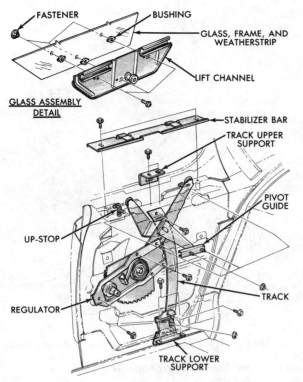

1974 Imperial, Chrysler, Fury & Monaco,
1975 Imperial, Chrysler, Gran Fury & Monaco
Two Door Hardtop Quarter Window Adjustment

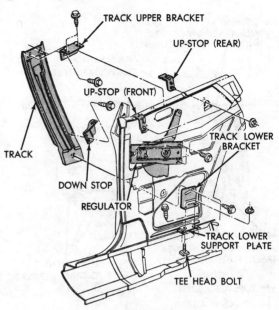

1974 Satellite & Charger
Two Door Hardtop & Special Quarter Window Adjustment

## QUARTER WINDOW ADJUSTMENTS

### Two Door Hardtop—Quarter

### 1974 Imperial, Chrysler, Fury and Monaco

### 1975 Imperial, Chrysler, Gran Fury and Monaco

1. Loosen all the threaded fasteners which secure the adjustable parts.
2. With the glass in the near UP position, loosen the stabilizer bar, up-stops, glass guide track upper support, track upper attachment and pivot guide.
3. Adjust the glass in and out by sliding the track upper support in and out. Tighten the support attaching screws.
4. Adjust the glass fore and aft to seal it with the front door glass by moving the track attachment fore and aft then tighten the nut.
5. Adjust the pivot guide (tilt glass fore or aft) until the top edge of the glass is parallel to the roof rail. Tighten the pivot guide nuts.
6. Crank the glass up so that it seals against the roof rail. Position up-stops to seat on the glass lift channel. Tighten the up-stop screws.

### Two Door Hardtop Special and Sedan—Quarter

### 1974 Satellite and Charger

1. Loosen all threaded fasteners which secure the adjustable parts.
2. With the door closed and the glass raised adjust the quarter window track, at the upper bracket, until the glass lightly touches the outer belt weatherstrip. Tighten the retaining screws.
3. With the top of the glass against the roof rail weatherstrip, and the front of the window level with the top of the front door glass; adjust the track fore or aft on the upper bracket and lower bracket until the front of the window is aligned with the rear of the front door window. Tighten the retaining screws.
4. Adjust the track inboard or outboard on the lower bracket until a seal is obtained at the roof weatherstrip. Tighten the retaining screws.
5. Position the front and rear up-stops against the glass lower frame and tighten the nuts.
6. Lower the window until the top of the glass is even with or slightly below the outer panel belt line.

### Two Door Sedan, Special and Hardtop—Quarter

### 1975 Fury and Coronet

1. Loosen the plate and channel assembly to glass nuts, the glass track assembly at the upper bracket retaining screws and the glass track lower bracket to sill retaining screws.
2. Loosen the glass stabilizer screw, the upstop retaining nuts at belt and the glass downstop nut.
3. Raise the glass to the full UP position.
4. Move the belt mounted glass stabilizer outboard to contact the glass and lower lip of the outer belt weatherstrip.
5. Tighten the attaching screws.
6. Align the front edge of the glass assembly to the rear of front door glass and parallel to the roof rail weatherstrip seal retainer, along the top edge of the glass. Do this by moving the glass on the plate and channel assembly fore-aft, or by tilting.
7. Tighten the attaching nuts.
8. Align the glass to the proper in-out position, to obtain a seal at

# Chrysler Corporation

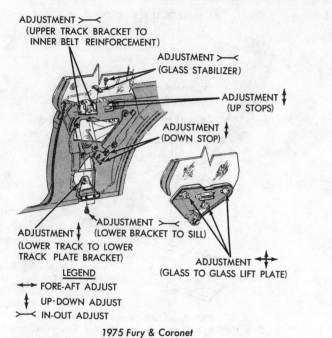

*1975 Fury & Coronet*
*Two Door Sedan, Special & Hardtop Quarter Window Adjustment*

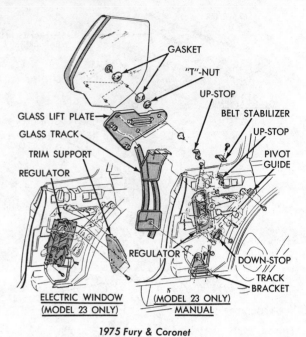

*1975 Fury & Coronet*
*Two Door Sedan, Special & Hardtop Quarter Window Regulator*

the roof, by moving the glass track assembly in or out at the upper bracket to belt attaching screws. Tighten the attaching screws.

9. Move the upstops down to contact the upper surface of the plate and channel assembly and tighten the nuts.

10. Lower the glass to the down position (glass upper edge at belt) and move the downstop bracket and bumper assembly up against the regulator drive arm. Tighten the retaining nut.

11. Tighten the glass track lower bracket to sill retaining screws. (This attachment is self-positioned in rotation during adjustment of the glass track assembly at its upper bracket.)

## Hardtop and Convertible—Quarter

### 1969-73 Chrysler, Imperial, Fury, Polara and Monaco

1. Loosen all adjustments. After each adjustment, tighten the adjusting nuts or screws involved in the operation. Adjust the upper end of the rear track so the rear of the glass seals properly with the weatherstrip's outer panel.

2. Raise the glass until the top is seated fully against the roof rail weatherstrip and the top front

of the glass is on the same level as the top rear of the door glass. Then, adjust the upper front track attachment so the front of the quarter glass and rear of the door glass are properly aligned at the belt line.

3. Adjust the lower front track attachment so the front of the glass is aligned with the rear of the front door glass at the roof rail.

4. Adjust the pivot bracket so the glass will seal with the adjusting bead on the roof rail weatherstrip.

5. Move the upper rear track attachment forward until the weatherstrip and front of the glass are snugly against the rear of the front door glass.

6. Readjust the pivot bracket as necessary to compensate for the adjustment above.

7. Adjust the front and rear stops downward against the glass frame.

8. Lower the glass until the top is flush with the belt line. Tighten the lower rear track adjusting screw.

9. Move the regulator plate stop against the stop on the sector and tighten the adjusting nut.

10. Position down stops against their bumpers and tighten the adjusting screws.

11. Tighten all remaining adjustments.

## Hardtop—Quarter

### 1971-73 Satellite, Coronet, and Charger

1. Loosen all adjustments. Retighten adjusting nuts and screws as appropriate after each operation or as specified in the instructions.

2. Raise the window until the top of the glass is seated against the roof rail weatherstrip and the top of the window is level with the top of the front door window.

3. Adjust the upper track so the front of the window is parallel with the rear of the front door window.

4. Position the lower front of the window so that the front of the window is aligned with the rear of the front door window at the roof rail.

5. Adjust the pivot bracket so the top of the window is parallel with and seals properly with the roof rail weatherstrip. Do not tighten bracket nuts.

6. Move the upper track attachment forward until the quarter window weatherstrip is against the front window. Tighten the attachment.

7. Tighten the pivot bracket nuts.

8. Adjust the front and rear up stops so they are against the glass lower frame.

9. Lower the window until the top of the glass is even with the belt

# Chrysler Corporation

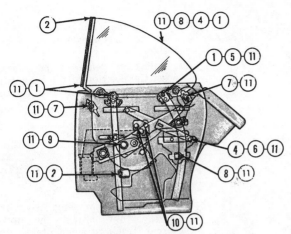

*1969-73 Imperial, Chrysler, Fury, Polara & Monaco
Quarter Window Adjustments*

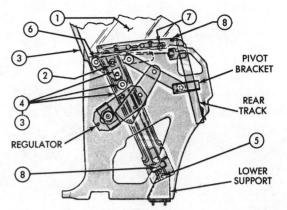

*1970-73 Barracuda & Challenger
Quarter Window Adjustments*

line.
10. Adjust the regulator stop so it rests against the sector stop.
11. Adjust the down stop so it rests against the bumper.

## 1970-73 Barracuda and Challenger—Quarter

1. Loosen all adjustments. Retighten adjusting screws and nuts as appropriate or as specified after each operation.
2. Put the window half way up. Adjust the front track upper attachment so that the glass will touch lightly against the weatherstrip at the bolt. Tighten the locknut on the upper adjusting screw.
3. Raise the glass all the way seating the top firmly against the roof rail weatherstrip. Adjust the front of the window so it is flush with the top of the rear edge of the front door glass. Tighten the jam nut located at the upper adjusting nut.
4. Adjust the lower front track attachment so the front of the window is aligned with the rear edge of the front door. This is edge of the front door. This is accomplished by sliding the track adjusting stud in the support slot.
5. Turn the adjusting screw in or out as required for an effective secondary seal. Secure the jam nut.
6. Adjust the front up stop so it contacts the lower frame.
7. Adjust the rear up stop down against the stop on the glass.

8. Lower the glass until the top edge is just even with the quarter panel belt line. Adjust the down stop bracket located on the lower front track upward as far as it will go.

## Hardtop and Convertible—Quarter

### 1968-70 Belvedere, Satellite, Coronet and Charger

1. Loosen all adjustments. Retighten adjusting screws and nuts as appropriate or as specified after each operation.
2. Close the door and adjust the upper rear track until the rear of the glass just touches the belt line weatherstrip. Adjustment is by means of a sleeve nut.

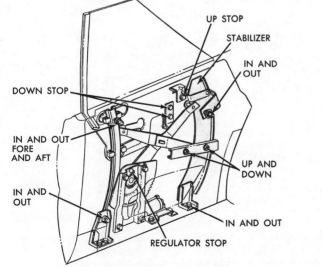

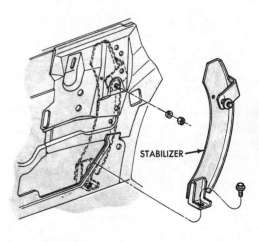

*1968-70 Belvedere, Satellite, Coronet & Charger Convertible Quarter Window Adjustments*

# Power Windows

## Chrysler Corporation

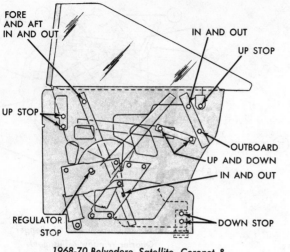

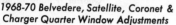

*1968-70 Belvedere, Satellite, Coronet &
Charger Quarter Window Adjustments*

14. Lower the window until the top of the glass is even with the belt line.
15. Allow the weight of the glass to set the position of the lower stabilizer attachment and tighten the attaching screw.

### Hardtop—Quarter

### 1968 Chrysler, Fury, Polara and Monaco

1. Close the door and, using the sleeve nut, adjust the upper rear track attachments so the rear of the window will lightly touch the belt line weatherstrip.
2. Raise the window, seating the top of the glass snugly against the roof rail weatherstrip and the front of the window flush with the top of the front door window.
3. Adjust the upper front track attachment so the front of the window is aligned with the rear of the front door window at the belt line.
4. Adjust the lower front track attachment so the front of the window is aligned with the rear of the front window at the top.
5. Adjust the pivot bracket so the top of the window seals with the roof rail.
6. Move the upper front track attachment forward so the weatherstrip of the window contacts the front door window.
7. Adjust the up stops so they rest against the lower frame of the window.

3. Raise the window until the top of the glass seats against the roof rail weatherstrip and the front of the window is level with the top of the front door window.
4. Adjust the upper front track until the front of the window is parallel with the rear of the front door window. Turn the sleeve nut in or out to accomplish this.
5. Adjust the lower front track so the front of the window is aligned with the rear of the front window at the roof rail.
6. Adjust the pivot bracket so the window is against and parallel to the weatherstrip along the top. Do not tighten the mounting nuts.
7. Move the upper front track attachment so the window weath-

erstrip seals with the front door window and tighten the mounts.
8. Tighten the pivot bracket nuts.
9. Adjust the front and rear stops so they rest against the glass lower frame.
10. Lower the window until the top of the glass is even with the belt line. Turn the lower track sleeve nut counter-clockwise until its boss contacts the outboard side of the inner panel. Tighten the nut.
11. Adjust the regulator stop so it contacts the sector stop.
12. Position the down stop against the bumper.

On Convertibles:

13. Close the door and lower the window ¼ of the way. Adjust the upper stabilizer attachment so the rear of the window just touches the belt line weather-

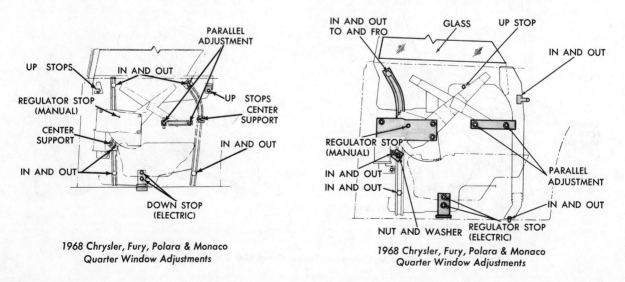

*1968 Chrysler, Fury, Polara & Monaco
Quarter Window Adjustments*

*1968 Chrysler, Fury, Polara & Monaco
Quarter Window Adjustments*

# Chrysler Corporation

8. Run the window down so the top of the glass is even with the belt line.

9. Adjust the lower rear track attachment so the boss is against the outer side of the inboard panel.

10. On manually operated regulators, position the stop, located on the regulator, so it rests directly against the bumper.

11. Adjust the front track center support so it is positioned against the brace.

## Convertible—Quarter

### 1968 Fury, Chrysler, Polara and Monaco

1. Close the front door and raise the window ¾ of the way.

2. Adjust the upper stabilizer so the rear of the window just touches the belt line weatherstrip.

3. Raise the window all the way so the front is flush with the top of the front of the door window and the lower frame is parallel with the belt line of the outside panel. Adjust the upper track attachment so the front of the window is aligned with the rear of the door window at the belt line, using the sleeve nut.

4. Adjust the lower track attachment so the front window is aligned with the rear of the door window at the top. This adjustment is also made with a sleeve nut.

5. Adjust the pivot bracket so the front of the window is parallel with the rear of the door window and the bottom is parallel with the outside quarter panel at the belt line.

6. Adjust the upper track attachment forward so the weatherstrip is against the front door window.

7. Adjust the up stop downward as far as it will go.

8. Lower the window until the top of the glass is just level with the belt line.

9. Adjust the lower stabilizer attachment in or out as required. Adjust the down stop so it rests against the bumper.

10. Adjust the center support inward until it rests against the inside panel.

## REMOVAL AND INSTALLATION PROCEDURES
## WINDOW LIFT SWITCH

### Removal

1. Slide a thin blade behind the switch housing from front to rear. This will depress the retaining clips that hold the switch in place.

2. Pull the switch off the panel. Separate the terminal block from the switch body.

3. Remove the switch.

### Installation

1. Install the terminal block onto the body of the switch. Make sure it is installed firmly.

2. Test switch operation. If satisfactory, install it in the panel.

## WINDOW LIFT REGULATOR AND MOTOR
## 1973-75 All Windows

### Removal

1. Remove the three (3) fasteners which engage the regulator drive arm and the cross shafts to the connecting lift channel and the pivot bracket.

2. Remove the fasteners holding the lift channel and pivot bracket. Disconnect the motor at the pigtail connector.

3. Pull the regulator out of the door.

4. Energize the motor and operate the regulator until it is in what would be the full up position.

5. Lock the regulator sector and plate securely in a vise and remove the counterbalance spring.

6. Remove the motor.

### Installation

1. Install the motor onto the regulator.

2. Install the counterbalance spring.

3. Remove the regulator from the vise and connect the motor electrical connection. Operate the regulator to ensure the counterbalance spring winds up as regulator is operated toward the down position.

4. Position the regulator in the middle of its travel, and then install it in the door and replace the fasteners, torquing them to 95 inch pounds.

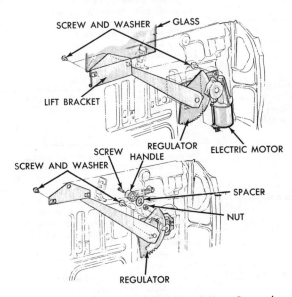

*1968-72 Front Door Window Regulator & Motor Removal*

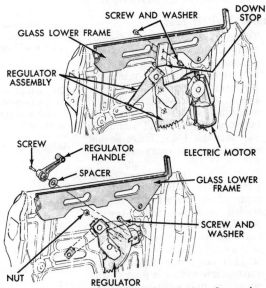

*1968-72 Rear Door Window Regulator & Motor Removal*

## Chrysler Corporation

5. Engage the drive arm and cross arms to the connecting lift channel and pivot bracket. Adjust the lift channel and pivot bracket as described in the section on adjustments.
6. Complete other adjustments as necessary to ensure proper window operation.

### 1968-72 Front Window

#### Removal

1. Lower the glass all the way. Disconnect the motor wiring.
2. Remove the screws and washers attaching the regulator to the door panel.
3. Slide the regulator rearward to disengage it from the lift bracket and guide assembly.
4. *Clamp the regulator assembly securely in a vise so the assist spring will not drive the mounting bracket around the lift pivot when the motor is removed.*

5. Remove the motor.

#### Installation

1. Install the motor on the regulator.
2. Lubricate the area of the sector gear teeth that comes in contact with the motor drive gear. Remove the regulator from the vise.
3. Put the regulator in the door and then slide it forward to engage the lift bracket and guide. Connect the motor wiring. Adjust the mechanism as required.

### 1968-72 Rear and Quarter Window

#### Removal

1. Support the glass assembly with a suitable prop. Disconnect the motor wiring.
2. Remove the attaching screws and washers.
3. Remove the spring nut which

retains the roller on the regulator front arm.
4. Remove the regulator. *Clamp the regulator assembly securely in a vise so the assist spring will not drive the mounting bracket around the lift pivot when the motor is removed.*
5. Remove the motor.

#### Installation

1. Install the motor.
2. Remove the regulator from the vise. Lubricate the outboard side of the regulator sector gear tooth contact area so as to form a belt about ½ in. wide. Lubricate the studs on the front and rear arms.
3. Position the regulator and install the roller spring nut and the attaching screws and washers.
4. Connect the motor wiring and remove the prop. Adjust the mechanism as necessary.

## Ford Motor Company

## DIAGNOSTIC TESTS

### 1971-75 Ford, Lincoln & Mercury

#### Power Test

1. Test for voltage to terminal (2) of the power window switch. If there is no voltage, check for faulty wiring between the power switch and the ignition switch.

#### Master Switch Test

1. Testing should be performed using a self powered test light or an ohmmeter. The switch must be removed from the vehicle to perform the test.
2. Leave switches in the neutral position and test for continuity between pin (3) and terminals (4) through (11). There should be continuity in every case. Otherwise, replace the switch.
3. Push each switch forward (as if pushing the switch toward the front of the car when in the installed position) while testing for continuity between pin (3) and the odd numbered pin for that switch. If pin (5), (7), (9), or (11) has continuity when the appropriate switch is pushed forward, the unit must be replaced.
4. Push each switch rearward while

## TROUBLESHOOTING CHART

| Condition | Possible Cause |
|---|---|
| None of the windows operate | Battery charge inadequate<br>Poor battery terminal connections<br>Circuit breaker inoperative<br>Short or open in main power feed wiring<br>Malfunctioning relay (if applicable)<br>Inoperative master switch<br>Loose wires in main power feed |
| One window does not operate (Neither master nor door control switch will activate it) | Faulty wiring to or from motor<br>Faulty motor<br>Faulty coupling or transmission between motor and window<br>Binding window |
| One window responds only to one of the control switches (One switch activates it, but the other does not) | Faulty switch<br>Faulty feed wire |
| Window operates sluggishly | Binding in window run or transmission<br>Frayed insulation or improper ground<br>Faulty motor |
| Window operates only in one direction | Faulty switch (May be checked by operating window with both master switch and door switch. If the problem exists at only one switch, that switch is faulty)<br>Faulty wiring |
| Window operates intermittently | Faulty wiring (loose connections)<br>Faulty circuit breakers<br>Faulty switch |

# Ford Motor Company

testing for continuity between pin (3) and the even numbered pin for that switch. If pin (4) (6), (8), or (10) has continuity when the appropriate switch is pushed rearward, the unit must be replaced.

5. Test for continuity between pin (2) and every other pin on the switch assembly with the switches in neutral position. There should be continuity only between pins (1) and (2).

6. Push each switch forward while testing for continuity between pin (2) and its odd numbered pin (3), (5), (7), (9), (11). If continuity is lacking at any pin, replace the switch assembly.

2. The switch should have continuity between terminals 1 and 3, 2 and 5, and 4 and 6 when it is in the neutral position.

3. When the switch is pushed downward it should have continuity between 2, 4 and 5 and 1 and 3. The 6 terminal should be isolated from the others.

4. There should be continuity between terminals 2, 3 and 5 and 4 and 6 when the switch is in the upward position. The 1 terminal now should be isolated from the others.

5. If in performing any of these tests the switch does not test as stated it is defective and should be replaced.

## 1968–70 Ford

### Power Test

1. Make sure that the battery is fully charged and turn the ignition switch to the accessory position.

2. Connect a voltmeter or test lamp between the power window relay black wire and ground. This wire is connected to the 20 ampere circuit breaker which is supplied by the battery terminal of the starting motor relay. If there is no voltage, either the circuit breaker or the relay must be replaced.

3. Connect a voltmeter or test lamp from the red wire of the power

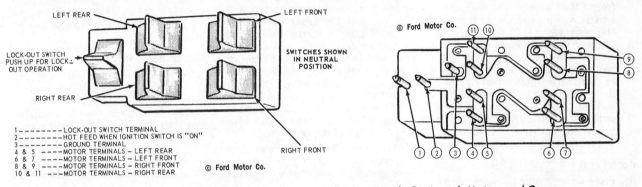

1 - - - - - - - LOCK-OUT SWITCH TERMINAL
2 - - - - - - - HOT FEED WHEN IGNITION SWITCH IS "ON"
3 - - - - - - - GROUND TERMINAL
4 & 5 - - - - MOTOR TERMINALS – LEFT REAR
6 & 7 - - - - MOTOR TERMINALS – LEFT FRONT
8 & 9 - - - - MOTOR TERMINALS – RIGHT FRONT
10 & 11 - - - MOTOR TERMINALS – RIGHT REAR

© Ford Motor Co.

*Power Window Switch Pin Connections and Locations—All Except Lincoln Continental, Mustang and Cougar*

7. Push each switch backward while testing for continuity between its even numbered pin and pin (2). If pin (4), (6), (8), or (10) lacks continuity, replace the switch assembly.

### Motor Test

Connect the motor to a fully charged battery with an ammeter in series between the motor and the positive battery post. With no load, the current draw should be a steady 5 amps or less at 12.8 volts.

### Single Switch Test—All Models

1. To test the window switch use a self powered test-light or an ohm meter.

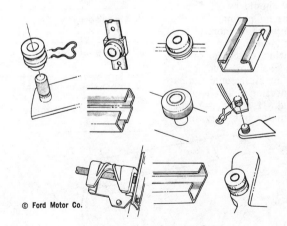

*Power Window Lubrication Points*

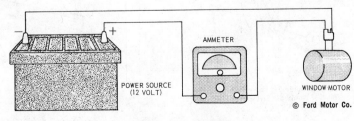

*Power Window Current Draw Test*

# Ford Motor Company

window relay to ground. If there is no voltage, the ignition switch or wire between the relay and switch must be replaced.

4. Check for voltage at the black-white wire of the relay. If there is no voltage, but voltage was encountered in step 3, replace the relay.

5. Check for voltage at the blue wire at the master control switch. If there is no voltage, the black-white wire is faulty.

### Switch Test

1. Check operation of the window from both the master switch and the door switch. If the window operates normally from one switch, but only in one direction from the other, replace the switch which produces only partial response.

2. If there is no response from the motor, disconnect the wires at the motor and check for voltage at each wire while actuating the individual switch. If there is no voltage, check for voltage at the switch feed wire. If the feed wire is hot but the wires to the motor are dead, replace the switch.

### Motor Test

1. Place an ammeter in series with the grounded battery connection, and operate the window. Current draw should be 12 amperes or less during normal operation and 20 amperes or more at stall. If current is too high during normal operation, check for binding in the mechanism. Too low an amperage at stall could indicate poor connections. These should be checked. If the motor operates normally, but only in one

direction, the wiring or switches are faulty.

### Lubrication

The mechanism should be lubricated, as shown in the illustration, whenever operating difficulties are experienced and each time it is disassembled.

# ADJUSTMENTS DOOR WINDOWS

## 1972 Ford, Mercury Four Door Sedan—Front

1. Remove the trim panel and watershield.
2. Loosen lower rear guide retaining nut, the screws at top and bottom of the front guide, and the 2 screws at the top of the rear guide.
3. Lower the glass until the top of it is about an inch below the top of the glass opening. Then adjust the set screw at the bottom of the rear guide so that the rear edge of the glass is aligned with the center of the rear run.
4. Raise the glass all the way. Position the front run and its retainer so they are snug against

the glass, and then tighten the two attaching screws to 6-11 ft. lbs.

5. Tighten the two rear guide attaching screws to 6-11 ft. lbs.
6. Lower the glass until the top is about 4 in. below the belt line.
7. Push the rear guide set screw forward and tighten the nut to 6-11 ft. lbs.
8. Reinstall the watershield and door trim panel.

## 1972 Ford and Mercury Except Four Door Sedans, 1972-74 Lincoln Continental— Front

The in-out tilt and upper rear stop position can be adjusted without removing the door trim panel. For complete adjustment procedures, see below.

### Upper Rear Stop

To adjust the upper rear stop, put the window in the full up position, place the upper rear stop down against the stop on the glass channel, and then tighten the two stop attaching screws.

### In-Out Tilt

1. Loosen the attaching screws that

| 1. | Glass position-fore and aft | Perform if glass has been moved or if door hinges have been adjusted to a great extent |
|----|------------------------------|----------------------------------------------------------------------------------------|
| 2. | Stabilizers | Adjust if glass is not properly supported at the belt line |
| 3. | Glass in-out tilt | Perform if glass does not seal effectively at the top |
| 4. | Upper stop adjustment | Adjust if glass does not rise to the proper situation |
| 5. | Lower stop adjustment | Adjust if glass does not lower to the proper position |

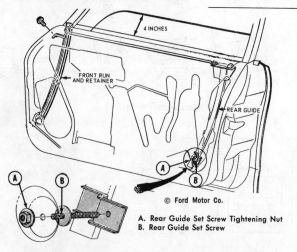

A. Rear Guide Set Screw Tightening Nut
B. Rear Guide Set Screw

*1972-73 Ford & Mercury, Front Door Window Adjustment*

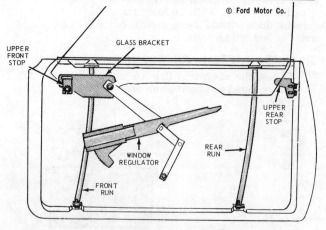

*1972-73 Ford & Mercury, Except Four Door, Front Door Window Adjustments*

# Ford Motor Company

hold the bottoms of the front and rear runs in place.

2. Put the glass in the up position. Then move the glass inboard or outboard as necessary to ensure proper engagement of the glass with the weatherstrip in the roof rail. The window must also be flush with the quarter window glass.

3. Tighten the two retainer attaching screws.

4. Run the glass up and down to check for binding. If the glass binds, lower the glass, loosen the front run lower attaching screw, allow the run to move to its most natural position, and retighten the screw.

## Complete Adjustment

1. Remove the watershield and door trim panel.

2. Loosen the nut at the rear of the glass bracket.

3. Loosen all adjusting screws as described below:
   a. upper front stop adjusting screw
   b. lower mechanism adjusting screw
   c. the lower front and rear run attaching screws
   d. the two upper rear stop attaching screws

4. Raise the glass all the way and then move it forward or rearward

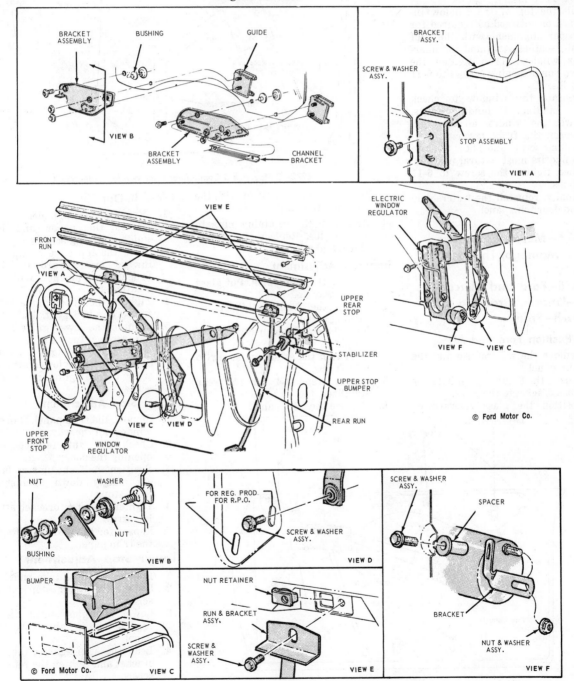

*1972-73 Ford & Mercury Front Door Window Mechanism*

# Ford Motor Company

as required for it to seal tightly against the (A) pillar.

5. Tighten the nut mentioned in step 2 and the screw that holds the lower mechanism in place.

6. Position the upper front stop so it rests firmly against the glass bracket. Then tighten its mounting screw to 6-11 ft. lbs.

7. Move the rear stop firmly downward as far as it will go and tighten the two mounting screws to 6-11 ft. lbs.

8. Tilt the top of the window inward or outward as required for proper alignment with the roof rail weather strip and the quarter window. Then tighten the two run-attaching screws to 6-11 ft. lbs.

9. Operate the window to check for binding. If binding exists, lower the window all the way. Loosen the front lower run attaching screw and allow the run to find its most natural position. Then tighten the screw to 6-11 ft. lbs.

10. Finally, reinstall the watershield and door trim panel.

## 1972-75—Mustang, Cougar, Torino, Montego, Thunderbird, Mark IV
## 1973-75—Ford and Mercury
## 1975—Lincoln, Granada and Monarch—Front

### Glass Position Fore and Aft

1. Remove the watershield and the trim panel.
2. Loosen the 3 nuts which hold the glass bracket to the glass.
3. Position the glass forward or

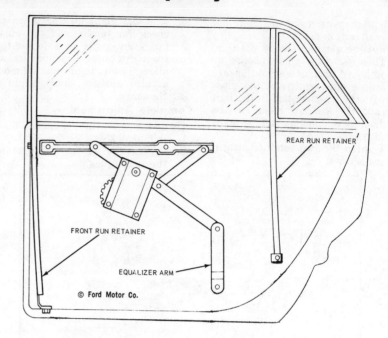

1972-73 Maverick & Comet Rear Door Window Adjustment

rearward for the best fit with the weatherstripping.

4. Retighten the retaining nuts to 6-11 ft. lbs. Replace the watershield and trim panel.

### Stabilizer Adjustment

1. Remove the trim panel. Put glass all the way up.
2. Loosen the front stabilizer attaching screw.
3. Push the stabilizer firmly against the glass.
4. Retighten the attaching screw to 6-11 ft. lbs.
5. Repeat steps 2-4 for the rear stabilizer.
6. Replace the trim panel.

### Glass In-Out Tilt

1. Remove the trim panel.
2. Loosen the upper and lower guide attaching screws.
3. Move the top edge of the glass inward or outward to obtain proper alignment with the weatherstrip.
4. Tighten the upper guide attaching screws to 6-11 ft. lbs.
5. Tighten the lower guide attaching screws to 6-11 ft. lbs. If working on the right hand door, tighten the rear lower attaching screw before tightening the front screw.

### Upper Stop Adjustment

1. Remove the trim panel. Raise the window all the way.
2. Check for interference when opening the door.
3. Position the front up-stop brackets snugly down against the glass stops.
4. Tighten the stop bracket attaching screw.
5. Repeat for the rear stop. Replace the trim panel.

### Lower Stop Adjustment

1. Remove the door trim panel.
2. Loosen the lower stop retainer screw.
3. Lower the glass until the top edge is 1¼ in. above the outer panel.
4. Lean the stop against the glass bracket and tighten the retaining screw.
5. Replace the door trim panel.

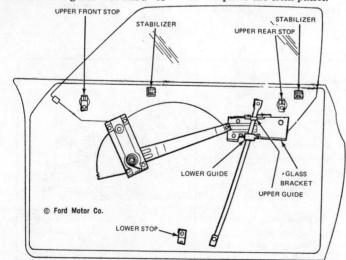

1972-73 Single Tubular Run Front Door Window Adjustment

# Ford Motor Company

## 1972 Maverick and Comet Four Door Sedan—Rear

1. Remove the trim panel and watershield.
2. Loosen all mechanism adjusting screws.
3. Raise the glass all the way.
4. Tighten the front run retainer attaching screw to 6-11 ft. lbs. and the equalizer arm attaching screw to 8-20 in. lbs.
5. Lower the glass until the top is approximately 4 in. above the belt line. Tighten the front run lower retainer attaching screw to 6-11 ft. lbs.
6. Locate the rear run and its retainer so that it is firmly against the glass. Tighten the attaching screw to 3-7 ft. lbs.
7. Reinstall the watershield and door trim panel.

## 1972 Ford, Mercury, Four Door Sedan, Station Wagon— Rear

1. Loosen the 2 screw and washer assemblies, accessible at the back of the rear door, that retain the rear run.
2. Lower the glass until it is about 4 in. above the belt line.
3. Tighten the screw and washer assemblies to 6-11 ft. lbs.

## 1972 Ford, Mercury, Four Door Sedan and Hardtop 1972-74 Lincoln—Rear

The in-out tilt and upper stop adjustments can be made without removing the door panel. If the glass does not align properly with the weatherstrip at the top, perform the in-out tilt adjustment. If it does not rise to the proper position, perform the upper stop adjustments. Otherwise, perform the complete adjustment as outlined below.

### Upper Front Stop

1. Raise the glass all the way. Loosen the two stop mounting screws, accessible from the front of the door.
2. Move the stop down until it firmly contacts the glass channel. Tighten the screws to 6-11 ft lbs.

### Upper Rear Stop

1. Loosen the two stop attaching screws, accessible from the rear of the door.
2. Put the window all the way up. Put the rear stop down against the glass channel. Tighten the

two attaching screws to 6-11 ft. lbs.

### In-Out Tilt

1. Put the glass all the way up. Loosen the front and rear guide attaching screws. These are accessible from underneath the door.
2. Move the glass inboard or outboard until it lines up properly with the roof rail weatherstrip and is flush with the weatherstrip which seals the front.
3. Tighten the attaching screws to 6-11 ft. lbs.
4. Raise and lower the glass to check for binding. If binding exists, lower the window, loosen the front run attaching screw, allow the run to move to its most natural position, and retighten the screw to 6-11 ft. lbs.

## Complete Adjustment Except 1972-74 Lincoln

1. Remove the door panel and watershield.
2. Loosen all adjusting nuts and screws as below:
   a. Front run and rear guide attaching screws, upper and lower.
   b. Front and rear stop attaching screws.
   c. Equalizer arm bracket attaching screws.
   d. Rear guide roller, and stabilizer attaching screw.
3. Raise the glass all the way. Position the glass forward or rearward until it fits snugly against the weatherstripping at the top and rear.
4. Tighten the nut to 6-11 ft. lbs.
5. Position the upper front stop down firmly against the glass channel. Tighten the screws to 6-11 ft. lbs.
6. Move the glass inboard or outboard until it seals efficiently at the top and front. Then tighten the front run and rear guide lower attaching screws to 6-11 ft. lbs.
7. Move the bottom of the glass inboard or outboard until an effective seal exists at the front. Then tighten the front guide upper attaching screw to 6-11 ft. lbs.
8. Raise and lower the glass to check for binding. If binding exists, lower the window, loosen the front run attaching screw, allow the run to move to its most natural position, and retighten the screw to 6-11 ft. lbs.
9. Raise the glass to within about

1½ in. from the full-up position.
10. Move the inside stabilizer outboard until it is snugly against the inside surface of the glass. Tighten the stabilizer attaching screw to 6-11 ft lbs.
11. Reinstall the watershield and door panel.

## Complete Adjustment 1972-74 Lincoln Continental

1. Remove the door panel and watershield.
2. Remove the seal from the lock pillar at the belt line.
3. Loosen all adjustments as listed below:
   a. Rear guide roller nut.
   b. Front run and rear guide upper and lower attaching screws.
   c. Front and rear upper stop attaching screws.
   d. Stabilizer attaching screw.
4. Move the front upper stop downward until it is snugly in contact with the glass stop. Tighten the attaching screws to 6-11 ft. lbs.
5. Move the rear stop downward until it snugly contacts the glass stop. Tighten the attaching screws to 6-11 ft. lbs.
6. Adjust the position of the top of the glass inboard or outboard as necessary to obtain a good seal with the weatherstrip on the roof rail.
7. Holding the glass in the proper position, tighten the front run and rear guide lower attaching screws to 6-11 ft. lbs.
8. Move the glass in or out to obtain a good seal at the front. Then, holding it in place, tighten the upper front run attaching screw to 6-11 ft. lbs.
9. Operate the window to check for binding. If binding occurs:
   a. Loosen the rear guide lower attaching screw.
   b. Allow the rear guide to come to its most natural position.
   c. Retorque the screw to 6-11 ft. lbs.
10. Reinstall the door panel and the watershield.

## 1972-75 Torino and Montego 1973-75 Ford and Mercury 1975 Lincoln, Granada and Monarch—Rear

### Glass Position Fore and Aft

1. Remove the watershield and trim panel.

# Ford Motor Company

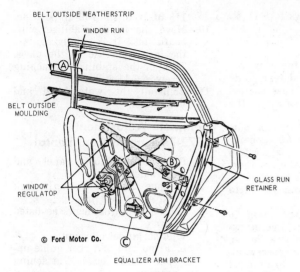

*1972-73 Ford & Mercury Rear Door Window Mechanism*

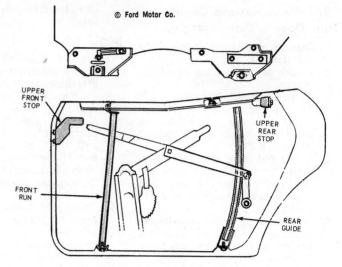

*1972-73 Lincoln Continental Rear Door Window Adjustment*

2. Loosen the 3 nuts which hold the glass bracket to the glass.
3. Position the glass forward or rearward for the best fit with the weatherstripping.
4. Retighten the retaining nuts to 6-11 ft. lbs. Replace watershield and trim panel.

## Stabilizer Adjustment

1. Remove the trim panel. Put glass all the way up.
2. Loosen the front stabilizer attaching screw.
3. Push the stabilizer firmly against the glass.
4. Retighten the attaching screw to 6-11 ft. lbs.
5. Repeat steps 2-4 for the rear stabilizer.
6. Replace the trim panel.

## Glass In-Out Tilt

1. Remove the trim panel.
2. Loosen the upper and lower guide attaching screws.
3. Move the top edge of the glass inward or outward to obtain proper alignment with the weatherstrip.
4. Tighten the upper guide attaching screws to 6-11 ft. lbs.
5. Tighten the lower guide attaching screws to 6-11 ft. lbs. If working on the right hand door, tighten the rear lower attaching screw before tightening the front screw.
6. Readjust the in-out tilt if leakage occurs.

## Upper Stop Adjustment

1. Remove the trim panel. Raise the window all the way.
2. Check for interference when opening the door.

| | |
|---|---|
| **1. Glass position-fore and aft** | Perform if glass has been moved or if door hinges have been adjusted to a great extent |
| **2. Stabilizers** | Adjust if glass is not properly supported at the belt line |
| **3. Glass in-out tilt** | Perform if glass does not seal effectively at the top |
| **4. Upper stop adjustment** | Adjust if glass does not rise to the proper situation |
| **5. Lower stop adjustment** | Adjust if glass does not lower to the proper position |

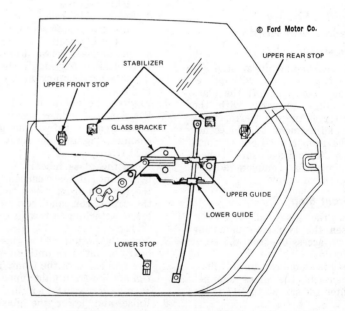

*1972-73 Single Tubular Rear Door Window Adjustment*

3. Position the front up-stop brackets snugly down against the glass stops.
4. Tighten the stop bracket attaching screw.
5. Repeat for the rear stop. Replace the trim panel.

## Lower Stop Adjustment

1. Remove the door trim panel.

# Ford Motor Company

2. Loosen the lower stop retainer screw.
3. Lower the glass until the top edge is 1¼ in. above the outer panel.
4. Lean the stop against the glass bracket and tighten the retaining screw.
5. Replace the door trim panel.

## QUARTER WINDOWS

### 1972–73 Mustang and Cougar

1. Remove the trim panel and the watershield.
2. Loosen the seven adjusting screws. Raise the window all the way.
3. Move the glass forward or rearward and tilt it until it seals effectively with the front door glass and top height the same. The adjusting screw at the top front of the quarter panel should be adjusted to ensure proper alignment.
4. Tighten the locking nut for the screw adjusted in the above step, the screw at the rear of the upper portion of the panel, and the guide lower bracket adjusting screw at (D).
5. Move the front and rear upper stops down as far as they will go and tighten the attaching screws.
6. Move the guide lower bracket in or out until the top of the window seals effectively with the roof or top, and tighten the adjusting screw.

7. Install the watershield and trim panel.

### 1972 Torino and Montego Two Door Hardtop or Fastback

NOTE: *All adjustments must be performed with the trim panel and watershield removed. They may be performed individually if only certain adjustments are required, or in the order in which they are given, if a complete adjustment is necessary.*

1. Loosen the three guide upper support-to-inner panel attaching screws (A, B, and E). Move the glass forward or to the rear until it seals effectively with the weatherstrip of the front door glass. Tighten the three screws.
2. Loosen the support upper attaching screws and move the glass in

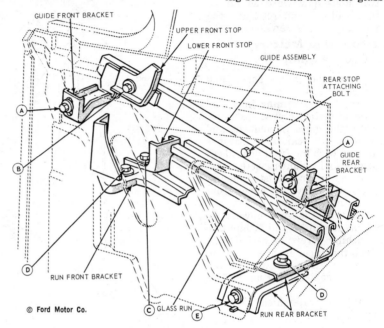

© Ford Motor Co.

*1972-73 Torino, Montego, Thunderbird and Mark IV Quarter Window Adjustments*

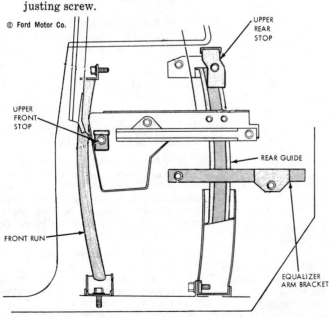

© Ford Motor Co.

*1972-73 Ford & Mercury Quarter Window Adjustment*

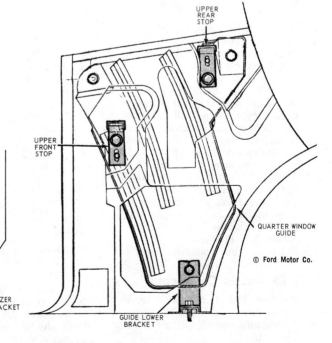

© Ford Motor Co.

*1972-73 Mustang & Cougar Quarter Window Adjustment*

# Ford Motor Company

or out as required to ensure good sealing.

3. Loosen the guide lower bracket-to-floor bracket attaching screw (H). Tilt the glass in or out as required to seal with the roof or top weatherstrip, and retorque (H).

4. Loosen the two upper stop adjusting screws. Close the window so it seals effectively, move the two stops downward as far as they will go, and retighten the stop adjusting screws.

## 1972 Ford and Mercury Two Door Hardtop

1. Remove the trim panel and watershield.
2. Loosen the retaining nut and nine adjusting screws.
3. Move the glass in and out and forward and rearward until it is aligned with the front door glass. Tighten all mounting screws except the upper rear stop mounting screw (leave the upper front mounting nut loose, also).
4. Push the rear stop upward as far as it will go and tighten the attaching screw to 6-11 ft lbs. Push the upper front stop downward as far as it will go and tighten the attaching nut to 6-11 ft lbs.
5. Install the watershield and trim panel.

## 1972 Ford Convertible

1. Remove the trim panel and watershield.
2. Loosen all five adjusting screws.
3. Move the glass up and down and forward and rearward until its height matches that of the door glass and there is an effective seal with the top. Tilt the glass in and out until it aligns with the door glass. Torque all but the top screws as follows: guide lower bracket: 3-7 ft lbs.; front run lower attaching screw: 6-11 ft lbs.; equalizer arm-to-quarter screw: 6-11 ft lbs.; rear guide upper attaching screw: 3-7 ft lbs.
4. Push the front and rear upper stops upward as far as they will go and tighten the attaching screws to 6-11 ft lbs.
5. Reinstall the watershield and trim panel.

## 1972-75 Lincoln Continental

1. Remove the trim panel and watershield.
2. Loosen all seven adjusting screws and nuts.
3. Raise the glass until it is flush

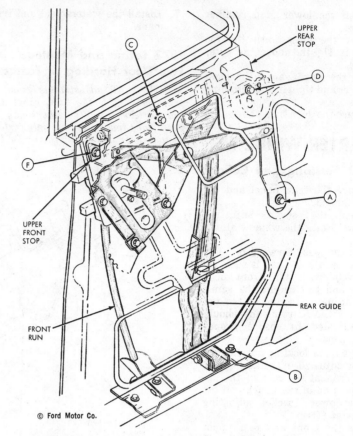

© Ford Motor Co.

*1972-75 Torino & Montego Two Door Quarter Window Adjustment*

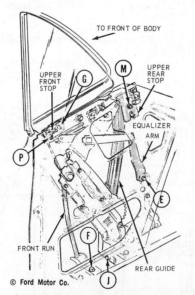

© Ford Motor Co.

*1972-75—Lincoln Continental Quarter Window Adjustment*

with the front door window and seals with the roof rail weatherstrip. Move the glass front and back and in and out until it is properly aligned and sealed with the door glass.

4. Tighten the upper and lower front run and rear guide attaching screws to 6-11 ft lbs.
5. Move the upper front stop firmly downward as far as it will go, and tighten the attaching screw to 6-11 ft lbs. Do the same with the upper rear stop, and then tighten its mounting screw and the equalizer arm attaching screw to 6-11 ft. lbs.
6. Reinstall the trim panel and watershield.

## 1972-75 Torino, Montego, Thunderbird, Mark IV

*NOTE: All adjustments must be performed with the trim panel and watershield removed. They may be performed individually if only certain adjustments are required, or in the order in which they are given, if a complete adjustment is necessary.*

1. Remove the trim panel and watershield.
2. Raise the glass all the way. Loosen the front and rear guide attaching screws.
3. Move the glass up or down until it seals effectively with the roof

# Ford Motor Company

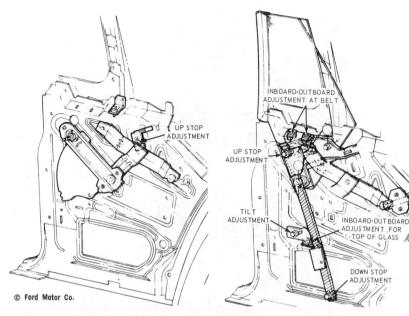

© Ford Motor Co.

*1973-75 Ford, Mercury & Meteor Quarter Window Adjustment*

weatherstripping and with the rear edge of the door glass. Tighten the guide attaching screws.

4. Loosen the upper and lower front stop attaching screws. Move the quarter glass toward the door glass just until a good seal is obtained. Move both stops until they are against the glass and tighten the attaching screws.

5. Loosen the glass run front and rear bracket attaching screws. Move the lower edge of the quarter glass in or out until it is in alignment with the door glass. Tighten the run attaching screws.

## 1973-75 Ford, Mercury and Meteor Hardtop

### Belt In-Out Adjustment

1. Remove the trim panel and watershield.
2. Loosen the two screws that hold the guide to the inner panel.
3. Move the glass in or out as required to align the glass with the door glass at the belt line.
4. When the glass is aligned tighten the two screws.

### Glass Tilt Adjustment

1. Loosen the lower quarter window guide bracket-to-inner panel attaching screw.
2. To obtain a parallel fit between the door glass and the quarter glass, tilt the quarter. When the proper fit is obtained tighten the two attaching screws.

### Up-Stop Adjustment

1. Loosen the two up-stop screws and raise the glass until the glass is against the door glass and roof rail weatherstrip.
2. Put the front up-stop firmly against the glass bracket and tighten the attaching screw.

### Down-Stop

1. Loosen the attaching screw for the down-stop.
2. Lower the glass into the body until the top edge of the glass is flush with the bottom of the glass opening.
3. Position the down-stop against the glass roller and tighten the attaching screw.

# ADJUSTMENTS DOOR WINDOWS

## 1971 Torino and Montego Front Door with Ventless Glass

In-out tilt and the upper rear stop can be adjusted without removing the door panel. If it appears that making either or both of these adjustments will cure the problem, make the adjustment(s) before removing the panel. If making these adjustments does not cure the problem, or if it appears that a more complete adjustment is required, see the procedure for complete adjustment below.

### In-Out Tilt

1. Loosen the attaching screws at the bottoms of the front and rear runs, accessible from under the door.
2. Tilt the top of the glass in or out as necessary to ensure a good seal with the groove of the roof rail weatherstrip. The window must also be flush with the quarter glass.
3. Tighten the attaching screws.

### Upper Rear Stop

1. Raise the window all the way.
2. Loosen the two upper rear stop attaching screws, accessible from the rear of the door.
3. Position the stop downward as far as it will go, and tighten the screws to 6-11 ft. lbs.

### Complete Adjustment

1. Remove the trim panel and watershield.
2. Loosen the adjusting nut and all five adjusting screws.
3. Raise the glass all the way.
4. Move the glass forward and backward until its location is just right to ensure a good seal with the A pillar. Hold in position and tighten the nut in the center of the glass bracket to 6-11 ft. lbs.
5. Move the upper front stop bracket until it firmly contacts the glass bracket. Hold the bracket in position and tighten the screw to 6-11 ft. lbs.
6. Position the upper rear stop downward, hold it, and tighten the two adjusting screws to 6-11 ft. lbs.
7. Move the top of the glass inboard or outboard as necessary to ensure a good seal with the roof rail weatherstrip. Tighten the lower run attaching screws to 6-11 ft. lbs. of torque.
8. Operate the glass to check for binding. If binding occurs, loosen the front lower attaching screw, allow the run to come to its most natural position, and then retighten the screw to 6-11 ft. lbs.
9. Reinstall the trim panel and watershield.

## 1971 Torino and Montego Hardtop

### In-Out Tilt

*NOTE: This adjustment can be made without removing the door panel.*

1. Raise the window all the way.
2. Loosen the screws at the bottoms

# Ford Motor Company

of the front and rear runs. These screws are under the door.

3. Move the glass inboard or outboard until it seals effectively at the top and front.

4. Tighten the screws at the bottoms of the runs to 6-11 ft. lbs.

### Belt Line In-Out Adjustment

1. Loosen the two screws which fasten the bracket at the top of the rear guide.

2. Move the glass until the rear edge is flush with the rear door glass.

3. Tighten the adjusting screws.

### Upper Stop Adjustment

1. Loosen the retaining screws for the front and rear upper stops.

2. Raise the glass to the proper up-position.

3. Tighten the retaining screws.

### Equalizer Adjustment

1. Put the window all the way up.

2. Loosen the four equalizer arm bracket screws (two at either end).

3. Raise or lower either end of the bracket until the top edge of the glass is parallel to the roof side rail.

4. Tighten the bracket nuts while carefully holding the bracket stationary.

### 1971 Torino and Montego Wagon

1. Remove the door panel and watershield.

2. Loosen the front run retaining nut and all adjusting screws.

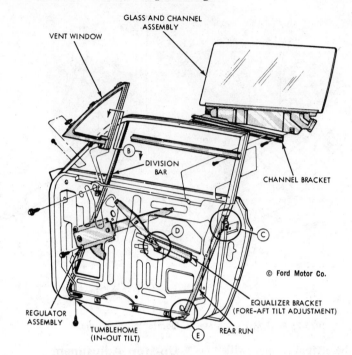

1971—Torino & Montego with Vented Glass Front Door Mechanism

3. Lower the glass until the top edge is about 4 in. from the belt line.

4. Adjust the position of the front run with the front run retainer adjusting screw until it is aligned with the rear run.

5. Tighten the front run retaining nut and the rear run lower attaching screw to 6-11 ft. lbs.

6. Lower the window until the top of the glass is right on the level of the belt line. Tighten the lower stop attaching screws to 6-11 ft. lbs.

7. Reinstall the door panel and watershield.

### 1971 Torino and Montego Four Door Sedan

1. Loosen the front and rear run retainer screws to 6-11 ft. lbs.

2. Lower the glass until the top edge is about 4 in. higher than the belt line.

3. Tighten the front and rear retainer screws to 6-11 ft. lbs.

## 1971 Lincoln Continental, Ford and Mercury with Ventless Glass

In-out tilt and the upper rear stop can be adjusted without removing the door panel. Make these adjustments first and then, if window does not perform properly, make the complete adjustment.

### Upper Rear Stop

1. Loosen the two screws which attach the rear stop to the rear of the door.

2. Put the window all the way up.

3. Place the stop down tightly against the stop on the glass channel and tighten the two attaching screws.

### In-Out Tilt

1. Loosen the screws which hold the front and rear run retainers in place.

2. Raise the glass all the way.

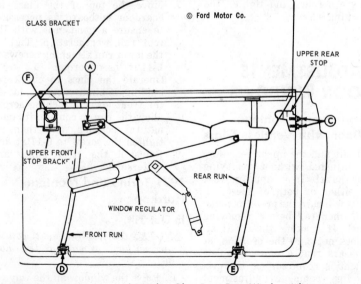

1971 Torino & Montego with Ventless Glass Front Door Window Adjustments

# Ford Motor Company

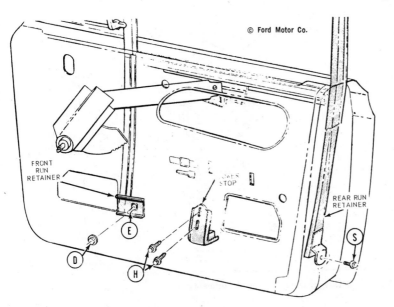

*1971 Torino & Montego Four Door Front Window Adjustments*

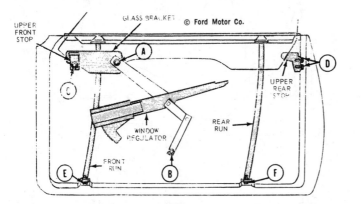

*1971 Ford, Mercury & Lincoln Continental with Ventless Glass Front Door Window Adjustments*

3. Move the top edge of the glass in and out as required to ensure a good seal with the weatherstrip on the roof rail and the quarter window glass.
4. Tighten the two retainer attaching screws.

## Complete Adjustment

1. Remove the door panel and watershield.
2. Loosen the adjusting nut and five screws.
3. Raise the glass all the way.
4. Move the glass forward or back until it seals effectively with the A pillar. Then tighten the adjusting nut at the lower center of the door to 6-11 ft. lbs.
5. Move the front stop until it firmly contacts the glass bracket, and tighten the fastening screw to 6-11 ft. lbs.

6. Move the rear stop down firmly against the glass bracket, and tighten the two attaching screws to 6-11 ft. lbs.
7. Move the top of the glass in or out to ensure a good seal with the roof rail weatherstrip and the quarter window. Then tighten the two lower run attaching screws.
8. Operate the window to check for binding. If binding occurs, lower the window, loosen the front lower run attaching screw, allow the run to come to its most natural position, and retorque the screw.
9. Replace the watershield and door trim panel.

## 1971 Ford, Mercury Four Door Sedan and Wagon

1. Remove the door panel and watershield.
2. Loosen the four lower guide retaining screws and the retaining nut.
3. Lower the glass until it is 1 in. below the top of the glass opening, and then adjust the rear guide set screw to move the rear edge of the glass until it aligns with the center of the rear door frame run.
4. Raise the glass all the way.
5. Position the front run so it is snugly against the glass. Then tighten the two front run retain-attaching screws to 6-11 ft. lb.
6. Tighten the two rear guide attaching screws to 6-11 ft. lbs.
7. Lower the glass until it is about 4 in. above the belt line.
8. Push the rear guide set screw forward and hold it while tightening the nut to 6-11 ft. lbs.

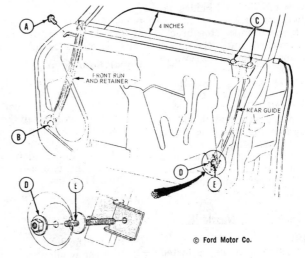

*1971 Ford & Mercury Four Door Front Door Window Adjustments*

# Ford Motor Company

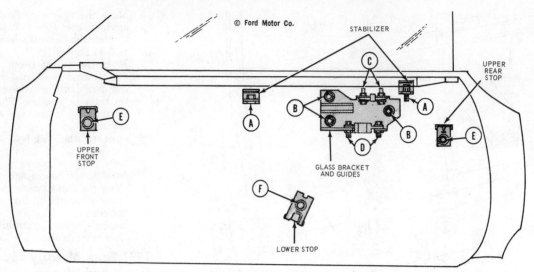

1971 Mustang & Cougar Door Window Adjustments

9. Operate the glass to test the adjustments. Repeat the adjustments if binding is noted.
10. Reinstall the inner door panel and watershield.

## 1971 Mustang and Cougar

1. Remove the door trim panel and watershield.
2. Loosen all adjusting screws and nuts.
3. Raise the glass all the way.
4. Position the glass so it rests firmly against the belt outer weatherstrip.
5. Move the inner stabilizers so they rest against the glass, and tighten their mounting screws to 6-11 ft. lbs.
6. Tilt the glass in and out until it seals effectively with the roof rail weatherstrip. Then torque the four screws and three nuts on the glass bracket and guides assembly to 6-11 ft. lbs.
7. Move the two upper stop brackets downward until they seat firmly and tighten the screws to 6-11 ft. lbs.
8. Lower the glass so the top is about $1/4$ in. above the belt weatherstrip. Move the lower stop upward as far as it will go and tighten the attaching screw to 6-11 ft. lbs.
9. Check for proper operation and readjust as necessary. Then reinstall the door panel and the watershield.

## 1971 Thunderbird, Mark III

In-out tilt and the position of the upper rear stop can be adjusted without removing the door trim

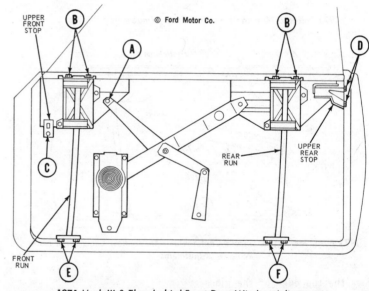

1971 Mark III & Thunderbird Front Door Window Adjustments

panel. Make these adjustments, and, if they do not cure the problem, proceed with the complete adjustment.

### Upper Rear Stop

1. Loosen the two attaching screws for the stop which is accessible at the rear of the door.
2. Put the window all the way up.
3. Move the stop firmly down against the stop on the glass channel and hold it while tightening the two attaching screws to 6-11 ft. lbs.

### In-Out Tilt

1. Loosen the run retainer attaching screws which are located under the door.
2. Put the window glass all the way up.

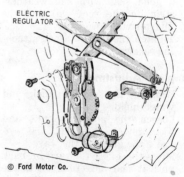

Window Motor and Drive

3. Move the window in or out until it seals effectively with the roof rail weatherstrip and quarter window.

# Ford Motor Company

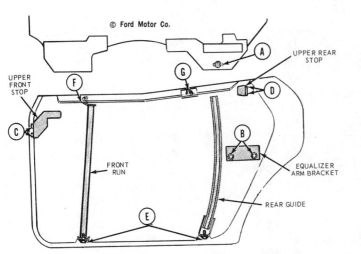

© Ford Motor Co.

*1971 Ford & Mercury Rear Door Window Adjustments*

4. Tighten the retainer attaching screws.
5. Operate the window to be sure it is free of binding. If binding occurs, lower the window, loosen the front run attaching screws, and allow the run to move to its most natural position. Then retorque the attaching screws.

## Complete Adjustment

1. Remove the door panel and watershield.
2. Loosen the adjusting nut and all adjusting screws.
3. Raise the glass all the way.
4. Push the glass forward or rearward until it seals effectively with the A pillar. Then, tighten the adjusting nut to 6-11 ft. lbs.
5. Move the bottom of the glass in or out until an effective seal is made at the belt outside weatherstrip and the quarter window. Then tighten the four upper rear run attaching screws to 6-11 ft. lbs.
6. Force the upper front stop bracket firmly downward and hold it while tightening the mounting screw to 6-11 ft. lbs.
7. Force the upper rear stop downward and hold it while tightening the two attaching screws to 6-11 ft. lbs.
8. Move the top edge of the glass in or out until it seals effectively with the roof rail weatherstrip and the quarter window.
9. Tighten the front and rear run lower attaching screws to 6-11 ft. lbs.
10. Operate the window to check for binding. If it binds, lower it

all the way, loosen the front run lower attaching screws, allow the front run to come to its most natural position, and retorque the attaching screws.
11. Reinstall the door panel and watershield.

## Rear Door

### 1971 Ford, Mercury Four Door Sedan

In-out tilt and upper stop adjustments can be made without removing the door panel. Make these adjustments and, if they do not cure the problem, proceed with the complete adjustment.

### Upper Front Stop

1. Raise the glass all the way.
2. Loosen the two stop attaching screws, which can be reached from the front of the door.
3. Move the stop downward until it firmly contacts the glass channel and tighten the two screws while holding it in place.

### Upper Rear Stop

1. Loosen the two stop attaching screws, accessible at the rear of the door.
2. Raise the window all the way.
3. Move the stop downward until it rests snugly against the stop on the glass channel and hold it while tightening the attaching screws.

### In-Out Tilt

1. Loosen the front run and rear

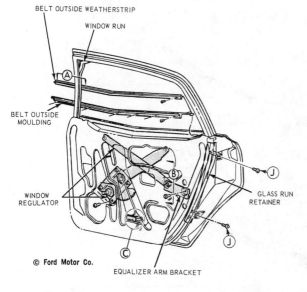

© Ford Motor Co.

*1971 Ford & Mercury Four Door Rear Door Window Adjustments*

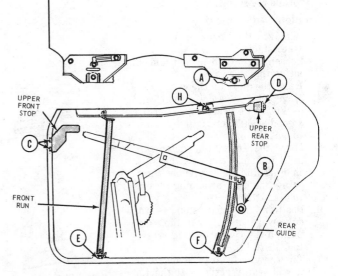

© Ford Motor Co.

*1971 Lincoln Continental Rear Door Window Adjustments*

# Ford Motor Company

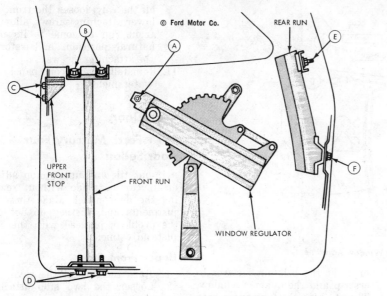

*1971 Thunderbird Rear Window Adjustments*

guide attaching screws, accessible from the underside of the door.

2. Raise the glass all the way and move the top in or out as necessary to ensure a tight seal with the roof rail weatherstrip and front door window or center pillar.

3. Tighten the two attaching screws carefully, to avoid disturbing the adjustment.

4. Raise and lower the glass to check for binding. If binding exists, raise the window all the way, loosen the front run attaching screw, allow the run to find its most natural position, and retorque the screw.

## Complete Adjustment

1. Remove the door panel and watershield.

2. Loosen the adjusting nut and all adjusting screws.

3. Raise the glass all the way.

4. Move the glass forward and backward as necessary to ensure a good seal. Then tighten the nut to 6-11 ft. lbs.

5. Move the front stop downward until it firmly contacts the glass channel and hold it while tightening the two attaching screws to 6-11 ft. lbs.

6. Position the rear stop as far downward as it will go, and tighten the two attaching screws to 6-11 ft. lbs.

7. Tilt the glass top in or out until it will seal effectively at the top and front. Then hold its position while tightening the front and

rear guide attaching screws to 6-11 ft. lbs.

8. Move the lower portion of the glass to obtain a good seal at the front in the belt area. Tighten the front guide upper screw to 6-11 ft. lbs.

9. Operate the glass and check for binding. If the glass binds, lower it all the way. Then loosen the front run lower attaching screw, allow the run to move to its most natural position, and retorque the screw.

10. Raise the glass to within about 1½ in. of the full up position.

11. Push the inside stabilizer outward until it rests snugly against the inside of the glass. Then tighten the attaching screw for the stabilizer to 6-11 ft. lbs.

12. Reinstall the inner door panel.

## 1971 Ford, Mercury 4 Door Sedan and Wagon

1. Loosen the rear run retainer screws.

2. Lower the glass until its top edge is about 4 in. above the belt line.

3. Torque the rear run retaining screws to 6-11 ft. lbs.

## 1971 Lincoln Continental

1. Remove the inner door panel and watershield.

2. Loosen the adjusting nut and all the adjusting screws.

3. Raise the glass all the way.

4. Swivel the glass forward or rearward as necessary to ensure good sealing. Then tighten the rear guide swivel retaining nut to 6-11 ft. lbs.

5. Move the front upper stop downward as far as it will go and tighten the attaching screws to 6-11 ft. lbs.

6. Repeat step 5 for the rear stop.

7. Tilt the top of the glass in or out as required to obtain a good seal with the roof rail weatherstrip.

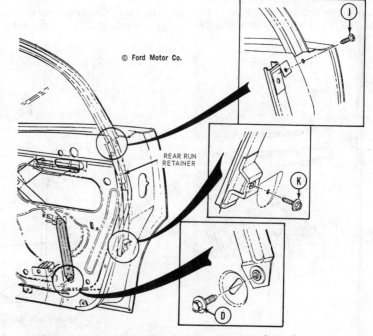

*1971 Torino & Montego Four Door Rear Door Window Adjustments*

## Ford Motor Company

Then tighten the lower attaching screws for the front run and rear guide.

8. Loosen the upper attaching screw on the front run. Move the lower portion of the glass in or out as required to provide a tight seal at the front belt.
9. Tighten the front run upper attaching screw to 6-11 ft. lbs.
10. Push the inside stabilizer out against the lower side of the glass. Tighten the attaching screw to 6-11 ft. lbs.
11. Operate the glass to check for binding.
12. If binding occurs, lower the glass, loosen the lower rear guide attaching screw, allow the guide to come to its most natural position, and retorque the screw.
13. Replace the watershield and door trim panel.

### 1971 Thunderbird

In-out tilt and upper stop adjustments can be made without removing the inner door panel. Make these adjustments and, if they do not cure the problem, proceed with the complete adjustment.

#### Upper Front Stop

1. Raise the glass all the way.
2. Loosen the two stop attaching screws which can be reached from the front of the door.
3. Move the stop downward until it firmly contacts the glass channel and tighten the two screws while firmly holding it in place.

#### In-Out Tilt

1. Loosen the lower attaching screws for the front run, located under the door, and for the rear run, located at the rear of the door.
2. Tilt the glass in or out as required for it to seal efficiently at the top and front.
3. Tighten the attaching screws.

#### Complete Adjustment

1. Remove the door panel and watershield.
2. Loosen all adjusting nuts and screws.
3. Raise the glass all the way.
4. Tilt the glass to the front or rear as necessary to ensure a good seal with the center pillar.
5. Hold the glass in position and tighten the regulator-to-glass channel pivot nut.
6. Move the front run in and out via the upper run adjusting screws until the glass seals effec-

tively with the belt outside weatherstrip.
7. Tighten the front run upper attaching screws to 6-11 ft. lbs.
8. Move the upper front stop down as far as it will go and tighten the attaching screws to 6-11 ft. lbs.
9. Torque the front run lower attaching screws to 6-11 ft. lbs.
10. Torque the rear run upper retaining nut to 3-7 ft. lbs.
11. Lower the glass and then tighten the rear run lower attaching screw to 6-11 ft. lbs.
12. Finally, reinstall the door panel and watershield.

### 1971 Torino and Montego Four Door Sedan

1. Remove the door panel and watershield.
2. Loosen all rear run retainer attaching screws and the equalizer arm attaching screw.
3. Lower the window until the top of the glass is about 4 in. above the belt line. Tighten the rear run retaining screws to 3-7 ft. lbs.
4. Raise the window all the way.
5. Tilt the glass forward and rearward until it seals tightly at the top and front. Then tighten the equalizer arm attaching screw to 6-11 ft. lbs.
6. Reinstall the door panel and watershield.

### 1971 Torino and Montego Station Wagons

1. Remove the door panel and watershield.
2. Loosen the screws that hold the rear run lower bracket and front run retaining bracket in place.
3. Lower the window until the top edge of the glass is about 4 in. above the belt line.
4. Torque the rear run attaching screws to 3-7 ft. lbs., and the front run lower attaching screw to 6-11 ft. lbs.
5. Reinstall the door panel and watershield.

### 1971 Torino, Montego Hardtops

1. Remove the door panel and watershield.
2. Loosen all adjusting screws and nuts.
3. Raise the glass all the way and then tilt it forward or rearward until it seals effectively with the front door glass.
4. Tighten the equalizer arm at-

taching screw and the rear guide upper attaching screws to 6-11 ft. lbs.
5. Position both upper stops downward as far as they will go and torque their attaching screws to 6-11 ft. lbs.
6. Move the top of the glass in or out until it fits flush with the front door glass and seals at the top.
7. Torque the front and rear guide lower attaching screws to 6-11 ft. lbs.
8. Install the watershield and inner door panel.

## QUARTER WINDOWS

### 1971 Mustang and Cougar Hardtop and Convertible

1. Remove the trim panel and watershield.
2. Loosen all adjusting bolts and the adjusting screw locknut. Raise the glass all the way.
3. Adjust the window forward and backward and tilt it as required for alignment with the front door window and equal height. Adjust the tilt with the adjusting screw. Then tighten the tilt adjusting screw locknut, and the upper and lower guide bracket bolts to 6-11 ft. lbs., leaving the lower guide bracket mounting bolt loose.
4. Slide the lower guide bracket in or out to ensure proper alignment of the glass with the roof rail. Tighten the mounting bolt.
5. Slide both upper stops downward as far as they will go and

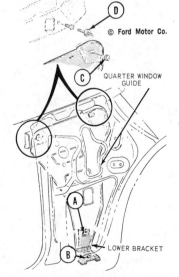

© Ford Motor Co.

QUARTER WINDOW GUIDE

LOWER BRACKET

*1971 Mustang Sportsroof Quarter Window Adjustments*

# Ford Motor Company

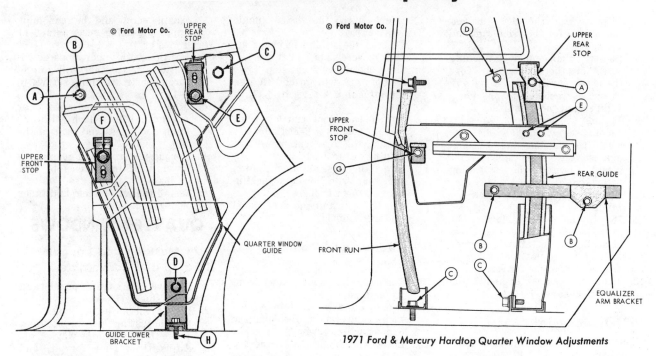

1971 Mustang & Cougar Hardtop Quarter Window Adjustments

1971 Ford & Mercury Hardtop Quarter Window Adjustments

tighten the mounting bolts to 6-11 ft. lbs.

6. Install the watershield and trim panel.

### 1971 Mustang Two Door With Sportsroof

1. Remove the trim panel and watershield.

2. Loosen the two guide-adjusting screws and the adjusting nut.

3. Adjust the in-out tilt with the adjusting screw until the window aligns with the roof rail weatherstrip. Move the glass up and down and forward and rearward to ensure a good seal with the door glass. Tighten the adjusting screws and the adjusting nut.

4. Install the watershield and trim panel.

### 1971 Torino, Montego, Thunderbird

*NOTE: On Montego and Torino, in-out tilt and belt line in-out adjustments may be made without removing the trim panel.*

1. Remove the trim panel.

2. Loosen the lower guide plate retaining bolt.

3. Tilt the top of the glass in or out until it seals with the weatherstrip at the top. Retighten the bolt.

4. Loosen the two set screws at the inside belt line on Torinos and Montegos, and the locknut at the upper front corner of the

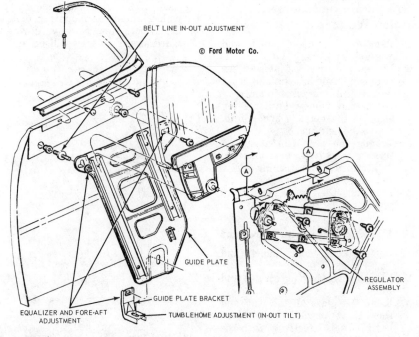

1971 Thunderbird Quarter Window Mechanism

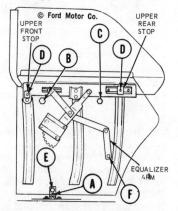

1971 Torino & Montego Quarter Window Adjustments

# Ford Motor Company

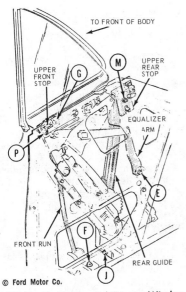

© Ford Motor Co.

*1971 Lincoln Continental Quarter Window Adjustments*

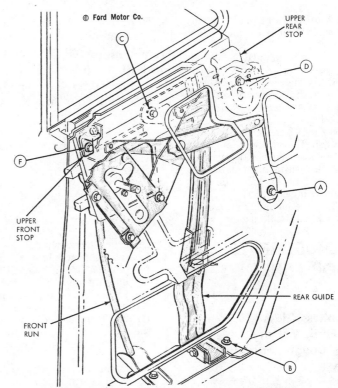

© Ford Motor Co.

*1971 Ford Convertible Quarter Window Adjustments*

guide plate on Thunderbirds. Move the glass in or out until it is flush with the door glass. On Thunderbirds, this involves turning the adjusting screw. Then tighten the screws or adjusting screw locknut.

5. Loosen the upper stop attaching bolts. Move the glass until the window is raised just enough to ensure proper sealing. Then tighten the stop attaching bolts.

6. On Montegos and Torinos, loosen the bolt which attaches the equalizer arm to the inner panel. On Thunderbirds, loosen the bolt at the upper rear corner of the guide plate and the bolt which attaches the guide plate to the lower guide plate bracket. Move the glass until the top is parallel with the roof rail weatherstrip. Tighten the adjusting bolt on Montegos and Torinos.

7. On Montegos and Torinos, loosen the upper and lower guide plate attaching bolts. Move the glass fore and aft to ensure a good seal without binding of the door window. Then, tighten all adjusting bolts.

8. Reinstall the trim panel.

## 1971
## Two Door Hardtop

1. Remove the trim panel and the watershield. Loosen the upper front stop retaining nut and the five adjusting screws.

2. Raise the glass until the top edge is flush with the door glass,

and it seals effectively with the roof rail weatherstrip. Then move the glass forward and backward and in and out until it is aligned with the door glass. Torque the four run-adjusting screws to 6-11 ft. lbs.

3. Push the upper rear stop as far upward as it will go and tighten the attaching screw. Push the upper front stop downward as far as it will go and tighten its attaching nut. Both must be torqued to 6-11 ft. lbs.

4. Install the watershield and trim panel.

## 1971 Ford Convertible

1. Remove the trim panel and watershield.

2. Loosen the five adjusting screws. Position the glass vertically so it seals with the folding top and it is flush with the door glass.

3. Then move the glass front and back and in and out until it aligns with the door glass. Tighten all but the stop attaching screws to 6-11 ft. lbs.

4. Push both stops upward all the way and tighten the attaching screws to 6-11 ft. lb.

5. Install the watershield and trim panel.

## 1971 Lincoln Continental

1. Remove the trim panel and watershield.

2. Loosen all seven adjusting screws and nuts.

3. Raise the glass until the top is flush with the door glass and will seal with the roof rail weatherstrip. Move it forward or backward and in and out until it is aligned with the door glass. Tighten the four run-attaching screws to 6-11 ft. lbs.

4. Position the upper front stop upward all the way and tighten the retaining nut to 6-11 ft. lbs. Position the upper rear stop downward all the way and tighten its attaching screw to 6-11 ft. lbs.

5. Tighten the equalizer attaching screw to 6-11 ft. lbs.

6. Install the watershield and trim panel.

## 1971 Mark III

1. Remove the rear seat cushion and seat back and the quarter trim panel.

2. Close the window all the way.

3. Loosen the screw and washer assemblies labeled (X) in view (B). Move the window frontward or backward until there is

# Ford Motor Company

a 5/32 to 3/16 in. parallel gap between the quarter and door windows.

4. Loosen the two nuts labeled (Y). Move the window up and down until it fits the roof rail weatherstrip and the gap between the quarter glass and door window is parallel.

5. Adjust the two set screws labeled (Z) until the window fits the roof rail and belt weatherstrips. When the adjustment is complete, tighten the locknuts and the screws labeled (X).

6. Install the quarter trim panel, seat back, and seat cushion.

# ADJUSTMENTS DOOR WINDOWS

## IN-OUT TILT

### Front Ventless Glass—1970 Lincoln, Ford, Mercury, Mustang, Cougar, Fairlane, Montego

### Rear Door Glass—1970 Thunderbird, Fairlane and Montego Hardtop

This adjustment may be performed with the door panel in place.

1. Loosen the front and rear run bottom attaching screws, accessible from the underside of the door.

2. Put the glass all the way up. Then move the top of the glass in or out until it seals tightly with the roof rail weatherstrip.

3. Retighten the lower run attaching screws.

### Front Ventless Glass—1970 Mark III, Thunderbird
### Rear Door Glass—Lincoln, Ford and Mercury Four Door Hardtops

1. Loosen the front and rear run lower attaching screws. These are accessible from the underside or the rear of the door. The inner door panel need not be removed.

2. Move the glass inboard or outboard as necessary until it seals effectively with the roof rail weatherstrip and the windshield pillar or quarter window.

3. Operate the window to check for binding. If the window does not operate smoothly, lower the glass. Loosen the front run lower retainer attaching screw on Mark III and Thunderbird models and the rear run lower retaining screw on Lincoln, Ford, and Mercury models.

4. Allow the loose run to come to its most natural position and then retorque the screw.

## UPPER STOP

### Front Ventless Glass—1970 Lincoln, Ford, Mercury, Mustang, Cougar, Fairlane, Montego

A partial adjustment may be made without removing the inner door panel. If this does not produce satisfactory results, perform the complete adjustment.

**Partial Adjustment**

1. Loosen the two bolts which hold the upper rear stop to the rear of the door. Lower the window all the way.

2. Using a 7/16 in. socket on an extension, loosen the top bolt on the upper front stop. The window travel may then be adjusted by moving the stop up and down on its bracket. Slide the stop up and down to restrict the travel of the window and slide it up to allow it to lift further for a tighter seal.

3. Retorque the mounting bolt.

**Complete Adjustment**

1. Loosen the two bolts which retain each of the stops (front and rear).

2. Alternately adjust the stops and operate the window until the adjustment is correct, lowering the position of the stop to further restrict window travel and raising it to allow the window to lift farther.

3. When the adjustment is correct, retorque the retaining bolts.

### Upper Front Stop—1970 Thunderbird and Mark III—Front

1. Lower the glass all the way. Insert a 7/16 in. socket into the opening between the door panels, and loosen the upper stop attaching screw.

2. Slide the stop toward the rear of the door to allow the window to rise farther, or toward the front of the door to further restrict its travel.

3. Test operation of the window to ensure correct operation. Ensure that the upper stop attaching screw is properly tightened.

### Upper Rear Stop—Front—1970 Thunderbird and Mark III Front and Rear Stop Adjustments—Rear—1970 Lincoln, Ford, Mercury, Thunderbird

1. Loosen the two upper stop attaching screws on both front and rear stops. Raise the window all the way.

2. Move the stop down tight against the glass channel or stop, and tighten the mounting screws.

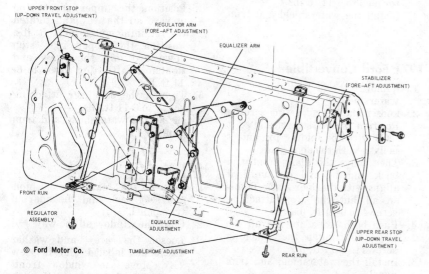

UPPER FRONT STOP (UP–DOWN TRAVEL ADJUSTMENT)

REGULATOR ARM (FORE–AFT ADJUSTMENT)

EQUALIZER ARM

STABILIZER (FORE–AFT ADJUSTMENT)

FRONT RUN

REGULATOR ASSEMBLY

EQUALIZER ADJUSTMENT

© Ford Motor Co.

TUMBLEHOME ADJUSTMENT

REAR RUN

UPPER REAR STOP (UP–DOWN TRAVEL ADJUSTMENT)

*1970 Ford & Mercury with Ventless Glass Front Door Window Mechanism*

# Ford Motor Company

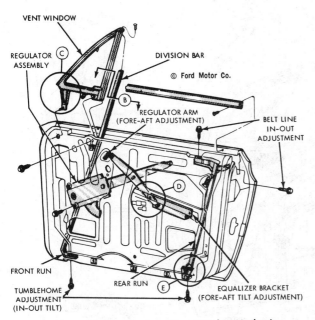

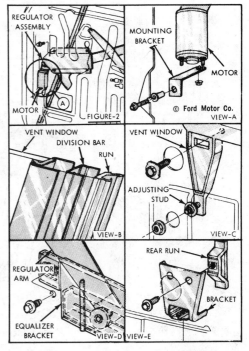

1970 Fairlane & Montego Front Door Window Mechanism

## FORE AND AFT ADJUSTMENT

**Front Door Ventless—1970
Thunderbird and Mark III
Front Door—Ford, Mercury
Four Door Sedan and Wagon
Rear Door—Lincoln, Ford,
Mercury, Thunderbird**

1. Remove the door panel.
2. Raise the window all the way.
3. Loosen the regulator arm retaining nut.
4. Move the glass fore and aft until a good seal is secured.
5. Retighten the nut and replace the door panel.

**Front Door Ventless—1970
Lincoln, Ford, Mercury,
Mustang, Cougar, Fairlane,
Montego**

1. Loosen the regulator front arm retaining nut. Raise the window all the way.
2. On two door models, move the glass fore and aft until a good seal is secured and then tighten the nut.
3. On four door models, loosen the front arm retaining bolt and the stabilizer attaching bolt.
4. Then move the window back and forth until it seals properly and put the front stabilizer fork into a position that causes it to just touch the rear stop ledge. Tighten all nuts and bolts.

## BELT LINE IN-OUT ADJUSTMENT

**Front Ventless Glass—1970
Lincoln, Ford, Mercury,
Mustang, Cougar, Fairlane,
Montego
Rear Door Glass—1970 Lincoln,
Ford, Mercury**

1. On front door glass, loosen the two screws on the bracket at the top of the rear run. On rear doors, loosen the screw at the top of the front run.

2. Move the glass in or out until front and rear glass are flush. Retighten the mounts.

## EQUALIZER ADJUSTMENT

**Front Ventless—1970 Lincoln,
Ford, Mercury, Mustang,
Cougar, Fairlane, Montego,
Thunderbird, Mark III
Rear Door—1970 Lincoln, Ford,
Mercury Four Door Hardtop,
Thunderbird**

1. Put the window all the way up.

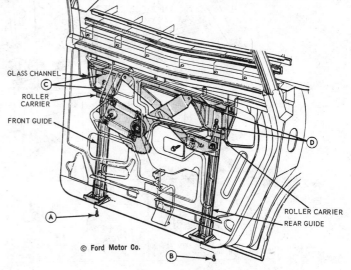

1970 Fairlane & Montego Rear Window Adjustments

# Ford Motor Company

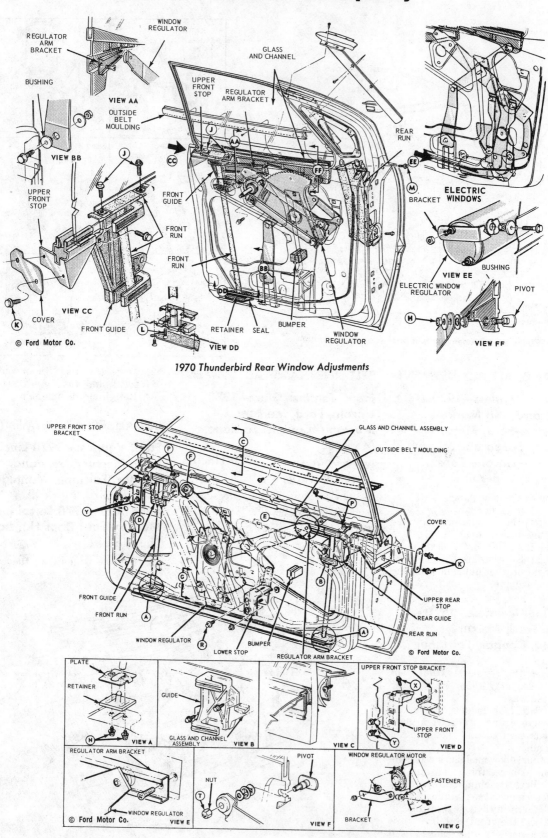

REGULATOR ARM BRACKET

WINDOW REGULATOR

GLASS AND CHANNEL

BUSHING

VIEW AA

OUTSIDE BELT MOULDING

UPPER FRONT STOP

REGULATOR ARM BRACKET

REAR RUN

VIEW BB

UPPER FRONT STOP

FRONT GUIDE

FRONT RUN

FRONT RUN

VIEW CC

COVER

FRONT GUIDE

RETAINER

SEAL

BUMPER

WINDOW REGULATOR

ELECTRIC WINDOWS

BRACKET

VIEW EE

BUSHING

ELECTRIC WINDOW REGULATOR

PIVOT

VIEW FF

VIEW DD

© Ford Motor Co.

*1970 Thunderbird Rear Window Adjustments*

UPPER FRONT STOP BRACKET

GLASS AND CHANNEL ASSEMBLY

OUTSIDE BELT MOULDING

COVER

FRONT GUIDE

FRONT RUN

UPPER REAR STOP

REAR GUIDE

REAR RUN

WINDOW REGULATOR

LOWER STOP

BUMPER

REGULATOR ARM BRACKET

© Ford Motor Co.

PLATE

RETAINER

VIEW A

GUIDE

GLASS AND CHANNEL ASSEMBLY

VIEW B

VIEW C

UPPER FRONT STOP BRACKET

UPPER FRONT STOP

VIEW D

REGULATOR ARM BRACKET

WINDOW REGULATOR

VIEW E

NUT

PIVOT

VIEW F

WINDOW REGULATOR MOTOR

FASTENER

BRACKET

VIEW G

© Ford Motor Co.

*1970 Fairlane & Montego Rear Window Adjustments*

# Ford Motor Company

Loosen the equalizer retaining nut or bolt (on Fairlane and Montego hardtops, loosen the two screws at either end of the equalizer arm bracket).

2. Move the equalizer up or down as necessary to tilt the window fore and aft for a good fit with the roof rail weatherstripping.

3. Retighten the equalizer fastener(s).

## Front Door Glass—1970 Falcon, Fairlane, Montego Four Door Sedan and Station Wagon

1. Remove the trim panel and watershield. Loosen the rear run lower attaching nut.

2. Lower the glass until the top edge is 4 in. above the belt line.

3. Adjust the screw at the bottom of the rear run until the rear run is in alignment with the front run. Tighten the nut to 8-23 ft. lbs.

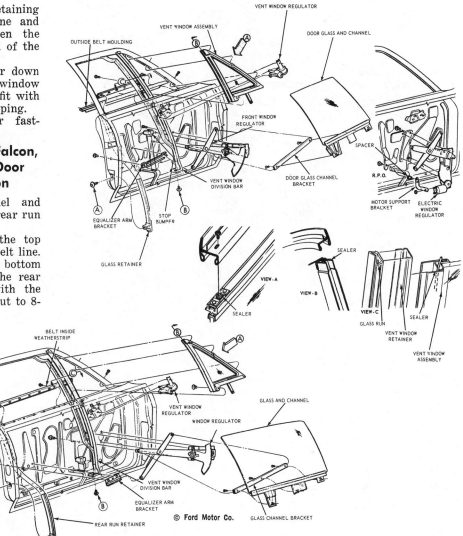

*1970 Ford & Mercury Front Door Window Mechanism*

4. Loosen the two lower stop attaching screws. Lower or raise the glass until it is just at the level of the belt line. Then position the lower stop tightly against the glass channel. Retighten the attaching screws.

## Front Door Glass—1970 Falcon Two Door Sedan

1. Remove the door panel and pull back the watershield.

2. Loosen the nut that retains the front run and the screw which retains the rear run.

3. Lower the glass until the top edge is about 4 in. above the belt line. Turn the screw at the bottom of the front run until the

window aligns with the vent window division bar and door window frame for smooth operation. Then tighten the run retaining screws.

4. Lower the window until it is just flush with the belt line. Then raise the lower stop as far as it will go and tighten the mounting screws.

5. Reinstall the inner door panel and watershield.

## Front Door Glass—1970 Ford, Mercury

1. Loosen the front and rear run retaining screws.

2. Lower the window until the top of the glass is about 4 in. above the belt line. This will allow the runs to come to their most nat-

ural position and ensure proper alignment with the window division bar and door window frame.

3. Tighten the run retaining screws.

## COMPLETE ADJUSTMENT
## Rear Door Glass—1970 Falcon

1. Remove the trim panel and watershield.

2. Loosen the nut which attaches the rear run retainer to the door.

3. Lower the window all the way and then rotate the adjusting screw as necessary to ensure alignment between the lower run and the door window frame. Then tighten the attaching nut.

4. Replace the trim panel and watershield.

# Ford Motor Company

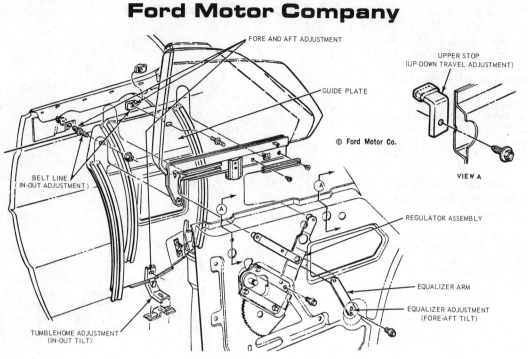

*1969 Fairlane & Montego Quarter Window Mechanism*

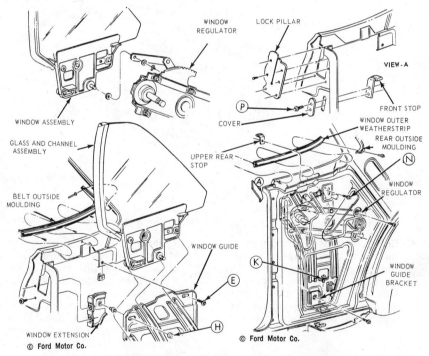

*1970 Mustang & Cougar Quarter Window Mechanism*

## Rear Door Glass—1970 Ford, Mercury

1. Loosen the two screws which retain the lower rear run and then lower the glass until it is about 4 in. above the belt line.
2. Tighten the two retaining screws.

## Rear Door Glass—1970 Fairlane and Montego Wagon

1. Remove the trim panel and watershield.
2. Loosen the screws which retain front and rear run retainers.
3. Raise the window all the way.
4. Tighten the screws and replace the trim panel and watershield.

# ADJUSTMENTS QUARTER WINDOW

## 1970 Fairlane and Montego

*NOTE: In-out tilt, belt line in-out tilt, and the upper front stop adjustments can be made without removing the trim panel.*

1. Loosen the lower guide plate retaining bolt. Tilt the glass in or out as necessary to ensure a good seal at the roof rail. Tighten the retaining bolt.
2. Loosen the set screws at the inside belt line. Move the glass in or out as required to ensure proper alignment and a tight seal with the front door glass.
3. Loosen the upper front stop attaching bolt. Raise the glass just until it seals properly. Tighten the retaining bolt.
4. Remove the trim panel. Loosen the equalizer-to-inner panel attaching bolt.
5. Tilt the glass to that its top is parallel with the roof side rail. Tighten the bolt.
6. Loosen the upper rear stop attaching bolt. Raise the glass until it seals properly at the top. Retighten the attaching bolt.
7. Loosen the lower guide plate attaching bolt and the two upper guide plate attaching bolts. Move the glass forward or backward as necessary to ensure a good seal and tighten the three bolts.

# Ford Motor Company

## 1970 Mustang and Cougar

NOTE: *The upper front stop may be adjusted without removing the trim panel.*

1. Loosen the two screws which retain the upper front stop. Raise the glass just until a proper seal is ensured. Tighten the top mounting screws.
2. Remove the quarter trim panel. Loosen the guide bracket-to-body screw.
3. Tilt the glass in or out until it seals against the roof rail weatherstrip. Tighten the guide bracket-to body screw.
4. Loosen the two screws which hold the top of the guide plate in place.
5. Move the lower portion of the window in or out until it is flush with the door window. Move it forward or rearward to ensure a good seal with the front door window. Tighten the screws.
6. Loosen the screw located at the lower guide plate bracket. Loosen the two screws located at the top of the guide plate. Tilt the glass to the front or rear until it is parallel with the roof rail. Tighten the screws.
7. Loosen the retaining bolts for both the upper front and upper rear stops. Raise the glass all the way. Then retighten the bolts.

## 1970 Ford Two Door Sedan

1. Remove the trim panel and watershield.
2. Lower the window all the way. Loosen the screw which fastens the lower run retainer in place.
3. Move the run retainer over against the window. Tighten the screw finger tight.
4. Raise the window all the way. Loosen the upper run retaining screw. Move the upper part of the run retainer against the window glass. Tighten the upper and lower retaining screws.
5. Lower the window until the top is flush with the belt line. Loosen the lower stop retaining screw, raise the stop until it contacts the lower edge of the window channel and tighten the screw.
6. Install the watershield and trim panel.

## 1970 Two Door Hardtop

1. Remove the trim panel and watershield.
2. Loosen the five adjusting bolts.

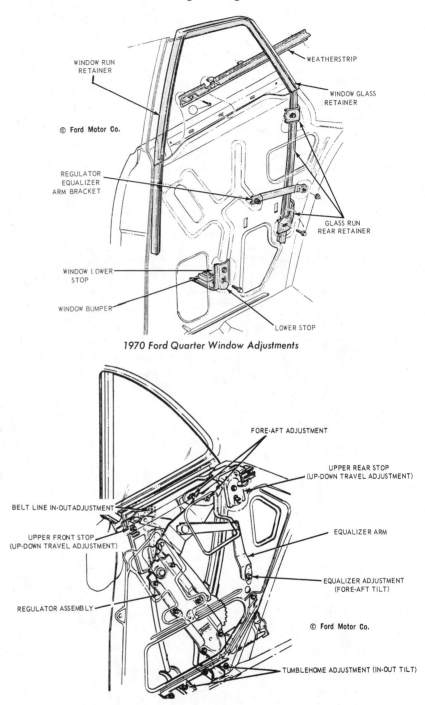

*1970 Ford Quarter Window Adjustments*

*1969 Ford, Mercury & Lincoln Continental Quarter Window Adjustments*

3. Raise the glass to a position that will permit good sealing with the roof rail. Slide it back and forth until it seals effectively with the front door glass. Then tighten the lower run mounting bracket screws and the upper rear run mounting screws.
4. Lower the window all the way and tighten the other adjusting screws.
5. Install the watershield and trim panel.

## 1970 Lincoln Ford and Mercury Two Door Hardtop and Convertible

NOTE: *In-out tilt, belt line in-out tilt, and upper front stop adjustments*

## Ford Motor Company

can be made without removing the door trim panel.

1. Using a 24 in. extension and socket wrench, loosen the front run lower retaining bolt. Move the run in and out until the window seals effectively with the roof rail weatherstrip. Tighten the run retaining bolt.

2. Loosen the front run at the top. Move the glass in or out until it is flush with the door glass. Tighten the retaining bolt.

3. Loosen the retaining bolt for the upper front stop. Adjust the position of the stop until the window will just reach a fully closed position. Tighten the retaining bolt.

4. Remove the door trim panel. If additional in-out tilt adjustment is required, loosen the rear run lower retaining bolt, tilt the run in or out as required, and retighten the bolt.

5. Loosen the equalizer attaching

bolt. Tilt the glass forward or backward until the top is parallel with the roof rail. Tighten the bolt.

6. Loosen the upper front and rear stop attaching bolts. Raise the window until it seals properly at the top. Tighten the retaining bolts.

7. Loosen the two regulator arm-to-glass channel retaining nuts. Move the glass forward or rearward until it seals effectively

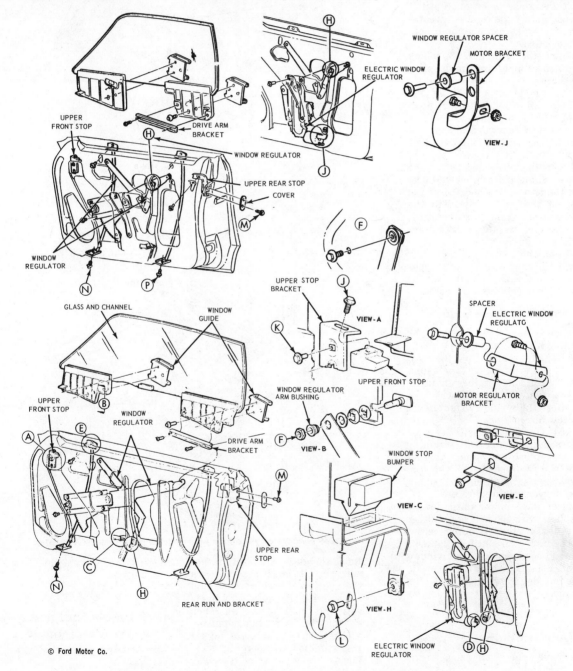

© Ford Motor Co.

*1969 Ford & Mercury with Ventless Glass, Front Door Window Mechanism*

# Ford Motor Company

with the door glass without causing the door glass to bind. Tighten the retaining nuts.

### 1970 Mark III, Thunderbird

See appropriate section of 1971 procedures.

# ADJUSTMENTS DOOR WINDOWS

## UPPER FRONT STOP
**Front Ventless—1969 Ford, Mercury, Mustang, Cougar, Fairlane, Montego, Thunderbird, Mark III**

1. Lower the glass all the way.
2. Using a 7/16 in. socket on an extension, loosen the upper front stop attaching screw. Access to the screw is through the slot between inner and outer door panels.
3. Adjust the stop to provide for proper window travel. Move the stop rearward to allow the window to rise farther, forward to further limit its travel.
4. Tighten the stop lightly and operate the window to test the adjustment. Repeat as necessary.

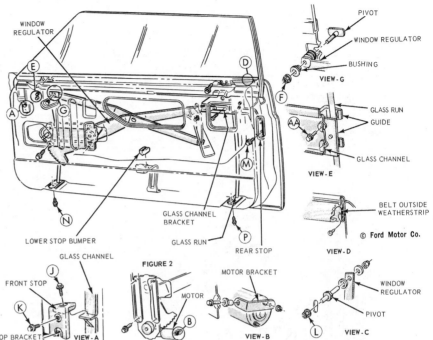

*1969 Mustang & Cougar with Ventless Glass, Front Door Window Mechanism*

5. When the adjustment is correct, tighten the stop screws snugly.

### Rear Door—1969 Ford, Mercury Four Door Sedan

1. Raise the glass all the way.
2. Loosen the stop attaching screws.
3. Push the stop downward as far as it will go, and hold it while tightening the screws.

## UPPER REAR STOP
**Front Ventless—1969 Ford, Mercury, Mustang, Cougar, Fairlane, Montego, Thunderbird, Mark III, Ford, Mercury Four Door Sedans**

1. Raise the window all the way and loosen the two stop attaching screws.

*1969 Fairlane & Montego with Ventless Glass, Front Door Window Mechanism*

# Ford Motor Company

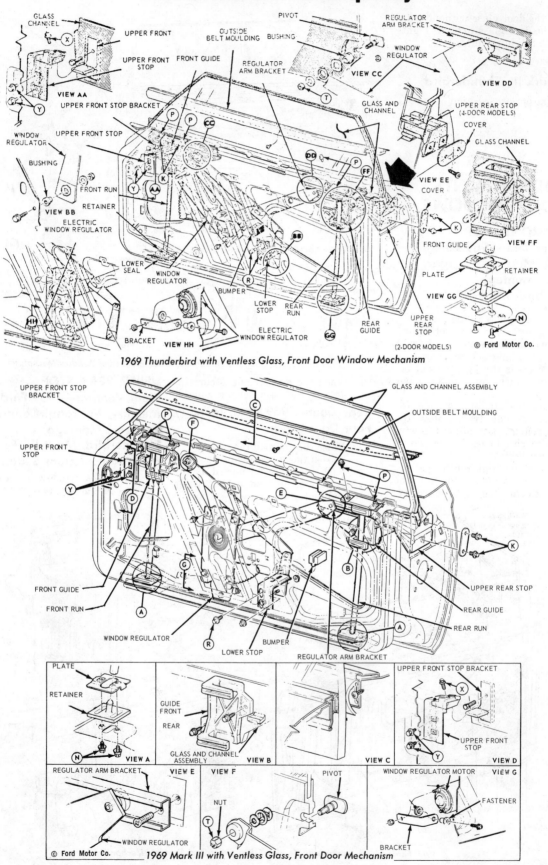

*1969 Thunderbird with Ventless Glass, Front Door Window Mechanism*

*1969 Mark III with Ventless Glass, Front Door Mechanism*

# Ford Motor Company

2. Move the stop downward as far as it will go and hold it while tightening the two attaching screws.

## DOOR GLASS TILT
### Front Ventless—1969 Ford, Mercury, Mustang, Cougar, Fairlane, Montego, Thunderbird, Mark III

1. Loosen all run retainer attaching screws.
2. Tilt the top of the glass in or out as necessary to ensure a good seal at the roof rail weatherstrip and the quarter window.
3. Tighten all run retainer attaching screws.
4. Run the glass up and down to check for binding. Binding may be corrected by putting the glass all the way up and loosening the front run retainer attaching screw. Allow the front run to come to its most natural position and then retorque the attaching screw.

## COMPLETE ADJUSTMENT
### Front Ventless—1969 Ford, Mercury, Mustang, Cougar, Fairlane, Montego,

1. Remove the trim panel and watershield. Loosen all adjusting nuts and screws. Raise the glass all the way.
2. Move the glass forward or to-

ward the rear of the car until it aligns with the body opening. Then tighten the equalizer arm attaching nuts.
3. Position both front and rear stops down as far as they will go and hold them while tightenthe attaching screws.
4. Tilt the glass in or out until it will seal effectively with the roof rail weatherstrip and quarter window. Then tighten the front and rear run mounting screws.
5. Raise and lower the glass to test it for binding. If binding is found, lower the glass, loosen the front run lower attaching screw, allow the run to come to its most natural position, and retorque the screw.
6. Reinstall the watershield and trim panel.

### Front Ventless—1969 Ford, Thunderbird, Mark III

1. Remove the trim panel and watershield, and guide retainer seals.
2. Loosen the adjusting nut and all adjusting screws.
3. Raise the window. Then move the glass forward or rearward until it aligns with the body. Tighten the adjusting nut.
4. Move the glass in or out until it seals with the outside door belt weatherstripping. Then tighten the four upper arm attaching screws.

5. Position the upper front and rear stops down as far as they will go. Make sure that the rear stop anti-rattle unit contacts the glass and channel assembly. Tighten all stop mounting screws.
6. Tilt the top of the window in or out until it seals with the roof rail and quarter window. Then tighten the rear run lower mounting screws.
7. Position the window so the top of the glass is just flush with the belt line. Move the lower stop and bumper downward until it rests firmly against the bottom of the glass and hold it while tightening the two mounting screws.
8. Operate the window to check it for binding. If it binds, lower it, loosen the front run lower attaching screws, allow the run to come to its most natural position, and retorque the screws.
9. Replace the guide retainer seals, the watershield, and the trim panel.

### Front Door Window—1969 Falcon, Fairlane and Montego

1. Remove the inner door panel and watershield.
2. Loosen the front run lower attaching nut and the rear run lower attaching screw. Lower the window until it is about 4 in. above the belt line.
3. Turn the front run lower adjust-

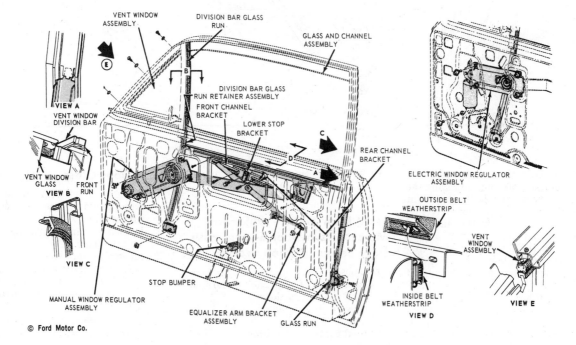

© Ford Motor Co.

*1969 Falcon Front Door Window Mechanism*

# Ford Motor Company

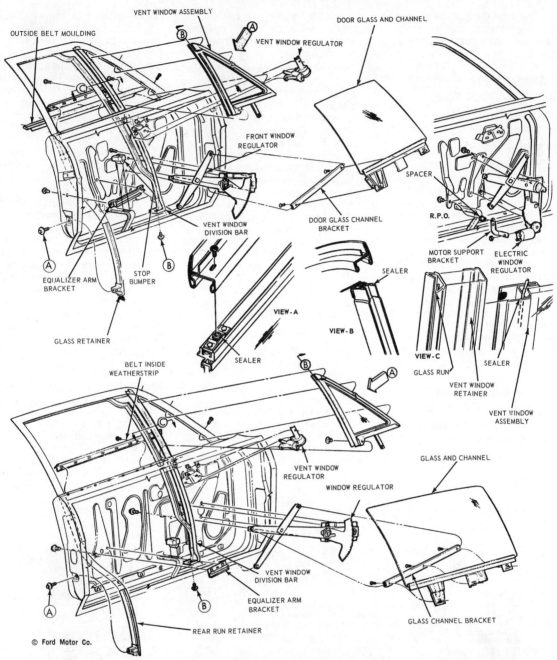

OUTSIDE BELT MOULDING

VENT WINDOW ASSEMBLY

VENT WINDOW REGULATOR

DOOR GLASS AND CHANNEL

FRONT WINDOW REGULATOR

SPACER

R.P.O.

MOTOR SUPPORT BRACKET

ELECTRIC WINDOW REGULATOR

VENT WINDOW DIVISION BAR

DOOR GLASS CHANNEL BRACKET

EQUALIZER ARM BRACKET

STOP BUMPER

GLASS RETAINER

VIEW - A

SEALER

VIEW - B

SEALER

VIEW - C

GLASS RUN

SEALER

VENT WINDOW RETAINER

VENT WINDOW ASSEMBLY

BELT INSIDE WEATHERSTRIP

VENT WINDOW REGULATOR

WINDOW REGULATOR

GLASS AND CHANNEL

VENT WINDOW DIVISION BAR

EQUALIZER ARM BRACKET

REAR RUN RETAINER

GLASS CHANNEL BRACKET

© Ford Motor Co.

*1969 Ford & Mercury Front Door Window Adjustments*

ing screw in or out until the front and rear runs align and the lower front run is in alignment with the vent window division bar. Then tighten the nuts and screw to 8-23 ft. lbs.

4. Loosen the lower stop attaching screws and lower the window until it is just flush with the belt line.

5. Move the stop upward until it rests snugly against the glass channel and tighten the mount-screws to 8-23 ft. lbs.

6. Reinstall the inner door panel and watershield.

## Front Door Glass—1969 Ford, Mercury Two Door Sedan, Four Door Sedan, Station Wagon

1. Loosen the screws which are accessible from the underside and rear of the door.

2. Lower the window until it is about 4 in. above the belt line, and retorque the screws.

## Front Door Glass—1969 Lincoln

1. Remove the trim panel and watershield. Raise the window all the way.

2. Loosen all nine adjusting screws and the locknut.

3. Move the glass outward until it is in alignment with the outside door belt molding. Then tighten the two upper run attaching screws.

4. Tilt the glass forward or rear-ward as necessary to ensure that

# Ford Motor Company

the top is parallel with the roof rail weatherstrip. Hold the proper position while tightening the inboard rear guide lower adjusting bracket screw.

5. Adjust the upper front stop so that it contacts the glass channel and tighten the mounting screw.

6. Position the vent window frame so that it is parallel to the front pillar and seals tightly against the door window. Then tighten the two vent window frame screws and the front run lower attaching screw.

7. Tilt the vent window frame in or out, using the adjusting screw, until it seals effectively at the front. Then tighten the locknut and the front and rear run lower attaching screws.

8. Lower the window until the top of the glass is just at the level of the outside belt moulding. Position the window stop lower bracket against the stop bumper and tighten the mounting screw.

## Rear Door Glass—1969 Falcon

1. Remove the trim panel and watershield. Lower the window all the way.

2. Loosen the locknut at the lower rear of the door and adjust the screw in or out until the rear run and the division bar are aligned.

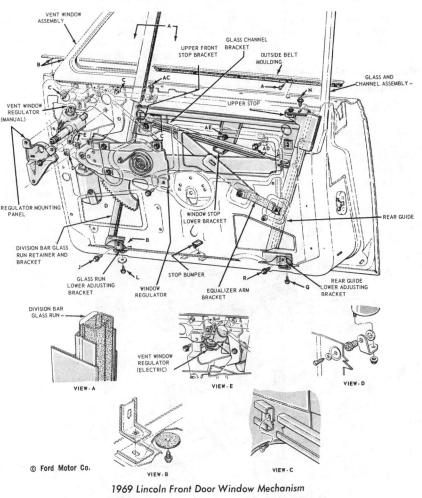

© Ford Motor Co.

*1969 Lincoln Front Door Window Mechanism*

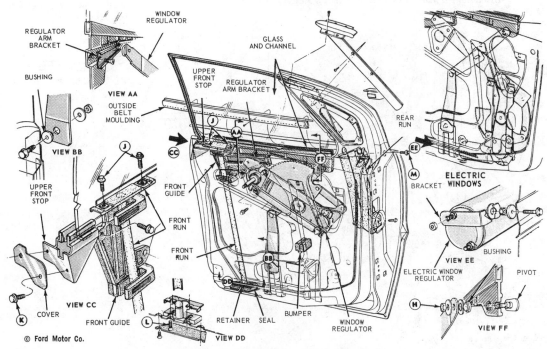

© Ford Motor Co.

*1969 Thunderbird Rear Door Window Mechanism*

# Ford Motor Company

3. Retorque the locknut and replace the trim panel and watershield.

## Rear Door Glass—1969 Ford, Mercury Four Door Hardtop

NOTE: *If the door glass tilt requires adjustment, the adjustment may be accomplished without removing the door trim panel, using the appropriate portions of the procedures below.*

1. Remove the trim panel and watershield.

2. Loosen all adjusting screws and the adjusting nut. Raise the window all the way.

3. Move the glass forward or backward until it is aligned at the top and front. Then tighten the adjusting nut.

4. Lower the front and rear upper stops until they rest snugly against the glass channel. Hold them while tightening the attaching screws.

5. Tilt the glass in or out until it seals with the roof rail and vent glass and then tighten the front and rear run attaching screws.

6. Operate the glass and, if binding occurs, lower it all the way, loosen the rear run lower attaching screw, and allow the run to come to its most natural position. Then retighten the mounting screw.

7. Replace the watershield and trim panel.

## Rear Door Glass—1969 Thunderbird

NOTE: *The upper front stop, rear run, and in-out tilt can be adjusted without removing the inner door panel.*

1. Remove the trim panel and weathershield. Remove the two rear run attaching screws.

2. Loosen the pivot adjusting nut and the four adjusting screws.

3. Raise the glass all the way. Then tilt the glass forward or backward until it seals effectively with the front door window. Tighten the pivot nut.

4. Move the upper front run in or out until the window is properly positioned in relation to the outside belt weatherstrip. Tighten the upper run attaching screws.

5. Adjust the upper front stop by sliding it down against the glass channel and then tightening the screws.

6. Install the upper rear run attaching screw. Lower the window and then install the lower rear run attaching screw.

7. Install the weathershield and trim panel.

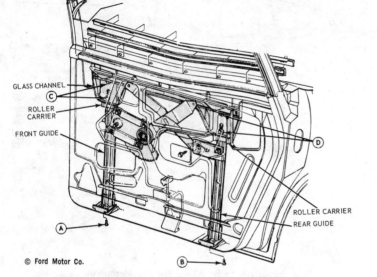

*1969 Fairlane & Montego Rear Door Window Adjustments*

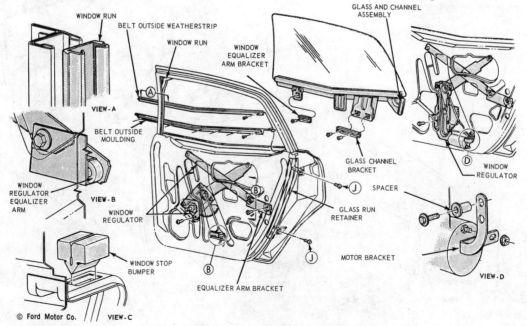

*1969 Ford & Mercury Rear Door Window Mechanism*

# Ford Motor Company

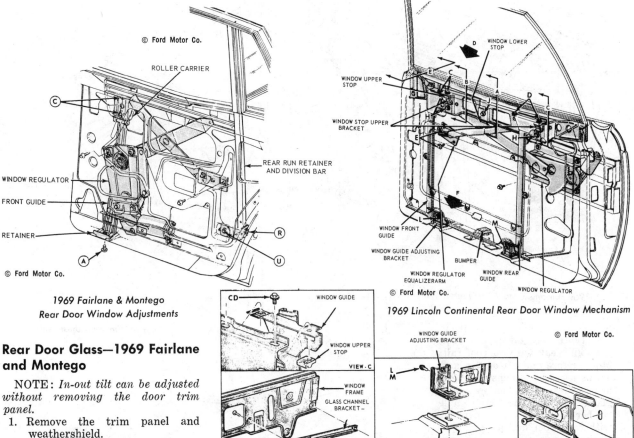

© Ford Motor Co.

ROLLER CARRIER

WINDOW REGULATOR

FRONT GUIDE

RETAINER

© Ford Motor Co.

REAR RUN RETAINER AND DIVISION BAR

*1969 Fairlane & Montego
Rear Door Window Adjustments*

WINDOW LOWER STOP

WINDOW UPPER STOP

WINDOW STOP UPPER BRACKET

WINDOW FRONT GUIDE

WINDOW GUIDE ADJUSTING BRACKET

BUMPER

WINDOW REGULATOR EQUALIZER ARM

WINDOW REAR GUIDE

WINDOW REGULATOR

© Ford Motor Co.

*1969 Lincoln Continental Rear Door Window Mechanism*

WINDOW GUIDE

WINDOW UPPER STOP

VIEW-C

WINDOW FRAME

GLASS CHANNEL BRACKET

VIEW-D

© Ford Motor Co.

WINDOW GUIDE ADJUSTING BRACKET

VIEW-F

MOULDING

VIEW-E

© Ford Motor Co.

## Rear Door Glass—1969 Fairlane and Montego

NOTE: *In-out tilt can be adjusted without removing the door trim panel.*

1. Remove the trim panel and weathershield.
2. Loosen the four adjusting screws. Raise the window all the way.
3. Tighten the upper stop attaching screws.
4. Lower and raise the window. Adjust the guides in or out until the glass aligns properly with the glass run. Then tighten the lower attaching screws.
5. Reinstall the watershield and trim panel.

## Rear Door Glass—1969 Ford, Mercury Four Door Sedan and Wagon

1. Loosen the two adjusting screws at the rear of the door.
2. Lower the glass until it is about 4 in. above the belt line and then tighten the adjusting screws.

## Rear Door Glass—1969 Fairlane and Montego Wagon

1. Remove the trim panel and watershield.
2. Loosen the five adjusting screws.
3. Raise the window all the way. Then tighten the two front run upper attaching screws.
4. Lower and raise the glass and

then tighten the front run lower attaching screw.
5. Lower the window until it is about half way down. Move the rear run retainer and window division bar until they are properly aligned with the door window frame. Then tighten the two lower run attaching screws.
6. Replace the trim panel and watershield.

## Rear Door Window Glass— 1969 Lincoln

1. Remove the trim panel and watershield.
2. Loosen all eight adjusting screws. Raise the window all the way.
3. Move the window until the in-out tilt and forward and rear-ward tilt are properly adjusted. Then tighten the upper and lower front and rear guide attaching screws.
4. Move the front and rear upper stops as far as they will go and tighten the attaching screws.

5. Move the equalizer arm bracket down firmly against the window regulator roller. Tighten the two attaching screws.
6. Move the lower front guide in or out until the front of the window seals effectively with the center pillar and there is a good seal at the top. Then tighten the lower front guide attaching screws.
7. Lower the window until the top of the glass is at the belt line. Move the lower stop until it is against the lower stop bumper and tighten the attaching screw.
8. Tighten the two screws at the rear run lower mounting bracket

# ADJUSTMENTS QUARTER WINDOWS

## 1969 Fairlane and Montego Four Door Hardtop and Convertible

1. Remove the trim panel and watershield. Loosen the seven adjusting screws.

# Ford Motor Company

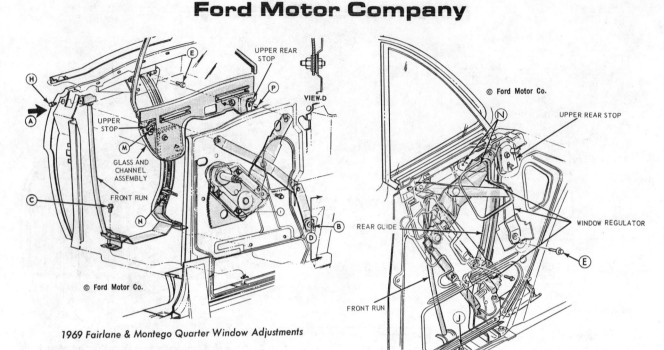

1969 Fairlane & Montego Quarter Window Adjustments

1969 Ford & Mercury Quarter Window Adjustments

2. Raise the window until it is flush with the top of the door glass and seals with the roof rail. Move it fore and aft and in and out as necessary to ensure alignment with the door window glass. Tighten the screw and washer assemblies not involved with the upper and lower stops.
3. Push the upper stops all the way up and tighten their mounting screws.
4. Lower the window just until the top is flush with the belt line. Tighten the lower stop attaching screw. Install the watershield and trim panel.

## 1969 Ford and Mercury Two Door Hardtop and Convertible

1. Remove the trim panel and watershield.
2. Loosen the three adjusting screws. On convertibles, loosen the upper front and rear stop attaching screws also.
3. Raise the glass until it seals effectively with the roof rail weatherstrip. Position the glass forward or rearward until the front edge is parallel with the rear edge of the door glass. Tighten the mechanism adjusting screws.
4. On convertibles, push the front and rear stops upward all the way and tighten the attaching screws.
5. Install the watershield and trim panel.

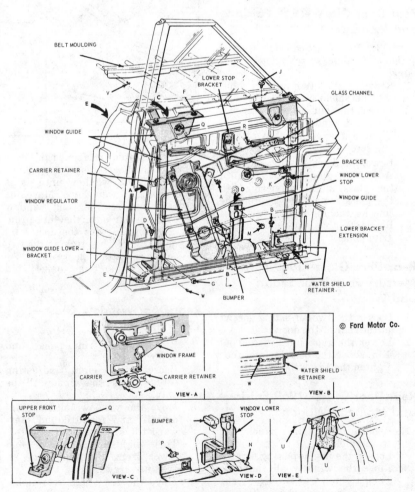

1969 Lincoln Continental Quarter Window Adjustments

# Ford Motor Company

### 1969 Thunderbird, Mark III

1. Remove the seat cushion and the seat back. Remove the trim panel and close the window all the way.
2. Loosen the screws marked (X) in the illustration. Move the window forward or backward as necessary to obtain a 5/32-3/16 in. uniform gap between it and the door window.
3. Loosen the units which are labeled (Y) in the illustration. Move the window vertically as required to obtain a tight seal with the roof rail and maintain a parallel relationship with the front door window.
4. Turn the two screws labeled (Z) until a proper fit with the roof rail and belt weatherstrip is created. Tighten (X) and items (Y).
5. Install the trim panel, seat back, and cushion.

### 1969 Lincoln Continental

1. Remove the trim panel and watershield. Raise the window all the way.
2. Loosen all the adjustment screws shown in the illustration.
3. Position the window so it aligns with the rear edge of the front door window, the rod rail weatherstrip, and the outside belt weatherstrip.
4. Tighten the screws marked (F), (G), and (J) in the illustration.
5. Raise the front and rear stops as far as they will go and tighten their mounting screws.
6. Tilt the front and rear guides in or out until the window glass aligns with the door glass and roof rail weatherstrip. Tighten the front rear run lower attaching screws.
7. Lower the glass until the top is flush with the beltline. Raise the lower stop until it contacts the lower edge of the glass and tighten the mounting bolt. Tighten the screw at point (H).
8. Install the watershield and door trim panel.

### 1969 Mustang, Cougar, Ford Two Door, Ford and Mercury Two Door Hardtop

See appropriate headings under "Adjustment for 1970."

# ADJUSTMENTS DOOR WINDOWS

### 1968 Ford Four Door Sedan, Two Door Sedan and Station Wagon—Front

1. Remove the door panel and watershield.
2. Loosen the front and rear run lower attaching screws and the two equalizer arm bracket attaching screws. Lower the window until the top of the glass is about 4 in. above the belt line and then tighten the four screws.
3. Lower the window until the top of the glass is just flush with the belt line. Loosen the adjustment on the lower stop, raise the stop as far as it will go, and retorque the stop. Test and readjust the stop, if necessary.
4. Replace the inner door panel and watershield.

### 1968 Ford Four Door Hardtop, Two Door Hardtop and Convertible—Front

1. Remove the door panel and the watershield.
2. Loosen all attaching screws and nuts. Raise the window all the way.
3. Align the window properly with the outside belt weatherstrip. Then tighten the upper rear guide attaching screw.

4. Tilt the window until the top of the glass is parallel with the weatherstrip on the roof rail. Tighten the lower rail guide attaching nut.
5. Adjust the upper stops in or out until the window properly engages the window channel. Then tighten the four upper stop mounting screws.
6. Move the equalizer down until it firmly contacts the regulator roller and tighten the equalizer arm bracket nut.
7. Tilt the vent assembly until it is parallel at the front with the body pillar and permits the window to operate smoothly. Then tighten the vent window assembly mounting screw.
8. Tilt the entire window assembly in or out, with the three adjusting nuts, so it will seal effectively with the roof rail weatherstrip. Then tighten the three locknuts.
9. Tighten the two vent window regulator mounting screws and the regulator-to-shaft screw.
10. Lower the window until the top of the glass is flush with the belt line. Then adjust the lower stop upward as far as it will go and tighten the mounting screw. Replace the door panel and watershield.

### 1968 Fairlane, Montego Two Door Hardtop, Convertible

NOTE: *Upper stop adjustments*

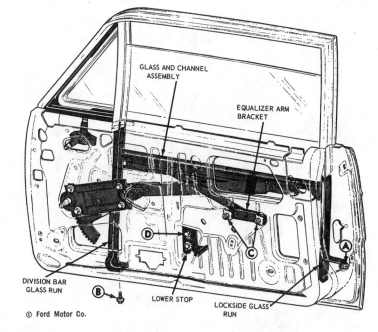

*1968 Ford & Mercury Front Door Window*

# Ford Motor Company

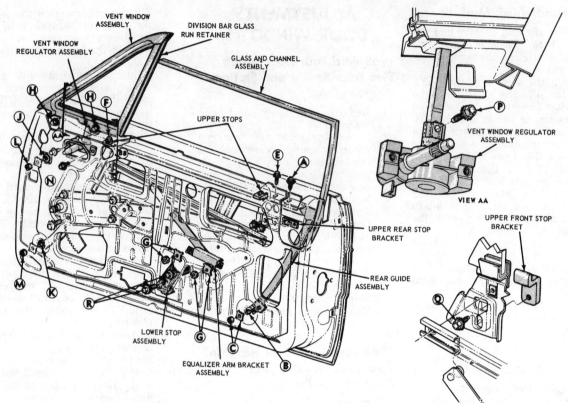

*1968 Ford & Mercury Hardtop & Convertible Door Window Adjustments*

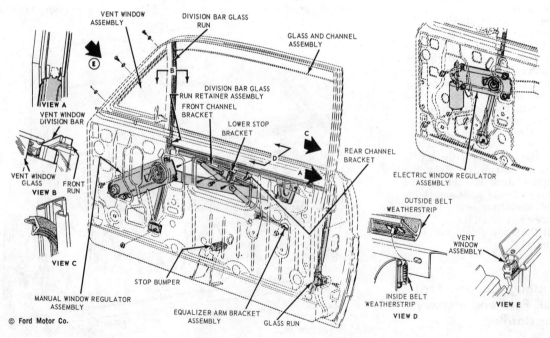

© Ford Motor Co.

*1968 Falcon Two Door Window Mechanism*

# Ford Motor Company

*and the in-out tilt adjustment can be accomplished without removing the door panel. The latter requires a 7/16 in. socket wrench and extension.*

1. Remove the door panel and the watershield. Loosen all adjusting nuts and screws.
2. Raise the glass all the way and then position it forward or rearward until it is in alignment at the top and front. Tighten the equalizer arm attaching nuts.
3. Move the upper front stop down as far as it will go and tighten the mounting screw. Repeat the process for the rear stop and tighten its two attaching screws.
4. Tilt the glass in or out until it seals effectively with the roof rail and quarter glass weatherstripping. Then, tighten the front and rear run attaching screws.
5. Test the operation of the window. If binding occurs, lower the window, loosen the front run lower attaching screw, and retighten it. Install the door panel and watershield.

## 1968 Falcon, Fairlane, Montego Four Door Sedan and Wagon—Front

1. Remove the trim panel and watershield.
2. Loosen the lower division bar attaching nut and lower rear run attaching screw. Lower the glass until the top is 4 in. above the belt line.
3. Turn the lower division bar adjusting screw in or out until the front run is aligned with the rear run. Tighten the adjusting screw locknut and the lower rear run attaching screw to 8-23 ft. lbs.
4. Lower the glass until it is just flush with the beltline. Then raise the lower stop until it contacts the glass channel and tighten the attaching screws to 8-23 ft. lbs. Reinstall the watershield and inner door panel.

## 1968 Falcon Two Door Sedan— Front

1. Remove the door panel and watershield.
2. Loosen the locknut at the lower end of the front lower run and loosen the screw at the lower end of the rear run.
3. Lower the window until it is about four in. above the belt line. Turn the adjusting screw at the bottom of the front run in or out as required to align the glass runs with the vent window divi-

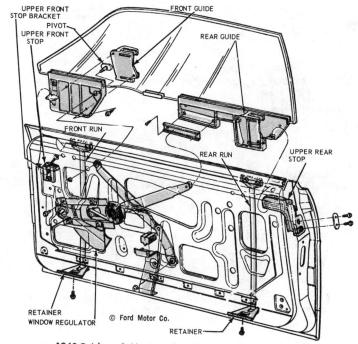

*1968 Fairlane & Montego Front Door Window Adjustments*

sion bar. Then tighten the nut and screw.
4. Lower the window and adjust the lower stop up or down via the adjusting screw until the window can drop just until it is flush with the beltline at the top. Reinstall the watershield and door panel.

## 1968 Mustang and Cougar— Front

1. Remove the door panel and watershield.
2. Loosen the six adjusting screws and the two locknuts.
3. Raise the window all the way. Move it in or out at the belt line for alignment with the outside belt weatherstrip. Then tighten the screw at the top of the rear of the door.
4. Tilt the window front or back until it aligns with the roof rail and then tighten the rear guide locknut.
5. Adjust the upper stops so that the window seals with the roof rail when raised all the way and then tighten the upper stop attaching screws.
6. Tilt the vent window so it seals tightly with the main door window at the rear and is parallel to the windshield post. Then tighten the two attaching screws.
7. Adjust the three tilt adjusting screws (at the bottoms of the

runs and at the bottom of the vent window mounting bracket) so that both windows seal properly with the roof rail weatherstrip. Tighten the three locknuts and the rear guide adjusting screw.
8. Reinstall the watershield and door panel.

## 1968 Lincoln Continental—Front

1. Remove the door panel and watershield. Raise the window all the way.
2. Loosen the nine adjusting screws and the locknut.
3. Adjust the glass in or out at front and rear so it is in alignment with the weatherstripping at the belt line. Tighten the upper run attaching screws.
4. Tilt the glass fore or aft until it is parallel with the roof rail. Tighten the lower rear run attaching screw which is accessible from the inside of the door.
5. Adjust the upper front stop so that it contacts the glass channel and tighten its attaching screw.
6. Position the vent window frame so that it is parallel with the front body pillar and seals with the main window. Then tighten its mounting screw and the lower front run attaching screw which is accessible from the inside of the door.

# Ford Motor Company

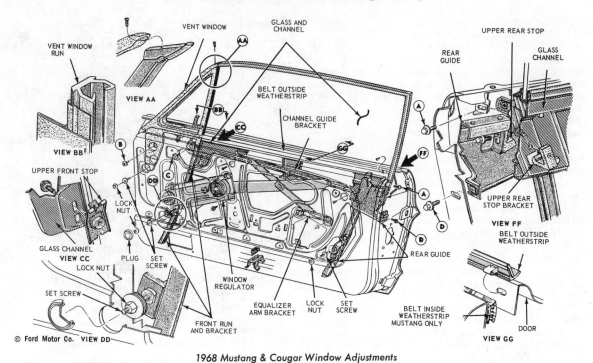

*1968 Mustang & Cougar Window Adjustments*

7. Tilt the vent window frame in or out with the adjusting screw until it seals tightly with the roof side rail weatherstrip. Then tighten the locknut and the lower run attaching screws which are accessible from under the door.

8. Lower the window until it is flush with the belt line and then position the lower stop against the window stop bumper. Tighten the mounting screw.

9. Replace the watershield and door panel.

## 1968 Ford Four Door Sedan and Station Wagon—Rear

1. Remove the door panel and watershield. Raise the window all the way.

2. Adjust the position of the equalizer arm bracket so that it is at the mid point in the slots and tighten the adjusting nuts.

3. Position the lower stop as far down as it will go in its slot and tighten the mounting screws. Replace the door panel and watershield.

## 1968 Ford Four Door Hartop—Rear

1. Remove the door panel and watershield. Loosen all attaching screws and nuts.

2. Tilt the window front or back until it aligns with the front door

window and the roof rail. Then tighten the window guide panel attaching screws.

3. Position the upper stops against the brackets on the window assembly and tighten their mounts.

4. Move the window regulator bracket assembly downward until it firmly contacts the regulator roller and hold it while tightening the assembly mounting nuts.

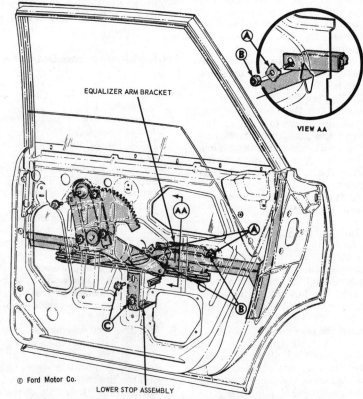

*1968 Ford & Mercury Sedan and Wagon Rear Door Window Adjustments*

# Ford Motor Company

5. Tighten the screws and washers that hold the guide adjusting bracket to the window guide.
6. Tilt the window guide panel in or out until the window seals with the front door window and the roof side rail and tighten the guide adjusting bracket screws.
7. Lower the window and adjust the position of the lower stop so that the top of the glass is flush with the beltline. Tighten the stop mounting screws.
8. Install the watershield and door trim panel.

## 1968 Falcon—Rear Door

1. Remove the trim panel and watershield.
2. Loosen the unit which locks the adjusting screw at the bottom of the rear glass run retainer and division bar and then lower the window. Adjust the screw until the retainer and division bar lines up with the window frame. Tighten the locknut.
3. Install the trim panel and watershield.

## 1968 Fairlane and Montego Four Door Sedan—Rear

NOTE: *In-out tilt can be adjusted without removing the door trim panel if that is the only adjustment required. See appropriate steps below.*

1. Remove the inner door panel and watershield.
2. Loosen the four adjusting screws. Raise the window all the way.
3. Tighten the upper guide attaching screws.

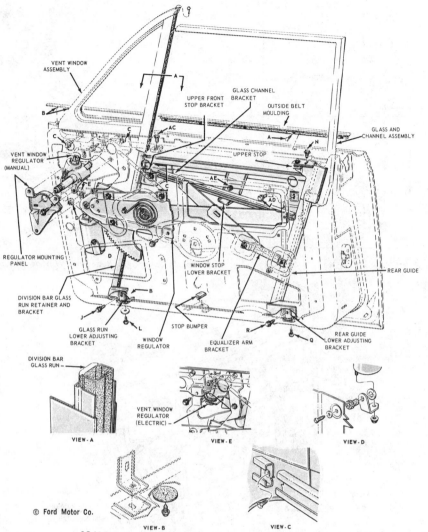

© Ford Motor Co.

*1968 Lincoln Continental Front Door Window Mechanism*

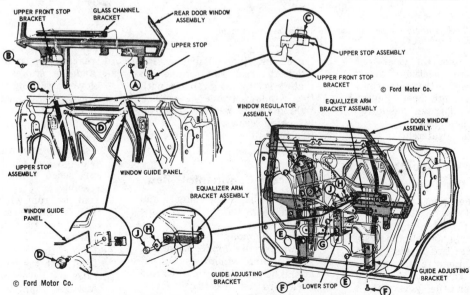

© Ford Motor Co.

*1968 Ford & Mercury Hardtop Rear Door Window Mechanism*

# Ford Motor Company

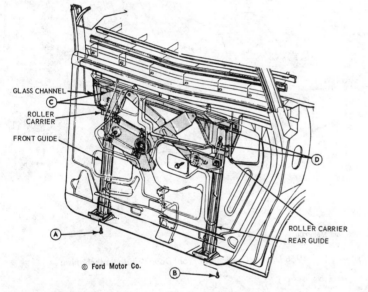

1968 Lincoln Continental Rear Door Window Mechanism

1968 Fairlane & Montego Rear Door Window Adjustments

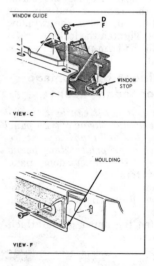

4. Lower and raise the glass and then adjust the position of front and rear lower attaching screws to permit smooth operation of the window. Tighten the lower run attaching screws.

5. Replace the watershield and trim panel.

## 1968 Fairlane and Montego Station Wagon—Rear

1. Remove the trim panel and watershield.

2. Loosen the five adjusting screws. Raise the window all the way.

3. Tighten the two upper front guide attaching screws.

4. Lower and raise the glass, and then tighten the lower front guide attaching screw.

5. Lower the window half way. Position the rear run retainer so that it is aligned properly with the window frame and then tighten the two lower rear run attaching screws.

6. Replace the trim panel and watershield.

## 1968 Lincoln Continental—Rear

1. Remove the trim panel and watershield. Raise the window all the way.

2. Loosen all mounting screws according to the applicable figure.

3. Position the window in or out at the belt line and forward and backward as necessary for a tight seal. Tighten the front and

rear run upper attaching screws and, on sedans, the front run lower attaching screw.

4. Adjust both upper stops as far down as they will go and tighten their attaching screws.

5. Push the equalizer arm bracket assembly downward as far as it will go and tighten the mounting screw while holding the assembly.

6. Tilt the front window guide in or out for proper alignment at the front and tighten the mounting screw.

7. Lower the window until it is flush with the belt line and then raise the lower stop as far as it will go. Tighten the mounting screw.

# Ford Motor Company

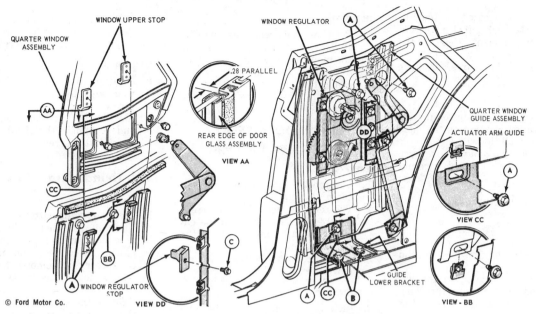

© Ford Motor Co.

*1968 Mustang & Cougar Quarter Window Adjustments*

8. Tighten the rear run upper and lower attaching screws.
9. Install the watershield and inner door panel.

## ADJUSTMENTS QUARTER WINDOWS

### 1968 Mustang and Cougar— Quarter

1. Remove the rear seat back and cushion, the trim panel, and the watershield.
2. Loosen the five regulator and lower guide adjusting screws.
3. Adjust the guide to the front or rear and up or down as necessary to obtain a 0.28 in. uniform gap between the front edge of the quarter window and the rear of the door window.
4. Move the guide in or out as necessary in order to ensure a proper seal at the top of the glass. Then tighten the five adjusting screws.
5. Raise the window all the way and then turn the regulator handle an additional ⅛ in. Adjust the regulator stop so that it contacts the arm of the regulator and then tighten the stop attaching screw.
6. Reinstall the trim panel and seat parts.

### 1968 Fairlane and Montego— Quarter

1. Remove the trim panel and watershield.

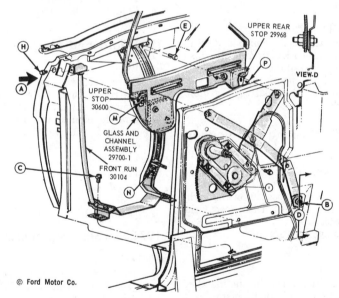

© Ford Motor Co.

*1968 Fairlane & Montego Quarter Window Adjustments*

2. Loosen all the adjusting screws.
3. Raise the window all the way. Move it until it is flush with the top of the door glass and seals with the roof rail.
4. Move the window fore and aft and inboard and outboard until it aligns with the door window. Tighten screws (B), (C), (E), and (H).
5. Push the upper stops up all the way and tighten their mounts. Lower the window all the way and tighten the lower stop attaching screw.

6. Install the watershield and quarter panel.

## REMOVAL AND INSTALLATION PROCEDURES

### POWER WINDOW RELAY
### 1972-75 Torino and Montego
### 1974-75 Cougar

**Removal**

1. Disconnect the battery ground cable.

# Ford Motor Company

2. The relay is located on the left side of the dash panel in the engine compartment. Remove the two mounting screws.
3. Disconnect the wires. Remove the relay.

**Installation**

1. Place the relay in approximately its installed location on the dash panel. Install the wires.
2. Install the two mounting screws.
3. Connect the battery ground cable.

## 1972-75 Ford, Mercury, and Meteor

**Removal**

1. Disconnect the battery ground cable.
2. The relay is located in the engine compartment on the dash panel. Remove the retaining screws.
3. Remove the wires. Remove the relay.

**Installation**

1. Place the relay approximately in its installed location on the dash panel. Install the wires.
2. Install the mounting screws.
3. Connect the battery ground cable.

## 1972-73 Mustang and Cougar

**Removal**

1. Disconnect the battery ground cable.
2. The relay is located on the right spring tower. Disconnect the wires.
3. Remove the retaining screws. Remove the relay.

**Installation**

1. Place the relay in its installed position and then install the mounting screws.
2. Reinstall the wires.
3. Connect the battery ground cable.

## 1972-75 Lincoln, Continental Mark IV, and Thunderbird

**Removal**

1. Disconnect the battery ground cable.
2. The relay is located in the engine compartment on the dash panel. Disconnect the multiple wiring connector.
3. Remove the mounting screws and then remove the relay.

**Installation**

1. Position the relay in the installed location and then install the mounting screws.
2. Reconnect the multiple wiring connector.
3. Connect the battery ground cable.

## POWER WINDOW RELAY
## 1971 Torino and Montego

**Removal**

1. Disconnect the battery ground cable.
2. The relay is located on the right side of the dash panel in the engine compartment. Remove the two attaching screws.
3. Disconnect the wires and remove the relay.

**Installation**

1. Install the relay with the two mounting screws.
2. Reconnect the wires.
3. Connect the battery ground cable.

## 1971 Ford and Mercury

**Removal**

1. Disconnect the battery. Locate the relay which is in the engine compartment on the dash panel.
2. Pull the connectors from the relay and remove the retaining screws. The relay may now be removed.

**Installation**

1. Place the relay on the dash panel. Push on the connectors.
2. Connect the battery.

## 1971 Lincoln Continental

**Removal**

1. The relay is located in the luggage compartment on the package tray. Disconnect the multiple connector.
2. Remove the retaining screws. Remove the relay.

**Installation**

1. Install the relay with the retaining screws. Connect the multiple connector.

## 1971 Mustang and Cougar

**Removal**

1. Disconnect the battery.
2. The relay is located on the right wheel well. Disconnect its two plug on connectors.
3. Loosen the screw which attaches the third connector and

pull the connector off.
4. Remove the relay retaining screws and remove the relay.

**Installation**

1. Position the relay on the wheel well and install the retaining screws.
2. Install the push-on connectors and reconnect the third connector with the screw.
3. Connect the battery.

## 1971 Thunderbird, Mark III

**Removal**

1. Disconnect the battery.
2. The relay is located in the engine compartment on the dash panel. Disconnect the multiple connector and remove the screw which holds the wires to the dash.
3. Remove the screws which retain the relay and remove the relay.

**Installation**

1. Position the relay and install the retaining screws.
2. Install the snap-on connectors and fasten the wires to the dash.
3. Connect the battery.

## POWER WINDOW RELAY
## 1970 Falcon, Fairlane, Montego

**Removal**

1. Disconnect the battery ground.
2. The relay is located on the right side of the dash panel in the engine compartment.
3. Disconnect the wires and remove the relay.

**Installation**

1. Connect the wiring.
2. Install the relay with the attaching screws. Connect the battery ground.

## 1970 Ford, Mercury

**Removal**

1. Disconnect the battery. The relay is located in the engine compartment on the dash panel.
2. Disconnect the wiring connectors and remove the relay.

**Installation**

1. Install the relay and fasten the push-on connectors.
2. Reconnect the battery cables.

## 1970 Lincoln Continental

**Removal**

1. The relay is located in the luggage compartment on the pack-

# Ford Motor Company

age tray. Disconnect the electrical connector, remove the retaining screws, and pull the relay off.

### Installation

1. Locate the relay on the package tray and install the retaining screws. Connect the multiple connector.

### 1970 Cougar

**Removal**

1. Disconnect the battery.
2. The relay is located on the right wheel well. Remove the plug-on connectors and screw-held connector. Remove the relay.

### Installation

1. Position the relay on the wheel well. Install the retaining screws.
2. Connect the snap-on connectors and install the remaining connector under the retaining screw.
3. Connect the battery.

### 1970 Thunderbird and Mark III

**Removal**

1. Disconnect the battery. The relay is located in the engine compartment on the dash.
2. Remove the screw which retains the wires to the dash and pull off the multiple connector. Remove the screws which retain the relay and pull it off.

### Installation

1. Mount the relay on the dash with the retaining screws. Plug in the multiple connector and mount the wires to the dash.
2. Connect the battery.

## POWER WINDOW RELAY
### 1969 Falcon, Fairlane, Montego

**Removal**

1. Disconnect the battery ground.
2. The relay is located on the right side of the dash panel in the engine compartment.
3. Disconnect the wires and remove the relay.

### Installation

1. Connect the wiring.
2. Install the relay with the attaching screws. Connect the battery ground.

### 1969 Ford, Mercury

**Removal**

1. Disconnect the battery. The relay is located in the engine compartment on the dash panel.

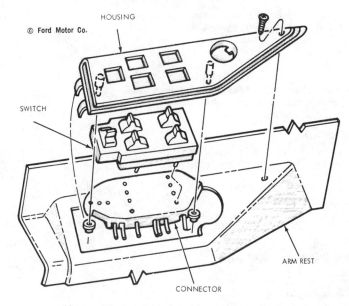

© Ford Motor Co.

*Mercury Hardtop & Mark III & IV Switch Installation*

2. Disconnect the wiring connectors and remove the relay.

### Installation

1. Install the relay and fasten the push-on connectors.
2. Reconnect the battery cables.

### 1969 Lincoln Continental

**Removal**

1. The relay is located in the luggage compartment on the package tray. Disconnect the electrical connector, remove the retaining screws, and pull off the relay.

### Installation

1. Locate the relay on the package tray and install the retaining screws. Connect the multiple connector.

### 1969 Cougar

**Removal**

1. Disconnect the battery.
2. The relay is located on the right wheel well. Remove the plug-on connectors and the screw-held connector. Remove the relay.

### Installation

1. Position the relay on the wheel well. Install the retaining screws.
2. Connect the snap-on connectors and install the remaining connector under the retaining screw.
3. Connect the battery.

### 1969 Thunderbird and Mark III

**Removal**

1. Disconnect the battery. The re-

lay is located in the engine compartment on the dash.
2. Remove the screw which retains the wires to the dash and pull off the multiple connector. Remove the screws which retain the relay and pull it off.

### Installation

1. Mount the relay on the dash with the retaining screws. Plug in the multiple connector and mount the wires to the dash.
2. Connect the battery.

## POWER WINDOW RELAY
### 1968 Falcon, Fairlane, and Montego

**Removal**

1. Disconnect the battery ground.
2. The relay is located on the right side of the dash panel in the engine compartment. Disconnect the wiring and remove the relay.

### Installation

1. Put the relay in position, install the mounting screws, and connect the wiring.
2. Connect the battery ground cable.

## POWER WINDOW SWITCH
### 1972-73 Mercury 2 and 4 Door Hardtops, 4 Door Hardtop Sedan, and Mark IV
### 1974-75 Lincoln Continental

**Removal**

1. Remove the bezel screw. Then lift the front end of the bezel up

# Ford Motor Company

and pull it from the arm rest. On the left front door, the bezel and its nut must also be removed from the mirror remote control.

2. Remove the two switch mounting nuts from the underside of the bezel and pull the switch from the connector.

### Installation

1. Press the switch firmly onto the connector. Install the two retaining nuts.
2. Replace the bezel for the mirror remote control.
3. Install the bezel on the arm rest and then install the retaining screw.

## 1972-75 Ford, Torino, and Montego
## 1973-75 Cougar

### Removal

1. Remove the bezel retaining screw. Pivot the lower edge of the bezel out and up and then remove it.
2. Pry the switch gently off the connector with a small screwdriver.

### Installation

1. Gently press the switch onto the connector.
2. Reposition the bezel in reverse order of the removal procedures and then replace the bezel retaining screw.

## 1972 Mustang and Cougar

### Removal

1. Remove the door trim panel.
2. Disconnect the power window switch wiring.
3. Remove the switch retaining screws and then remove the switch from the panel.

### Installation

1. Position the switch in the door panel. Install the retaining screws.
2. Connect the wiring. Install the trim panel.

## 1972-73 Lincoln Continental

### Removal

1. Remove the arm rest. Remove the switch retaining screws from the underside of the arm rest.
2. Disconnect the switch and remove it from the arm rest.

### Installation

1. Position the switch on the arm

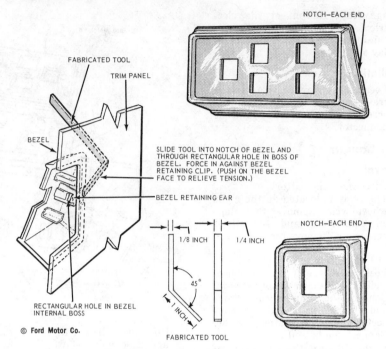

Ford & Mercury Typical Switch Removal

rest and then install the retaining screws.
2. Install the multiple connector and then reinstall the arm rest.

## POWER WINDOW SWITCH
## 1971 Mercury 2 and
## 4 Door Hardtop

### Removal

1. Remove the screw from the front of the bezel and lift it and the switch away from the arm rest.
2. Remove the two nuts from the studs on the bezel and pull off the switches.
3. Disconnect the electrical connector.

### Installation

1. Firmly install the connector onto the switch.
2. Position the switches on the bezel and then install their retaining nuts.
3. Position the switch and the bezel on the arm rest and install the retaining screw.

## 1971 Ford and Mercury Except
## 2 and 4 Door Hardtop

### Removal

1. Fabricate a tool as shown in the figure. It should be made from metal ⅛ in. thick and ¼ in.

wide. Make sure it is clean and has no sharp edges.
2. Insert the tool into either the front or rear notch in the bezel, aligning it with the retangular slot behind the bezel. Push the retaining clip from the retainer ear at the top of the rectangular slot.

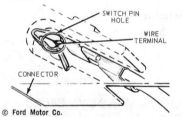

Ford & Mercury Typical Switch Connector Wire Terminal Removal

3. Repeat the process outlined in step 2 for the other retaining clip.
4. Use a small screwdriver to carefully pry the switch off the connecting and mounting pins.

### Installation

1. Position the switch on the connector and carefully press it downward into place. Then install the bezel.

## 1971 Torino, Montego, Mustang, Cougar

### Removal

1. Remove the trim panel. Discon-

# Ford Motor Company

nect the wire connector from the window switch.

2. Remove the attaching screws and remove the switch.

**Installation**

1. Position the switch and its retainer on the trim panel and install the attaching screws. Connect the wiring to the switch and install the trim panel.

### 1971 Mark III and Lincoln

**Removal**

1. Remove the arm rest. Remove the switch retaining screws.
2. Disconnect the switch and remove it.

**Installation**

1. Position the switch in the arm rest and install the retaining screws.
2. Connect the multiple connector and install the arm rest.

### 1971 Thunderbird

**Removal**

1. Remove the finish panel from the arm rest by removing the attaching screws and pulling it off.
2. Remove the radio speaker, if the vehicle is so equipped.
3. Remove the bezel and nut from the remote control lever for the mirror, if working on the left front door.
4. Remove the six armrest attaching screws. Pull the armrest away from the trim panel.
5. Disconnect the power window switch wiring and power door lock hoses. Feed the mirror control cable out of the armrest, if the vehicle is so equipped.
6. Remove the two switch mounting screws and remove the switch.

**Installation**

1. Position the switch on the armrest and install the attaching screws.
2. Position the armrest and, if necessary, route the mirror control. Install the bezel and nut.
3. Connect the power door lock vacuum lines and the window electric wiring.
4. Install the arm rest and attaching screws. Install the speaker and finish panel.

### POWER WINDOW SWITCH
### 1970 Ford and Mercury

**Removal**

1. Insert a screwdriver into the

notch at either end of the bezel and depress the locking tab to release it.

2. Pry the switch out of the retainer with a screwdriver. Work carefully to avoid damaging it.

**Installation**

1. Reverse the procedures above.

### 1970 Fairlane, Montego, and Cougar

**Removal**

1. Remove the trim panel.
2. Disconnect the window switch wire.
3. Remove the attaching screws and remove the switch from the panel.

**Installation**

1. Position the switch and its retainer to the trim panel and then install the attaching screws.
2. Connect the wire connector and install the trim panel.

### 1970 Thunderbird, Mark III, Lincoln

**Removal**

1. Remove the armrest.
2. From the underside of the armrest, remove the retaining screws and then remove the switch. Disconnect the multiple connector.

**Installation**

1. Position the switch, install the retaining screws, and install the connector.
2. Install the armrest.

### POWER WINDOW AND DOOR LOCK SWITCH
### 1970 Thunderbird

**Removal**

1. Remove the armrest finish panel by removing the attaching screws and pulling it off.
2. Remove the speaker from the armrest if there is one.
3. If working on the left front door, remove the bezel and nut from the mirror remote control.
4. Remove the six screws which attach the armrest and pull it from the door.
5. Disconnect the power window switch wires and vacuum switch hoses. Feed the mirror control cable out of the armrest, if the door has one.
6. Remove the two screws and remove the switch.

**Installation**

1. Install the switch on the armrest with the two attaching screws.
2. Position the armrest and route the mirror control. Install the bezel and nut.
3. Connect the door lock switch vacuum hoses and the power window switch wiring.
4. Install the armrest attaching screws. Install the speaker, if necessary.
5. Install the finish panel.

### POWER WINDOW SWITCH
### 1969 Ford and Mercury

**Removal**

1. Insert a screwdriver into the notch at either end of the bezel and depress the locking tab to release it.
2. Pry the switch out of the retainer with a screwdriver. Work carefully to avoid damaging it.

**Installation**

1. Reverse the above procedures.

### 1969 Fairlane, Montego, and Cougar

**Removal**

1. Remove the trim panel.
2. Disconnect the window switch wire.
3. Remove the attaching screws and remove the switch from the panel.

**Installation**

1. Position the switch and its retainer to the trim panel and install the attaching screws.
2. Connect the wire connector and install the trim panel.

### 1969 Thunderbird, Mark III, Lincoln

**Removal**

1. Remove the armrest.
2. From the underside of the armrest, remove the retaining screws and then remove the switch. Disconnect the multiple connector.

**Installation**

1. Position the switch, install the retaining screws, and install the connector.
2. Install the armrest.

### POWER WINDOW AND DOOR LOCK SWITCH
### 1969 Thunderbird

**Removal**

1. Remove the armrest finish panel

# Ford Motor Company

by removing the attaching screw and pulling it off.

2. Remove the speaker from the armrest if there is one.

3. If working on the left front door, remove the bezel and nut from the mirror remote control.

4. Remove the six screws which attach the armrest and pull it from the door.

5. Disconnect the power window switch wires and the vacuum switch hoses. Feed the mirror control cable out of the armrest, if the door has one.

6. Remove the two screws and remove the switch.

## Installation

1. Install the switch on the armrest with the two attaching screws.

2. Position the armrest and route the mirror control. Install the bezel and nut.

3. Connect the door lock switch vacuum hoses and the power window switch wiring.

4. Install the armrest attaching screws. Install the speaker, if necessary.

5. Install the finish panel.

## POWER WINDOW SWITCH CONNECTOR WIRE REMOVAL
### 1971-75 All Models

If necessary, a wire leading to the switch connector can be replaced without completely disassembling the connector.

### Removal

Insert a very small, sharp object into the pin hole to bend the terminal inward. The wire and terminal can then be pulled from the connector.

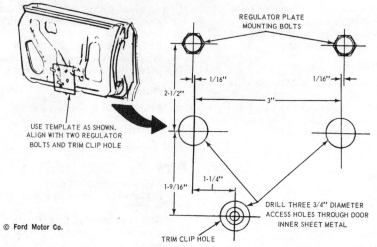

© Ford Motor Co.

*1972-73 U-Run & Channel Guide Type Front Door Motor Removal Template Dimensions*

### Installation

Open the terminal and then insert it into the wire hole.

## POWER WINDOW SWITCH BUTTONS
### 1972-73 All Models

#### Removal

1. Remove the switch from the arm rest or door panel.

2. Lift the rubber water seal off the switch.

3. With a sharp instrument, press inward and upward on the pivot which retains the switch. This will release the button.

4. Remove the button.

#### Installation

1. Locate the button carefully in the switch housing so that the pivot pins are directly above the holes. Then press firmly downward on the button until it snaps into place.

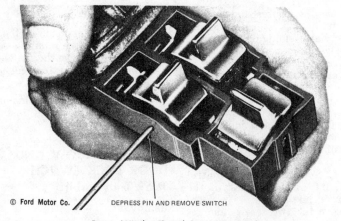

© Ford Motor Co.    DEPRESS PIN AND REMOVE SWITCH

*Power Window Switch Button Removal*

2. Install the water seal and then reinstall the switch.

## WINDOW MOTOR AND DRIVE
### 1972 Ford and Mercury
### 1972-75 Lincoln Continental—Front and Rear
### 1975

#### Removal

1. Remove the trim panel and watershield.

2. If there are vacuum hoses, remove their retainer clips and then position them so that there will be adequate working clearance. If there are any radio speakers mounted in the door, remove them.

3. Using the appropriate illustration, manufacture a template that conforms to the required dimensions. (Reverse the template for use on left hand doors.)

4. Position the template on the door and mark the centerpoint of each drill location with a center punch.

5. Raise the glass all the way and then drill the holes with a ¾ in. hole saw. The pilot drill on the saw should be approximately ¼ in. long in order to avoid damage to the mechanism.

6. Disconnect the motor wires and then remove the motor support bracket.

7. Remove the three screws that hold the motor and drive to the window regulator. Remove the assembly.

#### Installation

1. Place the motor and drive in

# Power Windows

## Ford Motor Company

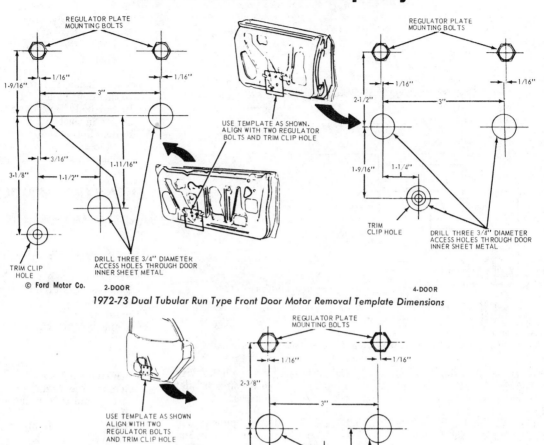

REGULATOR PLATE MOUNTING BOLTS

1-9/16"  1/16"  3"  1/16"

3-1/8"  3/16"  1-1/2"  1-11/16"

TRIM CLIP HOLE

© Ford Motor Co.  2-DOOR

USE TEMPLATE AS SHOWN. ALIGN WITH TWO REGULATOR BOLTS AND TRIM CLIP HOLE

DRILL THREE 3/4" DIAMETER ACCESS HOLES THROUGH DOOR INNER SHEET METAL

REGULATOR PLATE MOUNTING BOLTS

2-1/2"  1/16"  3"  1/16"

1-9/16"  1-1/4"

TRIM CLIP HOLE

DRILL THREE 3/4" DIAMETER ACCESS HOLES THROUGH DOOR INNER SHEET METAL

4-DOOR

*1972-73 Dual Tubular Run Type Front Door Motor Removal Template Dimensions*

USE TEMPLATE AS SHOWN ALIGN WITH TWO REGULATOR BOLTS AND TRIM CLIP HOLE

REGULATOR PLATE MOUNTING BOLTS

1/16"  1/16"

2-3/8"  3"

2-9/16"  1-1/2"  1-7/16"

1-1/8"

DRILL THREE 3/4" DIAMETER ACCESS HOLES THROUGH DOOR INNER PANEL SHEET METAL

© Ford Motor Co.

*1972-73 Dual U-Run Type Rear Door Motor Removal Template Dimensions*

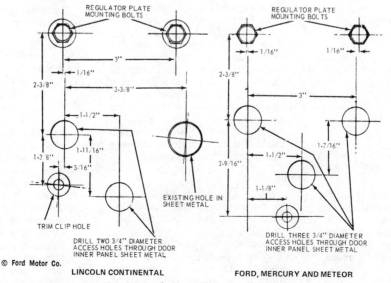

REGULATOR PLATE MOUNTING BOLTS

3"  1/16"

2-3/8"  3-3/8"

1-1/2"

1-2/8"  1-11/16"  3/16"

TRIM CLIP HOLE

EXISTING HOLE IN SHEET METAL

DRILL TWO 3/4" DIAMETER ACCESS HOLES THROUGH DOOR INNER PANEL SHEET METAL

© Ford Motor Co.

**LINCOLN CONTINENTAL**

REGULATOR PLATE MOUNTING BOLTS

1/16"  1/16"

2-3/8"  3"

2-9/16"  1-1/2"  1-7/16"

1-1/8"

DRILL THREE 3/4" DIAMETER ACCESS HOLES THROUGH DOOR INNER PANEL SHEET METAL

**FORD, MERCURY AND METEOR**

*1972-73 Tubular Run & Channel Guide Type Rear Door Motor Removal Template Dimensions*

# Ford Motor Company

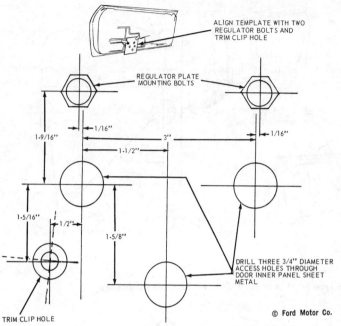

ALIGN TEMPLATE WITH TWO
REGULATOR BOLTS AND
TRIM CLIP HOLE

REGULATOR PLATE
MOUNTING BOLTS

1-9/16"

1/16"

3"

1/16"

1-1/2"

1-5/16"

1/2"

1-5/8"

DRILL THREE 3/4" DIAMETER
ACCESS HOLES THROUGH
DOOR INNER PANEL SHEET
METAL

TRIM CLIP HOLE

© Ford Motor Co.

*1972-73 Single Tubular Run Type Door Motor Removal Template Dimensions*

the proper position on the regulator and then install the mounting screws just until they will hold the unit in place.

2. Reconnect the motor wires. Cycle the glass up and down several times.
3. Tighten the motor and drive attaching screws.
4. Install the motor support bracket and then cover the three holes with body tape.
5. Replace radio speakers and relocate and clip vacuum hoses, as necessary.
6. Install the watershield and trim panel.

## 1972-75 Mustang, Cougar, Torino, Montego, Thunderbird, Mark IV—Front
## Torino, Montego—Rear
## 1973-75 Ford and Mercury

### Removal

1. Remove the inner door panel and watershield. Unclip and reposition vacuum hoses as necessary.
2. Remove door mounted radio speakers.
3. When working on 1972-73 Mustang and Cougar front doors, make a template as shown in the illustration. The template must be reversed for use on left hand doors. Using the template, mark the centers of the drill locations with a centerpunch. Then, raise

the glass and drill the holes with a ¾ in. hole saw using a pilot drill ¼ in. long or less.

All other 1972-73 models have holes already punched in the door panel for motor and drive. When working on 1974-75 models, all have holes punched except Ford, Mercury and Meteor. In these models it is necessary to drill a ¾ inch hole for the lower attaching screw at the dimple in the inner panel.

4. Disconnect the multiple connector from the motor. On 1973 models, except Ford, Mercury and Meteor, using a drift punch, remove the center pin from the rivet which attaches the support bracket to the inner door panel. Then drill out the rivet with a ¼ in. drill.
5. On models so equipped, remove the motor support bracket from the motor. On all other models, remove the three screws which hold the motor and drive to the regulator, gaining access through the holes in the door. Remove the assembly from the door.

### Installation

1. Position the motor and drive and then screw in the mounting screws just until they will hold the unit in place.
2. Reconnect the multiple connector and then operate the unit through its cycle several times until the gears are fully engaged.

Then tighten the mounting screws fully.

3. Install the motor support bracket. Use a screw and washer assembly to replace the rivet which holds the motor bracket to the inner panel.
4. Install body tape over the holes drilled in the body.
5. Reinstall the radio speaker and vacuum hose clips as necessary. Replace the inner door panel and watershield.

# QUARTER WINDOWS

## WINDOW MOTOR AND DRIVE
### 1972-73 Mustang and Cougar

### Removal

1. Remove the trim panel and watershield. Disconnect the motor wires.
2. While holding the glass up, remove the spring retainer and washer from the glass bracket stud. Then remove the regulator arm and washer.
3. Remove the regulator attaching screws and then remove the regulator.
4. After the regulator assembly is removed, the motor may be removed from the regulator.

### Installation

1. Mount the motor on the regulator assembly. Connect the motor wires.
2. Position the regulator and then install the attaching screws.
3. Install the washer, regulator arm, washer, and spring retainer, in that order, on the glass bracket stud.
4. Install the trim panel and watershield.

## 1972-75 Lincoln Continental
## 1972 Ford 2 Door Hardtop and Convertible

### Removal

1. Raise the top slightly on convertibles. Remove the trim panel and watershield. Remove the front retainer bracket for the trim panel.
2. Remove the equalizer arm-to-inner panel attaching screw. Lower the glass.
3. Remove the front guide and rear upper stop.
4. While holding the glass up, remove the glass channel bracket.
5. Disconnect the motor wires and the motor support bracket.

# Ford Motor Company

6. Remove the regulator attaching screws and then disengage the regulator arm roller from the glass channel.

7. Raise the glass enough to clear the rear guide and then remove the glass and the guide. Then remove the regulator.

8. Mount the regulator in a vise and then drill a 5/16 in. hole through the sector gear and regulator plate. Install a 1/4 in bolt and nut through the holes just drilled. Remove the motor assembly.

**Installation**

1. Lubricate the mechanism. Position the regulator in its installed position and install the attaching screws. Install the rear guide.

2. Install the motor support bracket and connect the motor wires.

3. Install the glass channel bracket.

4. Lower the glass part way and install the front guide. Install the upper rear stop.

5. Install the equalizer arm on the inner panel. Adjust as necessary.

6. Install the trim panel and watershield.

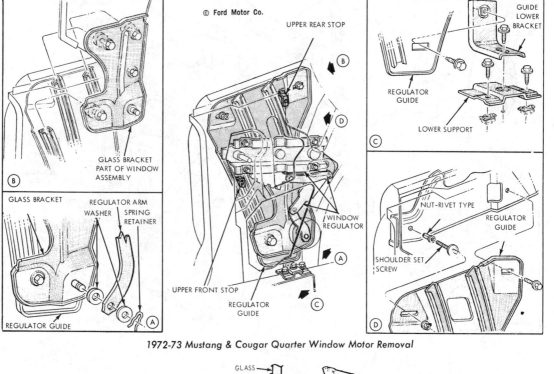

© Ford Motor Co.

*1972-73 Mustang & Cougar Quarter Window Motor Removal*

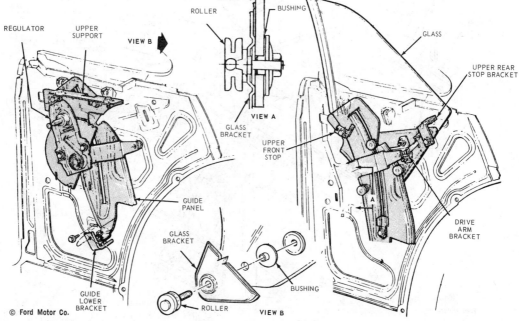

© Ford Motor Co.

*1972-73 Torino & Montego Quarter Window Motor Removal*

# Ford Motor Company

## 1972 Mercury
## 2 Door Hardtop

### Removal

1. Remove the quarter trim panel and watershield. Disconnect the motor wiring.
2. Remove the two equalizer arm bracket mounting screws.
3. Remove the nuts which hold the drive arm bracket to the glass bracket and then pull the drive arm bracket off the glass bracket.
4. Hold the glass up and remove the four regulator attaching screws. Then remove the regulator and the drive arm bracket from the panel area.
5. Separate the drive arm bracket from the regulator. The motor may now be removed.

### Installation

1. Install the motor and the drive arm bracket.
2. Position the regulator and then install the attaching screws.
3. Install the drive arm bracket and its two attaching nuts.

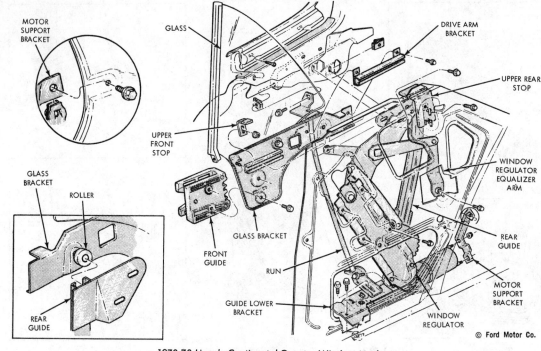

*1972-73 Lincoln Continental Quarter Window Mechanism*

© Ford Motor Co.

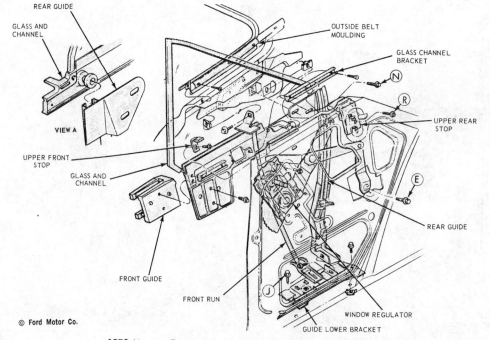

© Ford Motor Co.

*1972 Mercury Two Door and Convertible Quarter Window Mechanism*

# Ford Motor Company

4. Position the equalizer arm bracket and install its two attaching screws. Connect the motor wiring.
5. Adjust the unit as described in the "Adjustments" section.
6. Install the watershield and trim panel.

## 1972-75 Torino, Montego, Thunderbird, Mark IV

### Removal

1. Remove the trim panel and watershield.
2. Using a drift punch, remove the center pins in the four rivets which hold the regulator to the inner panel.
3. Drill the rivets out with a 1/4 in. drill. Disconnect the motor wires.
4. Disengage the window regulator arm from the drive arm bracket and then remove the regulator.
5. Remove the motor and drive from the regulator.

### Installation

1. Position the motor and drive assembly on the regulator and install four nut and retainer assemblies.
2. Position the regulator on the inner panel and install four screw and washer assemblies. Engage the regulator arm with the drive arm bracket.
3. Connect the motor wiring. Install the watershield and trim panel.

## 1973-75 Ford, Mercury and Meteor Hardtop

### Removal

1. Remove the trim panel and the watershield.
2. Raise the glass to the up position and locate two dimples on the inner quarter panel.
3. At the dimples drill a 3/4 inch hole.

4. Disconnect the wires from the motor at the connector.
5. Remove the three screws that hold the motor and drive assembly to the regulator and remove the assembly from the inner panel.

### Installation

1. Install the motor and drive assembly on the regulator and in-

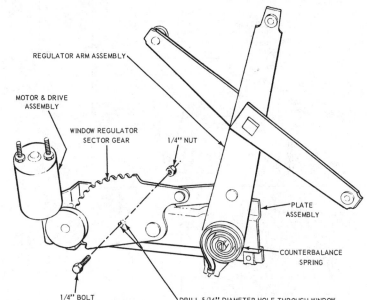

© Ford Motor Co.

*1970-73 Tubular Run and Channel Guide Type Quarter Window Motor Removal Precautions*

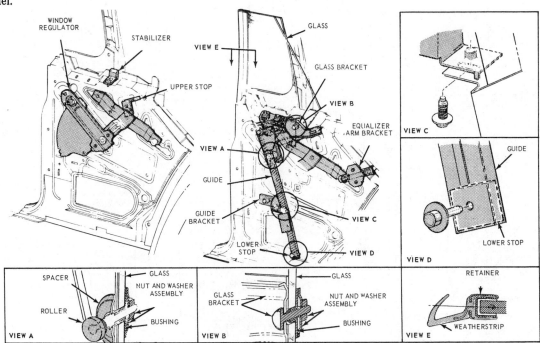

© Ford Motor Co.

*1973-75 Ford, Mercury & Meteor Quarter Window Mechanism*

# Ford Motor Company

stall the three retaining screws making them snug—not tight.

2. Reconnect the motor wires at the connector and cycle the glass

to make sure the gears are engaging properly.

3. Tighten the three motor retaining screws.

4. Put body tape over the two ¾ inch holes drilled in the inner panel.

5. Reinstall the trim panel and the watershield.

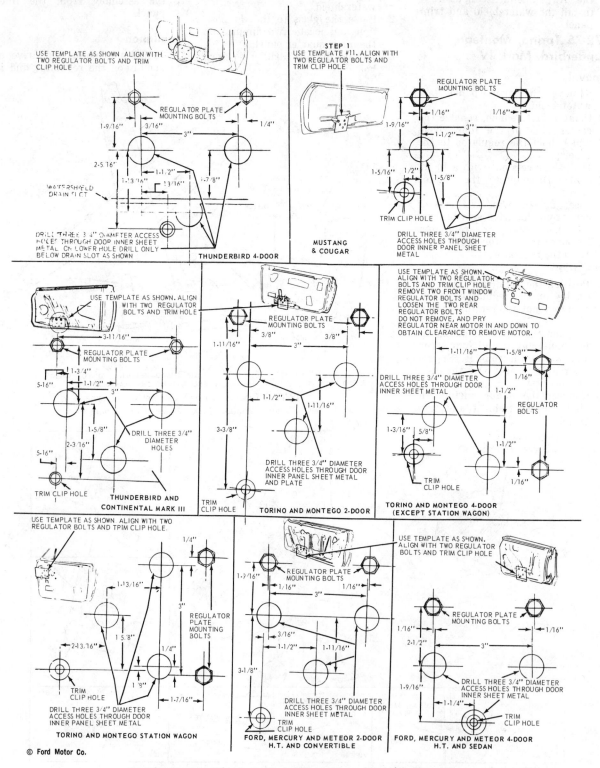

*1971 Ford Products Front Door Window Motor Removal Template Dimensions*

© Ford Motor Co.

# Ford Motor Company

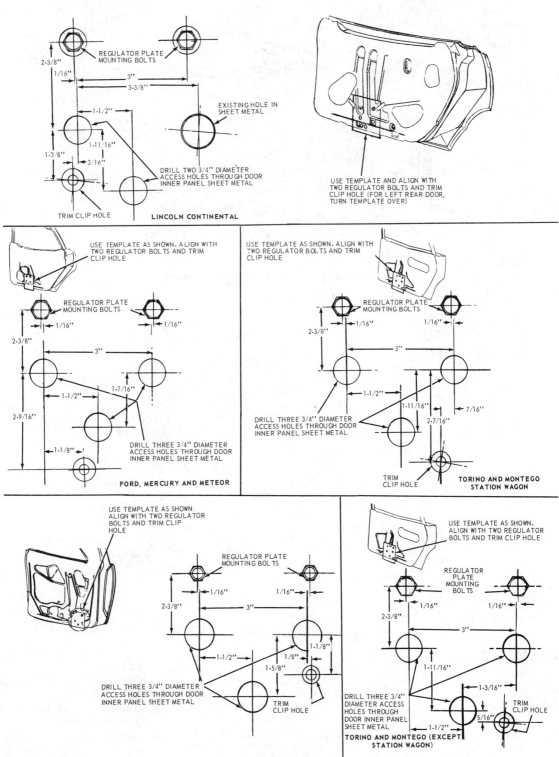

REGULATOR PLATE
MOUNTING BOLTS

2-3/8"

1/16"

3"

3-3/8"

1-1/2"

EXISTING HOLE IN
SHEET METAL

1-11/16"

1-3/8"

3/16"

DRILL TWO 3/4" DIAMETER
ACCESS HOLES THROUGH DOOR
INNER PANEL SHEET METAL

TRIM CLIP HOLE

**LINCOLN CONTINENTAL**

USE TEMPLATE AND ALIGN WITH
TWO REGULATOR BOLTS AND TRIM
CLIP HOLE (FOR LEFT REAR DOOR,
TURN TEMPLATE OVER)

USE TEMPLATE AS SHOWN. ALIGN WITH
TWO REGULATOR BOLTS AND TRIM
CLIP HOLE

REGULATOR PLATE
MOUNTING BOLTS

1/16"       1/16"

2-3/8"

3"

1-7/16"

1-1/2"

2-9/16"

1-1/8"

DRILL THREE 3/4"
ACCESS HOLES THROUGH DOOR
INNER PANEL SHEET METAL

**FORD, MERCURY AND METEOR**

USE TEMPLATE AS SHOWN. ALIGN WITH
TWO REGULATOR BOLTS AND TRIM
CLIP HOLE

REGULATOR PLATE
MOUNTING BOLTS

1/16"       1/16"

2-3/8"

3"

1-1/2"

1-11/16"

7/16"

2-7/16"

DRILL THREE 3/4" DIAMETER
ACCESS HOLES THROUGH DOOR
INNER PANEL SHEET METAL

TRIM
CLIP HOLE

**TORINO AND MONTEGO
STATION WAGON**

USE TEMPLATE AS SHOWN.
ALIGN WITH TWO REGULATOR
BOLTS AND TRIM CLIP
HOLE

REGULATOR PLATE
MOUNTING BOLTS

1/16"       1/16"

2-3/8"

3"

1-1/2"

1-1/8"

1/8"

1-5/8"

DRILL THREE 3/4" DIAMETER
ACCESS HOLES THROUGH DOOR
INNER PANEL SHEET METAL

TRIM
CLIP HOLE

USE TEMPLATE AS SHOWN.
ALIGN WITH TWO REGULATOR
BOLTS AND TRIM CLIP HOLE

REGULATOR
PLATE
MOUNTING
BOLTS

1/16"       1/16"

2-3/8"

3"

1-11/16"

1-3/16"

DRILL THREE 3/4"
DIAMETER ACCESS
HOLES THROUGH
DOOR INNER PANEL
SHEET METAL

1-1/2"

5/16"

TRIM
CLIP HOLE

**TORINO AND MONTEGO (EXCEPT
STATION WAGON)**

© Ford Motor Co.

*1971 Ford Product Rear Door Window Motor Removal Template Dimensions*

# Ford Motor Company

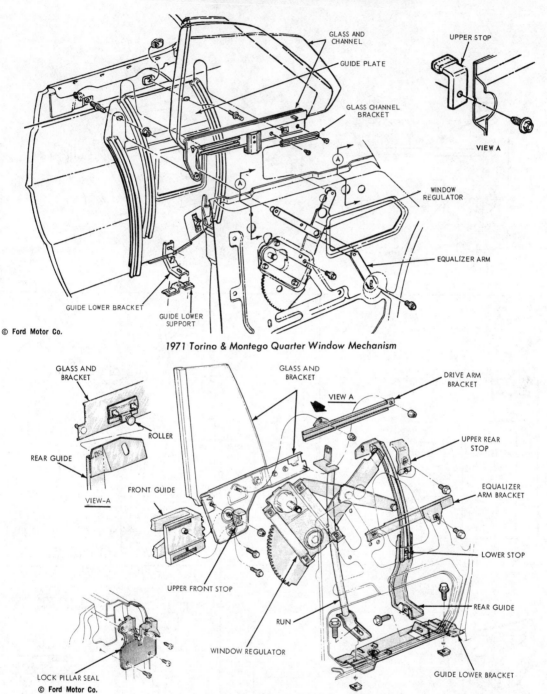

GLASS AND CHANNEL

GUIDE PLATE

GLASS CHANNEL BRACKET

UPPER STOP

VIEW A

WINDOW REGULATOR

EQUALIZER ARM

GUIDE LOWER BRACKET

GUIDE LOWER SUPPORT

© Ford Motor Co.

*1971 Torino & Montego Quarter Window Mechanism*

GLASS AND BRACKET

GLASS AND BRACKET

DRIVE ARM BRACKET

VIEW A

ROLLER

REAR GUIDE

UPPER REAR STOP

FRONT GUIDE

EQUALIZER ARM BRACKET

VIEW-A

LOWER STOP

UPPER FRONT STOP

REAR GUIDE

RUN

WINDOW REGULATOR

GUIDE LOWER BRACKET

LOCK PILLAR SEAL

© Ford Motor Co.

*1971 Ford & Mercury Quarter Window Mechanism*

## WINDOW MOTOR AND DRIVE
### Front and Rear Doors
### 1971 All Models
#### Removal

1. Remove the trim panel and watershield.
2. Remove vacuum hose retainer clips and then move the hoses out of the way.

3. Remove door mounted radio speakers if so equipped.
4. Make a template using the appropriate illustration. The template must be reversed for use on left hand doors.
5. Position the template on the door and use a center punch to mark the drill locations.
6. Raise the window all the way. Drill the holes with a ¾ in. hole

saw with a pilot drill about ¼ in. long.
7. Disconnect the motor wire multiple connector.
8. Remove the bracket which supports the motor.
9. Remove the three screws which attach the motor and drive to the regulator, working through the three holes. The motor and drive may now be removed.

# Ford Motor Company

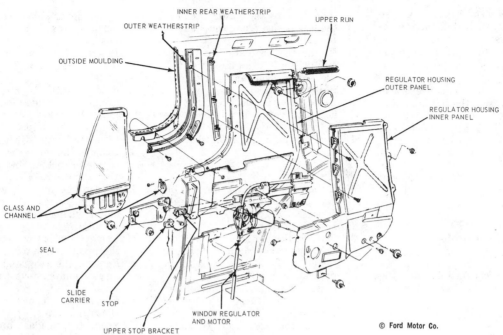

INNER REAR WEATHERSTRIP
OUTER WEATHERSTRIP
UPPER RUN
OUTSIDE MOULDING
REGULATOR HOUSING OUTER PANEL
REGULATOR HOUSING INNER PANEL
GLASS AND CHANNEL
SEAL
SLIDE CARRIER
STOP
UPPER STOP BRACKET
WINDOW REGULATOR AND MOTOR
© Ford Motor Co.

*1971 Mark III Quarter Window Mechanism*

## Installation

1. Put the motor and drive in position and install the mounting screws finger tight.
2. Connect the wires and then operate the window up and down to ensure that the gears are properly engaged. Then tighten the screws snugly.
3. Install the motor support bracket and then put body tape over the holes.
4. Install the radio speaker and relocate and clip vacuum hose retainer clips as necessary. Install the watershield and trim panel.

## WINDOW MOTOR AND DRIVE
### Quarter Windows
### 1971 Torino, and Montego
#### Removal

1. Remove the trim panel and watershield.
2. Remove the attaching screw which holds the equalizer arm to the inner panel.
3. Remove the rear glass channel bracket and disconnect the motor wires.
4. Remove the four regulator attaching screws.
5. Disengage the four regulator arm rollers from the glass channel and remove the regulator.
6. Mount the regulator in a vise. Drill a 5/16 in. hole through

the sector gear and regulator plate as shown in the illustration. Install a 1/4 in. bolt in the hole and screw a nut onto the end to hold the sector gear in place after the motor is removed.
7. Remove the motor.

## Installation

1. Install the motor on the regulator.
2. Position the window regulator and put the rollers through the glass channel brackets.
3. Replace the four regulator attaching screws.
4. Install the glass channel bracket. Connect the motor wiring.
5. Position the equalizer arm on the inner panel and then install the attaching screw.
6. Adjust the mechanism as described in the section on adjustments.
7. Install the watershield and quarter trim panel.

## 1971 Mustang and Cougar
### Removal

1. Remove the trim panel and watershield.
2. Hold the glass up while removing the spring retainer and the washer from the glass bracket stud.
3. Remove the regulator arm and washer from the stud.
4. Remove the regulator mounting

screws and then remove the regulator.

## Installation

1. Install the regulator with the four attaching screws.
2. Place the washer, regulator arm, another washer, and the spring retainer in that order (see illustration) on the glass bracket stud.
3. Install the watershield and trim panel.

## 1971 Ford and Mercury 2 Door Sedan
### Removal

1. Remove the trim panel and watershield.
2. Remove the equalizer arm-to-quarter inner panel attaching screws.
3. Remove the two nuts which hold the drive arm bracket onto the glass bracket and remove the bracket.
4. Hold the glass up all the way and remove the regulator attaching screws. Remove the regulator and drive arm bracket. Remove the drive arm bracket from the regulator.

## Installation

1. Install the bracket on the window regulator arms.
2. Put the regulator in position on the quarter panel and position

# Ford Motor Company

the drive arm bracket on the glass bracket. Install the attaching screws.

3. Install the nuts which hold the drive arm bracket to the glass bracket.

4. Reposition the equalizer arm bracket. Install the two attaching screws.

5. Remove the glass support and adjust the window mechanism as described in the section on adjustments.

6. Reinstall the watershield and trim panel.

## 1971 Lincoln 2 Door and Ford Convertible

### Removal

1. Raise the convertible top. Remove the trim panel and watershield.

2. Remove the trim panel front retainer bracket.

3. Remove the equalizer arm-to-inner panel attaching screw.

4. Lower the window. Remove the front guide and rear stop.

5. While holding the glass up, remove the glass channel bracket.

6. Disconnect the motor wires and the motor support bracket.

7. Remove the regulator attaching screws and then disengage the arm roller from the glass channel.

8. Raise the glass to permit removal of the rear guide and

then remove the guide. Remove the regulator from the quarter panel.

9. Mount the regulator in a vise and drill a 5/16 in. hole through the sector gear and plate. (see illustration)

10. Install a 1/4 in. bolt through the hole and screw a nut onto the other side.

11. Remove the motor from the regulator.

### Installation

1. Install the regulator on the inner panel with the attaching screws.

2. Install the rear guide.

3. Connect the motor wires and install the motor support bracket.

4. Install the glass channel bracket.

5. Lower the glass and install the front guide. Install the upper rear stop.

6. Install the regulator equalizer arm to the inner panel with the attaching screw.

7. Position the equalizer arm on the inner panel with the attaching screw. Adjust as necessary. (see the section on adjustments)

8. Install the watershield and trim panel.

## 1971 Mark III

### Removal

1. Remove the trim panel and

watershield. This requires removal of the rear seat back and cushion.

2. Pry the light from the roof quarter trim panel and remove the panel.

3. Remove the headlining from around the window opening. Remove the tacking strip.

4. Remove the nuts and washers from the lower adjusting screws.

5. Remove the screws that hold the regulator panel in place and then remove it.

6. Loosen the quarter window retaining screws. Disconnect the motor wiring and remove the assembly.

7. Remove the screws and separate the inner and outer door panels.

8. Remove the two stop attaching screws and remove the window stop.

9. Remove the cable clamp from the regulator.

10. Separate the glass and its carrier from the regulator.

11. Drill a 5/16 in. hole through the sector gear and plate of the regulator. Install a 1/4 in. bolt through the hole and place a nut on the end.

12. Remove the motor assembly.

### Installation

1. Lubricate the regulator, if necessary. Put the glass and the slide carrier on the regulator channel.

2. Install the stop and the cable clamp.

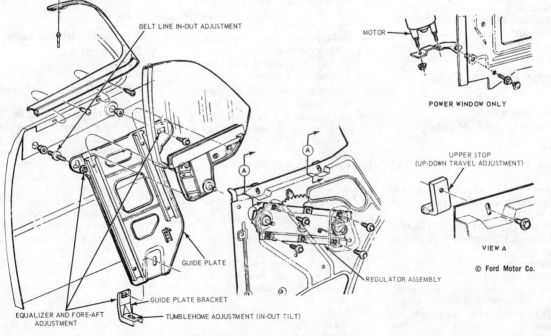

BELT LINE IN-OUT ADJUSTMENT

MOTOR

POWER WINDOW ONLY

GUIDE PLATE

GUIDE PLATE BRACKET

EQUALIZER AND FORE-AFT ADJUSTMENT

TUMBLEHOME ADJUSTMENT (IN-OUT TILT)

REGULATOR ASSEMBLY

UPPER STOP (UP-DOWN TRAVEL ADJUSTMENT)

VIEW A

© Ford Motor Co.

*1971 Thunderbird Quarter Window Mechanism*

# Ford Motor Company

3. Put the inner panel on the quarter window outer panel and install the attaching screws.
4. Install the assembly in the vehicle with the retaining screws. Tighten the two pillar screws and connect the motor wires.
5. Install the regulator panel. Install the headlining tacking strip. Attach the headlining to the strip.
6. Install the nuts and washers on the lower adjusting screws. Adjust the window as described under "Adjustments."
7. Install the roof quarter trim panel and the light.
8. Install the watershield and quarter trim panel.

## 1971 Thunderbird

### Removal

1. Remove the trim panel and watershield.
2. Disconnect the power window wiring.
3. Remove the window glass as below:
   a. Remove the belt line dust seal and both upper stops.
   b. Remove the clip that retains the regulator arm.
   c. Remove the nuts from the upper front and rear corners of the guide plate.
   d. Remove the bolts which hold the guide plate to the guide mounting bracket.
   e. Remove the glass assembly.
4. Remove the guide plate retaining bolts and remove the guide plate.
5. Remove the regulator arm-to-glass channel retaining clip. Remove the regulator retaining bolts.
6. While supporting the glass, detach the regulator arm from the glass and pull the regulator out.
7. Mount the regulator in a vise and drill a 5/16 in. hole through the sector gear and the regulator plate. Put a 1/4 in. bolt through the hole and install a nut in the other side. The motor may now be removed.

### Installation

1. Install the motor. Put the regulator in place and install the four mounting bolts. Remove the sector gear safety bolt installed during disassembly.
2. Connect the motor wiring. Push the pin on the regulator arm through the glass channel and then install the retaining pin.
3. Install the trim panel and watershield in reverse order of above.

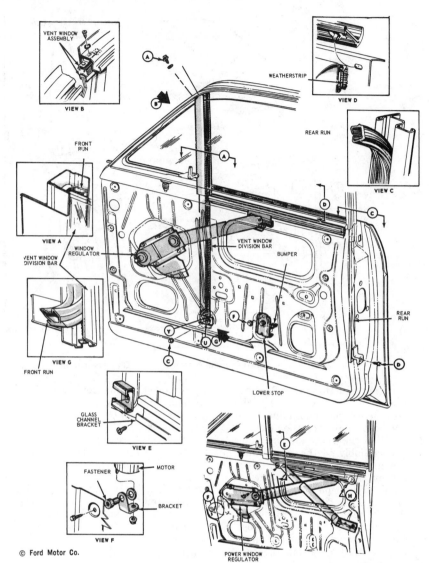

© Ford Motor Co.

*1970 Fairlane & Montego Front Door Window Mechanism*

## WINDOW REGULATOR AND MOTOR—FRONT DOOR
### 1970 Montego and Fairlane 4 Door Sedan and Wagon
#### Removal

1. Remove the trim panel and watershield.
2. Remove the regulator arm roller bracket attaching screws and then remove the bracket.
3. Disconnect the motor wires.
4. Remove the motor bracket inner attaching screw.
5. Remove the locknut and washer from the vent window division bar lower adjusting screw.
6. Remove the four screws which hold the window regulator to the inner door panel. While supporting the glass and channel assembly, disengage the regulator arm from the glass channel. Lay the regulator in the bottom of the door panel.
7. Remove the lower stop from the inner panel.
8. Lower the glass. Pull the front run and its retainer out of the vent window division bar.
9. Remove the regulator assembly. Mount it in a vise, and drill a 5/16 in. hole through the sector gear and regulator plate. Install a 1/4 in. bolt and screw a safety nut onto the other side.
10. Remove the motor.

#### Installation

1. Place the motor and transmission on the regulator and install the attaching screws.

## Ford Motor Company

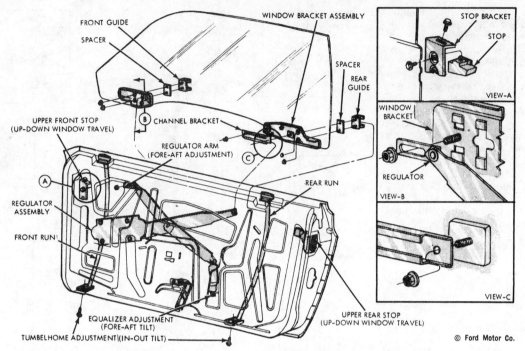

*1970 Fairlane & Montego Two Door Front Door Window Mechanism*

2. Put the regulator in its final position in the door. Insert the front run and its retainer into the vent window division bar.
3. Position the glass and the channel assembly in the runs. Raise the glass and support it. Place the nut and washer on the vent window division bar lower adjusting screw.
4. Put the regulator arm roller into the glass channel bracket. Position the regulator on the inner door panel and install the four attaching screws.
5. Install the regulator arm roller bracket with the two attaching screws.
6. Install the motor bracket on the inner door panel with the attaching screw. Adjust the window as described in the section on adjustments.
7. Install the lower stop. Connect the wiring, and install the watershield and trim panel.

### 1970 Ford and Mercury 2 and 4 Door Sedans and Wagons

#### Removal

1. Remove the trim panel and watershield.
2. Remove the glass channel retaining screws and secure the window in the up position.
3. Disconnect the motor bracket and wires.

4. Remove the equalizer bracket.
5. Remove the regulator attaching bolts and pull the regulator from the door.
6. Mount the regulator in a vise and drill a 5/16 in. hole through the regulator plate and sector gear.
7. Install a 1/4 in. bolt through the hole and install a nut on the other side. Remove the motor assembly.

#### Installation

1. Install the motor assembly. Remove the safety bolt.
2. Position the regulator in the door. Engage the equalizer arm in the arm bracket and install the retaining bolts.
3. Remove the prop used to secure the window in the up position. Position the glass channel bracket and install the screws that hold it in place on the glass channel.
4. Connect the motor wires and install the motor bracket. Install the watershield and trim panel.

### 1970 Montego and Fairlane 2 Door Hardtop, Ranchero, and Convertible

#### Removal

1. Remove the trim panel and weathersheet.

2. Remove the retaining nuts for the regulator channel bracket. Remove the bracket.
3. Remove the nut which holds the regulator arm to the pivot stud.
4. Remove the regulator arm-to-door inner panel nut.
5. Move the glass up all the way and support it.
6. Remove the regulator assembly mounting bolts and the motor mounting bracket bolt.
7. Disconnect the motor wires and remove the regulator and motor out through the access hole.
8. Drill a 5/16 in. hole through the regulator plate and sector gear and install a 1/4 in. bolt through the hole. Install a nut on the other side. Remove the motor assembly.

#### Installation

1. Position the regulator and motor in the door and install the mounting bolts. Install the motor mounting bracket and connect the motor wires.
2. Install the regulator arm attaching bolt.
3. Position the regulator arm onto the pivot stud and install the nut and washer.
4. Put the channel bracket in position and install the nut and washer.
5. Adjust the window according to the section on adjustments.

# Ford Motor Company

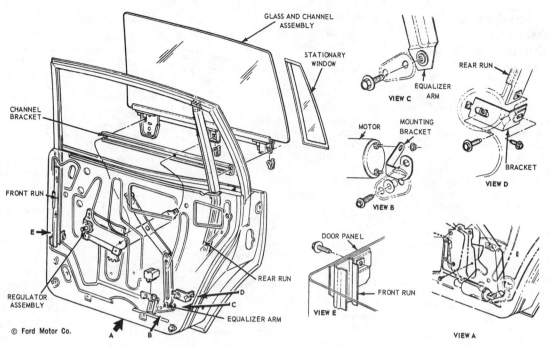

*1970 Thunderbird Front Door Window Mechanism*

6. Install the weathersheet and trim panel.

## 1970 Ford, Mercury, Mustang, and Cougar—Ventless Glass

### Removal

1. Remove the trim panel and watershield. Remove the motor bracket and disconnect the wires.
2. Disconnect the window regulator arms at the pivots. Disconnect the glass channel bracket where it mounts onto the glass channel.
3. Disconnect the remote control rod from the door latch.
4. Remove the rear weatherstrip cap. Remove the upper rear stop and the belt weatherstrip and moulding.
5. Remove the regulator attaching screws and remove the regulator.
6. Drill a 5/16 in. hole through the regulator and sector gear and install a 1/4 in. bolt and nut. Remove the motor assembly.

### Installation

1. Install the regulator, the belt weatherstrip, and the moulding.
2. Connect the regulator to the door at the pivots.
3. Place the glass channel bracket on the arm roller and install the bracket onto the glass channel.
4. Install the upper rear stop.
5. Connect the remote control rod to the door latch. Install the

motor bracket and connect the wires.
6. Install the rear weatherstrip cap and adjust the position of the glass and the stops and guides as described in the section on adjustments.
7. Install the watershield and door trim panel.

## 1970 Thunderbird and Mark III

### Removal

1. Remove the trim panel and watershield.
2. Position the glass so it is about half way down and support it there.
3. Remove the two screws and remove the glass channel bracket from the glass channel.
4. Remove the regulator arm-to-glass channel pivot by removing the nut and washer and pulling them off. Raise the glass all the way up and support it there.
5. Disconnect the regulator arm pivot from the inner panel.
6. Remove the four regulator mounting screws and the screw, retainer, and washer for the regulator and the motor bracket.
7. Disconnect the door latch remote control link. Remove one screw which attaches the link retaining clip to the inner panel and then let the rod hang from the latch.

8. Disconnect the wires at the connector and remove the motor and regulator. Remove the motor and transmission assembly.

### Installation

1. Position the motor and transmission onto the regulator and install the attaching screws.
2. Install the regulator with the four attaching screws.
3. Position the motor bracket and install the screw, washer, and retainer. Tighten the screws for the regulator and motor bracket.
4. Connect the door latch remote control link. Install the retaining clip.
5. Lower the glass until it is about half way down and support it there.
6. Position the regulator arm onto the glass channel. Install the pivot.
7. Put the regulator arm drive bracket in position and install the two attaching screws.
8. Remove the window support and attach the regulator arm pivot to the inner door panel.
9. Raise the window all the way, move it to the proper fore and aft position, and then tighten the pivot nut.
10. Connect the motor wires and install the watershield and trim panel.

# Ford Motor Company

## Window Regulator and Motor—Rear Door
### 1970 Fairlane and Montego 4 Door Sedan

### Removal

1. Remove the trim panel and watershield.
2. Disconnect the motor wiring connector. Remove the equalizer arm bracket.
3. Prop the glass and channel up and remove the glass channel bracket attaching screws. Separate the channel bracket and regulator arm rollers.
4. Remove the motor bracket attaching screw and the four regulator attaching screws and remove the regulator.
5. Drill a 5/16 in. hole through the sector gear and the regulator plate. Put a 1/4 in. bolt through the hole and install a nut onto the other end.
6. Remove the motor and drive.

### Installation

1. Install the motor and drive onto the regulator.
2. Position the regulator inside the door and engage the regulator arm rollers with the glass channel bracket.
3. Install the four attaching screws which hold the regulator to the inner door panel. Install the motor bracket attaching screw.
4. Install the equalizer arm bracket over the regulator arm roller and onto the inner door panel. Install the two attaching screws.
5. Install the glass channel bracket onto the glass channel.
6. Connect the motor wiring.
7. Install the watershield and trim panel.

### 1970 Fairlane and Montego Station Wagon
#### Removal

1. Remove the trim panel and watershield.

2. Lower the glass.
3. Remove the screw which mounts the lower division bar bracket and remove the bracket.
4. Remove the upper attaching screw from the division bar bracket.
5. Remove the division bar and rear run assembly.
6. Remove the stationary glass and weatherstrip.
7. Remove the four window regulator attaching screws and the equalizer arm bracket attaching screws. Remove the screws which hold the front roller carrier to the glass channel.
8. Remove the glass channel bracket-to-glass channel retaining screws.
9. Remove the glass and channel assembly. Remove the window regulator and motor.
10. Drill a 5/16 in. hole through the sector gear and regulator plate. Install a 1/4 in. bolt into the hole and install a nut onto

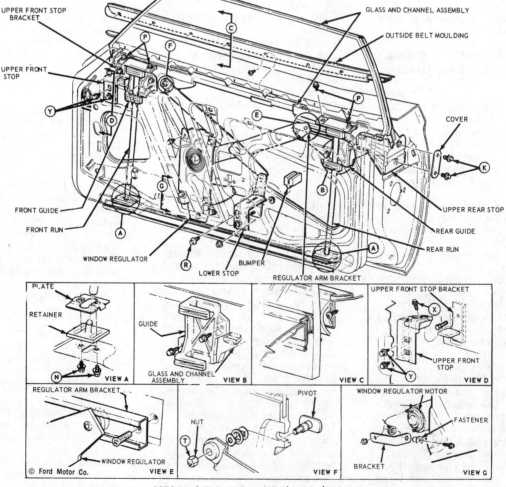

*1970 Mark III Front Door Window Mechanism*

# Ford Motor Company

the other end. Remove the motor and drive assembly.

## Installation

1. Install the motor and drive onto the regulator.
2. Lubricate the mechanism if necessary.
3. Position the regulator and drive within the door and then install the attaching screws.
4. Position the glass channel bracket onto the window rollers and then install the glass and channel assembly.
5. Install the glass channel bracket attaching screws.
6. Align the front roller carrier with the glass channel and install the attaching screws.
7. Install the stationary window glass and weatherstrip. (The factory recommends coating the weatherstrip with silicone before assembly.)
8. Install the division bar and rear run and install the upper attaching screw.
9. Install the division bar lower bracket with the two attaching screws.
10. Adjust the window as described in the section on adjustments.
11. Install the watershield and trim panel.

## 1970 Lincoln, Ford, and Mercury 4 Door Hardtops

### Removal

1. Remove the trim panel and watershield.

2. Prop the glass up and then remove the glass channel bracket.
3. Remove the glass channel pivot nut and its bushing.
4. Remove the equalizer arm-to-inner door panel attaching screw.
5. Disconnect the motor wires.
6. Remove the regulator attaching screws and pull it from the door.
7. Drill a 5/16 in. hole through the sector gear and plate of the regulator. Install a 1/4 in. bolt in the hole and screw a nut onto the other side. Remove the motor assembly.

### Installation

1. Install the motor and remove the safety bolt.
2. Install the regulator with the four attaching screws.
3. Install the motor bracket attaching screw and connect the wiring.
4. Connect the equalizer arm to the door panel.
5. Connect the regulator arm to the glass channel pivot with the nut and bushing.
6. Position the channel bracket to the regulator arm roller and the glass channel and then install the attaching screws.
7. Adjust the window as described in the section on adjustments.
8. Install the watershield and trim panel.

## 1970 Ford and Mercury 4 Door Sedan and Wagon

### Removal

1. Remove the trim panel and watershield.

2. Prop the glass and channel in the up position.
3. Remove the glass channel attaching screws. Disconnect the motor bracket and wires.
4. Remove the window regulator attaching screws. Separate the regulator arm rollers from the equalizer arm brackets. Remove the regulator. The motor may now be removed.

### Installation

1. Put the regulator in position, engaging the equalizer arm brackets, and install the attaching screws.
2. Put the glass channel bracket in position and engage it with the regulator arm rollers. Install the attaching screws.
3. Install the bracket and connect the wires. Remove the window glass support.
4. Install the watershield and trim panel.

## 1970 Thunderbird

### Removal

1. Remove the trim panel and the watershield.
2. Position and then support the glass about 3/4 of the way down.
3. Remove the regulator arm brackets from the glass channels.
4. Remove the regulator arm-to-glass channel pivot and its bushing and washer.
5. Remove the pivot-to-door inner panel nut, washer, screw, and bushing.

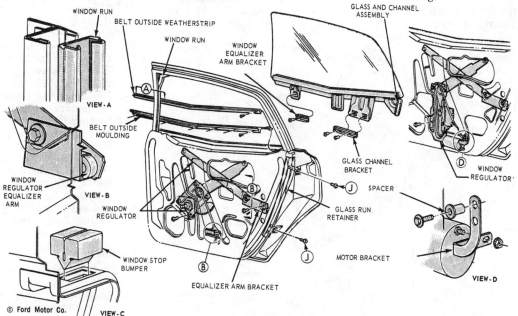

*1970 Ford & Mercury Rear Door Window Mechanism*

# Ford Motor Company

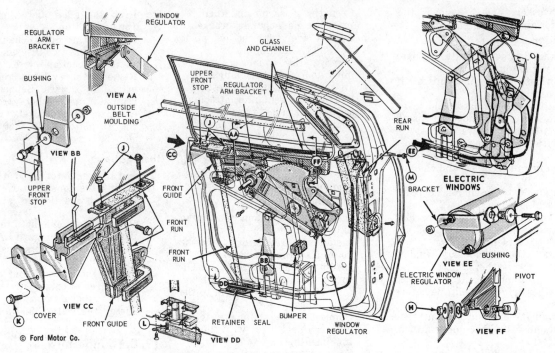

*1970 Thunderbird Rear Door Window Mechanism*

6. Raise the glass all the way and support it there.
7. Remove the regulator attaching screws and remove the regulator from the door.
8. Drill a 5/16 in. hole through the sector gear and plate of the regulator and install a 1/4 in. bolt through the hole. Screw a nut onto the other side. Remove the motor assembly.

## Installation

1. Position the regulator and install the attaching screws.

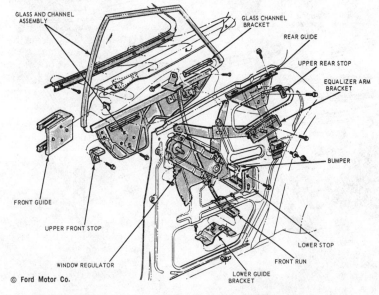

*1970 Ford & Mercury Two Door Hardtop Quarter Window Mechanism*

2. Lower the glass until it is 3/4 of the way down and support it there.
3. Install the regulator arm bracket with the attaching screws.
4. Position the regulator arm onto the glass channel via the pivot, bushing, washers and nuts.
5. Remove the glass support and attach the regulator arm pivot to the inner door panel.
6. Attach the equalizer arm to the inner door panel via the screw, bushing, washer and nut.

7. Raise the window all the way, adjust the fore and aft position as required for proper fit, and tighten the pivot nut.
8. Install the watershield and trim panel.

## QUARTER WINDOW REGULATOR AND MOTOR
## 1970 Ford and Mercury
## 2 Door Hardtop

### Removal

1. Remove the trim panel and watershield.
2. Remove the equalizer arm bracket. Remove the front guide.
3. Prop the glass up and then remove the glass channel brackets.
4. Disconnect the motor wiring and the motor support bracket.
5. Remove the window regulator attaching screws.
6. Disengage the regulator arm roller and remove the regulator.
7. Drill a 5/16 in. hole through the sector gear and side plate of the regulator and install a 1/4 in. bolt and nut to hold the gear in place during motor removal. Remove the motor assembly.

### Installation

1. Put the regulator in position and install the attaching screws.
2. Connect the motor wires. Install the motor support bracket.
3. Install the glass channel bracket and front guide.

# Ford Motor Company

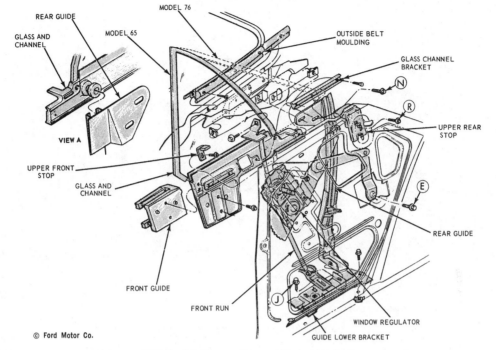

REAR GUIDE

GLASS AND CHANNEL

MODEL 65

MODEL 76

OUTSIDE BELT MOULDING

GLASS CHANNEL BRACKET

VIEW A

UPPER FRONT STOP

GLASS AND CHANNEL

FRONT GUIDE

FRONT RUN

UPPER REAR STOP

REAR GUIDE

WINDOW REGULATOR

GUIDE LOWER BRACKET

© Ford Motor Co.

*1970 Ford & Mercury Quarter Window Mechanism*

4. Install the equalizer arm bracket and adjust it as necessary.
5. Install the watershield and trim panel.

## 1970 Lincoln, Ford and Mercury, 2 Door Hardtop Formal and Convertible

### Removal

1. Raise the convertible top part way if applicable. Remove the quarter trim panel and the watershield.
2. Remove the front retainer
3. Remove the screw which at-bracket from the trim panel. taches the equalizer arm to the inner door panel.
4. Lower the glass and remove the front guide and upper rear stop.
5. Support the glass and remove the glass channel bracket.
6. Disconnect the motor wires and support bracket.
7. Remove the regulator attaching screws. Disengage the regulator arm roller.
8. Raise the glass part way and remove it. Remove the rear guide and then remove the regulator from the quarter panel.
9. Drill a 5/16 in. hole through the sector gear and plate of the regulator. (See illustration) Install

a ¼ in. bolt and nut to keep the gear from moving when the motor is removed. Remove the motor.

### Installation

1. Install the regulator with the four attaching screws.
2. Install the rear guide, connect the motor wires, and install the motor support bracket.
3. Install the glass channel bracket.
4. Lower the glass partway and install the front guide. Install the upper rear stop.
5. Install the equalizer arm with the attaching screw. Adjust the equalizer arm as described in the section on adjustments.
6. Install the watershield and trim panel.

## 1970 Mark III

### Removal

1. Remove the trim panel and watershield.
2. Remove the quarter roof panel overhead light and then remove the roof panel.
3. Remove the headlining and tacking strip.
4. Remove the two locknuts and their washers from the lower adjusting screws.
5. Remove the regulator panel attaching screws and then remove the panel.

6. Loosen the two screws which retain the quarter window assembly at the pillar and remove the quarter window assembly attaching screws.
7. Disconnect the wiring and then remove the assembly.
8. Remove the outer panel-to-inner panel attaching screws and separate the two panels. Remove the stop attaching screws and remove the stop.
9. Remove the regulator cable clamp.
10. Remove the glass and carrier.
11. Drill a 5/16 in. hole through the sector gear and regulator plate. Install a ¼ in. bolt and nut through the hole. Then remove the motor.

### Installation

1. Install the motor assembly on the regulator and remove the safety bolt.
2. Put the glass and side carrier into position on the regulator channel.
3. Install the cable clamp and the stop.
4. Position the inner panel onto the outer panel and install the attaching screws.
5. Tighten the two screws at the pillar and connect the motor wires.
6. Install the regulator panel and

# Ford Motor Company

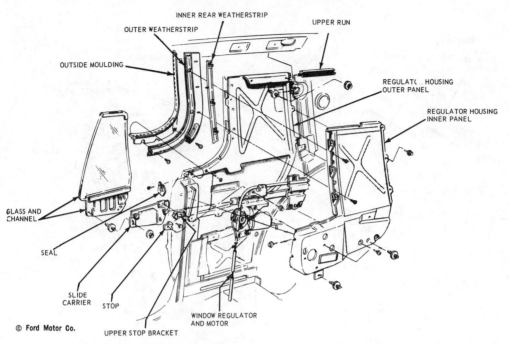

*1970 Mark III Quarter Window Mechanism*

headlining tacking strip. Attach the headlining to the strip.

7. Install the lower adjusting screw nuts and lockwashers.
8. Adjust the window as described in the section on adjustments.
9. Install the roof quarter panel and light, the quarter trim panel, and the watershield.

## 1970 Thunderbird

### Removal

1. Remove the trim panel and weathersheet. Disconnect the motor wiring.
2. Remove the belt line dust seal and both upper stops.
3. Remove the regulator arm-to-glass channel assembly retainer clip.
4. Remove the nuts from the upper front and rear corners of the guide plate. Remove the two bolts at the bottom. Remove the glass assembly from the guide plate.
5. Remove the guide plate. Remove

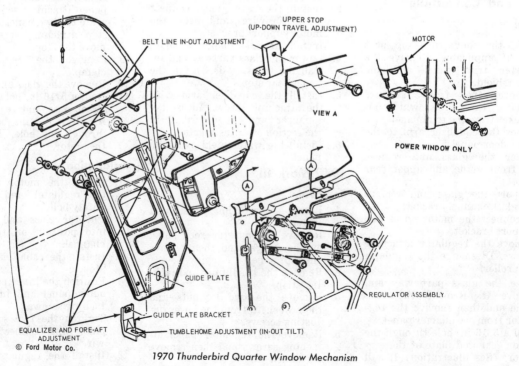

*1970 Thunderbird Quarter Window Mechanism*

# Ford Motor Company

the regulator retaining bolts.

6. Prop the glass up, remove the regulator arm from the glass and then remove the regulator.

7. Drill a 5/16 in. hole through the regulator sector gear and plate and install a 1/4 in. bolt and nut. Remove the motor assembly.

## Installation

1. Install the motor on the regulator and remove the safety bolt.

2. Put the regulator into position and replace the mounting bolts. Connect the motor wiring.

3. Replace the guide plate with the mounting bolts.

4. Position the glass properly and install the upper guide plate attaching bolts.

5. Position the regulator arm to the glass channel and install the retaining clip. Install the upper stops.

6. Adjust the mechanism as described in the section on adjustments.

7. Replace the watershield and trim panel.

## WINDOW REGULATOR AND MOTOR—FRONT DOOR

### 1969 Montego and Fairlane 4 Door Sedan and Wagon

#### Removal

1. Remove the trim panel and watershield.

2. Remove the regulator arm roller bracket attaching screws and then remove the bracket.

3. Disconnect the motor wires

4. Remove the motor bracket inner attaching screw.

5. Remove the locknut and washer from the vent window division bar lower adjusting screw.

6. Remove the four screws which hold the window regulator to the inner door panel. While supporting the glass and channel assembly, disengage the regulator arm from the glass channel. Lay the regulator in the bottom of the door panel.

7. Remove the lower stop from the inner panel.

8. Lower the glass. Pull the front run and its retainer out of the window division bar.

9. Remove the regulator assembly and mount it in a vise. The motor and transmission may now be removed.

#### Installation

1. Install the motor and transmission onto the regulator.

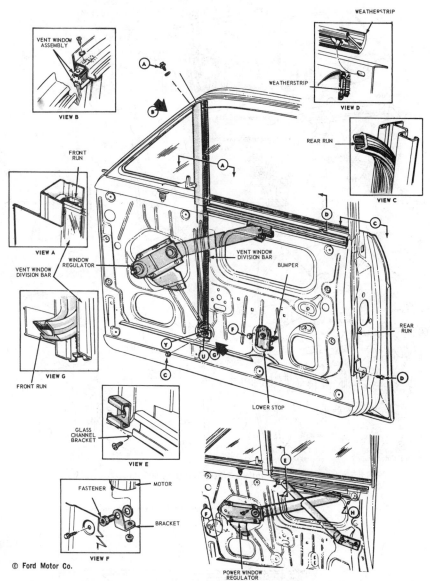

© Ford Motor Co.

*1969 Fairlane & Montego Front Door Window Mechanism*

2. Put the regulator in its final position on the door. Insert the front run and its retainer into the vent window division bar.

3. Position the glass and channel assembly in the runs. Raise the glass and support it. Place the nut and washer on the vent window division bar lower adjusting screw.

4. Put the regulator arm roller into the glass channel bracket. Position the regulator on the inner door panel and install the four attaching screws.

5. Install the regulator arm roller bracket with the two attaching screws.

6. Install the motor bracket on the

inner door panel with the attaching screw. Adjust the window as described in the section on adjustments.

7. Install the lower stop. Connect the wiring and install the watershield and trim panel.

### 1969 Ford and Mercury 2 and 4 Door Sedans and Wagons

#### Removal

1. Remove the trim panel and watershield.

2. Remove the glass channel retaining screws and secure the window in the up position.

3. Disconnect the motor bracket and wires.

# Ford Motor Company

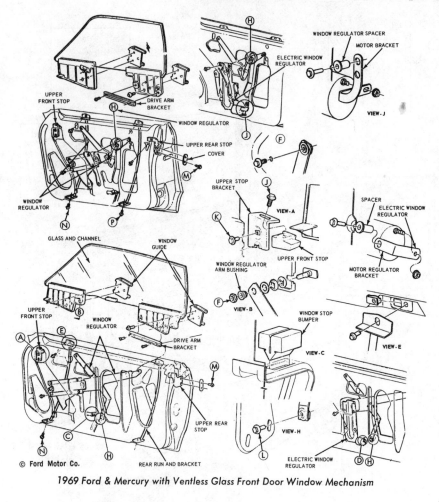

© Ford Motor Co.

*1969 Ford & Mercury with Ventless Glass Front Door Window Mechanism*

4. Remove the equalizer bracket.
5. Remove the regulator attaching bolts and remove the regulator from the door.
6. Mount the regulator in a vise and drill a 5/16 in. hole through the regulator plate and sector gear.
7. Install a 1/4 in. bolt through the hole and install a nut on the other side. Remove the motor assembly.

## Installation

1. Install the motor assembly. Remove the safety bolt.
2. Position the regulator in the door. Engage the equalizer arm in the arm bracket and install the retaining bolts.
3. Remove the prop used to secure the window in the up position. Position the glass channel bracket and install the screws that hold it in place on the glass channel.
4. Connect the motor wires and install the motor bracket. Install the watershield and trim panel.

## 1969 Montego and Fairlane 2 Door and Convertible

### Removal

1. Remove the trim panel and watershield.
2. Prop the glass in the up position. Remove the regulator arm pivot nut and bolt.

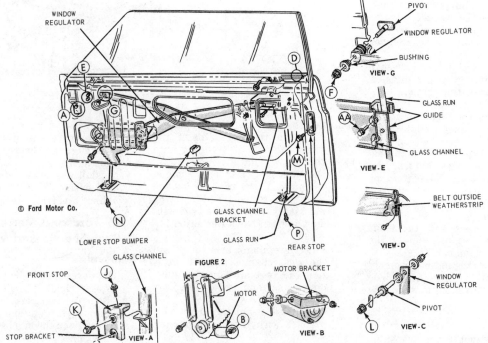

© Ford Motor Co.

*1969 Mustang & Cougar Door Window Mechanism*

# Ford Motor Company

3. Remove the screws which attach the glass channel bracket to the glass channel and remove the bracket.
4. Disconnect the motor wires at the connector and remove the window regulator equalizer arm and retaining nut.
5. Remove the screws which attach the regulator and motor to the inner door panel and remove the regulator.
6. Remove the motor attaching screws and remove the motor.

## Installation

1. Put the motor in position and install the retaining screws.
2. Put the regulator and motor in the door and install the attaching screws.
3. Position the equalizer arm and install the retaining nut.
4. Position the glass channel bracket, engage the regulator arm, and install the retaining nut.

5. Connect the motor wires at the multiple connector.
6. Install the pivot into the glass channel, position the window regulator arm, and install the pivot retaining nut.
7. Remove the prop used to hold the glass up and install the watershield and trim panel.

## 1969 Ventless Glass—Ford, Mercury, Mustang, and Cougar

### Removal

1. Remove the trim panel and watershield.
2. Remove the power window motor bracket and disconnect the wiring. Disconnect the regulator arms at the pivots.
3. Disconnect the glass channel bracket. Disconnect the door latch remote control rod.
4. Remove the rear weatherstrip cap.
5. Remove the upper rear stop and

the belt weatherstrip and molding.
6. Remove the regulator attaching screws and remove the regulator.
7. Remove the motor from the regulator.

## Installation

1. Install the motor on the regulator. Position the regulator and install the attaching screws.
2. Install the belt weatherstrip and molding.
3. Connect the regulator arms at the pivots.
4. Attach the glass channel bracket to the glass channel and engage it with the regulator arm roller.
5. Install the upper rear stop. Connect the remote control rod to the door latch.
6. Install the motor bracket and connect the wiring.
7. Install the rear weatherstrip cap, align the glass, and adjust the stops and guides as described in the section on adjustments.

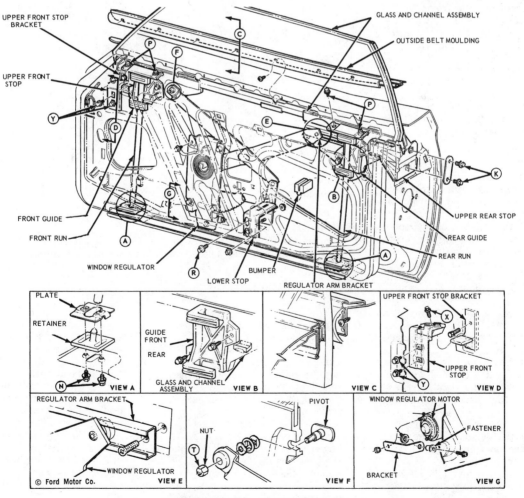

*1969 Mark III Door Window Mechanism*

# Ford Motor Company

8. Install the watershield and trim panel.

## 1969 Thunderbird and Mark III

### Removal

1. Remove the trim panel and watershield.
2. Support the glass so it is about half way down. Remove the regulator arm drive bracket-to-glass channel screws and remove the bracket.
3. Disassemble the regulator arm-to-glass channel pivot and remove it.
4. Raise the glass all the way and support it there. Disconnect the regulator arm-to-inner panel pivot.
5. Remove the screws which attach the regulator to the inner door panel.
6. Remove the screw which attaches the motor bracket to the inner panel and the associated retainer and washer.
7. Disconnect the door latch remote control link from the remote control. Remove one of the link retaining clip screws and allow the rod to hang from the latch.
8. Disconnect the motor wiring connector and remove the regulator assembly.
9. Place the regulator in a vise. The motor and transmission may then be removed.

### Installation

1. Install the motor and transmission onto the regulator.
2. Install the regulator in the door without fully tightening the screws.
3. Install the motor bracket onto the inner panel with the screw, retainer, and washer. Then, tighten motor and bracket attaching screws.
4. Connect the door latch remote control link.
5. Lower the glass half way and support it.
6. Install the regulator arm-to-glass channel pivot.
7. Install the regulator arm bracket onto the glass channel and engage it with the regulator arm. Install the bracket attaching screws.
8. Remove the glass support and install the regulator arm pivot onto the door inner panel with the attaching nut.
9. Raise the window all the way and adjust the fore and aft position as required. Then tighten the pivot nut.

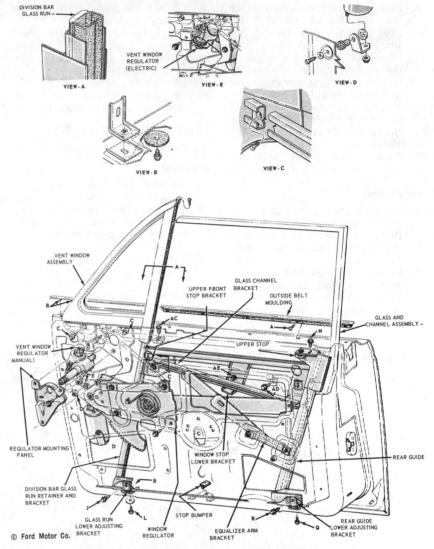

© Ford Motor Co.

*1969 Lincoln Continental Door Window Mechanism*

10. Connect the motor wires and install the watershield and trim panel.

## 1969 Lincoln Continental

### Removal

1. Remove the trim panel, watershield, and access cover.
2. Remove the window regulator equalizer arm bracket by removing the retaining nuts and then removing the bracket.
3. Disconnect the wiring connector, remove the retaining clip, and remove the motor bracket retaining screw.
4. Lower the window and remove the glass channel bracket.
5. Remove the front run lower retaining bolt and lean the run outboard.
6. Remove the regulator assembly.

7. Place the assembly in a vise and remove the motor and drive assembly.

### Installation

1. If the regulator is being replaced, move the mechanism against the spring until it is in the same position as the old one —before installing the motor.
2. Install the motor.
3. Install the assembly in the door with the retaining bolts. Install the motor bracket retaining screw.
4. Install the glass channel bracket. Reposition the front run and install the lower retaining bolt.
5. Connect the motor wiring connector and install the wiring clip.
6. Install the equalizer arm brack-

# Ford Motor Company

et. Install the access cover, watershield, and trim panel.

## WINDOW REGULATOR AND MOTOR—REAR DOOR
### 1969 Fairlane and Montego 4 Door Sedan
#### Removal

1. Remove the trim panel and watershield.

2. Disconnect the motor wires. Remove the equalizer arm bracket.
3. Support the glass and channel. Remove the three channel bracket attaching screws. Remove the glass channel bracket from the regulator arm rollers.
4. Remove the motor bracket attaching screw.
5. Remove the regulator attaching screws and remove the regulator.

6. Remove the motor.

#### Installation

1. Install the motor. Put the regulator in place and engage the arm rollers with the glass channel bracket.
2. Line up the screw holes and install the attaching screws.
3. Install the motor bracket attaching screw.

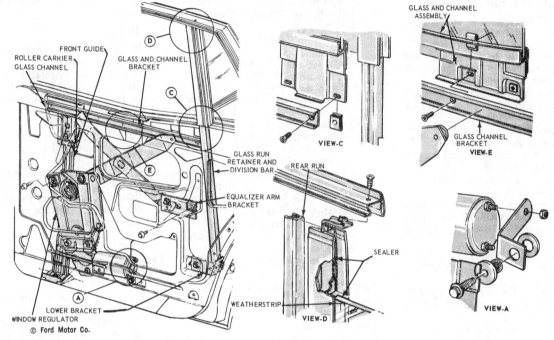

*1969 Fairlane & Montego Rear Door Window Mechanism*

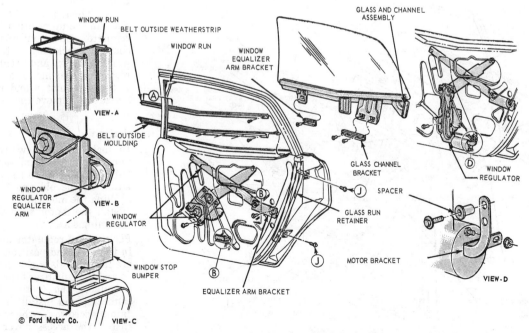

*1969 Ford & Mercury Rear Door Window Mechanism*

# Ford Motor Company

4. Position the regulator arm roller into the slot in the equalizer arm bracket and then install the bracket onto the inner panel.
5. Position the glass channel bracket and install the attaching screws.
6. Connect the motor wires.
7. Remove the window support and install the watershield and trim panel.

## 1969 Fairlane and Montego Station Wagons

### Removal

1. Remove the trim panel and watershield. Lower the glass all the way.
2. Remove the division bar lower bracket attaching screws and remove the bracket.
3. Remove the division bar upper attaching screw. Remove the division bar and rear run assembly from the door.
4. Remove the stationary glass and weatherstrip.
5. Remove the window regulator attaching screws and the equalizer arm bracket attaching screws.
6. Remove the roller front carrier-to-glass channel attaching screws.
7. Remove the glass channel bracket-to-glass channel attaching screws.
8. Remove the window glass and channel from the door.

9. Remove the regulator and motor assembly and then remove the motor and drive from the regulator.

### Installation

1. Install the motor and drive on the regulator.
2. Install the regulator and drive into the door.
3. Position the glass channel bracket on the regulator arm rollers.
4. Position the window glass and channel and install the glass channel bracket attaching screws.
5. Align the front roller carrier with the glass channel and install the attaching screws.
6. Lubricate the stationary window glass weatherstrip with silicone and then position the glass and weatherstrip in the door.
7. Put the division bar and rear run into position. Install the division bar upper attaching screw.
8. Put the lower division bar bracket into position and install the attaching screws.
9. Adjust the mechanism as described in the section on adjustments.
10. Install the watershield and trim panel.

## 1969 Ford and Mercury 4 Door Hardtop

### Removal

1. Remove the trim panel and watershield.
2. Prop the glass and channel assembly in the up position.
3. Remove the glass channel-to-bracket attaching screws.
4. Disconnect the motor bracket and wires.
5. Remove the window regulator mounting screws, disengage the regulator from the regulator arm rollers, and remove the unit.
6. Remove the motor from the regulator.

### Installation

1. Install the motor onto the regulator assembly.
2. Position the regulator into the proper position in the door and in relation to the equalizer arm brackets. Install the attaching screws.
3. Put the glass channel bracket into position and install the two attaching screws.
4. Install the motor bracket and connect the wiring.
5. Remove the support for the window glass. Install the watershield and trim panel.

## 1969 Lincoln Continental

### Removal

1. Remove the trim panel, watershield, and access cover.
2. Disconnect the motor electrical connector and remove the wiring retainer clip and screw.
3. Remove the regulator retaining bolts. Then prop the window glass in the up position, slide the regulator rollers out of the glass channel brackets and the equalizer bracket, and remove the regulator and motor assemblies.
4. Put the regulator and motor in a vise and remove the motor and drive.

### Installation

1. If installing a new regulator, move the mechanism against the spring until it is in the same position as the old one before installing the motor.
2. Install the motor with the three retaining screws.
3. Position the regulator and motor in the door and position the rollers into the glass channel bracket and the equalizer bracket.
4. Reconnect the motor electrical connector and install the clip retaining screws for the wiring.
5. Install the access cover, watershield, and trim panel.

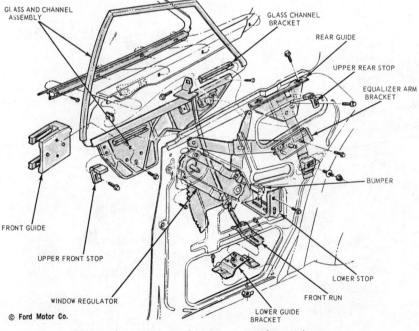

GLASS AND CHANNEL ASSEMBLY
GLASS CHANNEL BRACKET
REAR GUIDE
UPPER REAR STOP
EQUALIZER ARM BRACKET
BUMPER
FRONT GUIDE
UPPER FRONT STOP
WINDOW REGULATOR
© Ford Motor Co.
LOWER GUIDE BRACKET
FRONT RUN
LOWER STOP

*1969 Ford & Mercury Hardtop Quarter Window Mechanism*

# Ford Motor Company

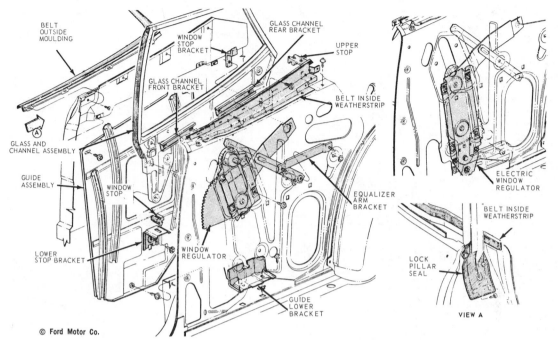

*1969 Ford & Mercury Quarter Window Mechanism*

## QUARTER WINDOW REGULATOR AND MOTOR
### 1969 Ford and Mercury
### 2 Door Hardtop

#### Removal

1. Remove the trim panel and watershield.
2. Remove the equalizer arm bracket.
3. Remove the front guide.
4. Support the glass and remove the glass channel brackets.
5. Disconnect the motor wires and support bracket.
6. Remove the regulator attaching screws, disengage the regulator arm roller, and remove the regulator. Remove the motor.

#### Installation

1. Position the regulator into the door and install the attaching screws.
2. Connect the motor wiring. Install the motor support bracket.
3. Install the glass channel bracket. Replace the front guide.
4. Install the equalizer arm bracket and adjust it.
5. Install the watershield and trim panel.

### 1969 Ford and Mercury
### 2 Door and Convertible

#### Removal

1. Raise convertible tops partially. Remove the trim panel and watershield.

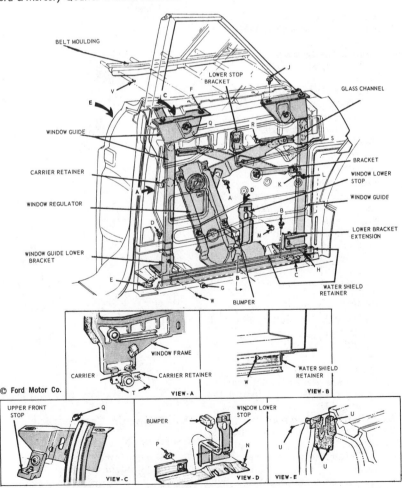

*1969 Lincoln Continental Quarter Window Mechanism*

# Ford Motor Company

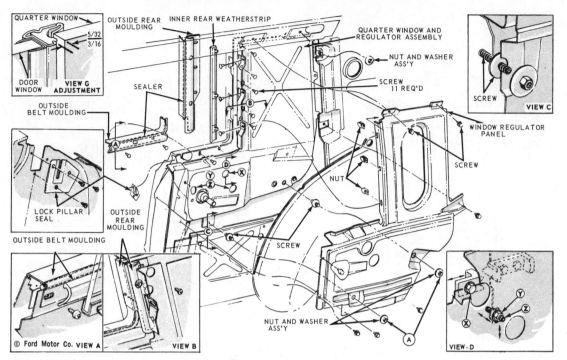

*1969 Thunderbird Quarter Window Installation*

2. Remove the front retainer bracket from the trim panel.
3. Remove the screw which attaches the equalizer arm to the inner panel.
4. Lower the glass. Remove the upper front guide and rear stop.
5. Support the glass with a prop and remove the glass channel bracket.
6. Disconnect the motor wiring and support bracket.
7. Remove the window regulator attaching screws and disengage the regulator arm roller where it engages the glass channel.
8. Remove the glass from the rear guide by raising it part way. Remove the rear guide and then remove the regulator from the quarter panel.

## Installation

1. Position the regulator and install the attaching screws.
2. Install the rear guide.
3. Connect the wiring and install the motor support bracket.
4. Install the glass channel bracket.
5. Lower the glass and install the front guide.
6. Install the upper rear stop.
7. Connect the equalizer arm to the inner panel with the attaching screw. Adjust it as necessary.
8. Lower the top on convertibles. Install the watershield and trim panel.

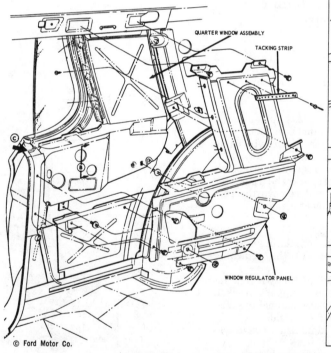

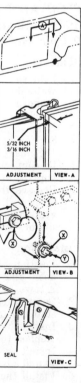

*1969 Mark III Quarter Window Installation*

## 1969 Lincoln Continental

### Removal

1. Remove the trim panel and watershield.
2. Disconnect the motor leads.
3. Remove the retaining nuts for

the equalizer bracket and then remove the bracket.
4. Remove the lower stop.
5. Remove the regulator retaining bolts and then prop the window in position. Slide the regulator rollers out of the window glass

# Ford Motor Company

channel brackets and remove the regulator assembly.

6. Clamp the regulator assembly in a vise. Remove the motor.

### Installation

1. Install the motor on the regulator.
2. Put the regulator assembly into position, engaging the rollers with the glass channel brackets. Install the mounting bolts.
3. Install the lower stop.
4. Install the equalizer bracket.
5. Connect the motor leads and then adjust the lower stop and the equalizer bracket.
6. Install the watershield and trim panel.

## 1969 Thunderbird and Mark III

### Removal

1. Remove the trim panel and watershield.
2. Remove the light from the quarter roof panel. Remove the quarter roof panel.
3. Pull the headlining out of the window opening tacking strip and then remove the tacking strip.
4. Remove the locknuts and their washers from the lower adjusting screws.
5. Remove the window regulator panel.
6. Loosen the two window assembly screws at the pillar and then

remove the ten other assembly attaching screws. Disconnect the motor wires and remove the assembly.

7. Remove the outer panel to inner panel screws and separate the two panels.

8. Remove the stop from the slide carrier.
9. Remove the regulator cable clamp.
10. Separate the glass and carrier from the regulator. The motor may now be removed.

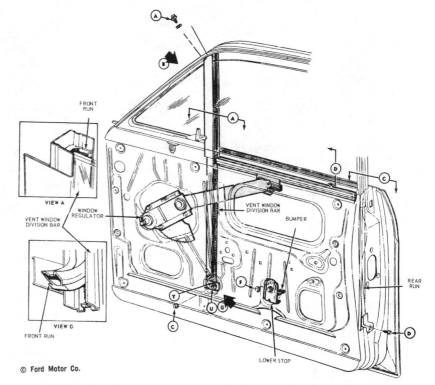

© Ford Motor Co.

*1968 Fairlane & Montego Four Door Sedan Front Door Window Mechanism*

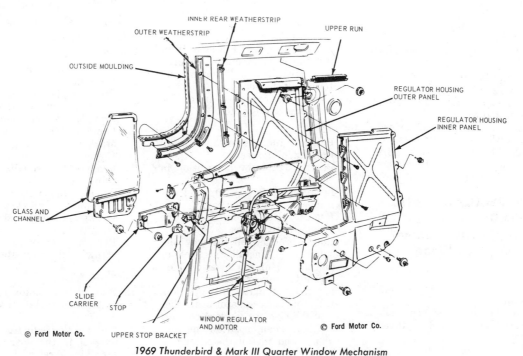

© Ford Motor Co.    © Ford Motor Co.

*1969 Thunderbird & Mark III Quarter Window Mechanism*

# Ford Motor Company

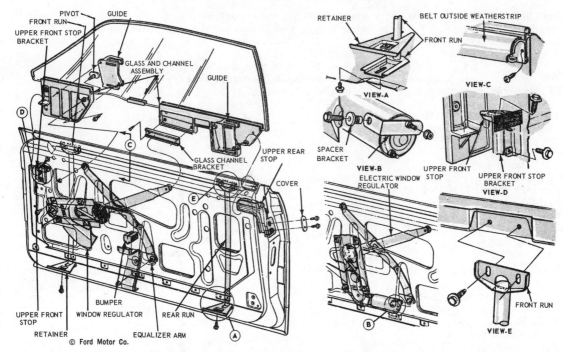

1968 Fairlane & Montego Hardtop Front Door Window Mechanism

## Installation

1. Install the motor.
2. Position the glass and slide carrier onto the regulator.
3. Install the stop and the cable clamp.
4. Put the inner panel into position on the outer panel and install the attaching screws.
5. Put the assembly into position in the vehicle and install the attaching screws. Tighten the two screws at the pillar.
6. Connect the motor wiring.
7. Install the window regulator panel.
8. Install the tacking strip and attach the headlining to it.
9. Install the lower adjusting screw locknuts and washers.
10. Adjust the window as described in the section on adjustments.
11. Install the roof quarter trim panel and light, and the watershield and trim panel.

## WINDOW REGULATOR AND MOTOR—FRONT DOOR
### 1968 Montego and Fairlane 4 Door Sedan and Wagon
#### Removal

1. Remove the trim panel and watershield.
2. Remove the regulator arm roller bracket from the door inner panel.
3. Disconnect the motor wires.

4. Remove the motor bracket attaching screw.
5. Remove the locknut and washer from the lower adjusting screw of the vent window division bar.
6. Remove the window regulator attaching screws, prop the glass and channel assembly in position, and disengage the regulator arm roller from the glass channel. Lay the regulator in the bottom of the door.
7. Remove the lower stop.
8. Lower the glass. Pull the front run and retainer out of the division bar. Then pull the regulator out of the door.
9. Clamp the regulator in a vise and remove the motor.

#### Installation

1. Position the motor and install the attaching screws.
2. Put the regulator in position in the door.
3. Locate the front run and retainer in the division bar.
4. Put the glass in position in the front and rear runs.
5. Raise the glass all the way and support it. Install the locknut and washer on the lower division bar adjusting screw.
6. Move the regulator into position, inserting the regulator arm roller into the slot in the glass channel bracket. Then, position the regulator and install the attaching screws.

7. Install the regulator arm roller bracket.
8. Install the motor bracket on the inner door panel.
9. Install the lower stop and then adjust the window as described in the section on adjustments.
10. Connect the motor wires, and install the watershield and trim panel.

## 1968 Montego and Fairlane 2 Door, 2 Door Hardtop, and Convertible
### Removal

1. Remove the trim panel and watershield.
2. Prop the glass in the up position and then remove the regulator arm pivot nut and bolt.
3. Remove the glass channel bracket from the glass channel.
4. Disconnect the motor wiring.
5. Remove the equalizer arm retaining nut.
6. Remove the window regulator and motor bracket attaching screws and remove the assembly from the door.
7. Remove the motor attaching screws and remove the motor.

### Installation

1. Position the motor on the regulator and install the attaching screws.
2. Position the regulator and motor bracket in the door. Install the attaching screws.

# Ford Motor Company

3. Put the equalizer arm in position and install the retaining nut.
4. Engage the glass channel bracket with the regulator arm and install the bracket onto the glass channel.
5. Connect the motor wiring.
6. Connect the window regulator arm to the glass channel via the pivot and pivot nut.
7. Remove the glass support and install the watershield and trim panel.

## WINDOW REGULATOR AND MOTOR—FRONT OR REAR
### 1968 Ford and Mercury
### 4 Door Sedan, 2 Door Sedan, and Station Wagon

### Removal

1. Remove the trim panel and watershield.
2. Prop the glass and channel assembly in the up position.
3. Remove the glass channel bracket attaching screws.
4. Disconnect the motor wires.
5. Remove the motor support bracket mounting screw.
6. Remove the regulator attaching screws, disengage the regulator arm rollers from the glass channel bracket, and pull the regulator and motor from the door.
7. Remove the motor from the regulator.

### Installation

1. Install the motor.
2. Put the regulator assembly into position in the door and install the attaching screws.
3. Install the motor support bracket attaching screw.
4. Position the glass channel bracket so that the regulator arm rollers are engaged in its slots and then install the bracket onto the glass channel.
5. Connect the motor wiring.
6. Remove the prop used to hold the glass up.
7. Install the watershield and trim panel.

## WINDOW REGULATOR AND MOTOR—REAR DOOR
### 1968 Ford and Mercury
### 4 Door Hardtop

### Removal

1. Remove the trim panel and watershield.
2. Remove the two upper stops.
3. Remove the glass channel bracket from the glass and pull the glass out of the door.
4. Remove the rear door guide panel retaining bolts and remove the panel from the door.
5. Remove the regulator assembly retaining screws and remove the assembly from the door.
6. Clamp the regulator in a vise, remove the motor, and remove the motor bracket.

### Installation

1. Put the motor and bracket in position and install the retaining screws.
2. Put the regulator into position in the door and install the retaining screws.
3. Connect the motor wiring.
4. Put the door glass into position and install the channel bracket screws.
5. Install the upper stops. Adjust the stops and guide as described in the section on adjustments.
6. Install the watershield and trim panel.

## 1968 Fairlane and Montego
### 4 Door Sedan

### Removal

1. Remove the trim panel and watershield.
2. Disconnect the motor wires.
3. Remove the equalizer arm bracket.
4. Support the glass and channel assembly with a suitable prop and remove the glass channel bracket.
5. Remove the motor bracket attaching screw.
6. Remove the regulator attaching screws and remove the regulator.

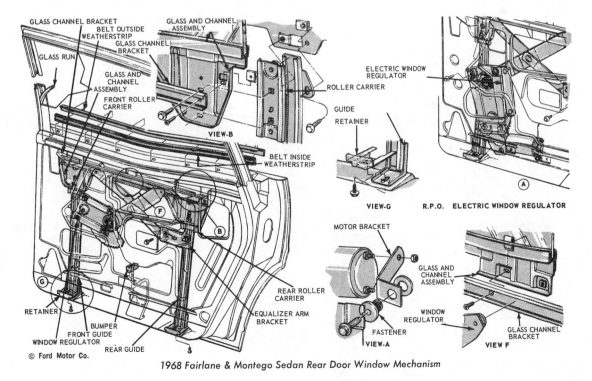

1968 Fairlane & Montego Sedan Rear Door Window Mechanism

# Ford Motor Company

7. Remove the motor from the regulator.

## Installation

1. Install the motor.
2. Install the regulator in the door, positioning the regulator arm rollers in the glass channel bracket slots before installing the attaching screws.
3. Install the motor bracket.
4. Install the equalizer arm bracket by positioning the equalizer arm roller in the slot and then mounting the bracket onto the inner panel.
5. Attach the glass channel bracket to the glass channel.
6. Connect the motor wiring.
7. Remove the window support and install the watershield and trim panel.

## Fairlane and Montego Station Wagon

### Removal

1. Remove the trim panel and watershield. Lower the window.
2. Remove the division bar lower bracket attaching screws and remove the bracket.
3. Remove the upper division bar attaching screw. Remove the division bar and rear run.
4. Remove the stationary window glass and weatherstrip.
5. Remove the window regulator

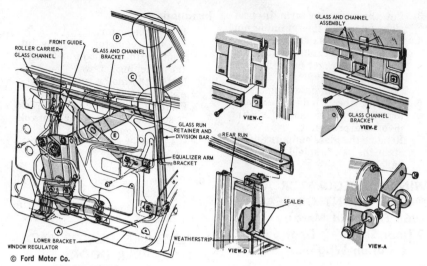

*1968 Fairlane & Montego Wagon Rear Door Window Mechanism*

mounting screws, the equalizer arm bracket mounting screws, and the roller front carrier attaching screws.

6. Remove the glass channel bracket attaching screws and remove the glass and channel assembly from the door.
7. Remove the window regulator and motor assembly.
8. Remove the motor and drive from the regulator.

### Installation

1. Install the motor and drive onto the regulator.

2. Position the regulator and drive into the door and install the attaching screws.
3. Position the glass channel bracket so the regulator arm rollers are properly positioned in the slots.
4. Put the glass and channel assembly in the door and install the glass channel bracket screws.
5. Align the roller front carrier with the glass channel and install it.
6. Coat the stationary window

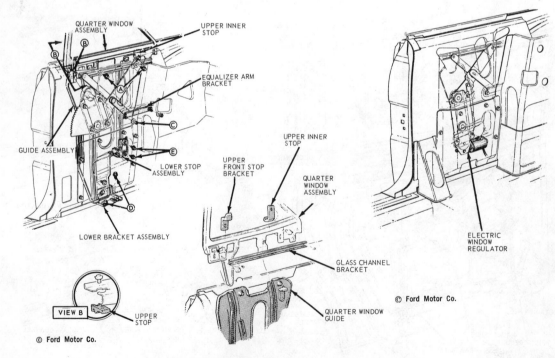

*1968 Ford & Mercury Convertible Quarter Window Mechanism*

# Ford Motor Company

glass weatherstrip with silicone and then install the weatherstrip and stationary window.

7. Position the division bar and rear run and install the upper attaching screw.

8. Install the division bar lower bracket.

9. Adjust the window as described in the section on adjustments.

10. Install the watershield and trim panel.

## REGULATOR AND MOTOR— QUARTER WINDOW
## 1968 Ford Convertible
### Removal

1. Remove the trim panel and watershield.

2. Remove the screws that attach the access hole cover to the regulator and lower stop.

3. Remove the remaining attaching screws, and remove the cover.

4. Remove the regulator attaching screws.

5. Disconnect the motor wiring and slide the regulator arm rollers out of the channel bracket and equalizer bracket.

6. Remove the regulator and motor. Remove the motor from the regulator.

### Installation

1. Install the motor on the regulator.

2. Position the regulator assembly, inserting the regulator arm roll-

ers into the channel bracket and equalizer arm bracket.

3. Align the front end of the channel bracket with the glass channel. Install the front attaching screw.

4. Connect the motor wiring at the connector.

5. Install the two upper regulator attaching screws.

6. Put the access hole cover into position and install the attaching screws. Install the remaining lower stop attaching screw.

7. Install the regulator-to-access hole cover attaching screws.

8. Adjust the lower stop so the window just drops to the beltline and then install the trim panel and watershield.

# General Motors

## Description

Power windows are operated by a 12 volt series wound motor with an internal circuit breaker and a self locking rubber coupled gear drive. Circuit wiring is protected by a circuit breaker located at the fuse panel on all models except 1968-71 Chevrolet, 1972 Chevelle and 1968-70 Oldsmobile. On these models the circuit breaker is located at the engine compartment bulkhead.

A relay is used in the circuit to prevent window operation until the ignition switch is turned "ON" in all models except 1971-75 Cadillac which uses a feed circuit through the ignition switch. The relay is located in the left shroud area or the steering column lower support.

## Electrical Tests
## Checking Feed Circuit at Circuit Breaker

Connect one test light lead to battery side of circuit breaker and ground other lead. If tester does not light, there is an open or short circuit to circuit breaker.

## Checking Circuit Breaker

Disconnect output feed wire from circuit breaker. Using test light, check terminal from which wire was disconnected. If tester does not light, circuit breaker is defective.

## Checking Relay

Check relay feed with test light. If

## TROUBLESHOOTING CHART

| Condition | Correction |
|---|---|
| **None of the windows will operate.** | a. Check circuit breaker. <br> b. Check relay at left cowl. <br> c. Check feed connection to power harness beneath instrument panel. <br> d. Check feed circuit for possible short or open circuit. <br> e. Check cut-out switch. <br> f. Check window lock-out switch (Cadillac) <br> g. Check console switch. |
| **Right rear door window does not operate from master control switch or right rear door switch. Left door window operates.** | a. Check harness connections beneath outer end of instrument panel. <br> b. Check wires in power window front harness for short or open circuit. <br> c. Check operation of rear door window control switch. <br> d. Check circuit from window control switch to window motor for short or open circuit. <br> e. Check window regulator and channels for mechanical failure or bind. <br> f. Check motor. |
| **Right door windows will operate from left door master control switch but will not operate from right door control switch. Left door windows operate.** | a. Check feed wire in front harness for possible short or open circuit. |

tester does not light, there is an open or short circuit between relay and circuit breaker. Turn ignition switch on and check output terminal of relay. If tester does not light, relay is defective or there is an open or short circuit between ignition switch and relay. (Check fuse.)

## Checking Window Lock-Out Switch (Cadillac only)

With ignition switch "ON," insert one end of No. 12 gauge jumper wire into terminal with red-white stripe wire and other end into terminal with pink-black stripe wire.

# General Motors

Operate control switches. If any windows operate with jumper wire, but not with lock-out switch, switch is defective.

## Checking Feed Circuit at Window Control Switch

Connect one test light lead to feed terminal of switch block and ground other tester lead to body metal. If tester does not light, there is an open or short circuit between switch and power source.

## Checking Window Control Switch

Insert one end of No. 12 gauge jumper wire into switch feed terminal and other end into one of motor lead terminals in switch block. Repeat check for other motor lead terminal. If window operates with jumper wire, but not with switch, switch is defective.

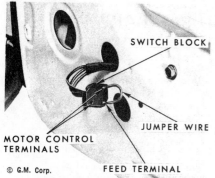

Checking Window Control Switch

## Checking Wires Between Window Switch and Window Motor

Disengage harness connector from window motor. Insert one end of No. 12 gauge jumper wire into switch feed terminal and other end into one of the motor lead terminals in the switch block. Using a test light, check for current at motor harness connector terminal being tested. If tester does not light, there is an open or short circuit in harness and connector. Check other terminal.

## Checking Window Motor

Check window regulator and channels for possible binding condition. Check window motor for effective ground. Connect one end of No. 12 gauge jumper wire to power source and other end to one of terminals on window motor. Check other terminal in same motor. If motor fails to operate with jumper wire, motor is defective.

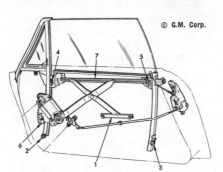

Front Door Glass Adjustment Locations—Typical

1. Inner Panel Cam
2. Front Glass Run Adjusting Stud
3. Rear Glass Run Adjusting Stud
4. Window Front Up-Travel Stop
5. Window Rear Up-Travel Stop
6. Sector Gear Up-Stop
7. Sash Channel Cam

## Door Glass Adjustments

Adjustments are provided to relieve binding glass due to misalignment of the glass run channel. The glass can also be adjusted to correct a cocked window assembly and up and down travel.

In and out adjustments are made at the glass run adjusting studs.

A cocked window is corrected by moving the inner panel cam adjusting bolts to the desired position. Elongated holes in the panel are provided for this adjustment.

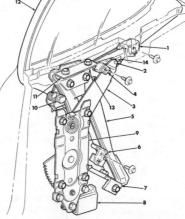

Quarter Window Glass Adjustment Locations—Typical

1. Rear Up-Stop
2. Regulator Lift Arm Roller
3. Regulator Lift Arm
4. Front Up-Stop
5. Window Guide
6. Down Stop
7. Lower Guide Support Bracket
8. Electric Motor
9. Regulator Assembly
10. Front Roller
11. Upper Guide Support Bracket
12. Front Vertical Weatherstrip
13. Rear Roller
14. Sash Channel Cam

Up and down adjustments are made at the travel stops. (See illustrations for typical adjustment locations.)

## Quarter Window Glass Adjustments

Adjustments for quarter window glass vary according to the year and model.

In and out and fore and aft adjustments are made at the window guides. Up and down adjustments are made at the travel stops. On some models the regulator can be rotated to provide further adjustment. (See illustration for typical adjustment locations.)

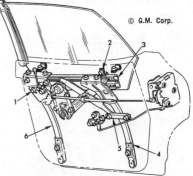

Rear Door Glass Adjustment Locations—Typical

1. Window Front Up-Travel Stop
2. Window Rear Up-Travel Stop
3. Lower Sash Channel Cam
4. Rear Guide
5. Inner Panel Cam
6. Front Guide

## Front Door Glass—Closed Styles with Ventilator Assembly

### Removal and Installation

1. With door window in full up position, remove trim panel and water deflector.
2. Disconnect ventilator motor wire harness connector on models so equipped.
3. Through access hole in inner panel, remove ventilator T-shaft bolt.
4. Remove ventilator regulator attaching bolts.
5. Pull regulator down to disengage from ventilator T-shaft and remove regulator through access hole.
6. Remove door window down stop.
7. Lower windows to full down position and remove bolt ventilator lower frame to door panel.

## General Motors

8. Remove division channel lower adjusting stud nut.
9. Remove ventilator to door upper frame attaching screws.
10. Disengage upper front end of glass run channel from door upper frame.
11. Tilt vent assembly rearward and remove from door. On some models it may be necessary to rotate vent assembly for removal.
12. Loosen window glass run channel lower attaching volt.
13. Remove inner panel cam bolts.
14. Slide window lower sash channel cam off window regulator lift arm and remove window through upper door frame.
15. To install, reverse removal procedure.

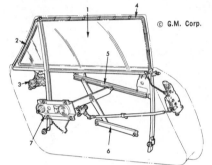

*Front Door Window Removal—Closed Styles With Ventilator Assembly—Typical*

1. Window Assembly
2. Ventilator Assembly
3. Ventilator Regulator
4. Window Glass Run Channel
5. Lower Sash Channel Cam
6. Inner Panel Cam
7. Window Regulator

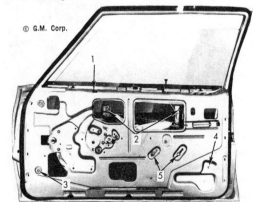

*Front Door Window Removal—Closed Styles Without Ventilator Assembly—Typical*

1. Window Anti-Rattle Strip
2. Window to Lower Sash Channel Cam to Glass Attaching Stud Nuts
3. Front Glass Run Channel Attaching Bolt
4. Rear Glass Run Channel Attaching Bolt
5. Inner Panel Cam Bolts

### Closed Styles without Ventilator Assembly

#### Removal and Installation

1. Remove trim panel and water deflector.
2. Operate window to gain access to lower sash channel cam to glass attaching stud nuts through access holes.
3. Remove nuts and disengage sash channel from studs.
4. Tilt front edge of glass downward to disengage from run channel.
5. Remove window through upper door frame.
6. To install, reverse removal procedure.

### Hardtop and Convertible Styles With Ventilator Assembly

#### Removal and Installation

1. Remove trim panel and water deflector.
2. Open window to a one-quarter down position.
3. Remove front up travel stop from lower sash channel.
4. Remove rear stop from rear guide.
5. Loosen rear guide to door inner panel attaching bolts.
6. Operate window to a three-quarter down position.
7. Remove screws securing lower sash channel cam to lower sash channel.

8. Support window and disengage lower sash channel cam from regulator lift. Balance arm rollers.
9. Push regulator lift arm inboard to clear glass sash channel.
10. Remove window by lifting straight up.
11. To install, reverse removal procedure.

### Two Door Hardtop and Convertible Styles Without Ventilator Assembly

#### Removal and Installation

1. Remove trim panel and water deflector.
2. Remove front and rear up-travel stops. Intermediate models on window assembly. Full size models on inner panel. (See illustration.)
3. On intermediate models, remove trim and adjusting plate. On all models, remove stabilizer strips.
4. Remove lower sash guide bolts.
5. Tilt upper edge of glass inboard to disengage glass from guide.
6. Remove window from door by lifting straight up.
7. To install, reverse removal procedure.

### Four Door Hardtop Without Ventilator Assembly

#### Removal and Installation

1. Remove trim panel and water deflector.

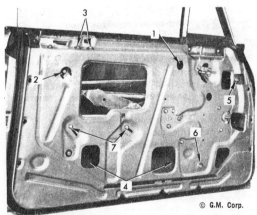

*Front Door Window Removal—Hardtop and Convertible Styles With Ventilator Assembly—Typical*

1. Window Front Upper Stop Access Hole
2. Window Rear Upper Stop Bolt
3. Rear Guide Upper Attaching Bolts
4. Lower Sash Channel Cam Attaching Screws Access Holes
5. Ventilator Lower Frame Adjusting Stud and Nut
6. Ventilator Division Channel Lower Adjusting Stud and Nut
7. Inner Panel Cam Attaching Bolts

# General Motors

2. Remove front and rear up-travel stops.
3. Loosen front and rear stabilizer strips.
4. Operate window to three-quarter down position and remove sash channel to glass attaching nuts.
5. Remove window by lifting straight up and aligning rollers with notches in door inner panel.
6. To install, reverse removal procedure.

## Rear Door Glass— Closed Styles— Intermediate Models

### Removal and Installation

1. Remove trim panel and water deflector.
2. Operate window to three-quarter down position and remove lower sash channel cam attaching screws.
3. Loosen rear glass run channel upper and lower attaching screws.
4. Rotate rear edge of glass downward and remove window by lifting front of glass upward outboard of upper door frame.
5. To install, reverse removal procedure.

© G.M. Corp.

*Front Door Window Removal—Two Door Hardtop and Convertible Styles Without Ventilator Assembly—Typical*

1. Front Up-Travel Stop (Intermediate Models)
2. Rear Up-Travel Stop (Intermediate Models)
3. Front Up-Travel Stop (Full Size Models)
4. Rear Up-Travel Stop (Full Size Models)
5. Trim Pad Adjusting Plate
6. Strip Stabilizer
7. Lower Sash Guide Plate Bolts
8. Lower Sash Guide Upper Bolts
9. Lower Sash Guide Lower Bolts
10. Front Bumper Support Bolt
11. Rear Window Support Bolt

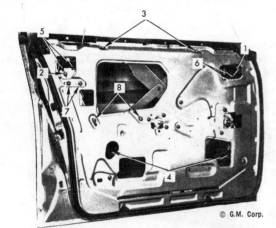

© G.M. Corp.

*Front Door Window Removal—Four Door Hardtop Without Ventilator Assembly— Typical*

1. Front Up-Travel Stop Bolt
2. Rear Up-Travel Stop Bolt
3. Stabilizer Strip Bolts
4. Window Lower Sash Channel Cam Nuts Access Holes
5. Rear Guide Upper Bracket Bolts
6. Front Guide Upper Bolts
7. Rear Guide to Guide Up Bracket Bolts
8. Inner Panel Cam Bolts

© G.M. Corp.

*Rear Door Window Removal—Four Door Hardtop— Intermediate Models—Typical*

1. Front Up-Travel Stop
2. Rear Up-Travel Stop
3. Front and Rear Stabilizer Strips
4. Lower Sash Channel Cam Stud Nuts
5. Front Guide Upper Support Attaching Bolts
6. Rear Guide Upper Attaching Bolts
7. Front Guide to Upper Support Bracket Attaching Bolts
8. Inner Panel Cam Attaching Bolts

# General Motors

© G.M. Corp.

*Rear Door Window Removal—Closed Styles—
Intermediate Models—Typical*

1. *Lower Sash Channel Cam Attaching Screw Access Holes*
2. *Rear Glass Run Upper and Lower Attaching Bolts*
3. *Inner Panel Cam Attaching Bolts*

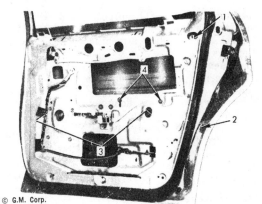

© G.M. Corp.

*Rear Door Window Removal—Closed Styles—
Full Size Models—Typical*

1. *Rear Glass Run Channel Upper Attaching Bolt*
2. *Rear Glass Run Channel Lower Attaching Bolt*
3. *Lower Sash Channel Cam Stud Nuts Access Holes*
4. *Inner Panel Cam Bolts*

## Closed Styles—Full Size Models
### Removal and Installation

1. Remove trim panel and water deflector.
2. Through 1970, remove front and rear run channel attaching bolts located on inner edges of door. From 1971, remove glass run upper and lower attaching bolts located at rear of door and remove channel.

3. Partially lower door window and remove lower sash channel cam to glass attaching stud nuts.
4. Press lower sash channel cam inboard to disengage from attaching studs.
5. Lower window to full open position.
6. Tilt front edge of glass downward and remove through door upper frame, rear edge first, then front edge.

7. To install, reverse removal procedure.

## Four Door Hardtop—Intermediate Models

### Removal and Installation

1. Remove trim panel and water deflector.
2. Remove window front up-stop from guide and rear up-stop from door inner panel.
3. Loosen front and rear stabilizer strip assembly bolts and remove stabilizer strips.

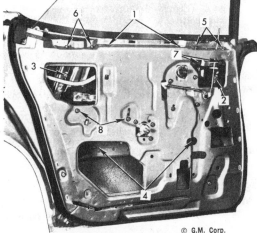

© G.M. Corp.

*Rear Door Window Removal—Four Door Hardtop—Full Size Models—Thru 1970*

1. *Stabilizer Strip Bolts*
2. *Front Up-Travel Stop Bolt*
3. *Rear Up-Travel Stop Bolt*
4. *Lower Sash Channel Cam Stud Nuts Access Holes*
5. *Front Guide Upper Support Bracket Bolts*
6. *Rear Guide Upper Bolts*
7. *Front Guide to Upper Support Bracket Bolts*
8. *Inner Panel Cam Bolts*

© G.M. Corp.

*Rear Door Window Removal—Four Door Hardtop—Full Size Models—From 1971*

1. *Stabilizer Strip Bolts*
2. *Front Up-Travel Stop Bolt*
3. *Rear Up-Travel Stop Bolt*
4. *Guide Cam Support Bolts*
5. *Guide Cam to Upper Support Bolts*
6. *Guide Cam Lower Bolt*
7. *Stud Nuts*

# General Motors

4. Operate window to full up position and remove lower sash channel cam to glass attaching stud nuts.
5. Disengage front roller from front guide, then rear roller from rear guide.
6. Remove window from door by aligning rollers with notches in inner panel. Remove rear end of window first, then front end.
7. To install, reverse removal procedure.

## Four Door Hardtop— Full Size Models— Through 1970

### Removal and Installation

1. Remove trim panel and water deflector.
2. Remove front and rear stabilizer strips.
3. Remove front and rear up-travel stops.
4. Operate window to a three-quarter down position and remove lower sash channel cam to glass attaching stud nuts.
5. Lift window upward and remove from door.
6. To install, reverse removal procedure.

## Four Door Hardtop— Full Size Models— From 1971

### Removal and Installation

1. Remove upper trim panel.
2. Operate glass to a partial down position.
3. Loosen front and rear stabilizer strips and up-travel stops. Rotate stops to allow glass to bypass stops when removing.
4. Remove lower sash guide plate to glass attaching stud nuts.
5. Tilt upper edge of glass inboard to disengage guide plate studs from glass.
6. Remove glass door by lifting rear edge of glass upward, then slide glass rearward to align guide plate studs with notch at rear of door inner panel.

## Front Door Window Regulator All Models Except 1968-69 Camaro and Firebird 1970-75 Two Door Hardtop and Convertible

### Removal and Installation

1. Remove trim panel, water deflector, window assembly and inner panel cam.

2. Disconnect wire harness connector at window regulator motor.
3. Remove window regulator attaching bolts and remove regulator through access hole.
4. To install, reverse removal procedure.

## 1968-69 Camaro and Firebird

### Removal and Installation

1. Remove trim panel and water deflector.
2. Operate window to gain access to lower sash channel cam. On 1968, support glass and remove sash channel cam. On 1969, remove cam attaching stud nut.
3. Support window in a full up position and remove inner panel cam.
4. Disconnect wire harness connector at regulator motor.
5. Remove window regulator attaching bolts and remove regulator through access hole.
6. To install, reverse removal procedure.

## 1970-75 Two Door Hardtop and Convertible

### Removal and Installation

1. Remove trim panels and water deflector.
2. Disconnect wire harness from regulator motor.
3. Remove door lock remote control locking rod.
4. Lower window to half-down position and remove regulator attaching bolts.
5. Disengage regulator lift arm roller from lower sash channel cam and prop window in full up position.
6. Rotate regulator assembly clockwise so that motor comes out access hole first.
7. To install, reverse removal procedure.

## Rear Door Window Regulator 1973-75 Intermediate Models— Rear

### Removal and Installation

1. Remove door window assembly.
2. Remove regulator attaching bolts.
3. Disengage regulator lift arm from sash plate guide cam assembly.
4. Remove upper and lower guide tube assembly attaching screws.
5. Remove guide tube and lower sash guide plate assembly from door.

6. Disengage wire harness from regulator motor.
7. Remove regulator from door, lift arm first.
8. To install, reverse removal procedure.

## Closed Styles 1971-75 Full Size Models—Rear

### Removal and Installation

1. Remove trim panels and water deflector.
2. Lower window and remove lower sash channel cam to glass attaching stud nuts.
3. Disengage cam from rollers on regulator lift and balance arms and remove cam.
4. Support glass in full up position.
5. Remove inner panel cam attaching bolts.
6. Disconnect wire harness from regulator motor.
7. Remove regulator attaching bolts and remove regulator through access hole.
8. To install, reverse removal procedure.

## Hardtop Styles 1971-75 Full Size Models—Rear

### Removal and Installation

1. Remove trim panels and water deflector.
2. Position window in full up position.
3. Remove center guide cam upper and lower attaching bolts.
4. Pull guide downward to disengage from window lower sash plate roller assembly. Remove guide.
5. Remove regulator attaching bolts.
6. Slide regulator lift arm roller out of lower sash channel cam and remove regulator through access hole.
7. To install, reverse removal procedure.

## 1969-70 All Models—Rear 1971-72 Intermediate Models— Rear

### Removal and Installation

1. Remove door window assembly.
2. Remove inner panel arm attaching bolts.
3. Disconnect wire harness from regulator motor.
4. On Intermediate Hardtop Models, remove window rear guide.
5. Remove regulator attaching bolts and remove regulator through access hole.

# General Motors

6. To install, reverse removal procedure.

## 1968 All Models—Rear

### Removal and Installation

1. Remove trim panel and water deflector.
2. Lower window and remove lower glass sash channel cam attaching screws.
3. Disengage cam from rollers on regulator lift and balance arms and remove cam.
4. Support glass in full-up position.
5. Remove inner panel cam attaching bolts.
6. Disconnect wire harness from regulator motor.
7. On Intermediate Hardtop Models, remove window rear guide.
8. Remove regulator attaching bolts and remove regulator through access hole.
9. To install, reverse removal procedure.

## Quarter Window Regulator Hardtop and Convertible 1971-73 Full Size Models— Quarter

### Removal and Installation

1. Remove glass and guide assembly.
   a. Remove rear seat cushion, seat back, trim panel and water deflector. On convertible, lower top.
   b. Lower glass to half down position.
   c. Remove rear up-travel stop.
   d. Remove lower down travel stop.

e. Remove upper support attaching bolts.
f. Remove lower guide support attaching bolts.
g. Disengage regulator and remove glass and guide as an assembly.
2. Disconnect wire at motor.
3. Remove regulator attaching bolts and remove regulator through access hole.
4. To install, reverse removal procedure.

## Closed Styles
## 1968-73 All Models

### Removal and Installation

1. Remove trim panel and water deflector.
2. Disconnect feed wire from regulator motor.
3. Disengage clip retainer from pivot pin on window lower sash channel.
4. Support window in full-up position.
5. Remove regulator through access hole.
6. To install, reverse removal procedure.

## Hardtop and Convertible 1968-70 Full Size Models Except Riviera, Eldorado, Toronado and Grand Prix

### Removal and Installation

1. Remove trim panel and access hole cover or water deflector.
2. Disconnect feed wire at motor or in-line connector.
3. Remove rear up-stop.

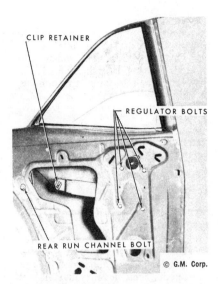

© G.M. Corp.

*Rear Quarter Hardware Attachment —Closed Styles*

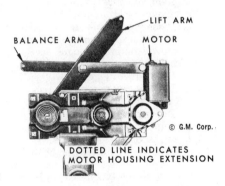

© G.M. Corp.

DOTTED LINE INDICATES MOTOR HOUSING EXTENSION

*Window Regulator and Elector Motor Assembly*

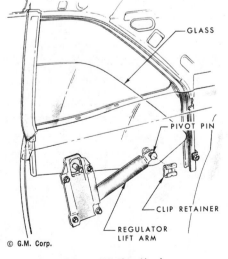

© G.M. Corp.

*Rear Quarter Window Hardware, Intermediate Models (Typical)*

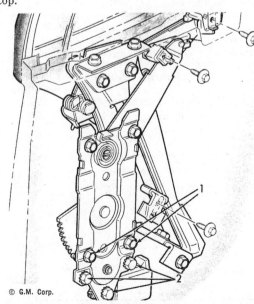

© G.M. Corp.

*Rear Quarter Window Hardware, Intermediate Models (Electric)*

# General Motors

4. Remove down-stop.
5. Support window and remove regulator attaching bolts.
6. Disengage lift arm roller from window lower sash channel cam.
7. Remove regulator through access hole.
8. To install, reverse removal procedure.

## Hardtop and Convertible
## 1968-73 Intermediate Models
## 1968-73 Riviera, Eldorado, Toronado and Grand Prix

### Removal and Installation

1. Remove trim panel and access hole cover or water deflector.
2. Disconnect feed wire at motor.
3. On Riviera, Eldorado and Toronado, remove rear quarter window.
   a. Raise window to full-up position.
   b. Remove rear guide upper and lower attaching bolts.
   c. Disengage guide from roller on window assembly and remove guide through access hole.
   d. Partially lower window.
   e. Remove nuts securing regulator lift arm cam to lift arm and remove cam.
   f. Remove front guide attaching bolts and lower guide.
   g. Remove window assembly inboard.
4. On all other models, support window in full up position.
5. Remove window guide attaching bolts.
6. Remove regulator to inner panel attaching bolts.
7. Disengage lift arm roller from sash channel cam and remove regulator. If necessary, loosen upper attaching points of front guide to gain additional clearance.
8. To install, reverse removal procedure.

## Window Regulator Motor
## 1968-75 All Models—
## All Windows

### Removal and Installation

*Caution:* The regulator lift arm is under tension from the counterbalance spring. Do not attempt to remove the motor from the regulator without locking the sector gear with a bolt and nut.

1. Remove regulator assembly and clamp assembly in a vise.
2. Drill a hole through regulator back plate and sector gear. Hole should be drilled a sufficient distance from edge of sector gear. Do not drill through motor housing extension.
3. Install a bolt through drilled hole and install a nut. Do not tighten nut.
4. Remove motor attaching bolts and remove motor from regulator.
5. To install, reverse removal procedure. Make certain motor pinion gear meshes properly with regulator sector gear. Remove nut and bolt from drilled hole.

### Installation

1. Wash the regulator with a cleaning solvent and dry it with compressed air. Apply a high temperature white lithium grease to the gear teeth and spring and to the glass bottom slide.
2. Install the regulator arm guide to the glass bottom channel.
3. Install the regulator mounting panel but do not install its screws.
4. Mount the regulator to the panel and then install the panel sheet metal attaching screws.
5. Connect the motor to the harness and install the operating switch.
6. Remove the glass support. In-

stall the water dam paper, trim panel, and switch escutcheon.
7. Install the armrest and switch escutcheon.

## Regulator Motor

### Removal

1. Remove window regulator as previously described.
2. Remove the two mounting nuts and pull the motor away from the regulator.

### Installation

1. Align the flat sides of the coupling and transmission shaft.
2. When alignment permits the shaft to slide into the coupling, push the two together, position the motor, and install the mounting nuts.

## Regulator Transmission

### Removal

NOTE: *Follow instructions precisely to ensure proper retention of regulator spring tension. Otherwise, injury may result.*

1. Remove the window regulator from the door.
2. Drill a hole in the mounting bracket through one of the holes in the sector gear. Install a bolt and nut to securely fasten the sector gear in place. Remove the regulator motor from the drive unit.
3. Insert a screw driver blade into the motor coupling and turn the shaft until all tension on the transmission is relieved.
4. Remove the three mounting bolts and remove the transmission.

### Installation

1. Position the transmission, engaging it with the sector gear.
2. Install the mounting bolts.
3. Remove the safety bolt.

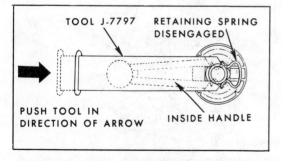

Door Inside Handle Removal

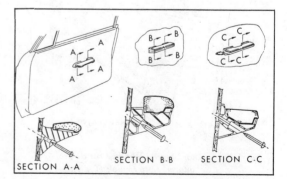

Typical Applied-Type Door Arm Rests

# Power Vent Windows

## Chrysler Corporation

### 1968-1973 Chrysler Power Vent Windows— Chrysler and Imperial

#### Electrical Tests

Before any tests are performed the battery should be fully charged and the terminals clean and tight. Check wire connections at the ammeter and accessory circuit breaker, located on or behind the left cowl trim panel.

Vent wing motors have two separate field windings (split series). Direction of rotation is controlled by energizing either field with the switch. Fields are grounded to the body through the motor housing. The switch completes the circuit back to ground when it is actuated.

#### Circuit Breaker Test

Connect one lead of a test light to circuit breaker output terminal and other lead to a good ground. The test bulb should light, if not, and wiring is not faulty, replace circuit breaker.

#### Vent Wing Switch Test

Insert a thin blade behind switch housing (front and back) to depress retaining clips, remove switch housing. Separate multiple terminal block from switch body. Connect one lead of a test light to tan feed wire terminal of terminal block and other lead to a good ground. If bulb does not light, inspect for broken or loose wire to circuit breaker.

If bulb does light, remove test light and connect a jumper wire between Tan feed wire in multiple connector and OPEN terminal wire. If vent operates, replace switch body. If vent does not operate, inspect for broken or loose wires or a faulty motor. Repeat test on CLOSE terminal, if first test opens vent wing.

#### Vent Wing Motor Test

Connect a jumper wire from positive post of a test battery to one of the two motor terminals. Connect a second jumper wire from battery negative post to motor housing. The motor should move in one direction. To reverse direction of motor, connect positive jumper wire to other motor terminal. If motor fails to operate in either direction, replace the motor.

### Vent Wing Regulator and Motor

#### Removal

1. Raise door main glass to full up position.
2. Remove trim panel and access hole cover.
3. With vent wing open, remove regulator to door inner panel attaching screws.
4. Remove shaft to coupling screw.
5. Move regulator off of vent wing pivot shaft.
6. Remove regulator through access hole in door panel.

#### Installation

1. Through access hole, position and align sleeve on regulator coupling over vent wing pivot shaft.
2. Align regulator body to door inner panel and install attaching screws.
3. Install shaft to coupling screw.
4. Install access hole cover and trim panel.

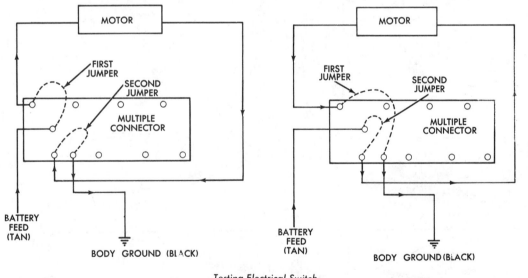

*Testing Electrical Switch*

## Ford Motor Company

### 1968-1969 Lincoln 1968 Mercury

#### Power Vent Windows

The power vent window circuit is similar to the power window circuit. Diagnosis for power windows may also be used for power vent windows.

### Vent Window Regulator and Motor

#### Removal

1. Raise door main glass to full up position.
2. Remove door trim panel and peel back water shield.
3. Disconnect motor wiring connector.
4. Remove vent glass pivot to motor and drive bolt.
5. Remove motor and regulator assembly retaining screws, and remove assembly.

#### Installation

1. Position motor and regulator as-

sembly to vent glass pivot.

2. Install pivot bolt and assembly retaining screws.
3. Connect motor wiring connector.
4. Install watershield and trim panel.

### 1973-75
### Power Mini-Vent Window

The mini-vent mechanism employs a single tubular run with a slide-down vent glass. The operation of both the main glass, and the vent window is controlled by a single switch. When the switch is moved to the down position the vent glass lowers into the door and only after the vent glass is all the way down will the door glass lower. When raising the glass they operate in the opposite way with the door glass raising first and the vent glass following. The vent or main glass may be stopped in any position.

The electrical tests for the operation of the motor and related electrical parts are similar to the standard ones used for the regular power windows. Refer to electrical tests in the front of the Ford power window section.

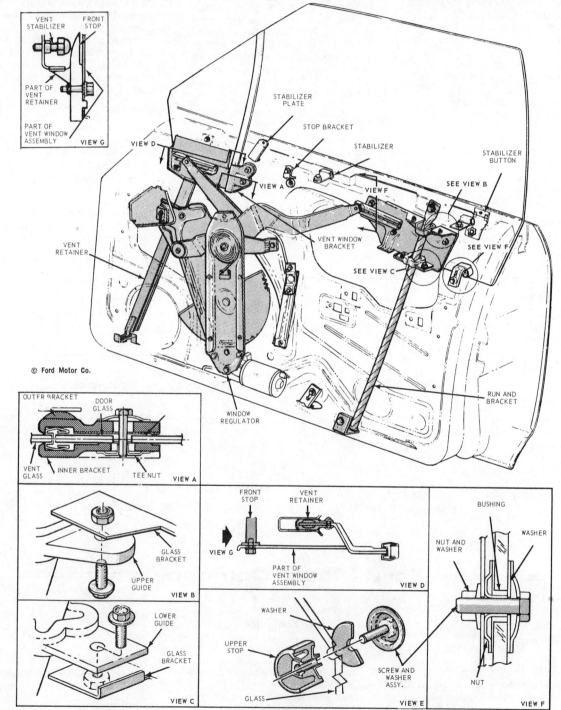

*1973-75 Mini-Vent Window Mechanism*

# Ford Motor Company

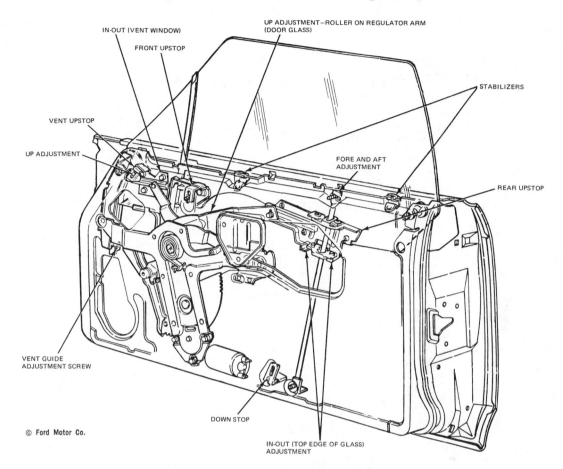

UP ADJUSTMENT—ROLLER ON REGULATOR ARM (DOOR GLASS)

IN-OUT (VENT WINDOW)

FRONT UPSTOP

STABILIZERS

VENT UPSTOP

UP ADJUSTMENT

FORE AND AFT ADJUSTMENT

REAR UPSTOP

VENT GUIDE ADJUSTMENT SCREW

© Ford Motor Co.

DOWN STOP

IN-OUT (TOP EDGE OF GLASS) ADJUSTMENT

*1973-75 Mini-Vent Window Mechanism*

## Main Glass Adjustments

*NOTE: When the vent glass reaches the end of its up cycle, the main glass shifts slightly. If adjustments were made to the main glass when the vent glass was down, they would change when the vent glass raised. So make sure the vent glass is RAISED when checking or making any adjustments.*

## Fore and Aft Adjustments

When any adjustment of the run is made for fore and aft movement, it must be followed by adjusting the tilt to maintain a good fit to the A-post. Do not try and adjust the glass parallel to the B-pillar.

1. Remove the trim panel and watershield from the door.
2. Loosen the upper glass run attaching screws and the screws for the front and rear up-stops.
3. Move the glass forward or backwards as required to obtain a good fit.
4. When proper fit is obtained tighten the attaching screws for the front and rear up-stops and the upper glass run.

## In-Out and Tilt Adjustment

1. To tilt the glass forward or backward loosen the front and rear up stops.
2. Loosen the screws for the lower plastic run guide to guide plate.
3. Move the glass forward or backward as necessary to obtain the proper seal and fit.
4. The in-out adjustment is to insure a good seal at the top of the window. Move the window in or out and when a good seal is obtained tighten the guide screws and the front and rear up-stop screws.

## Up Adjustment

1. With the main window all the way up raise the vent glass until the cap of the vent window is just above the door belt line.
2. Loosen the up stops and the regulator arm roller attachment.
3. With your hand lift the door glass bracket assembly until the glass has a good seal with the weatherseal or the top of the door, especially at the rear upper corner of the glass.

4. Tighten all of the screws to 6-11 ft. lbs.

## Upper Stop Adjustment

1. With the glass in the up position make sure there is a good seal at the top of the window.
2. Loosen the screw for the front upper stop and position the stop bracket down against the stop. Tighten the attaching screw.
3. Repeat the same procedure with the rear upper stop.

## Stabilizer Adjustment

1. The stabilizer is used to help support the glass at the door belt line.
2. Adjust the stabilizers by raising the glass to the up position and loosening the stabilizer attaching screw.

## Down Stop Adustment

1. Adjust the down stop so that the window is between flush and ¼ inch above the weatherstrip when the window is in the full down position.

# Ford Motor Company

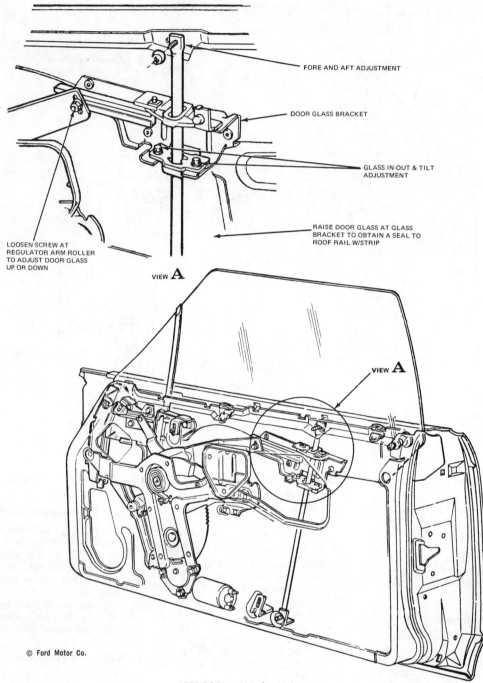

FORE AND AFT ADJUSTMENT

DOOR GLASS BRACKET

GLASS IN-OUT & TILT ADJUSTMENT

RAISE DOOR GLASS AT GLASS BRACKET TO OBTAIN A SEAL TO ROOF RAIL W/STRIP

LOOSEN SCREW AT REGULATOR ARM ROLLER TO ADJUST DOOR GLASS UP OR DOWN

VIEW **A**

VIEW **A**

© Ford Motor Co.

*1973-75 Door Window Adjustments*

## Front Door Vent Window Guide Adjustment

1. The guide is held in position by a retainer attached to the door pillar.
2. Adjust the guide by loosening the attaching screw and lowering the door and vent windows into the door.
3. The guide locates itself in the adjustment slot when the win-dows are lowered.
4. Check the position of the vent glass in the front guide and tighten the retaining screw.

## Vent Glass Adjustment
### In-Out Adjustment

1. The vent window should be adjusted so that the vent glass is parallel to the belt line of the door. Sometimes it is necessary to position the glass to the inside so that it has a good seal on the A-post.
2. To adjust the vent, first remove the end cap of the weatherstrip from the front edge of the door.
3. Using a 7/16 inch wrench inserted through the access opening in the front of the door, adjust the acorn-head adjusting bolt in or out as necessary.
4. Make sure when you are adjust-

# Ford Motor Company

ing the vent in or out that the window is in the full up position.

If the glass does not go all the way up, adjust the up-stop first and then adjust the in-out adjustment.

## Up-Stop Adjustment

1. Remove the trim panel and adjust the up-stop through the access hole in the inner panel.
2. Adjust the stop so that the vent glass is flush with the leading top edge of the door glass. The division bar cap will be slightly

above the two pieces of glass when they are flush.
3. Recheck the in-out adjustment after adjusting the up-stop. When a main glass adjustment is made, the vent glass may have to be adjusted to maintain flushness between the vent and main glass.

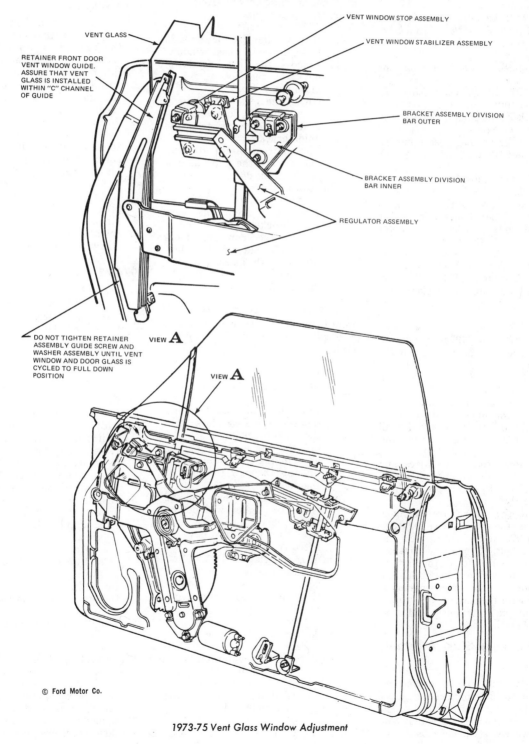

VENT GLASS

RETAINER FRONT DOOR VENT WINDOW GUIDE. ASSURE THAT VENT GLASS IS INSTALLED WITHIN "C" CHANNEL OF GUIDE

VENT WINDOW STOP ASSEMBLY

VENT WINDOW STABILIZER ASSEMBLY

BRACKET ASSEMBLY DIVISION BAR OUTER

BRACKET ASSEMBLY DIVISION BAR INNER

REGULATOR ASSEMBLY

DO NOT TIGHTEN RETAINER ASSEMBLY GUIDE SCREW AND WASHER ASSEMBLY UNTIL VENT WINDOW AND DOOR GLASS IS CYCLED TO FULL DOWN POSITION

VIEW A

VIEW A

© Ford Motor Co.

*1973-75 Vent Glass Window Adjustment*

# Ford Motor Company

## Drive and Motor Assembly

### Removal

1. Remove the door trim panel and watershield.
2. At the dimple located near the lower edge of the door opposite the window drive motor, drill a ¾ inch hole.

*NOTE: Make sure that the hole saw pilot is no more than ¼ inch beyond the saw.*

3. Disconnect the wires from the motor.
4. On 1973-74 models remove the center pin from the rivet that attaches the motor support to the inner panel.
5. After the pin has been removed, drill out the rivet with a ¼ inch drill.
6. Disregard steps 4 and 5 on 1975 models.
7. Working through the three holes in the inner panel remove the three bolts that hold the motor and drive to the regulator.
8. Remove the motor and drive assembly from the door.
9. On 1973 and 1974 models remove the support bracket from the motor.

### Installation

1. On 1973 and 1974 models install the support bracket on the motor.
2. On 1973 and 1974 models install a nut and retainer assembly on the motor support bracket.
3. Install the motor and drive assembly in the door and install the three attaching bolts making them just snug, not tight.
4. Reconnect the motor wires and cycle the glass and check to make sure the gears are meshing correctly.
5. When the gears are engaged, tighten the three screws securely.
6. On 1973 and 1974 models install a bolt, ½ inch long, that has the same thread as the nut on the motor support and attach the support to the inner panel of door with the bolt.
7. Install the watershield and trim panel on the door.

## Door and Vent Glass Assembly

### Removal

1. Remove the trim panel and the watershield from the door.
2. At the front and rear end of the door remove the screws that hold the weatherstrip end caps.

3. If so equipped, remove the assist handle support bracket from the inner panel.
4. Move the weatherstrip aside and remove the outside belt moulding.
5. Loosen the stabilizer screws and move the stabilizers away from the glass.
6. Remove the upper front and rear stop brackets.
7. On 1973 models:
   a. Remove the plastic up-stop from the vent glass window.
   b. Remove the three retaining nuts for the door glass to glass bracket.
   c. Lower the glass all the way down into the door and separate the door glass from the guide bracket.
   d. Lift the rear of the glass up and remove the glass assembly from the door.
8. On 1974 models:
   a. Remove the up-stop for the vent glass from the vent glass bracket.
   b. Remove the center pin from the rivets that hold the glass bracket to the glass.
   c. Drill out the rivets with a ¼ inch drill.

*CAUTION: DO NOT attempt to pry or break the rivets from the glass. This will result in breakage of the glass.*

   d. Push the rivets out of the glass and the glass bracket.
   e. Lower the vent glass all the way down into the door and separate the door glass from the glass bracket.
   f. Lift the rear end of the glass up bringing the white plastic up-stop through the end of the door.
   g. Keep lifting the door and the vent glass roller will detach from the channel. The window assembly can now be lifted from the door.
9. On 1975 models:
   a. Put the vent glass in the full down position and remove the vent roller from vent guide.
   b. Lower the door glass about three inches.
   c. Remove the center pin from three door-glass to glass-bracket retaining rivets and then drill out the rivets with a ¼ inch drill.

*CAUTION: DO NOT attempt to*

pry or break the rivets from the glass as this can result in the glass breaking.

   d. Lift the door glass and vent as an assembly out of the rear of the door.

### Installation

#### 1973 Models

1. Insert the door and vent glass assembly in the door positioning the vent glass bracket into the front guide and the door glass into the glass bracket.
2. Install three bolts and nuts into the glass bracket and tighten securely.
3. Install the upper rear stop, front up stop for the vent glass and the upper front stop bracket.
4. Adjust the door glass and vent glass as necessary to obtain proper fit and window operation.
5. Install the bracket for the inner panel support and the weatherstrip.
6. Install the door trim panel and the watershield.

#### 1974-75 Models

1. Position the vent glass half way down before positioning the glass assembly in the door.
2. Install the vent through the door first, in the wide part of the opening, and guide the vent channel onto its rollers.
3. The door regulator arm should be about three inches from the full up position.
4. Bring the rear end of the glass, with the rear up-stop attached to it, through the door opening.
5. Making sure the vent glass is in its guide, secure the glass to the glass bracket with three bolts and nuts of the proper size.
6. Install the vent glass up-stop, upper rear stop and the upper front stop bracket.
7. Make all the adjustments that are necessary to get the proper fit and operation from the main glass and the vent glass.
8. Install the support bracket for the inner panel and the weatherstrip.
9. Install the trim panel and the watershield.

## Window Regulator

### Removal

1. Remove the glass and vent assembly from the door.
2. Remove the upper and lower attaching screws for the door glass

# Ford Motor Company

run and remove the run, glass bracket and the guides from the door.

3. On 1973-74 models remove the screw that holds the equalizer arm to the inner panel.
4. Remove the wires from the regulator motor.
5. On 1973-74 models remove the seven rivets that hold regulator and motor support to the inner panel.
6. On 1975 models remove the four rivets holding the door and regulator reinforcement and the nine rivets securing the regulator and motor support to the inner panel.

*NOTE: On all models when removing the rivets, first remove the center pin and then drill out the rivet with a ¼ inch drill.*

7. On 1975 models remove the reinforcement plate from the door.
8. Remove the regulator assembly from the door using the upper rear opening with the motor out first.
9. Remove the remains of the rivets from the inside of the door.
10. Put the regulator in a vise and drill a 5/16 inch hole through the regulator sector gear and the regulator plate.
11. Install a ¼ inch bolt through the hole and install a nut on the bolt to hold the regulator from moving when the motor is removed.
12. Remove the motor and drive assembly from the regulator.

© Ford Motor Co.

*1973-75 Window Regulator Installation*

## Installation

1. On 1973-74 models install seven nut and retainer assemblies on the regulator and motor support bracket.
2. With the regulator in the collapsed position, insert the regulator in the door upside down turning the regulator as you put it in.
3. With the regulator arms partially open, on 1973-74 models install seven bolts that match the nuts used in step one and starting with the upper and lower front attachments, secure the regulator assembly to the door inner panel.

On 1975 models use five nuts and bolts of the proper size and install them in the five holes across the top of the regulator and through the door inner panel. Do not tighten the nuts.
4. Connect the wires to the motor.
5. On 1975 models operate the motor as required and move the gear to gain access to the four remaining holes in the regulator and install four bolts and nuts of the proper size. Now tighten all nine of the nuts to 6-11 ft. lbs.

*NOTE: All of the nut and bolt assemblies must be installed with the head of the bolt to the inside of the inner panel. This prevents the thread part of the bolt from interfering with the regulator operation.*

6. On 1975 models install four metal screws to the door and regulator reinforcement and tighten securely.
7. Install the run, glass bracket and guides in the door.
8. Install the glass and vent assembly in the door.
9. On 1973-75 models attach the equalizer arm to the inner panel.
10. Adjust the window as necessary.
11. Install the trim panel and the watershield.

© Ford Motor Co.

*1973-75 Inserting Window Regulator into Door*

# Power Vent Windows

### 1968—General Motors

### Power Vent Windows

The power ventilators are operated by a 12 volt series-wound motor with an internal circuit breaker. Some ventilator motors have a locking type connector which should not be disengaged. When testing or removing the motor, the in-line connector located inside of the inner panel should be

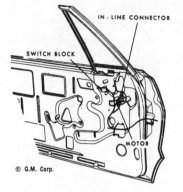

© G.M. Corp.

*Power Ventilator Wiring Installation—Typical*

disengaged. Tests are made at this location on those styles.

The power ventilator circuit is similar to the power window circuit. Diagnosis for power windows may also be used for the power ventilator circuit.

The ventilator harness is separate on Pontiac models. On all other series, the harness is an integral part of the power window harness.

## Power Tailgate Windows

## American Motors

### Description

To raise or lower the tailgate window with the instrument panel rear window control switch, the ignition switch must be in either accessory or ignition position on early models and the ignition position only on late models.

The tailgate window can also be operated by inserting the ignition key in the tailgate lock. Turn the key to left to lower and right to raise.

When the glass is completely lowered, a safety catch is released. The tailgate can then be opened. A plunger type safety switch is mounted on the left auxiliary floor panel to prevent raising the glass when the tailgate is open.

### Electrical Tests

To test for a defective circuit, connect a 12 volt test lamp across the circuit breaker wires supplying the circuit. (refer to wiring diagrams). Operate the switch in the circuit, the test lamp should light if the circuit is complete at this point.

CAUTION: The tailgate circuit has a central ground wire. Do not connect the test lamp to the chassis as incorrect indications will result.

### Tailgate Glass Alignment

The tailgate glass can be aligned to fit the body opening by removing the trim panel and access hole covers.

Loosening the regulator attaching screws will allow the regulator assembly to be shifted up or down on either one or both sides.

The glass slide channel lower mounting holes in the tailgate are elongated to allow for in or out adjustment of the glass for alignment into the upper glass slide channel.

Make certain that the tailgate is properly aligned before making any adjustment to the glass and regulator

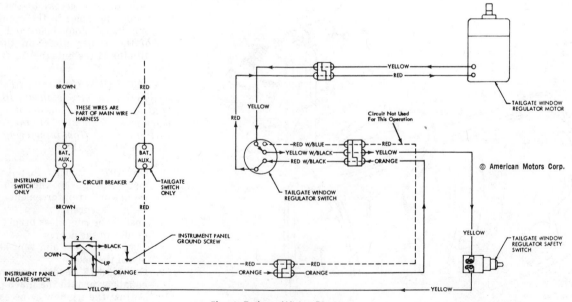

*Electric Tailgate Wiring Diagram*

# American Motors

assemblies. Any realignment of the tailgate will affect the fit of the glass in the upper slide channel.

## Circuit Breakers

The tailgate motor and wiring harness are protected by two 20 ampere circuit breakers located on the lower flange of the instrument panel next to the ash receiver.

## Rear Window Switch

The rear window switch is mounted on the instrument panel. Note the switch wire color code before disconnecting the wire connectors.

## Tailgate Switch

### Removal

1. Remove tailgate remote control handles, trim panel and access hole covers.
2. Raise glass to full up position.
3. Remove wire retainer that secures switch to key lock assembly.
4. Remove switch through access hole and disconnect wires at connectors.

### Installation

1. Connect wires and insert switch on key lock assembly.
2. Insert wire retainer and lower glass into tailgate.
3. Install access hole covers, trim panel and remote control handles.

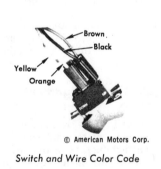

Switch and Wire Color Code

## Tailgate Glass Assembly Removal

### Glass stuck in "UP" position

1. Disconnect battery.
2. Remove remote control handles, trim panel and access hole covers.
3. Remove screws that retain regulator arm slide channels to glass bottom channel.
4. Hold glass in place and force slide channel out of glass bottom channel retaining brackets.
5. Lower window into tailgate.
6. Open tailgate and remove glass assembly.

### Glass stuck in "DOWN" position

1. Disconnect battery.
2. Remove remote control handles, trim panel and access hole covers.
3. Remove screws that retain regulator arm slide channels to glass bottom channel.
4. Remove rubber stop bumpers from inside bottom of door.
5. Insert a screwdriver to pry slide channels from glass bottom channel brackets.
6. Remove glass assembly.

## Tailgate Window Regulator

### Removal

1. Remove tailgate glass assembly.
2. Remove access hole covers.

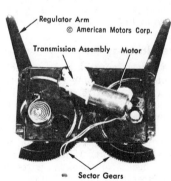

Tailgate Regulator

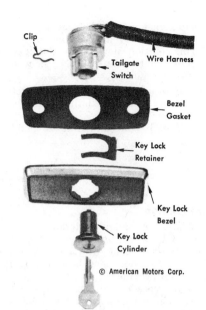

Key Lock and Switch Assembly

3. Move regulator arms to a horizontal position.
4. Disconnect motor wiring from harness.
5. Mark regulator position for installation.
6. Remove regulator mounting bolts.
7. Remove regulator assembly through access opening.

### Installation

1. Insert regulator into access opening and align with marks made on removal.
2. Install regulator mounting bolts.
3. Move regulator arms to full up position.
4. Install glass assembly.
5. Check glass alignment and operation.

## Motor to Window Regulator Transmission

### Removal

1. Remove two motor to transmission mounting nuts.
2. Pull motor away from transmission to expose coupling.

### Installation

1. Align flat side of coupling with flat side of transmission shaft.
2. Insert two mounting studs into transmission and install nuts.

## Window Regulator Transmission

### Removal

CAUTION: The regulator is under

Slide Channel    Regulator Arm    © American Motors Corp.

Removing Glass Assembly

## American Motors

spring tension from the regulator coil spring. To prevent possible injury, spring tension must be maintained before the transmission is removed from the regulator.

1. Drill a hole in mounting bracket under one of existing holes in sector gear.
2. Install bolt and nut to hold

spring tension.

3. Remove regulator motor and insert a screwdriver into coupling and turn until remaining tension on transmission is relieved.
4. Remove mounting bolts holding transmission to regulator and remove transmission. Transmission is serviced as an assembly.

Removing Tailgate Window Regulator

## Chrysler Corporation

### Description

The power tailgate window is controlled by a key operated switch at the tailgate and a front control switch. On some models a roof rail switch is provided.

Two types of tailgate motors are used. The permanent magnet type is grounded through the front control switch by a black lead attached to the body metal. The wound field type has two windings which are grounded to the body through the motor housing. The switch completes the circuit back to ground when it is actuated.

The tailgate wiring circuit is protected by a 30 ampere circuit breaker located on the fuse block.

### Electrical Tests

Before making electrical tests check for a binding condition between the glass and run channels. Align glass if binding condition exists.

### Circuit Breaker Test

Connect one lead of a test light to output terminal of circuit breaker and other lead to a good ground. The test bulb should light, if not and wiring is not faulty, replace circuit breaker.

### Control Switch Test 1968-73

Disconnect black wire at control switch and hold against yellow wire on control switch, glass should lower. Repeat test with brown wire, glass should rise. If glass operates during tests, but fails to operate with switch, switch is at fault. If glass fails to move during tests, check wiring harness.

### Instrument Panel Switch Test 1974-75

1. Place a test light across the terminals of the female connector attached to the tailgate wiring harness.

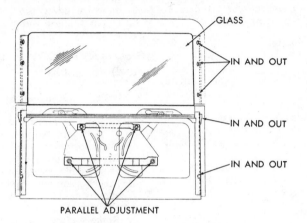

Tailgate Glass Adjustments—Thru 1970

2. Activate the instrument panel switch and the test light should light, if not, either the switch is defective, or there is an open or short circuit in the wiring harness or there is a poor ground connection at the switch.

### Wire Harness Test

Disconnect wire harness connector at motor. Connect one lead of a test light to brown wire and other lead to a good body ground. Position control switch to "UP", test bulb should light. Repeat test with yellow wire and switch in "DOWN" position, test bulb should light. If bulb fails to light, check for broken wires or faulty circuit breaker. If bulb fails to light in both tests, perform motor test.

### Tailgate Motor Test (Permanent Magnet Type)

Connect positive lead from test battery to one terminal of motor. Connect negative lead from test battery to other terminal of motor. Motor should rotate in one direction. Reverse battery leads and motor should rotate in other direction. If motor does not rotate in both directions, replace motor.

### Tailgate Motor Test (Wound Field Type)

Connect positive lead from test battery to one motor field terminal. Connect negative lead to motor case. Motor should rotate in one direction. Move positive battery lead to other field terminal and motor should rotate in opposite direction. If motor does not rotate in both directions, replace motor.

### Tailgate Glass Alignment Thru 1970

1. Remove tailgate trim panel.
2. Loosen regulator and run channel attaching screws and nuts.
3. With tailgate open, adjust upper attachments of lower run channels so glass lightly touches outer belt weatherstrip.
4. Close tailgate and run glass half way closed.
5. Adjust upper run channel and tighten two top screws.
6. Tighten lower nut on bottom of lower run channel.
7. Run glass up to about 1/8 inch below glass run.
8. Raise or lower regulator so top of glass is parallel to glass run.
9. Tighten all attaching screws and nuts and install trim panel.

# Chrysler Corporation

### 1971-73—All
### 1974—Satellite and Coronet

1. Open tailgate to gate position and remove trim panel.
2. Loosen all glass related attaching screws and nuts.
3. Push glass against belt inner weatherstrip and tighten upper screws of lower glass run channel.
4. Glass can be moved from side to side by loosening jam nut and adjusting sleeve nut. Tighten jam nut.
5. Close tailgate and raise glass to about $1/8$ inch below roof rear glass run.
6. Adjust regulator so top of glass is parallel to roof glass run.
7. Open tailgate to gate position and tighten nuts on lower glass run.
8. Tighten all attaching screws and nuts.
9. Close tailgate and test for operation and alignment. Install trim panel.

### 1974-75 exc. 1974 Satellite and Coronet

1. Open the tailgate and remove the inner trim panel cover.
2. Close the tailgate. Raise the glass to approximately $1/4$ inch below the weatherstrip.

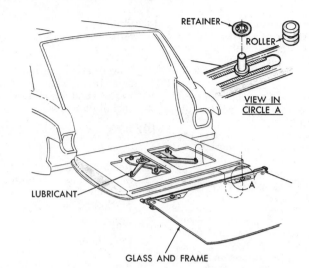

*Tailgate Glass Attachment—Thru 1969*

3. If the top edge of the glass is not parallel to the weatherstrip, loosen the corner window regulator mounting bolts. Twist the regulator base to bring the top edge of the glass parallel to the weatherstrip and tighten the mounting bolts.
4. Raise the glass all the way up and check for side fit. The glass should be centered in the body opening. If the glass is not centered an alignment bracket which is attached to the top of the right hand glass track should be adjusted.
5. Loosen the jam nut, adjust the bracket sleeve then tighten the jam nut.
6. In order to form a tight seal against the top weatherstrip the right and left up-stops should be adjusted.
7. Check that the glass does not raise too high causing a sheet metal interference with the body when the tailgate is opened as a door.

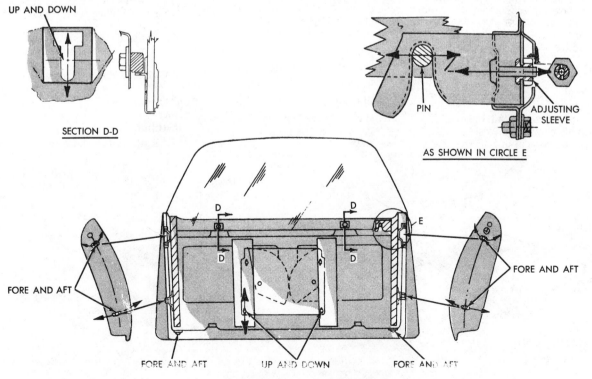

*1974-75 Tailgate Window Adjustment*

8. Open the tailgate as a gate and remove the trim panel cover.
9. Raise the glass about half way up and loosen the bolts that secure the right and left glass runs.
10. To obtain a glass seal at the roof, move the glass inward or outward as follows:
    a. Grasp the bottom edge of the glass and pull it upward to bring the top of the glass away from the roofline or push the glass downward to bring the glass closer to the roofline.
    b. Tighten the lower glass run bolt. Repeat for the other side.
    c. Close the tailgate and raise the glass carefully to the full up position and check to see if it seals properly at the roof.
    d. Tighten all the bolts which secure the glass run channels.

## Tailgate Glass Assembly Thru 1969

### Removal and Installation

1. Remove trim panel.
2. Remove retainers from ends of regulator arm studs.
3. Remove regulator arm studs from rollers in glass lower frame.
4. Remove glass assembly from tailgate.
5. To install, reverse removal procedures.

## 1970

### Removal

1. Remove trim panel.
2. Support glass and remove glass to lift channel screws.
3. Slide glass out of tailgate.

### Installation

1. Lubricate lift channels and sliding blocks.
2. Lower glass into glass runs, align holes in lift channels with holes in glass and install screws.
3. Install trim panel.

## 1971-73

### Removal

1. Remove trim panel.
2. Support glass and remove glass to frame channel screws.
3. Slide glass out of tailgate.

### Installation

1. Lubricate regulator sliding blocks.
2. Force slides outward and push glass in runs so that centering pin hole is aligned with pin.
3. Install gasket, frame channel and glass attaching screws, gaskets, and nuts.
4. Install trim panel.

## 1974—Fury, Chrysler, Monaco
## 1975—Gran Fury, Chrysler, Monaco

### Removal

1. Open the tailgate as a gate and remove the trim panel cover.
2. Raise the glass about half way up.
3. Reach through the access holes and remove the screws which secure the lift channels to the glass.
4. Remove the lift channels from the window regulator and pull the glass out of the tailgate.

### Installation

1. With the tailgate opened as a gate, guide the glass into the run channels.

*NOTE: A slight pressure will be required to push the glass past the indentations at the top of the run channel.*

2. Lubricate the lift channel brackets properly and slide the lift channels into the regulator. The regulator arms should be adjusted to approximately the mid position.
3. Attach the lift channels to the glass.

*NOTE: The lift channel with the slot for lateral adjustment must be installed on the left side.*

4. Adjust the glass as required. (See the Glass Adjustment procedure).

## 1974-75—Satellite, Coronet
## 1975—Fury, Coronet

### Removal

1. Run the glass to the full down position and open the tailgate.
2. Run the glass up and out of the tailgate until the glass lift channel screws are visible in the access holes.
3. Remove the glass lift channel attaching screws and disconnect the glass from the channel assembly.
4. Slide the glass out of the belt opening.
5. Remove the "T" nuts, gasket and rubber tubes from inside the tailgate.
6. Remove the retaining screws and remove the slides from the glass.

*NOTE: There are four slides, note which ones are fixed and which have wedges.*

### Installation

1. Position the slides in the edge of

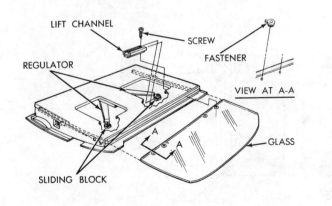

*Tailgate Glass Attachment—1970*

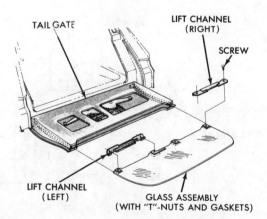

*1974-75 Tailgate Glass Removal*

# Chrysler Corporation

the glass and lubricate the slides.

2. Position the glass into the tailgate, forcing the spring loaded slides wedges outward to start them easily into the vertical glass tracks at each end of the gate.
3. Position the glass lift channels to the glass and install the "T" nuts, gaskets and rubber tubes in the glass holes.
4. Align the glass as required. (See the Glass Adjustment procedure).

## Tailgate Regulator

### 1974—Fury, Chrysler, Monaco
### 1975—Gran Fury, Chrysler, Monaco

#### Removal and Installation

1. Remove tailgate glass.
2. Disconnect electrical leads at regulator.
3. Remove regulator to inner tailgate panel attaching screws.
4. Remove regulator through access hole.
5. Install, reverse removal procedures.

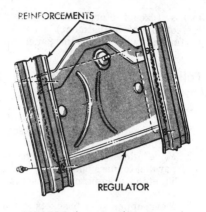

*1974-75 Tailgate Regulator Removal*

### 1974—Satellite, Coronet
### 1975—Fury, Coronet

#### Removal

1. Remove the glass (see glass removal).
2. Remove the lock linkage and position the regulator arms in the three-quarter up position.
3. Remove the regulator attaching bolts.
4. Disengage the serrated regulator crankshaft from the window reg-

ulator handle by lifting vertically up.

5. Disconnect the electrical leads and remove the regulator through the access hole.

*NOTE: Never remove the electric motor or counter balance spring from the regulator assembly without locking the unit in a bench vise.*

#### Installation

1. Install the regulator through the access hole.
2. Press the window regulator handle down on the regulator crankshaft.
3. Install the regulator attaching screws and connect the electrical leads.
4. Install and adjust the lock leads.

## Tailgate Motor
#### Removal and Installation

1. Remove regulator assembly.
2. Lock unit in bench vise to avoid injury from counter balance spring.
3. Remove motor attaching bolts and remove motor.
4. To install, reverse removal procedures.

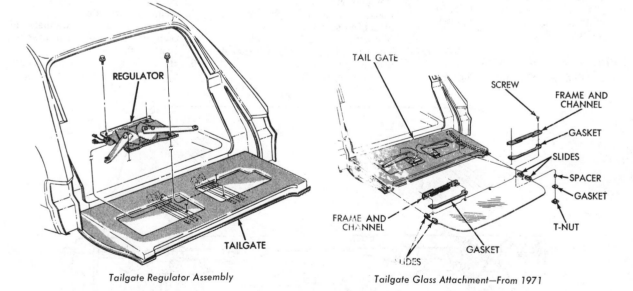

*Tailgate Regulator Assembly*

*Tailgate Glass Attachment—From 1971*

# Ford Motor Company

## Ford
### Description

The power tailgate window is operated by a reversible electric motor and a window regulator mechanism in the tailgate. Control of the window is through a key operated lock switch on the tailgate outer panel, and a switch on the left front door or instrument panel. A limit switch located at the tailgate prevents operation of the window when the tailgate is open.

## Troubleshooting
### Window will not operate with either switch

1. Check connection at window relay for tailgate switch.
2. Check primary ground circuit

## Ford Motor Company

through front control switch and to ground attachment.

3. Check for feed to front control switch from window relay with ignition switch at accessory.
4. Check circuit continuity of front control switch.
5. Connect front control switch and check feed circuits with ammeter while actuating switch. If motor labors and draws current, front control switch is operating.
6. Perform motor test.

### Window will not operate with front control switch

1. Check circuit breaker.
2. Check for power to switch.
3. Check switch for proper operation.
4. Check for feed through relay.
5. Check circuits from front control switch to tailgate switch connector.

### Window does not operate with tailgate key switch

1. Check circuit breaker.
2. Check for power to key switch connector.
3. Check key switch.
4. Check limit switch.
5. Place a test light across tailgate motor connector and operate switch.

### Tailgate Glass Alignment

All window mechanism adjustments (except Ford, Mercury and Meteor in-out adjustment) must be performed with the trim panel removed.

### Full-Up Adjustment

1. Remove trim panel.
2. Loosen each upper stop bracket attaching screw. Check glass fit.
3. Loosen window regulator attaching bolts.
4. Move glass until top edge is parallel to glass opening.
5. Tighten regulator attaching bolts.
6. Move upper stop brackets down firmly against stops and tighten attaching screws.
7. Install trim panel.

### Side to Side Adjustment

#### Ford, Mercury and Meteor

1. Remove trim panel.
2. Loosen two right guide to glass attaching screws.
3. Move glass to desired position.
4. Tighten guide attaching screws.
5. Install trim panel.

#### Torino and Montego

1. Remove trim panel.
2. Loosen glass to glass bracket attaching screws.
3. Move glass to desired position.
4. Tighten glass to glass bracket attaching screws.
5. Install trim panel.

### In and Out Adjustment

#### Ford, Mercury and Meteor

1. Loosen glass run lower attaching screws.
2. Move glass run lower ends forward or rearward, as necessary to obtain good glass seal against weatherstrip.
3. Tighten glass run lower attaching screws.

#### Torino and Montego

1. Remove trim panel.
2. Loosen guide attaching screws.
3. Move top edge of glass inward or outward as necessary to obtain a good glass seal against weatherstrip.
4. Tighten guide attaching screws.
5. Install trim panel.

### Tailgate Window Glass Emergency Lowering Procedure

#### Models with tailgate channeled upper glass runs

1. Remove trim panel screws.
2. Remove glass opening side garnish mouldings.
3. Insert two wire hooks in upper side screw holes and slide trim panel up and off tailgate.
4. Remove water shield.
5. Remove nuts and washers attaching regulator arm brackets to glass channel.
6. Hold glass and disengage regulator arm brackets from glass

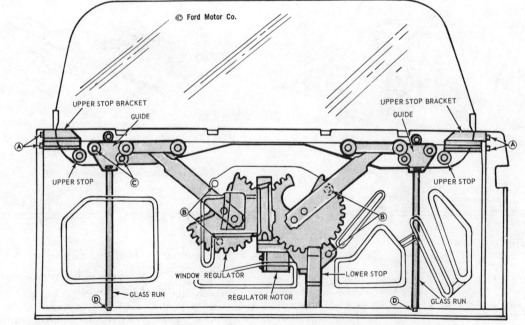

*Tailgate Window Mechanism—Ford, Mercury*

# Ford Motor Company

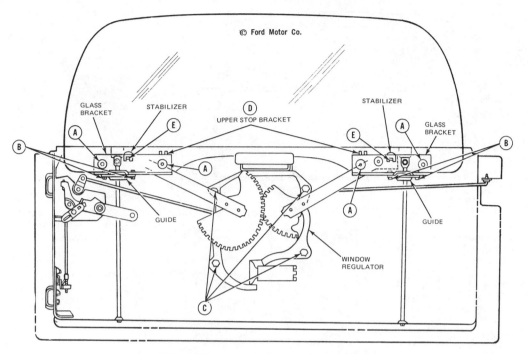

*Tailgate Window Mechanism—Torino and Montego*

channel and regulator rollers.
7. Lower glass into tailgate.

## Tailgate Power Window Switch
## Single Action Tailgate

### Removal and Installation

1. Remove tailgate glass and regulator assembly.
2. Remove nuts retaining lock and switch.
3. Remove lock and switch and disconnect switch wires from tailgate wiring harness. Remove switch and wires.
4. To install, reverse removal procedures.

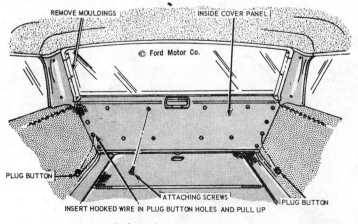

*Tailgate Emergency Opening*

## Dual Action Tailgate
## Ford, Mercury and Meteor

### Removal and Installation

1. Remove tailgate inside cover and watershield.
2. Disconnect tailgate latch rod from switch.
3. Remove switch clip.
4. Remove lock set retainer.
5. Disconnect switch wires and remove wire clips.
6. Remove switch and wire assembly.
7. To install, reverse removal procedures.

## Fairlane, Torino and Montego
## 1969-71

### Removal and Installation

1. Remove trim panel and access hole cover.
2. Remove glass and channel assembly.
3. Insert a small rod into two holes in switch assembly and spread spring clips outward.
4. Slide switch assembly off latch outside handle.
5. To install, reverse removal procedures.

## Torino and Montego—1972-75

### Removal and Installation

1. Remove trim panel and access hole cover.
2. Disconnect rod at bellcrank.
3. Remove spring retainer and remove switch assembly from lock cylinder assembly.
4. Disconnect multiple connectors and remove switch and wire assembly.
5. To install, reverse removal procedures.

## Tailgate Window Regulator and Motor
## Ford, Mercury and Meteor—1969-70

### Removal and Installation

1. Remove tailgate glass.

## Ford Motor Company

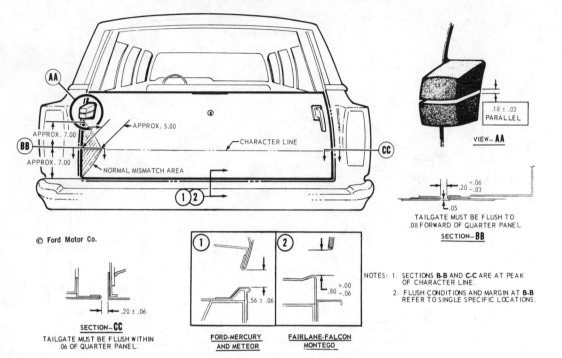

© Ford Motor Co.

VIEW- **AA**

TAILGATE MUST BE FLUSH TO
.08 FORWARD OF QUARTER PANEL
**SECTION- BB**

SECTION-**CC**
TAILGATE MUST BE FLUSH WITHIN
.06 OF QUARTER PANEL.

FORD-MERCURY
AND METEOR

FAIRLANE-FALCON
MONTEGO

NOTES: 1. SECTIONS **B-B** AND **C-C** ARE AT PEAK
OF CHARACTER LINE.
2. FLUSH CONDITIONS AND MARGIN AT **B-B**
REFER TO SINGLE SPECIFIC LOCATIONS.

*Tailgate Switch and Lock Cylinder—Single Action Tailgate*

2. Remove glass channel brackets from regulator arm rollers.
3. Disconnect motor wires at connector.
4. Remove regulator attaching screws and remove regulator from tailgate.
5. Remove motor from regulator.
6. To install, reverse removal procedures.

### Ford, Mercury and Meteor—1971-75

#### Removal and Installation

1. Remove tailgate glass.

2. Remove regulator arm brackets from regulator arm rollers.
3. Disconnect motor wires at connector.
4. Remove regulator attaching screws and remove regulator from tailgate.
5. Drill a hole through regulator sector gear and regulator plate.
6. Install a bolt through hole to prevent sector gear from moving when motor and drive assembly is removed from regulator.
7. Remove motor assembly from regulator.
8. To install, reverse removal pro-

cedures. Remove bolt from drilled hole.

### Fairlane, Torino and Montego—1969-70

#### Removal

1. Open and temporarily support tailgate.
2. Disconnect tailgate hinge supports at tailgate.
3. Remove trim panel.
4. Remove window regulator arm roller retaining pins, disconnect arms from rollers, and remove rollers from glass channel.

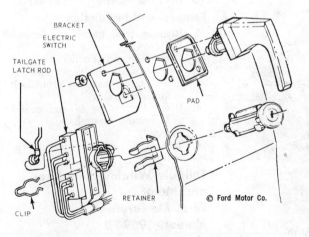

*Tailgate Window Switch—Ford, Mercury*

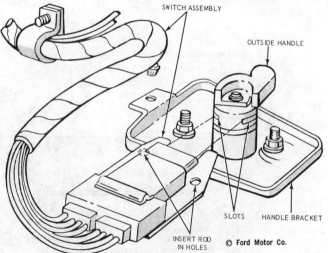

*Tailgate Window Switch—Torino and Montego (Thru 1971)*

# Ford Motor Company

5. Remove window assembly.
6. Disconnect motor leads from wire harness.
7. Mark regulator mounting location, remove regulator retaining bolts and remove regulator with motor attached.
8. Unload regulator counterbalance spring by placing spring in vise so that spring cannot unwind. Disconnect spring from outer retaining tab, and slowly loosen vise.
9. Remove screws retaining regulator drive assembly and motor to regulator and remove motor and drive assembly.
10. To install, reverse removal procedures.

## Torino and Montego—1971-75

### Removal and Installation

1. Remove tailgate trim panel.
2. Remove window assembly.

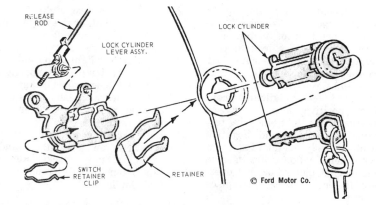

*Tailgate Window Switch—Torino and Montego (From 1972)*

3. Disconnect motor leads from wire harness.
4. Mark regulator mounting location, remove regulator retaining bolts.
5. Slide the regulator to one side and disengage the arm rollers from the glass brackets and remove the regulator through the recess hole in the door.
6. To install, reverse removal procedures.

# General Motors

## Non-Retractable Type

## General Motors

### Description

The power operated tailgate window is equipped with a 12 volt reversible direction motor with an internal circuit breaker and a self-locking drive gear. In addition, to the internal circuit breaker the wiring circuit is protected by a 40 ampere circuit breaker.

The circuit breaker locations are as follows:

Buick and Pontiac—in fuse block
Chevrolet and Oldsmobile—engine compartment bulk-head.

The power tailgate window can be operated by any one of three switches. One on the instrument panel, a key operated switch at the tailgate lock cylinder and on some models a switch on the wheelhouse cover panel (down only).

All tailgates are equipped with an electrical safety switch that prevents movement of the window with the gate in any position other than fully closed.

### Electrical Tests

Before performing checking procedures, check all connections for proper installation. Checking procedures may be used to check the operation of a switch or motor after the cause of electrical failure has been isolated. Refer to circuit diagrams.

### Checking Feed Circuit at Circuit Breaker

Connect one test light lead to battery side of circuit breaker, ground other lead. If tester does not light, there is an open or short circuit in feed circuit to breaker.

### Checking Circuit Breaker

Connect one test light lead to output terminal and ground other lead. If tester does not light, circuit breaker is faulty.

*NOTE: On 1968-69 models, disconnect output feed wire from breaker before connecting test light.*

### Checking Relay Assembly

1. With test light, check relay feed. If tester does not light, there is an open or short circuit in feed circuit to breaker.
2. Turn ignition switch on and with test light check output terminal of relay. If tester does not light, the relay is inoperative or there is an open or short circuit between ignition switch and relay. (check fuse).

### Checking Feed Circuit at Control Switch on Instrument Panel

Disconnect harness connector from switch. Connect one test light lead to feed terminal of switch connector and ground other lead to body metal.

If tester does not light, there is an open or short circuit between switch and power source.

### Checking Control Switch at Instrument Panel

1. Disconnect harness connector from switch.
2. Insert one end of a #12 gauge jumper wire into feed terminal and other end into one of the other terminals. Tailgate motor should operate.
3. Repeat procedure for the other terminal. If tailgate motor operates with jumper wire, but does not operate with control switch, the switch is defective.

### Checking Control Switch on Tailgate

1. Remove the tailgate switch.
2. Disengage connector from switch and test for current at terminal block with test light.
3. Use a #12 gauge jumper wire and perform same checking procedure as outlined for control switch at instrument panel.

### Checking Tailgate Motor

1. Disengage harness connector from motor.
2. On single acting tailgates—connect positive lead of power source to light blue wire terminal on motor and negative lead to white-dark green (ground)

# General Motors

wire terminal on motor. Motor should operate. To check reverse operation of motor, connect power source lead to tan-white terminal on motor. If motor does not operate in both directions, replace motor.

3. On dual acting tailgates—connect positive lead of power source to one light blue wire terminal on motor and negative lead to body metal. Test tan-white terminal on motor in same manner. If motor does not operate in both directions, replace motor.

## Checking Safety Switch

### Single Action Tailgates

1. With tailgate open, depress safety switch arm to simulate tailgate being closed.
2. Operate control switch. If motor does not operate, either switch is defective or circuit is open from motor to switch.
3. To check for defective switch, connect one lead of test light to power source and other lead to safety switch terminal. If tester lights when switch lever is depressed, the switch is operative.

*NOTE: Safety switch completes the ground circuit from motor.*

### Dual Acting Tailgates

CAUTION: Before actuating safety switch, apply tape over "DOOR" remote control handle so it cannot be used.

1. With tailgate open as a tailgate, manually trip upper right and left lock assemblies to lock position to simulate tailgate being closed.

2. Connect one test light lead to ground and other to switch input connector. If lamp does not light inspect for open or short circuit.
3. Connect test light to output connector. If lamp does not light, and switch is properly adjusted (1/16" clearance between switch plunger and locking lever) replace switch.
4. Before closing tailgate, actuate "GATE" remote control handle to unlock upper locks. Remove tape from "DOOR" remote control handle.

## Tailgate Glass Alignment

The tailgate glass run channels can be adjusted to relieve a binding glass. If the glass is misaligned, remove the tailgate inner panel, water deflector and access hole covers. Loosen window regulator attaching screws and rotate the regulator clockwise or counter clockwise as required.

## Tailgate Window Assembly

### Single Acting Tailgates

#### Removal and Installation

1. Remove tailgate inner panel cover, water deflector and both access hole covers.
2. Engage safety switch.
3. Using tailgate key switch, operate window to a point that cam attaching bolts are accessible.
4. Remove right and left cam attaching bolts. Slide cams to disengage from lift arm rollers and remove cams from tailgate.
5. Pull window straight out from tailgate.
6. To install, reverse removal procedures and align window assembly.

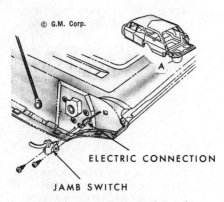

*Single Action Tailgate Jamb Switch*

## Dual Acting Tailgates

### Removal and Installation

1. Open tailgate to gate position.
2. Remove tailgate inner panel cover, water deflector and both access hole covers.
3. Apply tape over "DOOR" remote control handle so it cannot be used. If "DOOR" handle is actuated after upper locks are engaged, tailgate could drop from right lower lock.
4. Manually lock both upper locks. Right upper lock is engaged by pivoting fork bolt to its full clockwise limits. Left upper lock is engaged by depressing locking lever to full engagement.
5. Engage safety switch.
6. Using tailgate key switch, operate window to a point that cam attaching bolts are accessible.
7. Remove right and left cam attaching bolts. Slide cams free of regulator lift arm rollers and remove cams from tailgate.
8. Pull window straight out from tailgate.

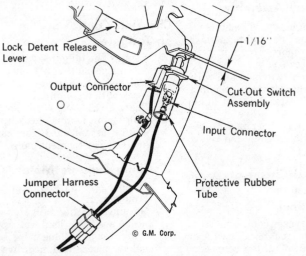

*Dual Action Tailgate Cut-Out Switch*

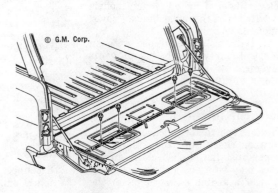

*Tailgate Inner Panel Cam Attachments*

# General Motors

9. To install, reverse removal procedures.
10. Unlock right and left upper locks by actuating "GATE" inside remote control handle.
11. Remove tape from "DOOR".
12. Close tailgate and check glass alignment.

## Tailgate Window Regulator

### Removal and Installation

1. Remove tailgate window.
2. Disconnect electric harness at regulator motor connector.
3. Remove bolts securing regulator to support.
4. Remove regulator, with motor attached from tailgate.

CAUTION: See tailgate window regulator motor for motor removal.

5. To install, reverse removal procedures.

## Tailgate Window Regulator Motor

### Removal

1. Open tailgate and remove tailgate inner cover panel, water deflector and on Single Acting Tailgates, the right access hole cover. Dual Acting tailgates, the left cover.

*NOTE: If window motor fails with tailgate closed and glass in up position, remove covers and sash channel cams and manually lower glass to bottom of gate.*

2. Disconnect wire harness connector from motor.

CAUTION: The following procedure must be performed if window is removed or disengaged from regulator lift arms. Lift arms are under tension from counter-balance spring. Injury may result if motor is removed

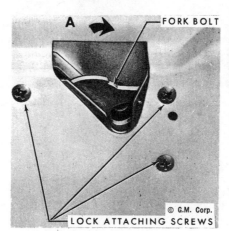

Dual Action Tailgate Upper Lock Engagement

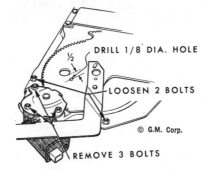

Tailgate Regulator Motor Assembly

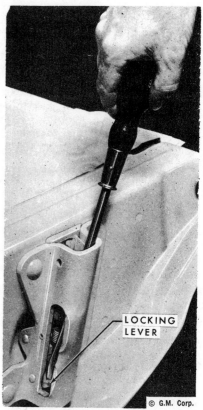

Dual Action Tailgate Left Lock Engagement

without locking sector gears in position.

Drill a hole through regulator sector gear and back plate. Do not drill hole closer than ½" to edge of sector gear or back plate. Install sheet metal tapping screw in drilled hole to lock sector gears.

3. Loosen regulator attaching bolts.
4. Remove regulator motor attaching bolts and remove motor from assembly.

### Installation

1. Lubricate motor drive gear and

regulator sector teeth with cold weather approved lube.

2. With tailgate in open position, install motor to regulator. Make sure motor pinion gear teeth mesh properly with sector gear teeth. Install motor attaching bolts.
3. Tighten regulator attaching bolts and remove screw (if used) which locks sector gears.
4. Connect wire harness to motor.
5. Cycle glass alignment before installing access hole cover, water deflector and cover panel.

## ══════ POWER TAILGATE WINDOWS AND GATES ══════

### Retractable Type

#### Description

The retractable back window raises upward and into the space between the roof inner and outer panels. The window can be operated by either of two switches; one on the instrument panel and one (key operated) on the rear of the quarter panel, next to the tailgate.

The tailgate window is independent of the tailgate, all glass support and operating components are mounted in the body shell. The window motor is mounted to the rear of the spare tire well and delivers torque to the window regulator assembly through a drive cable. The window regulator drives another cable that is attached to the right upper glass roller support and moves the glass along the guide cams.

The retractable tailgate is designed

to lower into the under body. The power tailgate is operated by the exterior switch. On some models an instrument panel switch is also provided.

A lift arm and hinge assembly with an electric motor is mounted to the left quarter inner construction and to the left upper inner corner of the gate. The assembly mounting holes are elongated to allow for adjustments.

# General Motors

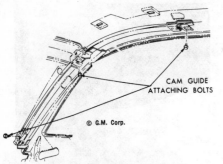

*Tailgate Left Guide Cam Attachment*

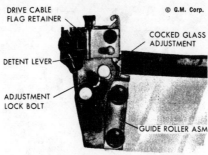

*Window Guide Roller Assembly*

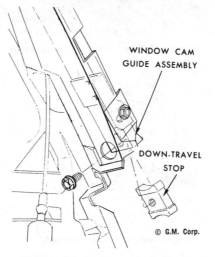

*Tailgate Window Down-Travel Stop*

## Retractable Tailgate and Window

### General Motors

### Electrical Tests

Before performing checking procedures, check all connectors for proper installation. Checking procedures may be used to check the operation of a switch or motor after the cause of electrical failure has been isolated. Refer to circuit diagrams.

### Checking Feed Circuit at Circuit Breaker

Connect one test light lead to battery side of circuit breaker, ground other lead. If tester does not light, there is an open or short circuit in feed circuit to breaker.

### Checking Circuit Breaker

Connect one test light lead to output terminal and ground other lead. If tester does not light, circuit breaker is faulty.

### Checking Relay Assembly

1. With test light, check relay feed. If tester does not light, there is an open or short circuit between relay and circuit breaker.
2. Turn ignition switch on and with test light check output terminal of relay. If tester does not light, put test light on relay coil feed and if tester lights, replace relay. If tester does not light at relay coil feed there is an open or short circuit between ignition switch and relay. (check fuse)

### Checking Feed Circuit at Control Switch on Instrument Panel

Turn ignition switch on and disconnect harness connector from instrument panel switch. Connect one test light lead to feed terminal of switch connector and ground other lead to body metal. If tester does not light, there is an open or short circuit between switch and power source.

### Checking Control Switch at Instrument Panel

1. Turn ignition switch on and disconnect harness connector from instrument panel switch.
2. Insert one end of #12 gauge jumper wire into feed terminal and other end into one of the other terminals. Tailgate window motor should operate.
3. Repeat procedure for the other terminal. If tailgate window motor operates with jumper wire but does not operate with control switch, the switch is defective.

### Checking Key Operated Control Switch on Quarter Panel

This procedure applies to power operated windows and power operated tailgates.

1. Remove key switch assembly.

2. Disengage connector from switch and test for current at feed terminal.
3. Use a #12 gauge jumper wire and perform same checking procedure as outlined for control switch at instrument panel.

### Checking Tailgate Window and Tailgate Motors

1. Disengage harness connector from motor.
2. Connect positive side of power source to one of motor terminals and negative side to body metal. Motor should operate.
3. To check reverse operation of motor, connect power soruce to other motor terminal.
4. If motor does not operate in both directions, replace motor.

### Tailgate Glass Alignment

Fore and aft adjustment of window for proper weatherstrip contact is made by adjusting both right and left window guide cams at rear and midway attaching locations.

A cocked window adjustment is performed by loosening and rotating right upper roller support.

Window down travel is controlled by adjustable stops in lower end of window guide cams.

### Tailgate Window Regulator

#### Removal and Installation

1. Remove spare tire cover and tire.
2. Disengage window motor cable at regulator assembly.
3. Disengage window drive cable clip at upper end of regulator and remove cable conduit at lower end of regulator.
4. Remove regulator attaching screws. Rotate regulator clockwise off lower end of drive cable.
5. To install, reverse removal procedure.

### Tailgate Window Motor

#### Removal and Installation

1. Remove spare tire cover and tire.
2. Disconnect motor wire and disengage cable at upper end of motor.
3. Remove motor mounting plate attaching screws and remove plate and motor as an assembly.
4. Remove motor from mounting plate.
5. To install, reverse removal procedures.

## American Motors

## Rear Window Heater/Defogger System 1971-1975

The heated rear window employs a grid of horizontal lines, composed of silver-impregnated ceramic enamel, fused to the inside of the rear window glass. It is activated at the dash panel by a control switch, with an indicator light to tell when the system is operating. Also in the system is a timer-relay which allows operation of the system for 3–7 minutes at a time, depending on the existing ambient temperature. The unit can be recycled by the control switch.

The feed to the relay is supplied by a wire, with an in-line fuse, from the battery side of the starter solenoid. The relay connects to two vertical buss bars, each of which have braided copper wire soldered to them at 2½ in. intervals, which in turn supply voltage to the grid. The feed buss bar is located on the driver's side and the ground buss bar on the passenger's side.

To operate the system, the ignition switch must be in the "on" position and the engine must be running. This is necessary because of the current draw.

## 1. Systems Tests
### A. Switch

Disconnect the feed-to-switch and switch feed-to-relay wires. Resistance across the terminals should be 200 ohms with the switch off and 0 ohms with the switch on.

### B. Indicator Light

Connect jumper wires from the accessories terminal of the fuse panel to the bulb and from the bulb to a known ground. Turn the ignition switch to ACC. The bulb should light.

### C. Relay-Timer
1. Disconnect the 3-wire plug from the relay.
2. Connect known feed from the accessories terminal of the fuse panel to the (X) terminal of the relay.
3. Connect another known feed from the accessories terminal of the fuse panel to the input terminal of the control switch.
4. Connect another known feed from the output side of the switch to the (P) terminal of the relay.
5. Connect a known 12V test lamp from the (L) terminal of the relay to a known ground.
6. Turn the ignition switch to ACC. The lamp should *not* light.
7. Turn the defogger switch to ON. The lamp should light and remain lit for 3–7 minutes.

*NOTE: The battery should be fully charged for this test.*

### D. Grid

The most obvious indication of the grid not working is a patch of lingering ice or frost. The patch will appear over the break in the grid.

The system test is as follows:

Turn the ignition switch to ON and, with the engine runing–
1. Connect a 12V DC voltmeter to the vertical busses, positive lead to the left buss; negative lead to the right buss. Voltage drop should be 11-13V.
2. Connect the negative lead to a known ground. Voltage drop should remain constant.
3. Keep the negative lead connected to the known ground and, with the positive lead, carefully contact each grid line at the midpoint of the window. A reading of 6V, one half maximum load, is normal. A complete drop indicates a break between the positive lead and the ground. No drop in voltage indicates a break between the positive lead and feed.
4. To find the exact location of the break, move the positive lead to the left or right as necessary. A sudden change in voltage will indicate the break.

## 2. Grid Repair

A broken grid can be repaired by application of an air-dry silver preparation available from the manufacturer.
1. When the break is found, mark its location on the *outside* of the glass.
2. Turn the control switch to OFF.
3. Clean the inside area at the break with fine steel wool and alcohol.
4. Using cellulose tape, place two strips along the top and bottom of the broken line, touching the edge of the line, and extending at least one inch to either side of the break.
5. Mix the repair solution thoroughly.
6. Using a fine brush, paint on a heavy coat, overlapping ¼ in. on either side of the break.
7. After the first coat has dried, apply a second heavy coat.
8. After the second coat has dried, remove the tape and check voltage.

*NOTE: Do not touch the repaired area. Do not clean the repaired area with solvents.*

## 3. Relay-Timer Removal

### 01 Series

The relay-timer is located on the right side of the brake pedal support bracket.

### 10-80 Series

The relay-timer is located on the inside wall of the intake plenum chamber above the steering column. Removal is made easier by removal of the instrument cluster.

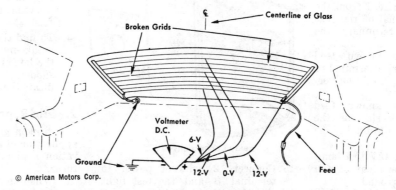

© American Motors Corp.

*Voltmeter Connections and Voltage Drop for Grid Continuity*

# Chrysler Corporation

## HEATED REAR WINDOW SYSTEM

The heated rear window employs a grid of horizontal lines composed of silver-impregnated ceramic enamel fused to the inside of the rear window glass. It is activated at the dash panel by a control switch, with an indicator light to tell when the system is operating. Also in the system is a timer-relay which allows operation of the system for 3–7 minutes at a time, depending on the existing ambient temperature. The unit can be recycled by the control switch.

The feed to the relay is supplied by a wire with an in-line fuse from the special 60 amp alternator. The relay connects to two vertical buss bars, each of which have braided copper wire soldered to them at 2½ in. intervals, which in turn supply voltage to the grid. The feed buss bar is located on the driver's side and the ground buss bar on the passenger's side.

To operate the system, the ignition switch must be in the ON position and the engine must be running. This is necessary because of the current draw.

### 1. System Tests

#### A. Switch

Disconnect the feed-to-switch and switch feed-to-relay wires. Resistance across the terminals should be 200 ohms with the switch off and 0 ohms with the switch on.

#### B. Indicator Light

Connect jumper wires from the accessories terminal of the fuse panel to the bulb and from the bulb to a known ground. Turn the ignition switch to ACC. The bulb should light.

#### C. Relay-Timer—1973-74

1. Disconnect the 3-wire plug from the relay.
2. Connect a known feed from the accessories terminal of the fuse panel to the (X) terminal of the relay.
3. Connect another known feed from the accessories terminal of the fuse panel to the input terminal of the control switch.
4. Connect another known feed from the output side of the switch to the (P) terminal of the relay.
5. Connect a known 12V test lamp from the (L) terminal of the relay to a known ground.
6. Turn the ignition switch to ACC. The lamp should *not* light.

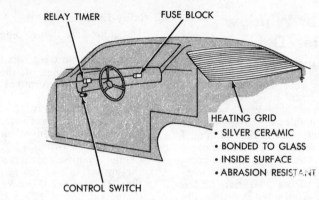

*Basic System*

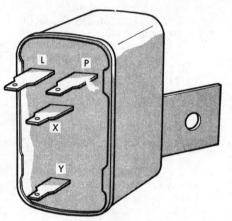

*Time Delay Relay*

7. Turn the defogger switch to ON. The lamp should light and remain lit for 3–7 minutes.

#### Relay-Timer—1975

1. Ground the relay case and connect a jumper wire between terminals B and Y. Connect a 12 volt test light between L and ground.

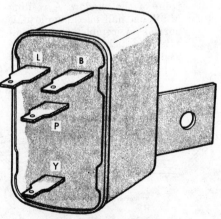

*Relay Connections—1975*

2. Connect 12 bolts of power to terminal B and the test light should not light. If it does light, replace the relay.

3. Momentarily short the B and P terminals. The test light should come on and stay on for 8½-11½ minutes for the timer relay and indefinitely for the continuous relay.

*NOTE: The battery should be fully charged for this test.*

#### D. Grid

The most obvious indication of the grid not working is a patch of lingering ice or frost. The patch will appear over the break in the grid.

The system test is as follows:

Turn the ignition switch to ON and, with the engine running,

1. Connect a 12V DC voltmeter to the vertical busses, positive lead to the left buss, negative lead to the right buss. Voltage drop should be 11–13V.
2. Connect the negative lead to a known ground. Voltage drop should remain constant.
3. Keep the negative lead connected to the known ground and, with the positive lead, carefully contact each grid line at the midpoint of the window. A reading of 6V, one half maximum load, is normal. A complete drop indicates a break between the positive lead and the ground. No drop in voltage indicates a break between the positive lead and feed.
4. To find the exact location of the break, move the positive lead to the left or right as necessary. A sudden change in voltage will indicate the break.

### 2. Grid Repair

A broken grid can be repaired by application of an air-dry silver preparation available from the manufacturer.

1. When the break is found, mark its location on the *outside* of the glass.

## Chrysler Corporation

2. Turn the control switch to OFF.

3. Clean the inside area at the break with fine steel wool and alcohol.

4. Using cellulose tape, place two strips along the top and bottom of the broken line, touching the edge of the line, and extending at least one inch to either side of the break.

5. Mix the repair solution thoroughly.

6. Using a fine brush, paint on a heavy coat overlapping ¼ in. on either side of the break.

7. After the first coat has dried, apply a second heavy coat.

8. After the second coat has dried, remove the tape and check voltage.

*NOTE: Do not touch the repaired area. Do not clean the repaired area with solvents.*

## Ford Motor Company

### HEATED REAR WINDOW SYSTEM

**1972-75 All—except Maverick and Comet**
**1971 All—except Maverick, Comet, and Pinto**
**1969-70 Ford, Mercury, Continental, Mark III, and Thunderbird**

The heated rear window system is composed of a control switch, a relay, an indicator light, and a silver wire grid, horizontally bonded to the inside of the rear window glass. The relay on all 1969–70, 1971–73 Ford, Mercury and Meteor, and 1972–73 Montego and Torino is a time relay unit. All others are latching relays.

The latching relay is so called because it remains latched in the energized position until either the control switch or the ignition switch is turned off. The time delay relay allows the grid to function for a specified period of time: 6–14 minutes on Torino and Montego; 3–7 minutes on all others. The timer-relay can be recycled by the control switch. It is recommended that the engine be running during use because of the current draw.

### System Tests

#### Grid Test

The most obvious test of a grid is its operation under weather conditions. A lingering patch of ice or frost on the window indicates a break in the grid.

1. Inspect the grid by placing a strong light inside the vehicle. Observe the grid from the outside. A break will appear as a brown spot.

2. With the engine running and the switch ON, connect a 12V DC voltmeter with the positive lead to the broad, vertical silver strip on the driver's side of the rear window (feed side), and connect the negative lead to the broad, vertical silver strip on the passenger's side of the rear window (ground side). A reading of 10–13 volts should be recorded. Anything less will indicate a loose ground connection.

3. Connect the negative lead of the voltmeter to a known ground. The reading should not change.

4. Carefully using the positive lead, contact each grid line at the center point of the window. A reading of 6 volts, half the maximum load, should be observed. A reading of 0 indicates a break in the line between the midpoint and the driver's side. A reading of 12V indicates a break in the line between the midpoint and the passenger's side. To precisely locate the break, move the positive lead to the left or right, as indicated, along the line. A sudden change in voltage will occur at the point of the break.

*NOTE: On the 1972-74 Pinto three door and the 1974 Mustang II three door the slower defrosting of the bottom four grids on the heated back window is a normal condition related to grid pattern coverage requirements, voltage drop and alternator output capabilities. The widened spacing of the lower grids is an intended design.*

### Relay Test
### Latching Type

1. Connect the relay to a known ground.

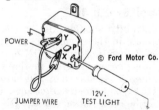

*Ford & Mercury Time Delay Relay Test*

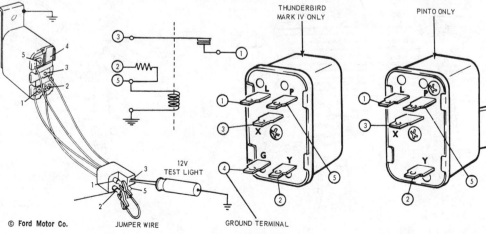

*Latching Relay Test*

## Ford Motor Company

2. Using a wire, connect pins (1) & (2).
3. Connect a 12V test light between pin (3) and ground.
4. Short pins (2) & (5). The light should come on and stay on after the short is removed.

### Time Delay Type

1. Connect the relay to a known ground.
2. Using a wire, connect terminals (X) & (Y).
3. Connect a 12V test light between terminal (L) and ground.
4. Activate the unit at the switch. The lamp should not light.
5. Short terminals (X) & (P). The light should come on and stay on for 3–7 or 6–14 minutes after the short is removed.

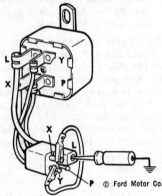

*Torino & Montego Time Delay Relay Test*

### Control Switch Test

Continuity should exist between 2 terminals in the normal position; between 3 terminals in the ON or high position; between none in the OFF position. A resistance of 200 ohms in the OFF position should occur. There should be no resistance in the ON position.

### Grid Repair

A broken grid line can be repaired with an air-dry silver preparation available from the manufacturer.

1. When the break is found, mark its location on the *outside* of the glass.
2. Turn switch to OFF.
3. Clean the inside area at the break with fine steel wool and alcohol.
4. Using cellulose tape, place two strips along the top and bottom of the grid line at the break, touching the edges of the line and extending at least one inch on either side of the break.
5. Mix the repair solution thoroughly.
6. Using a fine brush, paint on a heavy coat, overlapping about ¼ in. on either side of the break.
7. After the first coat has dried, apply a second heavy coat.
8. After the second coat has dried, remove the tape and check the voltage.

*NOTE: Do not touch the repaired area. Do not clean the repaired area with solvents.*

### Relay Removal and Installation

**1972-75—Ford, Mercury**
Relay is located on a panel attached to the lower edge of the instrument panel, above and left of the drive tunnel.

**1972-75—Torino and Montego**
Relay is mounted on the instrument panel above the light switch. The instrument panel pad must be removed.

**1972—Pinto**
Relay is mounted on the far lower edge of the instrument panel.

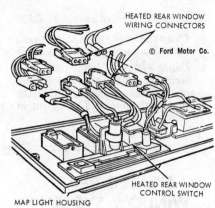

MAP LIGHT HOUSING

*Typical Switch Pin Connections and Location*

**1972-75—Mustang and Cougar**
Relay is mounted on a panel at the upper right corner of the instrument panel, behind the glove box.

**1972-75—Thunderbird and Mark IV**
Relay plugs into a connector on a bracket behind the glove box.

**1972—Lincoln Continental**
Relay is mounted on a bracket behind the glove box. The instrument panel pad must be removed.

**1971—Lincoln Continental and Mark III**
Relay is mounted on the brake pedal support bracket.

**1971—Mustang and Cougar**
Relay is mounted on the instrument panel upper right corner.

**1971—All others**
Relay is mounted under the instrument panel on the right side.

*NOTE: To remove relay, remove two attaching screws and disconnect relay wires. The instrument panel pad on the Continental must be removed.*

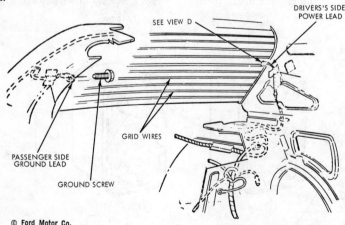

© Ford Motor Co.

VIEW SHOWING REAR HEATED BACK-LITE

*Typical System*

# Ford Motor Company

**1969-70—Continental Mark III and Thunderbird**

Relay is mounted on the brake pedal support bracket.

**1969-70—Ford**

Relay is mounted under the instrument panel near the ash tray.

**1969-70—Lincoln Continental and Mercury**

Relay is mounted under the instrument panel on the right side.

**1973-74—Lincoln Continental**

The relay is mounted to a bracket on the package tray support at the left hand side in the luggage compartment area.

**1973-74—Pinto**

The relay is mounted on the upper right hand part of the instrument panel above the glove box.

*NOTE: To remove relay, remove two attaching screws and disconnect relay wires. On Continental, the instrument panel pad must be removed.*

## Control Switch Removal and Installation

Due to model design and interior changes, the control switch on Ford products 1969-73 varies widely in location. To list all variations would be lengthy and unnecessary, since location in all models is obvious, as the switch is labeled, and removal is simple. All have the following procedure in common:

1. Remove knob from switch except where switch knob is integral.
2. Remove retaining screws and/or nuts.

3. Remove switch and disconnect multiple connector.

*NOTE: Some switches are integrated into other assemblies which must be removed at the same time.*

## Quick Defrost Winshield and Rear Window—Thunderbird and Continental Mark III 1974

### Description

The heater elements used in the windshield and rear window are composed of metallic gold, deposited in a thin film so that almost the entire glass is heated uniformly.

Since voltage approaching 120 volts is required for the heater elements to defrost the glass effectively, red plastic shielded wiring, with high voltage warning tags at each junction is used from the alternator output to the heating elements in the glass. This isolates the high voltage system from the cars normal electrical system.

The control switch located on the dash has three positions off, normal, on. The on and off positions are spring loaded and return to normal when released.

When the switch is pushed to the right to turn the system on, the indicator light will go on. Current flows from the battery to a timer which limits the high heat output from the alternator to approximately ten minutes, then it automatically cuts the voltage to a low heat output. The supplemental alternator that is used is mounted on a bracket above the

charging system alternator. The alternator output is unregulated and does not use a regulator or a rectifier.

### High Voltage Alternator Test

*NOTE: It is suggested that all repairs to the high voltage alternator be made by Ford and Lincoln Mercury dealers.*

*CAUTION: Since the high voltage used in this system presents a danger of electrical shock, all tests must be performed with the engine stopped, the field lead disconnected and using an ohmmeter.*

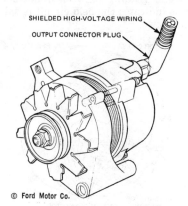

© Ford Motor Co.

*High Voltage Alternator Assembly*

For safety reasons, do not attempt to read the output voltage at the three alternator output terminals. The system output can better be determined by performing the Field Circuit Voltage test.

### Alternator Field Coil Test

Connect an ohmmeter to the field

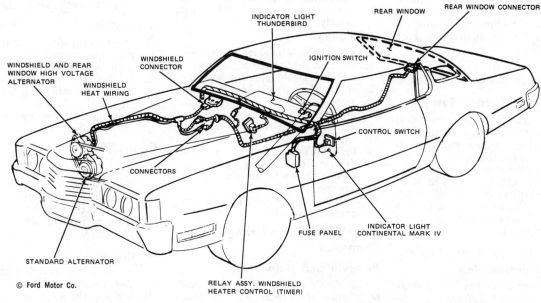

© Ford Motor Co.

*Quick Defrost Windshield and Rear Window System*

# Ford Motor Company

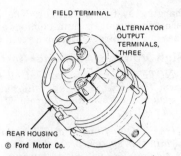

*High Voltage Alternator Terminals*

terminal stud, and the rear housing. A meter reading between 3 and 250 ohms indicates the field circuit is satisfactory.

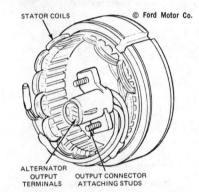

*High Voltage Alternator Stator Assembly*

## Stator Coil Test

Stator coil resistances between any two of the three output terminals in the connector should be equal and approximately one ohm. Check all three of the coils by moving around the three terminals with the ohmmeter to the highest range. Connect the ohmmeter prods to any stator terminal and to the rear housing. A reading of infinity indicates a good coil.

*CAUTION: Be careful not to touch prods or terminals with hands.*

## Field Circuit Voltage Test

Remove the push-on type field terminal connector, touch one voltmeter lead wire to the metal termination, and connect the other voltmeter lead wire to the alternator rear housing. System voltage of 12-13 volts should be indicated with the switch in the on (normal) position. Zero volts should appear with the switch in the off position.

## Windshield and Rear Window Electrical System Test

*CAUTION: Since the high voltage used in this system presents a danger of electrical shock, all tests must*

be performed with the engine stopped, with the field lead disconnected and using an ohmmeter. Also, refer to the electrical wiring diagram.

1. Check the drive belt tension on the supplemental alternator.
2. Check all electrical connectors at the glass and alternator to see if they are firmly connected.
3. Check the two connectors at the rear of the right front fender apron for tight connections.
4. Check to see if the indicator light glows when the engine and control switch are on.
5. Allow the system to operate approximately four minutes at 1500 rpm, then touch both sides of the glass and verify the system is operating.

## Windshield and Hinged Connector

### Removal and Installation

*CAUTION: Before removal and installation the engine must be shut off and Quick Defrost alternator field circuit disconnected or a dangerous electrical shock may result.*

### Removal

1. Disconnect the harness from the heat filament extension which is part of the glass assembly.
2. Remove the three screws from the hinged connector.
3. Release the three tabs and open the hinged connector.
4. Remove the two screws that connect the bracket to the cowl and pull the connector from the windshield heat element.
5. Remove the windshield assembly.

### Installation

1. Install the windshield assembly.
2. Position the hinged connector to the windshield element and install the two brackets to cowl screws.
3. Snap the hinged connector together and lock the three tabs.
4. Install the three hinged connector attaching screws.
5. Connect the field terminal to the high voltage alternator and start the engine.
6. Activate the control switch and check the system.

## Rear Window and Hinged Connector

### Removal and Installation

*CAUTION: Before removal and installation the engine must be shut off and the Quick defrost alternator*

field circuit disconnected or a dangerous electrical shock may result.

1. Disconnect the harness from the heat filament extension which is part of the glass assembly.
2. Remove the hinged connector shield.
3. Pop out the two pins.
4. Remove the one retaining screw and release the two tabs and open the hinged connector.
5. Pull the connector from the heat element.
6. Remove the rear window.

### Installation

1. Install the rear window.
2. Position the hinged connector to the rear window element.
3. Snap the hinged connector together and lock the tabs.
4. Install the one attaching screw.
5. Position the shield pin drives into the holes and snap it down to the locked position.
6. Connect the field terminal to the high voltage alternator and start the engine.
7. Activate the control switch and check the system.

## Alternator

### Removal

1. Disconnect by pulling apart the output connector plug from the alternator.
2. Remove the push-on terminal from the field circuit terminal.
3. Loosen the alternator mounting bolts and remove the adjustment arm bolt from the alternator.
4. Remove the alternator belt.
5. Remove the alternator pivot bolt and remove the alternator.

### Installation

1. Position the alternator to the engine and install the alternator pivot bolt finger tight.
2. Replace the adjusting arm and install the attaching bolt finger tight.
3. Reconnect all terminals and replace the belt.

## Control Switch

### Removal

1. Remove the switch knob.
2. Disconnect the electrical connector from the switch.
3. Remove the one switch attaching screw.

### Installation

1. Position the switch and install the attaching screw.
2. Connect the electrical connector.
3. Install the knob.

# Ford Motor Company

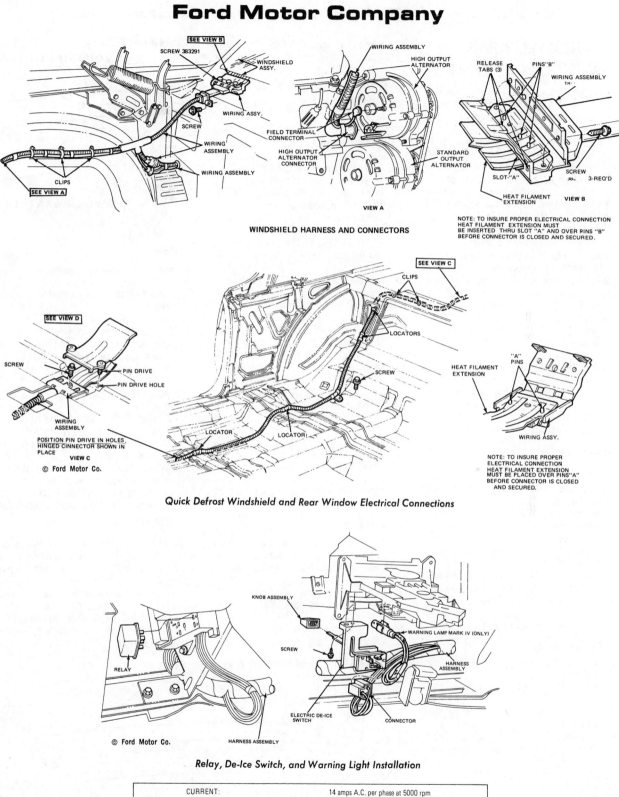

**WINDSHIELD HARNESS AND CONNECTORS**

NOTE: TO INSURE PROPER ELECTRICAL CONNECTION HEAT FILAMENT EXTENSION MUST BE INSERTED THRU SLOT "A" AND OVER PINS "B" BEFORE CONNECTOR IS CLOSED AND SECURED.

NOTE: TO INSURE PROPER ELECTRICAL CONNECTION HEAT FILAMENT EXTENSION MUST BE PLACED OVER PINS "A" BEFORE CONNECTOR IS CLOSED AND SECURED.

*Quick Defrost Windshield and Rear Window Electrical Connections*

*Relay, De-Ice Switch, and Warning Light Installation*

| | |
|---|---|
| CURRENT: | 14 amps A.C. per phase at 5000 rpm |
| POWER: | 2200 watts at 5000 rpm |
| OUTPUT: | Three-phase A.C. |
| ROTOR: | 2.8 ohm coil; 4.3 amps at 12 volts |
| STATOR: | WYE connected coils |

*High Voltage Alternator Specifications*

## General Motors

## HEATED REAR WINDOW SYSTEM

The heated rear window system is composed of a grid of horizontal lines which are made up of silver-impregnated ceramic enamel bonded to the inside of the rear window glass. It is activated at the dash panel by a control switch with an indicator light to tell when the system is operating. Also in use is a relay-timer which allows the system to operate from 6–14 minutes at a time, depending on the ambient temperature. The unit can be recycled at the control switch.

The feed to the relay is supplied by a wire with an in-line fuse from the fuse block. The relay connects to two vertical buss bars on either side of the back window. These supply voltage to the grid. The feed buss is on the driver's side; the ground buss is on the passenger's side.

To operate the system, it is recommended that the engine be running because of the current draw. The switch is spring loaded to return to a midposition. The ON position activates the timer-relay; the OFF position deactivates it.

### System Tests

#### A. Switch

Disconnect the feed-to-switch and switch feed-to-relay wires. Resistance across the terminals should be 200 ohms with the switch off and 0 ohms with the switch on.

#### B. Indicator Light

Connect jumper wires from the accessories terminal of the fuse panel to the bulb and from the bulb to a good ground. Turn the ignition switch to ACC. The bulb should light.

#### C. Relay-Timer

1. Disconnect the three-wire plug from the relay.
2. Connect a known feed from the accessories terminal of the fuse panel to the (X) terminal of the relay. ((H) on Oldsmobile)
3. Connect another known feed from the accessories terminal of the fuse panel to the input terminal of the control switch.
4. Connect another known feed from the output side of the switch to the (P) terminal of the relay. ((B) on Oldsmobile).
5. Connect a 12V test lamp from the (L) terminal of the relay to a good ground.
6. Turn the ignition switch to ACC. The lamp should *not* light.

7. Turn the switch to ON. The lamp should light and remain lit for 6–14 minutes.

*NOTE: The battery should be fully charged for these tests.*

#### D. Grid

The most obvious indication of the grid not working is a patch of lingering ice or frost. The patch will appear over the break in the grid.

The system test is as follows:
1. With the engine running and the switch on, connect a 12V DC voltmeter to the vertical busses, positive lead to the left buss, negative lead to the right buss. A reading of 11–13 volts should occur.
2. Connect the negative lead to a known ground. Voltage drop should remain constant.
3. Keep the negative lead connected to the known ground and, with the positive lead, carefully contact each grid line at the midpoint of the window. A reading of 6 volts, half the maximum load, is normal. A complete drop indicates a break between the positive lead and ground. No voltage drop indicates a break between the positive lead and feed.
4. To find the exact location of the break, move the lead to the left or right as required. A sudden change in voltage will occur at the break.

### Grid Repair

A broken grid line can be repaired by the application of an air-dry silver preparation available from the manufacturer.
1. When the break is found, mark its location on the *outside* of the glass.
2. Turn the switch to OFF.
3. Clean the inside area at the

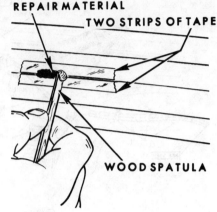

© G.M. Corp.

*Applying Repair Material to Broken Grid Line*

break with fine steel wool and alcohol.
4. Using cellulose tape, place two strips, one on top and one below the broken line, extending at least 1 in. to either side of the break, and touching the edge of the line.
5. Mix the repair solution thoroughly.
6. Using a fine brush, paint on a heavy coat of preparation extending about ¼ in. to either side of the break.
7. When the first coat has dried, apply a second heavy coat.
8. When the second coat has dried, remove the tape and check the voltage.

*NOTE: Do not touch the repaired area. Do not clean the repaired area with solvents. Use of a heat gun applying 500–700°F for about 3 min. is recommended to establish a good conductivity factor. When using this heat, take care to protect surrounding trim. In any case, allow 24 hrs before activating grid.*

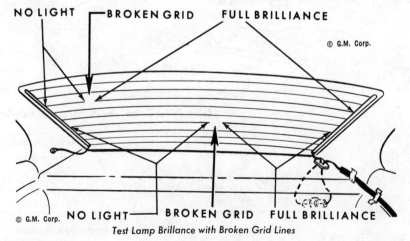

© G.M. Corp.

*Test Lamp Brillance with Broken Grid Lines*

## General Motors

### Relay—Cadillac 1974-75

**Removal**

1. Disconnect the negative battery cable.
2. Remove the lower steering column cover.
   a. Remove the four screws which retain the cover to the lower steering column cover reinforcement.
   b. Remove the four screws which retain the cover to the instrument panel horizontal support.
   c. Remove the lower cover.
3. Remove the two screws that secure the relay to the steering column.
4. Disconnect the electrical connectors.
5. Remove the relay.

**Installation**

1. Connect the wire connectors to the relay.
2. Position the relay to the steering column and install the two retaining screws.
3. Position the lower cover and install the four screws securing it to the instrument panel horizontal support.
4. Install the four remaining cover screws to the reinforcement.
5. Connect the negative battery cable.

### Control Switch-Cadillac 1974-75

**Removal**

1. Remove the instrument panel pad.
   a. Disconnect the negative battery cable.
   b. Remove the right, left and right center climatic control air outlet grilles by compressing the release tabs and rotating the grille upward and out.
   c. Reach through the outlet openings and remove the three pad to panel support fasteners.
   d. Remove the screws which hold the pad to panel horizontal support.
   e. Pull the pad outward and disconnect the wiper switch electrical connection.
   f. If necessary place the transmission shift lever in low range and if equipped with a tilt steering wheel, place the wheel in the lowest position.
   g. Remove the pad.

2. Remove the right hand insert and applique.
   a. Remove the radio knobs, wave washers, control rings and left hex nut.
   b. Reach through the opening in the top of the glove box and remove the attaching screws from the rear of the insert.
3. Push the switch, until it snaps from the housing.
4. Remove the wiring terminals from the switch.

**Installation**

1. Connect the wire terminals to the switch.
2. Snap the switch back into the housing.
3. Install the right hand insert and applique and install the screw.
   a. Install the left hex nut, control tings, wave washers and radio knobs.
4. Install the instrument panel pad.
   a. Position the pad to the panel and connect the wiper switch.
   b. Install the screws retaining the pad to the horizontal support.
   c. Reach through the climate control outlet openings and install the three fasteners which hold the pad to the panel support.
   c. Reach through the climate control outlet openings and install the three fasteners which hold the pad to the panel support.
5. Install the air outlet grilles.
   a. Position grille and press the release tabs.
   b. Snap the tabs into the retaining holes.
6. Connect negative battery terminal.

### Oldsmobile—1974-75
### Instrument Panel Switch 88, 98, Toronado

**Removal**

1. Remove the radio knobs.
2. Remove the applique.
3. Disconnect the wires from the back of the switch.
4. Use a screwdriver and pry the switch out.

**Installation**

1. Snap switch back into position.
2. Connect the wire leads.
3. Install applique.
4. Replace the radio knobs.

### Instrument Panel Switch Cutlass

**Removal**

1. Disconnect the wire terminals.
2. Push from behind the dash panel to remove the switch.

### Instrument Panel Switch Omega

**Removal**

1. Disconnect the ground cable from the battery.
2. Disconnect the switch wire connections.
3. Remove the two nuts which attach the switch to the bezel.
4. Remove the switch.

**Installation**

1. Position the switch and connect the two nuts attaching it to the bezel.
2. Connect the switch wires.
3. Connect the battery ground cable.

### Station Wagons—All
### Heated Tailgate Window Rear Wire Harness Assembly

**Description**

The wire harness for the heated tailgate window is coiled to allow it to extend whenever the window is raised or lowered.

**Removal**

1. Remove the back body opening upper trim finishing moulding and inner filler strip.
2. Remove the left rear pillar finishing moulding and inner filler strip.
3. Remove the left quarter window upper garnish moulding and detach the head lining over the quarter glass enough to reveal the access hole.
4. Disconnect the heated window rear harness at the front junction and tie a four foot cord to the harness for installation.
5. Lower the tailgate all the way down for access to the harness terminal on the glass. (On Manual tailgates, snap the tailgate lock to the lock position in order to lower the window fully).
6. Pull the harness from the body leaving the cord in the body cavity for installation purposes.

## General Motors

**Installation**

1. Pull the cord to guide the harness into position.
2. Connect the wire harness at the front junction.
3. Position the headlining and replace the left quarter window upper garnish moulding.
4. Replace the left rear pillar finishing moulding and inner filler strip.
5. Replace the back body opening upper trim finishing moulding and the inner filler strip.

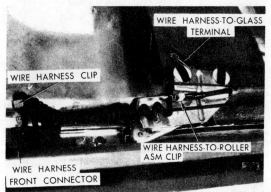

© G.M. Corp.

*Heated Window Rear Wire Harness*

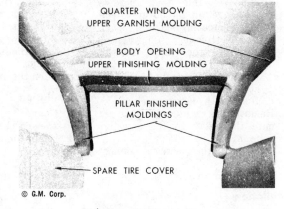

© G.M. Corp.

*Body Rear Finishing Moldings*

| STYLE | GROUND WIRE LOCATION | FEED WIRE LOCATION | CONNECTOR LOCATION | TRIM REMOVAL REQUIRED TO DISCONNECT WIRES FOR GLASS R & I |
|---|---|---|---|---|
| "A" STYLES | Right Side | Left Side | Rear Compartment at Rear Seat Back Panel | Disconnect in Rear Compartment - Lift Rear Corners of Rear Seat to Back Window Trim Panel to Pull Wire Through |
| "F" STYLES | Right Side | Left Side | Rear Compartment | Rear Seat Cushion and Back, Shelf Trim and Right Quarter Upper Trim Panel |
| "B-C-E" STYLES Except Station Wagons & Convertibles | Right Side to Rear Compartment Lid Hinge Box | Left Side | Rear Compartment Under Shelf | Rear Seat Cushion and Back and Shelf Trim |
| STATION WAGONS | Right Side | Left Side | Left Upper Corner on Glass | Standard Glass Removal Operation |
| CONVERTIBLES | Right Side | Left Side | Exposed - Below Right and Left Lower Corners of Glass | None |
| "H" "11" STYLES | Right Side to Rear Seat Back Panel | Left Side | Rear Compartment | Rear Seat Cushion and Back |
| "H" "05,07,15,77" STYLES | Right Side | Left Side | Left and Right Upper Corner of Glass | Standard Glass Removal Operation |

**Connector Location - Optional Rear Window Electric Grid Defogger**

## Chrysler Corporation

### Rear Window Defogger— Blower Type

#### Description

All of the blower type rear window defoggers are basically the same. The defogger is designed to operate at either high or low speeds. Air is drawn into the defogger unit and is directed against the rear window through an outlet located in the rear compartment shelf.

#### Defogger Assembly

**Removal**

1. From inside the luggage compartment disconnect the outlet hose and wire connector.
2. Remove the mounting screws from the mounting clips on the shelf panel and remove the assembly from the car.

**Disassembly**

1. Remove the screws which attach the blower motor adapter plate to the housing and remove the motor and fan assembly from the housing.
2. Loosen the fan hub set screw and remove the fan from the motor.
3. Remove the motor mounting nuts from the adapter plate and remove the motor.

### TROUBLESHOOTING CHART

#### Rear Window Defogger
#### Chrysler Corp.—All Models—1968-75

| Condition | Possible Cause |
|---|---|
| 1. Blower operates but no air movement | a. Obstructions at the air outlet or inlet |
| 2. Defogger does not operate at all | a. Defective control switch<br>b. Open or short circuit between the power supply, switch or motor<br>c. Defective motor |
| 3. Blower motor does not operate at both speeds | a. Defective switch<br>b. Open or short circuit in the wiring |

**Assembly**

1. Place the adapter plate on the motor studs and install the mounting nuts.
2. Install the fan on the motor shaft and insert the assembly in the housing.
   (a) Adjust the fan to housing clearance and tighten the fan set screw.
3. Position the blower motor adapter plate to the housing and install the attaching screws.

**Installation**

1. Install the defogger assembly to the shelf panel and replace the mounting screws.
2. Connect the outlet hose and the wire connector.

#### Defogger Switch

**Removal**

1. Disconnect the negative battery terminal.
2. On air conditioned vehicles remove the transition ducts and left spot cooler ducts.
3. From behind the panel disconnect the electrical leads.
4. Remove the switch mounting screws and remove the switch.

**Installation**

1. Position the switch to the panel and install the mounting screws.
2. Connect the switch electrical leads.
3. On air conditioned vehicles replace the ducts.
4. Connect the negative battery terminal.

## Ford Motor Company

### Rear Window—Defogger— Blower Type

#### Description

All of the blower type rear window defoggers are basically the same. The defogger is designed to operate at either high or low speeds. Air is drawn into the defogger unit and is directed against the rear window through an outlet located in the rear compartment shelf. The defogger blower switch is located next to the heater or heater-air conditioner blower switch on the instrument panel on all models except the Lincoln Continental. The blower switch is located in the instrument panel map light housing on the Lincoln Continental.

#### Defogger Motor

**Removal**

1. Open the trunk and disconnect the motor wires.

### TROUBLESHOOTING CHART

#### Ford—Rear Window Defogger

| Condition | Possible Cause |
|---|---|
| 1. Blower operates but no air movement | a. Obstructions at the air outlet or inlet |
| 2. Defogger does not operate at all | a. Defective control switch<br>b. Open or short circuit between the power supply, switch or motor<br>c. Defective motor |
| 3. Blower motor does not operate at both speeds | a. Defective switch<br>b. Open or short circuit in the wiring |

2. Remove the package tray trim panel.
3. Remove the four defogger retaining clips by twisting them 1/4 turn.
4. Disconnect the ground wire and remove the defogger from the package tray support.

5. Remove the clips and separate the motor and wheel from the housing.

**Installation**

1. Transfer the blower wheel to the new motor.
2. Install the blower and wheel to the new housing.

# Ford Motor Company

3. Position the defogger to the package tray.
4. Install the ground wire and tighten the retaining screw.
5. Install the four defogger mounting clips.
6. Route the power lead through the hole in the tray and connect it to the motor.

## Defogger Switch—
## Ford, Meteor and Mercury

### Removal

1. Remove the knob from the defogger switch.
2. From behind the instrument panel, disconnect the multiple connector from the switch.

CLIPS

DEFOGGER BLOWER MOTOR AND WHEEL ASSY.

GROUND LEAD

PACKAGE TRAY PANEL

© Ford Motor Co.

← FRONT OF VEHICLE

POWER LEAD

**Typical Defogger Motor Installation**

3. Remove the two switch to heater or A/C control screws and remove the switch.
*NOTE: On some models it may be necessary to remove the heater or A/C control unit then remove the switch.*

## Defogger Switch—Thunderbird, Continental Mark III and Mark IV

### Removal

1. Remove the inspection hole

DEFOGGER AIR OUTLET GRILLE

DEFOGGER AIR INLET

REAR VENT INLET

PACKAGE TRAY TRIM PANEL

LEFT REAR VENT ASSEMBLY (RIGHT SYMMETRICALLY OPPOSITE)

DEFOGGER BLOWER MOTOR AND WHEEL ASSEMBLY

REAR WINDOW PACKAGE TRAY

VIEW A

VACUUM HOSE CONNECTION

PURPLE FROM REAR VENT SWITCH SEE VIEW B

UPPER INSTRUMENT PANEL

BLACK TO SOURCE

PURPLE TO REAR VENT

DEFOGGER SWITCH

SWITCH RETAINING CLIPS

MAP LAMP HOUSING ASSEMBLY

REAR VENT VACUUM SWITCH

© Ford Motor Co.

PULL OUT

PUSH IN

DEPRESS BOTH RETAINING CLIPS AND PULL SWITCH OUT OF PLATE ASSEMBLY

PULL FOR "LOW-MED-HIGH" BLOWER SPEED

H M L

PUSH TO CLOSE

PULL TO OPEN

PUSH TO "OFF" POSITION

VIEW C

VIEW B

**Rear Window Defogger and Vent System—Lincoln Continental**

## Ford Motor Company

cover plate from below the steering column.
2. Pull off the blower switch knob.
3. Remove the left register and face plate assembly by removing the four screws. The register will slide out of the left air duct.
4. Remove defogger switch retaining nut from the front of the panel.
5. Disconnect the electrical wire connector and remove the switch.

**Installation**

1. Position the new switch to the panel and install the wire connector and mounting nut.
2. Replace the switch knob.
3. Install the left register and face plate assembly and inspection hole cover plate.

### Defogger Switch— Lincoln Continental

**Removal**

1. Remove the map light housing from the instrument panel.
2. Disconnect the multiple wire connector from the switch.

3. Depress the two switch retaining clips and pull the switch from the map light housing.

**Installation**

1. Place the new switch into the map light housing and snap into place.
2. Connect the multiple wire connector to the switch.
3. Position the map light housing to the instrument housing and install the three remaining screws.

## General Motors

### Rear Window Defogger— Blower Type General Motors

**Description**

All of the blower type rear window defoggers are basically the same. The defogger is designed to operate at either high or low speeds. Air is drawn into the defogger unit and is directed against the rear window through an outlet located in the rear compartment shelf.

## TROUBLESHOOTING CHART

### General Motors—Rear Window Defogger

| Condition | Possible Cause |
|---|---|
| 1. Blower operates but no air movement | a. Obstructions at the air outlet or inlet |
| 2. Defogger does not operate at all | a. Defective control switch<br>b. Open or short circuit between the power supply, switch or motor<br>c. Defective motor |
| 3. Blower motor does not operate at both speeds | a. Defective switch<br>b. Open or short circuit in the wiring |

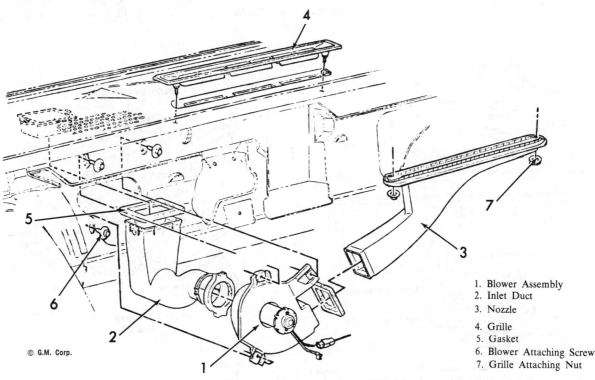

© G.M. Corp.

1. Blower Assembly
2. Inlet Duct
3. Nozzle
4. Grille
5. Gasket
6. Blower Attaching Screw
7. Grille Attaching Nut

Blower Installation - Chevrolet *1968-73*

## General Motors

### Circuit Testing Procedures:

**Blower Motor Test**

1. Check to see if the blower motor is properly grounded.
2. Disconnect the blower motor feed wire.
3. Using a 12 volt power source, connect the negative lead to the blower motor ground wire.
4. Connect the positive lead to the motor feed wire.
5. If the blower does not operate replace the blower assembly.

*NOTE: A resistor is used in the circuit to provide the difference be-* *tween high and low speeds. If the switch connector contains only one output feed wire, the resistor is located in the switch. If two output feed wires are found in the connector, the resistance is included in the low speed wire harness.*

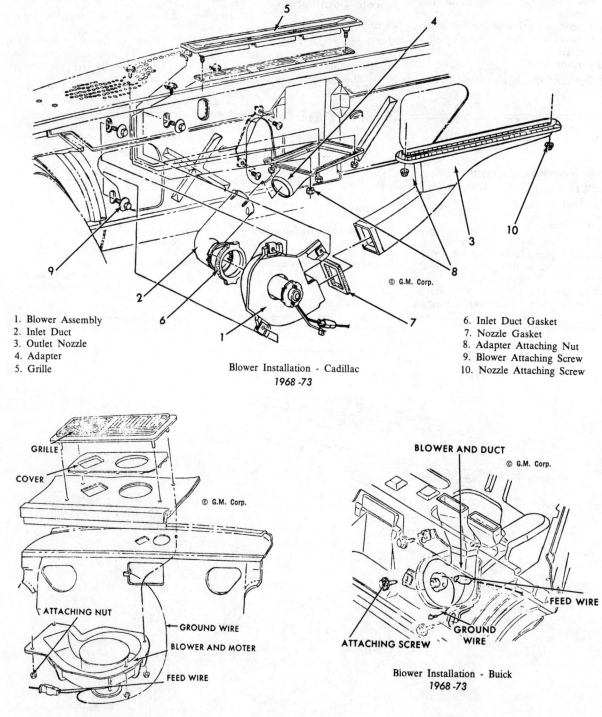

1. Blower Assembly
2. Inlet Duct
3. Outlet Nozzle
4. Adapter
5. Grille
6. Inlet Duct Gasket
7. Nozzle Gasket
8. Adapter Attaching Nut
9. Blower Attaching Screw
10. Nozzle Attaching Screw

© G.M. Corp.

Blower Installation - Cadillac
*1968 -73*

GRILLE
COVER
© G.M. Corp.
ATTACHING NUT
GROUND WIRE
BLOWER AND MOTER
FEED WIRE

Blower Installation
Chevrolet, Pontiac and Buick

BLOWER AND DUCT
© G.M. Corp.
FEED WIRE
GROUND WIRE
ATTACHING SCREW

Biower Installation - Buick
*1968 -73*

## General Motors

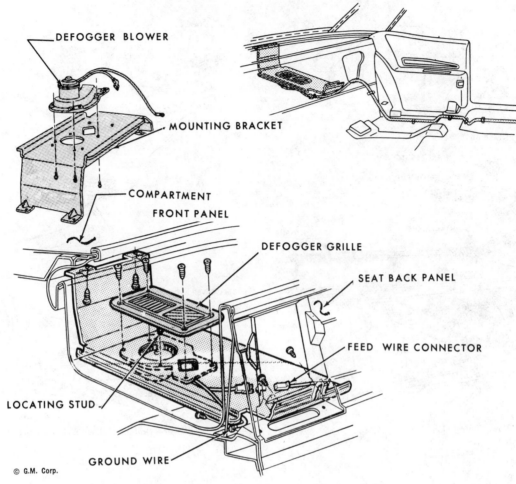

DEFOGGER BLOWER

MOUNTING BRACKET

COMPARTMENT
FRONT PANEL

DEFOGGER GRILLE

SEAT BACK PANEL

FEED WIRE CONNECTOR

LOCATING STUD

GROUND WIRE

© G.M. Corp.

*Blower Installation—Chevrolet Caprice Classic—1974-75*

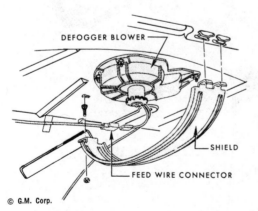

DEFOGGER BLOWER

SHIELD

FEED WIRE CONNECTOR

© G.M. Corp.

*Blower Installation—Chevelle, LeMans, Grand Prix,
Grand Am, Cutlass, Century—1974-75*

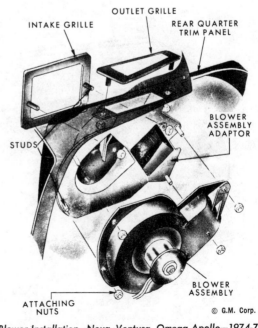

INTAKE GRILLE

OUTLET GRILLE

REAR QUARTER
TRIM PANEL

BLOWER
ASSEMBLY
ADAPTOR

STUDS

BLOWER
ASSEMBLY

ATTACHING
NUTS

© G.M. Corp.

*Blower Installation—Nova, Ventura, Omega Apollo—1974-75*

## General Motors

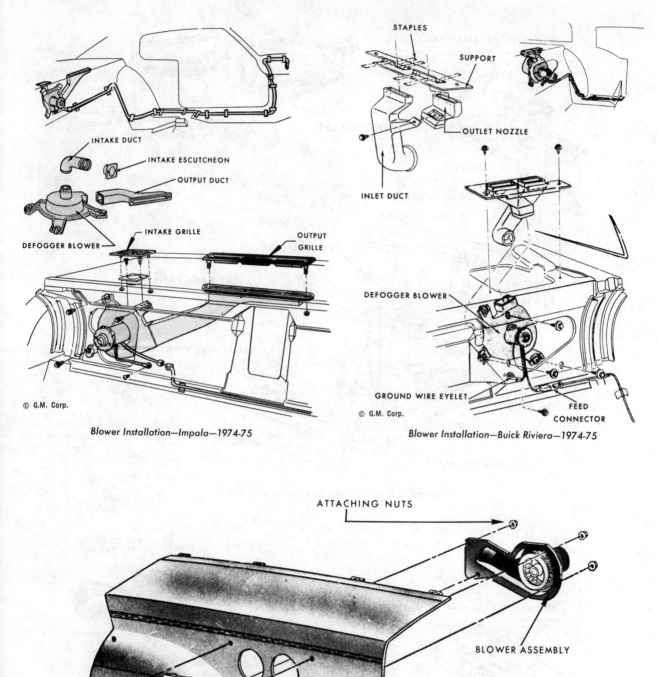

© G.M. Corp.

*Blower Installation—Impala—1974-75*

INTAKE DUCT

INTAKE ESCUTCHEON

OUTPUT DUCT

DEFOGGER BLOWER

INTAKE GRILLE

OUTPUT GRILLE

STAPLES

SUPPORT

OUTLET NOZZLE

INLET DUCT

DEFOGGER BLOWER

GROUND WIRE EYELET

FEED CONNECTOR

© G.M. Corp.

*Blower Installation—Buick Riviera—1974-75*

ATTACHING NUTS

BLOWER ASSEMBLY

QUARTER TRIM ASSEMBLY

COVER AND SCREEN

GRILLE ASSEMBLY

© G.M. Corp.

*Blower Installation—Station Wagons (Typical)*

## American Motors

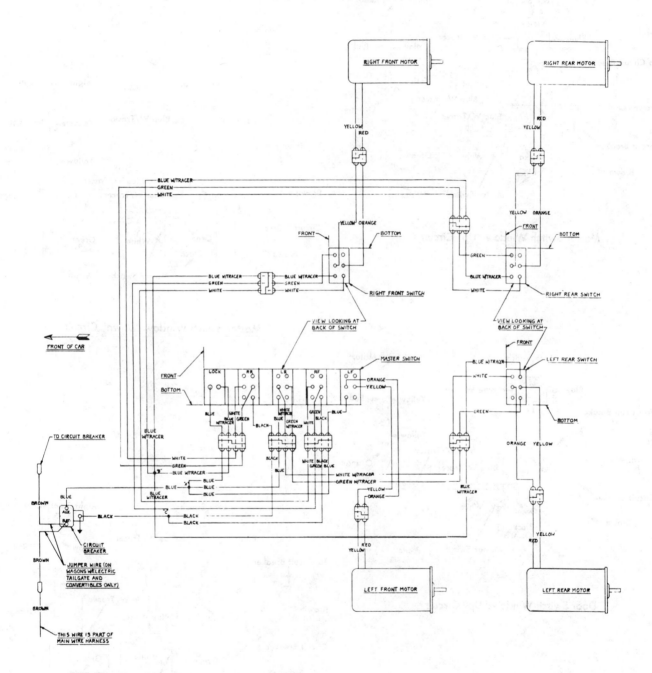

**1968-69 —AMBASSADOR**

# Power Window Wiring

## American Motors

Master Switch Window "Up" Circuit

Master Switch Window "Down" Circuit

Door Switch Window "Up" Circuit

Door Switch Window "Down" Circuit

1970-75

# Power Window Wiring

## Chrysler Corporation

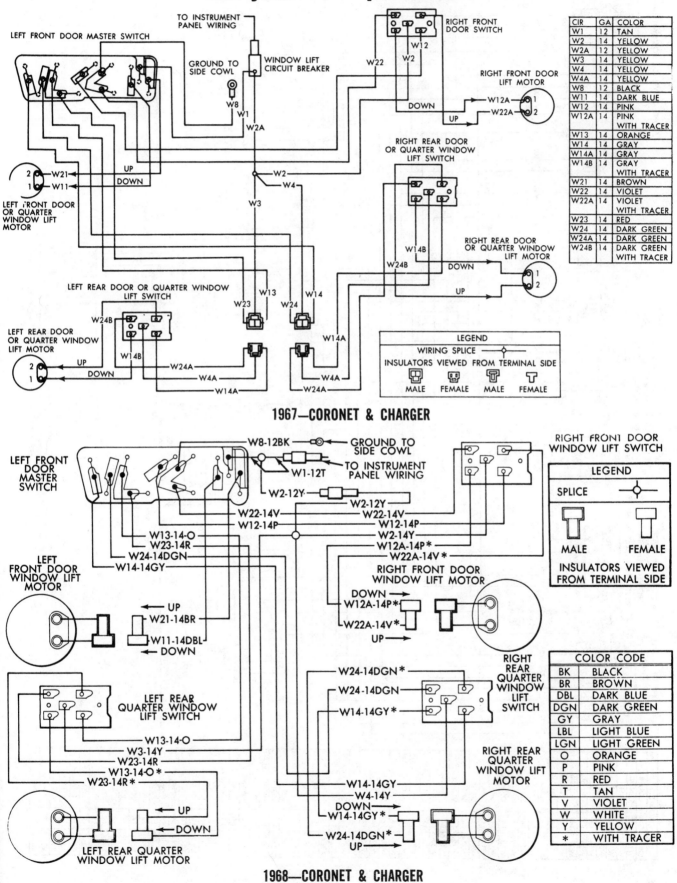

| CIR | GA | COLOR |
|---|---|---|
| W1 | 12 | TAN |
| W2 | 14 | YELLOW |
| W2A | 12 | YELLOW |
| W3 | 14 | YELLOW |
| W4 | 14 | YELLOW |
| W4A | 14 | YELLOW |
| W8 | 12 | BLACK |
| W11 | 14 | DARK BLUE |
| W12 | 14 | PINK |
| W12A | 14 | PINK WITH TRACER |
| W13 | 14 | ORANGE |
| W14 | 14 | GRAY |
| W14A | 14 | GRAY |
| W14B | 14 | GRAY WITH TRACER |
| W21 | 14 | BROWN |
| W22 | 14 | VIOLET |
| W22A | 14 | VIOLET WITH TRACER |
| W23 | 14 | RED |
| W24 | 14 | DARK GREEN |
| W24A | 14 | DARK GREEN |
| W24B | 14 | DARK GREEN WITH TRACER |

LEGEND

WIRING SPLICE

INSULATORS VIEWED FROM TERMINAL SIDE

MALE  FEMALE  MALE  FEMALE

**1967—CORONET & CHARGER**

LEGEND

SPLICE

MALE  FEMALE

INSULATORS VIEWED FROM TERMINAL SIDE

| | COLOR CODE |
|---|---|
| BK | BLACK |
| BR | BROWN |
| DBL | DARK BLUE |
| DGN | DARK GREEN |
| GY | GRAY |
| LBL | LIGHT BLUE |
| LGN | LIGHT GREEN |
| O | ORANGE |
| P | PINK |
| R | RED |
| T | TAN |
| V | VIOLET |
| W | WHITE |
| Y | YELLOW |
| * | WITH TRACER |

**1968—CORONET & CHARGER**

# Power Window Wiring

## Chrysler Corporation

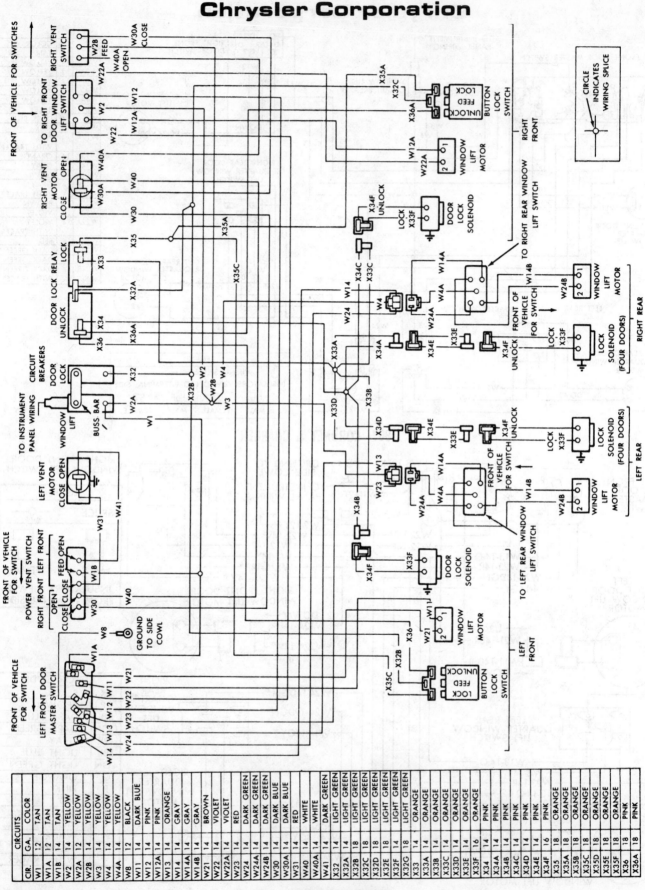

| CIRCUITS | | |
|---|---|---|
| CIR. | GA. | COLOR |
| W1 | 12 | TAN |
| W1A | 12 | TAN |
| W1B | 14 | TAN |
| W2 | 12 | YELLOW |
| W2A | 12 | YELLOW |
| W2B | 14 | YELLOW |
| W3 | 14 | YELLOW |
| W4 | 14 | YELLOW |
| W4A | 14 | YELLOW |
| W8 | 12 | BLACK |
| W11 | 14 | DARK BLUE |
| W12 | 14 | PINK |
| W12A | 14 | PINK |
| W13 | 14 | ORANGE |
| W14 | 14 | GRAY |
| W14A | 14 | GRAY |
| W14B | 14 | GRAY |
| W21 | 14 | BROWN |
| W22 | 14 | VIOLET |
| W22A | 14 | VIOLET |
| W23 | 14 | RED |
| W24 | 14 | DARK GREEN |
| W24A | 14 | DARK GREEN |
| W24B | 14 | DARK GREEN |
| W30 | 14 | DARK BLUE |
| W30A | 14 | DARK BLUE |
| W31 | 14 | RED |
| W40 | 14 | WHITE |
| W40A | 14 | WHITE |
| W41 | 14 | DARK GREEN |
| X32 | 14 | LIGHT GREEN |
| X32A | 14 | LIGHT GREEN |
| X32B | 18 | LIGHT GREEN |
| X32C | 18 | LIGHT GREEN |
| X32D | 18 | LIGHT GREEN |
| X32E | 18 | LIGHT GREEN |
| X32F | 14 | LIGHT GREEN |
| X32G | 18 | LIGHT GREEN |
| X33 | 14 | ORANGE |
| X33A | 14 | ORANGE |
| X33B | 14 | ORANGE |
| X33C | 14 | ORANGE |
| X33D | 14 | ORANGE |
| X33E | 18 | ORANGE |
| X33F | 16 | ORANGE |
| X34 | 14 | PINK |
| X34A | 14 | PINK |
| X34B | 14 | PINK |
| X34C | 14 | PINK |
| X34D | 14 | PINK |
| X34E | 18 | PINK |
| X34F | 16 | PINK |
| X35 | 18 | ORANGE |
| X35A | 18 | ORANGE |
| X35B | 18 | ORANGE |
| X35C | 18 | ORANGE |
| X35D | 18 | ORANGE |
| X35E | 18 | ORANGE |
| X36 | 18 | PINK |
| X36A | 18 | PINK |

**1968—PLYMOUTH**

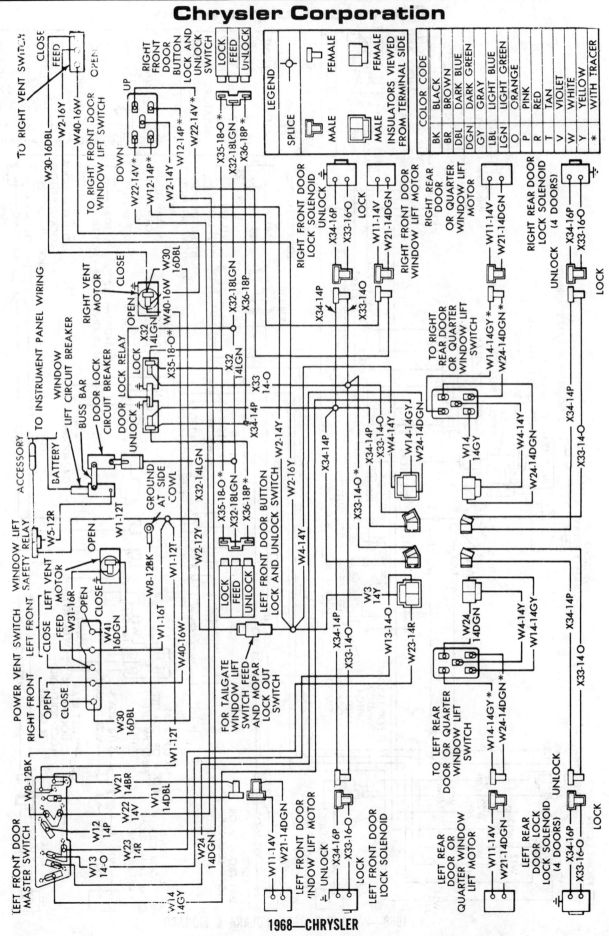

**1968—CHRYSLER**

# Power Window Wiring
## Chrysler Corporation

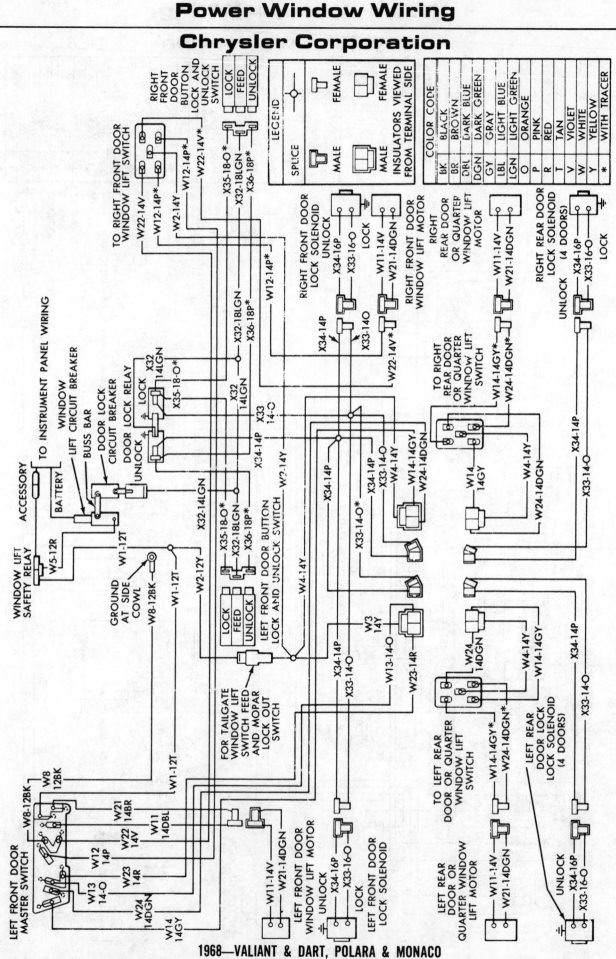

1968—VALIANT & DART, POLARA & MONACO

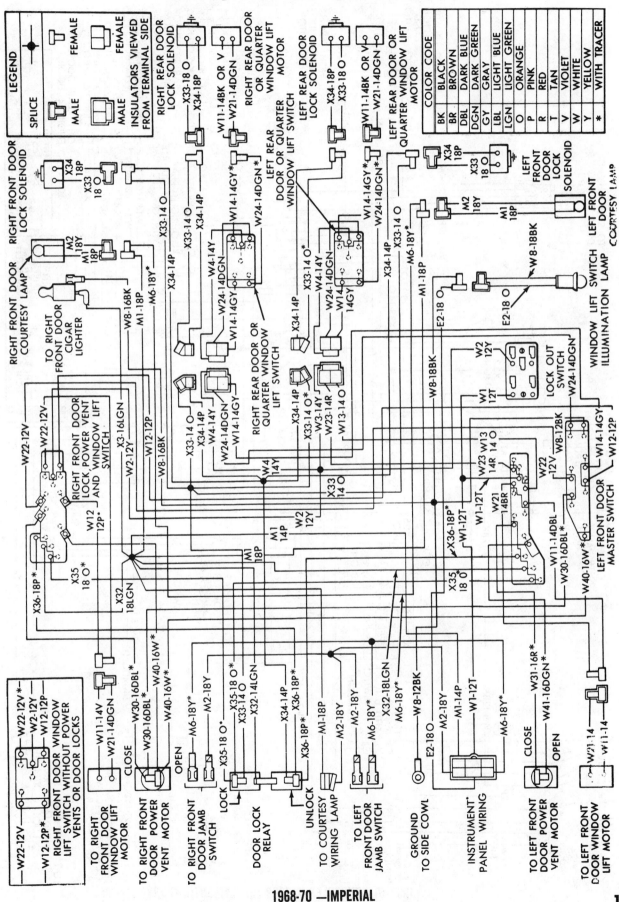

# Power Window Wiring
## Chrysler Corporation

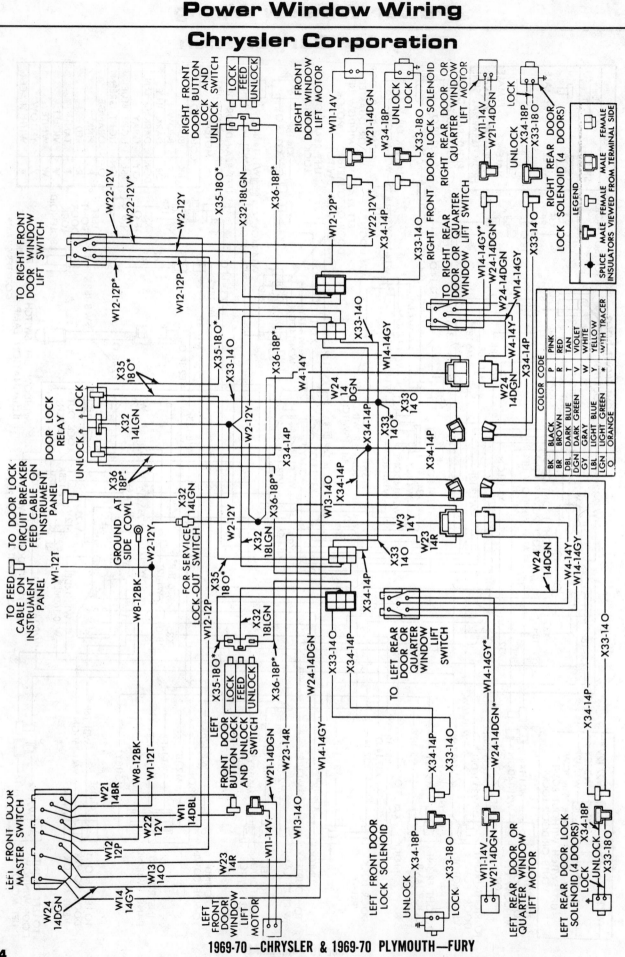

1969-70—CHRYSLER & 1969-70 PLYMOUTH—FURY

## Chrysler Corporation

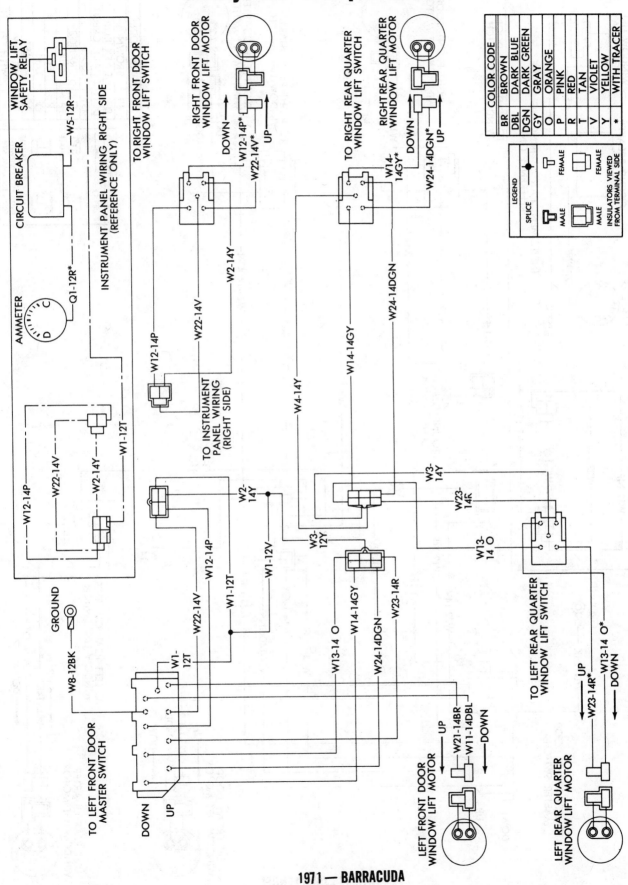

1971 — BARRACUDA

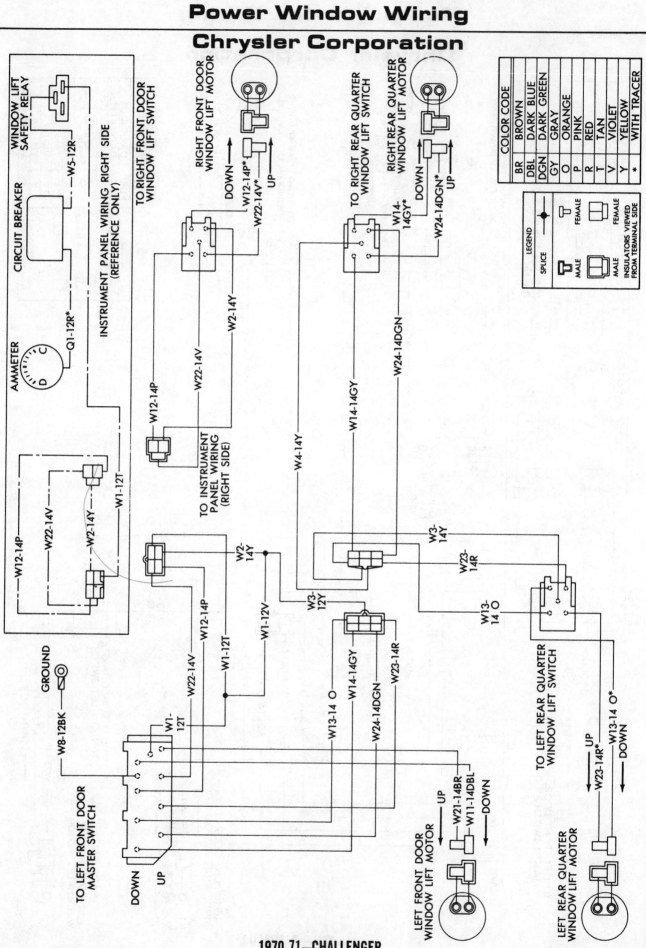

1970-71—CHALLENGER

## Chrysler Corporation

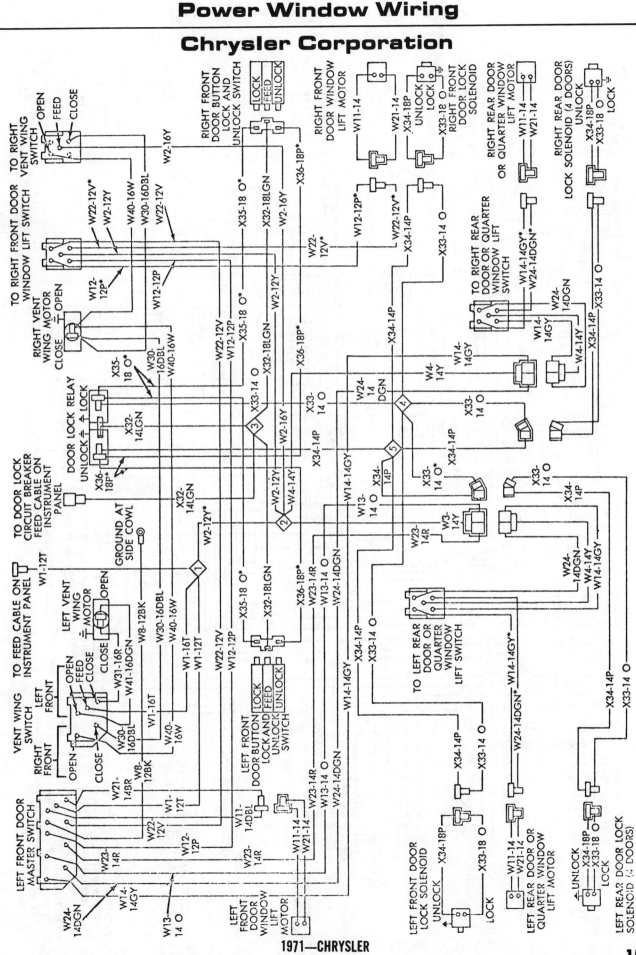

**1971—CHRYSLER**

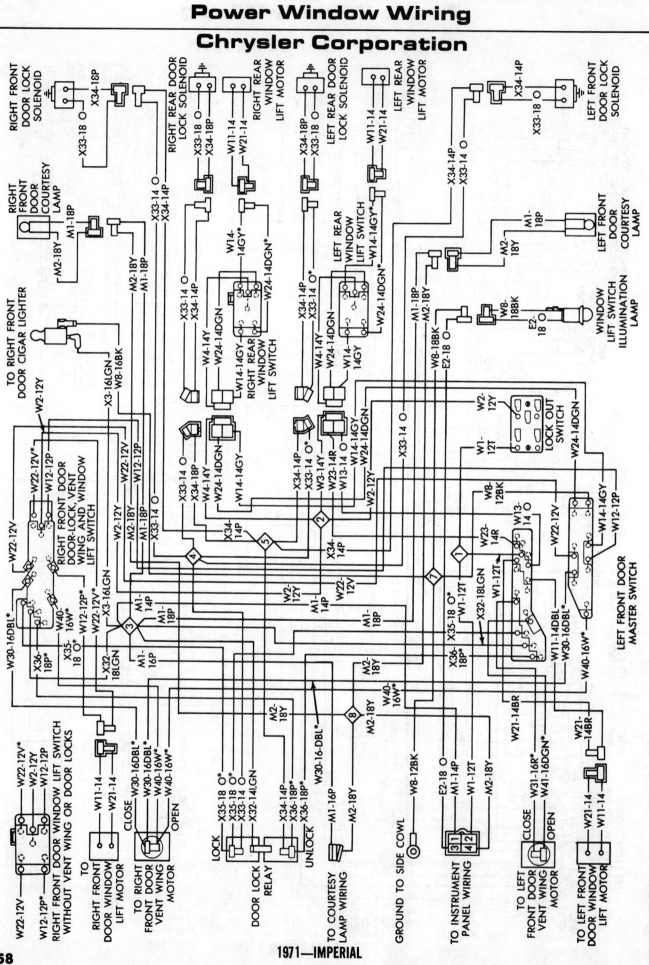

1971—Imperial

# Power Window Wiring
## Chrysler Corporation

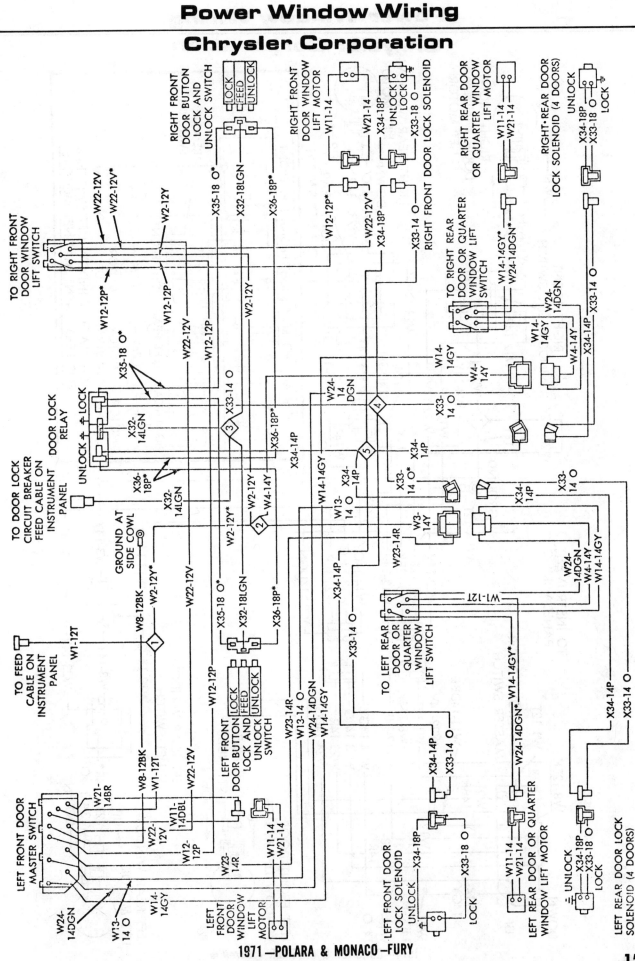

1971—POLARA & MONACO—FURY

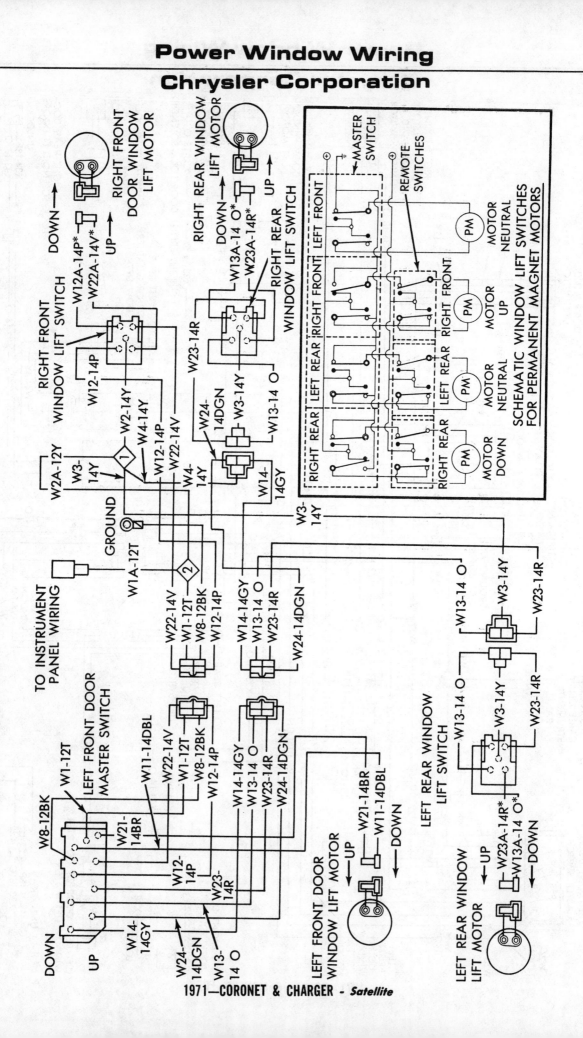

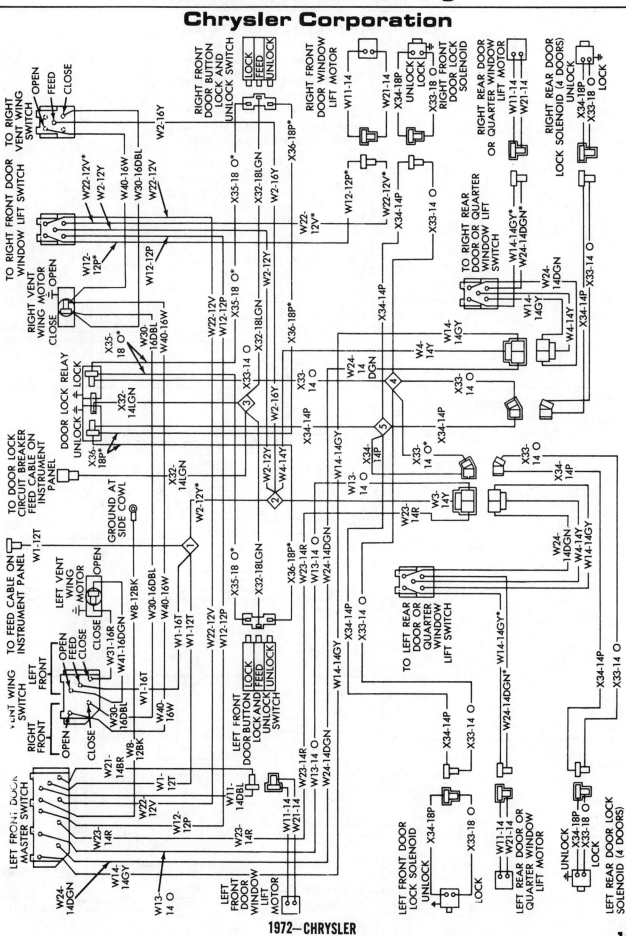

**1972—CHRYSLER**

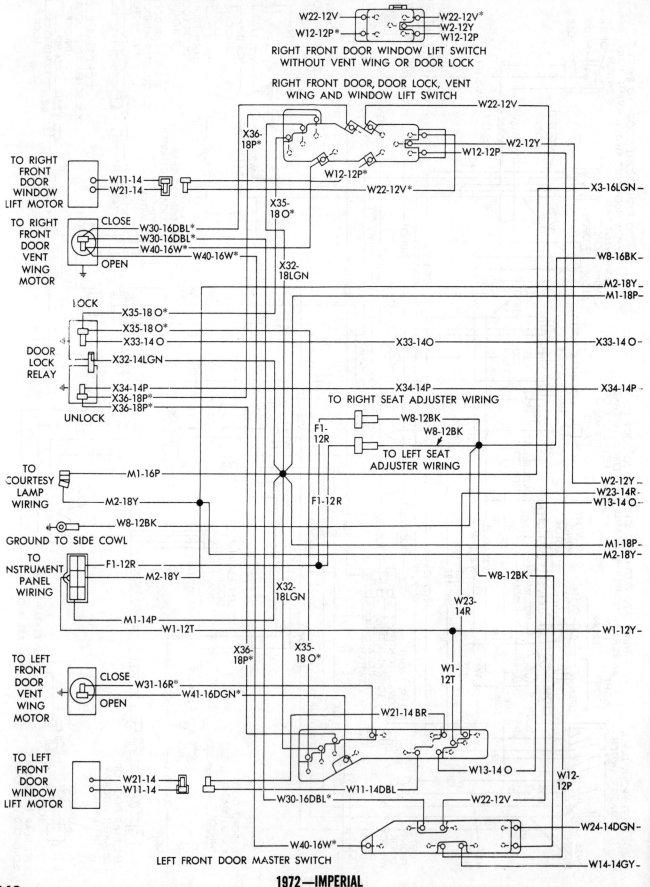

RIGHT FRONT DOOR WINDOW LIFT SWITCH
WITHOUT VENT WING OR DOOR LOCK

RIGHT FRONT DOOR, DOOR LOCK, VENT
WING AND WINDOW LIFT SWITCH

W22-12V
W12-12P*
W22-12V*
W2-12Y
W12-12P

TO RIGHT
FRONT
DOOR
WINDOW
LIFT
MOTOR

W11-14
W21-14

X36-18P*

W12-12P*
W22-12V
W22-12V*
W2-12Y
W12-12P

X3-16LGN

X35-18 O*

TO RIGHT
FRONT
DOOR
VENT
WING
MOTOR

CLOSE
W30-16DBL*
W30-16DBL*
W40-16W*
W40-16W*
OPEN

X32-18LGN

W8-16BK
M2-18Y
M1-18P

LOCK
X35-18 O*
X35-18 O*
X33-14 O
X32-14LGN
X34-14P
X36-18P*
X36-18P*
UNLOCK

DOOR
LOCK
RELAY

X33-14O
X33-14 O

X34-14P
X34-14P
TO RIGHT SEAT ADJUSTER WIRING

F1-12R
W8-12BK
W8-12BK
TO LEFT SEAT
ADJUSTER WIRING

TO
COURTESY
LAMP
WIRING

M1-16P
M2-18Y

W2-12Y
W23-14R
W13-14 O

W8-12BK
GROUND TO SIDE COWL

F1-12R

M1-18P
M2-18Y

TO
NSTRUMENT
PANEL
WIRING

F1-12R
M2-18Y

W8-12BK

M1-14P
W1-12T

X32-18LGN

W23-14R

W1-12Y

X36-18P*
X35-18 O*

W1-12T

TO LEFT
FRONT
DOOR
VENT
WING
MOTOR

CLOSE
W31-16R*
W41-16DGN*
OPEN

W21-14 BR

W13-14 O
W12-12P

TO LEFT
FRONT
DOOR
WINDOW
LIFT
MOTOR

W21-14
W11-14

W11-14DBL
W30-16DBL*
W22-12V

W24-14DGN

W40-16W*

W14-14GY

LEFT FRONT DOOR MASTER SWITCH

**1972—Imperial**

# Power Window Wiring

## Chrysler Corporation

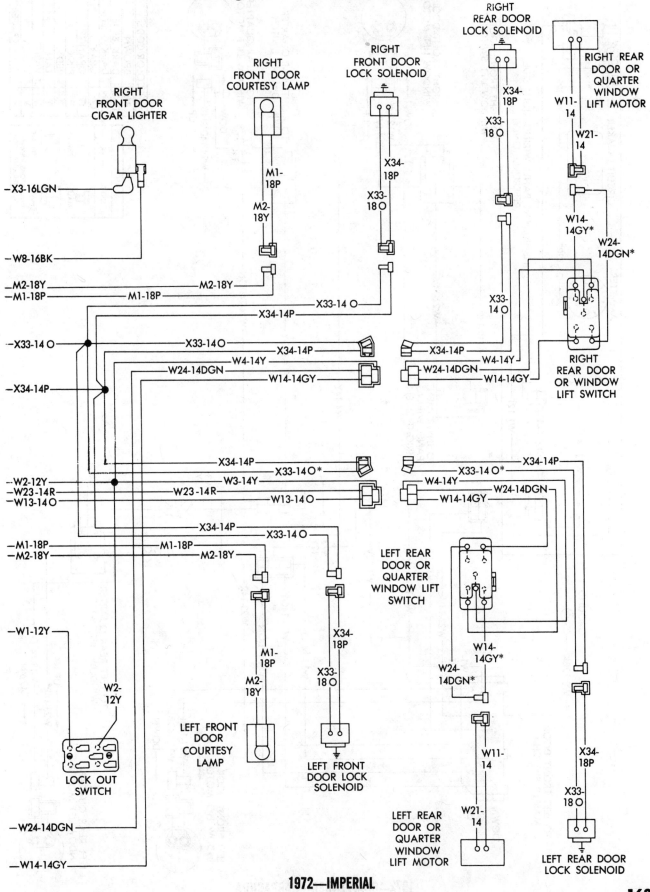

RIGHT
REAR DOOR
LOCK SOLENOID

RIGHT
FRONT DOOR
COURTESY LAMP

RIGHT
FRONT DOOR
LOCK SOLENOID

RIGHT REAR
DOOR OR
QUARTER
WINDOW
LIFT MOTOR

RIGHT
FRONT DOOR
CIGAR LIGHTER

—X3-16LGN—

—W8-16BK—

—M2-18Y—
—M1-18P—

M2-18Y
M1-18P

M1-
18P

M2-
18Y

X34-
18P

X33-
18 O

X34-
18P

X34-
18P

X33-
18 O

X33-14 O

X34-14P

W11-
14

W21-
14

W14-
14GY*

W24-
14DGN*

—X33-14 O—

X33-14 O

X34-14P

W4-14Y

W24-14DGN

W14-14GY

X34-14P

W4-14Y

W24-14DGN

W14-14GY

X33-
14 O

RIGHT
REAR DOOR
OR WINDOW
LIFT SWITCH

—X34-14P—

X34-14P

X33-14 O*

W3-14Y

W23-14R

W13-14 O

X34-14P

X33-14 O*

W4-14Y

W24-14DGN

W14-14GY

—W2-12Y—
—W23-14R—
—W13-14 O—

W23-14R

X34-14P

X33-14 O

—M1-18P—
—M2-18Y—

M1-18P

M2-18Y

LEFT REAR
DOOR OR
QUARTER
WINDOW LIFT
SWITCH

M1-
18P

M2-
18Y

X34-
18P

X33-
18 O

W14-
14GY*

W24-
14DGN*

W11-
14

X34-
18P

X33-
18 O

—W1-12Y—

W2-
12Y

LOCK OUT
SWITCH

LEFT FRONT
DOOR
COURTESY
LAMP

LEFT FRONT
DOOR LOCK
SOLENOID

LEFT REAR
DOOR OR
QUARTER
WINDOW
LIFT MOTOR

W21-
14

LEFT REAR DOOR
LOCK SOLENOID

—W24-14DGN—

—W14-14GY—

**1972—IMPERIAL**

163

# Power Window Wiring
## Chrysler Corporation

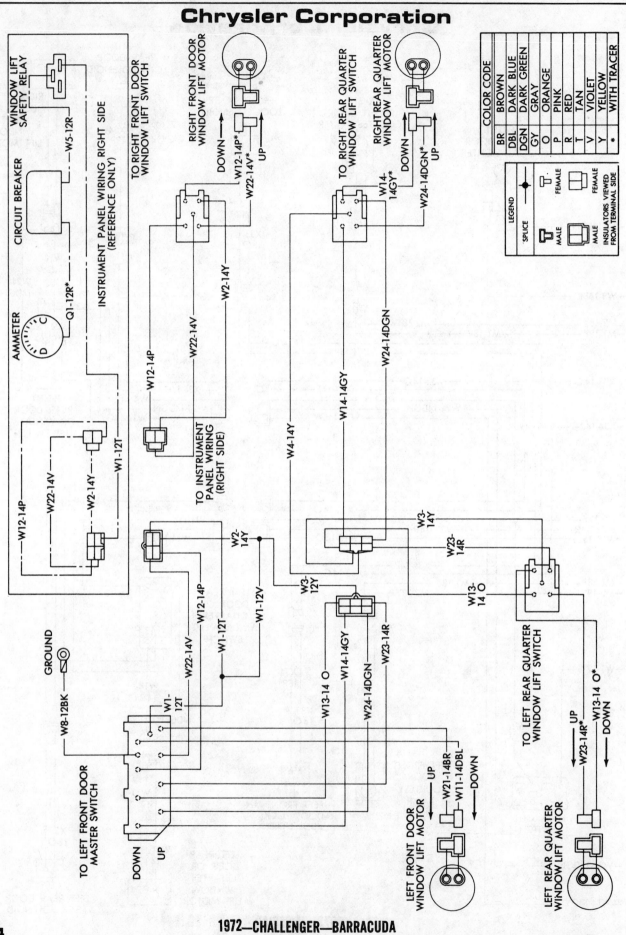

**1972—CHALLENGER—BARRACUDA**

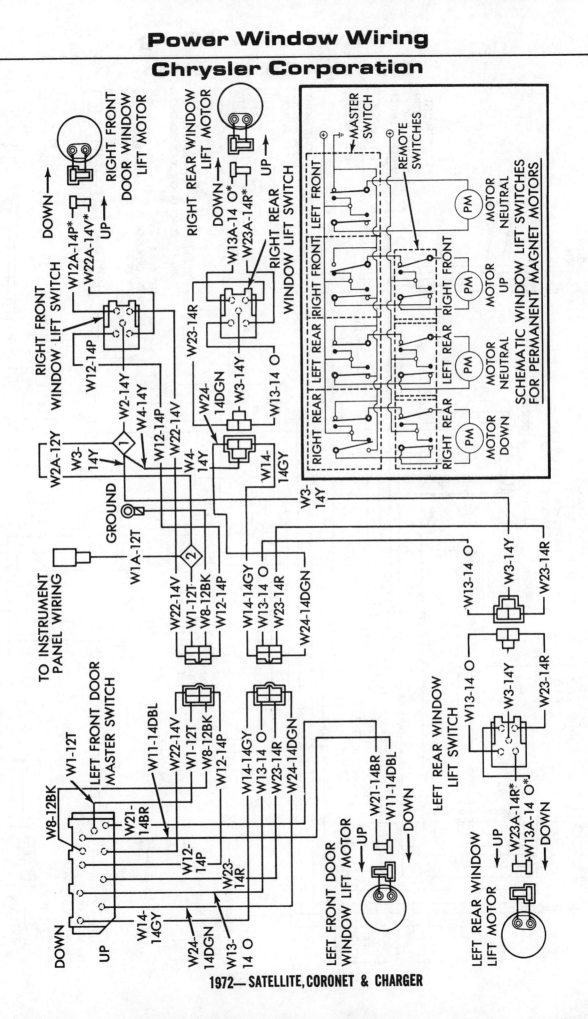

1972— SATELLITE, CORONET & CHARGER

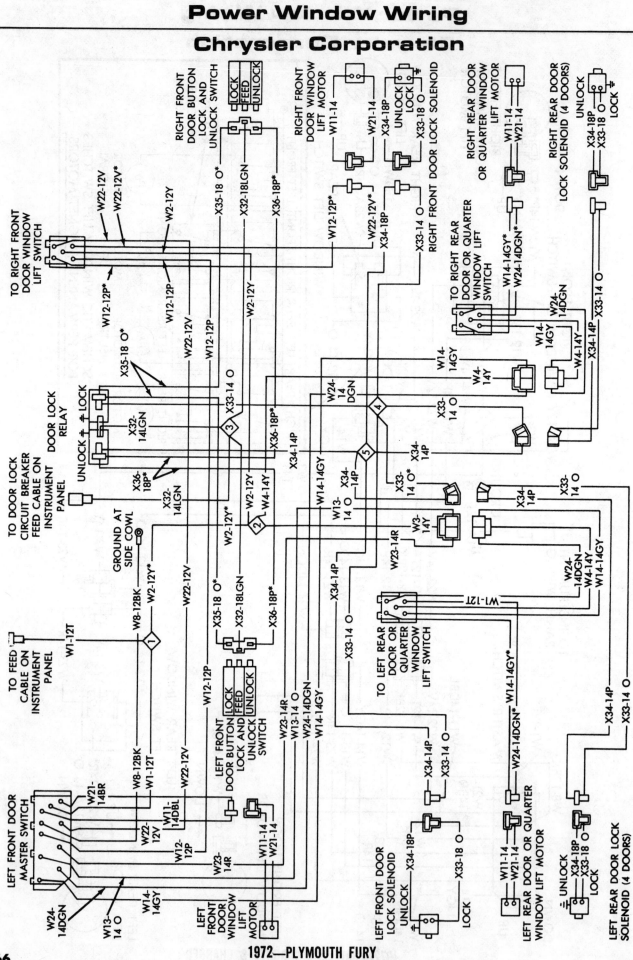

1972—PLYMOUTH FURY

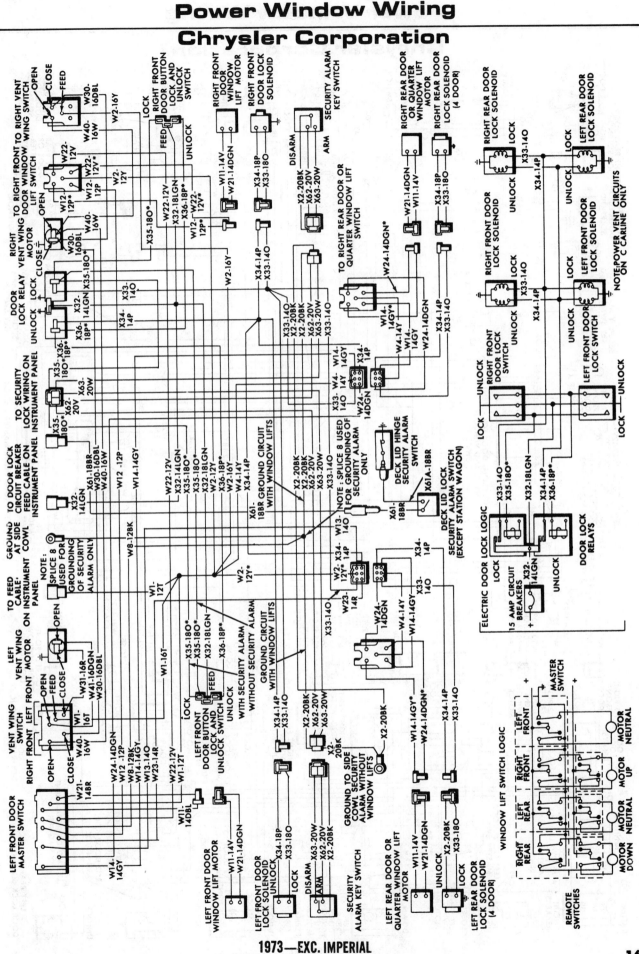

**1973—EXC. IMPERIAL**

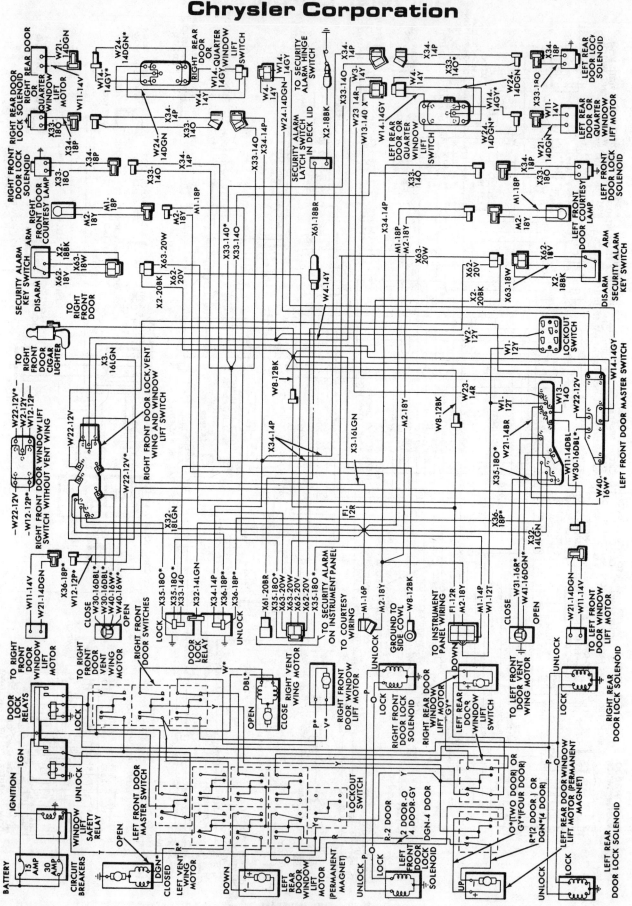

**1973—IMPERIAL**

# Power Window Wiring

## Chrysler Corporation

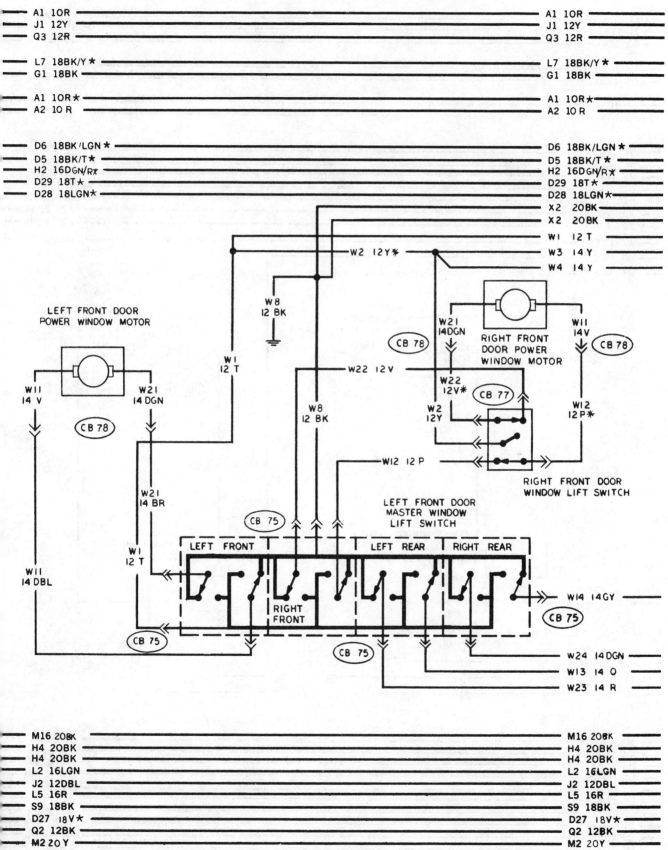

A1 1OR
J1 12Y
Q3 12R

L7 18BK/Y ★
G1 18BK

A1 1OR★
A2 10 R

D6 18BK/LGN ★
D5 18BK/T ★
H2 16DGN/R×
D29 18T★
D28 18LGN★

A1 1OR
J1 12Y
Q3 12R

L7 18BK/Y ★
G1 18BK

A1 1OR★
A2 10 R

D6 18BK/LGN ★
D5 18BK/T ★
H2 16DGN/R×
D29 18T★
D28 18LGN★
X2 20BK
X2 20BK
W1 12 T
W3 14 Y
W4 14 Y

W2 12Y✳

LEFT FRONT DOOR
POWER WINDOW MOTOR

W8
12 BK

W21
14DGN

CB 78

W22 12V

RIGHT FRONT
DOOR POWER
WINDOW MOTOR

W11
14 V

CB 78

W11
14 V

W21
14 DGN

CB 78

W1
12 T

W8
12 BK

W22
12V✳

CB 77

W2
12Y

W12
12P✳

W12 12 P

W21
14 BR

RIGHT FRONT DOOR
WINDOW LIFT SWITCH

W11
14 DBL

W1
12 T

CB 75

LEFT FRONT DOOR
MASTER WINDOW
LIFT SWITCH

LEFT FRONT    LEFT REAR    RIGHT REAR

RIGHT
FRONT

W14 14GY

CB 75

CB 75

CB 75

W24 14DGN
W13 14 O
W23 14 R

M16 20BK
H4 20BK
H4 20BK
L2 16LGN
J2 12DBL
L5 16R
S9 18BK
D27 18V★
Q2 12BK
M2 20 Y

M16 20BK
H4 20BK
H4 20BK
L2 16LGN
J2 12DBL
L5 16R
S9 18BK
D27 18V★
Q2 12BK
M2 20 Y

1974-1

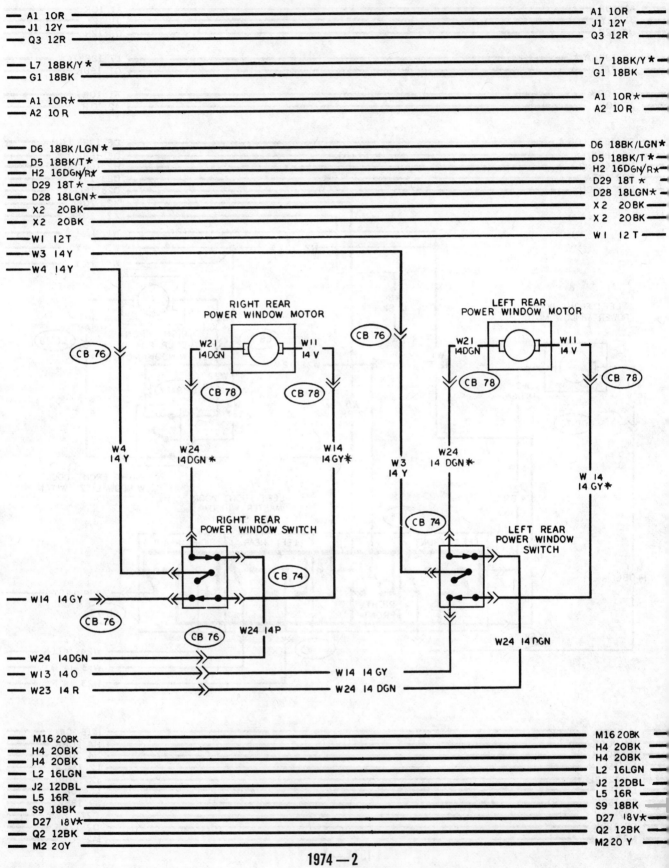

A1 1OR
J1 12Y
Q3 12R

L7 18BK/Y ★
G1 18BK

A1 1OR★
A2 10 R

D6 18BK/LGN ★
D5 18BK/T★
H2 16DGN/R★
D29 18T ★
D28 18LGN★
X2 20BK
X2 20BK

W1 12T
W3 14Y
W4 14Y

A1 1OR
J1 12Y
Q3 12R

L7 18BK/Y ★
G1 18BK

A1 1OR★
A2 10 R

D6 18BK/LGN ★
D5 18BK/T ★
H2 16DGN/R★
D29 18T ★
D28 18LGN★
X2 20BK
X2 20BK
W1 12T

RIGHT REAR
POWER WINDOW MOTOR

LEFT REAR
POWER WINDOW MOTOR

CB 76

W21 14DGN    W11 14 V

W21 14DGN    W11 14 V

CB 76

CB 78    CB 78

CB 78    CB 78

W4 14 Y

W24 14DGN ★

W14 14GY★

W3 14 Y

W24 14 DGN★

W 14 14 GY★

CB 74

RIGHT REAR
POWER WINDOW SWITCH

LEFT REAR
POWER WINDOW
SWITCH

W14 14GY

CB 74

CB 76

CB 76    W24 14P

W24 14DGN

W13 14 O

W23 14 R

W14 14 GY

W24 14 DGN

W24 14 DGN

M16 20BK
H4 20BK
H4 20BK
L2 16LGN
J2 12DBL
L5 16R
S9 18BK
D27 18V★
Q2 12BK
M2 20Y

M16 20BK
H4 20BK
H4 20BK
L2 16LGN
J2 12DBL
L5 16R
S9 18BK
D27 18V★
Q2 12BK
M2 20 Y

1974—2

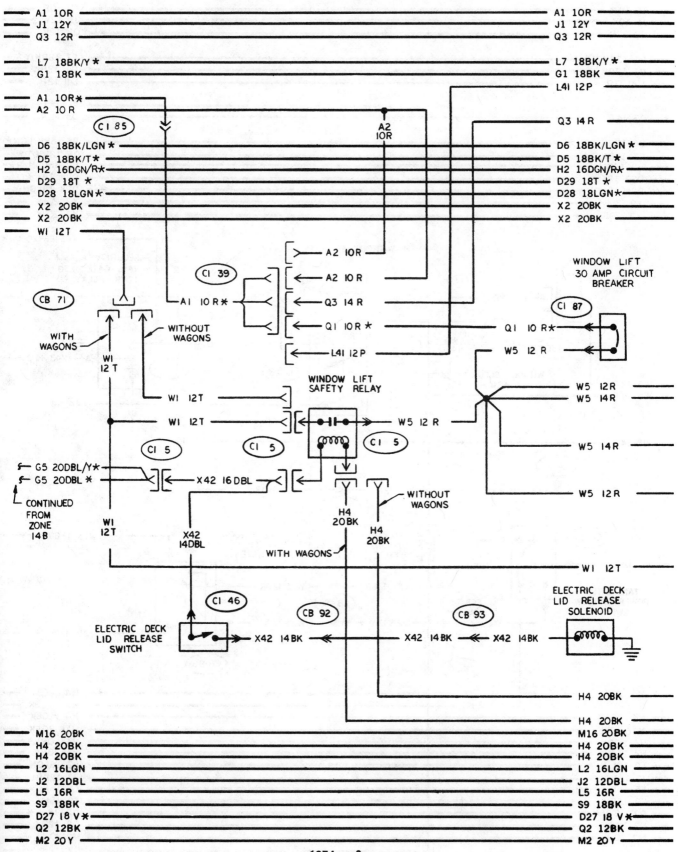

# Chrysler Corporation

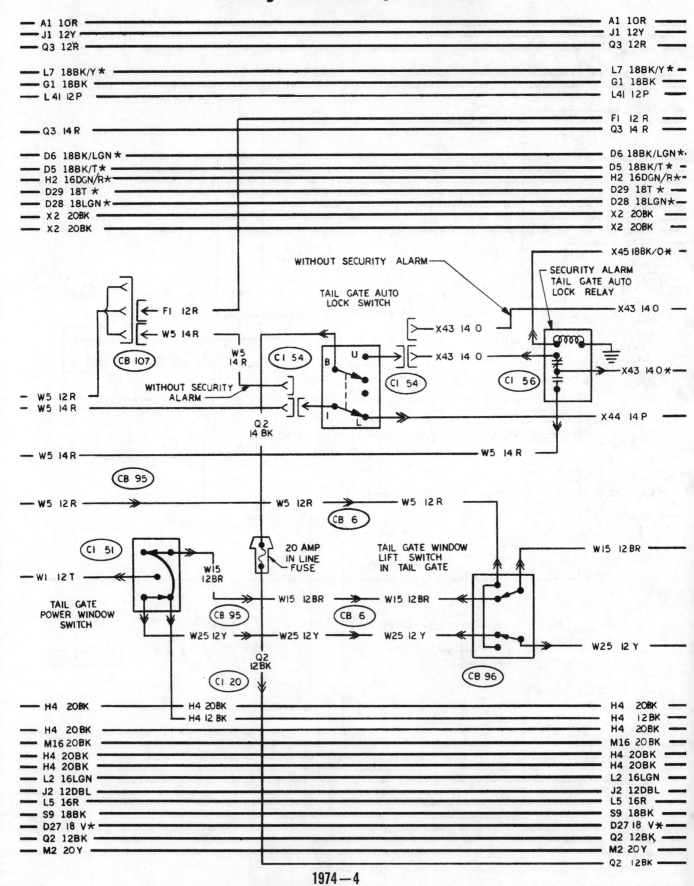

— A1 10R
— J1 12Y
— Q3 12R

— L7 18BK/Y *
— G1 18BK
— L41 12P

— Q3 14R

— D6 18BK/LGN *
— D5 18BK/T *
— H2 16DGN/R *
— D29 18T *
— D28 18LGN *
— X2 20BK
— X2 20BK

A1 10R —
J1 12Y —
Q3 12R —

L7 18BK/Y * —
G1 18BK —
L41 12P —

F1 12R —
Q3 14R —

D6 18BK/LGN *
D5 18BK/T * —
H2 16DGN/R *
D29 18T * —
D28 18LGN *—
X2 20BK —
X2 20BK —

X45 18BK/O *

WITHOUT SECURITY ALARM

SECURITY ALARM
TAIL GATE AUTO
LOCK RELAY

TAIL GATE AUTO
LOCK SWITCH

F1 12R
W5 14R

CB 107

W5 14R

WITHOUT SECURITY ALARM

— W5 12R
— W5 14R

CI 54

B          U
X43 14 0

CI 54

X43 14 0

X43 14 0

CI 56

X43 14 0 *

I          L

Q2 14BK

X44 14 P

— W5 14R

W5 14R

CB 95

— W5 12R

W5 12R          W5 12R

CB 6

W15 12BR

CI 51

20 AMP IN LINE FUSE

TAIL GATE WINDOW LIFT SWITCH IN TAIL GATE

W15 12BR

— W1 12T

W15 12BR

W15 12BR          W15 12BR

TAIL GATE POWER WINDOW SWITCH

CB 95          CB 6

W25 12Y

W25 12Y          W25 12Y          W25 12Y

CB 96

Q2 12BK

CI 20

— H4 20BK          H4 20BK
H4 12 BK

— H4 20BK
— M16 20BK
— H4 20BK
— H4 20BK
— L2 16LGN
— J2 12DBL
— L5 16R
— S9 18BK
— D27 18 V *
— Q2 12BK
— M2 20Y

H4 20BK —
H4 12BK —
H4 20BK —
M16 20BK —
H4 20BK —
H4 20BK —
L2 16LGN —
J2 12DBL —
L5 16R —
S9 18BK —
D27 18 V * —
Q2 12BK —
M2 20Y —
Q2 12BK —

1974—4

## Chrysler Corporation

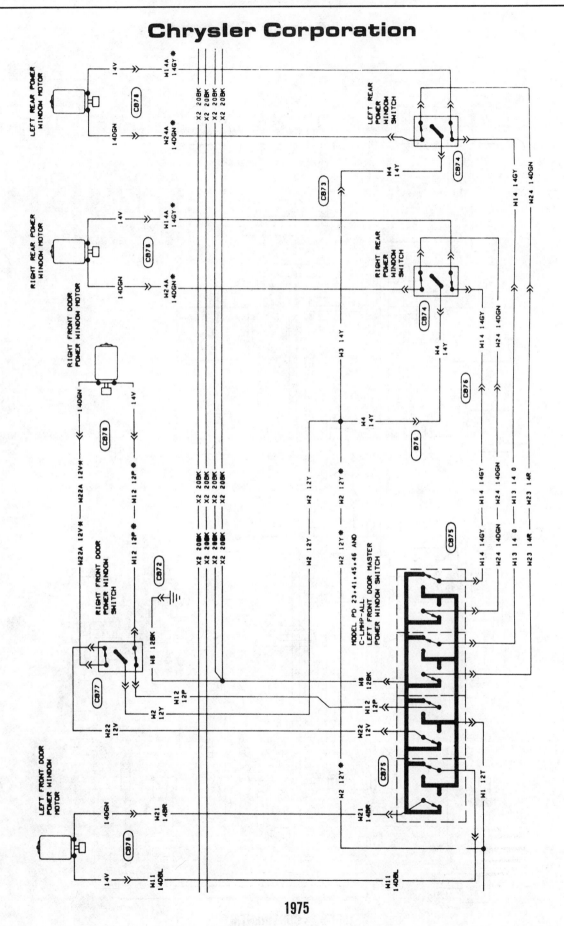

1975

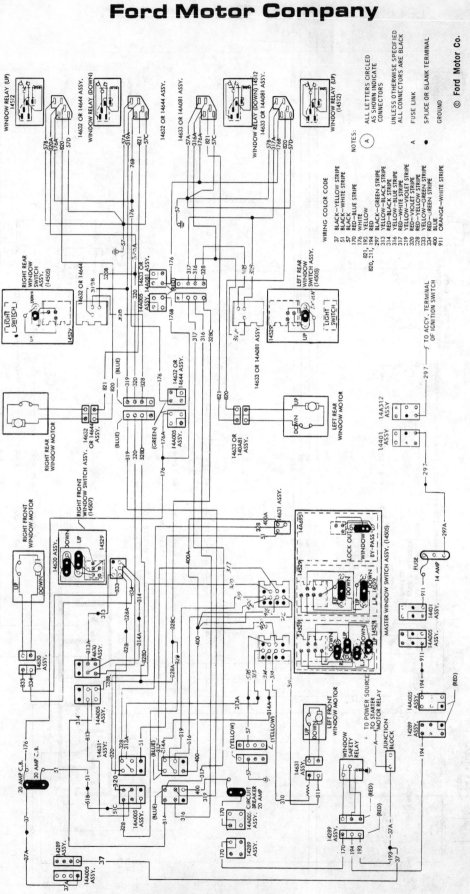

## Ford Motor Company

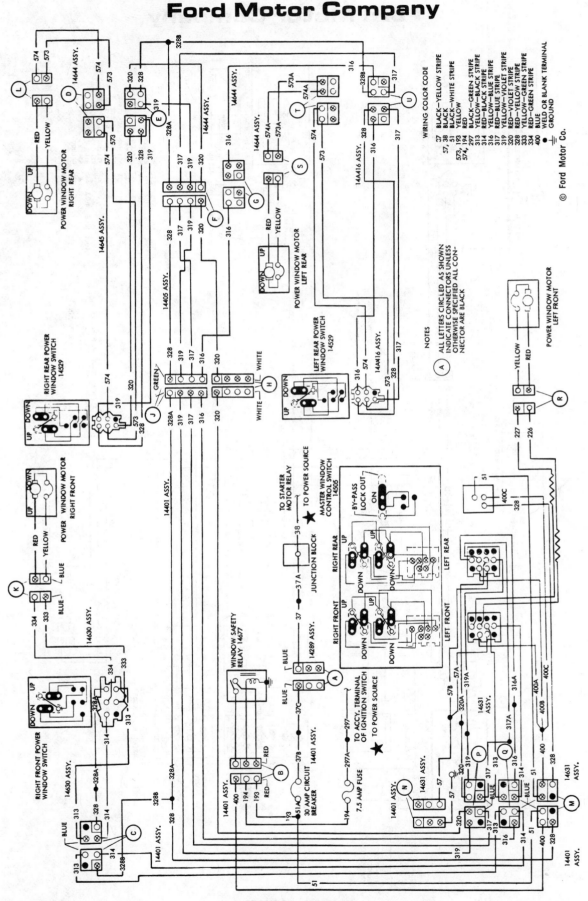

**1968-69—Mark III**

# Ford Motor Company

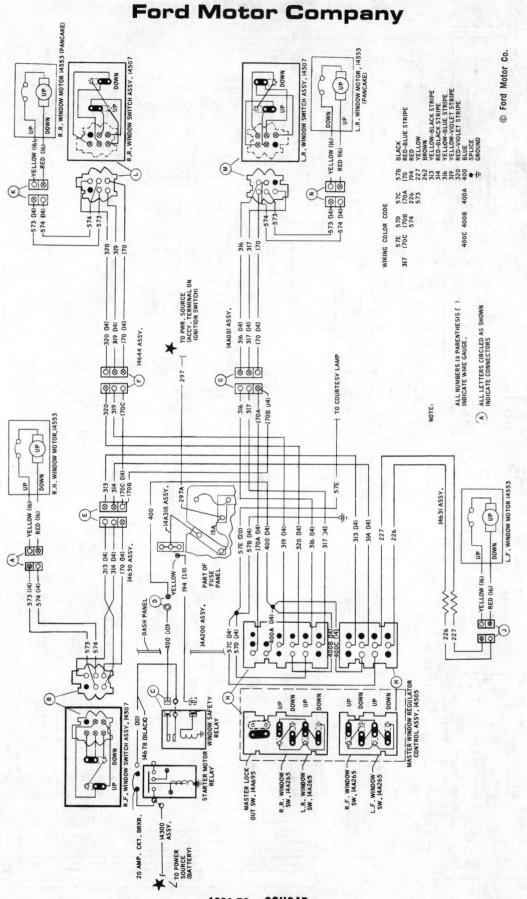

© Ford Motor Co.

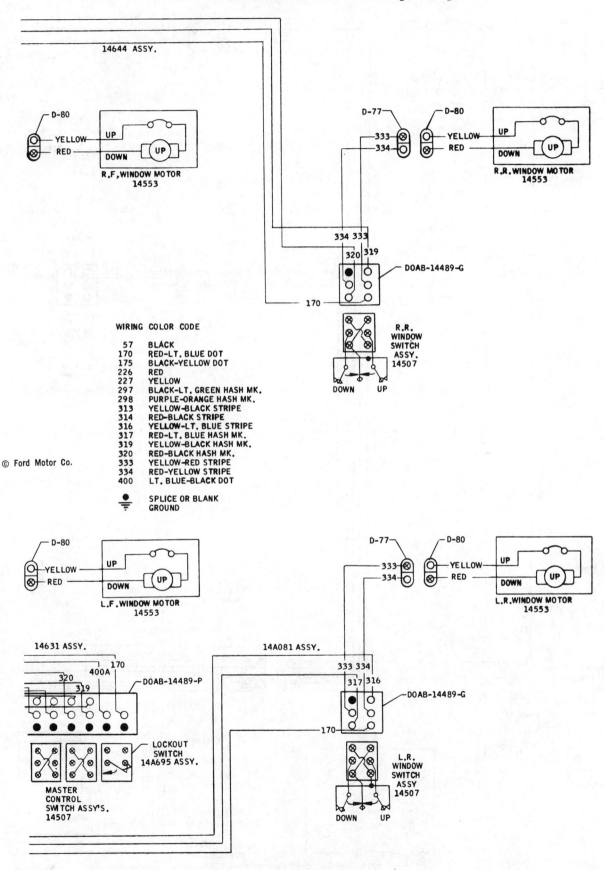

WIRING COLOR CODE

| | |
|---|---|
| 57 | BLACK |
| 170 | RED-LT. BLUE DOT |
| 175 | BLACK-YELLOW DOT |
| 226 | RED |
| 227 | YELLOW |
| 297 | BLACK-LT. GREEN HASH MK. |
| 298 | PURPLE-ORANGE HASH MK. |
| 313 | YELLOW-BLACK STRIPE |
| 314 | RED-BLACK STRIPE |
| 316 | YELLOW-LT. BLUE STRIPE |
| 317 | RED-LT. BLUE HASH MK. |
| 319 | YELLOW-BLACK HASH MK. |
| 320 | RED-BLACK HASH MK. |
| 333 | YELLOW-RED STRIPE |
| 334 | RED-YELLOW STRIPE |
| 400 | LT. BLUE-BLACK DOT |

© Ford Motor Co.

SPLICE OR BLANK
GROUND

**1971—COUGAR**

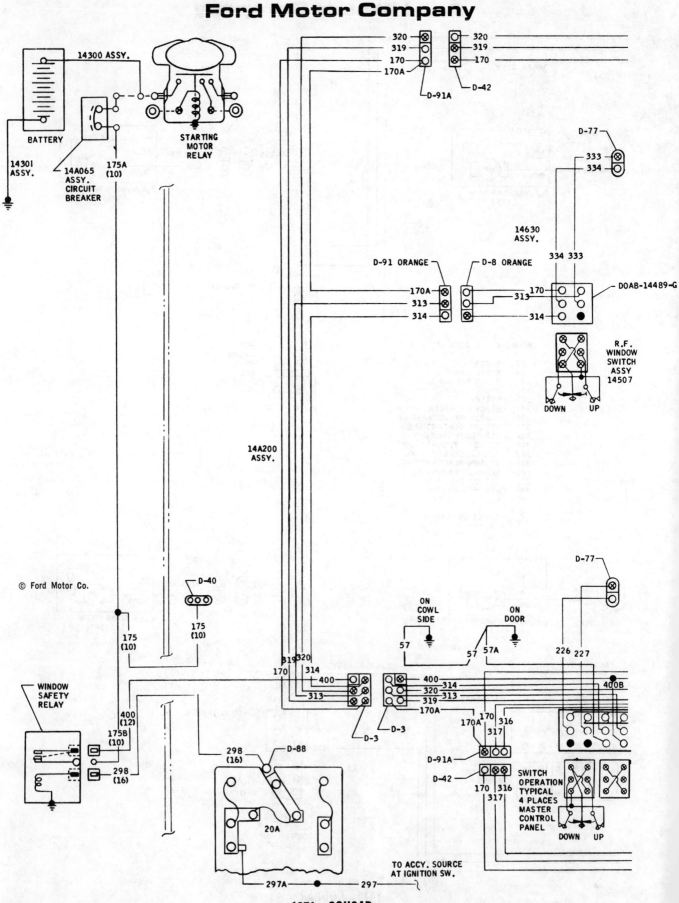

© Ford Motor Co.

**1971—COUGAR**

## Ford Motor Company

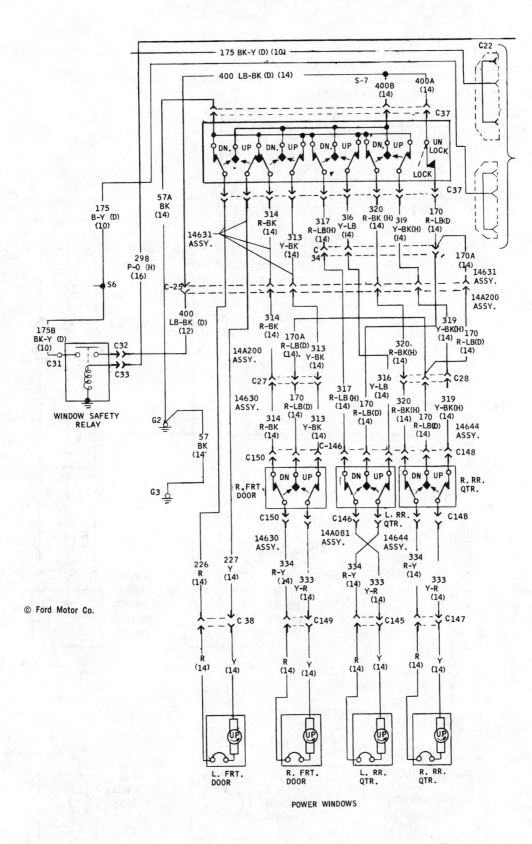

POWER WINDOWS

**1972—COUGAR**

## Ford Motor Company

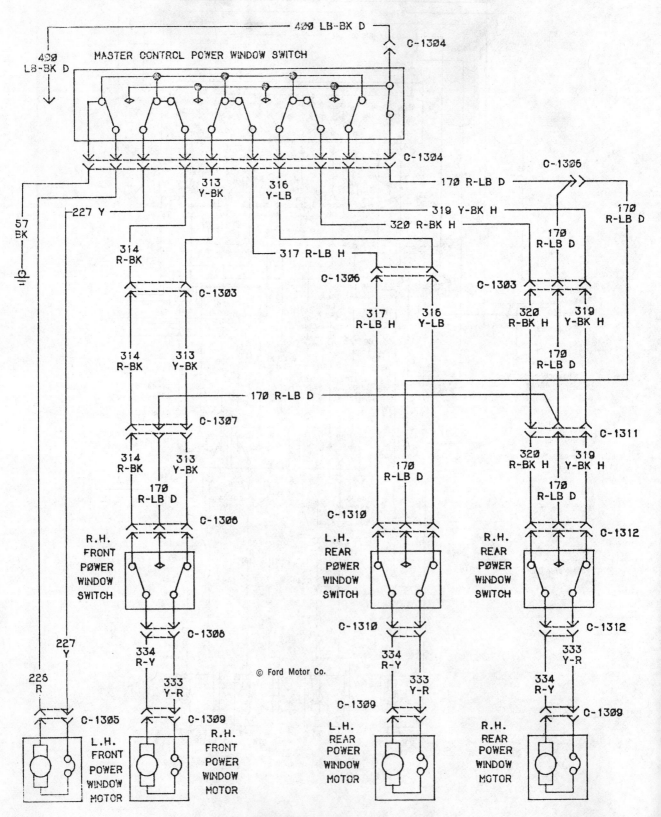

© Ford Motor Co.

**1973—COUGAR**

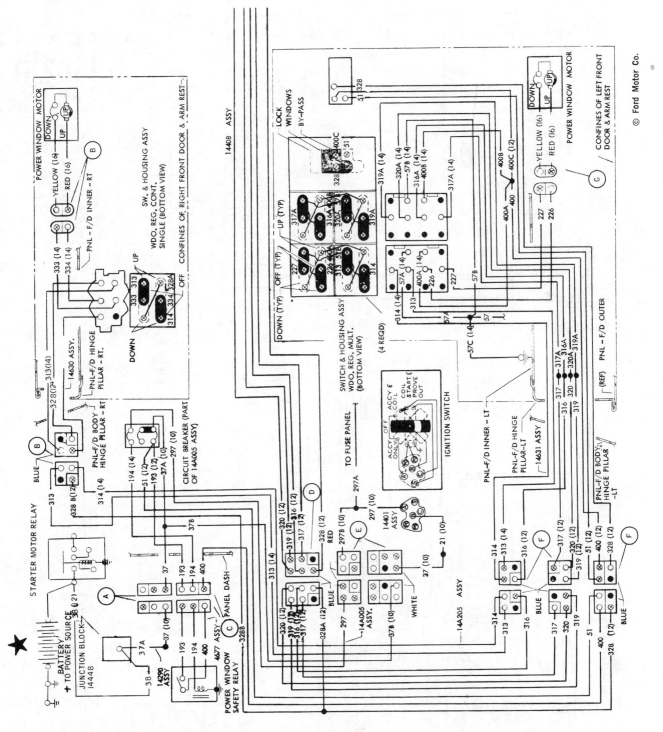

© Ford Motor Co.

**FRONT SECTION**
**1968-69—THUNDERBIRD**

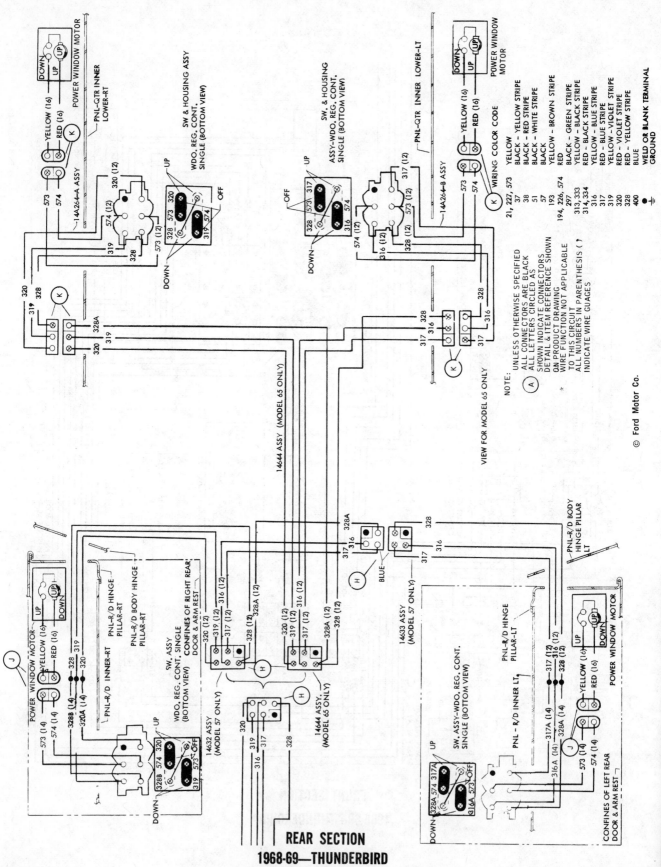

**REAR SECTION**
**1968-69—THUNDERBIRD**

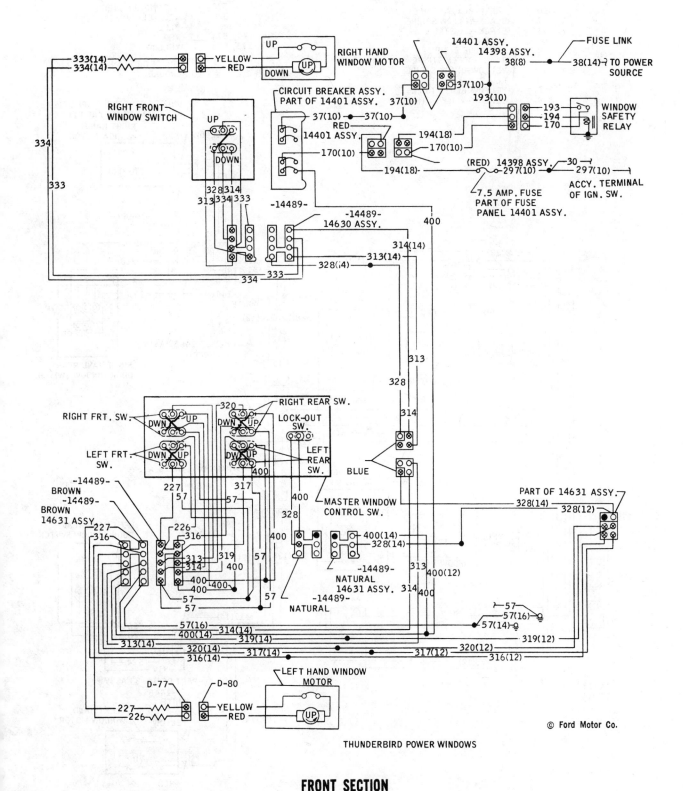

THUNDERBIRD POWER WINDOWS

© Ford Motor Co.

# FRONT SECTION

## 1970—THUNDERBIRD

# Ford Motor Company

WIRING COLOR CODE

| | | | | |
|---|---|---|---|---|
| 30 | GREEN-BLACK STRIPE | | 320 | RED-VIOLET STRIPE |
| 37 | BLACK-YELLOW STRIPE | | 328 | RED-YELLOW STRIPE |
| 38 | BLACK-RED STRIPE | | 400 | BLUE |
| 57 | BLACK | | 226, 194, 574 | RED |
| 317, 170 | RED-BLUE STRIPE | | 227, 193, 573 | YELLOW |
| 297 | BLACK-GREEN STRIPE | | | |
| 333, 313 | YELLOW-BLACK STRIPE | | ⏚ | SPLICE OR BLANK TERMINAL GROUND |
| 334, 314 | RED-BLACK STRIPE | | | |
| 316 | YELLOW-BLUE STRIPE | | | |
| 319 | YELLOW-VIOLET STRIPE | | | |

NOTE:
UNLESS OTHERWISE SPECIFIED,
ALL CONNECTORS ARE BLACK

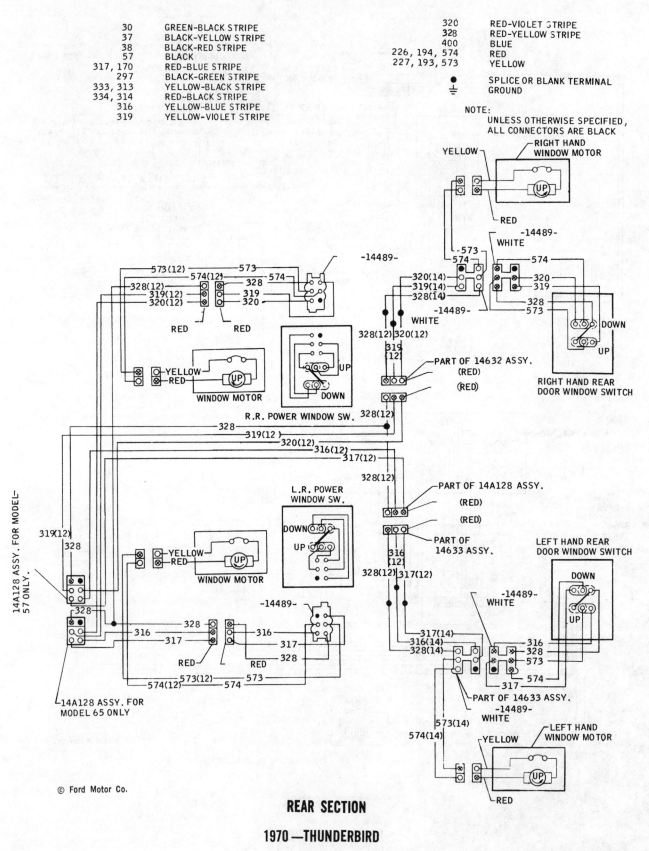

© Ford Motor Co.

**REAR SECTION**

**1970 —THUNDERBIRD**

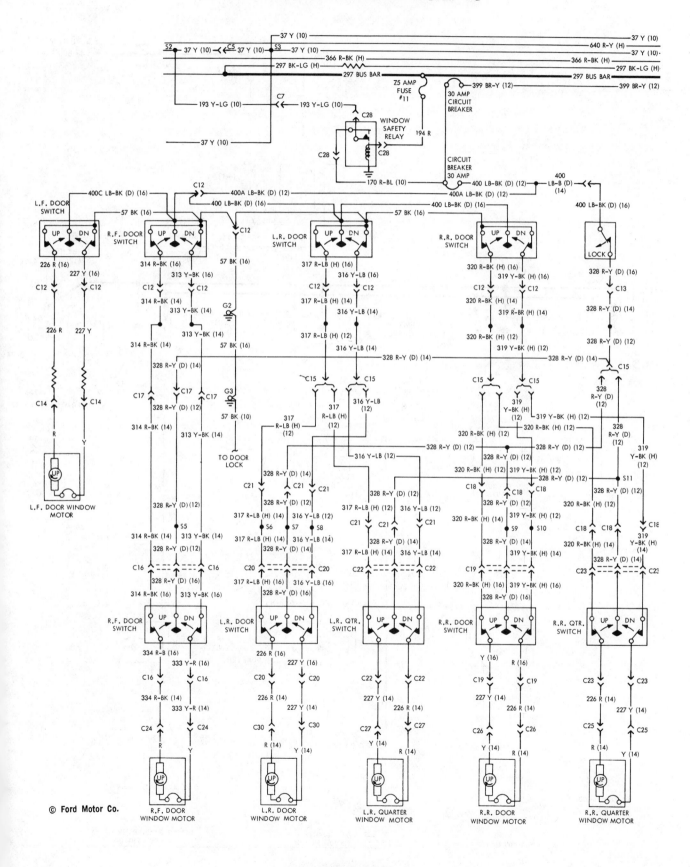

**1971—Thunderbird**

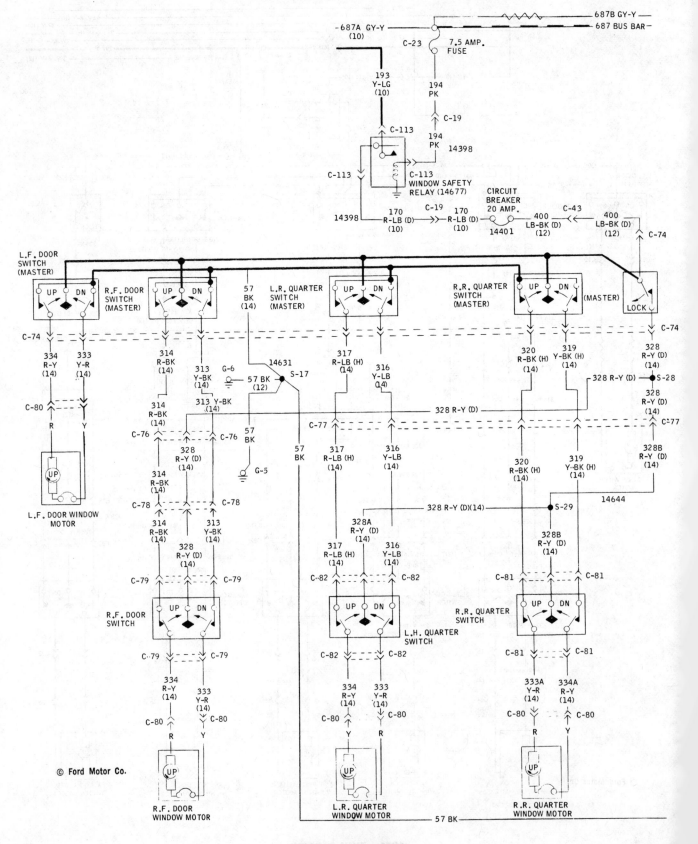

© Ford Motor Co.

**1972 —THUNDERBIRD**

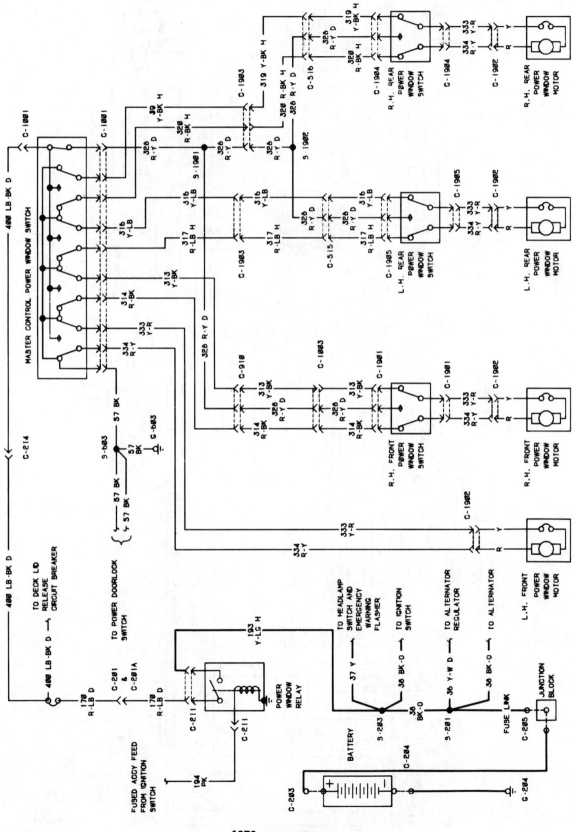

**1973 —THUNDERBIRD**

© Ford Motor Co.

# Ford Motor Company

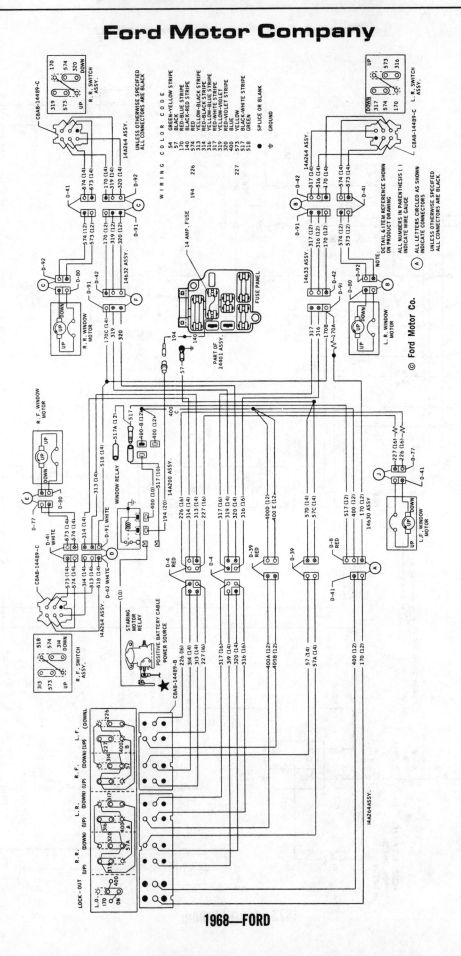

1968—FORD

## Ford Motor Company

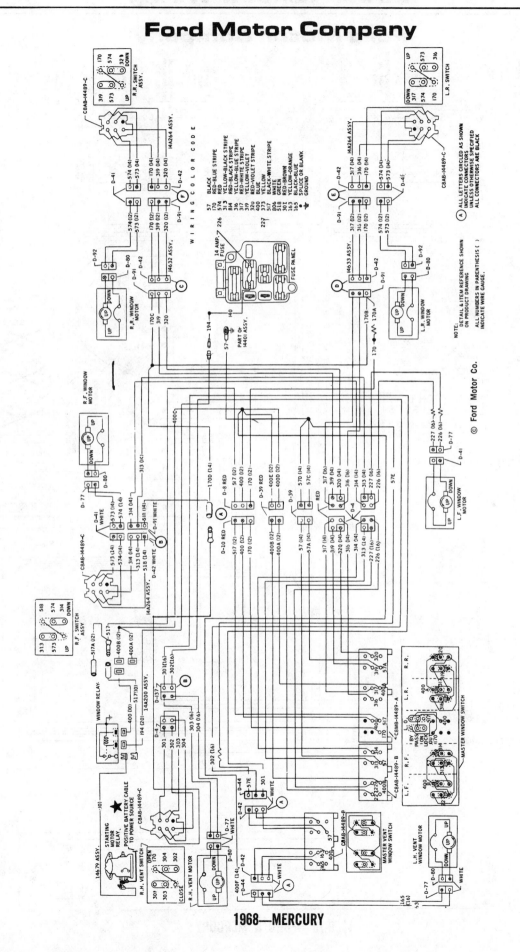

**1968—MERCURY**

## Ford Motor Company

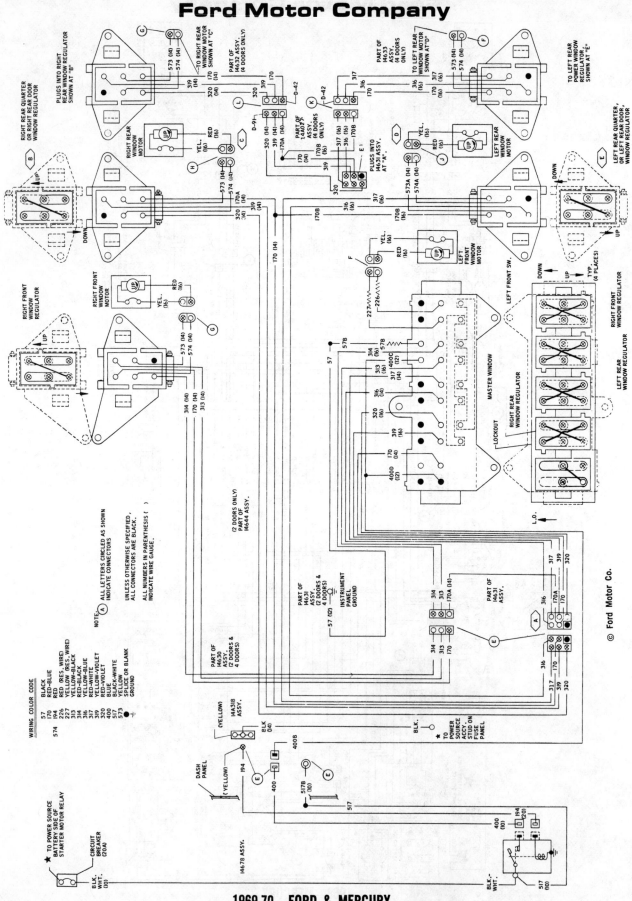

© Ford Motor Co.

**1969-70 —Ford & MERCURY**

# Ford Motor Company

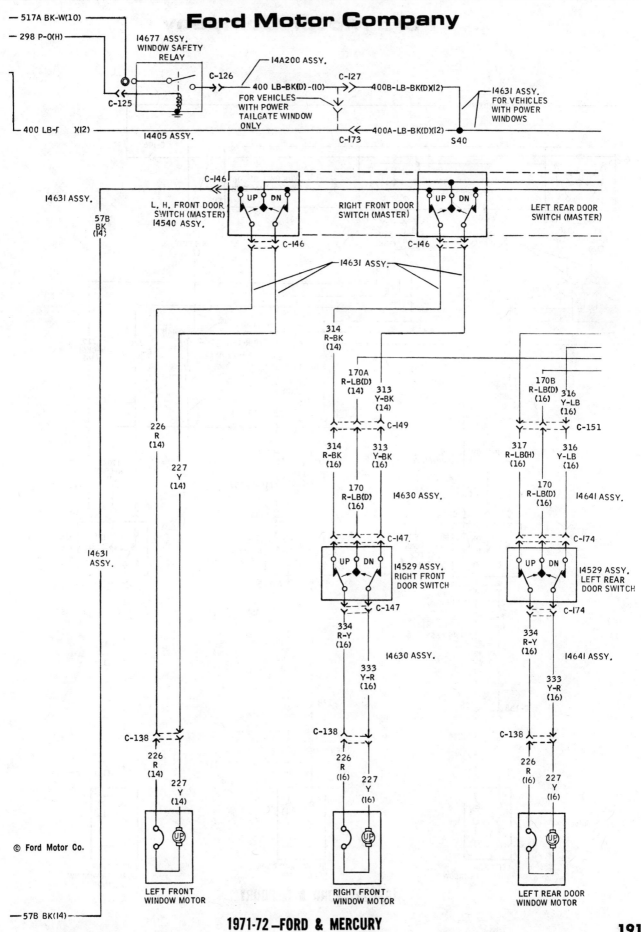

© Ford Motor Co.

**1971-72 – Ford & Mercury**

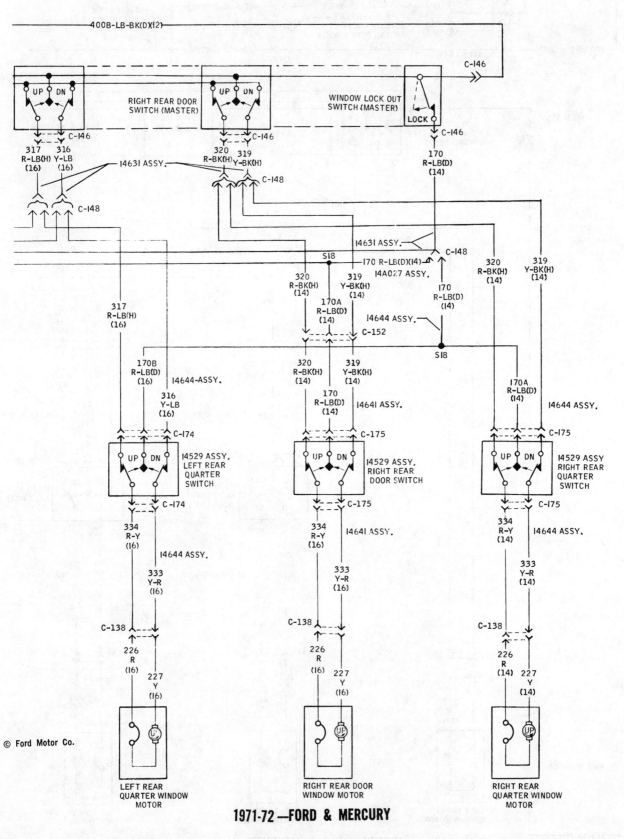

© Ford Motor Co.

LEFT REAR
QUARTER WINDOW
MOTOR

RIGHT REAR DOOR
WINDOW MOTOR

RIGHT REAR
QUARTER WINDOW
MOTOR

**1971-72 — FORD & MERCURY**

## Ford Motor Company

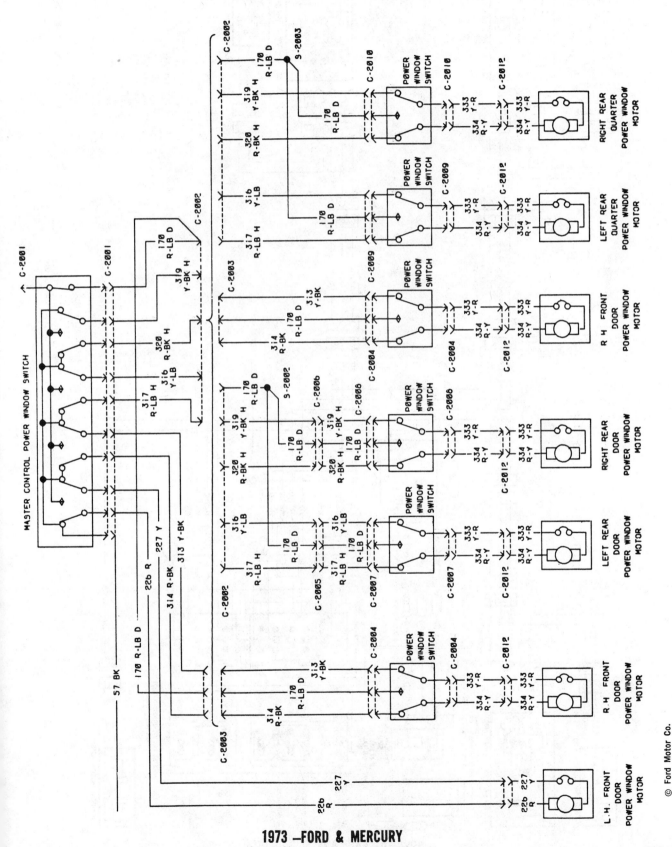

**1973 —FORD & MERCURY**

© Ford Motor Co.

# Ford Motor Company

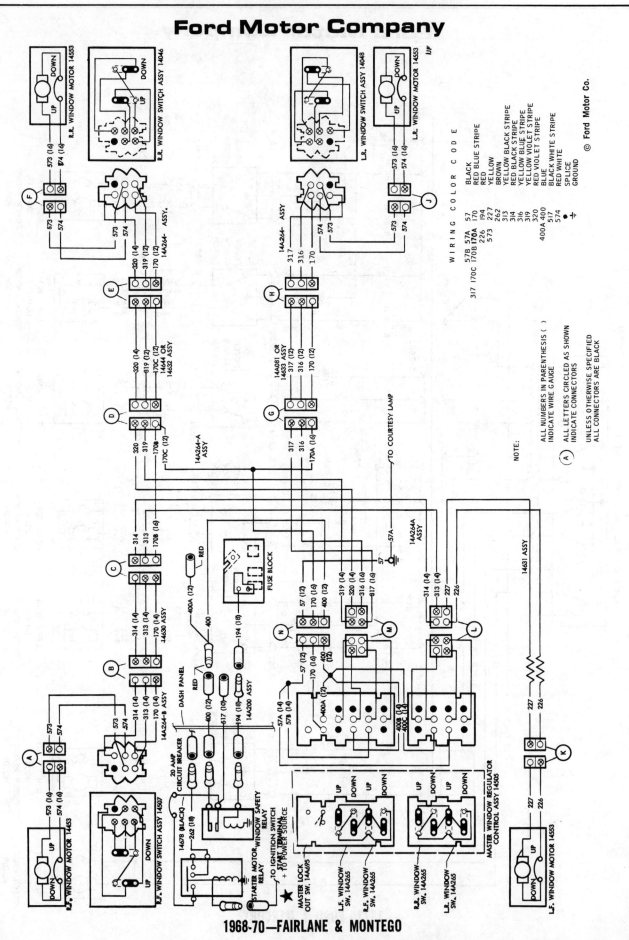

**WIRING COLOR CODE**

| | |
|---|---|
| 57 | BLACK |
| 170 | RED BLUE STRIPE |
| 194 | RED |
| 227 | YELLOW |
| 262 | BROWN |
| 313 | YELLOW BLACK STRIPE |
| 314 | RED BLACK STRIPE |
| 316 | YELLOW BLUE STRIPE |
| 319 | YELLOW VIOLET STRIPE |
| 320 | RED VIOLET STRIPE |
| 400A 400 | BLUE |
| 517 | BLACK WHITE STRIPE |
| 574 | RED WHITE |
| | SPLICE |
| | GROUND |

© Ford Motor Co.

**NOTE:**

ALL NUMBERS IN PARENTHESIS ( ) INDICATE WIRE GAUGE

(A) ALL LETTERS CIRCLED AS SHOWN INDICATE CONNECTORS

UNLESS OTHERWISE SPECIFIED ALL CONNECTORS ARE BLACK

**1968-70—FAIRLANE & MONTEGO**

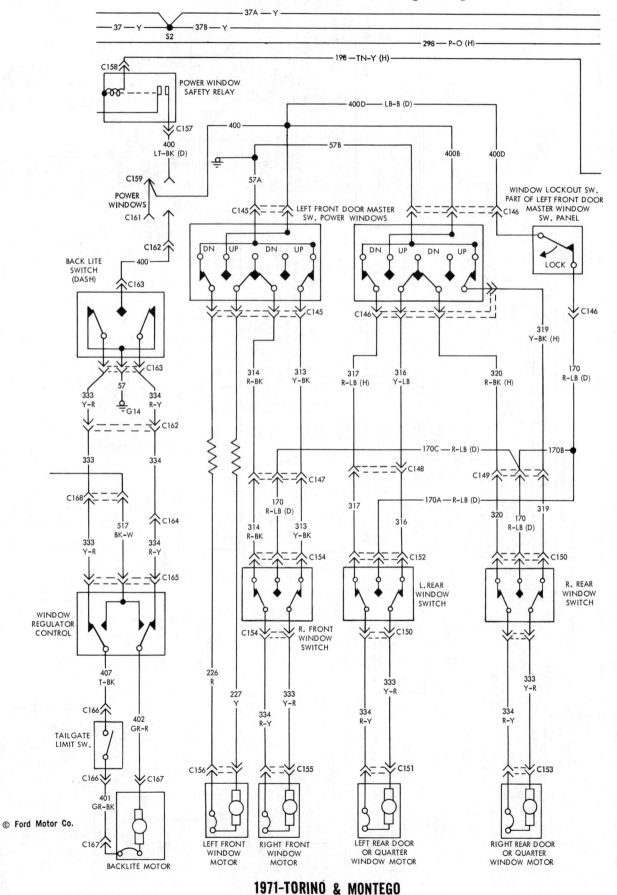

### 1971-TORINO & MONTEGO

© Ford Motor Co.

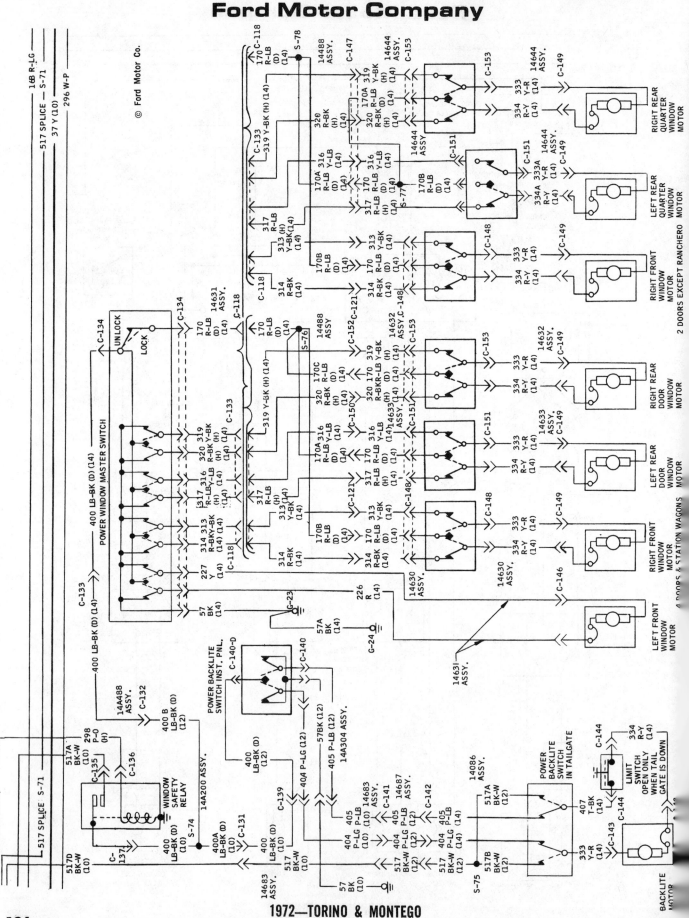

© Ford Motor Co.

1972—TORINO & MONTEGO

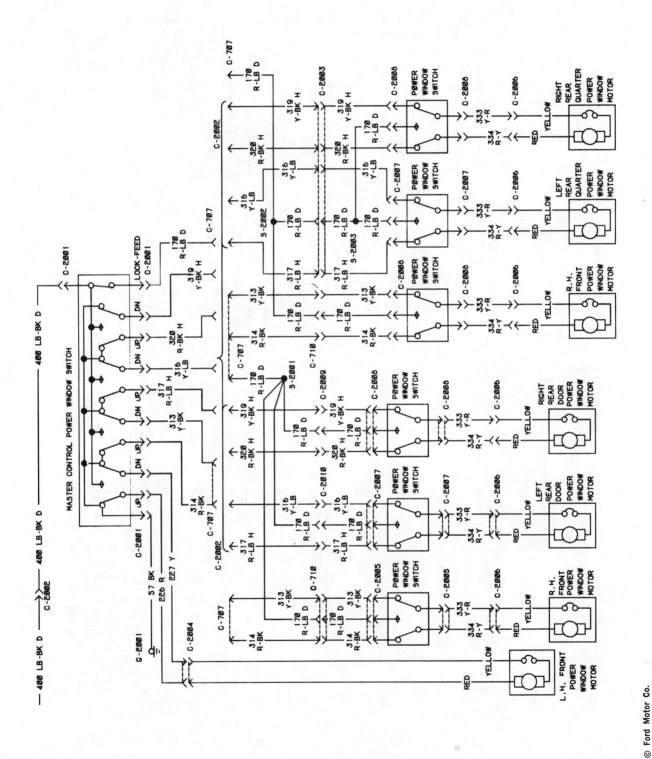

**1973—TORINO & MONTEGO**

# Ford Motor Company

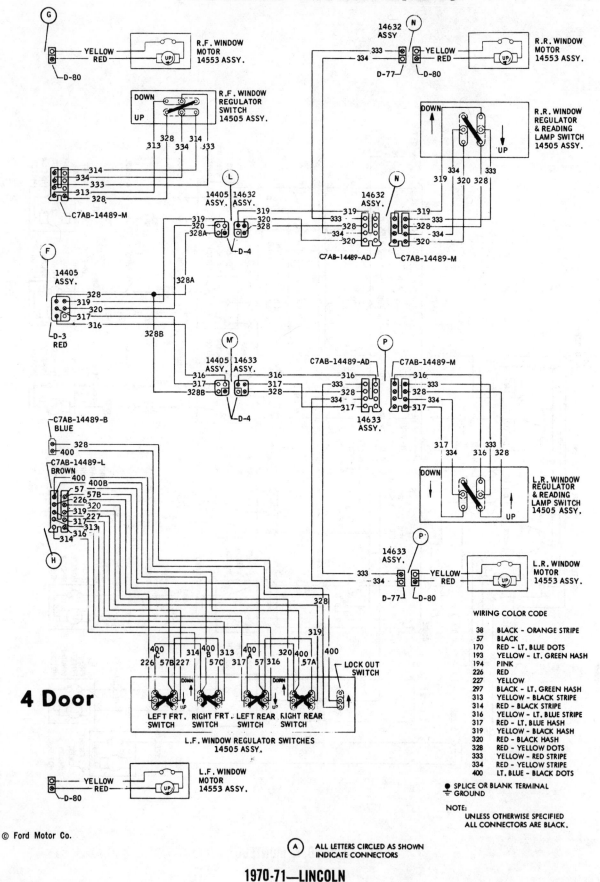

**4 Door**

### WIRING COLOR CODE

| | |
|---|---|
| 38 | BLACK - ORANGE STRIPE |
| 57 | BLACK |
| 170 | RED - LT. BLUE DOTS |
| 193 | YELLOW - LT. GREEN HASH |
| 194 | PINK |
| 226 | RED |
| 227 | YELLOW |
| 297 | BLACK - LT. GREEN HASH |
| 313 | YELLOW - BLACK STRIPE |
| 314 | RED - BLACK STRIPE |
| 316 | YELLOW - LT. BLUE STRIPE |
| 317 | RED - LT. BLUE HASH |
| 319 | YELLOW - BLACK HASH |
| 320 | RED - BLACK HASH |
| 328 | RED - YELLOW DOTS |
| 333 | YELLOW - RED STRIPE |
| 334 | RED - YELLOW STRIPE |
| 400 | LT. BLUE - BLACK DOTS |

● SPLICE OR BLANK TERMINAL
⏚ GROUND

NOTE:
UNLESS OTHERWISE SPECIFIED
ALL CONNECTORS ARE BLACK.

© Ford Motor Co.

(A) ALL LETTERS CIRCLED AS SHOWN
INDICATE CONNECTORS

## 1970-71—LINCOLN

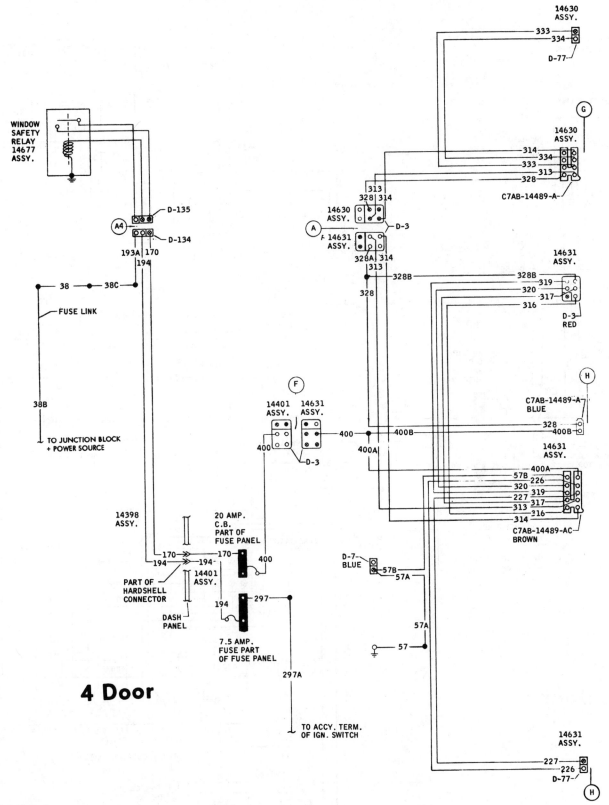

**4 Door**

## Ford Motor Company

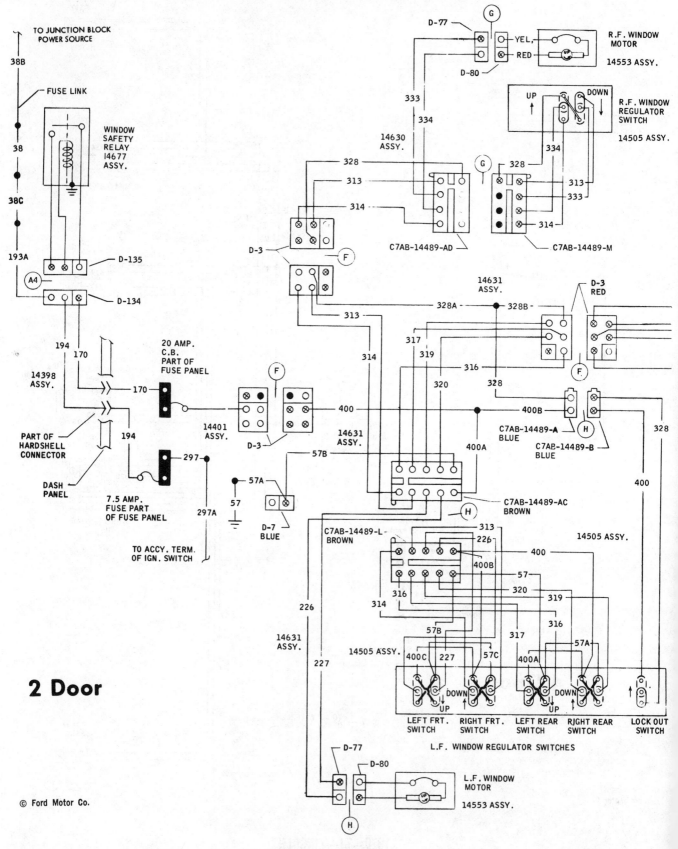

**2 Door**

© Ford Motor Co.

**1970—71—LINCOLN**

# Power Window Wiring

## Ford Motor Company

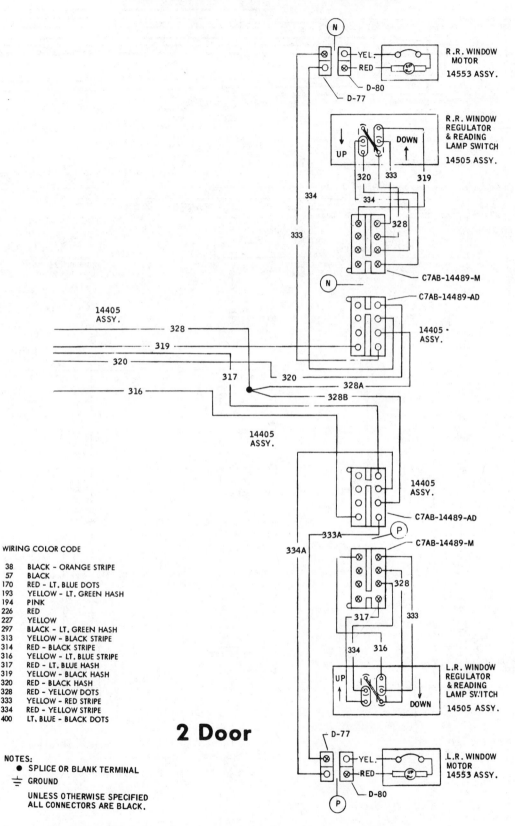

R.R. WINDOW
MOTOR
14553 ASSY.

R.R. WINDOW
REGULATOR
& READING
LAMP SWITCH
14505 ASSY.

UP   DOWN

320   333   319

334

C7AB-14489-M

C7AB-14489-AD

14405
ASSY.

14405 ·
ASSY.

328

319

320

317

320

328A

316   328B

14405
ASSY.

14405
ASSY.

C7AB-14489-AD

333A   P   C7AB-14489-M

334A   328

317   333

334   316

L.R. WINDOW
REGULATOR
& READING
LAMP SWITCH
14505 ASSY.

UP   DOWN

D-77

YEL.   L.R. WINDOW
RED    MOTOR
       14553 ASSY.

D-80

**WIRING COLOR CODE**

| | |
|---|---|
| 38 | BLACK – ORANGE STRIPE |
| 57 | BLACK |
| 170 | RED – LT. BLUE DOTS |
| 193 | YELLOW – LT. GREEN HASH |
| 194 | PINK |
| 226 | RED |
| 227 | YELLOW |
| 297 | BLACK – LT. GREEN HASH |
| 313 | YELLOW – BLACK STRIPE |
| 314 | RED – BLACK STRIPE |
| 316 | YELLOW – LT. BLUE STRIPE |
| 317 | RED – LT. BLUE HASH |
| 319 | YELLOW – BLACK HASH |
| 320 | RED – BLACK HASH |
| 328 | RED – YELLOW DOTS |
| 333 | YELLOW – RED STRIPE |
| 334 | RED – YELLOW STRIPE |
| 400 | LT. BLUE – BLACK DOTS |

## 2 Door

NOTES:
- ● SPLICE OR BLANK TERMINAL
- ⏚ GROUND

UNLESS OTHERWISE SPECIFIED
ALL CONNECTORS ARE BLACK.

© Ford Motor Co.

Ⓐ ALL LETTERS CIRCLED AS SHOWN
INDICATE CONNECTORS

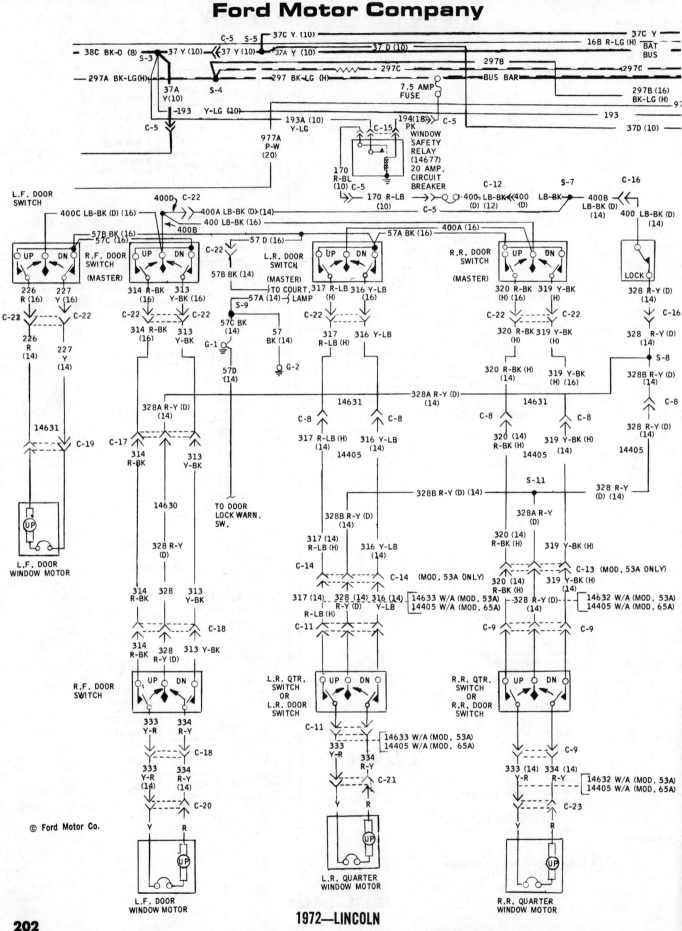

© Ford Motor Co.

**1972—LINCOLN**

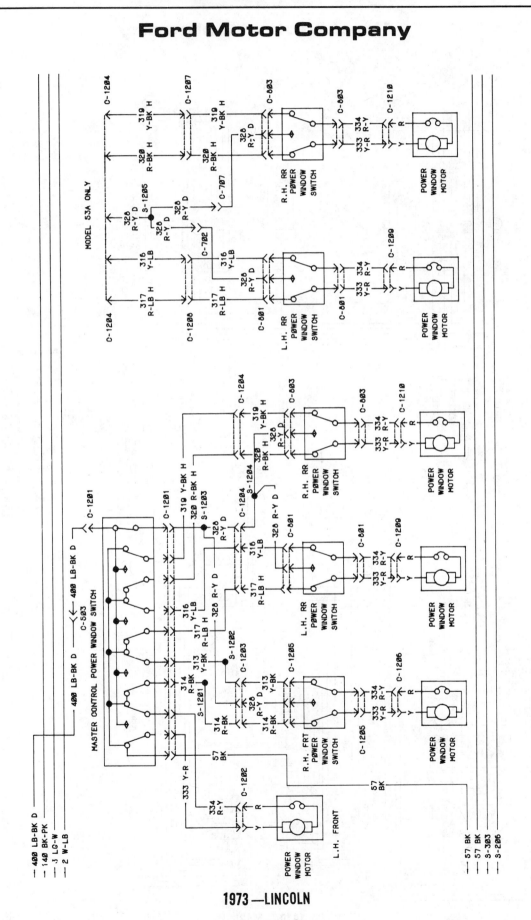

1973 —LINCOLN

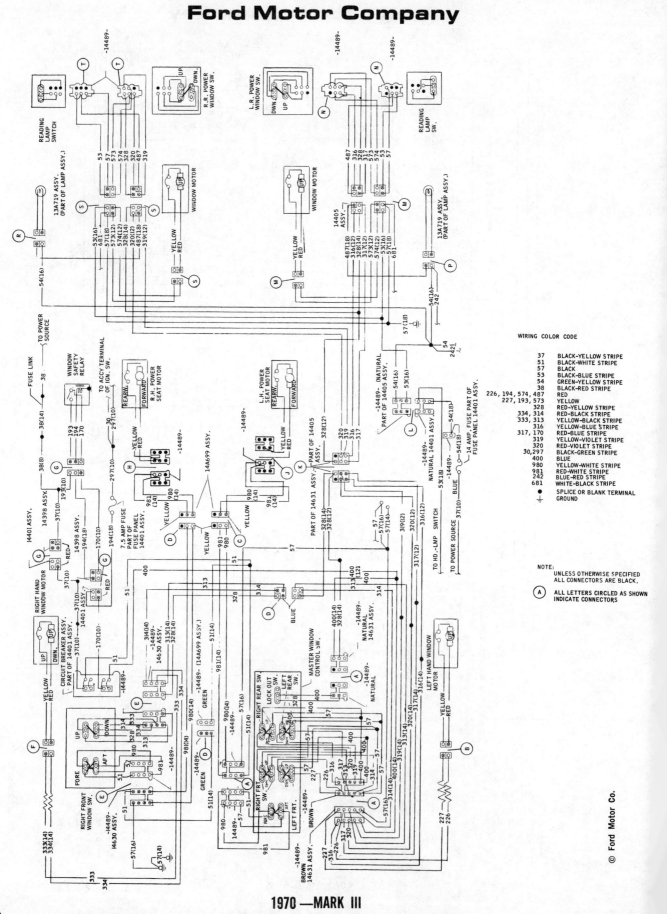

1970 — MARK III

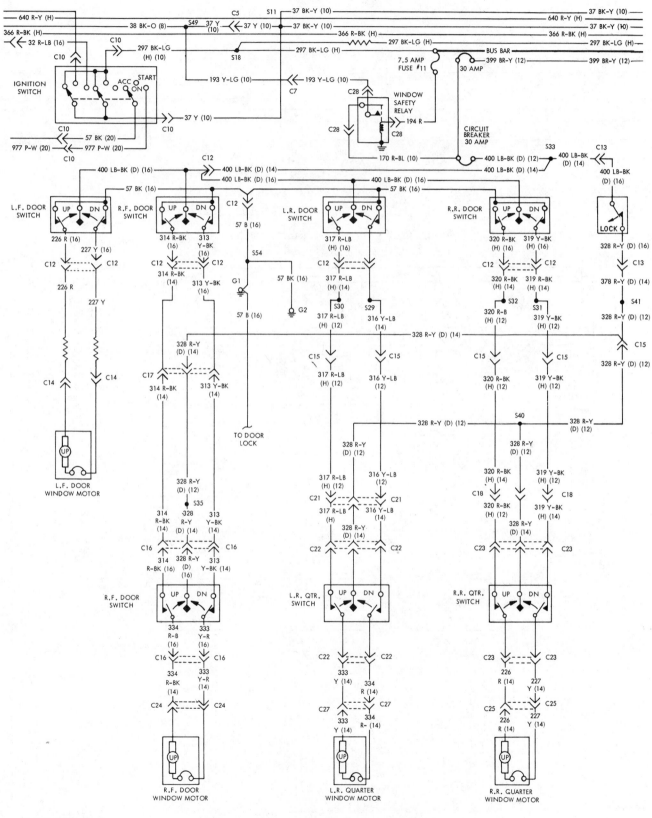

**1971—MARK III**

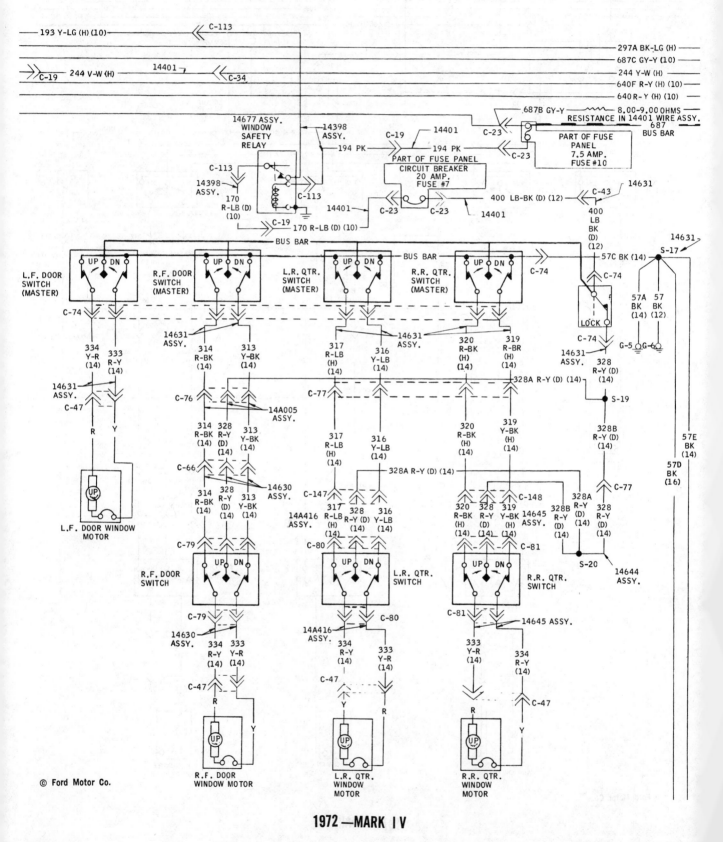

**1972—Mark IV**

# Power Window Wiring

## Ford Motor Company

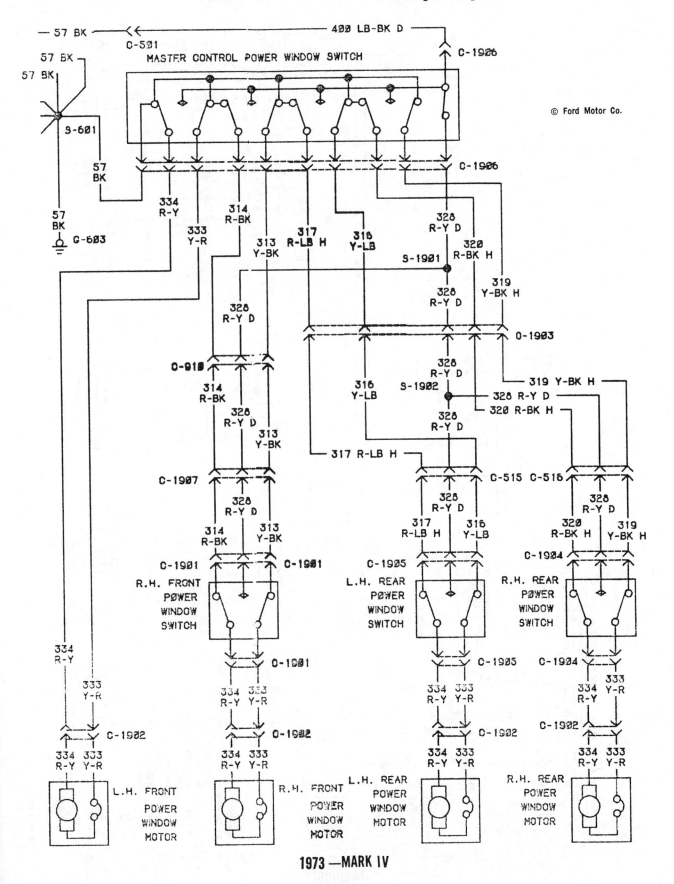

© Ford Motor Co.

**1973 — MARK IV**

## Ford Motor Company

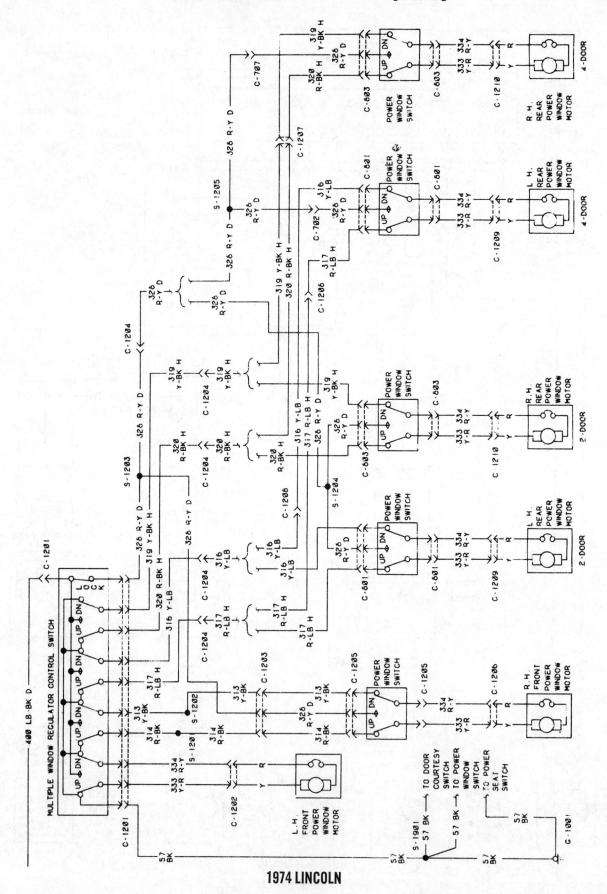

**1974 LINCOLN**

© Ford Motor Co.

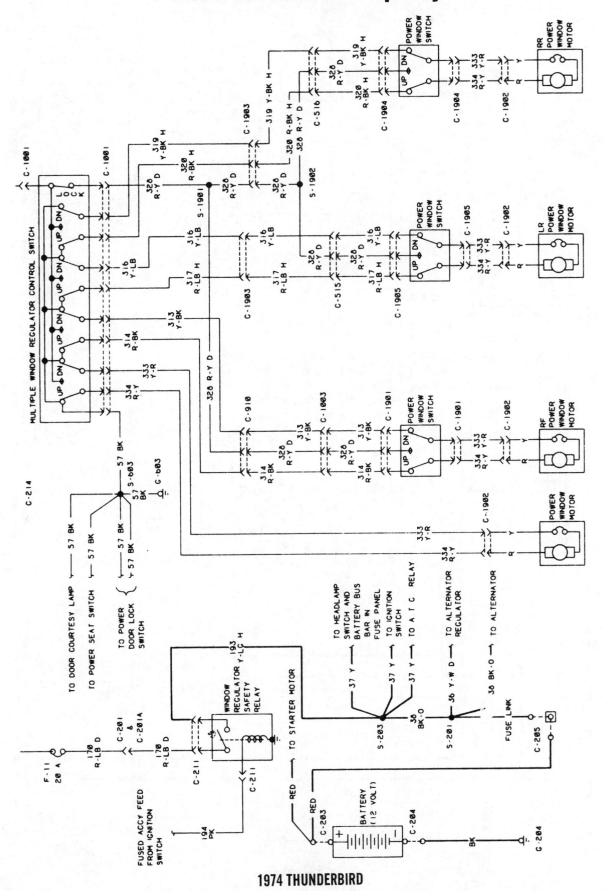

**1974 THUNDERBIRD**

## Ford Motor Company

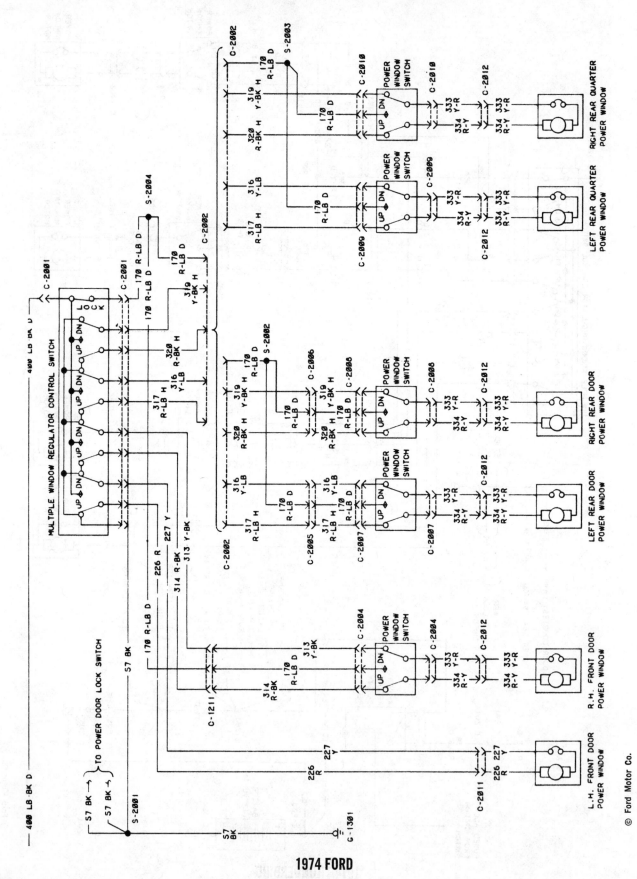

**1974 FORD**

© Ford Motor Co.

## Ford Motor Company

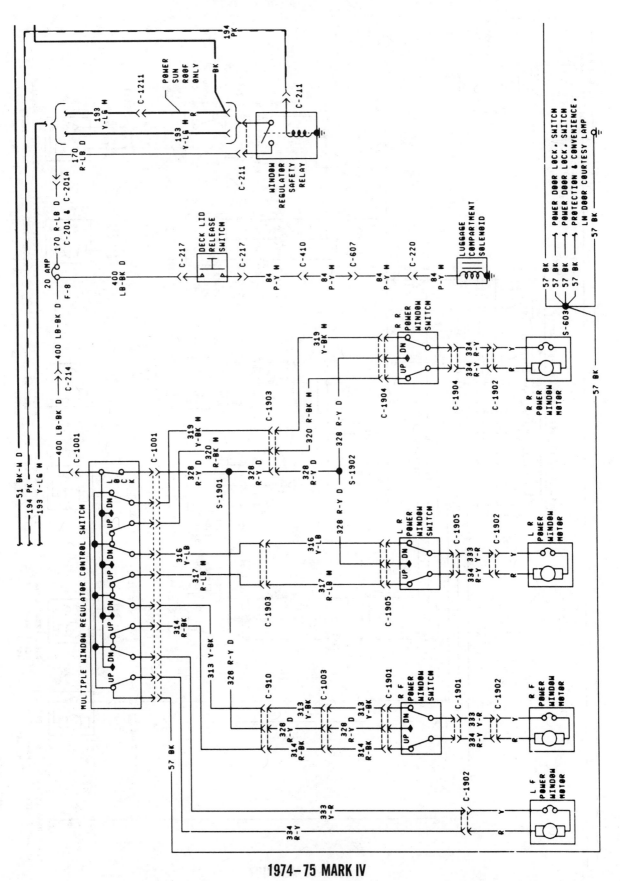

**1974–75 MARK IV**

© Ford Motor Co.

211

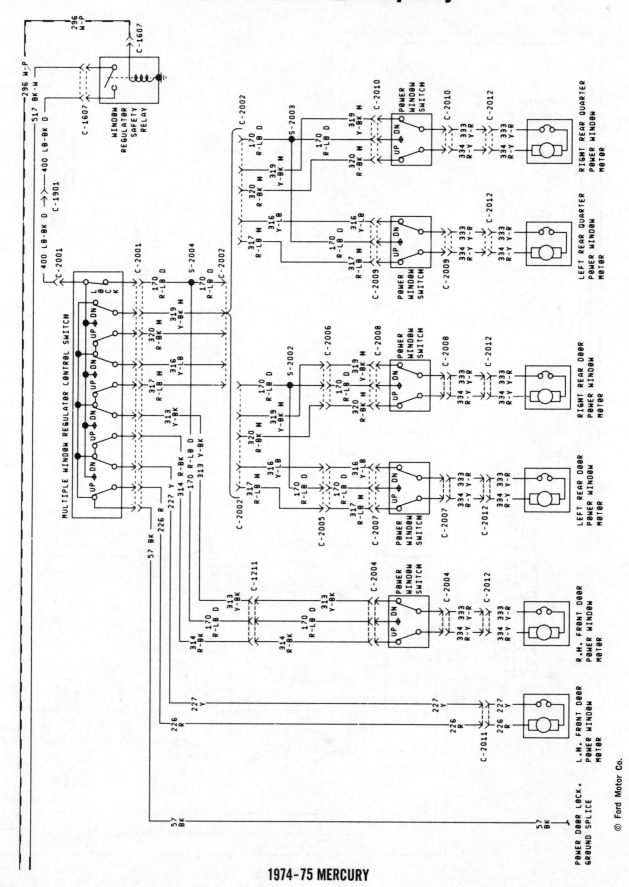

**1974-75 MERCURY**

© Ford Motor Co.

# Power Window Wiring

## Ford Motor Company

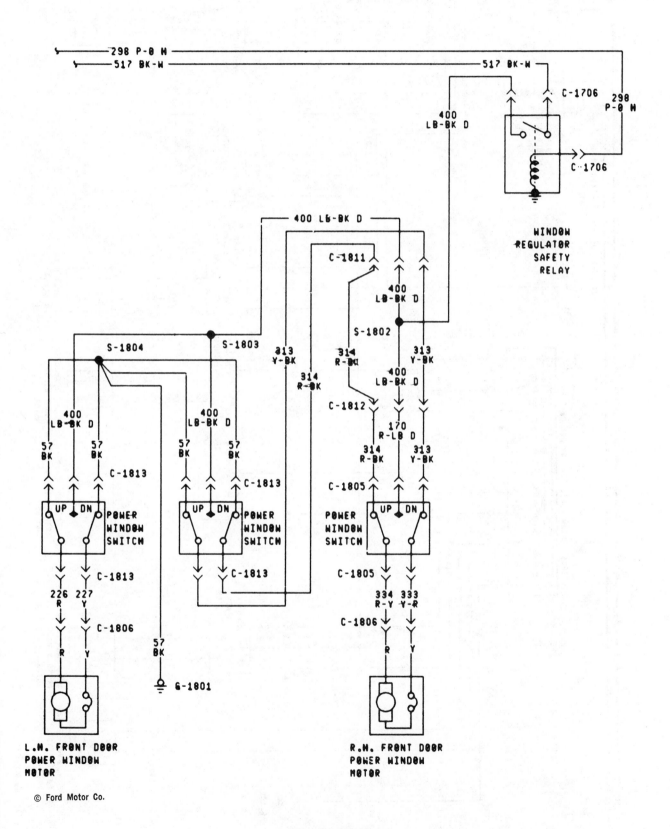

**1974-75 COUGAR**

## Ford Motor Company

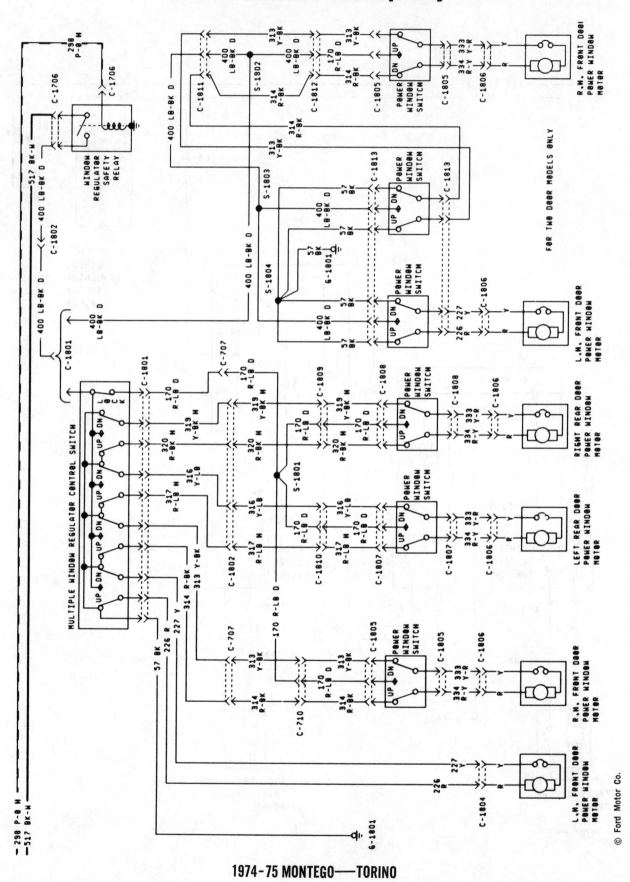

FOR TWO DOOR MODELS ONLY

**1974-75 MONTEGO—TORINO**

© Ford Motor Co.

## Ford Motor Company

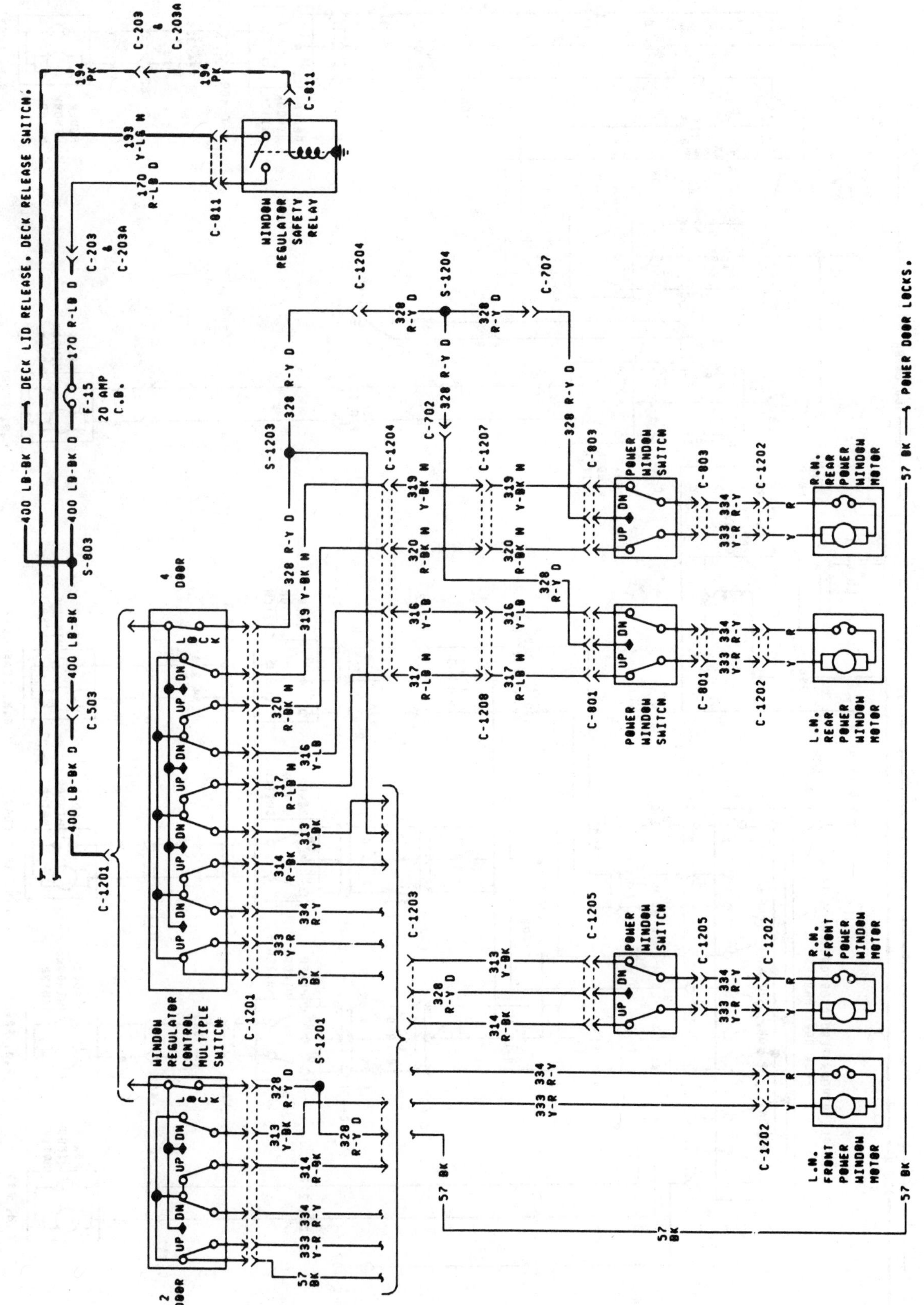


1975 LINCOLN

# Power Window Wiring

## Ford Motor Company

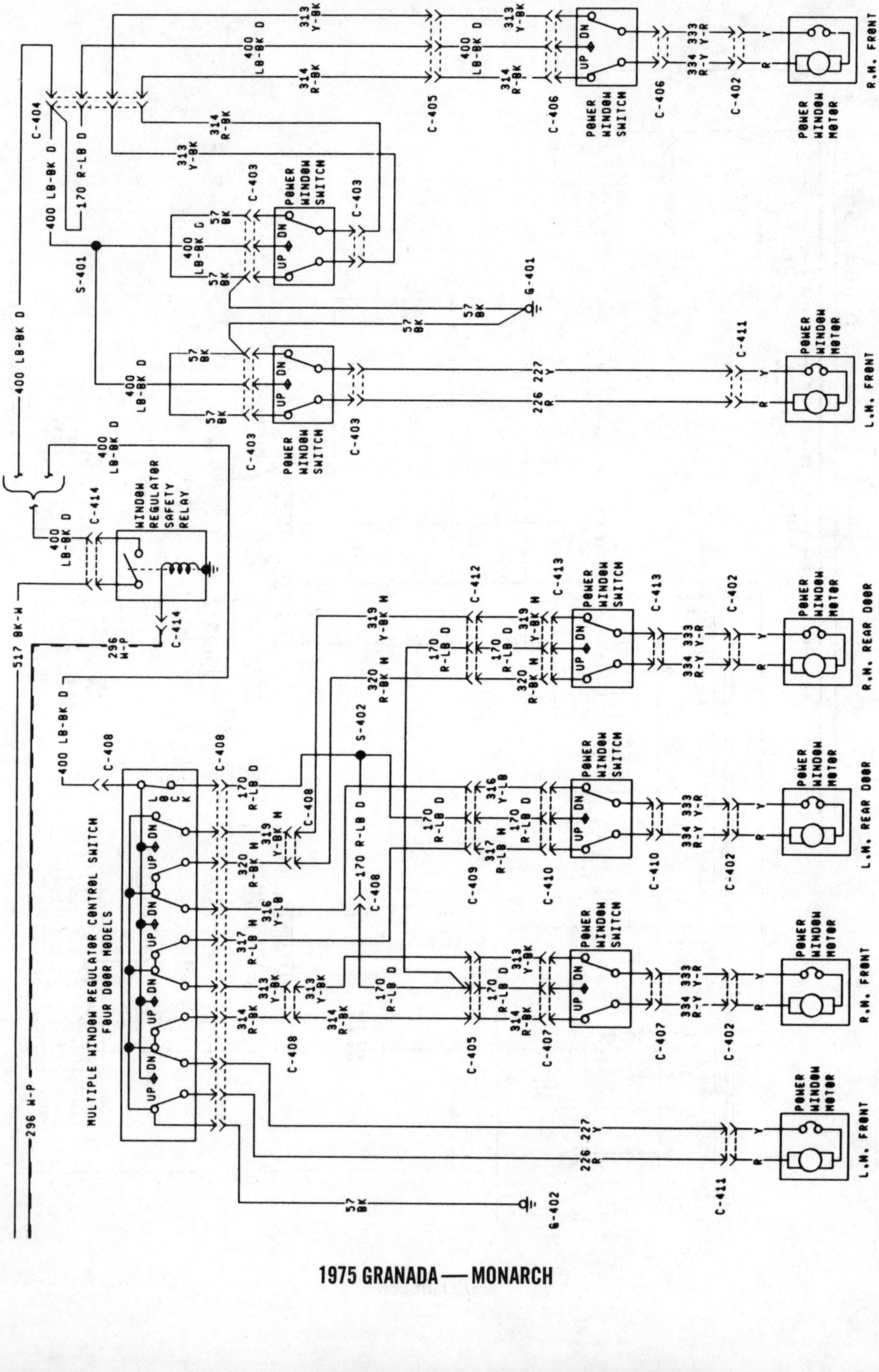




1975 GRANADA — MONARCH

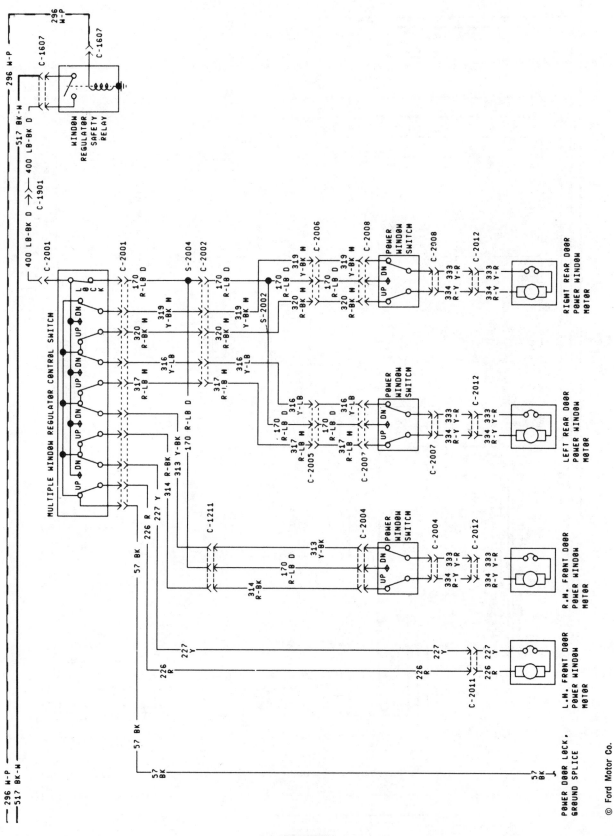

## Ford Motor Company

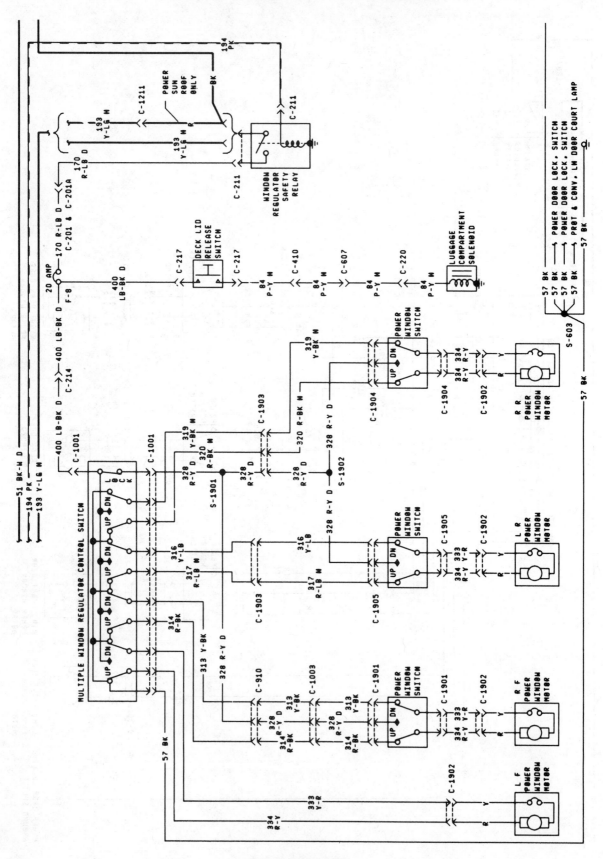

**1975 THUNDERBIRD**

© Ford Motor Co.

# Power Window Wiring

## General Motors

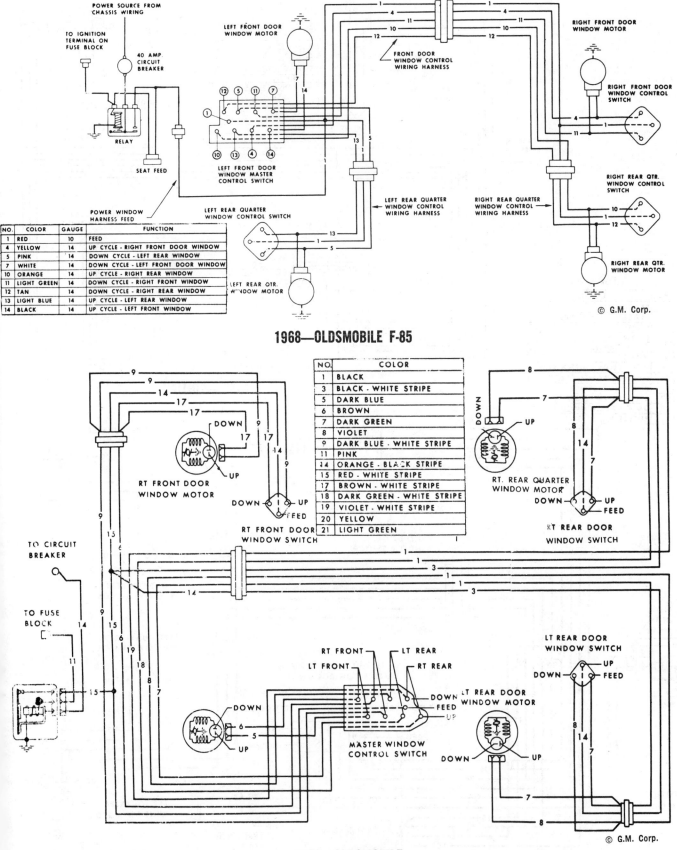

| NO. | COLOR | GAUGE | FUNCTION |
|---|---|---|---|
| 1 | RED | 10 | FEED |
| 4 | YELLOW | 14 | UP CYCLE - RIGHT FRONT DOOR WINDOW |
| 5 | PINK | 14 | DOWN CYCLE - LEFT REAR WINDOW |
| 7 | WHITE | 14 | DOWN CYCLE - LEFT FRONT DOOR WINDOW |
| 10 | ORANGE | 14 | UP CYCLE - RIGHT REAR WINDOW |
| 11 | LIGHT GREEN | 14 | DOWN CYCLE - RIGHT FRONT WINDOW |
| 12 | TAN | 14 | DOWN CYCLE - RIGHT REAR WINDOW |
| 13 | LIGHT BLUE | 14 | UP CYCLE - LEFT REAR WINDOW |
| 14 | BLACK | 14 | UP CYCLE - LEFT FRONT WINDOW |

© G.M. Corp.

**1968—OLDSMOBILE F-85**

| NO. | COLOR |
|---|---|
| 1 | BLACK |
| 3 | BLACK - WHITE STRIPE |
| 5 | DARK BLUE |
| 6 | BROWN |
| 7 | DARK GREEN |
| 8 | VIOLET |
| 9 | DARK BLUE - WHITE STRIPE |
| 11 | PINK |
| 14 | ORANGE - BLACK STRIPE |
| 15 | RED - WHITE STRIPE |
| 17 | BROWN - WHITE STRIPE |
| 18 | DARK GREEN - WHITE STRIPE |
| 19 | VIOLET - WHITE STRIPE |
| 20 | YELLOW |
| 21 | LIGHT GREEN |

© G.M. Corp.

**1968—OLDSMOBILE**

## General Motors

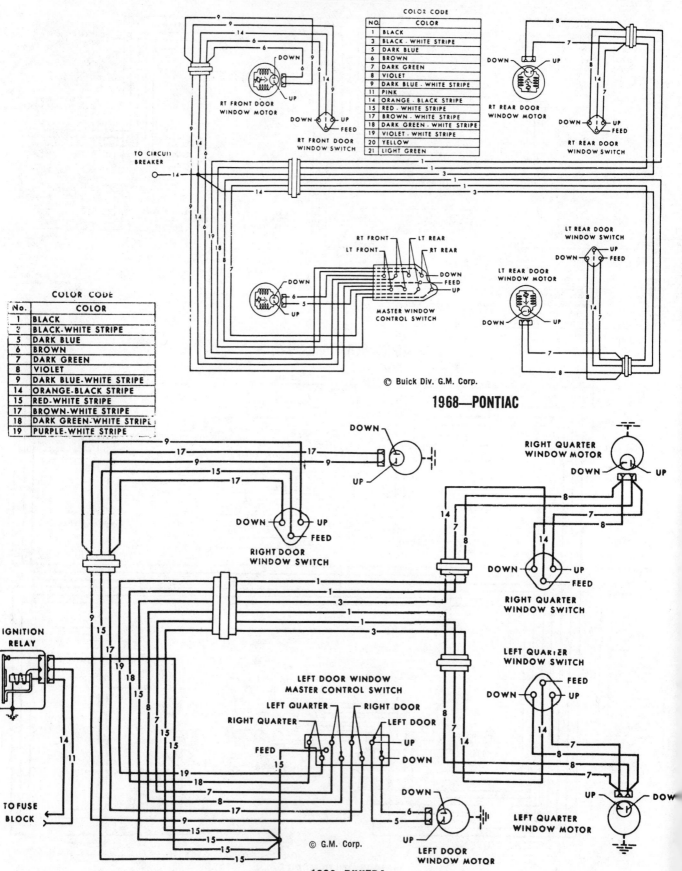

| COLOR CODE | |
|---|---|
| NO. | COLOR |
| 1 | BLACK |
| 3 | BLACK - WHITE STRIPE |
| 5 | DARK BLUE |
| 6 | BROWN |
| 7 | DARK GREEN |
| 8 | VIOLET |
| 9 | DARK BLUE - WHITE STRIPE |
| 11 | PINK |
| 14 | ORANGE - BLACK STRIPE |
| 15 | RED - WHITE STRIPE |
| 17 | BROWN - WHITE STRIPE |
| 18 | DARK GREEN - WHITE STRIPE |
| 19 | VIOLET - WHITE STRIPE |
| 20 | YELLOW |
| 21 | LIGHT GREEN |

| COLOR CODE | |
|---|---|
| No. | COLOR |
| 1 | BLACK |
| 3 | BLACK-WHITE STRIPE |
| 5 | DARK BLUE |
| 6 | BROWN |
| 7 | DARK GREEN |
| 8 | VIOLET |
| 9 | DARK BLUE-WHITE STRIPE |
| 14 | ORANGE-BLACK STRIPE |
| 15 | RED - WHITE STRIPE |
| 17 | BROWN-WHITE STRIPE |
| 18 | DARK GREEN-WHITE STRIPE |
| 19 | PURPLE-WHITE STRIPE |

© Buick Div. G.M. Corp.

**1968—PONTIAC**

© G.M. Corp.

**1968—RIVIERA**

## General Motors

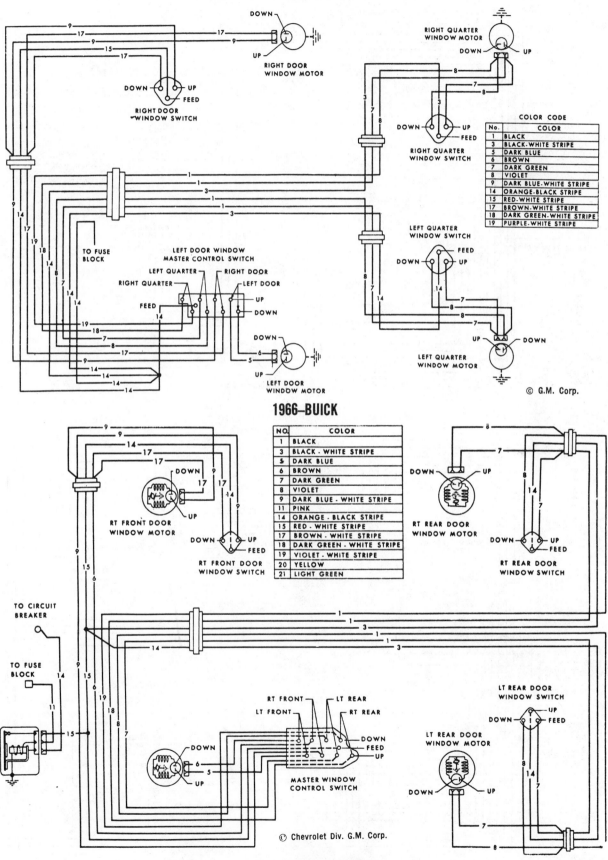

| No. | COLOR CODE<br>COLOR |
|-----|-------|
| 1 | BLACK |
| 3 | BLACK-WHITE STRIPE |
| 5 | DARK BLUE |
| 6 | BROWN |
| 7 | DARK GREEN |
| 8 | VIOLET |
| 9 | DARK BLUE-WHITE STRIPE |
| 14 | ORANGE-BLACK STRIPE |
| 15 | RED-WHITE STRIPE |
| 17 | BROWN-WHITE STRIPE |
| 18 | DARK GREEN-WHITE STRIPE |
| 19 | PURPLE-WHITE STRIPE |

© G.M. Corp.

**1966–BUICK**

| NO. | COLOR |
|-----|-------|
| 1 | BLACK |
| 3 | BLACK - WHITE STRIPE |
| 5 | DARK BLUE |
| 6 | BROWN |
| 7 | DARK GREEN |
| 8 | VIOLET |
| 9 | DARK BLUE - WHITE STRIPE |
| 11 | PINK |
| 14 | ORANGE - BLACK STRIPE |
| 15 | RED - WHITE STRIPE |
| 17 | BROWN - WHITE STRIPE |
| 18 | DARK GREEN - WHITE STRIPE |
| 19 | VIOLET - WHITE STRIPE |
| 20 | YELLOW |
| 21 | LIGHT GREEN |

© Chevrolet Div. G.M. Corp.

**1967-68—BUICK**

221

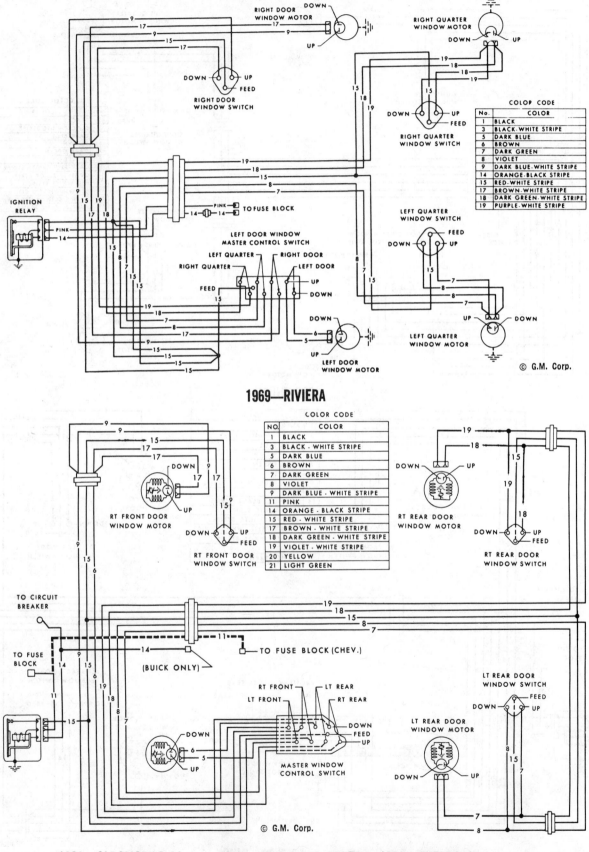

**1969—RIVIERA**

**1969—OLDSMOBILE 88     1969—BUICK EXC. RIVIERA  1968—CHEVROLET**

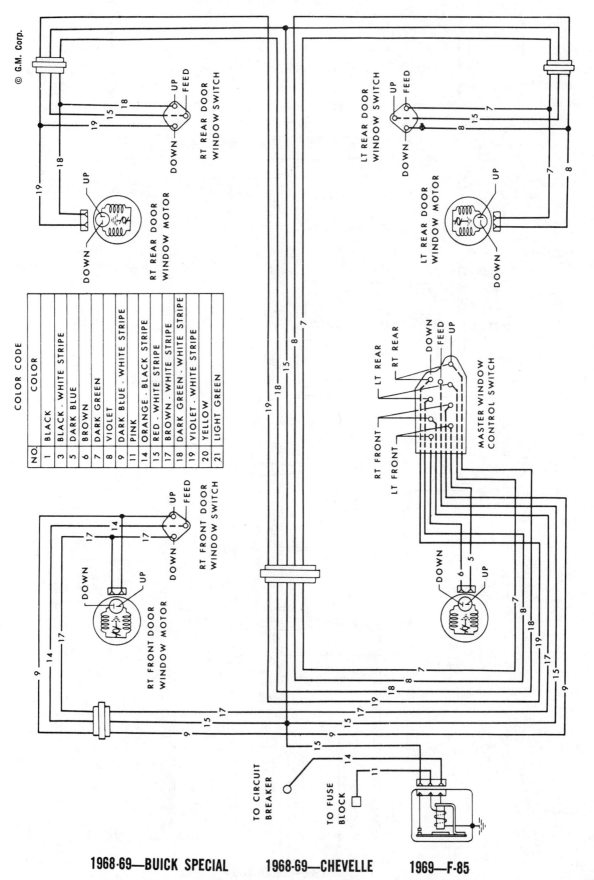

© G.M. Corp.

| COLOR CODE | |
|---|---|
| NO. | COLOR |
| 1 | BLACK |
| 3 | BLACK - WHITE STRIPE |
| 5 | DARK BLUE |
| 6 | BROWN |
| 7 | DARK GREEN |
| 8 | VIOLET |
| 9 | DARK BLUE - WHITE STRIPE |
| 11 | PINK |
| 14 | ORANGE - BLACK STRIPE |
| 15 | RED - WHITE STRIPE |
| 17 | BROWN - WHITE STRIPE |
| 18 | DARK GREEN - WHITE STRIPE |
| 19 | VIOLET - WHITE STRIPE |
| 20 | YELLOW |
| 21 | LIGHT GREEN |

1968-69—BUICK SPECIAL    1968-69—CHEVELLE    1969—F-85

# General Motors

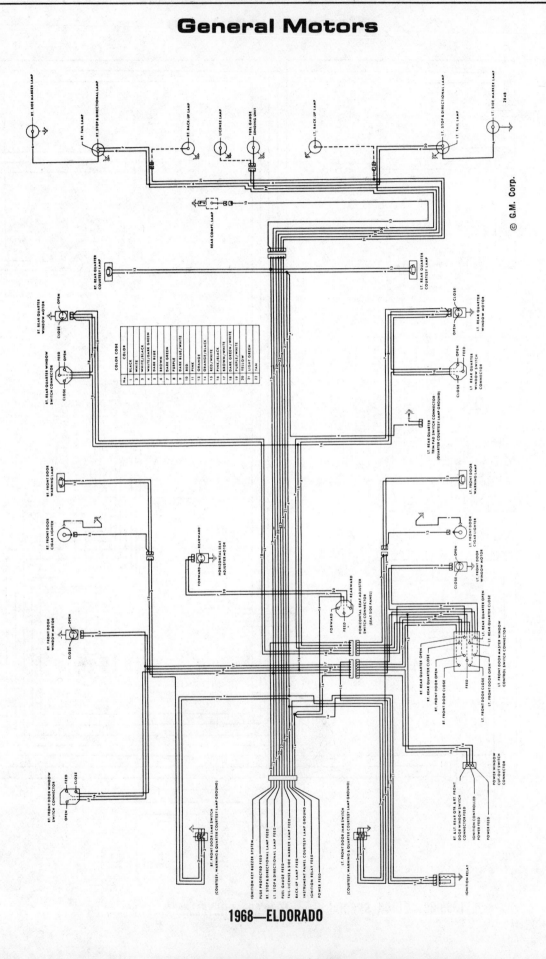

© G.M. Corp.

| COLOR CODE | |
|---|---|
| No. | Color |
| 1 | BLACK |
| 2 | WHITE |
| 3 | WHITE/BLACK |
| 4 | WHITE/DARK GREEN |
| 5 | DARK BLUE |
| 6 | BROWN |
| 7 | DARK GREEN |
| 8 | PURPLE |
| 9 | DARK BLUE/WHITE |
| 10 | RED |
| 11 | PINK |
| 12 | ORANGE |
| 13 | ORANGE/BLACK |
| 14 | RED/WHITE |
| 15 | BROWN/WHITE |
| 16 | PINK/BLACK |
| 17 | DARK GREEN/WHITE |
| 18 | PURPLE/WHITE |
| 19 | PURPLE/WHITE |
| 20 | YELLOW |
| 21 | LIGHT GREEN |
| 22 | TAN |

## 1968—ELDORADO

## General Motors

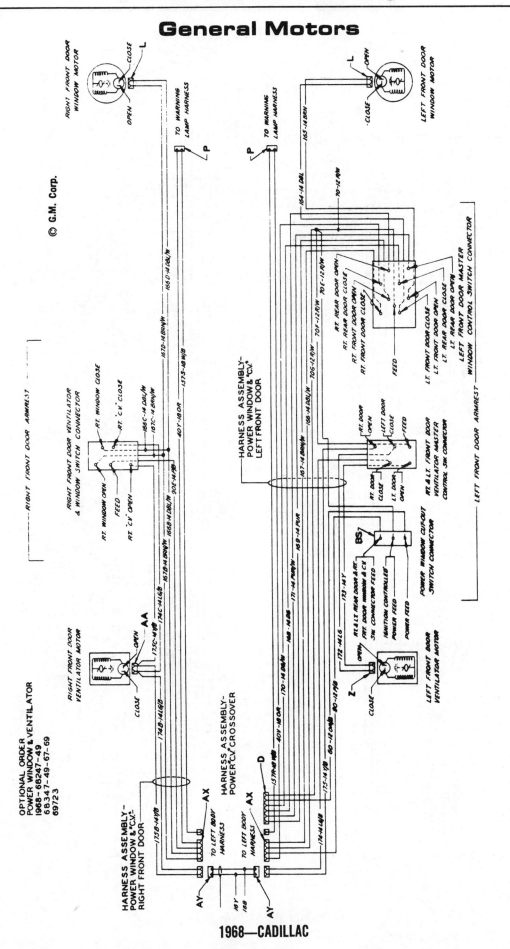

© G.M. Corp.

**1968—CADILLAC**

## General Motors

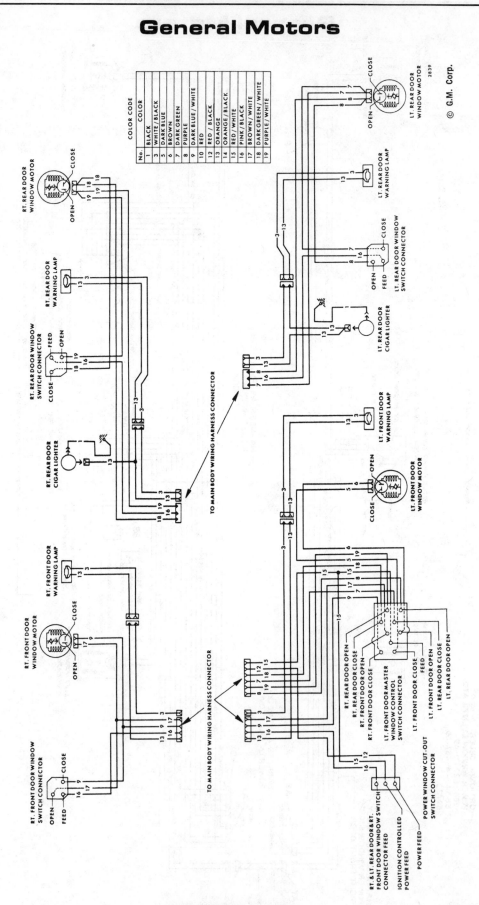

| COLOR CODE | |
|---|---|
| No. | COLOR |
| 1 | BLACK |
| 3 | WHITE / BLACK |
| 5 | DARK BLUE |
| 6 | BROWN |
| 7 | DARK GREEN |
| 8 | PURPLE |
| 9 | DARK BLUE / WHITE |
| 10 | RED |
| 12 | RED / BLACK |
| 13 | ORANGE |
| 14 | ORANGE / BLACK |
| 15 | RED / WHITE |
| 16 | PINK / BLACK |
| 17 | BROWN / WHITE |
| 18 | DARK GREEN / WHITE |
| 19 | PURPLE / WHITE |

© G.M. Corp.

**1968—CADILLAC (4 DR.)**

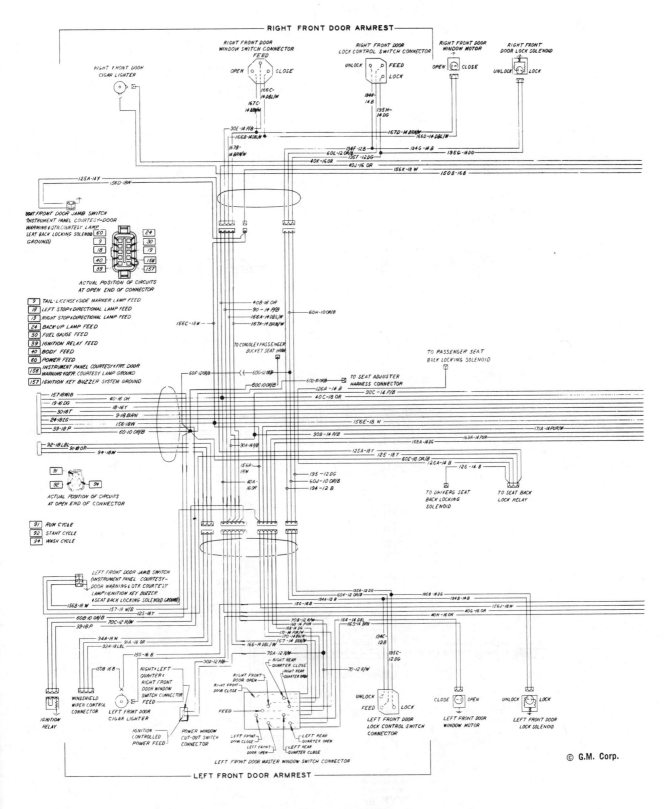

1969—ELDORADO

© G.M. Corp.

## General Motors

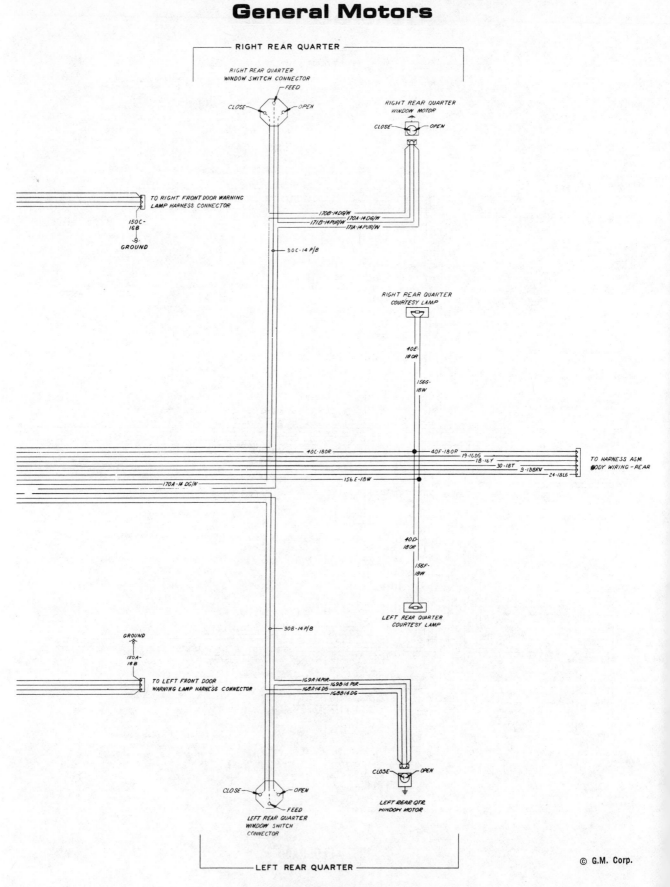

© G.M. Corp.

## 1969—ELDORADO

## General Motors

┌─ RIGHT FRONT DOOR ARMREST ─┐

RIGHT FRONT DOOR
WINDOW SWITCH CONNECTOR

RIGHT FRONT DOOR
CIGAR LIGHTER

FEED   OPEN — CLOSE

RIGHT FRONT DOOR
WINDOW MOTOR
OPEN — CLOSE

RIGHT FRONT DOOR
COURTESY LAMP

RIGHT REAR QUARTER
COURTESY LAMP
(TRIM PANEL)

150D-16B

166B   40J

167B   90E

156F-18W
40G-180R

166C-14 DBL/W
167C-14 BRN/W

170A-14 DG/W   40H-16OR
90CA 14 P/B

90-E-14P/B
166B-14DBL/W
167B-14 BRN/W

166D-14DBL/W
167D-14BRN/W

40J-16OR
156L-18W

156D-18W

REAR RADIO
SPEAKER FEED

HARNESS ASM. RIGHT FRONT
DOOR WINDOW WIRING

RIGHT FRONT DOOR JAMB SWITCH
(INSTRUMENT PANEL COURTESY-DOOR
WARNING & QTR COURTESY LAMP GROUND)

HARNESS ASM. SEAT ADJUSTER
HORIZONTAL

157  39
156  40
19   18
30   9
24   60

ACTUAL POSITION OF CIRCUITS
AT OPEN END OF CONNECTOR

166A-14 D BL/W

176-12DG   177-12Y

FORWARD — REARWARD

167A-14 BRN/W

HORIZONTAL SEAT
ADJUSTER MOTOR

9   TAIL & LICENSE LAMP FEED
18  LEFT STOP & DIRECTIONAL LAMP FEED
19  RIGHT STOP & DIRECTIONAL LAMP FEED
24  BACK-UP LAMP FEED
30  FUEL GAUGE SENDING UNIT FEED
39  IGNITION RELAY FEED
40  FUSE PROTECTED FEED
60  POWER FEED
156 INSTRUMENT PANEL COURTESY & DOOR WARNING &
    QUARTER COURTESY LAMP GROUND
157 IGNITION KEY BUZZER SYSTEM GROUND

156C-18W

40B-16OR
90A-14P/B

HARNESS ASM-LEFT
BODY WIRING

60A-10 OR/B

TO PASSENGER SEAT
ADJUSTER HARNESS

157-18W/B
40-16OR
19-16DG
18-16Y
30-18T
9-18BRN

60B10 OR/B

40F-16OR
170A-14 DG/W
90C-14P/B   171A-14PUR/W

163-12 PUR

24-18LG
156-18W
39-18P

40J-18OR

156F-18W

156E-18 W

92-18LBL
9I-18OR
94-18W

162-12GY
163-12 PUR

60-10 OR/B

60H-10 OR/B

168A-14DG
90B-14P/B
169-14 PUR

40C-16OR

91   92   94

ACTUAL POSITION OF
CIRCUITS AT OPEN END
OF CONNECTOR

91   RUN CYCLE
92   START CYCLE
94   WASH CYCLE

90-12 P/B
40A-18OR
60D-12 OR/B

156A-18W

60R-12 OR/B

WIRE ASM FRONT SEAT
GROUND

151-12B

SCREW TO SEAT   ADJUSTER TO FLOOR
FRAME         PAN ATTACHING BOLT

FRONT SEAT GROUND WIRE

163   162
DOWN      UP
60H
FEED

FORWARD

FEED

REARWARD

HORIZONTAL SEAT ADJUSTER
SWITCH CONNECTOR (SEAT
SIDE PANEL)

168A
169A   BLANK
170A   70C
171A

40A   166A
167A   30

LEFT FRONT DOOR JAMB
SWITCH (INSTRUMENT PANEL
COURTESY-DOOR WARNING-QTR
COURTESY LAMP & IGNITION KEY
BUZZER SYSTEM GROUND)

HARNESS ASM-LEFT FRONT
DOOR WINDOW WIRING

168A-14DG
169A-14PUR   40E-16OR

156B-18W
157-18W/B   70C-12R/W

60C-10 OR/B
39-18P

40G-16OR   156K-18W

70B-12R/W   169-14PUR

40G-18OR
156K-18W

90D-12P/B

168-14DG   171-14PUR/W
170-14DG/W   167-14BRN/W
166-14DBL/W
70A-12R/W

64-14DBL
165-14BRN

94A-18W
91A-18OR
92A-18LBL

150B-16B

RIGHT & LEFT REAR QTR
& RIGHT FRONT DOOR
WINDOW SWITCH
CONNECTOR FEED

IGNITION CONTROLLED
POWER FEED

34A

CLOSE — OPEN

RIGHT REAR QTR OPEN
RIGHT REAR QTR CLOSE
RIGHT FRONT DOOR OPEN
RIGHT FRONT DOOR CLOSE

FEED

LEFT FRONT DOOR
WARNING LAMP

156 E-18 W
40 D-18 OR

LEFT FRONT DOOR
WINDOW MOTOR

LEFT REAR QUARTER
COURTESY LAMP
(TRIM PANEL)

IGNITION
RELAY

39

60C

70C

WINDSHIELD WIPER
CONTROL

91A

92A   150B

POWER WINDOW
CUT-OUT SWITCH
CONNECTOR

LEFT FRONT DOOR CLOSE
LEFT FRONT DOOR OPEN
LEFT REAR QTR CLOSE
LEFT REAR QTR OPEN

© G.M. Corp.

LEFT FRONT DOOR ARMREST

## 1969—CADILLAC DEVILLE CONVERTIBLE

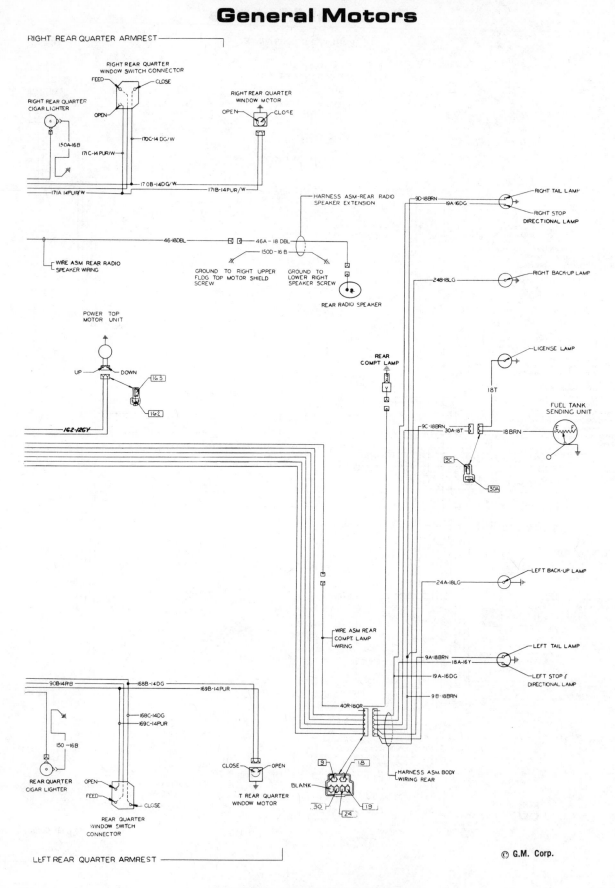

## General Motors

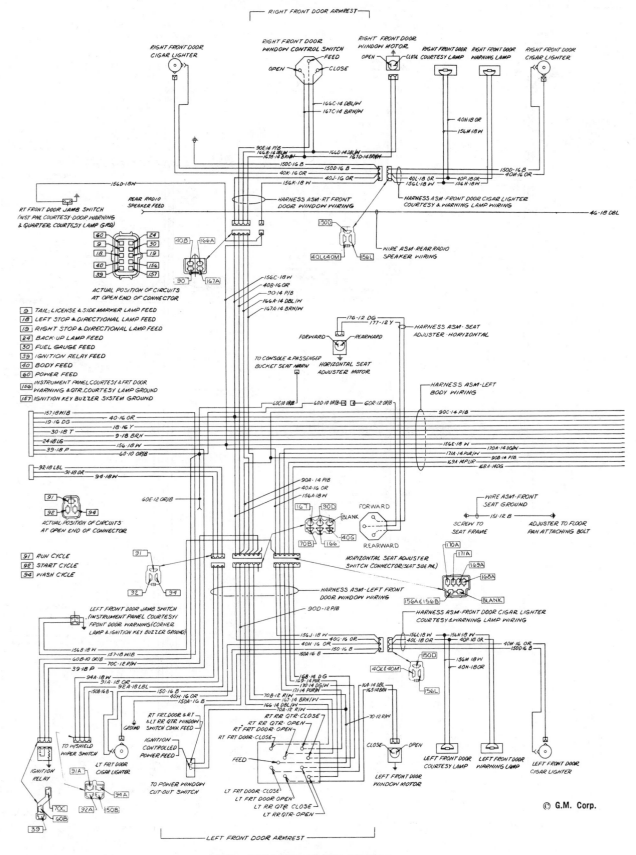

1969—CADILLAC COUPE DEVILLE

© G.M. Corp.

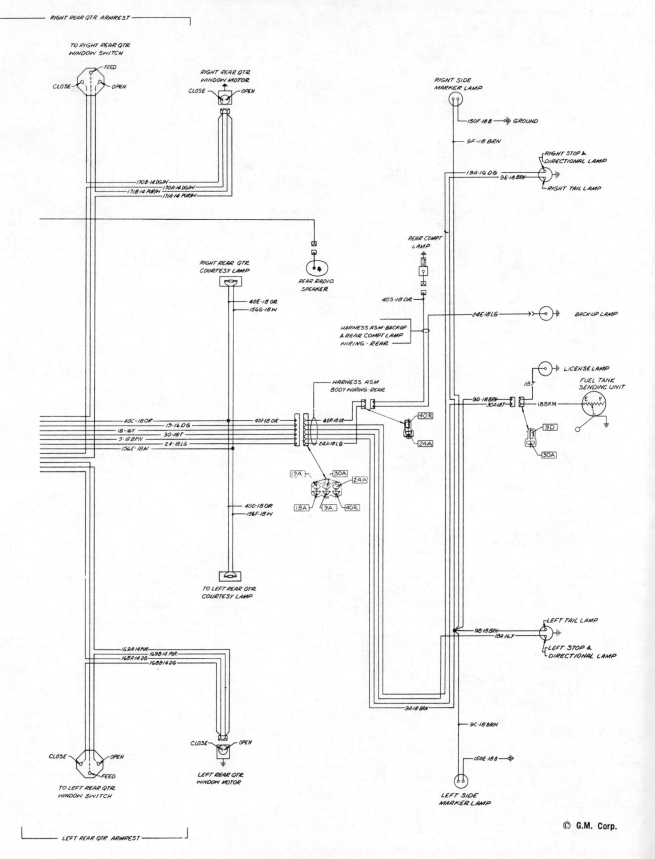

## 1969—CADILLAC COUPE DEVILLE

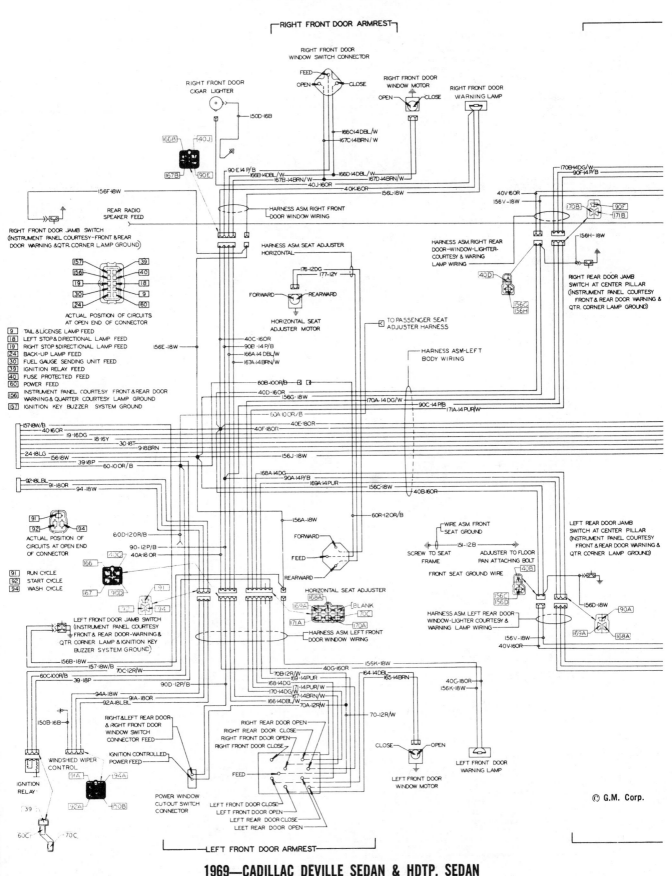

**1969—CADILLAC DEVILLE SEDAN & HDTP. SEDAN**

© G.M. Corp.

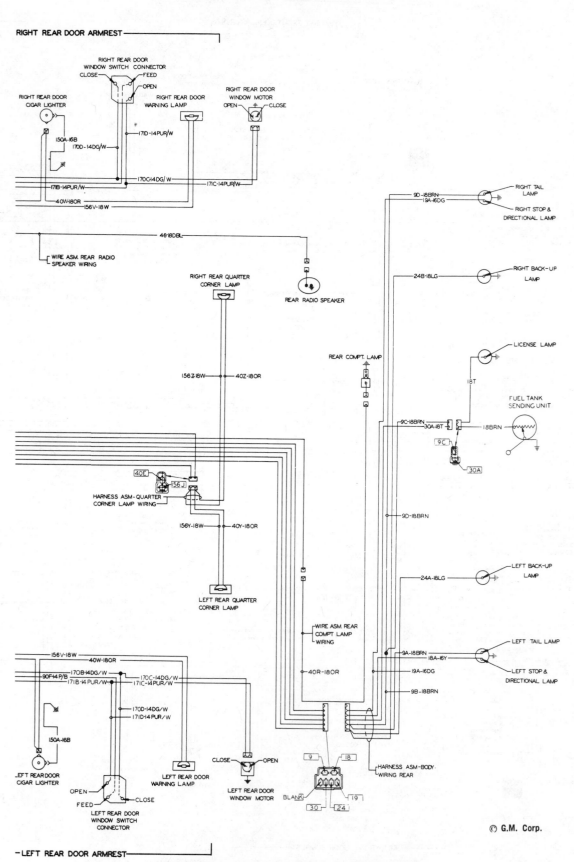

**1969—CADILLAC DEVILLE SEDAN & HDTP. SEDAN**

© G.M. Corp.

# General Motors

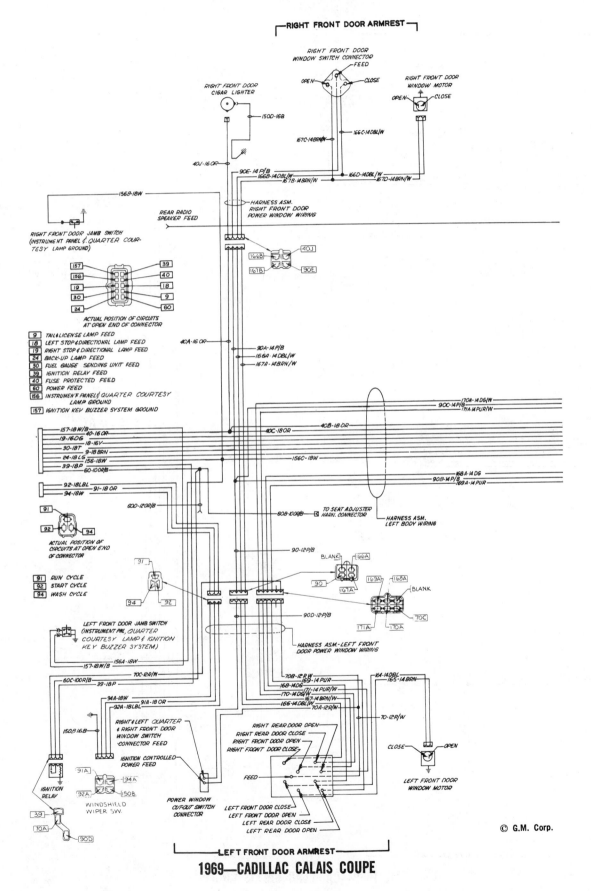

RIGHT FRONT DOOR ARMREST

RIGHT FRONT DOOR
WINDOW SWITCH CONNECTOR
FEED

RIGHT FRONT DOOR
WINDOW MOTOR

RIGHT FRONT DOOR
CIGAR LIGHTER

OPEN    CLOSE

OPEN    CLOSE

150D-16B

167C-14BRN/W    166C-14DBL/W

40J-16 OR

90E-14 P/B
166B-14DBL/W
167B-14BRN/W

166D-14DBL/W    167D-14BRN/W

156B-18W

HARNESS ASM.
RIGHT FRONT DOOR
POWER WINDOW WIRING

REAR RADIO
SPEAKER FEED

RIGHT FRONT DOOR JAMB SWITCH
(INSTRUMENT PANEL & QUARTER COUR-
TESY LAMP GROUND)

166B    40J

161B    90E

| 157 | | 39 |
| 156 | | 40 |
| 19 | | 18 |
| 30 | | 9 |
| 24 | | 60 |

ACTUAL POSITION OF CIRCUITS
AT OPEN END OF CONNECTOR

4CA-16 OR

90A-14 P/B
166A-14DBL/W
167A-14BRN/W

9    TAIL & LICENSE LAMP FEED
18    LEFT STOP & DIRECTIONAL LAMP FEED
19    RIGHT STOP & DIRECTIONAL LAMP FEED
24    BACK-UP LAMP FEED
30    FUEL GAUGE SENDING UNIT FEED
39    IGNITION RELAY FEED
40    FUSE PROTECTED FEED
60    POWER FEED
156    INSTRUMENT PANEL & QUARTER COURTESY
LAMP GROUND
157    IGNITION KEY BUZZER SYSTEM GROUND

90C-14P/B    170A-14 DG/W
171A-14 PUR/W

157-18 W/B
19-16 DG
30-18 T
24-18 LS
39-18 P
92-18 LBL
94-18 W

40-16 OR
18-16 Y
9-18 BRN
156-18W
60-100 R/B
91-18 OR

40C-18 OR    40B-18 OR

156C-18W

168A-14 DG
90B-14P/B
169A-14 PUR

91

92    94

ACTUAL POSITION OF
CIRCUITS AT OPEN END
OF CONNECTOR

91    RUN CYCLE
92    START CYCLE
94    WASH CYCLE

60D-12OR/B

60B-100R/B

TO SEAT ADJUSTER
HARN. CONNECTOR

HARNESS ASM.
LEFT BODY WIRING

90-12P/B

BLANK    166A

90

169A    168A

167A

BLANK

94    92

171A    170A    70C

LEFT FRONT DOOR JAMB SWITCH
(INSTRUMENT PNL, QUARTER
COURTESY LAMP & IGNITION
KEY BUZZER SYSTEM)

90D-12P/B

HARNESS ASM.-LEFT FRONT
DOOR POWER WINDOW WIRING

157-18W/B    156A-18W

70C-12R/W

60C-100R/B    39-18P

9A-18W    91A-18 OR
92A-18LBL

150B,16B

RIGHT & LEFT QUARTER
& RIGHT FRONT DOOR
WINDOW SWITCH
CONNECTOR FEED

IGNITION CONTROLLED
POWER FEED

91A

94A

92A    150B

IGNITION
RELAY

39

70A

90D

WINDSHIELD
WIPER SW.

POWER WINDOW
CUT-OUT SWITCH
CONNECTOR

70B-12 R/W    164-14DBL
169-14 PUR    165-14 BRN
168-14 DG
170-14 DG/W    171-14 PUR/W
167-14 BRN/W
166-14 DBL/W    70A-12R/W

RIGHT REAR DOOR OPEN
RIGHT REAR DOOR CLOSE
RIGHT FRONT DOOR OPEN
RIGHT FRONT DOOR CLOSE

70-12R/W

FEED

CLOSE    OPEN

LEFT FRONT DOOR
WINDOW MOTOR

LEFT FRONT DOOR CLOSE
LEFT FRONT DOOR OPEN
LEFT REAR DOOR CLOSE
LEFT REAR DOOR OPEN

© G.M. Corp.

LEFT FRONT DOOR ARMREST

## 1969—CADILLAC CALAIS COUPE

# General Motors

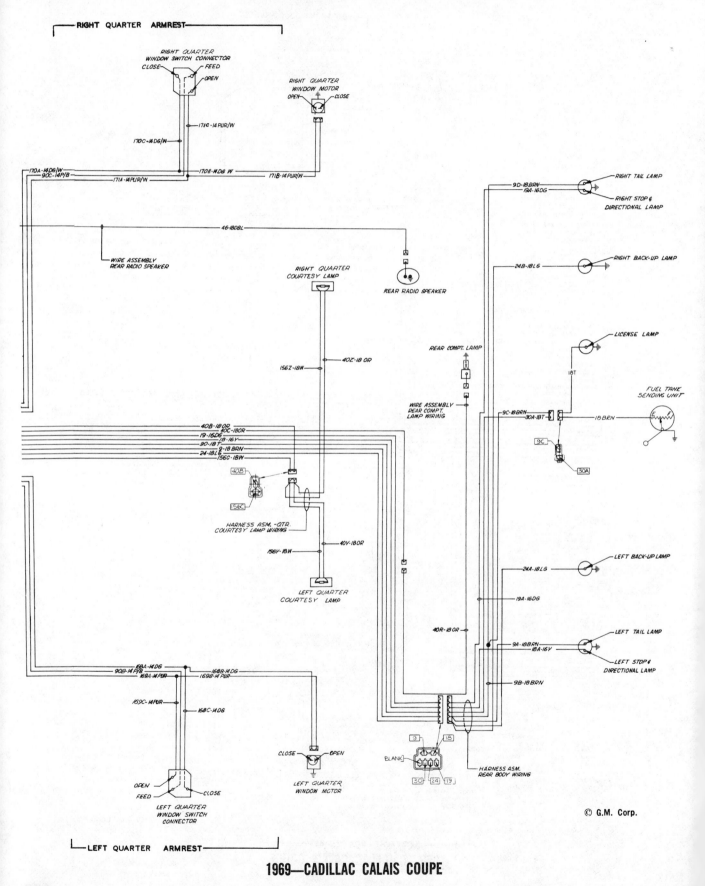

**1969—CADILLAC CALAIS COUPE**

© G.M. Corp.

# General Motors

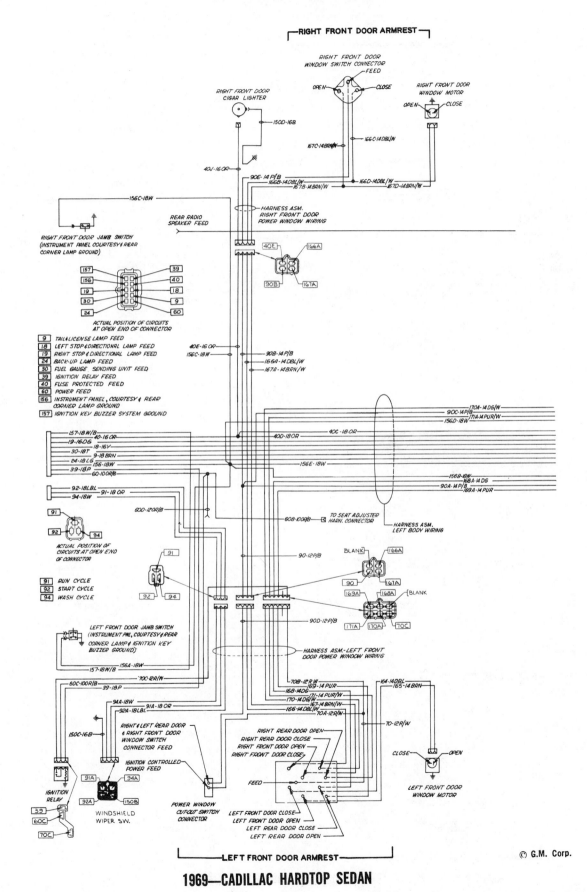

1969—CADILLAC HARDTOP SEDAN

© G.M. Corp.

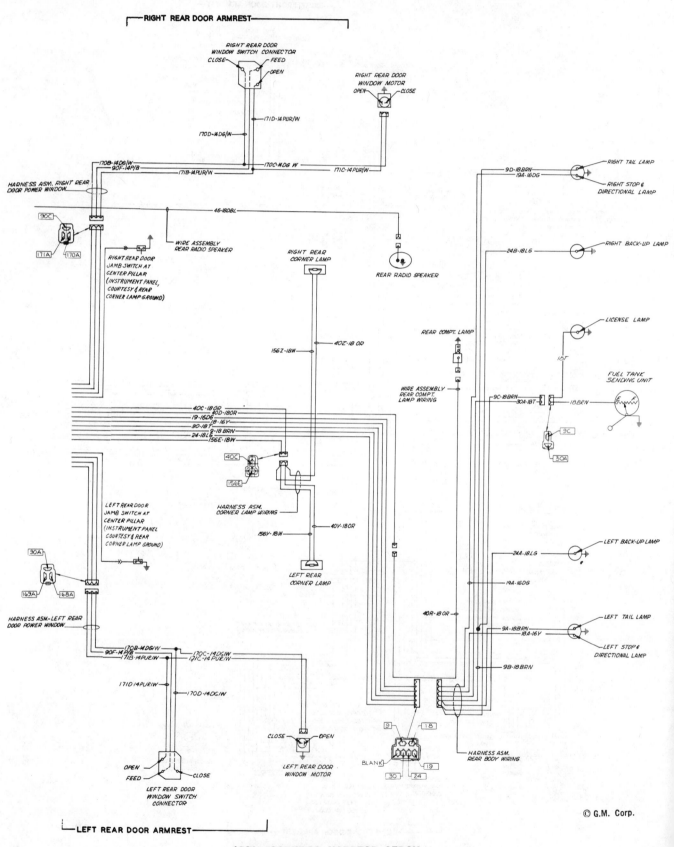

## 1969—CADILLAC HARDTOP SEDAN

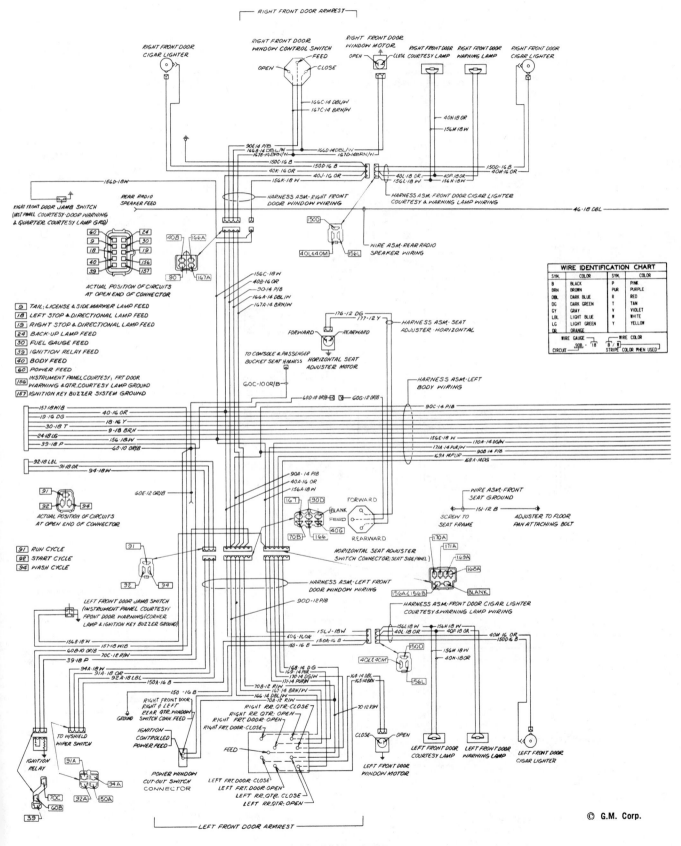

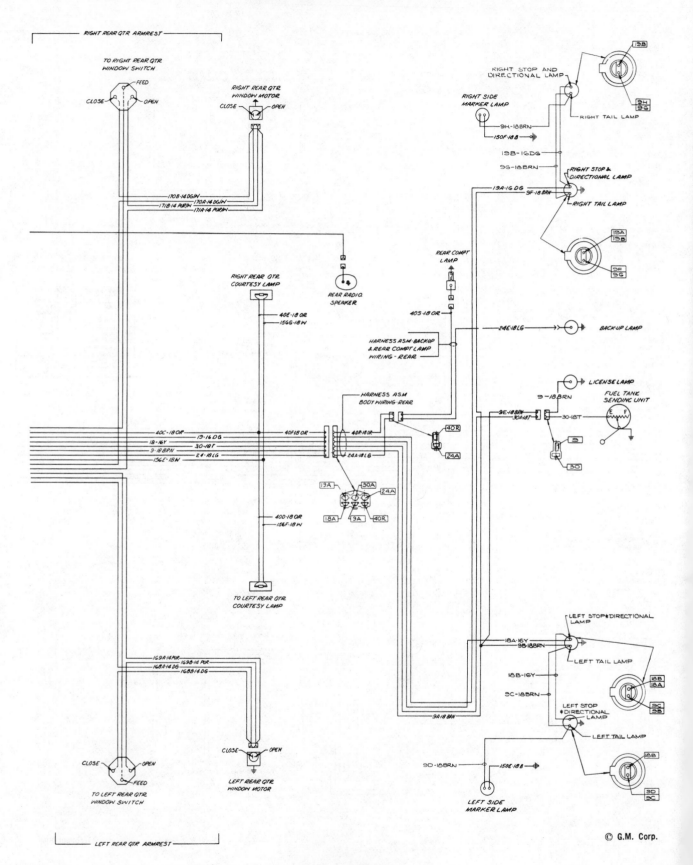

## 1970 —ELDORADO

# Power Window Wiring

## General Motors

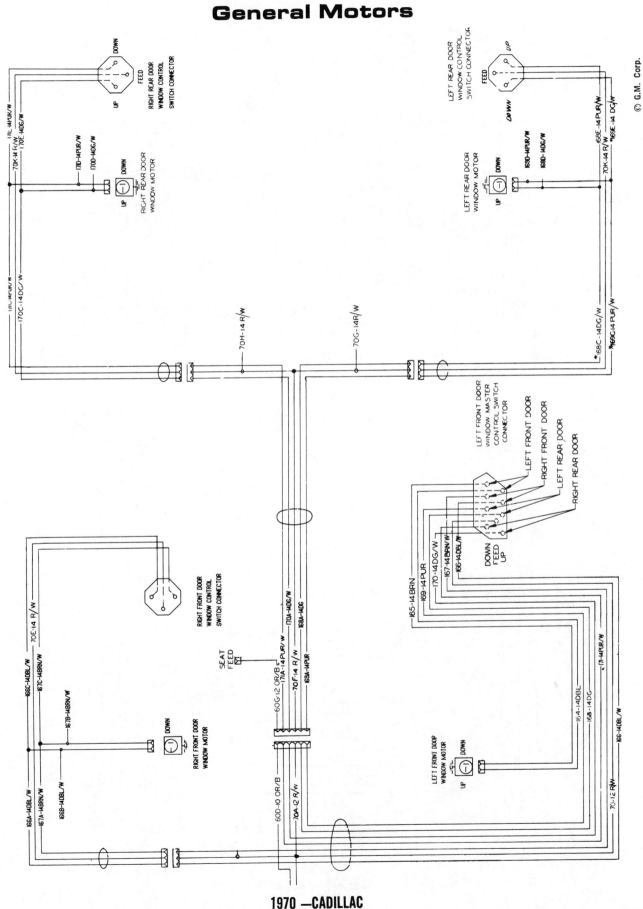

© G.M. Corp.

**1970 —CADILLAC**

## General Motors

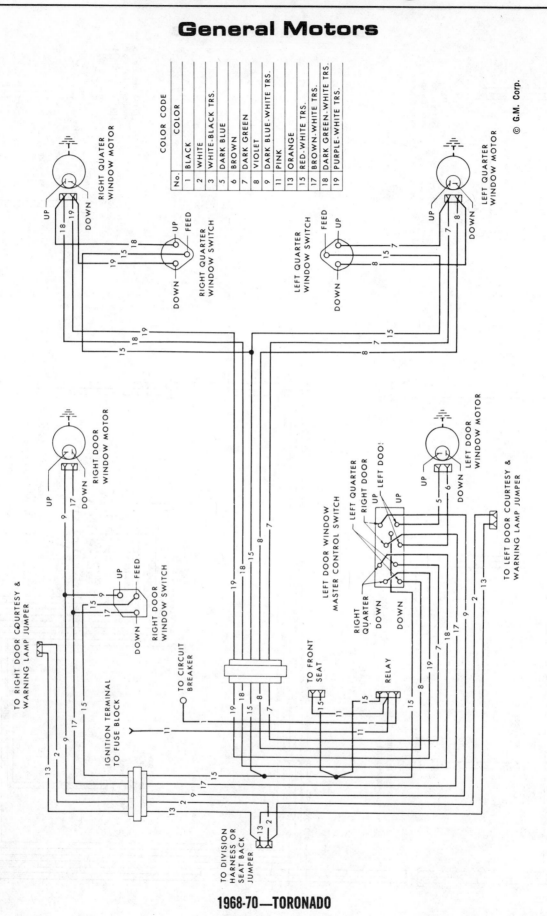

| No. | COLOR |
|-----|-------|
| 1 | BLACK |
| 2 | WHITE |
| 3 | WHITE-BLACK TRS. |
| 5 | DARK BLUE |
| 6 | BROWN |
| 7 | DARK GREEN |
| 8 | VIOLET |
| 9 | DARK BLUE-WHITE TRS. |
| 11 | PINK |
| 13 | ORANGE |
| 15 | RED-WHITE TRS. |
| 17 | BROWN-WHITE TRS. |
| 18 | DARK GREEN-WHITE TRS. |
| 19 | PURPLE-WHITE TRS. |

COLOR CODE

© G.M. Corp.

**1968-70—TORONADO**

## General Motors

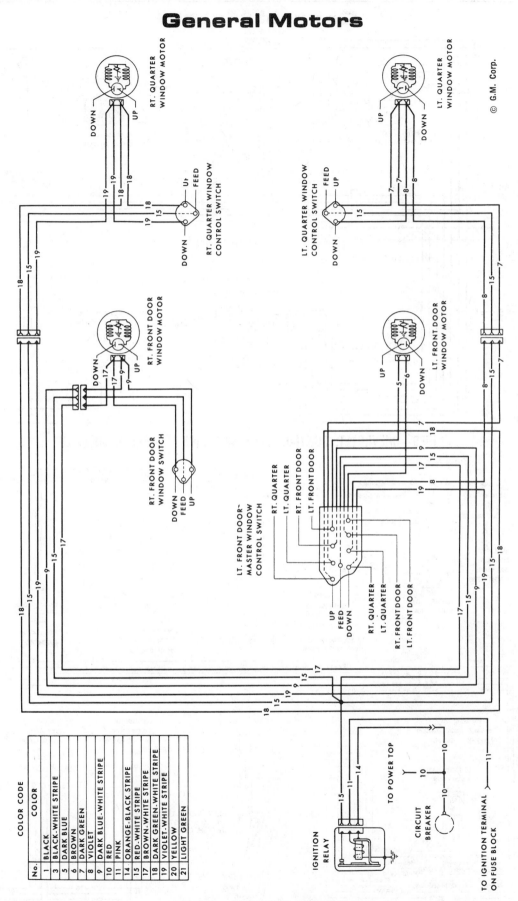

© G.M. Corp.

**1968-70—CAMARO & FIREBIRD**

| No. | COLOR |
|---|---|
| 1 | BLACK |
| 3 | BLACK-WHITE STRIPE |
| 5 | DARK BLUE |
| 6 | BROWN |
| 7 | DARK GREEN |
| 8 | VIOLET |
| 9 | DARK BLUE-WHITE STRIPE |
| 10 | RED |
| 11 | PINK |
| 14 | ORANGE-BLACK STRIPE |
| 15 | RED-WHITE STRIPE |
| 17 | BROWN-WHITE STRIPE |
| 18 | DARK GREEN-WHITE STRIPE |
| 19 | VIOLET-WHITE STRIPE |
| 20 | YELLOW |
| 21 | LIGHT GREEN |

COLOR CODE

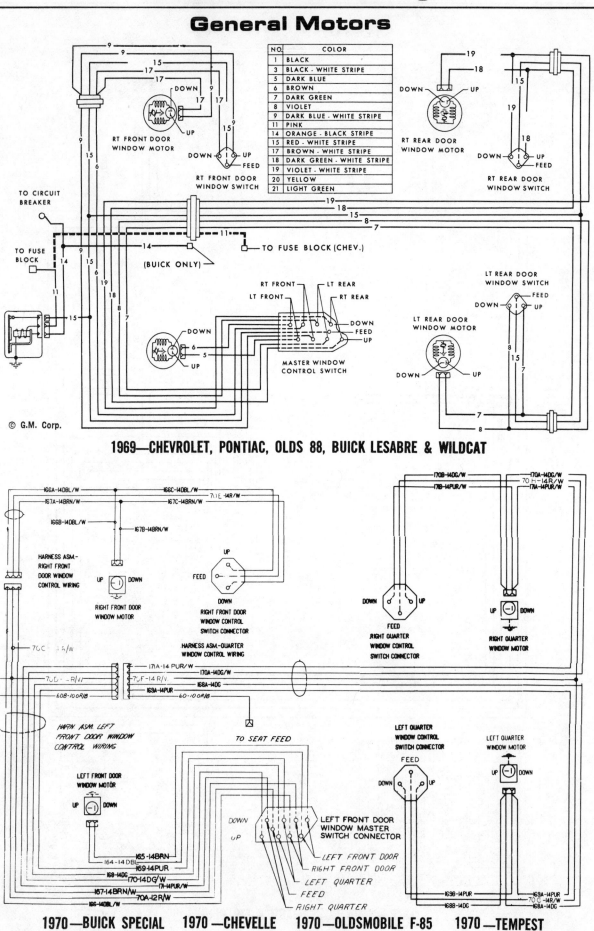

| NO. | COLOR |
|-----|-------|
| 1 | BLACK |
| 3 | BLACK - WHITE STRIPE |
| 5 | DARK BLUE |
| 6 | BROWN |
| 7 | DARK GREEN |
| 8 | VIOLET |
| 9 | DARK BLUE - WHITE STRIPE |
| 11 | PINK |
| 14 | ORANGE - BLACK STRIPE |
| 15 | RED - WHITE STRIPE |
| 17 | BROWN - WHITE STRIPE |
| 18 | DARK GREEN - WHITE STRIPE |
| 19 | VIOLET - WHITE STRIPE |
| 20 | YELLOW |
| 21 | LIGHT GREEN |

© G.M. Corp.

**1969—CHEVROLET, PONTIAC, OLDS 88, BUICK LESABRE & WILDCAT**

**1970—BUICK SPECIAL   1970—CHEVELLE   1970—OLDSMOBILE F-85   1970—TEMPEST**

## General Motors

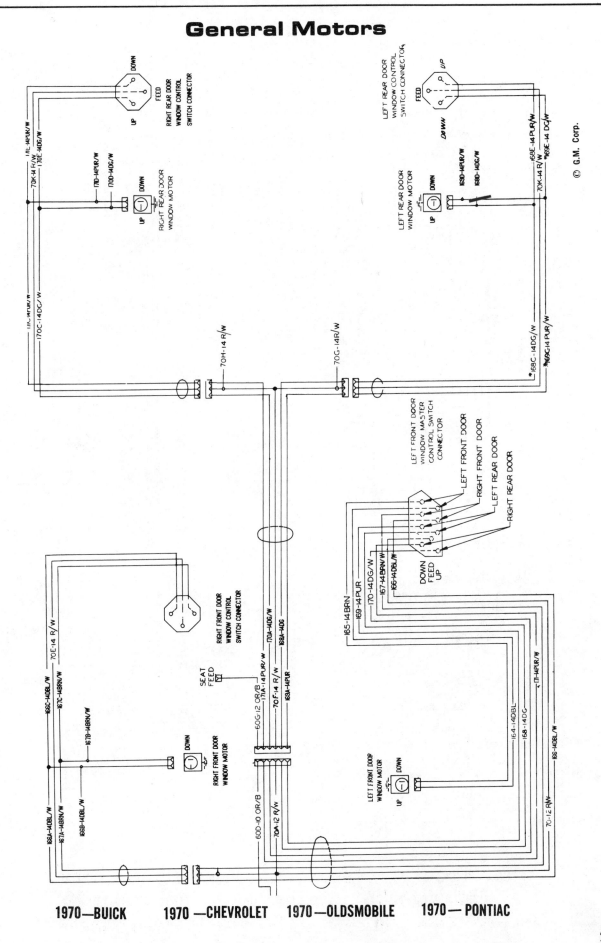

© G.M. Corp.

1970—BUICK     1970—CHEVROLET     1970—OLDSMOBILE     1970—PONTIAC

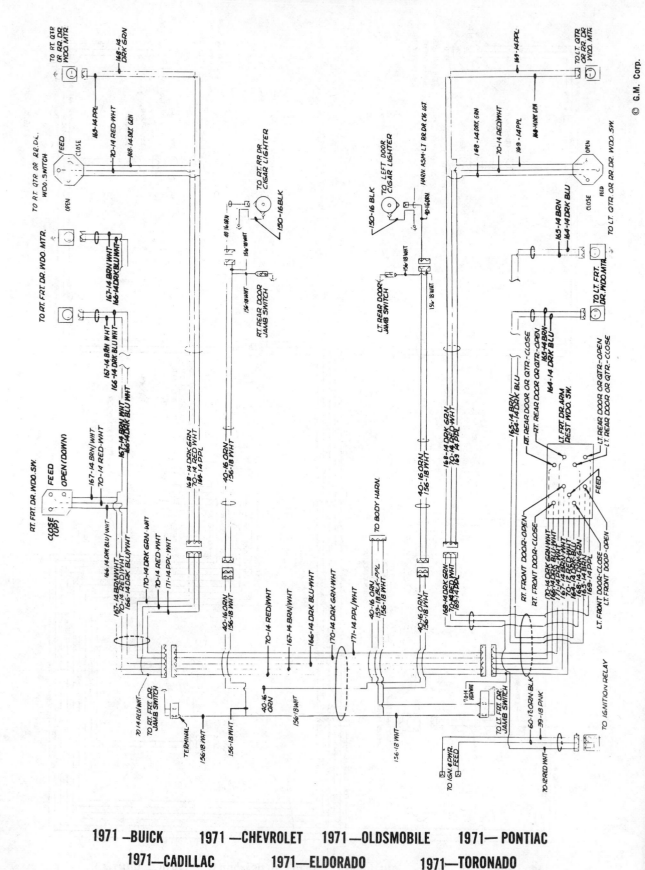

1971 —BUICK     1971 —CHEVROLET     1971 —OLDSMOBILE     1971— PONTIAC

1971—CADILLAC     1971—ELDORADO     1971—TORONADO

# Power Window Wiring

## General Motors

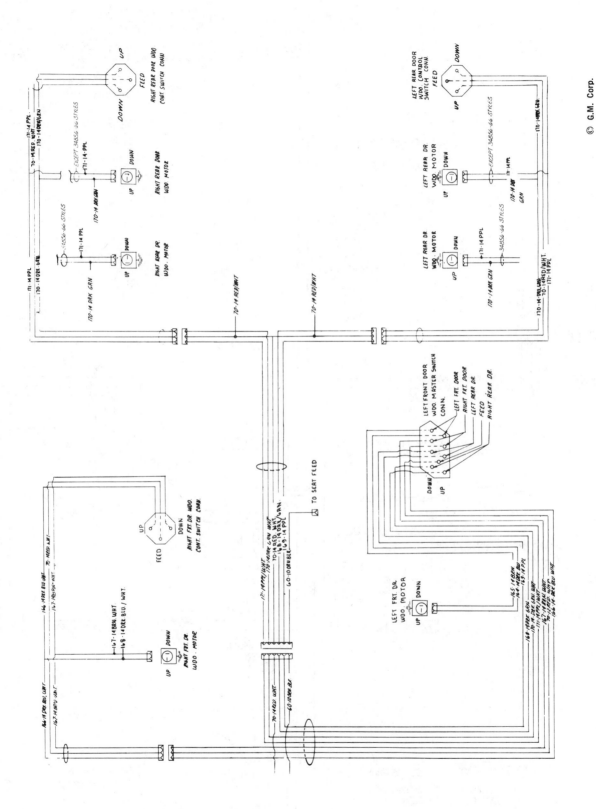

© G.M. Corp.

**1971—BUICK SPECIAL    1971—CHEVELLE    1971—OLDSMOBILE F-85    1971—TEMPEST**

## General Motors

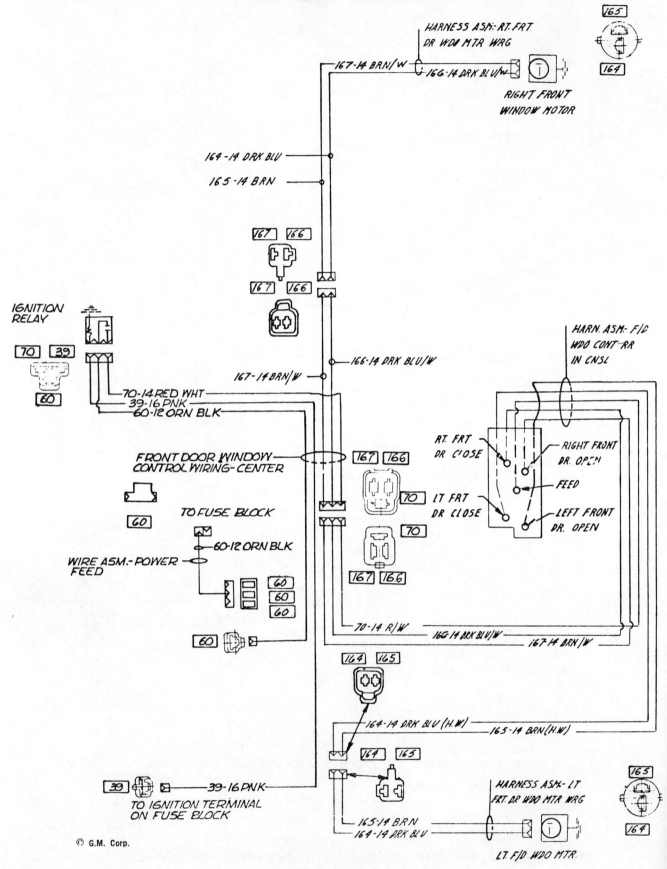

**1971 — FIREBIRD**

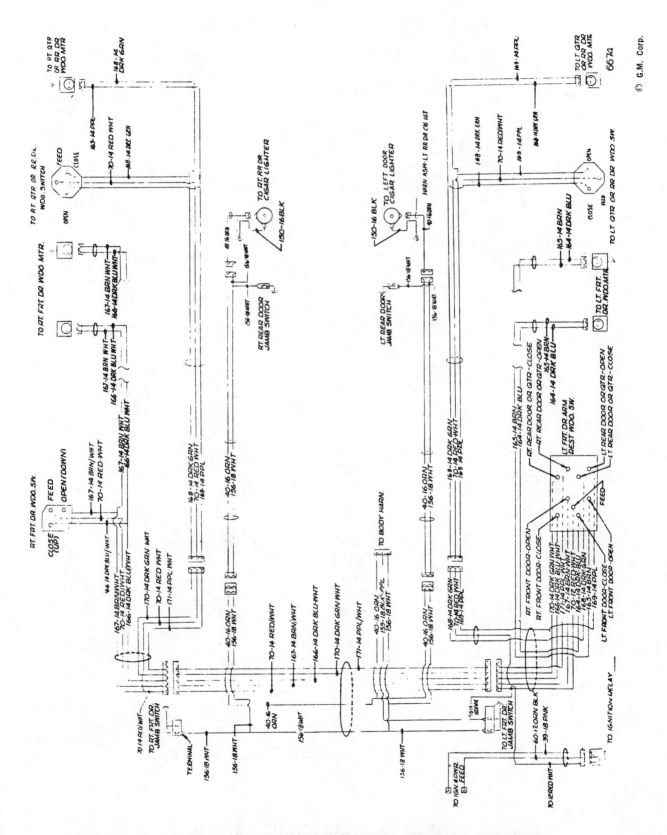

**1972-73—BUICK EXC. BUICK SPECIAL, CADILLAC, PONTIAC, CHEVROLET, OLDSMOBILE**

© G.M. Corp.

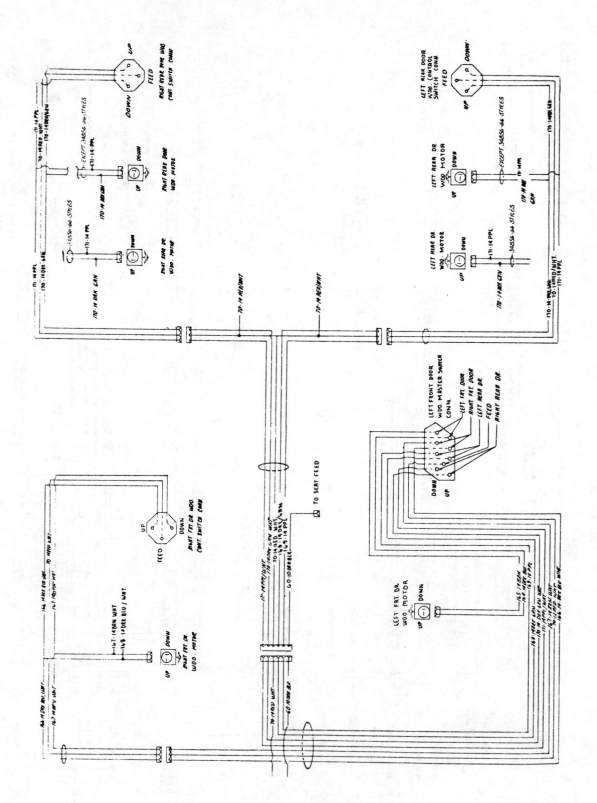

**1972—BUICK SPECIAL, CHEVELLE, F-85, LE MANS**

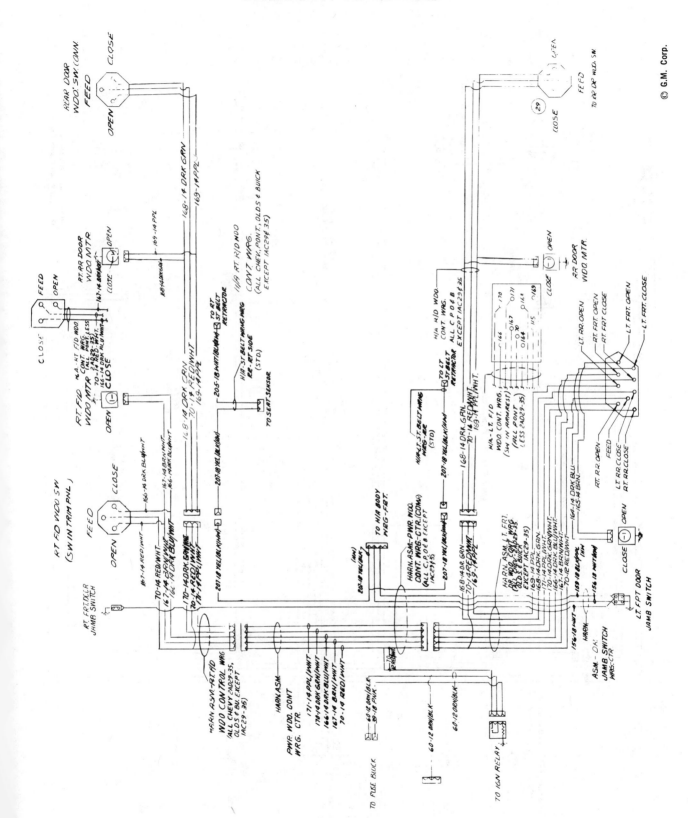

**1973—BUICK SPECIAL, CHEVELLE, F-85, LE MANS**

© G.M. Corp.

© G.M. Corp.

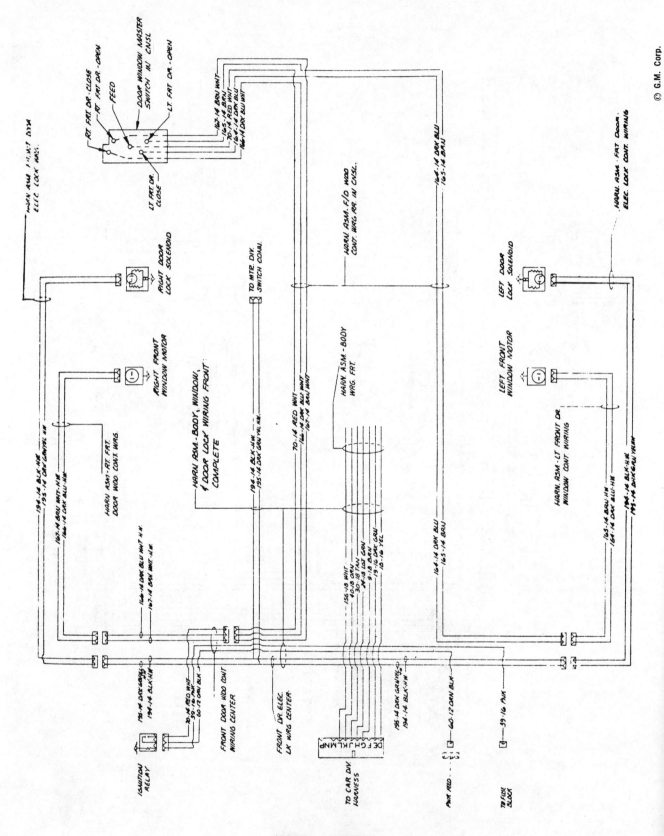

**1972-73 —FIREBIRD**

## General Motors

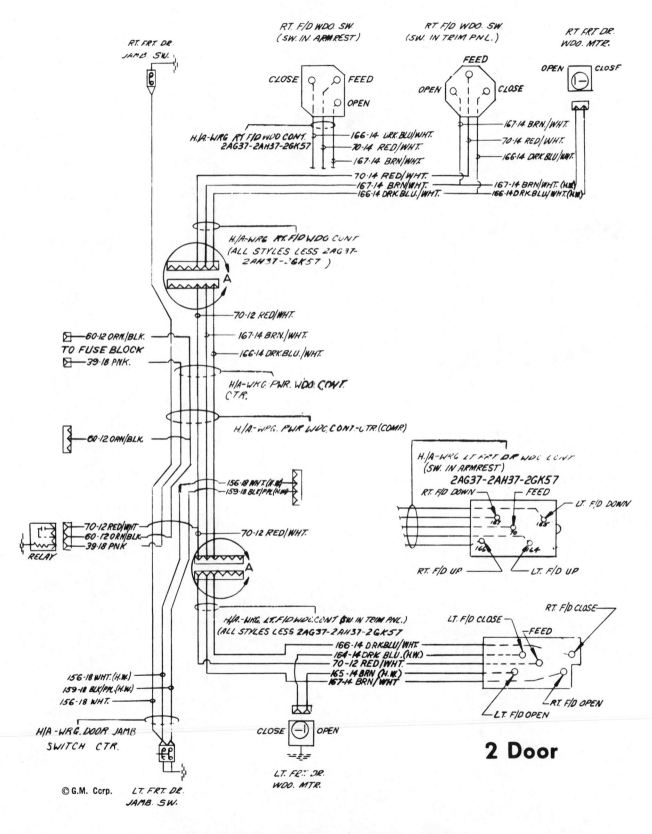

**1974 LE MANS— CUTLASS —CHEVELLE—CENTURY**

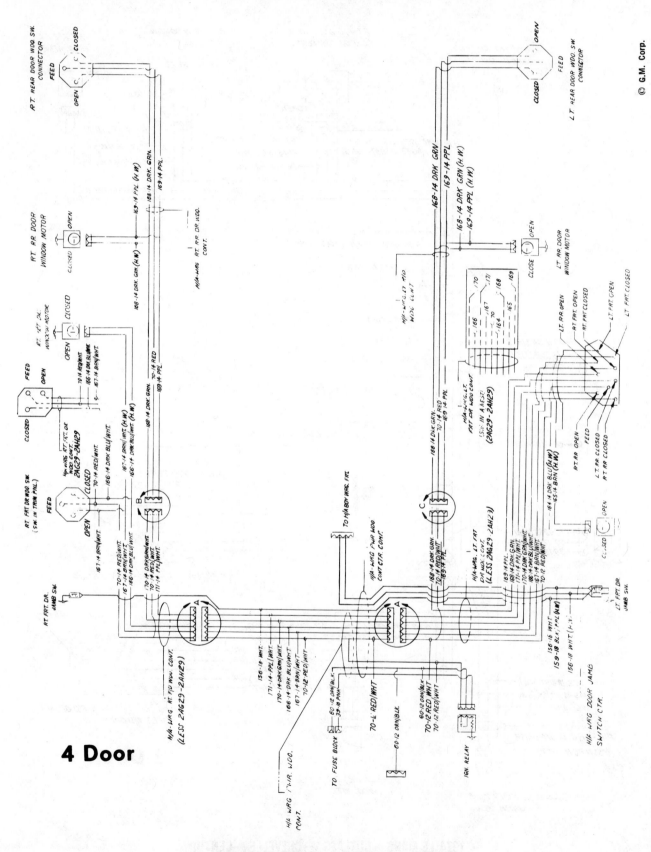

**4 Door**

**1974 LE MANS — CUTLASS — CHEVELLE — CENTURY**

## General Motors

© G.M. Corp.

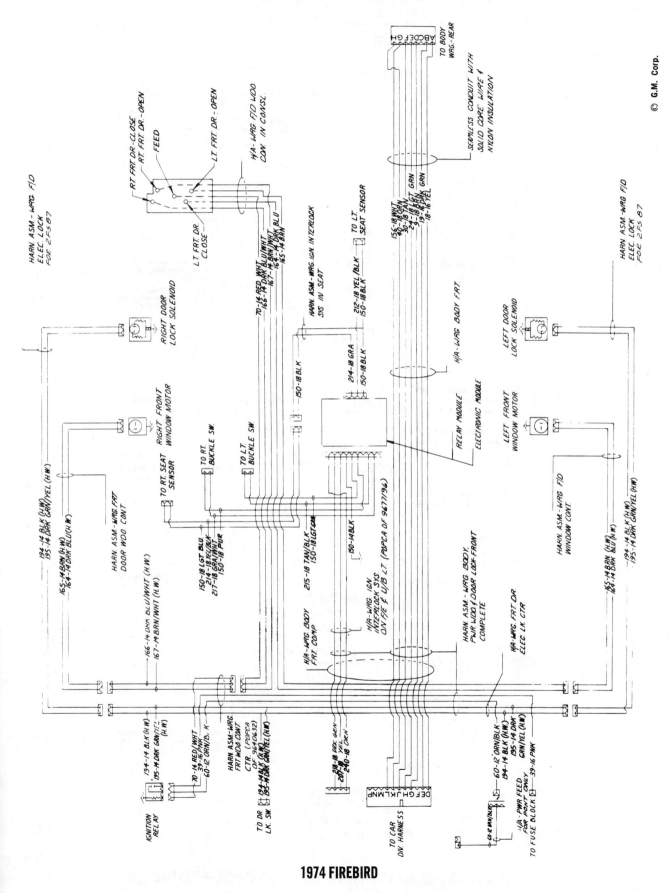

**1974 FIREBIRD**

## General Motors

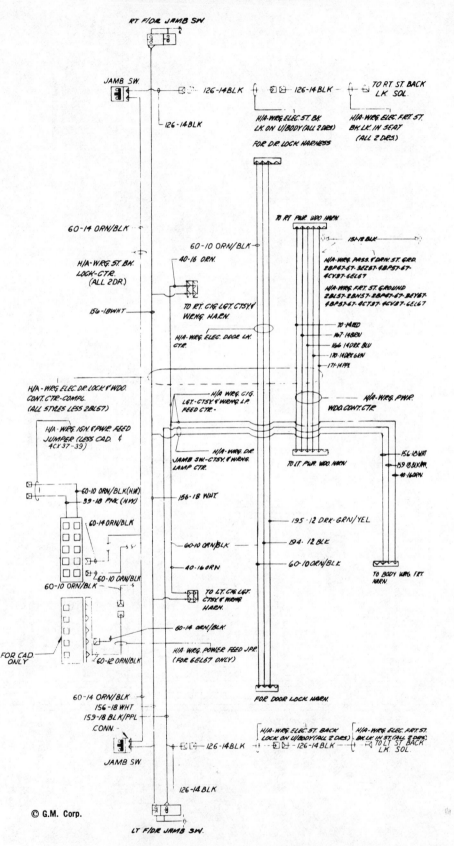

**1974 BUICK—CADILLAC—CHEVROLET—OLDSMOBILE—PONTIAC**

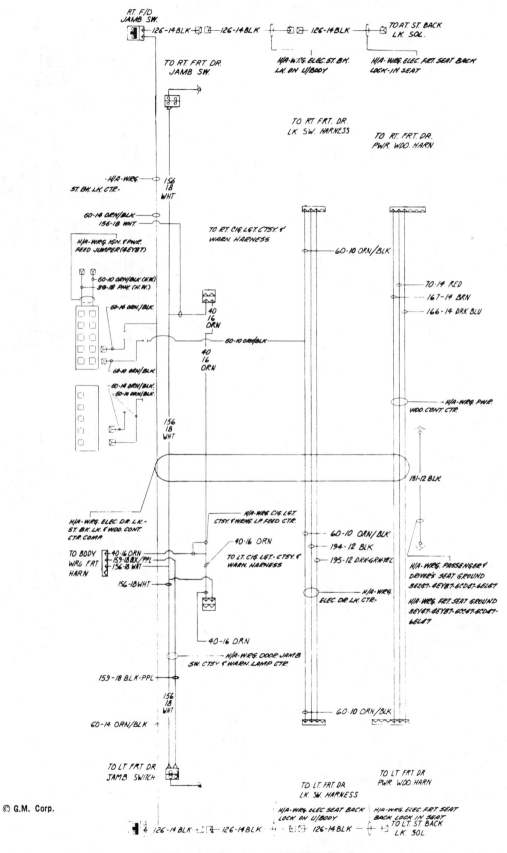

**1974 ELDORADO**

© G.M. Corp.

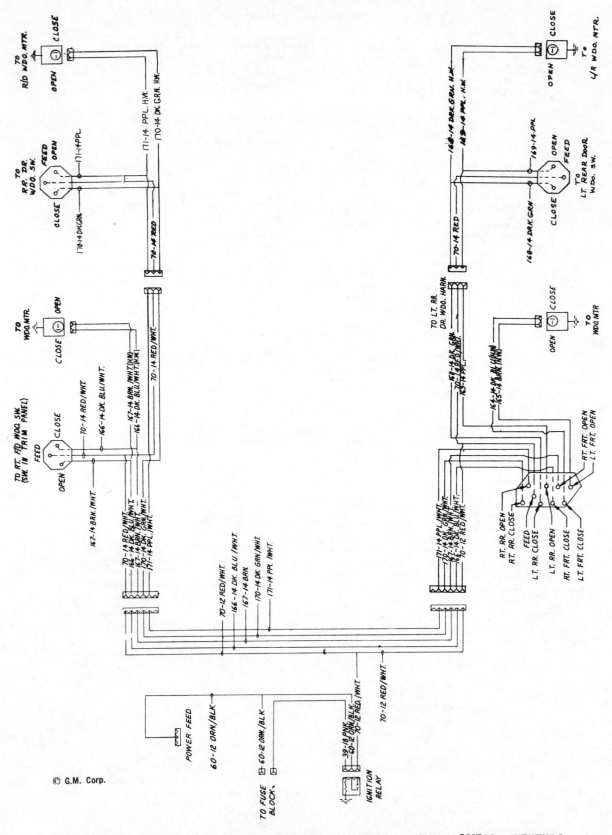

1975 APOLLO — CENTURY — CHEVELLE — CUTLASS — LE MANS — NOVA — OMEGA — VENTURA

© G.M. Corp.

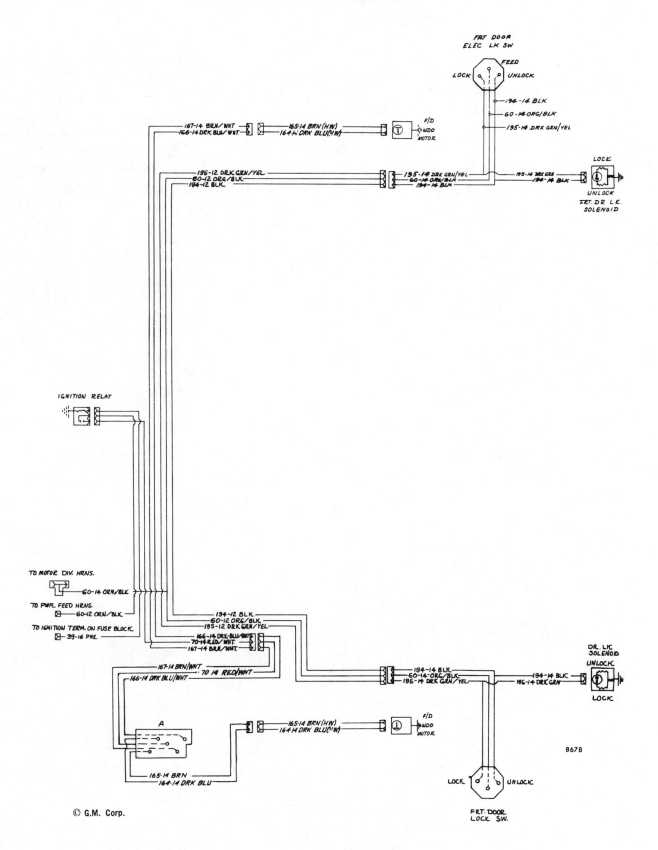

© G.M. Corp.

**1975 CAMARO**

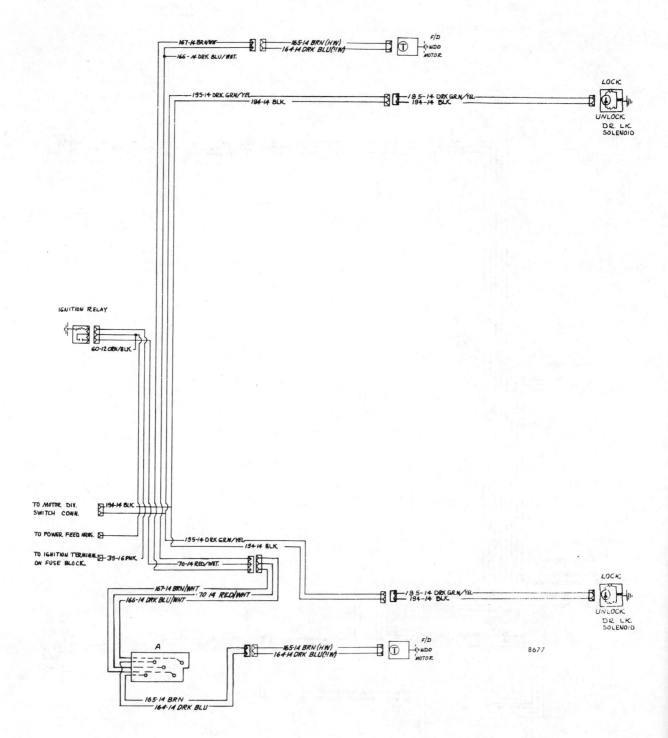

© G.M. Corp.

**1975 FIREBIRD**

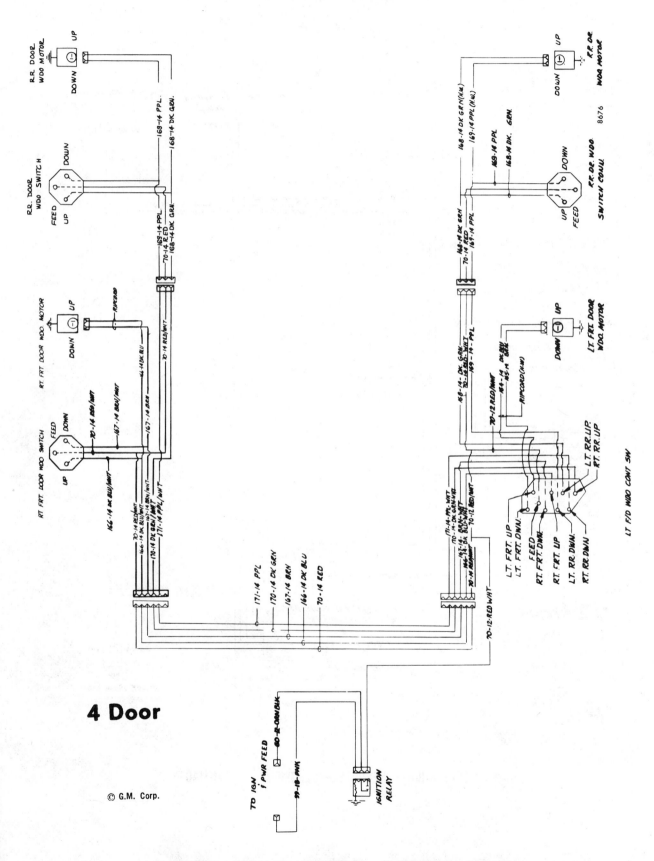

**4 Door**

© G.M. Corp.

**1975 BUICK — CADILLAC — CHEVROLET — OLDSMOBILE — PONTIAC**

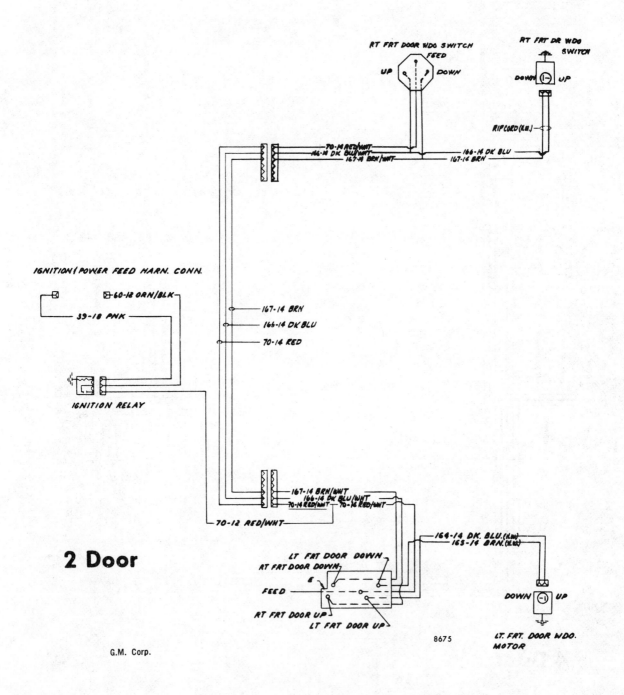

**2 Door**

G.M. Corp.

8675

**1975 BUICK—CHEVROLET—OLDSMOBILE—PONTIAC**

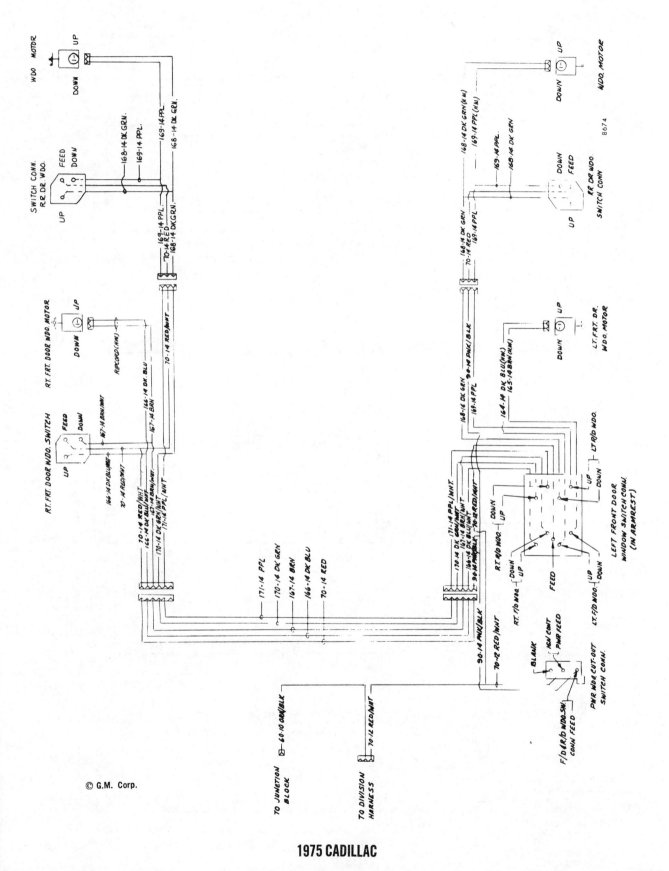

© G.M. Corp.

**1975 CADILLAC**

# Power Tailgate Window Wiring

## American Motors

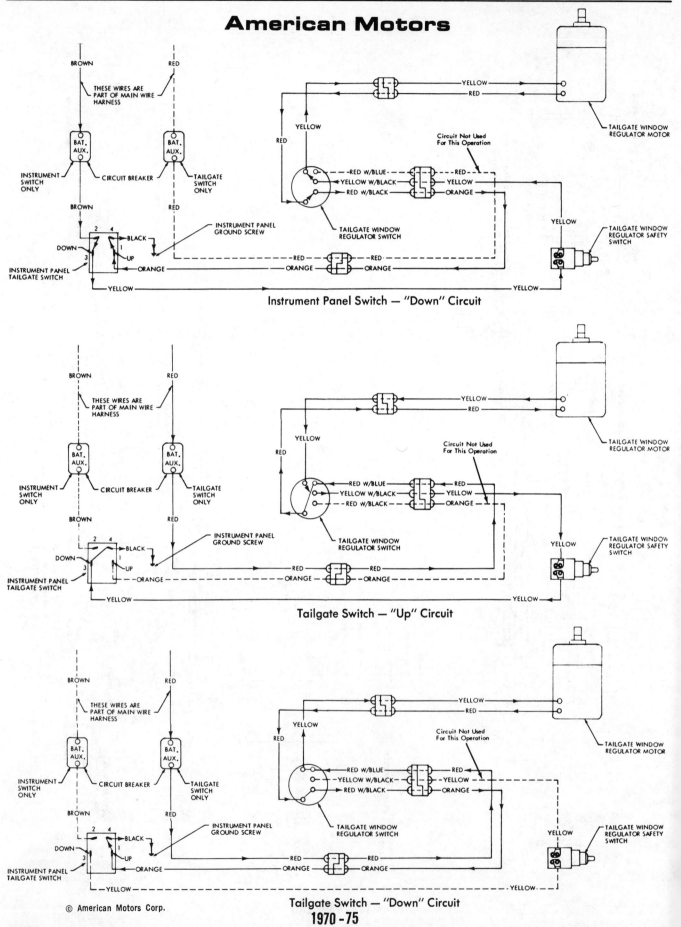

Instrument Panel Switch — "Down" Circuit

Tailgate Switch — "Up" Circuit

Tailgate Switch — "Down" Circuit
1970-75

© American Motors Corp.

## American Motors

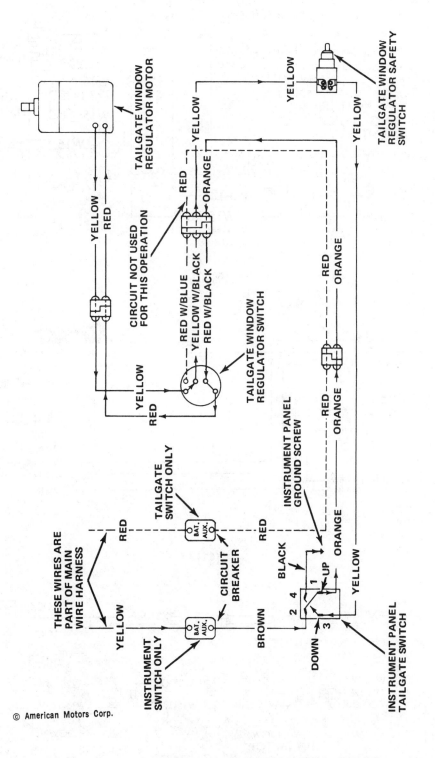

*Instrument Panel Switch—"Up" Circuit*

© American Motors Corp.

## Chrysler Corporation

## Chrysler

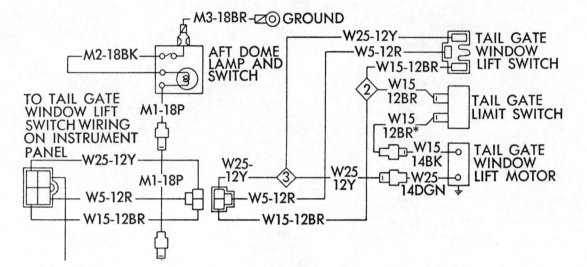

**1969-70**

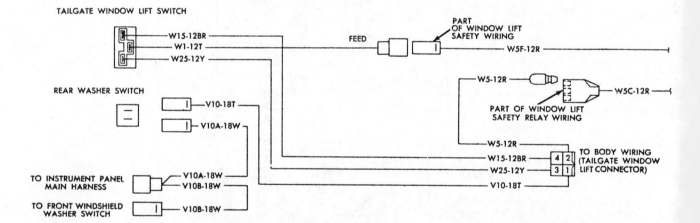

**1971**

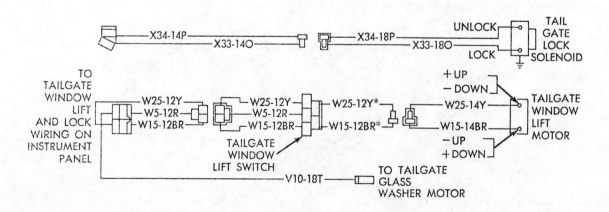

**1972**

# Power Tailgate Window Wiring

## Chrysler

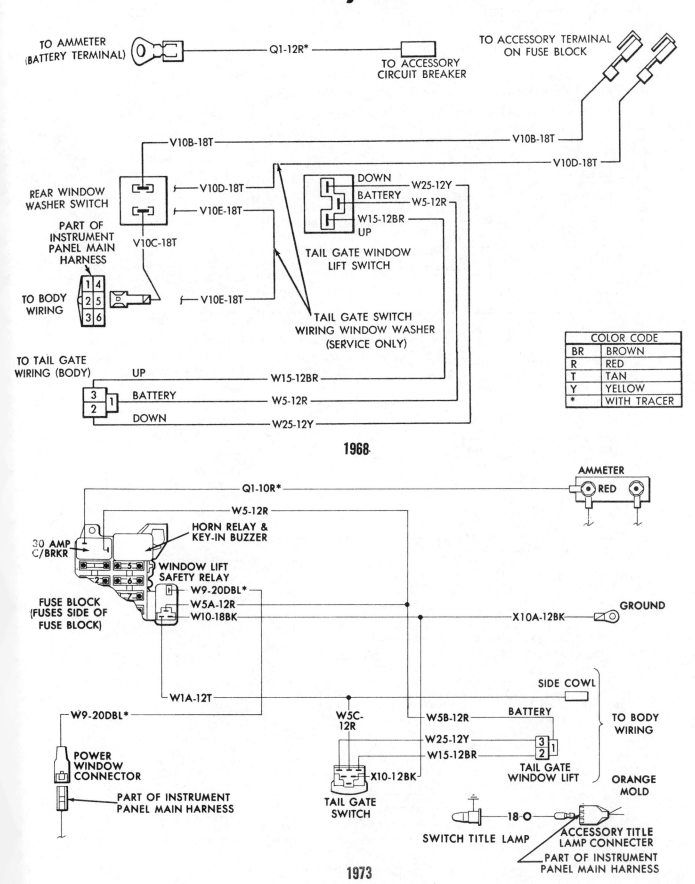

**1968**

**1973**

## Dodge

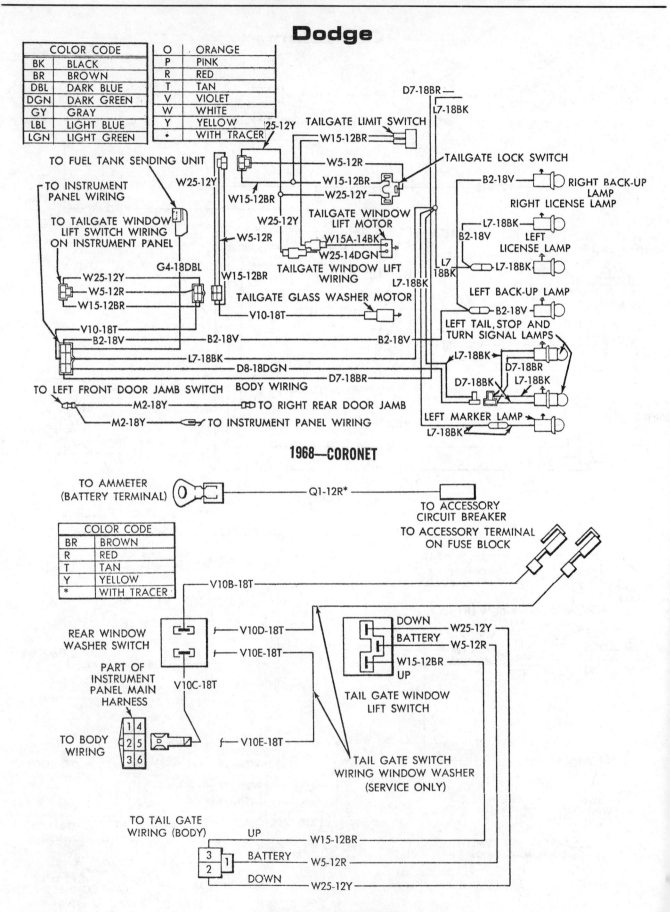

| COLOR CODE | |
|---|---|
| BK | BLACK |
| BR | BROWN |
| DBL | DARK BLUE |
| DGN | DARK GREEN |
| GY | GRAY |
| LBL | LIGHT BLUE |
| LGN | LIGHT GREEN |

| O | ORANGE |
|---|---|
| P | PINK |
| R | RED |
| T | TAN |
| V | VIOLET |
| W | WHITE |
| Y | YELLOW |
| * | WITH TRACER |

TO FUEL TANK SENDING UNIT

TO INSTRUMENT PANEL WIRING

TO TAILGATE WINDOW LIFT SWITCH WIRING ON INSTRUMENT PANEL

W25-12Y

'25-12Y

W15-12BR — TAILGATE LIMIT SWITCH

W5-12R

W15-12BR — TAILGATE LOCK SWITCH

W25-12Y

W15-12BR

W25-12Y

W5-12R

TAILGATE WINDOW LIFT MOTOR

W15A-14BK

W25-14DGN

TAILGATE WINDOW LIFT WIRING

W15-12BR

TAILGATE GLASS WASHER MOTOR

V10-18T

G4-18DBL

W25-12Y

W5-12R

W15-12BR

V10-18T

B2-18V — B2-18V — B2-18V

L7-18BK

D8-18DGN

D7-18BR

BODY WIRING

TO LEFT FRONT DOOR JAMB SWITCH

M2-18Y — TO RIGHT REAR DOOR JAMB

M2-18Y — TO INSTRUMENT PANEL WIRING

D7-18BR —
L7-18BK

B2-18V — RIGHT BACK-UP LAMP
RIGHT LICENSE LAMP

L7-18BK

B2-18V — LEFT LICENSE LAMP

L7-18BK

L7-18BK

LEFT BACK-UP LAMP

B2-18V

LEFT TAIL, STOP AND TURN SIGNAL LAMPS

L7-18BK

L7-18BK

D7-18BR

D7-18BK

L7-18BK

LEFT MARKER LAMP

L7-18BK

### 1968—CORONET

TO AMMETER (BATTERY TERMINAL) — Q1-12R* — TO ACCESSORY CIRCUIT BREAKER

TO ACCESSORY TERMINAL ON FUSE BLOCK

| COLOR CODE | |
|---|---|
| BR | BROWN |
| R | RED |
| T | TAN |
| Y | YELLOW |
| * | WITH TRACER |

V10B-18T

REAR WINDOW WASHER SWITCH

V10D-18T

V10E-18T

DOWN

BATTERY

UP

W25-12Y

W5-12R

W15-12BR

TAIL GATE WINDOW LIFT SWITCH

PART OF INSTRUMENT PANEL MAIN HARNESS

V10C-18T

TO BODY WIRING

| 1 | 4 |
| 2 | 5 |
| 3 | 6 |

V10E-18T

TAIL GATE SWITCH WIRING WINDOW WASHER (SERVICE ONLY)

TO TAIL GATE WIRING (BODY)

| 3 | 1 |
| 2 | |

UP — W15-12BR

BATTERY — W5-12R

DOWN — W25-12Y

### 1968—POLARA & MONACO

## Dodge

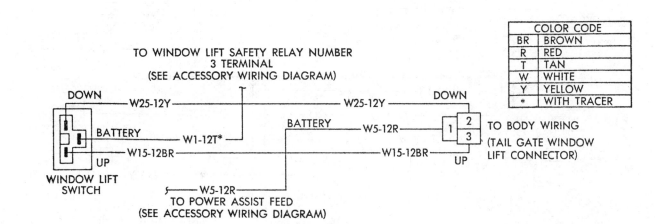

TO WINDOW LIFT SAFETY RELAY NUMBER
3 TERMINAL
(SEE ACCESSORY WIRING DIAGRAM)

DOWN — W25-12Y — W25-12Y — DOWN

BATTERY — W1-12T* — BATTERY — W5-12R

W15-12BR — W15-12BR

UP — UP

WINDOW LIFT
SWITCH

W5-12R
TO POWER ASSIST FEED
(SEE ACCESSORY WIRING DIAGRAM)

TO BODY WIRING
(TAIL GATE WINDOW
LIFT CONNECTOR)

| COLOR CODE | |
|---|---|
| BR | BROWN |
| R | RED |
| T | TAN |
| W | WHITE |
| Y | YELLOW |
| * | WITH TRACER |

**1969-70**

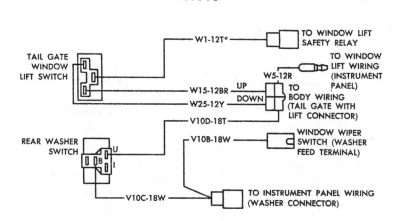

W1-12T* — TO WINDOW LIFT
SAFETY RELAY

TAIL GATE
WINDOW
LIFT SWITCH

TO WINDOW
LIFT WIRING
(INSTRUMENT
PANEL)

W5-12R

W15-12BR — UP — TO
BODY WIRING
W25-12Y — DOWN — (TAIL GATE WITH
LIFT CONNECTOR)

V10D-18T

V10B-18W — WINDOW WIPER
SWITCH (WASHER
FEED TERMINAL)

REAR WASHER
SWITCH

V10C-18W — TO INSTRUMENT PANEL WIRING
(WASHER CONNECTOR)

**1971— POLARA & MONACO —W/ REAR WINDOW WASHER**

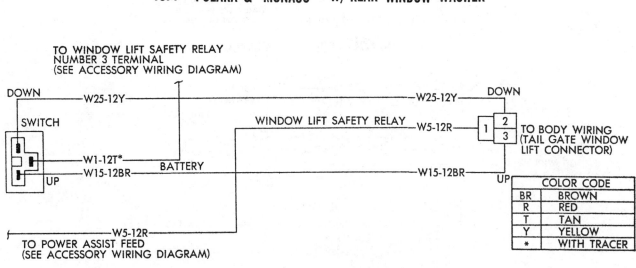

TO WINDOW LIFT SAFETY RELAY
NUMBER 3 TERMINAL
(SEE ACCESSORY WIRING DIAGRAM)

DOWN — W25-12Y — W25-12Y — DOWN

SWITCH

WINDOW LIFT SAFETY RELAY — W5-12R

W1-12T* — BATTERY

W15-12BR — W15-12BR

UP — UP

TO BODY WIRING
(TAIL GATE WINDOW
LIFT CONNECTOR)

W5-12R
TO POWER ASSIST FEED
(SEE ACCESSORY WIRING DIAGRAM)

| COLOR CODE | |
|---|---|
| BR | BROWN |
| R | RED |
| T | TAN |
| Y | YELLOW |
| * | WITH TRACER |

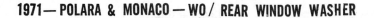

**1971— POLARA & MONACO —WO/ REAR WINDOW WASHER**

## Dodge

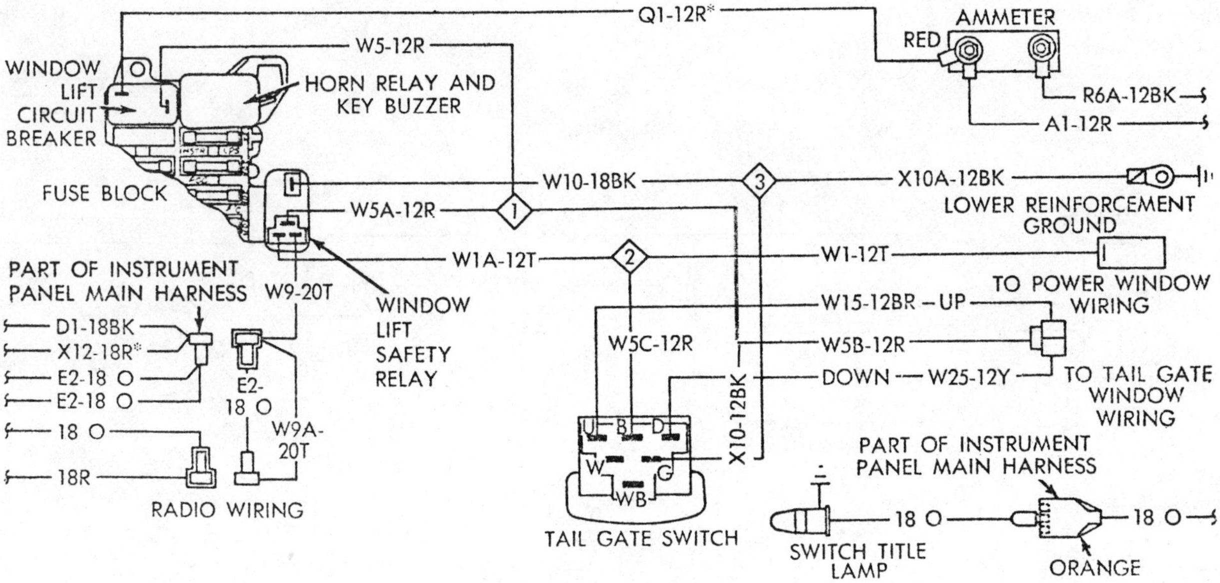

**1971—CORONET & CHARGER**

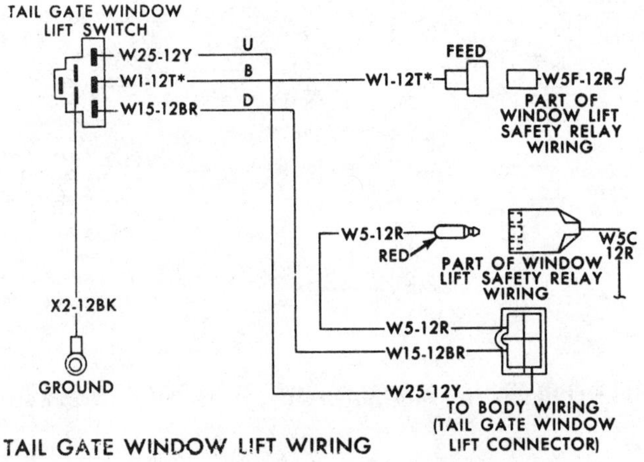

**1972-73— POLARA & MONACO**

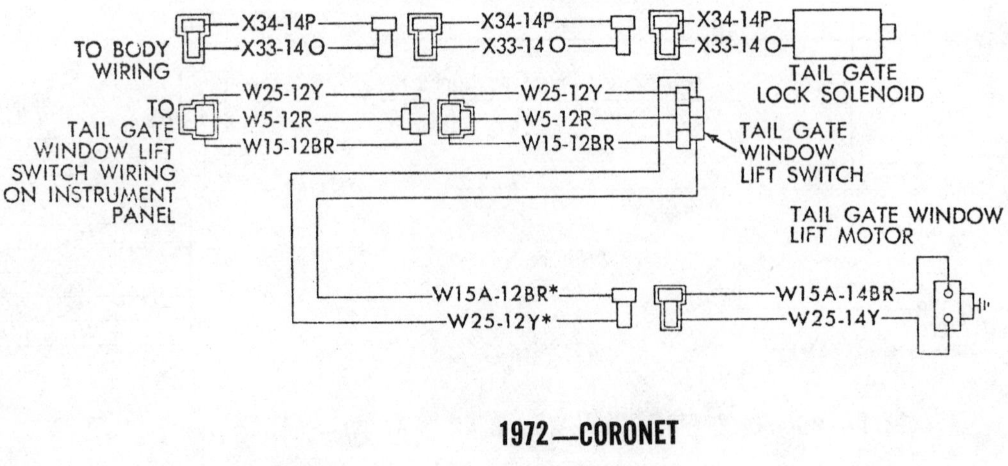

**1972—CORONET**

# Dodge

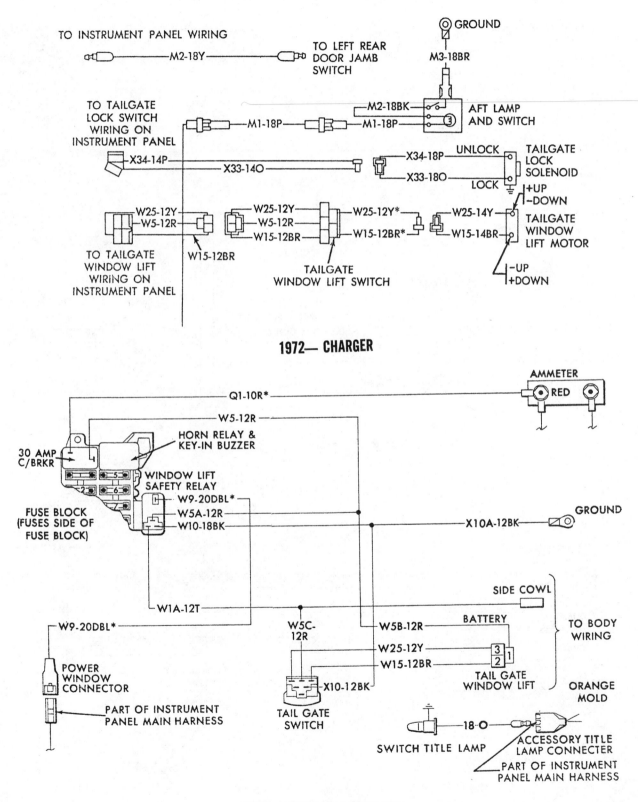

**1972— CHARGER**

**1973—CORONET & CHARGER**

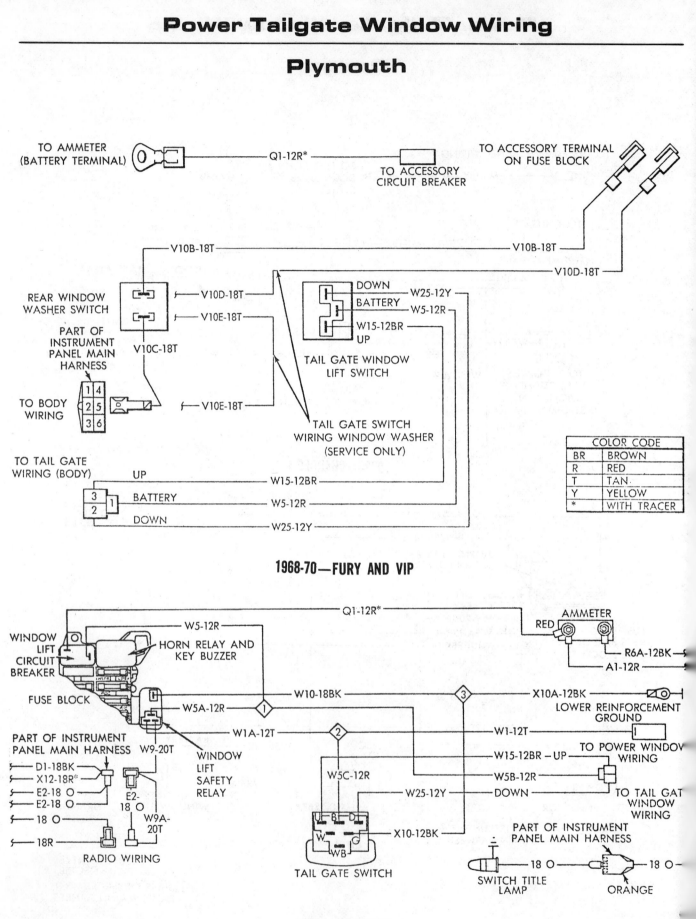

**1968-70—FURY AND VIP**

| COLOR CODE | |
|---|---|
| BR | BROWN |
| R | RED |
| T | TAN. |
| Y | YELLOW |
| * | WITH TRACER |

**1971—SATELLITE**

## Plymouth

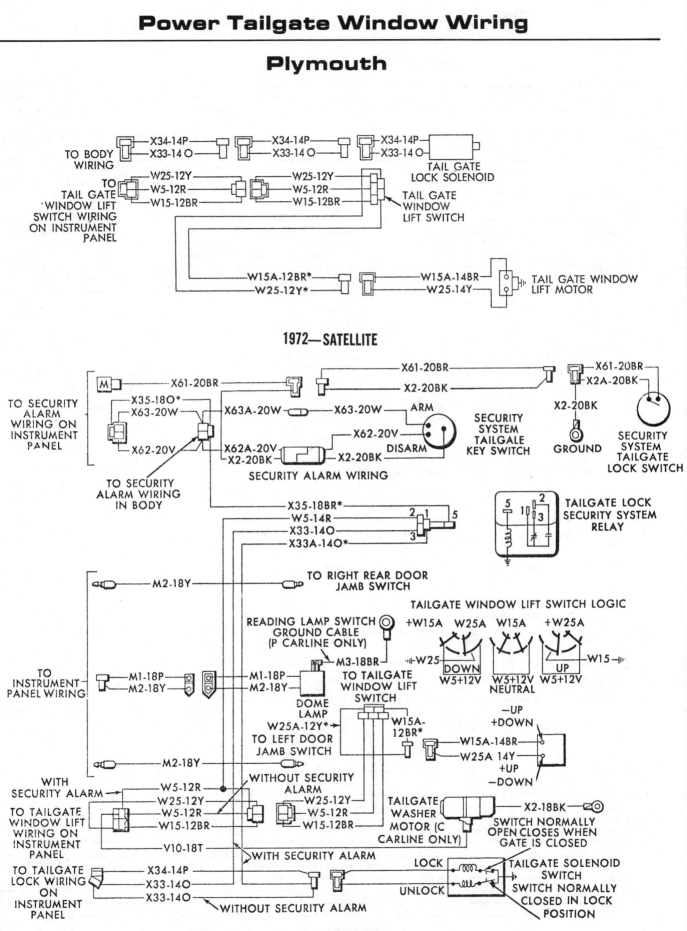

**1972—SATELLITE**

**1973**

## Chrysler Corporation

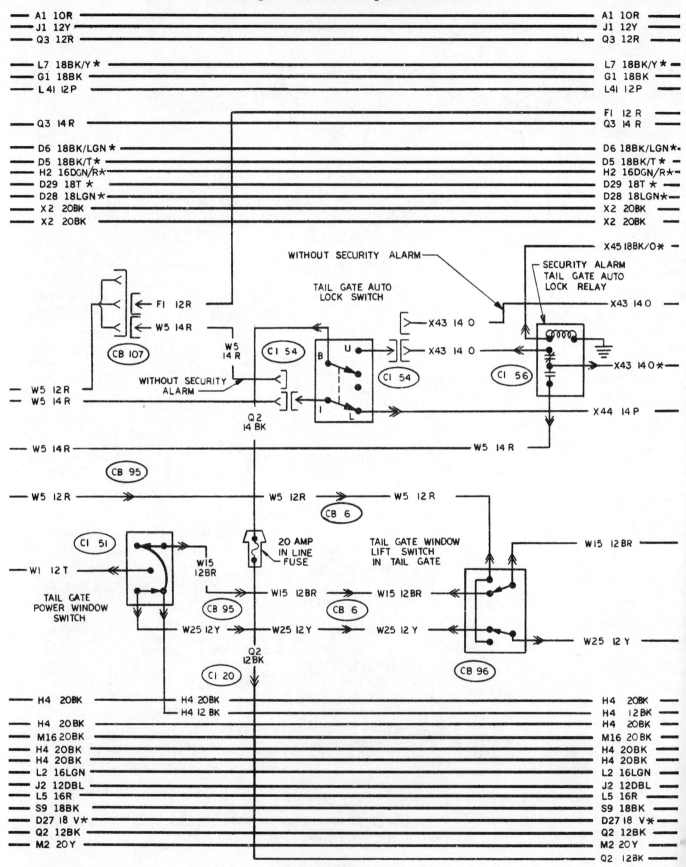

1974

## Ford Motor Company

## Falcon

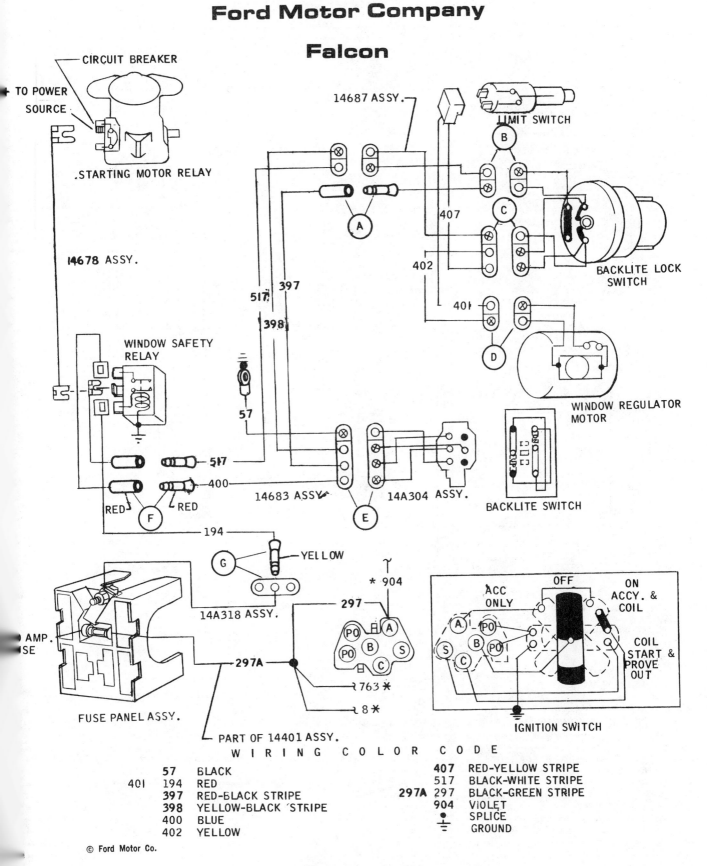

WIRING COLOR CODE

| | | | | |
|---|---|---|---|---|
| | **57** | BLACK | **407** | RED-YELLOW STRIPE |
| **401** | **194** | RED | **517** | BLACK-WHITE STRIPE |
| | **397** | RED-BLACK STRIPE | **297A 297** | BLACK-GREEN STRIPE |
| | **398** | YELLOW-BLACK STRIPE | **904** | VIOLET |
| | **400** | BLUE | ⊥ | SPLICE |
| | **402** | YELLOW | ⏚ | GROUND |

© Ford Motor Co.

**1970—Single Action**

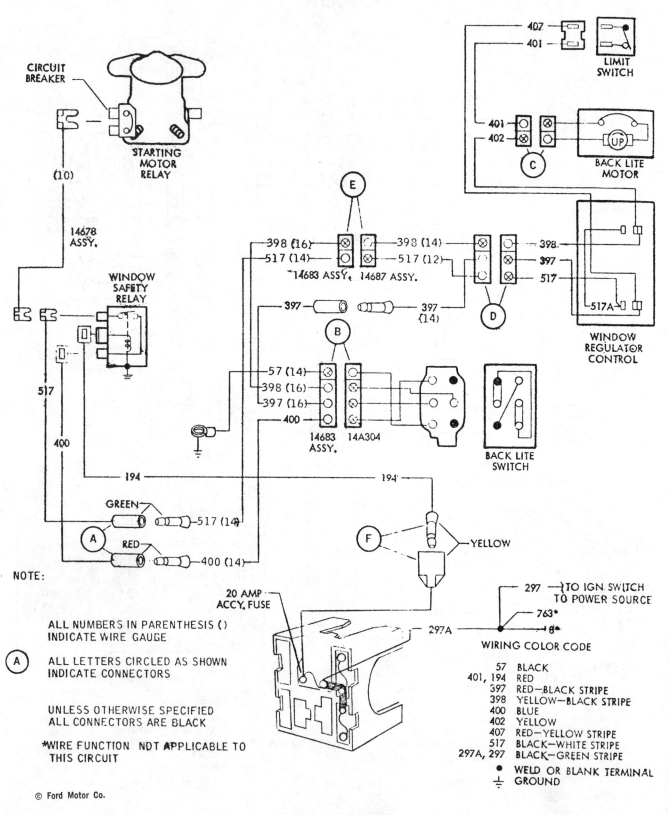

**1970—DUAL ACTION**

CIRCUIT BREAKER

STARTING MOTOR RELAY

(10)

14678 ASSY.

WINDOW SAFETY RELAY

517

400

194

GREEN

RED

517 (14)

400 (14)

A

LIMIT SWITCH

407
401

401
402

C

BACK LITE MOTOR

E

398 (16)
517 (14)

398 (14)
517 (12)

14683 ASSY.   14687 ASSY.

398
397
517

517A

WINDOW REGULATOR CONTROL

D

397

397 (14)

B

57 (14)
398 (16)
397 (16)
400

14683 ASSY.   14A304

BACK LITE SWITCH

194

F

YELLOW

20 AMP ACCY. FUSE

297   TO IGN. SWITCH
TO POWER SOURCE

763*

297A   8*

**WIRING COLOR CODE**

| | |
|---|---|
| 57 | BLACK |
| 401, 194 | RED |
| 397 | RED—BLACK STRIPE |
| 398 | YELLOW—BLACK STRIPE |
| 400 | BLUE |
| 402 | YELLOW |
| 407 | RED—YELLOW STRIPE |
| 517 | BLACK—WHITE STRIPE |
| 297A, 297 | BLACK—GREEN STRIPE |
| ● | WELD OR BLANK TERMINAL |
| ⏚ | GROUND |

NOTE:

ALL NUMBERS IN PARENTHESIS ( )
INDICATE WIRE GAUGE

A   ALL LETTERS CIRCLED AS SHOWN
INDICATE CONNECTORS

UNLESS OTHERWISE SPECIFIED
ALL CONNECTORS ARE BLACK

*WIRE FUNCTION NOT APPLICABLE TO
THIS CIRCUIT

© Ford Motor Co.

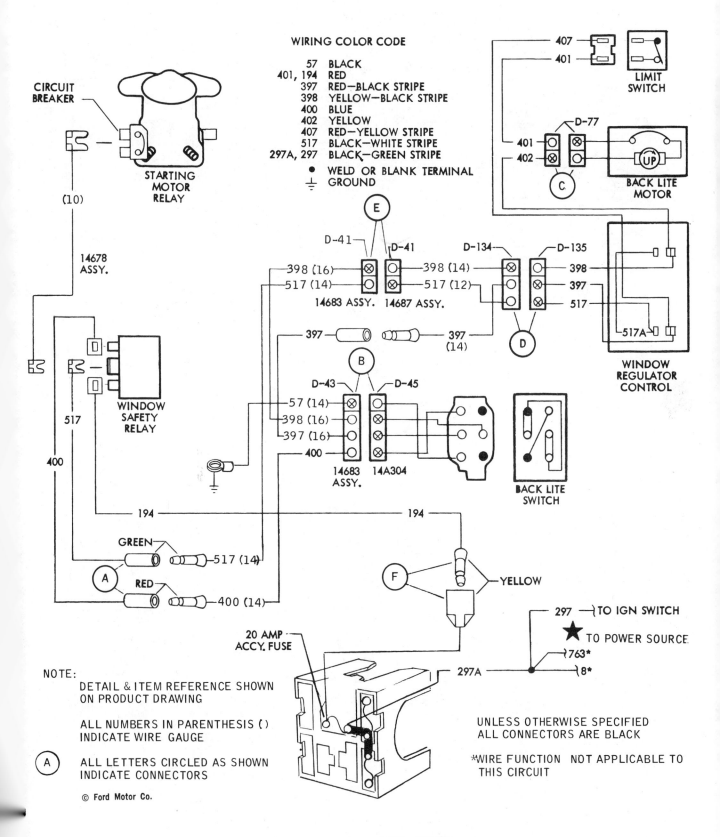

**WIRING COLOR CODE**

| 57 | BLACK |
| 401, 194 | RED |
| 397 | RED—BLACK STRIPE |
| 398 | YELLOW—BLACK STRIPE |
| 400 | BLUE |
| 402 | YELLOW |
| 407 | RED—YELLOW STRIPE |
| 517 | BLACK—WHITE STRIPE |
| 297A, 297 | BLACK—GREEN STRIPE |

● WELD OR BLANK TERMINAL
⏚ GROUND

CIRCUIT BREAKER

STARTING MOTOR RELAY

(10)

14678 ASSY.

WINDOW SAFETY RELAY

517

400

LIMIT SWITCH

407
401

D-77

401
402

C

BACK LITE MOTOR

E

D-41          D-41          D-134          D-135

398 (16)      398 (14)      398
517 (14)      517 (12)      397
                            517

14683 ASSY.   14687 ASSY.

517A

WINDOW REGULATOR CONTROL

397          397 (14)

D

B

D-43          D-45

57 (14)
398 (16)
397 (16)
400

14683 ASSY.   14A304

BACK LITE SWITCH

194                    194

GREEN ——517 (14)

A

RED ——400 (14)

F          YELLOW

297 →TO IGN SWITCH

★ TO POWER SOURCE

763*

297A          8*

20 AMP ACCY. FUSE

**NOTE:**

DETAIL & ITEM REFERENCE SHOWN ON PRODUCT DRAWING

ALL NUMBERS IN PARENTHESIS ( ) INDICATE WIRE GAUGE

(A) ALL LETTERS CIRCLED AS SHOWN INDICATE CONNECTORS

© Ford Motor Co.

UNLESS OTHERWISE SPECIFIED ALL CONNECTORS ARE BLACK

*WIRE FUNCTION NOT APPLICABLE TO THIS CIRCUIT

**1968—STA. WAG.—DUAL ACTION**

# Power Tailgate Window Wiring

## Falcon

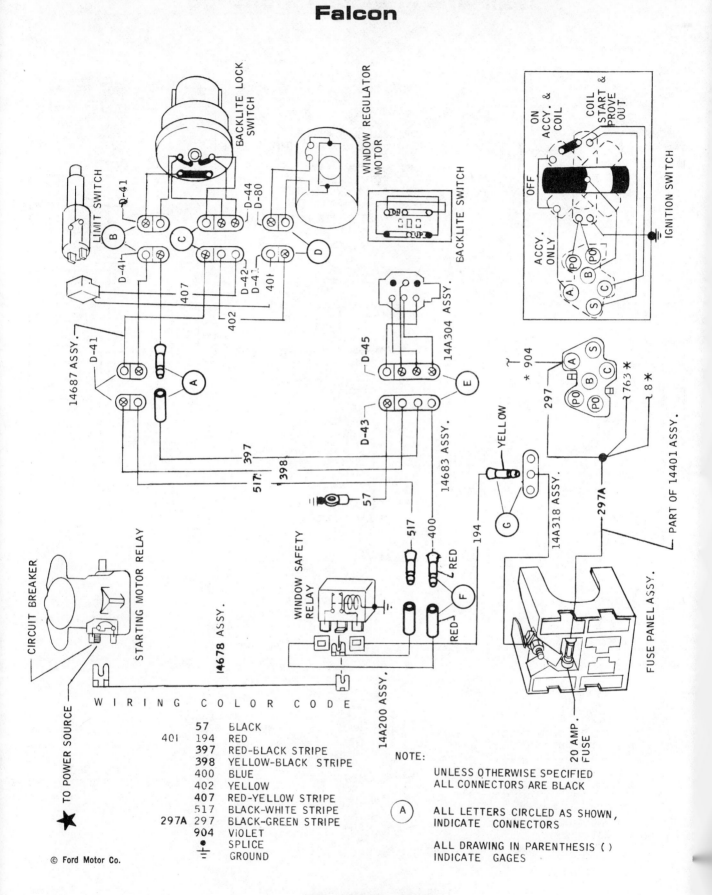

WIRING COLOR CODE

| | 57 | BLACK |
| 401 | 194 | RED |
| | 397 | RED-BLACK STRIPE |
| | 398 | YELLOW-BLACK STRIPE |
| | 400 | BLUE |
| | 402 | YELLOW |
| | 407 | RED-YELLOW STRIPE |
| | 517 | BLACK-WHITE STRIPE |
| 297A | 297 | BLACK-GREEN STRIPE |
| | 904 | VIOLET |
| | ⊥ | SPLICE |
| | ⏚ | GROUND |

© Ford Motor Co.

NOTE:

UNLESS OTHERWISE SPECIFIED
ALL CONNECTORS ARE BLACK

(A) ALL LETTERS CIRCLED AS SHOWN,
INDICATE CONNECTORS

ALL DRAWING IN PARENTHESIS ( )
INDICATE GAGES

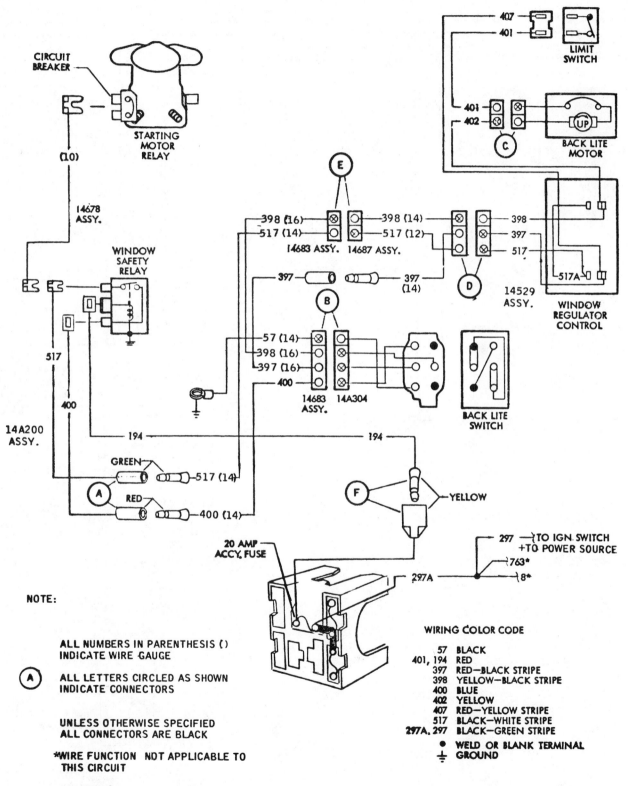

CIRCUIT BREAKER

STARTING MOTOR RELAY

(10)

14678 ASSY.

WINDOW SAFETY RELAY

517

400

14A200 ASSY.

GREEN
517 (14)

RED
400 (14)

LIMIT SWITCH

407
401

401
402

BACK LITE MOTOR

UP

C

E

398 (16)  398 (14)  398
517 (14)  517 (12)  397
14683 ASSY.  14687 ASSY.  517

D

517A

14529 ASSY.

WINDOW REGULATOR CONTROL

397  397 (14)

B

57 (14)
398 (16)
397 (16)
400

14683 ASSY.  14A304

BACK LITE SWITCH

194  194

F

YELLOW

297 → TO IGN. SWITCH
+ TO POWER SOURCE

763*

8*

20 AMP ACCY. FUSE

297A

**NOTE:**

**A**  ALL NUMBERS IN PARENTHESIS ( )
INDICATE WIRE GAUGE

ALL LETTERS CIRCLED AS SHOWN
INDICATE CONNECTORS

UNLESS OTHERWISE SPECIFIED
ALL CONNECTORS ARE BLACK

*WIRE FUNCTION NOT APPLICABLE TO
THIS CIRCUIT

© Ford Motor Co.

**WIRING COLOR CODE**

| | |
|---|---|
| 57 | BLACK |
| 401, 194 | RED |
| 397 | RED—BLACK STRIPE |
| 398 | YELLOW—BLACK STRIPE |
| 400 | BLUE |
| 402 | YELLOW |
| 407 | RED—YELLOW STRIPE |
| 517 | BLACK—WHITE STRIPE |
| 297A, 297 | BLACK—GREEN STRIPE |

● WELD OR BLANK TERMINAL
⏚ GROUND

1970

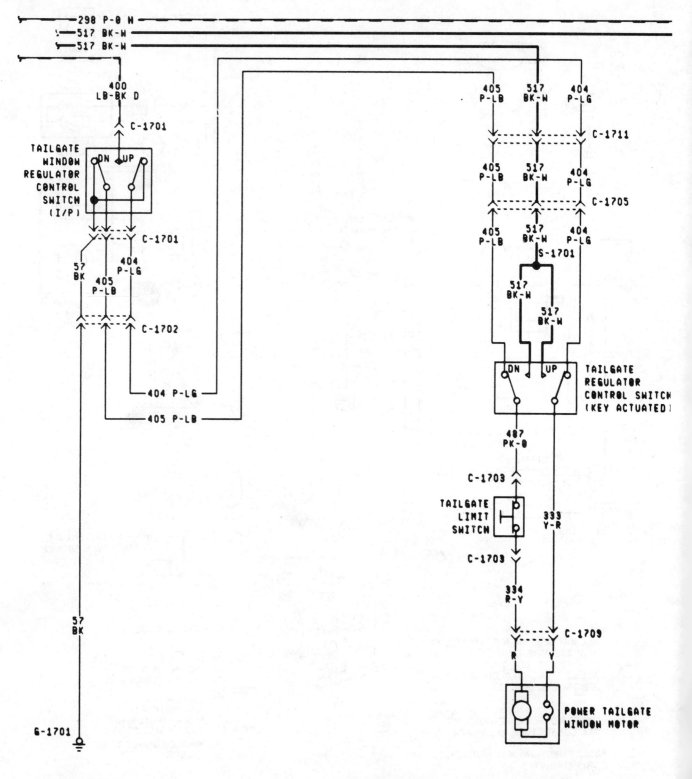

**1974–75 MONTEGO — TORINO**

# Ford

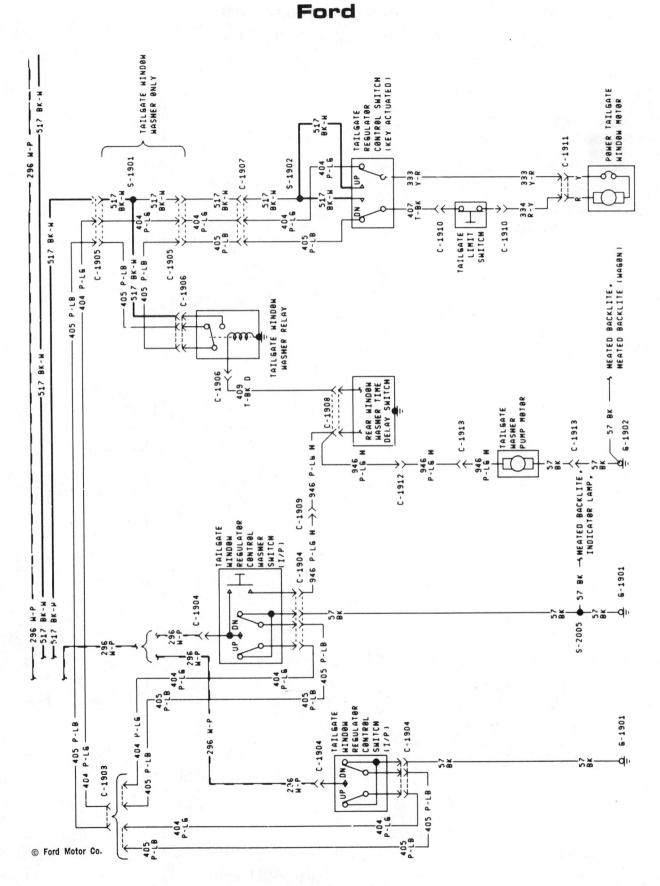

© Ford Motor Co.

**1974-75 FORD — MERCURY**

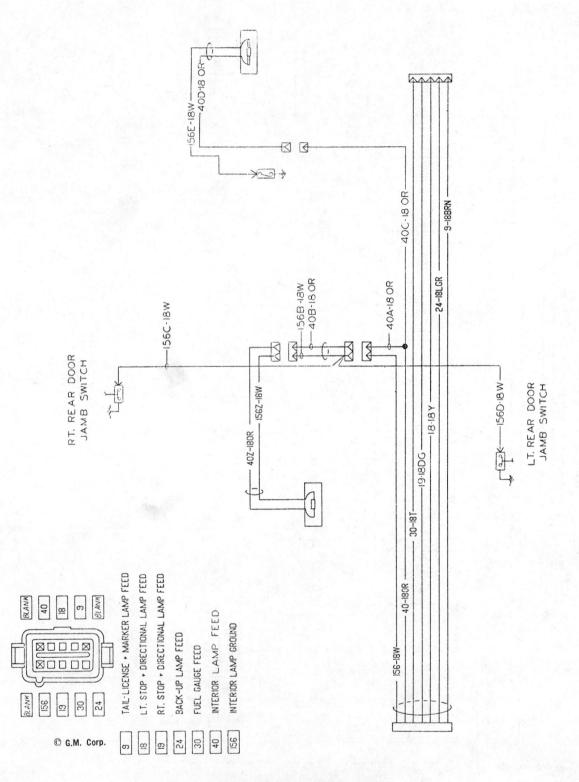

**1969-71—BUICK SPECIAL—FRONT WIRING**

RT. REAR DOOR JAMB SWITCH

LT. REAR DOOR JAMB SWITCH

156C-18W

156E-18W

40D-18 OR

156B-18W

40B-18 OR

40A-18 OR

40C-18 OR

9-18BRN

24-18LGR

18-18Y

19-18DG

30-18T

40-18OR

156-18W

156D-18W

56Z-18W

40Z-18OR

© G.M. Corp.

| | | |
|---|---|---|
| BLANK | | |
| 40 | TAIL-LICENSE + MARKER LAMP FEED | |
| 18 | LT. STOP + DIRECTIONAL LAMP FEED | |
| 9 | RT. STOP + DIRECTIONAL LAMP FEED | |
| BLANK | BACK-UP LAMP FEED | |
| BLANK | FUEL GAUGE FEED | |
| 156 | INTERIOR LAMP FEED | |
| 19 | INTERIOR LAMP GROUND | |
| 30 | | |
| 24 | | |

9  18  19  24  30  40  156

## General Motors

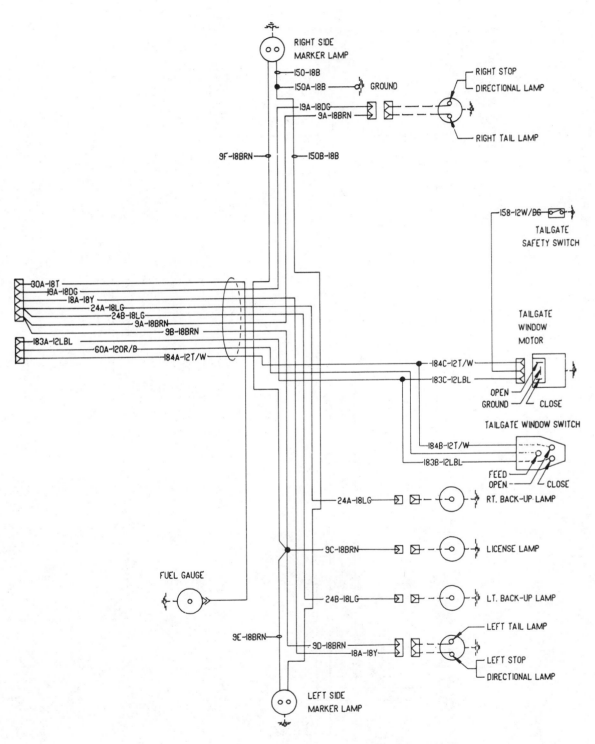

© G.M. Corp.

**1969-71 — BUICK SPECIAL — REAR WIRING**

## General Motors

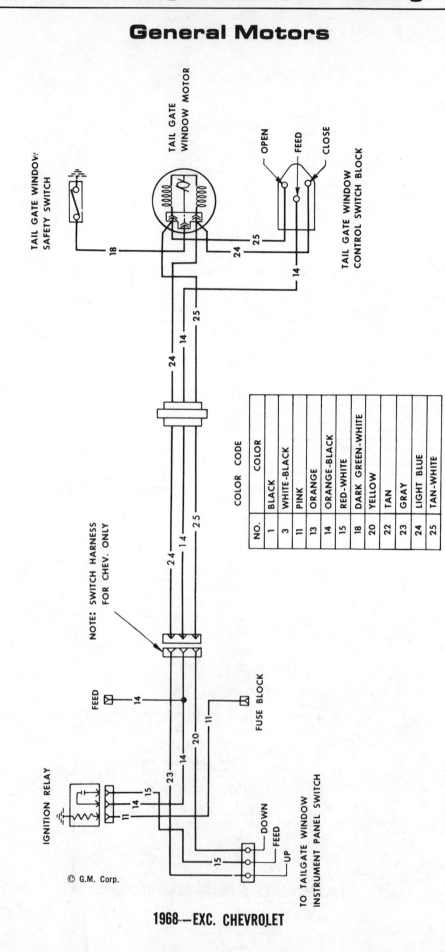

| COLOR CODE | |
|---|---|
| NO. | COLOR |
| 1 | BLACK |
| 3 | WHITE-BLACK |
| 11 | PINK |
| 13 | ORANGE |
| 14 | ORANGE-BLACK |
| 15 | RED-WHITE |
| 18 | DARK GREEN-WHITE |
| 20 | YELLOW |
| 22 | TAN |
| 23 | GRAY |
| 24 | LIGHT BLUE |
| 25 | TAN-WHITE |

TAIL GATE WINDOW SAFETY SWITCH

TAIL GATE WINDOW MOTOR

OPEN   FEED   CLOSE

TAIL GATE WINDOW CONTROL SWITCH BLOCK

NOTE: SWITCH HARNESS FOR CHEV. ONLY

FEED

FUSE BLOCK

IGNITION RELAY

DOWN
FEED
UP

TO TAILGATE WINDOW INSTRUMENT PANEL SWITCH

© G.M. Corp.

## 1968—EXC. CHEVROLET

# General Motors

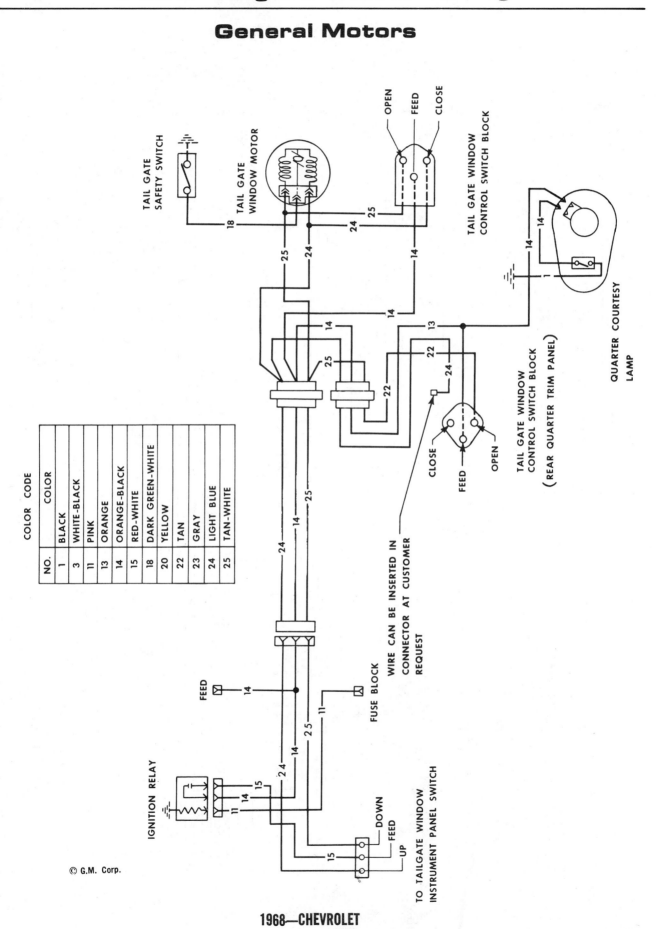

COLOR CODE

| NO. | COLOR |
|-----|-------|
| 1 | BLACK |
| 3 | WHITE-BLACK |
| 11 | PINK |
| 13 | ORANGE |
| 14 | ORANGE-BLACK |
| 15 | RED-WHITE |
| 18 | DARK GREEN-WHITE |
| 20 | YELLOW |
| 22 | TAN |
| 23 | GRAY |
| 24 | LIGHT BLUE |
| 25 | TAN-WHITE |

TAIL GATE SAFETY SWITCH

TAIL GATE WINDOW MOTOR

TAIL GATE WINDOW CONTROL SWITCH BLOCK

OPEN    FEED    CLOSE

QUARTER COURTESY LAMP

TAIL GATE WINDOW CONTROL SWITCH BLOCK (REAR QUARTER TRIM PANEL)

CLOSE    OPEN

FEED

WIRE CAN BE INSERTED IN CONNECTOR AT CUSTOMER REQUEST

FEED

FUSE BLOCK

IGNITION RELAY

DOWN    FEED    UP

TO TAILGATE WINDOW INSTRUMENT PANEL SWITCH

© G.M. Corp.

**1968—CHEVROLET**

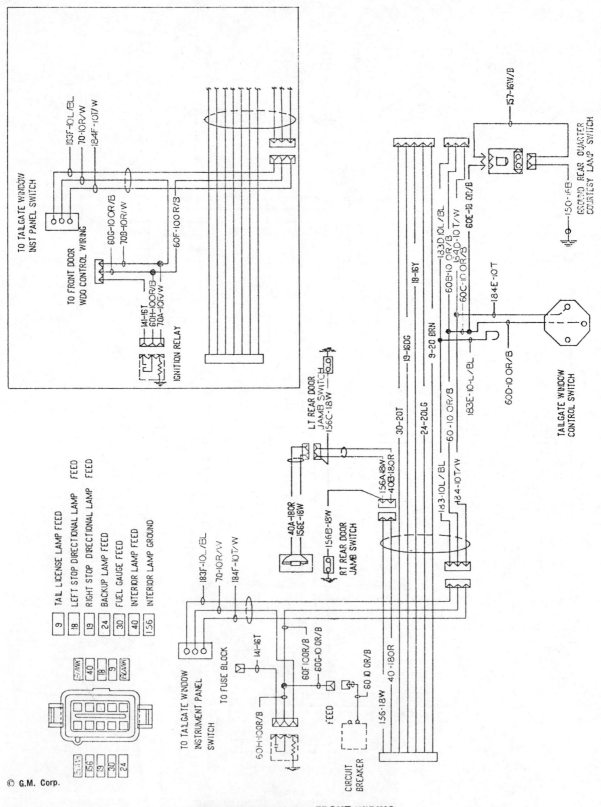

**1969-71—CHEVROLET—FRONT WIRING**

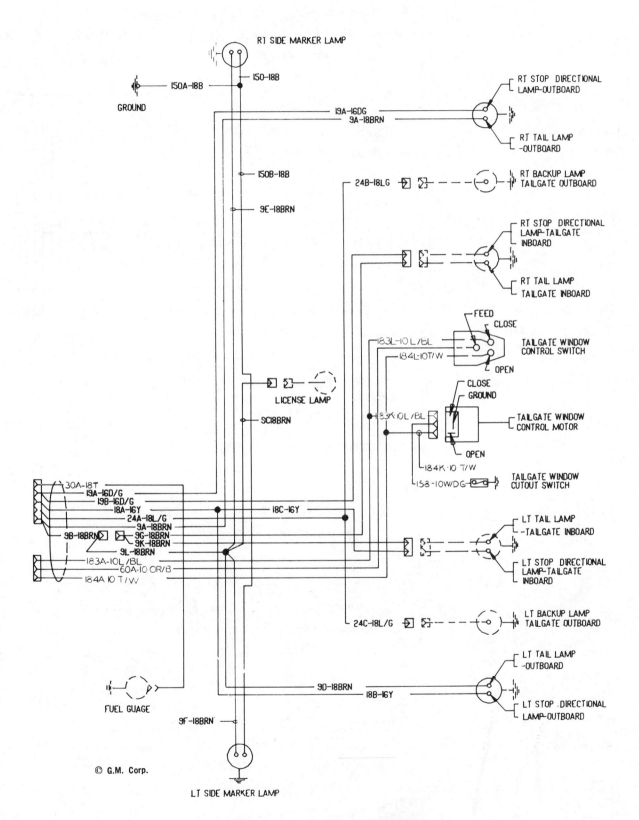

**1969-71—CHEVROLET—REAR WIRING**

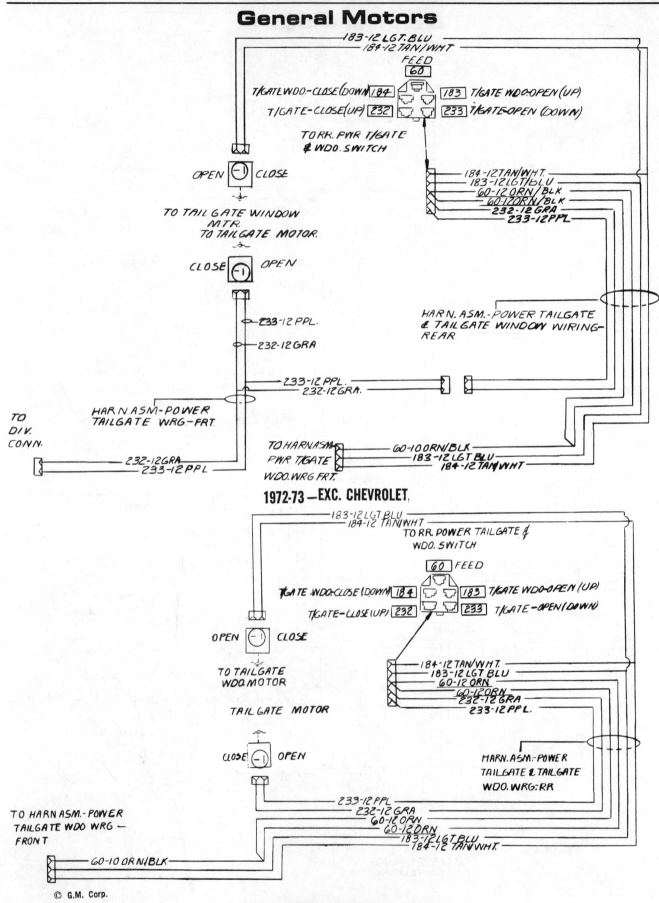

**1972-73—EXC. CHEVROLET.**

**1972-73—CHEVROLET**

© G.M. Corp.

## General Motors

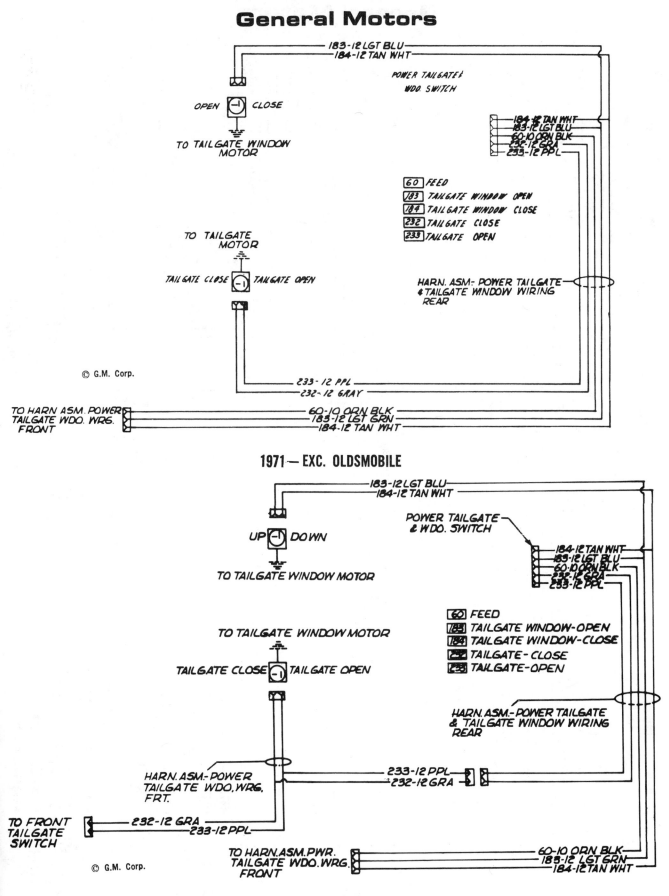

© G.M. Corp.

**1971— EXC. OLDSMOBILE**

© G.M. Corp.

**1971—OLDSMOBILE**

## General Motors

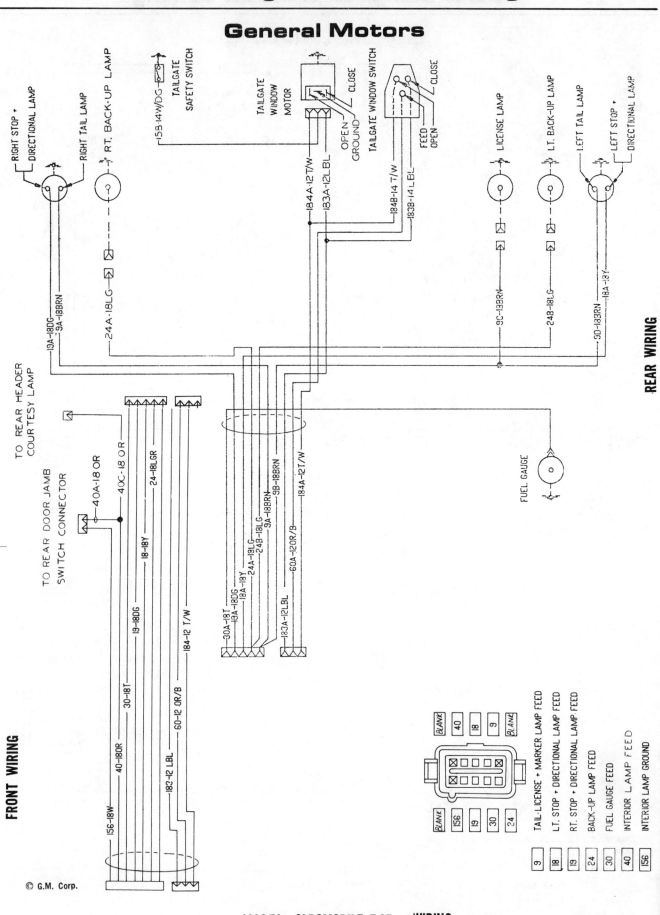

**FRONT WIRING**

**REAR WIRING**

TO REAR HEADER COURTESY LAMP

TO REAR DOOR JAMB SWITCH CONNECTOR

RIGHT STOP + DIRECTIONAL LAMP

RIGHT TAIL LAMP

RT. BACK-UP LAMP

TAILGATE SAFETY SWITCH

TAILGATE WINDOW MOTOR

TAILGATE WINDOW SWITCH

LICENSE LAMP

LT. BACK-UP LAMP

LEFT TAIL LAMP

LEFT STOP + DIRECTIONAL LAMP

CLOSE

OPEN

GROUND

CLOSE

FEED

OPEN

FUEL GAUGE

158-14W/DG

184A-12T/W

183A-12LBL

184B-14 T/W

183B-14 LBL

9C-18BRN

24B-18LG

9D-18BRN

18A-18Y

19A-18DG

9A-18BRN

24A-18LG

40A-18 OR

40C-18 OR

24-18LGR

18-18Y

19-18DG

30-18T

40-18OR

156-18W

183-12 LBL

60-12 OR/B

184-12 T/W

30A-18T

18A-18Y

24A-18LG

24B-18LG

9A-18BRN

9B-18BRN

184A-12T/W

183A-12LBL

60A-12OR/B

TAIL-LICENSE + MARKER LAMP FEED

LT. STOP + DIRECTIONAL LAMP FEED

RT. STOP + DIRECTIONAL LAMP FEED

BACK-UP LAMP FEED

FUEL GAUGE FEED

INTERIOR LAMP FEED

INTERIOR LAMP GROUND

BLANK | 40 | 18 | 9 | BLANK

BLANK | 156 | 19 | 30 | 24

9 | 18 | 19 | 24 | 30 | 40 | 156

© G.M. Corp.

**1969-71—OLDSMOBILE F-85 — WIRING**

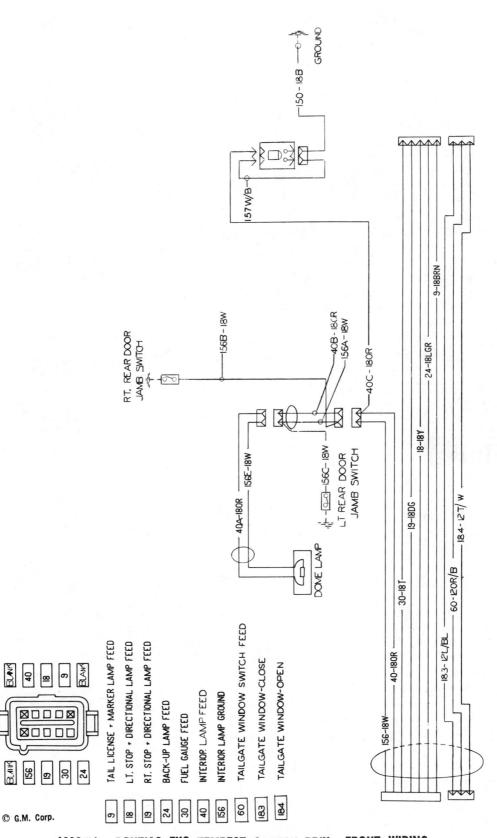

GROUND

150 - 18B

157 W/B

RT. REAR DOOR
JAMB SWITCH

156B - 18W

40B - 18CR

156A - 18W

40C - 18OR

9 - 18BRN

24 - 18LGR

18 - 18Y

156E - 18W

40A - 18OR

156C - 18W

LT REAR DOOR
JAMB SWITCH

DOME LAMP

19 - 18DG

30 - 18T

60 - 12OR/B

18-4 - 12T/W

40 - 18OR

18-3 - 12L/BL

156 - 18W

| | | | | |
|---|---|---|---|---|
| BLANK | 40 | 18 | 9 | BLANK |

| | | | | |
|---|---|---|---|---|
| BLANK | 156 | 19 | 30 | 24 |

| | |
|---|---|
| 9 | TAIL LICENSE - MARKER LAMP FEED |
| 18 | LT. STOP - DIRECTIONAL LAMP FEED |
| 19 | RT. STOP - DIRECTIONAL LAMP FEED |
| 24 | BACK-UP LAMP FEED |
| 30 | FUEL GAUGE FEED |
| 40 | INTERIOR LAMP FEED |
| 156 | INTERIOR LAMP GROUND |
| 60 | TAILGATE WINDOW SWITCH FEED |
| 183 | TAILGATE WINDOW-CLOSE |
| 184 | TAILGATE WINDOW-OPEN |

© G.M. Corp.

## 1969-71—PONTIAC EXC. TEMPEST & GRAN PRIX—FRONT WIRING

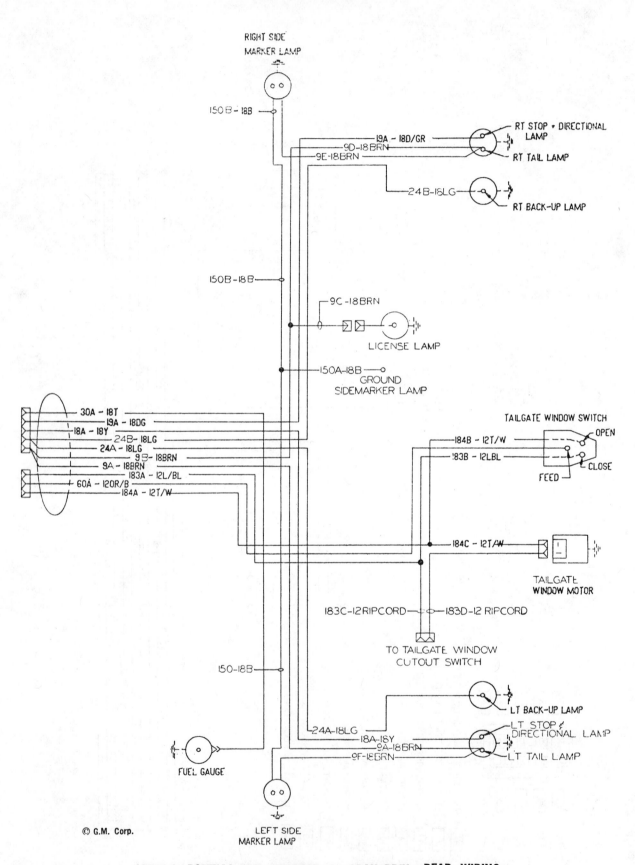

RIGHT SIDE
MARKER LAMP

150 B - 18B

19A - 18D/GR — RT STOP + DIRECTIONAL LAMP
9D-18BRN
9E-18BRN — RT TAIL LAMP

24B-18LG — RT BACK-UP LAMP

150B-18B

9C -18BRN

LICENSE LAMP

150A-18B
GROUND
SIDEMARKER LAMP

30A - 18T
19A - 18DG
18A - 18Y
24B - 18LG
24A - 18LG
9B - 18BRN
9A - 18BRN
183A - 12L/BL
60A - 120R/B
184A - 12T/W

TAILGATE WINDOW SWITCH
184B - 12T/W — OPEN
183B - 12LBL — CLOSE
FEED

184C - 12T/W

TAILGATE
WINDOW MOTOR

183C - 12 RIPCORD — 183D-12 RIPCORD

TO TAILGATE WINDOW
CUTOUT SWITCH

150-18B

LT BACK-UP LAMP

24A-18LG
18A-18Y — LT STOP & DIRECTIONAL LAMP
9A-18BRN
9F-18BRN — LT TAIL LAMP

FUEL GAUGE

LEFT SIDE
MARKER LAMP

© G.M. Corp.

**1969-71—PONTIAC EXC. TEMPEST & GRAN PRIX—REAR WIRING**

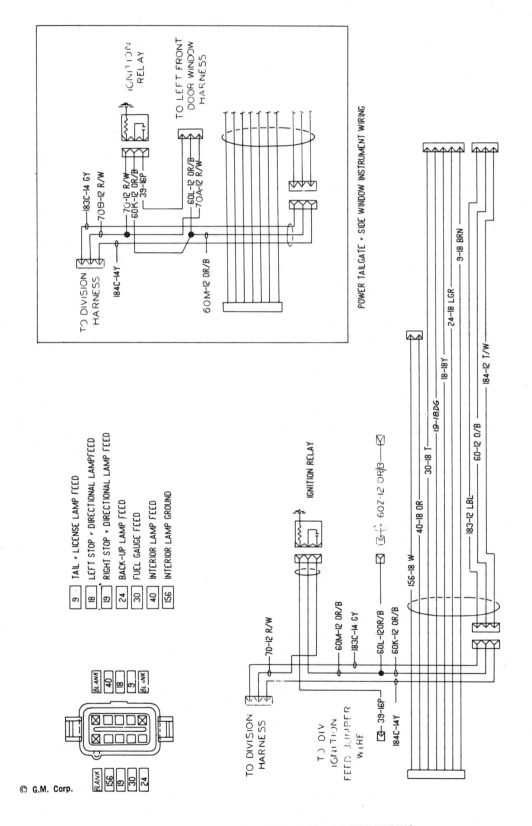

© G.M. Corp.

**1969-71—TEMPEST & GRAN PRIX —FRONT WIRING**

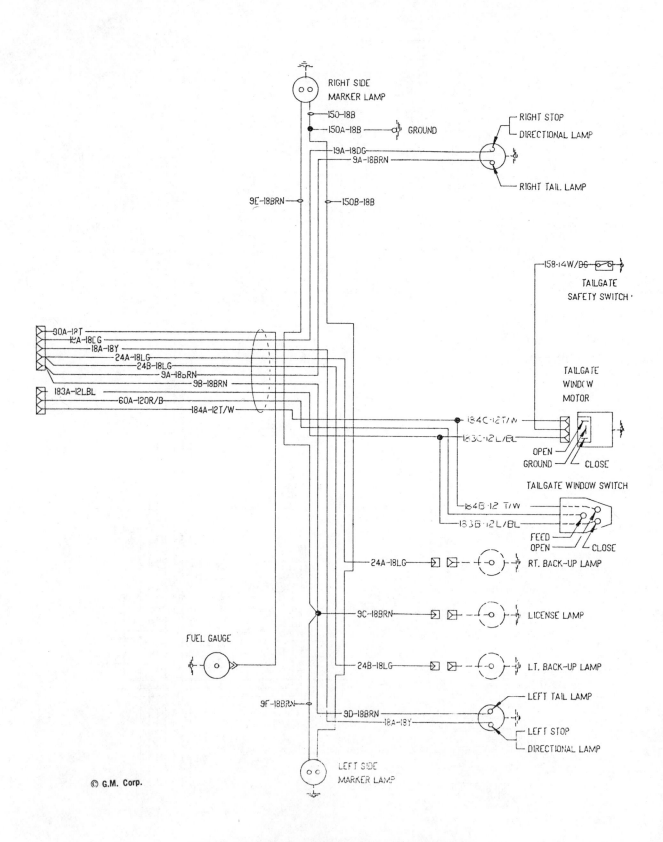

RIGHT SIDE
MARKER LAMP

150-18B

150A-18B — GROUND

19A-18DG

9A-18BRN

RIGHT STOP
DIRECTIONAL LAMP

RIGHT TAIL LAMP

9E-18BRN

150B-18B

158-14W/DG

TAILGATE
SAFETY SWITCH

30A-12T

12A-18LG

18A-18Y

24A-18LG

24B-18LG

9A-18BRN

9B-18BRN

183A-12LBL

60A-120R/B

184A-12T/W

TAILGATE
WINDOW
MOTOR

184C-12T/W

183C-12L/BL

OPEN
GROUND      CLOSE

TAILGATE WINDOW SWITCH

184B-12 T/W

183B-12L/BL

FEED
OPEN      CLOSE

24A-18LG      RT. BACK-UP LAMP

9C-18BRN      LICENSE LAMP

FUEL GAUGE

24B-18LG      LT. BACK-UP LAMP

LEFT TAIL LAMP

9F-18BRN

9D-18BRN

18A-18Y

LEFT STOP
DIRECTIONAL LAMP

LEFT SIDE
MARKER LAMP

© G.M. Corp.

## 1969-71—Tempest & Gran Prix —Rear Wiring

## General Motors

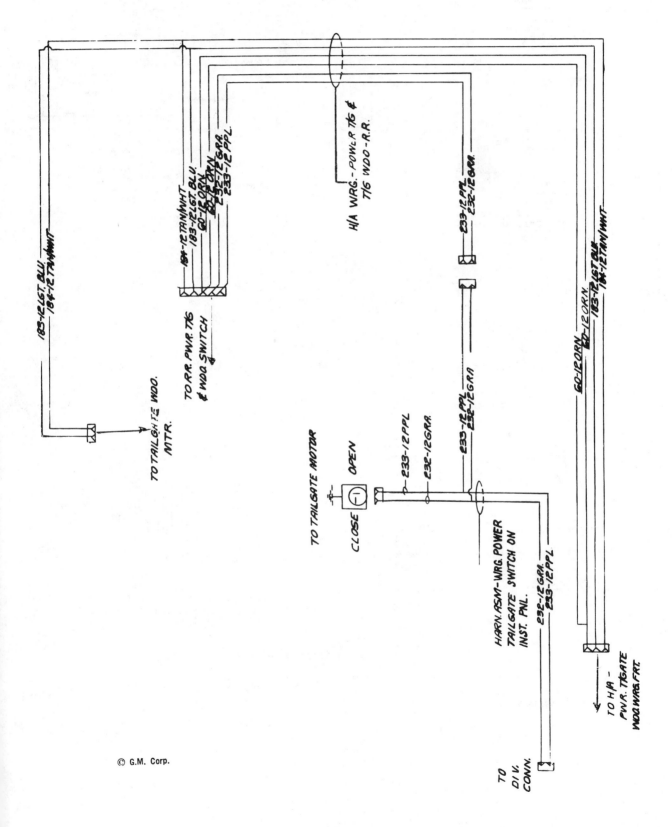

1974-75

## American Motors

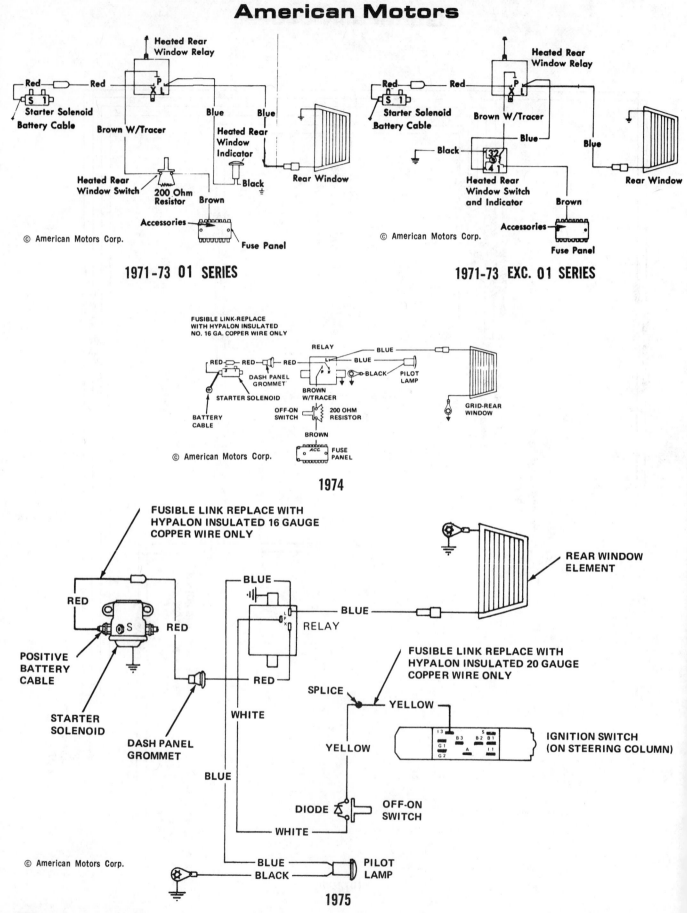

1971-73 01 SERIES

1971-73 EXC. 01 SERIES

1974

1975

## Chrysler Corporation

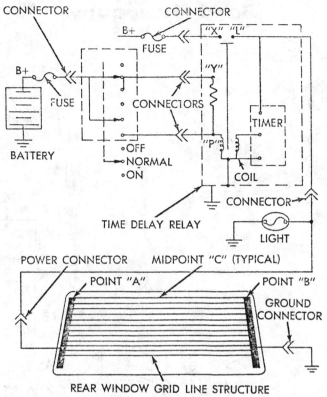

**1973-74—CHRYSLER**

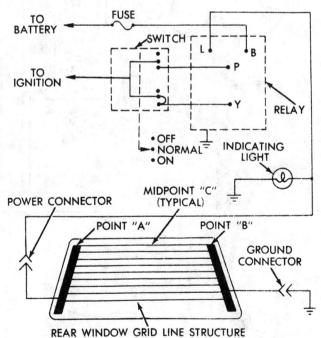

**1975 CHRYSLER**

## Ford Motor Company
## Ford · Mercury

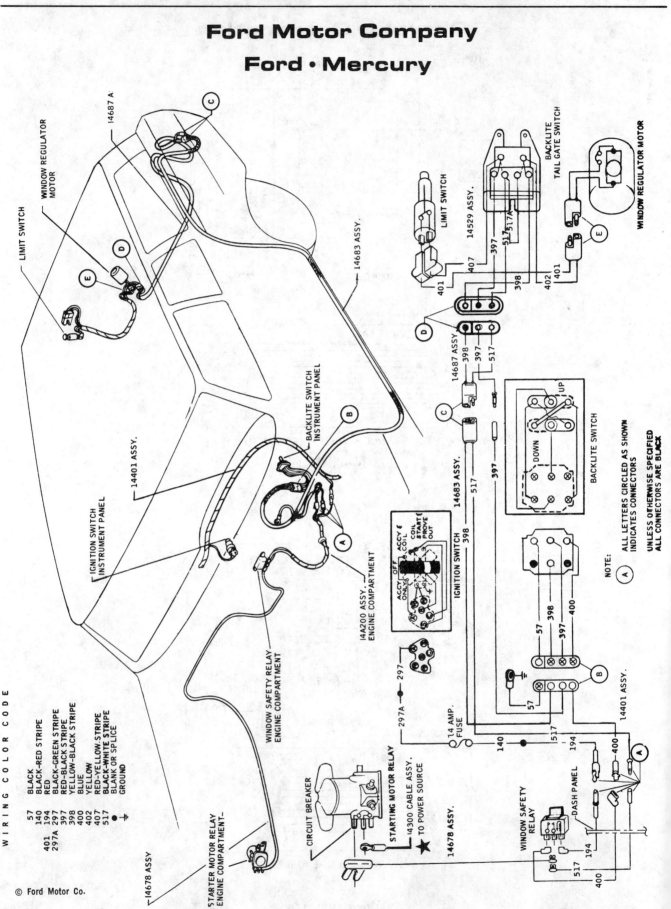

WIRING COLOR CODE

| | |
|---|---|
| 57 | BLACK |
| 140 | BLACK-RED STRIPE |
| 194 | RED |
| 297 | BLACK-GREEN STRIPE |
| 297A | RED-BLACK STRIPE |
| 398 | YELLOW-BLACK STRIPE |
| 400 | BLUE |
| 401 | |
| 402 | YELLOW |
| 407 | RED-YELLOW STRIPE |
| 517 | BLACK-WHITE STRIPE |
| ● | BLANK OR SPLICE |
| ⏚ | GROUND |

NOTE:
Ⓐ ALL LETTERS CIRCLED AS SHOWN INDICATES CONNECTORS

UNLESS OTHERWISE SPECIFIED ALL CONNECTORS ARE BLACK

**1968—STATION WAGON**

© Ford Motor Co.

## Ford • Mercury

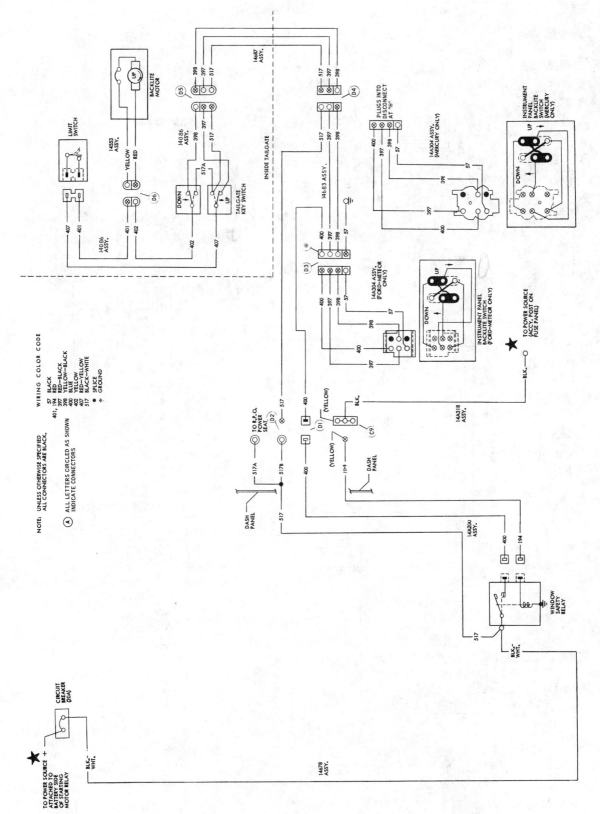

© Ford Motor Co.

1969

## Ford

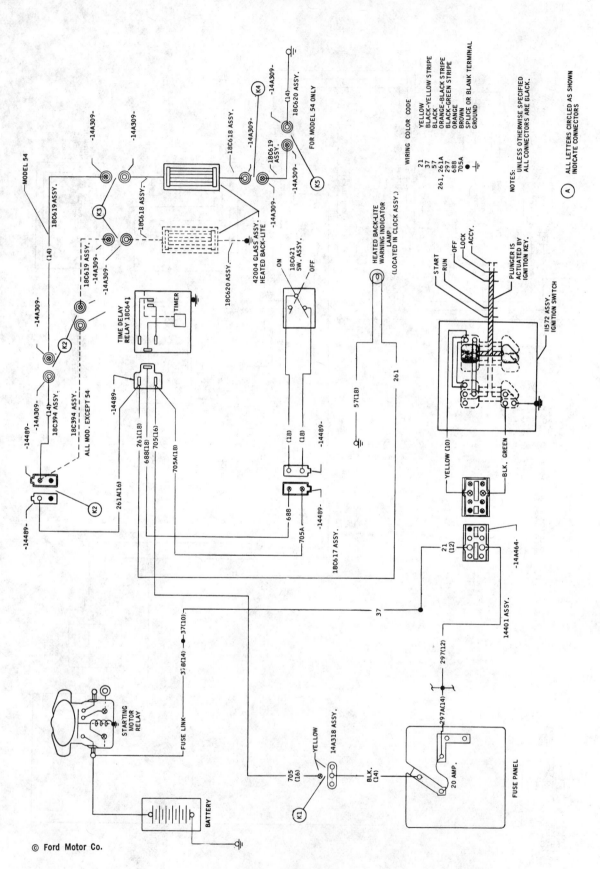

© Ford Motor Co.

1970

## Mercury

WIRING COLOR CODE

| | |
|---|---|
| 21 | YELLOW |
| 37 | BLACK-YELLOW STRIPE |
| 261, 261A | ORANGE-BLACK STRIPE |
| 297 | BLACK-GREEN STRIPE |
| 688 | ORANGE |
| | BROWN |
| 705, 705A | VIOLET |
| 904 | SPLICE OR BLANK |
| | GROUND |

NOTES:

UNLESS OTHERWISE SPECIFIED ALL CONNECTORS ARE BLACK.

(A) ALL LETTERS CIRCLED AS SHOWN INDICATE CONNECTORS AND ARE GRAPHICALLY LOCATED.

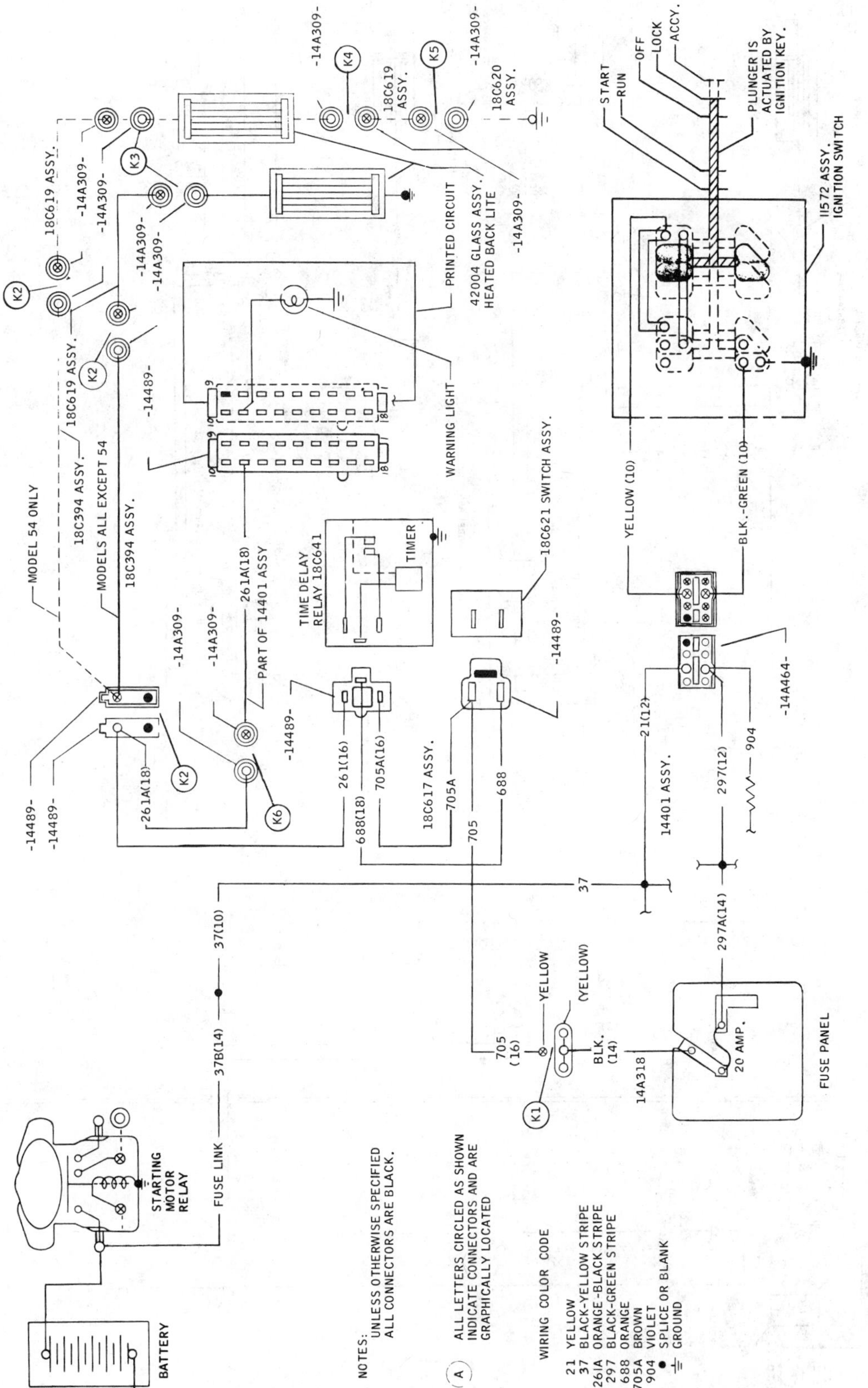

© Ford Motor Co.

1970

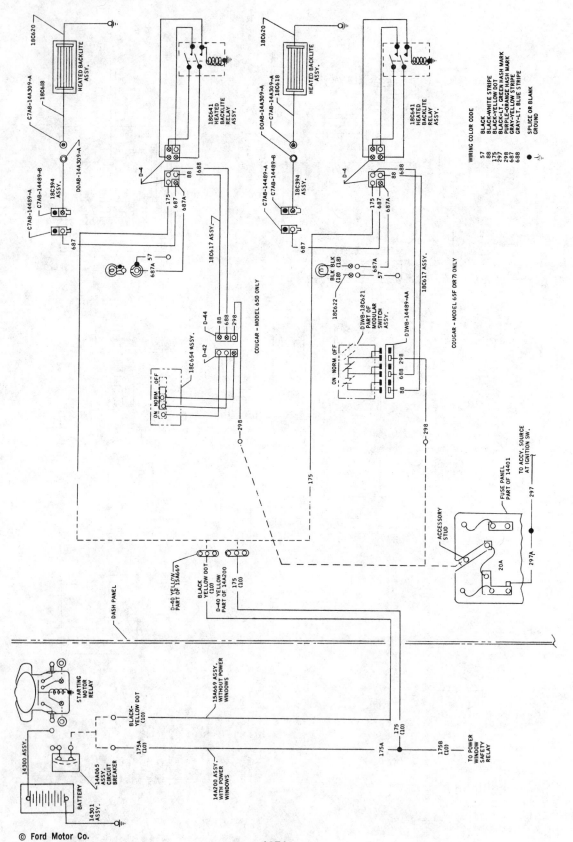

© Ford Motor Co.

## Lincoln·Continental

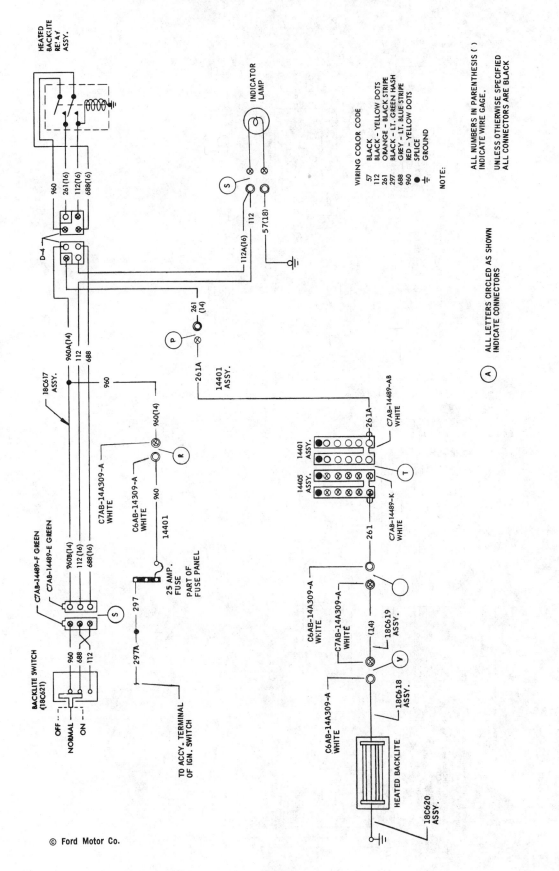

© Ford Motor Co.

## Thunderbird

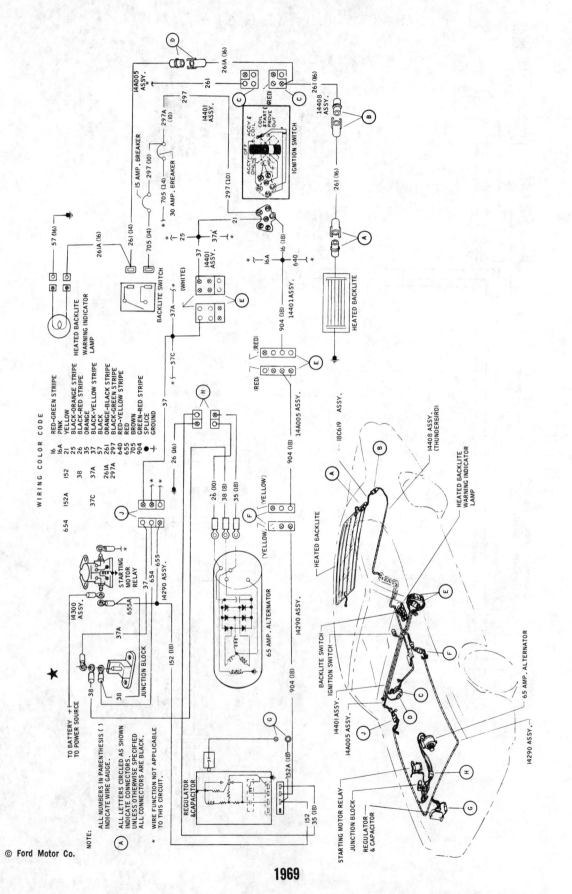

© Ford Motor Co.

1969

## Thunderbird

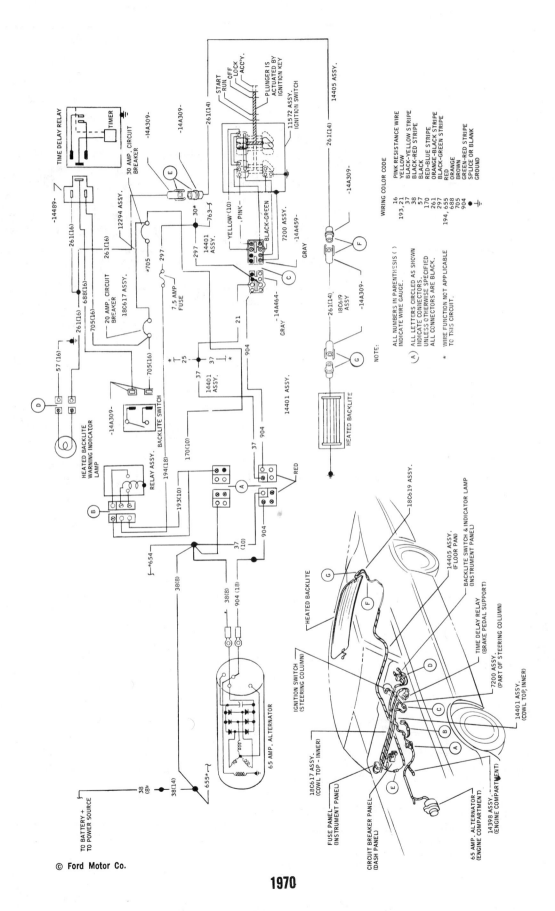

WIRING COLOR CODE

| 16 | PINK RESISTANCE WIRE |
| 193, 21 | YELLOW |
| 37 | BLACK-YELLOW STRIPE |
| 38 | BLACK-RED STRIPE |
| 57 | BLACK |
| 170 | RED-BLUE STRIPE |
| 261 | ORANGE-BLACK STRIPE |
| 297 | BLACK-GREEN STRIPE |
| 194, 655 | RED |
| 688 | ORANGE |
| 705 | BROWN |
| 904 | GREEN-RED STRIPE |
| — | SPLICE OR BLANK |
| ⏚ | GROUND |

NOTE:

ALL NUMBERS IN PARENTHESIS ( )
INDICATE WIRE GAUGE.

(A) ALL LETTERS CIRCLED AS SHOWN
INDICATE CONNECTORS.
UNLESS OTHERWISE SPECIFIED
ALL CONNECTORS ARE BLACK.

*  WIRE FUNCTION NOT APPLICABLE
TO THIS CIRCUIT.

**1970**

## Ford Motor Company

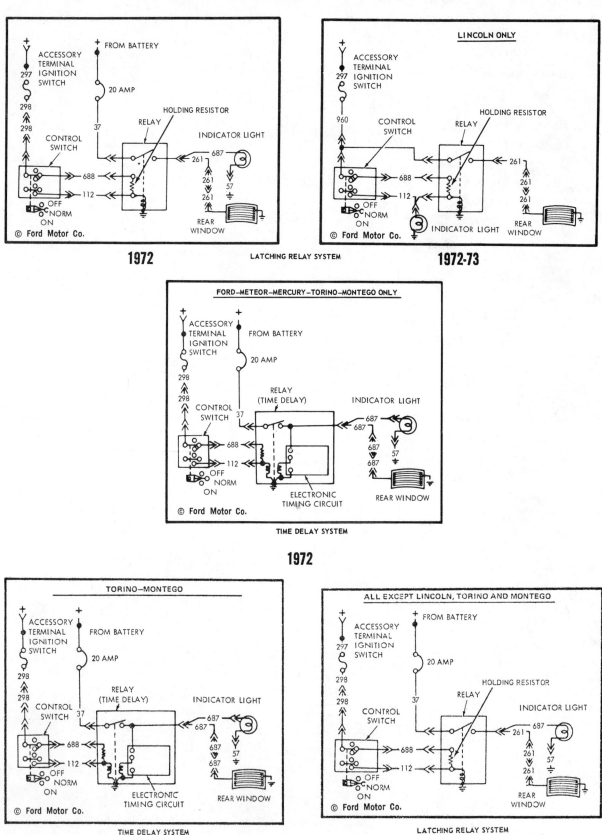

# Heated Back Window Wiring

## Ford Motor Company

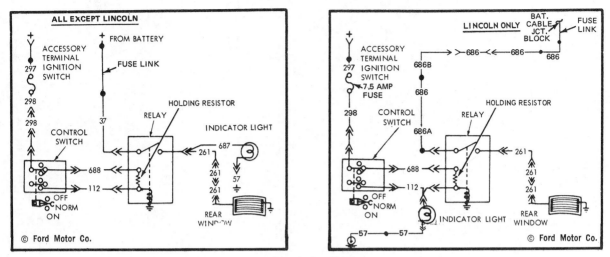

*Latching Relay System*

**1974-75**

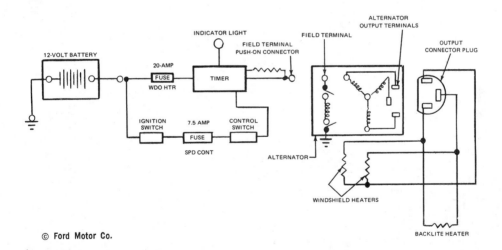

*Quick Defrost Windshield and Rear Window Electrical Circuit*

**1974-75**

# Ford Motor Company

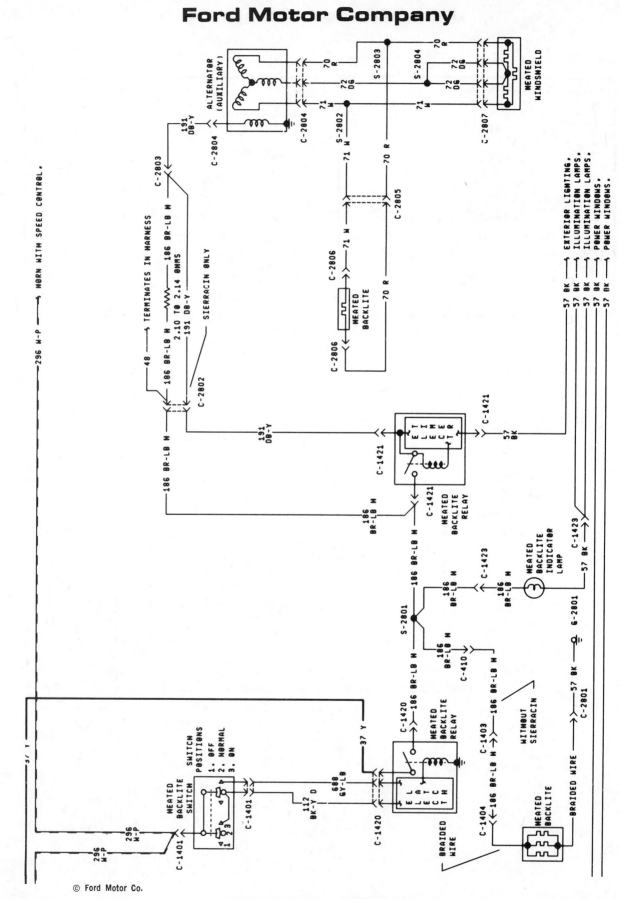

**1974-75 MARK IV—THUNDERBIRD**

## Ford Motor Company

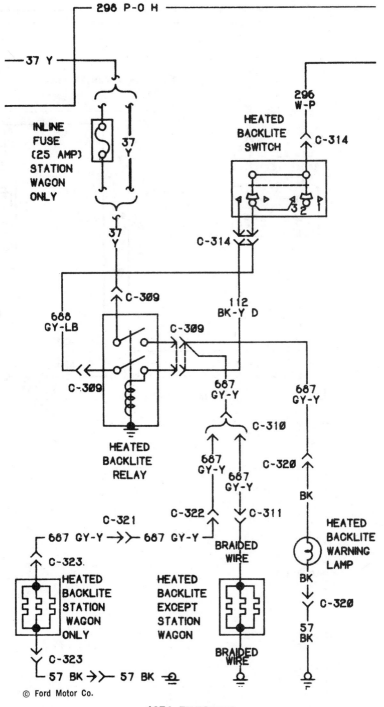

**1974-75 TORINO**

© Ford Motor Co.

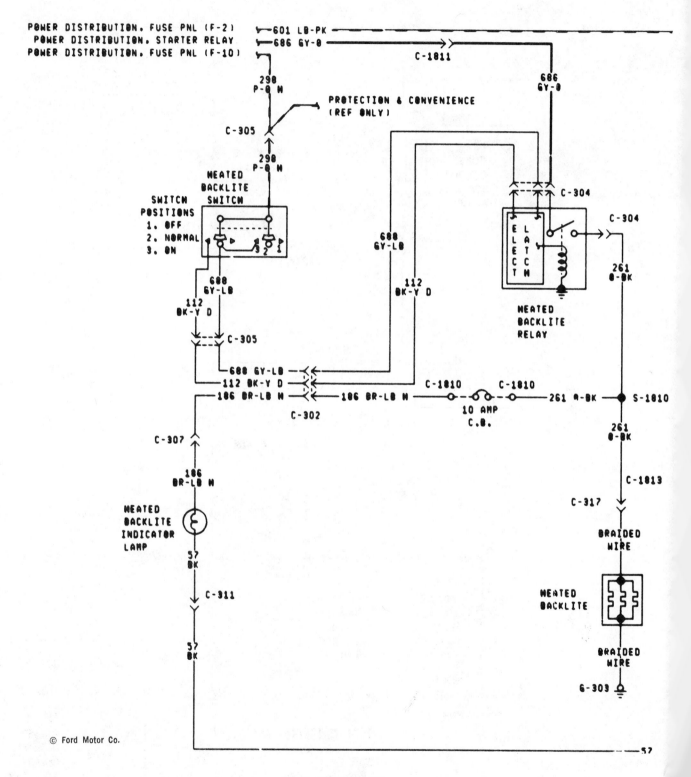

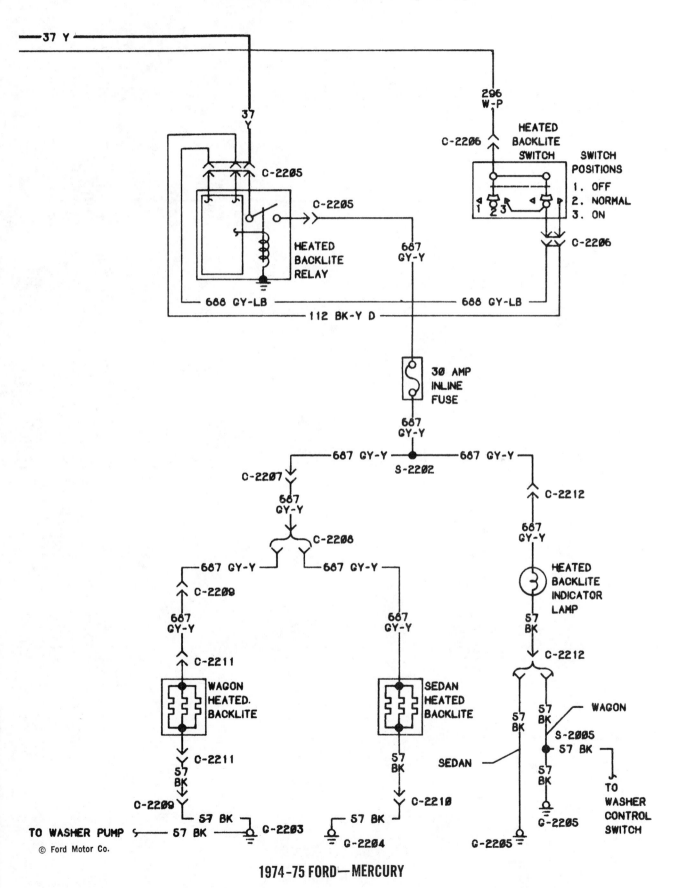

© Ford Motor Co.

**1974-75 FORD—MERCURY**

# Ford Motor Company

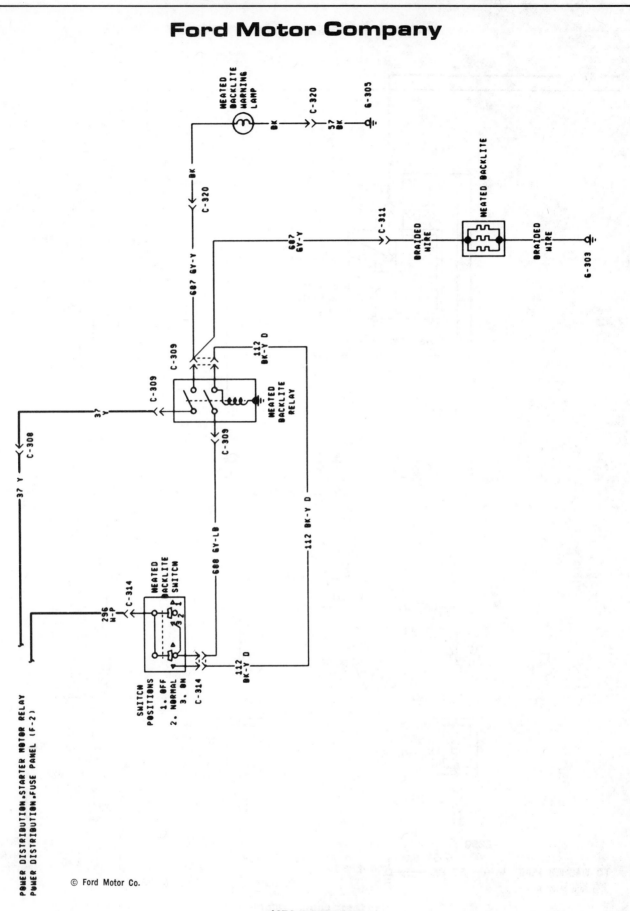

© Ford Motor Co.

**1974–75 COUGAR**

## Ford Motor Company

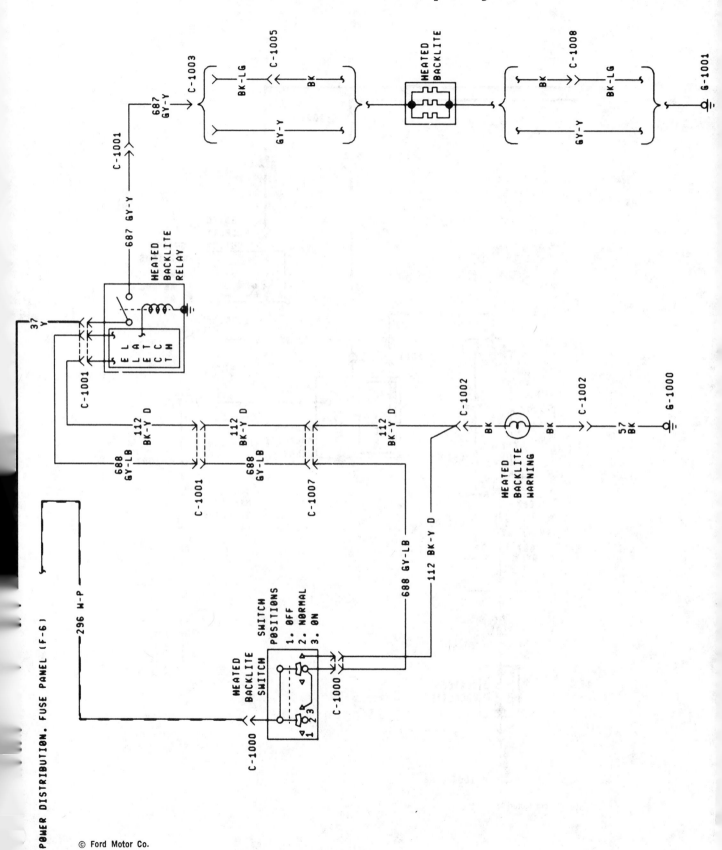

© Ford Motor Co.

**1974-75 MUSTANG**

# Ford Motor Company

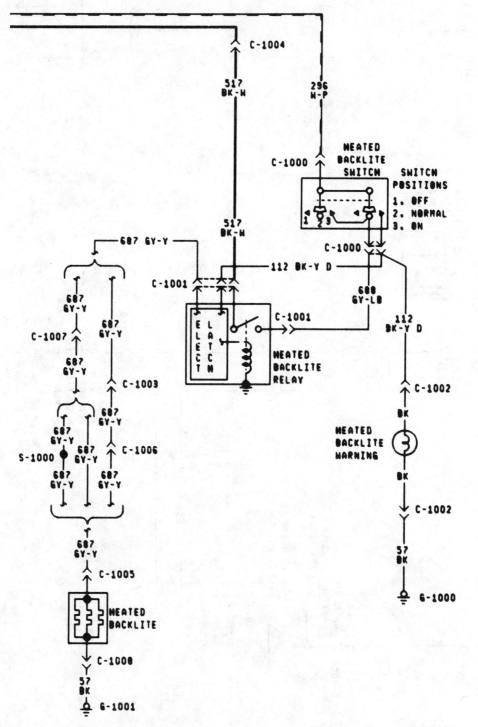

© Ford Motor Co.

**1974-75 PINTO**

## General Motors

## Buick

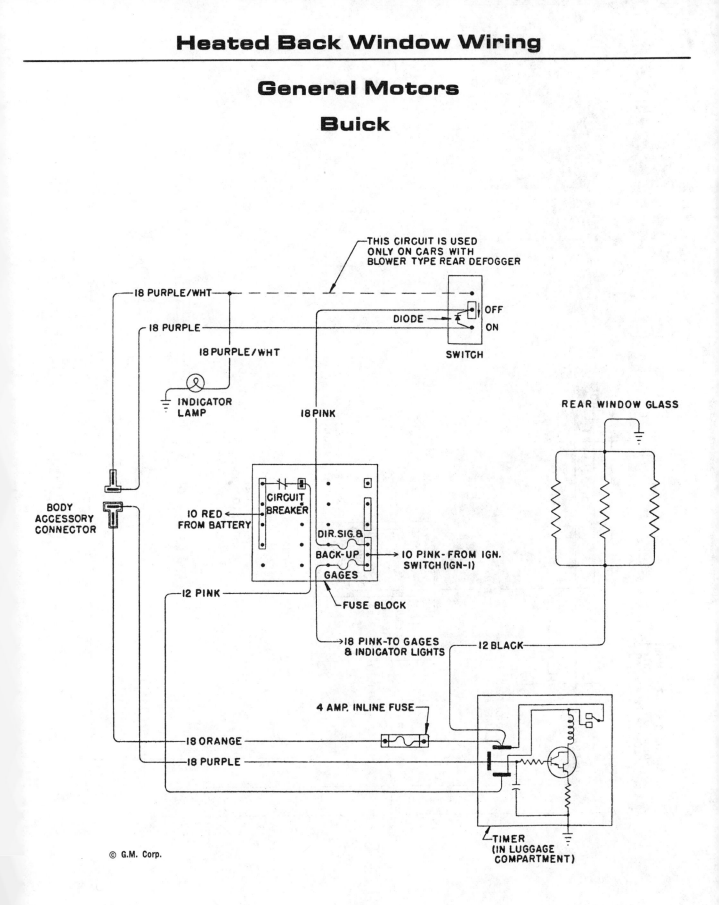

THIS CIRCUIT IS USED
ONLY ON CARS WITH
BLOWER TYPE REAR DEFOGGER

18 PURPLE/WHT

18 PURPLE

18 PURPLE/WHT

OFF

DIODE

ON

SWITCH

INDICATOR
LAMP

18 PINK

REAR WINDOW GLASS

CIRCUIT
BREAKER

10 RED
FROM BATTERY

DIR. SIG. &

BACK-UP

10 PINK-FROM IGN.
SWITCH (IGN-1)

GAGES

FUSE BLOCK

BODY
ACCESSORY
CONNECTOR

12 PINK

18 PINK-TO GAGES
& INDICATOR LIGHTS

12 BLACK

4 AMP. INLINE FUSE

18 ORANGE

18 PURPLE

TIMER
(IN LUGGAGE
COMPARTMENT)

© G.M. Corp.

1969

# Heated Back Window Wiring

## Buick

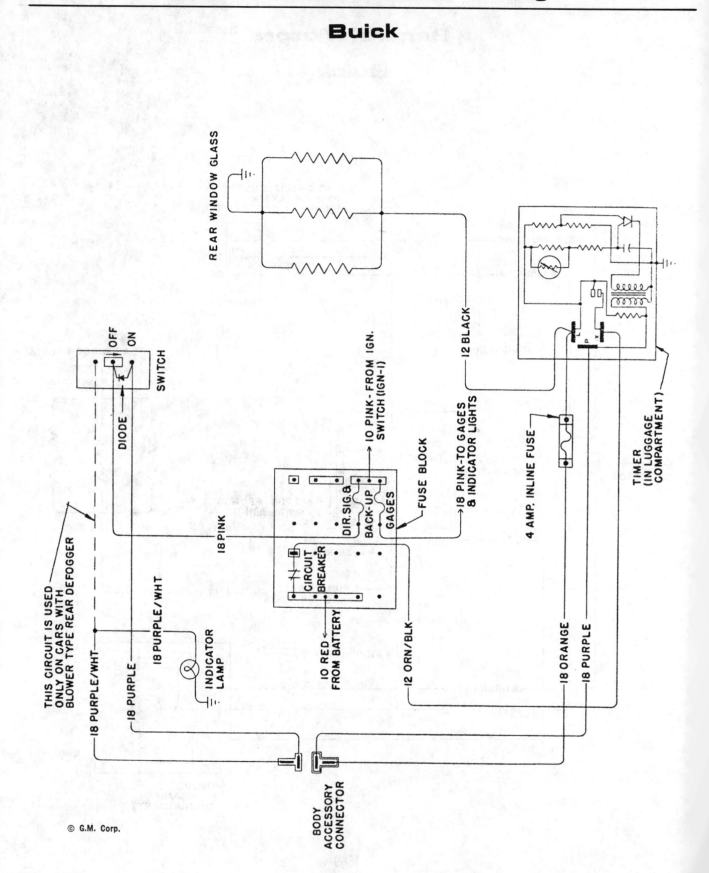

© G.M. Corp.

1970

## Buick

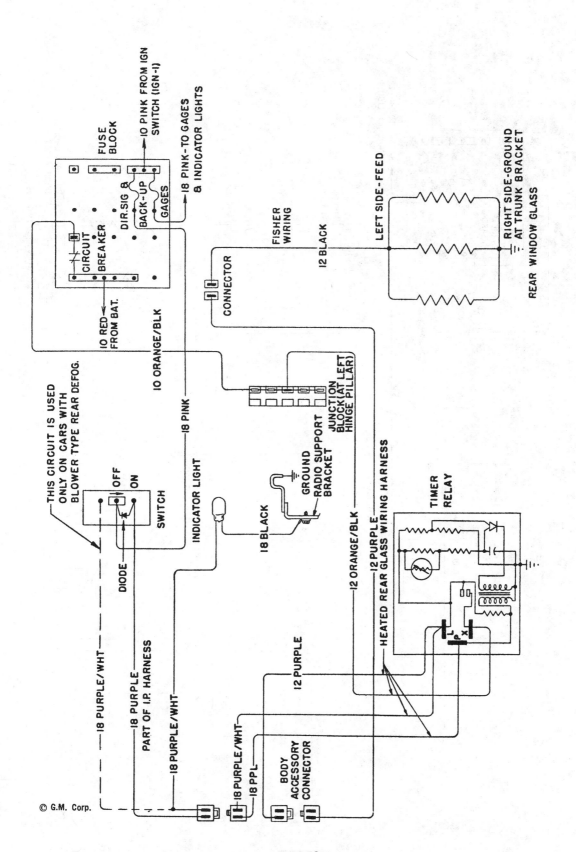

**1971-72**

## Buick

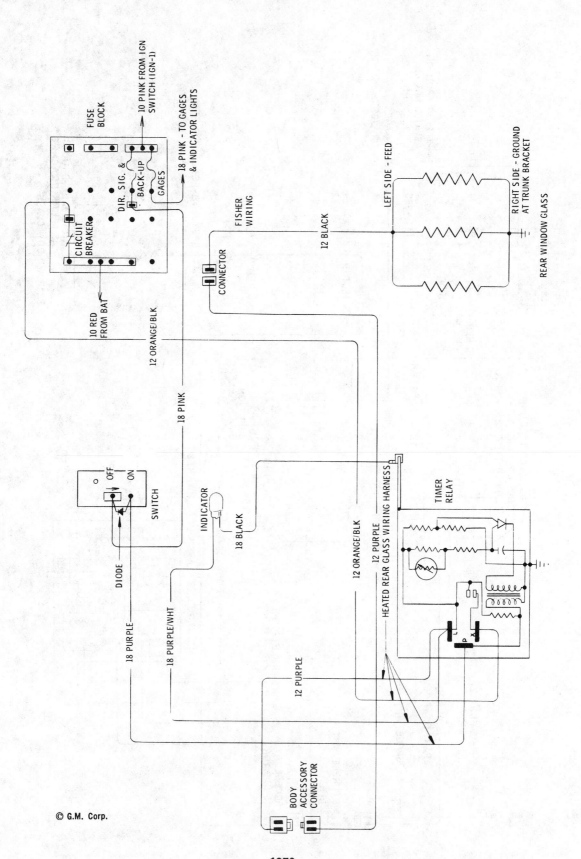

1973

# Buick

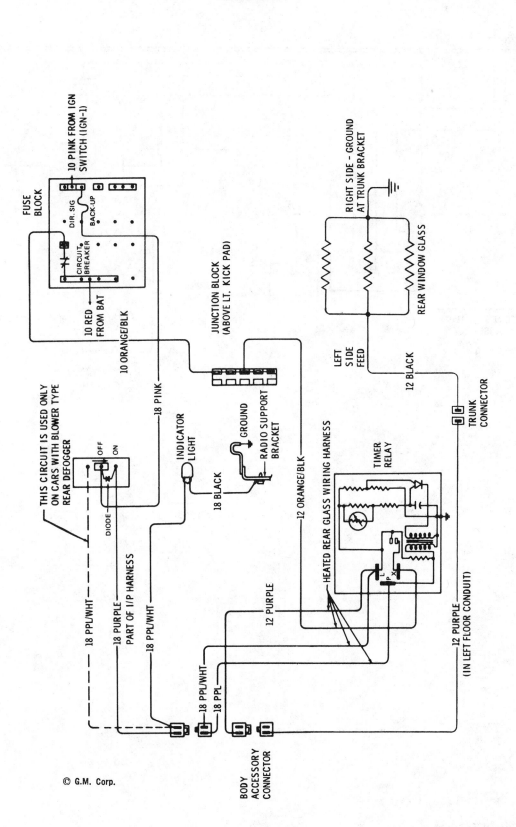

© G.M. Corp.

1974-75

## Vega

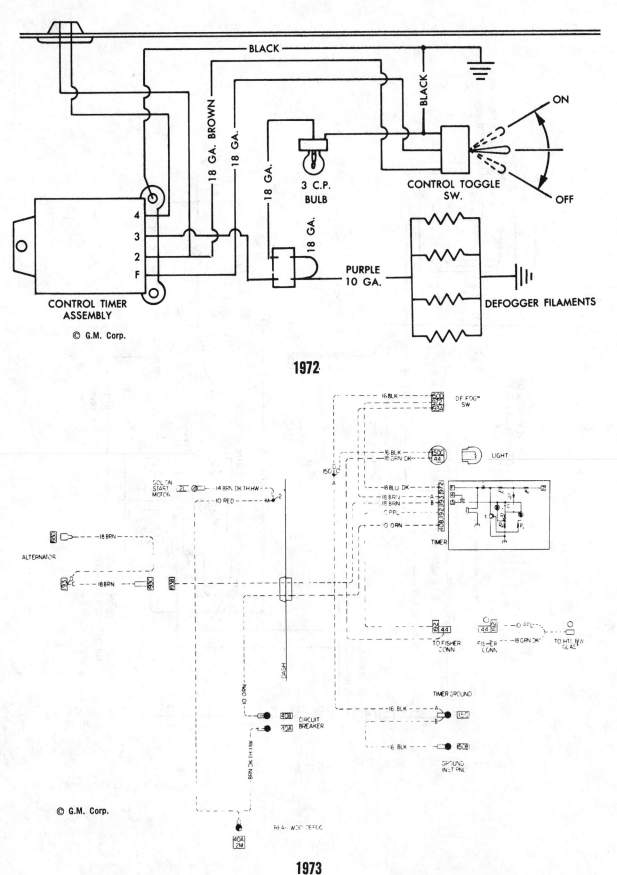

© G.M. Corp.

**1972**

© G.M. Corp.

**1973**

## Vega

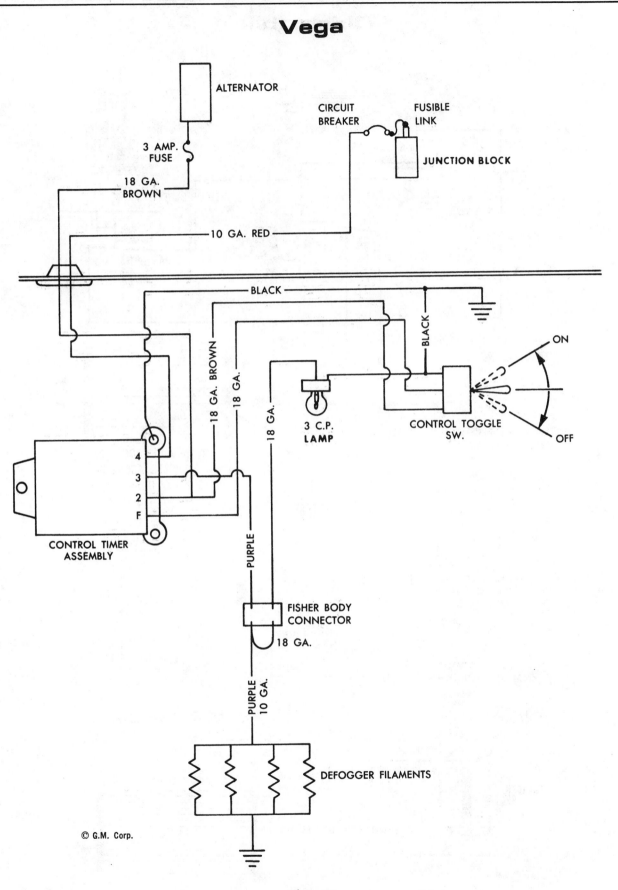

1974-75

## Oldsmobile

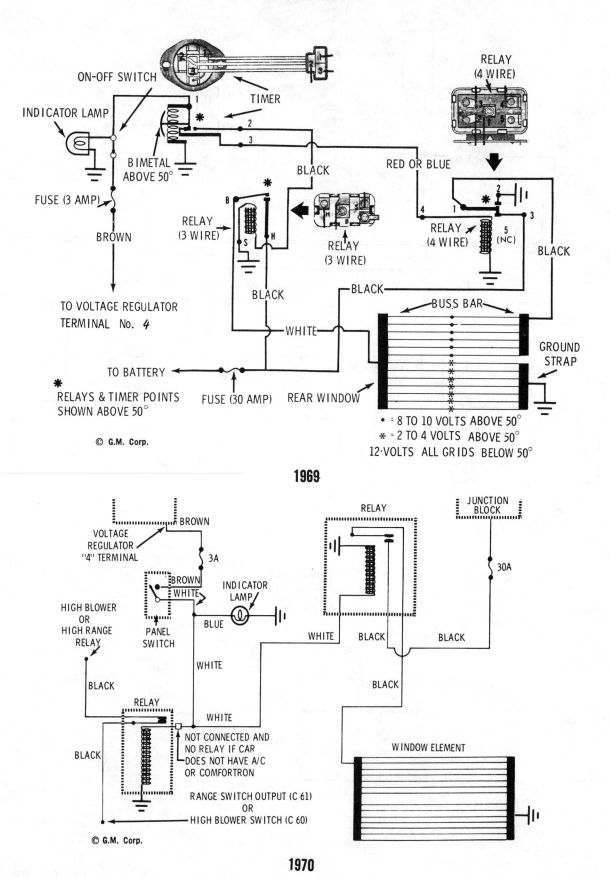

**1969**

**1970**

# Heated Back Window Wiring

## Oldsmobile

### TROUBLE DIAGNOSIS CHART

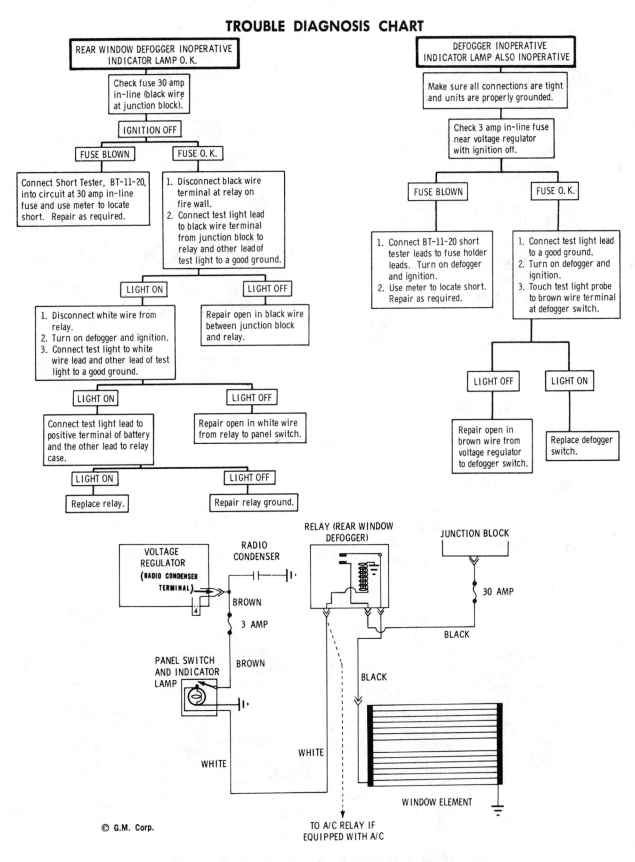

REAR WINDOW DEFOGGER INOPERATIVE
INDICATOR LAMP O. K.

Check fuse 30 amp in-line (black wire at junction block).

IGNITION OFF

FUSE BLOWN

Connect Short Tester, BT-11-20, into circuit at 30 amp in-line fuse and use meter to locate short. Repair as required.

FUSE O. K.

1. Disconnect black wire terminal at relay on fire wall.
2. Connect test light lead to black wire terminal from junction block to relay and other lead of test light to a good ground.

LIGHT ON

1. Disconnect white wire from relay.
2. Turn on defogger and ignition.
3. Connect test light to white wire lead and other lead of test light to a good ground.

LIGHT OFF

Repair open in black wire between junction block and relay.

LIGHT ON

Connect test light lead to positive terminal of battery and the other lead to relay case.

LIGHT OFF

Repair open in white wire from relay to panel switch.

LIGHT ON

Replace relay.

LIGHT OFF

Repair relay ground.

DEFOGGER INOPERATIVE
INDICATOR LAMP ALSO INOPERATIVE

Make sure all connections are tight and units are properly grounded.

Check 3 amp in-line fuse near voltage regulator with ignition off.

FUSE BLOWN

1. Connect BT-11-20 short tester leads to fuse holder leads. Turn on defogger and ignition.
2. Use meter to locate short. Repair as required.

FUSE O. K.

1. Connect test light lead to a good ground.
2. Turn on defogger and ignition.
3. Touch test light probe to brown wire terminal at defogger switch.

LIGHT OFF

Repair open in brown wire from voltage regulator to defogger switch.

LIGHT ON

Replace defogger switch.

VOLTAGE REGULATOR
(RADIO CONDENSER TERMINAL)

RADIO CONDENSER

RELAY (REAR WINDOW DEFOGGER)

JUNCTION BLOCK

30 AMP

BROWN

3 AMP

PANEL SWITCH AND INDICATOR LAMP

BROWN

BLACK

BLACK

WHITE

WHITE

WINDOW ELEMENT

© G.M. Corp.

TO A/C RELAY IF EQUIPPED WITH A/C

**1971**

## Oldsmobile

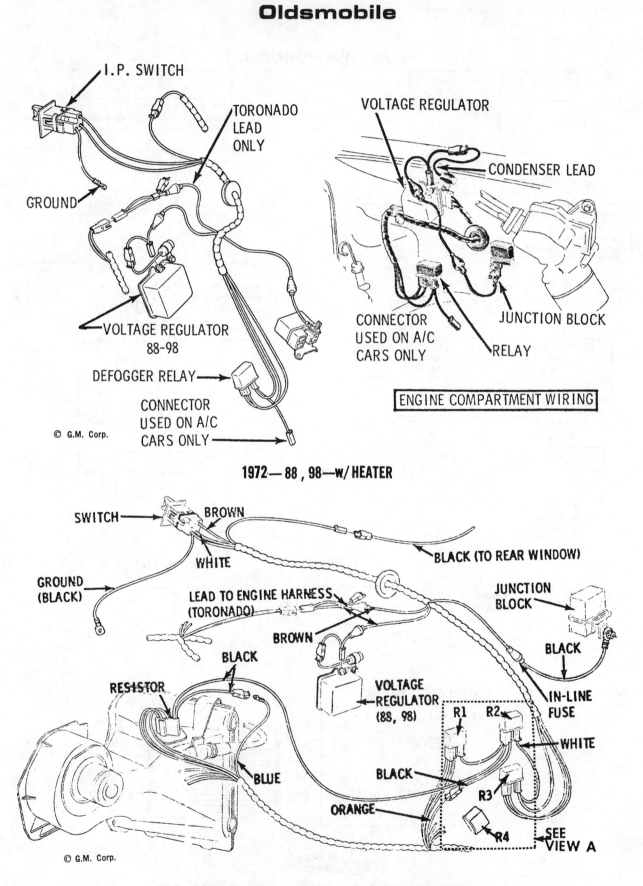

I.P. SWITCH

TORONADO LEAD ONLY

GROUND

VOLTAGE REGULATOR 88-98

DEFOGGER RELAY

CONNECTOR USED ON A/C CARS ONLY

© G.M. Corp.

VOLTAGE REGULATOR

CONDENSER LEAD

CONNECTOR USED ON A/C CARS ONLY

RELAY

JUNCTION BLOCK

ENGINE COMPARTMENT WIRING

**1972—88 , 98—w/HEATER**

SWITCH

BROWN

WHITE

BLACK (TO REAR WINDOW)

GROUND (BLACK)

LEAD TO ENGINE HARNESS (TORONADO)

BROWN

JUNCTION BLOCK

BLACK

RESISTOR

BLACK

VOLTAGE REGULATOR (88, 98)

IN-LINE FUSE

R1    R2

WHITE

BLACK

BLUE

R3

ORANGE

R4

SEE VIEW A

© G.M. Corp.

**1972—88, 98 & TORONADO—w/MANUAL AIR CONDITIONER**

## Oldsmobile

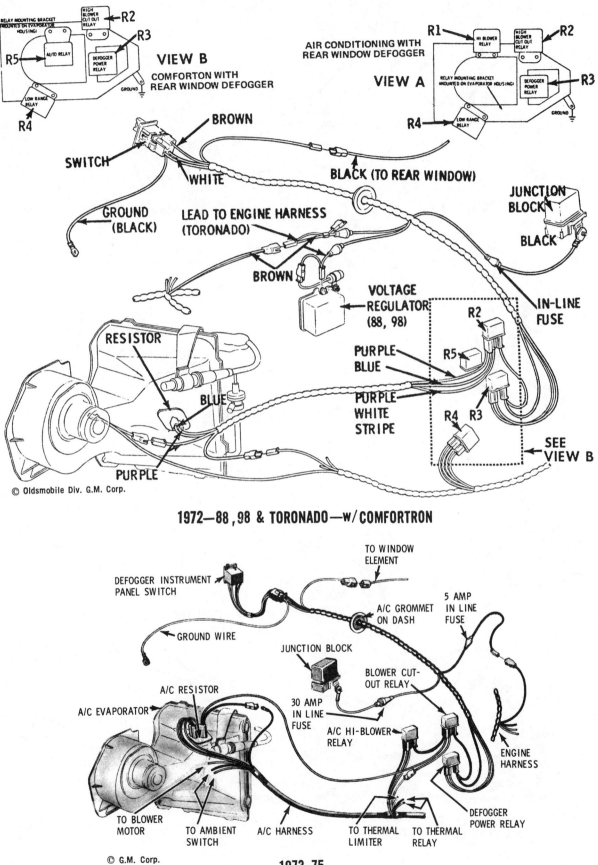

VIEW B

COMFORTON WITH
REAR WINDOW DEFOGGER

AIR CONDITIONING WITH
REAR WINDOW DEFOGGER

VIEW A

RELAY MOUNTING BRACKET
(MOUNTED ON EVAPORATOR HOUSING)

HIGH BLOWER CUT OUT RELAY

AUTO RELAY

DEFOGGER POWER RELAY

GROUND

LOW RANGE RELAY

R2
R3
R5
R4

HI BLOWER RELAY

R1
R2
R3
R4

SWITCH

BROWN

WHITE

BLACK (TO REAR WINDOW)

JUNCTION BLOCK

BLACK

GROUND (BLACK)

LEAD TO ENGINE HARNESS (TORONADO)

BROWN

VOLTAGE REGULATOR (88, 98)

IN-LINE FUSE

RESISTOR

PURPLE BLUE

PURPLE WHITE STRIPE

R2
R5
R4  R3

SEE VIEW B

BLUE

PURPLE

© Oldsmobile Div. G.M. Corp.

### 1972—88,98 & TORONADO—w/COMFORTRON

DEFOGGER INSTRUMENT PANEL SWITCH

TO WINDOW ELEMENT

A/C GROMMET ON DASH

5 AMP IN LINE FUSE

GROUND WIRE

JUNCTION BLOCK

BLOWER CUT-OUT RELAY

A/C RESISTOR

A/C EVAPORATOR

30 AMP IN LINE FUSE

A/C HI-BLOWER RELAY

ENGINE HARNESS

TO BLOWER MOTOR

TO AMBIENT SWITCH

A/C HARNESS

TO THERMAL LIMITER

TO THERMAL RELAY

DEFOGGER POWER RELAY

© G.M. Corp.

### 1973-75

## Oldsmobile

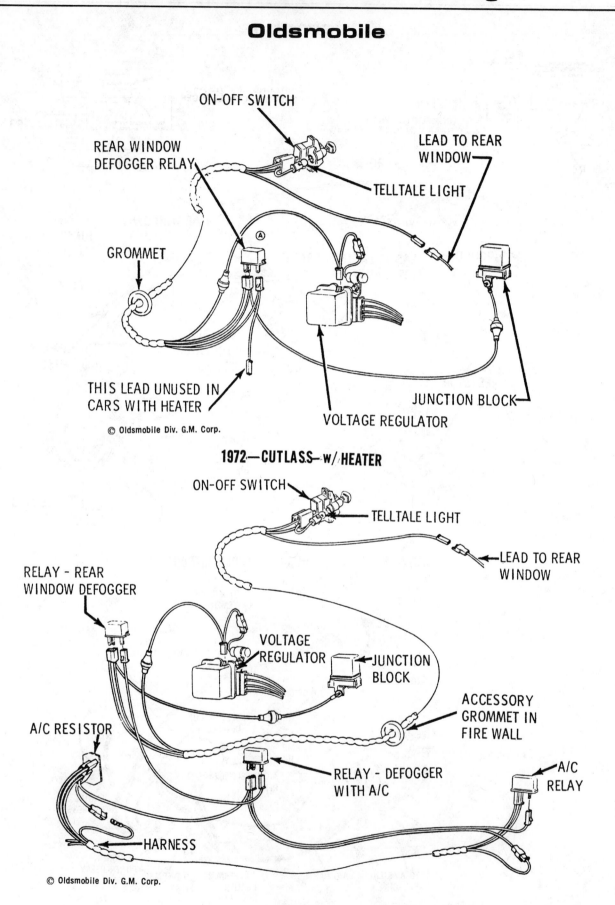

ON-OFF SWITCH

REAR WINDOW
DEFOGGER RELAY

LEAD TO REAR
WINDOW

TELLTALE LIGHT

GROMMET

Ⓐ

THIS LEAD UNUSED IN
CARS WITH HEATER

JUNCTION BLOCK

VOLTAGE REGULATOR

© Oldsmobile Div. G.M. Corp.

**1972—CUTLASS—w/ HEATER**

ON-OFF SWITCH

TELLTALE LIGHT

LEAD TO REAR
WINDOW

RELAY - REAR
WINDOW DEFOGGER

VOLTAGE
REGULATOR

JUNCTION
BLOCK

ACCESSORY
GROMMET IN
FIRE WALL

A/C RESISTOR

RELAY - DEFOGGER
WITH A/C

A/C
RELAY

HARNESS

© Oldsmobile Div. G.M. Corp.

**1972—CUTLASS—w/ AIR CONDITIONER**

# Heated Back Window Wiring

## Pontiac

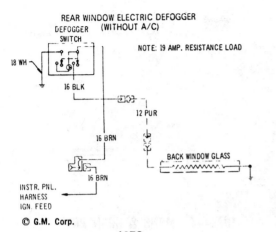

REAR WINDOW ELECTRIC DEFOGGER
(WITHOUT A/C)

DEFOGGER SWITCH

NOTE: 19 AMP. RESISTANCE LOAD

18 WH

16 BLK

12 PUR

16 BRN

16 BRN

BACK WINDOW GLASS

INSTR. PNL. HARNESS IGN. FEED

© G.M. Corp.

**1972**

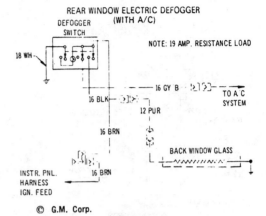

REAR WINDOW ELECTRIC DEFOGGER
(WITH A/C)

DEFOGGER SWITCH

NOTE: 19 AMP. RESISTANCE LOAD

18 WH

16 BLK

16 GY B    TO A C SYSTEM

12 PUR

16 BRN

BACK WINDOW GLASS

INSTR. PNL. HARNESS IGN. FEED

© G.M. Corp.

**1970**

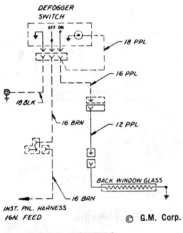

DEFOGGER SWITCH

OFF  ON

18 PPL

16 PPL

18 BLK

16 BRN

12 PPL

BACK WINDOW GLASS

16 BRN

INST. PNL. HARNESS IGN. FEED

© G.M. Corp.

**1971—PONTIAC**

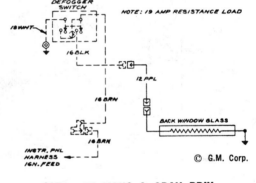

DEFOGGER SWITCH

NOTE: 19 AMP RESISTANCE LOAD

18 WHT

16 BLK

12 PPL

16 BRN

BACK WINDOW GLASS

16 BRN

INSTR. PNL. HARNESS IGN. FEED

© G.M. Corp.

**1971— LE MANS & GRAN PRIX**

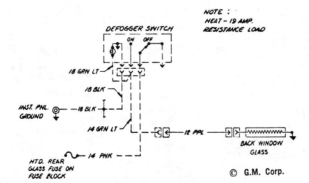

NOTE :
HEAT - 19 AMP. RESISTANCE LOAD

DEFOGGER SWITCH

ON    OFF

18 GRN LT

18 BLK

INST. PNL. GROUND    18 BLK

14 GRN LT

12 PPL

BACK WINDOW GLASS

HTD. REAR GLASS FUSE ON FUSE BLOCK    14 PNK

© G.M. Corp.

**1971—FIREBIRD**

327

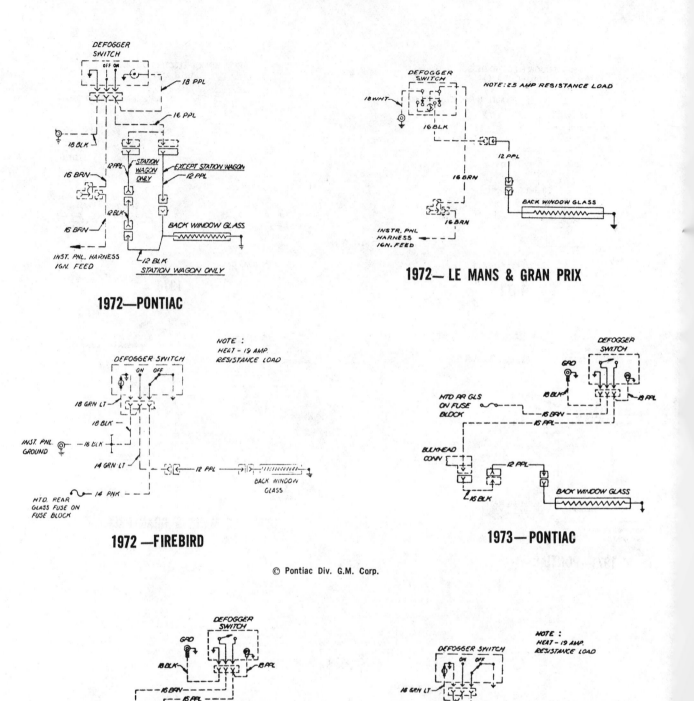

1972—PONTIAC

1972— LE MANS & GRAN PRIX

1972 —FIREBIRD

1973— PONTIAC

© Pontiac Div. G.M. Corp.

1973-75 LE MANS & GRAN PRIX

1973-75 FIREBIRD

## General Motors

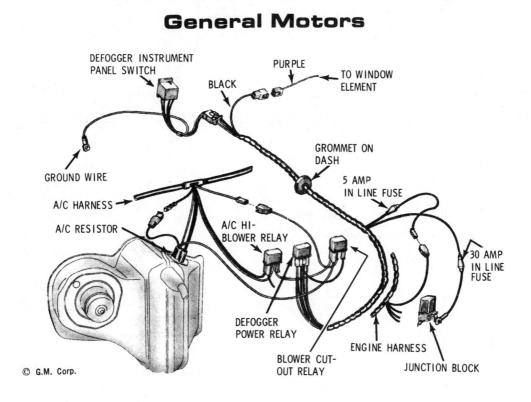

DEFOGGER INSTRUMENT PANEL SWITCH

PURPLE

BLACK

TO WINDOW ELEMENT

GROUND WIRE

GROMMET ON DASH

5 AMP IN LINE FUSE

A/C HARNESS

A/C RESISTOR

A/C HI-BLOWER RELAY

30 AMP IN LINE FUSE

DEFOGGER POWER RELAY

ENGINE HARNESS

BLOWER CUT-OUT RELAY

JUNCTION BLOCK

© G.M. Corp.

*1974-75—Cutlass with A/C*

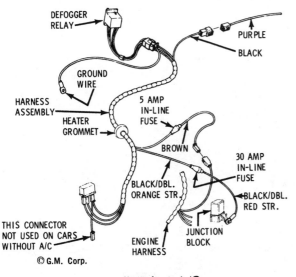

DEFOGGER RELAY

PURPLE

BLACK

GROUND WIRE

HARNESS ASSEMBLY

HEATER GROMMET

5 AMP IN-LINE FUSE

BROWN

30 AMP IN-LINE FUSE

BLACK/DBL. ORANGE STR.

BLACK/DBL. RED STR.

THIS CONNECTOR NOT USED ON CARS WITHOUT A/C

ENGINE HARNESS

JUNCTION BLOCK

© G.M. Corp.

*1973-75 All Without A/C.*

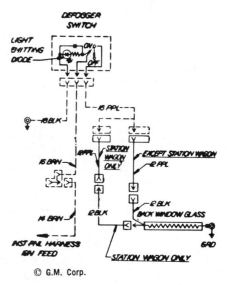

REAR WINDOW DEFOGGER (HEATED BACK-LITE)

DEFOGGER SWITCH

LIGHT EMITTING DIODE

ON

OFF

Y-Y-Y

18 BLK

18 PPL

18 BRN

STATION WAGON ONLY

EXCEPT STATION WAGON

12 PPL

12 BLK

12 BLK

BACK WINDOW GLASS

14 BRN

GRD

INST PNL HARNESS IGN FEED

STATION WAGON ONLY

© G.M. Corp.

*1974-75—Pontiac*

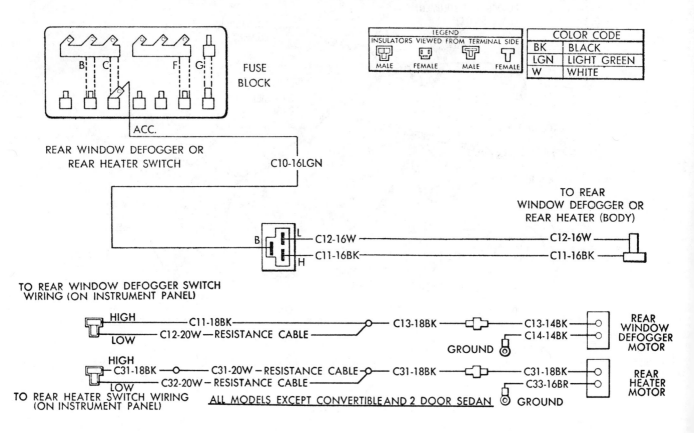

**1968-71**

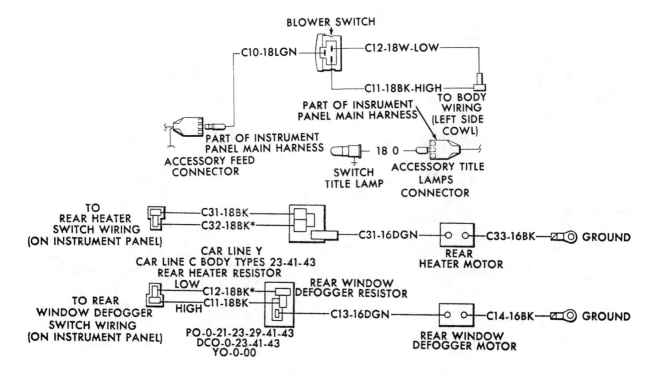

**1972-73**

## Ford Motor Company
## Ford

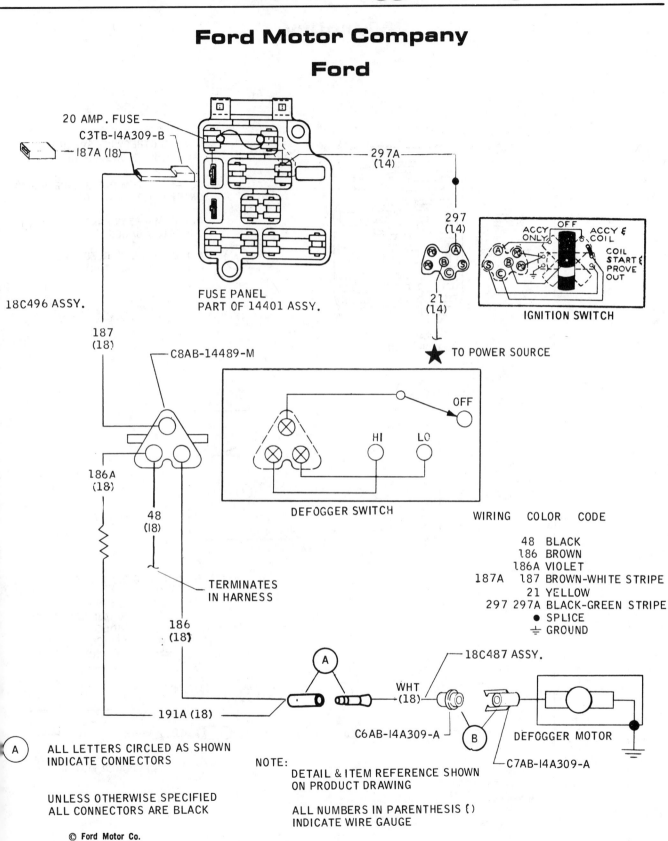

20 AMP. FUSE
C3TB-14A309-B
187A (18)

FUSE PANEL
PART OF 14401 ASSY.

18C496 ASSY.

297A (14)

297 (14)

21 (14)

IGNITION SWITCH

ACCY ONLY    OFF    ACCY & COIL
COIL START & PROVE OUT

TO POWER SOURCE

187 (18)

C8AB-14489-M

OFF
HI    LO

DEFOGGER SWITCH

186A (18)

48 (18)

TERMINATES IN HARNESS

186 (18)

WIRING   COLOR   CODE

|  | 48 | BLACK |
|  | 186 | BROWN |
|  | 186A | VIOLET |
| 187A | 187 | BROWN-WHITE STRIPE |
|  | 21 | YELLOW |
| 297 | 297A | BLACK-GREEN STRIPE |
|  | ● | SPLICE |
|  | ⏚ | GROUND |

A

18C487 ASSY.

WHT (18)

C6AB-14A309-A

B

DEFOGGER MOTOR

C7AB-14A309-A

191A (18)

A  ALL LETTERS CIRCLED AS SHOWN
INDICATE CONNECTORS

UNLESS OTHERWISE SPECIFIED
ALL CONNECTORS ARE BLACK

© Ford Motor Co.

NOTE:

DETAIL & ITEM REFERENCE SHOWN
ON PRODUCT DRAWING

ALL NUMBERS IN PARENTHESIS ( )
INDICATE WIRE GAUGE

**1968**

## Mercury

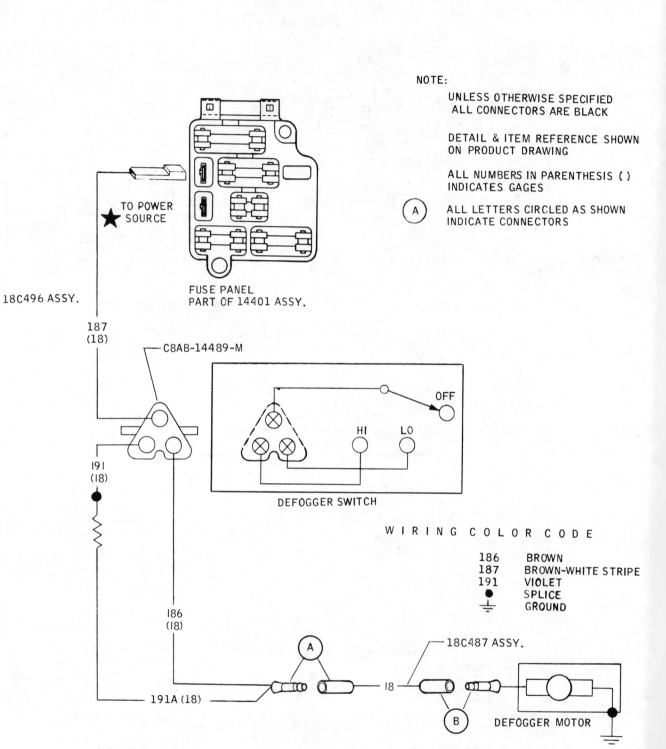

NOTE:

UNLESS OTHERWISE SPECIFIED
ALL CONNECTORS ARE BLACK

DETAIL & ITEM REFERENCE SHOWN
ON PRODUCT DRAWING

ALL NUMBERS IN PARENTHESIS ( )
INDICATES GAGES

(A) ALL LETTERS CIRCLED AS SHOWN
INDICATE CONNECTORS

TO POWER
SOURCE

FUSE PANEL
PART OF 14401 ASSY.

18C496 ASSY.

187
(18)

C8AB-14489-M

191
(18)

OFF

HI        LO

DEFOGGER SWITCH

W I R I N G   C O L O R   C O D E

| 186 | BROWN |
| 187 | BROWN-WHITE STRIPE |
| 191 | VIOLET |
| ● | SPLICE |
| ⏚ | GROUND |

186
(18)

(A)

18C487 ASSY.

191A (18)

18

(B)

DEFOGGER MOTOR

© Ford Motor Co.

1968

## Ford • Mercury

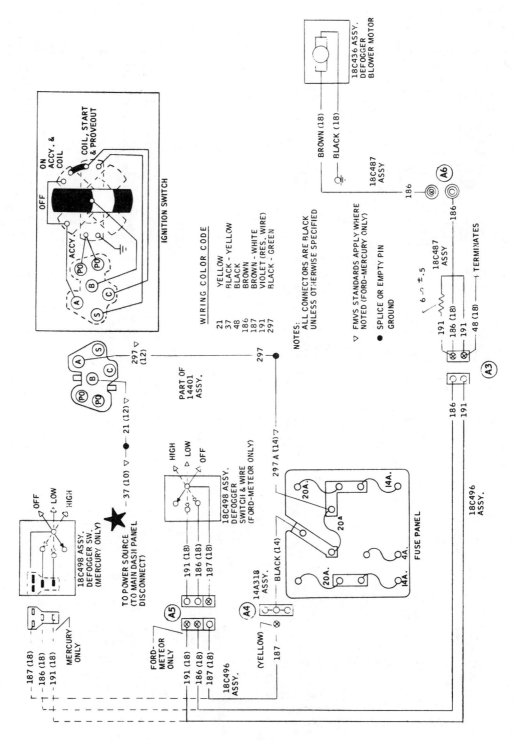

WIRING COLOR CODE

| | |
|---|---|
| 21 | YELLOW |
| 37 | BLACK – YELLOW |
| 48 | BLACK |
| 186 | BROWN |
| 187 | BROWN – WHITE |
| 191 | VIOLET (RES. WIRE) |
| 297 | BLACK – GREEN |

NOTES:
ALL CONNECTORS ARE BLACK
UNLESS OTHERWISE SPECIFIED

▽ FMVS STANDARDS APPLY WHERE
NOTED (FORD–MERCURY ONLY)

● SPLICE OR EMPTY PIN
⏚ GROUND

© Ford Motor Co.

1969

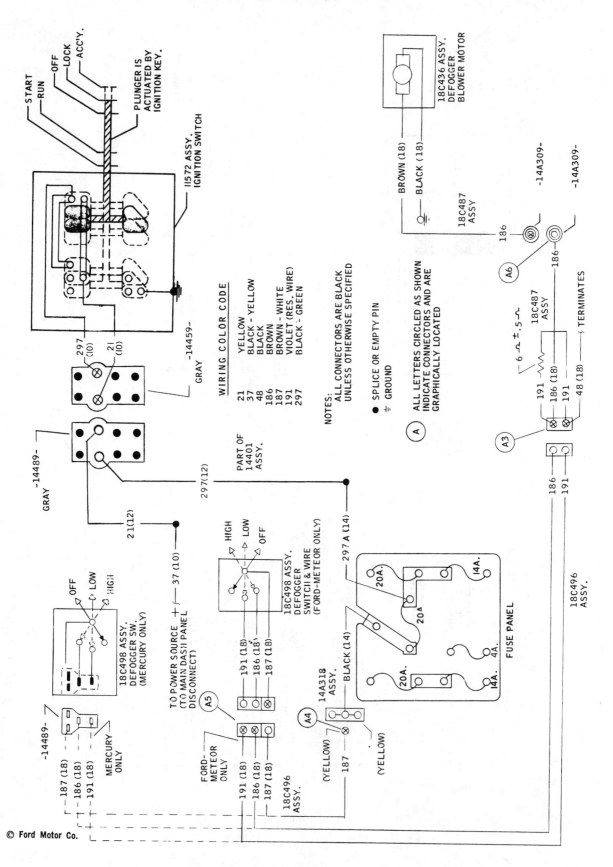

WIRING COLOR CODE

| | |
|---|---|
| 21 | YELLOW |
| 37 | BLACK - YELLOW |
| 48 | BLACK |
| 186 | BROWN |
| 187 | BROWN - WHITE |
| 191 | VIOLET (RES. WIRE) |
| 297 | BLACK - GREEN |

NOTES:
ALL CONNECTORS ARE BLACK
UNLESS OTHERWISE SPECIFIED

● SPLICE OR EMPTY PIN
⏚ GROUND

Ⓐ ALL LETTERS CIRCLED AS SHOWN
INDICATE CONNECTORS AND ARE
GRAPHICALLY LOCATED

© Ford Motor Co.

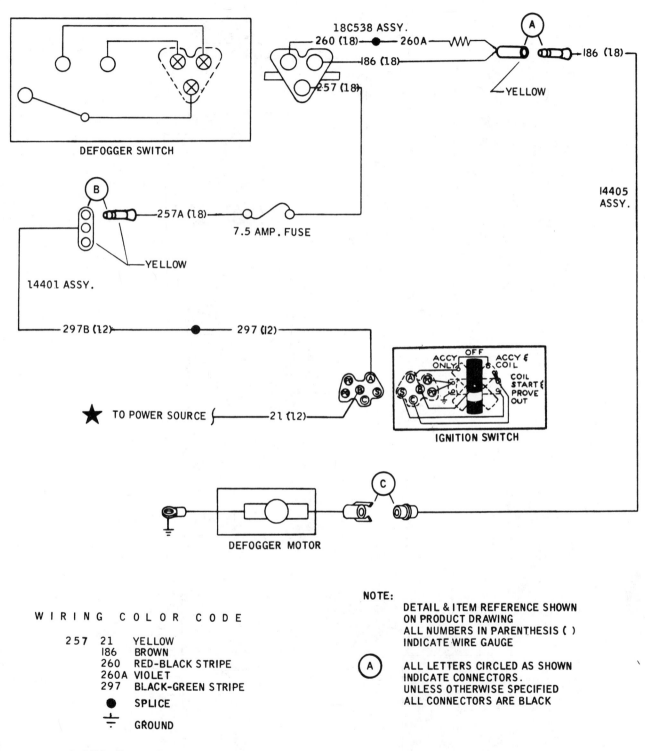

18C538 ASSY.
260 (18) — 260A
186 (18)
257 (18)
YELLOW
186 (18)
14405 ASSY.

DEFOGGER SWITCH

B
257A (18)
7.5 AMP. FUSE
YELLOW
14401 ASSY.

297B (12) — 297 (12)

★ TO POWER SOURCE — 21 (12)

ACCY ONLY
OFF
ACCY & COIL
COIL START & PROVE OUT

IGNITION SWITCH

C

DEFOGGER MOTOR

WIRING COLOR CODE

257 21 YELLOW
186 BROWN
260 RED-BLACK STRIPE
260A VIOLET
297 BLACK-GREEN STRIPE
● SPLICE
⏚ GROUND

NOTE:

DETAIL & ITEM REFERENCE SHOWN
ON PRODUCT DRAWING
ALL NUMBERS IN PARENTHESIS ( )
INDICATE WIRE GAUGE

A ALL LETTERS CIRCLED AS SHOWN
INDICATE CONNECTORS.
UNLESS OTHERWISE SPECIFIED
ALL CONNECTORS ARE BLACK

© Ford Motor Co.

**1968**

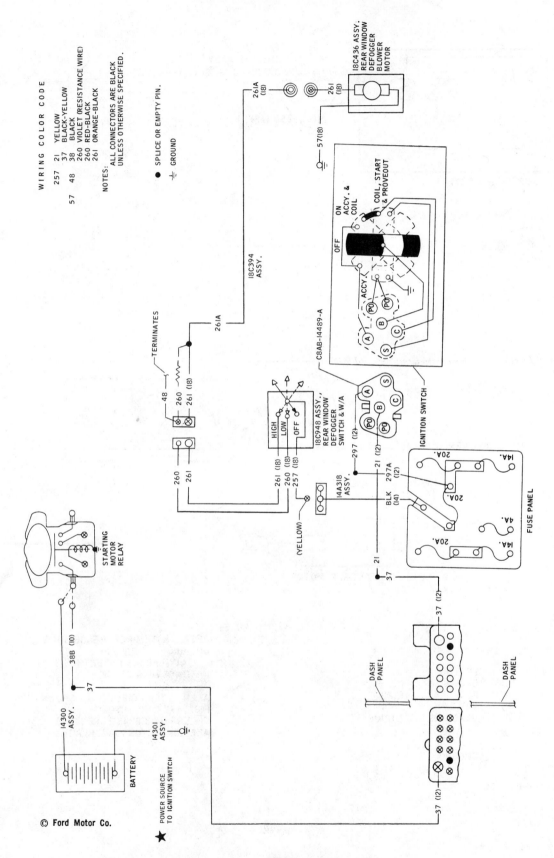

1969

# Rear Window Defogger Wiring

## Fairlane • Falcon • Montego

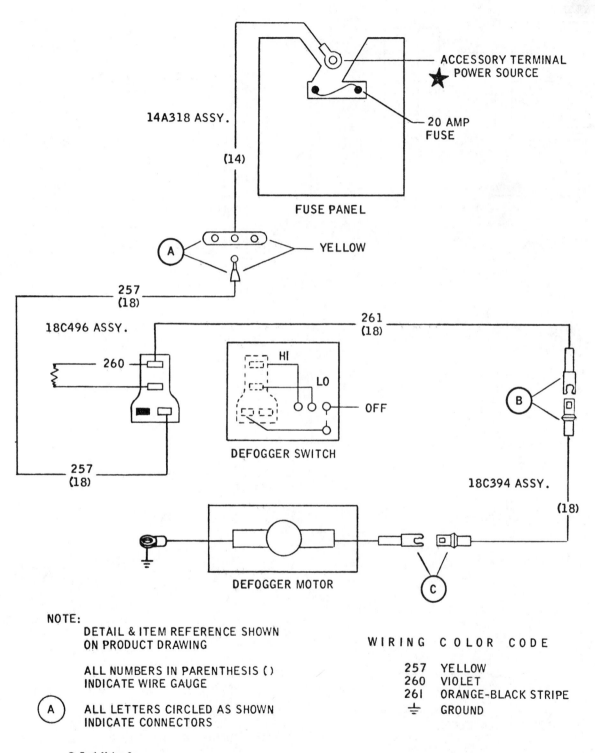

ACCESSORY TERMINAL
POWER SOURCE

14A318 ASSY.

20 AMP
FUSE

(14)

FUSE PANEL

A          YELLOW

257
(18)

18C496 ASSY.          261
(18)

260                    HI

LO

OFF                    B

DEFOGGER SWITCH

257
(18)                                   18C394 ASSY.

(18)

DEFOGGER MOTOR          C

NOTE:

DETAIL & ITEM REFERENCE SHOWN
ON PRODUCT DRAWING

ALL NUMBERS IN PARENTHESIS ( )          WIRING  COLOR  CODE
INDICATE WIRE GAUGE
                                        257   YELLOW
                                        260   VIOLET
A   ALL LETTERS CIRCLED AS SHOWN         261   ORANGE-BLACK STRIPE
    INDICATE CONNECTORS                  ⏚    GROUND

© Ford Motor Co.

**1970**

## Lincoln·Continental

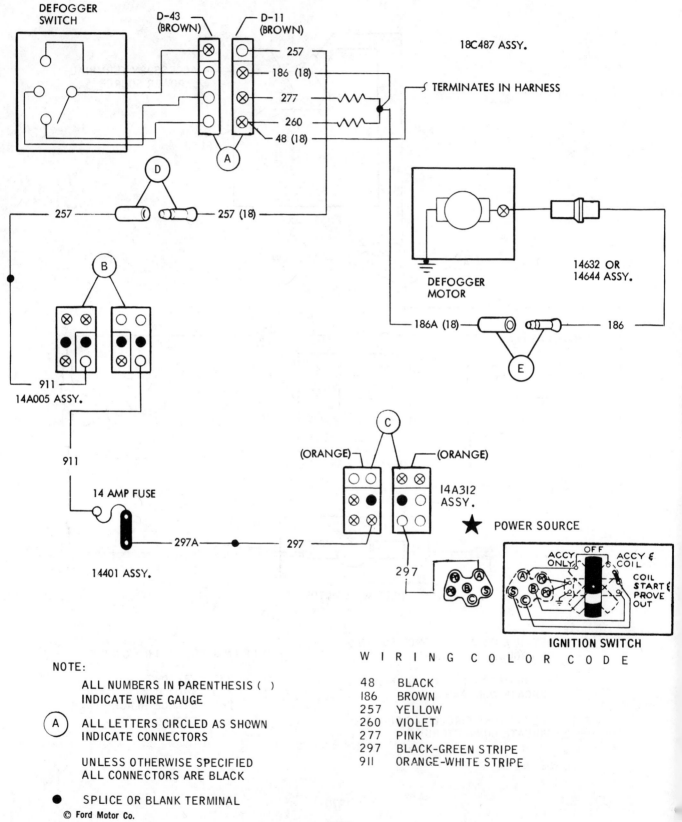

NOTE:

ALL NUMBERS IN PARENTHESIS ( )
INDICATE WIRE GAUGE

(A) ALL LETTERS CIRCLED AS SHOWN
INDICATE CONNECTORS

UNLESS OTHERWISE SPECIFIED
ALL CONNECTORS ARE BLACK

● SPLICE OR BLANK TERMINAL

© Ford Motor Co.

WIRING COLOR CODE

| | |
|---|---|
| 48 | BLACK |
| 186 | BROWN |
| 257 | YELLOW |
| 260 | VIOLET |
| 277 | PINK |
| 297 | BLACK-GREEN STRIPE |
| 911 | ORANGE-WHITE STRIPE |

**1968**

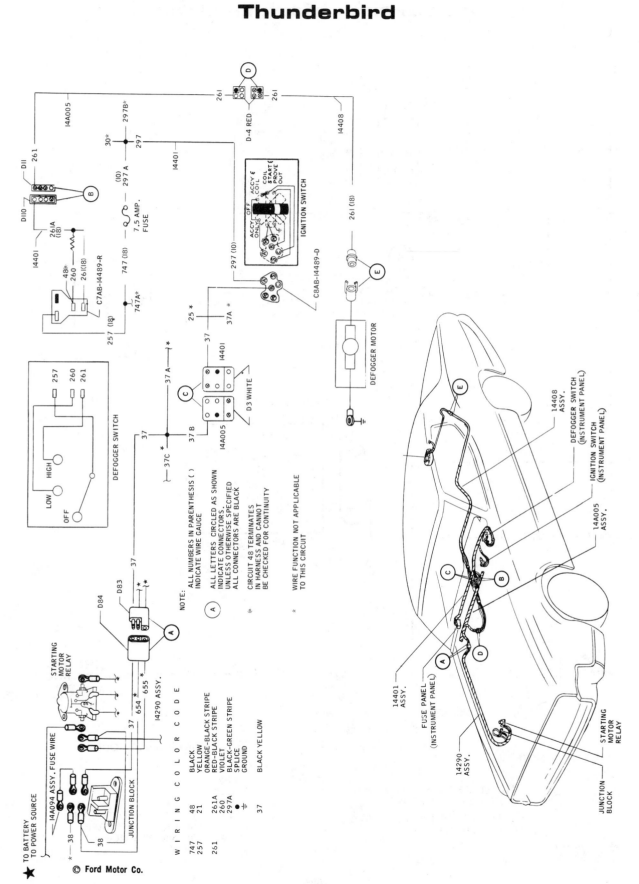

© Ford Motor Co.

1968

## Thunderbird• Mark III•Lincoln

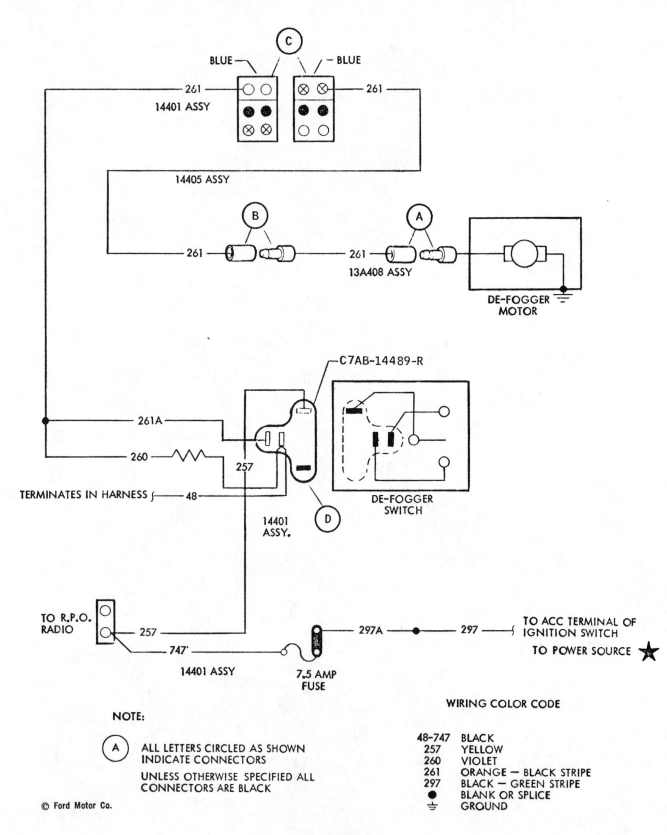

NOTE:

(A) ALL LETTERS CIRCLED AS SHOWN
INDICATE CONNECTORS

UNLESS OTHERWISE SPECIFIED ALL
CONNECTORS ARE BLACK

© Ford Motor Co.

WIRING COLOR CODE

| 48-747 | BLACK |
| 257 | YELLOW |
| 260 | VIOLET |
| 261 | ORANGE — BLACK STRIPE |
| 297 | BLACK — GREEN STRIPE |
| ● | BLANK OR SPLICE |
| ⏚ | GROUND |

1969

## Thunderbird • Mark III

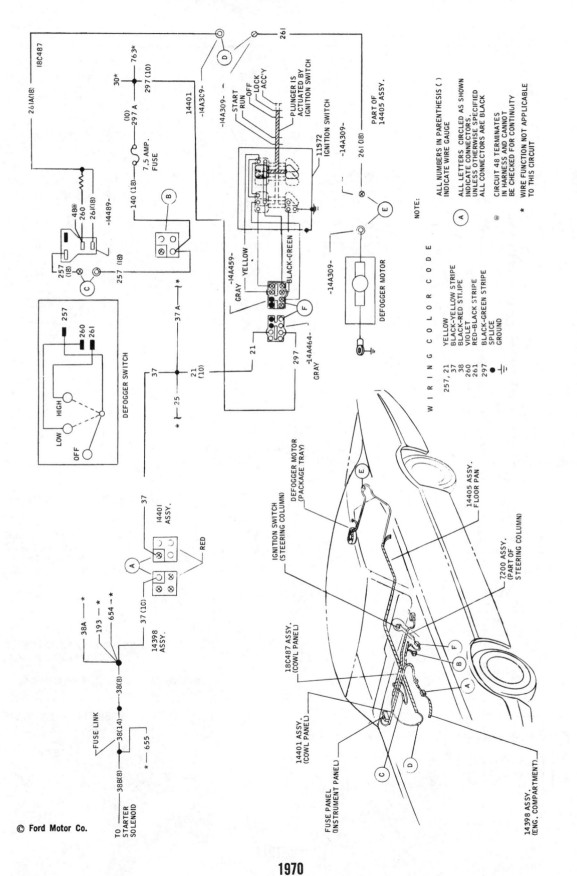

© Ford Motor Co.

**1970**

## Thunderbird • Mark III

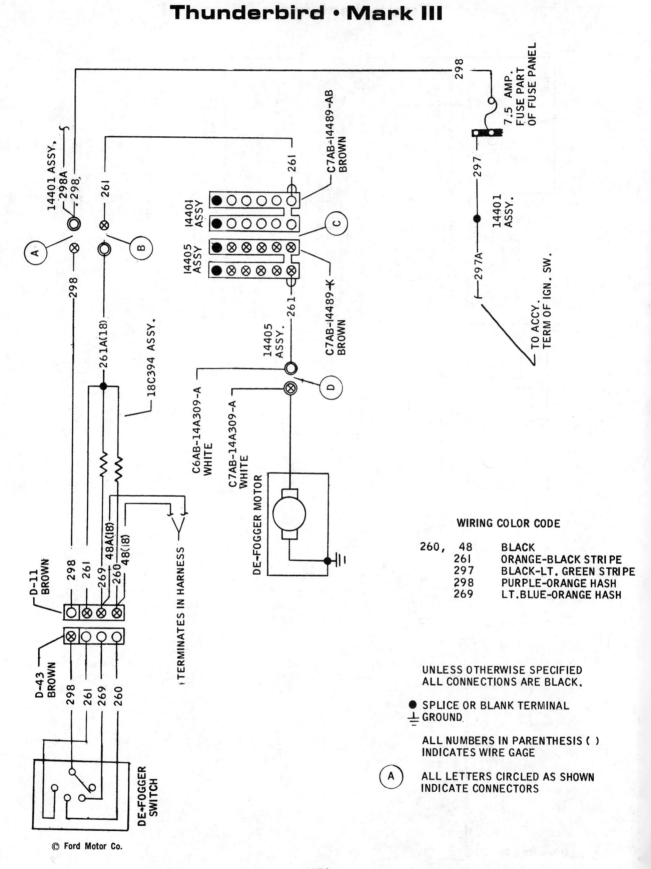

**WIRING COLOR CODE**

| 260, | 48 | BLACK |
|---|---|---|
| | 261 | ORANGE-BLACK STRIPE |
| | 297 | BLACK-LT. GREEN STRIPE |
| | 298 | PURPLE-ORANGE HASH |
| | 269 | LT.BLUE-ORANGE HASH |

UNLESS OTHERWISE SPECIFIED
ALL CONNECTIONS ARE BLACK.

● SPLICE OR BLANK TERMINAL
⏚ GROUND

ALL NUMBERS IN PARENTHESIS ( )
INDICATES WIRE GAGE

(A) ALL LETTERS CIRCLED AS SHOWN
INDICATE CONNECTORS

© Ford Motor Co.

1971

## Ford

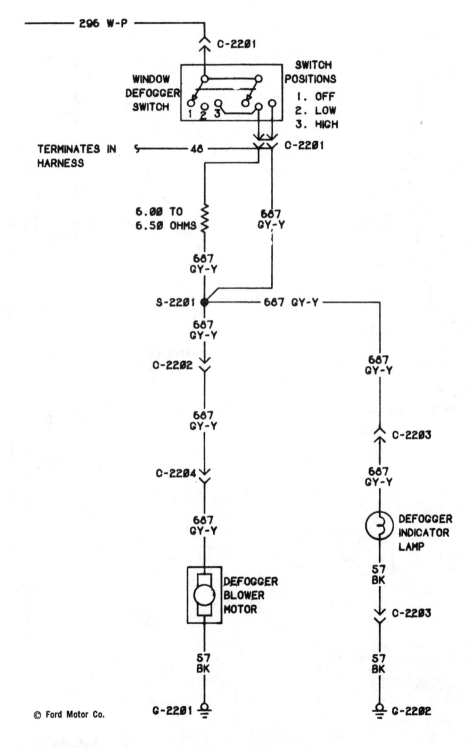

**1974-75 FORD**

# Ford Motor Company

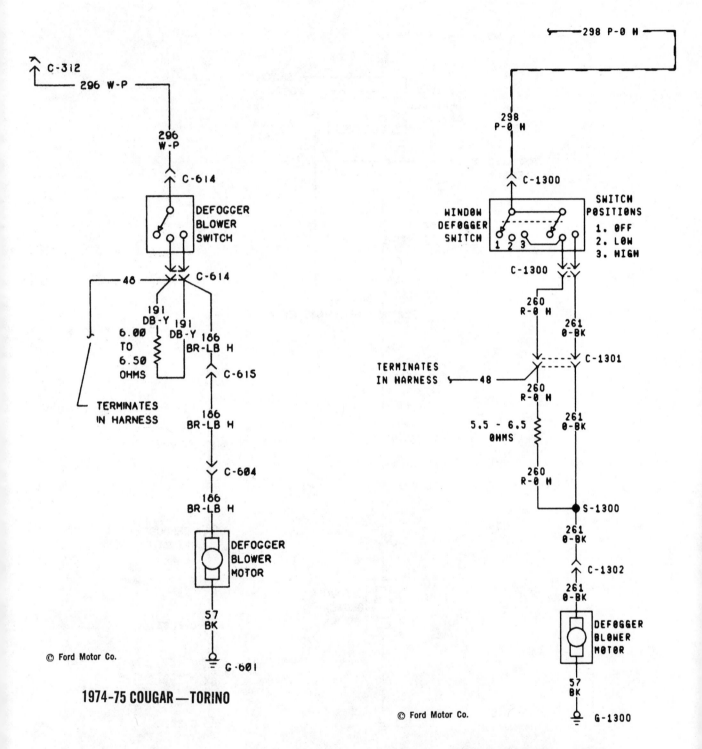

**1974-75 COUGAR — TORINO**

**1974-75 MAVERICK — PINTO**

© Ford Motor Co.

© Ford Motor Co.

## General Motors
## Buick

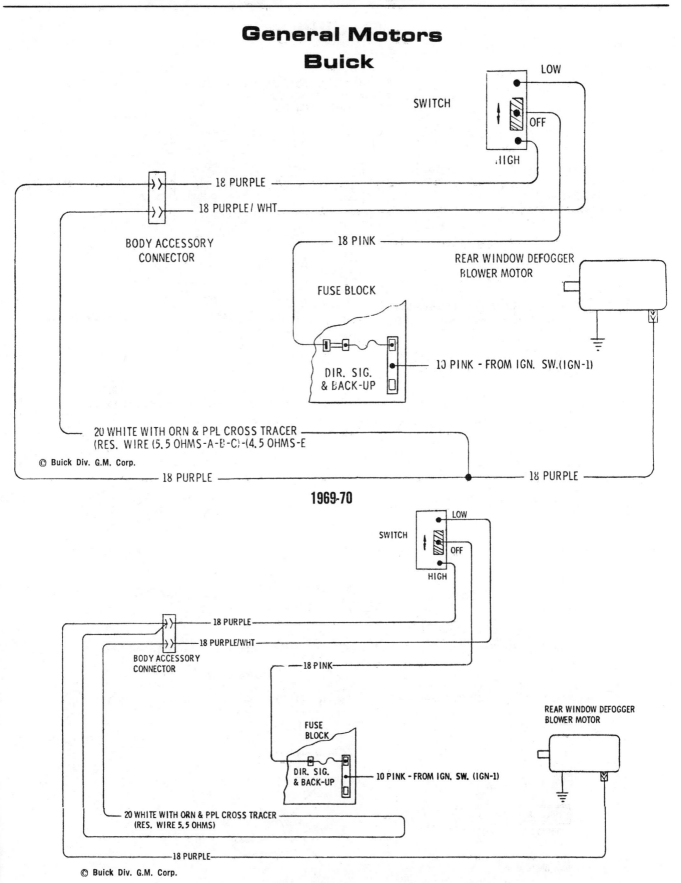

SWITCH

LOW

OFF

HIGH

18 PURPLE

18 PURPLE / WHT

BODY ACCESSORY
CONNECTOR

18 PINK

REAR WINDOW DEFOGGER
BLOWER MOTOR

FUSE BLOCK

DIR. SIG.
& BACK-UP

10 PINK - FROM IGN. SW.(IGN-1)

20 WHITE WITH ORN & PPL CROSS TRACER
(RES. WIRE (5.5 OHMS-A-B-C)-(4.5 OHMS-E

© Buick Div. G.M. Corp.

18 PURPLE

18 PURPLE

**1969-70**

SWITCH

LOW

OFF

HIGH

18 PURPLE

18 PURPLE/WHT

BODY ACCESSORY
CONNECTOR

18 PINK

REAR WINDOW DEFOGGER
BLOWER MOTOR

FUSE
BLOCK

DIR. SIG.
& BACK-UP

10 PINK - FROM IGN. SW. (IGN-1)

20 WHITE WITH ORN & PPL CROSS TRACER
(RES. WIRE 5.5 OHMS)

18 PURPLE

© Buick Div. G.M. Corp.

**1971-73**

## Cadillac

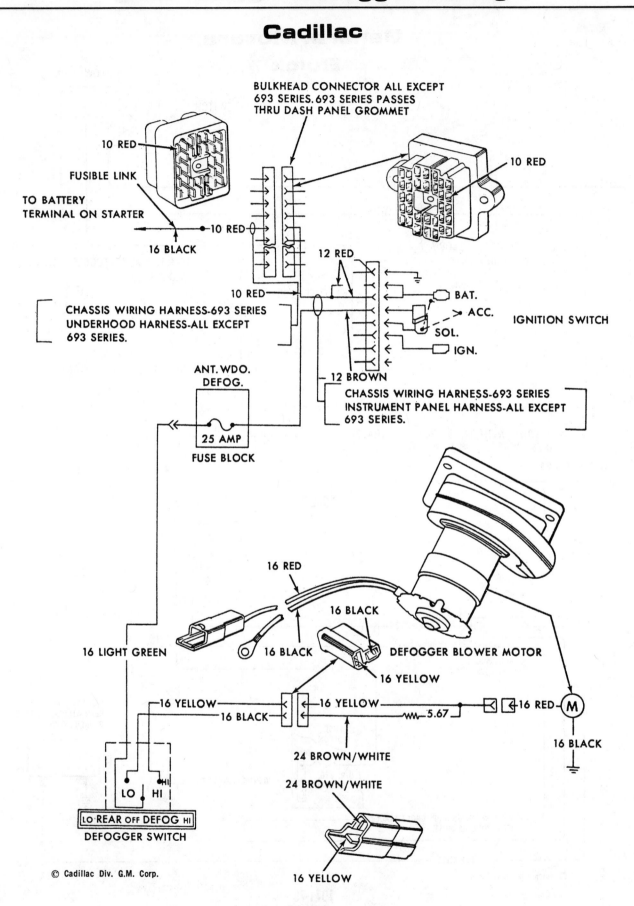

BULKHEAD CONNECTOR ALL EXCEPT
693 SERIES. 693 SERIES PASSES
THRU DASH PANEL GROMMET

10 RED

FUSIBLE LINK

TO BATTERY
TERMINAL ON STARTER

16 BLACK

10 RED

10 RED

10 RED

12 RED

BAT.

ACC.

IGNITION SWITCH

SOL.

IGN.

CHASSIS WIRING HARNESS-693 SERIES
UNDERHOOD HARNESS-ALL EXCEPT
693 SERIES.

12 BROWN

CHASSIS WIRING HARNESS-693 SERIES
INSTRUMENT PANEL HARNESS-ALL EXCEPT
693 SERIES.

ANT. WDO.
DEFOG.

25 AMP

FUSE BLOCK

16 RED

16 BLACK

16 BLACK

16 BLACK

DEFOGGER BLOWER MOTOR

16 YELLOW

16 LIGHT GREEN

16 YELLOW

16 YELLOW

16 BLACK

5.67

16 RED

M

16 RED

LO    HI

LO REAR OFF DEFOG HI

DEFOGGER SWITCH

16 BLACK

24 BROWN/WHITE

24 BROWN/WHITE

© Cadillac Div. G.M. Corp.

16 YELLOW

**1968**

## Cadillac

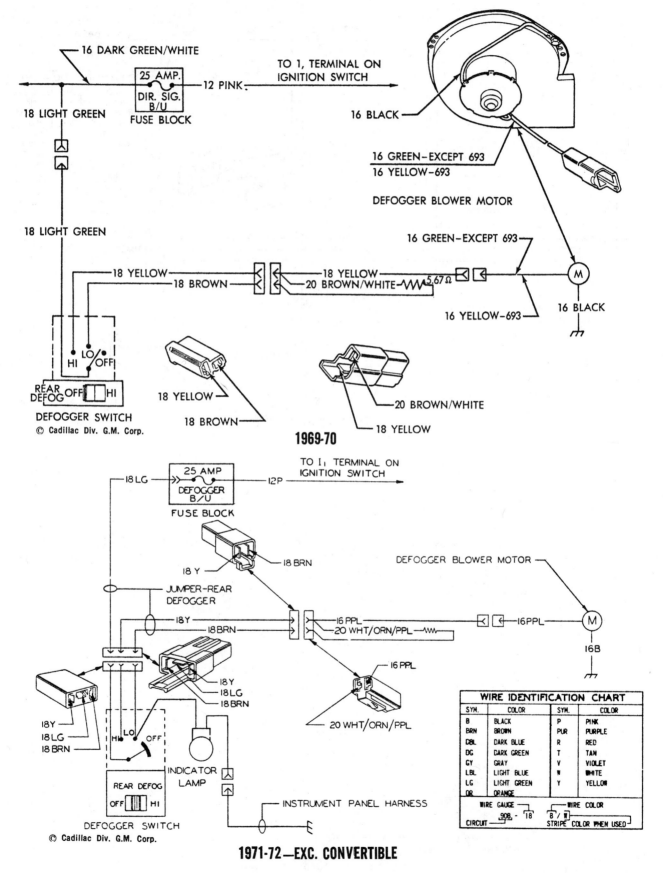

16 DARK GREEN/WHITE

25 AMP. DIR. SIG. B/U FUSE BLOCK

12 PINK

TO 1, TERMINAL ON IGNITION SWITCH

18 LIGHT GREEN

16 BLACK

16 GREEN—EXCEPT 693
16 YELLOW—693

DEFOGGER BLOWER MOTOR

18 LIGHT GREEN

16 GREEN—EXCEPT 693

18 YELLOW
18 BROWN
18 YELLOW
20 BROWN/WHITE—5.67 Ω

16 YELLOW—693

M

16 BLACK

LO OFF
HI

REAR DEFOG OFF HI

DEFOGGER SWITCH

© Cadillac Div. G.M. Corp.

18 YELLOW

18 BROWN

20 BROWN/WHITE

18 YELLOW

**1969-70**

18 LG

25 AMP DEFOGGER B/U FUSE BLOCK

12 P

TO I, TERMINAL ON IGNITION SWITCH

18 BRN

18 Y

JUMPER-REAR DEFOGGER

DEFOGGER BLOWER MOTOR

18 Y
18 BRN

16 PPL
20 WHT/ORN/PPL

16 PPL

M

16 B

18 Y
18 LG
18 BRN

16 PPL

18 Y
18 LG
18 BRN

20 WHT/ORN/PPL

HI LO OFF

INDICATOR LAMP

REAR DEFOG OFF HI

DEFOGGER SWITCH

© Cadillac Div. G.M. Corp.

INSTRUMENT PANEL HARNESS

| WIRE IDENTIFICATION CHART | | | |
|---|---|---|---|
| SYM. | COLOR | SYM. | COLOR |
| B | BLACK | P | PINK |
| BRN | BROWN | PUR | PURPLE |
| DBL | DARK BLUE | R | RED |
| DG | DARK GREEN | T | TAN |
| GY | GRAY | V | VIOLET |
| LBL | LIGHT BLUE | W | WHITE |
| LG | LIGHT GREEN | Y | YELLOW |
| OR | ORANGE | | |
| WIRE GAUGE | | WIRE COLOR | |
| .908 - 18 | | B / W | |
| CIRCUIT | | STRIPE COLOR WHEN USED | |

**1971-72—EXC. CONVERTIBLE**

## Cadillac

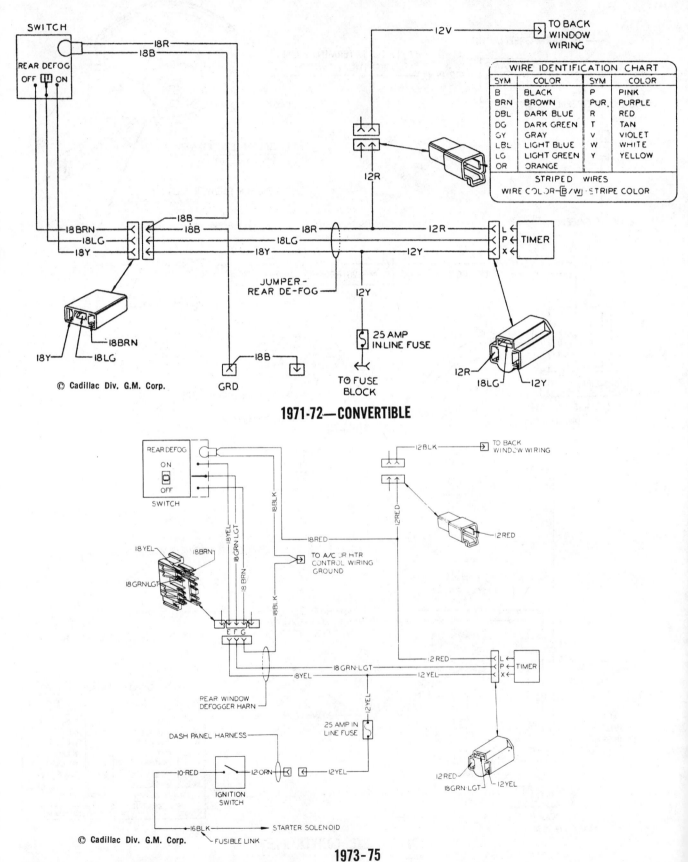

### 1971-72—CONVERTIBLE

### 1973-75

## Chevrolet

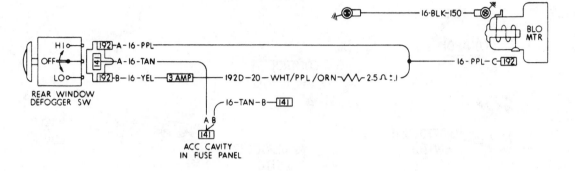

**1972-75—CORVETTE**

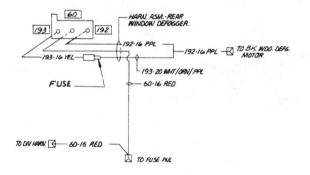

**1972-75—CAMARO**

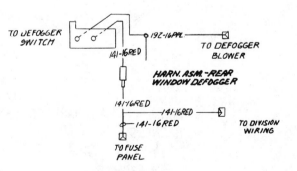

**1972-75—NOVA**

© Chevrolet Div. G.M. Corp.

## Oldsmobile

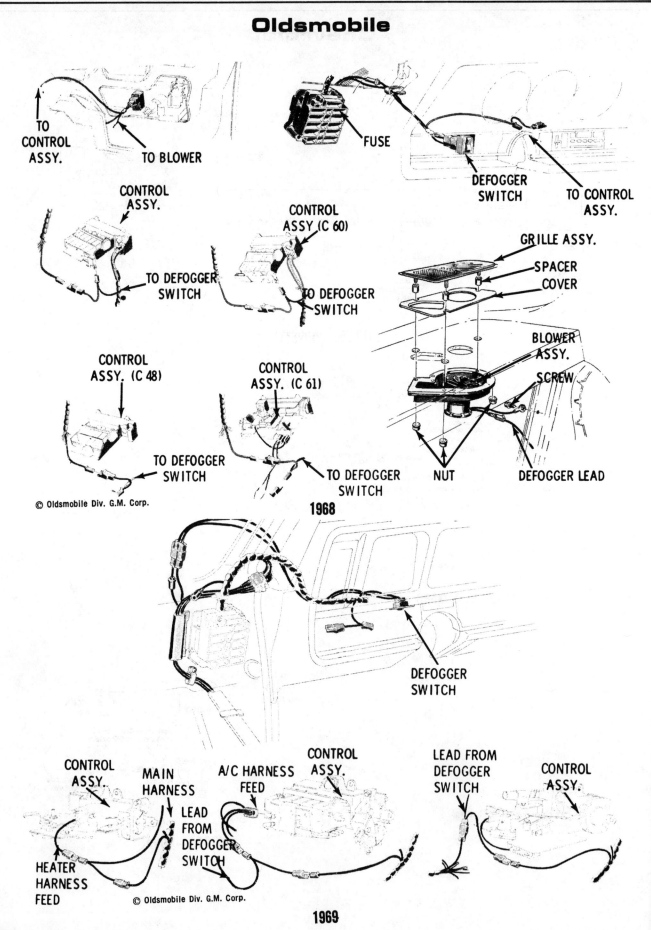

TO CONTROL ASSY.

TO BLOWER

FUSE

DEFOGGER SWITCH

TO CONTROL ASSY.

CONTROL ASSY.

TO DEFOGGER SWITCH

CONTROL ASSY (C 60)

TO DEFOGGER SWITCH

GRILLE ASSY.

SPACER

COVER

CONTROL ASSY. (C 48)

TO DEFOGGER SWITCH

CONTROL ASSY. (C 61)

TO DEFOGGER SWITCH

BLOWER ASSY.

SCREW

NUT

DEFOGGER LEAD

© Oldsmobile Div. G.M. Corp.

**1968**

DEFOGGER SWITCH

CONTROL ASSY.

MAIN HARNESS

A/C HARNESS FEED

CONTROL ASSY.

LEAD FROM DEFOGGER SWITCH

CONTROL ASSY.

LEAD FROM DEFOGGER SWITCH

HEATER HARNESS FEED

© Oldsmobile Div. G.M. Corp.

**1969**

## Oldsmobile F-85

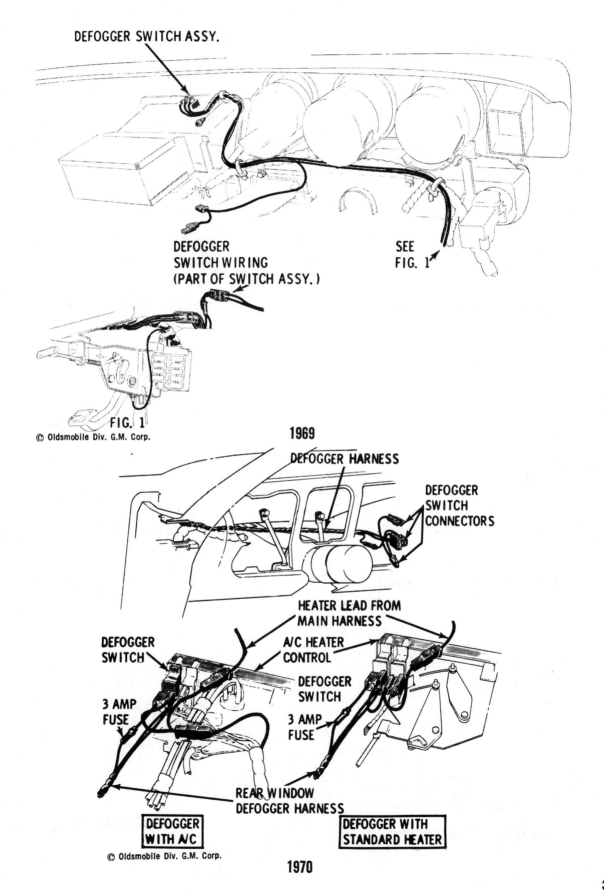

DEFOGGER SWITCH ASSY.

DEFOGGER
SWITCH WIRING
(PART OF SWITCH ASSY. )

SEE
FIG. 1

FIG. 1

© Oldsmobile Div. G.M. Corp.

1969

DEFOGGER HARNESS

DEFOGGER
SWITCH
CONNECTORS

HEATER LEAD FROM
MAIN HARNESS

DEFOGGER
SWITCH

A/C HEATER
CONTROL

DEFOGGER
SWITCH

3 AMP
FUSE

3 AMP
FUSE

REAR WINDOW
DEFOGGER HARNESS

DEFOGGER
WITH A/C

DEFOGGER WITH
STANDARD HEATER

© Oldsmobile Div. G.M. Corp.

1970

## Pontiac

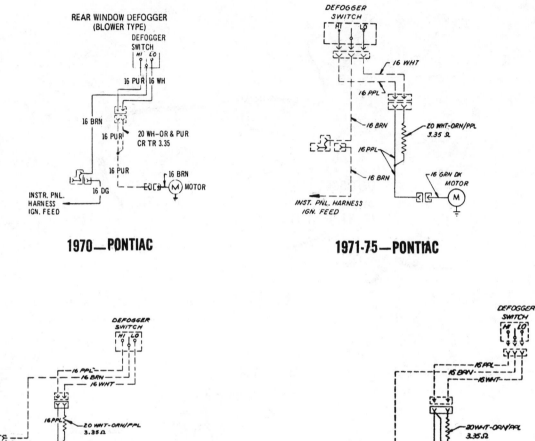

**1970—PONTIAC**

**1971-75—PONTIAC**

**1971-72—LE MANS & GRAN PRIX**

**1973-75—LE MANS & GRAN PRIX**

© Pontiac Div. G.M. Corp.

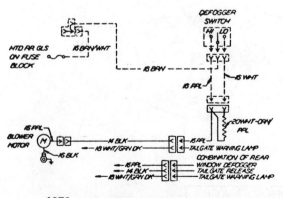

**1973—LE MANS STATION WAGON**

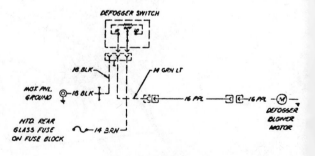

**1971-75—FIREBIRD**

## General Motors

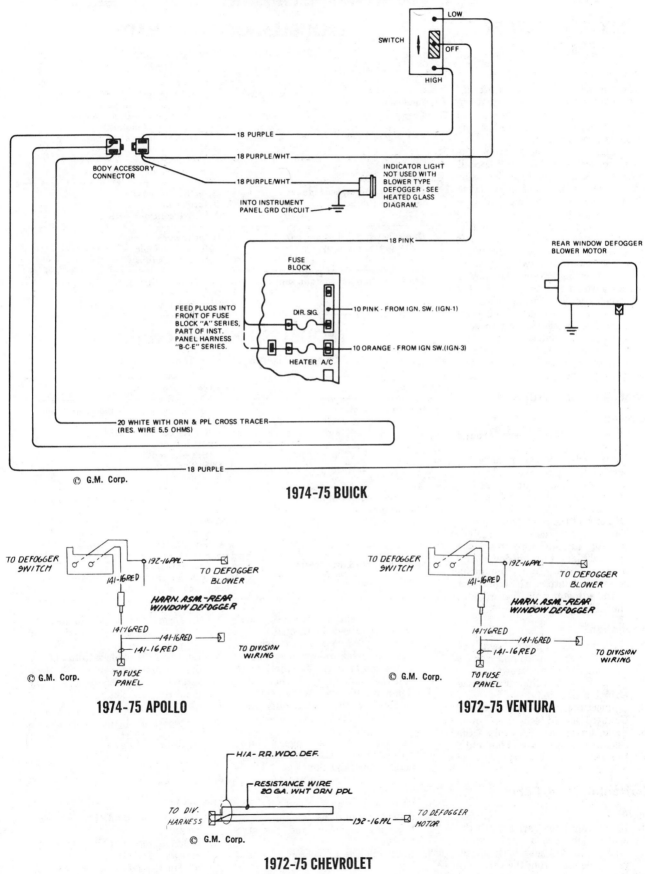

**1974-75 BUICK**

**1974-75 APOLLO**

**1972-75 VENTURA**

**1972-75 CHEVROLET**

## Chrysler Corporation

# SIX-WAY POWER SEAT 1968

## Description

The power seat has six different movements. Forward, back, up, down and the front and rear of the seat can be moved up or down to give it a forward or rearward tilt.

A single wire comes from the power source to a 30 AMP circuit breaker located on the fuse block side of the cowl panel, left of the steering column. Power is then supplied to a control switch through a relay.

The seat adjusters are activated by the control switch, located on the left side panel of the front seat. Six wires are connected to the switch. One of the wires comes from the power source. Two wires connect to the motor field, which also actuates the relay for motor armature current. The last three wires connect to solenoids located in the drive unit. Cables connect the solenoids to jack units located in the seat tracks and control the various movements.

## Front Seat and Adjuster

### Removal

1. Disconnect the battery ground cable.
2. From under the car, remove the seat-to-floor pan attaching nuts.
3. Tilt the complete seat forward.
4. Disconnect the control switch wires.
5. Disconnect the red feed wire.
6. Take the seat assembly, including the adjuster unit, from the car and place it upside down.
7. Remove the four mounting screws that attach the front seat to the adjuster unit, then remove the adjuster unit.

### Installation

1. With the seat upside down, put the adjuster in place and replace the four mounting screws.
2. Place the seat in the car with the adjuster mounted.
3. Connect the control switch wires.
4. Connect the red feed wire.
5. From under the car, replace the seat-to-floor pan attaching nuts.
6. Connect the battery ground cable.

## Horizontal Drive Cable

### Removal

1. From under the car, remove the seat-to-floor pan attaching nuts.
2. Either tip the seat back or remove the seat from the car. (Be-

# TROUBLESHOOTING CHART

### 1968 Chrysler Six Way Power Seat

| Condition | Possible Cause |
|---|---|
| 1. Inoperative motor | a. Open or short circuit between power supply and circuit breaker, relay, switch, or motor<br>b. Defective switch<br>c. Defective relay<br>d. Bad ground<br>e. Defective motor |
| 2. Operative motor, seat moves in only one direction | a. Defective solenoid<br>b. Defective cable<br>c. Defective control switch |
| 3. Operative motor, but no seat movement either way. | a. Defective drive unit<br>b. Defective solenoid<br>c. Defective control switch |
| 4. Seat operation not smooth, binds | a. Improper lubrication<br>b. Defective drive unit<br>c. Defective cable |

# TROUBLESHOOTING CHART

### Chrysler Six-Way Power Seat 1969-75

| Condition | Possible Cause |
|---|---|
| 1. Inoperative motor | a. Open or short circuit between switch and power supply<br>b. Defective control switch<br>c. Open or short circuit between switch and motor<br>d. Defective motor<br>e. Bad ground |
| 2. Operative motor but no seat movement | a. Defective control switch<br>b. Defective drive cable<br>c. Defective transmission<br>d. Improper alignment of adjusters<br>e. Open or short circuit |
| 3. Seat binds, hard movement | a. Improper lubrication<br>b. Defective transmission<br>c. Improper alignment of adjusters |

fore the seat is removed, the wires must be disconnected.)
3. Remove the two screws which secure the cable mounting bracket at the motor drive assembly and pull the cable from the housing.
4. Remove the drive rack assembly.
   a. Remove the cotter pins and drive the horizontal drive out gear pin.
5. Remove the six cover plate screws on the drive gear housing and lift the cable out.

### Installation

1. Replace the square-end of the drive cable into the housing.
2. Replace the cover and the six screws.
3. Re-install the drive rack assembly.

a. Insert the pivot pin and install the washers and cotter pins.
4. Reinstall the cable into the motor drive unit and replace the two screws which secure the cable mounting bracket.

*NOTE: The horizontal racks must be synchronized. Adjustments can be made by turning the cables to move the upper slide either way.*

## Front Jack

### Removal

1. Move the seat all the way backward.
2. Remove the four jack-retaining screws.
   a. On the left side of cars with

# Chrysler Corporation

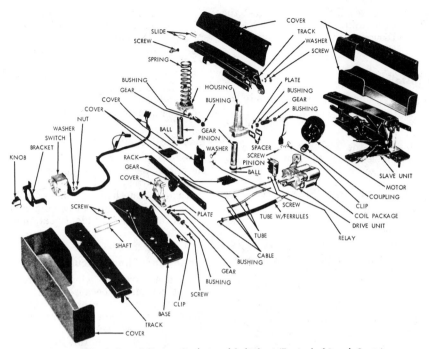

*Electric Seat Adjuster—Bucket and Split Seat (Typical of Bench Seats)*

bucket seats, the two screws which retain the spacer to the base must be removed first.

3. Remove the cotter pin and washer from the upper slide.
4. Drive out the upper retaining clevis pin from the lower side.
5. Remove the four screws from under the base plate.
6. Pull the jack foward to separate it from the drive cable and tube.
7. Keep the base plate under the jack in order to keep the worm and bushing in place.

### Installation

1. Place the jack into position.

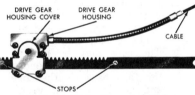

*Horizontal Drive Gear and Rack*

2. Connect the drive cable and tube.
3. Replace the four base plate screws.
4. Turn the worm shaft with a small screwdriver to run the jack up and down to align the clevis pin holes.
5. Drive the clevis pin through the

lower slide and replace the cotter pin and washer.
6. Replace the four jack-retaining screws.
7. Check operation of the seat.

### Rear Jack

#### Removal

1. Remove front seat and adjuster.
   a. Disconnect the battery ground cable.
   b. From under the car, remove the seat-to-floor pan attaching nuts.
   c. Tilt the complete seat forward.
   d. Disconnect the control switch wires and the red feed wire.
   e. Take the seat assembly, including the adjuster unit, from the car and place it upside down.
   f. Remove the four mounting screws that attach the front seat to the adjuster unit, then remove the adjuster unit.
2. Disconnect the cables from the drive unit.
3. Place the seat track in a vise.
4. Using a C-clamp, clamp the base of the adjuster to the upper slide.
5. Tighten the C-clamp just enough to keep it in place.
6. Drive the roll pin out of the slide assembly.
7. From under the base, remove the four jack-mounting screws.
8. Remove the coil spring from between the slide and base after slowly loosening the clamp.

#### Installation

1. Adjust the worm shaft with a small screwdriver to run the jack up and down in order to align the roll pin holes.
2. Slide the jack onto the base.

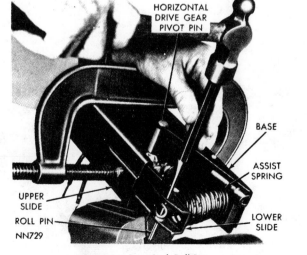

*Removing Rear Jack Roll Pin*

*Motor Removal*

# Chrysler Corporation

3. Place the cable end into the worm shaft.
4. From under the base, replace the four jack-mounting screws.
5. Place the spring over the jack.
6. Install the C-clamp between the base and the upper slide.
7. Tighten just enough to align the roll pin holes.
8. Drive the roll pin through while placing the washers on either side of the jackhead.
9. Lubricate the slides properly.
10. Connect the cables to the drive unit.
11. Put the seat adjuster assembly in place on the seat and install the four mounting screws.
12. Place the seat in the car with the adjuster mounted.
13. Connect the control switch wires and the red feed wire.
14. From under the car, replace the seat-to-floor pan attaching nuts.
15. Connect the battery ground cable.

## Rear Jack Assist Spring

Removal procedure is the same as the rear jack previously described.

*NOTE: The jacks must be synchronized. Adjustments can be made by turning the cables to raise or lower the jack.*

## Control Switch
### Removal

1. Remove the four mounting screws that attach the seat to the seat adjusters.
2. Tilt the seat forward and disconnect the wire terminals from the solenoid and relay.
3. Remove the two switch mounting nuts from the studs and remove the switch.

### Installation

1. Place the switch on the mounting studs and install the nuts.
2. Connect the wire terminals to the solenoids and relay.
3. Realign the seat on the adjusters and replace the mounting screws.

## Motor
### Removal

1. Remove the two screws that attach the front seat to the adjuster on the left side.
2. Prop up the left side of the seat cushion.
3. Remove the two nuts that attach the motor to the drive unit.

4. Remove the motor from the drive unit.
5. Disconnect the motor wires from the relay.

### Installation

1. Reconnect the motor wires to the relay.
2. Connect the motor to the drive unit.
3. Place the seat cushion back on the seat adjuster and install the two screws.

## Drive Unit and Solenoid Assembly
### Disassembly

1. From under the car, remove the seat-to-floor pan attaching nuts.
2. Either tip the seat back or remove the seat from the car. (Before the seat is removed, the wires must be disconnected.)
3. Remove the cables and the drive unit. (See "Horizontal drive cable removal")
4. Remove the solenoid assembly from the drive unit.
   a. Remove the two screws from the plate that holds the solenoid to the drive unit.
   b. The coils may be removed from the solenoid by bending the tabs back on the cover and unsoldering the ground wire at one of the tabs.
   c. The clutch lever and shaft may be removed from the solenoid by removing the cover-to-drive unit retaining screws.

### Assembly

1. Replace the clutch lever and shaft.
2. Replace the cover and screws.

3. Place the coil into the coil cover and position the ground wire to one of the tabs.
4. Align the cover tabs with the slots on the coil plate.
5. Bend the tabs over and resolder the coil ground wire to the tab and plate.
6. Replace the solenoid springs.

## Electrical Circuit

Before performing any extensive electrical testing procedures, make sure the battery is in good shape and there are no mechanical failures. Also refer to the power seat wiring diagrams for the proper identification of wires.

### Open and Short Circuits

An open circuit is when the circuit is not completed because of a poor terminal contact or a broken wire. A short circuit is when the current is being grounded before it reaches a particular unit. When this happens, it actuates a circuit breaker or blows a fuse. The 30 AMP circuit breaker that is used, is located on the fuse block on the inside of the cowl panel and to the left of the steering column.

### Improper Ground

Many times perfectly good operating units, such as motors, are considered defective and are replaced because of a bad ground.
1. Attach one end of a jumper wire to the body of an inoperative unit.
2. Connect the other end to a good ground, such as a bare metal panel.
3. Switch on the unit. If it operates, the original ground is defective.

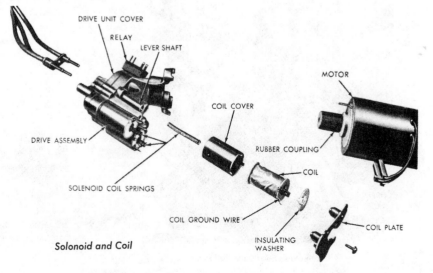

*Solenoid and Coil*

# Power Seats

## Chrysler Corporation

### Testing the Motor and Relay

1. Disconnect the red, black and green motor wires from the relay.
2. Connect a jumper wire from the red wire to either the black or green wire coming from the motor.
3. Connect another jumper wire to the red feed-in wire on the relay. If the motor does not run it should be replaced. If the motor runs the relay should be replaced.

### Testing the Solenoid and Switch

1. Remove all the leads from the solenoids.
2. Connect one end of a jumper wire to the red feed-in lead.
3. Touch the other end to a solenoid terminal, one at a time and listen for a distinct click. If the click is not heard, the solenoid is defective. If all the solenoids click, then the switch is defective.

### Testing the Relay

1. Connect a jumper wire from the red feed-in wire to either the green or black wire terminal on the relay.
2. If the motor doesn't run the relay is defective.

## ═══ SIX-WAY POWER SEAT 1969-1975 ═══

### Description

The seat adjusters are controlled by a three lever switch located on the left side panel of the driver's seat. The control switch activates a three armature permanent magnet reversible motor. The motors are connected by cables to a rack and pinion assembly which is located in the seat track. The cables control the various seat movement.

The seat adjusters can be moved in six directions. The front lever on the switch by moving up and down, raises or lowers the front seat. The center lever by moving up and down raises or lowers the complete seat. It also moves the complete seat forward and backward. The rear lever raises and lowers the back of the seat by moving it up and down.

The electrical circuit is protected by a 30 AMP circuit breaker located on the fuse block on the inside cowl panel.

### Front Seat Assembly

#### Removal

1. Disconnect the battery ground cable.
2. Remove the seat-to-floor pan attaching nuts from under the car.
3. Tilt the seat back and remove the wiring harness connector.
4. Remove the seat from the car.

#### Installation

1. Place the seat in the car.
2. Replace the wiring harness.
3. Replace and tighten the seat-to-floor pan attaching nuts.
4. Connect the battery ground cable.

### Front Seat Adjuster

#### Removal

1. Remove the front seat.
   a. Disconnect the battery ground cable.
   b. Remove the seat-to-floor pan attaching nuts from under the car.
   c. Tilt the seat back and remove the wiring harness connector.
   d. Remove the seat from the car and place it upside down.
2. Remove the adjuster-to-seat attaching bolts.

#### Installation

1. Place the seat upside down.
2. Place the adjuster in the proper position and install the adjuster-to-seat attaching bolts.
3. Place the seat in the car and connect the wiring harness.
4. Replace and tighten the seat-to-floor pan attaching nut.

5. Connect the battery ground cable.

### Motor

#### Removal

1. Remove the front seat.
   a. Disconnect the battery ground cable.
   b. Remove the seat-to-floor pan attaching nuts from under the car.
   c. Tilt the seat back and remove the wiring harness connector.
   d. Remove the seat from the car and place it upside down.
2. Remove the motor-to-support bolt.
3. Remove the motor mounting screws located on either side of the cables.
4. Disconnect the cables from the motor, then remove the seat motor.

#### Installation

1. Put the motor in place.
2. Connect the cables to the motor.
3. Replace the motor mounting screws.
4. Install the motor-to-support bolt.
5. Place the seat in the car and connect the wiring harness.
6. Replace and tighten the seat-to-floor pan attaching nuts.

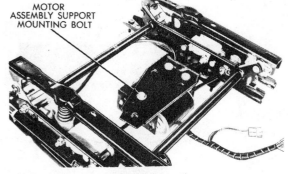

*Mounting Bolt Location*

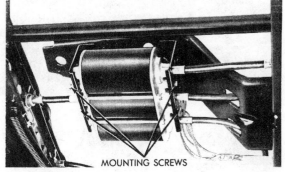

*Mounting Screw Location*

# Power Seats

## Chrysler Corporation

### Drive Cables

#### Removal

1. Remove the front seat.
   a. Disconnect the battery ground cable.
   b. Remove the seat-to-floor pan attaching nuts from under the car.
   c. Tilt the seat back and remove the wiring harness connector.
   d. Remove the seat from the car and place it upside down.
2. Remove the motor.
   a. Remove the motor-to-support bolt.
   b. Remove the motor mounting screws located on either side of the cables.
   c. Disconnect the cables and remove the motor.
3. Remove the clamp from the adjuster side of the cable housing.
4. Slide the cable and housing from the connector.

#### Installation

1. Replace the cable and housing into the connector, then replace the clamp.
2. Replace the motor.
   a. Connect the cables together.
   b. Replace the motor mounting screws and the motor-to-support bolt.
3. Replace the seat.
   a. Place the seat in the car and connect the wiring harness.
   b. Replace and tighten the seat-to-floorpan attaching nuts.

### Horizontal and Vertical Transmission

#### Removal

1. Remove the front seat.
   a. Disconnect the battery ground cable.
   b. Remove the seat-to-floor pan attaching nuts from under the car.

   c. Tilt the seat back and remove the wiring harness connector.
   d. Remove the seat from the car and place it upside down.
2. Remove motor.
   a. Remove the motor-to-support bolt.
   b. Remove the motor mounting screws located on either side of the cables.
   c. Disconnect the cables and remove the motor.
3. Using a C-clamp to reduce the tension, clamp the mounting base to the upper channel.
4. Remove the cotter key and front clevis pin.
5. Remove the C-clamp slowly.
6. Remove the cotter key, rear clevis pin and upper channel assembly.
7. Remove the horizontal spring.
8. Remove the bolts from the ends of the side rail.
9. Remove the bolts which secure the transmission assemblies.
10. Separate the rails and transmission assemblies.

#### Installation

1. Place the transmission between the side rails and install the bolts and nuts.
2. Replace the pin and install the bolts in each end.
3. Replace the horizontal spring.
4. Position the rails to the ends of the torsion bar.
5. Position the holes with the upper channel and replace the rear clevis pin and key.
6. Replace the vertical spring, apply a C-clamp and align the holes in the mounting base and the upper channel.
7. Install the front clevis pin and cotter key.
8. Install the motor.
   a. Put the motor in place.
   b. Connect the cables to the motor.
   c. Replace the motor mounting screws and motor-to-support bolt.
9. Replace the seat.
   a. Place the seat in the car and connect the wiring harness.

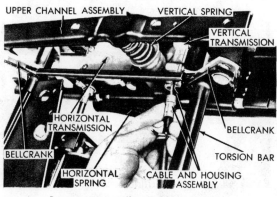

*Removing or Installing Cable and Housing*

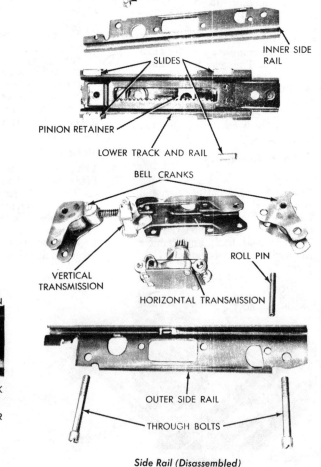

*Side Rail (Disassembled)*

# Chrysler Corporation

b. Replace and tighten the seat-to-floor pan attaching nuts.

*NOTE: It is important to keep tracks and rails aligned properly to insure smooth operation.*

### Electrical Circuit

Before performing any extensive electrical testing procedures, make sure the battery is in good shape and there are no mechanical failures. An easy check for this would be to turn the dome light on and operate the seat control switch. If the dome light dims while the seat is trying to move but can't, there is most likely a mechanical problem. Also refer to the power seat wiring diagrams for the proper identification of wires.

### Open and Short Circuits

An open circuit is when the circuit is not completed because of a poor terminal contact or a broken wire. A short circuit is when the current is being grounded before it reaches a particular unit. When this happens, it actuates a circuit breaker or blows a fuse, due to the overload created.

The 30 AMP circuit breaker is located on the fuse block on the inside of the cowl panel and to the left of the steering column.

### Circuit Testing Procedures

Testing for current in the instrument panel feed wire.
1. Disconnect the wire from the circuit breaker at the fuse block side of the cowl.
2. Connect one test light lead to the end of the wire and ground the other lead.
3. If the test lamp lights, the feed wire is good.

### Testing for Current in the Seat Wiring Harness

1. Disconnect the wiring harness connector on the harness.
2. If the test lamp lights, the seat harness is good.

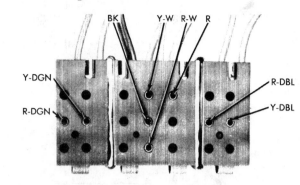

*Electrical Test Area Location*

### Testing the Circuit Breaker

1. Make sure that the wire on the fuse block side of the circuit breaker is connected.
2. Disconnect the other breaker wire.
3. Connect a test lamp in a series between the circuit breaker and a good ground.
4. If the circuit breaker is good, the test lamp will light.

### Testing for Defective Front Motor

1. In the front section, connect a jumper wire between the (R) red terminal and either the (R-DGN) red with dark green terminal or the (Y-DGN) yellow with dark green terminal.
2. Connect another jumper wire between the (BK) terminal in the center section, with an open connector found in the front section.
3. Reverse the wires in the front section if the motor does not operate.
4. If the motor still does not operate, and the harness is good, the complete three-motor assembly should be replaced.

### Testing for a Defective Center Motor

1. In the center section, connect a jumper wire between the (R)

red terminal and either the (R-W) red with white or the (Y-W) yellow with white terminal.
2. In the center section, connect another jumper wire between the (B-K) black terminal and an open connection.
3. Reverse the jumper wires (R-W) and (Y-W) if the motor does not operate.
4. If the motor still does not operate, and the harness is good, the complete three-motor assembly should be replaced.

### Testing for a Defective Rear Motor

1. Connect a jumper wire between the (R) red terminal in the center section with either the (R-DBL) red with dark blue terminal or the (Y-DBL) yellow with dark blue terminal in the rear section.
2. Reverse the jumper wires in the rear section if the motor does not operate.
3. If the motor still does not operate, and the harness is good, the complete three-motor assembly should be replaced.

*NOTE: If all the motors operate properly after applying the above tests, the control switch is probably defective.*

# Ford Motor Company

## TWO WAY POWER SEAT ALL 1969-1975 FORD EXC. 1969 LINCOLN CONTINENTAL

### Description

The seat adjusters are controlled by a toggle switch located on the left side panel of the driver's seat. The

switch activates a 12 volt reversible motor. Cables are connected to the right and left ends of the motor shaft and the rotation of the shaft controls the direction of the seat. The other end of the cable connects to a transmission and horizontal rack on each seat track.

A 30 amp circuit breaker mounted on the instrument panel protects the electrical system. The circuit breaker can be reached by removing the glove

box filler. The Cougar has a 20 amp circuit breaker located in the engine compartment at the starter motor relay or junction block.

### Front Seat Assembly

#### Removal

1. From under the car, remove the four seat track-to-floorpan attaching nuts and washers.
2. Tilt the seat backward and dis-

# Ford Motor Company

connect the seat motor wiring harness.

3. Remove the seat assembly from the car.

## Installation

1. Place the seat assembly back in the car.
2. Reconnect the seat motor wiring harness.
3. Align the seat track mounting bolts to the floorpan holes.
4. Replace the four seat track-to-floorpan attaching nuts and washers. (Torque to 12–25 ft lbs)

## Seat Track

### Removal

1. From under the car, remove the four seat track-to-floorpan attaching nuts and washers.
2. Tilt the seat backward and disconnect the seat motor wiring harness.
3. Remove the seat assembly from the car and remove the seat side panel.
4. Disconnect the drive cable from each of the transmissions.
5. Remove the two bolts that hold the transmission to the seat track.
6. The tracks will now move freely and expose the seat cushion-to-track attaching bolts.
7. Remove the bolts and separate the track from the seat cushion.

### Installation

1. Replace the five anti-squeak pads between the track and the cushion.
2. Replace the seat cushion and install the attaching bolts. (Torque to 12–25 ft lbs)
3. Reconnect the drive cables to the transmission assembly. Install the retaining clips.
4. Replace the seat side panel.
5. Place the seat assembly back in the car.
6. Reconnect the seat motor wiring harness.
7. Align the seat track mounting bolts to the floorpan holes and replace the attaching nuts. (Torque to 12–25 ft lbs)

## Motor and Drive Cables

### Removal

1. From under the car, remove the four seat track-to-floorpan attaching nuts and washers.
2. Tilt the seat backward and disconnect the seat motor wiring harness.

## TROUBLESHOOTING CHART

### All 1969-75 Ford Exc. 1969 Lincoln Continental

| Condition | Possible Cause |
|---|---|
| 1. Inoperative motor | a. Open or short circuit between power supply and circuit breaker, relay, switch, or motor<br>b. Defective switch<br>c. Defective circuit breaker<br>d. Defective motor<br>e. Bad ground<br>f. Defective relay |
| 2. Operative motor, seat moves in only one direction | a. Defective relay<br>b. Defective switch<br>c. Defective cable<br>d. Defective seat transmission |
| 3. Operative motor but seat does not move either way | a. Open or short circuit between motor, switch, or transmission<br>b. Defective switch<br>c. Defective seat transmission<br>d. Defective relay |
| 4. Seat operation not smooth, binds | a. Improper lubrication<br>b. Defective cable<br>c. Defective transmission |

3. Remove the seat assembly from the car.
4. Disconnect the drive cable from each of the transmissions.
5. Remove the two screws that attach the motor to the mounting bracket.
6. Separate the motor and drive cables from the track.
7. Remove the retaining bracket that connects the drive cable to the right end of the motor.
8. Pull the drive cables out of the tubes.

## Installation

1. Insert the drive cables into the tubes.
2. Reconnect the drive cable assemblies to the right end of the motor and replace the retaining bracket.
3. Secure the motor and drive cable assembly to the mounting

*Two Way Power Seat Track—Continental Mark III*

# Ford Motor Company

bracket with the two attaching screws.

4. Connect the drive cables to the transmission assemblies and reinstall the clips.
5. Place the seat assembly back into the car.
6. Reconnect the seat motor wiring harness.
7. Align the seat track mounting bolts to the floorpan holes and replace the attaching nuts. (Torque to 12–25 ft lbs)

## Transmission and Rack Assembly

### Removal

1. From under the car, remove the

four seat track-to-floorpan attaching nuts and washers.

2. Tilt the seat backward and disconnect the seat motor wiring harness.
3. Remove the seat assembly from the car.
4. Disconnect the drive cable from the transmission to be removed.
5. Remove the two transmission mounting bolts and remove the transmission, bushing, spacer, and spring clip.
6. Remove the rack from the seat track by pulling the cotter pin out at the end of the rack.

### Installation

1. Position the rack to the seat

track and replace the cotter pin and washer.

2. Position the transmission to the track and replace the bushing, spacer, and spring clip.
3. Replace the two transmission mounting bolts.
4. Connect the drive cable to the transmission and install the cable tube clamp.
5. Place the seat assembly back in the car.
6. Reconnect the seat motor wiring harness.
7. Align the seat track bolts to the mounting holes.
8. Replace the four seat track-to-floorpan attaching nuts and washers. (Torque to 12–25 ft lbs)

# ═══ TWO WAY POWER SEAT 1969 ═══

# LINCOLN CONTINENTAL

## Bucket Seat

### Description

The seat adjusters are controlled by a switch mounted on the left seat side panel. The switch activates a 12 volt motor which couples on both sides to an actuator or drivescrew assembly. The drivescrews direct the front and rear movement of the seat.

The electrical circuit has a three way protection against an overload. The first is a fusible link wire connected between the battery terminal of the starter motor relay and the junction block. The second is a 30 amp circuit breaker mounted on the instrument panel. The circuit breaker can be reached by removing the glove box filler. The third protection is a circuit breaker built into the power seat motor.

## Front Seat Assembly

### Removal

1. From under the car, remove the seat track-to-floor pan retaining nuts and bolts.
2. Tilt the seat up and disconnect the motor wires.
3. Lift the seat assembly from the car.

### Installation

1. Place the seat assembly in the car.
2. Connect the motor wires.
3. Position the seat track to the floor pan and install the retaining bolts and nuts from under the car.

# TROUBLESHOOTING CHART

## 1969 Lincoln Continental
## Bucket Seat

| Condition | Possible Cause |
|---|---|
| 1. Inoperative motor | a. Defective circuit breaker<br>b. Defective control switch<br>c. Open or short circuit between the power supply and circuit breaker, switch or motor<br>d. Defective motor<br>e. Bad ground |
| 2. Operative motor but no seat movement | a. Foreign object stuck under seat<br>b. Defective switch<br>c. Defective actuator |
| 3. Seat operation not smooth, binds | a. Improper lubrication<br>b. Foreign object stuck under seat<br>c. Defective actuator |

# TROUBLESHOOTING CHART

## 1969 Lincoln Continental
## Bench Seat

| Condition | Possible Cause |
|---|---|
| 1. Inoperative motor | a. Defecive circuit breaker<br>b. Defective control switch<br>c. Open or short circuit between the power supply and circuitbreaking switch or motor<br>d. Defective motor<br>e. Bad ground |
| 2. Operative motor, but no seat movement | a. Foreign object stuck under seat<br>b. Defective cable<br>c. Defective switch<br>d. Defective actuator |
| 3. Seat operation not smooth, binds | a. Improper lubrication<br>b. Foreign object stuck under seat<br>c. Defective actuator |

# Ford Motor Company

## Seat Track Assembly

### Removal

1. From under the car, remove the seat track-to-floor pan retaining nuts and bolts.
2. Tilt the seat up and disconnect the motor wires.
3. Lift the seat assembly from the car.
4. Disconnect the seat control wires.
5. Remove the four seat track-to-cushion attaching screws and remove the cushion.

### Installation

1. Position the cushion on the seat track and install the four retaining screws.
2. Connect the seat control wires.
3. Place the seat assembly in the car and connect the motor wires.
4. From under the car, install the seat track-to-floor pan attaching nuts and bolts.

## Motor

### Removal

1. From under the car, remove the seat track-to-floor pan retaining nuts and bolts.
2. Tilt the seat up and disconnect the motor wires.
3. Lift the seat assembly from the car.
4. Remove the four seat track-to-

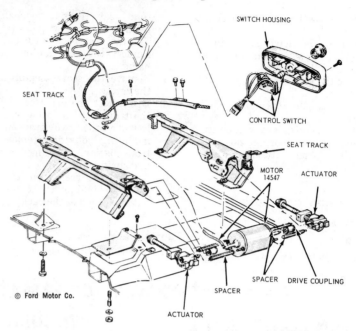

Two-Way Power Bucket Seat Track Disassembled—Lincoln Continental

cushion retaining nuts and remove the cushion.
5. Remove the four seat track-to-motor retaining nuts.
6. Remove the motor mounting studs and rubber drive blocks.

### Installation

1. Replace the motor mounting studs and rubber drive blocks.

2. Install the four seat track-to-motor retaining nuts.
3. Place the cushion on the track assembly and install the four attaching screws.
4. Place the seat assembly in the car.
5. From under the car, install the seat track-to-floor pan attaching nuts and bolts.

## ═══════TWO-WAY POWERED SEAT 1969═══════

# LINCOLN CONTINENTAL

## Bench Seat

### Description

The seat adjusters are controlled by a switch mounted on the left side panel. The switch activates a 12 volt motor which is connected to the horizontal actuator by a flexible cable on the right side and on the left side by a drive coupling. The horizontal actuators attach to each seat track to direct the front and rear movement of the seat.

The electrical circuit has a three-way protection against an overload.

The first is a fusible link wire connected between the battery terminal of the starter motor relay and the junction block. The second is a 30 amp circuit breaker mounted on the instrument panel. The circuit breaker can be reached by removing the glove box filler.

The third protection is a circuit breaker built in to the power seat motor.

## Front Seat Assembly

### Removal

1. Disconnect the ground cable from the battery.
2. Remove the nuts which retain the front of the seat track to the floor pan.
3. Remove the cap screws from the rear of each seat track.
4. Disconnect the wiring harness.
5. Lift the seat assembly from the car.
6. The seat track assembly may be removed by removing the four screws which retain the track assembly to the cushion.

### Installation

1. Position the seat cushion to the track assembly and replace the four retaining screws.
2. Place the seat in the car and align the seat track holes to the floor pan.
3. Install the front seat track retaining nuts and the seat track rear cap screws to the floor pan.

4. Connect the wiring harness.
5. Connect the battery ground cable.

## Motor

### Removal

1. Disconnect the ground cable from the battery.
2. Remove the nuts which retain the front of the seat track to the floor pan.
3. Remove the capscrews from the rear of each seat track.
4. Disconnect the wiring harness.
5. Lift the seat assembly from the car and place it upside down.
6. Remove the four seat track-to-cushion retaining screws.
7. Remove the two screws that attach the drive cable cover and motor to the right side track and actuator.
8. Disconnect the motor drive coupling from the right side track and actuator.
9. Disconnect the motor feed wires and separate the motor from the seat.

# Ford Motor Company

## Installation

1. Position the motor in the right side track and actuator.
2. Replace the two screws that attach the drive cable cover and motor to the right side seat track and actuator.
3. Connect the motor feed wires.
4. Position the cushion and replace the four seat track-to-cushion retaining screws.
5. Place the seat assembly back in the car.
6. Connect the main wiring harness.
7. Install the front seat track retaining nuts and the seat track rear cap screws to the floor pan.
8. Connect the ground cable to the battery.

## Seat Track and Actuator

1. Disconnect the ground cable from the battery.
2. Remove the nuts which retain the front of the seat track to the floor pan.
3. Remove the cap screws from the rear of each seat track.
4. Disconnect the main wiring harness.
5. Lift the seat assembly from the car.
6. Remove the four seat track-to-cushion screws and remove the cushion.
7. Remove the two drive cable cover-to-seat track attaching screws.

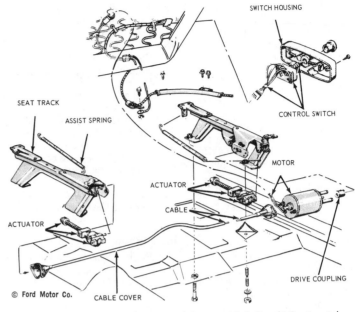

*Two-Way Power Bench Seat Track Disassembled—Lincoln Continental*

8. Separate the motor and cable from the seat track.
9. Remove the four screws that connect the actuator to the track and remove the actuator.

## Installation

1. Replace the four actuator-to-seat track retaining screws.
2. Position the drive cable cover and the motor to the seat track and install the two retaining screws.
3. Place the cushion on the seat track and install the four retaining screws.
4. Place the seat assembly in the car and connect the main wiring harness.
5. Replace the seat track-to-floor pan retaining nuts and bolts.
6. Connect the battery ground cable.

# FOUR WAY POWER SEAT 1968-73

## MONTEGO, TORINO

### Bench Seat

#### Description

The seat adjusters are controlled by a four-way switch, located on the left side of the seat. The switch through two relays activates a 12 volt reversible motor. The motor transmits its power to three solenoids located in the seat transmission. Three cables are engaged by the solenoids and connect to the seat track. These cables determine the direction of the seat movement.

A 20 amp circuit breaker, mounted on the starting motor relay in the engine compartment, protects the electrical system.

### Front Seat Assembly

#### Removal

1. Remove the two inner seat belt retaining bolts.
2. From under the car, remove the

## TROUBLESHOOTING CHART
### Four-Way Power Bench Seat
### 1968-73 Montego and Torino

| Condition | Possible Cause |
|---|---|
| **1 Inoperative motor** | a. Defective motor<br>b. Bad ground<br>c. Defective circuit breaker<br>d. Defective relay<br>e. Defective switch<br>f. Open or short circuit between power supply and circuit breaker, relay, switch, and motor |
| **2. Operative motor but no seat movement** | a. Open or short circuit between control switch and solenoid in transmission<br>b. Defective switch<br>c. Defective drive cable<br>d. Defective relay<br>e. Defective solenoid in transmission<br>f. Foreign object stuck under seat |
| **3. Seat operation not smooth, binds** | a. Improper lubrication<br>b. Defective drive cable<br>c. Defective seat transmission<br>d Foreign object stuck under seat |

# Ford Motor Company

four seat track-to-floor pan retaining nuts.
3. Tilt the seat up and disconnect the seat wiring harness.
4. Remove the seat assembly from the car.

### Installation

1. Replace the seat assembly in the car.
2. Connect the seat wiring harness.
3. Align the seat track bolts to the floor pan holes and replace the four retaining nuts. (Torque to 9–25 ft lbs)
4. Install the two inner seat belt retaining bolts.

## Seat Track

### Removal

1. Remove the two inner seat belt retaining bolts.
2. From under the car, remove the four seat track-to-floor pan retaining nuts.
3. Tilt the seat up and disconnect the wiring harness.
4. Remove the seat assembly from the car.
5. Remove the four screws that hold the seat cushion to the track.
6. Disconnect the wiring harness that comes from the control switch.
7. Remove the seat track.

### Installation

1. Connect the seat control switch wiring harness.
2. Position the track to the seat cushion and replace the four retaining screws.
3. Place the seat assembly back in the car.
4. Connect the wiring harness.
5. Align the seat track bolts to the floor pan holes and replace the four retaining nuts.
6. Install the two inner seat belt retaining bolts.

## Transmission and Drive Unit

### Removal

1. Remove the two inner seat belt retaining bolts.

2. From under the car, remove the four seat track-to-floor pan retaining nuts.
3. Tilt the seat up and disconnect the seat wiring harness.
4. Remove the seat assembly from the car.
5. Release the tension on the assist springs on the seat track.
6. Separate the three drive units from the track assembly by removing the six retaining screws and disconnecting the wires.
7. Remove the transmission retaining screws and disconnect the wires to the transmission.
8. Remove the transmission.

### Installation

1. Replace the transmission assembly to the seat track bracket and install the two retaining screws.
2. Reconnect the transmission wires.
3. Position the three drive units on the seat track assembly and replace the six retaining screws.
4. Replace the assist springs on the seat tracks.
5. Place the seat assembly back in the car.
6. Connect the wiring harness.
7. Align the seat track bolts to the floor pan holes and replace the four retaining nuts.
8. Install the two inner seat belt retaining nuts.

## Motor

### Removal

1. From under the car, remove the four seat track-to-floor pan retaining nuts.
2. Tilt the seat backward and disconnect the main wiring harness.
3. Disconnect the wires to the transmission.
4. Remove the two transmission retaining bolts and lay the transmission and drive assembly to one side.
5. Remove the two motor retaining nuts and remove the motor.

### Installation

1. Place the motor in its mounting bracket and replace the two nuts.
2. Replace the transmission and drive assembly to the motor and install the two retaining bolts.
3. Connect the main wiring harness.
4. Place the seat back in the car.
5. Align the seat track bolts to the floor pan holes and replace the four retaining nuts. (Torque to 9–25 ft lbs)

## Horizontal and Vertical Drive

### Removal

1. Raise the seat all the way up if possible.
2. Remove the four attaching screws that connect the seat cushion to the track.
3. Remove the horizontal cable and the vertical cable and tube from the drive assemblies.
4. Remove the seat track assist spring.
5. Remove the two screws that attach the horizontal drive assembly to the track.
6. Remove the roll pin which attaches the horizontal drive unit to its support.
7. Remove the roll pin at the attaching bracket and remove the vertical drive assembly by unscrewing the drive screw out of the vertical nut.

### Installation

1. Screw the drive screw into the vertical nut and replace the roll pin at the attaching bracket.
2. Slide the upper track into the lower track.
3. Replace the horizontal support attaching screws and replace the roll pin in the drive assembly.
4. Replace the seat track assist spring.
5. Place the cushion in the car and replace the four cushion-to-seat track attaching screws.
6. Check the seat for operation.

---

# ═══ FOUR WAY POWER SEAT 1971-73 ═══

## COUGAR

### Bucket Seat
#### Description

The seat adjusters are controlled by a four-way switch, located under the left front edge of the seat. The seat assembly moves forward and backward and the front of the seat moves up and down to give it a tilting action. The switch activates a dual electric motor coupled with two gear boxes. Flexible cables connect the motor to vertical and horizontal drive units located on the adjusters.

A 20 amp circuit breaker, mounted on the starting motor relay in the engine compartment, protects the electrical system.

### Seat Assembly
#### Removal

1. If possible, raise the seat all the way up and back.

# Ford Motor Company

2. Remove the attaching screws located in the rear of the seat track.
3. Remove the outer front seat track attaching screws and the inner seat track attaching nuts.
4. Disconnect the wiring harnesses and remove the seat from the car.

## Installation

1. Place the seat in the car and reconnect the wiring harnesses.
2. Replace all attaching screws and nuts. (Torque the nuts to 18-32 ft lbs)

## Seat Track Assembly

### Removal

1. If possible, raise the seat all the way up and back.
2. Remove the attaching screws located in the rear of the seat track.
3. Remove the outer front seat track attaching screws and the inner seat track attaching nuts.
4. Disconnect the wiring harnesses.
5. Remove the seat and track assembly from the car and place upside down.
6. Remove the seat track-to-cushion attaching screws and separate the track assembly from the cushion.

### Installation

1. On a bench, replace the seat track-to-cushion attaching screws.
2. Place the seat in the car and reconnect the wiring harnesses.
3. Replace the seat track-to-floor attaching screws and nuts and torque the nuts to 18–32 ft lbs.
4. Check the seat operation.

## Motor

### Removal

1. Raise the seat all the way up if possible.
2. Remove the four attaching screws that connect the seat cushion to the track. The screws are located at each corner of the seat cushion.
3. Remove the cables and tubes from the motor.
4. Remove the two nuts that attach the motor to the mounting bracket.
5. Remove the motor.

### Installation

1. Position the motor and replace the two motor mounting nuts.
2. Reconnect the drive cables and tubes.
3. Place the seat cushion in the car and replace the four attaching screws.
4. Reconnect the control switch wiring harness.

## TROUBLESHOOTING CHART

### Four Way Power Seat Cougar 1971-73

| Condition | Possible Cause |
|---|---|
| 1. Inoperative motor | a. Defective motor<br>b. Bad ground<br>c. Defective circuit breaker<br>d. Open or short circuit between power supply, circuit breaker, relay switch, and motor |
| 2. Operative motor but no seat movement | a. Defective drive cable<br>b. Foreign object stuck under seat<br>c. Defective switch<br>d. Defective drive unit |
| 3. Seat operation not smooth, binds | a. Foreign object stuck under seat<br>b. Defective drive cable<br>c. Improper lubrication<br>d. Defective slides<br>e. Defective drive unit |

Seat Track Assembly—Cougar Four-Way Power Driver's Seat

# Six-Way Power Seat

## All 1968-75 Except 1969 Lincoln Continental

### Bench and Bucket

#### Description

The adjusters are controlled by three switches, located on the outer seat side panels on the bucket seat and on the left seat side panel on the bench seat.

The center switch controls the horizontal and vertical movement of the seat. The forward switch controls the vertical tilt of the front of the seat and the rear switch controls the vertical tilt of the rear of the seat.

The switches activate a reversible three-armature motor which drives the vertical drive units and the horizontal drive units by flexible cables.

When the center switch is moved forward or rearward it activates the

# Ford Motor Company

ward. When the center switch is moved up and down it activates both the front and rear armatures of the tri-motor. The armatures' drive cables, which are connected to the vertical worm drive gears, are located in center armature in the tri-motor which, through a drive cable, drives the horizontal rack and pinion and moves the seat forward and rear-the rear of the right track and the front of the left track. The worm gears drive the seat up and down.

The front switch activates the front armature of the tri-motor which drives the front vertical worm gear only and tilts the seat by moving the front of the seat up and down. The rear switch activates the rear armature of the tri-motor which drives the rear vertical worm gear only and tilts the seat by moving the rear of the seat up and down.

The electrical circuit is protected by a 20 amp circuit breaker mounted on the starter solenoid on every model but the Thunderbird, Lincoln Continental, and Continental Mark IV, which have their circuit breakers located on the fuse panel.

## Front Seat Assembly

### Removal

1. Remove the seat track-to-floor-pan attaching nuts and bolts.
2. Lift the seat up and disconnect the seat motor wires.
3. Remove the seat from the car.

### Installation

1. Place the seat in the car.
2. Connect the motor wires.
3. Install the seat track-to-floor pan attaching nuts and bolts (Tighten to 14–32 ft lbs)

## Seat Track Assembly

### Removal

1. Remove the seat track-to-floor pan attaching nuts and bolts.
2. Lift the seat up and disconnect the seat motor wires.
3. Remove the seat assembly from the car and place it upside down.
4. Disconnect the switch wires.
5. Remove the outer seat cushion shield.
6. Remove the four seat track-to-cushion retaining screws and separate the seat track from the cushion.

### Installation

1. Place the seat cushion on the track assembly and install the four retaining screws.
   a. Measure between the track base channels to be sure they are parallel.

## TROUBLESHOOTING CHART

### Six-Way Power Seat All 1968-75 Except 1969 Lincoln Continental

| Condition | Possible Cause |
|---|---|
| 1. Inoperative motor | a. Defective motor<br>b. Defective control switch<br>c. Defective circuit breaker<br>d. Bad ground<br>e. Open or short circuit between power and circuit breaker, switch, and motor |
| 2. Operative motor but seat will not move forward or rearward | a. Defective switch<br>b. Defective cable<br>c. Foreign object stuck under seat<br>d. Defective horizontal rack and pinion |
| 3. Operative motor but seat will not move up or down | a. Defective switch<br>b. Defective cable<br>c. Defective vertical drive unit |
| 4. Seat operation not smooth | a. Improper lubrication<br>b. Defective cable<br>c. Foreign object stuck under seat<br>d. Defective horizontal or vertical drive units |

2. Replace the seat cushion side shield.
3. Connect the control switch wires.
4. Place the seat assembly in the car and connect the motor wires.
5. Install the seat track-to-floor pan attaching nuts and bolts. (Tighten to 14–32 ft lbs)

## Motor and Drive Cables

### Removal

1. Remove the seat track-to-floor pan retaining nuts and bolts.
2. Lift the seat up and disconnect the motor wires.
3. Remove the motor mounting bracket attaching bolts.
4. Remove the drive cables from the seat tracks by removing the retaining clamps.
5. Remove the wire retaining straps and the cable retaining brackets to the motor.
6. Remove the drive cables from the motor.

### Installation

1. Position the motor to the mounting bracket and the cables to the motor and seat track.
2. Install the cable retaining screws and the motor mounting bracket attaching bolts.
3. Install the cable-to-seat track retaining clamps.
4. Place the seat in the car and connect the motor wires.
5. Install the seat track-to-floor

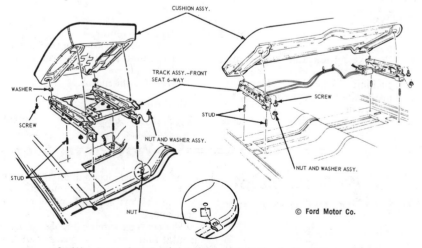

*Six-Way Power Seat Tracks—Bench and Split Bench—Ford, Mercury, and Lincoln Continental*

© Ford Motor Co.

# Ford Motor Company

pan attaching nuts and bolts. (Tighten to 14–31 ft lbs)

6. Check seat operation.

## Primary and Secondary Seat Track

The primary seat track is the name given to the seat track which contains a vertical assist spring, cup assembly, the seat motor, and the mounting bracket. The opposite seat track is referred to as the secondary seat track.

## Primary Seat Track

### Removal

1. Remove the seat track-to-floor pan retaining nuts and bolts.
2. Lift the seat up and disconnect the motor wiring harness.
3. Remove the seat assembly from the car.
4. Remove the right and left cushion side shields.
5. Disconnect the drive cables from the seat tracks by removing the retaining clamps.
6. Remove the motor mounting bracket retaining screws and remove the motor and bracket from the track.
7. Bucket and split bench seats only —remove the front and rear torsion bars from the end of each track by removing the cotter keys and pivot pins.
8. Remove the two seat track-to-cushion retaining screws.

### Disassembly

1. Raise the track upper channel to the full up position if possible.
   a. To raise the channel, insert the square end of the drive cable into the vertical transmission coupling and turn it counter clockwise.
2. If the vertical transmission will not operate, move the horizontal track to the full forward position.
   a. To move the track horizontally and to the full forward position, insert the drive cable into the horizontal transmission coupling and turn it counter clockwise.
3. Apply pressure to the upper channel against the vertical assist spring and remove the front clevis pin.
4. Release the pressure slowly and remove the rear clevis pin, upper channel, spring, and cup.
5. Remove the front and rear pivot bolts and nuts and the roll pin from the rear end of the two side rails.
6. Remove the two bolts and nuts

*Turning Vertical Transmission to Up Position*

*Removing Upper Channel*

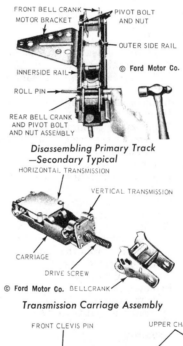

*Disassembling Primary Track —Secondary Typical*

*Transmission Carriage Assembly*

that retain the horizontal transmission and motor mounting bracket to the side rails and remove the bracket.

7. Spread the side rails apart slightly and slide the outer side rail forward and off of the base channel.
8. Lift the transmission carriage and transmission assembly out of the base channel.
9. Lift the inner side rail from the base channel.
10. Lift the horizontal transmission from the carriage and turn the bell crank off the vertical transmission drive screw.
11. If the transmission is defective it may be taken apart by removing the cover to expose the internal parts.

### Assembly

1. Install the bellcrank to the vertical transmission by turning it on to the left-hand threaded screw drive.
2. Install the horizontal transmission to the carriage.
3. Position the four horizontal slide blocks and the pinion retainer block on the base channel.
   a. The ridges on the blocks should be aligned with the grooves on the channel.
4. Install the transmission and carriage assembly to the base channel.
   a. Make sure that the horizontal pinion engages the horizontal rack.
5. Slide the outer rail onto the base channel.
6. Slide the inner rail onto the base channel.
7. Replace the two through bolts and nuts that hold the motor

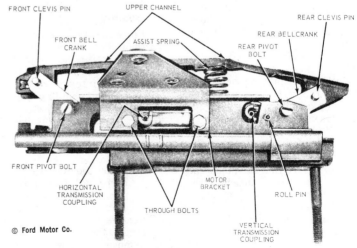

*Primary Track Assembly—Continental Mark IV, Typical of All*

# Ford Motor Company

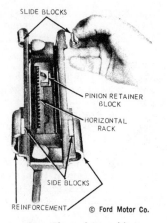

SLIDE BLOCKS

PINION RETAINER BLOCK

HORIZONTAL RACK

SIDE BLOCKS

REINFORCEMENT    © Ford Motor Co.

*Base Channel Assembly*

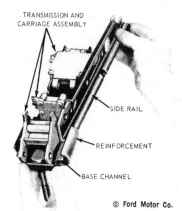

TRANSMISSION AND CARRIAGE ASSEMBLY

SIDE RAIL

REINFORCEMENT

BASE CHANNEL

© Ford Motor Co.

*Installing Outer Side Rail on Base Channel —Primary Track*

bracket, horizontal transmission, and the side rails together.

8. Install the roll pin at the rear end of the two side rails.
9. Install the front bellcrank between the side rails and replace the pivot bolt and nut.
10. Swing the rear bellcrank into alignment with the bolt holes and install the pivot bolt and nut.
11. Assemble the rear end of the upper channel to the rear bellcrank and install the clevis pin.
12. Install the vertical assist spring and cup assembly into the transmission carriage.
13. Install the wear plates—one on each side of the front end of the upper channel.
    a. Make sure that the upper end of the spring fits into the spring seat in the upper channel.
    b. Force the channel down against the spring and secure the forward end to the front bellcrank with the clevis pin.

## Installation

1. Position the cushion to the seat track and replace the retaining screws.
2. Bucket and split bench only—replace the front and rear torque bars to the front and rear ends of each track using the pivot pins and cotter pins.
3. Position the motor and bracket assembly and replace the retaining screws.
4. Connect the drive cables to the seat track and install the retaining clamps.
5. Replace the cushion side shield.
6. Place the seat assembly in the car and connect the motor wires.
7. Install the seat track-to-floor pan attaching nuts and bolts. (Tighten to 14–3 ft lbs)

## Secondary Seat Track

### Removal

1. Remove the seat track-to-floor pan retaining nuts and bolts.
2. Lift the seat up and disconnect the motor wiring harness.
3. Remove the seat assembly from the car.
4. Remove the cushion side shield.
5. Disconnect the drive cables from the seat tracks by removing the retaining clamps.
6. Remove the three motor-to-bracket retaining screws and remove the motor and cables together.
7. Bucket and split bench seats only—remove the front and rear torsion bars from the end of each track by removing the cotter keys and pivot pins.
8. Remove the two seat track-to-cushion retaining screws and separate the seat track.

### Disassembly

1. Raise the track upper channel to the full up position if possible.
   a. To raise the channel, insert the square end of the drive cable into the vertical transmission coupling and turn it counter clockwise.
2. If the vertical transmission will not operate, move the horizontal track to the full forward position.
   a. Insert the drive cable into the horizontal transmission coupling and turn it counter clockwise.
3. Remove the two clevis pins and remove the upper channel.
4. Remove the roll pin from the rear end of the two side rails and

remove the front and rear pivot bolts and nuts.
5. Remove the two side rail bolts and nuts.
6. Lift the transmission and carriage assembly out of the base channel.
7. Lift the horizontal transmission from the carriage and turn the bellcrank off of the vertical transmission drive screw.
8. If the transmission is defective, it may be taken apart by removing the cover to expose the internal parts.

## Assembly

1. Install the bellcrank to the vertical transmission by turning it on to the left-hand threaded screw drive.
2. Install the horizontal transmission to the carriage.
3. Position the four horizontal slide blocks and the pinion retainer block on the base channel.
   a. The ridges on the blocks should be aligned with the grooves on the channel.
4. Mount the two side rails to the base channel.
5. Install the two through bolts and nuts that hold the horizontal transmission and side rails together.
6. Install the roll pin at the rear end of the two side rails.
7. Install the rear bellcrank between the slide rails and replace the pivot bolt and nut.
8. Swing the front bell crank into alignment with the bolt holes and install the pivot bolt and nut.
9. Install the wear plates and connect the forward end of the upper channel to the front bellcrank with a clevis pin.

## Installation

1. Position the cushion to the seat track and replace the retaining screws.
2. Bucket and split bench only—replace the front and rear torsion bars to the front and rear ends of each track using the pivot pins and cotter pins.
3. Place the motor and the cables into position and replace the three motor-to-bracket screws.
4. Connect the drive cables to the seat track and install the retaining clamps.
5. Replace the cushion side shield.
6. Place the seat assembly in the car and connect the motor wires.
7. Install the seat track-to-floor pan attaching nuts and bolts. (Tighten to 14–32 ft lbs)

# Ford Motor Company

## Ford 1968-1975 Two, Four, and Six-Way Seat

### Electrical Circuits

Before performing any extensive electrical testing procedures, make sure the battery is in good shape and there are no mechanical failures. Also, refer to the power seat wiring diagrams for proper identification of wires.

### Open and Short Circuits

An open circuit is when the circuit is not completed because of a poor terminal contact or a broken wire A short circuit occurs when the current is being grounded before it reaches a particular unit. When this happens, it actuates a circuit breaker or blows a fuse because of the overload created. Use a test light to detect the location of a short.

A 30 amp circuit breaker is used on most models and is mounted on the instrument panel behind the glove box. It can be reached by removing the glove box filler. Others use a 20 amp circuit breaker mounted on the starting motor relay in the engine compartment.

### Improper Ground

Many times perfectly good operating units, such as motors, are considered defective and are replaced because of a bad ground. To test for an improper ground, perform the following:

1. Attach one end of a jumper wire to the body of an inoperative unit.
2. Connect the other end to a good ground, such as a bare metal panel.
3. Switch on the unit. If it operates, the original ground is defective.

### Four-Way Power Seat Switch Test

1. Disconnect the four terminal wire connectors. The single wire connector remains connected.
2. Using a 12 volt test light, connect one test light wire to a good ground.
3. With the other test light wire,

check for power at each of the four terminal connectors using the following combinations:

| Switch position | Terminal |
|---|---|
| Up | Lt. green/Yellow dot and white |
| Down | Orange/Yellow dot and white |
| Forward | Lt. green/Yellow dot and lt. blue |
| Rearward | Orange/Yellow dot and lt. blue |

### Six-Way Power Seat Switch Test Except Lincoln

1. Disconnect the wire connector from the switch.
2. Using a self-powered test light, check for power between the black (ground) wire and each of the red and yellow wires. With the switches in the center position, the test light should light.
3. Connect the self-powered test light to the black and white striped wire and to each of the red and yellow wires. With the switches in their center positions, the test light should not light.
4. With the self-powered test light connected to the black and white striped wire, check for power at the terminals of the connectors as follows:

| Switch position | Wire color |
|---|---|
| Forward up | Red/Lt. blue stripe |
| Forward down | Yellow/Lt. blue stripe |
| Rear up | Red/Lt. green stripe |
| Rear down | Yellow/Lt. green stripe |
| Center up | Yellow/Lt. blue stripe and green stripe |
| Center down | Yellow/Lt. blue stripe and Yellow/Lt. green stripe |
| Center forward | Red/White stripe |
| Center rearward | Yellow/White stripe |

### Seat Control Solenoid Test

1. Disconnect the wiring harness from each solenoid.
2. Connect 12 volts of power to the solenoid connector terminals, one at a time. Listen for a clicking noise.

### Six-Way Power Seat Switch Test for Lincoln

1. Disconnect the wiring harness from the switch connectors.
2. Keep the power connector con-

nected (Two terminals—yellow and red/white).

3. Connect a 12-volt test light to a good ground and check for power at the terminals of the connectors as follows:

| Switch position | Terminal |
|---|---|
| Front up | Brown-Yellow |
| Front down | Brown-Red |
| Rear up | Green-Yellow |
| Rear down | Green-Red |
| Center up | White-Yellow |
| Center down | White |
| Center forward | Red-Blue |
| Center rearward | Yellow-Blue |

### Seat Motor Test

1. Disconnect the motor leads from the circuit.
2. Connect a ground and a positive lead wire from the battery to the motor.
3. Reverse the leads at the motor connector to see if the motor will operate in the reverse direction.

### Seat Directional Control Relay Test

1. Disconnect the solenoids from the harness.
2. Disconnect the center switch from the harness.
3. Connect 12 volts of power to the white wire terminal of the center switch connector.
4. Using a test light, test for power at the brown and green wire terminals of the wiring connector for the solenoids.

## Six-Way Power Seat 1969

## Lincoln Continental

### Bench and Bucket
#### Description

The seat adjusters are controlled by three switches mounted on the left seat side panel. The center switch controls the horizontal and vertical movement of the seat. The forward switch controls the tilting of the front of the seat and the rear switch controls the tilting of the rear of the seat.

When the switches are activated

for a desired movement they transmit power to the solenoids by way of relays, except for horizontal movement which is controlled directly from the switch to the solenoid. The solenoids engage the gears in the transmission and drive the actuators by way of

# Ford Motor Company

flexible cables.

A 30 amp circuit breaker protects the electrical circuit and is mounted on the starter solenoid.

## Front Seat Assembly (Bucket)

### Removal

1. From under the car, remove the two seat track front retaining nuts and the two seat track rear retaining bolts.
2. Tilt the seat assembly up and disconnect the seat track motor wires.
3. Lift the seat assembly from the car.

### Installation

1. Place the seat in the car.
2. Connect the seat track motor wires.
3. Install the two seat track front retaining nuts and the two seat track rear retaining bolts to the floor pan.

## Seat Track Assembly (Bucket)

### Removal

1. From under the car, remove the two seat track front retaining nuts and the two seat track rear retaining bolts.
2. Tilt the seat assembly up and disconnect the seat track motor wires.
3. Lift the seat assembly from the car.
4. Disconnect the seat control wires.
5. Remove the four cushion-to-seat track retaining screws and separate the seat track from the cushion.

### Installation

1. Position the cushion to the seat track and replace the four retaining screws.
2. Connect the seat control wires.
3. Place the seat assembly in the car.
4. Connect the seat track motor wires.
5. Install the two seat track front retaining nuts and the two seat track rear retaining bolts to the floor pan.

## Motor (Bucket)

### Removal

1. From under the car, remove the two seat track front retaining nuts and the two seat track rear retaining bolts.
2. Tilt the seat assembly up and disconnect the motor wires at the connection.

## TROUBLESHOOTING CHART

### 1969 Lincoln Continental
### Bench and Bucket

| Condition | Possible Cause |
|---|---|
| 1. Inoperative motor | a. Defective motor<br>b. Defective switch<br>c. Defective circuit breaker<br>d. Open or short circuit between power source and circuit breaker, switch, motor<br>e. Bad ground |
| 2. Operative motor but seat will not move forward or rearward | a. Defective switch<br>b. Defective actuator<br>c. Defective solenoid<br>d. Open or short circuit between switch and solenoid |
| 3. Operative motor but seat will not move up or down | a. Defective switch<br>b. Defective relay<br>c. Defective cable<br>d. Defective actuator<br>e. Open or short circuit between switch and relay or solenoid |
| 4. Seat operation not smooth, binds | a. Improper lubrication<br>b. Defective cable<br>c. Foreign object stuck under seat |

3. Remove the two motor-to-bracket retaining nuts.
4. Remove the drive coupling from the motor and remove the motor.

### Installation

1. Replace the drive coupling on the motor shaft.
2. Connect the motor and coupling to the mounting bracket and install the retaining nuts.
3. Connect the motor wires.
4. Position the seat to the floor pan and install the two seat track front retaining nuts and the two seat track rear retaining bolts.

## Front Seat Asembly (Bench)

### Removal

1. Disconnect the ground cable from the battery.
2. From under the car, remove the two seat track front retaining nuts and the two seat track rear retaining bolts.
3. Remove the motor mounting bracket to the floor pan nut and washer.

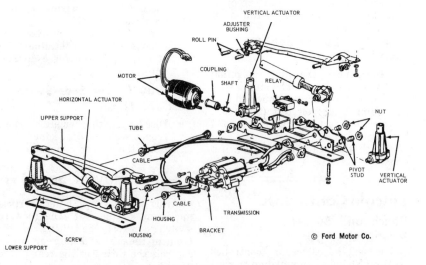

*Six-Way Power Bucket Seat Track Disassembled—Lincoln Continental*

# Ford Motor Company

4. Disconnect the main wiring harness.
5. Lift the seat from the car.

## Installation

1. Place the seat back in the car.
2. Connect the wiring harness.
3. Replace the motor mounting bracket-to-floor pan nut.
4. Position the seat to the floor pan and install the two seat track front retaining nuts and the two seat track rear retaining bolts.
5. Connect the ground cable to the battery.

## Seat Track Assembly (Bench)

### Removal

1. Disconnect the ground cable from the battery.
2. From under the car, remove the two seat track front retaining nuts and the two seat track rear retaining bolts.
3. Remove the motor mounting bracket-to-floor pan nut and washer.
4. Disconnect the main wiring harness.
5. Lift the seat from the car.
6. Remove the four cushion-to-seat track retaining screws and remove the cushion.

### Installation

1. Position the cushion to the seat track and replace the four retaining screws.

2. Place the seat assembly in the car.
3. Replace the motor mounting bracket-to-floor pan nut.
4. Position the seat to the floor pan and install the two seat track front retaining nuts and the two seat track rear retaining bolts.
5. Connect the ground cable to the battery.

## Motor (Bench)

### Removal

1. From under the car, remove the two seat track front retaining nuts and the two seat track rear retaining bolts.
2. Tilt the seat up and disconnect the motor wires.
3. Remove the two motor-to-mounting bracket nuts.
4. Remove the motor from the drive coupling and mounting bracket.

### Installation

1. Position the motor and drive coupling to the mounting bracket and install the attaching nuts.
2. Connect the motor wires.
3. Install the seat track-to-floor pan attaching nuts and bolts.

## Seat Relay (Bench and Bucket)

### Removal

1. From under the car, remove the

two seat track front retaining nuts and the two seat track rear retaining bolts.
2. Disconnect the main wiring harness.
3. Lift the seat from the car.
4. Disconnect the wire connector at the relay.
5. Remove the relay-to-mounting bracket retaining screws.

### Installation

1. Connect the relay to the mounting bracket.
2. Connect the wire connector to the relay.
3. Place the seat in the car.
4. Connect the main wiring harness.
5. Position the seat to the floor pan and install the two seat track front retaining nuts and the two seat track rear retaining bolts.

## Transmission (Bench and Bucket)

### Removal

1. From under the car, remove the two seat track front retaining nuts and the two seat track rear retaining bolts.
2. Tilt the seat up and disconnect the wiring harness.
3. Lift the seat assembly from the car.
4. From both sides of the transmission, remove the cable housing retainers.

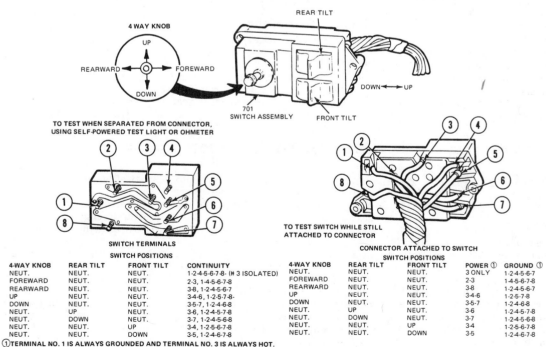

4-WAY KNOB
UP
REARWARD — FOREWARD
DOWN

REAR TILT

DOWN ← → UP

701
SWITCH ASSEMBLY          FRONT TILT

TO TEST WHEN SEPARATED FROM CONNECTOR,
USING SELF-POWERED TEST LIGHT OR OHMETER

SWITCH TERMINALS

TO TEST SWITCH WHILE STILL
ATTACHED TO CONNECTOR

CONNECTOR ATTACHED TO SWITCH

| SWITCH POSITIONS | | | | SWITCH POSITIONS | | | | |
| --- | --- | --- | --- | --- | --- | --- | --- | --- |
| 4-WAY KNOB | REAR TILT | FRONT TILT | CONTINUITY | 4-WAY KNOB | REAR TILT | FRONT TILT | POWER ① | GROUND ① |
| NEUT. | NEUT. | NEUT. | 1-2-4-5-6-7-8- (# 3 ISOLATED) | NEUT. | NEUT. | NEUT. | 3 ONLY | 1-2-4-5-6-7 |
| FOREWARD | NEUT. | NEUT. | 2-3, 1-4-5-6-7-8 | FOREWARD | NEUT. | NEUT. | 2-3 | 1-4-5-6-7-8 |
| REARWARD | NEUT. | NEUT. | 3-8, 1-2-4-5-6-7 | REARWARD | NEUT. | NEUT. | 3-8 | 1-2-4-5-6-7 |
| UP | NEUT. | NEUT. | 3-4-6, 1-2-5-7-8- | UP | NEUT. | NEUT. | 3-4-6 | 1-2-5-7-8 |
| DOWN | NEUT. | NEUT. | 3-5-7, 1-2-4-6-8 | DOWN | NEUT. | NEUT. | 3-5-7 | 1-2-4-6-8 |
| NEUT. | UP | NEUT. | 3-6, 1-2-4-5-7-8 | NEUT. | UP | NEUT. | 3-6 | 1-2-4-5-7-8 |
| NEUT. | DOWN | NEUT. | 3-7, 1-2-4-5-6-8 | NEUT. | DOWN | NEUT. | 3-7 | 1-2-4-5-6-8 |
| NEUT. | NEUT. | UP | 3-4, 1-2-5-6-7-8 | NEUT. | NEUT. | UP | 3-4 | 1-2-5-6-7-8 |
| NEUT. | NEUT. | DOWN | 3-5, 1-2-4-6-7-8 | NEUT. | NEUT. | DOWN | 3-5 | 1-2-4-6-7-8 |

① TERMINAL NO. 1 IS ALWAYS GROUNDED AND TERMINAL NO. 3 IS ALWAYS HOT.

*Power Seat Switch Test—Armrest Mounted Switch—6 Way*

# Power Seats

## Ford Motor Company

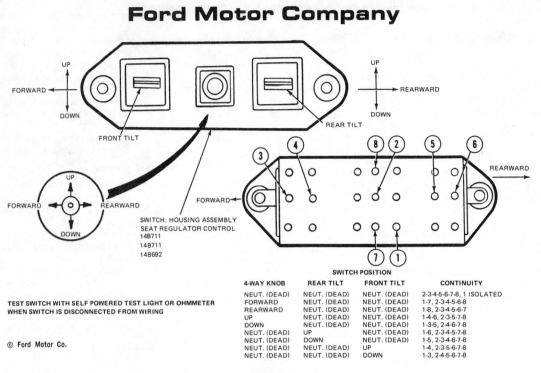

TEST SWITCH WITH SELF POWERED TEST LIGHT OR OHMMETER
WHEN SWITCH IS DISCONNECTED FROM WIRING

© Ford Motor Co.

| | SWITCH POSITION | | |
|---|---|---|---|
| 4-WAY KNOB | REAR TILT | FRONT TILT | CONTINUITY |
| NEUT. (DEAD) | NEUT. (DEAD) | NEUT. (DEAD) | 2-3-4-5-6-7-8, 1 ISOLATED |
| FORWARD | NEUT. (DEAD) | NEUT. (DEAD) | 1-7, 2-3-4-5-6-8 |
| REARWARD | NEUT. (DEAD) | NEUT. (DEAD) | 1-8, 2-3-4-5-6-7 |
| UP | NEUT. (DEAD) | NEUT. (DEAD) | 1-4-6, 2-3-5-7-8 |
| DOWN | NEUT. (DEAD) | NEUT. (DEAD) | 1-3-5, 2-4-6-7-8 |
| NEUT. (DEAD) | UP | NEUT. (DEAD) | 1-6, 2-3-4-5-7-8 |
| NEUT. (DEAD) | DOWN | NEUT. (DEAD) | 1-5, 2-3-4-6-7-8 |
| NEUT. (DEAD) | NEUT. (DEAD) | UP | 1-4, 2-3-5-6-7-8 |
| NEUT. (DEAD) | NEUT. (DEAD) | DOWN | 1-3, 2-4-5-6-7-8 |

*Power Seat Switch Test—Seat Mounted Switch—6 Way*

5. Remove the bolts which attach the left seat track to the frame and remove the track, motor, and transmission as a unit.
6. Remove the bolts which attach the transmission to its mounting bracket and separate the transmission from the cable housing and cables.
7. Disconnect the solenoid wires and separate the transmission.

### Installation

1. Connect the motor and drive coupling to the transmission and replace the two retaining nuts.
2. Connect the solenoid wires.
3. Position the transmission to the right and left drive cables and

install the retainers.
4. Install the two transmission-to-bracket retaining bolts.
5. Position the left track to the frame and replace the attaching bolts.
6. Place the seat in the car and install the two seat track front retaining nuts and the two seat track rear retaining bolts.

### Cable and Housing (Bench and Bucket)

#### Removal

1. From under the car, remove the two seat track front retaining nuts and the two seat track rear retaining bolts.

2. Remove the seat assembly from the car and place it upside down.
3. Remove the cable housing retaining screws and separate the cables from the track and the transmission.
4. Remove the two seat track-to-frame retaining bolts.

### Installation

1. Install the cable housing retainers at the seat track and the transmission.
2. Install the two seat track-to-frame retaining bolts.
3. Place the seat in the car and install the two seat track front retaining nuts and the two seat track rear retaining bolts.

## General Motors

### GM—Two-, Four-, or Six-Way Power Seats

#### Description

The seat adjusters are operated by a 12 volt, reversible motor with a built-in circuit breaker (located directly under the seat).

The motor is activated by a toggle switch usually located in the left seat side panel or arm rest. Current is supplied from the circuit breaker to a junction block (located behind the left kick panel) by way of the power seat wiring harness.

When the toggle switch is put into position, it engages one of the transmission solenoids (located inside the seat transmission).

A solenoid coupled with two drive cables controls the desired movement of the seat. A four-way seat has a total of two solenoids and four cables. The combination of one solenoid and two cables is used for horizontal movement and the other solenoid and the two other cables are used for vertical movement of the seat. A six-way seat has a total of three solenoids and six cables. The third solenoid coupled with two cables controls

vertical movement of the rear of the seat.

When one of the solenoids is activated, it engages a drive gear dog (located at the drive end of the solenoid shaft inside the transmission). Current then flows through a relay coil and closes the contacts between the relay power source and the armature feed wire which then operates the motor under the seat. Power is then transmitted through the transmission shaft on bench seats. (Cars with bucket seats use a pulley on the motor and transmission connected by a belt.)

# Power Seats

## General Motors

The drive gear at the end of the transmission then rotates the cables which in turn control the adjusters for each desired movement. When the seat reaches its limit of travel, the cables stop rotating and the torque is absorbed by a rubber coupler (between the motor and transmission on bench seats and through the pulleys on bucket seats). When the pressure on the control switch is released, a spring returns the solenoid plunger to its original position, disengaging the drive gear dog which stops the operation.

## ═══ Two-Way Power Seat (bench and bucket) ═══

### Front Seat Assembly

**Removal**

1. Remove the front seat retaining bolts. (On some models it may be necessary to remove the door sill plates and turn back the floor mat to gain access to these bolts.)
   a. On seats with electrical equipment, tilt the seat back in order to disconnect the wire connectors.
   b. On cars with front inner seat belts, it may be necessary to remove the seat belt-to-floor bolts.

**Installation**

1. Reverse removal procedures.
   a. Make sure that both seat adjusters are parallel and synchronized. (One adjuster does not reach its maximum point of travel before the other.)

### Front Seat Adjuster Assembly

**Removal**

1. Remove the front seat (previously described).
2. Disconnect drive cables at the adjuster.
   a. On cars with split bench or bucket seats, remove the bolt that holds the motor and transmission to the adjuster.
3. Remove the adjuster from the seat bottom frame.

**Installation**

1. Reverse removal procedures.
   a. Make sure that both seat adjusters are parallel and synchronized during operation.

### Electric Motor

**Removal and Installation**

1. If possible, move the seat to midway position.
2. Remove the seat and tilt backward.
   a. Full width bench seats—Disconnect both drive cables from the motor.
   b. Split bench seat—Disconnect the seat adjuster from the seat bottom, then disconnect the drive cables from the motor.
   c. Bucket seats—Remove the belt cover and motor-to-transmission drive belt.
3. Remove the motor support from the seat bottom frame, then remove the motor.
4. To install, reverse the removal procedures.

### Horizontal Gearnut

**Removal**

1. Remove the front seat with the adjuster attached.
2. Disconnect the drive cable at the gearnut end.
3. Remove the gearnut from the upper slide portion of the seat adjuster (two "clutch" type shoulder bolts).
4. Rotate the jack screw upward to expose the cotter pin.
   a. Remove the cotter pin, washer, and the rubber bumper at the end of the jack screw and then remove the gearnut.

## TROUBLESHOOTING CHART
### GM-Two, Four-, Six-Way Power Seat

| Condition | Possible Cause |
|---|---|
| **1. Inoperative motor** | a. Open or short circuit between switch and power supply<br>b. Defective control switch<br>c. Open or short circuit between switch and motor<br>d. Defective motor<br>e. Bad ground |
| **2. Operative motor but no seat movement either way** | a. Damage of internal transmission parts<br>b. Defective control switch<br>c. Defective solenoid<br>d. Check pulley belt (bucket seat only) |
| **3. Operative motor, seat moves in only one direction** | a. Defective solenoid<br>b. Defective cable<br>c. Defective actuator<br>d. Open or short circuit |
| **4. Seat operation not smooth—either binds or too loose** | a. Lack of lubrication<br>b. Actuator gear out of adjustment<br>c. Defective actuator shoes<br>d. Loose pulley belt (bucket seat only) |

**Installation**

1. Reverse removal procedures
   a. Make sure that both seat adjusters are parallel and synchronized during operation. (see "adjustment of seat adjusters.")

### Horizontal Jack Screws

**Removal and Installation**

1. Remove the front seat with the adjusters attached.
2. Disconnect the drive cable at the gearnut end.
3. Remove the gearnut from the upper slide portion of the seat adjuster (two "clutch" type shoulder bolts).
4. Remove the retainer and cross-pin that holds the stop bracket to the front adjuster support.
5. Remove the jack screw from the adjuster.
6. To install, reverse removal procedures.

*NOTE: When replacing the jack screw, the old attaching parts from the front and rear end of the jack screw must be used.*

# Power Seats

## General Motors

### Plastic Slides

#### Removal

1. Remove the front seat adjuster. (See "Front seat adjuster removal and installation.")
2. Remove the upper channel gearnut from the seat adjuster (two "clutch" type shoulder bolts).
3. Slide the lower track and base portion of the seat adjuster forward, with gearnut and jack screw attached, until it separates from the upper channel.
   a. The four plastic slides may now be separated from the lower track.

#### Installation

1. Reverse removal procedure.
   a. Make sure that the thinner section of the slide shows above the track surface when the groove of the plastic slide is slipped onto the lower track.

### Horizontal Drive Cable

#### Removal

1. Remove the front seat. (See "Front seat removal").
2. Place the seat upside down and detach the cable.

#### Installation

1. Reverse removal procedure.
   a. Check the seat for full limit of operation.

### Adjustment of Seat Adjusters

When replacing the seat in the car, one horizontal or vertical adjuster should not be ahead of the other when in operation. If one is not mov-

© G.M. Corp.

*Front Seat Adjusters—Power Operated Horizontal—Oldsmobile and Cadillac*

1. Seat Adjuster to Floor Pan Attaching Bolts
2. Horizontal Drive Cables
3. Adjuster Horizontal Gear Nut and Shoulder Screws
4. Adjuster Jack Screw
5. Jack Screw Support Pin
6. Electric Motor
7. Motor to Seat Frame Attaching Screws
8. Horizontal Drive Cable Straps
9. Seat Frame to Adjuster Ground Strap
10. Adjuster to Seat Frame Bolts

ing parallel with the other, adjust as follows:

### Horizontal Movement

1. Actuate the seat switch and move the seat all the way forward.
2. Remove the cable from the horizontal adjuster that is moved all the way forward.
3. Activate the seat switch again and move the other horizontal adjuster all the way forward.
4. Attach the cable and check movement again. Repeat if necessary.

### Front or Rear Vertical Movement

1. Activate the seat switch and move the vertical adjusters all the way up, at both front and rear ends.
2. Remove the front and rear vertical cables from the adjuster that has reached the top first.
3. Activate the seat switch and raise the other vertical adjuster until it is parallel to the other.
4. Connect both front and rear cables and check movement again. Repeat if necessary.

## ═══════ Four-Way Power Seat (Bench and Bucket) ═══════

### Front Seat Assembly

#### Removal

1. Remove the front seat retaining bolt. (On some models it may be necessary to remove the door sill plates and turn back the floor mat to gain access to the bolt.)
   a. On seats with electrical equipment, tilt the seat back in order to disconnect the wire connectors.
   b. On cars with front inner seat belts, it may be necessary to remove the seat belt-to-floor bolts.

#### Installation

1. Reverse removal procedures.

   a. Make sure that both seat adjusters are parallel. Make sure one adjuster does not reach its maximum point of travel before the other. (see "adjustment of seat adjuster")

### Front Seat Adjuster Assembly

#### Removal

1. Remove the front seat.
2. Disconnect the drive cables at the adjuster.
   a. On cars with the split bench or bucket seats, remove the bolt that holds the motor and transmission to the adjuster.
3. Remove the adjuster from the

seat bottom frame.

#### Installation

1. Reverse removal procedures.
   a. Connect the black cable from the front of the transmission to the horizontal actuator.
   b. Connect the blue cable from the rear of the transmission to the rear vertical gearnut.
   c. Make sure that the seat travels to its full limit either way.

### Transmission

#### Removal

1. Remove the seat assembly from the body, keeping the adjusters, motor, and transmission at-

# General Motors

tached. (See "Front seat removal")

2. Disconnect the wire harness from the transmission.
3. Remove the cables from both sides of the transmission by removing the screws from the end plate.
4. Remove the bolts that connect the transmission to the transmission support and separate the transmission from the rubber coupler.

## Installation

1. Reverse removal procedure.
   a. Connect the black cables from the front of the transmission to the horizontal actuator.
   b. Connect the blue cable from the rear of the transmission to the rear vertical gearnut.

## Disassembly of Transmission

1. Remove the transmission from the seat. (See "Transmission removal")
2. Remove the screws and separate the gear solenoid housings, exposing the internal gears.

## Assembly of Transmission

1. Reverse disassembly procedure.
   a. Lubricate gears before assembly.

## Transmission and Motor Drive Belts and Pulleys

## (Bucket Seat Only)

### Removal

1. Remove the drive belt cover screws and remove the cover located at the front of the seat.
2. Remove the belt.
3. Pull the pulley from the shafts.

### Installation

1. Reverse removal procedure.
   a. Make sure that the seat travels its full limit both ways.

## Adjustment of Seat Adjusters

When replacing the seat in the car, one horizontal or vertical adjuster should not be ahead of the other when in operation. If one is not moving parallel with the other, adjust as follows:

## Horizontal Movement

1. Actuate the seat switch and move the seat all the way forward.
2. Remove the cable from the horizontal adjuster that is moved all the way forward.

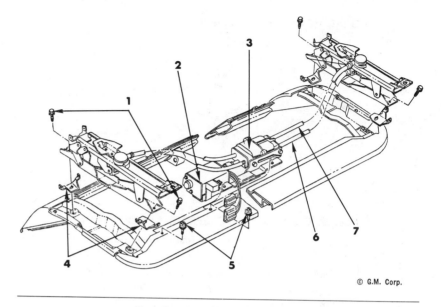

© G.M. Corp.

*Front Seat Assembly—Four Way Tilt*

1. Adjuster to Seat Frame Attaching Bolts
2. Motor Assembly
3. Transmission Assembly
4. Track Cover Supports
5. Motor and Transmission Support Attaching Screws
6. Vertical Cable (Yellow)
7. Horizontal Cable (Black)

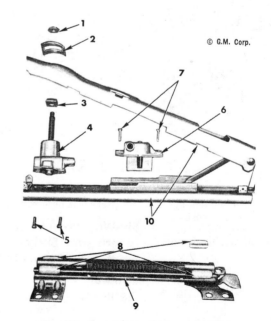

© G.M. Corp.

*Four-Way Seat Adjuster Components—Buick*

1. Upper Channel to Gearnut Attaching Nut
2. Vertical Gearnut Tension Spring
3. Vertical Gearnut Shoulder Nuts
4. Vertical Gearnut
5. Vertical Gearnut Attaching Screws
6. Horizontal Actuator
7. Horizontal Actuator Attaching Screws
8. Plastic Shoes
9. Lower Channel
10. Upper Channel

## General Motors

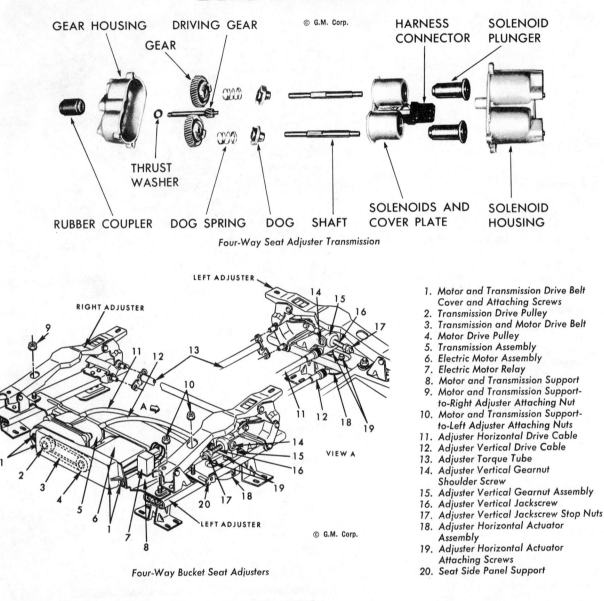

GEAR HOUSING    DRIVING GEAR    © G.M. Corp.    HARNESS CONNECTOR    SOLENOID PLUNGER

GEAR

THRUST WASHER

RUBBER COUPLER    DOG SPRING    DOG    SHAFT    SOLENOIDS AND COVER PLATE    SOLENOID HOUSING

*Four-Way Seat Adjuster Transmission*

LEFT ADJUSTER

RIGHT ADJUSTER

VIEW A

© G.M. Corp.

*Four-Way Bucket Seat Adjusters*

1. Motor and Transmission Drive Belt Cover and Attaching Screws
2. Transmission Drive Pulley
3. Transmission and Motor Drive Belt
4. Motor Drive Pulley
5. Transmission Assembly
6. Electric Motor Assembly
7. Electric Motor Relay
8. Motor and Transmission Support
9. Motor and Transmission Support-to-Right Adjuster Attaching Nut
10. Motor and Transmission Support-to-Left Adjuster Attaching Nuts
11. Adjuster Horizontal Drive Cable
12. Adjuster Vertical Drive Cable
13. Adjuster Torque Tube
14. Adjuster Vertical Gearnut Shoulder Screw
15. Adjuster Vertical Gearnut Assembly
16. Adjuster Vertical Jackscrew
17. Adjuster Vertical Jackscrew Stop Nuts
18. Adjuster Horizontal Actuator Assembly
19. Adjuster Horizontal Actuator Attaching Screws
20. Seat Side Panel Support

3. Activate the seat switch again and move the other horizontal adjuster all the way forward.
4. Attach the cable and check movement again.

### Front or Rear Vertical Movement

1. Activate the seat switch and move the vertical adjusters all the way up, at both front and rear ends.
2. Remove the front and rear vertical cables from the adjuster that has reached the top first.
3. Activate the seat switch and raise the other vertical adjuster until it is parallel to the other.
4. Connect both front and rear cables and check movement again.

Repeat if necessary.

### Six-Way Power Seat (Bench and Bucket) Front Seat Assembly

#### Removal

1. Remove the front seat retaining bolts. (On some models, it may be necessary to remove the door sill plates and turn back the floor mat to gain access to these bolts.)
   a. On seats with electrical equipment, tilt the seat back in order to disconnect the wire connectors.
   b. On cars with front inner seat belts, it may be necessary to remove the seatbelt-to-floor bolts.

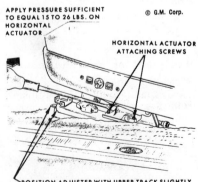

APPLY PRESSURE SUFFICIENT TO EQUAL 15 TO 26 LBS. ON HORIZONTAL ACTUATOR    © G.M. Corp.

HORIZONTAL ACTUATOR ATTACHING SCREWS

POSITION ADJUSTER WITH UPPER TRACK SLIGHTLY REARWARD OF LOWER TRACK AND CHECK (OBSERVE) FOR HORIZONTAL CHUCK

*Horizontal Actuator Adjustment—*
*Six-Way Seat Adjusters*

# General Motors

## Installation

1. Reverse removal procedures.
   a. Make sure that both seat adjusters are parallel and synchronized. (One adjuster does not reach its maximum point of travel before the other.) (See "Adjustment of seat adjusters")

## Front Seat Adjuster Assembly

### Removal

1. Remove the front seat as previously described.
2. Disconnect the drive cables at the adjuster.
   a. On cars with split-bench or bucket seats, remove the bolt that holds the motor and transmission to the adjuster.
3. Remove the adjuster from the seat bottom frame.

### Installation

1. Reverse removal procedure.
   a. Make sure that both seat adjusters are parallel and synchronized. (See "Adjustment of seat adjuster")

## Electric Motor

### Removal

1. Remove the front seat assembly. (See "Front seat removal")
2. Disconnect the wires from the motor relay.
3. Unbolt the motor and transmission support which attaches to the seat frame.
4. Move the motor away from the transmission and separate it at the rubber coupling.

### Installation

1. Reverse removal procedure.
   a. Make sure that the rubber coupling is properly connected.
   b. Check for full seat movement.

## Vertical Gearnut

### Removal

1. Move the seat all the way forward.
2. Remove the seat from the car. (See "Front seat removal")
3. Separate the three drive cables from the adjuster.
4. Remove the seat adjuster from the seat bottom frame.
5. Remove the two nuts and tension springs from the top of the adjuster which threads on to the vertical gearnut shaft.
6. Remove the two screws from the

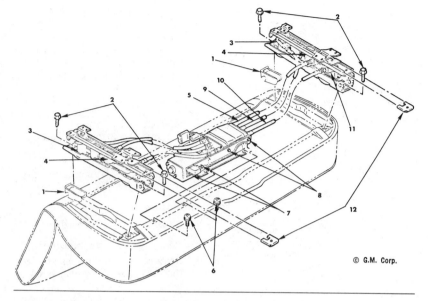

*Front Seat Assembly—Six-Way*

1. Track Cover
2. Adjuster-to-Seat Attaching Bolts
3. Rear Vertical Gearnut
4. Horizontal Actuator
5. Horizontal Cables—Black
6. Motor and Transmission
7. Motor Attaching Screws
8. Transmission Screws
9. Rear Vertical Cables
10. Front Vertical Cables
11. Front Vertical Gearnut
12. Carpet Retainers

© G.M. Corp.

bottom of each gearnut which attaches it to the bottom of the adjuster.
   a. When replacing the gearnut, be sure to transfer the shoulder nuts and tension spring.

*Six-Way Seat Adjuster Components*

1. Upper Channel Assembly
2. Upper Channel to Gearnut Attaching Bolts
3. Gearnut Tension Springs
4. Gearnut Shoulder Nuts
5. Rear Vertical Gearnut and Attaching Screws
6. Horizontal Actuator
7. Front Vertical Gearnut and Attaching Screws
8. Plastic Shoes
9. Lower Channel

© G.M. Corp.

### Installation

1. Reverse removal procedure.
   a. Make sure that both seat adjusters are parallel and synchronized during operation. (See "Adjustment of seat adjuster")

## Horizontal Actuator

### Removal

1. Remove the seat. (See "Seat removal")
2. Separate the three drive cables from the adjuster.
3. Remove the seat adjuster from the seat bottom frame.
4. Remove the two nuts and tension springs from the top of the adjuster which thread onto the vertical gearnut shafts.
5. Lift the top of the adjuster upward in order to expose the screws which hold the actuator to the adjuster.
   a. Remove the screws and actuator from the adjuster.

### Installation

1. Reverse removal procedure.
   a. Adjust the actuator so that the drive gear teeth fully contact the lower channel. When the actuating screws are tightened, there should be no free motion between the upper and lower channel. Re-

# General Motors

## Upper or Lower Channel and Plastic Slides

### Removal

1. Remove the seat. (See "Front seat removal")
2. Remove all three drive cables from the adjuster.
3. Remove the adjuster from the seat assembly.
4. Remove the two nuts and tension springs from the top of the adjuster which thread onto the vertical gearnut shafts.
5. Lift the top of the adjuster upward in order to expose the screws which hold the actuator to the adjuster.
6. Remove the screws and actuator from the adjuster.
7. Slide the lower channel until it is separated from the upper channel, then remove the plastic slides.

### Installation

1. Reverse removal procedures.
   a. Transfer old vertical slides when replacing the lower channel.
   b. Transfer the vertical gearnuts when replacing the upper channel.
   c. Lubricate sliding surfaces properly.
   d. Make sure that the seat adjusters are both parallel and synchronized during operation. (See "Adjustment of seat adjusters.")

## Horizontal and Vertical Drive Cables

### Removal

1. Remove the front seat. (See "Front seat removal")
2. Place the seat upside down and detach the cables from the seat adjuster. (Note the color code of the cables for installation.)
3. Remove the screws which secure the end plates from the transmission end of the cables.

### Installation

1. Reverse removal procedures.

## Transmission

### Removal

1. Remove the front seat with ad-

move free motion by readjusting the actuator.
   b. Make sure that the seat adjusters are both parallel and synchronized during operation. (See "Adjustment of seat adjusters.")

justers, motor and transmission attached. (See "Front seat removal.")
2. Place the seat upside down and remove the right side seat adjuster and disconnect the wiring harness from the transmission.
3. Remove the screw which secure the end plates from the transmission end of the cables.
4. Remove the attaching bolts that hold the transmission to the support.
5. Separate the transmission from the motor at the coupling.

### Installation

1. Reverse removal procedures.

### Disassembly of Transmission

1. Remove the transmission from the seat. (See "Transmission removal)
2. Remove the screws and separate the gear and solenoid housings exposing the internal gears.

### Assembly of Transmission

1. Reverse disassembly procedures.
   a. Lubricate gears before assembly.

## Transmission and Motor Drive Belt and Pulleys

## (Bucket Seat Only)

### Removal

1. Remove the drive belt cover screws and remove the cover located at the front of the seat.
2. Remove the belt.
3. Pull the pulleys from the shafts.

### Installation

1. Reverse removal procedures.
   a. Make sure that the seat travels to its full limit in all directions.

## Adjustment of Seat Adjusters

When replacing the seat in the car, one horizontal or vertical adjuster should not be ahead of the other when in operation. If one is not moving parallel with the other, adjust as follows:

## Horizontal Movement

1. Actuate the seat switch and move the seat all the way forward.
2. Remove the cable from the horizontal adjuster that is moved all the way forward.
3. Activate the seat switch again and move the other horizontal adjuster all the way forward.

4. Attach the cable and check movement again.

## Front or Rear Vertical Movement

1. Activate the seat switch and move the vertical adjusters all the way up, at both front and rear ends.
2. Remove the front and rear vertical cables from the adjuster that has reached the top first.
3. Activate the seat switch and raise the other vertical adjuster until it is parallel to the other.
4. Connect both front and rear cables and check movement again. Repeat if necessary.

## Seat Torque Specifications

The following torque specifications should be used when servicing seat assemblies:

## Bolt or Nut Location and Torque-Foot Pounds

*NOTE: Some service replacement assemblies such as seat cushion and back frame assemblies and rear compartment pan assembly may have unthreaded nuts for attachment of seat adjusters, seat back and lap belts. These unthreaded nuts must be tapped with proper size and threaded tap or either the original or a new thread forming bolt must be used. If thread forming bolts are used, apply 15 to 20 pounds of straight in pressure to start thread forming action of bolt.*

1. Seat Adjuster and Folding Seat Back-to-Floor Pan Bolts or Nuts —12-18 foot pounds.
2. Seat Adjuster-to-Seat Frame Bolts—12-18 foot pounds.
3. Seat Back to Cushion Frame Bolts—16-22 foot pounds.
4. Seat Back Hinge Bolts—12-18 foot pounds.
5. Seat Back Lock Attaching Screws—12-18 foot pounds.
6. Seat Back Lock Striker and Inner Side Bar top—12-18 foot pounds.
7. Lap Belt-to-Floor Pan Anchor Bolts—20-45 foot pounds.

*WARNING: Seat attaching parts such as seat adjuster-to-floor pan bolts or nuts, seat adjuster-to-seat frame bolts, seat cushion frame-to-seat back frame bolts, seat back lock bolts, seat back lock striker, etc. are important attaching parts in that they could affect the performance of vital components and systems. They must be replaced with one of the same part number or with an equiv-*

# Power Seats

## General Motors

*alent part if replacement becomes necessary. Do not use a replacement* *part of lesser quality or substitute design. Torque values must be used as* *specified during reassembly to assure proper retention of these parts.*

## ELECTRICAL TESTS

### Two-, Four-, and Six-Way Power Seat

Before performing any extensive electrical testing procedures, check for mechanical failures. Make sure that the drive cables, located between the seat transmission and seat adjusters, are properly attached. Also refer to the power seat wiring diagrams.

#### Open and Short Circuits

An open circuit is when the circuit is not completed because of a poor terminal contact or a broken wire. A short circuit is when the current is being grounded before it reaches a particular unit. When this happens, it actuates the circuit breaker or blows a fuse, due to the overload created.

The 40 ampere circuit breaker plugs into the fuse panel on every car but Chevrolet. Chevrolet's bolts on the dash panel in the engine compartment.

#### Circuit Testing Procedures

##### Testing for Current between Seat Switch and Motor Relay

1. Disconnect the wiring harness from the seat transmission.
2. Connect one test light lead to the end of wiring harness and ground the other lead.
3. Turn on the seat switch and if the tester does not light, there is no current at the end of the wire. This is caused by an open or short circuit in the wire.
4. Check all other wires the same way.

##### Testing for Current between Seat Switch and Motor Relay

1. Disconnect the wiring harness from the motor relay.
2. Insert one test light lead into either the dark green or yellow wire slot on the wiring harness connector. Ground the other test light lead.
3. Turn the seat switch on and if the tester does not light there is an open or short circuit between the end of the wire and the switch.

##### Testing for Current at Motor Relay

1. Disconnect the wiring harness

from the relay.
2. Insert one test light lead into the orange/black wire slot on the wiring harness connector. Ground the other test light lead.
3. If the tester does not light, there is an open or short circuit.

#### Testing for Current at Seat Switch

1. Insert one test light lead into the feed terminal (See illustration for location) on the switch block. Ground the other test wire. If the tester does not light, there is an open or short circuit between the power source and the seat switch.

### Testing Procedures for Defective Parts

#### Testing for Defective Relay

1. Disconnect the wire connector from the relay.
2. Connect one end of a jumper wire to the motor field feed terminal on the relay and ground the other end.
3. Connect one wire of a test light to the motor armature feed terminal on the relay and ground the other wire.
4. Connect a hot jumper wire to the other field terminal which is not grounded. The relay is defective if the test light does not light.

*NOTE: See motor relay illustration for the proper terminal identification.*

#### Testing for Defective Motor

1. Check the seat ground wire to see if it is grounded.
2. Disconnect the motor wire connectors to the relay.
3. Connect one end of a jumper wire to the positive battery pole and the other end to both the armature wire and one of the motor field wires. (See seat motor relay illustration for wire identification.)
4. Check the other motor field wire the same way. If the motor does not operate, it is defective.

#### Testing for Defective Solenoid

1. Check the seat ground wire to see if it is grounded.
2. Connect one end of the jumper wire to the positive side of the

battery and the other end to the suspected defective solenoid.

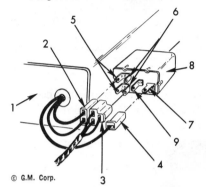

© G.M. Corp.

*Seat Adjuster Motor Control Relay*

1. Seat Adjuster Motor
2. Motor Field Connector
3. Control Switch to Relay Connector
4. Motor Armature Connector
5. Motor Field Feed Studs
6. Relay Coils Studs
7. Armature Feed Stud
8. Motor Control Relay
9. Relay Input Stud

3. Activate the seat switch, but for no longer than one minute in order to prevent damage to the solenoid.
4. If the adjusters do not operate, the solenoid is defective, unless there is a mechanical failure of the adjusters.
   a. A click is heard when the solenoid is operating properly.
5. Check the other solenoids the same way.

#### Testing for Defective Seat Switch

1. If a new switch isn't available, make a three way jumper wire by using two pieces of wire five inches long and twisting one end together.
2. Insert the joined end into the switch feed slot on the switch block.
3. Insert one of the other ends into one of the solenoid slots on the switch block.
4. Insert the remaining wire end into one of the field feed slots. (See illustration of seat block for proper location of wires for specific movements.)
5. If the seat adjusters now operate, the switch is defective.

# General Motors

## Jumper Wire Location Four-Way Power Seat (Seat Panel Switch or Arm Rest Switch)

1. To raise seat, insert jumper wires in (A), (B), and (A).
2. To lower seat, insert jumper wires in (A), (D), and (E).
3. To move seat forward, insert jumper wires in (A), (C), and (D).
4. To move seat backward, insert jumper wires in (A), (B), and (C).

## Jumper Wire Location Six-Way Power Seat (Seat Panel Switch)

1. To raise front edge of seat, insert jumper wires (A), (F), and (E).
2. To lower front edge of seat, insert jumper wires in (A), (C), and (E).
3. To raise rear edge of seat, insert jumper wires (A), (F), and (D).
4. To lower rear edge of seat, insert jumper wires (A), (C), and (D).
5. To move seat forward, insert jumper wires in (A), (B), and (F).
6. To move seat backward, insert jumper wires in (A), (C), and (B).

## (Arm Rest Switch)

1. To raise front edge of seat, insert jumper wires in (A), (F), and (E).
2. To lower front edge of seat, insert jumper wires in (A), (C), and (E).
3. To raise rear edge of seat, insert jumper wires (A), (C), and (D).
4. To lower rear edge of seat, insert jumper wires in (A), (F), and (D).
5. To move seat forward, insert jumper wires in (A), (C), and (B).
6. To move seat backward, insert jumper wires in (A), (F), and (B).

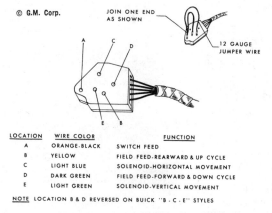

© G.M. Corp.

JOIN ONE END AS SHOWN

12 GAUGE JUMPER WIRE

| LOCATION | WIRE COLOR | FUNCTION |
|---|---|---|
| A | ORANGE-BLACK | SWITCH FEED |
| B | YELLOW | FIELD FEED-REARWARD & UP CYCLE |
| C | LIGHT BLUE | SOLENOID-HORIZONTAL MOVEMENT |
| D | DARK GREEN | FIELD FEED-FORWARD & DOWN CYCLE |
| E | LIGHT GREEN | SOLENOID-VERTICAL MOVEMENT |

NOTE LOCATION B & D REVERSED ON BUICK "B - C - E" STYLES

*Four-Way Seat Switch Block in Trim Panel*

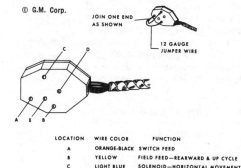

© G.M. Corp.

JOIN ONE END AS SHOWN

12 GAUGE JUMPER WIRE

| LOCATION | WIRE COLOR | FUNCTION |
|---|---|---|
| A | ORANGE-BLACK | SWITCH FEED |
| B | YELLOW | FIELD FEED—REARWARD & UP CYCLE |
| C | LIGHT BLUE | SOLENOID—HORIZONTAL MOVEMENT |
| D | DARK GREEN | FIELD FEED—FORWARD & DOWN CYCLE |
| E | LIGHT GREEN | SOLENOID—VERTICAL MOVEMENT |

*Four-Way Seat Switch Block in Arm Rest*

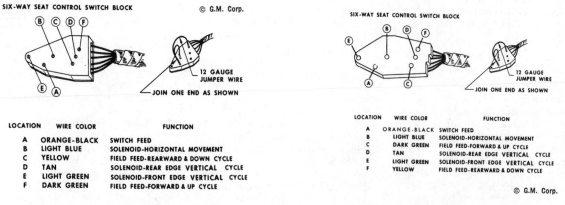

SIX-WAY SEAT CONTROL SWITCH BLOCK

© G.M. Corp.

12 GAUGE JUMPER WIRE

JOIN ONE END AS SHOWN

| LOCATION | WIRE COLOR | FUNCTION |
|---|---|---|
| A | ORANGE-BLACK | SWITCH FEED |
| B | LIGHT BLUE | SOLENOID-HORIZONTAL MOVEMENT |
| C | YELLOW | FIELD FEED-REARWARD & DOWN CYCLE |
| D | TAN | SOLENOID-REAR EDGE VERTICAL CYCLE |
| E | LIGHT GREEN | SOLENOID-FRONT EDGE VERTICAL CYCLE |
| F | DARK GREEN | FIELD FEED-FORWARD & UP CYCLE |

*Six-Way Seat Switch Block in Seat Side Panel*

SIX-WAY SEAT CONTROL SWITCH BLOCK

12 GAUGE JUMPER WIRE

JOIN ONE END AS SHOWN

| LOCATION | WIRE COLOR | FUNCTION |
|---|---|---|
| A | ORANGE-BLACK | SWITCH FEED |
| B | LIGHT BLUE | SOLENOID-HORIZONTAL MOVEMENT |
| C | DARK GREEN | FIELD FEED-FORWARD & UP CYCLE |
| D | TAN | SOLENOID-REAR EDGE VERTICAL CYCLE |
| E | LIGHT GREEN | SOLENOID-FRONT EDGE VERTICAL CYCLE |
| F | YELLOW | FIELD FEED-REARWARD & DOWN CYCLE |

© G.M. Corp.

*Six-Way Seat Switch Block in Arm Rest*

## Chrysler Corporation

### Six Way

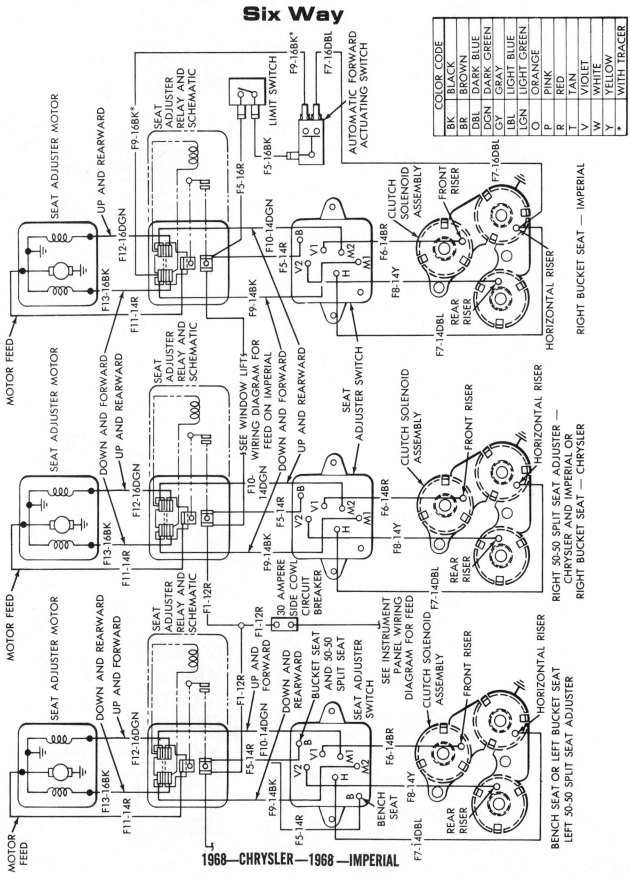

| COLOR CODE | |
|---|---|
| BK | BLACK |
| BR | BROWN |
| DBL | DARK BLUE |
| DGN | DARK GREEN |
| GY | GRAY |
| LBL | LIGHT BLUE |
| LGN | LIGHT GREEN |
| O | ORANGE |
| P | PINK |
| R | RED |
| T | TAN |
| V | VIOLET |
| W | WHITE |
| Y | YELLOW |
| * | WITH TRACER |

1968—CHRYSLER—1968—IMPERIAL

## Chrysler Corporation

### Six Way

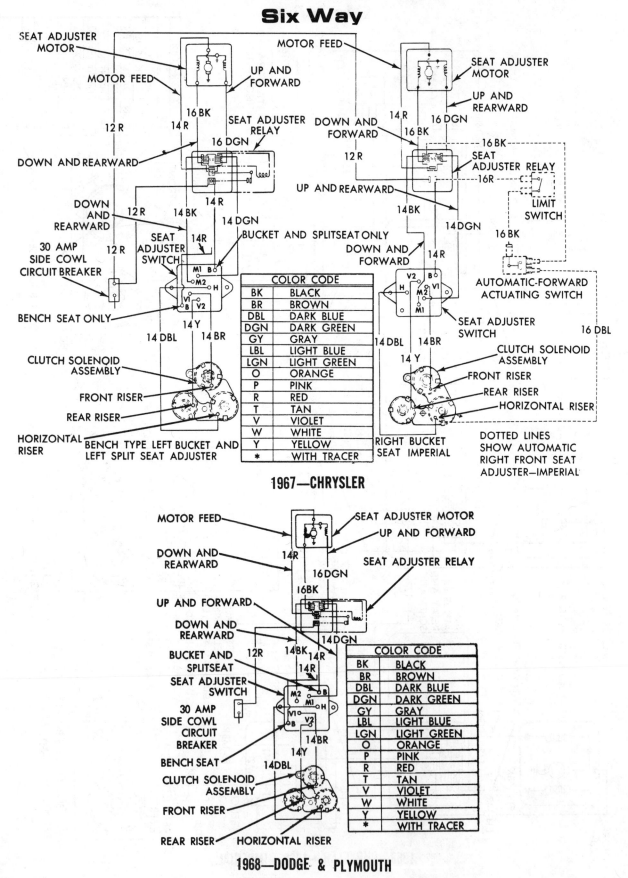

SEAT ADJUSTER MOTOR

MOTOR FEED

MOTOR FEED

UP AND FORWARD

SEAT ADJUSTER MOTOR

UP AND REARWARD

16 BK

14 R

14 R

16 DGN

SEAT ADJUSTER RELAY

16 DGN

DOWN AND FORWARD

16 BK

16 BK

12 R

SEAT ADJUSTER RELAY

16 R

12 R

DOWN AND REARWARD

14 R

UP AND REARWARD

14 BK

14 DGN

LIMIT SWITCH

16 BK

DOWN AND REARWARD

12 R

14 BK

14 DGN

DOWN AND FORWARD

14 R

16 BK

30 AMP SIDE COWL CIRCUIT BREAKER

12 R

SEAT ADJUSTER SWITCH

14 R

BUCKET AND SPLITSEAT ONLY

AUTOMATIC-FORWARD ACTUATING SWITCH

BENCH SEAT ONLY

M1  B
M2
V1  H
B  V2

V2  B
H  V1
M2
M1

SEAT ADJUSTER SWITCH

16 DBL

14 DBL

14 BR

14 Y

| COLOR CODE | |
|---|---|
| BK | BLACK |
| BR | BROWN |
| DBL | DARK BLUE |
| DGN | DARK GREEN |
| GY | GRAY |
| LBL | LIGHT BLUE |
| LGN | LIGHT GREEN |
| O | ORANGE |
| P | PINK |
| R | RED |
| T | TAN |
| V | VIOLET |
| W | WHITE |
| Y | YELLOW |
| * | WITH TRACER |

14 DBL

14 BR

14 Y

CLUTCH SOLENOID ASSEMBLY

FRONT RISER

REAR RISER

HORIZONTAL RISER

CLUTCH SOLENOID ASSEMBLY

FRONT RISER

REAR RISER

HORIZONTAL RISER

BENCH TYPE LEFT BUCKET AND LEFT SPLIT SEAT ADJUSTER

RIGHT BUCKET SEAT IMPERIAL

DOTTED LINES SHOW AUTOMATIC RIGHT FRONT SEAT ADJUSTER—IMPERIAL

**1967—CHRYSLER**

MOTOR FEED

SEAT ADJUSTER MOTOR

UP AND FORWARD

DOWN AND REARWARD

14 R

16 DGN

SEAT ADJUSTER RELAY

16 BK

UP AND FORWARD

DOWN AND REARWARD

14 DGN

BUCKET AND SPLITSEAT

12 R

14 BK

14 R

14 R

SEAT ADJUSTER SWITCH

30 AMP SIDE COWL CIRCUIT BREAKER

M2  B
M1
V1  H
B  V2

BENCH SEAT

14 BR

CLUTCH SOLENOID ASSEMBLY

14 Y

14 DBL

FRONT RISER

REAR RISER

HORIZONTAL RISER

| COLOR CODE | |
|---|---|
| BK | BLACK |
| BR | BROWN |
| DBL | DARK BLUE |
| DGN | DARK GREEN |
| GY | GRAY |
| LBL | LIGHT BLUE |
| LGN | LIGHT GREEN |
| O | ORANGE |
| P | PINK |
| R | RED |
| T | TAN |
| V | VIOLET |
| W | WHITE |
| Y | YELLOW |
| * | WITH TRACER |

**1968—DODGE & PLYMOUTH**

## Chrysler Corporation

## Six Way

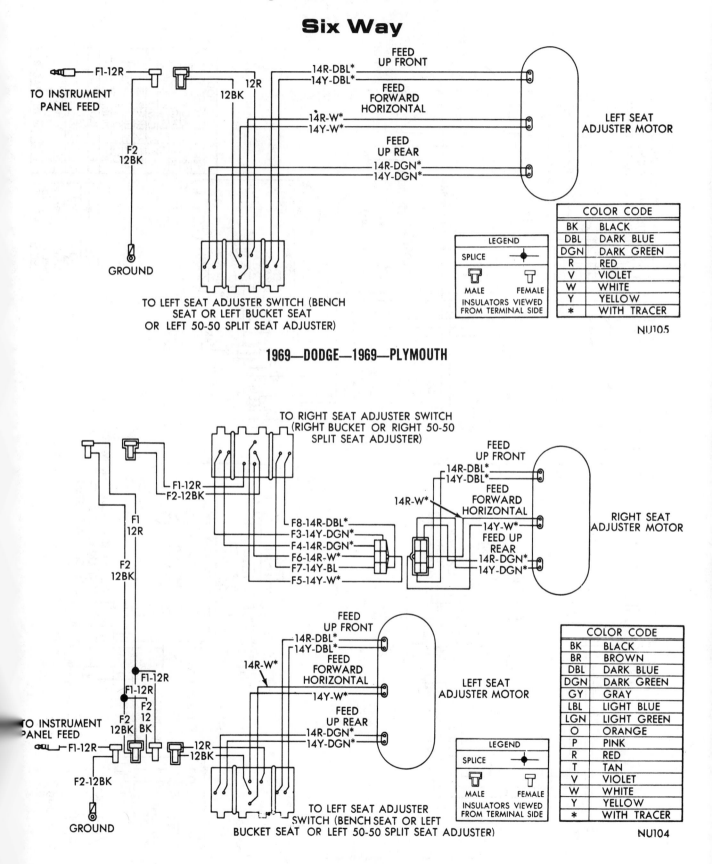

**1969—DODGE—1969—PLYMOUTH**

**1969—CHRYSLER**

## Chrysler Corporation
## Six Way

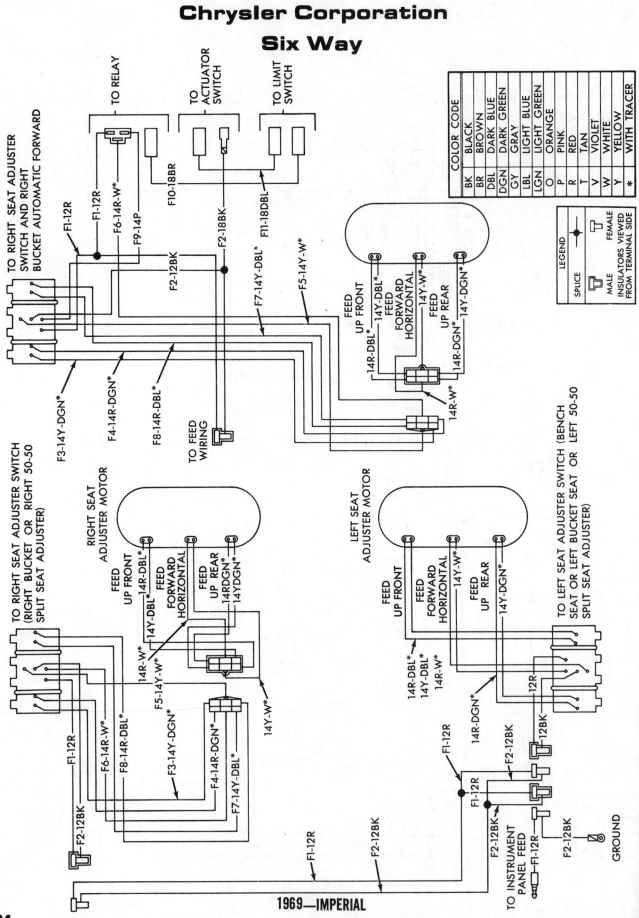

1969—IMPERIAL

## Chrysler Corporation
## Six Way

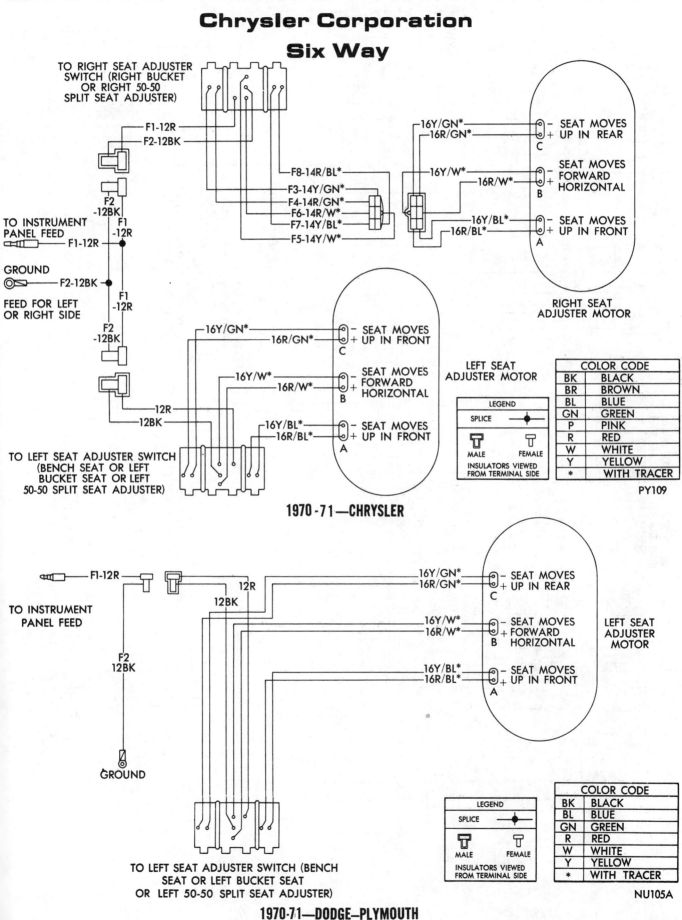

1970-71—CHRYSLER

1970-71—DODGE-PLYMOUTH

## Chrysler Corporation

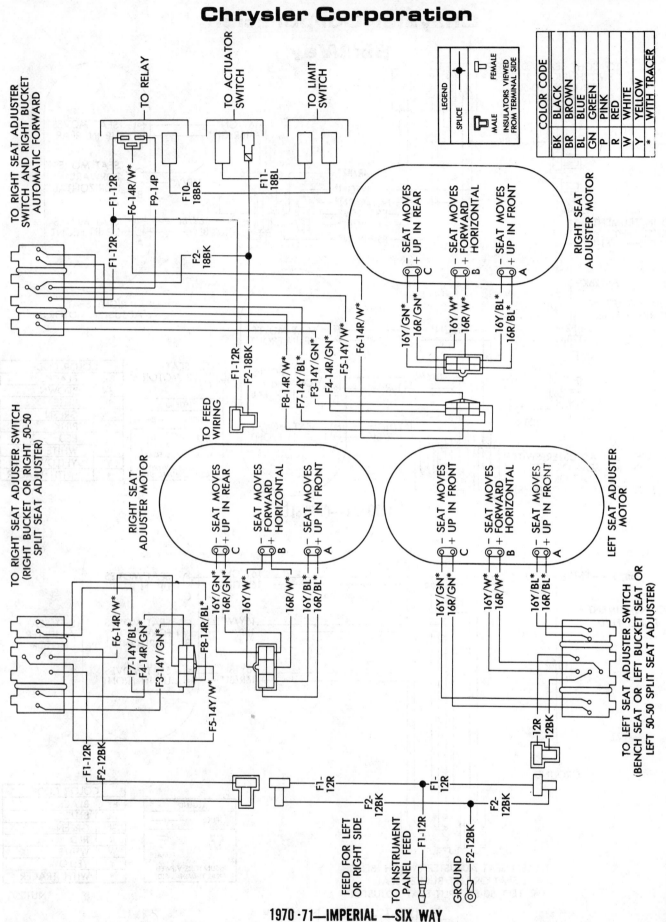

1970-71—IMPERIAL —SIX WAY

## Chrysler Corporation

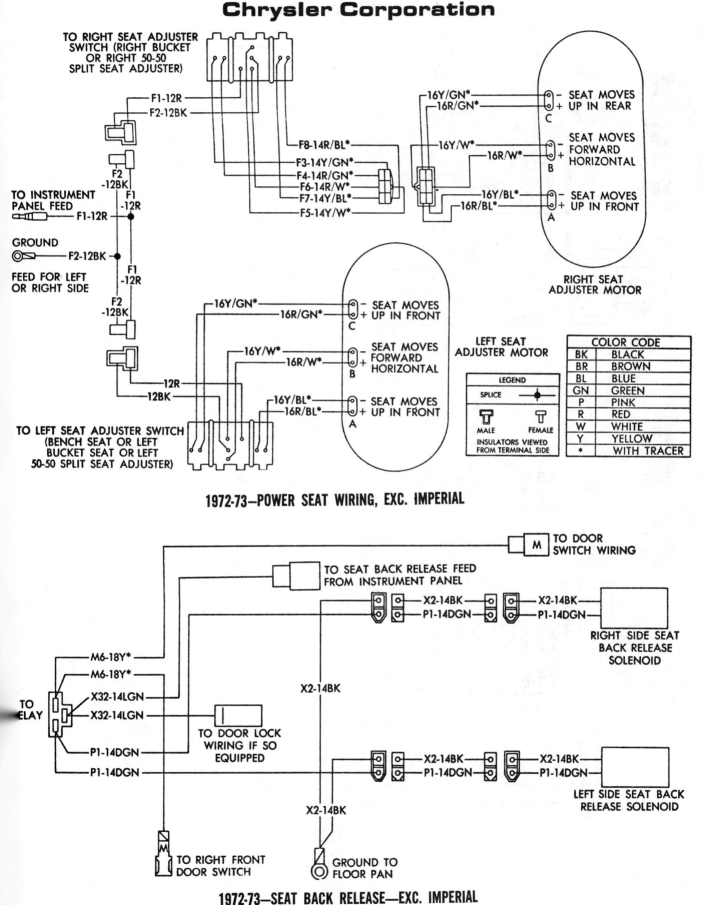

**1972-73—POWER SEAT WIRING, EXC. IMPERIAL**

TO RIGHT SEAT ADJUSTER SWITCH (RIGHT BUCKET OR RIGHT 50-50 SPLIT SEAT ADJUSTER)

F1-12R
F2-12BK

F8-14R/BL*
F3-14Y/GN*
F4-14R/GN*
F6-14R/W*
F7-14Y/BL*
F5-14Y/W*

F2-12BK
F1-12R

TO INSTRUMENT PANEL FEED
F1-12R

GROUND
F2-12BK

FEED FOR LEFT OR RIGHT SIDE

F1-12R
F2-12BK

16Y/GN*
16R/GN*
C — SEAT MOVES + UP IN REAR

16Y/W*
16R/W*
B — SEAT MOVES + FORWARD HORIZONTAL

16Y/BL*
16R/BL*
A — SEAT MOVES + UP IN FRONT

RIGHT SEAT ADJUSTER MOTOR

16Y/GN*
16R/GN*
C — SEAT MOVES + UP IN FRONT

16Y/W*
16R/W*
B — SEAT MOVES + FORWARD HORIZONTAL

16Y/BL*
16R/BL*
A — SEAT MOVES + UP IN FRONT

LEFT SEAT ADJUSTER MOTOR

12R
12BK

TO LEFT SEAT ADJUSTER SWITCH (BENCH SEAT OR LEFT BUCKET SEAT OR LEFT 50-50 SPLIT SEAT ADJUSTER)

| COLOR CODE | |
|---|---|
| BK | BLACK |
| BR | BROWN |
| BL | BLUE |
| GN | GREEN |
| P | PINK |
| R | RED |
| W | WHITE |
| Y | YELLOW |
| * | WITH TRACER |

**LEGEND**

SPLICE

MALE    FEMALE

INSULATORS VIEWED FROM TERMINAL SIDE

---

**1972-73—SEAT BACK RELEASE—EXC. IMPERIAL**

M — TO DOOR SWITCH WIRING

TO SEAT BACK RELEASE FEED FROM INSTRUMENT PANEL

X2-14BK
P1-14DGN

X2-14BK
P1-14DGN

RIGHT SIDE SEAT BACK RELEASE SOLENOID

M6-18Y*
M6-18Y*
X32-14LGN
X32-14LGN

TO RELAY

P1-14DGN
P1-14DGN

TO DOOR LOCK WIRING IF SO EQUIPPED

X2-14BK

X2-14BK

X2-14BK
P1-14DGN

X2-14BK
P1-14DGN

LEFT SIDE SEAT BACK RELEASE SOLENOID

M — TO RIGHT FRONT DOOR SWITCH

GROUND TO FLOOR PAN

387

# Chrysler Corporation

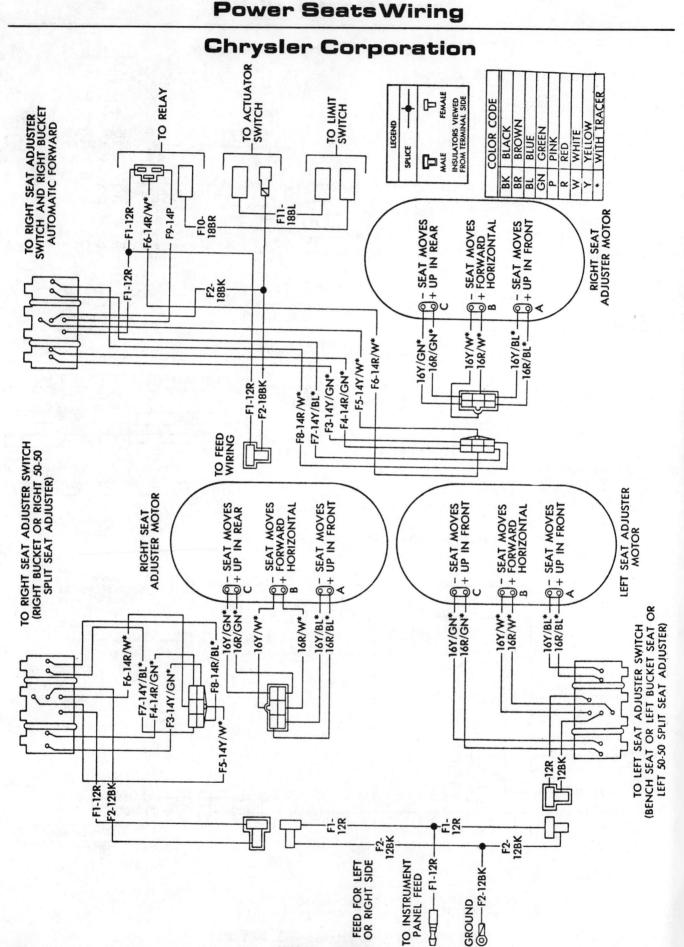

# Power Seat Wiring

## Chrysler Corporation

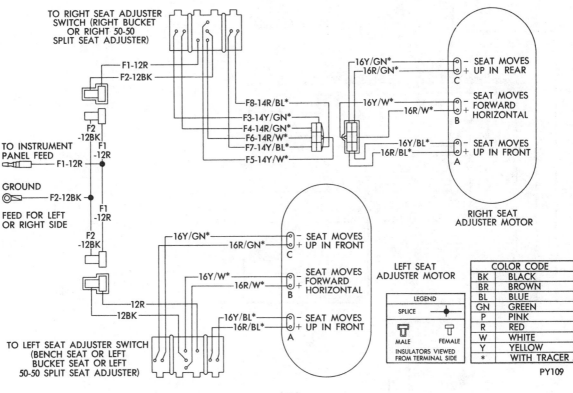

1973

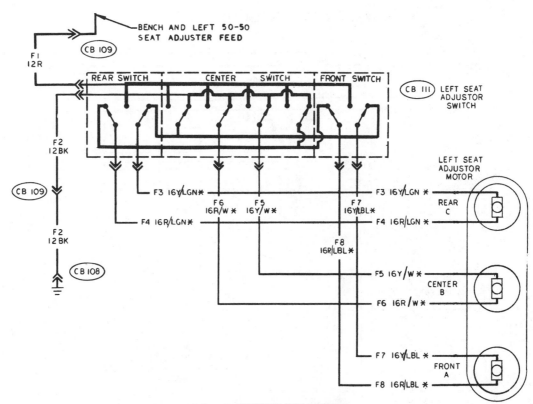

**1974-75 CHRYSLER AND IMPERIAL**

# Power Seat Wiring

## Chrysler Corporation

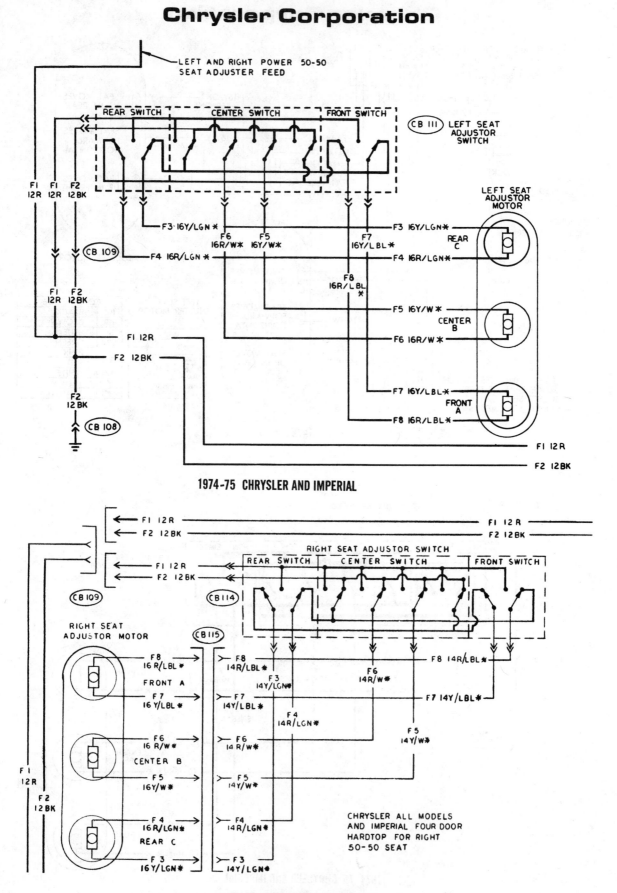

**1974-75 CHRYSLER AND IMPERIAL**

**1974-75 CHRYSLER AND IMPERIAL**

## Chrysler Corporation

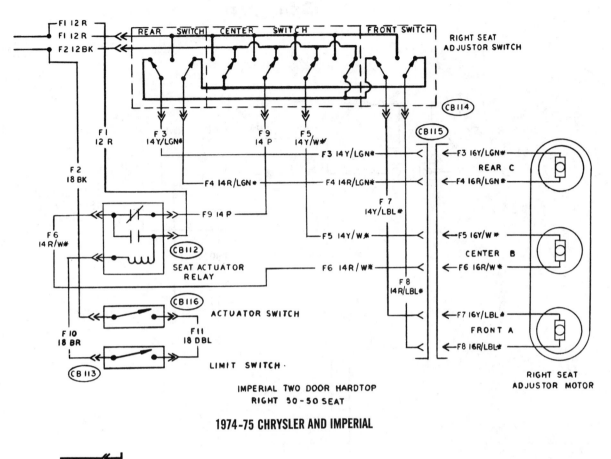

IMPERIAL TWO DOOR HARDTOP
RIGHT 50-50 SEAT

**1974-75 CHRYSLER AND IMPERIAL**

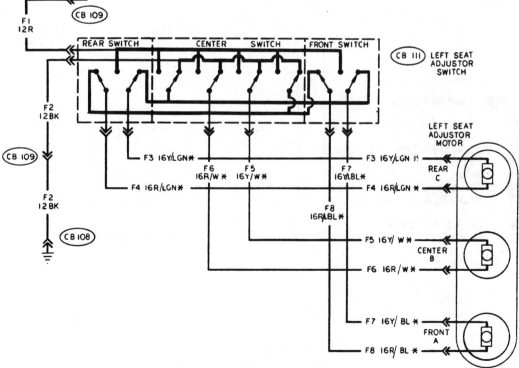

**1974-75 DODGE — PLYMOUTH**

# Ford Motor Company

# Cougar

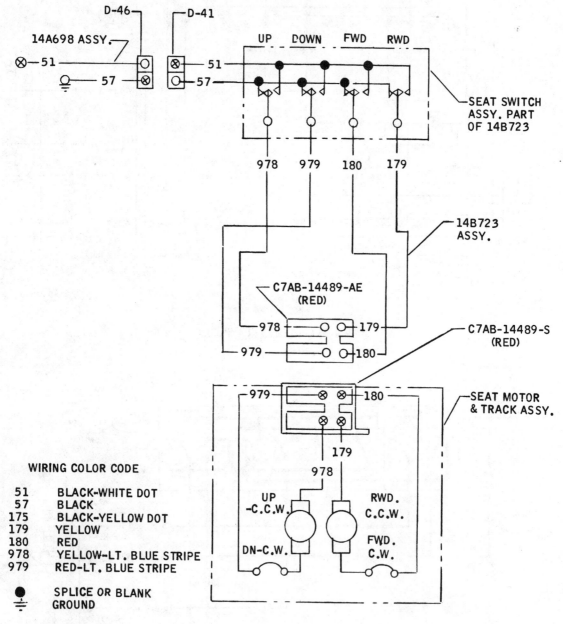

**WIRING COLOR CODE**

| | |
|---|---|
| 51 | BLACK-WHITE DOT |
| 57 | BLACK |
| 175 | BLACK-YELLOW DOT |
| 179 | YELLOW |
| 180 | RED |
| 978 | YELLOW-LT. BLUE STRIPE |
| 979 | RED-LT. BLUE STRIPE |

● SPLICE OR BLANK
⏚ GROUND

© Ford Motor Co.

1971

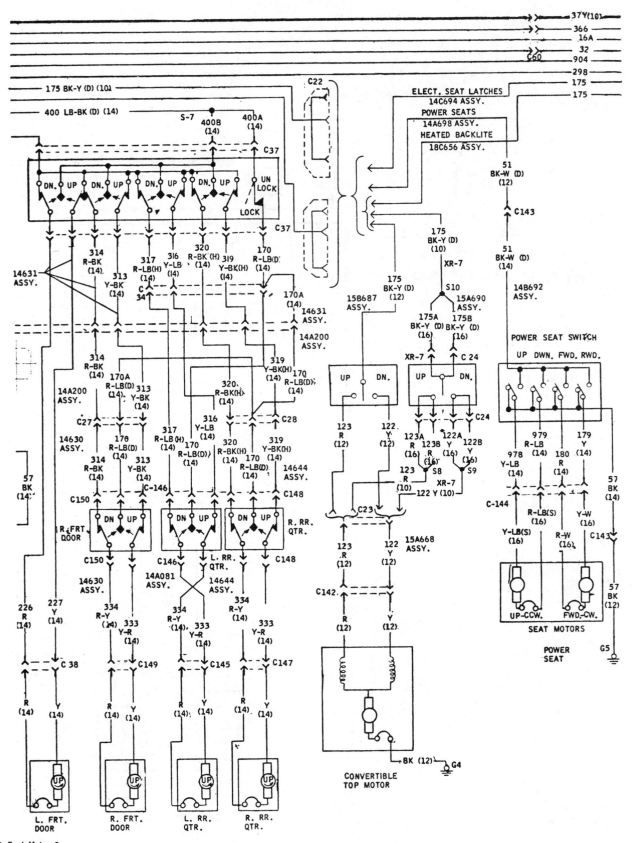

Power Seats Wiring — Cougar

© Ford Motor Co.                    POWER WINDOWS

1972

## Cougar

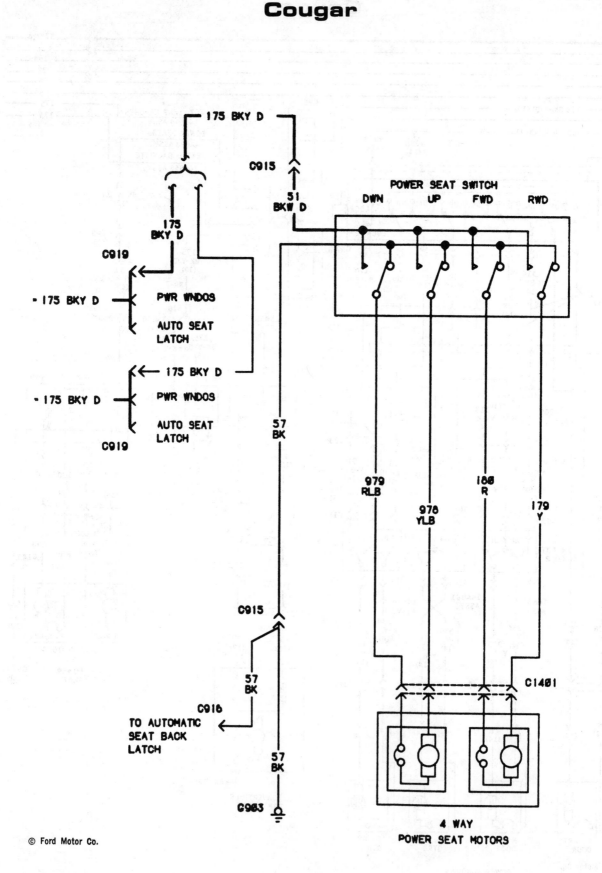

© Ford Motor Co.

1973

## Cougar

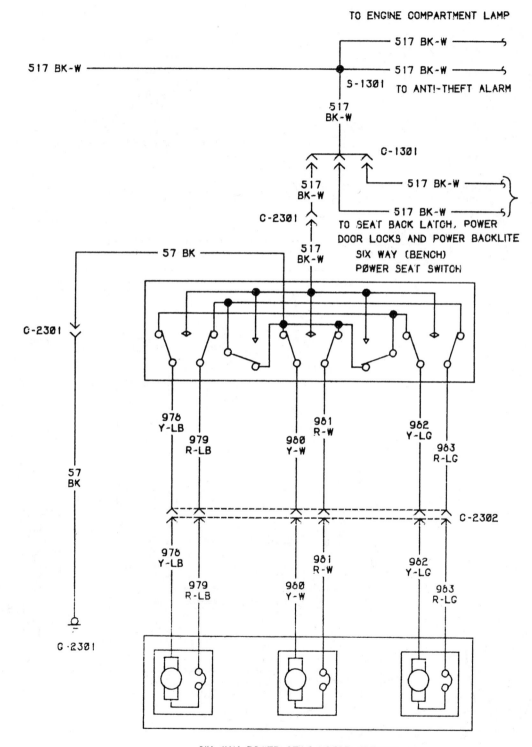

TO ENGINE COMPARTMENT LAMP

517 BK-W

517 BK-W ──────────────── 517 BK-W
S-1301    TO ANTI-THEFT ALARM

517 BK-W

C-1301

517 BK-W

C-2301

517 BK-W ─── 517 BK-W

TO SEAT BACK LATCH, POWER
DOOR LOCKS AND POWER BACKLITE

57 BK

SIX WAY (BENCH)
POWER SEAT SWITCH

517 BK-W

C-2301

978 Y-LB    981 R-W    982 Y-LG
979 R-LB    980 Y-W    983 R-LG

57 BK

C-2302

978 Y-LB    981 R-W    982 Y-LG
979 R-LB    980 Y-W    983 R-LG

G-2301

© Ford Motor Co.

SIX WAY POWER SEAT MOTOR (BENCH)

1973

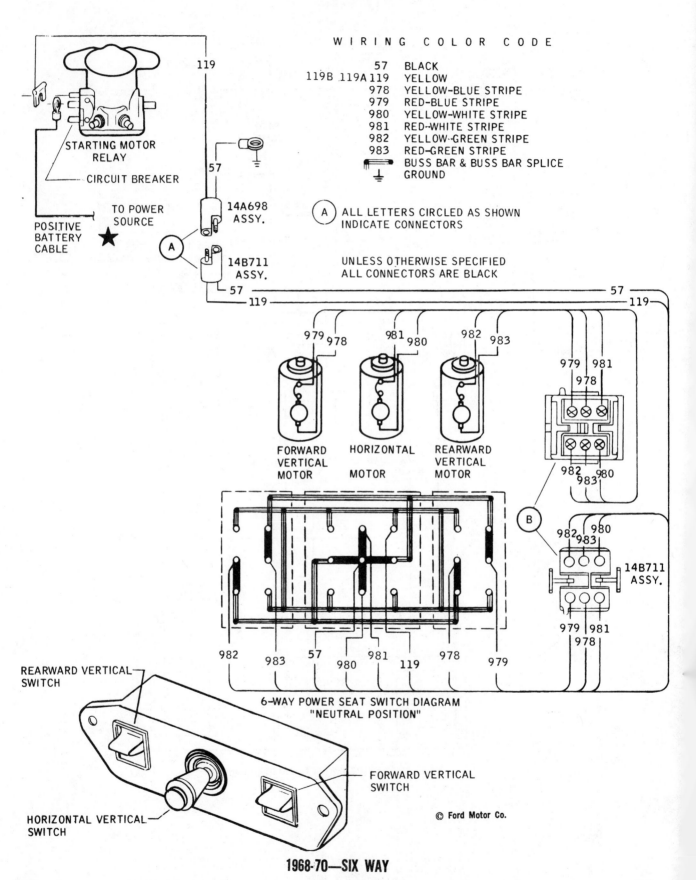

WIRING COLOR CODE

| | |
|---|---|
| 57 | BLACK |
| 119B 119A 119 | YELLOW |
| 978 | YELLOW-BLUE STRIPE |
| 979 | RED-BLUE STRIPE |
| 980 | YELLOW-WHITE STRIPE |
| 981 | RED-WHITE STRIPE |
| 982 | YELLOW-GREEN STRIPE |
| 983 | RED-GREEN STRIPE |
| | BUSS BAR & BUSS BAR SPLICE |
| | GROUND |

(A) ALL LETTERS CIRCLED AS SHOWN INDICATE CONNECTORS

UNLESS OTHERWISE SPECIFIED ALL CONNECTORS ARE BLACK

STARTING MOTOR RELAY

CIRCUIT BREAKER

POSITIVE BATTERY CABLE

TO POWER SOURCE

14A698 ASSY.

14B711 ASSY.

FORWARD VERTICAL MOTOR

HORIZONTAL MOTOR

REARWARD VERTICAL MOTOR

14B711 ASSY.

6-WAY POWER SEAT SWITCH DIAGRAM "NEUTRAL POSITION"

REARWARD VERTICAL SWITCH

HORIZONTAL VERTICAL SWITCH

FORWARD VERTICAL SWITCH

© Ford Motor Co.

**1968-70—SIX WAY**

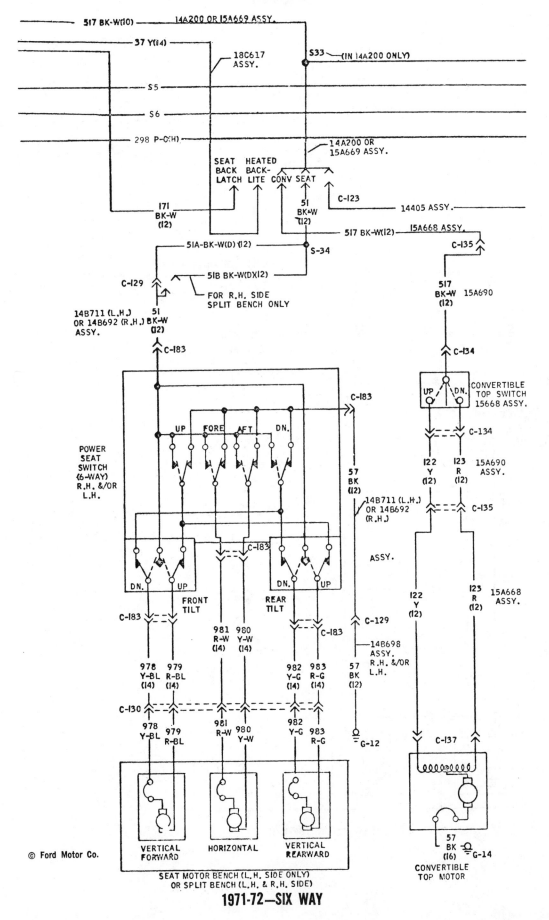

© Ford Motor Co.

SEAT MOTOR BENCH (L.H. SIDE ONLY)
OR SPLIT BENCH (L.H. & R.H. SIDE)

**1971-72—SIX WAY**

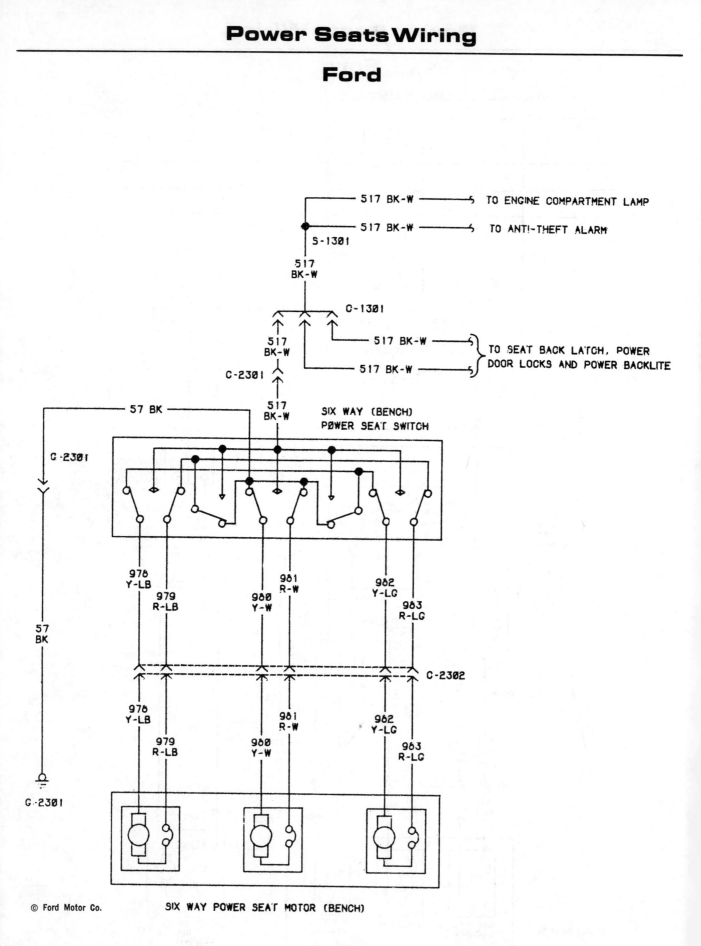

© Ford Motor Co.  SIX WAY POWER SEAT MOTOR (BENCH)

**1973**

## Montego

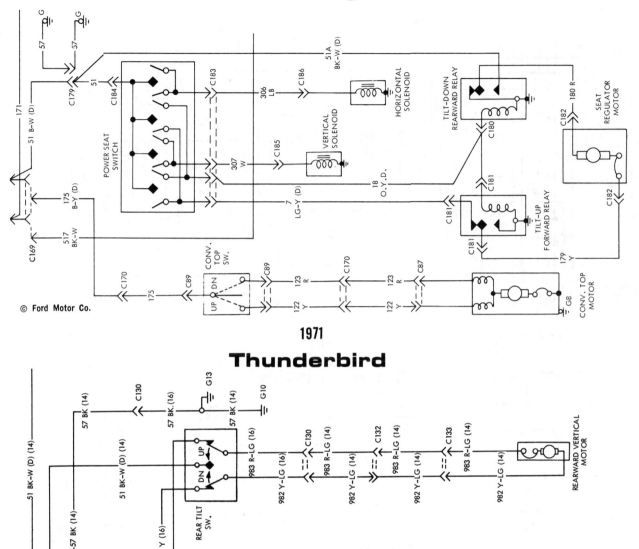

© Ford Motor Co.

**1971**

## Thunderbird

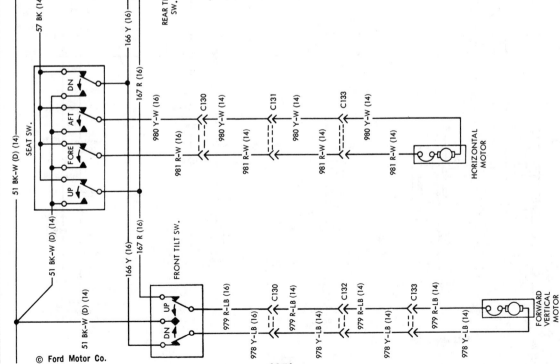

© Ford Motor Co.

**1971**

## Montego

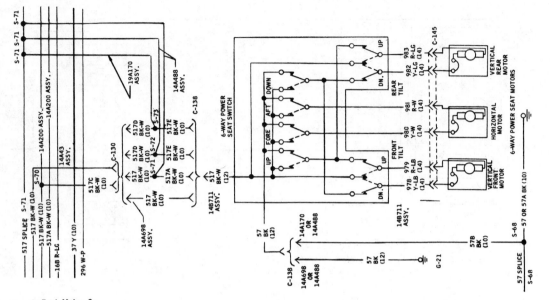

© Ford Motor Co.

**1972**

## Thunderbird

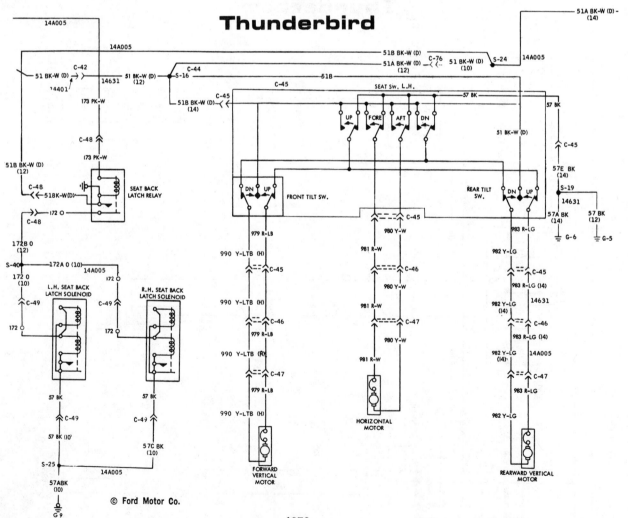

© Ford Motor Co.

**1972**

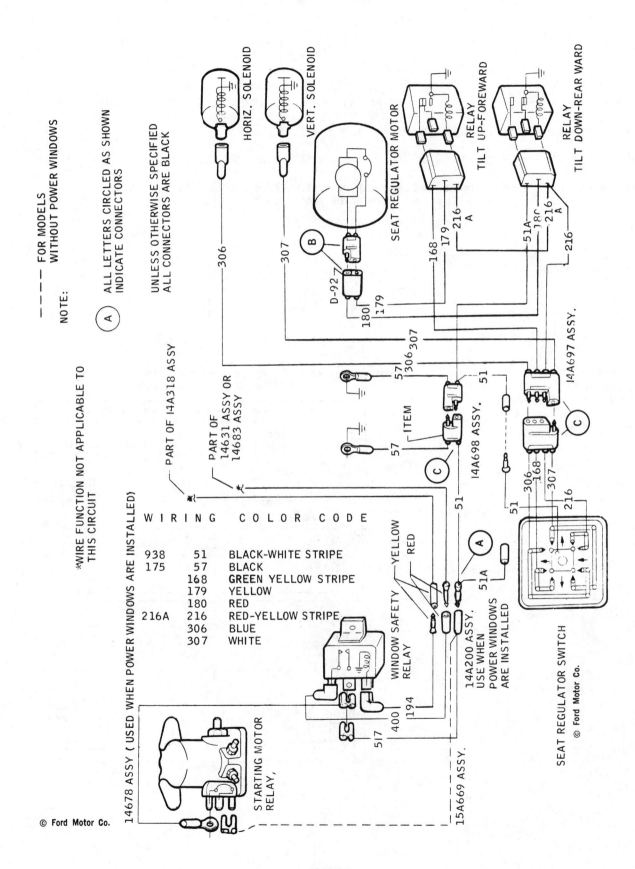

## Montego

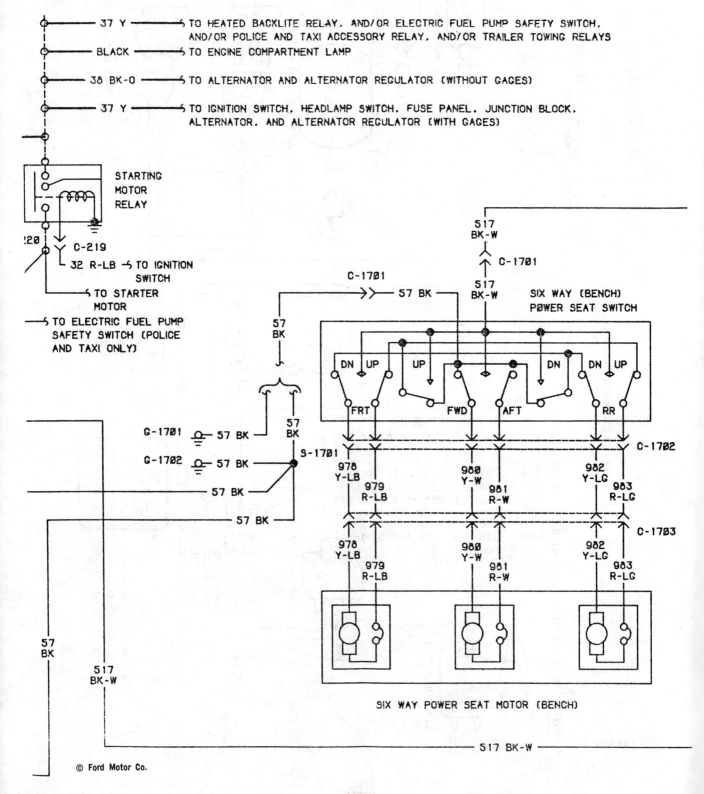

37 Y ——→ TO HEATED BACKLITE RELAY, AND/OR ELECTRIC FUEL PUMP SAFETY SWITCH,
AND/OR POLICE AND TAXI ACCESSORY RELAY, AND/OR TRAILER TOWING RELAYS

BLACK ——→ TO ENGINE COMPARTMENT LAMP

38 BK-O ——→ TO ALTERNATOR AND ALTERNATOR REGULATOR (WITHOUT GAGES)

37 Y ——→ TO IGNITION SWITCH. HEADLAMP SWITCH. FUSE PANEL. JUNCTION BLOCK.
ALTERNATOR. AND ALTERNATOR REGULATOR (WITH GAGES)

STARTING
MOTOR
RELAY

220  C-219

32 R-LB —→ TO IGNITION
SWITCH

——→ TO STARTER
MOTOR

——→ TO ELECTRIC FUEL PUMP
SAFETY SWITCH (POLICE
AND TAXI ONLY)

517
BK-W

C-1701

C-1701

57 BK

517
BK-W

SIX WAY (BENCH)
POWER SEAT SWITCH

57
BK

DN UP    UP    DN    DN UP

FRT    FWD    AFT    RR

G-1701    57 BK

57
BK

C-1702

G-1702    57 BK

S-1701

978
Y-LB

980
Y-W

982
Y-LG

57 BK

979
R-LB

981
R-W

983
R-LG

57 BK

C-1703

978
Y-LB

980
Y-W

982
Y-LG

979
R-LB

981
R-W

983
R-LG

57
BK

517
BK-W

SIX WAY POWER SEAT MOTOR (BENCH)

517 BK-W

1973

## Thunderbird

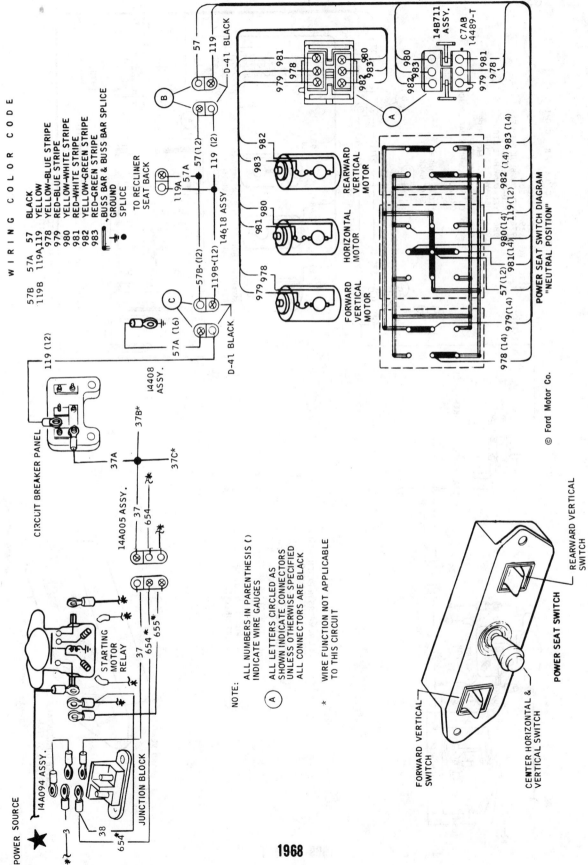

© Ford Motor Co.

**WIRING COLOR CODE**

| | |
|---|---|
| 57 | BLACK |
| 57A | YELLOW |
| 119 | YELLOW–BLUE STRIPE |
| 978 | RED–BLUE STRIPE |
| 979 | YELLOW–WHITE STRIPE |
| 980 | RED–WHITE STRIPE |
| 981 | YELLOW–GREEN STRIPE |
| 982 | RED–GREEN STRIPE |
| 983 | BUSS BAR & BUSS BAR SPLICE |
| 57B | GROUND |
| 119B | SPLICE |

NOTE:

ALL NUMBERS IN PARENTHESIS ( ) INDICATE WIRE GAUGES

(A) ALL LETTERS CIRCLED AS SHOWN INDICATE CONNECTORS UNLESS OTHERWISE SPECIFIED ALL CONNECTORS ARE BLACK

* WIRE FUNCTION NOT APPLICABLE TO THIS CIRCUIT

**1968**

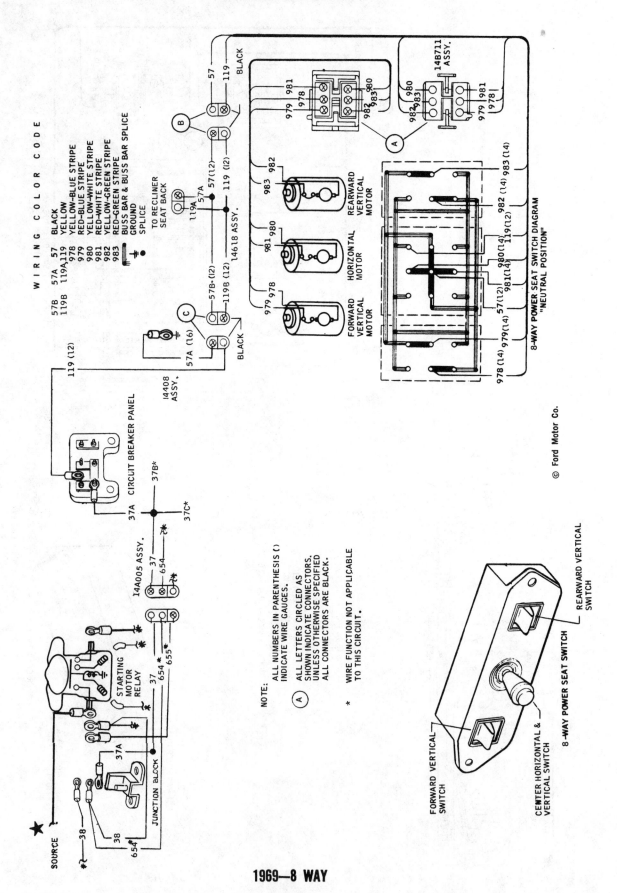

WIRING COLOR CODE

| | | |
|---|---|---|
| 57 | BLACK | |
| 57A | YELLOW | |
| 119A | YELLOW-BLUE STRIPE | |
| 119 | | |
| 978 | RED-BLUE STRIPE | |
| 979 | YELLOW-WHITE STRIPE | |
| 980 | RED-WHITE STRIPE | |
| 981 | YELLOW-GREEN STRIPE | |
| 982 | RED-GREEN STRIPE | |
| 983 | BUSS BAR & BUSS BAR SPLICE | |
| 57B | GROUND | |
| 119B | SPLICE | |

8-WAY POWER SEAT SWITCH DIAGRAM "NEUTRAL POSITION"

© Ford Motor Co.

NOTE:

ALL NUMBERS IN PARENTHESIS ( ) INDICATE WIRE GAUGES.

ⓐ ALL LETTERS CIRCLED AS SHOWN INDICATE CONNECTORS. UNLESS OTHERWISE SPECIFIED ALL CONNECTORS ARE BLACK.

* WIRE FUNCTION NOT APPLICABLE TO THIS CIRCUIT.

REARWARD VERTICAL SWITCH

FORWARD VERTICAL SWITCH

CENTER HORIZONTAL & VERTICAL SWITCH

8-WAY POWER SEAT SWITCH

**1969—8 WAY**

## Thunderbird

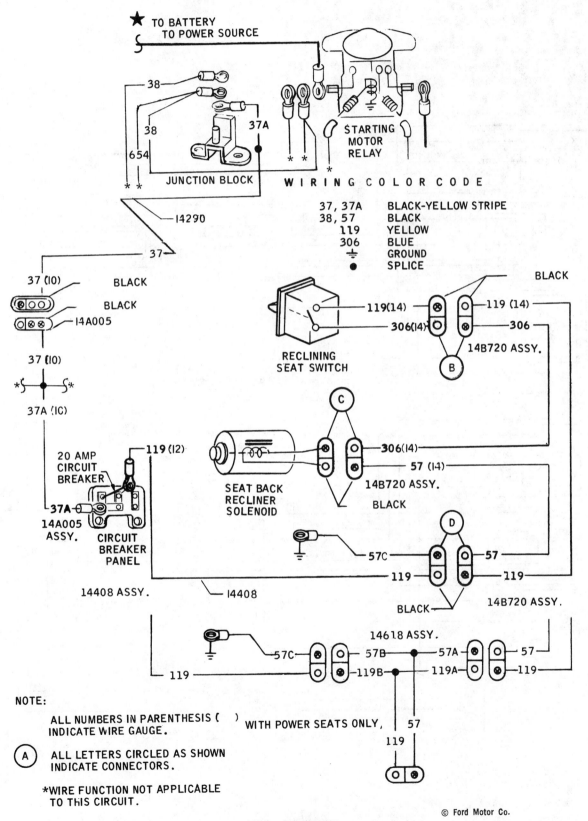

★ TO BATTERY
TO POWER SOURCE

38

38

654

37A

JUNCTION BLOCK

STARTING
MOTOR
RELAY

WIRING COLOR CODE

| 37, 37A | BLACK-YELLOW STRIPE |
| 38, 57 | BLACK |
| 119 | YELLOW |
| 306 | BLUE |
| ⏚ | GROUND |
| ● | SPLICE |

14290

37

37 (10)     BLACK

BLACK

14A005

37 (10)

*⌇        ⌇*

37A (10)

20 AMP
CIRCUIT
BREAKER

119 (12)

37A

14A005
ASSY.

CIRCUIT
BREAKER
PANEL

14408 ASSY.          14408

RECLINING
SEAT SWITCH

119(14)

306(14)

BLACK

119 (14)

306

14B720 ASSY.

B

C

SEAT BACK
RECLINER
SOLENOID

306(14)

57 (14)

14B720 ASSY.

BLACK

57C

57C

119

57

119

D

57

119

BLACK          14B720 ASSY.

14618 ASSY.

119        57B    57A    57

57C

119B    119A    119

BLACK

NOTE:

ALL NUMBERS IN PARENTHESIS (   )
INDICATE WIRE GAUGE.

Ⓐ     ALL LETTERS CIRCLED AS SHOWN
INDICATE CONNECTORS.

*WIRE FUNCTION NOT APPLICABLE
TO THIS CIRCUIT.

WITH POWER SEATS ONLY.

119        57

© Ford Motor Co.

**1969—RECLINING**

# Thunderbird

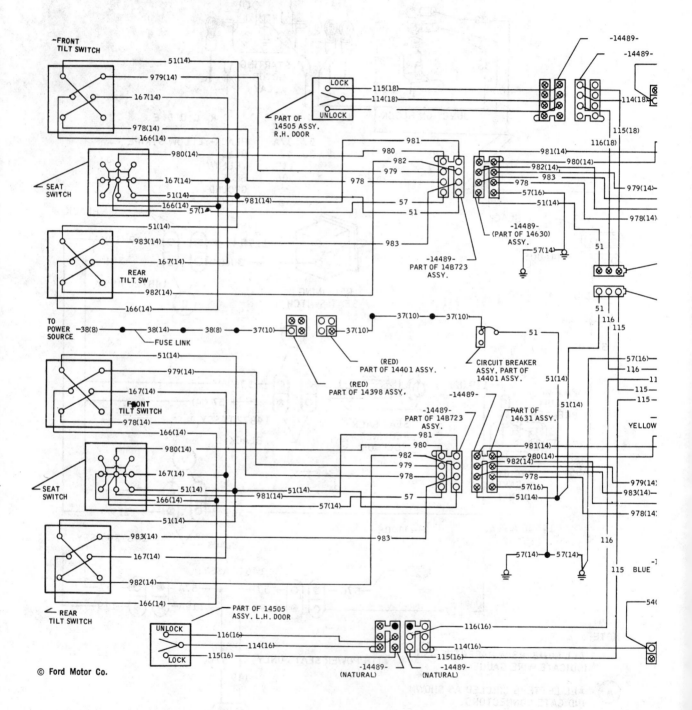

© Ford Motor Co.

**1970**

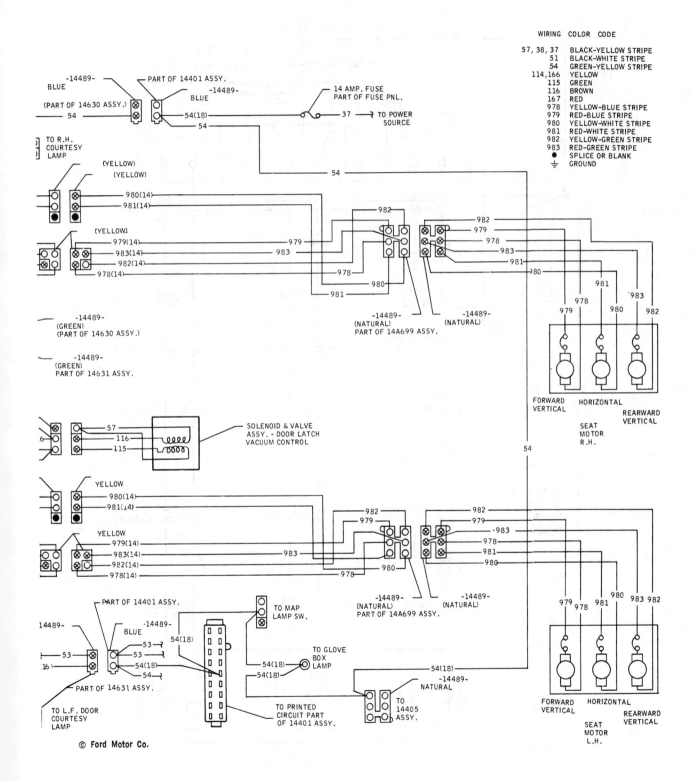

| WIRING | COLOR CODE |
|---|---|
| 57, 38, 37 | BLACK-YELLOW STRIPE |
| 51 | BLACK-WHITE STRIPE |
| 54 | GREEN-YELLOW STRIPE |
| 114,166 | YELLOW |
| 115 | GREEN |
| 116 | BROWN |
| 167 | RED |
| 978 | YELLOW-BLUE STRIPE |
| 979 | RED-BLUE STRIPE |
| 980 | YELLOW-WHITE STRIPE |
| 981 | RED-WHITE STRIPE |
| 982 | YELLOW-GREEN STRIPE |
| 983 | RED-GREEN STRIPE |
| ● | SPLICE OR BLANK |
| ⏚ | GROUND |

© Ford Motor Co.

# Thunderbird

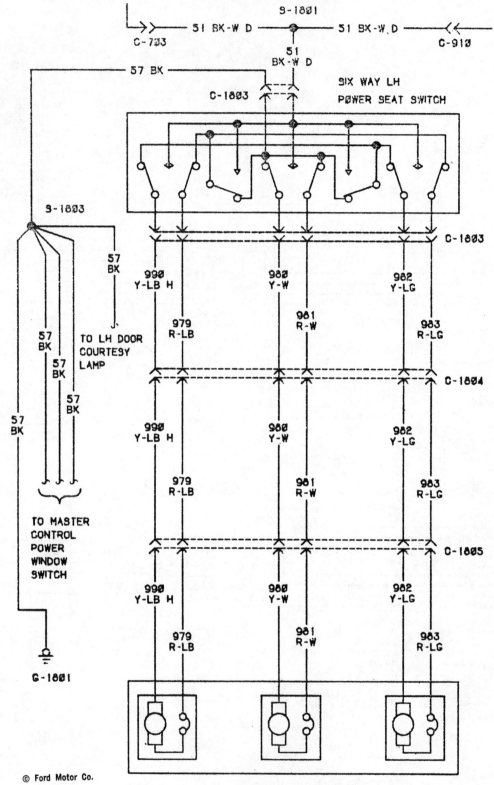

© Ford Motor Co.

LH POWER SEAT MOTORS

**1973**

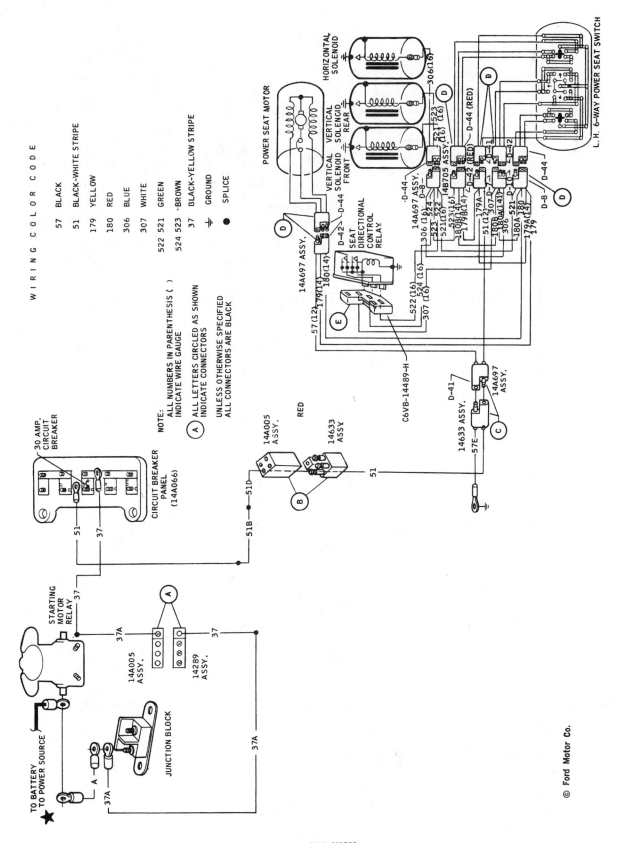

1968—SIX WAY

© Ford Motor Co.

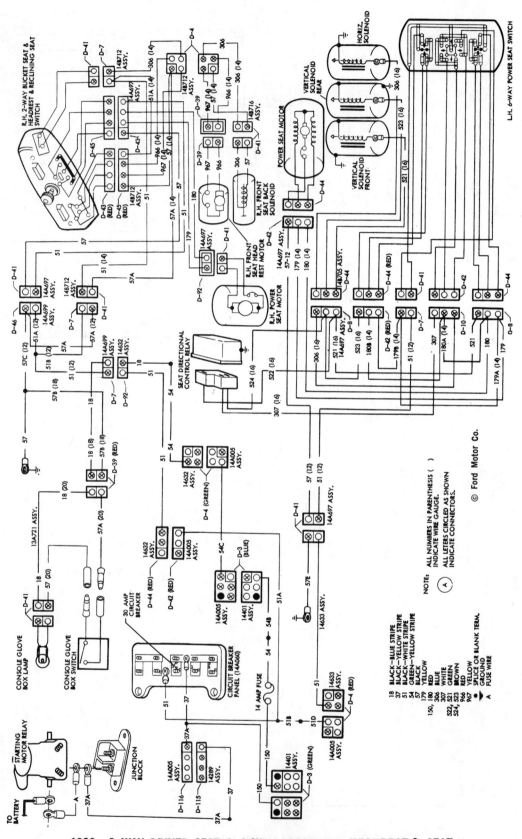

**1968—6 WAY DRIVER SEAT & 2 WAY PASSENGER HEADREST & SEAT**

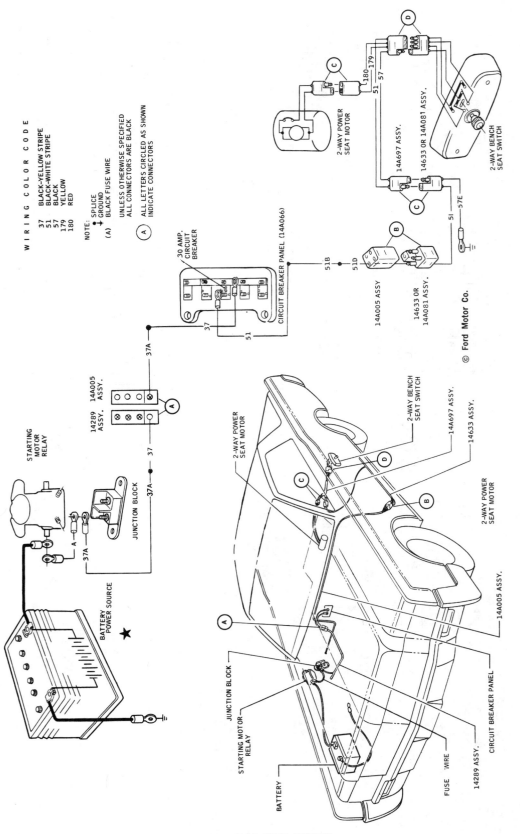

**1969—TWO WAY BENCH**

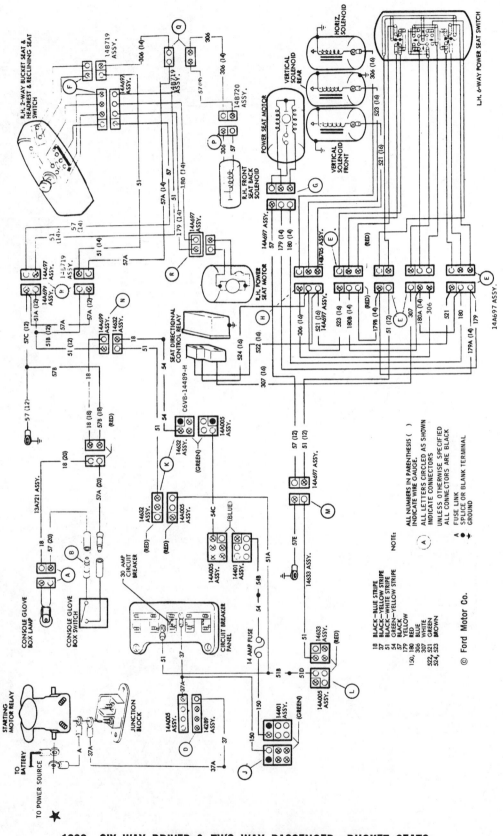

**1969—SIX WAY DRIVER & TWO WAY PASSENGER—BUCKET SEATS**

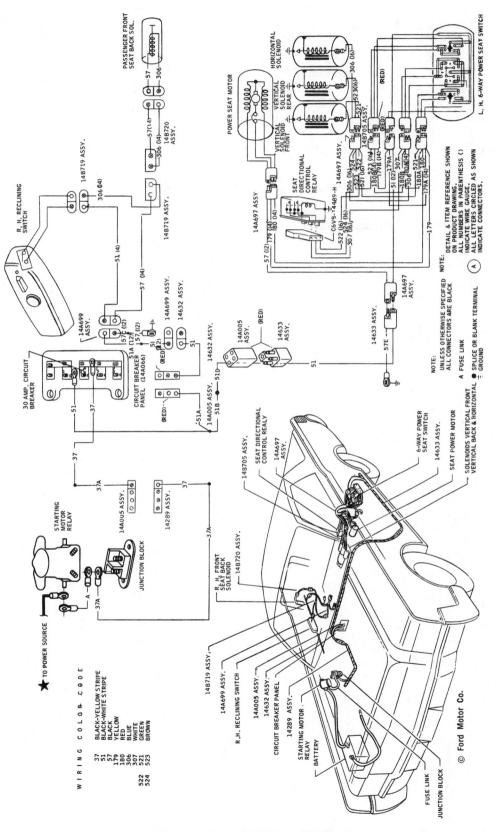

**1969—SIX WAY BENCH & RECLINING**

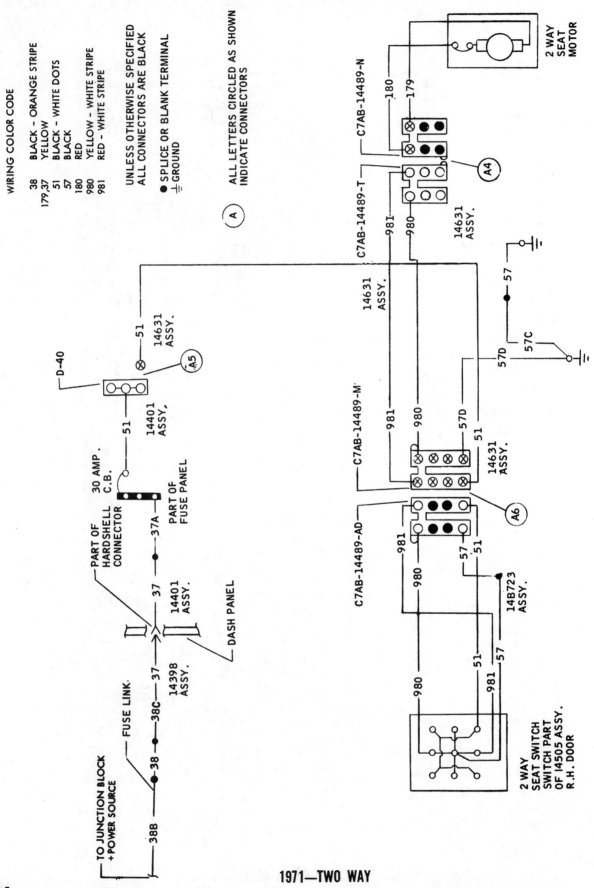

WIRING COLOR CODE

| 38 | BLACK – ORANGE STRIPE |
| 179,37 | YELLOW |
| 51 | BLACK – WHITE DOTS |
| 57 | BLACK |
| 180 | RED |
| 980 | YELLOW – WHITE STRIPE |
| 981 | RED – WHITE STRIPE |

UNLESS OTHERWISE SPECIFIED
ALL CONNECTORS ARE BLACK

● SPLICE OR BLANK TERMINAL
⏚ GROUND

Ⓐ ALL LETTERS CIRCLED AS SHOWN
INDICATE CONNECTORS

2 WAY SEAT MOTOR

C7AB-14489-N

180
179

14631 ASSY.

Ⓐ4

C7AB-14489-T

981
980

14631 ASSY.

57
57C
57D

51

14631 ASSY.

D-40

14631 ASSY.

Ⓐ5

14401 ASSY.

PART OF HARDSHELL CONNECTOR

30 AMP. C.B.

51

PART OF FUSE PANEL

37    37A

14401 ASSY.

DASH PANEL

FUSE LINK

14398 ASSY.

38    38C    37

C7AB-14489-M

981    980    57D    51

14631 ASSY.

C7AB-14489-AD

981    980    57    51

Ⓐ6

14B723 ASSY.

51    57

980    981

2 WAY SEAT SWITCH SWITCH PART OF 14505 ASSY. R.H. DOOR

TO JUNCTION BLOCK + POWER SOURCE

38B

**1971—TWO WAY**

## Lincoln·Continental

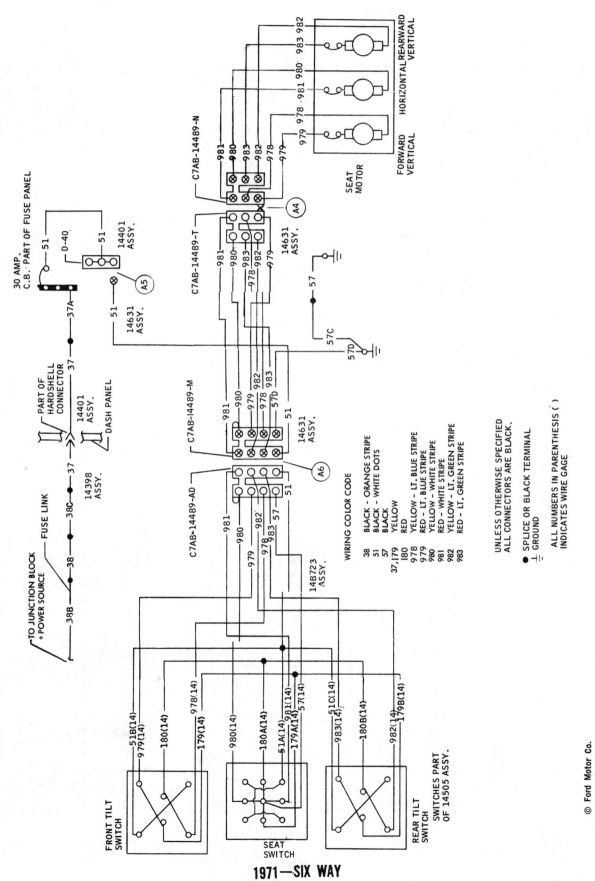

WIRING COLOR CODE

| | |
|---|---|
| 38 | BLACK – ORANGE STRIPE |
| 51 | BLACK – WHITE DOTS |
| 57 | BLACK |
| 37,179 | YELLOW |
| 180 | RED |
| 978 | YELLOW – LT. BLUE STRIPE |
| 979 | RED – LT. BLUE STRIPE |
| 980 | YELLOW – WHITE STRIPE |
| 981 | RED – WHITE STRIPE |
| 982 | YELLOW – LT. GREEN STRIPE |
| 983 | RED – LT. GREEN STRIPE |

UNLESS OTHERWISE SPECIFIED
ALL CONNECTORS ARE BLACK.

● SPLICE OR BLACK TERMINAL
⏚ GROUND

ALL NUMBERS IN PARENTHESIS ( )
INDICATES WIRE GAGE

© Ford Motor Co.

1971—SIX WAY

## Lincoln·Continental

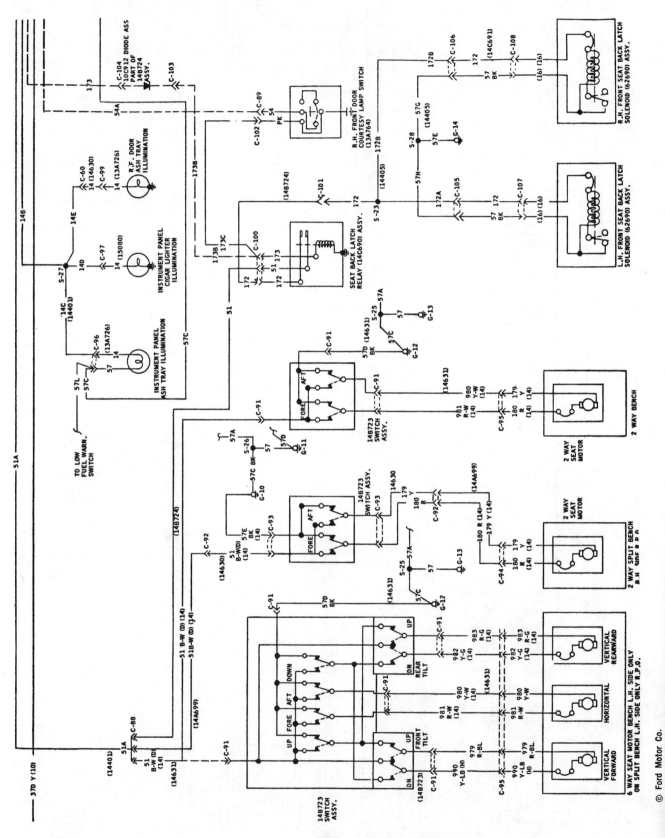

© Ford Motor Co.

**1972**

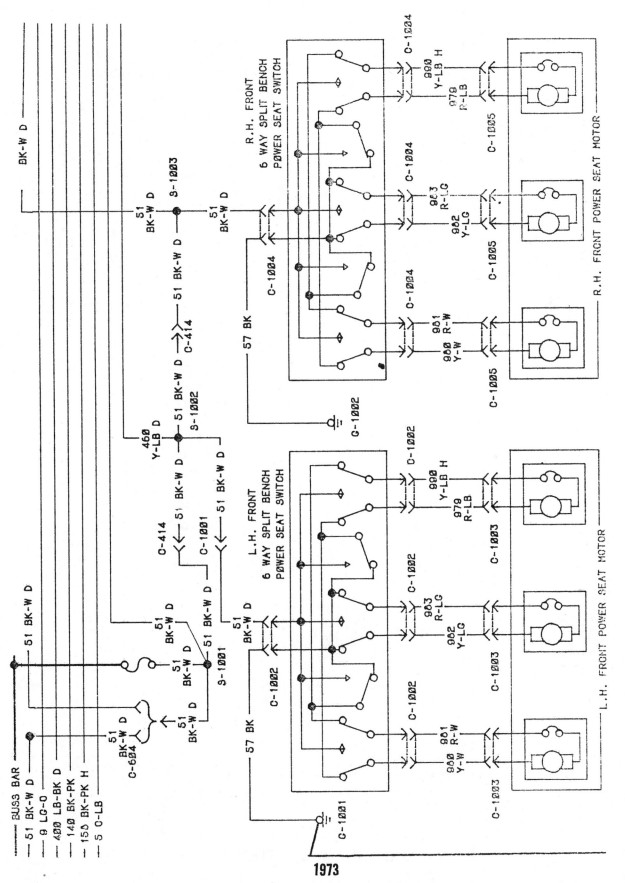

1973

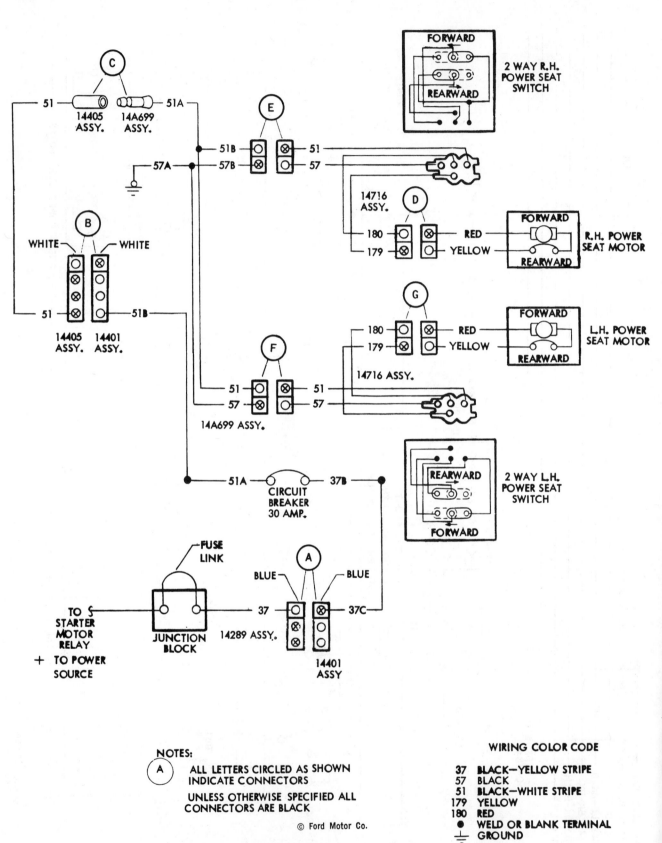

**1969—TWO WAY SPLIT BENCH**

## Mark III

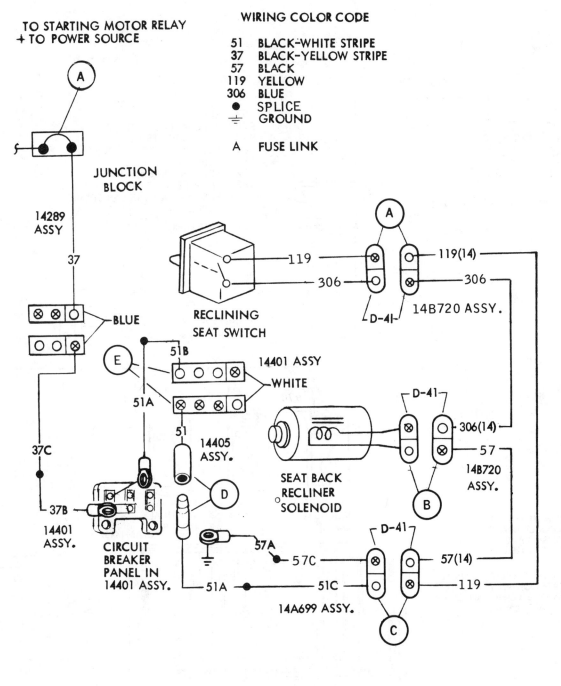

TO STARTING MOTOR RELAY
+ TO POWER SOURCE

(A)

JUNCTION
BLOCK

14289
ASSY

37

BLUE

37C

37B

14401
ASSY.

CIRCUIT
BREAKER
PANEL IN
14401 ASSY.

E

51B

51A

51

14405
ASSY.

D

57A

51A

WIRING COLOR CODE

| 51 | BLACK-WHITE STRIPE |
| 37 | BLACK-YELLOW STRIPE |
| 57 | BLACK |
| 119 | YELLOW |
| 306 | BLUE |
| ● | SPLICE |
| ⏚ | GROUND |
| A | FUSE LINK |

RECLINING
SEAT SWITCH

119

306

14401 ASSY

WHITE

SEAT BACK
RECLINER
SOLENOID

(A)

119(14)

306

D-41

14B720 ASSY.

D-41

306(14)

57

14B720
ASSY.

(B)

57C

51C

14A699 ASSY.

D-41

57(14)

119

(C)

NOTE:

DETAIL & ITEM REFERENCE SHOWN ON
PRODUCT DRAWING

ALL NUMBERS IN PARENTHESIS ( )
INDICATE WIRE GAUGE

(A) ALL LETTERS CIRCLED AS SHOWN
INDICATE CONNECTORS

© Ford Motor Co. UNLESS OTHERWISE SPECIFIED ALL
CONNECTORS ARE BLACK

**1969—RECLINING**

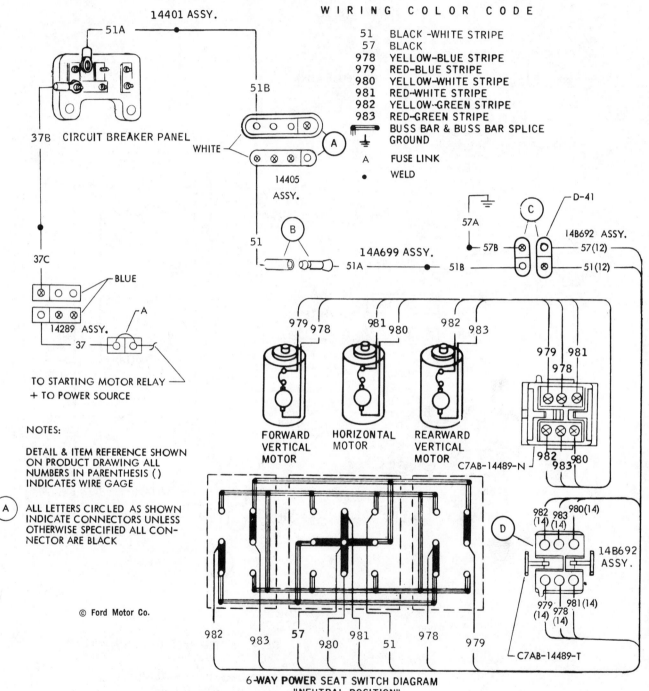

WIRING COLOR CODE

| | |
|---|---|
| 51 | BLACK -WHITE STRIPE |
| 57 | BLACK |
| 978 | YELLOW-BLUE STRIPE |
| 979 | RED-BLUE STRIPE |
| 980 | YELLOW-WHITE STRIPE |
| 981 | RED-WHITE STRIPE |
| 982 | YELLOW-GREEN STRIPE |
| 983 | RED-GREEN STRIPE |
| | BUSS BAR & BUSS BAR SPLICE |
| | GROUND |
| A | FUSE LINK |
| • | WELD |

14401 ASSY.

51A

37B   CIRCUIT BREAKER PANEL

WHITE

14405 ASSY.

51B

A

B

51

51A   14A699 ASSY.   51B

57A

57B   C

D-41

14B692 ASSY.

57(12)

51(12)

37C

BLUE

14289 ASSY.

A

37

TO STARTING MOTOR RELAY
+ TO POWER SOURCE

NOTES:

DETAIL & ITEM REFERENCE SHOWN
ON PRODUCT DRAWING ALL
NUMBERS IN PARENTHESIS ( )
INDICATES WIRE GAGE

A   ALL LETTERS CIRCLED AS SHOWN
INDICATE CONNECTORS UNLESS
OTHERWISE SPECIFIED ALL CON-
NECTOR ARE BLACK

© Ford Motor Co.

979 978   981 980   982 983

FORWARD
VERTICAL
MOTOR

HORIZONTAL
MOTOR

REARWARD
VERTICAL
MOTOR

979 981
978
C7AB-14489-N
982 983 980

D

982 980(14)
(14) 983 (14)
(14)
14B692
ASSY.

979 981(14)
(14) 978
(14)

C7AB-14489-T

982   983   57   981   978   979
980   51

6-WAY POWER SEAT SWITCH DIAGRAM
"NEUTRAL POSITION"

## Mark III

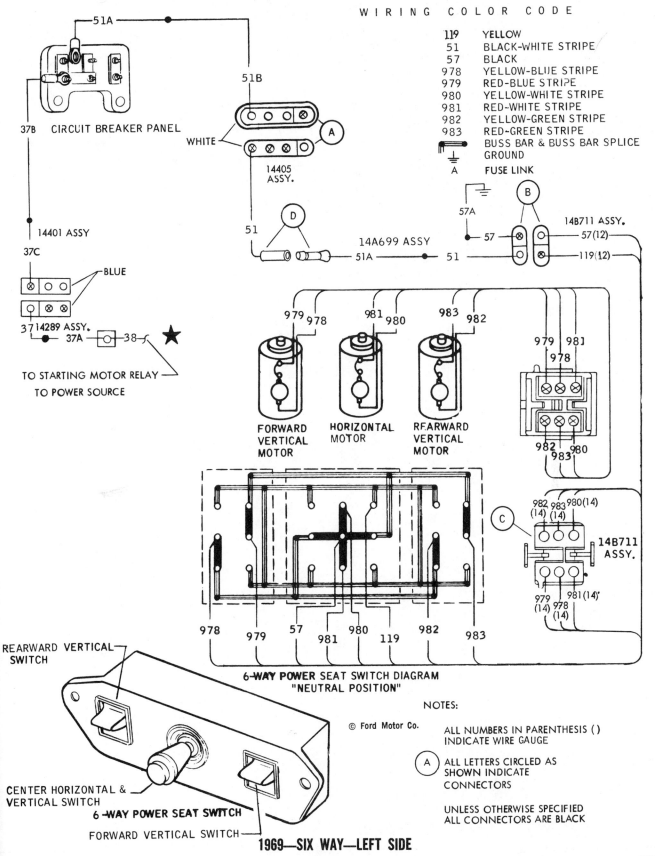

WIRING COLOR CODE

| | |
|---|---|
| 119 | YELLOW |
| 51 | BLACK-WHITE STRIPE |
| 57 | BLACK |
| 978 | YELLOW-BLUE STRIPE |
| 979 | RED-BLUE STRIPE |
| 980 | YELLOW-WHITE STRIPE |
| 981 | RED-WHITE STRIPE |
| 982 | YELLOW-GREEN STRIPE |
| 983 | RED-GREEN STRIPE |
| | BUSS BAR & BUSS BAR SPLICE GROUND |
| A | FUSE LINK |

51A

51B

37B    CIRCUIT BREAKER PANEL

WHITE

14405 ASSY.

14401 ASSY

37C

BLUE

3714289 ASSY.

37A — 38

TO STARTING MOTOR RELAY
TO POWER SOURCE

D

51

51A

14A699 ASSY

51

57A

57

B

57(12)

119(12)

14B711 ASSY.

979 978    981 980    983 982

979 981
978
982 983 980

FORWARD VERTICAL MOTOR

HORIZONTAL MOTOR

REARWARD VERTICAL MOTOR

982 983 980(14)
(14) (14)

C    14B711 ASSY.

979 981(14)
(14) 978
(14)

978    979    57    981    980    119    982    983

6-WAY POWER SEAT SWITCH DIAGRAM
"NEUTRAL POSITION"

REARWARD VERTICAL SWITCH

CENTER HORIZONTAL & VERTICAL SWITCH

6-WAY POWER SEAT SWITCH

FORWARD VERTICAL SWITCH

1969—SIX WAY—LEFT SIDE

NOTES:

© Ford Motor Co.

ALL NUMBERS IN PARENTHESIS ( ) INDICATE WIRE GAUGE

A    ALL LETTERS CIRCLED AS SHOWN INDICATE CONNECTORS

UNLESS OTHERWISE SPECIFIED ALL CONNECTORS ARE BLACK

## Mark III

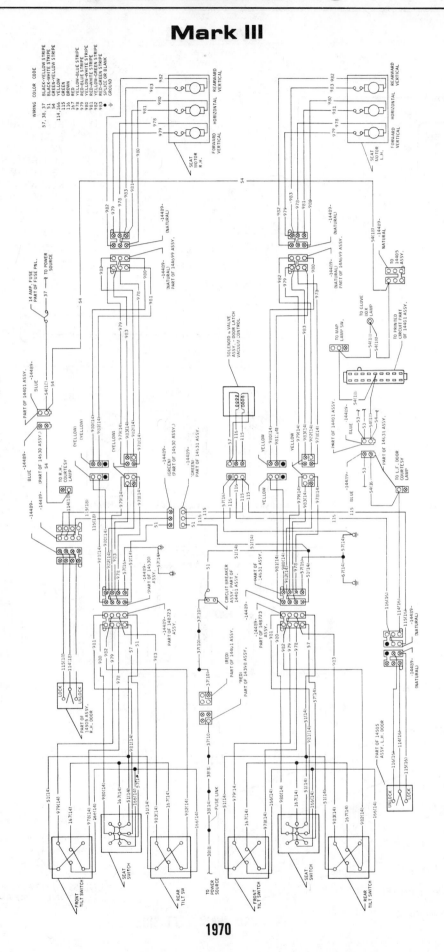

© Ford Motor Co.

1970

## Mark III

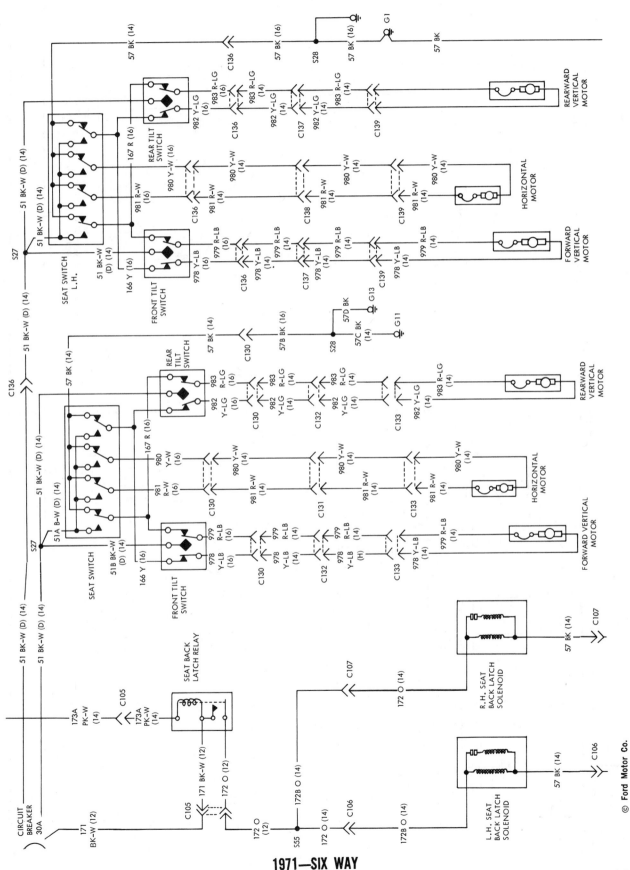

**1971—SIX WAY**

© Ford Motor Co.

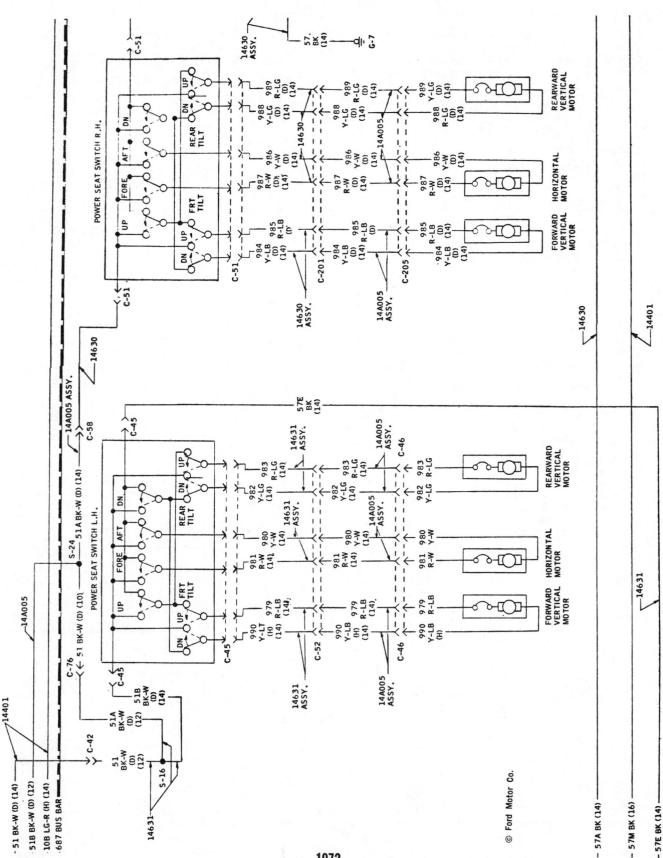

© Ford Motor Co.

1972

## Mark IV

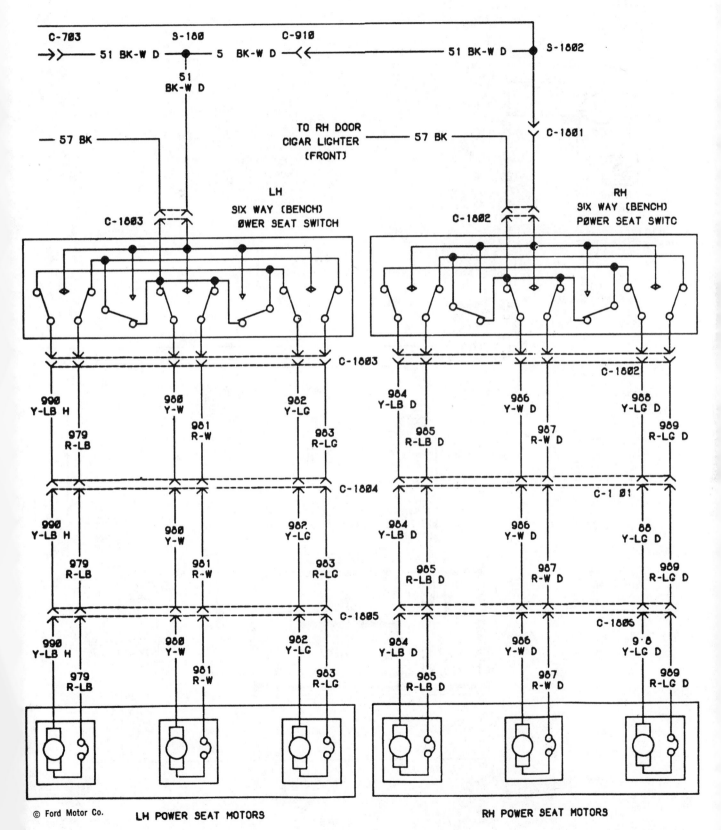

© Ford Motor Co.  LH POWER SEAT MOTORS

RH POWER SEAT MOTORS

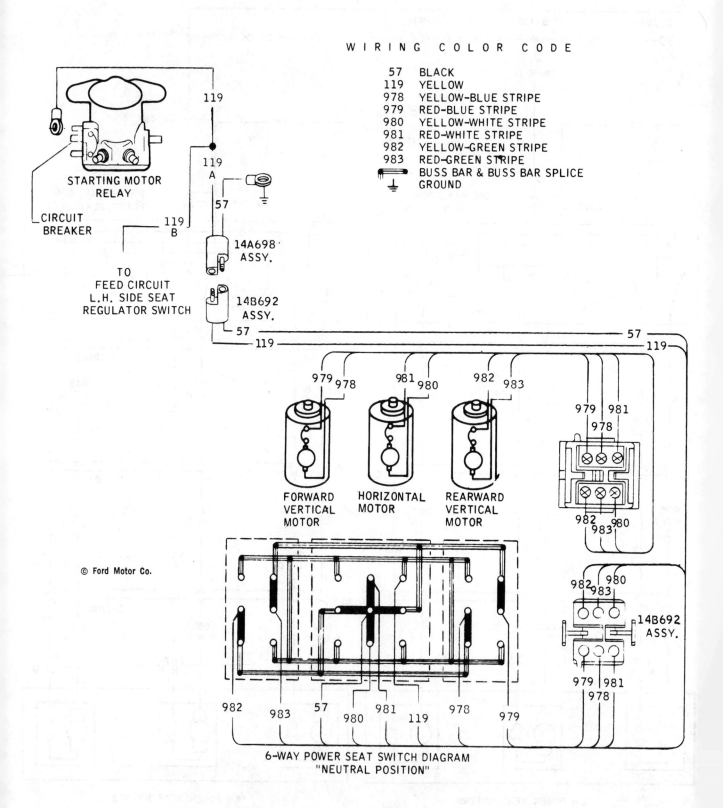

WIRING COLOR CODE

| 57  | BLACK |
| 119 | YELLOW |
| 978 | YELLOW-BLUE STRIPE |
| 979 | RED-BLUE STRIPE |
| 980 | YELLOW-WHITE STRIPE |
| 981 | RED-WHITE STRIPE |
| 982 | YELLOW-GREEN STRIPE |
| 983 | RED-GREEN STRIPE |
| | BUSS BAR & BUSS BAR SPLICE |
| | GROUND |

STARTING MOTOR RELAY

CIRCUIT BREAKER

119

119 A

119 B

57

14A698 ASSY.

14B692 ASSY.

57

119

TO FEED CIRCUIT L.H. SIDE SEAT REGULATOR SWITCH

© Ford Motor Co.

FORWARD VERTICAL MOTOR

HORIZONTAL MOTOR

REARWARD VERTICAL MOTOR

14B692 ASSY.

6-WAY POWER SEAT SWITCH DIAGRAM "NEUTRAL POSITION"

**1968-70—SIX WAY**

## Mercury

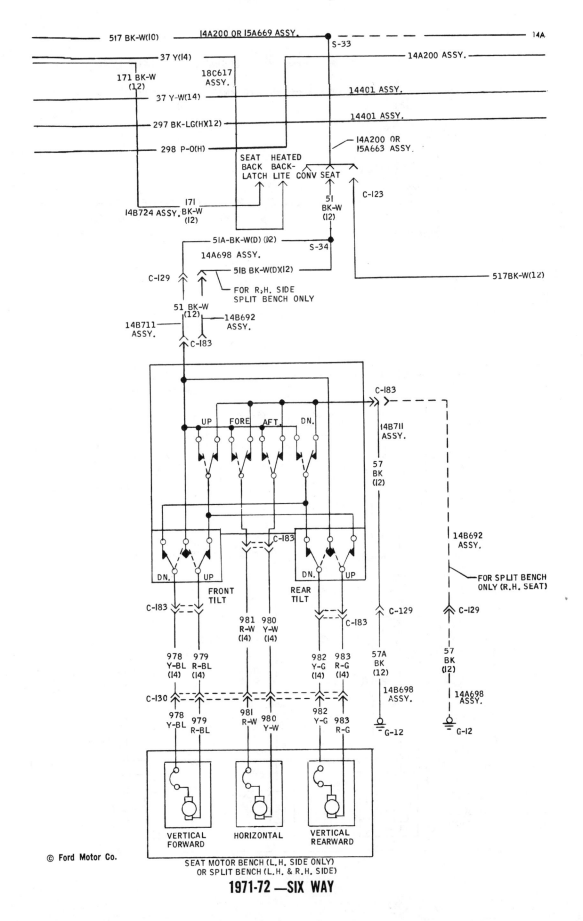

© Ford Motor Co.

SEAT MOTOR BENCH (L.H. SIDE ONLY)
OR SPLIT BENCH (L.H. & R.H. SIDE)

## 1971-72 —SIX WAY

# Power Seats Wiring

## Mercury

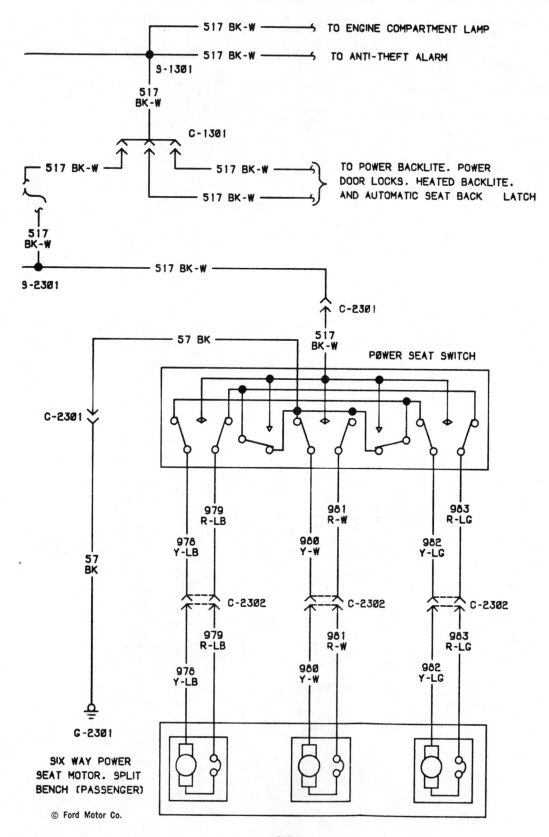

517 BK-W → TO ENGINE COMPARTMENT LAMP

517 BK-W → TO ANTI-THEFT ALARM

S-1301

517
BK-W

C-1301

517 BK-W

517 BK-W → TO POWER BACKLITE, POWER
DOOR LOCKS, HEATED BACKLITE,
AND AUTOMATIC SEAT BACK    LATCH

517 BK-W

517
BK-W

S-2301

517 BK-W

C-2301

57 BK

517
BK-W

POWER SEAT SWITCH

C-2301

57
BK

979
R-LB

981
R-W

983
R-LG

978
Y-LB

980
Y-W

982
Y-LG

C-2302

C-2302

C-2302

979
R-LB

981
R-W

983
R-LG

978
Y-LB

980
Y-W

982
Y-LG

G-2301

SIX WAY POWER
SEAT MOTOR, SPLIT
BENCH (PASSENGER)

© Ford Motor Co.

1973

428

## Mercury

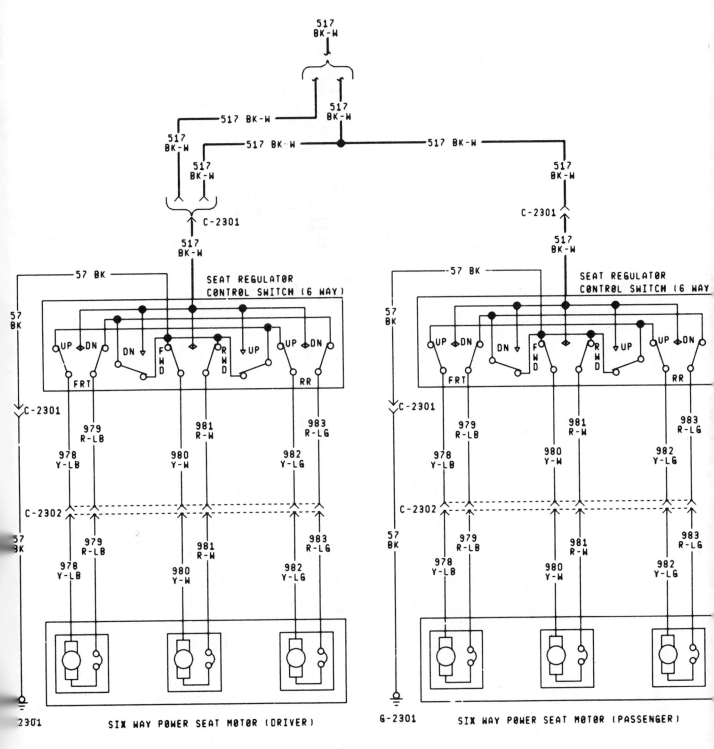

SIX WAY POWER SEAT MOTOR (DRIVER)     SIX WAY POWER SEAT MOTOR (PASSENGER)

© Ford Motor Co.

**1974-75**

## Ford

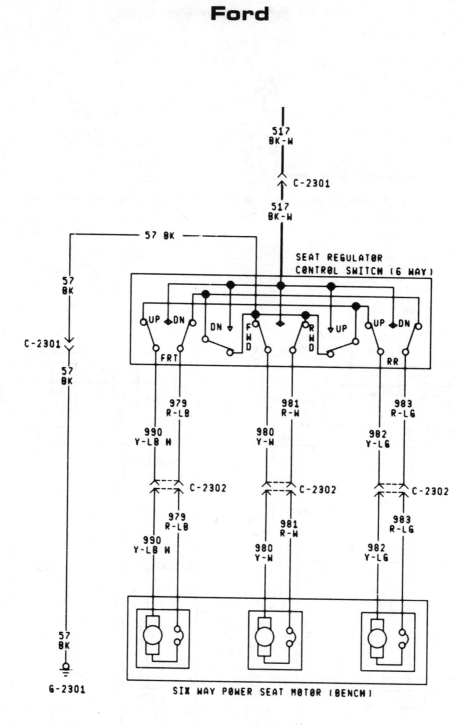

© Ford Motor Co.

**1974-75**

## Torino—Montego

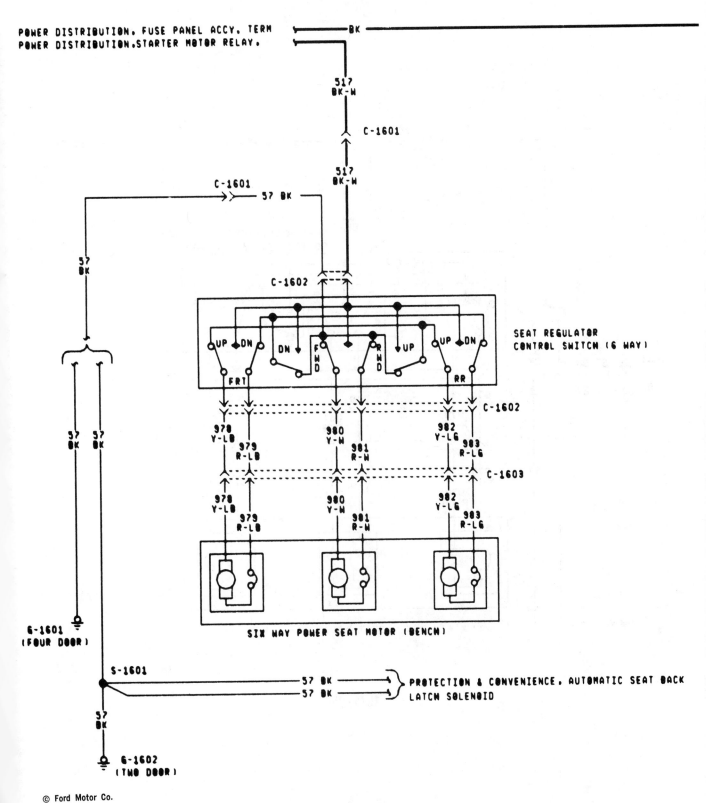

POWER DISTRIBUTION, FUSE PANEL ACCY, TERM
POWER DISTRIBUTION, STARTER MOTOR RELAY.

BK

517
BK-W

C-1601

517
BK-W

C-1601          57 BK

57
BK

C-1602

UP    DN         DN    F        R    UP        UP    DN
                       W             W
                       D             D

FRT                                              RR

SEAT REGULATOR
CONTROL SWITCH (6 WAY)

57    57
BK    BK

C-1602

978          980          982
Y-LB         Y-W          Y-LG
     979          981          983
     R-LB         R-W          R-LG

C-1603

978          980          982
Y-LB         Y-W          Y-LG
     979          981          983
     R-LB         R-W          R-LG

SIX WAY POWER SEAT MOTOR (BENCH)

G-1601
(FOUR DOOR)

S-1601

57 BK          PROTECTION & CONVENIENCE, AUTOMATIC SEAT BACK
57 BK          LATCH SOLENOID

57
BK

G-1602
(TWO DOOR)

© Ford Motor Co.

1974-75

## Cougar

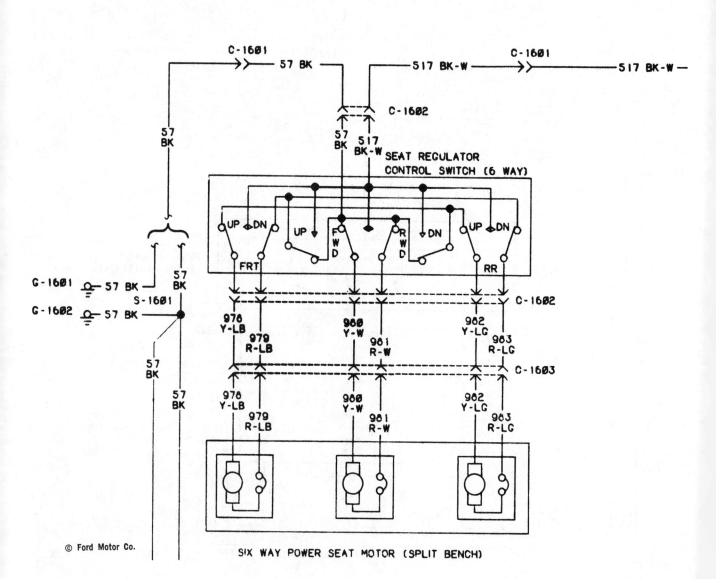

© Ford Motor Co.

SIX WAY POWER SEAT MOTOR (SPLIT BENCH)

1974-75

# Power Seats Wiring

## Lincoln

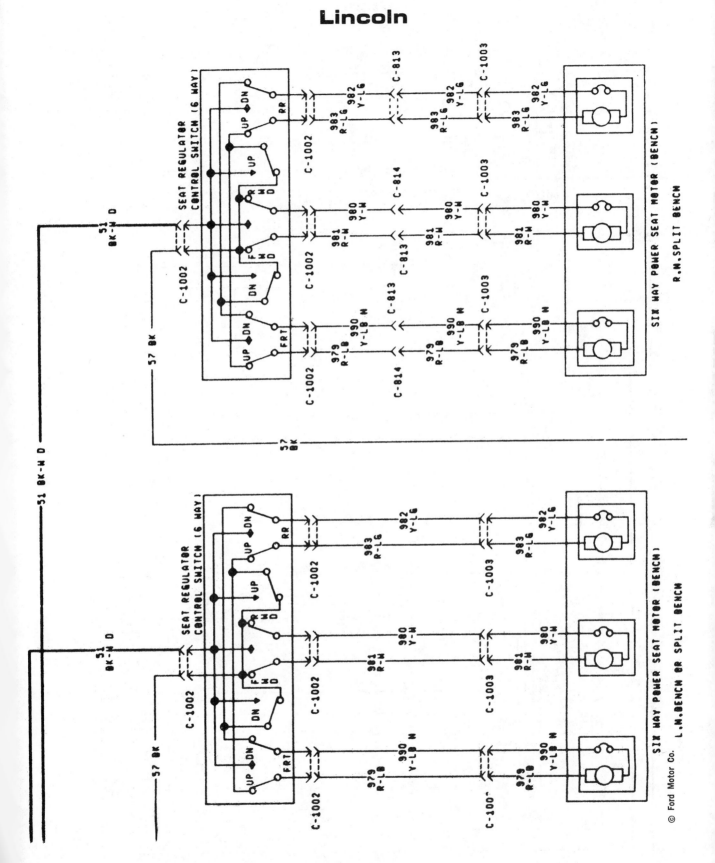

## Thunderbird

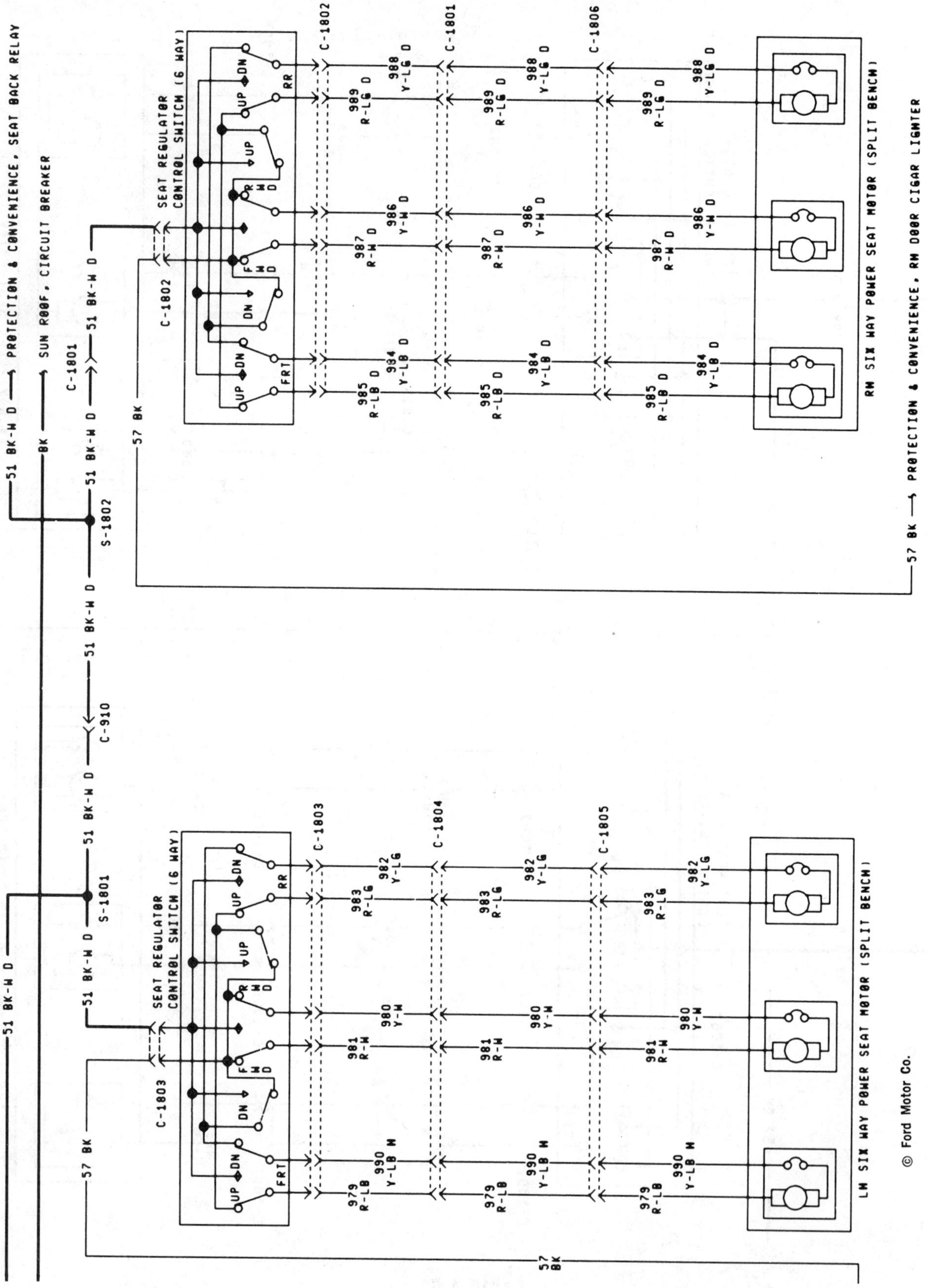
51 BK-W D
PROTECTION & CONVENIENCE, SEAT BACK RELAY
BK
SUN ROOF, CIRCUIT BREAKER
C-1801
S-1802
S-1801
C-910
57 BK
SEAT REGULATOR CONTROL SWITCH (6 WAY)
UP
DN
RR
FRT
R W D
F W D
C-1802
C-1801
C-1806
988 Y-LG D
989 R-LG D
986 Y-W D
987 R-W D
984 Y-LB D
985 R-LB D
RH SIX WAY POWER SEAT MOTOR (SPLIT BENCH)
57 BK
PROTECTION & CONVENIENCE, RH DOOR CIGAR LIGHTER
C-1803
C-1804
C-1805
982 Y-LG
983 R-LG
980 Y-W
981 R-W
990 Y-LB W
979 R-LB
LH SIX WAY POWER SEAT MOTOR (SPLIT BENCH)
© Ford Motor Co.

1974-75

# Mark IV

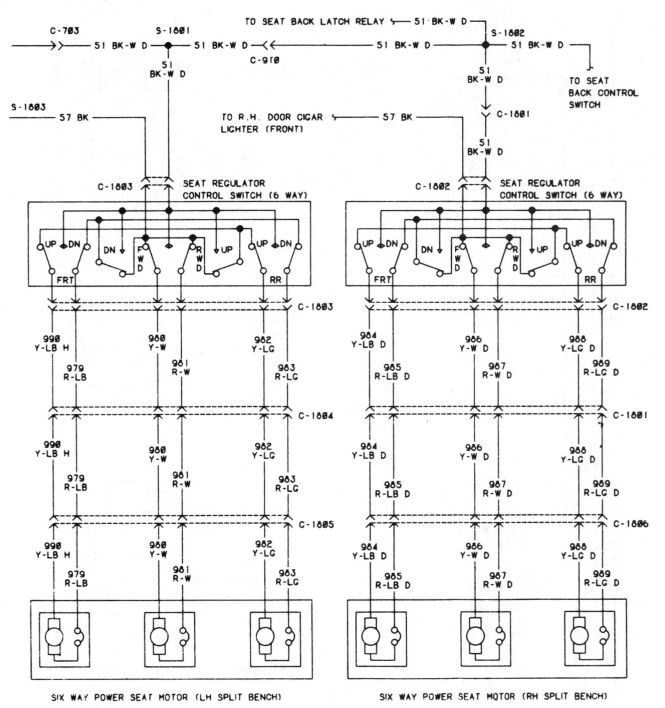

SIX WAY POWER SEAT MOTOR (LH SPLIT BENCH)

SIX WAY POWER SEAT MOTOR (RH SPLIT BENCH)

© Ford Motor Co.

1974

## Mark IV

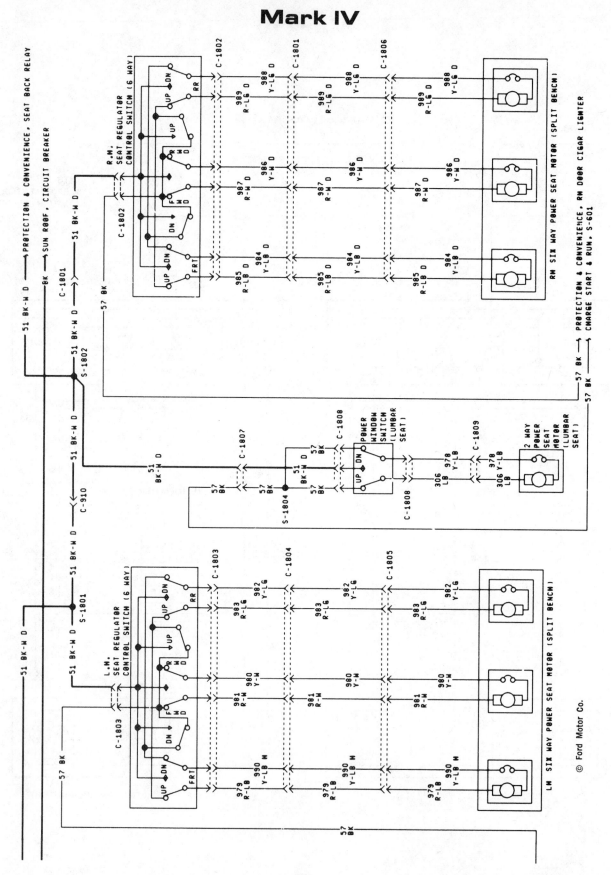

1975

## General Motors

### Two Way

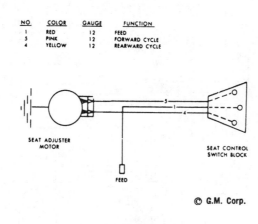

| NO | COLOR | GAUGE | FUNCTION |
|----|-------|-------|----------|
| 1 | RED | 12 | FEED |
| 5 | PINK | 12 | FORWARD CYCLE |
| 4 | YELLOW | 12 | REARWARD CYCLE |

SEAT ADJUSTER MOTOR

SEAT CONTROL SWITCH BLOCK

FEED

© G.M. Corp.

**1968—Oldsmobile**

### Four Way

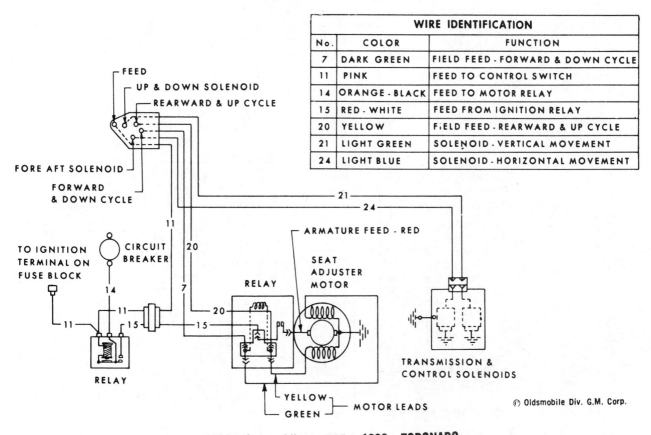

| WIRE IDENTIFICATION | | |
|---|---|---|
| No. | COLOR | FUNCTION |
| 7 | DARK GREEN | FIELD FEED - FORWARD & DOWN CYCLE |
| 11 | PINK | FEED TO CONTROL SWITCH |
| 14 | ORANGE - BLACK | FEED TO MOTOR RELAY |
| 15 | RED - WHITE | FEED FROM IGNITION RELAY |
| 20 | YELLOW | FIELD FEED - REARWARD & UP CYCLE |
| 21 | LIGHT GREEN | SOLENOID - VERTICAL MOVEMENT |
| 24 | LIGHT BLUE | SOLENOID - HORIZONTAL MOVEMENT |

FEED
UP & DOWN SOLENOID
REARWARD & UP CYCLE

FORE AFT SOLENOID
FORWARD & DOWN CYCLE

TO IGNITION TERMINAL ON FUSE BLOCK

CIRCUIT BREAKER

RELAY

ARMATURE FEED - RED

SEAT ADJUSTER MOTOR

TRANSMISSION & CONTROL SOLENOIDS

RELAY

YELLOW
GREEN
MOTOR LEADS

© Oldsmobile Div. G.M. Corp.

**1968— Oldsmobile & F-85 —1968—TORONADO**

## General Motors

## Six Way

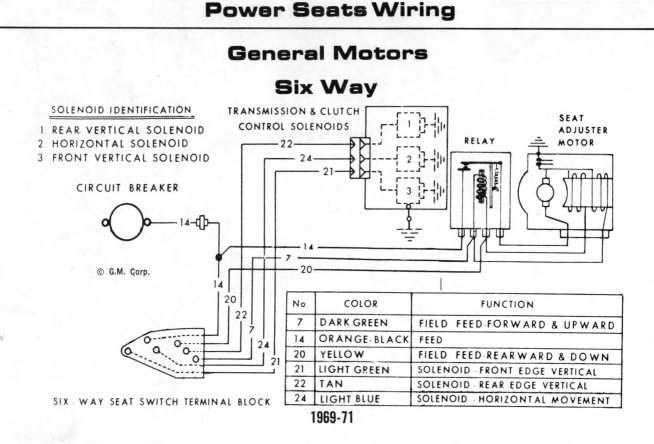

**SOLENOID IDENTIFICATION**

1. REAR VERTICAL SOLENOID
2. HORIZONTAL SOLENOID
3. FRONT VERTICAL SOLENOID

CIRCUIT BREAKER

© G.M. Corp.

SIX - WAY SEAT SWITCH TERMINAL BLOCK

TRANSMISSION & CLUTCH CONTROL SOLENOIDS

RELAY

SEAT ADJUSTER MOTOR

| No. | COLOR | FUNCTION |
|-----|-------|----------|
| 7 | DARK GREEN | FIELD FEED-FORWARD & UPWARD |
| 14 | ORANGE-BLACK | FEED |
| 20 | YELLOW | FIELD FEED-REARWARD & DOWN |
| 21 | LIGHT GREEN | SOLENOID - FRONT EDGE VERTICAL |
| 22 | TAN | SOLENOID - REAR EDGE VERTICAL |
| 24 | LIGHT BLUE | SOLENOID - HORIZONTAL MOVEMENT |

**1969-71**

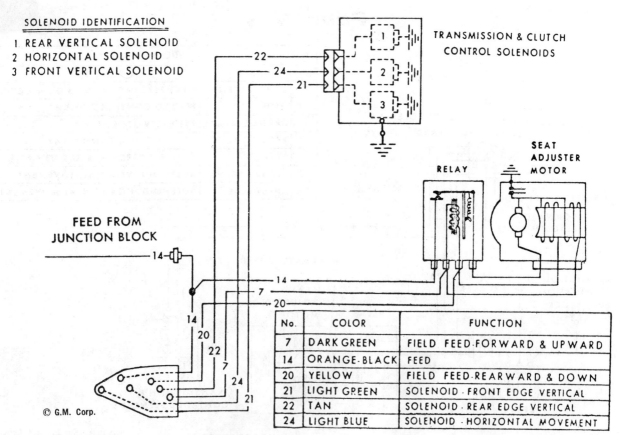

**SOLENOID IDENTIFICATION**

1. REAR VERTICAL SOLENOID
2. HORIZONTAL SOLENOID
3. FRONT VERTICAL SOLENOID

TRANSMISSION & CLUTCH CONTROL SOLENOIDS

SEAT ADJUSTER MOTOR

RELAY

FEED FROM JUNCTION BLOCK

© G.M. Corp.

SIX - WAY SEAT SWITCH TERMINAL BLOCK

| No. | COLOR | FUNCTION |
|-----|-------|----------|
| 7 | DARK GREEN | FIELD FEED-FORWARD & UPWARD |
| 14 | ORANGE-BLACK | FEED |
| 20 | YELLOW | FIELD FEED-REARWARD & DOWN |
| 21 | LIGHT GREEN | SOLENOID - FRONT EDGE VERTICAL |
| 22 | TAN | SOLENOID - REAR EDGE VERTICAL |
| 24 | LIGHT BLUE | SOLENOID - HORIZONTAL MOVEMENT |

**1972-73**

# Power Seats Wiring

## General Motors
## Six Way

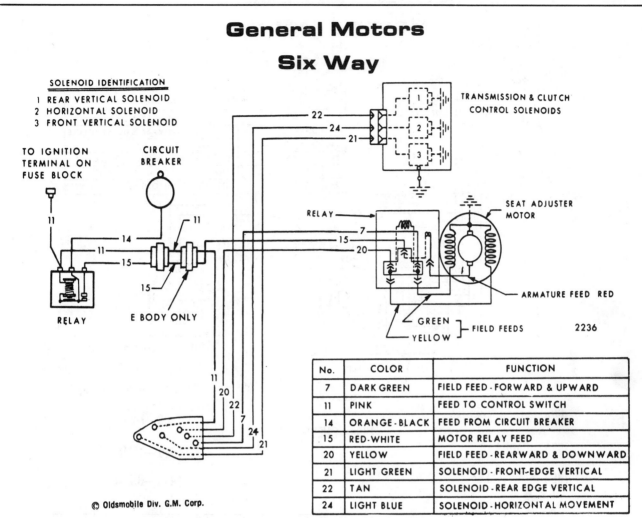

SOLENOID IDENTIFICATION
1. REAR VERTICAL SOLENOID
2. HORIZONTAL SOLENOID
3. FRONT VERTICAL SOLENOID

TO IGNITION TERMINAL ON FUSE BLOCK

CIRCUIT BREAKER

RELAY

E BODY ONLY

TRANSMISSION & CLUTCH CONTROL SOLENOIDS

RELAY

SEAT ADJUSTER MOTOR

ARMATURE FEED RED

GREEN ⎱ FIELD FEEDS
YELLOW ⎰

2236

© Oldsmobile Div. G.M. Corp.

| No. | COLOR | FUNCTION |
|-----|-------|----------|
| 7 | DARK GREEN | FIELD FEED - FORWARD & UPWARD |
| 11 | PINK | FEED TO CONTROL SWITCH |
| 14 | ORANGE - BLACK | FEED FROM CIRCUIT BREAKER |
| 15 | RED - WHITE | MOTOR RELAY FEED |
| 20 | YELLOW | FIELD FEED - REARWARD & DOWNWARD |
| 21 | LIGHT GREEN | SOLENOID - FRONT-EDGE VERTICAL |
| 22 | TAN | SOLENOID - REAR EDGE VERTICAL |
| 24 | LIGHT BLUE | SOLENOID - HORIZONTAL MOVEMENT |

### 1968—OLDSMOBILE & TORONADO

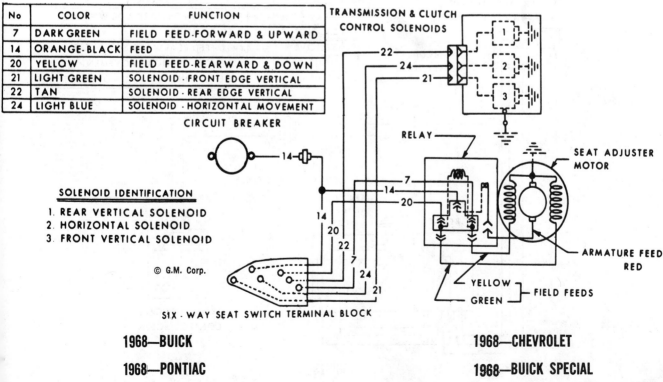

| No | COLOR | FUNCTION |
|----|-------|----------|
| 7 | DARK GREEN | FIELD FEED-FORWARD & UPWARD |
| 14 | ORANGE-BLACK | FEED |
| 20 | YELLOW | FIELD FEED-REARWARD & DOWN |
| 21 | LIGHT GREEN | SOLENOID - FRONT EDGE VERTICAL |
| 22 | TAN | SOLENOID - REAR EDGE VERTICAL |
| 24 | LIGHT BLUE | SOLENOID - HORIZONTAL MOVEMENT |

CIRCUIT BREAKER

SOLENOID IDENTIFICATION
1. REAR VERTICAL SOLENOID
2. HORIZONTAL SOLENOID
3. FRONT VERTICAL SOLENOID

© G.M. Corp.

SIX - WAY SEAT SWITCH TERMINAL BLOCK

TRANSMISSION & CLUTCH CONTROL SOLENOIDS

RELAY

SEAT ADJUSTER MOTOR

ARMATURE FEED RED

YELLOW ⎱ FIELD FEEDS
GREEN ⎰

### 1968—BUICK
### 1968—PONTIAC

### 1968—CHEVROLET
### 1968—BUICK SPECIAL

439

## General Motors

## Four Way

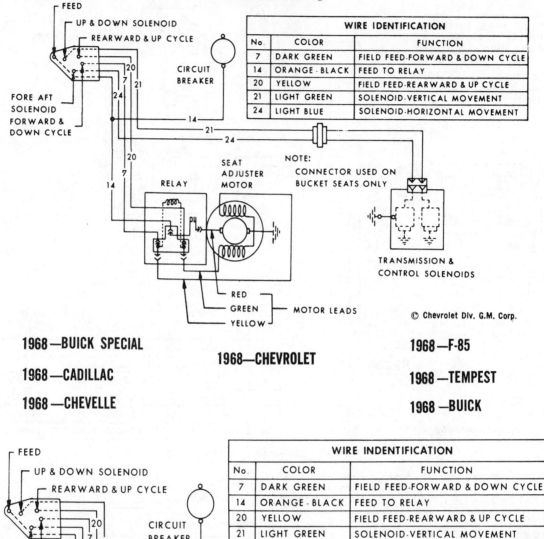

| WIRE IDENTIFICATION | | |
|---|---|---|
| No. | COLOR | FUNCTION |
| 7 | DARK GREEN | FIELD FEED-FORWARD & DOWN CYCLE |
| 14 | ORANGE-BLACK | FEED TO RELAY |
| 20 | YELLOW | FIELD FEED-REARWARD & UP CYCLE |
| 21 | LIGHT GREEN | SOLENOID-VERTICAL MOVEMENT |
| 24 | LIGHT BLUE | SOLENOID-HORIZONTAL MOVEMENT |

NOTE:
CONNECTOR USED ON
BUCKET SEATS ONLY

© Chevrolet Dlv. G.M. Corp.

**1968—BUICK SPECIAL**

**1968—CADILLAC**

**1968—CHEVELLE**

**1968—CHEVROLET**

**1968—F-85**

**1968—TEMPEST**

**1968—BUICK**

| WIRE INDENTIFICATION | | |
|---|---|---|
| No. | COLOR | FUNCTION |
| 7 | DARK GREEN | FIELD FEED-FORWARD & DOWN CYCLE |
| 14 | ORANGE-BLACK | FEED TO RELAY |
| 20 | YELLOW | FIELD FEED-REARWARD & UP CYCLE |
| 21 | LIGHT GREEN | SOLENOID-VERTICAL MOVEMENT |
| 24 | LIGHT BLUE | SOLENOID-HORIZONTAL MOVEMENT |

NOTE:
CONNECTOR USED ON
BUCKET SEATS ONLY

© G.M. Corp.

**1969-73**

## General Motors

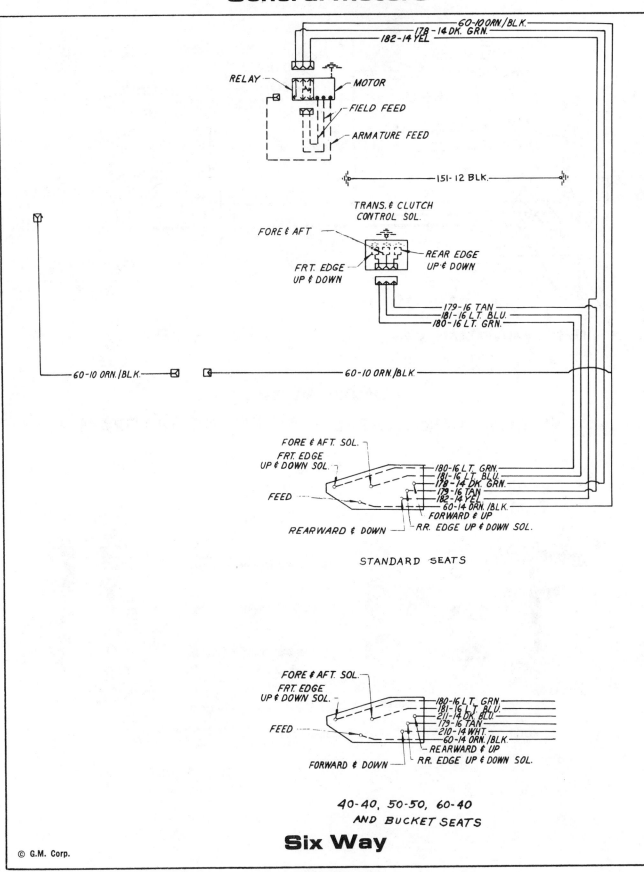

RELAY

MOTOR

FIELD FEED

ARMATURE FEED

60-10 ORN./BLK.
178-14 DK. GRN.
182-14 YEL

151-12 BLK.

TRANS. & CLUTCH
CONTROL SOL.

FORE & AFT

REAR EDGE
UP & DOWN

FRT. EDGE
UP & DOWN

179-16 TAN
181-16 LT. BLU.
180-16 LT. GRN.

60-10 ORN./BLK.

60-10 ORN./BLK.

FORE & AFT. SOL.
FRT. EDGE
UP & DOWN SOL.

FEED

180-16 LT. GRN.
181-16 LT. BLU.
178-14 DK. GRN.
179-16 TAN
182-14 YEL
60-14 ORN./BLK.
FORWARD & UP
RR. EDGE UP & DOWN SOL.

REARWARD & DOWN

STANDARD SEATS

FORE & AFT. SOL.
FRT. EDGE
UP & DOWN SOL.

FEED

180-16 LT. GRN.
181-16 LT. BLU.
211-14 DK. BLU.
179-16 TAN
210-14 WHT.
60-14 ORN./BLK.
REARWARD & UP
RR. EDGE UP & DOWN SOL.

FORWARD & DOWN

40-40, 50-50, 60-40
AND BUCKET SEATS

## Six Way

**1974-75**

## General Motors

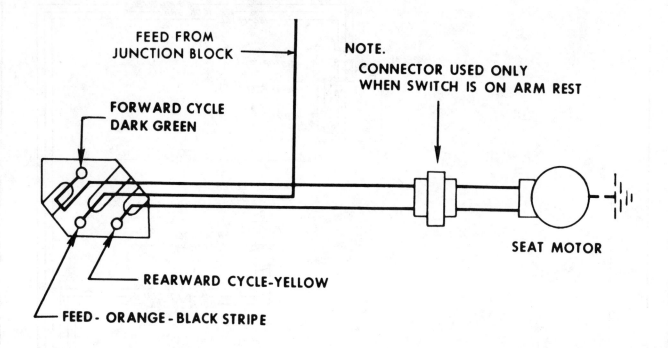

FEED FROM
JUNCTION BLOCK

NOTE.
CONNECTOR USED ONLY
WHEN SWITCH IS ON ARM REST

FORWARD CYCLE
DARK GREEN

SEAT MOTOR

REARWARD CYCLE-YELLOW

FEED - ORANGE - BLACK STRIPE

## Four Way
## ELECTRIC HORIZONTAL SEAT CIRCUIT DIAGRAM

© G.M. Corp.

### 1974-75

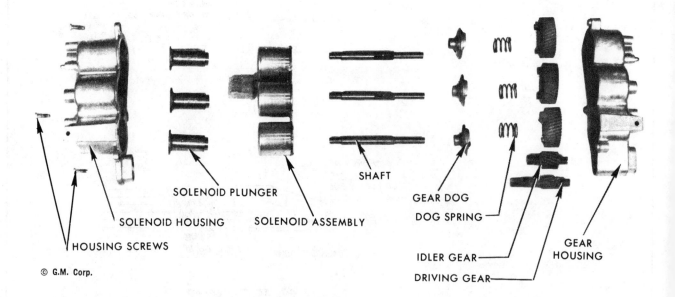

SHAFT

GEAR DOG

DOG SPRING

SOLENOID PLUNGER

SOLENOID HOUSING

SOLENOID ASSEMBLY

IDLER GEAR

GEAR
HOUSING

HOUSING SCREWS

DRIVING GEAR

© G.M. Corp.

Six-Way Seat Adjuster Transmission

## Chrysler Corporation

## Chrysler—Electric Door Locks—All 1968-75

### Description

All the doors can be locked and unlocked at once by pushing down or pulling up on the front door lock buttons. The only exception is the Imperial which uses a switch mounted in the front door arm rest. In the event of a power failure, the left front door can be unlocked manually with the inside remote control handle. The right front door can be locked or unlocked mechanically with the lock push button.

The left door lock button is connected to a toggle switch located behind the door trim panel. When the lock button is pushed down, it closes the contacts in the switch and completes the circuit between the circuit breaker located on the fuse block, and the door locking relay, located behind the right front cowl trim panel. The relay completes the circuit to a solenoid, located in each door. The solenoid is connected to the door locking mechanism by a link rod. When the plunger inside the solenoid moves up

## TROUBLESHOOTING CHART

### Chrysler—Electric Door Locks—All 1968-75

| Condition | Possible Cause |
|---|---|
| 1. Electric door lock system does not operate at all | a. Mechanical binding<br>b. Open or short circuit between the power source, fuse block, switch, or solenoid |
| 2. All but one door lock operates | a. Defective solenoid<br>b. Improper solenoid adjustment<br>c. Mechanical binding<br>d. Open or short circuit in wiring |
| 3. Electric door lock does not operate in both positions | a. Defective switch<br>b. Mechanical binding<br>c. Defective solenoid<br>d. Open or short circuit in wiring |

and down it locks or unlocks the doors.

### Electrical Test Procedures

Before performing any extensive electrical testing procedures, make sure that the battery has a good charge and that there are no mechanical binds. Also, refer to the door lock wiring diagrams for the proper identification of wires. If the inside door panel has been removed, check the toggle switch and make sure the spring is not corroded. This condition could possibly cause the switch contacts to stick and burn out the solenoids.

### Open and Short Circuits

An open circuit occurs when the circuit is not completed because of a poor terminal contact or a broken

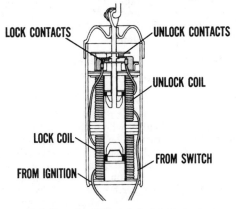

*Pushing Button Down Activates Switch*

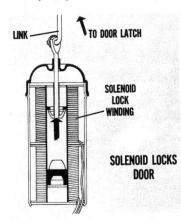

*Relay Completes Circuit to Solonoid*

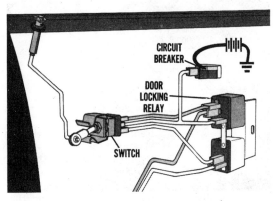

*Coils Energized Through Switch Contacts*

*Solonoid Connected to Door Latch by Link*

# Chrysler Corporation

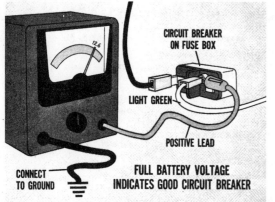

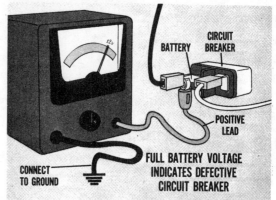

Circuit Breaker Test No. 1

Circuit Breaker Test No. 2

wire. A short circuit occurs when the current is being grounded out before it reaches a particular unit.

## Improper Ground

Often, perfectly good operating units and parts are considered defective and are replaced because of a bad ground.

### Testing for an Improper Ground

1. Attach one end of a jumper wire to the part or unit.
2. Connect the other end to a good ground, such as a bare metal panel.
3. Activate the switch. If it operates, the original ground is defective.

## Door Lock Relay Test

1. With a voltmeter, connect the positive lead to the buss bar (the metal connection between the two relays).
2. Connect the negative lead to a good ground.
3. The voltmeter should read full battery voltage until the locks are activated, then it should decrease by one-half volts.
4. If no reading is obtained, check the circuit breaker.

## Circuit Breaker Test

1. Using a voltmeter, connect the positive lead to the light green terminal of the circuit breaker.
2. Ground the other voltmeter lead.
3. If a full battery reading is not obtained, connect the positive lead to the battery terminal on the circuit breaker.
4. I the voltmeter now reads fully charged, the circuit breaker is defective and should be replaced.
5. If a full battery reading is not obtained from either terminal,

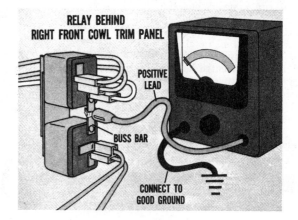

Test for Door Lock and Unlock Relay

check for an open or short circuit in the wiring.

## Door Lock Solenoid
### Adjustment

1. Disconnect the battery.
2. Remove the door trim inner panel.
3. Loosen the two solenoid retaining screws.
4. Push the solenoid all the way down.
5. While holding the solenoid down, carefully pull up on the solenoid link until the door locks.
6. Hold the solenoid in this position and tighten the retaining screws.

## Solenoid
### Removal

1. Remove the door inner trim panel.
2. Disconnect the solenoid link at the solenoid.
3. Remove the solenoid wires.
4. Remove the solenoid attaching screws and remove the solenoid.

### Installation

1. Position the solenoid to the retaining bracket.
2. Replace but do not tighten the retaining screws.
3. Connect the link to the solenoid.
4. Replace the wires.
5. While carefully holding the solenoid down, pull up on the solenoid link until the door locks.
6. Hold the solenoid in this position and tighten the retaining screws.
7. Replace the door inner trim panel.

## Tailgate Electric Door Lock Chrysler 1971-75

### Description

The tailgate door locks automatically when the ignition switch is turned on. The tailgate may be unlocked electrically with the ignition switch on, by actuating the unlock switch on the instrument panel. Hold the spring loaded switch in position until the tailgate has been opened. When the switch is released the tail-

# Chrysler Corporation

gate will lock. With the ignition switch on, the tailgate can also be locked by using the tailgate key or the locking button.

## Tailgate Solenoid Adjustment
## Fury, Chrysler, Monaco

1. Loosen the solenoid mounting screws.
2. Push the solenoid toward the bottom of the tailgate and hold it lightly while pushing the push-button to the locked position.
3. Position the solenoid correctly and tighten the mounting screws.

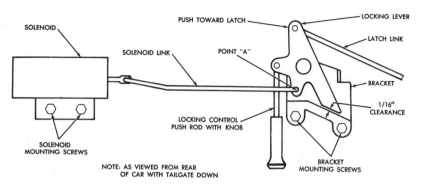

*Tailgate Autolock—Satellite, Charger, Coronet*

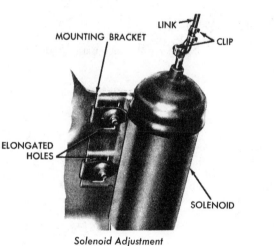

*Solenoid Adjustment*

## Tailgate Electric Test
## Fury, Chrysler, Monaco

1. Check for correct solenoid adjustment.
2. Disconnect the wiring connectors at the tailgate solenoid.
3. Connect a test lamp to the orange lead at the connector.
4. Turn the ignition switch on or in the accessory position and the test lamp should light.
5. Actuate the tailgate unlock switch to the unlock position and hold it there. The test lamp should go out.
6. Connect the test lamp lead to the pink lead in the connector and the test lamp should be out.

Release the tailgate unlock switch and the test lamp should light.

## Tailgate Solenoid Test
## Fury, Chrysler, Monaco

1. Connect a hot lead to the orange wire in the solenoid connector and the solenoid link should extend.
2. Move the hot lead to the pink wire in the connector and the solenoid link should retract.

## Tailgate Solenoid Adjustment
## Satellite, Coronet, Charger

1. Loosen the solenoid mounting screws.
2. Attach the solenoid link to the locking control assembly.
3. Push the solenoid toward the locking control assembly.
4. Hold the solenoid firmly and push the locking control push button until it bottoms out in the locked position.
5. Hold the solenoid in this position and tighten the mounting screws.
6. With the locking button pulled to the unlocked position there

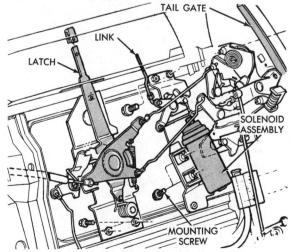

*Tailgate Solenoid Mounting—Fury, Chrysler, Monaco*

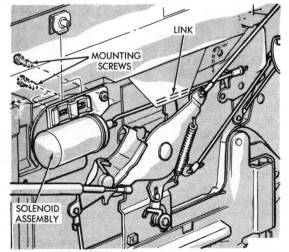

*Tailgate Solenoid Mounting—Satellite, Charger, Coronet*

# Chrysler Corporation

should be a 1/16" clearance between the locking lever and the tab.

## Tailgate Electrical Test
### Satellite, Coronet, Charger

1. Adjust the solenoid correctly.
2. If after adjusting the solenoid the tailgate still does not lock or unlock electrically perform the following circuit test:
   a. Disconnect the wiring connector at the tailgate solenoid.
   b. Connect a rest lamp to the pink lead at the connector.
   c. Turn the ignition switch on or in the accessory position and the test lamp should light.
   d. Actuate the tailgate unlock switch to the unlock position. The test lamp should go out.
   e. Connect the test lamp lead to the orange lead in the connector and the test lamp should be out. Release the tailgate unlock switch and the test lamp should light.

## Electric Seat Back Release
### Imperial and New Yorker Brougham

#### Description

The seatback latches are released

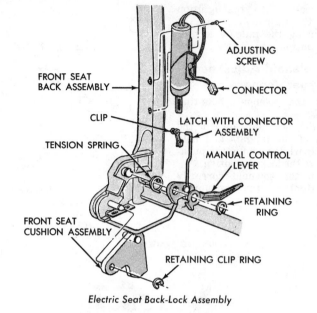

*Electric Seat Back-Lock Assembly*

*Door Lock Relays—Plymouth, Dodge, Chrysler*

electrically whenever either front door is opened. When the seat back is placed in the upright position and the door is closed the latch will again lock. The seat backs can also be released by a manual lever located at the outer area of the seat cushion.

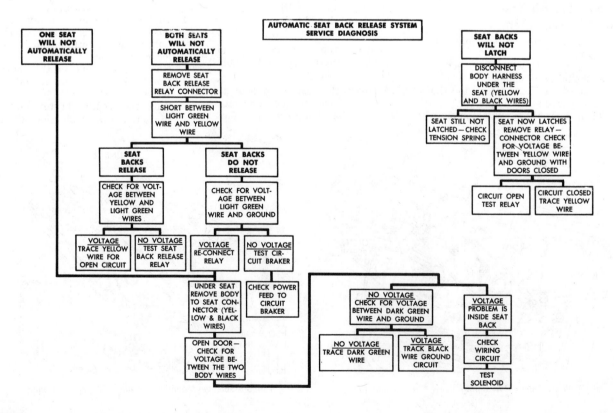

## Ford Motor Company

### Vacuum Power Door Locks 1968-69 Ford, Mercury and Meteor

#### Description

Vacuum is supplied by the intake manifold and by way of a check valve is stored in a reservoir tank which is mounted on the left front fender cavity. The tank contains enough vacuum for one lock and unlock cycle after the engine has been turned off. A hose connects the check valve to a tee in the passenger compartment. From there it connects to a control valve and the door lock control switch, usually located on the lower edge of the instrument panel.

A green hose connects the switch to the locking side of the control valve and a white hose connects the switch to the unlocking side of the control valve, located under the instrument panel.

The control valve is connected to a door lock actuator, one in each door. A yellow hose connects to the locking side of the actuator, and an orange hose connects to the unlocking side of the actuator. The actuator, when supplied with vacuum, moves a link which operates the locking mechanism to the desired position.

### 1968-69 Lincoln Continental

#### Description

Vacuum is supplied by the engine manifold. A hose comes from a seven way connector at the manifold to a check valve and a tee, and from there to the vacuum reservoir tank, located under the right front fender, forward of the wheel. A green hose connects the tee to a multiple connector, located on the dash panel. A red hose connects the multiple connector to a four way connection to the control valve and to the control switches at each front door.

When a control switch is activated to the lock position, it supplies vacuum to the locking side of the control valve. The control valve then applies vacuum to the locking side of an actuator located in each door. When a control switch is activated to the unlock position, it supplies vacuum to the unlocking side of the control valve. The control valve then applies vacuum to the unlocking side of an actuator. A link rod connects the actuators to the door locking mechanisms. When the actuator pushes the rod down, it locks the door or when it pushes the rod up until it unlocks the doors.

### 1968-69 Thunderbird and Mark III

#### Description

Vacuum is supplied by the engine manifold and by way of a check valve is stored in a reservoir tank, which is located under the right front fender. A hose, routed along the fender, connects the tank to a tee connection at the dash panel. A hose connects the tee to a multiple connector mounted on the dash panel. A red hose comes from the multiple connector, passes through the dash panel and connects to another tee connection. From the tee connection, one red hose goes to the lock side of the control valve and another goes to the unlock side of the control valve. A third red hose is connected to the control switch on the left front door.

When the control switch is activated to the lock position, it supplies vacuum to the locking side of the control valve. The control valve then applies vacuum to the locking side of the actuator, located in each door. When a control switch is activated to the unlock position, it supplies vacuum to the unlocking side of the control valve. The control valve then applies vacuum to the unlocking side of an actuator

A link rod connects the actuators to the door locking mechanisms. When the actuator pushes the rod down, it locks the door and when it pushes the rod up, it unlocks the doors.

#### One Door Will Not Unlock— Two-Door Models

1. Remove the orange hose from

the cowl side panel connector.
2. Attach a vacuum gauge to the hose.
3. Start the engine.
4. Move the control switch to the unlock position.
5. Hold the switch in the unlock position all during the test.
6. If no vacuum is present, check the hose for kinks or leaks.
7. If vacuum is available, reconnect the orange hose to the connector.
8. Remove the door trim panel.
9. Remove the orange hose from the vacuum actuator.
10. Connect a vacuum gauge to the orange hose.
11. Move the door switch to the unlock position.
12. If no vacuum is available, check the hose for kinks or leaks.
13. If vacuum is available, check for binding at the locking mechanisms and also for a defective vacuum actuator.

#### One Door Will Not Lock— Four-Door Models

1. Remove the door trim panel.
2. Connect a vacuum gauge to the yellow hose connected to the vacuum actuator.
3. Move to the lock position and hold it there.
4. If no vacuum is available, check the hose for kinks or leaks.
5. If vacuum is available, check for binding at the locking mechanisms and also for a defective vacuum actuator.

#### One Door Will Not Unlock— Four-Door Models

1. Remove the door trim panel.
2. Connect a vacuum gauge to the orange hose connected to the vacuum actuator.
3. Start the engine, move the control switch to the unlock position and hold it there.
4. If no vacuum is available, check the hose for kinks or leaks.

## TROUBLESHOOTING CHART

| Condition | Possible Cause |
|---|---|
| 1. Inoperative system | a. Pinched hose at the control valve or reservoir tank<br>b. Disconnected vacuum hose at the tank, control valve, or manifold<br>c. Leaking remote control valve |
| 2. One door lock will not lock or unlock | a. Actuator hoses pinched or disconnected<br>b. Defective actuator<br>c. Mechanical binding<br>d. Defective switch |

# Ford Motor Company

5. If vacuum is available, check for binding at the locking mechanisms and also for a defective vacuum actuator.

## Vacuum Door Lock Testing Procedures

### Completely Inoperative System

1. Start the engine.
2. Attach a vacuum and fuel pump tester and test for vacuum at the check valve.
3. If no vacuum is present, check for a defective check valve.
4. Check the hose that connects the check valve to the manifold.
5. If vacuum is present, check for vacuum at check valve on the dash panel.
6. Replace kinked, pinched or cracked hoses.
7. If vacuum is present at the dash connector, check the four way connector located above the control valve.
8. Replace kinked, pinched or broken hoses.
9. If vacuum is present at the four way connector, check for vacuum at the red hose connection of the switches.
10. Replace kinked, pinched or cracked hoses.
11. If vacuum is present at both the door control switches, replace the control valve.

### One Door Will Not Lock— Two-Door Models

1. Remove the vacuum hose from the cowl side panel connector.
2. Attach a vacuum gauge to the hose.
3. Start the engine.
4. Move one of the door control switches to the lock position.
5. Hold the switch in the lock position all during the test.
6. If no vacuum is present, check the yellow hose for kinks.
7. If vacuum is present, reconnect the hose to the connector.
8. Remove the yellow hose from the locking mechanism vacuum motor.
9. Connect the vacuum gauge to the yellow hose.
10. Move the control switch to the lock position.
11. If vacuum is not available, check the hose for kinks or leaks.
12. If vacuum is available at the yellow hose, check the locking mechanism and the vacuum actuator for binding.

### All Doors Will Not Lock Using One Control Switch

1. Remove the door trim panel.
2. Move the control switch to the lock position.
3. Check for vacuum at the green hose connector of the control switch.
4. If vacuum is not available, replace the control switch.
5. If vacuum is available, check for kinks or leaks in the hose.

### All Doors Will Not Unlock Using One Control Switch

1. Remove the door trim panel.
2. Move the control switch to the unlock position.
3. Check for vacuum at the white hose connector of the control switch.
4. If no vacuum is available, replace the control switch.
5. If vacuum is available, check for kinks or leaks in the white hose.

### All Doors Will Not Lock Using Either Control Switch

1. Disconnect the two green hoses from the control switches at the tee located below the control valve.
2. Connect a vacuum gauge to one of the green hoses.
3. Start the engine and move the one control switch to lock position and check for vacuum.
4. If no vacuum is present, move the other door control switch to the lock position.
5. If vacuum is available, note which switch is connected to the hose and connect the vacuum hose to the other green hose.
6. Move the other door switch to the lock position.
7. If there is no vacuum at one hose, check for damage between the gauge and the control switch.
8. If vacuum is available at both hoses, check for a defective hose-to-control valve or a defective control valve.

### All Doors Will Not Unlock Using Either Control Switch

1. Disconnect the two white hoses coming from the door control switches at the tee located below the control valve.
2. Connect a vacuum gauge to one of the hoses.
3. Start the engine.
4. Move one of the control switches to the unlock position and check for vacuum.

5. If vacuum is not available, move the other control switch to the unlock position.
6. If vacuum is available, note which switch is connected to the hose and connect the vacuum gauge to the other white hose.
7. Move the other control switch to the unlock position.
8. If vacuum is not available, the hose is damaged between the gauge and the control switch.
9. If vacuum is available at both hoses, the hose-to-control valve must be replaced.

## 1970 Ford and Mercury

### Description

Vacuum is supplied by the engine intake manifold and stored in a reservoir tank located in the engine compartment. A red hose channels the vacuum from a check valve, through the dash panel and directly to the control switch.

When the control is switched to the lock position, the lock vacuum hose port is opened and vacuum is channeled into the yellow (lock) hose to the locking side of the door lock actuator. The actuator is connected to the door locking mechanisms by a link rod. The actuator pulls the link down and locks the doors.

When the control is switched to the unlock position, the unlock vacuum hose port is opened and vacuum is channeled into the orange (unlock) hose to the unlocking side of the door lock actuator. The actuator pushes the link rod up and unlocks the doors.

### None of the Doors Will Lock or Unlock

1. Start the engine.
2. Check for vacuum at the check valve's nipple that connects to the red hose which runs into the passenger compartment.
3. If vacuum is not available, check for vacuum at the intake manifold connection.
4. Check for vacuum coming from the reservoir tank.
5. If vacuum is present at both input connections of the check valve, but not at the red hose connection to the passenger compartment, replace the check valve.
6. If vacuum is available up to this point, check for vacuum at the red hose connection of the control switch.
7. If vacuum is available, check for vacuum at both the lock-yellow

## Ford Motor Company

and unlock-orange hoses at the switch connections.

   a. Hold the switch in both the lock and unlock positions during the test.

8. Replace the switch if vacuum is not available.
9. If vacuum is present and the switch is not defective, check for kinked or cracked orange and yellow hoses that connect to the actuators.

### One Door Lock Does Not Work

1. Remove the lock push button and check for binding at the trim panel.
2. Connect a vacuum gauge to the lock-yellow and the unlock-orange hoses at the door lock actuator to determine whether it is a vacuum loss or a mechanical problem.
3. Repair or replace cracked or kinked hoses.

### All Doors Will Unlock, But Not Lock

1. Check for vacuum through the yellow hose at the switch when held in the lock position.
2. If vacuum is not available, replace the switch.
3. If vacuum is available, check for leaks or kinks in the yellow hoses that connect to the door lock actuators.

### All Doors Will Lock, But Not Unlock

1. Check for vacuum through the orange hose at the switch when held in the unlock position.
2. If vacuum is not available, replace the switch.
3. If vacuum is available, check for leaks or kinks in the orange hoses that connect to the door lock actuators.

### Door Lock Control Switch

#### Removal

1. Pry the switch from the opening.
2. Disconnect the vacuum hose.
3. Release the spring clips and remove the switch from the housing.

#### Installation

1. Position the switch to the housing and connect the vacuum hoses.

### Vacuum Actuator

#### Removal

1. Remove the door trim panel and watershield.
2. Disconnect the link connecting the actuator to the bellcrank on rear doors or to the door latch on front doors.
3. Remove the two actuator-to-door retaining screws.
4. Disconnect the vacuum hoses from the actuator.
5. Remove the two actuators.

#### Installation

1. Connect the vacuum hoses to the actuator.
2. Connect the actuator rod to the latch or bellcrank.
3. Position the actuator to the door and install the attaching screws.
4. Replace the watershield and the door trim panel.

### Vacuum Actuator (Tailgate)

#### Removal

1. Remove the tailgate trim panel and watershield.
2. Remove the two actuator-to-tailgate inner panel retaining screws.
3. Disconnect the actuator rod from the bellcrank.
4. Remove the actuator.

#### Installation

1. Position the actuator to the tailgate panel.
2. Replace the two retaining screws and connect the actuator rod to the bellcrank.

3. Connect the vacuum hoses.
4. Replace the tailgate trim panel.

## 1971-1972 Ford and Mercury

### Description

Vacuum is supplied by the engine manifold and stored in a reservoir tank in the engine compartment.

The doors are locked by pushing down on either of the front door push buttons. When a button is pushed down, it closes a set of contacts within the electric switch and completes the electrical circuit to the solenoid valve. When the solenoid valve is activated, it opens a valve and supplies vacuum to the lock side of all the door lock actuators, one in each door. When the push button is released, it opens the circuit to the solenoid valve. The vacuum port of the valve closes, and the doors stay locked.

The doors are unlocked by lifting up on the door lock push button. When the button is lifted up, it closes the circuit to the solenoid valve. The valve supplies vacuum to the unlock side of the door lock actuators to unlock the doors.

### None of the Actuators Will Lock or Unlock

1. Start the engine and quickly check the vacuum supply at the check valve connected to the supply hose which runs into the passenger compartment.

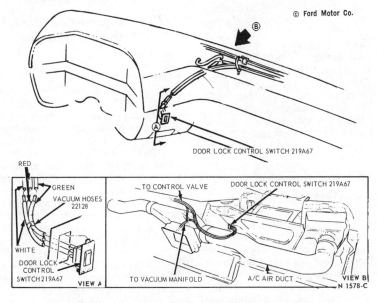

© Ford Motor Co.

Vacuum Door Lock Control Switch Installation and Hoses—Ford

# Ford Motor Company

2. Check the vacuum supply hose to the control valve for any leaks or kinks.
3. Check the output hoses at the control valve with the switch held in both the lock and unlock position.
4. Check the hoses that come from the control valve toward the doors for kinks or leaks.
5. Check for electrical power to the control valve switches while held in the lock and unlock positions.
6. Check wires back through the switches to the power source for shorts.
7. Check to see if the control valve is grounded properly.
8. If all of the above checks out properly replace the control valve.

## All Doors Will Lock But Not Unlock

1. Check for vacuum at the control valve, at the orange connections, with the switch held in the unlock position.
2. Check the orange hoses from the control valve toward the doors for leaks and kinks.
3. Check for electrical power to the control valve with the switch held in the unlock position.
4. Check the circuit back through the switches to the power source.
5. Replace the control valve if necessary.

## All Doors Will Unlock, But Not Lock

1. Check for vacuum at the control valve at the yellow connections with the switch held in the lock position.
2. Check the yellow hoses from the control valve toward the door for leaks and kinks.
3. Check for electrical power to the control valve with the switch held in the lock position.
4. Check the circuit back through the switches to the power source.
5. Replace the control valve if necessary.

## Not All the Actuators Will Operate

1. Remove the lock push buttons and check for binding at the trim panel.
2. Connect a vacuum tester to the lock-yellow and the unlock-orange hoses at the door lock actuator to determine whether it is a vacuum loss or a mechanical problem.

3. Repair or replace cracked or kinked hoses.

## Vacuum Door Lock Actuator

### Removal

1. Remove the door trim panel and watershield.
2. Disconnect the vacuum actuator link from the bellcrank on rear doors and from the door latch on front doors.
3. Remove the three actuator-to-door retaining screws.
4. Remove the vacuum hoses and remove the actuator.

### Installation

1. Position the actuator to the door and replace the three retaining screws.
2. Replace the vacuum hoses.
3. Connect the actuator link to the bellcrank on rear doors and to the door latch on front doors.
4. Install the watershield and the door trim panel.

## Door Lock Switch

### Removal

1. Remove the door trim panel and watershield.
2. Remove the button from the top of the rod.
3. Unplug the wires from the switch.
4. Separate the push button rod from the latch.

# VACUUM POWER DOOR LOCKS

### 1970-72 Lincoln Continental 1970-72 Thunderbird and Mark III

### Description

Vacuum is supplied by the engine intake manifold and stored in a reservoir tank by way of a check valve. A combination electric-vacuum control valve is used and it is located under the instrument panel next to the glove compartment. The valve consists of a valve body, two solenoids, and two plungers.

The door lock control switch is located in the arm rest on each front door on every model except the Thunderbird which has the switch mounted on a panel on the left front door. When the control switch is activated to the desired position, it sends current to either the lock or unlock solenoid. The solenoid pulls a plunger which opens either the lock or unlock

vacuum port. The vacuum is then supplied to the door lock actuators. The vacuum pulls the actuators up or down to lock or unlock the doors.

## Door Lock Solenoid Valve

### Removal

1. Remove the glove compartment liner.
2. Remove the vacuum hoses from the solenoid valve.
3. Remove the solenoid valve retaining screws.

### Installation

1. Position the solenoid valve and replace the retaining screws.
2. Replace the vacuum hoses.
3. Install the glove compartment liner.

## Vacuum Door Lock Actuator

### Removal

1. Remove the door trim panel and watershield.
2. Disconnect the vacuum actuator link from the bellcrank on rear doors and from the door latch on front doors.
3. Remove the three actuator-to-door retaining screws.
4. Remove the vacuum hoses and remove the actuator.

### Installation

1. Position the actuator to the door and replace the three retaining screws.
2. Replace the vacuum hoses.
3. Connect the actuator link to the bellcrank on rear doors and to the door latch on front doors.
4. Install the watershield and the door trim panel.

## Door Lock Control Switch

### Removal

1. Remove the control panel from the arm rest.
2. Release the spring clips and remove the switch from the control panel.

### Installation

1. Position the switch to the control panel.
2. Replace the control panel in the arm rest.

## All Doors Will Not Lock, But Will Unlock

1. Check for vacuum at the control valve.
2. Hold the switch in the lock position.

# Power Door Locks

## Ford Motor Company

3. If vacuum is available, check the hoses toward the doors for leaking or kinks or replace the valve.
4. If vacuum is not available at the control valve, check for electrical power to the control valve with the switch held in the lock position.
5. Also, trace the circuit back to the power source for an open or closed circuit.

### All Doors Will Not Unlock, But Will Lock

1. Check for vacuum at the control valve.
2. Hold the switch in the unlock position.
3. If vacuum is available, check the hoses toward the doors for leaks or kinks.
4. If the hoses are not defective, replace the control valve.
5. If vacuum is not present at the control valve, check for electrical power at the control valve with the switch held in the unlock position.
6. Also, trace the circuit to the electrical power source for an open or closed circuit.

### Not All The Actuators Will Operate

1. Remove the lock push buttons and check for binding at the trim panel.
2. Connect a vacuum tester to the lock-yellow and the unlock-or-ange hoses at the door lock actuator to determine whether it is a vacuum loss or a mechanical problem.
3. Repair or replace cracked or kinked hoses.

### None of the Actuators Will Lock or Unlock

1. Start the engine and quickly check the vacuum supply at the check valve connected to the hose which runs into the passenger compartment.
2. Check the vacuum supply hose to the control valve for leaks or kinks.
3. Check the output nipples on the control valve with the control switch held in both the lock and unlock position.
4. Check for electrical power to the control valve with the switch held in the lock and unlock positions.
5. Trace the circuit back to the power source and check for an open or closed circuit.

6. Check for a proper ground at the control valve.
7. If all of the above check out OK, replace the control valve.

## ELECTRIC POWER DOOR LOCKS

### 1972-75—All Models

#### Description

The electric door lock system is controlled by switches which are activated by the front door lock push buttons (Torino, Montego and Cougar) and rocker type switches located in the arm rest on all other models. When one of the door lock buttons is pushed down or an arm rest switch is activated the contacts close in the switch and completes the circuit to one of two relays. The contacts in the relays close and direct current to the door lock actuators which operate the locking mechanisms. Relays are only used on Torino, Montego, Cougar and all four door models. Each individual door can be locked or unlocked from the outside by using the key.

### Motor Tests (Actuators)—All Models

1. Connect 12 volts to one of the motor (actuator) connectors and ground the other terminal.
2. The motor (actuator) gear should finish its travel in less than one second.
3. Use an ammeter and check to see that it draws no more than six amps.
4. Reverse the power and ground leads and check the amp draw again.

### Relay Location

Torino, Montego and Cougar—Brake pedal support.
Four Door and Station Wagon—Mounted under the drivers seat.

### Relay Tests

1. Remove both relay connectors.
2. Check to see that terminal (B) is grounded on each relay.
3. If not, check the relay cases-to-ground bolts for tightness.
4. Apply power to terminals (A) and (C) on each relay.
5. Connect a 12 volt test light between terminal (B) and ground (no longer than two minutes).
6. If the test light does not light, replace the relay.

### Switch Test—Torino, Montego, Cougar

1. Use a self powered test lamp.
2. Continuity should exist between terminals (A) and (B) with the switch held in one position.
3. Continuity should exist between terminals (B) and (C) with the switch held in the other position.

### Electric Door Lock Motor—All Models (Actuator)

#### Removal

1. Remove the door trim panel and watershield.
2. Disconnect the motor (actuator) link from the door latch.
3. Remove the two (actuator) motor-to-door attaching screws.
4. Disconnect the wiring and remove the motor.

#### Installation

1. Connect the actuator wires.
2. Position the actuator and replace the two attaching screws.

## TROUBLESHOOTING CHART

### Electric Power Door Locks 1972-75 All Models

| Condition | Possible Cause |
|---|---|
| 1. Electric door lock system does not work at all | a. Mechanical binding<br>b. Open or short circuit between the power source, relays, switches, and actuator<br>c. Defective switch |
| 2. One door lock does not operate | a. Defective relay<br>b. Improper relay ground<br>c. Mechanical binding<br>d. Open or short circuit in wiring<br>e. Defective actuator<br>f. Defective switch |

# Ford Motor Company

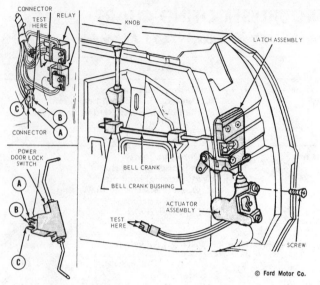

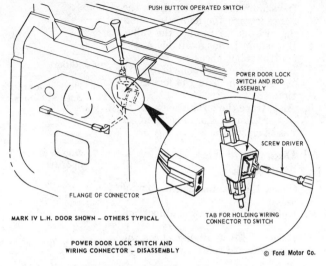

*Rear Door Lock Switch and Connector*

*Power Door Lock Actuator, Switch and Relay—Thunderbird and Continental Mark IV*

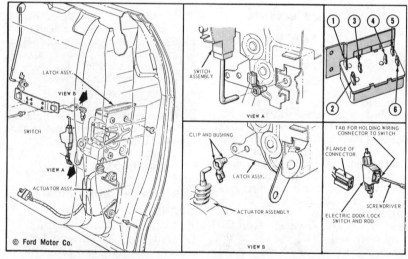

*Power Door Lock Actuator, Switch and Relay—Torino and Montego*

3. Connect the actuator link to the door latch.
4. Replace the water shield and door trim panel.

## Door Lock Control Switch— Torino, Montego, Cougar

### Removal

1. Remove the door trim panel and watershield.
2. Remove the button from the top of the rod.
3. Unplug the wires from the switch by unprying the locking tab.
4. Separate the push button rod from the latch.

### Installation

1. Connect the push button rod to the latch.
2. Connect the wires to the switch.

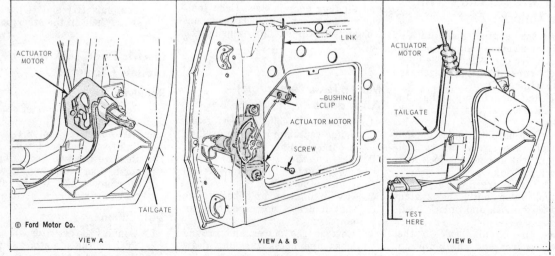

*Tailgate Actuator Motor Assembly*

# Ford Motor Company

3. Replace the button on top of the rod.
4. Replace the watershield and door trim panel.

## Door Lock Control Switch
## Ford, Mercury, Meteor, Lincoln Continental, Thunderbird and Continental Mark IV
### Removal

1. Remove the control panel from the armrest.
2. Release the connector attaching nuts.
3. Remove the switch from the control panel.

### Installation

1. Reverse the removal procedures.

## Tailgate Lock Actuator
## Ford, Mercury, Meteor, Torino and Montego—Station Wagons
### Removal

1. Remove the tailgate trim panel and watershield.
2. Remove the two screws or rivets retaining the lock actuator to the tailgate inner panel.
3. Disconnect the lock actuator rod from the latch.
4. Disconnect the wiring connector and remove the actuator.

### Installation

1. Reverse the removal procedure.

## Seat Back Lock Release
## 1970-75—All Models
### Description

When either front door is opened the switch located in the front door hinge pillar completes the circuit from the battery to a relay switch. The relay closes and sends power to two solenoids, one mounted on each seat back. The solenoid plunger releases the latch when it is energized. The seat back lock can be released manually by moving the seat back release handle.

### Relay—Location

1970-74 Lincoln Continental—on the brake pedal support bracket.
1970 Fairlane—on the left cowl inner side panel.
1970-71 Torino and Montego—on the left cowl inner side panel.
1970-71 Thunderbird and Continental Mark III—mounted along the circuit breaker panel on the right passenger side of the dash panel.

1971-73 Mustang and Cougar—above the glove box door opening.
1972-74 Thunderbird and Continental Mark III—on the brake pedal support bracket to the right of the fuse panel.
1970-74 Ford, Mercury, and Meteor—on the front part of the floor near the No. 1 crossmember.
1970-74 Torino and Montego, 1974 Cougar—on the brake pedal support bracket.

### Relay Test

1. Note the color of the three wires at each terminal and disconnect the relay connector.
2. Remove the relay.
3. Connect the positive post of the battery to the red (1970-71), pink-white (1972-74) wire terminal of the relay and the negative post to the relay case.
4. Connect a self-powered test light between the two other relay terminals.
5. If the test light does not light, replace the relay.

### Solenoid Test

1. Remove the solenoid.
2. Connect the battery power to the connector terminal.
3. Ground the case of the solenoid

assembly to the negative side of the battery.
4. If the solenoid does not operate replace the solenoid.

### Relay
#### Removal

1. Disconnect the negative battery cable.
2. Disconnect the wires from the relay noting the color and terminals.
3. On 1972-74 Lincoln Continentals disconnect the pigtail and the in line connector from the relay.
4. Remove the mounting screws.

#### Installation

1. Position the relay and install the mounting screws.
2. Connect the wires to the proper terminals.
3. Connect the battery terminal.

### Solenoid
### 1970-71—All Models
#### Removal

1. Remove the seat back trim cover far enough for access to the solenoid.
2. Disconnect the wires at the conconnector plug.
3. Disconnect the solenoid plunger from the latch pawl by removing the clip.

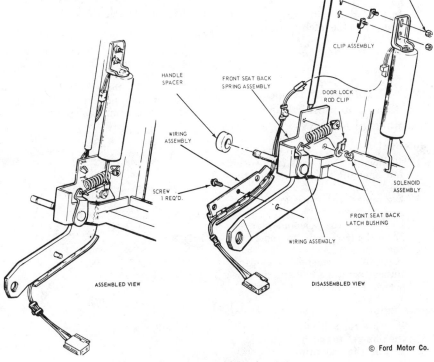

*Automatic Seat Back-Latch—1970*

© Ford Motor Co.

# Ford Motor Company

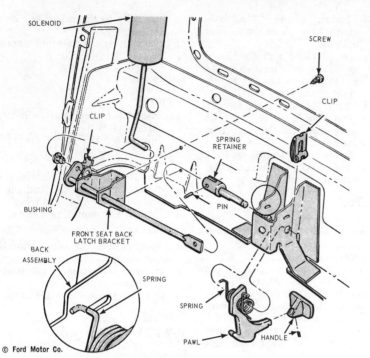

*Automatic Seat Back-Latch—Mustang, Cougar—1971-74*

4. Remove the solenoid mounting nuts or screws and disengage the solenoid from the latch pawl.

## Installation

1. Position the solenoid and engage the plunger to the latch pawl.
2. Install the mounting screws or nuts.
3. Install the clip securing the plunger to the latch pawl.
4. Connect the wires.
5. Install the trim panel.

## Solenoid
### 1972-73 All except Torino, Montego, Thunderbird and Continental Mark IV

### Removal

1. Remove the seat back trim cover far enough for access to the solenoid.
2. Disconnect the wires at the connector plug.
3. Disconnect the solenoid plunger from the latch pawl by removing the clip.
4. Remove the solenoid mounting nuts or screws and disengage the solenoid from the latch pawl.

### Installation

1. Position the solenoid and engage the plunger to the latch pawl.
2. Install the mounting screws or nuts.

3. Install the clip securing the plunger to the latch pawl.
4. Connect the wires.
5. Install the trim panel.

## Solenoid
### 1972-75—Torino, Montego, Cougar, Thunderbird and Continental Mark IV

### Removal

1. Cut the hog rings from the carpet to gain access to the solenoid assembly.
2. Remove the three shield retaining screws and disconnect the wires at the connector plug.

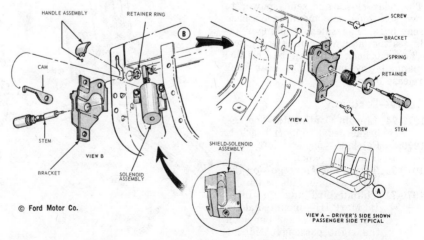

*Automatic Seat Back-Latch—Torino, Montego, Thunderbird, Continental Mark IV—1972-74*

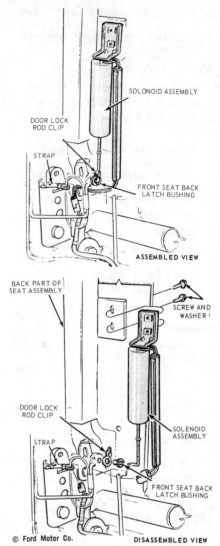

*Automatic Seat Back-Latch—Lincoln—1970-74*

3. Remove the solenoid retaining screws.

## Ford Motor Company

4. Loosen the two back pivot bracket assembly screws and slide the solenoid from the seat back latch handle stem.

### Installation

1. Slide the solenoid into the seat back latch handle stem and tighten the two back pivot bracket screws.

2. Install the solenoid retaining screws.
3. Connect the wires at the connector plug and install the three shield retaining screws.

## General Motors

## GM—VACUUM DOOR LOCKS ALL—1968-69

### Description

Vacuum is stored in a tank which is mounted in the engine compartment and is refilled by the engine manifold through a hose connection. A red hose comes from the tank and connects to a remote control valve located under the instrument panel. The remote control valve momentarily releases, through the red hose, vacuum to the entire system.

A selector valve is located in each front door trim assembly. When either selector valve is actuated upward, vacuum is supplied through white hoses which opens the ports to momentarily supply vacuum into the orange (unlock) hoses. When either selector valve is actuated downward, vacuum is supplied through the white hoses which opens the ports to momentarily supply vacuum into the yellow (lock) hoses. The orange and yellow hoses are connected to actuators, one in each door. The actuators are double acting vacuum diaphragms and are attached by screws to the door lock pillar below the lock on the front doors and at the front of the inner panel on the rear doors. Vacuum is supplied to either side of the diaphragm to lock or unlock the door. The diaphragm moves a rod that operates the locking lever of the lock to the desired position.

### Front Door Selector Valves

*NOTE: Before replacing the selector valve because of leakage, first tighten the screws on the back of the valve. Then recheck for leakage.*

### Removal

1. Remove the front door inner trim panel.
2. Disconnect the vacuum hoses from the selector valve.
   a. Note the color code of the hoses.
3. Separate the valve assembly from the door trim assembly.

## TROUBLESHOOTING CHART

### GM Vacuum Door Locks All 1968-69

| Condition | Possible Cause |
|---|---|
| 1. Inoperative system | a. Pinched vacuum hoses at the remote control valve<br>b. Disconnected vacuum hose at tank, control valve, or manifold<br>c. Leaking remote control diaphragm<br>d. Crossed hoses |
| 2. One door lock will not lock or unlock | a. Actuator hoses pinched or disconnected<br>b. Kinked or flattened hoses under front door carpet plate |
| 3. One door lock lags behind the other when locking or unlocking | a. Linkage binding<br>b. Improper lubrication of lock and linkage |
| 4. System will not hold vacuum for more than two days | a. Leaking remote valve<br>b. Leaking storage tank<br>c. Leaking door valves |

### Installation

1. Position the selector valve to the door trim assembly.
2. Attach the hoses to the proper connections.
3. Check the lock operation, then replace the inner trim panel.

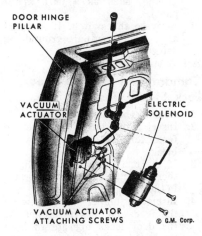

DOOR HINGE PILLAR

VACUUM ACTUATOR

ELECTRIC SOLENOID

VACUUM ACTUATOR ATTACHING SCREWS © G.M. Corp.

*Front Door Lock Vacuum Actuator*

### Door Lock Actuator

#### Removal

1. Raise the window all the way up.

2. Remove the door inner trim panel.
3. Remove the inner panel water deflector.
4. Disconnect the hoses from the actuator.
   a. Note the color code of the hoses.
5. On front doors, remove the actuator-to-door lock pillar attaching screws.
6. Disconnect the rod and remove the actuator through the access hole.
7. On rear doors, remove the actuator-to-door inner panel attaching screws.
8. Disconnect the rod and remove the actuator through the access hole.

#### Installation

1. Position the actuator inside the door panel and replace the attaching screws.
2. Connect the link rod to the actuator.
3. Attach the hoses to the proper connections.
4. Check the operation of the door locks.
5. Install the inner panel water deflector.

# General Motors

6. Replace the door inner trim panel.

## Remote Control Assembly

### Removal

1. From under the right side of the dash, remove the vacuum hoses noting the color codes of the hoses and the connectors.
2. Remove the remote control attaching screws.

### Installation

1. Position the remote control under the dash and install the attaching screws.
2. Replace the vacuum hoses to the proper connections.

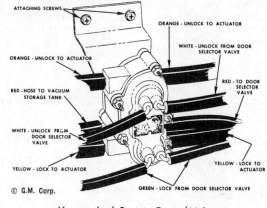

© G.M. Corp.

*Vacuum Lock Remote Control Valve*

## GM—ELECTRIC
## DOOR LOCKS 1969-75

### Description

All the doors lock and unlock electrically and are activated by control switches mounted on each door on all models except the Firebird and Camaro which have one instrument panel switch. When the switch is activated it completes the circuit to a solenoid located in each door. The solenoid is connected to the door latch mechanism by a link rod. When the plunger in the solenoid moves up and down it moves the link rod which in turn locks and unlocks the door. Each solenoid has an internal circuit breaker which, under extreme conditions, may require up to three minutes to reset.

In case of a power failure all the door lock buttons may be operated manually.

### Electrical Test Procedures

Before performing any extensive electrical testing procedures, make sure the battery is in good shape and there are no mechanical failures. Also, refer to the door lock wiring diagrams for the proper identification of wires.

### Open and Short Circuits

An open circuit is a circuit which is not completed because of a poor terminal contact or a broken wire. A short circuit occurs when the current is being grounded before it reaches the switch or solenoid.

### Improper Ground

Often, perfectly good operating units and parts are considered defective and are replaced because of a bad ground.

## TROUBLESHOOTING CHART

### GM—Electric Door Locks 1969-75

| Condition | Possible Cause |
|---|---|
| 1. Electric door lock system does not operate at all | a. Mechanical binding<br>b. Open or short circuit between the power source and the fuse block, switch, or solenoid<br>c. Bad fuse |
| 2. Electric door lock does not operate in both positions | a. Defective switch<br>b. Defective solenoid<br>c. Improper solenoid ground<br>d. Open or short circuit in wiring<br>e. Mechanical binding |

### Testing for Improper Ground

1. Attach one end of a jumper wire to the part or unit.
2. Connect the other end to a good ground, such as a bare metal panel.
3. Activate the switch. If it operates, the original ground is defective.

### All GM Models—Except Camaro and Firebird—Door Lock Switch Test

1. Remove the door trim panel.
2. Insert a test lamp lead into the feed terminal of the switch block.
3. If the test lamp does not light, there is an open or short circuit in the orange/black wire.
4. Insert a jumper wire between the feed and lock terminals. If the door locks operate in both the lock and unlock positions, the switch is defective and should be replaced.

### Front Door Lock Solenoid Test

1. Remove the door inside trim panel.

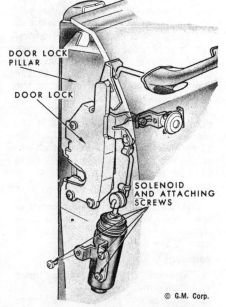

© G.M. Corp.

*Front Door Lock Electric Solonoid Installation*

2. Disconnect the wire connector at the solenoid.

# General Motors

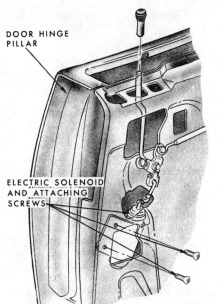

*Rear Door Lock Electric Solenoid Installation*

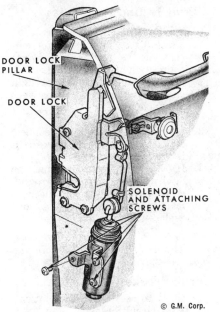

*Front Door Lock Electric Solenoid Installation*

3. Make sure that the solenoid is properly grounded.
4. Activate the switch and if the test lamp lights at both terminals, the solenoid should be replaced.
5. If the test lamp does not light at both terminals, there is an open or short circuit in the black or dark green wire.

## Rear Door Lock Solenoid Test

1. On all GM intermediate models, remove the center pillar trim panel.
2. Insert the test lamp lead into the center pillar (black and dark green) wire connector.
3. If the test lamp does not light, there is an open or short circuit in the black and dark green wires.
4. On all models, remove the rear door trim inner panel.
5. Disconnect the wire connector at the solenoid.
6. Make sure that the solenoid is properly grounded.
7. Activate the switch and if the test lamp lights at both terminals, the solenoid should be replaced.

## Electric Door Lock Solenoid Front Door

### Removal

1. Raise the door window all the way.
2. Remove the door inner trim panel.

3. Remove the door inner panel water deflector.
4. Disconnect the wiring harness from the solenoid.
5. Remove the door inner panel-to-solenoid attaching screws.
6. Remove the connecting rod link attaching clip.
7. Remove the solenoid through the access hole.

### Installation

1. Position the solenoid to the door inner panel and replace the attaching screws.
2. Connect the link and replace the attaching clip.
3. Connect the wiring harness to the solenoid.
4. Replace the door inner panel water deflector.
5. Replace the door inner trim panel.

## Camaro and Firebird

### Door Lock Switch Test

1. Insert a test light lead into the feed wire insulation at the base of the switch.
   a. If the test lamp does not light, there is an open or short circuit in the feed wire coming from the circuit breaker.
2. Disconnect the door lock switch wiring harness connector (black and dark green wires) from the door lock center wiring harness connector.

3. Insert a test lamp lead into the black wire-unlock connectors, and the dark green wire-lock connectors, of the switch wiring harness.
   a. If the test lamp does not light at both terminals, check for an open wire or replace the switch.

## Door Lock Solenoid

### Removal

1. Raise the door window all the way.
2. Remove the door inner trim panel.
3. Remove the door inner panel water deflector.
4. Disconnect the wiring harness from the solenoid.
5. Remove the solenoid-to-lock pillar attaching screws.
6. Disconnect the rod and remove the solenoid through the access hole.

### Installation

1. Place the solenoid inside the lock pillar and replace the attaching screws.
2. Connect the link rod.
3. Connect the wiring harness to the solenoid.
4. Replace the door inner panel water deflector.
5. Replace the door inner trim panel.

## Door Lock Center Harness Test

1. Remove the left shroud side finishing panel.
2. Disconnect the door lock center harness from the door lock solenoid harness.
3. Connect a jumper wire from the circuit breaker output at the fuse block to the door lock center harness feed connector.
4. Insert a test lamp into the left shroud side connector opposite the feed terminal.
   a. If the test lamp does not light, check for an open or short circuit.
   b. If a short circuit exists, a click will be heard in the circuit breaker.

## Door Lock Solenoid and Solenoid Harness Test

1. Remove the door inner trim panel.
2. Disconnect the solenoid harness from the solenoid.
3. Connect a jumper wire from the circuit breaker output at the

# General Motors

fuse block to one of the solenoid terminals, then to the other.

4. If the solenoid operates, there is an open or short circuit in the solenoid harness.

5. If the solenoid does not operate and is properly grounded, replace the solenoid.

## GM—Electric Seat Back Lock Release

### Description

The electric seat back lock release is optional on all two door models that are equipped with electric door locks.

The system uses two insulated "flow through" type jamb switches which are attached to the front body hinge pillar on each side of the car.

When the door is opened the switch completes the circuit from the power source to an internally grounded solenoid on each seat back and releases the seat back lock.

When the door is closed the solenoid de-energizes and allows the seat back lock to return to the lock position. The seat back locks also have a manual override release.

## Circuit Testing Procedures
### Solenoid Test

1. Using a test lamp check for current at the feed (black wire) connection on the solenoid.

2. If the test lamp does not light check for a short circuit between the solenoid and the power source.

3. If the test lamp lights connect an extra ground wire to see if it is grounded properly.

4. If the test lamp continues to light and the solenoid is grounded properly and has no mechanical binds but still does not work replace the solenoid.

*NOTE: On Strato-Seats the solenoid is part of the lock assembly and must be replaced as a unit.*

### Circuit Breaker Test

1. Check to see if there is current to the circuit breaker.
   a. Connect a test lamp to the input side of the circuit breaker (at the left shroud).
   b. Ground the other lead.
   c. If the test lamp does not light there is an open or short circuit in the feed wire.

2. Check the circuit breaker.
   a. Connect a test lamp to the output side of the circuit breaker.
   b. Ground the other lead.
   c. If the test lamp does not light the circuit breaker is defective.

### Jamb Switch Test

1. Remove the jamb switch from the pillar.
2. Touch a test lamp to the orange wire terminal.
   a. If the test lamp does not light check for an open circuit.
3. Connect a jumper wire between the orange and yellow wires.
   a. If the seat back lock release operates replace the jamb switch.

### Jamb Switch Adjustment

When installing a new jamb switch the adjustment is automatically made by slowly closing the door which positions the collar correctly into the retainer.

*NOTE: After the initial adjustment no outward adjustment of the jamb switch is possible.*

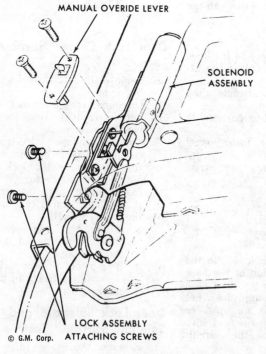

Front Seat Back Electrically Operated Lock

MANUAL OVERIDE LEVER
SOLENOID ASSEMBLY
© G.M. Corp.
LOCK ASSEMBLY ATTACHING SCREWS

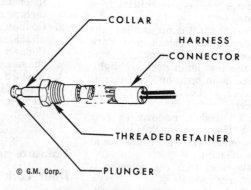

Flow Through Type Jamb Switch

COLLAR
HARNESS CONNECTOR
THREADED RETAINER
PLUNGER
© G.M. Corp.

# General Motors

### ELECTRIC SEAT BACK LOCK DIAGNOSIS CHART

| CONDITION | APPARENT CAUSE | CORRECTION |
|---|---|---|
| 1. Seat back lock does not lock when doors are closed. | 1. Current at actuator solenoid does not cut off - jamb switch remains open.<br><br>2. Seat back relay contacts sticking.<br><br>3. Seat back does not return to upright position far enough to trip lock into locked position. Check for excessive trim build-up; also check inboard bumper clearance. | 1. Refer to Electrical Checking Procedure - where required, install new jamb switch.<br><br>2. Refer to Electrical Checking Procedure - where required, install new relay.<br><br>3. Specified inboard bumper clearance 1/16″ - where required install thinner bumper. Locking effort applied rearward at upper outboard corner of seat back is 0-10 lbs. maximum. |
| 2. Seat back lock will not unlock when door(s) are open. | 1. No current at actuator solenoid - blown fuse, defective jamb switch or seat back relay, or short in wiring.<br><br>2. Bind in lock or lock linkage. | 1. Refer to Electrical Checking Procedure.<br><br>2. Locate and eliminate bind or, where required, install new lock assembly. |
| 3. Seat back lock unlocks but solenoid flutters or solenoid circuit breaker cuts in and out. | 1. Bind in lock or linkage which does not allow solenoid plunger to completely deactivate pull in coil.<br><br>2. Actuator solenoid plunger is not completely deactivating pull in coil with no bind present in lock or linkage. Lock operates okay manually. | 1. Locate bind or interference and eliminate, or where required install new lock.<br><br>2. Check solenoid as described under "Electrical Checking Procedure" - Check if solenoid is adjusted properly on lock - see "Seat Back Electric Lock Solenoid and Support Assembly" - Step 3 and 4. Where required replace solenoid assembly. |

## Chrysler Corporation

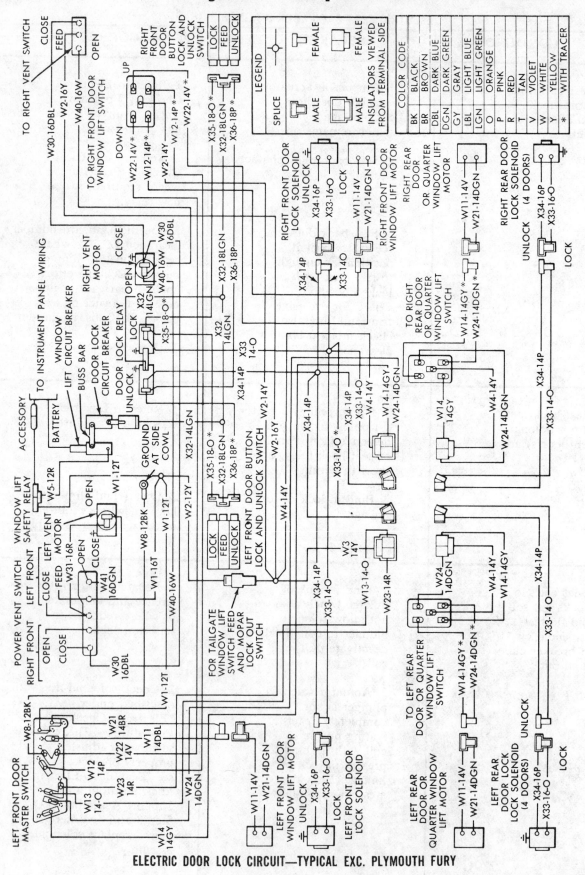

**ELECTRIC DOOR LOCK CIRCUIT—TYPICAL EXC. PLYMOUTH FURY**

# Chrysler Corporation

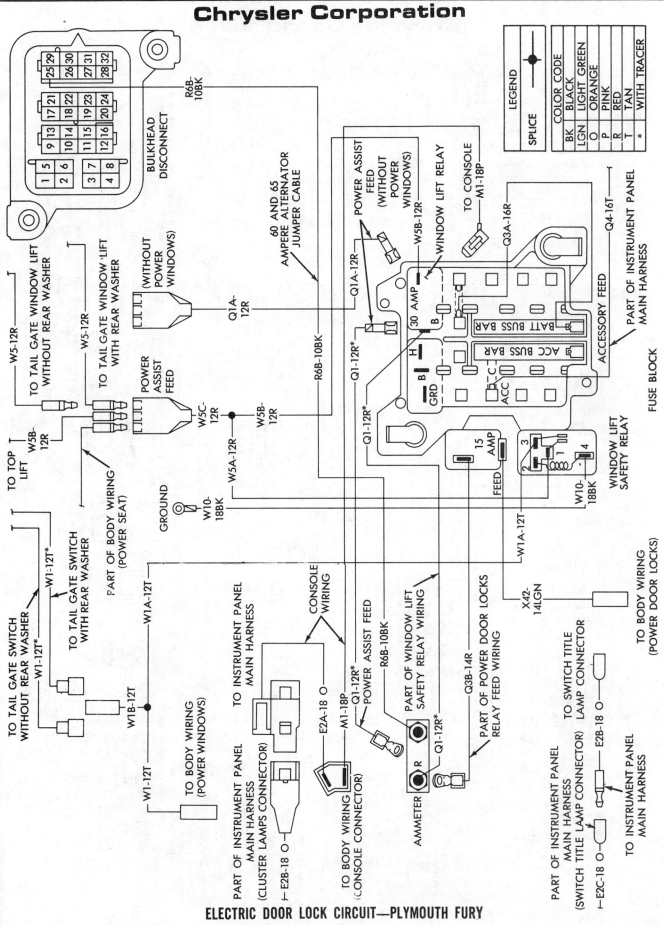

ELECTRIC DOOR LOCK CIRCUIT—PLYMOUTH FURY

461

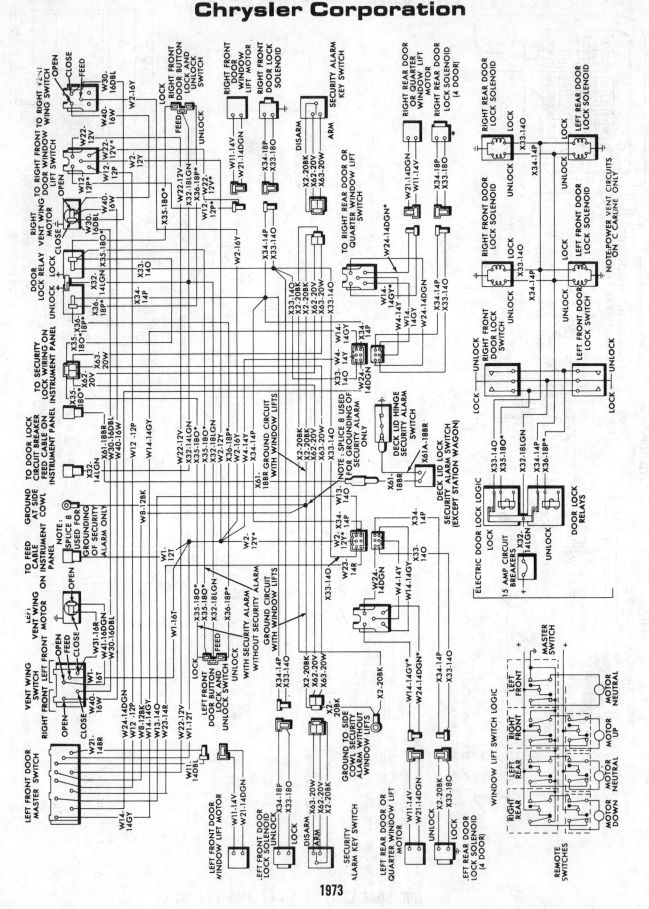

1973

## Chrysler Corporation

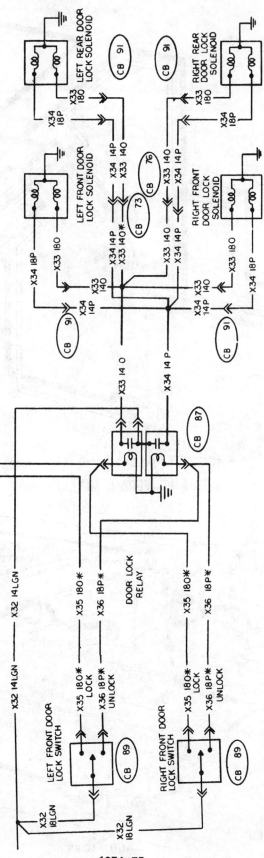

**1974-75**

## Ford Motor Company

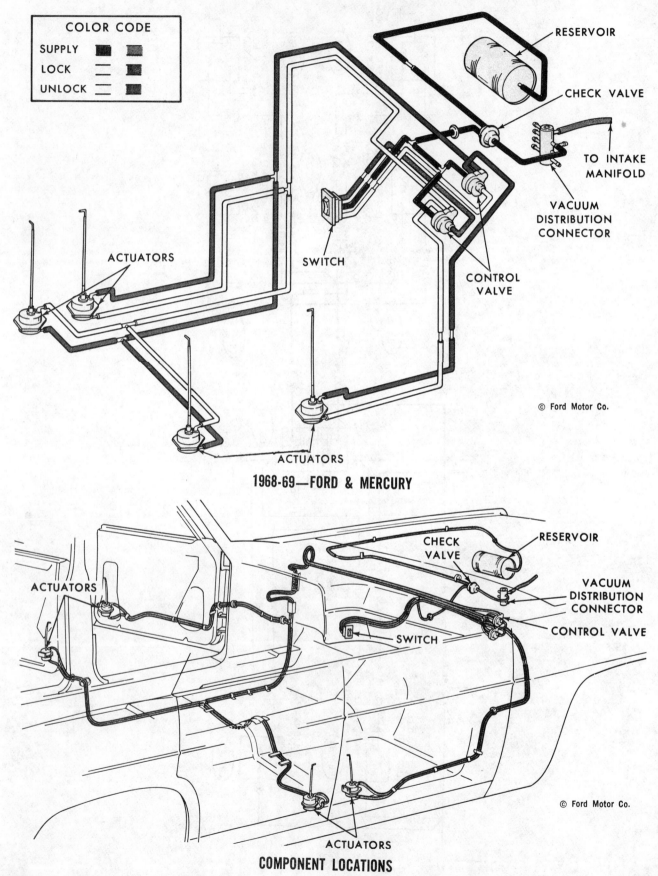

COLOR CODE

SUPPLY

LOCK

UNLOCK

RESERVOIR

CHECK VALVE

TO INTAKE MANIFOLD

VACUUM DISTRIBUTION CONNECTOR

CONTROL VALVE

SWITCH

ACTUATORS

ACTUATORS

© Ford Motor Co.

**1968-69—FORD & MERCURY**

CHECK VALVE

RESERVOIR

VACUUM DISTRIBUTION CONNECTOR

CONTROL VALVE

ACTUATORS

SWITCH

ACTUATORS

© Ford Motor Co.

**COMPONENT LOCATIONS**

## Ford Motor Company

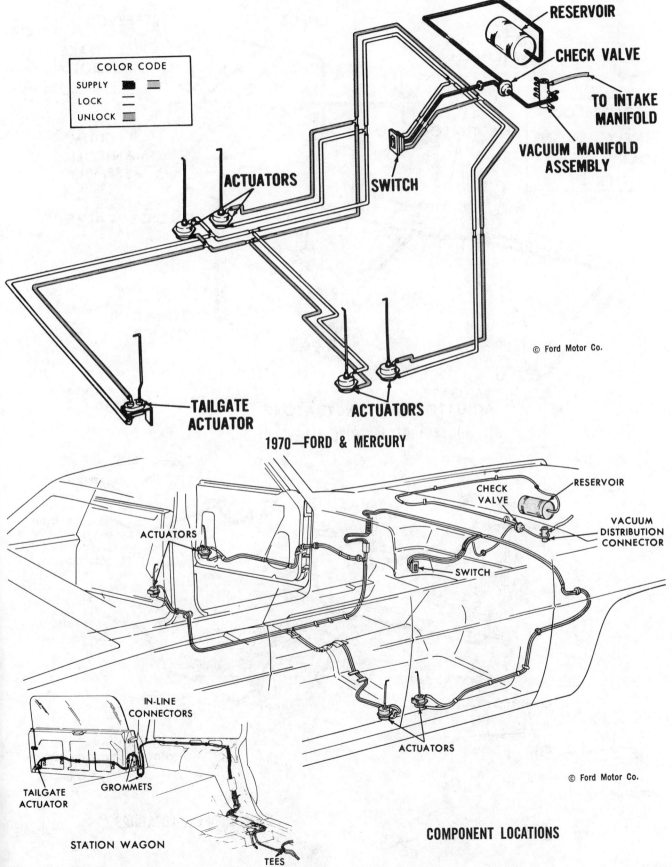

COLOR CODE

SUPPLY

LOCK

UNLOCK

RESERVOIR

CHECK VALVE

TO INTAKE MANIFOLD

VACUUM MANIFOLD ASSEMBLY

ACTUATORS

SWITCH

© Ford Motor Co.

TAILGATE ACTUATOR

ACTUATORS

1970—FORD & MERCURY

CHECK VALVE

RESERVOIR

VACUUM DISTRIBUTION CONNECTOR

ACTUATORS

SWITCH

IN-LINE CONNECTORS

ACTUATORS

TAILGATE ACTUATOR

GROMMETS

© Ford Motor Co.

STATION WAGON

TEES

**COMPONENT LOCATIONS**

# Ford Motor Company

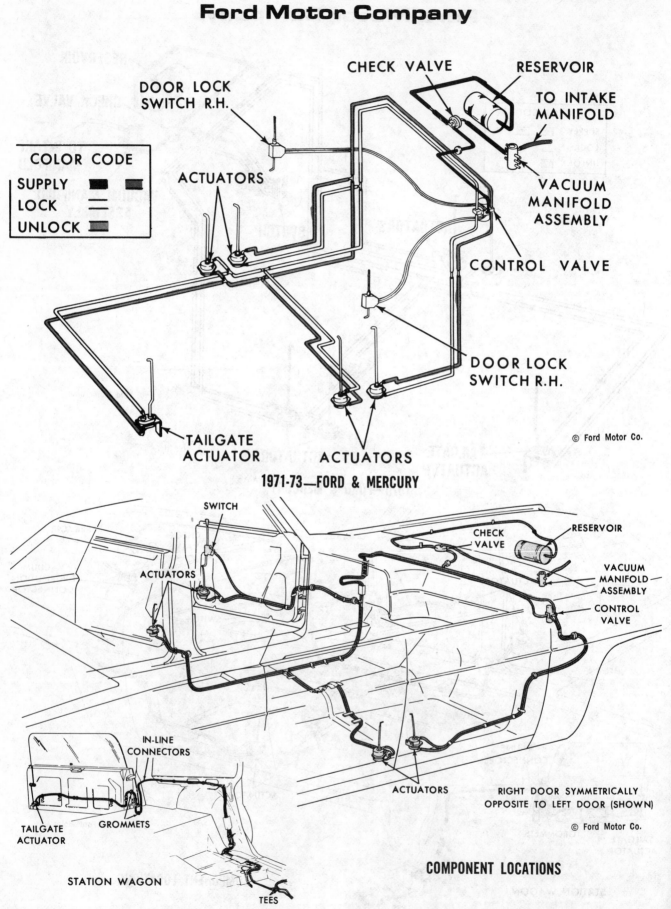

CHECK VALVE

RESERVOIR

TO INTAKE MANIFOLD

DOOR LOCK SWITCH R.H.

COLOR CODE
SUPPLY
LOCK
UNLOCK

ACTUATORS

VACUUM MANIFOLD ASSEMBLY

CONTROL VALVE

DOOR LOCK SWITCH R.H.

© Ford Motor Co.

TAILGATE ACTUATOR

ACTUATORS

**1971-73—FORD & MERCURY**

SWITCH

CHECK VALVE

RESERVOIR

ACTUATORS

VACUUM MANIFOLD ASSEMBLY

CONTROL VALVE

IN-LINE CONNECTORS

ACTUATORS

RIGHT DOOR SYMMETRICALLY OPPOSITE TO LEFT DOOR (SHOWN)

TAILGATE ACTUATOR

GROMMETS

© Ford Motor Co.

STATION WAGON

TEES

**COMPONENT LOCATIONS**

# Ford Motor Company

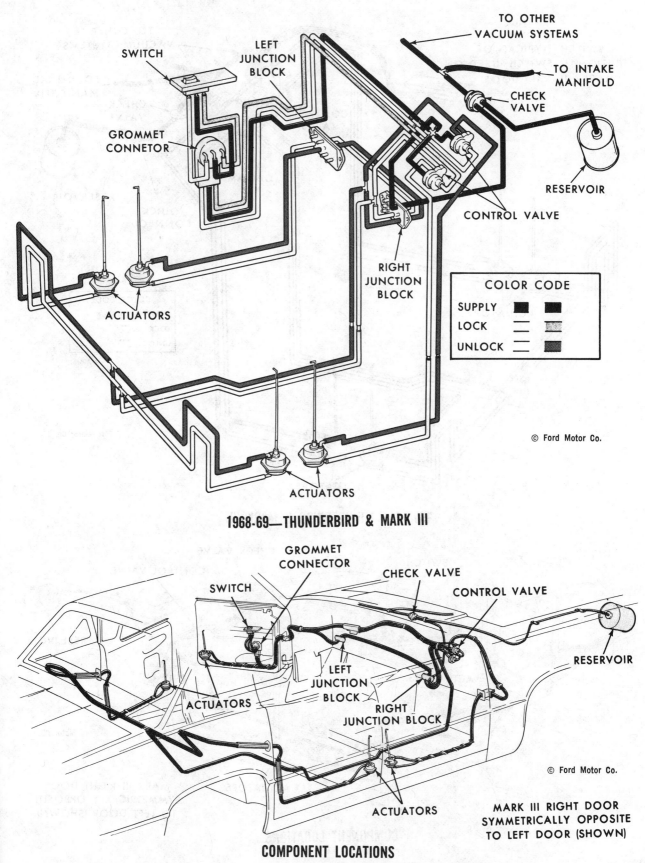

**1968-69—THUNDERBIRD & MARK III**

**COMPONENT LOCATIONS**

# Ford Motor Company

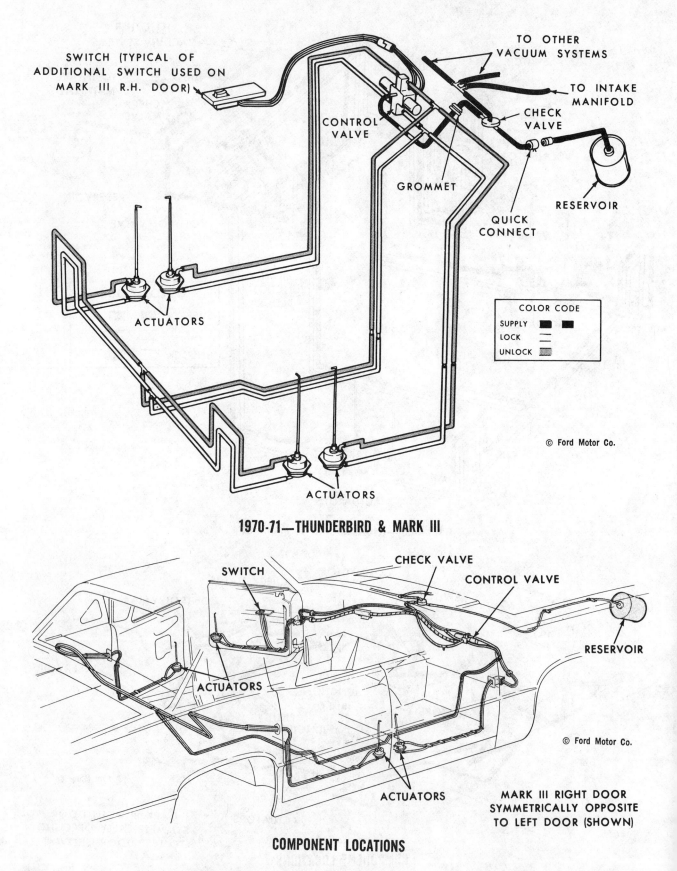

SWITCH (TYPICAL OF ADDITIONAL SWITCH USED ON MARK III R.H. DOOR)

TO OTHER VACUUM SYSTEMS

TO INTAKE MANIFOLD

CONTROL VALVE

CHECK VALVE

GROMMET

RESERVOIR

QUICK CONNECT

ACTUATORS

COLOR CODE

SUPPLY

LOCK

UNLOCK

© Ford Motor Co.

ACTUATORS

**1970-71—THUNDERBIRD & MARK III**

SWITCH

CHECK VALVE

CONTROL VALVE

RESERVOIR

ACTUATORS

© Ford Motor Co.

ACTUATORS

MARK III RIGHT DOOR SYMMETRICALLY OPPOSITE TO LEFT DOOR (SHOWN)

**COMPONENT LOCATIONS**

# Ford Motor Company

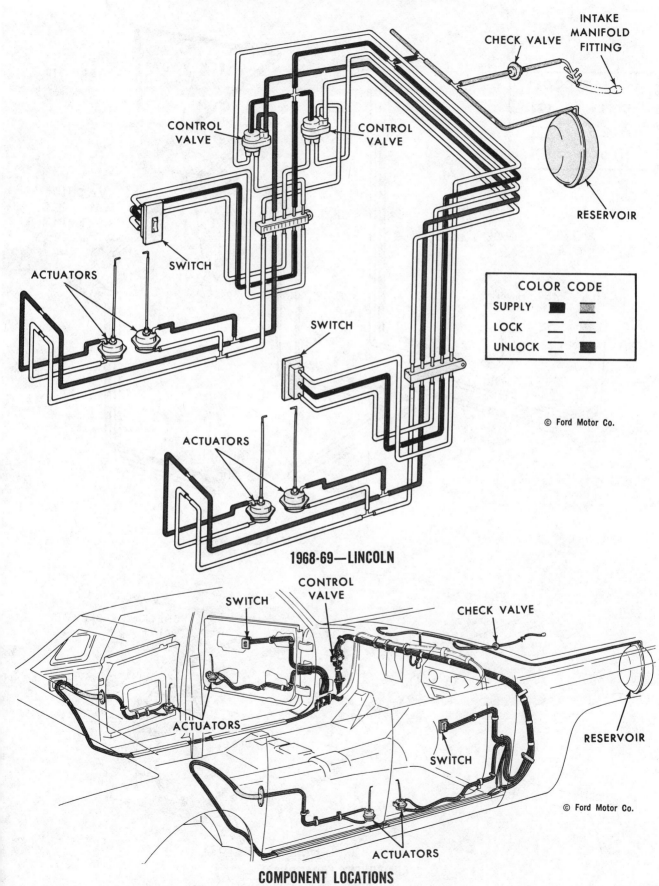

1968-69—LINCOLN

**COMPONENT LOCATIONS**

# Ford Motor Company

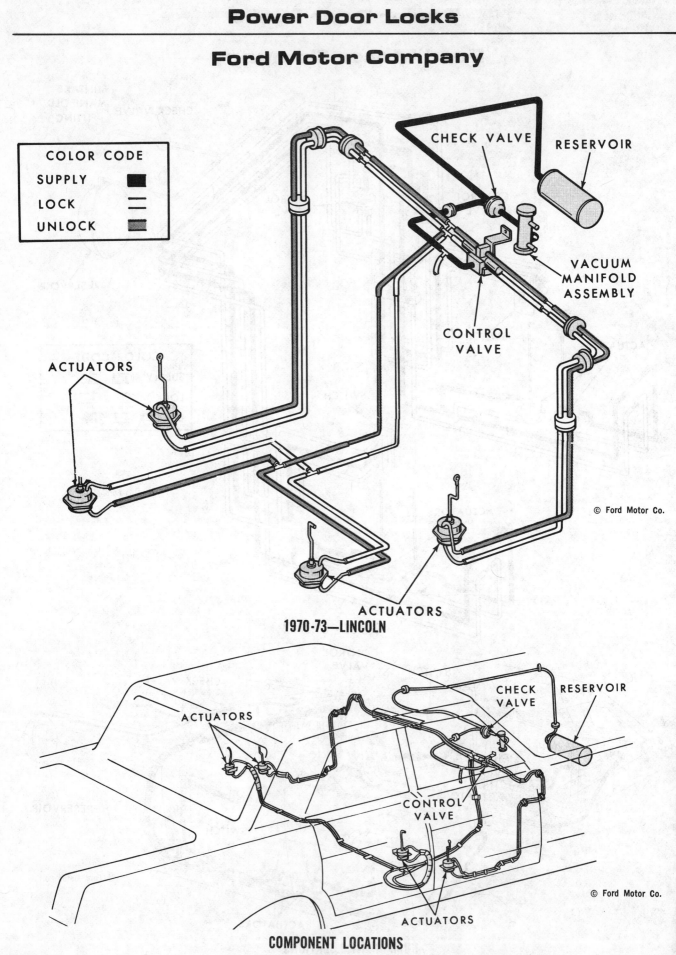

COLOR CODE
SUPPLY
LOCK
UNLOCK

CHECK VALVE

RESERVOIR

VACUUM
MANIFOLD
ASSEMBLY

CONTROL
VALVE

ACTUATORS

ACTUATORS

© Ford Motor Co.

1970-73—LINCOLN

CHECK
VALVE

RESERVOIR

ACTUATORS

CONTROL
VALVE

ACTUATORS

© Ford Motor Co.

COMPONENT LOCATIONS

# Ford Motor Company

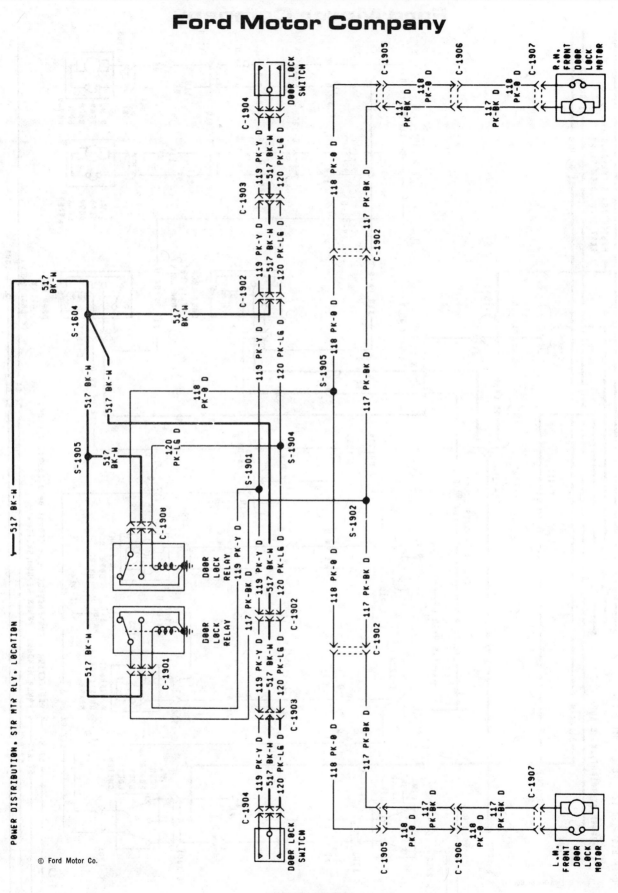

**1974-75 COUGAR**

© Ford Motor Co.

## Ford Motor Company

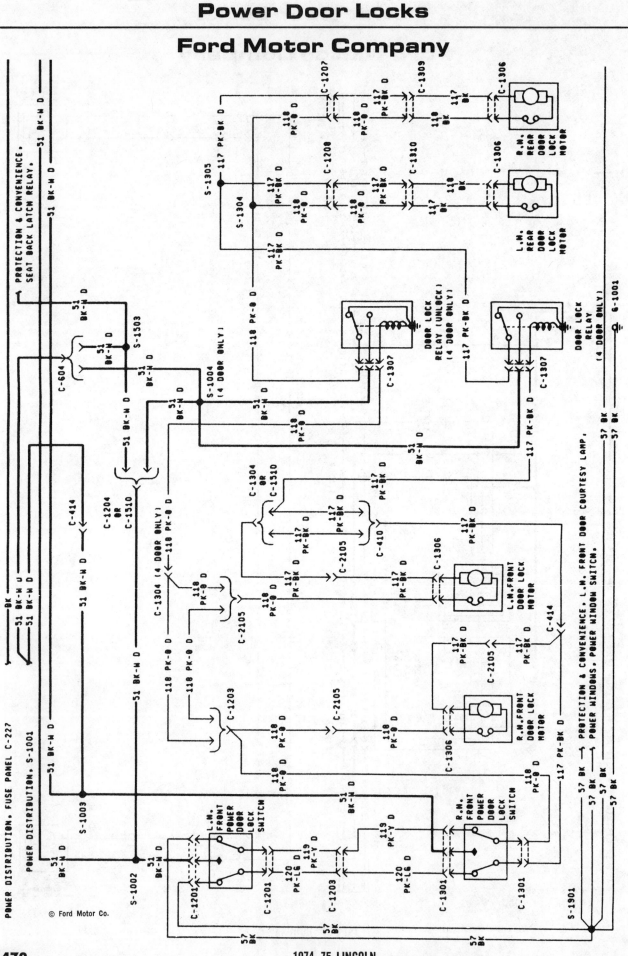

© Ford Motor Co.

## Ford Motor Company

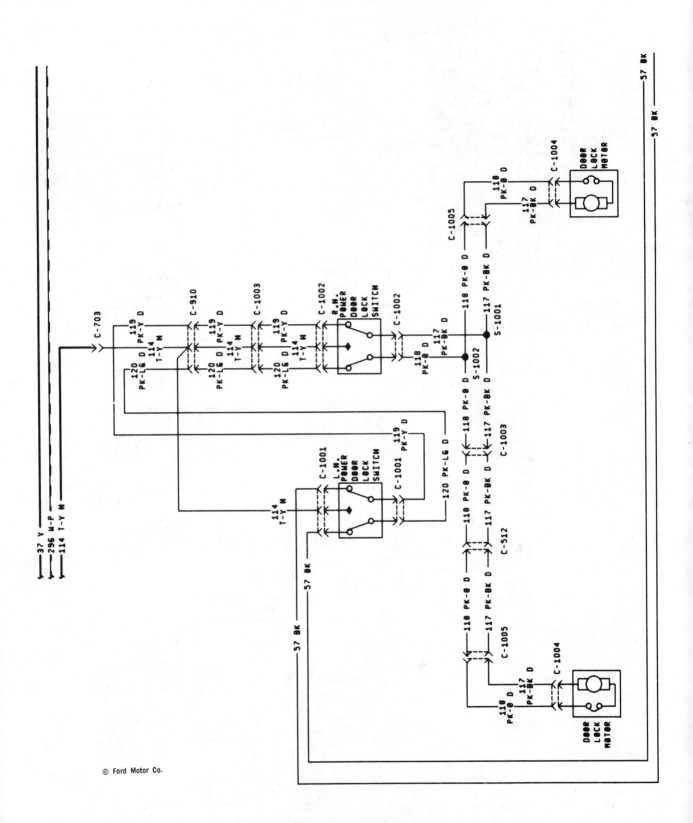

© Ford Motor Co.

**1974-75 THUNDERBIRD — MARK IV**

# Ford Motor Company

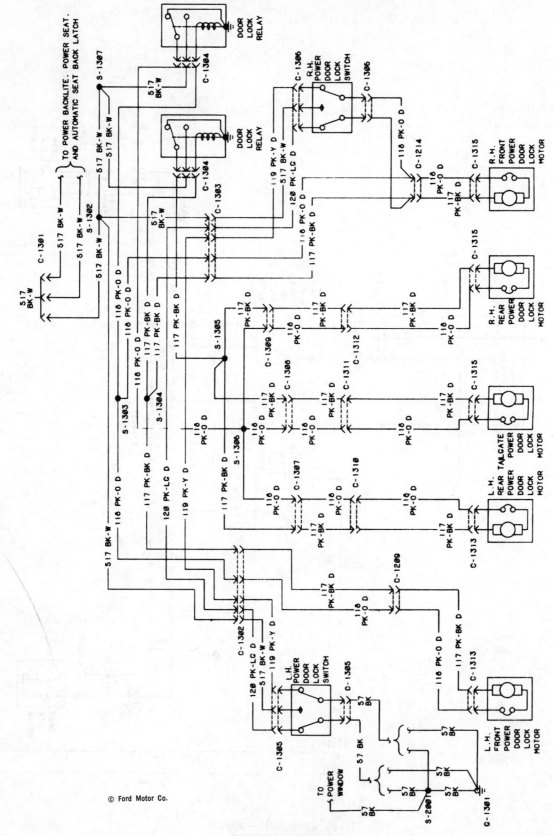

© Ford Motor Co.

**1974 Ford — Mercury**

## Ford Motor Company

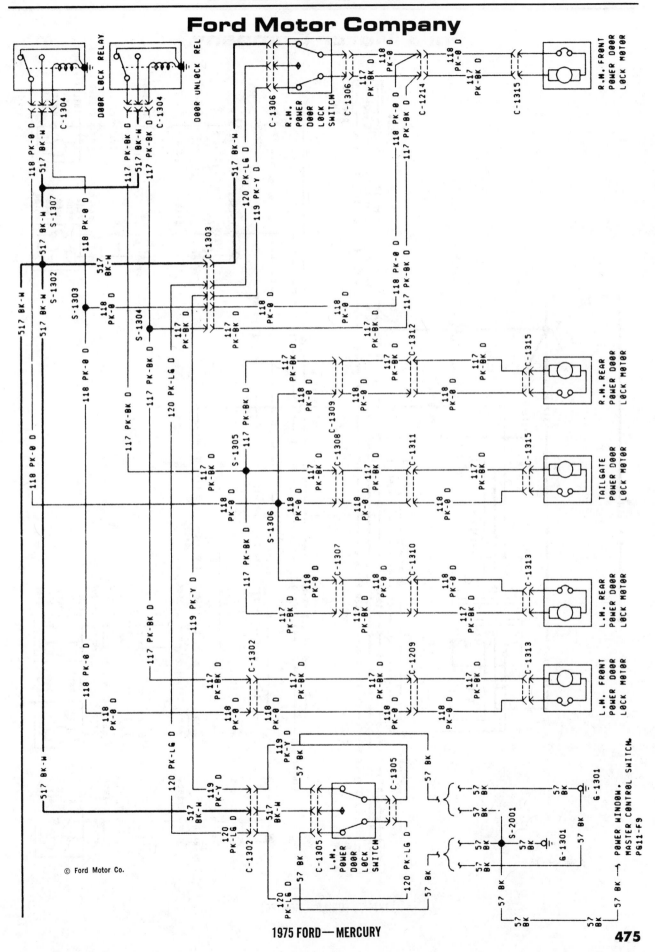

© Ford Motor Co.

## Ford Motor Company

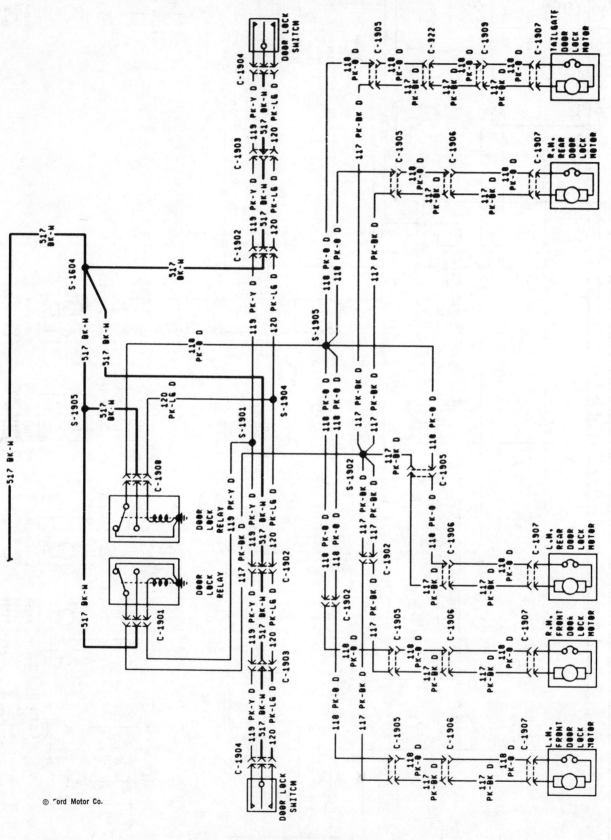

© Ford Motor Co.

**1974-75 TORINO—MONTEGO**

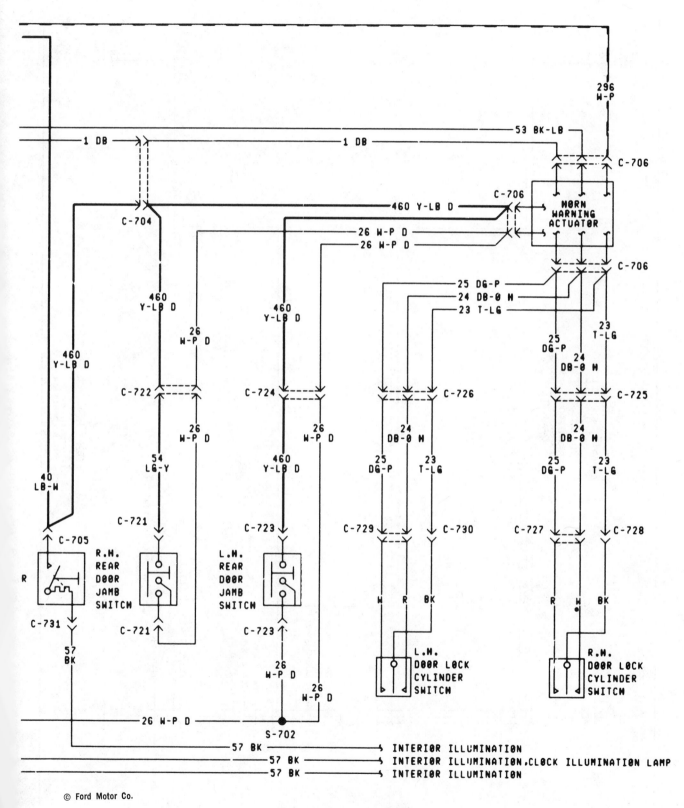

1975 GRANADA — MONARCH

© Ford Motor Co.

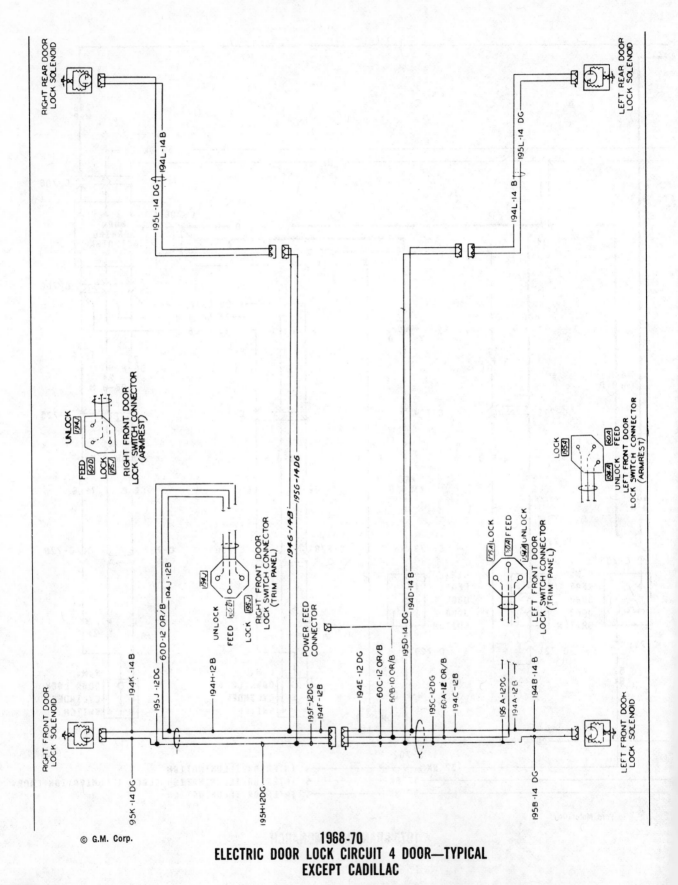

© G.M. Corp.

**1968-70**
**ELECTRIC DOOR LOCK CIRCUIT 4 DOOR—TYPICAL**
**EXCEPT CADILLAC**

# General Motors

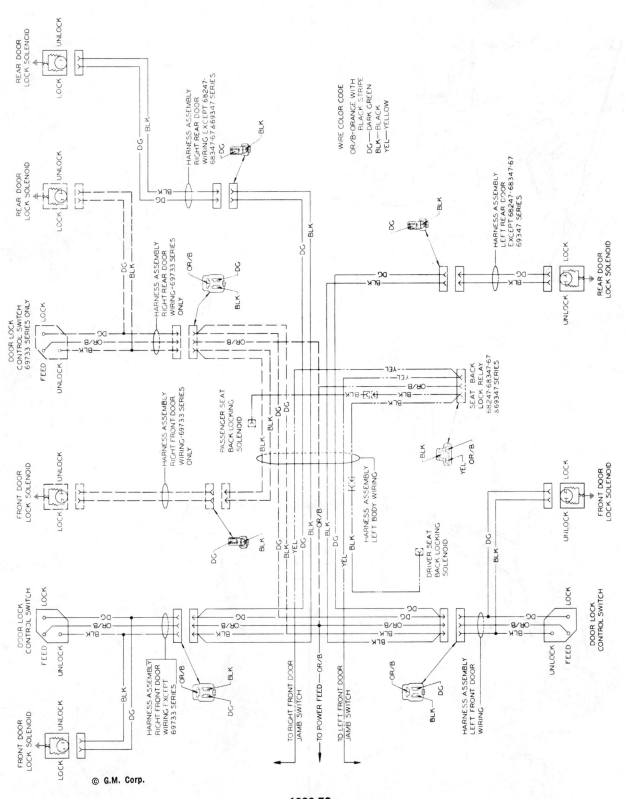

© G.M. Corp.

**1968-70
ELECTRIC DOOR LOCK CIRCUIT—CADILLAC**

## General Motors

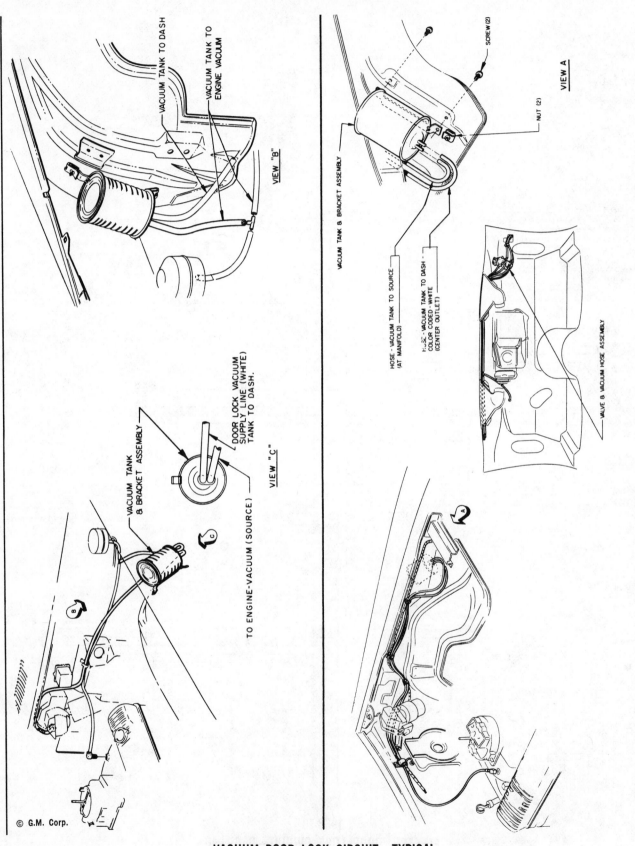

**VACUUM DOOR LOCK CIRCUIT—TYPICAL**

© G.M. Corp.

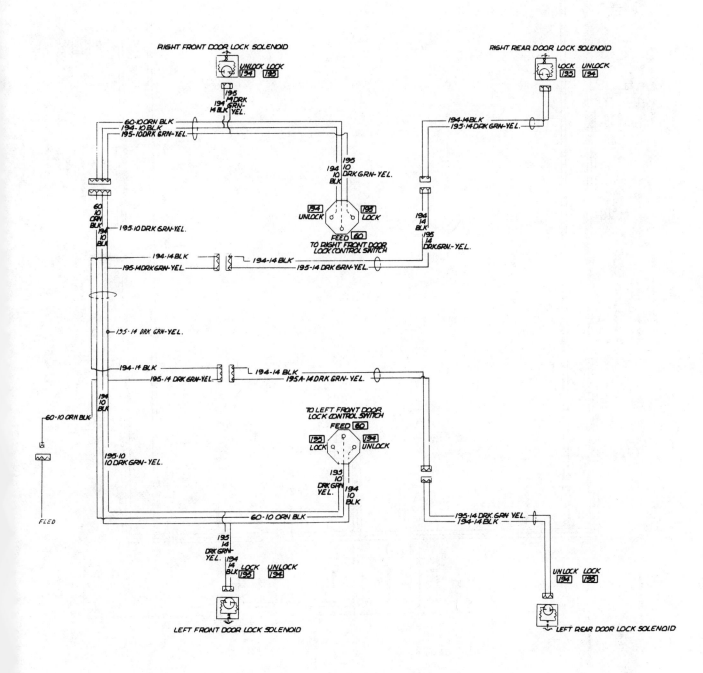

**1971—BUICK SPECIAL    1971—CHEVELLE    1971—OLDSMOBILE F-85    1971—TEMPEST**

## General Motors

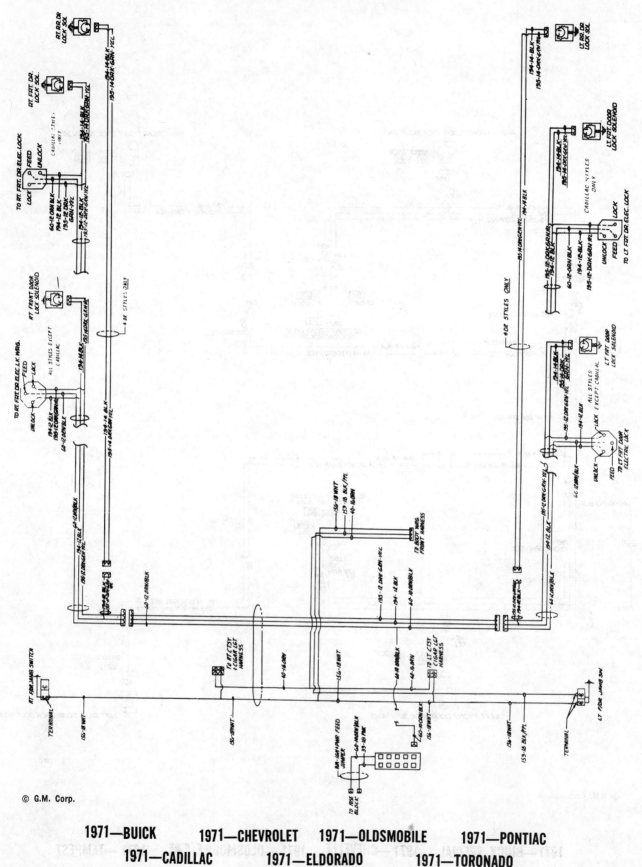

**1971—BUICK      1971—CHEVROLET      1971—OLDSMOBILE      1971—PONTIAC**

**1971—CADILLAC      1971—ELDORADO      1971—TORONADO**

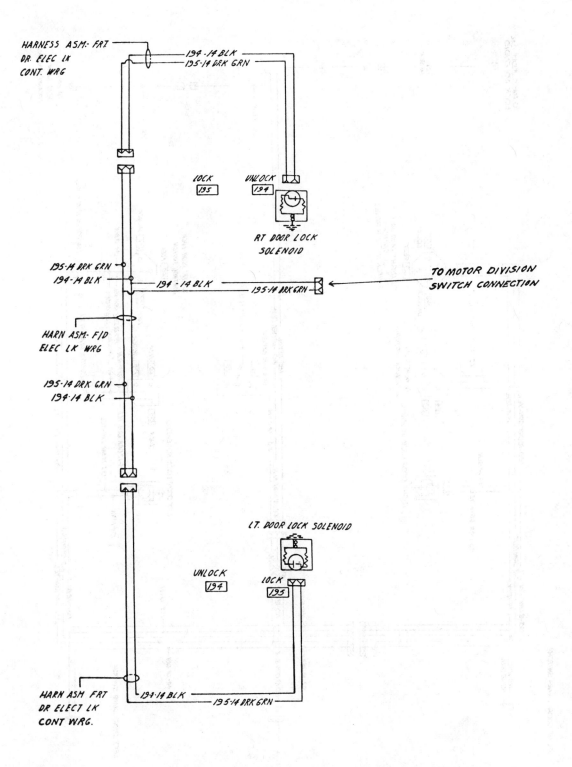

HARNESS ASM: FRT
DR. ELEC LK
CONT. WRG

194-14 BLK
195-14 DRK GRN

LOCK
195

UNLOCK
194

RT DOOR LOCK
SOLENOID

195-14 DRK GRN
194-14 BLK

194-14 BLK

195-14 DRK GRN

TO MOTOR DIVISION
SWITCH CONNECTION

HARN ASM: F/D
ELEC LK WRG

195-14 DRK GRN
194-14 BLK

LT. DOOR LOCK SOLENOID

UNLOCK
194

LOCK
195

HARN ASM FRT
DR ELECT LK
CONT WRG.

194-14 BLK

195-14 DRK GRN

**1971—FIREBIRD**

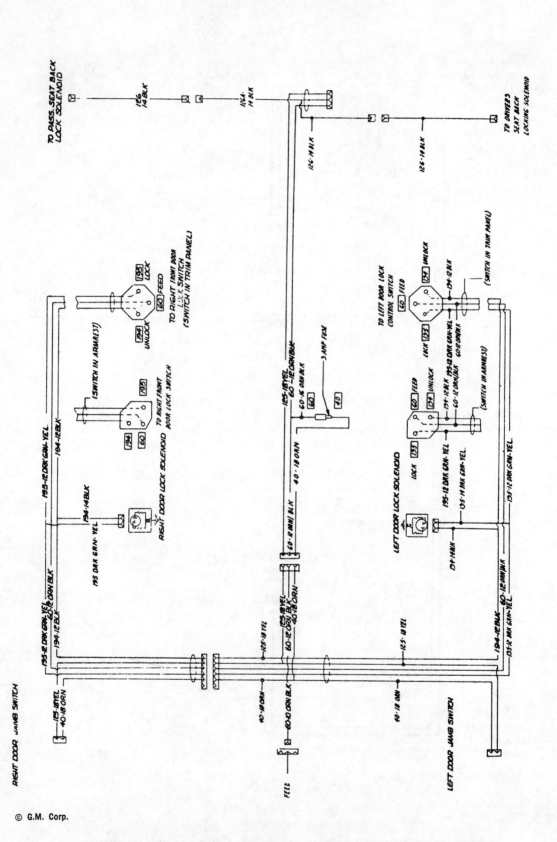

**1972—BUICK SPECIAL—1972—CHEVELLE—OLDSMOBILE F85—1972—TEMPEST**

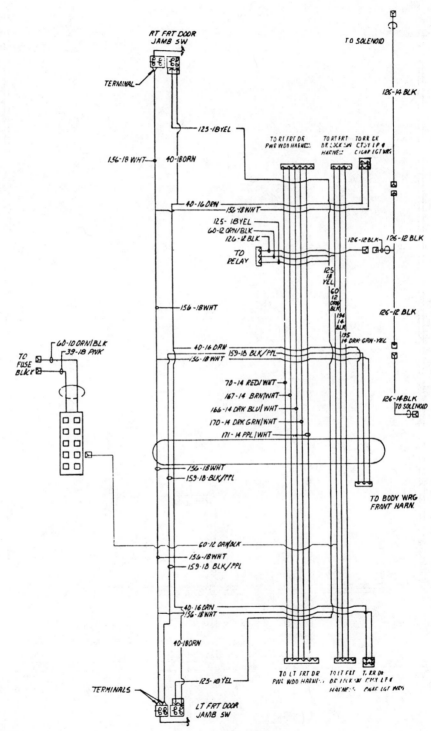

**1972—BUICK—1972—CADILLAC 1972—CHEVROLET—1972—OLDSMOBILE 1972—PONTIAC**

## General Motors

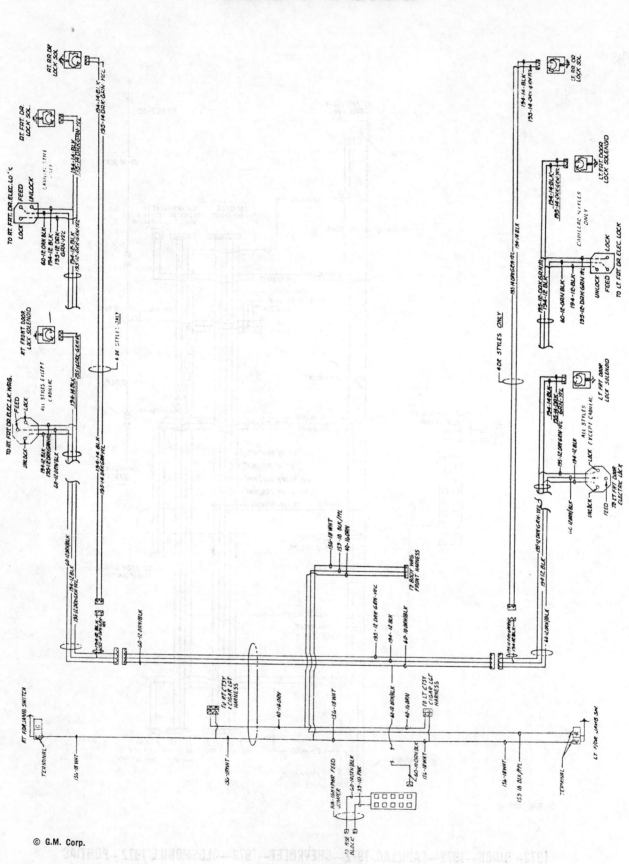

© G.M. Corp.

**1973—EXC. FIREBIRD**

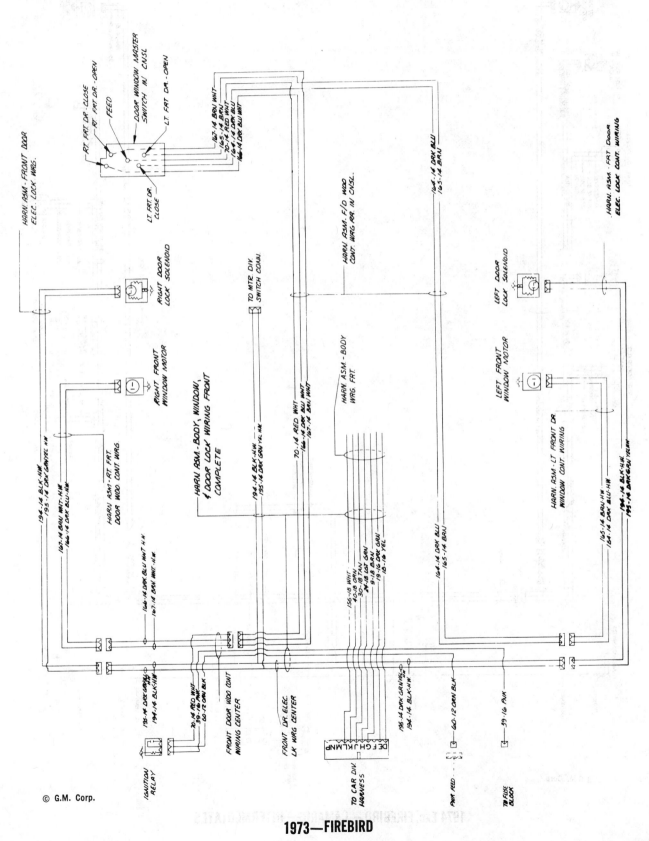

**1973—FIREBIRD**

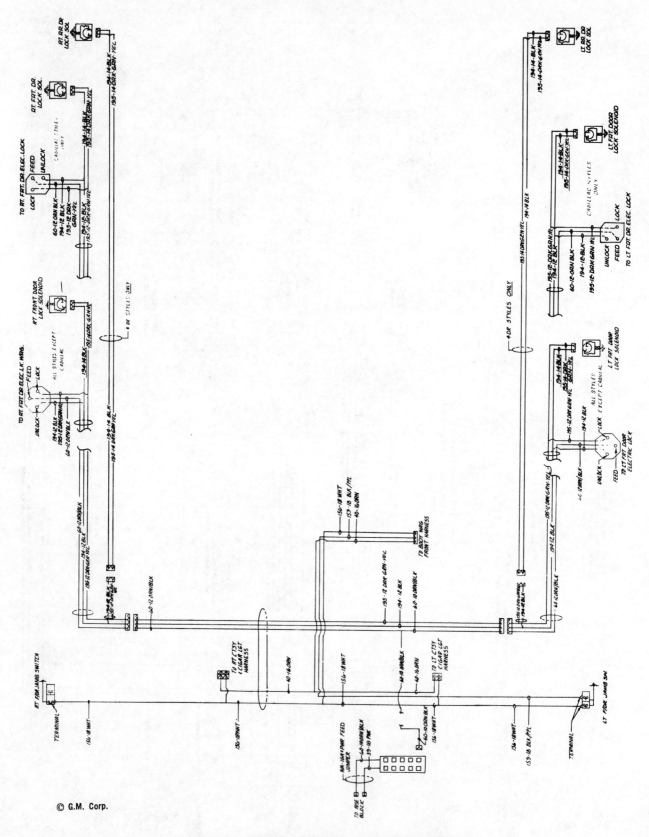

**1974 Exc. FIREBIRD—CAMARO—INTERMEDIATES**

© G.M. Corp.

## General Motors

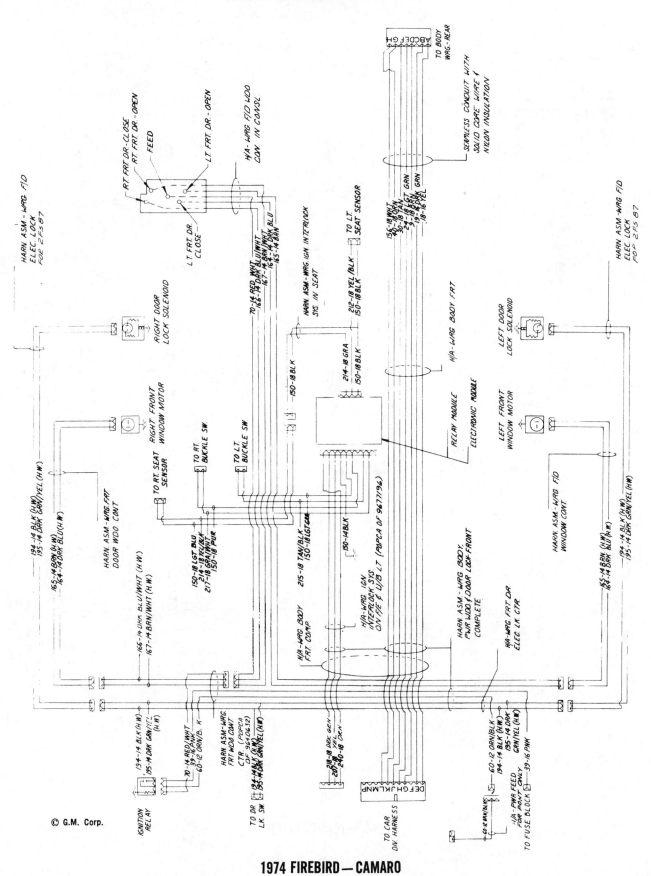

© G.M. Corp.

**1974 FIREBIRD—CAMARO**

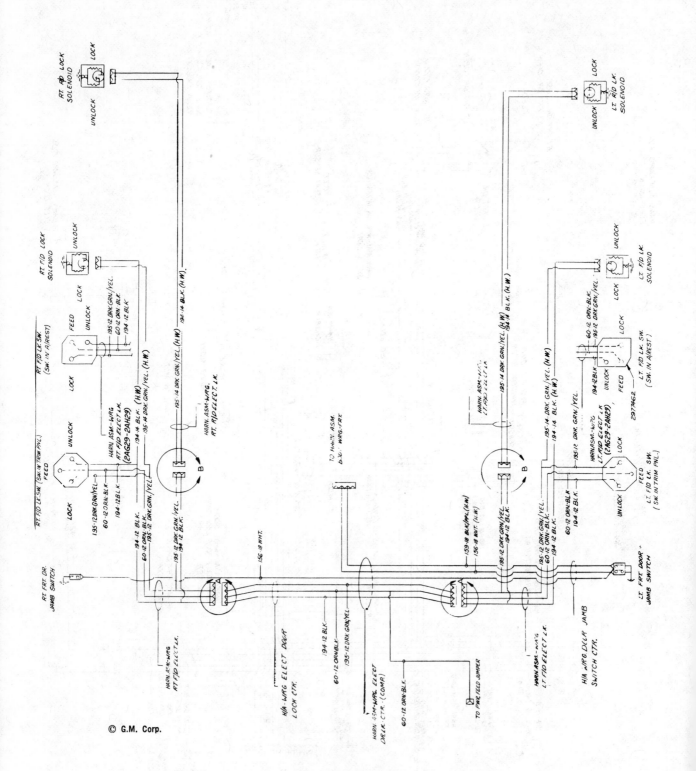

© G.M. Corp.

**1974 INTERMEDIATES**

## General Motors

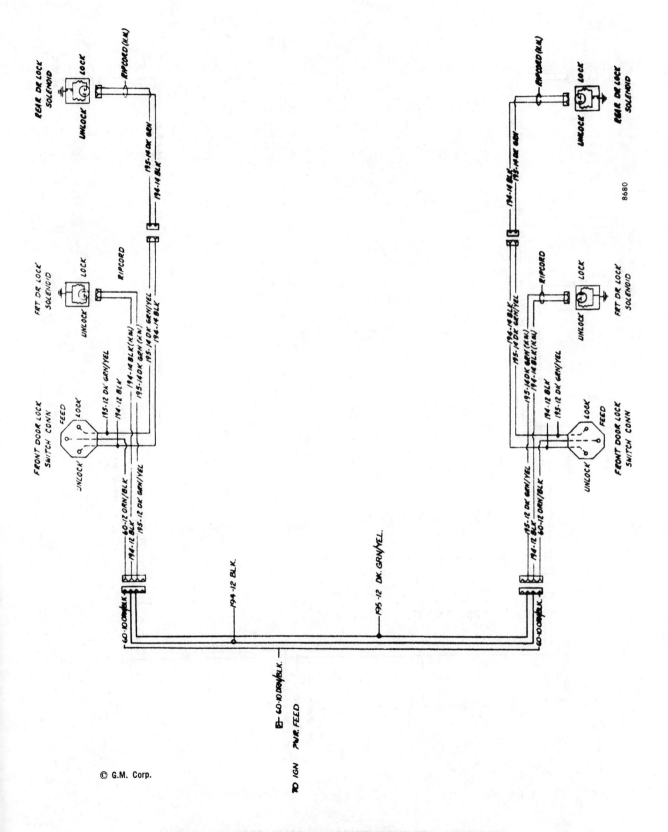

**1975 Exc. FIREBIRD — CAMARO — INTERMEDIATES — COMPACTS**

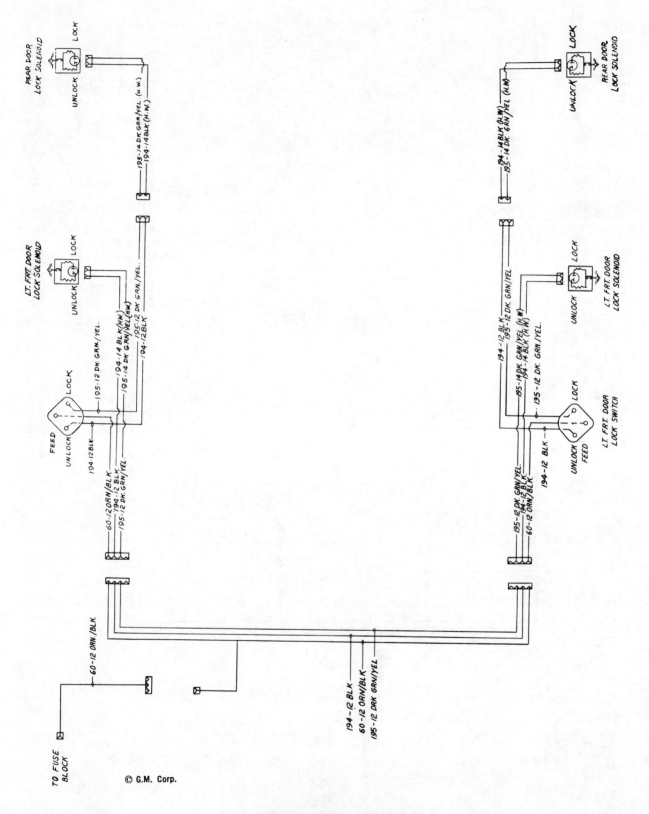

© G.M. Corp.

**1975 INTERMEDIATES — COMPACTS**

492

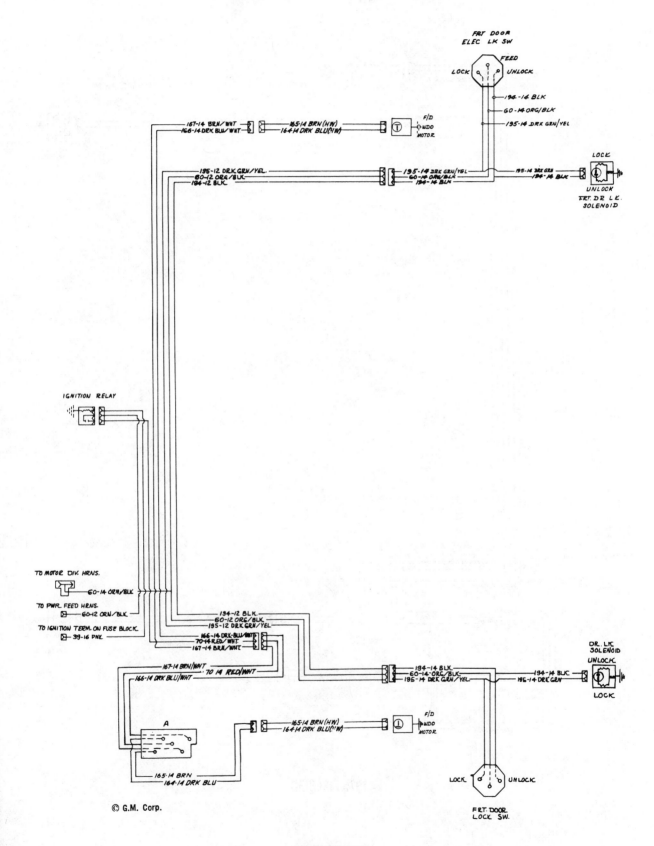

© G.M. Corp.

## 1975 Camaro

# Power Door Locks

## General Motors

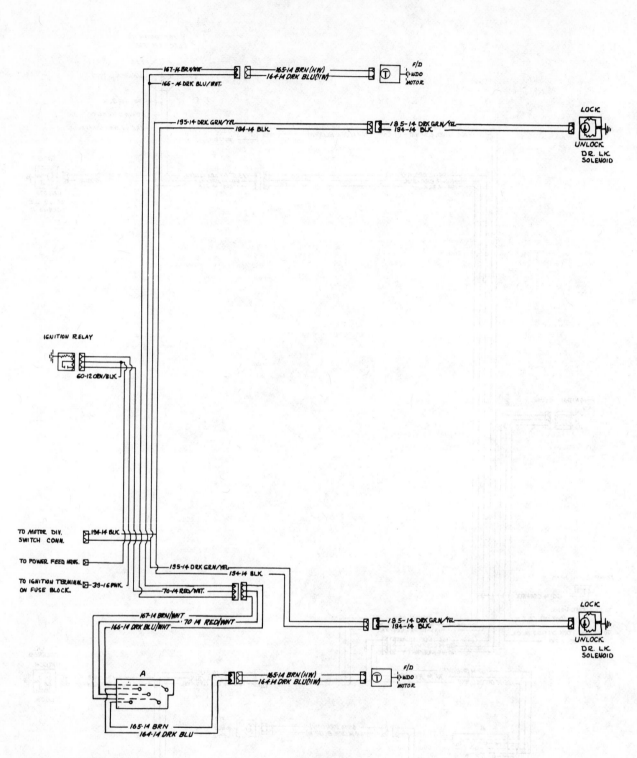

© G.M. Corp.

**1975 FIREBIRD**

# Seat Back Locks

## Chrysler Corporation

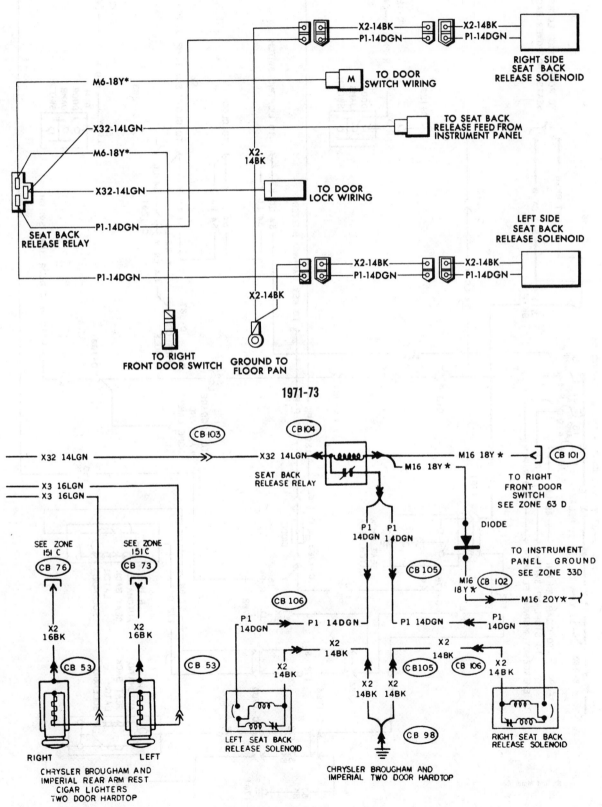

**1971-73**

**1974-75**

## Ford Motor Company

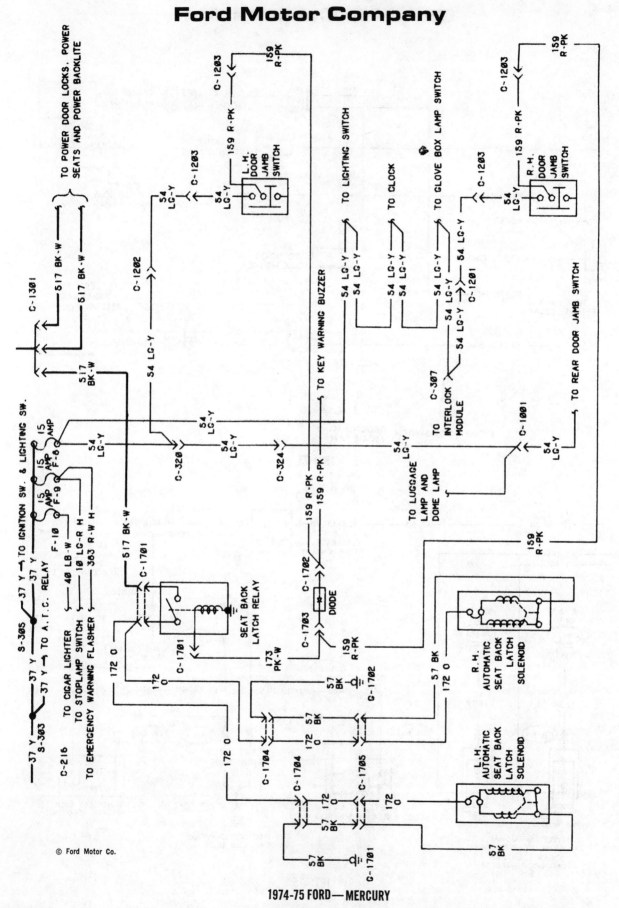

**1974-75 FORD — MERCURY**

## Ford Motor Company

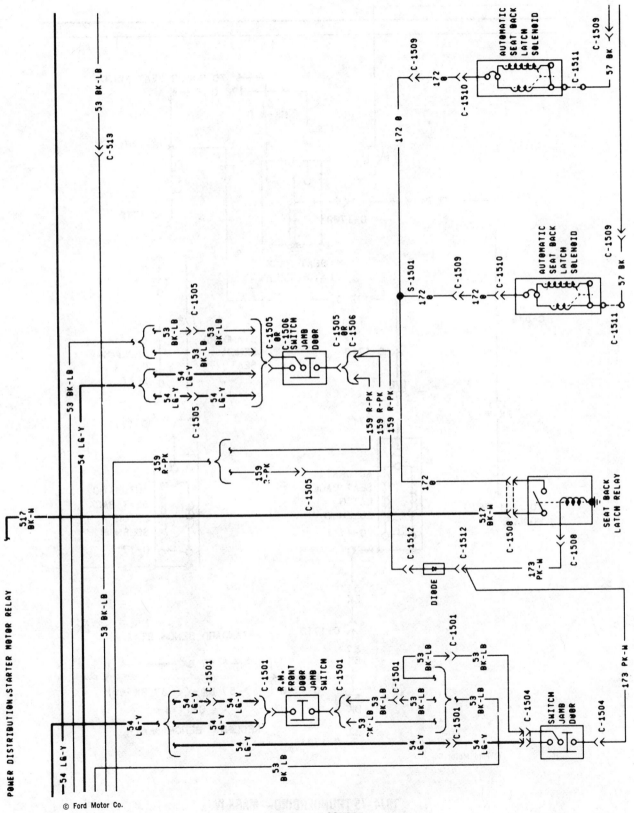

**1974-75 COUGAR**

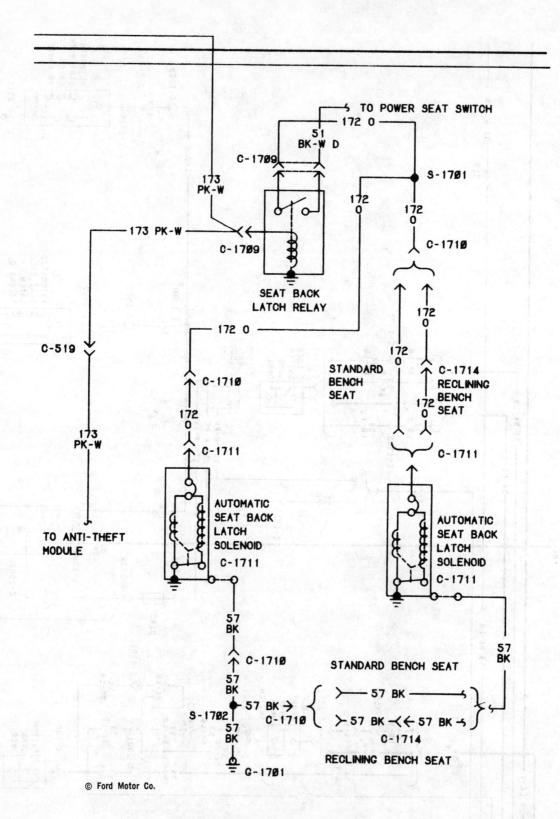

TO POWER SEAT SWITCH

172 O

51
BK-W D

C-1709

S-1701

173
PK-W

172
O

173 PK-W

C-1709

172
O

C-1710

SEAT BACK
LATCH RELAY

172 O

172
O

172
O

C-519

C-1710

STANDARD
BENCH
SEAT

172
O

C-1714

RECLINING
BENCH
SEAT

173
PK-W

172
O

172
O

C-1711

C-1711

TO ANTI-THEFT
MODULE

AUTOMATIC
SEAT BACK
LATCH
SOLENOID

C-1711

AUTOMATIC
SEAT BACK
LATCH
SOLENOID

C-1711

57
BK

57
BK

C-1710

STANDARD BENCH SEAT

57
BK

57 BK

S-1702

57 BK

C-1710

57 BK

57 BK

C-1714

57
BK

RECLINING BENCH SEAT

G-1701

© Ford Motor Co.

## 1974-75 THUNDERBIRD—MARK IV

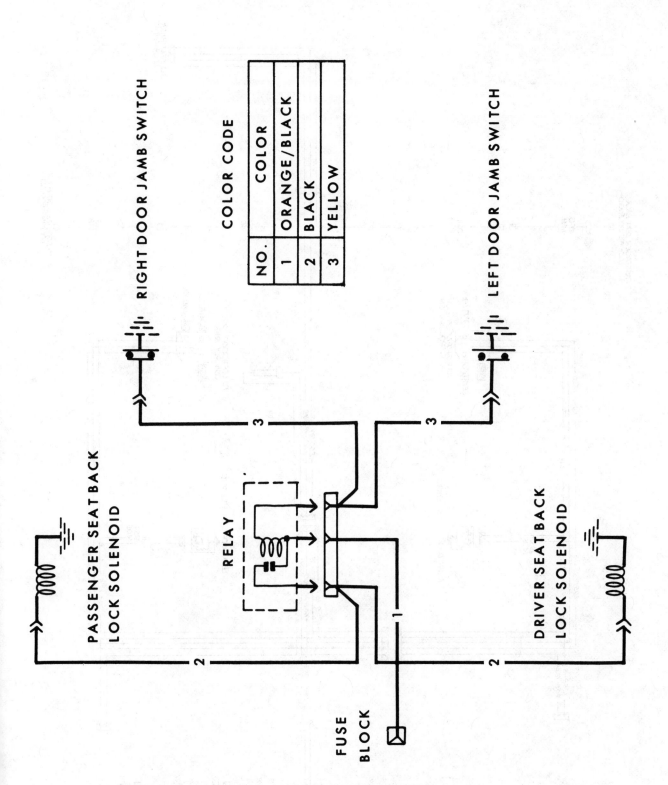

COLOR CODE

| NO. | COLOR |
|-----|-------|
| 1 | ORANGE/BLACK |
| 2 | BLACK |
| 3 | YELLOW |

RIGHT DOOR JAMB SWITCH

LEFT DOOR JAMB SWITCH

PASSENGER SEAT BACK LOCK SOLENOID

DRIVER SEAT BACK LOCK SOLENOID

RELAY

FUSE BLOCK

© G.M. Corp.

1969

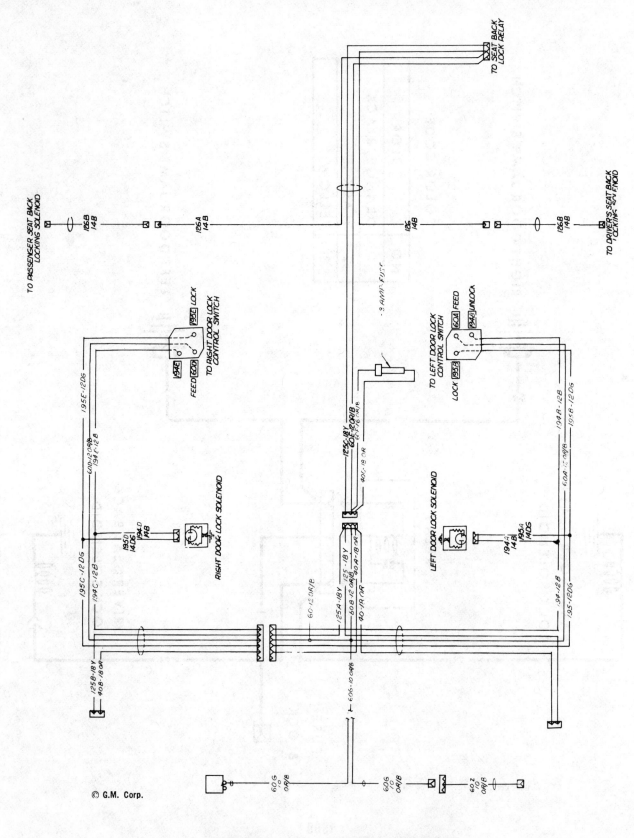

**1970 BUICK RIVIERA—OLDSMOBILE TORONADO**

© G.M. Corp.

## General Motors

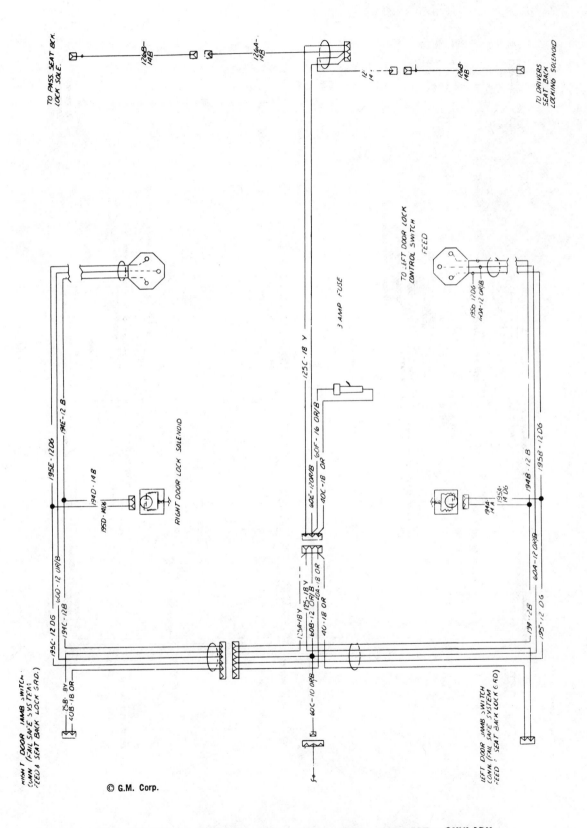

© G.M. Corp.

## 1970 CHEVELLE—CUTLASS—F-85—GRAND PRIX—TEMPEST—SKYLARK

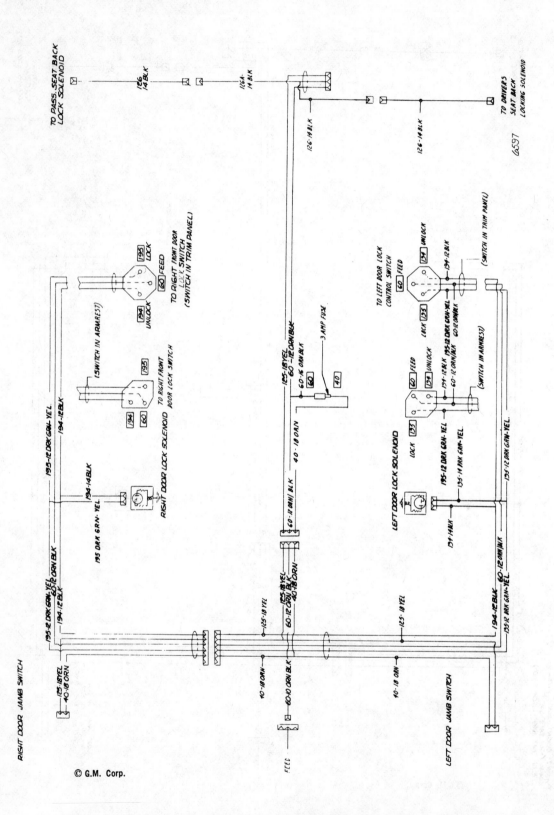

© G.M. Corp.

**1971-73 CHEVELLE—CUTLASS—F-85—GRAND PRIX—LE MANS—SKYLARK**

# General Motors

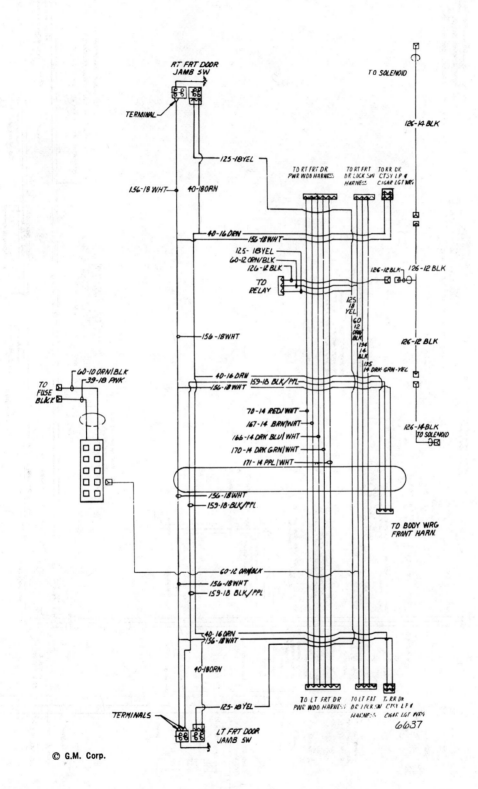

**1971-73 Exc. CHEVELLE — CUTLASS — F-85 — GRAND PRIX — LE MANS — SKYLARK**

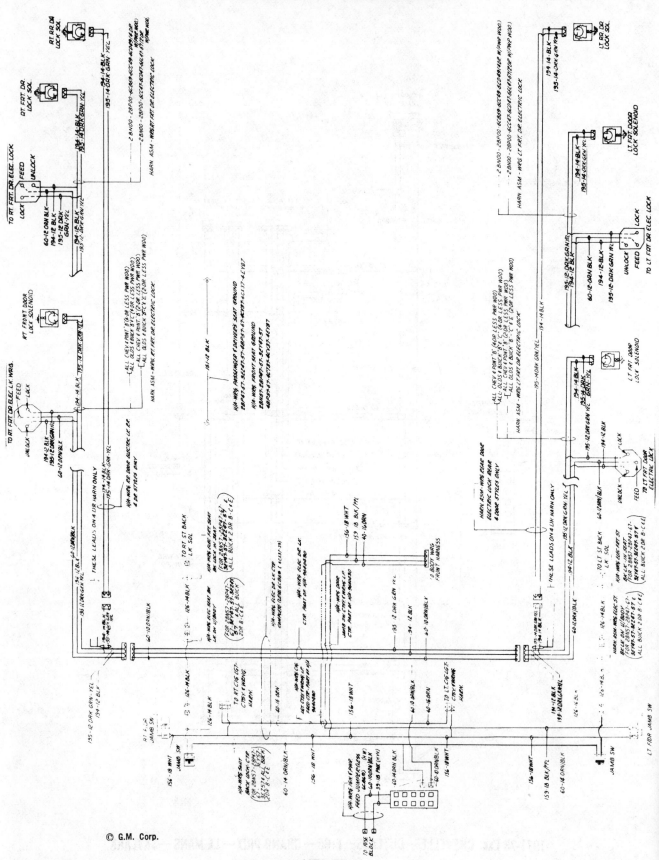

© G.M. Corp.

**1974-75**

## ELECTRIC OPERATED HEADLAMP DOORS

### 1968-75 Chrysler All Models

#### Description

Power is supplied by a single electric motor which is mounted behind the center of the grille.

On the upper end of the motor armature shaft, a worm gear drives a pinion gear which has a rectangular shaped slot in the center. A torsion bar extends into the slot and is mechanically connected to the hinged headlamp doors.

When the ignition is on and the headlight switch is turned on, a circuit is completed through the headlight switch to the upper end of the relay coil. The lower end is connected to the ignition circuit. A spring pulls the relay plunger down, completing a circuit through the "open door" contacts of the relay. The circuit then feeds the motor actuating cam which opens the door opening limit switch. The limit switch cuts off the feed to the motor when the head light doors reach the full open position.

When the ignition is on and the headlight switch is turned off, the circuit branches into two parallel circuits. One branch goes to the relay operating coil and the other is grounded through the filament in the sealed beam. The relay feeds the motor and opens the door closing limit switch. The limit switch cuts off the feed to the motor when the headlamp doors reach the full closed position.

To open the doors in the event of an electrical failure, disconnect the motor leads first, then rotate the hand wheel located at the lower end of the motor clockwise until the headlamp doors are fully opened. Care must be taken not to rotate the wheel after the doors reach the end of travel or the motor may be damaged permanently.

### Torsion Bar and Motor

#### Removal

1. Disconnect the battery ground strap.
2. Disconnect the motor leads and the harness ground wire.
3. Open the headlamp doors half-way by rotating the wheel on the motor.
4. Remove the clips from the crank assemblies.
5. Remove the torsion bar from the rectangular slots in the cranks by wiggling the door up and down with one hand and pulling the bar from the slot with your other.
6. On Imperial and Fury models, remove the two motor mounting bracket-to-vertical lock support bolts.
7. Remove the three motor screws from the mounting bracket to the torsion bar.

#### Installation

1. Insert the torsion bar into the rectangular slot in the motor and position the clips on the bar.
2. Attach the motor to the mounting bracket and install the screws.
   a. The motor should be in the half-way open position. (See the illustration of the alignment of indicators).

## TROUBLESHOOTING CHART

### 1968-75—All Models

| Condition | Possible Cause |
|---|---|
| 1. Inoperable headlight doors | a. Defective motor |
| | b. Defective headlight switch or relay |
| | c. Open or short between power supply, switch, or motor |
| | d. Torsion bar disconnected or bent |
| | e. Faulty circuit breaker |
| 2. Headlamp doors won't open and close together | a. Missing crank screw |
| | b. Torsion bar bent or twisted |
| 3. Noisy operation of headlamp doors | a. Stripped motor plastic drive gear |
| | b. Rubber bumpers may need replacement |
| | c. Door pivot bushings either missing or damaged |
| | d. Torsion spring damaged or broken |
| | e. Improper lubrication |

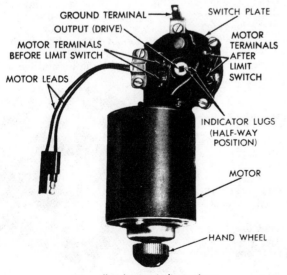

GROUND TERMINAL
OUTPUT (DRIVE)
SWITCH PLATE
MOTOR TERMINALS BEFORE LIMIT SWITCH
MOTOR TERMINALS AFTER LIMIT SWITCH
MOTOR LEADS
INDICATOR LUGS (HALF-WAY POSITION)
MOTOR
HAND WHEEL

*Manually Aligning Indicator Lugs*

CRANK
HEADLAMP DOOR
SPRING
TORSION BAR

*Removing Torsion Bar From Headlamp Door Crank—Typical*

## Chrysler Corporation

    b. Tighten the screws to 75–115 in. lbs.
3. On Imperial and Fury models, position the motor mounting bracket to the vertical lock support.
    a. Tighten the bolts to 220 in. lbs.
4. Position and insert the torsion bars in the cranks.
5. Compress the clips and position them over the cranks and the torsion bar.
6. Connect the motor wiring harness.
7. Connect the battery ground strap.

### Headlamp Doors

#### Removal

1. Disconnect the motor wiring harness.
2. Open the headlamp doors halfway by rotating the wheel on the motor.
    a. The indicator lug on the motor switch plate and the lug on the gear near the rectangular hole should align together.
3. Compress the torsion bar to the headlamp door crank clip and slide the clip from the crank.
4. Remove the torsion bar from the crank arm slot by wiggling the door up and down with one hand and pulling the bar out of the slot with your other.
5. Remove the inboard sealed beams.
    a. On Imperial models, remove the headlamp bezels.
6. Remove the crank assembly retaining clip.
7. On the inboard side of the headlamp door, remove the screw which holds the crank assembly to the door arm.
8. On Imperial and Fury models, remove the idler pin from the outboard side of the door.
9. Remove the headlamp door from the opening.

#### Installation

1. Position the door into the grille opening.
2. Align the crank assembly holes and insert the crank.
3. On Imperial and Fury models, install the idler pin.
4. Make sure that the crank arm and the idler bushings are in place.
5. Install the retainer on the crank.
6. Attach the crank assembly to the door and install the retaining screw.

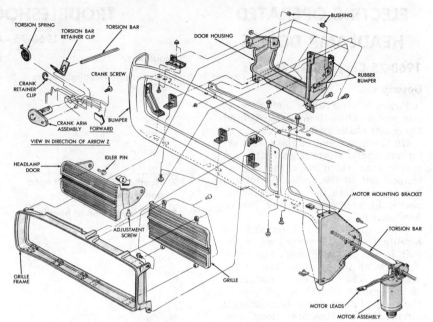

*Concealed Headlamp Door Adaption—Typical*

    a. Tighten to 25–45 in. lbs.
7. Position the torsion bar and insert it into the slotted portion of the crank.
    a. Check to see if the motor is in the halfway open position.
8. Compress and position the clip over the crank and torsion bar.
9. On Imperial models, install the headlamp bezels.
10. Connect the motor wiring harness.

### Electrical Testing Procedures

Before performing any extensive electrical testing procedures check to see that all terminals are connected properly and free of dirt and corrosion. Also make sure there are no mechanical failures.

The motor should not be operated on a bench or without the headlamp doors attached because without the load it can be damaged.

### Motor and Wiring Test

1. Using jumper wires, test the motor by using the battery as a direct source of power.
    a. Apply power to the terminals after the limit switches.
2. If the motor draws current but does not operate in either direction, the motor has a locked armature or an internal short circuit.
3. If the motor does not draw any current, then there is an open circuit and the motor should be replaced.
4. Using a jumper wire, test for

voltage at each wire connector at the sealed beams.
5. If there is no voltage at either sealed beam connector when the switch is on or off, check for loose connections at the headlight switch, headlight motor relay, or a defective circuit breaker.

### Gear and Limit Switch

#### Removal

1. Remove the torsion bar and motor.
    a. Disconnect the battery ground strap.
    b. Disconnect the motor leads and the harness ground wire.
    c. Open the headlamp doors halfway by rotating the wheel on the motor.
    d. Remove the clips from the crank assemblies.
    e. Remove the torsion bar from

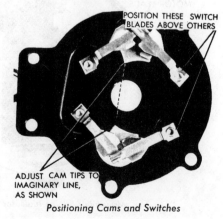

*Positioning Cams and Switches*

# Chrysler Corporation

*Switches Open*

*Testing Switch Operation*

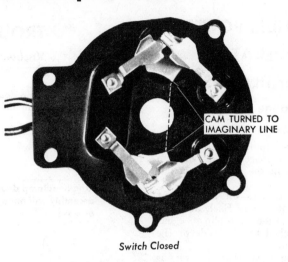

*CAM TURNED TO IMAGINARY LINE*

*Switch Closed*

INDICATOR LUG ON GEAR SHAFT

LIMIT SWITCH ACTUATING CAM

*Gear Assembly*

the rectangular slots in the cranks by wiggling the door up and down with one hand and pulling the bar from the slot with your other.

f. On Imperial and Fury models, remove the two motor mounting bracket-to-vertical lock support bolts.

g. Remove the three motor screws from the mounting bracket and separate the torsion bar.

2. Remove the screws from the switch plate.

3. Check to see that the indicator lugs are lined up.

4. Hold the gear in place by pushing the output drive then carefully remove the switch plate.

5. Remove the gear and examine for chipped or worn teeth.

## Limit Switch Test

1. Make sure that the switch blade contact surfaces are clean.

2. Insert the cam side of the gear assembly into the switch plate.

3. Rotate the gear assembly while pressing it against the switch plate.

   a. Do not over rotate since the cam may damage the limit switch.

4. While rotating, observe the operation of the limit switches when they open and close.

5. Before removing the gear assembly, return the limit switches to the closed position.

## Gear and Limit Switch

### Installation

1. Properly clean and lubricate the teeth of the gears.

2. Install the gears into the housing and make sure that the indicator lugs will line up when the switch plate is installed.

3. Install the switch plate and gasket to the housing while keeping the switch blades in the closed position.

4. Install the switch plate retaining screws.

5. Install the torsion bar and motor.

   a. Insert the torsion bar into

the rectangular slot in the motor and position the clips onto the bar.

b. Attach the motor to the mounting bracket and install the screws. The motor should be in the halfway open position. (See illustration of the alignment of indicator lugs.)

c. Tighten the screws to 75–115 in. lbs.

d. On Imperial and Fury models, position the motor mounting bracket to the vertical lock support. (Tighten the bolts to 220 in. lbs.)

e. Position and insert the torsion bars in the cranks.

f. Compress the clips and position them over the cranks and the torsion aar.

g. Connect the motor wiring harness and the battery ground strap.

## Chrysler Corporation

### VACUUM POWER OPERATED HEADLAMPS

#### 1968-69 Dodge Charger

#### Description

Vacuum is supplied by the intake manifold and stored in a vacuum tank located in the engine compartment.

The system uses an actuator at each headlamp door. Each actuator shaft is connected by a clip to a bar that is attached to each side of the headlight door.

When the headlight switch is turned on, the open port of the vacuum valve, mounted on the back of the headlight switch, supplies vacuum to the open or top side of each actuator and the doors are opened.

When the headlight switch is turned off, the close port of the vacuum valve supplies vacuum to the closed side or bottom of each actuator and the doors are closed.

#### Vacuum Actuator

#### Removal

1. Remove each vacuum hose, noting the color codng.
2. Remove the screw which attaches the actuator shaft to the clip on the actuator bar.
3. Remove the two actuator-to-mounting plate attaching nuts.
4. Lift the actuator from the car.

#### Installation

1. Position the actuator to the mounting plate and install the two retaining nuts.
2. Connect the actuator shaft to the clip on the actuator bar and install the screw.
3. Connect the proper color coded hoses to the actuator, replacing any that are cracked or kinked.

### TROUBLESHOOTING CHART

#### Vacuum Power Operated Headlamps

| Condition | Possible Cause |
|---|---|
| 1. Both headlamp doors or assemblies will not open or close | a. Defective relay valve<br>b. Kinked or split hoses between headlight switch, vacuum tank, and relay valve<br>c. Defective vacuum valve at headlight switch<br>d. Vacuum tank leakage |
| 2. One headlamp door or assembly will not open or close | a. Defective actuator<br>b. Defective relay valve<br>c. Kinked or split hoses between relay valve and actuator<br>d. Mechanical binding<br>e. System should contain 14 in. of vacuum |

*Chrysler Actuator Application*

## Ford Motor Company

#### 1968-75 Ford—All Models

#### General Description

Vacuum is supplied by the intake manifold and is distributed, by a valve through an orange hose, to a check valve which is used in the vacuum source line to prevent vacuum from leaking from the reservoir back through the engine. On Lincoln Continental models, the check valve is part of the vacuum manifold assembly.

A white hose connects the check valve to the vacuum reservoir tank which stores enough vacuum to permit limited operation of the headlight covers without the car engine running.

Another white hose comes from the check valve and supplies vacuum to the center connector on the distribution valve mounted on the back of the headlight switch. When the switch is pulled out, it actuates the distribution valve and supplies vacuum through the green hose to the open side port of the vacuum motor and opens the headlight covers.

When the switch is pushed in to turn the headlights off, it actuates the distribution valve and supplies vacuum through the yellow hose to

## Ford Motor Company

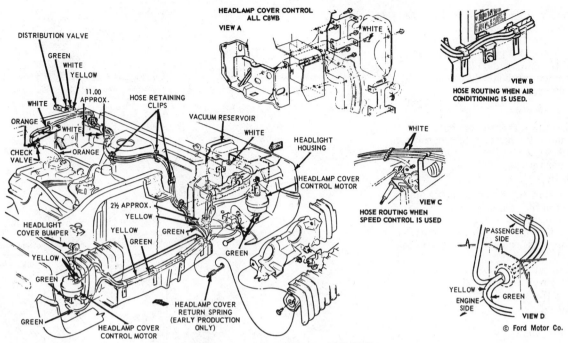

*Headlight Covers and Vacuum System—1968-69 Cougar*

the closed side port of the vacuum motor and closes the headlight covers.

### 1968-69 Ford, Mercury, Cougar

### 1970-71 Ford, Fairlane, Lincoln Continental, Mercury, Cougar, and Montego

### 1972 Mercury and Continental Mark IV

### 1973-74 Continental Mark IV Vacuum Failure

A cover hinge spring, attached to each cover helps to hold the covers in the opened or closed position. The vacuum supplied to each side of the motor overcomes the spring tension. In case of vacuum loss the covers can be opened or closed manually by hand. A by-pass valve is also provided to vent the system and allow the covers to open.

### 1969 Continental Mark III and Thunderbird

### 1970-71 Continental Mark III
### 1973 Mercury

### 1974 Mercury and Lincoln

### 1975 LTD Landau

### Vacuum Failure

Each cover motor is equipped with an internal spring which will automatically open the headlight cover in case of vacuum failure. On 1973 and 1974 models a by-pass valve is also provided to vent the system and allow the covers to open. The valve is located in the vacuum lines between the headlight switch and the vacuum motor.

### 1972-74 Lincoln Continental Vacuum Failure

A spring attached to the center shaft will automatically open the cov-

ers in the event the system should lose vacuum. A by-pass valve is also provided to vent the system and allow the covers to open. The valve is located in the vacuum lines between the headlight switch and the vacuum motor.

### 1968-71 Cougar Vacuum Motor
#### Removal

1. Remove the spring clip that con-

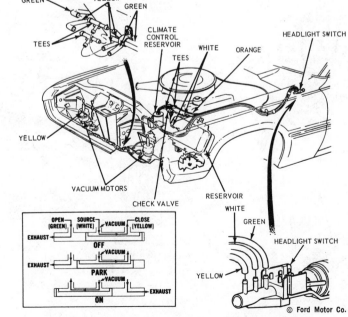

*Headlight Covers and Vacuum System—1968-69 Thunderbird*

nects the motor push rod to the cover actuating shaft.

  a. Push the clip tab out to release the clip and then pull the clip up and off.

2. Remove the bolts that retain the bumper lower extension and let it hang on the parking light leads.

3. Disconnect the vacuum hoses.

4. Remove the motor attaching nuts and remove the motor from under the car.

## Installation

1. Position the vacuum motor and install the retaining nuts.

2. Connect the vacuum hoses.

3. Position the bumper lower extension and replace the retaining bolts.

4. Connect the motor push rod to the cover actuating shaft and install the spring clip.

## 1968-71 Ford

## 1968-74 Mercury

## 1970-74 Lincoln Continental

## 1972-74 Continental Mark IV

## 1975 LTD Landau
### Vacuum Motor
#### Removal

1. Disconnect the hoses from the vacuum motor.

2. Remove the spring clip that connects the motor push rod to the cover actuating shaft and remove the rod and shaft.

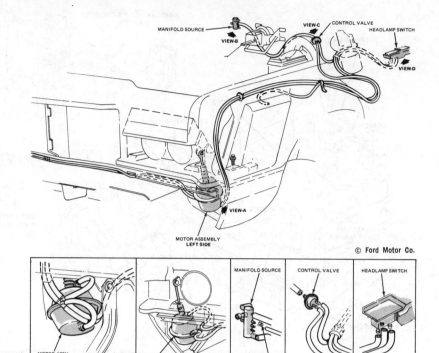

*Headlight Covers and Vacuum System—1973-74 Mercury*

3. Remove the two motor-to-support attaching nuts and remove the motor through the opening at the bottom of the car.

#### Installation

1. Position the motor to the support and install the retaining nuts.

2. Connect the motor push rod to the cover actuating shaft and install the spring clip.

3. Connect the vacuum hoses to the motor, green on top and yellow on the bottom.

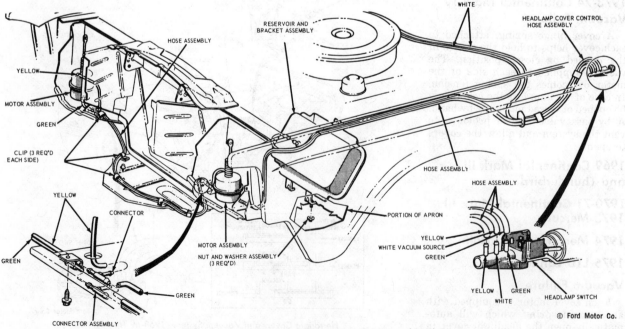

*Headlight Covers and Vacuum System—1968 Continental Mark III*

# Ford Motor Company

## 1968-69 Thunderbird

## 1968-71 Continental Mark III

## Vacuum Motor

### Removal

1. Operate the covers to the closed position.
2. Separate the motor rod pin from the cover actuator bracket by removing the retaining clip.
3. From under the car, remove the four motor lower support plate retaining screws and washers.
4. Pull the motor and support plate down and disconnect both vacuum hoses.
5. Separate the motor and support plate by removing the retaining pin and nut.

### Installation

1. Position the vacuum motor to the support plate, facing the hose connections toward the proper direction.
2. Install the motor-to-support plate retaining pin and nut.
3. Connect the yellow hose to the top of the vacuum motor and the green hose to the bottom.
4. Place the motor and support plate into position and install the four lower support plate retaining screws and washers.
5. Run the engine to extend the vacuum motor actuating rod. Lubricate properly and attach the rod pin to the cover actuator bracket with the clip.

## 1968-71 Montego

## 1970-71 Fairlane

## Vacuum Motor

### Removal

1. Separate the motor control rod from the headlight cover shaft by removing the retaining clip.
2. Remove seven of the ten valance-to-bumper retaining bolts and allow the valance panel to hang.
3. Disconnect the hoses from the vacuum motor.
4. Remove the two motor-to-support retaining nuts and remove the motor.

### Installation

1. Position the motor to the support and replace the retaining nuts.
2. Connect the yellow hose to the top of the motor and the green hose to the bottom.
3. Install the seven valance-to-bumper retaining bolts.

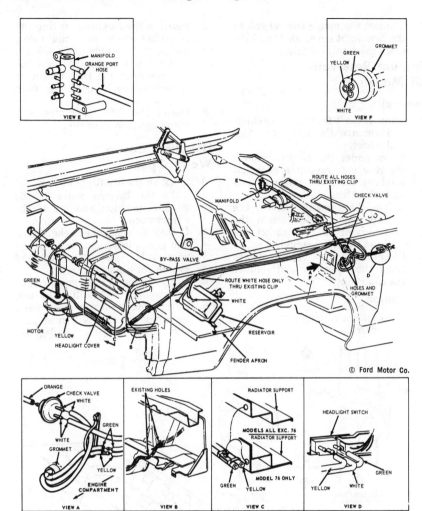

*Headlight Covers and Vacuum System—1970-72 Mercury, 1970-71 Ford and Cougar—Typical*

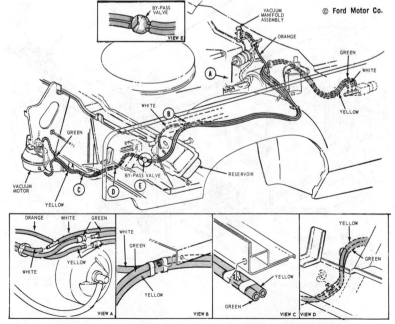

*Headlight Covers and Vacuum System—1971-73 Lincoln Continental*

# Ford Motor Company

4. Connect the motor control rod to the headlight cover shaft and replace the retaining clip.

## Vacuum Reservoir— All Models

### Removal

1. Raise the left front of the vehicle and remove the left front tire and wheel.
2. From under the fender, remove the reservoir retaining nuts and washers from the fender apron and wheel housing.
   a. On the Cougar, remove the four bolts which retain the reservoir to the bracket behind the left headlights.
3. Disconnect the vacuum hose from the reservoir and remove the reservoir.

### Installation

1. Connect the vacuum hose to the reservoir.

---

2. Position the reservoir, fitting the retaining studs into the holes, and install the nuts and washers.
   a. On the Cougar, position the reservoir to the retaining bracket and install the four retaining bolts.
3. Install the left front tire and wheel and lower the car.

## Headlight Covers Won't Open

1. Turn on the headlight switch.
2. Turn the by-pass valve to the parallel position and see if the covers open.
3. If they do open, check the yellow and green hoses between the by-pass valve and the headlight switch for kinks or cracks.
4. If the hoses are in good condition, replace the headlight switch.
5. If the covers do not open when the by-pass valve is turned parallel, check the yellow and green

---

hoses between the by-pass valve and the vacuum motor or motors for kinks or cracks.
6. If the hoses are in good condition replace the by-pass valve.

*NOTE: On models not having a by-pass valve, check for a plugged venting hole on the headlight switch.*

## Headlight Covers Won't Close

1. If the car contains a by-pass valve located between the headlight switch and the motor or motors, make sure it is in the normal position.
2. Start the engine and check for vacuum at the orange hose that connects the intake manifold to the check valve.
3. If there is no vacuum available, check the orange hose for leaks or kinks.
4. If vacuum is available, turn off the headlight switch and leak test the white hose that connects the check valve to the headlight switch. Leak test it again with the switch on.
5. Leak test the vacuum motor, headlight switch, and vacuum reservoir and replace if necessary.
6. Check the yellow and green vacuum hoses, between each component, for kinks or leaks.
7. Check for a plugged venting hole on the headlight switch.

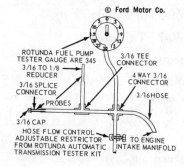

*Vacuum Test Probe*

## Vacuum Test Probe

A vacuum probe tester cannot be obtained commercially, but can be made easily.

1. Cut a length of 3/16 in. vacuum hose long enough to reach from the engine intake manifold to any part of the vacuum system.
2. Insert a four-way connector into the working end of the hose.
3. Attach a vacuum gauge to one of the four-way connector nipples.
4. Install a short length of 3/16 in.

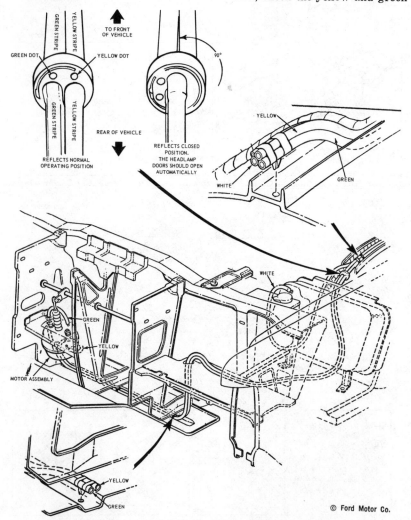

*Headlight Covers and Vacuum System—1972-74 Continental Mark IV*

## Ford Motor Company

hose, with an adjustable hose restrictor, onto another nipple of the four-way connector. An adjustable hose restrictor may be obtained from some automatic transmission tester kits.

5. Install a short length of hose onto the last nipple of the four-way connector. Insert a tee connector into this hose.
6. Install a short length of hose to the two open ends of the tee connector.
7. Install a 3/16–1/8 in. reducer in one hose and a 3/16 in. splice connector in the other hose.
8. By adding or removing connectors (splices) to these test probe hoses, they can be connected to any 3/16–1/8 in. hose, nipple, or connector, while the other test hose is plugged; or both the 3/16 and 1/8 in. tester probes can be used at the same time.
9. To adjust the probe to the required 14 in. of test vacuum, plug the test probe hoses into the vacuum source at the carburetor.
10. Adjust the hose restrictor until the vacuum gauge reads 14 in. (See illustration of vacuum test probe)

### Headlight Cover Vacuum System Leak Test

1. A leak test on any part or component of the headlight cover vacuum system can be done with the use of the vacuum test probe.
2. Plug the probe into the system at the desired point.
3. The reading on the gauge should momentarily fall below the pre-set valve of 14 in.
4. If there are no leaks in the part being checked, the gauge reading should come back to 14 in. of vacuum and hold.
5. If there is a leak in the part being checked, the gauge reading will not come up to 14 in. of vacuum.

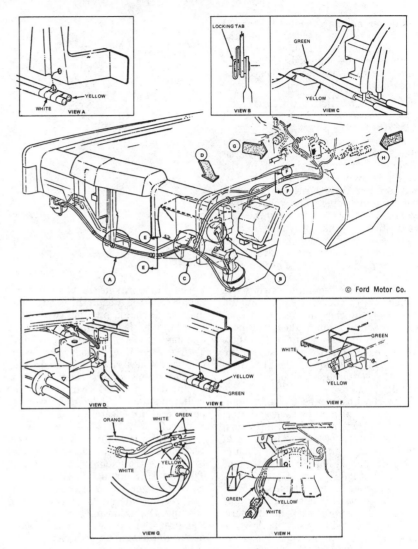

© Ford Motor Co.

*Headlight Covers and Vacuum System—1974 Lincoln Continental*

### Headlight Switch Leak Test

1. Connect the vacuum test probe to the center (white) port of the headlight switch.
2. Cap the two outside ports of the headlight switch.
3. Move the switch selector thru the OFF-PARK-ON positions.
4. The gauge should read 14 in. of vacuum in each position.
5. If the gauge reading should fall off at any position, the switch should be replaced.

## General Motors

### VACUUM POWER OPERATED HEADLAMPS

#### 1968-69 Buick Riviera
**Description**

Vacuum is supplied by the intake manifold and is stored in a vacuum reservoir tank by way of a check valve.

When the headlight switch is turned on, the vacuum valve at the switch shuts off the flow of vacuum and allows normal air pressure into the vacuum relay diaphragm. The diaphragm spring in the relay valve moves the valve and supplies vacuum to the upper end of each actuator through a green hose, while the lower ends are vented to normal air pressure. The vacuum forces the actuator shaft and rotates the headlamp assemblies so they point straight forward.

When the headlight switch is turned off, vacuum flows through the vacuum valve at the headlight switch and supplies vacuum to the vacuum diaphragm. A spring is compressed and opens the relay valve which supplies vacuum to the lower end of each actuator through a red hose, while

# General Motors

the upper ends are vented to normal air pressure. The vacuum forces the actuator shaft and rotates the headlamp assemblies upward. At the same time, the right and left grille sections line up with the main grille.

## 1968-69 Cadillac Eldorado

### Description

Vacuum is supplied by the intake manifold and is distributed by the vacuum valve which is part of the headlight switch.

There are three hoses connected to the vacuum valve. The yellow hose connects the vacuum valve to the vacuum storage tank, providing a constant source of vacuum. The green hose connects the vacuum valve to the vacuum port on the top of each actuator.

When the headlight switch is pulled out to turn the lights on, the open port of the vacuum valve supplies vacuum through the green hose to the top of each actuator. The bottom of each actuator is vented to the outside air, forcing up the piston inside the actuators and opening the headlight doors.

The red hose connects the vacuum valve to the bottom of each actuator. When the switch is pushed in to turn the headlamps off, the close port of the vacuum valve supplies vacuum through the red hose to the bottom of each actuator. The top of each actuator is vented to the outside air, forcing down the piston inside the actuator and closing the headlight doors.

The system employs a check valve to equalize the pressure between the

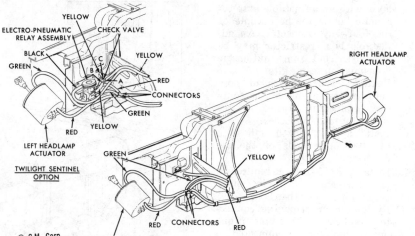

*Headlamp Door Vacuum Schematic*

ports. This provides a vacuum-tight system so the headlight doors may operate through one or two cycles with the engine not running.

Some models are equipped with Twilight Sentinel which uses every component described previously plus an electric-pneumatic relay which is mounted on the left rear side of the radiator support. It has four vacuum ports and an electrical lead to the relay coil.

When the twilight sentinel is energized, it completes an electrical circuit to the electro-pneumatic relay coil. The resulting magnetic field pulls the metal plunger into the center of the coil, sealing off the vacuum port and opening the atmospheric port. This equalizes the pressure on both sides of the diaphragm assembly.

## Vacuum Storage Tank— Eldorado

### Removal

1. Remove the upper attaching screw from the top of the storage tank.
2. Remove the vacuum hose through the access hole in the back of the radiator support.
3. Remove the two angle bracket-to-front wheel housing retaining nuts and washers and remove the angle bracket.
4. Remove the two lower attaching screws at the bottom of the radiator support.
5. Remove the vacuum tank.

### Installation

1. Position the vacuum tank to the radiator support and install the lower attaching screws.
2. Install the angle bracket to the front wheel housing and replace the retaining nuts and washers.
3. Replace the vacuum hose.
4. Install the upper tank attaching screws.

## Electric-Pneumatic Relay Control

### Removal

1. Disconnect the light blue feed wire from the control switch.
2. Remove the vacuum hoses, noting the color coding.
3. Remove the two attaching screws.

### Installation

1. Position the control to the radiator support.
2. Connect the correct color coded hoses to the control.
3. Connect the light blue feed wire to the control.

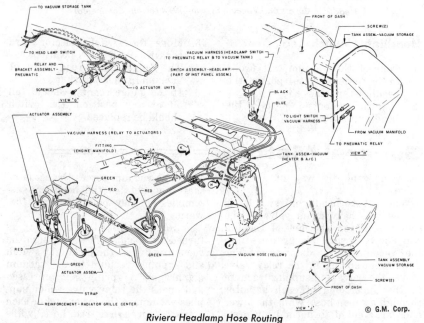

*Riviera Headlamp Hose Routing*

# General Motors

## Headlamp Actuator—Right or Left

### Removal

1. Remove the two bracket-to-wheel housing screws and remove the bracket.
2. Remove the rubber splash shield retaining clips from behind the radiator support.
3. Remove the vacuum hoses from the actuator, noting the color coding.
4. Remove the upper and lower cotter pins from each pivot and remove the actuator.

### Installation

1. Position the actuators to the upper and lower pivots and install the cotter pin and washer at the lower pivot.
2. Install the clevis pin and cotter pin at the upper pivot.
3. Connect the vacuum hoses.
4. Replace the rubber splash shield and retaining clips.

## 1968-69 Chevrolet and Camaro 1968-75 Corvette

### Description

Vacuum is supplied by the intake manifold and stored in a vacuum tank by way of a check valve.

When the headlight switch is turned on, the vacuum valve at the switch shuts off the flow of vacuum and allows normal air pressure into the relay valve diaphragm. (Corvette uses one relay valve for each actuator.) The diaphragm spring in the relay valve opens a valve and supplies vacuum to the upper end of each actuator through a green hose, while the lower ends are vented to normal air pressure. The vacuum forces the actuator shaft and rotates the headlamp assemblies forward on the Corvette and opens the grille doors on the Camaro and Chevrolet.

When the headlight switch is turned off, vacuum flows through the vacuum valve at the headlight switch and supplies vacuum to the relay valve. The relay valve opens and supplies vacuum to the lower end of each actuator through a red hose while the upper ends are vented to normal air pressure. The vacuum forces the actuator shaft and rotates the headlamp assemblies upward on the Corvette and closes the headlight doors on the Chevrolet and Camaro.

## Headlight Door—Chevrolet

### Removal

1. Open the headlight doors by sliding the valve inboard on top of the vacuum relay.
2. Remove the four screws on the lid.
3. Remove the three door cover attaching bolts and remove the cover.

### Installation

1. Position the door cover and install three attaching bolts.
2. Install the four screws onto the lid.

## Headlight Door—Corvette

### Removal

1. Open the headlamps.
2. Remove the radiator grille and attaching screws.
3. Remove the headlamp bezel.
4. Remove the inner and outer headlamp assemblies, using a small vise-grip or a hooked wire to remove the springs.
5. Remove the front screw and bushing which attaches the headlamp housing to the support assembly link.
6. Remove the "J" bar from the side of the headlamp housing which extends downward.
7. Remove the three cap screws that attach the bearing and headlamp assemblies to the support assemblies, by reaching in through the grille opening.
8. Lift the headlamp door forward and out of opening.

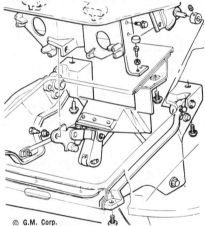

© G.M. Corp.
*Headlamp Door—Corvette*

### Installation

1. Position the headlamp door into the opening.
2. Reach through the grille opening and install the three cap screws which attach the bearing and headlamp housing assemblies to the support assemblies.
3. Replace the "J" bar on the side of the headlamp housing.
4. Replace the front screw and bushing which attaches the headlamp housing to the support assembly link.
5. Install the inner and outer headlamp assemblies and replace the retaining springs.
6. Install the headlight bezel.
7. Replace the radiator grille.

## Headlight Door—Camaro

### Removal

1. Close the doors.

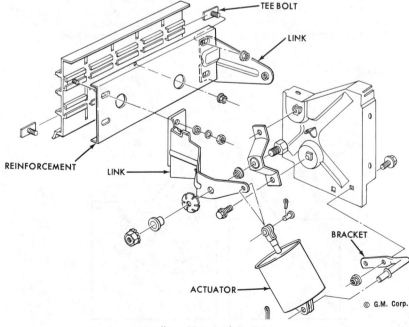

TEE BOLT

LINK

REINFORCEMENT

LINK

BRACKET

ACTUATOR

© G.M. Corp.

*Headlamp Vacuum Actuators*

2. Remove the two cover-to-plate screws.
3. Open the hood and slide the valve inboard on top of the vacuum relay to open the headlamp cover.
4. Open the door plate partially and reach inside of the opening to remove the nuts which attach the cover to the hinge.

### Installation

1. Attach the cover to the hinge and replace the nuts.
2. Install the two cover-to-plate screws.

### Actuator Assembly—Chevrolet

#### Removal

1. Remove the vacuum tank.
2. When removing the right side actuator, remove the battery.
3. Remove the actuator hoses, noting the color coding.
4. Remove the front pivot pin and retaining washers.
5. Remove the rear actuator pivot pin and retaining washers.
6. Lift out the actuator.

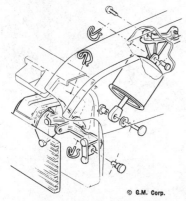

*Actuator Assembly—Chevrolet*

### Installation

1. Position the actuator in the car.
2. Install the front and rear actuator pivot pins and washers.
3. When replacing the right side actuator, replace the battery.
4. Install the vacuum tank and three retaining screws.

### Actuator Assembly—Corvette

#### Removal

1. Remove the radiator grille and screws.
2. Open the headlamps partially and remove the long spring on either side of the pivot link pin.
3. Remove the two actuator vacuum hoses, noting the color coding.
4. Free the actuator rod by removing the cotter pin and sliding out the pivot pin.

5. Remove the four actuator stud retaining nuts.
6. Move the actuator down and out of grille opening.

### Installation

1. Position the actuator and replace the four retaining nuts on the studs.
2. Attach the actuator rod and install the pivot pin and cotter pin.
3. Install the two long springs on either side of the pivot link pin.
4. Replace the two actuator vacuum hoses.
5. Replace the radiator grille and retaining screws.

### Actuator Assembly—Camaro

#### Removal

1. Remove the actuator vacuum hoses and identify for replacement.
2. Place the car on a lift and raise.
3. From under the car, remove the actuator shield from the front of the fender skirt.
4. Remove the actuator front pin and retainer.
5. Remove the actuator attaching rear bolt and remove the actuator.

### Installation

1. Position the actuator and install the rear attaching bolt and front pin and retainer.
2. Replace the actuator shield at the fender skirt.
3. Lower the car all the way down.
4. Replace the actuator vacuum hoses to the proper connections.

### Vacuum Relay—Corvette, Camaro, and Chevrolet

#### Removal

1. Raise the hood.
2. Remove the four hoses from the relay, noting the color coding.
3. Remove the two relay attaching screws.

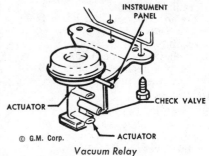

*Vacuum Relay*

### Installation

1. Position the relay and install the attaching screws.
2. Install the hoses to the relay at the proper connectors.

### Vacuum Tank—Chevrolet

#### Removal

1. Raise the hood.
2. Remove the vacuum relay retaining screws.
3. Remove the vacuum hose.
4. Remove the two vacuum tank-to-radiator support attaching bolts.

### Installation

1. Position the vacuum tank to the radiator support and install the two retaining bolts.
2. Replace the vacuum hose.

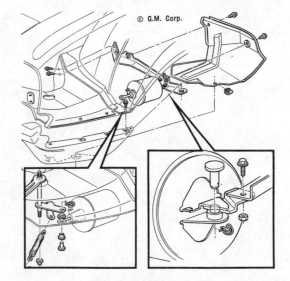

*Actuator Assembly—Camaro*

## General Motors

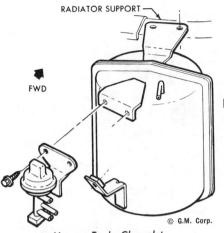

*Vacuum Tank—Chevrolet*

3. Replace the vacuum relay to the vacuum tank bracket with the two attaching screws.

### Vacuum Tank—Camaro

#### Removal

1. Raise the hood.
2. Remove the washer jar and bracket.
3. Remove the vacuum relay-to-tank retaining screws.
4. Remove the vacuum tank hose.
5. From under the left ender, remove the tank attaching bolts.

#### Installation

1. Position the tank to the fender skirt and install the attaching bolts.
2. Replace the vacuum hose to the tank.
3. Replace the vacuum relay to the vacuum tank.
4. Replace the washer jar and bracket.

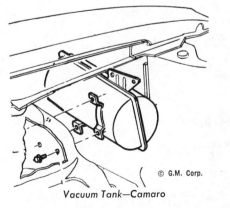

*Vacuum Tank—Camaro*

### Vacuum Tank—Corvette

#### Removal

1. Raise the hood.
2. Remove the master cylinder and power brake booster.

---

3. Remove the vacuum hoses, noting color coding.
4. Remove the vacuum tank retaining screws from under the left fender skirt.
5. Lift the vacuum tank out from the engine compartment.

#### Installation

1. Position the vacuum tank and install the retaining screws to the left fender skirt.
2. Replace the vacuum hoses to the proper connectors.

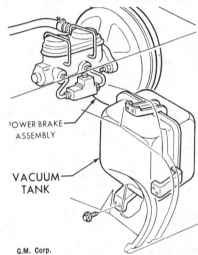

*Vacuum Tank—Corvette*

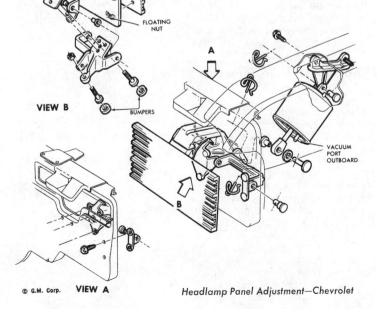

*Headlamp Panel Adjustment—Chevrolet*

---

3. Install the master cylinder and power brake booster.

### Headlamp Panel Adjustment —Chevrolet

1. Close the door and check the bottom edge of the door to the sheet metal.
2. Loosen the four screws on the door.
3. After loosening the locknut, turn the adjustment screw clockwise to move the lower edge of the door inward.

### Headlamp Panel Adjustment —Camaro

1. Align the cover with the radiator grille by adjusting the nuts on the back of the plate assembly.

### Headlamp Housing Alignment —Corvette

1. To align in and out, loosen the screws which fasten the slotted bracket to the underside of the headlamp housing assembly.
2. To adjust the headlamp cover down to the opening, turn the hex head screw fastened to the top of the pivot link.
3. To adjust the headlamp assembly to open all the way.
   a. Remove the spring and the cotter pin from the actuator rod pin.
   b. With the engine idling for vacuum and the actuator rod connecting link extended fully, turn the actuator rod until the bushing hole aligns to the forward end of the slot in the connecting link.

# General Motors

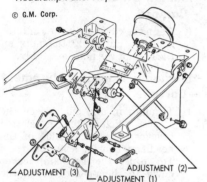

*Headlamp Panel Adjustment—Camaro*

© G.M. Corp.

© G.M. Corp.

*Headlamp Panel Adjustment—Corvette*

ADJUSTMENT (3) ADJUSTMENT (2)
ADJUSTMENT (1)

c. Shut the engine off and unscrew the actuator rod ½ turn to preload the actuator rod in the link.

4. To adjust the bezel to the opening upward, loosen the jamb nut and turn the bumper cover screw up or down to touch, then up 1–1½ turns more.

a. When the lights are fully extended, the micro switch linkage must shut off the warning lamp.

b. Before aiming the headlamps, make sure that the headlamp housing is properly aligned.

## 1968-69 Oldsmobile Toronado

### Description

Vacuum is supplied by the intake manifold. A green hose connects the intake manifold to a check valve. The check valve has to other connections. A black hose connects to the remote control valve and another black hose leads to a tee. At the tee, a blue hose connects to the vacuum reservoir and a green hose to the headlight switch.

When the headlight switch is turned on, the vacuum is cut off at the switch and at the closed side of the remote control valve through a yellow hose. Inside the remote control valve, spring pressure moves the valve to the open position and the

center port of the valve supplies vacuum to the open side of the actuator through a blue hose. The vacuum forces the actuator shaft up and opens the headlamp grilles.

When the headlight switch is turned off, vacuum is supplied through the switch, through a yellow hose to the control valve which closes; the center port supplies vacuum to the closed side of the actuator through an orange hose. The vacuum forces the actuator shaft down and closes the headlamp grilles.

### Headlamp Actuator Door

#### Removal

1. On the left side, remove the three vacuum tank attaching bolts.
2. Slide the vacuum tank over and remove the bolt and nut from the outer end of the door.
3. On the right side, remove the battery.
4. Remove the actuator pin retainer and remove the pin from the door.
5. Remove the two screws from the end of the inner grille.
6. Remove the nut from the inner end of the actuator door.
7. Open the actuator door to the full open position and remove.

#### Installation

1. Position the actuator door and install the inner door nut.
2. Install the two inner grille screws.
3. Install the actuator pin and retainer.
4. Replace the battery.
5. Install the bolt and nut at the outer end of the door.
6. Replace the vacuum tank and attaching bolts.

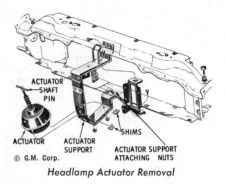

ACTUATOR SHAFT PIN

SHIMS

ACTUATOR  ACTUATOR SUPPORT
ACTUATOR SUPPORT ATTACHING NUTS

© G.M. Corp.

*Headlamp Actuator Removal*

### Vacuum Actuator

#### Removal

1. Remove the actuator shaft pin retaining clips and remove the pin from the actuator door arms.
2. Remove the lower radiator deflector.
3. Remove the vertical center brace.
4. Remove the actuator attaching nut and insulator.
5. Disconnect the vacuum hoses at the actuator, noting color code.
6. Remove the two bolts that connect the actuator support to the lower support.
7. Pull down on the actuator support and remove the actuator from the right side of the support.
8. Remove the center valence panel bolt and pull the panel down far enough to remove the actuator from the car.

#### Installation

1. Position the actuator and install the support bolts.
2. Replace the center valence panel bolt.
3. Connect the vacuum hoses to the

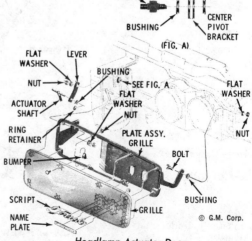

BOLT  BUSHING

BUSHING  CENTER PIVOT BRACKET

(FIG. A)

FLAT WASHER  LEVER

NUT  BUSHING

SEE FIG. A

ACTUATOR SHAFT  FLAT WASHER NUT  FLAT WASHER

RING RETAINER  NUT

PLATE ASSY. GRILLE  BOLT

BUMPER

SCRIPT  BUSHING

NAME PLATE  GRILLE  © G.M. Corp.

*Headlamp Actuator Door*

# General Motors

actuator: blue hose to the top, and orange to the bottom.

4. Install the actuator attaching nut and insulator.
   a. Torque the actuating attaching nut to 13 ft lbs. and make sure that the actuator moves freely in the lower insulator.
5. Install the vertical center brace.
6. Install the lower radiator deflector.
7. Install the actuator shaft pin to the actuator door arm and replace the retaining clips.

## Head Lamp Assembly

### Removal

1. Open the headlight grille and remove the headlamp door and inner grille.
2. Close the headlamp grille assembly and disconnect the wire connection at the headlamp.
3. Remove the three upper and lower attaching bolts.
   a. Two bolts are removed through an opening in the front bumper and one is removed from the rear of the bumper.
4. Slide the headlamp assembly to the center of the car and remove it through the opening between the upper bumper and upper radiator support.

### Installation

1. Place the headlight assembly through the opening in the center of the car between the upper bumper and upper radiator support.
2. Slide the headlight assembly over and into position.
3. Install the three upper and lower attaching bolts.
4. Connect the wire connector to the headlamp.
5. Replace the headlamp door and inner grille.

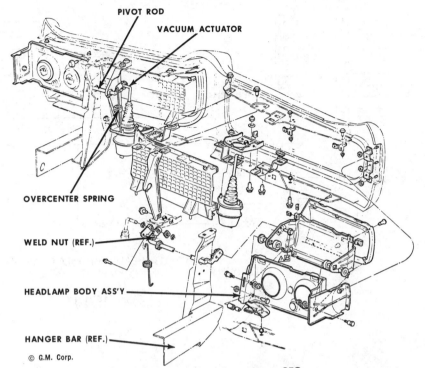

© G.M. Corp.

*Vacuum Operated Headlamp Doors—GTO*

## 1968-69 Pontiac GTO

### Description

Vacuum is supplied by the intake manifold and stored in a vacuum tank by way of a check valve.

When the headlight switch is pulled out to turn the headlamps on, it mechanically opens the open side of the vacuum valve located on the back of the headlight switch. The valve supplies vacuum first through a green stripe hose then through a dark green hose and finally through another green stripe hose which is connected to the open side of each actuator. The vacuum actuator shaft pushes a pivot rod up and opens the headlamp doors.

When the headlight switch is pushed in to turn the headlamps off, it mechanically opens the close side of the vacuum valve. This supplies vacuum through a black hose which is connected to the close side of each actuator. The vacuum actuator shaft pulls a pivot rod down and closes the headlamp doors.

Each door is equipped with an overcenter spring which is hooked to the actuator support on one end and a bracket on the pivot rod on the other. The overcenter spring holds each headlamp door in position and enables them to be opened mechanically in case of a vacuum failure.

### Vacuum Actuator

#### Removal

1. Remove the parking lamps and the valence panel.
2. Remove the vacuum hoses from the actuator, noting the color code.
3. Remove the actuator-to-bracket retaining screws.
4. Remove the clips which attach the actuator shaft to the pivot rod.

#### Installation

1. Position the actuator to the bracket and pivot rod.
2. Install the bracket screws and the pivot rod-to-actuator shaft retaining clip.
3. Replace the vacuum hoses to the actuator at the proper connections.
4. Replace the parking lamps and valance panel.

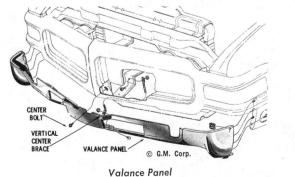

© G.M. Corp.

*Valance Panel*

## Chrysler Corporation

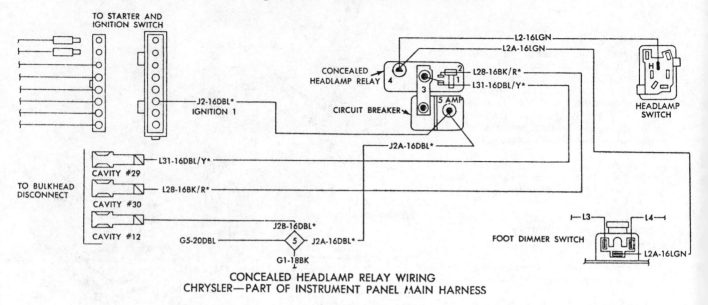

CONCEALED HEADLAMP RELAY WIRING
CHRYSLER—PART OF INSTRUMENT PANEL MAIN HARNESS

**1971-72**

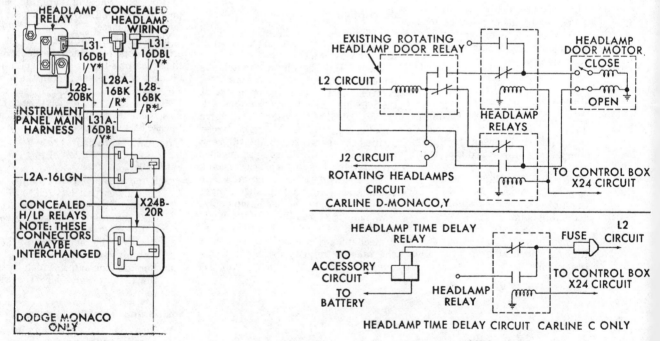

DODGE MONACO ONLY

**1973**

ROTATING HEADLAMPS CIRCUIT CARLINE D-MONACO, Y

HEADLAMP TIME DELAY CIRCUIT CARLINE C ONLY

**1973**

## Chrysler Corporation

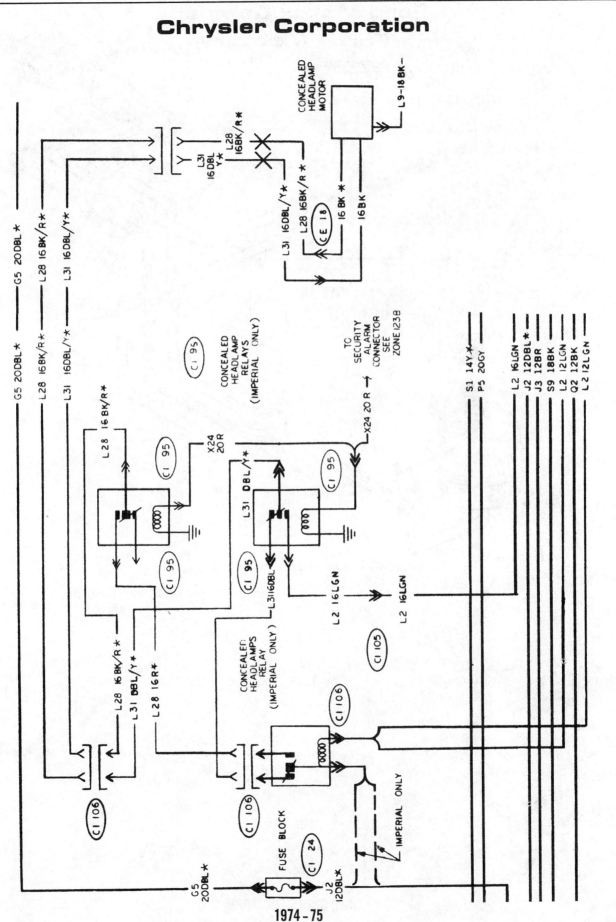

1974-75

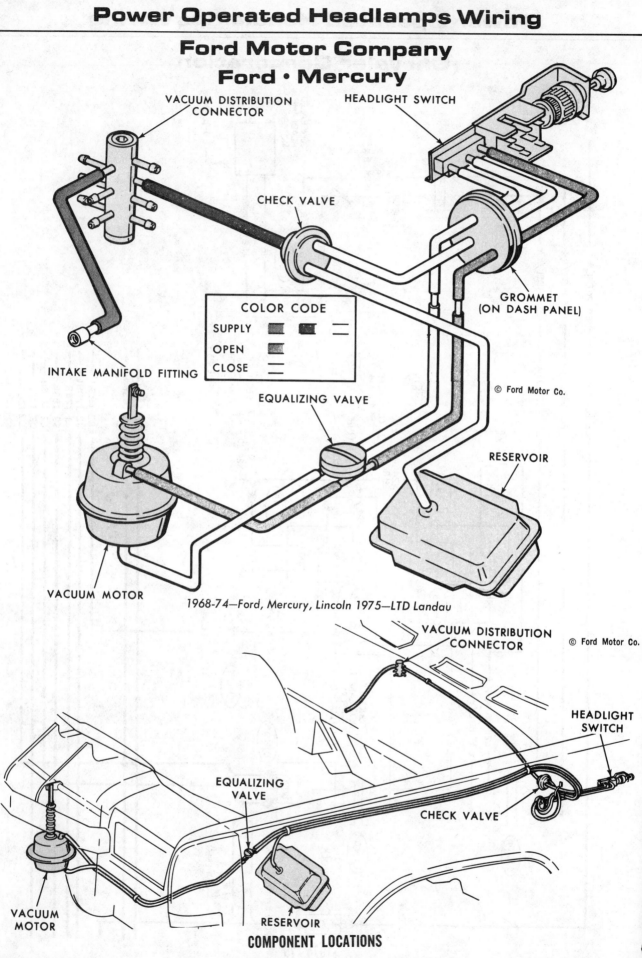

COLOR CODE

| | | |
|---|---|---|
| SUPPLY | ▐███▌ | ▭ |
| OPEN | ▐▒▒▌ | |
| CLOSE | ▭ | |

VACUUM DISTRIBUTION CONNECTOR

HEADLIGHT SWITCH

CHECK VALVE

GROMMET (ON DASH PANEL)

INTAKE MANIFOLD FITTING

EQUALIZING VALVE

© Ford Motor Co.

RESERVOIR

VACUUM MOTOR

*1968-74—Ford, Mercury, Lincoln 1975—LTD Landau*

VACUUM DISTRIBUTION CONNECTOR

© Ford Motor Co.

HEADLIGHT SWITCH

EQUALIZING VALVE

CHECK VALVE

VACUUM MOTOR

RESERVOIR

## COMPONENT LOCATIONS

## Thunderbird • Mark III • Mark IV

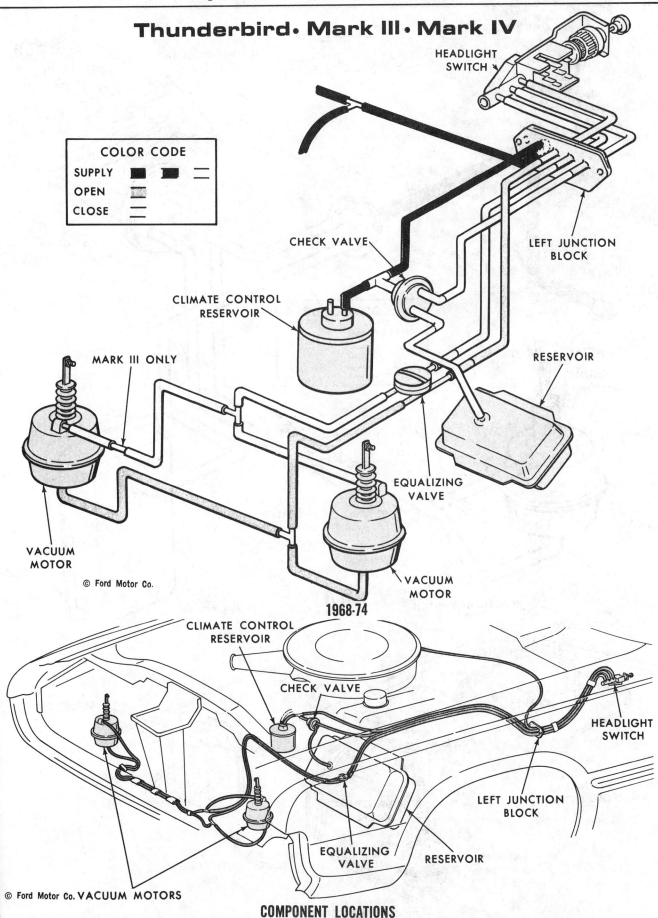

COLOR CODE

SUPPLY ▮ ▮ —

OPEN ▦

CLOSE —

HEADLIGHT SWITCH ↙

LEFT JUNCTION BLOCK

CHECK VALVE

CLIMATE CONTROL RESERVOIR

RESERVOIR

MARK III ONLY

EQUALIZING VALVE

© Ford Motor Co.

VACUUM MOTOR

VACUUM MOTOR

**1968-74**

CLIMATE CONTROL RESERVOIR

CHECK VALVE

HEADLIGHT SWITCH

LEFT JUNCTION BLOCK

EQUALIZING VALVE

RESERVOIR

© Ford Motor Co. **VACUUM MOTORS**

**COMPONENT LOCATIONS**

## Cougar

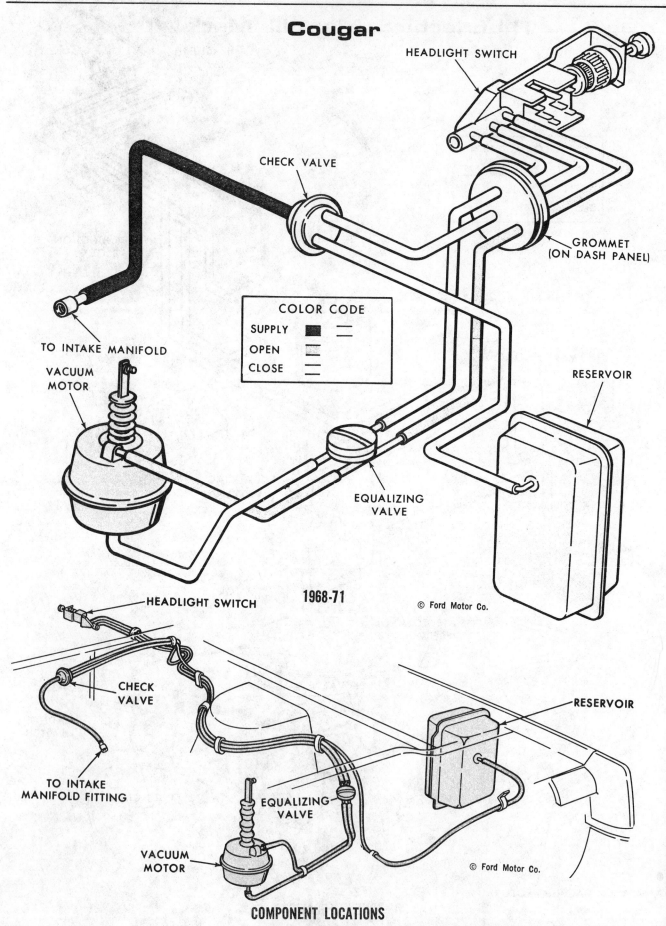

HEADLIGHT SWITCH

CHECK VALVE

GROMMET
(ON DASH PANEL)

COLOR CODE

SUPPLY

OPEN

CLOSE

TO INTAKE MANIFOLD

VACUUM
MOTOR

RESERVOIR

EQUALIZING
VALVE

HEADLIGHT SWITCH

1968-71

© Ford Motor Co.

CHECK
VALVE

RESERVOIR

TO INTAKE
MANIFOLD FITTING

EQUALIZING
VALVE

VACUUM
MOTOR

© Ford Motor Co.

**COMPONENT LOCATIONS**

# General Motors
# Buick

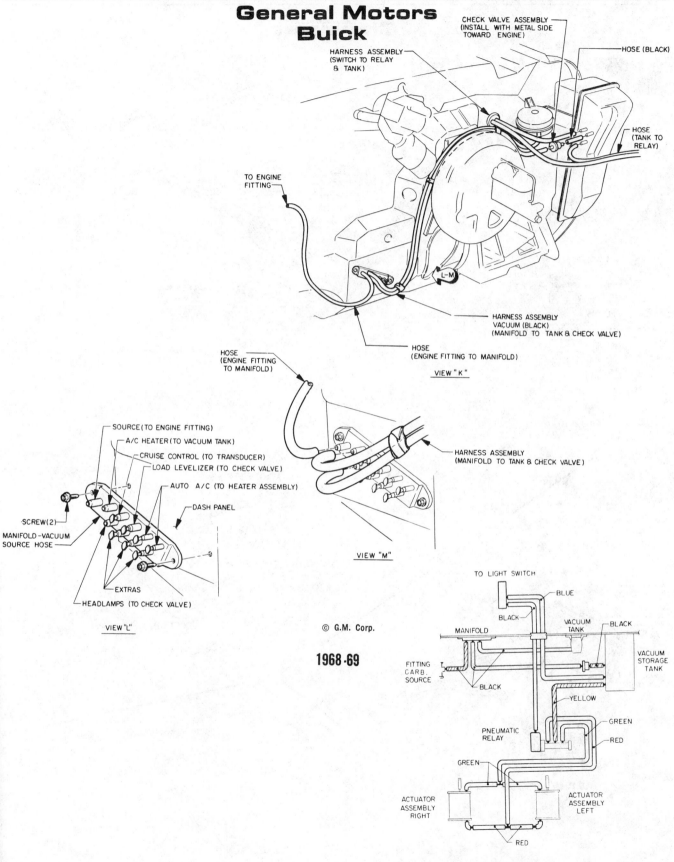

CHECK VALVE ASSEMBLY
(INSTALL WITH METAL SIDE
TOWARD ENGINE)

HARNESS ASSEMBLY
(SWITCH TO RELAY
& TANK)

HOSE (BLACK)

HOSE
(TANK TO
RELAY)

TO ENGINE
FITTING

L-M

HARNESS ASSEMBLY
VACUUM (BLACK)
(MANIFOLD TO TANK & CHECK VALVE)

HOSE
(ENGINE FITTING TO MANIFOLD)

VIEW "K"

HOSE
(ENGINE FITTING
TO MANIFOLD)

HARNESS ASSEMBLY
(MANIFOLD TO TANK & CHECK VALVE)

VIEW "M"

SOURCE (TO ENGINE FITTING)
A/C HEATER (TO VACUUM TANK)
CRUISE CONTROL (TO TRANSDUCER)
LOAD LEVELIZER (TO CHECK VALVE)
AUTO A/C (TO HEATER ASSEMBLY)
DASH PANEL

SCREW (2)

MANIFOLD-VACUUM
SOURCE HOSE

EXTRAS

HEADLAMPS (TO CHECK VALVE)

VIEW "L"

© G.M. Corp.

1968-69

TO LIGHT SWITCH

BLUE

BLACK

VACUUM
TANK

BLACK

MANIFOLD

FITTING
CARB.
SOURCE

BLACK

VACUUM
STORAGE
TANK

YELLOW

GREEN

PNEUMATIC
RELAY

RED

GREEN

ACTUATOR
ASSEMBLY
RIGHT

ACTUATOR
ASSEMBLY
LEFT

RED

VACUUM HOSE CHART

# Power Operated Headlamps Wiring

## Chevrolet

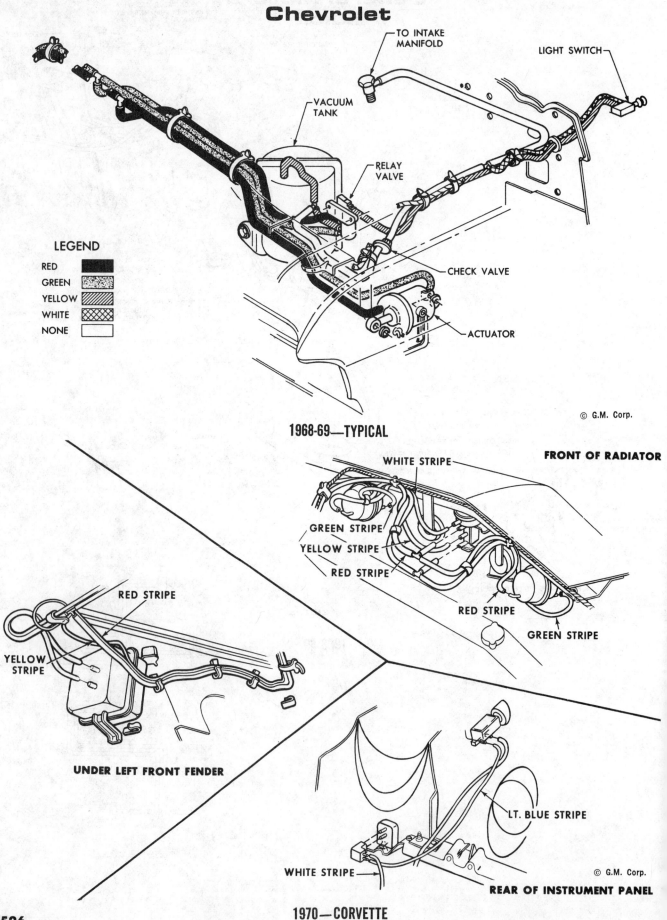

TO INTAKE MANIFOLD

LIGHT SWITCH

VACUUM TANK

RELAY VALVE

CHECK VALVE

ACTUATOR

LEGEND

RED
GREEN
YELLOW
WHITE
NONE

© G.M. Corp.

**1968-69—TYPICAL**

**FRONT OF RADIATOR**

WHITE STRIPE

GREEN STRIPE

YELLOW STRIPE

RED STRIPE

RED STRIPE

GREEN STRIPE

RED STRIPE

YELLOW STRIPE

**UNDER LEFT FRONT FENDER**

LT. BLUE STRIPE

WHITE STRIPE

© G.M. Corp.

**REAR OF INSTRUMENT PANEL**

**1970—CORVETTE**

# Power Operated Headlamps Wiring

## Corvette

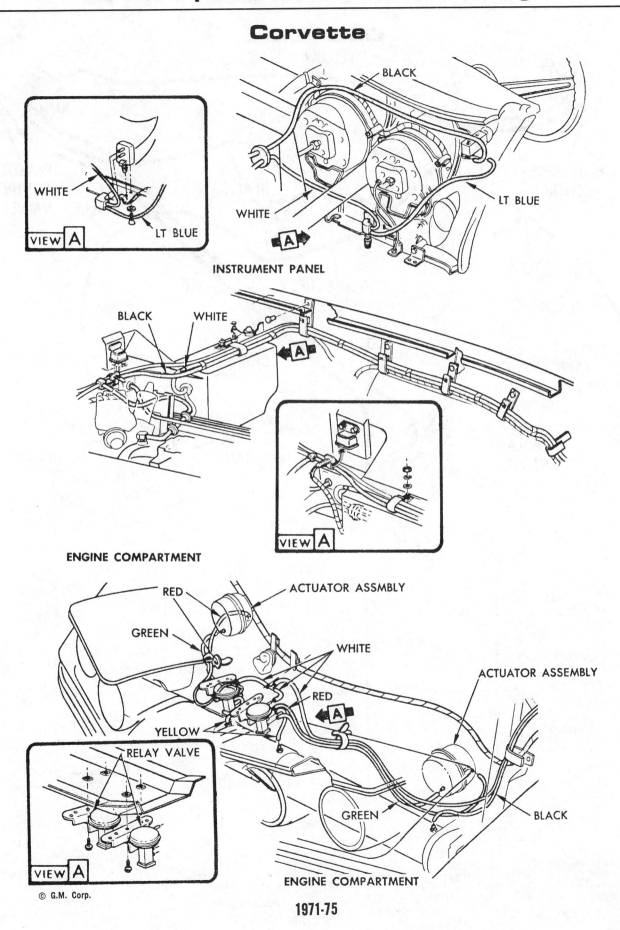

BLACK

WHITE

LT BLUE

WHITE

LT BLUE

VIEW A

A

INSTRUMENT PANEL

BLACK    WHITE

A

VIEW A

ENGINE COMPARTMENT

RED    ACTUATOR ASSMBLY

GREEN

WHITE

ACTUATOR ASSEMBLY

RED

A

YELLOW

RELAY VALVE

GREEN

BLACK

VIEW A

© G.M. Corp.

ENGINE COMPARTMENT

**1971-75**

# Power Operated Headlamps Wiring

## Oldsmobile

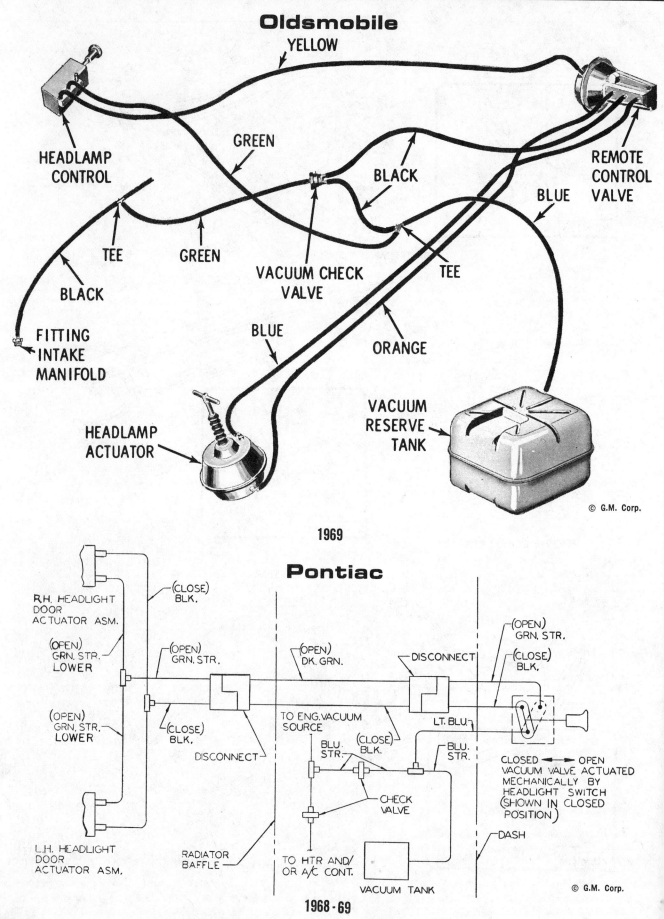

YELLOW

GREEN

BLACK

HEADLAMP
CONTROL

REMOTE
CONTROL
VALVE

BLUE

TEE

GREEN

TEE

BLACK

VACUUM CHECK
VALVE

FITTING
INTAKE
MANIFOLD

BLUE

ORANGE

HEADLAMP
ACTUATOR

VACUUM
RESERVE
TANK

© G.M. Corp.

1969

## Pontiac

R.H. HEADLIGHT
DOOR
ACTUATOR ASM.

(CLOSE)
BLK.

(OPEN)
GRN. STR.

(OPEN)
GRN. STR.
LOWER

(OPEN)
GRN. STR.

(OPEN)
DK. GRN.

DISCONNECT

(OPEN)
GRN. STR.

(CLOSE)
BLK.

(OPEN)
GRN. STR.
LOWER

(CLOSE)
BLK.

DISCONNECT

TO ENG. VACUUM
SOURCE

(CLOSE)
BLK.

LT. BLU.

BLU.
STR.

BLU.
STR.

CLOSED ←→ OPEN
VACUUM VALVE ACTUATED
MECHANICALLY BY
HEADLIGHT SWITCH
(SHOWN IN CLOSED
POSITION)

CHECK
VALVE

L.H. HEADLIGHT
DOOR
ACTUATOR ASM.

RADIATOR
BAFFLE

TO HTR AND/
OR A/C CONT.

DASH

VACUUM TANK

© G.M. Corp.

1968-69

**American Motors—
All Models—1968**
**Description**

The convertible top system uses a 12 volt reversible motor and a rotor type pump which is connected to two hydraulic lift cylinders by way of flexible hoses.

The motor and pump unit is installed in the body directly behind the rear seat assembly. Each hydraulic lift cylinder is located behind the convertible top compartment side trim panel.

The top is controlled by a three terminal switch mounted on the instrument panel. The right terminal of the control switch is the up circuit and the left terminal is the down circuit. The center terminal is connected to the battery by way of a 30 amp. circuit breaker, located on the back of the instrument panel, left of the ash tray.

When the control switch is actuated to raise the top, power is supplied through a red wire to the motor and pump unit. The motor drive shaft turns the rotors in the pump clockwise and forces the fluid under pressure to the bottom of each cylinder, forcing the piston rod upward and raising the top. The fluid that is above the cylinder piston is forced back into the pump and recirculated to the bottom of the cylinder.

When the control switch is actuated to lower the top, power is supplied through a yellow wire. The motor drive shaft turns the rotors counter clockwise and forces the fluid under pressure to the top of each cylinder, forcing the piston rod downward and lowering the top.

The fluid that is below the cylinder piston is forced back into the pump and recirculated to the top of each cylinder.

All the surplus fluid flows into the reservoir.

## Motor and Pump
### Removal

1. Raise the top fully.
2. Remove the rear seat cushion and seat back.
3. Disconnect the motor and ground wires.
4. In order to reduce the pressure within the hydraulic system, vent the reservoir by removing the filler plug, then re-install.
5. Place absorbent cloths under the hydraulic line connections at the pump.
6. Disconnect the hydraulic lines from the pump and plug the open fittings and lines.

## TROUBLESHOOTING CHART
### American Motors Power Operated Convertible Top

| Condition | Possible Cause |
|---|---|
| **1. Convertible top does not operate at all** | a. Improper motor ground<br>b. Circuit breaker at starter relay<br>c. Open or short circuit between power supply, switch, motor or pump<br>d. Defective control switch<br>e. Defective motor<br>f. Deficient pump pressure |
| **2. Convertible top operates sluggishly** | a. Improper ground<br>b. Defective motor<br>c. Kinked hydraulic hoses<br>d. Deficient pump pressure<br>e. One or both cylinders defective<br>f. Low voltage<br>g. Loss of fluid at hose connections<br>h. Improper lubrication of cylinder rods |
| **3. Convertible top binds while being raised or lowered** | a. Improper linkage adjustment or cylinder rods<br>b. Improper linkage adjustment or alignment |
| **4. Convertible top will operate in only the up direction** | a. Defective control switch<br>b. Open or short circuit in the motor yellow wire<br>c. Kinked top cylinder hoses |
| **5. Convertible top will operate in only the down direction** | a. Defective control switch<br>b. Open or short circuit in the motor red wire<br>c. Kinked lower cylinder hoses |

Filler Plugs      Ground Wire      Wire Connectors

© American Motors Corp.

Mounting Grommet      Supply Lines to Cylinders

*Power Unit and Supply Lines*

7. Remove the motor and pump to floor pan retaining nuts and washers.

### Installation

1. Unplug the hydraulic lines and fittings.
2. Position the motor and pump assembly to the floor pan.
3. Install the motor and pump mount nuts, rubber grommets and washers.
4. Connect the motor and ground wires.
5. Operate the top up and down to bleed air from the system.
6. Check the fluid level in the reservoir.
   (a) Raise the top to the full up position.
   (b) Fluid level should be within ¼ inch of filler plug opening.
   (c) Fill with automatic transmission fluid. Type "A"

### Motor and Pump

#### Disassembly

1. Remove the reservoir filler plug and the fluid into a clean container.
2. Scribe a line on the reservoir and pump body for proper reassembly.
3. Remove the reservoir cover center bolt.
4. Remove the reservoir cover and O-ring seal from the pump body.
5. Remove the hex head bolts that hold the valve body to the pump body.
6. Place a cloth under the unit and remove the valve body, making sure that the steel check balls are not lost.
7. Remove the inner and outer rotors and drive ball.

#### Assembly

1. Install the inner rotor on the armature shaft.
2. Place the outer rotor over the inner rotor.
3. Install the steel check balls in the motor body channels.
4. Position the valve body on the motor body.
5. Install the five valve body mounting bolts.
6. Install the valve body O-ring seal.
7. Using the line previously scribed on the reservoir and pump body, install the reservoir cover and center bolt.
   (a) Use a new seal on center bolt if possible.
8. Place the motor and pump unit

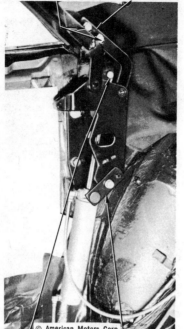

Balance Link Adjusting Screws    Balance Link

Cylinder Rod Pivot Pin    Trunnion Mounting Plate

© American Motors Corp.

*Cylinder Mounting*

in a horizontal position and fill the reservoir within ¼ inch of filler plug opening.

### Top Cylinder

#### Removal

1. Remove the rear seat.
2. Remove the rear quarter trim panel.
3. Remove the hairpin clip, washer, and clevis pin that attaches the upper end of the cylinder to the top linkage.
4. Remove the three cylinder mounting bolts at the bottom of the cylinder.
5. Pull the cylinder down and place absorbent cloths under the hydraulic line connections.

6. Disconnect the hydraulic lines and remove the cylinders.

### Installation

1. Install the hydraulic lines to the cylinder.
2. Position the bottom of the cylinder to the frame bracket and install the mounting bracket, two bushings and three bolts.
3. Position the top end of the cylinder to the linkage and install the clevis pin, washers, and hairpin.
4. Check the fluid level in the reservoir.
   (a) Raise the top to the full up position.
   (b) Fluid level should be within ¼ inch of filler plug opening.
   (c) Fill with automatic transmission fluid—Type "A".

### Control Switch

#### Removal

1. Remove the two self-threading nuts on the back of the switch bezel.
2. Disconnect the wires.
3. Remove the switch from the mounting bracket.

#### Installation

1. Position the switch to the mounting bracket.
2. Place the switch and mounting bracket to the dash and install chrome bezel.
3. Install the two self threading nuts on the back of the bezel.
4. Connect the wires.

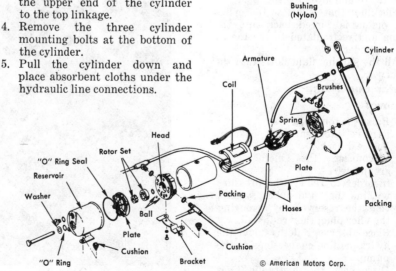

*Top Cylinder and Power Unit*

# Convertible Tops

## American Motors

### Hydraulic Checking Procedures

#### Checking fluid level

1. Remove the rear seat cushion and seat back.
2. Place an absorbent cloth below the reservoir filler plug.
3. Remove the plug. Fluid level should be even with the bottom of the filler plug hole.

#### Bleeding the system

1. Lower all the door and quarter windows.
2. Remove the filler plug and make sure the fluid level is even with the bottom of the filler plug hole.
3. Install the filler plug and tighten only one or two threads.
4. Run the engine and operate the top up and down a few times to purge the system of air pockets.
   (a) Excessive air can be seen in the transparent lines.
   (b) Replenish the reservoir to the proper level as necessary.
5. Tighten the filler plug.

### Electrical Testing Procedures

Before performing any extensive electrical testing procedures make sure there is no mechanical binding and the battery has a full charge.

#### Current Draw Test

1. Disconnect the black wire at the circuit breaker which is located on the starter relay and connect an ammeter in series in the circuit.

2. Operate the control switch and check to see that the maximum current draw is 28 amperes while operating and 40 to 50 amps stalled; with a voltage reading of 12.3 volts.
3. If the current is more than 75 amps. there is probably a frozen pump or cylinder.
4. A low amp. reading with no top movement and the motor running indicates a defective pump or a low fluid level in the reservoir.

#### Top Control Switch

1. Connect one lead of a test lamp to the black feed wire of the switch.
2. Ground the other test lamp lead.
3. If the test lamp does not light, there is an open or short circuit between the battery and the switch or a defective circuit breaker.
4. If the test lamp does light there is voltage to the switch.
5. Connect a jumper wire between the block feed wire and the red wire.
6. Then between the black wire and the yellow wire.
7. If the motor operates the switch is defective.

#### Circuit Breaker

1. Connect a jumper wire between the terminals of the circuit breaker, located on the starter relay.

2. Operate the switch.
3. If the top motor operates the circuit breaker is defective.
4. Check for voltage coming to the circuit breaker from the starter relay, through the black wire.

#### Switch to Motor Wires

1. Disconnect the yellow and the red switch to motor wires at the junction block near the motor.
2. Connect a test lamp between the red wire and a ground.
3. Operate the switch to lower the top.
4. Connect a test lamp between the yellow wire and a ground.
5. Operate the switch to raise the top.
6. If the test lamp does not light during either test, there is an open or short circuit in the wire from the junction block.

#### Motor Test

1. If the motor does not operate disconnect the motor wiring harness.
2. Check to see that the black wire is grounded properly.
3. Connect first the one motor lead then the other directly to the battery positive terminal.
4. If the motor does not operate replace the motor.
5. If the motor does operate, check the wiring harness for an open or short circuit.

## Chrysler Corporation

### Chrysler Corp.—All Models— 1968 to 1971

#### Description

The convertible top system uses a 12 volt reversible motor and a rotor type pump which is connected to two hydraulic lift cylinders by way of flexible hoses. The motor and pump unit is installed in the body directly behind the rear seat assembly. Each hydraulic lift cylinder is located behind the convertible top compartment side trim panel. The top is controlled by a double throw rotary switch and the motor and wiring are protected by a separate external circuit breaker. Power is supplied from the battery to the switch through a red wire.

When the control switch is actuated to raise the top current flows from the switch to the motor and pump unit through a brown wire. The motor drive shaft turns the rotors in the pump clockwise and forces the fluid under pressure to the bottom of

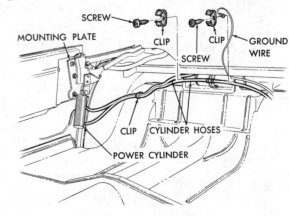

*Folding Top Mechanism*

531

# Chrysler Corporation

each cylinder, forcing the piston rod upward and raising the top. The fluid that is above the cylinder piston is forced back into the pump and re-circulated to the bottom of the cylinders.

When the control switch is actuated to lower the top current flows from the switch to the motor and pump unit through a yellow wire. The motor drive shaft turns the rotors counter clockwise and forces the fluid under pressure to the top of each cylinder, forcing the piston rod downward and lowering the top.

The fluid that is below the cylinder piston is forced back into the pump and recirculated to the top of each cylinder.

All the surplus fluid flows into the reservoir.

## Motor and Pump

### Removal

1. Raise the top fully.
2. Remove the rear seat cushion and seat back.
3. Disconnect the motor and ground wires.
4. In order to reduce the pressure within the hydraulic system, vent the reservoir by removing the filler plug, then re-install.
5. Place absorbent cloths under the hydraulic line connections at the pump.
6. Disconnect the hydraulic lines from the pump and plug the open fittings and lines.
7. Remove the motor and pump to floor pan retaining nuts and washers.

### Installation

1. Unplug the hydraulic lines and fittings.
2. Position the motor and pump assembly to the floor pan.
3. Install the motor and pump mount nuts, rubber grommets and washers.
4. Connect the motor and ground wires.
5. Operate the top up and down to bleed air from the system.
6. Check the fluid level in the reservoir.
   - (a) Raise the top to the full up position.
   - (b) Fluid level should be within $\frac{1}{4}$ inch of filler plug opening.
   - (c) Fill with automatic transmission fluid—Type "A".

## Motor and Pump

### Disassembly

1. Remove the reservoir filler plug

## TROUBLESHOOTING CHART

### Chrysler Corporation—Power Operated Convertible Top

| Condition | Possible Cause |
|---|---|
| 1. Convertible top does not operate at all | a. Improper ground<br>b. Circuit breaker at starter relay<br>c. Open or short circuit between power supply, switch, motor or pump<br>d. Defective control switch<br>e. Defective motor<br>f. Deficient pump pressure |
| 2. Convertible top operates sluggishly | a. Improper ground<br>b. Defective motor<br>c. Kinked hydraulic hoses<br>d. Deficient pump pressure<br>e. One or both cylinders defective<br>f. Low voltage<br>g. Loss of fluid at hose connections<br>h. Improper lubrication of cylinder rods |
| 3. Convertible top binds while being raised or lowered | a. Improper lubrication of hinges or cylinder rods<br>b. Improper linkage adjustment or alignment |
| 4. Convertible top will operate in only the up direction | a. Defective control switch<br>b. Open or short circuit in the motor yellow wire<br>c. Kinked top cylinder hoses |
| 5 Convertible top will operate in only the down direction | a. Defective control switch<br>b. Open or short circuit in the motor red wire<br>c. Kinked lower cylinder hoses |

and the fluid into a clean container.
2. Scribe a line on the reservoir pump body for proper reassembly.
3. Remove the reservoir cover center bolt.
4. Remove the reservoir cover and O-ring seal from the pump body.
5. Remove the hex head bolts that hold the valve body to the pump body.
6. Place a cloth under the unit and remove the valve body, making sure that the steel check balls are not lost.
7. Remove the inner and outer rotors and drive ball.

### Assembly

1. Install the inner rotor on the armature shaft.
2. Place the outer rotor over the inner rotor.
3. Install the steel check balls in the motor body channels.
4. Position the valve body on the motor body.
5. Install the five valve body mounting bolts.
6. Install the valve body O-ring seal.
7. Using the line preivously scribed

on the reservoir and pump body, install the reservoir cover and center bolt.
   - (a) Use a new seal on center bolt.
8. Place the motor and pump unit in a horizontal position and fill the reservoir within $\frac{1}{4}$ inch of filler plug opening.

## Top Cylinder

### Removal

1. Remove the rear seat.
2. Remove the rear quarter trim panel.
3. Remove the hairpin clip, washer, and clevis pin that attaches the upper end of the cylinder to the top linkage.
4. Remove the three cylinder mounting bolts at the bottom of the cylinder.
5. Pull the cylinder down and place absorbent cloths under the hydraulic line connections.
6. Disconnect the hydraulic lines and remove the cylinders.

### Installation

1. Install the hydraulic lines to the cylinder.
2. Position the bottom of the cylin-

# Chrysler Corporation

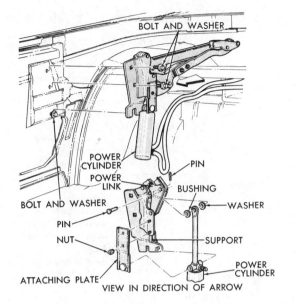

BOLT AND WASHER

POWER
CYLINDER
POWER
LINK
BOLT AND WASHER
PIN
NUT

PIN
BUSHING
WASHER
SUPPORT
POWER
CYLINDER
ATTACHING PLATE
VIEW IN DIRECTION OF ARROW

*Power Cylinder*

der to the frame bracket and install the mounting bracket, two bushings and three bolts.

3. Position the top end of the cylinder to the linkage and install the clevis pin, washers, and hairpin.

4. Check the fluid level in the reservoir.
   (a) Raise the top to the full up position.
   (b) Fluid level should be within ¼ inch of filler plug opening.
   (c) Fill with automatic transmission fluid—Type "A".

## Hydraulic Checking Procedures

### Checking fluid level

1. Remove the rear seat cushion and seat back.
2. Place an absorbent cloth below the reservoir filler plug.
3. Remove the plug. Fluid level should be even with the bottom of the filler plug hole.

### Bleeding the system

1. Lower all the door and quarter windows.
2. Remove the filler plug and make sure the fluid level is even with the bottom of the filler plug hole.
3. Install the filler plug and tighten only one or two threads.
4. Run the engine and operate the

top up and down a few times to purge the system of air pockets.
   (a) Excessive air can be seen in the transparent lines.
   (b) Replenish the reservoir to the proper level as necessary.

5. Tighten the filler plug.

## Electrical Testing Procedures

Before performing any extensive electrical testing procedures make sure there is no mechanical binding and the battery has a full charge.

### Current Draw Test

1. Disconnect the black wire at the circuit breaker which is located on the starter relay and connect an ammeter in series in the circuit.
2. Operate the control switch and check to see that the maximum current draw is 28 amps. while operating and 40 to 50 amps. stalled; with a voltage reading of 12.3 volts.
3. If the current is more than 75 amps. there is probably a frozen pump or cylinder.
4. A low amp. reading with no top movement and the motor running indicates a defective pump or a low fluid level in the reservoir.

### Top Control Switch

1. Connect one lead of a test lamp to the black feed wire of the switch.
2. Ground the other test lamp lead.
3. If the test lamp does not light, there is an open or short circuit between the battery and the switch or a defective circuit breaker.
4. If the test lamp does light there is voltage to the switch.
5. Connect a jumper wire between the black feed wire and the red wire.
6. Then between the black wire and the yellow wire.
7. If the motor operates the switch is defective.

### Circuit Breaker

1. Connect a jumper wire between the terminals of the circuit breaker, located on the starter relay.
2. Operate the switch.
3. If the top motor operates the circuit breaker is defective.
4. Check for voltage coming to the circuit breaker from the starter relay, through the black wire.

### Switch to Motor Wires

1. Disconnect the yellow and the red switch to motor wires at the junction block near the motor.
2. Connect a test lamp between the red wire and a ground.
3. Operate the switch to lower the top.
4. Connect a test lamp between the yellow wire and a ground.
5. Operate the switch to raise the top.
6. If the test lamp does not light during either test, there is an open or short circuit in the wire from the junction block.

### Motor Test

1. If the motor does not operate disconnect the motor wiring harness.
2. Check to see that the black wire is grounded properly.
3. Connect first the one motor lead then the other directly to the battery positive terminal.
4. If the motor does not operate replace the motor.
5. If the motor does operate, check the wiring harness for an open or short circuit.

# Ford Motor Company

### Ford—All Models

#### Description

The convertible top system uses a

12 volt reversible motor and a rotor type pump which is connected to two hydraulic lift cylinders by way of flexible hoses.

The motor and pump unit is installed in the body directly behind the rear seat assembly. Each hydraulic lift cylinder is located behind the

# Ford Motor Company

convertible top compartment side trim panel.

When the control switch is actuated to raise the top, power is supplied from the battery to the motor and pump unit through a red wire. The motor drive shaft turns the rotors in the pump clockwise and forces the fluid under pressure to the bottom of each cylinder, forcing the piston rod upward and raising the top. The fluid that is above the cylinder piston is forced back into the pump and recirculated to the bottom of the cylinders.

When the control switch is actuated to lower the top, power is supplied from the battery to the motor and pump unit through the yellow wire. The motor drive shaft turns the rotors counter clockwise and forces fluid under pressure to the top of each cylinder, forcing the piston rod downward and lowering the top.

The fluid that is below the cylinder piston is forced back into the pump and recirculated to the top of each cylinder. All the surplus fluid flows into the reservoir.

## Motor and Pump

### Removal

1. Raise the top fully.
2. Remove the rear seat cushion and seat back.
3. Disconnect the motor and ground wires.
4. In order to reduce the pressure within the hydraulic system, vent the reservoir by removing the filler plug, then re-install.
5. Place absorbent cloths under the hydraulic line connections at the pump.
6. Disconnect the hydraulic lines from the pump and plug the open fittings and lines.
7. Remove the motor and pump to floor pan retaining nuts and washers.

### Installation

1. Unplug the hydraulic lines and fittings.
2. Install the motor and pump assembly to the floor pan.
3. Install the motor and pump mount nuts, rubber grommets and washers.
4. Connect the motor and ground wires.
5. Operate the top up and down to bleed air from the system.
6. Check the fluid level in the reservoir.
   (a) Raise the top to the full up position.
   (b) Fluid level should be within ¼ inch of filler plug opening.
   (c) Fill with automatic transmission fluid. Type "A"

## Motor and Pump

### Disassembly

1. Remove the reservoir filler plug and the fluid into a clean container.
2. Scribe a line on the reservoir and pump body for proper reassembly.
3. Remove the reservoir cover center bolt.
4. Remove the reservoir cover and O-ring seal from the pump body.
5. Remove the hex head bolts that hold the valve body to the pump body.
6. Place a cloth under the unit and remove the valve body, making sure that the steel check balls are not lost.
7. Remove the inner and outer rotors and drive ball.

## TROUBLESHOOTING CHART

### Ford Power Operated Convertible Top

| Condition | Possible Cause |
|---|---|
| 1. Convertible top does not operate at all | a. Improper ground<br>b. Circuit breaker at starter relay<br>c. Open or short circuit between power supply, switch, motor or pump<br>d. Defective control switch<br>e. Defective motor<br>f. Deficient pump pressure |
| 2. Convertible top operates sluggishly | a. Improper ground<br>b. Defective motor<br>c. Kinked hydraulic hoses<br>d. Deficient pump pressure<br>e. One or both cylinders defective<br>f. Low voltage<br>g. Loss of fluid at hose connections<br>h. Improper lubrication of cylinder rods |
| 3. Convertible top binds while being raised or lowered | a. Improper lubrication of hinges or cylinder rods<br>b. Improper linkage adjustment or alignment |
| 4 Convertible top will operate in only the up direction | a. Defective control switch<br>b. Open or short circuit in the motor yellow wire<br>c. Kinked top cylinder hoses |
| 5. Convertible top will operate in only the down direction | a. Defective control switch<br>b. Open or short circuit in the motor red wire<br>c. Kinked lower cylinder hoses |

*Typical Motor and Pump Disassembled*

© Ford Motor Co.

# Ford Motor Company

## Assembly

1. Install the inner rotor on the armature shaft.
2. Place the outer rotor over the inner rotor.
3. Install the steel check balls in the motor body channels.
4. Position the valve body on the motor body.
5. Install the five valve body mounting bolts.
6. Install the valve body O-ring seal.
7. Using the line previously scribed on the reservoir and pump body, install the reservoir cover and center bolt.
   (a) Use a new seal on center bolt if possible.
8. Place the motor and pump unit in a horizontal position and fill the reservoir within $\frac{1}{4}$ inch of filler plug opening.

## Top Cylinder

### Removal

1. Remove the rear seat.
2. Remove the rear quarter trim panel.
3. Remove the hairpin clip, washer, and clevis pin that attaches the upper end of the cylinder to the top linkage.
4. Remove the three cylinder mounting bolts at the bottom of the cylinder.

5. Pull the cylinder down and place absorbent cloths under the hydraulic line connections.
6. Disconnect the hydraulic lines and remove the cylinders.

### Installation

1. Install the hydraulic lines to the cylinder.
2. Position the bottom of the cylinder to the frame bracket and install the mounting bracket, two bushings and three bolts.
3. Position the top end of the cylinder to the linkage and install the clevis pin, washers, and hairpin.
4. Check the fluid level in the reservoir.
   (a) Raise the top to the full position.
   (b) Fluid level should be within $\frac{1}{4}$ inch of filler plug opening.
   (c) Fill with automatic transmission fluid—Type "A".

## Hydraulic Checking Procedures

### Checking fluid level

1. Remove the rear seat cushion and seat back.
2. Place an absorbent cloth below the reservoir filler plug.
3. Remove the plug. Fluid level should be even with the bottom of the filler plug hole.

### Bleeding the system

1. Lower all the door and quarter windows.
2. Remove the filler plug and make sure the fluid level is even with the bottom of the filler plug hole.
3. Install the filler plug and tighten only one or two threads.
4. Run the engine and operate the top up and down a few times to purge the system of air pockets.
   (a) Excessive air can be seen in the transparent lines.
   (b) Replenish the reservoir to the proper level as necessary.
5. Tighten the filler plug.

## Electrical Testing Procedures

Before performing any extensive electrical testing procedures make sure there is no mechanical binding and the battery has a full charge.

### Current Draw Test

1. Disconnect the black wire at the circuit breaker which is located on the starter relay and connect an ammeter in series in the circuit.
2. Operate the control switch and check to see that the maximum current draw is 28 amps. while operating and 40 to 50 amps stalled; with a voltage reading of 12.3 volts.
3. If the current is more than 75 amps. there is probably a frozen pump or cylinder.
4. A low amp. reading with no top movement and the motor running indicates a defective pump or a low fluid level in the reservoir.

### Top Control Switch

1. Connect one lead of a test lamp to the black feed wire of the switch.
2. Ground the other test lamp lead.
3. If the test lamp does not light, there is an open or short circuit between the battery and the switch or a defective circuit breaker.
4. If the test lamp does light there is voltage in the switch.
5. Connect a jumper wire between the black feed wire and the red wire.
6. Then between the black wire and the yellow wire.
7. If the motor operates the switch is defective.

### Circuit Breaker

1. Connect a jumper wire between the terminals of the circuit breaker, located on the starter relay.

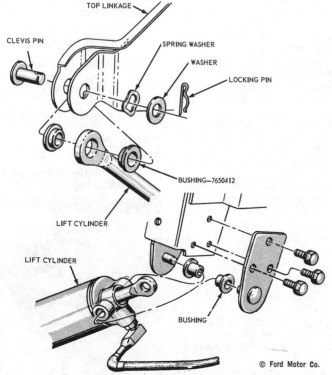

TOP LINKAGE

CLEVIS PIN

SPRING WASHER

WASHER

LOCKING PIN

BUSHING—7650412

LIFT CYLINDER

LIFT CYLINDER

BUSHING

© Ford Motor Co.

*Folding Top Lift Cylinder Installation*

# Ford Motor Company

2. Operate the switch.
3. If the top motor operates the circuit breaker is defective.
4. Check for voltage coming to the circuit breaker from the starter relay, through the black wire.

## Switch to Motor Wires

1. Disconnect the yellow and the red switch to motor wires at the junction block near the motor.
2. Connect a test lamp between the red wire and a ground.

3. Operate the switch to lower the top.
4. Connect a test lamp between the yellow wire and a ground.
5. Operate the switch to raise the top.
6. If the test lamp does not light during either test, there is an open or short circuit in the wire from the junction box.

## Motor Test

1. If the motor does not operate disconnect the motor wiring harness.
2. Check to see that the black wire is grounded properly.
3. Connect first the one motor load then the other directly to the battery positive terminal.
4. If the motor does not operate replace the motor.
5. If the motor does operate, check the wiring harness for an open or short circuit.

# General Motors

## General Motors—All Models— 1971-75 Actuator Type

### Description

The operation of the convertible top is controlled by a dash mounted switch and is powered by a 12 volt reversible motor coupled with a gear reduction unit. The reduction unit, motor and relay are accessible by removing the rear seat cushion and seat back.

The gear reduction unit has a drive cable attached to each side. Each cable is connected to an actuator, which is mounted to each main hinge on the side rail assembly of the top frame. Both actuator assemblies contain internal gear reduction units which multiply the power coming from the motor.

When the control switch is activated to the desired position the motor through the gear reduction unit drives the cables to each actuator and operates the top up and down.

## Actuator Drive Cable— Right Side

### Removal

1. Remove the rear seat cushion.
2. Remove the rear seat back.
3. Separate the drive cable from the top actuator assembly.
4. Separate the drive cable at the electric motor reduction unit.

### Installation

1. Connect the drive cable to the electric motor reduction unit.
2. Connect the drive cable to the top actuator assembly.
3. Install the rear seat back.
4. Install the rear seat cushion.

## Actuator Drive Cable— Left Side

### Removal

1. Remove the motor.

# TROUBLESHOOTING CHART

### GM—All Models—1971-75 Actuator Type

| Condition | Possible Cause |
|---|---|
| 1. Convertible top will not operate in either direction | a. Defective motor<br>b. Defective control switch<br>c. Open or short circuit between power supply, control switch, motor or relay<br>d. Defective actuator<br>e. Defective cable<br>f. Mechanical binding |
| 2. Convertible top will not operate in one direction | a. Defective control switch<br>b. Mechanical binding<br>c. Defective cable<br>d. Open or short circuit between switch and motor<br>e. Defective actuator |

a. Remove the rear seat cushion and seat back.
b. Separate the drive cable from the top actuator.
c. Separate the electric motor wire connectors from the relay.
d. Remove the relay attaching screw and remove the relay.
e. Remove the screw retaining the motor ground wire to the rear seat back panel.
f. Separate the rubber grommets retaining the motor support to the rear seat back panel.
2. Separate the drive cable from the electric motor reduction.

### Installation

1. Attach the drive cable to the electric motor reduction unit.
2. Install the motor.
   a. Apply a lubricant to the rubber grommets on the motor bracket and install to the rear seat back panel.
   b. Attach the motor ground wire to the rear seat back panel.

c. Install the relay and attaching screw.
d. Install the motor to relay wiring harness.
e. Attach the drive cable to the actuator.
f. Install the rear seat back and cushion.

## Electric Motor

### Removal

1. Remove the rear seat cushion and seat back.

*Drive Cable to Top Actuator Attachment*

# General Motors

2. Separate the drive cables from the actuator.
3. Separate the motor relay wiring harness.
4. Remove the screw retaining the motor ground wire to the rear seat back panel.
5. Separate the rubber grommets retaining the motor support to the rear seat back panel.
6. Separate the right and left drive cables from the electric motor reduction unit.
7. Remove the two motor to support attaching screws and remove the motor.

### Installation

1. Position the motor to the support and install the two retaining screws.
2. Install the right and left drive cables to the electric motor reduction unit.
3. Apply a lubricant to the rubber grommets on the motor and install to the rear seat back panel.
4. Attach the motor ground wire to the rear seat back panel.
5. Connect the motor relay wiring harness.
6. Attach the drive cables to the actuator.
7. Install the rear seat cushion and seat back.

## Relay

### Removal

1. Remove the rear seat cushion and seat back.
2. Separate the motor wiring harness from the relay.
3. Remove the relay attaching screw and remove the relay.

### Installation

1. Position the relay to back panel and install the retaining screw.
2. Connect the motor wiring harness to the relay.
3. Install the rear seat back and cushion.

## Top Actuator

### Removal

1. If possible lower the top.
2. Remove the rear seat cushion.
3. Remove the rear seat back.
4. Move the bottom of the main hinge cover panel to expose the actuator attaching screws.
5. Disconnect the drive cables from the actuator.
6. Remove the actuator to main hinge attaching screws.
7. Loosen the seat screw in the side rail actuator link.

8. Remove the shoulder bolt that connects the sector arm to the actuator link.

### Installation

1. Position the top actuator to the main hinge and install the

attaching screws. (Do not tighten).
2. Align the side rail actuator link with the sector arm.
3. Lubricate the shoulder bolt and install it through the actuator link and sector arm.

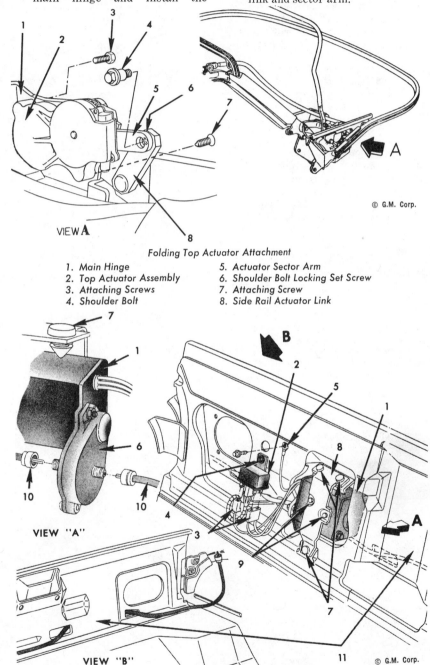

VIEW **A**

© G.M. Corp.

*Folding Top Actuator Attachment*

1. Main Hinge
2. Top Actuator Assembly
3. Attaching Screws
4. Shoulder Bolt
5. Actuator Sector Arm
6. Shoulder Bolt Locking Set Screw
7. Attaching Screw
8. Side Rail Actuator Link

VIEW "A"

VIEW "B"

© G.M. Corp.

*Folding Top Electric Motor and Relay*

1. Electric Motor
2. Relay
3. Electric Motor Connectors
4. Relay Attaching Screw
5. Motor Ground
6. Electric Motor Reduction Unit
7. Rubber Grommets
8. Motor Support
9. Motor Attaching Screw
10. Drive Cable
11. Seat Back Panel

## General Motors

4. Tighten the actuator link set screw.
5. Tighten the actuator to main hinge attaching screws.
6. Synchronize the actuators.
   a. Raise the top and lock at the windshield header.
   b. Disconnect each drive cable from the top actuators.
   c. Shake each side roof rail to equalize and position properly.
   d. Connect the drive cables to each actuator.
7. Replace the rear seat cushion and rear seat back.

### Synchronizing Top Actuators

1. Raise the top and lock at the windshield header.
2. Disconnect each drive cable from the top actuators.
3. Shake each side roof rail to equalize and position properly.
4. Connect the drive cables to each actuator.

### Front Roof Rail Lock

#### Removal

1. Unlock the front roof rail and hold several inches above the windshield header.
2. Hold the lock in the open position.
3. Unhook the coil spring.
4. Remove the lock attaching screws and remove the lock.

#### Installation

1. Position the lock to the roof rail and install the attaching screws.
2. Hook the coil spring.
3. Try operation of locks.
   a. Always lock the left side of top before locking the right side.

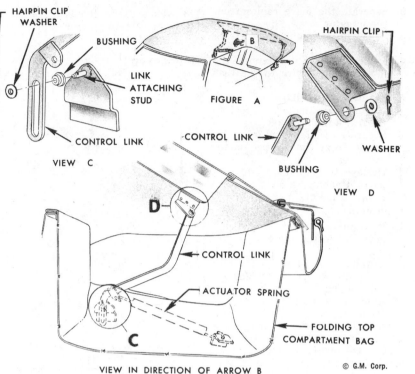

*Back Window Guide Control Link Attachment*

### Front Roof Rail Locating Pin

#### Removal

1. Lower the top either part way or completely.
2. Remove the locating pin attaching screw.

#### Installation

1. Position the plastic locating pin on the side roof front rail.
2. Install the locating pin attaching screw.

### Back Window Guide Control Link and Spring

#### Removal

1. Raise the top.
2. Remove the hair pin clip and washer from the link attaching stud at the back window.
3. Lift the control link which is under spring tension from the attaching bracket.
4. While carefully lowering the control link, lift the compartment bag over the control link and lay the control link on the floor.
5. Reach through the opening in the compartment bag and remove the actuator spring, first

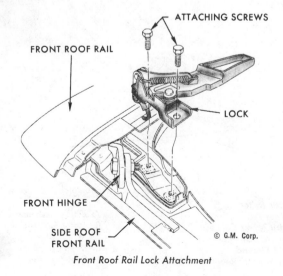

*Front Roof Rail Lock Attachment*

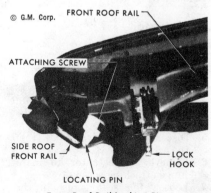

*Front Roof Rail Locking Pin*

## General Motors

from the link end, then from the floor bracket.

6. Through the compartment bag opening remove the control link hair pin clip and washer.

7. Remove the control link.

### Installation

1. Attach the control link to the front link attaching stud and install the hair pin clip and washer.

2. Connect the actuator spring from the floor bracket to the link end.

3. Install the hair pin clip and washer to the link attaching stud at the rear window.

## General Motors

### General Motors—All Models 1968-72 Hydraulic Pump Type

#### Description

The hydro-lectric Convertible Top system uses a 12 volt reversible motor and a rotor type pump which is connected to two hydraulic lift cylinders by way of flexible hoses.

The motor and pump unit is installed in the body directly behind the rear seat back support on all the intermediate models and on all full size models the unit is located in the body beneath the rear seat back panel. Each hydraulic lift cylinder is located behind the convertible top compartment side trim panel.

When the control switch is actuated to raise the top, power is supplied from the battery to the motor and pump unit through a red wire. The motor drive shaft turns the rotor in the pump clockwise and forces the fluid under pressure to the bottom of each cylinder, forcing the piston rod upward and raising the top. The fluid that is above the cylinder piston is forced back into the pump and recirculated to the bottom of the cylinders.

When the control switch is actuated to lower the top, power is supplied from the battery to the motor and pump unit through a green wire. The motor drive shaft turns the rotors counterclockwise and forces the fluid under pressure to the top of each cylinder, forcing the piston rod downward and lowering the top.

The fluid that is below the cylinder piston is forced back into the pump and recirculated to the top of each cylinder. All surplus fluid flows into the reservoir.

## TROUBLESHOOTING CHART

### Convertible Top Hydraulic Pump Type

| Condition | Possible Cause |
|---|---|
| 1. **Convertible top does not operate at all** | a. Open or short circuit between power supply, switch, motor or pump<br>b. Defective control switch<br>c. Defective motor<br>d. Deficient pump pressure |
| 2. **Convertible top operates sluggishly** | a. Kinked hydraulic hoses<br>b. Deficient pump pressure<br>c. One or both cylinders defective<br>d. Low voltage<br>e. Loss of fluid at hose connections<br>f. Improper lubrication of cylinder rods |
| 3. **Convertible top binds while being raised or lowered** | a. Improper lubrication of hinges or cylinder rods<br>b. Improper linkage adjustment or alignment |
| 4. **Convertible top will ioperate in only the up direction** | a. Defective control switch<br>b. Open or short circuit in the motor dark green wire<br>c. Kinked top cylinder hoses |
| 5. **Convertible top will operate in only the down direction** | a. Defective control switch<br>b. Open or short circuit in the motor red wire<br>c. Kinked lower cylinder hoses |

### Motor and Pump Assembly

#### Removal

1. Operate the top to the full up position.

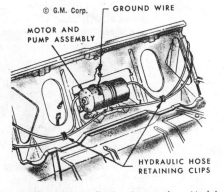

*Motor and Pump Installation—Intermediate Models*

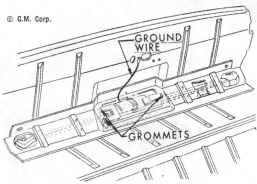

*Motor and Pump Installation—Full Size Models*

# General Motors

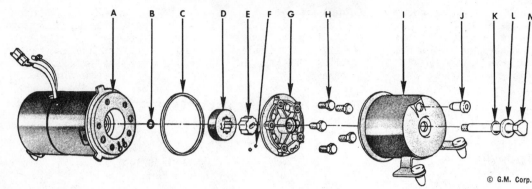

*Motor and Pump Components*

© G.M. Corp.

A. Motor Assembly
B. Motor Shaft "O" Ring Seal
C. Reservoir Seal
D. Outer Pump Rotor

E. Inner Pump Rotor
F. Fluid Control Valve Balls
G. Pump Cover Plate Assembly

H. Pump Cover Attaching Screws
I. Reservoir Tube and Bracket Assembly
J. Reservoir Filler Plug

K. Reservoir End Plate Attaching Bolt
L. Reservoir End Plate Attaching Bolt Washer
M. Reservoir End Plate Attaching Bolt

2. Disconnect the positive battery cable.
3. On all the intermediate models place a protective covering over the rear seat cushion.
4. On all the full size models including the Firebird and Camaro, remove the rear seat cushion and back.
5. From inside the car, detach the front edge of the folding top compartment bag from the rear seat back panel.
6. Remove the clips holding the wiring harness and hydraulic hose to the rear seat back panel and support.
7. Remove the pump to floor pan grommets.
   a. On the intermediate models remove the grommets from the rear seat back support.
8. To release pressure and keep the fluid from running out of disconnected lines remove the reservoir filler plug then reinstall.
9. Place absorbant cloths under the connections then disconnect the hydraulic lines.
   a. Cap all open fittings to prevent further fluid loss.

## Installation

1. Connect all hydraulic hoses.
2. Replace the floor pan and rear back panel pump attaching grommets.
3. Install the wiring harness and hose retaining clips.
4. Install the front edge of the folding top compartment bag.
5. On the full size models including the Firebird and Camaro replace the rear seat cushion and back.
6. Connect the positive battery cable.

*NOTE: When installing a replacement unit fill the reservoir with type "A" transmission fluid.*

## Reservoir Tube

### Dissassembly from the Motor and Pump Assembly

1. Remove the motor and pump assembly.
2. Scribe a line across the pump end plate and reservoir tube for proper reassembly. (see illustration)
3. Remove the reservoir filler plug.
4. Drain the fluid from the reservoir.

5. Remove the bolt from the end of the assembly and remove the reservoir tube.

### Assembly to Motor and Pump Assembly

1. Install the sealing ring on the pump and the reservoir tube according to the marker line drawn.
2. Install the attaching bolt.
3. Place the unit in a horizontal position and fill with fluid up to a ¼ in. of the lower edge of the filler plug.

## Folding Top Lift Cylinder

### Removal

1. Lock the top to the windshield header.
2. Disconnect the positive battery cable to prevent accidental operation of pump and loss of fluid.
3. Remove the rear seat cushion and seat back.
4. Remove the side trim panel on the folding top compartment.
5. Remove the cylinder rod upper end attaching nut, bolt, bushing and washer.
6. Remove the clips holding the hydraulic hose to the rear seat back panel.
7. Remove the inner and outer bolts that hold the cylinder to the hinge.
8. Move the cylinder to the inboard side of the top compartment brace, exposing the upper and lower hose to cylinder connections.
9. Disconnect the hose connectors.

### Installation

1. Transfer old connectors to the new cylinder and install hoses.
2. Position the cylinder to the hinge

RESERVOIR FILLER PLUG

© G.M. Corp.

ATTACHING BOLT    SCRIBE LINE

*Motor and Pump Assembly*

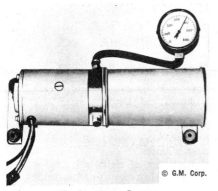

*Checking Pump Pressure*

© G.M. Corp.

and install the inner and outer bolts.

3. Connect the positive battery cable.
4. Using power, extend the cylinder piston rod all the way out.
5. Attach the cylinder rod to the linkage and install the nut, bolt, bushing and washer.
6. Check the level of the reservoir. Fluid level should be ¼ in. within the lower edge of the filler plug.
   a. Fill with type "A" transmission fluid.

## Hydraulic Checking Procedures

### Checking fluid level

1. Put the top up.
2. Separate the front edge of the top folding top compartment bag from the rear seat back panel.
3. Remove the clips holding the hydraulic hose to the rear seat back panel.
4. Separate the pump grommets from the floor pan holes.
5. Remove the filler plug using needle nose pliers.
6. Fluid level should be ¼ inch within the lower edge of the filler plug.
   a. Fill with type "A" transmission fluid.
7. Install filler plug.
8. Position the pump attaching grommets to the floor pan.
9. Install the clip holding the hydraulic hose to the rear seat back.
10. Install the front edge of the folding top compartment bag.

### Checking Operation of Lift Cylinders

1. Remove the rear seat cushion and seat back.
2. Remove the folding top compartment side panels.

3. Observe for the following conditions of the cylinders during up or down operation.
   a. If the cylinder movement is sluggish or uncoordinated, check the hydraulic hoses for kinks.
   b. If one cylinder rod moves slower than the other replace the slower cylinder.
   c. If both the cylinder rods move slowly or not at all check the pressure of the pump.

### Checking Pump Pressure

1. Remove the motor and pump assembly.
2. Install a plug in one port and a pressure gauge in the port to be checked.
3. Actuate the motor.
   a. With the applied terminal voltage between 9.5 and 11.0 volts the pressure gauge should read between 340 p.s.i. and 380 p.s.i.
4. Check the pressure in the other port.
   a. A difference in pressure readings is acceptable between the pressure port at the top of the cylinders and the pressure port at the bottom of the cylinders as long as the readings are between 340 p.s.i. and 380 p.s.i.
5. If the pressure is not between the specified limits, repair or replace the unit.

## Electrical Testing Procedure

### Testing For Current at the Control Switch

1. Disconnect the green motor feed wire at the switch.
2. Connect one wire of a test light to the center feed terminal of the switch terminal block.
3. Ground the other test light wire to the metal body.
4. If the test light does not light there is an open or short circuit between the switch and power source.

### Testing the Control Switch

1. Connect a 12 gauge jumper wire between the center feed terminal on the switch block and one motor wire terminal.
2. If the motor now operates but did not before, replace the control switch.

### Testing the Motor Lead Wires to Control Switch

1. Disconnect the green switch lead wire from the motor.

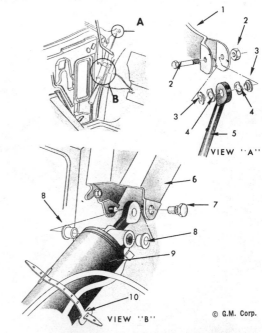

*Folding Top Lift Cylinder Attachment*

© G.M. Corp.

1. Side Roof Rear Rail
2. Piston Rod Attaching Bolt and Nut
3. Piston Rod Bushing
4. Piston Rod Anti-Rattle Washer
5. Piston Rod
6. Male Hinge
7. Cylinder Attaching Bolt
8. Cylinder Bushing
9. Top Lift Cylinder
10. Hydraulic Hose Retainer

## General Motors

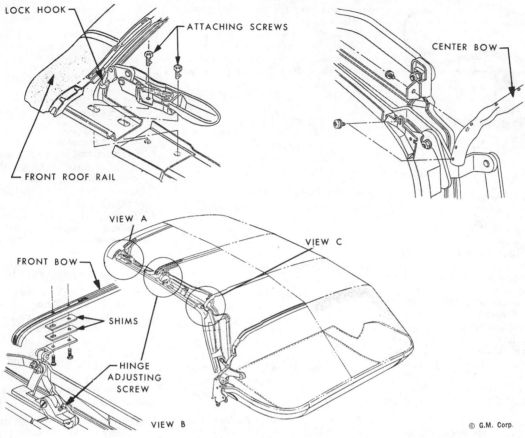

*Folding Top Adjustments*

© G.M. Corp.

2. Connect one test light wire to the motor terminal.
3. Ground the other test light wire to the metal body.
4. Operate the switch to the down position
   a. If the test light does not light there is an open or short circuit in the green wire.
5. Disconnect the red switch lead from the motor.
6. Connect one test light wire to the motor terminal.
7. Ground the other test light wire to the metal body.
8. Operate the switch to the up position.
   a. If the test light does not light there is an open or short circuit in the red wire.

### Motor Test

1. Check for a proper ground.
2. Connect a 12 gauge jumper wire

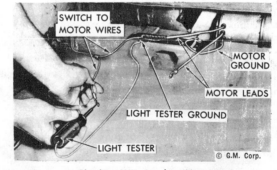

*Checking Wire Leads to Motor*

© G.M. Corp.

from the battery positive pole to the green lead terminal at the motor and lower the top.
3. Connect a jumper wire to the red lead terminal at the motor and raise the top.
4. If the motor fails to operate in

either direction it should be replaced.
5. If the motor operates using the jumper wire but not with the switch to motor wires check for an open or short circuit in the wires.

## Chrysler Corporation

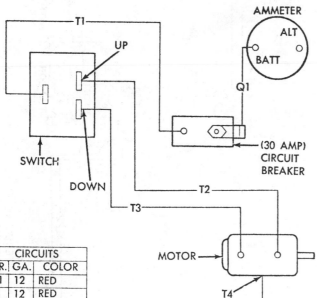

| CIRCUITS | | |
|---|---|---|
| CIR. | GA. | COLOR |
| Q1 | 12 | RED |
| T1 | 12 | RED |
| T2 | 12 | BROWN |
| T3 | 12 | YELLOW |
| T4 | 12 | BLACK |

**1968**

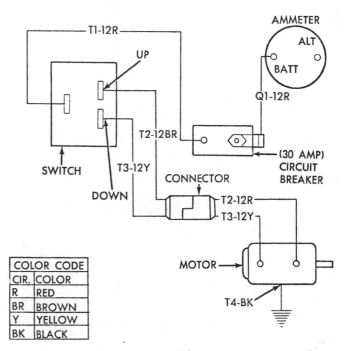

| COLOR CODE | |
|---|---|
| CIR. | COLOR |
| R | RED |
| BR | BROWN |
| Y | YELLOW |
| BK | BLACK |

**1969-71**

## Ford Motor Company
### Ford • Mercury

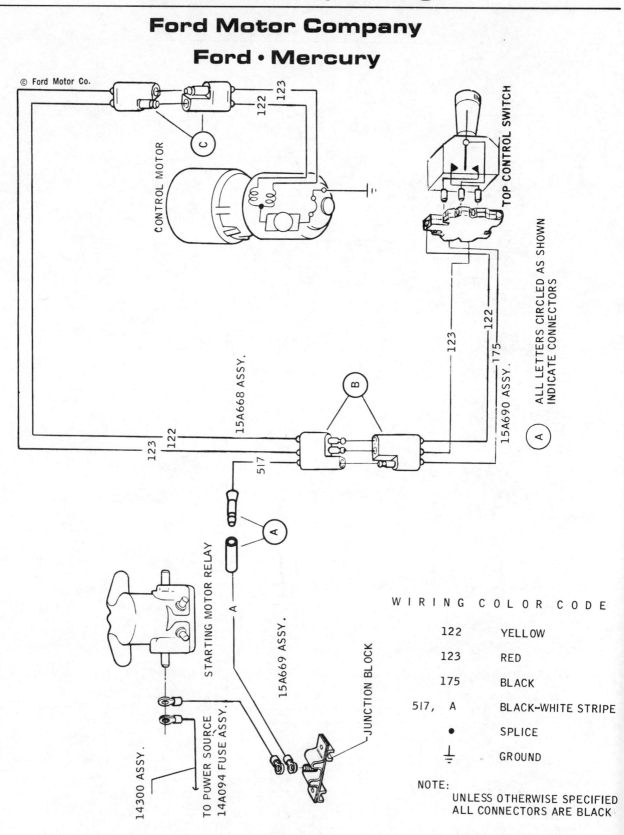

© Ford Motor Co.

CONTROL MOTOR

TOP CONTROL SWITCH

ALL LETTERS CIRCLED AS SHOWN
INDICATE CONNECTORS

122 123

15A668 ASSY.

15A690 ASSY.

15A669 ASSY.

STARTING MOTOR RELAY

JUNCTION BLOCK

14300 ASSY.

TO POWER SOURCE
14A094 FUSE ASSY.

WIRING COLOR CODE

| 122 | YELLOW |
|---|---|
| 123 | RED |
| 175 | BLACK |
| 517, A | BLACK-WHITE STRIPE |
| • | SPLICE |
| ⏚ | GROUND |

NOTE:
UNLESS OTHERWISE SPECIFIED
ALL CONNECTORS ARE BLACK

1968

## Ford • Mercury

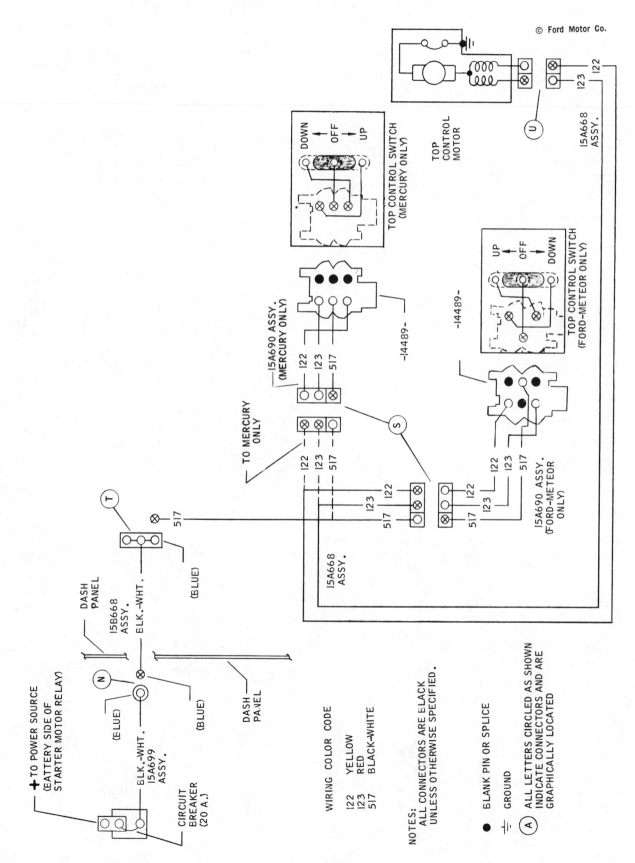

© Ford Motor Co.

1970

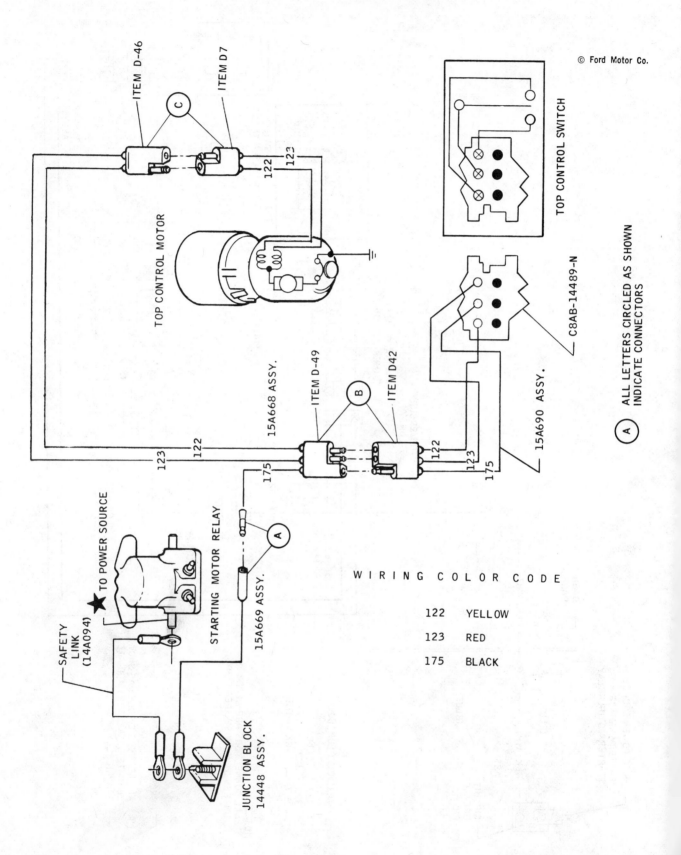

© Ford Motor Co.

TOP CONTROL SWITCH

C8AB-14489-N

(A) ALL LETTERS CIRCLED AS SHOWN INDICATE CONNECTORS

ITEM D-46

ITEM D7

(C)

122

123

TOP CONTROL MOTOR

15A668 ASSY.

ITEM D-49

(B)

ITEM D42

15A690 ASSY.

123

122

175

175

123

122

TO POWER SOURCE

★

SAFETY LINK (14A094)

STARTING MOTOR RELAY

15A669 ASSY.

(A)

JUNCTION BLOCK 14448 ASSY.

WIRING COLOR CODE

122    YELLOW

123    RED

175    BLACK

## Fairlane

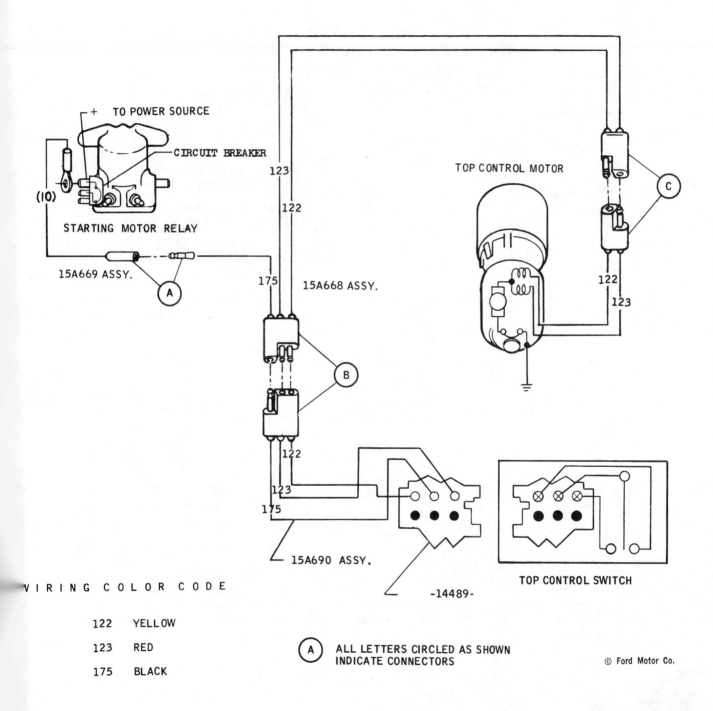

TO POWER SOURCE

CIRCUIT BREAKER

123

122

(10)

STARTING MOTOR RELAY

175

TOP CONTROL MOTOR

C

15A669 ASSY.

A

15A668 ASSY.

122

123

B

122

123

175

15A690 ASSY.

-14489-

TOP CONTROL SWITCH

WIRING COLOR CODE

122    YELLOW

123    RED

175    BLACK

(A)    ALL LETTERS CIRCLED AS SHOWN
        INDICATE CONNECTORS

© Ford Motor Co.

1970

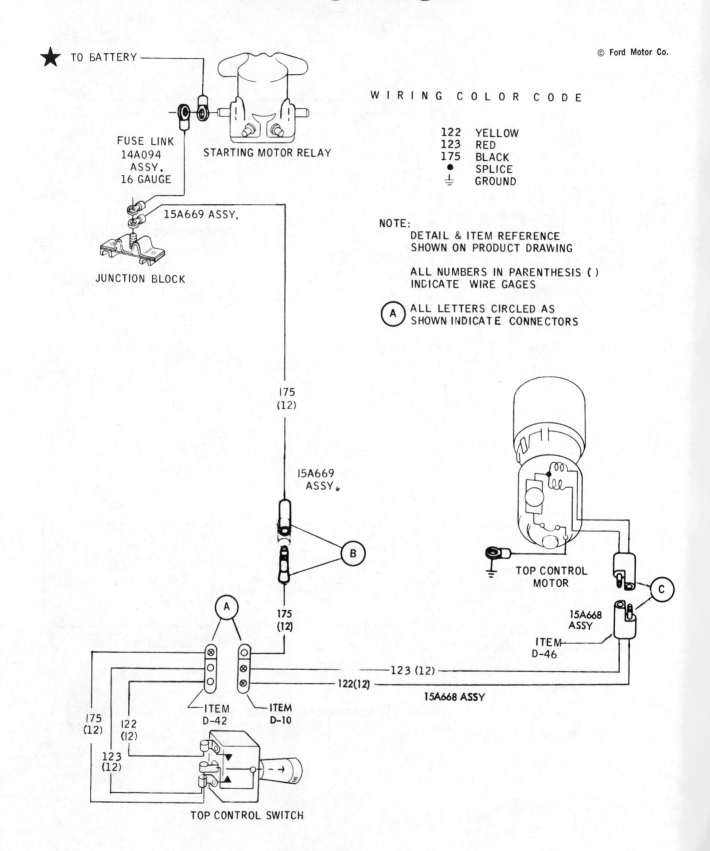

© Ford Motor Co.

TO BATTERY

FUSE LINK
14A094
ASSY.
16 GAUGE

STARTING MOTOR RELAY

15A669 ASSY.

JUNCTION BLOCK

WIRING COLOR CODE

122 YELLOW
123 RED
175 BLACK
• SPLICE
⏚ GROUND

NOTE:
DETAIL & ITEM REFERENCE
SHOWN ON PRODUCT DRAWING

ALL NUMBERS IN PARENTHESIS ( )
INDICATE WIRE GAGES

(A) ALL LETTERS CIRCLED AS
SHOWN INDICATE CONNECTORS

175
(12)

15A669
ASSY.

(B)

175
(12)

(A)

TOP CONTROL
MOTOR

15A668
ASSY

ITEM
D-46

(C)

123 (12)
122(12)
15A668 ASSY

ITEM
D-42

ITEM
D-10

175
(12)

122
(12)

123
(12)

TOP CONTROL SWITCH

1968

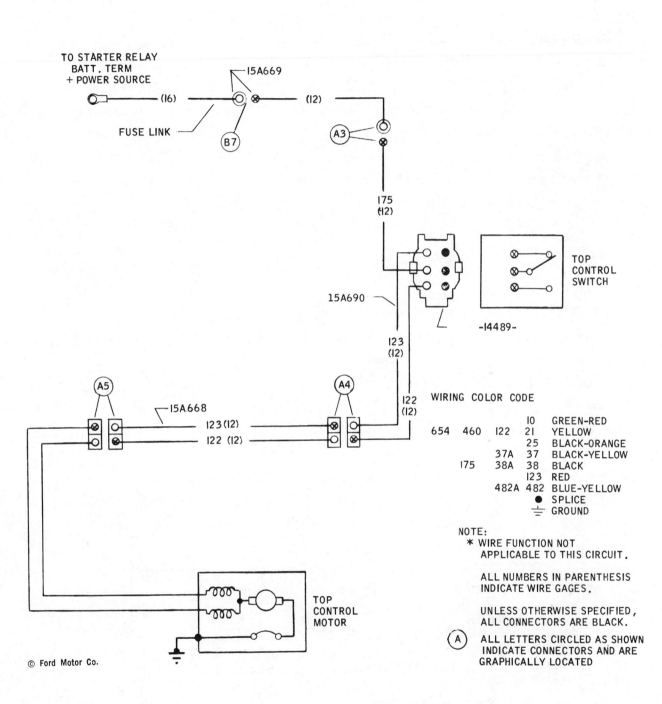

TO STARTER RELAY
BATT. TERM
+ POWER SOURCE

15A669

(16)

FUSE LINK

B7

(12)

A3

175
(12)

15A690

123
(12)

TOP
CONTROL
SWITCH

-14489-

122
(12)

A5

15A.668

A4

123 (12)

122 (12)

TOP
CONTROL
MOTOR

© Ford Motor Co.

WIRING COLOR CODE

| | | | 10 | GREEN-RED |
|---|---|---|---|---|
| 654 | 460 | 122 | 21 | YELLOW |
| | | | 25 | BLACK-ORANGE |
| | | 37A | 37 | BLACK-YELLOW |
| | 175 | 38A | 38 | BLACK |
| | | | 123 | RED |
| | | 482A | 482 | BLUE-YELLOW |
| | | | ● | SPLICE |
| | | | ⏚ | GROUND |

NOTE:
* WIRE FUNCTION NOT
  APPLICABLE TO THIS CIRCUIT.

ALL NUMBERS IN PARENTHESIS
INDICATE WIRE GAGES.

UNLESS OTHERWISE SPECIFIED,
ALL CONNECTORS ARE BLACK.

(A) ALL LETTERS CIRCLED AS SHOWN
INDICATE CONNECTORS AND ARE
GRAPHICALLY LOCATED

1970

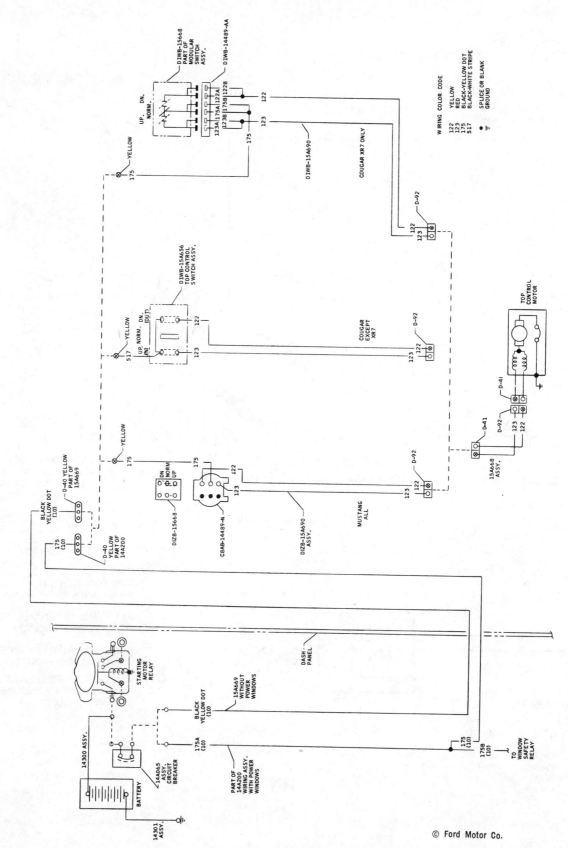

© Ford Motor Co.

1971

# Convertible Top Wiring

## General Motors
## Pontiac

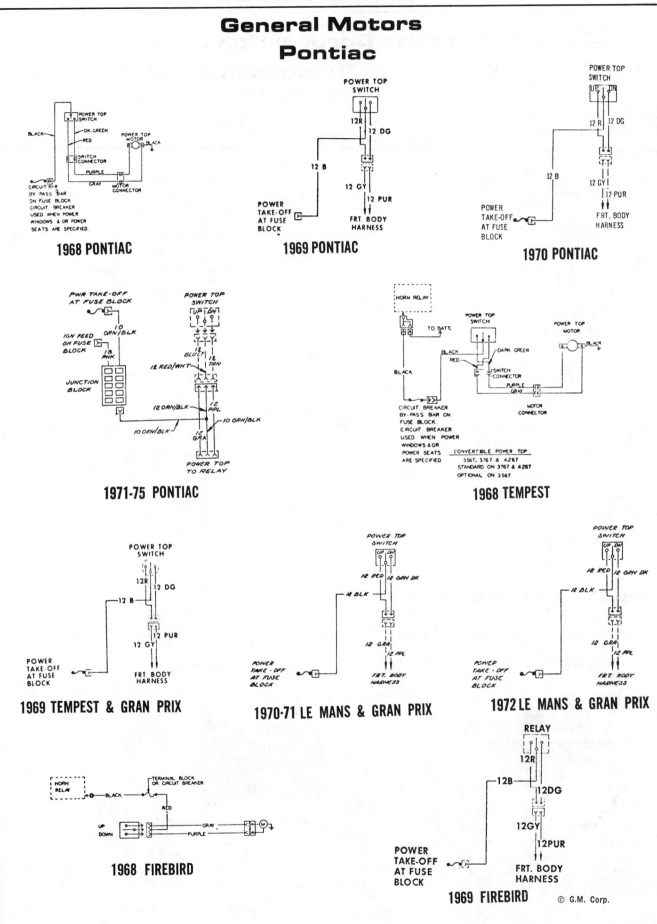

**1968 PONTIAC**

**1969 PONTIAC**

**1970 PONTIAC**

**1971-75 PONTIAC**

**1968 TEMPEST**

**1969 TEMPEST & GRAN PRIX**

**1970-71 LE MANS & GRAN PRIX**

**1972 LE MANS & GRAN PRIX**

**1968 FIREBIRD**

**1969 FIREBIRD**

© G.M. Corp.

## Chrysler Corporation

## POWER OPERATED SUNROOF

### Chrysler Corporation— All Models—1972-75

#### Description

The sunroof is controlled by a two position switch, located on the right side of the roof panel.

A 12 volt reversible motor with an integral gear drive mechanism is mounted to the roof panel, forward of the roof opening near the center of the windshield header area. The motor drives two flexible cables which are attached to the sunroof sliding panel.

When the switch is actuated to open the sunroof the panel retreats down and rearward on guide rails into a space between the headlining and the roof.

When the switch is actuated to close the sunroof the panel moves forward and upward on two ramps until the panel is flush with the roof's surface.

The electrical system is protected by a 25 amp. circuit breaker located on the left side kick panel. Power is supplied from the fuse block through a red wire to the circuit breaker. Another red wire is routed from the circuit breaker to the control switch.

Two wires are routed from the switch to the motor. One wire is for the open cycle and one for the close cycle. A wire is connected to the windshield header by a screw for a ground.

### Motor and Drive Gear Assembly

#### Removal

1. Open the sunroof to the three

## TROUBLESHOOTING CHART

### Chrysler Corp.—Power Operated Sunroof

| Condition | Possible Cause |
|---|---|
| 1. Sunroof will not operate at all with ignition on | a. Open or short circuit between power supply, switch, or motor<br>b. Defective circuit breaker<br>c. Defective ignition relay<br>d. Defective control switch<br>e. Defective motor<br>f. Mechanical binding |
| 2. Motor runs, but no panel movement | a. Panel alignment<br>b. Disconnected or damaged drive cables<br>c. Clutch slippage in drive gear assembly (see motor and drive gear installation) |
| 3. Panel moves sluggishly | a. Improper lubrication of cables, rails<br>b. Improper panel alignment |

quarter full open position.
2. Disconnect the negative battery cable.
3. Remove the windshield garnish mouldings from the left and right sides.
4. Remove the garnish mouldings from the roof side rails.
5. Remove both sun visor assemblies and the center sun visor bracket.
6. Carefully pull the headlining down enough to gain access to the motor and drive gear.
7. Remove the foam insulator padding in front of the roof panel opening next to the motor and drive gear assembly.
8. Disconnect the motor electrical connector.
9. Remove the drive cable housing cover.
10. Remove the left and right elbow corner guides.
11. Carefully pry up the drive cable retaining clip (hold hand over clip to keep from springing up.)
12. Pull the drive cables out of the upper and lower front guides noting routing for installation.
13. Remove the three drive cable housing screws and remove the housing.
14. Remove the two drive gear assembly retaining screws and remove the drive gear assembly and motor.

#### Installation

1. Push the plastic cover over the motor to the base of the drive gear assembly.
2. Position the motor and drive

MOTOR CONNECTION PIGTAIL

MOTOR

DRIVE CLUTCH SCREW

ELECTRIC MOTOR

DRIVE PINION

SWITCH

MOTOR TO SWITCH PIGTAIL

*Electric Motor*

## Chrysler Corporation

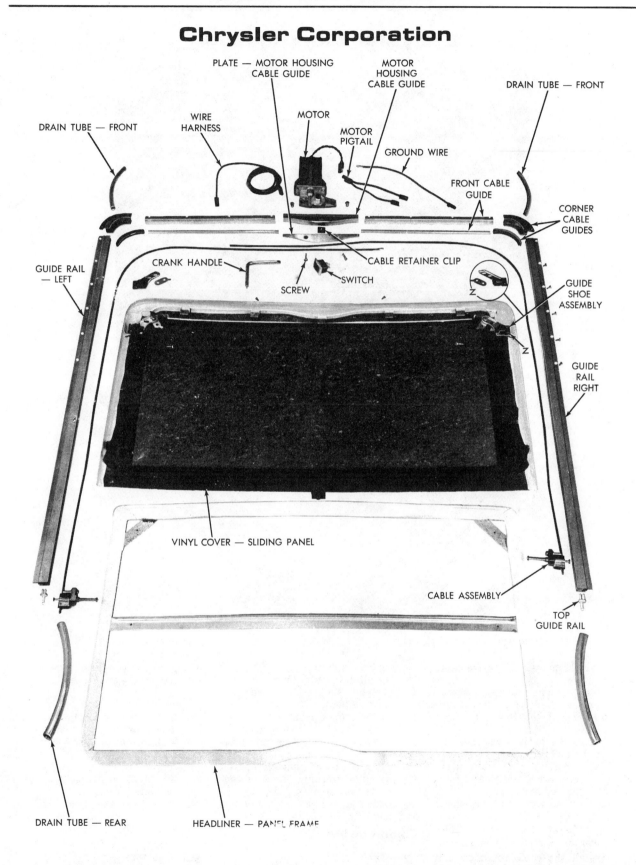

PLATE — MOTOR HOUSING CABLE GUIDE

MOTOR HOUSING CABLE GUIDE

DRAIN TUBE — FRONT

WIRE HARNESS

MOTOR

MOTOR PIGTAIL

GROUND WIRE

DRAIN TUBE — FRONT

DRAIN TUBE — FRONT

FRONT CABLE GUIDE

CORNER CABLE GUIDES

CABLE RETAINER CLIP

GUIDE RAIL — LEFT

CRANK HANDLE

SCREW

SWITCH

GUIDE SHOE ASSEMBLY

Z

Z

GUIDE RAIL RIGHT

VINYL COVER — SLIDING PANEL

CABLE ASSEMBLY

TOP GUIDE RAIL

DRAIN TUBE — REAR

HEADLINER — PANEL FRAME

*Roof Panel Disassembled*

# Chrysler Corporation

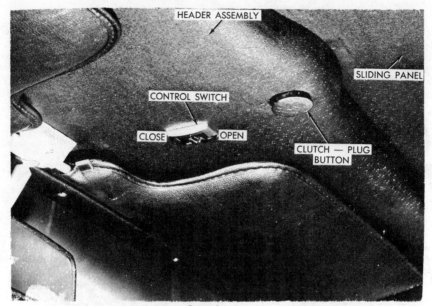

*Control Switch*

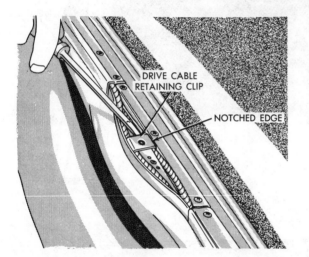

*Removing Drive Cable Retaining Clip*

*Headlining Panel Removal*

gear assembly in the drive cable housing.
3. Install the two retaining screws.
4. Replace the drive cable housing and install the three retaining screws.
5. Insert the cable ends into the guides and reroute.
   (a) Lubricate cables and drive gear with cold weather approved lube.
6. Install the right and left elbow corner guides.

*Note: The alignment of the lower elbow corner guide is very important.*

7. Install the cable retaining clip by pressing down firmly.
8. Install the drive cable housing cover.
9. Connect the motor electrical

wiring connector.
10. Install the battery terminal.
11. Cement the foam insulation padding in place.
12. Apply trim cement to the forward edge of the roof panel.
13. Starting from the center, position the headlining to the forward edge and smooth out all wrinkles, working from the center to the outboard ends.
14. Install all the garnish mouldings and both sun visors.

## Control Switch

### Removal

1. Pull instrument panel insert out of the bezel.
2. Disconnect the electrical feed wires from the wiring harness.

3. Remove the retaining screw and remove the switch.

### Installation

1. Install the switch to the instrument panel insert and secure with the one screw.
2. Connect the switch electrical connectors.
3. Install the instrument panel insert into the bezel.
   (a) Press the right side until secured by the spring catch.

## Sunroof Panel

### Removal

1. Open the sunroof approximately three inches.

## Chrysler Corporation

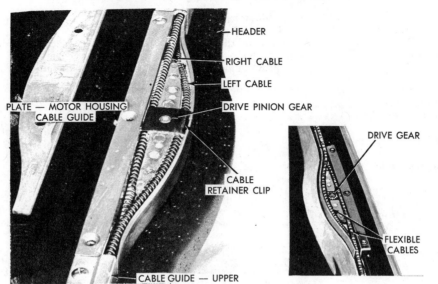

*Drive Pinion Gear and Cables*

2. Remove the two screws from the front of the headlining panel.
3. Slide the headlining panel forward and out of the retaining clips.
4. Close the roof and push the headlining panel to the full rearward position.
5. Remove the outboard screw from each front slide assembly.
6. Loosen the inboard screws and rotate both front slide assemblies inboard to clear the guide rail.
7. Pull each rear slide and cable assembly inboard and out of the slide retainer hole of the roof opening.
8. Lift the panel at the front edge and pull forward and out of the opening.

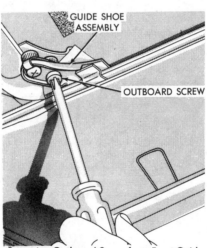

*Removing Outboard Screw from Front Guide Shoe.*

### Installation

1. While the headlining panel is in the full rearward position install the roof panel into the opening without damaging the headlining.
2. Move each front slide assembly outboard and install the slides on the guide rail upper tracks.
3. Install the outboard screws and tighten on each slide.
4. Push the roof panel to the full forward position.
5. Lift the rear of the roof panel upward and actuate the control switch to move the rear slides into alignment with the holes on the slide retainers.
6. Engage each rear slide pin into the retainer holes and install the retainer springplate on the slide pin.

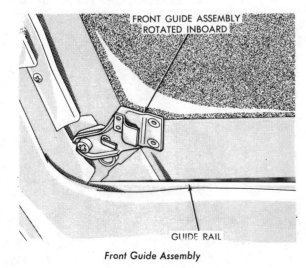

*Front Guide Assembly*

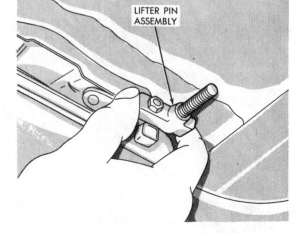

*Removing Lifter Pin and Cable Assembly*

## Chrysler Corporation

7. Adjust panel if necessary (see sunroof adjustments.)

### Rear Slide and Cable

#### Removal

1. Remove the sunroof panel. (see sunroof panel removal)
2. Remove the drive cable housing cover.
3. Remove both the front upper elbow guides.
4. Pry off the drive cable retaining clip.
5. Pull the free end of one cable out of the guide rail and drive housing, and pull the cable and rear slide assembly forward to the front corner.
6. Remove the slide from the guide track and pull the cable out of the front guide.

#### Installation

1. Position the left rear slide in the guide track and move the slide and cable assembly back until the slide is centered with the fifth side guide rail screw from the front.
2. Slide the free end of the cable into the upper front guide.
3. Route the cable through the curved front center track in the drive cable housing and into the lower track on the right side.
4. Check both front corner lower elbow guides for alignment with the front and side guides. (Shim, if necessary.)
5. Lubricate the cables with a cold weather approved lube at the elbow guide areas.
6. Install both the front corner upper elbow guides.
7. Check to make sure the rear slides are centered with the fifth screw from the front on the side guide rails, then engage the cables in the drive pinion teeth.
8. Lubricate the cables and drive pinion teeth with a cold weather approved lube.

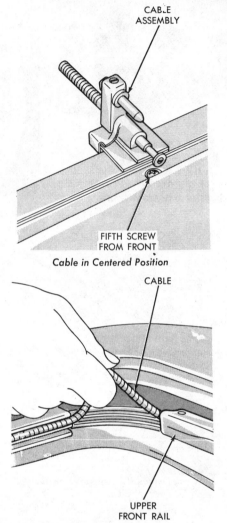

*Cable in Centered Position*

*Removing Cable Assemblies from Front Rails*

9. Install the drive cable retaining clip.
10. Install the drive cable housing cover.
11. Install the roof panel (see roof panel installation.)

### Sunroof Adjustments

#### Panel Alignment— Front, Left, or Right

1. To obtain a flush fit with the roof on one side of the front of the roof panel, loosen both front slide screws.
2. Turn the knurled nuts clockwise to raise the roof panel and counter-clockwise to lower the panel.
3. When the panel is aligned properly tighten the screws.
4. If necessary, adjust the opposite front slide in the same way.

#### Panel Alignment— Rear, Left, or Right

1. To obtain a flush fit with the roof on one side of the rear of the roof panel, loosen the 3/8 locknut on the rear slide.
2. Turn the adjusting screw clockwise to raise the roof panel and counter-clockwise to lower the panel.
3. After aligning the panel, properly tighten the locknut.
4. If necessary, adjust the opposite rear slide in the same way.

#### Ramp Adjustment

1. When the roof panel is being closed and does not rise into the roof opening, remove the headlining panel from the roof panel and open the roof panel to the full rearward position.
2. Examine the ramps in the drainage channel to see if they

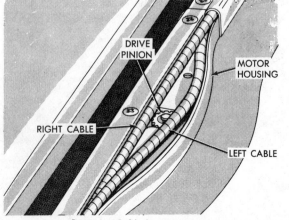

*Removing Cable from Housing*

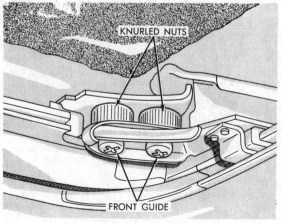

*Panel Alignment—Front*

# Chrysler Corporation

are properly aligned with the lifting elements at the rear of the panel.

   (a) The point where the lifting element makes contact with the ramp can be seen on the rearward slope of the ramp.

3. Pry the ramp up and move it from side to side until it is centered with the lifting element.
4. Close the roof panel and watch the lifting action of the panel.
5. If required, readjust the ramps up or down or side to side until proper lifting action is obtained.

## Panel Does Not Run True

1. Close the roof panel to see which side jams.
2. Open the roof panel.
3. Remove the drive housing center cover.
4. Pry off the drive cable retaining clip.

   (a) Hold a hand over the clip to keep it from flying upward.

5. To move the right side of the roof panel forward, lift the right cable at the front of the pinion and pull it one or more teeth to the left.
6. Install the retaining clip and the drive housing cover.
7. Move the left side of the roof panel in the same manner.

## Cable Guide Alignment

1. If the roof panel jams during operation, check both front corner lower elbow guides for alignment with the front and side guides.
2. If necessary, shim the lower elbow guides to move the guides inboard for alignment with the adjacent guides.

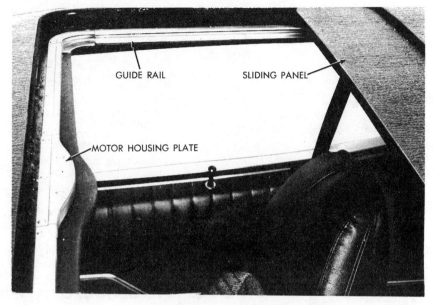

*Guide Rails—Sunroof Opened*

3. If the panel fails to rise, the joints of the cable slides are out of alignment and are jamming the cable drive.

   (a) Loosen the screws retaining the guide rails, corner and connector rails and drive cable housing.

   (b) While continually activating the drive mechanism, align the points where resistance is felt and retighten the screws one by one.

## Power Sunroof Electrical Testing Procedures

Before performing any extensive electrical testing procedures make sure the battery has a full charge and that there are no mechanical bindings. Also check all wire connections for proper contact.

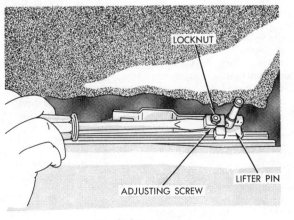

*Panel Alignment—Rear*

## Testing the Feed Wires to the Circuit Breaker

1. Connect one test light lead to the battery side of the circuit breaker.
2. Ground the other test light lead.
3. If the test light does not light, there is an open or short circuit in the feed wire to the circuit breaker.

## Circuit Breaker Test

1. Disconnect the output feed wire from the circuit breaker (the wire opposite the power feed wire to the circuit breaker.)
2. Using a test light, check the disconnected terminal.
3. If the test light does not light the circuit breaker is defective.

## Testing the Ignition Relay

1. Using a test light, check the relay feed wire.
2. If the test light does not light, there is an open or short circuit between the relay and circuit breaker.
3. Using a test light, check the output terminal of the relay while the ignition switch is turned on.
4. If the test light does not light, connect a test light on the ignition coil terminal.
5. If the test light lights, replace the ignition relay.
6. If the tester does not light, there is an open or short circuit in the power feed, and ignition to relay wires.

## Chrysler Corporation

### Testing for Current at the Control Switch

1. Connect one test light lead to the control switch feed terminal of the switch block.
2. Turn the ignition switch on.
3. Ground the other test lead.
4. If the test light does not light, there is an open or short circuit between the relay and control switch.

### Control Switch Test

1. Connect one end of a 12 gauge jumper wire to the red feed wire.
2. Connect the other end to the light green motor feed wire.
3. Use a second jumper wire and connect the black motor feed wire with the black switch ground wire.
4. If the motor does not operate with the switch but does with the jumper wires, check to see that the switch is grounded properly.
5. If the switch is grounded properly, replace the switch.

### Testing the Switch to Motor Wires

1. Disconnect the motor wire connectors.
2. Connect one end of a test light to ground.
3. Connect the other to one of the two motor feed wires.
4. Actuate the control switch, if the test lamp does not light, there is an open or short circuit between the control switch and the motor.
5. Test the other motor feed wire in the same manner.

### Motor Test

1. Disconnect the wire harness connector from the motor.
2. Connect one end of a test lamp to one of the two motor feed wire.
3. Connect the other test lamp lead to ground.
4. Actuate the control switch, if the test lamp lights, check to see that the switch is properly grounded.
5. If the switch is properly grounded then the motor is defective.

## Ford Motor Company

### Ford—Power Operated Sunroof—1969-74
### Power Operated Moonroof—1975

#### Description

The sunroof is controlled by a two position switch, located on the windshield header area.

A 12 volt reversible motor with an integral gear drive mechanism is mounted to the roof panel, forward of the roof opening near the center of the windshield header area. The motor drives two flexible cables which are attached to the sunroof sliding panel.

When the switch is actuated to open the sunroof the panel retreats down and rearward on guide rails into a space between the headlining and the roof.

When the switch is actuated to close the sunroof the panel moves forward and upward on two ramps until the panel is flush with the roof's surface.

#### Motor and Drive Coupling

##### Removal

1. Disconnect the battery ground cable.
2. Remove both sun visor assemblies and the center sun visor bracket.
3. On all Thunderbirds:
   (a) Remove the control switch from the convenience panel.
   (b) Remove the windshield upper and side garnish mouldings.
   (c) Remove the left side rail garnish mouldings.
   (d) Remove the convenience panel from the front edge of the roof panel.
4. On all Cougars:
   (a) Remove the windshield side garnish mouldings.
   (b) Remove the map light or convenience panel.
5. To gain access to the motor and drive coupling, carefully pull down the headlining from behind the windshield weatherstrip.
6. Disconnect the two motor wires and the motor ground wire connected to the windshield header.
7. Remove the two motor support bracket mounting bolts and slide the motor and bracket assembly off the drive coupling.
8. Slide the motor from the support bracket.

##### Installation

1. Connect the motor shaft to the drive coupling.
2. Position the motor and bracket assembly and install the two retaining bolts.
3. Connect the motor wires and secure the ground wire to the windshield header.
4. Connect the battery ground cable.
5. Apply cement to the forward edge of the headlining. Start from the center and position the

### TROUBLESHOOTING CHART

#### Ford—All Models—Power Operated Sunroof

| Condition | Possible Cause |
|---|---|
| 1. Sunroof will not operate at all with ignition on | a. Open or short circuit between power supply, switch, or motor<br>b. Defective circuit breaker<br>c. Defective ignition relay<br>d. Defective control switch<br>e. Defective motor<br>f. Mechanical binding |
| 2. Motor runs, but no panel movement | a. Panel alignment<br>b. Disconnected or damaged drive cables<br>c. Clutch slippage in drive gear assembly (see motor and drive gear installation) |
| 3. Panel moves sluggishly | a. Improper lubrication of cables, rails<br>b. Improper panel alignment |

# Ford Motor Company

headlining to the windshield header.

6. Install the windshield weatherstrip to retain the headlining in position.

7. On the Cougar Model, install the map light and/or convenience panel.

8. Install the windshield garnish mouldings.

9. On the Thunderbirds, install the roof side rail garnish mouldings and the control switch in the convenience panel.

10. Install both sun visors and the center bracket.

## Drive Pinion

### Removal

1. Open the sunroof panel to the full open position.

2. Remove the cable drive housing cover.

3. Remove the snap ring, flat washer and pinion from the shaft.

### Installation

1. Position the new pinion and in-

stall the flat washer and snap ring.

2. Re-engage the drive cables to the pinion and install the retaining clip.

3. Replace the drive cable housing center.

## Sunroof Panel

### Removal

1. Open the roof panel approximately three inches.

2. Remove the two screws that secure the headlining trim panel to the sliding roof panel at the front corners.

3. Slide the headlining trim panel forward and out of the trim retaining clips.

4. Move the trim panel to the full rearward posiiton.

5. Remove the outboard screw from each front slide assembly.

6. Loosen the inboard screws and rotate both front slide assemblies inboard to clear the guide rail.

7. Pull the left and right rear slide and cable assemblies out of the guide retainer holes at the rear of the panel.

8. Lift the front edge of the roof panel up and at the same time operate the switch to move the rear slide and cable assemblies forward one inch.

9. Pull the roof forward and out of the roof opening.

### Installation

1. Install the roof panel into the roof opening without damaging the headlining.

2. Position the left and right front slides out onto their guide rail upper tracks.

3. Install and tighten both outboard screws on the front slides.

4. Push the roof panel to the full forward position.

5. Lift the rear of the roof panel upward while actuating the control switch to bring the rear slides into alignment with the holes on the slide retainers.

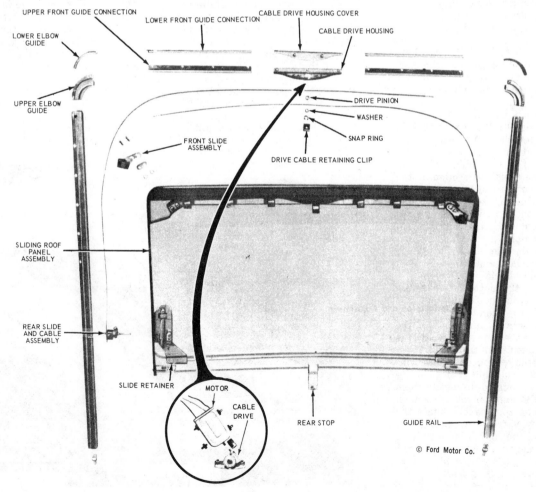

© Ford Motor Co.

*Roof Panel Disassembled*

# Ford Motor Company

6. Engage each slide pin into the retainer hole and install the retainer spring plate on the slide.

7. Adjust the sunroof panel if necessary. (see sunroof panel alignment)

8. While the sliding roof panel is in a partially open position, slide the headlining trim panel forward of the roof panel and then to the rear until the front edge of the headlining trim panel is retained by the clips mounted on the roof panel.

9. Install the two headlining trim panel retaining screws.

## Moon Roof Panel

### Removal

1. Remove the halo moulding.
   (a) Cycle the sunshade to the most rearward position.
   (b) Open the roof panel approximately half way.
   (c) Remove the three screws on the forward surface of of the halo moulding.
   (d) Operate the roof panel to a nearly closed position and pull downward on the forward center of the halo moulding so that the horizontal tabs at the front of the halo moulding are removed from the track mechanism.
   (e) Operate the roof panel to the full closed position and slide the halo moulding forward. Pull downward on the rearward section of the rearward section of the halo moulding so that the horizontal track slide surface is removed from the track assembly.
   (f) Slide the halo moulding forward and remove it from the vehicle.
2. Remove the outboard retaining screws from the front guide shoe assemblies, then loosen the inboard screws and rotate the shoes so that the slide portion is disengaged from the track.
3. Grasp the rear moon roof retainer pins and slide the pins inboard enough to disengage them from the guide pivot bracket on the moon roof panel. Rotate the pins away from the moon roof.
4. Remove the roof from outside of the vehicle.

### Installation

1. Reverse the removal procedure.

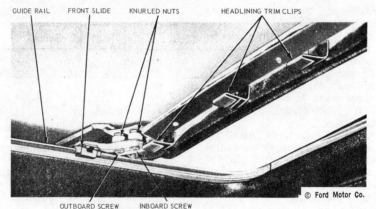

Front Slide Installation and Adjustment

GUIDE RAIL  FRONT SLIDE  KNURLED NUTS  HEADLINING TRIM CLIPS
OUTBOARD SCREW  INBOARD SCREW
© Ford Motor Co.

## Rear Slide and Cable Assembly

### Removal

1. Remove the sliding roof panel. (see sunroof panel removal.)
2. Remove the cable drive housing cover.
3. Remove both upper elbow guides at the front corners.
4. Pry off the drive cable retaining clip, while holding one hand over the clip to prevent it from popping up.
5. Pull the free end of one cable out of the guide rail and out of the center opening.
6. Pull the opposite end of the cable with the slide assembly forward to the front corner.
7. Remove the slide from the guide track and pull the slide and cable out of the guide front connection.
8. Remove the opposite cable the same way.

### Installation

1. Position the left rear slide on the guide track.
2. Move the slide and cable assembly back until the slide is on the center line with the fifth slide guide rail screw from the front.
3. Slide the free end of the cable into the guide front connection and route the cable through the curved front center track and into the lower track on the right side.
   (a) Do not engage the cable in the drive pinion teeth.
4. Check to see that both front

1975 Halo Moulding Removal

HALO MOULDING
REMOVE HALO MOULDING ATTACHING SCREWS
© Ford Motor Co.

## Ford Motor Company

lower elbow guides are aligned with the front and side guides and shim if necessary.

5. Install both of the front corner upper elbow guides.
6. Check again to see if the rear slides are centered with the fifth screw from the front on the guide rails. Proper alignment is important.
7. With the slides in position, carefully engage the cables in the drive pinion teeth.
8. Replace the drive cable housing cover and install the two retaining screws.
9. Actuate the switch and check the cable operation.
10. Return the rear slides to the fifth screw from the front of the guide rail and install the roof panel. (see sunroof installation.)

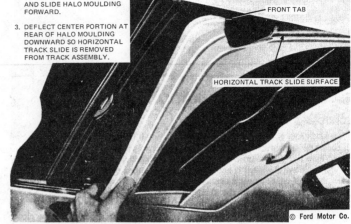

1. GRASP CENTER OF HALO MOULDING AND DEFLECT MOULDING DOWNWARD TO DISENGAGE FRONT TABS FROM TRACK.
2. CYCLE MOON ROOF CLOSED AND SLIDE HALO MOULDING FORWARD.
3. DEFLECT CENTER PORTION AT REAR OF HALO MOULDING DOWNWARD SO HORIZONTAL TRACK SLIDE IS REMOVED FROM TRACK ASSEMBLY.
4. SLIDE HALO MOULDING FORWARD AND REMOVE HALO MOULDING FROM VEHICLE.
5. HORIZONTAL TRACK SLIDE SURFACE MUST BE POSITIONED IN UPPER SLOT IN TRACK WHEN DISASSEMBLING.

FRONT TAB

HORIZONTAL TRACK SLIDE SURFACE

© Ford Motor Co.

*1975 Halo Moulding Removal*

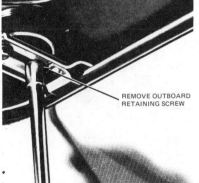

REMOVE OUTBOARD RETAINING SCREW

© Ford Motor Co.

*1975 Roof Panel Removal*

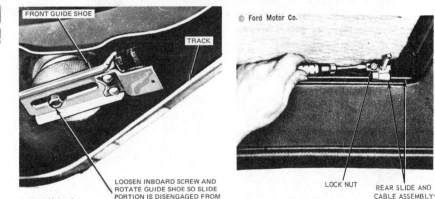

FRONT GUIDE SHOE

TRACK

LOOSEN INBOARD SCREW AND ROTATE GUIDE SHOE SO SLIDE PORTION IS DISENGAGED FROM TRACK

© Ford Motor Co.

*1975 Roof Panel Removal*

© Ford Motor Co.

LOCK NUT

REAR SLIDE AND CABLE ASSEMBLY

*Rear Slide Installation and Adjustment*

### Control Switch

#### Removal

1. Using fingers pull the switch down from the roof panel area.
2. Disconnect the wires.

#### Installation

1. Connect the wires.
2. Position the switch to the panel and push in until it snaps into place.

### Drive Unit Clutch Adjustment

If the motor spins, but the panel fails to close completely perform the following operation to eliminate slippage.

1. Remove the drive unit cover where the manual handle is used.
2. Tighten the clutch adjusting screw.
3. If necessary, add washers be-

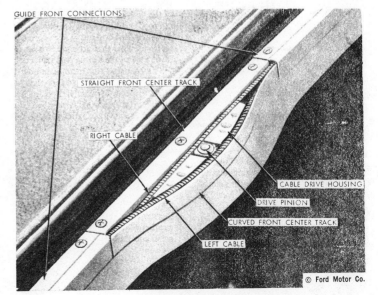

GUIDE FRONT CONNECTIONS

STRAIGHT FRONT CENTER TRACK

RIGHT CABLE

CABLE DRIVE HOUSING

DRIVE PINION

CURVED FRONT CENTER TRACK

LEFT CABLE

© Ford Motor Co.

*Drive Cable and Housing Installation*

# Ford Motor Company

hind the screw to eliminate slippage.

4. Make sure the screw is tight after adding additional washers.

## Sunroof Adjustments

### Panel Alignment—
### Front, Left or Right

1. To obtain a flush fit with the roof on one side of the front of the roof panel, loosen both front slide screws.
2. Turn the knurled nuts clockwise to raise the roof panel and counter-clockwise to lower the panel.
3. When the panel is aligned properly tighten the screws.
4. If necessary, adjust the opposite front slide in the same way.

### Panel Alignment—
### Rear, Left or Right

1. To obtain a flush fit with the roof on one side of the rear of the roof panel, loosen the 3/8 locknut on the rear slide.
2. Turn the adjusting screw clockwise to raise the roof panel and counter-clockwise to lower the panel.
3. After aligning the panel, properly tighten the locknut.
4. If necessary, adjust the opposite rear slide in the same way.

### Ramp Adjustment

1. When the roof panel is being closed and does not rise into the roof opening, remove the headlining panel from the roof panel

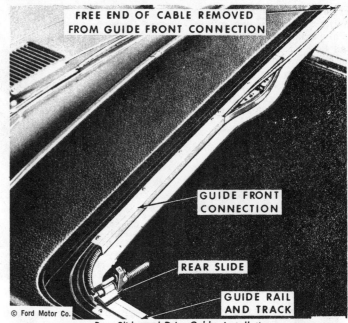

FREE END OF CABLE REMOVED FROM GUIDE FRONT CONNECTION

GUIDE FRONT CONNECTION

REAR SLIDE

GUIDE RAIL AND TRACK

© Ford Motor Co.

*Rear Slide and Drive Cable Installation*

and open the roof panel to the full rearward position.

2. Examine the ramps in the drainage channel to see if they are properly aligned with the lifting elements at the rear of the panel.
   (a) The point where the lifting element makes contact with the ramp can be seen on the rearward slope of the ramp.
3. Pry the ramp up and move it from side to side until it is cen-

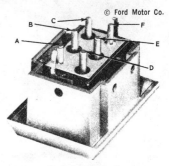

© Ford Motor Co.

B  C      F
A          E
          D

*Switch Terminals*

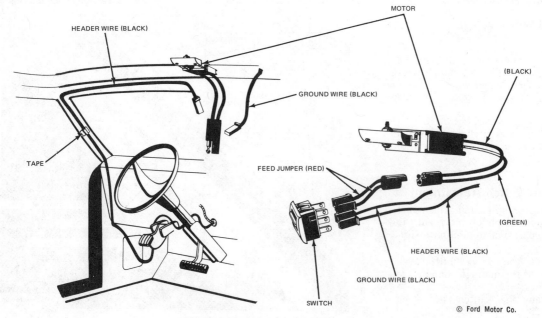

*1975 Moon Roof Motor and Switch—Removal*

MOTOR

HEADER WIRE (BLACK)

GROUND WIRE (BLACK)

(BLACK)

TAPE

FEED JUMPER (RED)

(GREEN)

HEADER WIRE (BLACK)

GROUND WIRE (BLACK)

SWITCH

© Ford Motor Co.

# Ford Motor Company

tered with the lifting element.

4. Close the roof panel and watch the lifting action of the panel.
5. If required, readjust the ramps up or down or side to side until proper lifting action is obtained.

### Panel Does Not Run True

1. Close the roof panel to see which side jams.
2. Open the roof panel.
3. Remove the drive housing center cover.
4. Pry off the drive cable retaining clip.
   (a) Hold a hand over the clip to keep it from flying upward.
5. To move the right side of the roof panel forward, lift the right cable at the front of the pinion and pull it one or more teeth to the left.
6. Install the retaining clip and the drive housing cover.
7. Move the left side of the roof panel in the same manner.

### Cable Guide Alignment

1. If the roof panel jams during operation, check both front corner lower elbow guides for alignment with the front and side guides.
2. If necessary, shim the lower elbow guides to move the guides inboard for alignment with the adjacent guides.
3. If the panel fails to rise, the joints of the cable slides are out of alignment and are jamming the cable drive.
   (a) Loosen the screws retaining the guide rails, corner and connector rails and drive cable housing.
   (b) While continually activating the drive mechanism, align the points where resistance is felt and retighten the screws one by one.

## Moonroof Adjustments

### Panel Alignment
### Rear Edge—Raise or Lower

1. Loosen the rear retainer pin assembly attaching nut which is located in the slotted link.
2. Position the moon roof up or down as required.
3. Tighten the pin retainer nut and torque to 20-23 in. lbs.

### Front Edge—Raise or Lower

1. Loosen the forward track shoe retaining screws.
2. Rotate the adjuster clockwise to lower the panel and counterclockwise to raise the panel.
3. Tighten the track shoe attaching screws and torque to 18-23 in. lbs.

### Parallel Alignment

1. Open the roof approximately ½ inch.
2. Sight down the ½" opening to see if the forward edge of the moon roof and the forward edge of the opening in the roof panel are parallel.
3. If not, open the moon roof panel approximately eight inches to gain access to the cable/drive gear mechanism.
4. Remove the two cable cover screws and remove the cover.
5. Pry the metal retaining clip off the cable drive gear mechanism.
6. Remove one of the cables from the track.
7. Adjust the moon roof slightly as required to obtain a parallel relationship between the front of the moon roof and the roof panel opening.

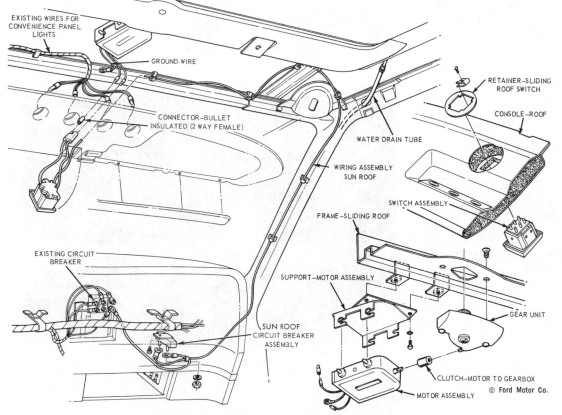

*Electric Wire Routing and Control Switch Installation*

# Ford Motor Company

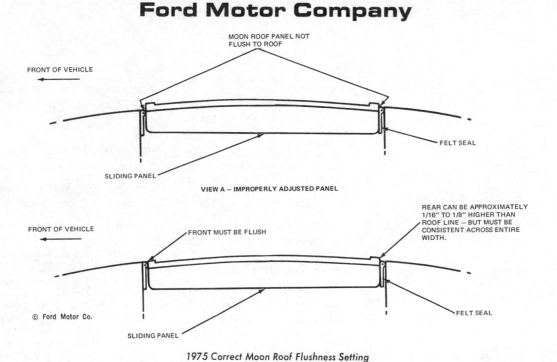

VIEW A – IMPROPERLY ADJUSTED PANEL

1975 Correct Moon Roof Flushness Setting

*NOTE: Do not activate the control switch while the covers or cables are removed from the track, as this could result in cable damage.*

8. Insert the cable into the track and position the clip so that the narrow side of the clip is facing the front of the vehicle and it is firmly seated into the notches in the track assembly.

*NOTE: If the clip is not properly positioned in the track, the down-*

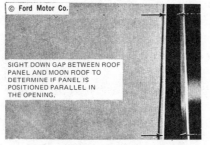

1975 Panel—Parallel Alignment

*standing flanges will not go into the grooves in the track and will result in extensive damage to the cables.*

9. Open the moon roof and check to see if the roof is parallel to the roof opening. If not repeat the above procedure.

## Electrical Testing Procedures 1969-75

Before performing any extensive electrical testing procedures make

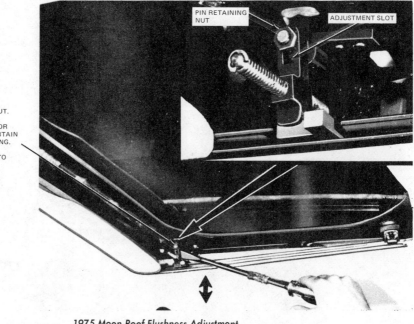

1. LOOSEN PIN RETAINING NUT.

2. POSITION MOON ROOF UP OR DOWN AS REQUIRED TO OBTAIN PROPER FLUSHNESS SETTING.

3. TORQUE RETAINING NUT TO 20-23 INCH LBS.

© Ford Motor Co.

1975 Moon Roof Flushness Adjustment

# Ford Motor Company

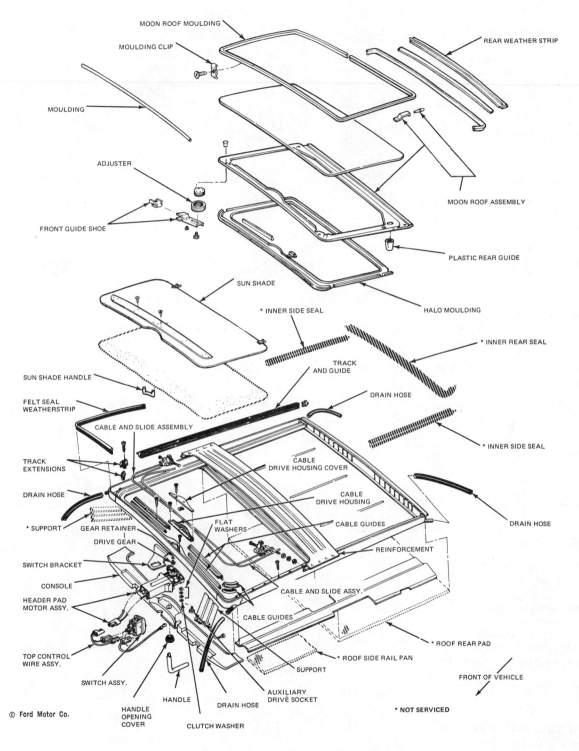

MOON ROOF MOULDING

MOULDING CLIP

REAR WEATHER STRIP

MOULDING

ADJUSTER

MOON ROOF ASSEMBLY

FRONT GUIDE SHOE

PLASTIC REAR GUIDE

SUN SHADE

* INNER SIDE SEAL

HALO MOULDING

* INNER REAR SEAL

SUN SHADE HANDLE

TRACK
AND GUIDE

DRAIN HOSE

FELT SEAL
WEATHERSTRIP

* INNER SIDE SEAL

CABLE AND SLIDE ASSEMBLY

TRACK
EXTENSIONS

CABLE
DRIVE HOUSING COVER

DRAIN HOSE

CABLE
DRIVE HOUSING

* SUPPORT

GEAR RETAINER

FLAT
WASHERS

CABLE GUIDES

DRAIN HOSE

DRIVE GEAR

REINFORCEMENT

SWITCH BRACKET

CONSOLE

CABLE AND SLIDE ASSY.

HEADER PAD
MOTOR ASSY.

CABLE GUIDES

* ROOF REAR PAD

TOP CONTROL
WIRE ASSY.

* ROOF SIDE RAIL PAN

SUPPORT

FRONT OF VEHICLE

SWITCH ASSY.

AUXILIARY
DRIVE SOCKET

HANDLE

© Ford Motor Co.

HANDLE
OPENING
COVER

DRAIN HOSE

* NOT SERVICED

CLUTCH WASHER

*1975 Moon Roof—Exploded View—Typical*

# Ford Motor Company

sure the battery has a full charge and that there are no mechanical bindings. Also check all wire connections for proper contact.

### Testing the Feed Wires to the Circuit Breaker

1. Connect one test light lead to the battery side of the circuit breaker.
2. Ground the other test light lead.
3. If the test light does not light, there is an open or short circuit in the feed wire to the circuit breaker.

### Circuit Breaker Test

1. Disconnect the output feed wire from the circuit breaker (the wire opposite the power feed wire to the circuit breaker.)
2. Using a test light, check the disconnected terminal.
3. If the test light does not light the circuit breaker is defective.

### Testing the Ignition Relay

1. Using a test light, check the relay feed wire.
2. If the test light does not light, there is an open or short circuit between the relay and circuit breaker.
3. Using a test light, check the output terminal of the relay while the ignition switch is turned on.
4. If the test light does not light, connect a test light on the ignition coil terminal.
5. If the test light lights, replace the ignition relay.
6. If the tester does not light, there is an open or short circuit in the power feed, and ignition to relay wires.

### Testing for Current at the Control Switch

1. Connect one test light lead to the control switch feed terminal of the switch block.
2. Turn the ignition switch on.
3. Ground the other test lead.
4. If the test light does not light, there is an open or short circuit between the relay and control switch.

### Control Switch Test—1974-75

1. Remove the switch from the car by pulling down from the roof and disconnecting the wires.
2. Use an ohmmeter or a self-powered test light.
3. Operate the switch in one direc-

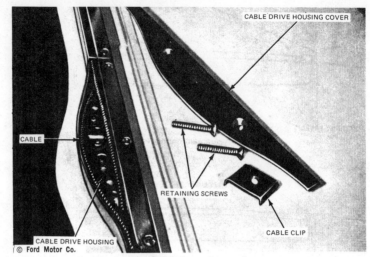

1975 Cable Cover Removal

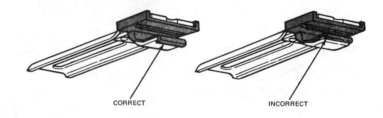

1975 Incorrect Track Shoe Plastic Insert. Installation can cause binding.

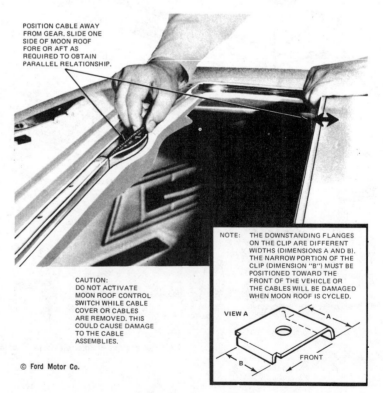

1975 Cable Clip Positioning

# Power Sun Roofs

## Ford Motor Company

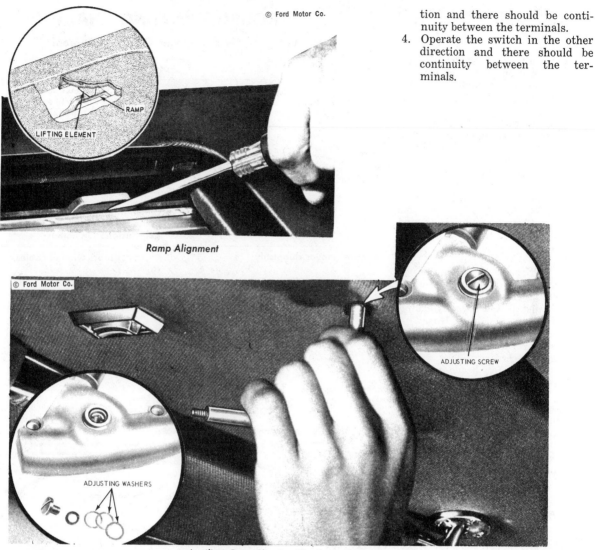

© Ford Motor Co.

RAMP

LIFTING ELEMENT

*Ramp Alignment*

© Ford Motor Co.

ADJUSTING SCREW

ADJUSTING WASHERS

*Auxiliary Drive Slipping Clutch Adjustment*

tion and there should be continuity between the terminals.

4. Operate the switch in the other direction and there should be continuity between the terminals.

## General Motors

### GENERAL MOTORS

#### All Models—1973-75

#### Cadillac—1971-75

#### Description

The sunroof is controlled by a two position switch which is located on the right side of the instrument cluster just above the radio or on the accessory switch panel on the Cadillac and on all other General Motors models is mounted in the windshield header safety pad area.

A 12 volt reversible motor with an integral gear drive mechanism is mounted to the roof panel, forward of the roof opening near the center of the windshield header area. The motor drives two flexible cables which are attached to the sunroof sliding panel.

When the switch is actuated to open the sunroof the panel retreats down and rearward on guide rails into a space between the headlining and the roof.

When the switch is actuated to close the sunroof the panel moves forward and upward on two ramps until the panel is flush with the roof's surface.

The electrical system is protected by a 25 amp. circuit breaker, located on the instrument panel center brace underneath the instrument panel top cover on the Cadillac. On all other

General Motors models a 40 amp. circuit breaker is used and is mounted on the fuse panel.

Two wires are routed from the switch to the motor, black for the open cycle and green for the close cycle.

### Motor and Drive Gear Assembly
### All except Cadillac

#### Removal

1. Open the sunroof panel.
2. Remove the headlining trim lace that runs across the front of the sunroof opening.
3. Remove the windshield upper and side garnish molding.

# Power Sun Roofs

## General Motors

4. At the center of the windshield remove the drive pinion cover button.
5. Remove the control switch:
   (a) Pull the switch toggle bezel out from the retainer in the headlining.
   (b) Disconnect the electrical connector.
6. Remove the headlining across the front of the opening.
7. Remove the front cable guide cover screws.
8. Remove the safety header pad.
9. Disconnect the electrical connectors from the motor.
10. Remove the two motor and drive gear attaching bolts and remove the motor from the housing.

### Installation

1. Position the motor and the drive gear assembly to the housing and install the two attaching bolts.
2. Connect the electrical leads.
3. Check operation of the roof and align if necessary.
4. Install the safety header pad.
5. Replace the headlining across the front of the opening.
6. Install the control switch and connect the wires.
7. Replace the drive pinion cover button at the center of the windshield.
8. Replace the headlining trim lace across the front of the sunroof opening.

*NOTE: Excessive clutch slippage may be corrected by adding clutch washers under the screw which is threaded into the drive pinion at the bottom side of the drive gear assembly.*

### Motor and Drive Gear Assembly Cadillac

#### Removal

1. Open the sunroof to the three quarter full open position.
2. Disconnect the negative battery cable.
3. Remove the windshield garnish mouldings from the left and right sides.
4. Remove the garnish mouldings from the roof side rails.
5. Remove both sun visor assemblies and the center sun visor bracket.
6. Carefully pull the headlining down enough to gain access to the motor and drive gear.
7. Remove the foam insulator padding in front of the roof panel

## TROUBLESHOOTING CHART
### General Motors—Power Operated Sunroof

| Condition | Possible Cause |
|---|---|
| **1. Sunroof will not operate at all with ignition on** | a. Open or short circuit between power supply, switch, or motor<br>b. Defective circuit breaker<br>c. Defective ignition relay<br>d. Defective control switch<br>e. Defective motor<br>f. Mechanical binding |
| **2. Motor runs, but no panel movement** | a. Panel alignment<br>b. Disconnected or damaged drive cables<br>c. Clutch slippage in drive gear assembly (see motor and drive gear installation note.) |
| **3. Panel moves sluggishly** | a. Improper lubrication of cables, rails<br>b. Improper panel alignment |

*Sunroof Disassembled*

© G.M. Corp.

## General Motors

opening next to the motor and drive gear assembly.

8. Disconnect the motor electrical connector.
9. Remove the drive cable housing cover.
10. Remove the left and right elbow corner guides.
11. Carefully pry up the drive cable retaining clip (hold hand over clip to keep from springing up.)
12. Pull the drive cables out of the upper and lower front guides noting routing for installation.
13. Remove the three drive cable housing screws and remove the housing.
14. Remove the two drive gear assembly retaining screws and remove the drive gear assembly and motor.

### Installation

1. Push the plastic cover over the motor to the base of the drive gear assembly.
2. Position the motor and drive gear assembly in the drive cable housing.
3. Install the two retaining screws.
4. Replace the drive cable housing and install the three retaining screws.
5. Insert the cable ends into the guides and reroute.
   (a) Lubricate cables and drive gear with cold weather approved lube.
6. Install the right and left elbow corner guides.
   *NOTE: The alignment of the lower elbow corner guide is very important.*
7. Install the cable retaining clip by pressing down firmly.
8. Install the drive cable housing cover.
9. Connect the motor electrical wiring connector.
10. Install the battery terminal.
11. Cement the foam insulation padding in place.
12. Apply trim cement to the forward edge of the roof panel.
13. Starting from the center position the headlining to the forward edge and smooth out all wrinkles, working from the center to the outboard ends.
14. Install all the garnish mouldings and both sun visors.

### Control Switch—Cadillac— 1971-73

#### Removal

1. Pull instrument panel insert out of the bezel.

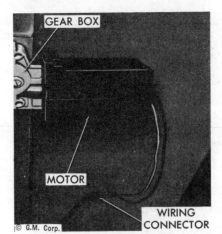

© G.M. Corp.

*Motor and Drive Unit Location*

2. Disconnect the electrical feed wires from the wiring harness.
3. Remove the retaining screw and remove the switch.

#### Installation

1. Install the switch to the instrument panel insert and secure with the one screw.
2. Connect the switch electrical connectors.
3. Install the instrument panel insert into the bezel.
   (a) Press the right side until secured by the spring catch.

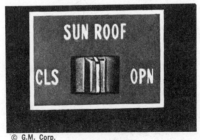

© G.M. Corp.

*Control Switch*

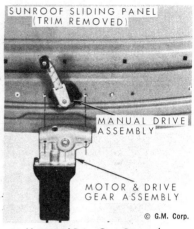

© G.M. Corp.

*Motor and Drive Gear Removal*

### Control Switch—Cadillac— 1974-75

#### Removal

1. Remove the instrument panel pad.
   a. Disconnect the negative battery cable.
   b. Remove the right, left and right center climatic control air outlet grilles by compressing the release tabs and rotating the grille upward and out.
   c. Reach through the outlet openings and remove the three pad to panel support fasteners.
   d. Remove the screws which hold the pad to panel horizontal support.
   e. Pull the pad outward and disconnect the wiper switch electrical connection.
   f. If necessary place the transmission shift lever in low range and if equipped with a tilt steering wheel, place the wheel in the lowest position.
   g. Remove the pad.

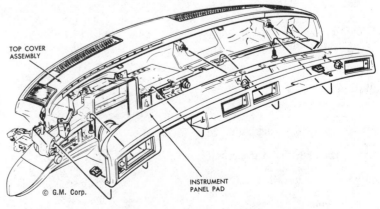

© G.M. Corp.

*Removing The Instrument Panel Pad—Cadillac—1974*

# General Motors

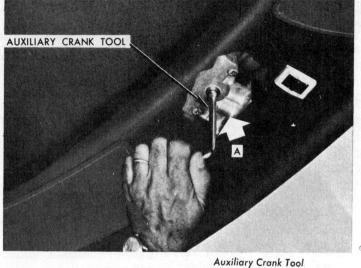

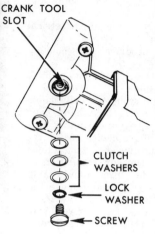

CRANK TOOL SLOT

CLUTCH WASHERS

LOCK WASHER

SCREW

© G.M. Corp. VIEW 'A'

AUXILIARY CRANK TOOL

*Auxiliary Crank Tool*

2. Remove the right hand insert and applique.

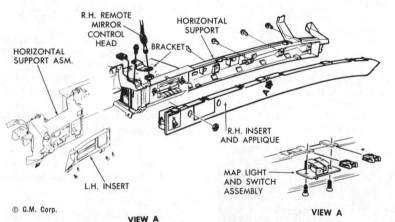

R.H. REMOTE MIRROR CONTROL HEAD

HORIZONTAL SUPPORT

BRACKET

HORIZONTAL SUPPORT ASM.

R.H. INSERT AND APPLIQUE

L.H. INSERT

MAP LIGHT AND SWITCH ASSEMBLY

© G.M. Corp.

VIEW A

VIEW A

*Inserts, Appliques and Accessory Switches—Cadillac—1974*

a. Remove the radio knobs, wave washers, control rings and left hex nut.
b. Reach through the opening in the top of the glove box and remove the attaching screws from the rear of the insert.
3. Push the switch, until it snaps from the housing.
4. Remove the wiring terminals from the switch.

## Installation

1. Connect the wire terminals to the switch.
2. Snap the switch back into the housing.
3. Install the right hand insert and applique and install the screw.
   a. Install the left Hex nut, control tings, wave washers and radio knobs.
4. Install the instrument panel pad.

a. Position the pad to the panel and connect the wiper switch.

b. Install the screws retaining the pad to the horizontal support.
c. Reach through the climate control outlet openings and install the three fasteners which hold the pad to the panel support.
5. Install the air outlet grilles.

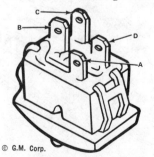

C

B

D

A

© G.M. Corp.

*Control Switch Terminals—1974*

a. Position grille and press the release tabs.
b. Snap the tabs into the retaining holes.
6. Connect negative battery terminal.

## Control Switch— All Except Cadillac

### Removal

1. Pull the switch toggle bezel out from the retainer in the headlining.
2. Disconnect the electrical connector.

### Installation

1. Install the wire connector to the switch.
2. Press the switch in place until the retaining clip engages.

## Sunroof Panel— All except Cadillac

### Removal

1. Open the sunroof approximately eight inches.
2. Remove the headlining panel and slide rearward into the sunroof housing for storage.
3. Close the sunroof panel.
4. Remove the outboard screw from each front guide shoe assembly.
5. Loosen the inboard guide shoe screw.
6. Rotate each front guide shoe assembly inboard to clear the guide rail.
7. Remove the rear guide retainer plates by removing the attaching bolts.

# General Motors

8. Disengage the rear slide tension springs from their rollers and pivot spring inboard.
9. Lift the roof panel at the front edge and pull the panel out of the roof opening.

**Installation**

1. While the headlining panel is in the full rearward position, install the roof panel into the roof opening.
2. Turn each front guide shoe outward and engage with the side guide rails.
3. Install each outboard screw and tighten on each guide.
4. Push the panel to the full forward position.
5. Lift the rear of the roof panel upward and actuate the control switch so that the cable assembly can be positioned to the rear guide attaching plate and to the holes on the roof panel.
6. Place the rear guide attaching plate retainer over the rear attaching plate and install the bolts.
7. Turn the rear slide tension spring outboard and place on the underside of the roller.
8. Install the headlining to the roof panel.

## Rear Guide and Cable Assembly— All except Cadillac

**Removal**

1. Remove the roof sliding panel and the motor and drive gear assembly. (See sunroof panel and motor and drive gear removal and installation.)
2. Detach the trim lace and headlining at the sides of the sunroof opening.
3. At the top edge of the sunroof opening, use a 5/32″ drill bit and remove only the heads of three blind rivets that hold each side guide rail and retainer.
4. Remove the heads of the ten rivets that retain the front guide cover.
5. Remove the remainder of each rivets with a drift punch.
6. Remove the two cable center guide bolts and the four screws that secure the cable front guide.
7. Disengage the side guide rail from the front rail and pull the rear guide and cable assembly forward and out of the side guide rail. (See illustration of sunroof hardware.)

DRIVE CABLE HOUSING COVER

© G.M. Corp.

*Removing Drive Cable Housing Gear*

**Installation**

1. Insert the guide and cable assembly into the proper channel of the side guide rail and move the guide rearward beyond location of the side guide rail retainer.
   (a) Insert the left cable into the inboard channel of the left guide rail and insert the right cable into the outboard channel of the right guide rail.
2. Connect the front guide with the side guide rail and install the guide attaching screws.
3. Install the side guide rail retainer.
   (a) Use 5/32 x 1/2 steel countersunk blind rivets.
4. Place the cable in the proper channel of the front guide.
5. Pull both right and left guide and cable assemblies against the rear edge of the side guide rail retainers.
6. Lubricate the cables and channels with cold weather approved lube, and install the center cable guide.

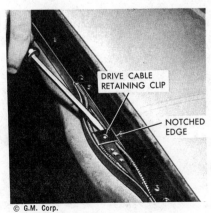

DRIVE CABLE RETAINING CLIP

NOTCHED EDGE

© G.M. Corp.

*Removing Drive Cable Retaining Clip*

7. Install the motor and drive assembly after making sure that both right and left rear slide and cable assemblies are positioned identically.
8. Install the sunroof panel.
9. Install the cable front guide cover using 15/32″ x 1/2″ steel countersunk blind rivets.
10. Replace all remaining trim material.

## Sunroof Panel—Cadillac

**Removal**

1. Open the sunroof approximately three inches.
2. Remove the two screws from the front of the headlining panel.
3. Slide the headlining panel forward and out of seven retaining clips.
4. Close the roof and push the headlining panel to the full rearward position.
5. Remove the outboard screw from each front slide assembly.
6. Loosen the inboard screws and rotate both front slide assemblies inboard to clear the guide rail.
7. Pull each rear slide and cable assembly inboard and out of the slide retainer hole of the roof opening.
8. Lift the panel at the front edge and pull forward and out of the opening.

**Installation**

1. While the headlining panel is in the full rearward position install the roof panel into the opening without damaging the headlining.
2. Move each front slide assembly outboard and install the slides on the guide rail upper tracks.
3. Install the outboard screws and tighten on each slide.
4. Push the roof panel to the full forward position.
5. Lift the rear of the roof panel upward and actuate the control switch to move the rear slides into alignment with the holes on the slide retainers.
6. Engage each rear slide pin into the retainer holes and install the retainer springplate on the slide pin.
7. Adjust panel if necessary (see sunroof adjustments.)

# General Motors

## Rear Slide and Cable— Cadillac

### Removal

1. Remove the sunroof panel. (see sunroof panel removal.)
2. Remove the drive cable housing cover.
3. Remove both the front upper elbow guides.
4. Pry off the drive cable retaining clip.
5. Pull the free end of one cable out of the guide rail and drive housing, and pull the cable and rear slide assembly forward to the front corner.
6. Remove the slide from the guide track and pull the cable out of the front guide.

*NOTE: If one cable is found to be defective replace both.*

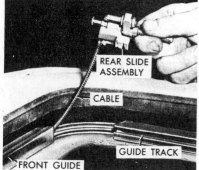

*Removing Rear Slide and Cable*

### Installation

1. Position the left rear slide in the guide track and move the slide and cable assembly back until the slide is centered with the fifth side guide rail screw from the front.
2. Slide the free end of the cable into the upper front guide.
3. Route the cable through the curved front center track in the drive cable housing and into the lower track on the right side.
4. Check both front corner lower elbow guides for alignment with the front and side guides. (Shim, if necessary.)
5. Lubricate the cables with a cold weather approved lube at the elbow guide areas.
6. Install both the front corner upper elbow guides.
7. Check to make sure the rear slides are centered with the fifth screw from the front on the side guide rails, then engage the cables in the drive pinion teeth.
8. Lubricate the cables and drive pinion teeth with a cold weather approved lube.
9. Install the drive cable retaining clip.
10. Install the drive cable housing cover.
11. Install the roof panel. (see roof panel installation.)

## Sunroof Adjustments— All except Cadillac

### Vertical Adjustment at the front of the panel

1. Detach the headlining panel and slide it rearward into the sunroof housing.
2. To obtain a flush fit with the roof, loosen the two bolts on the front guide shoes.
3. Turn the front guide adjusting nut clockwise to lower the roof panel and counter-clockwise to lift the panel.
4. When the panel is aligned properly, tighten the bolts.

### Vertical Adjustment at the Rear of the panel

1. Detach the headlining panel and slide it rearward into the sunroof housing.
2. To obtain a flush fit with the roof, loosen the lifter link attaching screw.
3. Raise or lower the panel to the desired height and tighten the lifter link screw.

### Parallel Adjustment to the Sides of the Panel

1. Close the roof panel.
2. Remove the motor and drive gear assembly.
3. Align the panel equally at both sides and replace the motor and drive gear unit.

### Cable Guide Alignment

1. If the panel jams during its travel, check the alignment of the front cable guide to the side guide rail.
2. If necessary, shim the front cable guide for alignment with the adjacent side guide rail.
3. If the panel fails to rise, check the battery for low voltage, or add more clutch washers.

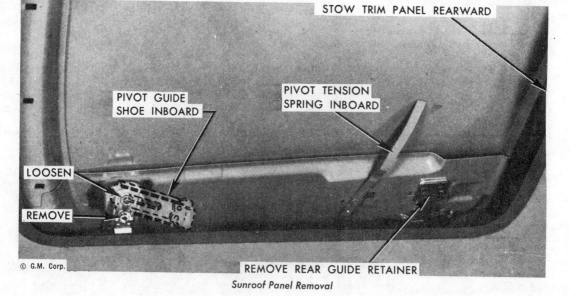

*Sunroof Panel Removal*

# General Motors

## Sunroof Adjustments—Cadillac

### Panel Alignment—Front, Left or Right

1. To obtain a flush fit with the roof on one side of the front of the roof panel, loosen both front slide screws.
2. Turn the knurled nuts clockwise to raise the roof panel and counter-clockwise to lower the panel.
3. When the panel is aligned properly tighten the screws.
4. If necessary, adjust the opposite front slide in the same way.

### Panel Alignment—Rear, Left or Right

1. To obtain a flush fit with the roof on one side of the rear of the roof panel, loosen the ⅜ locknut on the rear slide.
2. Turn the adjusting screw clockwise to raise the roof panel and counter-clockwise to lower the panel.
3. After aligning the panel, properly tighten the locknut.
4. If necessary, adjust the opposite rear slide in the same way.

### Ramp Adjustment

1. When the roof panel is being closed and does not rise into the roof opening, remove the headlining panel from the roof panel and open the roof panel to the full rearward position.
2. Examine the ramps in the drainage channel to see if they are properly aligned with the lifting elements at the rear of the panel.
   (a) The point where the lifting element makes contact with the ramp can be seen on the rearward slope of the ramp.
3. Pry the ramp up and move it from side to side until it is centered with the lifting element.
4. Close the roof panel and watch the lifting action of the panel.
5. If required, readjust the ramps up or down or side to side until proper lifting action is obtained.

### Panel Does Not Run True

1. Close the roof panel to see which side jams.
2. Open the roof panel.
3. Remove the drive housing center cover.
4. Pry off the drive cable retaining clip.
   (a) Hold a hand over the clip to keep it from flying upward.
5. To move the right side of the roof panel forward, lift the right cable at the front of the pinion and pull it one or more teeth to the left.
6. Install the retaining clip and the drive housing cover.
7. Move the left side of the roof panel in the same manner.

TO RAISE FRONT OF PANEL

TO LOWER FRONT OF PANEL

LIFTER LINK ATTACHING SCREW

RAISE - LOWER REAR OF PANEL HERE

VIEW A

FRONT GUIDE SHOE ATTACHING BOLTS

REAR GUIDE TENSION SPRING

A

© G.M. Corp.

*Sunroof Panel Installation*

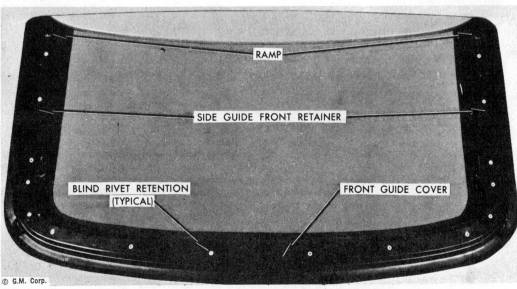

RAMP

SIDE GUIDE FRONT RETAINER

BLIND RIVET RETENTION (TYPICAL)

FRONT GUIDE COVER

© G.M. Corp.

*Front and Side Guide Rail Covers*

## General Motors

*Headlining Panel Removal*

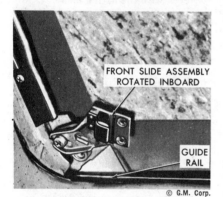

*Front Slide Assembly*

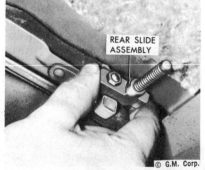

*Removing Rear Slide and Cable Assy. from Retainer*

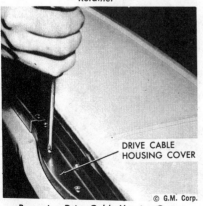

*Removing Drive Cable Housing Cover*

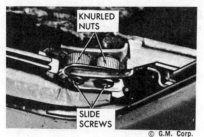

*Outboard Slide Screws*

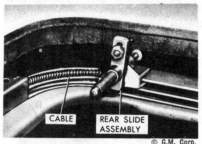

*Cable and Slide Assembly Pulled Forward*

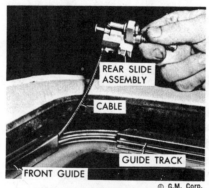

*Removing Rear Slide and Cable*

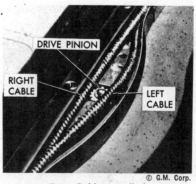

*Drive Cables Installed*

### Cable Cuide Alignment

1. If the roof panel jams during operation, check both front corner lower elbow guides for alignment with the front and side guides.
2. If necessary, shim the lower elbow guides to move the guides inboard for alignment with the adjacent guides.
3. If the panel fails to rise, the joints of the cable slides are out of alignment and are jamming the cable drive.
   (a) Loosen the screws retaining the guide rails, corner and connector rails and drive cable housing.
   (b) While continually activating the drive mechanism, align the points where resistance is felt and retighten the screws one by one.

### Power Sunroof Electric Testing Procedures

Before performing any extensive electrical testing procedures make sure the battery has a full charge and that there are no mechanical bindings. Also check all wire connections for proper contact.

### Testing the Feed Wires to the Circuit Breaker

1. Connect one test light lead to the battery side of the circuit breaker.
2. Ground the other test light lead.
3. If the test light does not light, there is an open or short circuit in the feed wire to the circuit breaker.

### Circuit Breaker Test

1. Disconnect the output feed wire from the circuit breaker (the wire opposite the power feed wire to the circuit breaker.)
2. Using a test light, check the disconnected terminal.
3. If the test light does not light the circuit breaker is defective.

### Testing the Ignition Relay

1. Using a test light, check the relay feed wire.
2. If the test light does not light, there is an open or short circuit between the relay and circuit breaker.
3. Using a test light, check the output terminal of the relay while the ignition switch is turned on.
4. If the test light does not light, connect a test light on the ignition coil terminal.
5. If the test light lights, replace the ignition relay.
6. If the tester does not light, there is an open or short circuit in the power feed, and ignition to relay wires.

## General Motors

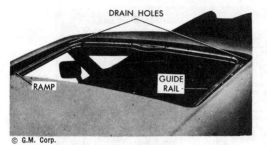

*Sunroof Fully Opened*

*Rear Panel Alignment*

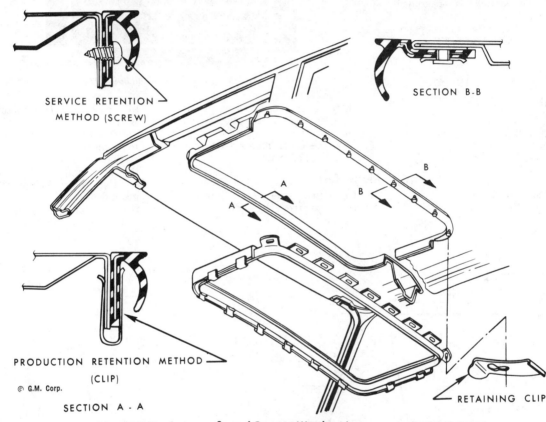

SERVICE RETENTION METHOD (SCREW)

SECTION B-B

PRODUCTION RETENTION METHOD (CLIP)

© G.M. Corp.

SECTION A - A

*Sunroof Opening Weatherstrip*

RETAINING CLIP

### Testing for Current at the Control Switch

1. Connect one test light lead to the control switch feed terminal of the switch block.
2. Turn the ignition switch on.
3. Ground the other test lead.
4. If the test light does not light, there is an open or short circuit between the relay and control switch.

### Control Switch Test— All except Cadillac

1. Connect one end of a 12 gauge jumper wire to the red and white switch feed wire.
2. Connect the other end to the

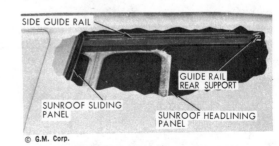

*Front Panel Alignment*

light green motor feed wire.
3. Use a second jumper wire and connect the black motor feed wire with the black switch ground wire.
4. If the motor does not operate

with the switch but does with the jumper wires, check to see that the switch is properly grounded.
5. If the switch is properly grounded, replace the switch.

## General Motors

### Control Switch Test—Cadillac

1. Connect one end of a 12 gauge jumper wire to the orange-black feed wire.
2. Connect the other end to the light green motor feed wire.
3. Use a second jumper wire and connect the black motor feed wire with the black switch ground wire.
4. If the motor does not operate with the switch but does with the jumper wires, check to see that the switch is grounded properly.
5. If the switch is grounded properly, replace the switch.

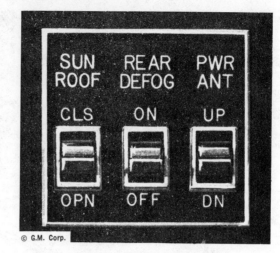

Accessory Switch Panel—Cadillac—1974

### Testing the Switch to Motor Wires

1. Disconnect the motor wire connectors.
2. Connect one end of a test light to ground.
3. Connect the other to one of the two motor feed wires.
4. Actuate the control switch. If the test lamp does not light, there is an open or short circuit between the control switch and the motor.
5. Test the other motor feed wire in the same manner.

### Motor Test

1. Disconnect the wire harness connector from the motor.
2. Connect one end of a test lamp to one of the two motor feed wires.
3. Connect the other test lamp lead to ground.
4. Actuate the control switch, if the test lamp lights, check to see that the switch is properly grounded.
5. If the switch is properly grounded then the motor is defective.

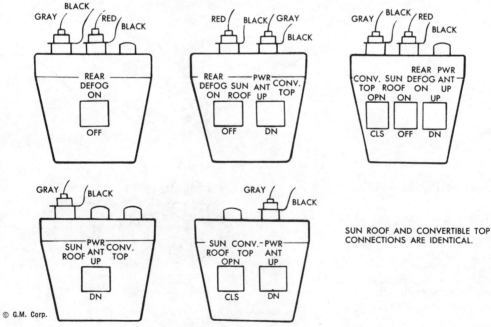

Accessory Switch Wiring—Cadillac—1974

## Chrysler Corporation

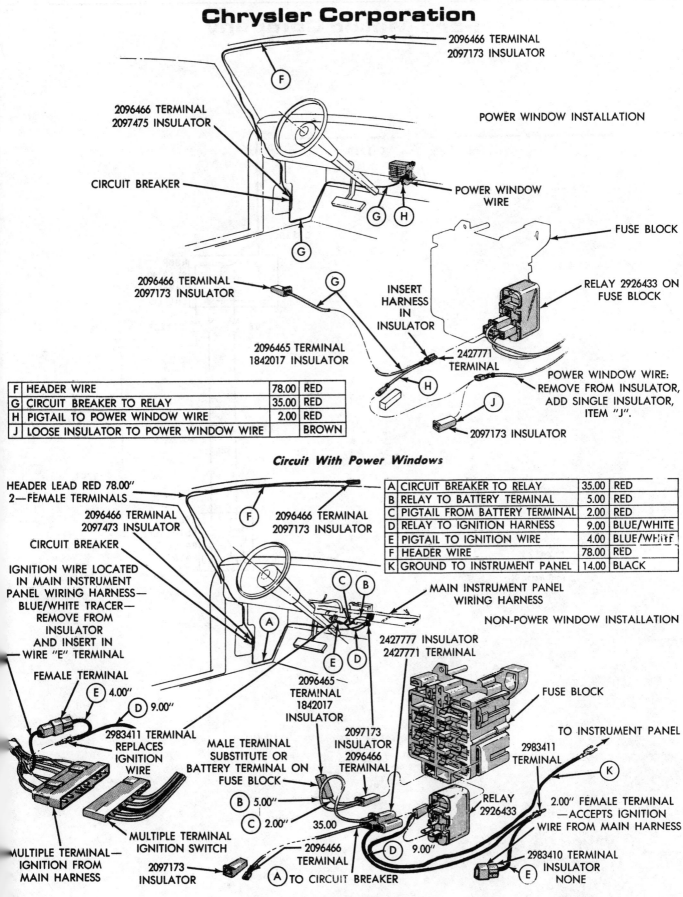

2096466 TERMINAL
2097173 INSULATOR

POWER WINDOW INSTALLATION

2096466 TERMINAL
2097475 INSULATOR

CIRCUIT BREAKER

POWER WINDOW WIRE

FUSE BLOCK

RELAY 2926433 ON FUSE BLOCK

2096466 TERMINAL
2097173 INSULATOR

INSERT HARNESS IN INSULATOR

2096465 TERMINAL
1842017 INSULATOR

2427771 TERMINAL

POWER WINDOW WIRE: REMOVE FROM INSULATOR, ADD SINGLE INSULATOR, ITEM "J".

2097173 INSULATOR

| F | HEADER WIRE | 78.00 | RED |
| G | CIRCUIT BREAKER TO RELAY | 35.00 | RED |
| H | PIGTAIL TO POWER WINDOW WIRE | 2.00 | RED |
| J | LOOSE INSULATOR TO POWER WINDOW WIRE | | BROWN |

*Circuit With Power Windows*

HEADER LEAD RED 78.00"
2—FEMALE TERMINALS

2096466 TERMINAL
2097473 INSULATOR

CIRCUIT BREAKER

IGNITION WIRE LOCATED IN MAIN INSTRUMENT PANEL WIRING HARNESS— BLUE/WHITE TRACER— REMOVE FROM INSULATOR AND INSERT IN WIRE "E" TERMINAL

2096466 TERMINAL
2097173 INSULATOR

| A | CIRCUIT BREAKER TO RELAY | 35.00 | RED |
| B | RELAY TO BATTERY TERMINAL | 5.00 | RED |
| C | PIGTAIL FROM BATTERY TERMINAL | 2.00 | RED |
| D | RELAY TO IGNITION HARNESS | 9.00 | BLUE/WHITE |
| E | PIGTAIL TO IGNITION WIRE | 4.00 | BLUE/WHITE |
| F | HEADER WIRE | 78.00 | RED |
| K | GROUND TO INSTRUMENT PANEL | 14.00 | BLACK |

MAIN INSTRUMENT PANEL WIRING HARNESS

NON-POWER WINDOW INSTALLATION

FEMALE TERMINAL

E 4.00"

D 9.00"

2983411 TERMINAL REPLACES IGNITION WIRE

2096465 TERMINAL 1842017 INSULATOR

2427777 INSULATOR
2427771 TERMINAL

FUSE BLOCK

TO INSTRUMENT PANEL

2983411 TERMINAL

K

MALE TERMINAL SUBSTITUTE OR BATTERY TERMINAL ON FUSE BLOCK

2097173 INSULATOR 2096466 TERMINAL

2.00" FEMALE TERMINAL —ACCEPTS IGNITION WIRE FROM MAIN HARNESS

B 5.00"

C 2.00"

35.00

RELAY 2926433

D 9.00"

MULTIPLE TERMINAL IGNITION SWITCH

2096466 TERMINAL

2983410 TERMINAL
INSULATOR NONE

E

MULTIPLE TERMINAL— IGNITION FROM MAIN HARNESS

2097173 INSULATOR

A TO CIRCUIT BREAKER

*Circuit Without Power Windows*

# Ford Motor Company

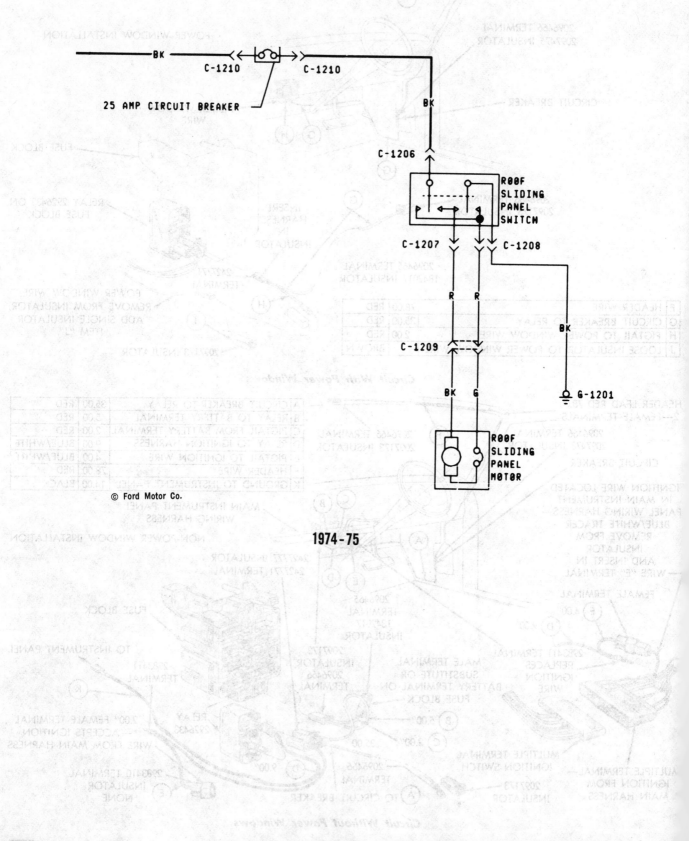

25 AMP CIRCUIT BREAKER

C-1210  C-1210

BK

C-1206

ROOF SLIDING PANEL SWITCH

C-1207  C-1208

R  R

C-1209

BK  G

G-1201

ROOF SLIDING PANEL MOTOR

© Ford Motor Co.

**1974-75**

## General Motors
## Buick

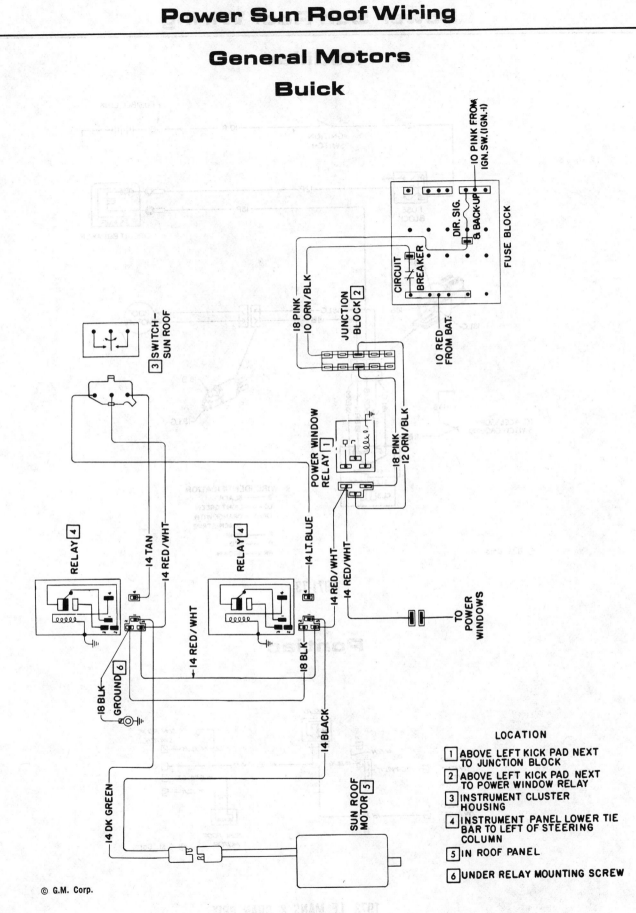

**LOCATION**

1. ABOVE LEFT KICK PAD NEXT TO JUNCTION BLOCK
2. ABOVE LEFT KICK PAD NEXT TO POWER WINDOW RELAY
3. INSTRUMENT CLUSTER HOUSING
4. INSTRUMENT PANEL LOWER TIE BAR TO LEFT OF STEERING COLUMN
5. IN ROOF PANEL
6. UNDER RELAY MOUNTING SCREW

© G.M. Corp.

1973

## Cadillac

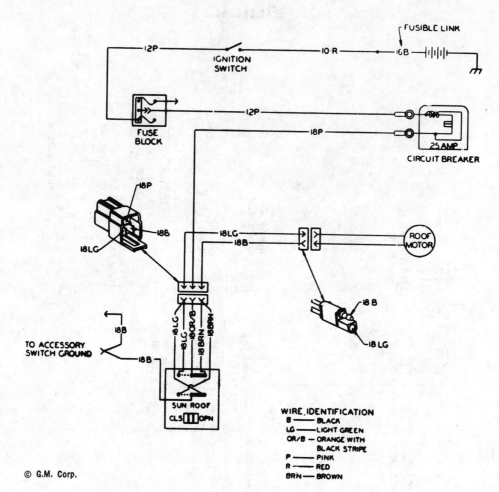

WIRE IDENTIFICATION
B ——— BLACK
LG ——— LIGHT GREEN
OR/B — ORANGE WITH
               BLACK STRIPE
P ——— PINK
R ——— RED
BRN — BROWN

© G.M. Corp.

**1971-73**

## Pontiac

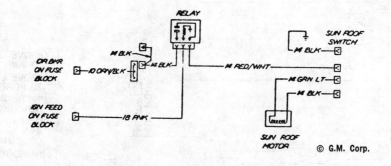

© G.M. Corp.

**1973 LE MANS & GRAN PRIX**

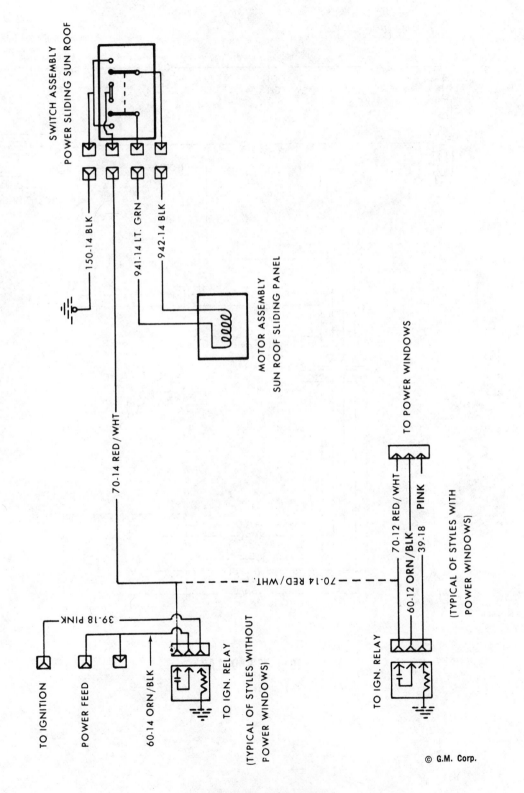

SWITCH ASSEMBLY
POWER SLIDING SUN ROOF

150-14 BLK

941-14 LT. GRN

942-14 BLK

MOTOR ASSEMBLY
SUN ROOF SLIDING PANEL

70-14 RED/WHT

TO POWER WINDOWS

70-12 RED/WHT

60-12 ORN/BLK

39-18 PINK

(TYPICAL OF STYLES WITH
POWER WINDOWS)

70-14 RED/WHT

39-18 PINK

TO IGNITION

POWER FEED

60-14 ORN/BLK

TO IGN. RELAY

(TYPICAL OF STYLES WITHOUT
POWER WINDOWS)

TO IGN. RELAY

© G.M. Corp.

**1973-75 INTERMEDIATES**

## Cadillac

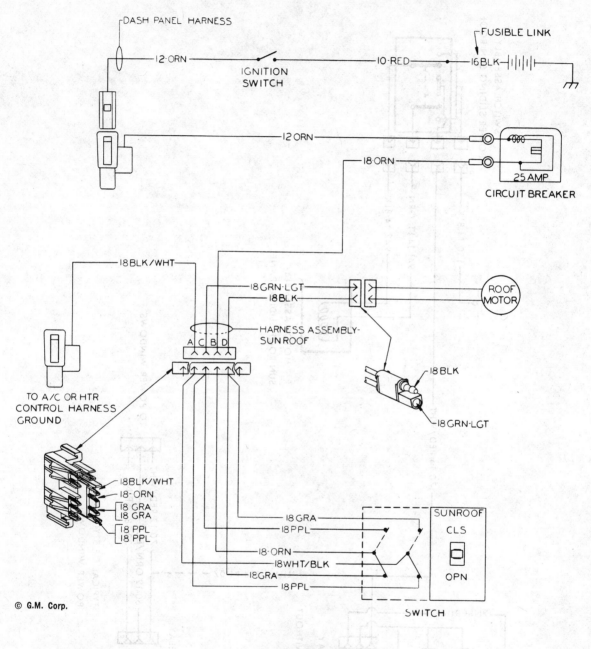

© G.M. Corp.

**1974-75 CADILLAC**

# Chrysler Corporation

NOTE: Provide a self-powered indicator light or ohmmeter or equivalent to test wiring continuity with car battery disconnected, a voltage indicator light or voltmeter or equivalent to test voltage levels with car battery connected. test lead jumper wire and wiring diagrams included in this unit.

## SERVICE DIAGNOSIS

| Condition | Possible Cause | Correction |
|---|---|---|
| **(1)**<br>**ALARM ON WHEN IT SHOULD BE OFF** | (a) Ignition Switch—switch causes alarm to go ON if it is moved to the ON or START position any time the doors have been locked with the key. | (a) Turn ignition switch to OFF, then using the key unlock the driver's door, alarm should turn OFF. |
| | (b) Lock Alarm Switch—switch should be open unless pushed and held. | (b) Remove connector to switch, then key unlock the driver's door, if alarm turns OFF replace the switch. |
| | (c) Alarm Control Unit—the alarm control unit decides when the alarm should be ON or OFF. | (c) Unplug all 3 harness connectors at the control unit, alarm should turn OFF. Attach a new alarm control unit to the 3 connectors, if alarm remains OFF, replace the faulty alarm control unit. |
| **(2)**<br>**DOME LAMP NOT OPERATING** | (a) Defective bulb or door switch. | (a) Check basic car wiring. |
| **ALARM GOES ON WHEN IT SHOULD REMAIN OFF** | (a) System ARMED—before test begins—should any of the doors be locked with the key before the test, alarm will go ON if the system senses any illegal entry. | (a) Unlock the driver's door with the key, alarm should turn OFF. |
| | (b) Alarm Control Unit | (b) Use Step 1 (Alarm Control Unit) |
| **(3)**<br>**ALARM ON WHEN IT SHOULD REMAIN OFF** | (a) Ignition Switch<br>(b) Alarm Control Unit | (a) Use Step 1—Ignition Switch<br>(b) Use Step 1—Alarm Control Unit |
| **(4)**<br>**ALARM OFF WHEN IT SHOULD GO ON** | (a) Alarm Control Unit | (a) Unplug all 3 connectors at the alarm control unit and attach a new unit. Lock the open driver's door with the key and turn the ignition to ON, if alarm goes ON, replace the alarm control unit. |
| **(5)**<br>**ALARM OFF WHEN IT SHOULD BE ON** | (a) Alarm Control Unit | (a) Unplug all 3 connectors at the alarm control unit and attach a new unit. Key lock door and turn ignition ON then OFF, if alarm remains ON, replace alarm control unit. |
| **(6)**<br>**HOOD RELEASE LEVER MOVES WHEN IT SHOULD NOT** | (a) Hood Latch—hood latch must be closed or hood blocker cannot operate and hood release lever will be free to move. | (a) If the latch is open, manually close it then repeat checking procedure steps 3 and 4. |
| | (b) Hood Open Switch—switch must open (disconnected or depressed) or alarm control unit will not cause hood blocker to operate. | (b) If the switch is closed, open or disconnect it and repeat checking procedure steps 3 and 4. |
| | (c) Disarm Switch Arm—switch is attached to the back of the key cylinder, arms and disarms the alarm system. Disarming the system turns OFF the alarm. | (c) Check continuity at switch terminals while slowly rotating key through total travel, first in one direction then the other.<br>(1) between the violet and the white wire, the circuit should always be OPEN. |

# Chrysler Corporation

| Condition | Possible Cause | Correction |
|---|---|---|
| | | (2) between the violet and the black wire, the circuit should be open except when the key is turned in the direction of:<br>—lock on the driver door or<br>—unlock on the passengers door.<br>(3) between the white and black wire, the circuit should be OPEN except when the key is turned in the direction of:<br>—unlock on the driver door, or<br>—lock on the passenger's door.<br>If the switch does not function as explained above, replace the switch. |
| | (d) Alarm Control Unit—the alarm control unit is the BRAIN that decides if and when the hood blocker should operate. | (d) Unplug all 3 connectors at the alarm control unit and attach a substitute alarm unit. Lock the open driver's door using the key, if the hood release lever does NOT MOVE, replace the alarm control unit. |
| | (e) Hood Blocker—the hood blocker prevents latch movement when the latch is closed and the alarm system is armed. When the system is disarmed the latch is free to be operated by the hood release lever. | (e) Check continuity at the 2 way connector on the Hood Blocker. If the circuit between either wire and ground is OPEN replace the Blocker. |
| **(7A)**<br>**HEADLAMPS ON WHEN ALARM IS OFF** | (a) Headlamp Time Delay By-Pass Relay—relay prevents the headlamp lamp time delay system, available on Carline C and Y, from operating during the alarm ON cycle. By-pass relay is located on the dash panel above the time delay relay. | (a) Turn the ignition switch ON. Turn the headlamp switch ON then OFF; Turn the ignition switch OFF, the headlamps should go OFF. If they remain ON, remove by-pass relay connector. If the headlamps go OFF, the relay is either not properly grounded or defective. |
| | (b) Alarm Control Unit—the alarm control unit causes the headlamp doors to open when the alarm starts. | (b) Unplug all 3 connectors at the alarm control unit and attach a new unit. Lock the driver's door using the key. Lift the door button and open; key unlock the door, if headlamps are OFF and the headlamps doors are open, replace the alarm control unit. |
| **(7B)**<br>**HEADLAMP DOORS CLOSED WHEN THEY SHOULD BE OPEN** | (a) Headlamp Doors Relays—two identical relays located on the right side of the brake support bracket—one relay functions as the headlamp door opening relay. The second relay functions as the holding relay to prevent the doors from closing. | (a) Headlamp Door Holding Relay. Remove connector which has two (2) dark blue lead wires. Lock the driver's door using the keys and then turn ignition to ON; if headlamp doors OPEN when alarm goes on, the relay is either not properly grounded or defective.<br>Headlamp Door Opening Relay. With no connector on the holding relay, move the connector from the opening relay which has a light green lead wire and connect this wire to the holding relay. Lock the driver's door using the key then turn ignition to ON; if the headlamp doors OPEN when the alarm goes on, the opening relay is either not properly grounded or it is defective. |

## Chrysler Corporation

| Condition | Possible Cause | Correction |
|---|---|---|
| | (b) Alarm Control Unit | (b) Use Step 10—Alarm Control Unit |
| **(8)** **ALARM ON WHEN IT SHOULD BE OFF** | (a) Arm-Disarm Switch <br> (b) Alarm Control | (a) Use Step 6—Arm-Disarm Switch <br> (b) Unplug all 3 connectors at the alarm control unit and attach new unit. Lock the driver's door using the key then close door, if alarm remains OFF, replace control unit. |
| **(9)** **ALARM OFF WHEN SYSTEM IS ARMED AND DOOR IS OPENED** | (a) Alarm Control Unit | (a) Unplug all 3 connectors at the alarm control unit and attach a new unit. Lock the driver's door using the key then if alarm goes ON, replace the alarm control unit. |
| **(10)** | SEE STEP 7 | |
| **(11)** **ALARM OFF WHEN HOOD IS OPENED** | (a) Hood Switch—Switch grounds when hood is opened. <br> (b) Alarm Control Unit | (a) Remove connector and short to ground. If alarm goes ON replace switch. <br> (b) Unplug the 3 connectors to the alarm control unit and substitute new units, disconnect or clamp hood switch open, lock the driver's door using the key. If alarm goes ON when the hood switch is reconnected or unclamped, replace the alarm control unit. |
| **(12)** **RIGHT SIDE DOORS NOT LOCKED** | | (a) Check basic car wiring. |
| **(12A)** **ALARM REMAINS ON WHEN PASSENGERS DOORS IS KEY UNLOCKED** | | (a) Use Step 6—Arm-Disarm Switch. |
| **(13A)** **ALARM REMAINS OFF WHEN HOOD IS OPENED** | | (a) Use Step 11—Alarm Control Unit. |
| **(13B)** **HEADLAMPS NOT FLASHING AND HORN NOT PULSING DURING ALARM** | (a) Headlamp Time Delay By-Pass Relay —headlamps ON all during alarm. <br> (b) Alarm Control Unit—headlamps and horn ON or OFF all during alarm. | (a) With alarm operating, remove connector from time delay relay if headlamps begin to flash. By-Pass relay is either not properly grounded or defective. <br> (b) Unplug all 3 connectors to the alarm control unit and substitute a new unit. Lock the driver's door using the key then open the door. If the headlamps now flash, and horn pulses, replace the alarm control unit. |
| **(14)** **DOME LAMP DOES NOT OPERATE** | | (a) Check basic car wiring. |
| **(15)** **ALARM REMAINS OFF WHEN LOCK ALARM SWITCH IS PUSHED** | (a) Lock Alarm Switch—operates alarm at anytime. <br> (b) Alarm Control Unit | (a) Remove the connector at switch and short the two harness leads together, if the alarm goes ON replace this switch. <br> (b) Unplug the 3 connectors at the alarm control unit and attach a new unit; push the lock alarm switch, if alarm goes ON, replace alarm control unit. |

# Chrysler Corporation

| Condition | Possible Cause | Correction |
|---|---|---|
| **(16)** **DOME LAMP DOES NOT OPERATE** | | (a) Check basic car wiring. |
| **(17)** **ALARM GOES ON WHEN TRUNK IS UNLOCKED AND OPENED** | (a) Latch Switch—This switch should be closed when the trunk latch is closed and open when the latch is open. | (a) Disconnect harness from switch leads and check continuity between switch leads. If switch is closed when trunk latch is open, or open when latch is closed, replace switch. |
| **(18A)** **ALARM REMAINS OFF WHEN LATCH IS CLOSED** | (a) Trunk Open Switch—this switch, operated by the left hinge, closes when the trunk is open. | (a) Disconnect the harness at the switch and ground harness lead. If the alarm goes ON, the switch is either not properly grounded or defective. |
| | (b) Latch Switch | (b) Use Step 17—Latch Switch. |
| | (c) Alarm Control Unit | (c) Unlock the trunk to open the latch; unplug all 3 connectors at the alarm control unit and attach a new unit. Lock the driver's door using the key, then close the latch again. If alarm goes ON replace alarm control unit. |
| **(18B)** **ALARM GOES OFF AFTER CLOSING TRUNK AND BEFORE DISARMING THE SYSTEM** | (a) Alarm Control Unit | (a) Unplug the 3 connectors at the alarm control unit and attach a new unit. Lock the passenger's door using the key and repeat checking procedures steps 16 and 17. If alarm remains ON, replace the alarm control unit. |
| **(19A)** **TAILGATE NOT LOCKED AFTER SYSTEM HAS BEEN ARMED** | (a) Tailgate Lock Relay—relay is mounted in right side cowl and provides power to lock tailgate everytime the system is armed. | (a) Remove relay connector. Using test lead, short orange wire with tracer to red wire. If tailgate locks, the relay is either not properly grounded or defective. |
| | (b) Alarm Control Unit. | (b) Unplug the 3 connectors to the alarm control unit and attach a new unit. Lock passenger door using the key, if the tailgate LOCKS, replace the alarm control unit. |
| **(19B)** **ALARM DOES NOT REMAIN ON WHEN BUTTON ON TAILGATE IS PUSHED DOWN** | (a) Alarm Control Unit. | (a) Use Step 19—Alarm Control Unit. |
| **(20)** **ALARM DOES NOT:** | (1) Go ON when tailgate is unlocked with the key. (2) Remain ON when the tailgate is locked using the key. | (a) Use Step 19—Alarm Control Unit. |
| **(21)** **ALARM DOES NOT REMAIN ON WHEN BUTTON ON TAILGATE IS PUSHED DOWN** | | (a) Use Step 19—Alarm Control Unit. |
| **(22A)** **HOOD BLOCKER PREVENTS LATCH MOVEMENT WHEN THE SYSTEM IS DISARMED** | | (a) Use Step 6—Hood Blocker. |

### Chrysler Corporation—
### All Models 1973-75

#### Description

The theft warning system is armed when either front door is locked with the key. When the system is armed, forced entry of the doors, hood, trunk, tailgate, or application of voltage to the accessory circuit of the ignition switch will activate the alarm. When one of the mechanisms is triggered the control unit flashes the headlamps, tail and side marker lamps and simultaneously sounds the horns at a rate of ninety times per minute. The alarm will continue to operate for three to five minutes or until the system is turned off by using the key.

#### Testing Procedures

1. If the hood cannot be opened because of a run down battery, the following steps must be taken to open the hood.
   a) Using jumper cables, attach the negative cable to a ground. Use the courtesy light door switch.
   b) Turn the door lock with the key and leave it in the unlock position.
   c) Clamp the positive jumper cable to a screwdriver and touch the screwdriver to the battery terminal of the firewall mounted fuse block.
   d) The hood should now open by pulling the hood release.

#### Checkout Procedures

The following conditions are required to use the checkout procedures effectively.

1. The ignition switch must be in the "off" or "lock" position.
2. The headlight switch should be in the "off" position.
3. All power headlight doors should be closed.
4. All doors should be closed and unlocked.
5. Put the driver's door and tailgate glass in the full down position.
6. The hood should be opened with the latch manually closed. The hood switch should either be disconnected or clamped open.
7. Keep the ignition and trunk key available.

Follow the checkout procedures step by step until the problem area is detected. Each number of the following checkout procedures corresponds with a number in the troubleshooting chart for possible causes and corrections.

1. With the alarm control unit not armed and all the wiring properly connected the alarm should stay off.
2. Open and close the left rear door and when the dome light goes on the alarm should stay off.
3. Open the driver's door and while open, lock the door with the key. The alarm should stay off.
4. Turn the ignition to the "on" position and the alarm should go on.
5. Turn the ignition to the "off"

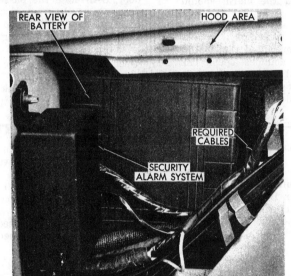

*Control Unit Location*

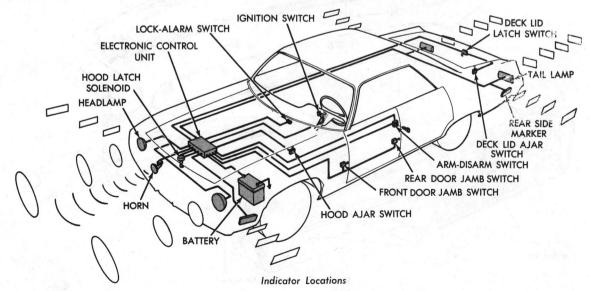

*Indicator Locations*

## Chrysler Corporation

position and the alarm should stay on.

6. The hood release lever when pulled should not release.

7. The headlamps should be off and if so equipped, the headlamp doors should be open.

8. Unlock the driver's door with a key, the alarm should turn off. Lock the driver's door with a key and the alarm should stay off.

9. Unlock the driver's door by lifting the door lock button. Open the door until the dome lamp turns on. The alarm should go on. Close the door and the alarm should remain on.

10. Unlock the driver's door with a key and the alarm should turn off. Lock the driver's door with the key and the alarm should remain off.

11. Connect the wiring harness lead to the hood switch if it is disconnected, or allow the switch to close if clamped open. The alarm should go on.

12. On the right side of the car both doors should be locked. Unlock the front door with the key. The alarm should turn off. Lock the door using the key.

13. Push the hood switch down, then release the switch and the alarm should go off. Disconnect the wiring harness connector or clamp the hood switch open. Headlamps should be flashing.

14. Unlock the passenger's door with the key and the alarm should turn off. Open the door and the alarm should stay off and the dome light should operate.

15. Press the lock alarm switch by reaching in the car and the alarm should go on.

16. Unlock the passenger's door with the key and the alarm should turn off. Unlock the rear door, then close the passenger's door. Open the rear door and observe the dome lamp operation. Lock the passenger's door with the key.

17. Open the trunk and the alarm should stay off.

18. Manually close the trunk latch, and the alarm should go on.

Unlock the latch and close the trunk. The alarm should stay on. (All models other than Stationwagons proceed to step #22.)

19. The tailgate should be locked. Unlock the tailgate by lifting the door lock button. The alarm should go on. Open the tailgate and push the door lock button down. The alarm should stay on.

20. Unlock the tailgate using the key and the alarm should stay on. Lock the tailgate using the key then close the tailgate. The alarm should stay on.

21. Unlock the tailgate by lifting the door lock button. The alarm should stay on.

22. Using a key, unlock the driver's door. The alarm should turn off. Pull the hood release and the handle should allow the hood latch to release. Turn the ignition key to "on" and the alarm should stay off. The headlamp doors should close.

23. Turn the ignition off and connect the wire to the hood switch. Close the hood.

## Ford Motor Company

### Ford and Mercury 1973-75

### Description

The theft warning system is armed by locking either front door with a key and then removing the key from the cylinder. When the trunk lid or doors are opened, the alarm is activated and the horns sound intermittently, for approximately five minutes. The horns can only be turned off by inserting the key in the ignition switch and turning it to the Accessory or Run position.

The hood latch release used with this system can only be opened from inside the car by using the trunk key and pulling on the hood release handle.

The warning system is controlled by a transistorized sensor (actuator) which is mounted to a bracket and located under the instrument panel top pad and above the glove com-

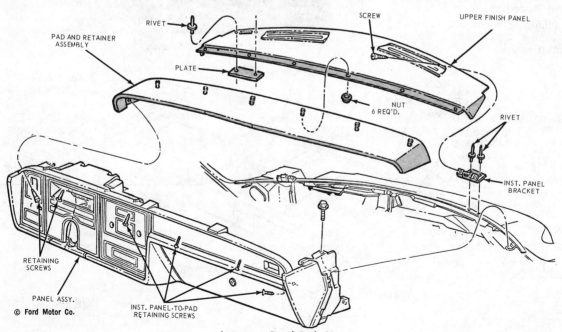

*Instrument Panel Pad—Mercury*

© Ford Motor Co.

# Ford Motor Company

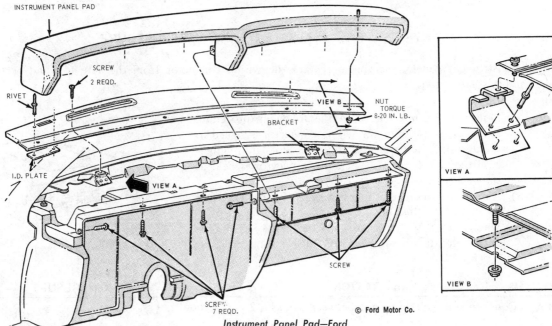

*Instrument Panel Pad—Ford*

© Ford Motor Co.

partment door. The sensor receives its power from the battery and is electrically connected to the trunk warning switch and door lock cylinder switches. The sensor unit cannot be repaired and must be replaced if found defective.

## Operation Test

1. Close the trunk, tailgate and all doors except the front passengers door.
2. Insert the ignition key into the opened passenger front door and turn it momentarily to the lock position. Wait about one to two minutes and the horn should sound.
3. Turn the key to the unlock position to stop the horns.
4. Open the trunk or tailgate and lock all the car doors. Leave the driver's window open and the door unlocked.
5. Lock the door with the key then remove the key.

*CAUTION: Do not overtravel when turning the key back to the center position in the lock cylinder. Overtravel may disarm the system. Wait about one to two minutes and the horns should sound.*

6. Reach through the open window and turn the ignition key to On or ACC to disarm the system.

## SENSOR (ACTUATOR)

### Ford 1973

#### Removal

1. Remove the instrument panel pad.

a) Remove one screw on each side of the defroster nozzle opening.
b) Remove the three screws on the ledge above the glove box door.
c) Remove the four screws around the instrument cluster opening and remove the instrument panel pad and the upper finish pad assembly.

2. Disconnect the wiring connector from the sensor.

3. Remove the four sensor bracket attaching screws and remove the sensor and bracket from the instrument panel.

## Installation

1. Position the sensor and bracket assembly to the instrument panel and install the four attaching screws.
2. Connect the wiring harness to the sensor.
3. Check for proper operation.
4. Install the instrument panel pad.

a) Position the instrument panel pad and the upper finish pad and install the four screws around the instrument cluster opening.
b) Install the three screws above the glove box door.
c) Install each screw on the sides of the defroster nozzle opening.

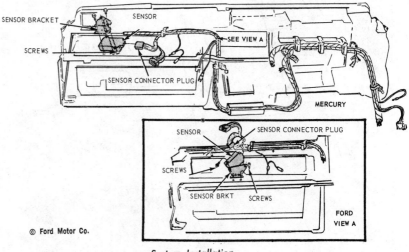

© Ford Motor Co.

*System Installation*

# Ford Motor Company

### ANTI—THEFT ALARM SYSTEM CHECKOUT PROCEDURE

Remove the instrument panel upper pad, separate the wiring connector from the actuator, and perform the following circuit isolation test.

**NOTE:** (A) Slot numbers referred to in the following procedure relate to the slots in the wiring connector attached to the anti-theft actuator assembly. The slots are numbered from left to right (when the connector is held as shown.)

(B) Any short circuits diagnosed in steps (F) thru (J) could be located in either front door.

(C) When necessary to trace and/or repair the various circuits refer to the respective vehicle wiring diagrams.

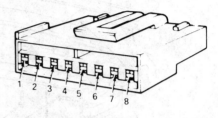

| OPERATION | RESULT |
|---|---|
| **Step A** – Connect a 12-volt test light between slot No. 2 and a good ground. | |

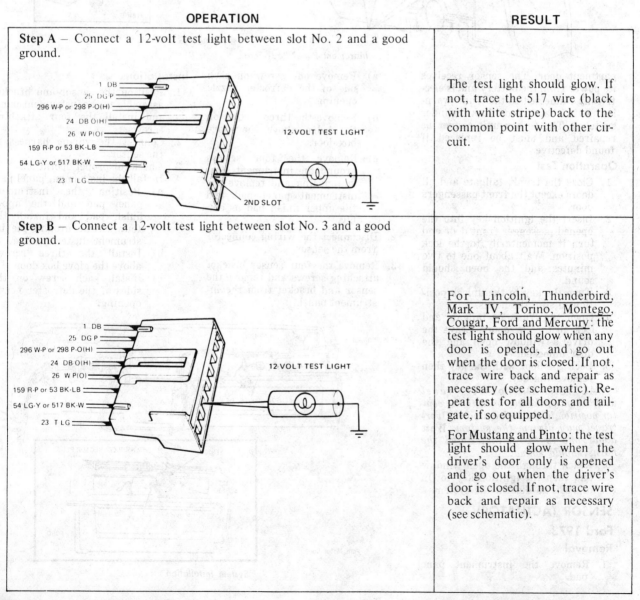

| OPERATION | RESULT |
|---|---|
| **Step A** | The test light should glow. If not, trace the 517 wire (black with white stripe) back to the common point with other circuit. |
| **Step B** – Connect a 12-volt test light between slot No. 3 and a good ground. | For Lincoln, Thunderbird, Mark IV, Torino, Montego, Cougar, Ford and Mercury: the test light should glow when any door is opened, and go out when the door is closed. If not, trace wire back and repair as necessary (see schematic). Repeat test for all doors and tailgate, if so equipped. |
| | For Mustang and Pinto: the test light should glow when the driver's door only is opened and go out when the driver's door is closed. If not, trace wire back and repair as necessary (see schematic). |

Step A diagram labels:
1 DB
25 DG P
296 W-P or 298 P-O(H)
24 DB O(H)
26 W P(O)
159 R-P or 53 BK-LB
54 LG-Y or 517 BK-W
23 T LG
12-VOLT TEST LIGHT
2ND SLOT

Step B diagram labels:
1 DB
25 DG P
296 W-P or 298 P-O(H)
24 DB O(H)
26 W P(O)
159 R-P or 53 BK-LB
54 LG-Y or 517 BK-W
23 T LG
12-VOLT TEST LIGHT

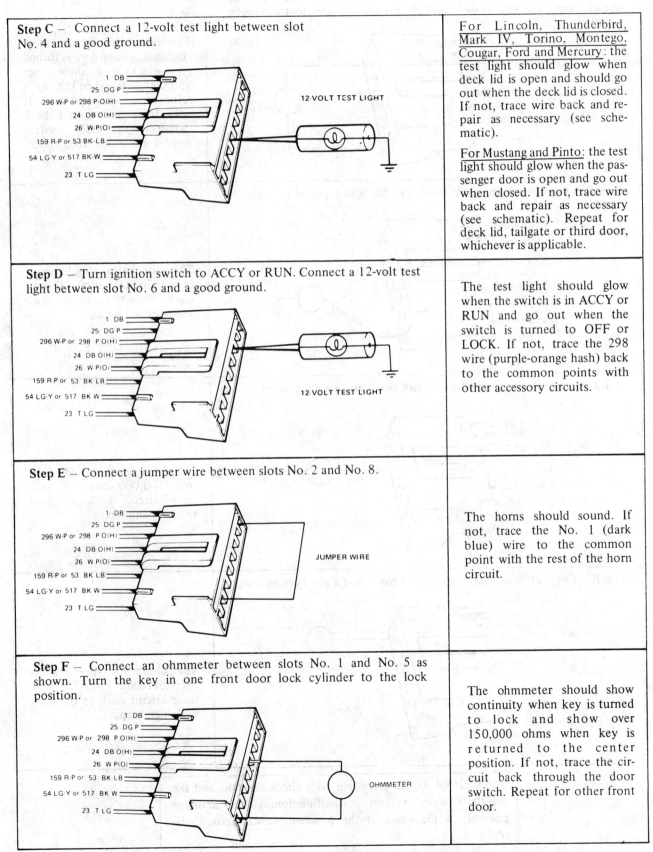

**Step C** – Connect a 12-volt test light between slot No. 4 and a good ground.

For Lincoln, Thunderbird, Mark IV, Torino, Montego, Cougar, Ford and Mercury: the test light should glow when deck lid is open and should go out when the deck lid is closed. If not, trace wire back and repair as necessary (see schematic).

For Mustang and Pinto: the test light should glow when the passenger door is open and go out when closed. If not, trace wire back and repair as necessary (see schematic). Repeat for deck lid, tailgate or third door, whichever is applicable.

**Step D** – Turn ignition switch to ACCY or RUN. Connect a 12-volt test light between slot No. 6 and a good ground.

The test light should glow when the switch is in ACCY or RUN and go out when the switch is turned to OFF or LOCK. If not, trace the 298 wire (purple-orange hash) back to the common points with other accessory circuits.

**Step E** – Connect a jumper wire between slots No. 2 and No. 8.

The horns should sound. If not, trace the No. 1 (dark blue) wire to the common point with the rest of the horn circuit.

**Step F** – Connect an ohmmeter between slots No. 1 and No. 5 as shown. Turn the key in one front door lock cylinder to the lock position.

The ohmmeter should show continuity when key is turned to lock and show over 150,000 ohms when key is returned to the center position. If not, trace the circuit back through the door switch. Repeat for other front door.

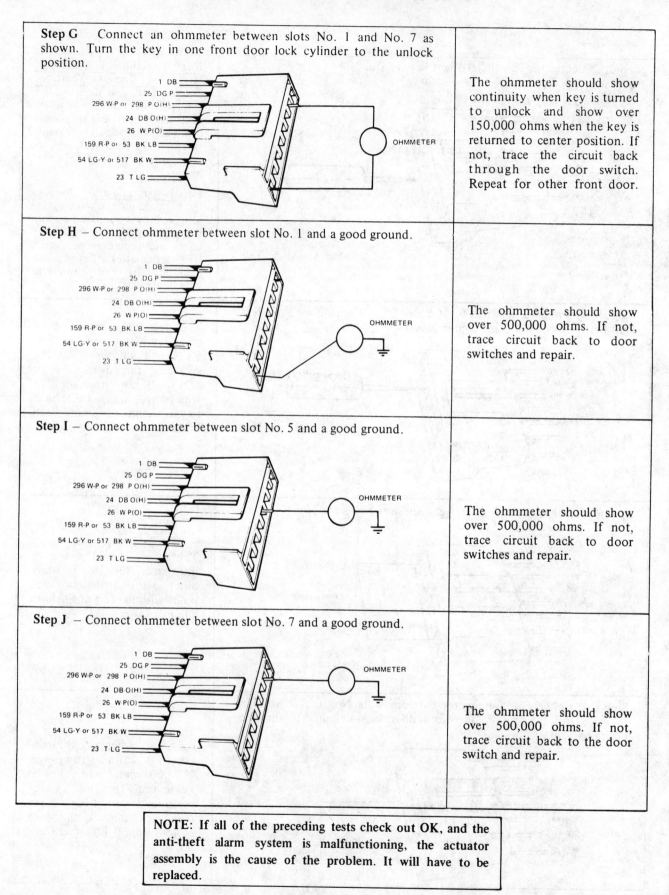

**Step G**  Connect an ohmmeter between slots No. 1 and No. 7 as shown. Turn the key in one front door lock cylinder to the unlock position.

The ohmmeter should show continuity when key is turned to unlock and show over 150,000 ohms when the key is returned to center position. If not, trace the circuit back through the door switch. Repeat for other front door.

**Step H** – Connect ohmmeter between slot No. 1 and a good ground.

The ohmmeter should show over 500,000 ohms. If not, trace circuit back to door switches and repair.

**Step I** – Connect ohmmeter between slot No. 5 and a good ground.

The ohmmeter should show over 500,000 ohms. If not, trace circuit back to door switches and repair.

**Step J** – Connect ohmmeter between slot No. 7 and a good ground.

The ohmmeter should show over 500,000 ohms. If not, trace circuit back to the door switch and repair.

**NOTE: If all of the preceding tests check out OK, and the anti-theft alarm system is malfunctioning, the actuator assembly is the cause of the problem. It will have to be replaced.**

# Ford Motor Company

## SENSOR (ACTUATOR)
### Mercury 1973
#### Removal

1. Remove the instrument panel pad.
   a) Remove one screw on each side of the defroster nozzle opening.
   b) Remove the four screws going up into the entire length of the pad.
   c) Remove the one screw at each end of the inboard side of the pad and remove the upper instrument panel pad and the upper finish panel assembly.
2. Disconnect the wiring harness from the sensor.
3. Remove the four sensor bracket attaching screws and remove the sensor and bracket from the instrument panel.

#### Installation

1. Position the sensor and bracket assembly to the instrument panel and install the four attaching screws.
2. Connect the wiring harness to the sensor.
3. Check for proper operation.
4. Install the instrument panel pad.
   a) Position the upper instrument panel pad and the upper finish panel assembly and install all the attaching screws.

## SENSOR (ACTUATOR)
### Ford 1974-75 All Models
#### Removal

1. Refer to the actuator location chart to gain access to the actuator assembly for each particular vehicle.
2. Remove the instrument panel pad.

3. Disconnect the wiring connector from the sensor.
4. Remove the four sensor bracket attaching screws and remove the sensor and bracket from the instrument panel.

#### Installation

1. If the sensor is being replaced transfer the old bracket to the new sensor.
2. Position the sensor and bracket assembly to the instrument panel and install the four attaching screws.
3. Install the instrument panel pad.

## TRUNK LID SWITCH
### Removal

1. Open the trunk lid.
2. Disconnect the wire connector from the switch.
3. Remove the one screw which attaches the switch and bracket to the left hinge support assembly.

### Installation

1. Position the switch to the left hinge support assembly and install the retaining screw.
2. Connect the wire connector to the switch.

| Passenger Cars | Actuator Locations |
|---|---|
| Lincoln | Instrument panel - to the right of the glove box |
| T-Bird, Mark IV | Instrument panel - to the right of the glove box |
| Ford, Mercury, Torino, Montego, Cougar, Mustang | Instrument panel - above glove box |
| Pinto | Instrument panel - on the top of brake pedal support bracket |

*Actuator Locations*

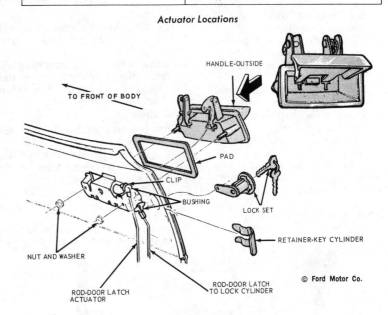

*Door Handle and Lock Cylinder Installation*

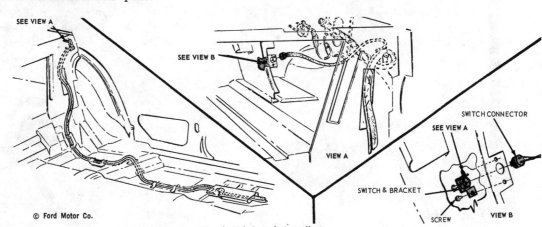

*Trunk Lid Switch Installation*

# Ford Motor Company

3. Close the trunk lid and check the operation of the switch.

## DOOR LOCK CYLINDER SWITCH

### Removal

1. Remove the door trim panel.

*NOTE: If some of the following steps do not apply to the particular model being worked on, proceed to the next step.*

  a) Remove the door lock push button and garnish moulding.

  b) Remove the window regulator handle screw access cover and remove the screw and handle.

  c) Remove the door latch handle retaining screw access cover, if so equipped, and remove the door latch handle screws.

  d) Remove the screws from the armrest door pull cup area, if so equipped.

  e) Remove the arm rest retaining screws and any wiring connectors and remove the arm rest.

  f) Remove the bezel nut from the mirror remote control.

  g) Remove the door trim panel retaining screws.

  h) Pry the trim panel retaining clips from the door inner panel and separate the panel.

2. Disconnect the lock cylinder switch connector from the harness.

3. Remove the lock cylinder.

  a) Disconnect the control rod at the cylinder arm.

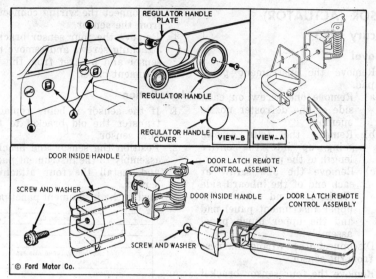

*Door and Window Regulator Handle Installation*

  b) Remove the door lock cylinder retainer and remove the lock cylinder.

4. Remove the spring retaining clip from the lock cylinder switch assembly and remove the switch from the lock cylinder.

### Installation

1. Position the switch to the lock cylinder.

2. Align the plastic arm of the switch to the metal tang on the back of the lock cylinder.

3. Install and lock securely the retaining clip to the switch housing tabs.

4. Install the lock cylinder and switch assembly to the door and make sure the locking arm points to the rear of the vehicle.

  a) Position the lock cylinder and install the retainer.

  b) Connect the control rod at the cylinder arm.

5. Test the alarm system for proper operation.

6. Install the door trim panel.

  a) If the watershield has been remove, position it correctly before installing the trim panel.

  b) Make sure that the arm rest retaining clips are properly positioned before installing the watershield.

  c) Position the trim panel to

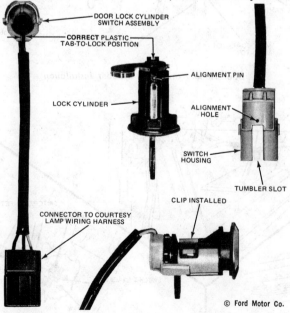

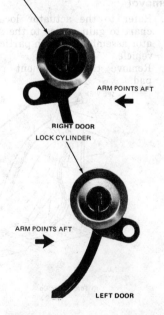

*Door Lock Cylinder and Switch Assembly*

## Ford Motor Company

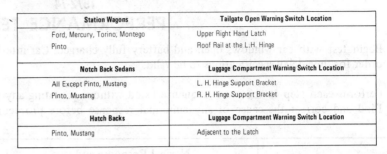

| Station Wagons | Tailgate Open Warning Switch Location |
|---|---|
| Ford, Mercury, Torino, Montego | Upper Right Hand Latch |
| Pinto | Roof Rail at the L.H. Hinge |
| **Notch Back Sedans** | **Luggage Compartment Warning Switch Location** |
| All Except Pinto, Mustang | L. H. Hinge Support Bracket |
| Pinto, Mustang | R. H. Hinge Support Bracket |
| **Hatch Backs** | **Luggage Compartment Warning Switch Location** |
| Pinto, Mustang | Adjacent to the Latch |

*Warning Switch Locations*

the door inner panel and connect any wiring and re-route the mirror control cable through the hole.

d) Push the trim panel and retaining clips into the inner door panel holes and install the retaining screws.

e) Install the bezel nut for the remote control mirror.

f) Position the arm rest to the trim panel, connect any wiring and install the retaining screws.

g) Install the arm rest finish panel, if so equipped.

h) Position the door latch and window regulator handles and install the retaining screws.

i) Tape the access cover back in place.

j) Install the garnish moulding and the lock push button control knob.

*NOTE: If for any reason the switch is separated from the lock cylinder a new switch must be installed.*

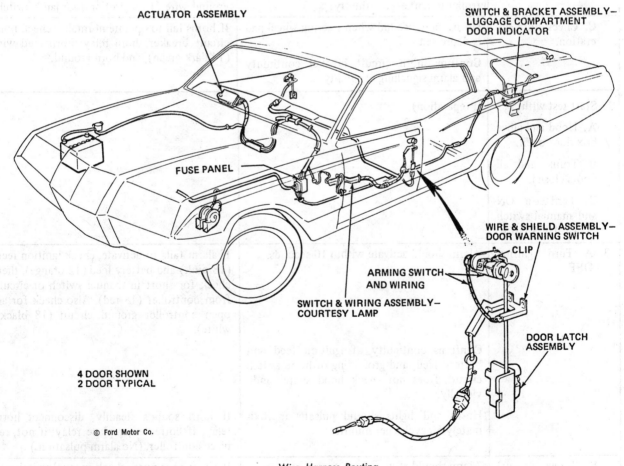

ACTUATOR ASSEMBLY

SWITCH & BRACKET ASSEMBLY—
LUGGAGE COMPARTMENT
DOOR INDICATOR

FUSE PANEL

WIRE & SHIELD ASSEMBLY—
DOOR WARNING SWITCH

CLIP

ARMING SWITCH
AND WIRING

SWITCH & WIRING ASSEMBLY—
COURTESY LAMP

DOOR LATCH
ASSEMBLY

**4 DOOR SHOWN
2 DOOR TYPICAL**

© Ford Motor Co.

*Wire Harness Routing*

# Theft Warning Systems

## General Motors

### 1972-74
### PERFORMANCE TEST

Begin test with car windows open and battery fully charged. Car interior should be at normal shop temperature in order for time delay specifications to be valid.

Perform each step in the exact sequence listed without actuating any electrical devices other than those indicated. Find and correct the cause of any abnormal response before proceeding to the next step.

| Steps | Normal Response and Circuits Confirmed | Abnormal Response and Items To Be Checked |
|---|---|---|
| 1. A. Open and close trunk. | Trunk light should operate normally. | If light fails to go on, check bulb, mercury switch, and feed wire continuity. |
|  | Confirms ability of trunk light to trigger alarm. | If light fails to shut off, check switch positioning. |
| B. Open and close each car door. | Courtesy lights should operate normally. | If lights fail to go on, check fuse and feed circuit. |
|  | Confirms courtesy light ground circuit to door jamb switches, but does not check controller to harness continuity. | If lights fail to shut off, check for shorts at ground wire (18 white) or door jamb switch. |
| C. Check horn operation. | Horns should sound when steering wheel pad is depressed. | If horns fail to operate normally, check horn circuit breaker, horn relay, horn feed wire (14 dark green), and horn ground. |
|  | Confirms horn circuit breaker continuity and alarm signalling capability. |  |
| 2. Start test with:<br><br>A. Hood and glove box door open.<br><br>B. Trunk and all doors closed.<br><br>C. Ignition ON and manual switch in ARM ENABLE. | (Preparation) |  |
| 3. A. Turn ignition OFF. | Alarm should activate within 10 seconds. | If alarm fails to activate, check ignition feed (18 pink) and battery feed (12 orange), then check for short in manual switch or circuit from controller (18 red). Also check for an open controller ground circuit (18 black/white). |
|  | Confirms continuity of ignition feed and battery feed, and grounding of hood switch circuit. Does not check hood switch individually. |  |
|  | Horns and lights should pulsate approximately 50 cycles per minute. | If horn sounds steadily, disconnect horn relay. If corrected, replace relay; if not, replace controller. (No alarm pulsation.) |
| B. Move manual switch to ARM PREVENT (not later than 30 seconds after ignition OFF). | Alarm should stop.<br><br>Confirms manual switch circuit continuity to ground. | If alarm continues, check manual switch positioning (wires to R.H. Side), switch and connector continuity, and check for open from 18 red wire to ground. |

© G.M. Corp.

## General Motors

### 1972-74
### PERFORMANCE TEST (Cont'd.)

| Steps | Normal Response and Circuits Confirmed | Abnormal Response and Items To Be Checked |
|---|---|---|
| C. Move manual switch back to ARM ENABLE. | Alarm should resume. (Same as 3A) | If alarm fails to activate, check for shorted manual switch. |
| D. Turn ignition to ACCESSORY, then to OFF. | Alarm should stop. Confirms either ignition or accessory feed circuit continuity. | If alarm continues, check continuity of accessory feed (18 yellow) to controller. |
| E. Wait 10 seconds. | No alarm should occur. Confirms accessory feed continuity to controller. | If alarm sounds, check for crossed ignition feed (18 pink) and accessory feed (18 yellow) wires to controller. |
| 4. A. Open door and exit from car. | (Preparation) | |
| 5. A. Turn ignition ON. | (Cancels temporary alarm lockout.) | |
| B. Turn ignition OFF. | (To begin arming.) | |
| C. Wait 10 seconds. | No alarm should occur. Confirms hood switch open and hood switch circuit not shorted. Also confirms horn breaker circuit continuity. | If alarm sounds, check for hood switch misadjustment or grounded circuit (18 black). Also check faulty or unplugged horn circuit breaker, or open in the circuit breaker wire to controller (18 purple). |
| D. Wait an additional 35 seconds (total of 45 seconds from ignition OFF.) | (Preparation) | |
| E. Depress brake pedal, then release. | No alarm should occur. Confirms arming time above minimum limit for normal voltage and temperature. | If alarm activates, replace controller (insufficient exit delay time). |
| 6. A. Wait an additional 75 seconds (total of 120 seconds from ignition OFF). | (Preparation) | |
| B. Turn courtesy lights ON, then OFF at headlight switch. | Alarm should activate after 15-20 second delay. Confirms arming time within maximum limit, and also confirms that entrance delay is within limits for normal voltage and temperature. | If alarm fails to activate within 30 seconds, open glove box or turn on map light for a substitute trigger. If alarm activates (immediately), check continuity of courtesy lamp ground to controller circuit (18 white). If alarm still fails to activate, replace controller (no arming). If alarm activates sooner than 13 seconds or later than 22 seconds after courtesy lights ON, replace controller (incorrect entrance delay). |

© G.M. Corp.

| Steps | Normal Response and Circuits Confirmed | Abnormal Response and Items To Be Checked |
|---|---|---|
| C. Allow alarm to continue flashing until automatic shutdown (less than 2 minutes), then wait at least 40 seconds longer. | (Preparation for re-arming test.) | |
| D. Open car door until courtesy lights come on, then close door. | Alarm should activate immediately. Confirms re-arming signal to driver of prior activation. Also reconfirms continuity of courtesy light ground circuit. | If alarm fails to activate, check continuity of courtesy light circuit (18 white) from door jamb switches to controller. If continuity OK, replace controller (no re-arming). If alarm activation is delayed (more than 5 seconds), replace controller (no rearming signal). |
| 7. A. Turn ignition ON, then OFF, and remove key. | (To enable normal arming.) | |
| B. Exit from car immediately and close all doors. | (Preparation for maximum signal duration test.) | |
| C. Wait 4-1/2 minutes after closing doors. | (To allow full arming.) | |
| D. Open trunk. | Alarm should activate immediately. Confirms voltage sensing from trunk light. | If alarm fails to activate, recheck trunk light bulb, mercury switch, and feed circuit as in Step 1A. |
| E. Check duration of alarm. | Alarm should continue for 3-5 minutes. Confirms signal duration within limits for normal voltage and temperature. Alarm should shut down after no longer than 7 minutes. | If alarm duration is shorter than 3 minutes or longer than 7 minutes, replace controller (incorrect alarm duration). |
| 8. A. Enter car and turn ignition ON; set manual switch to ARM PREVENT. | (Conclusion of test.) | |
| B. Open hood and reconnect horn feed wire connectors. Close hood. | No alarm should sound. | If alarm sounds, repeat checks under Steps 1C and 3B. |

© G.M. Corp.

© G.M. Corp.

Using a non-powered test light, start test with doors, hood and trunk closed and manual switch on "ARM ENABLE". Probe terminals of wiring harness connector.

| Wire Colors / Terminal Numbers | Brown 1 — Ext. Lamps | Yellow 2 — Acc. | Red 3 — Manual Switch | Pink 4 — Ign. | Orange 5 — Batt. | Lt. Blue 6 — Hd. Lamp Feed | Purple 7 — Horn Brkr. | White 8 — Courtesy Lamps | Black 9 — Hood | Dk. Green 10 — Horns | Black/White Extra — Separate Ground Connection |
|---|---|---|---|---|---|---|---|---|---|---|---|
| 1. Connect tester to known good ground on Inst. Panel and each terminal: | | | | | | | | | | | |
| A. Ign. "OFF" | OFF | OFF | OFF | OFF | ON | OFF | ON | ON | OFF | OFF | OFF |
| B. Ign. "ON" | | ON | | ON | | | | | | | |
| C. Ign. "ACC" | | ON | | OFF | | | | | | | |
| 2. Connect tester to known good ground on inst. panel and probe each terminal with ign. in off and: | | | | | | | | | | | |
| A. Sound horn. (NOTE: If 1B above checks OK then the dark green wire (10) should energize when the horn is sounded). | | | | | | | | | | | |
| B. Turn headlamps on. | ON | | | | | ON | | | | | |
| C. Turn courtesy lamps on. | | | | | | | | OFF | | | |
| 3. A. Ignition in off-clip connected to terminal #5 (Battery) | | | | | | | | | | | |
| B. Place manual switch in arm prevent | | | OFF | | | | | | | | |
| C. Open Hood | | | ON | | | | | | ON | ON | ON |

## General Motors

### 1975
## THEFT DETERRENT DIAGNOSIS CHART

Before using the "THEFT DETERRENT DIAGNOSIS CHART", check the following inter-related electrical components for proper operation:

1. Horns
2. Exterior Lamps
3. Trunk, Door Lock Adjustments
4. Electric door lock circuits

(NOTE: Some system malfunctions DO NOT affect the operation of the tell-tale light. Therefore, a complete testing of proper alarm function is required in order to detect some problems.)

| COMPLAINT | PROBABLE CAUSE | CORRECTION |
|---|---|---|
| System inoperative. | Open in one of the following wires:<br>1. Ground wire.<br>2. Battery feed.<br>3. Electric door lock wire.<br>4. Blown fuses. | Repair or replace as needed.<br><br><br><br>Same as above.<br>(If fuse in yellow wire is blown, horn only will activate. If fuse in black with red stripe wire is blown, system will not operate.) |
| | Check for loose connectors at controller to instrument panel harness or instrument panel harness to body harness. | Repair or replace as needed. |
| Unable to reverse arming process with "UNLOCK" switch. | Open in electric door "UNLOCK" wire. | Repair or replace as needed. |
| "S E C U R I T Y SYSTEM" tell-tale light inoperative. | Check body fuse.<br>Check bulb. | Repair or replace as needed. |
| System operates normally except <u>alarm will not activate when</u> hood opened. | Open in hood switch wire.<br><br>Inoperative hood switch.<br><br>Malfunctioning controller. | Repair or replace as needed.<br><br>Same as above.<br><br>Replace after investigating previously listed causes. |
| System operates normally except <u>does not disarm with door key.</u> | A. Try to disarm system by opening other door lock with key. If system disarms, check for:<br>1. Open light green wire.<br>2. Malfunctioning door lock switch. | Repair or replace as needed.<br>Same as above. |
| | B. If system cannot be disarmed from either door:<br>1. Check for open at 18 red wire at controller with door lock cylinder in unlock position. | Repair or replace as needed. |

© G.M. Corp.

# General Motors

## 1975

| COMPLAINT | PROBABLE CAUSE | CORRECTION |
|---|---|---|
| Security light will not go out upon closing doors, and system will not arm. | LOCK CYLINDER VIOLATED or unwanted ground at door jamb switches, door and trunk tamper switches or pinched wires leading to these components. | Repair or replace as needed. |
| | Door and trunk lock tamper switches out of adjustment. | Readjust or replace as necessary. |
| Alarm activates when depressing door lock button when equipped with illuminated lock cylinder option. | Unwanted ground at door jamb switch. | Remove wires from door jamb switch and install wires so that illuminated lock cylinder feed (18 white) is separated from theft deterrent wiring (18 blue). |
| Alarm activates by itself. | Check for too close adjustment of hood and door jamb switches. | Readjust or replace as necessary. |
| System cannot be armed - tell-tale O.K. | Check for ground at #18 red wire at controller. | Repair or replace as needed. |
| Drivers door only will not generate alarm. | Open diode in dash harness. | Replace diode. |
| Key buzzer activated by all doors. | Diode shorted. | Replace diode. |

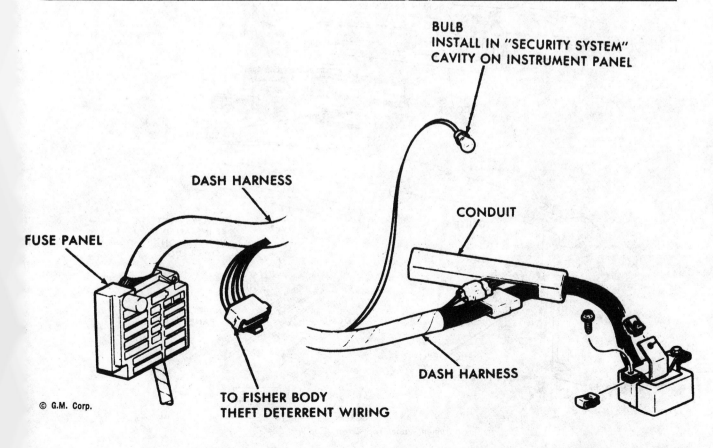

BULB
INSTALL IN "SECURITY SYSTEM"
CAVITY ON INSTRUMENT PANEL

DASH HARNESS

CONDUIT

FUSE PANEL

DASH HARNESS

© G.M. Corp.

TO FISHER BODY
THEFT DETERRENT WIRING

### Cadillac 1972-74

#### Description

The theft warning system is operated by the ignition switch. When the ignition is turned off, the system is automatically armed within one and a half minutes. The system is disarmed when the ignition is turned to the run position within fifteen seconds after any door is opened. After fifteen seconds the alarm will go off.

The system may be prevented from being armed by actuating a two position switch located in the glove compartment. When the switch is turned to the "Arm Prevent" position with the ignition switch on or within thirty seconds after the ignition is switched off, the system will remain disarmed until the switch is turned to the "Arm Enable" position. A second arm prevent method is by turning the ignition switch to the accessory position for five seconds before withdrawing the key. This will allow the car to be moved or parked one time without the alarm going off.

After the system is armed the alarm will be actuated electrically by seven different trigger mechanisms: (1) A plunger type switch is located on the left side of the radiator tie bar in a position where it can sense any small movement of the hood, (2) Within fifteen seconds after any door is opened, the door pillar switches activate the alarm, (3) When the trunk lid is lifted and the inside bulb goes on, (4) A special cover is placed over the fuse block and held in place by the horn and window circuit breakers. When the horn circuit breaker is removed the alarm goes off, (5) If a resistance-type electrical load is turned on, (6) When the glove box is opened, (7) If the control switch in the glove compartment is turned to the disarm position.

The electronic sensor or control box is mounted on the instrument panel center brace. Access to the control can only be made by removing the top instrument panel cover. The controller contains an internal timing circuit and relay which flash the parking, side marker, tail and license lamps and simultaneously sounds the horns at a rate of fifty cycles per minute.

In order to conserve the battery the alarm automatically shuts off after three to five minutes of operation then rearms itself.

### CONTROL BOX

#### Removal

1. Cycle the ignition switch slowly between "ACC" and the "lock" position.
2. Open the glove compartment door and move the manual switch to the "Arm Prevent" position.
3. Remove the instrument panel top cover.
   a) Disconnect the negative battery cable.
   b) Open the glove compartment and remove the two screws which secure the top cover to the instrument panel. On air conditioned cars, remove the aspirator hose from the sensor through the top of the glove compartment.
   c) Remove the our screws which secure the top cover to the instrument panel bezel assembly.
   d) Carefully lift up and pull the top cover rearward to separate it from the cowl.

*NOTE: On models equipped with a tilt wheel, removal can be accom-*

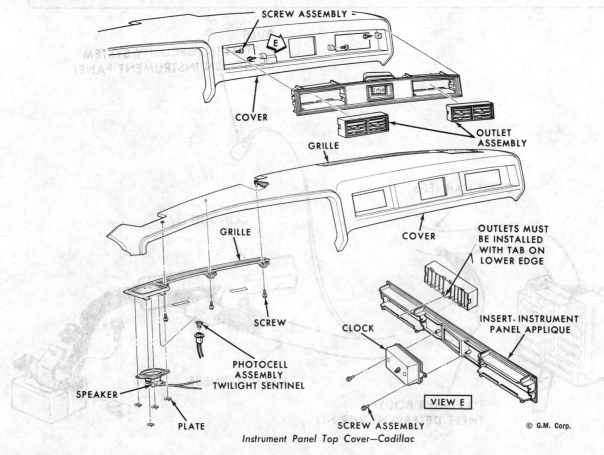

*Instrument Panel Top Cover—Cadillac*

© G.M. Corp.

# General Motors

*plished by placing the wheel in the low position.*

    e) Disconnect the speaker wires from the radio.

    f) Raise the top cover high enough to disconnect the Twilight Sentinel photocell at the left from speaker opening and sensor harness connector from the sensor, if so equipped.

    g) Disconnect the clock electrical feed wires and remove the top cover.

4. Remove the air conditioner center outlet duct hose.

5. Disconnect the control box wiring connectors from the wiring harness connectors.

6. Remove the two screws which secure the control box to the instrument panel center brace and remove the control box.

*NOTE: The control box cannot be repaired and must be replaced if defective.*

## Installation

1. Position the control box to the instrument panel center brace and install the two retaining screws.

2. Connect the control box wiring connectors to the wiring harness connectors.

3. Install the air condition center outlet duct hose.

4. Install the instrument panel top cover.

*NOTE: Install the screws in the following order to prevent damage to the plastic bosses if stresses are present in the panel.*

    a) Place the top cover over the instrument panel and connect the clock feed wires and lamp assembly, also connect the Twilight Sentinel photocell and sensor harness connector if so equipped.

    b) Connect the speaker wires at the radio.

    c) Position the top cover on the instrument panel so that the three clips engage at the windshield.

    d) Align the screw holes in the bezel and the glove compartment and install the four screws which attach the top cover to the bezel.

    e) From within the glove compartment, install the two top cover to instrument panel screws.

    f) On air conditioned models install the aspirator hose.

5. Open the glove compartment

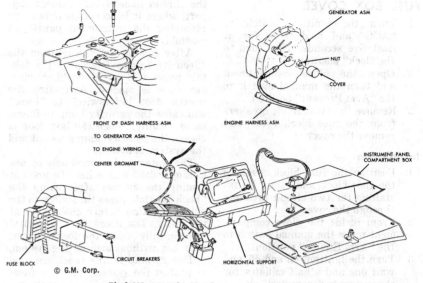

*Theft Warning System Components—Cadillac*

door and move the manual switch to the "Arm Enable" position.

6. Turn the ignition on and off and wait one and a half minutes to rearm the system.

## MANUAL CONTROL SWITCH

### Removal

1. Turn the ignition switch slowly between the "ACC" and "lock" position. (Hold at "ACC" for at least five seconds.)

2. Open the glove compartment door and turn the manual switch to the "Arm Prevent" position.

3. Hold the switch by reaching up through the access hole in the top of the glove box and turn the switch mounting nut off of the switch.

4. Disconnect the switch wiring connector and remove the switch.

### Installation

1. Connect the switch wiring connector.

2. Position the switch in the mounting hole and install the retaining nut.

3. Turn the switch to the "Arm Enable" position.

4. Turn the ignition on and off and wait one and a half minutes to rearm the system.

## HOOD SENSING SWITCH

### Removal

1. Turn the ignition switch slowly between the "ACC" and "lock" positions. (Hold at "ACC" for at least five seconds.)

2. Open the glove compartment door and turn the manual switch to the "Arm Prevent" position.

3. Open the hood and reach under the left hand side of the radiator tie bar.

4. Remove the switch to tie bar retaining nut and remove the switch.

### Installation

1. Position the switch to the tie bar and install the retaining nut.

2. Connect the wiring harness to the switch.

3. Close the hood.

4. Open the glove compartment door and turn the manual switch to the "Arm Enable" position.

5. Turn the ignition on and off and wait for one and a half minutes for the system to rearm itself.

6. Check the system by opening the hood.

## HOOD SENSING SWITCH ADJUSTMENT

### Removal

1. Make sure that the hood panel and latches are properly aligned.

2. Turn the ignition switch on and off and wait ten seconds.

3. With the hood locked, lift upward at the left front corner.

4. If the alarm sounds remove the switch and shim with washers as required.

5. Pull the hood release cable and open the hood.

6. If the alarm does not sound, stretch the hood pop-up spring to raise the hood fully to the secondary latch position.

## General Motors

### FUSE BOX COVER

1. Turn the ignition switch to "ACC" and hold there for at least five seconds. Then turn to the "lock" position.
2. Open the glove compartment and turn the manual switch to the "Arm Prevent" position.
3. Remove the two circuit breakers from the fuse block cover and remove the cover.

### Installation

1. Position the fuse block cover on the fuse block and retain by installing the two circuit breakers through the cover.
2. From inside the glove compartment move the manual switch to the "Arm Enable" position.
3. Turn the ignition on and off and wait one and a half minutes for the system to rearm itself.
   *NOTE: When using jumper cables or reconnecting battery cables to a car equipped with the theft warning system, it is normal for the alarm to be activated and the horns and lights to operate. The alarm may be shut off by turning the ignition switch to the accessory or run position.*

### Cadillac 1975

#### Description

The theft warning system provides additional protection for the vehicle in case the doors, trunk lid or hood is tampered with. When the system is armed properly and any of these areas are tampered with switches activate the alarm system and pulsate the vehicles horns at a rate of fifty cycles per minute, along with the simultaneous flashing of the low beam headlights, parking, tail, license and side marker lamps. In order to save battery power, the alarm shuts off after three to seven minutes of operation and re-arms if the locks have not been damaged. If a lock has been damaged the "Security System" light flashes when the ignition is off.

A plunger type hood switch is used and is located on the left side of the radiator tie bar in a position where it can sense a small movement of the hood. It is very similar to a door lock pillar switch.

The door and trunk locks use tamper switches. These switches will activate the alarm system if the lock cylinders are tampered with, either by attempting to pull out, push in or rotate from its normally installed position. The solid state controller contains electronic components and power relays and is located beneath the shroud panel reinforcement support, where it is accessible only after removing the instrument panel pad assembly.

After turning off the ignition the "Security System" lamp in the telltale panel will begin flashing when any door is opened. Activating the electric door lock switch to "Lock" will cause the security lamp to illuminate steadily. When the last door is closed, the security lamp goes out and the system is armed.

The system is disarmed only by unlocking a door with a key. To prevent arming the system after using the "Lock" switch, press the switch to the unlock position before closing all of the doors. The doors may be locked mechanically using the lock knob or door key without arming the system.

Two 25 amp in-line fuses are used to protect the system. The two fuses are located side-by-side above the radio. One is between the controller and the horn-battery feed and the other is between the controller and the external lamps battery feed.

### CONTROLLER

#### Removal

1. Unlock the door with a key.
2. Disconnect the negative battery cable.
3. Remove the instrument panel pad assembly.
   a) Remove the three climate control outlet grilles—right, left and right center by compressing the release tabs and rotating the grilles upward and out.
   b) Reach through the outlet openings and remove the three fasteners which secure the pad to the instrument panel support.
   c) Remove the three screws which secure the pad to the instrument panel horizontal support.
   d) Pull the pad outward and disconnect the electrical connector from the windshield wiper switch.
   e) Remove the pad.
4. Disconnect the controller wiring connectors from the wiring harness connectors, located just above the radio receiver.
5. Remove the mounting screw which secures the controller and mounting bracket to the support and remove the controller.

*NOTE: The control box cannot be repaired and must be replaced if defective.*

### Installation

1. Position the controller and mounting bracket and install the attaching screw.
2. Connect the controller wiring connectors to the wiring harness connectors.
3. Install the instrument panel pad.
4. Connect the battery cable.
5. Remain in the vehicle and lower the left front window.
6. Remove the ignition key, open the door, lock the door with the electric door lock switch then get out of the car and close the door. Lift the manual door locking button and open the door. The alarm should activate. To stop the alarm, insert the key in the door lock and turn it to the unlock position.

### HOOD SENSING SWITCH

#### Removal

1. Open the hood.
2. Reach under the left hand side of the radiator cradle tie bar and disconnect the wiring from the sensing switch.
3. Remove the nut which attaches the switch to the tie bar and remove the switch.

#### Installation

1. Position the switch through the tie bar and install the attaching nut.
2. Connect the wiring to the switch.
3. Close the hood.
4. Open the door and window and move the electric door lock switch to the "Lock" position and close the door. Check the system by opening the hood.

### SWITCH ADJUSTMENT

1. Make sure the hood panel and latches are properly aligned.
2. If the alarm sounds, remove the switch, adjust it upward and if required install shims and washers.
3. Lower the hood and rearm the system. Repeat steps 1 and 2 and the alarm should not sound.
4. Pull the hood release cable and the alarm should sound. If the alarm does not sound, stretch the hood pop-up spring to raise the hood fully to the secondary latch position.

### Corvette 1972-75

#### Description

The theft warning system is armed when the glove compartment and spare tire key is inserted into the tail panel lock cylinder and turned

## General Motors

clockwise ninety degrees. Plunger type switches are located in both the door jambs and under the right side of the hood. When the system is armed and the hood or doors are opened, the triggered switches complete the circuit and actuate the warning horn located above the left rear tire in the wheelhouse.

The only way to shut off the alarm is to insert the key into the tail panel lock cylinder and turn it ninety degrees counter-clockwise.

### LOCK CYLINDER CONTROL SWITCH

#### Removal

1. Remove the ground cable from the battery.
2. Remove the license plate.
3. Remove the two license lamp

housing retaining screws and remove the housing.
4. After the license lamp housing is removed, reach through the access hole created and pull the clip which retains the control switch.
5. Note the location of the switch wires and remove both from the switch.

#### Installation

1. Position the new switch and install the wires and retaining clip.
2. Position the license lamp housing and install the two retaining screws.
3. Replace the license plate.
4. Replace the ground cable on the battery.

### WARNING HORN

#### Removal

1. Raise the car and lower the left tail pipe assembly.
2. Remove the wiring connector from the horn.
3. Remove the bolt which retains the warning horn to the wheelhouse panel above the left rear tire.

#### Installation

1. Position the horn and install the retaining bolt.
2. Install the wire connector.
3. Check the operation of the system.
4. Raise the tailpipe and secure in place.

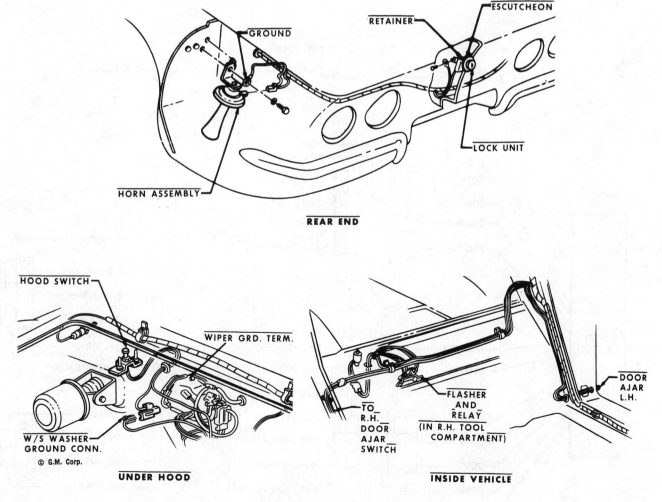

**REAR END**

**UNDER HOOD**  **INSIDE VEHICLE**

© G.M. Corp.

*Corvette Installation*

## Chrysler Corporation

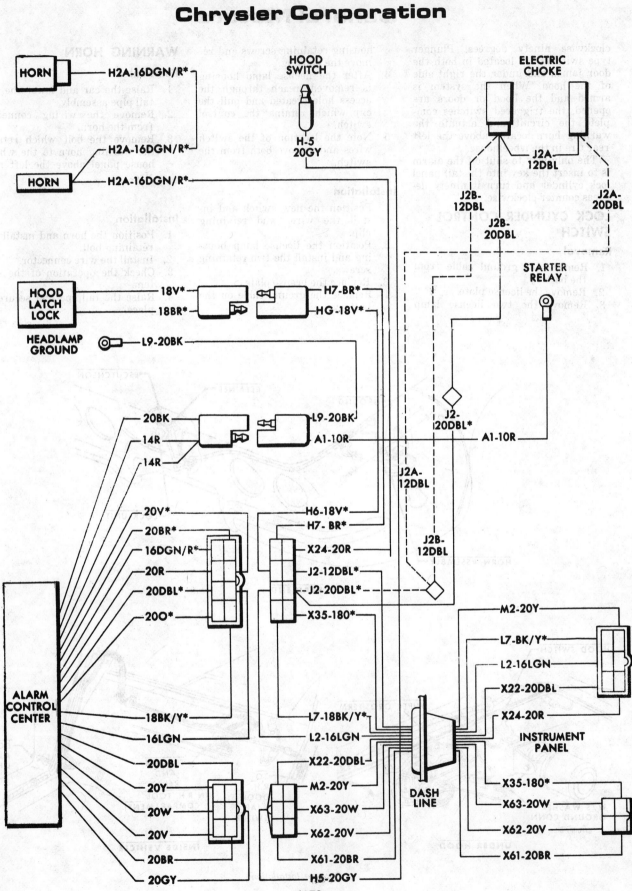

1973

## Chrysler Corporation

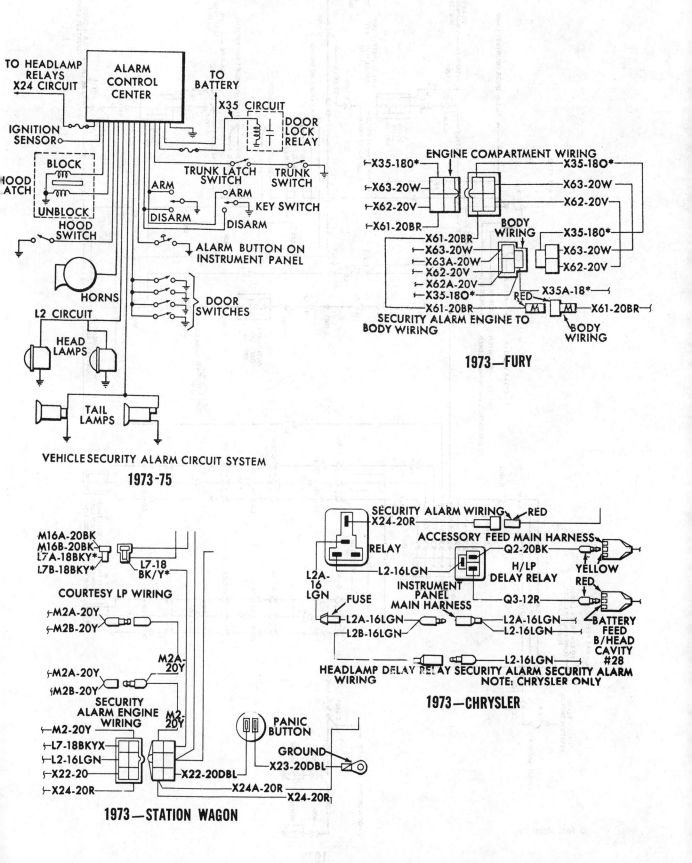

TO HEADLAMP RELAYS X24 CIRCUIT

ALARM CONTROL CENTER

TO BATTERY

X35 CIRCUIT

DOOR LOCK RELAY

IGNITION SENSOR

BLOCK

HOOD LATCH

UNBLOCK

HOOD SWITCH

TRUNK LATCH SWITCH

TRUNK SWITCH

ARM

ARM

DISARM

KEY SWITCH

DISARM

ALARM BUTTON ON INSTRUMENT PANEL

HORNS

DOOR SWITCHES

L2 CIRCUIT

HEAD LAMPS

TAIL LAMPS

VEHICLE SECURITY ALARM CIRCUIT SYSTEM
### 1973-75

ENGINE COMPARTMENT WIRING

X35-180*
X63-20W
X62-20V
X61-20BR

X35-180*
X63-20W
X62-20V

BODY WIRING

X61-20BR
X63-20W
X63A-20W
X62-20V
X62A-20V
X35-180*
X61-20BR

X35-180*
X63-20W
X62-20V

RED
X35A-18*

M M X61-20BR

SECURITY ALARM ENGINE TO BODY WIRING

BODY WIRING

### 1973—FURY

M16A-20BK
M16B-20BK
L7A-18BKY*
L7B-18BKY*

L7-18 BK/Y*

COURTESY LP WIRING

M2A-20Y
M2B-20Y

M2A-20Y
M2B-20Y

M2A-20Y

SECURITY ALARM ENGINE WIRING

M2-20Y

M2-20Y

M2-20Y
L7-18BKYX
L2-16LGN
X22-20
X24-20R

X22-20DBL

X24A-20R

PANIC BUTTON

GROUND
X23-20DBL

X24-20R

### 1973—STATION WAGON

SECURITY ALARM WIRING
X24-20R

RED

RELAY

ACCESSORY FEED MAIN HARNESS

Q2-20BK

YELLOW

H/LP DELAY RELAY

RED

L2A-16LGN

L2-16LGN

INSTRUMENT PANEL MAIN HARNESS

FUSE

L2A-16LGN

L2B-16LGN

Q3-12R

L2A-16LGN

L2-16LGN

BATTERY FEED B/HEAD CAVITY #28

L2-16LGN

HEADLAMP DELAY RELAY SECURITY ALARM SECURITY ALARM WIRING

NOTE: CHRYSLER ONLY

### 1973—CHRYSLER

## Ford Motor Company

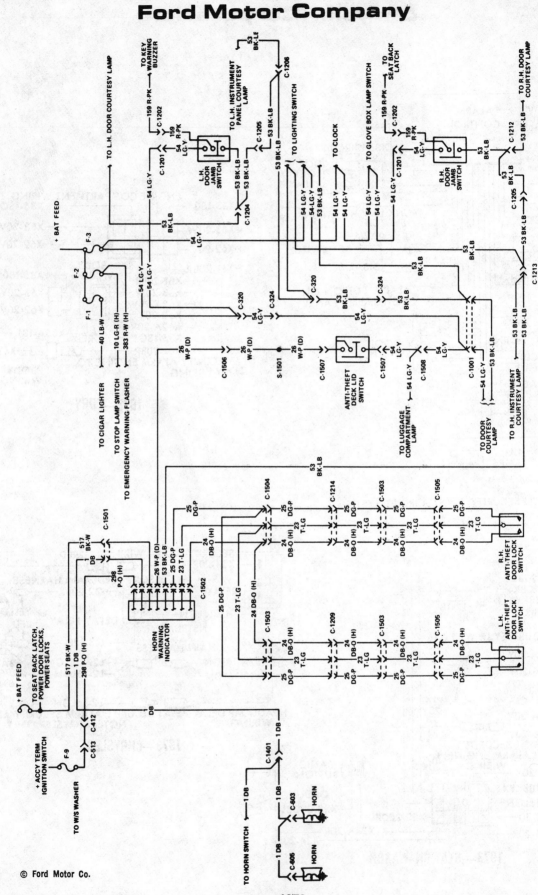

© Ford Motor Co.

1973

## Ford Motor Company

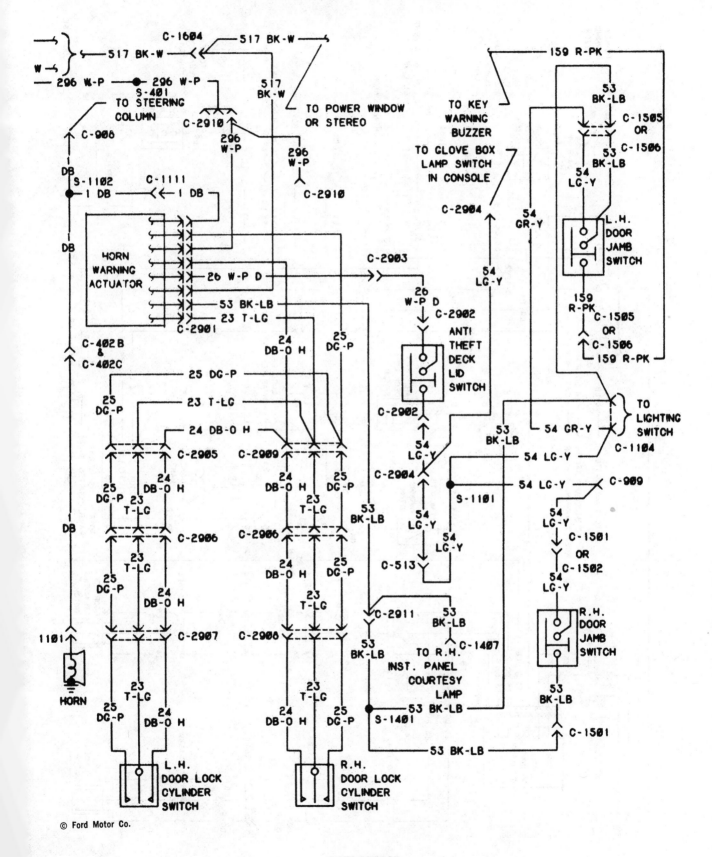

**1974 COUGAR**

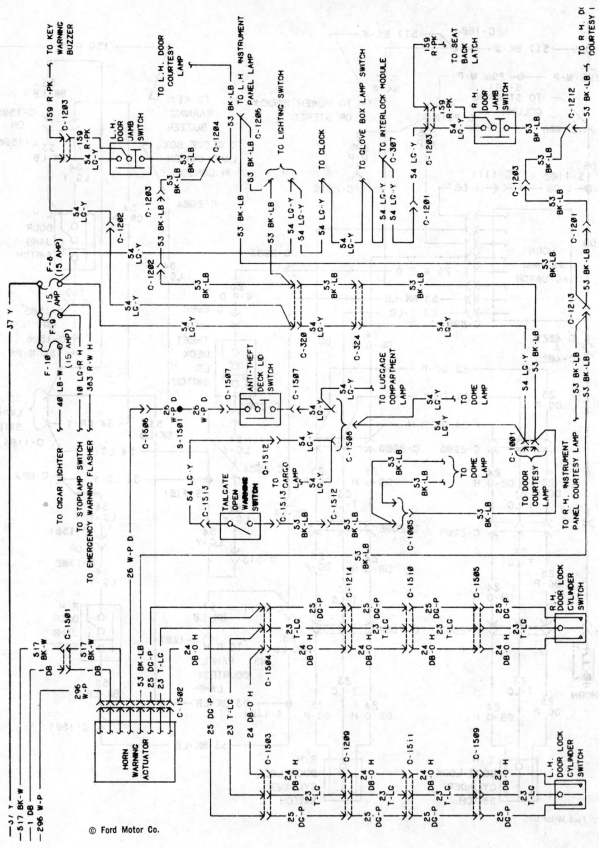

© Ford Motor Co.

**1974 FORD**

## Ford Motor Company

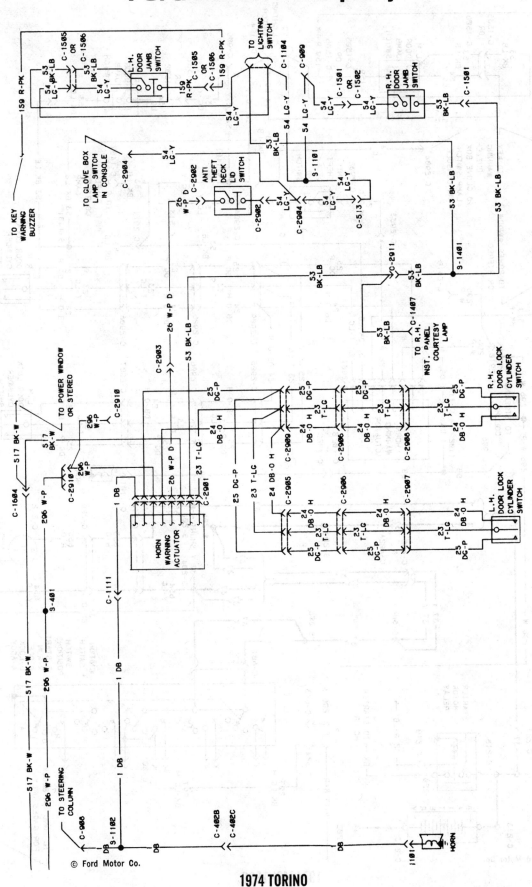

© Ford Motor Co.

**1974 TORINO**

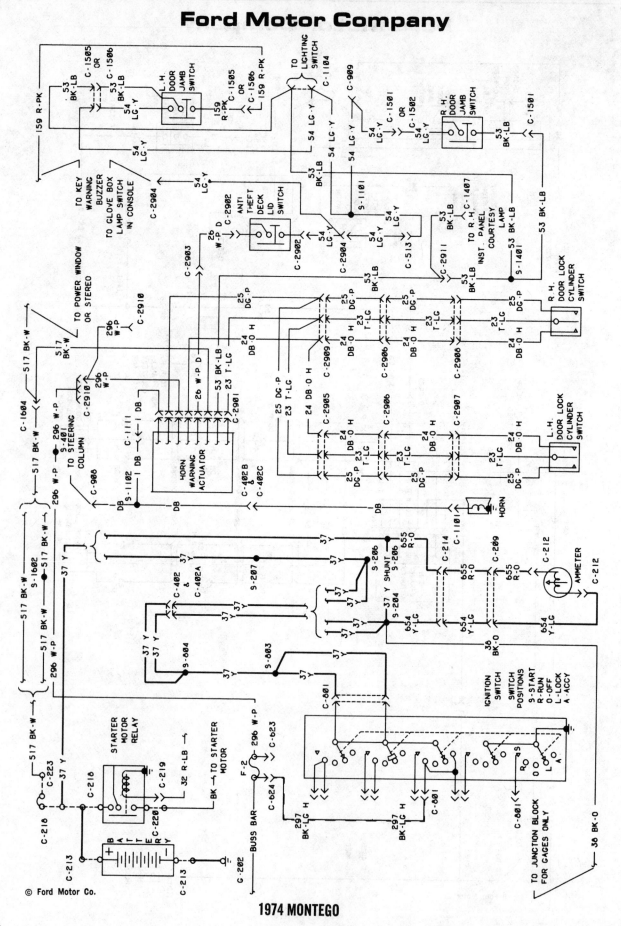

1974 MONTEGO

## Ford Motor Company

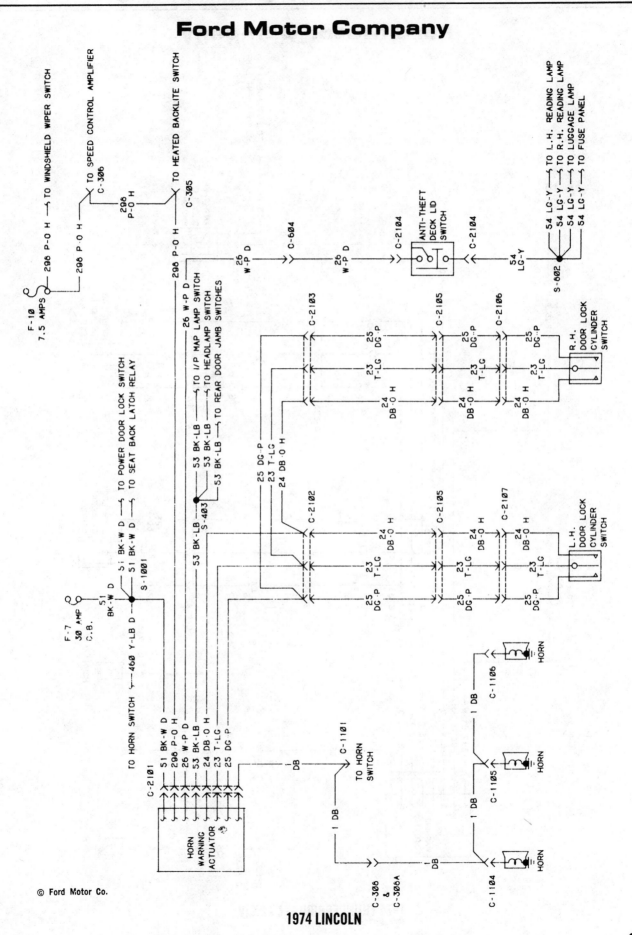

© Ford Motor Co.

**1974 LINCOLN**

## Ford Motor Company

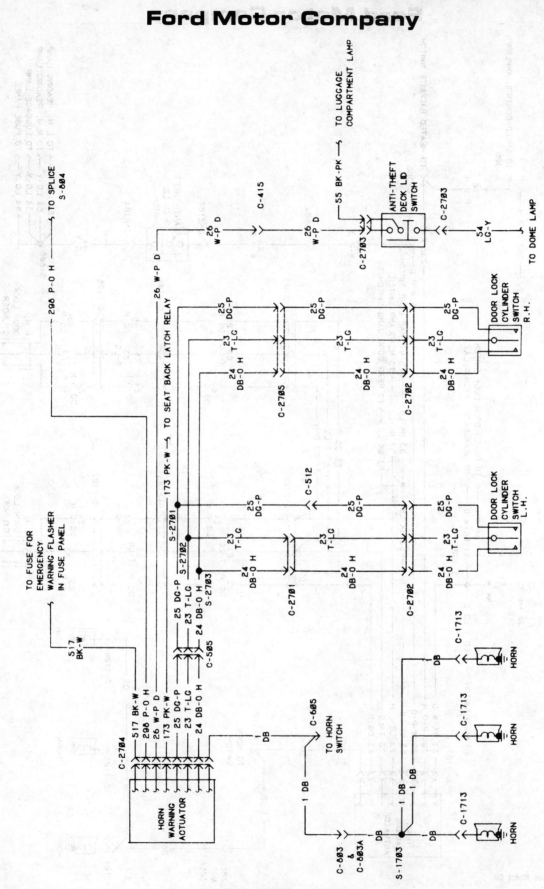

1974 THUNDERBIRD — Mark IV

# Ford Motor Company

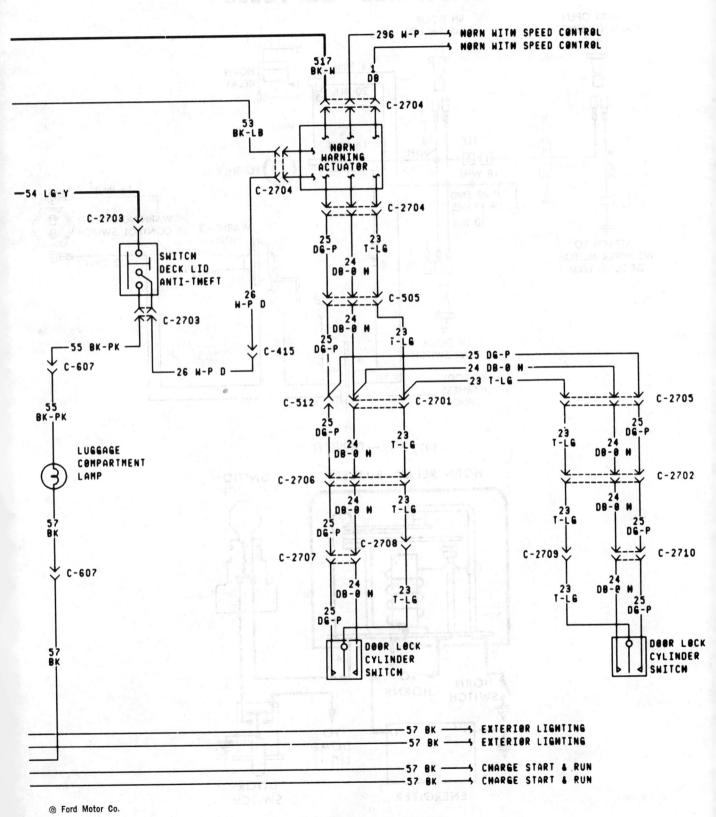

**1975 THUNDERBIRD— MARK IV**

## General Motors
## Chevrolet · Corvette

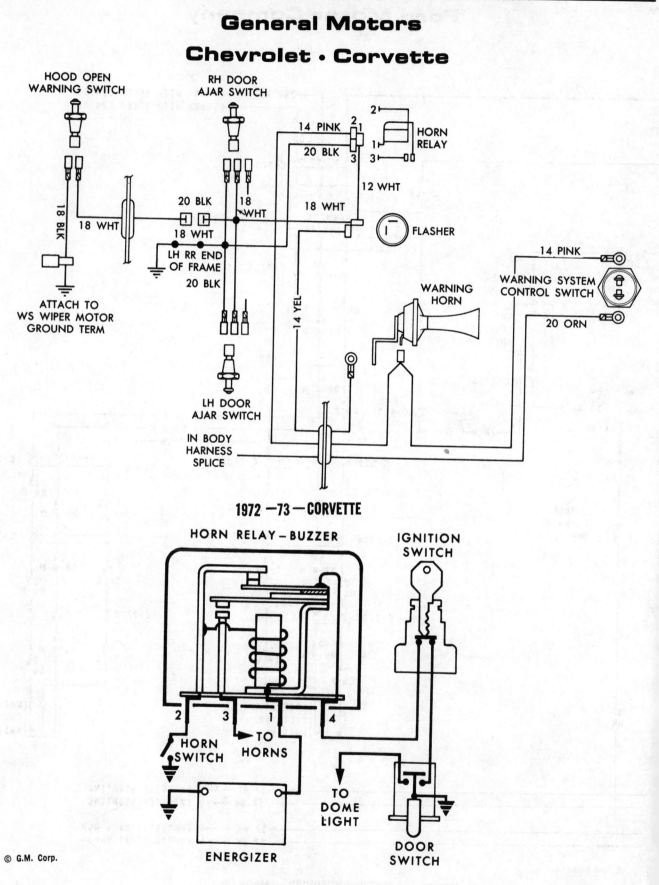

**HOOD OPEN WARNING SWITCH**

**RH DOOR AJAR SWITCH**

14 PINK

20 BLK

**HORN RELAY**

18 BLK

18 WHT

20 BLK

18 WHT

18 WHT

12 WHT

18 WHT

**LH RR END OF FRAME**

20 BLK

**ATTACH TO WS WIPER MOTOR GROUND TERM**

**FLASHER**

14 PINK

**WARNING SYSTEM CONTROL SWITCH**

20 ORN

14 YEL

**WARNING HORN**

**LH DOOR AJAR SWITCH**

**IN BODY HARNESS SPLICE**

### 1972 –73 – CORVETTE

**HORN RELAY – BUZZER**

**IGNITION SWITCH**

2     3     1     4

**HORN SWITCH**

**TO HORNS**

**TO DOME LIGHT**

**ENERGIZER**

**DOOR SWITCH**

### 1968-71 – CHEVROLET

# Cadillac

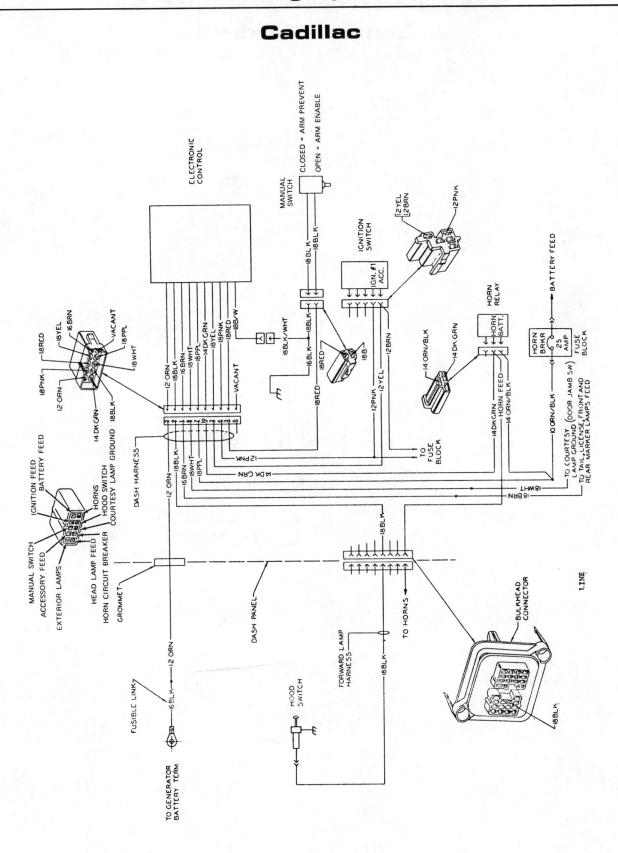

1973

## General Motors

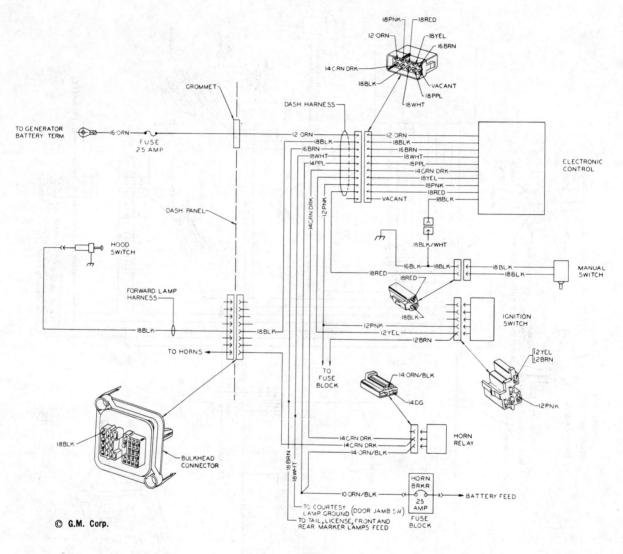

1974

© G.M. Corp.

# General Motors

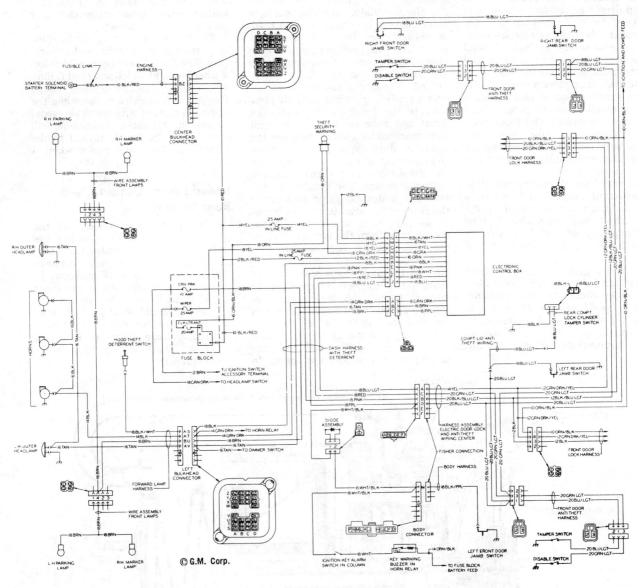

© G.M. Corp.

1975

## Chrysler Corporation

# SURE BRAKE SYSTEM

### General Description

This system is designed to prevent lockup of any of the four wheels during hard braking. Braking is faster and surer when the wheels are turning approximately at normal road speed because both tire adhesion and directional stability are increased.

The system employs a mechanically driven speed sensor in each wheel, a logic controller or computer which evaluates the signals, and three pressure modulators. One modulator serves both rear brakes, and each of the remaining modulators serves one front wheel.

The wheel speed sensors consist of a permanent magnet and coil in a case. A tone wheel is driven by the rear wheel and generates a tone the frequency of which is directly proportional to the speed of the wheel.

The tones generated in the wheel sensors are fed to the logic controller. This device interprets the signals and, when a rapid change is produced, indicating that a wheel is starting to lock up, the controller sends signals to the appropriate pressure modulator.

The pressure modulators, one for each front brake, and one for the two rear brakes, each contain a solenoid type bypass valve which converts the electrical signal into usable vacuum for the modulator. Another valve, a solenoid type air valve, is also used. A signal from the logic controller causes the vacuum bypass valve to close, causing the vacuum supply to the front of the modulator to be cut off. The signal also opens an air valve, supplying atmospheric air pressure to the front of the unit. The front and rear sections of the unit are separated by a diaphragm and the pressure differential resulting from the operation of the two valves forces the diaphragm to the rear, against spring pressure. The diaphragm operates a hydraulic valve located on the front of the modulator, which separates the brake which the modulator controls from the rest of the system hydraulically, and then provides additional space for the relief of pressure as the diaphragm moves to the rear. When the wheel comes up to normal speed, the logic controller sends a signal to the modulator which reverses the positions of the two valves. This causes an equal vacuum to exist on either side of the diaphragm and allows the spring to

return it to normal position, where hydraulic fluid flows to the brake cylinder in an unobstructed manner. During heavy braking, the actuator will cycle a number of times providing, in effect, an extremely rapid pumping of the brakes.

The brake warning light will come on when the modulators are in operation. The Sure Brake System also has a warning light which warns of failure within the system. The system will go through two exercise cycles when the engine is started with the brake pedal depressed. All three modulators will cycle when the key is turned to the "start" position, and again when it is turned to the "on" position.

### Speed Sensor Output Check Rear Sensors

1. Raise the rear wheels off the floor and use the engine to drive them at 5 to 6 miles per hour.
2. Measure the voltage between K-4 and K-3 in Connector B. Measure where the wires enter the back of the connectors. There should be at least .2 volts.
3. In a similar manner, measure the voltage between K-3 and K-5. There should also be .2 volts here.

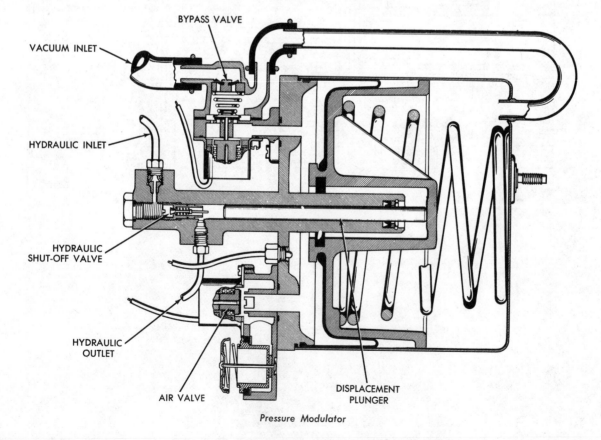

*Pressure Modulator*

## Chrysler Corporation

**TROUBLE DIAGNOSIS CHART**

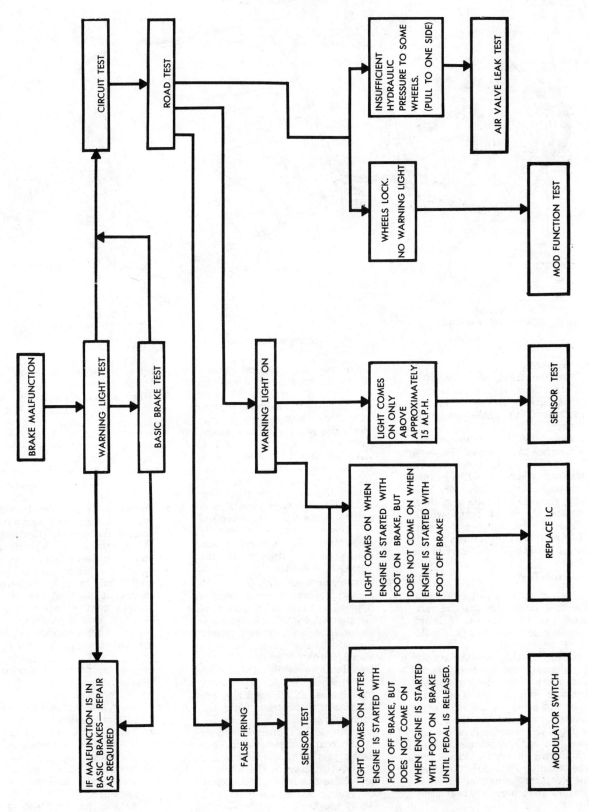

# Chrysler Corporation

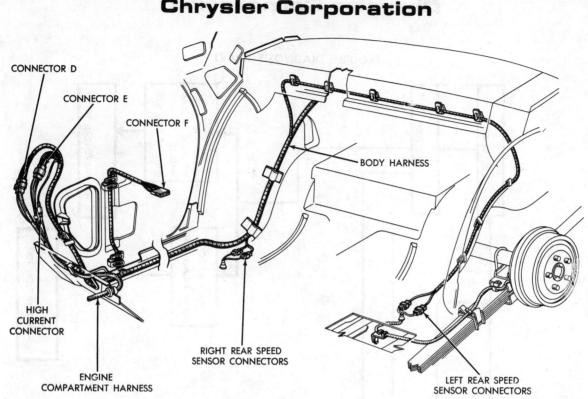

**CONNECTOR D**

**CONNECTOR E**

**CONNECTOR F**

**BODY HARNESS**

**HIGH
CURRENT
CONNECTOR**

**RIGHT REAR SPEED
SENSOR CONNECTORS**

**LEFT REAR SPEED
SENSOR CONNECTORS**

**ENGINE
COMPARTMENT HARNESS**

*Body Harness and Connections*

### Front Sensors

1. Raise the front wheels slightly off the floor. Rotate each front wheel at about one revolution per second during the test for its sensor.
2. Rotate the left front wheel. Measure the voltage between K-3 and K-15 in Connector B. Measure where the wires go into the back of the connector. Voltage should be .2 volts or higher.
3. Rotate the right front wheel. Measure the voltage between K-3 and K-12 in Connector B. Reading should be .2 volts or above.

### Modulator Test

1. Install a vacuum gauge between the rear modulator and the vacuum hose that leads to it. Start the engine. The gauge should read the normal engine vacuum reading. If this vacuum supply is adequate but all four wheels can lock up during heavy braking and the warning light does not come on, the logic controller is at fault. Continue with the test if vacuum is adequate, one, two, or three wheels can lock up during heavy braking, and the warning light does not come on. Perform the test for the modulators that permit wheel lock-up.

2. Disconnect the electrical connector to the modulator to be tested. Connect the vacuum gauge into the line to the modulator to be tested. Start the engine and check the reading on the gauge.
3. Connect a jumper from the positive terminal of the battery to the air valve terminal on the side of the connector leading to the modulator. *Do not make this connection for more than 30 seconds. Allow a two minute cooling off period between periods of connection.* The reading on the gauge should drop when the wiring is connected.
4. Connect another jumper between battery positive terminal and the bypass terminal on the side of the connector leading to the modulator. The gauge reading should increase to the reading noted in step 2. If there is no increase, the modulator is faulty. Otherwise, repeat the test for the other modulators. If all readings are satisfactory, proceed with the following steps.
5. Disconnect the connector leading to the rear modulator and connect a jumper to connectors K-2 and K-8 leading to the modulator. Raise the rear wheels, start the engine, and engage drive.
6. Apply the brakes with moderate

force. If the wheels do not stop, the modulator is faulty.
7. Have someone apply the other end of the jumper to K-2 and K-8 to the battery positive terminal. *Do not apply this jumper for more than 10 seconds.* The rear wheels should now begin to revolve if brake pressure is moderate. Otherwise, replace the modulator.
8. Disconnect either front modulator connector and connect a jumper to it. Raise the front wheels off the ground and make sure they can be rotated by hand.
9. Apply the brake with moderate force and then have someone connect the other end of the jumper to the battery positive terminal. Do not connect the lead for more than 10 seconds. Have someone attempt to turn the front wheel. If it cannot be turned, replace the modulator.
10. Repeat steps 8 and 9 for the other front modulator.
11. Perform a hydraulic test on each modulator as below:
    a. Connect one end of a jumper to the two terminals in the connector leading to the modulator. Start the engine and apply moderate brake pressure.
    b. Attach the other end of the

## Chrysler Corporation

LEFT FRONT MODULATOR

RIGHT FRONT MODULATOR

VACUUM HOSE

REAR MODULATOR

VACUUM TEE FITTING

VACUUM HOSE

INTAKE MANIFOLD FITTING

*Vacuum Hose Routing*

jumper to the battery positive post. Crack a bleed screw at the appropriate brake. Fluid should not rush out and the pedal should not sink for at least 30 seconds. Otherwise, replace the modulator in question.

c. Remove jumper and tighten bleed screw.

### Front Wheel Speed Sensor

#### Removal

1. Disconnect the speed sensor con-

nector in the engine compartment, and remove the sensor lead from the retaining clip.

2. Raise the car and remove the tire and wheel.

3. Separate the speed sensor lead from the clamp which retains it to the front suspension.

4. Disconnect the caliper without disconnecting the hydraulic lines. Support the caliper properly so that the weight is not placed on the brake hose.

5. Remove the hub and disc assem-

bly. (The tone wheel is part of the hub and disc.)

6. Remove the two bolts which attach the speed sensor to the splash shield.

7. Pull the speed sensor lead through the hole in the splash shield and remove the sensor.

#### Installation

1. Loosen the nut which secures the sensor to the mounting bracket, and position the sensor to provide maximum clearance be-

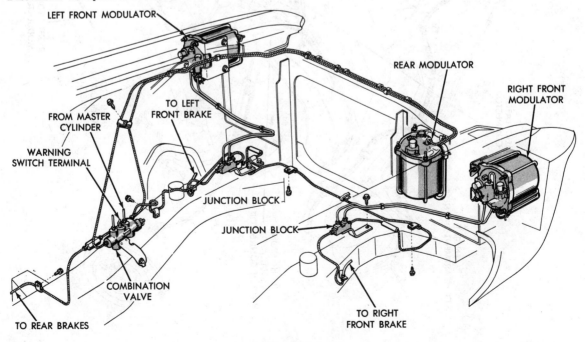

LEFT FRONT MODULATOR

REAR MODULATOR

RIGHT FRONT MODULATOR

FROM MASTER CYLINDER

TO LEFT FRONT BRAKE

WARNING SWITCH TERMINAL

JUNCTION BLOCK

JUNCTION BLOCK

COMBINATION VALVE

TO REAR BRAKES

TO RIGHT FRONT BRAKE

*Vacuum Hose Routing*

# Chrysler Corporation

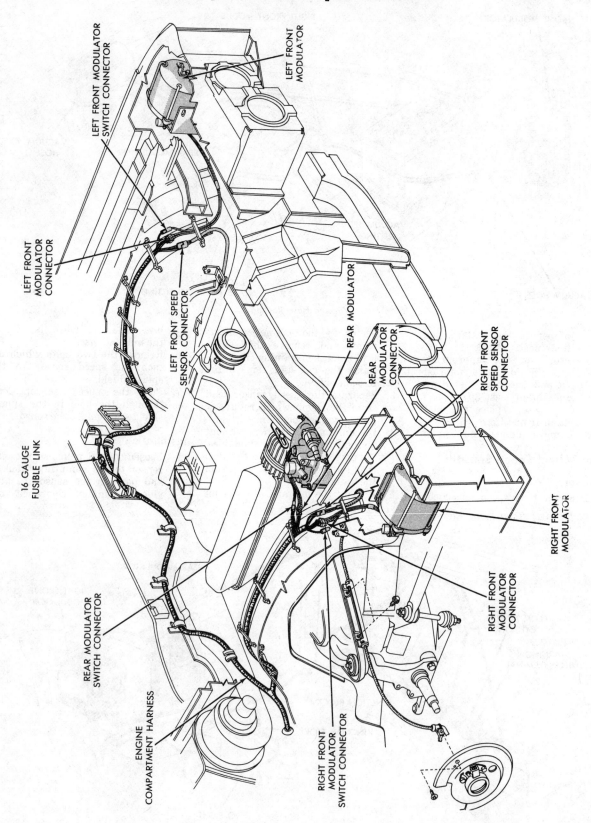

LEFT FRONT MODULATOR SWITCH CONNECTOR

LEFT FRONT MODULATOR

LEFT FRONT MODULATOR CONNECTOR

LEFT FRONT SPEED SENSOR CONNECTOR

REAR MODULATOR

REAR MODULATOR CONNECTOR

RIGHT FRONT SPEED SENSOR CONNECTOR

16 GAUGE FUSIBLE LINK

RIGHT FRONT MODULATOR

RIGHT FRONT MODULATOR CONNECTOR

REAR MODULATOR SWITCH CONNECTOR

ENGINE COMPARTMENT HARNESS

RIGHT FRONT MODULATOR SWITCH CONNECTOR

*Harness Routing and Connectors in the Engine Compartment*

# Chrysler Corporation

tween the sensor and the tone wheel.

2. Insert the sensor lead through the hole in the splash shield and mount the sensor and bracket to the shield and the wire clip with the two bolts.

3. Install the hub and disc assembly.

4. Working through the hole in the splash shield, slide the sensor in the mounting bracket slot and obtain a .020 clearance between the small magnets on the sensor and the tone wheel teeth. Use a ¼ in. wide feeler gauge to set the gap and tighten the nut to 70-90 in. lbs.

*NOTE: When a new sensor is being installed slide the sensor toward the tone wheel teeth until the plastic projections on each edge of the sensor case are against the tone wheel. The plastic projections will wear off during the first few revolutions of the tone wheel and provide the correct clearance of .020.*

5. Mount the caliper.

6. Secure the sensor lead to the suspension holding clamp and route to the engine compartment.

7. Install the tire and wheel and lower the car.

8. Connect the speed sensor lead in the engine compartment.

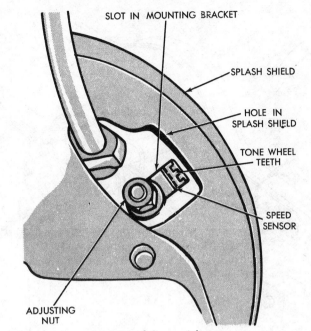

*Front Speed Sensor Adjustment*

4. Press the speed sensor toward the axle and remove the drive ring.

5. Through the hole in the axle flange, remove the two sensor retaining nuts.

6. Pull the sensor lead through the backing plate hole and the floor pan.

### Installation

1. Insert the sensor lead through the hole in the backing plate.

2. Reaching through the hole in the axle flange, place the sensor on the two bolts and install the retaining nuts.

*NOTE: Nothing should be between the speed sensor bracket and the backing plate. On the right wheel it may be necessary to move the axle lock to one of the other studs.*

3. Position the drive ring on the axle flange while pressing the speed sensor toward the axle.

4. Attach the sensor lead to the spring clamp and frame rail clip and route the lead through the floor pan.

5. Seat the grommets in the floor pan and backing plate.

### Rear Wheel Speed Sensor

#### Removal

1. Disconnect the speed sensor connectors located under the rear seat.

2. Raise the car and remove the tire, wheel, and drum.

3. Remove the speed sensor lead from the spring and the frame rail.

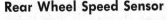

*Front Wheel Speed Sensor Installation*

# Chrysler Corporation

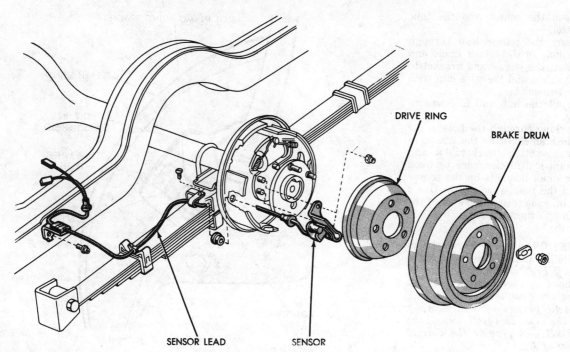

*Rear Wheel Speed Sensor Installation*

6. Install the drum, tire, and wheel and lower the car.
7. Connect the sensor connectors under the seat.

## Logic Controller

### Removal

1. Remove the right side lining in the trunk.
2. Remove the jack.
3. Disconnect the controller wire connectors.
4. Disconnect the ground wire by removing the bolt.
5. Remove the three controller to mounting bracket attaching screws.

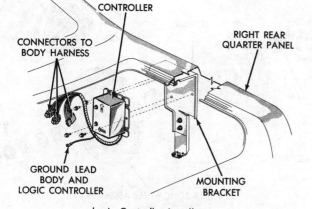

*Logic Controller Installation*

### Installation

1. Position the control to the mounting bracket and install the retaining screws.
2. Connect the wiring harness connectors.
3. Attach the ground wire securely.
4. Replace the side panel and replace the jack.

## Front Wheel Pressure Modulators

### Removal

1. Raise the hood and disconnect the electrical connectors at the modulator.
2. Remove the modulator attaching nuts.
3. Remove the wheelhouse outer panel to permit access to the modulator.
4. Disconnect the vacuum hose from the modulator.
5. Disconnect the hydraulic lines.
6. Pull the electrical lines through the housing.
7. Remove the two bolts which secure the modulator side bracket to the car and remove the modulator.

*WARNING: Do not attempt to disassemble the modulator. A heavy duty diaphragm return spring is compressed inside the modulator, and personal injury could result if any attempt is made to remove the "J" bolts and end plate.*

### Installation

1. Install the bracket to the modulator mounting bolts and nuts until all threads are started.
2. Align the modulator and slide studs on the end bracket and position through the hole in the panel and start a nut on each stud.
3. Attach the side bracket to the car with the two bolts.
4. Tighten all of the mounting bolts and nuts.
5. Route the wires into the engine compartment and connect the modulator wire connectors to the

# Chrysler Corporation

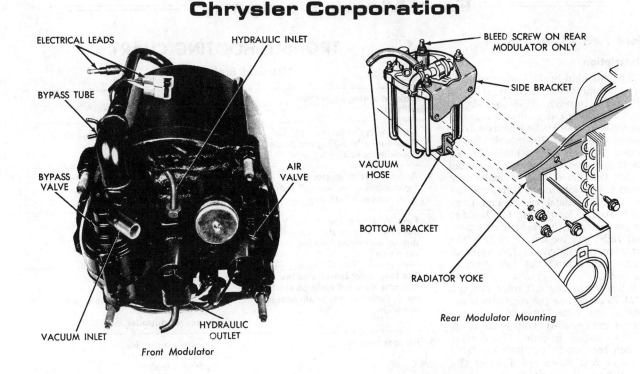

*Front Modulator*

*Rear Modulator Mounting*

engine wiring harness connectors.

6. Connect each hydraulic line to the same port from which it was disconnected.

7. Connect the vacuum hose to the modulator.

8. Bleed the hydraulic system to remove all air.

9. Install the wheelhouse outer panel.

## Rear Modulator

### Removal

1. Disconnect the electrical connectors from the modulator.

2. Disconnect the modulator bypass valve vacuum hose.

3. Disconnect both hydraulic lines from the modulator.

4. Remove the two nuts which retain the bottom bracket to the radiator yoke.

5. Remove the bolts that retain the modulator side bracket to the radiator yoke and remove the modulator.

*WARNING: Do not attempt to disassemble the modulator. A heavy duty diaphragm return spring is compressed inside the modulator, and personal injury could result if any attempt is made to remove the "J" bolts and end plate.*

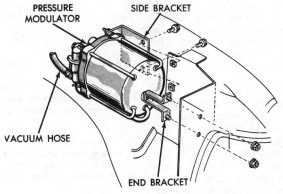

*Front Modulator Mounting*

### Installation

*NOTE: Do not tighten any of the modulator mounting nuts or bolts until all the threads are started.*

1. Position the side bracket on the modulator and install the two nuts and lockwashers.

2. Position the modulator and attach the bottom bracket to the radiator yoke with the two nuts.

3. Install the two side bracket bolts.

4. Tighten all of the modulator

mounting bolts and nuts.

5. Connect each hydraulic line to the same port from which it was disconnected.

6. Connect the modulator by-pass valve hose.

7. Connect the modulator electrical connectors to the engine wiring harness connectors.

8. Bleed the hydraulic system to remove all air. Also bleed the modulator hydraulic cylinder at the bleed screw located on the modulator.

## Ford Motor Company

### Ford 1969-75—All Models
#### Description

The non-skid brake system consists of three major components: (1) On all 1971 through 1975 models, a mechanically driven electromagnetic sensor is located at the rear axle drive pinion. All 1969-70 models use a sensor at each rear wheel, (2) An electronic control module mounted under the glove box or under the front seat on late model Mercurys, (3) On 1969-74 models a vacuum powered actuator is attached to a bracket on the inside of the right front frame rail under the toe board. In 1975 the actuator is located on the lefthand frame rail behind the No. 1 crossmember.

When the drive shaft rotates on the 1971-75 models or the rear wheels rotate on the 1969-70 models, the sensor(s) generate AC voltage impulses to the control module. The control module continually monitors the drive shaft or rear wheel speed. When the signal drops abruptly due to a maximum braking condition, the module sends an electrical signal to the actuator solenoid and increases the volume of pressure in the hydraulic brake chamber of the actuator. The increased chamber pressure reduces the line pressure and the rear brakes are released.

As the drive shaft or rear wheel revolutions increase the control module shuts off the electrical signal and de-energizes the solenoid.

A time delay switch which is mounted on the actuator above the solenoid will cause a three amp fuse, located in the fuse panel, to blow and the brake warning light to come on if the actuator diaphragm remains in the forward position for more than 60 seconds. The warning light will also come on if the fuse blows during a malfunction in the power supply system.

### Actuator Assembly
### 1969-74—All Models

#### Removal

1. From inside the passenger compartment, disconnect the harness connector at the intermediate harness.
2. Remove the grommet from the dash panel and push the wiring harness and connector through the opening.
3. From inside the engine compartment loosen the hose clamp and remove the air hose from the air filter.

## TROUBLESHOOTING CHART
### Non-Skid Brake System

| I. Brake Warning Light ON Condition | Possible Cause |
|---|---|
| 1. Actuator cycles on start up, but does not cycle during maximum breaking condition | a. Controller or sensor malfunction<br>b. Open circuit to solenoid |
| 2. Actuator cycles on start up. System functions, but will not cycle down to 5-10 m.p.h. | a. Defective sensor or sensor wires<br>b. Defective controller<br>c. Vacuum leak |
| 3. Fuse burns out. The system does not cycle on start up or during maximum braking condition | a. Defective actuator or controller<br>b. Open or short circuit in the actuator wing |
| 4. The fuse is not blown and the actuator does not cycle on start up or during a maximum braking condition | a Loose or broken controller connections<br>b. Defective controller or loose ground connection<br>c. Defective controller |
| 5. No rear brakes | a. Defective controller<br>b. Defective actuator<br>c. Hydraulic leak |

## TROUBLESHOOTING CHART
### Non-Skid Brake System—1969-74

| II. Brake Warning Light OFF Condition | Possible Cause |
|---|---|
| 1. The system operates during a normal braking condition | a. Defective controller<br>b. Defective sensor<br>c. Open or short circuit in sensor leads |
| 2. Fuse is blown and the actuator does not cycle on start up or during a maximum braking condition | a. Defective controller<br>b. Loose controller connection<br>c. Defective actuator<br>d. Defective solenoid |
| 3. No rear brakes | a. Defective controller<br>b. Defective actuator |
| 4. The actuator cycles slowly during a maximum braking condition | a. Defective actuator<br>b. Pinched vacuum hoses |

4. Remove the engine air cleaner and remove the air hose from the air filter.
5. Raise the car on a lift.
6. Disconnect the exhaust pipes at the exhaust manifolds and support with wires in order to provide access to the actuator assembly.
7. Disconnect the actuator ground wire by removing the bolt from the corner of the engine bank.
8. Loosen the hydraulic tube nuts and disconnect the hydraulic brake tubes from the valve housing.
9. Remove the three nuts which retain the actuator assembly to the actuator support bracket.
10. Remove the three actuator support bracket bolts and remove the support bracket from the side rail.
11. Place the actuator on a bench and remove the air and vacuum hoses.

*NOTE: The actuator is serviced as a unit and should not be disassembled.*

# Non Skid Brake Systems

# Ford Motor Company

THE 1975 HYDRAULIC SKID CONTROL SYSTEM DOES NOT HAVE THE AUDIBLE ACTUATOR CYCLE CHARACTERISTICS OF THE 1974 AND EARLIER SYSTEMS. INSTEAD, AS A PROVEOUT FUNCTION, THE BRAKE WARNING LIGHT WILL COME ON MOMENTARILY AS THE IGNITION SWITCH IS TURNED TO THE RUN POSITION. AT THE SAME TIME, THE ACTUATOR SOLENOID IS MOMENTARILY ENERGIZED: HOWEVER, IT USUALLY CAN NOT BE DETECTED UNLESS THE VEHICLE IS RAISED ON A HOIST AND A SECOND PERSON TOUCHES THE ACTUATOR AS IT CYCLES.

| CONDITION | CAUSE | CORRECTION |
|---|---|---|
| 1. Brake warning light comes on and stays on **immediately** (not 5 seconds later) after key is turned to **ON** or **ACCESSORY** position and:<br><br>• Actuator cycles and 4 amp fuse OK | • Differential valve shuttled.<br><br>• Short in brake warning light ground circuit.<br><br>• Inoperative computer module. | • Refer to Hydraulic Brake System Diagnostic Procedure.<br>• Remove plug C from module, turn ignition to **RUN.** If light comes on, locate and repair short.<br>• Replace computer module. |
| • Actuator does not cycle and 4 amp fuse "OK" | • Open B+ lead to module.<br><br>• Inoperative computer module. | • Check B+ wiring and connectors for open circuit and repair as required.<br>• Replace computer module. |
| • Actuator does not cycle and 4 amp fuse is blown | • Shorted B+ lead to module.<br><br>• Shorted actuator solenoid circuit.<br><br>• Defective computer module. | • Check B+ wiring and connectors for short circuit and repair as required.<br>• Perform Solenoid Test and repair as required.<br>• Replace computer module. |
| 2. Brake warning light comes on **4 to 6 seconds after** key is turned to **ON** or **START** position, 4 amp fuse **OK** and:<br>• Actuator cycles once when ignition switch is turned on (see note at beginning of Diagnostic Procedure) | • Open sensor circuit.<br><br><br>• Open failure switch connector.<br><br><br><br>• Closed differential failure switch in actuator.<br>• Defective computer module. | • Check sensor harness connections at computer module, in trunk, and at sensor and repair as required (See Sensor Test).<br>• Check failure switch connections at actuator, computer module, and in engine compartment and repair as required. (Perform Failure Switch Test).<br>• Perform Failure Switch Test.<br><br>• Replace module. |
| • Actuator does not cycle once when ignition switch is turned on | • Open actuator solenoid circuit.<br><br><br><br>• Inoperative computer module.<br><br><br>• Defective actuator. | • Check solenoid connections at computer module, in passenger compartment and at actuator and repair as required. (Perform Solenoid Test).<br>• Replace computer module — if problem still exists, re-install old computer module and continue check sequence.<br>• Replace actuator. |
| • Actuator has long cycle (energized when key is turned to **ON** or **START** and de-energized when light comes on) | • Defective computer module. | • Replace computer module. |
| 3. Skid control cycles once, brake light comes on 4-6 seconds after solenoid is energized and 4 amp fuse OK. | • Inoperative computer module. | • Replace computer module. |
| 4. Brake warning light off and:<br>• Actuator cycles while driving over rough roads or during normal braking conditions (false cycling). | • Loose ground connection.<br><br>• Loose sensor connection.<br><br><br><br>• Loose B+ and failure light connector at computer module.<br>• Defective computer module. | • Perform System Ground Test Procedure.<br>• Check sensor connection at computer module, in trunk and at sensor and repair as required. Perform Sensor Test.<br>• Check plug C and repair as required.<br><br>• Replace computer module. |
| • Actuator cycles after key is turned to **ON** or **ACCESSORY** position but does not cycle during a maximum braking condition. | • Shorted sensor circuit.<br><br>• Defective computer module. | • Perform Sensor Test.<br><br>• Replace computer module. |
| • Actuator cycles slowly or not at all during an impending skid braking condition. | • Plugged actuator filter. | • Replace actuator. |

## Ford Motor Company

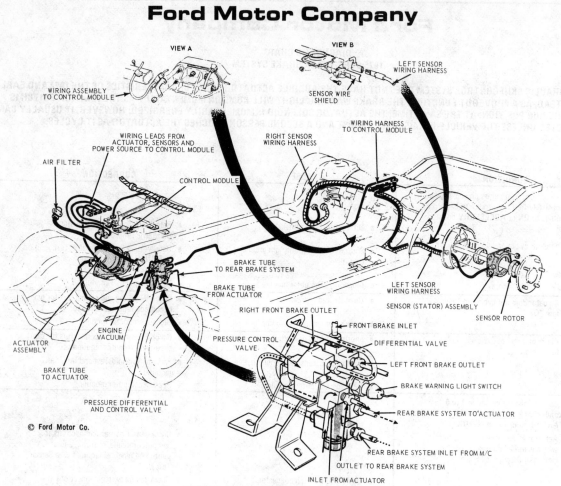

VIEW A

WIRING ASSEMBLY
TO CONTROL MODULE

VIEW B

LEFT SENSOR
WIRING HARNESS

SENSOR WIRE
SHIELD

WIRING HARNESS
TO CONTROL MODULE

WIRING LEADS FROM
ACTUATOR, SENSORS AND
POWER SOURCE TO CONTROL MODULE

RIGHT SENSOR
WIRING HARNESS

AIR FILTER

CONTROL MODULE

BRAKE TUBE
TO REAR BRAKE SYSTEM

BRAKE TUBE
FROM ACTUATOR

LEFT SENSOR
WIRING HARNESS

RIGHT FRONT BRAKE OUTLET

SENSOR (STATOR) ASSEMBLY

SENSOR ROTOR

ENGINE
VACUUM

PRESSURE CONTROL
VALVE

FRONT BRAKE INLET

DIFFERENTIAL VALVE

ACTUATOR
ASSEMBLY

LEFT FRONT BRAKE OUTLET

BRAKE TUBE
TO ACTUATOR

BRAKE WARNING LIGHT SWITCH

REAR BRAKE SYSTEM TO ACTUATOR

PRESSURE DIFFERENTIAL
AND CONTROL VALVE

REAR BRAKE SYSTEM INLET FROM M/C

© Ford Motor Co.

OUTLET TO REAR BRAKE SYSTEM

INLET FROM ACTUATOR

*1969-70 Anti-Skid Control System—Typical*

## Installation

1. Install the air and vacuum hoses on the actuator.
2. Position the actuator and route the air and vacuum hoses up between the engine and the fender apron.
3. Push the harness connectors through the hole in the firewall.
4. Connect the ground wire to the engine block.
5. Install the three bolts which attach the actuator and bracket to the frame side rail.
6. Connect the hydraulic tubes to the valve housing and tighten the nuts.
7. Connect the exhaust pipes to the manifolds.
8. Lower the car from the lift.
9. Pull the actuator solenoid and brake warning switch wiring harness through the hole in the dash panel from the inside the car.
10. Place the wiring harness grommet in the dash panel hole.
11. Connect the harness connector to the intermediate harness.
12. Connect the air hose, the air filter and position the hose clamp.

13. Connect the vacuum hose to the engine vacuum manifold fitting.
14. Install the engine air cleaner.
15. Bleed the rear brake system and centralize the pressure differential valve.
16. Raise the rear wheels and try the brakes while the rear wheels are turning to test the system. (see Non Skid System Test)

## Actuator Assembly
## 1975—All Models

### Removal

1. Raise the car on a lift.
2. Disconnect the solenoid and failure switch connectors from the actuator.
3. Disconnect and plug the power steering pressure connections at the actuator.
4. Disconnect the power steering return hose at the clamp and plug.
5. Disconnect the hydraulic brake lines at the actuator and cap the lines.
6. Remove the three bolts which attach the actuator to the frame

and lower the actuator around the stabilizer bar.

### Installation

1. Position the actuator in the vehicle and install the attaching bolts.
2. Connect the hydraulic brake tubes to the actuator and tighten the tube nuts.
3. Connect the power steering drain hose to the actuator and tighten the hose clamp.
4. Inspect the O-ring seals on the tube ends and replace any that may be damaged. Connect the power steering pressure hoses to the actuator and tighten the tube nuts.
5. Connect the solenoid and failure switch plugs at the actuator.
6. Bleed the rear brake system.
7. Check the power steering fluid and refill if necessary.
8. Remove the coil wire so the engine will not start. Fill the power steering pump reservoir and while engaging the starter, turn the steering wheel all the way one way and then the other and

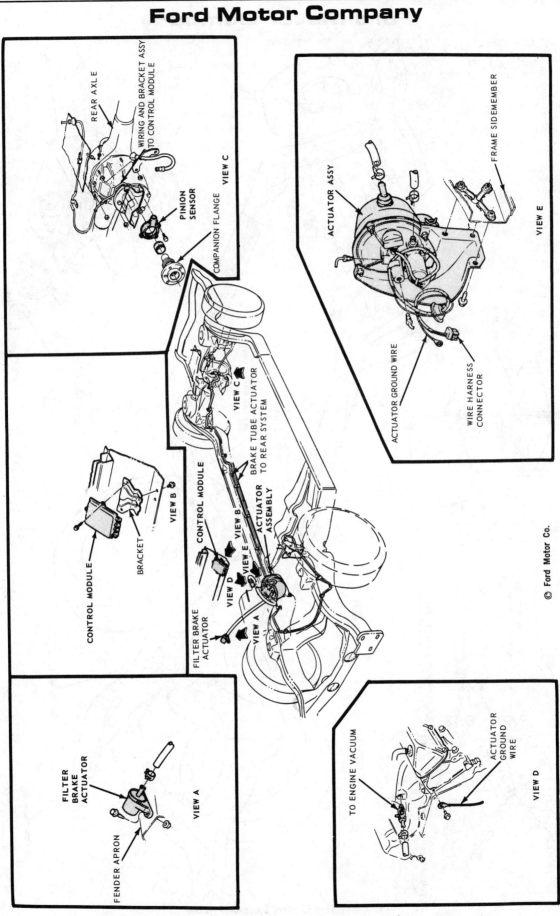

REAR AXLE

WIRING AND BRACKET ASSY
TO CONTROL MODULE

VIEW C

PINION SENSOR

COMPANION FLANGE

FRAME SIDEMEMBER

VIEW E

ACTUATOR ASSY

ACTUATOR GROUND WIRE

WIRE HARNESS CONNECTOR

VIEW C

BRAKE TUBE ACTUATOR TO REAR SYSTEM

CONTROL MODULE

VIEW B

CONTROL MODULE

BRACKET

VIEW B

VIEW E

ACTUATOR ASSEMBLY

VIEW D

VIEW A

FILTER BRAKE ACTUATOR

© Ford Motor Co.

FILTER BRAKE ACTUATOR

VIEW A

FENDER APRON

TO ENGINE VACUUM

ACTUATOR GROUND WIRE

VIEW D

*1971-73 Anti-Skid Control System—Typical*

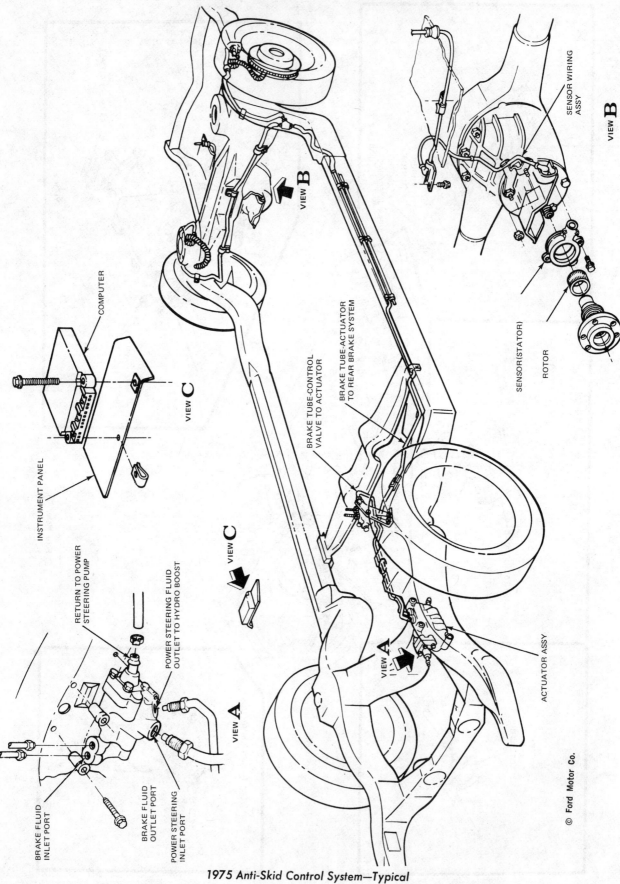

COMPUTER

INSTRUMENT PANEL

VIEW **C**

VIEW **B**

BRAKE TUBE-CONTROL
VALVE TO ACTUATOR

BRAKE TUBE-ACTUATOR
TO REAR BRAKE SYSTEM

SENSOR WIRING ASSY

VIEW **B**

SENSOR (STATOR)

ROTOR

RETURN TO POWER
STEERING PUMP

POWER STEERING FLUID
OUTLET TO HYDRO BOOST

VIEW **C**

VIEW **A**

VIEW **A**

ACTUATOR ASSY

BRAKE FLUID
INLET PORT

BRAKE FLUID
OUTLET PORT

POWER STEERING
INLET PORT

© Ford Motor Co.

*1975 Anti-Skid Control System—Typical*

# Ford Motor Company

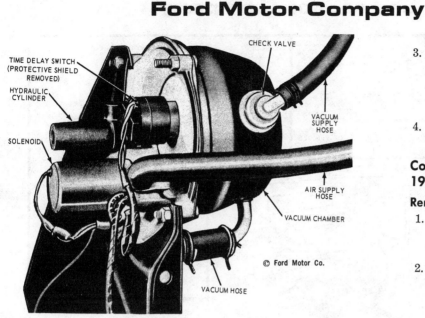

*Actuator Assembly Components*

© Ford Motor Co.

apply the brake to distribute the fluid. Check the fluid level and add if required. Install the coil wire.

9. Raise the rear wheels and try the brakes while the rear wheels are turning to test the system. (see Non Skid System Test)

## Control Module
## 1969-70 All Models

### Removal

1. Remove the wiring harnesses retaining strap.
2. Remove the screws that attach the forward end of the control

module and retainer to the support assembly.

3. Lower the forward end of the module and retainer and move it forward until the flange clears the slot in the support assembly.
4. Disconnect the five wiring harness plugs from the control module.
5. Remove the control module.

### Installation

1. Connect the five wiring harness plugs.
2. Position the control module in the retainer and insert the retainer flange into the slot at the

rear of the support assembly.

3. Move the retainer and control module upward and align the screw holes in the forward end of the retainer with the holes in the support bracket assembly. Install the retaining screws.
4. Secure the wiring harnesses with the retaining strap.

## Control Module
## 1971-74 Lincoln Continental

### Removal

1. Remove the screws that attach the control module to its mounting bracket and lower the module.
2. Depress the lock tabs on each side of the wiring harness connectors and separate the harness from the module, then remove the module.

### Installation

1. Connect the wiring harness to the module.
2. Position the control module on the mounting bracket and install the three attaching screws.

## Control Module—Thunderbird and Continental Mark IV 1971-74

### Removal

1. Disconnect the four wiring harness connector plugs from the control module.
2. Remove the two screws which attach the control module and

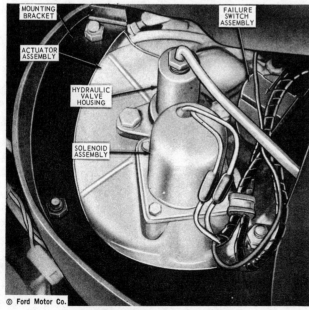

*Actuator Component Connections*

© Ford Motor Co.

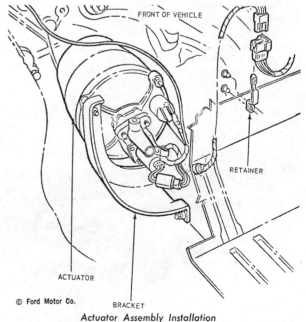

*Actuator Assembly Installation*

© Ford Motor Co.

# Ford Motor Company

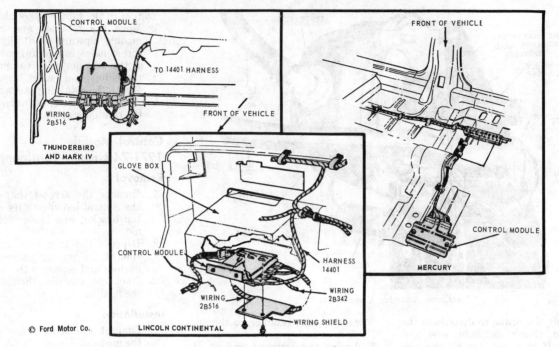

© Ford Motor Co.

*Control Module Removal*

mounting bracket assembly on the instrument panel lower channel.

3. Remove the glove box from the instrument panel.
4. Reach through the glove box opening and remove the control module and mounting bracket assembly from the car.
5. Separate the control module from the mounting bracket by removing the two retaining screws.

## Installation

1. Position the control module on the mounting bracket and install the two retaining screws.
2. Place the control module and mounting bracket assembly

through the glove box opening and position it to the lower instrument panel channel. Install the two retaining screws.

## Control Module
## 1971-74 Mercury
### Removal

1. Remove the front seat.
   (a) Remove the seat track to floor pan attaching nuts and bolts.

(b) If the seats are power operated lift the seat up enough to disconnect the seat sensor and motor wires.
   (c) Lift the seat from the car.
2. Disconnect the control module wiring harness.
3. Remove the two control module and bracket retaining screws and remove the assembly from the car.

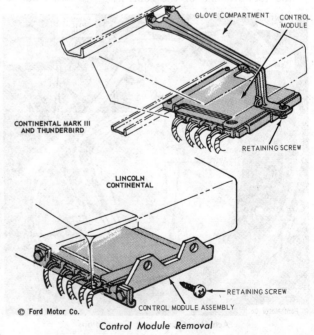

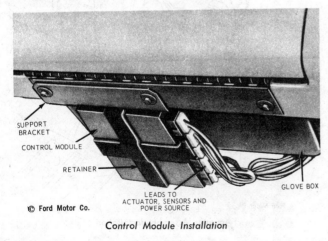

© Ford Motor Co.

*Control Module Installation*

© Ford Motor Co.

*Control Module Removal*

# Ford Motor Company

## Installation

1. Position the control module and bracket assembly to the floor and install.
2. Connect the control module wiring harness.
3. Position the seat in the car and connect the motor and seat sensor wires.
4. Install the seat track to floor pan, attaching nuts and bolts.

## Control Module
## 1975 Thunderbird, Continental and Mark IV

### Removal

1. Remove the applique panel above the glove box by removing the four screws.
2. Use a small screwdriver to lift the latching fingers on the connectors and pull the three wiring harness connector plugs from the module.
3. Remove the two screws which retain the module to the instrument panel and remove the module.

### Installation

1. Reconnect the three wiring harness plugs into the module.
2. Position the module and the instrument panel and install the attaching screws.
3. Raise the rear wheels and check the operation of the system. (see Non-Skid System Test)

## Control Module
## 1975 Lincoln Continental

### Removal

1. Remove the two screws that attach the control module to its mounting bracket and lower the module.
2. Raise the latching fingers with a screwdriver on each wiring harness connector and pull the connector from the control module.
3. Remove the control module from the vehicle.

### Installation

1. Reconnect the three wiring harness plugs into the module.
2. Position the module on the mounting bracket and install the two attaching screws.
3. Raise the rear wheels and check the operation of the system. (see Non-Skid System Test)

## Control Module
## 1975 Mercury

### Removal

1. Remove the two screws which retain the module to the instrument panel sight shield in front of the glove box and lower the module.
2. Use a small screwdriver to lift the latching fingers on the connectors and pull the three wiring harness connector plugs from the module.
3. Remove the module from the vehicle.

### Installation

1. Reconnect the three wiring harness plugs into the module.
2. Position the module on the sight shield mounting pads and install the two attaching screws.
3. Raise the rear wheels and check the operation of the system. (see Non-Skid System Test)

## Sensor Rotor and Stator Assembly
## 1969-70 All Models

### Removal

1. Raise the car up on a lift.
2. Remove the rear wheel and tire assembly.
3. Remove the three speed nuts and remove the brake drum.
4. Disconnect the sensor lead from the rear wiring harness.
5. Push the sensor lead grommet inside the brake assembly.
6. Remove the four sensor stator to backing plate nuts and pull the axle shaft.

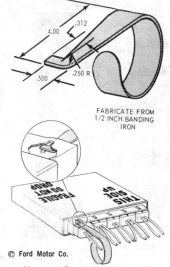

FABRICATE FROM 1/2 INCH BANDING IRON

© Ford Motor Co.

*Harness Connector Removal*

7. Remove the wheel bearing retainer ring and press the wheel bearing retainer and wheel bearing from the axle shaft.
8. Remove the sensor stator assembly.
9. Press the sensor rotor off of the axle shaft.

### Installation

1. Press the sensor rotor onto the axle shaft.
2. Install the sensor stator over the rotor and press the bearing and retainer onto the axle shaft.
3. Insert the axle shaft into the rear axle housing and feed the sensor lead through the hole in the backing plate.
4. Install the four backing plate retaining nuts.
5. Connect the sensor lead to the

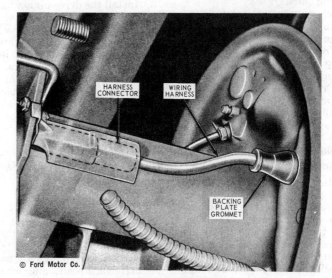

© Ford Motor Co.

*Sensor Wiring Harness Connection*

# Ford Motor Company

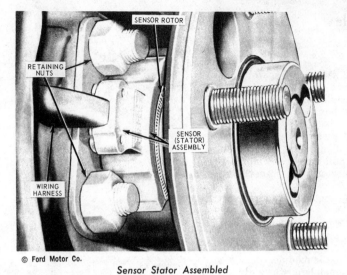

© Ford Motor Co.

*Sensor Stator Assembled*

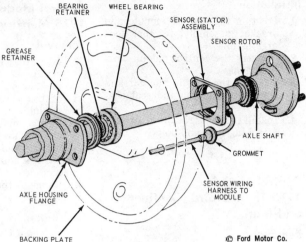

© Ford Motor Co.

*Sensor Stator Disassembled*

wiring harness and install the two retaining straps.

6. Position the rear brake drum and retain with the speed nuts.
7. Install the rear wheel and tire.
8. While the car is on the lift check the operation of the non-skid system. (See non-skid system test.)

## Sensor Rotor
### 1971-75 All Models

#### Removal

1. Raise the car up on a lift.
2. Using a center punch, mark the companion flange and the universal joint flange to maintain driveshaft positioning when reassembling.
3. Remove the four companion flange to drive pinion flange connecting bolts.
4. Attach a universal joint flange holding tool to the universal joint flange and remove the retaining nut from the drive pinion.
5. Using the drive pinion flange holding tool remove the flange and rotor assembly from the rear axle drive pinion.
6. Install the rotor removal tool on the flange and rotor assembly and press the rotor from the companion flange.

#### Installation

1. Position the drive pinion flange on a press, place the rotor and the rotor installer tool on the drive pinion flange and press onto the pinion flange until the flange end bottoms on the shoulder in the tool.
2. Install the drive pinion flange and rotor assembly on the drive

© Ford Motor Co.

*Sensor Rotor Installation*

pinion shaft splines. Position the flange replacer tool on the pinion shaft and press the flange on the pinion shaft.

3. Install the drive pinion flange retaining nut on the drive pinion shaft. Hold the flange with the holding tool and tighten the pinion nut to 180-220 ft. lb.
4. Position the companion flange and the universal joint flange and align the punch marks. Install the retaining nuts and bolts and torque to 70-90 ft. lbs.
5. Check the system. (See non-skid system test.)

## Sensor Assembly (Stator)
### 1971-75 All Models

#### Removal

1. Raise the car up on a lift.
2. Using a center punch, mark the companion flange and the universal joint flange to maintain driveshaft positioning when reassembling.

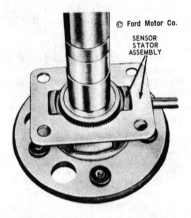

© Ford Motor Co.

*Sensor Stator Assembly Installation*

3. Remove the four companion flange to drive pinion flange connecting bolts.
4. Attach a universal joint flange holding tool to the universal joint flange and remove the retaining nut from the drive pinion.
5. Using the drive pinion flange

© Ford Motor Co.

*Pinion Shaft Nut Removal*

# Ford Motor Company

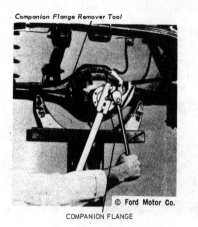

*Companion Flange Remover Tool*

© Ford Motor Co.

COMPANION FLANGE

*Companion Flange and Rotor Removal*

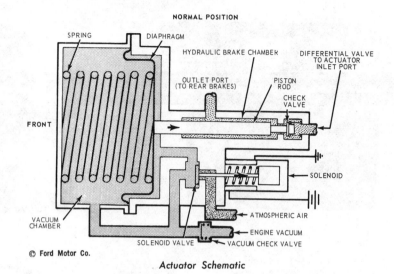

NORMAL POSITION

SPRING

DIAPHRAGM

HYDRAULIC BRAKE CHAMBER

DIFFERENTIAL VALVE
TO ACTUATOR
INLET PORT

OUTLET PORT
(TO REAR BRAKES)

PISTON
ROD

CHECK
VALVE

FRONT

SOLENOID

ATMOSPHERIC AIR

VACUUM
CHAMBER

ENGINE VACUUM

SOLENOID VALVE

VACUUM CHECK VALVE

© Ford Motor Co.

*Actuator Schematic*

holding tool remove the flange and rotor assembly from the rear axle drive pinion.
6. Remove the nut which retains the wiring harness tube assembly bracket on the pinion bearing retainer housing.
7. Remove the two nuts which retain the wiring harness and tube assembly bracket on the rear axle carrier assembly studs.
8. Move the wiring harness and bracket forward off the carrier studs and disconnect the plug from the sensor connector.
9. Remove the three bolts which attach the sensor assembly on the drive pinion bearing retainer housing.
10. Insert a screwdriver in the drain hole in the bottom of the pinion bearing retainer housing and pry the sensor assembly from the retainer housing.

*NOTE: Do not pry between the sensor wire connector and casting and the edge of the bearing retainer housing as damage to the wire connector could result.*

## Installation

1. Position the sensor assembly on the drive pinion bearing retainer housing and install the three attaching bolts. Torque to 16-24 ft. lbs.
2. Connect the wiring harness plug to the sensor wire connector.
3. Position the wiring harness and tube assembly bracket on the carrier studs and install the two nuts. Torque to 30-40 ft. lbs.
4. Install the wiring harness and tube bracket retaining screw at the pinion bearing retainer housing and tighten to 30-45 ft. lbs.
5. Install the drive pinion flange and rotor assembly on the drive

4. Place the transmission in the drive position and accelerate to approximately 25-30 m.p.h.
5. Watch the rear wheels while applying the brakes quickly and firmly. If the system is working properly, it will cycle five or six times or cycle until the brake pedal is released.

## Electric Control System Test 1969-74 All Models

When the ignition is turned *on* electrical power is provided to the system. The circuit is protected by a three amp fuse, located in the fuse panel on all models except the 1974 Mercury which is in line.

*NOTE: Do not use a fuse higher than a three amp or damage to the control module may result.*

## Sensor Test

1. Remove plug C from the module.
2. Connect an ohmmeter between the two contacts of the sensor lead plug. Resistance should be between 2400-3200 ohm.
3. Connect an ohmmeter between the chassis ground and one of the two contacts of the sensor lead plug. Resistance should be infinite.
4. If the resistance is not within the limits on both checks, disconnect the sensor lead plug from the sensor at the rear axle pinion housing.
5. Repeat the resistance checks at the sensor plug connector. If the resistance is within specifications the problem is in the wiring harness between the sensor and the module.

## Solenoid Test

1. Remove plugs A and B from the control module.
2. Replace the fuse in the fuse panel.
3. Turn the ignition switch to the on position.
4. Connect plug B and if the fuse blows, replace the module.
5. If the fuse does not blow when B is connected:
   (a) Connect an ohmmeter between the solenoid lead (red) and the system ground.
   (b) Resistance should be six plus or minus two ohms.
   (c) If the resistance is lower than four ohms, check to see if the solenoid wires are grounded out.
   (d) If the resistance is higher than eight ohms, check the solenoid wiring for an open condition.
   (e) If the wiring checks out okay, replace the actuator assembly.

## System Ground Test

1. Remove plug A from the module.
2. Connect an ohmmeter between the system ground plug sleeve (black) and a suitable chassis ground.
3. If the ohmmeter reading is less than one ohm, replace the module and check the system for normal operation.
4. If the reading is more than one ohm, check the ground system for a loose or broken wire.
5. With the ohmmeter still connected move the ground wires

# Ford Motor Company

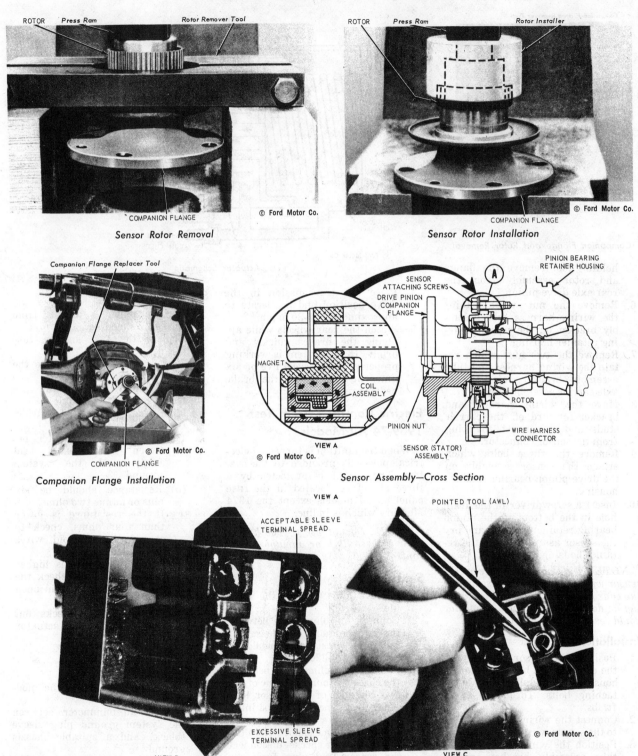

Sensor Rotor Removal

Sensor Rotor Installation

ROTOR    Press Ram    Rotor Remover Tool

COMPANION FLANGE

© Ford Motor Co.

ROTOR    Press Ram    Rotor Installer

COMPANION FLANGE

© Ford Motor Co.

Companion Flange Replacer Tool

COMPANION FLANGE

© Ford Motor Co.

Companion Flange Installation

PINION BEARING RETAINER HOUSING

SENSOR ATTACHING SCREWS

DRIVE PINION COMPANION FLANGE

MAGNET

COIL ASSEMBLY

VIEW A

© Ford Motor Co.

PINION NUT

SENSOR (STATOR) ASSEMBLY

ROTOR

WIRE HARNESS CONNECTOR

Sensor Assembly—Cross Section

VIEW A

ACCEPTABLE SLEEVE TERMINAL SPREAD

EXCESSIVE SLEEVE TERMINAL SPREAD

VIEW B

Actuator Wire Harness Connectors

POINTED TOOL (AWL)

© Ford Motor Co.

VIEW C

(black) at the actuator harness to the intermediate harness connector in and out. If the meter fluctuates, there is a poor connection.

(a) If a poor connection exists, separate the connector.

(b) Check the actuator wiring connector terminals for an oversize condition.

(c) If the terminal is oversize, use a pointed tool to force it together.

(d) Reinstall the connectors

and check the system for normal operation.

## 1975 All Models

When the ignition is turned to the run position the brake warning light will come on for a split second indi-

# Ford Motor Company

cating the sure-track system is working. The circuit is protected by a four amp fuse located on the fuse panel on all models except the Mercury which is in-line.

*NOTE: Do not use a fuse higher than a four amp or damage to the control module may result.*

The control module can detect an open sensor circuit, an open actuator solenoid circuit, an excessively long output pulse to the solenoid and an open failure switch connector at the actuator. If any of these conditions occur the brake warning light will come on around four to six seconds afterwards. When the ignition is turned to start and the sure track fuse is defective or the primary power is interrupted the warning light will also come on, but immediately afterward.

## Sensor Test

1. Calibrate an ohmmeter on the scale being used.
2. Remove sensor plug A from the module.
3. Connect an ohmmeter between pins two and three of the sensor connector. The resistance should be between 2400-3200 ohms.
4. Connect an ohmmeter between the chassis ground and either pin of the sensor connector. The resistance should be infinite.
5. If the resistance is not within the limits on both of the above checks, remove the connector from the sensor at the rear axle pinion housing.
6. Repeat the resistance checks in steps 3 and 4 at the terminals on the sensor. If the resistance is not within the limits, replace the sensor.

## Sensor Output Voltage Test

The following test must be made with a voltmeter capable of measuring AC voltage.
1. Disconnect plug A at the module.
2. Connect the AC voltmeter to pins two and three.
3. Raise the rear wheels off the ground and run at 30 mph and the voltage should be above 5 volts AC.

## Solenoid Test

1. Calibrate an ohmmeter on the RX1 scale.
2. Remove plug B from the module.
3. Connect an ohmmeter between pin six (solenoid high) and pin

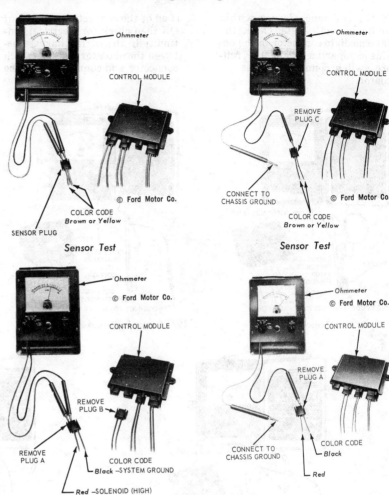

Sensor Test

Sensor Test

Solenoid Test

System Ground Test

*1969-74 Electrical Test*

four (system ground) of the plug. The resistance should be between two and eight ohms.
4. If the resistance is higher than eight ohms, connect an ohmmeter to the terminals on the solenoid.
5. If the resistance is between two and eight ohms check for an open circuit, or poor connections in the solenoid wiring harness.
6. If the resistance is not between two and eight ohms, replace the actuator assembly.

## System Ground Test

1. Calibrate an ohmmeter on the RX1 scale.
2. Remove plug B from the module.
3. Connect an ohmmeter between the chassis ground and the system ground (black lead of the plug). The resistance should be lower than one ohm.

4. If the resistance is higher than one ohm, check the system ground wiring for a loose or broken wire. The system ground is located at the right side of the cowl, at the top near the air conditioning blower motor on the Lincoln-Mercury and below- and outward of the fuse block on the Thunderbird and Mark IV.

## Failure Switch Test

1. Calibrate an ohmmeter on the scale being used.
2. Remove plug B from the module.
3. Connect the ohmmeter between pin five (dark green) failure switch and pin eight (red) failure switch. The resistance should be less than one ohm.
4. Connect an ohmmeter between the chassis ground and one of the two pins for the failure switch. The resistance should be infinite.

## Ford Motor Company

5. If the resistance is not within limits on both tests, check the intermediate connector in the engine compartment and the failure switch connector at the actuator.

6. If all of the connections check out OK then check for electrical continuity in the wiring harness between the actuator failure switch connector and connector B at the module. If continuity is OK and the failure switch has not been shuttled due to brake release during sure-track cycling, replace the actuator.

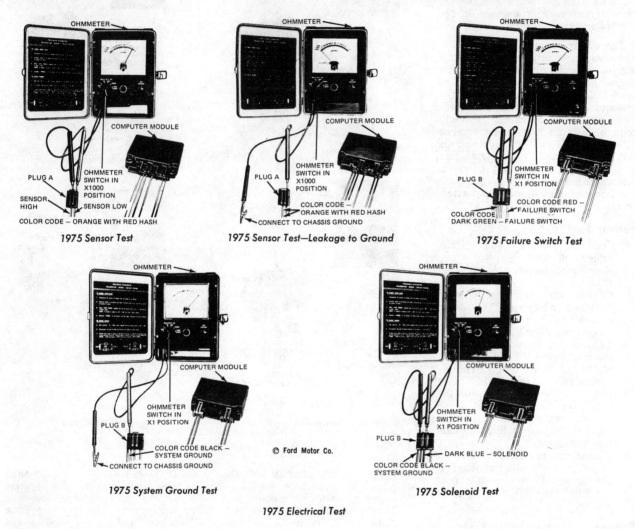

1975 Sensor Test

1975 Sensor Test—Leakage to Ground

1975 Failure Switch Test

1975 System Ground Test

© Ford Motor Co.

1975 Solenoid Test

1975 Electrical Test

## General Motors

### Oldsmobile
### 1970 Wheel Lock Control
### 1971-74 True Track

### Cadillac
### 1971-75 Track Master

### General Description

Non-skid braking systems are employed to control rear wheel lock-up. Lock-up occurs because of the shift of weight off the rear wheels during very heavy braking and the resultant loss of tire friction on the road. Rear wheel lockup is objectionable because stationary tires have less of a grip on the road than tires which are rolling, and almost no directional stability. Thus, keeping the rear wheels turning will make for a shorter stop and almost eliminate the tendency for the car to go into a skid.

Generally, the system monitors the speeds of the rear wheels and responds to a very sudden decrease in rotational speed with a decrease in hydraulic pressure to both rear wheels. Full pressure is restored as soon as rotating speed levels off.

The system employs a sensor at each rear wheel or, in the case of 1972 and 1973 Cadillacs with rear wheel drive, a sensor located in the rear portion of the transmission. The sensor generates an AC current through the interaction of a permanent magnet, a rotor, and a stator. The signal generated by the sensor is sent to the controller, an electronic computer which determines whether or not the signal is changing fast

## Oldsmobile
### TRUE-TRACK DIAGNOSIS

| CONDITION | POSSIBLE CAUSE | CORRECTION |
|---|---|---|
| Brakes grab, tire skids on city streets below 10 mph normal to moderate heavy pedal pressure. | Mechanical condition. | True track system is ineffective under these conditions. Check brake linings for contamination. |
| No brake light under any condition (Ignition "on"). System operates OK. | Burned out lamp (Bulb). | Check for cause. Replace bulb. |
| | Blown fuse. | Check for cause. Replace fuse. |
| | Open electrical leads to brake lamp circuit. | Check for continuity of leads and correct accordingly. |
| Immediate brake light when engine is started or ignition switch is turned "on". | Parking brake on. | Release parking brake. |
| | Shorted parking brake switch (System OK). | Replace parking brake switch. |
| | Short in electrical lead to parking brake switch and/or brake lamp (System OK). | Check continuity of leads. Correct as required. |
| | Shorted differential pressure switch (System OK). | Replace switch. |
| | Fuse blown (System inoperative). | Check harness and connectors for cause of blown fuse and correct. Replace fuse (Refer to following steps). |
| | Shorted solenoid lead to ground- blows fuse (System inoperative). | Repair or replace harness. |
| | Shorted solenoid - blows fuse (System inoperative). | Replace Solenoid. |
| | No + 12 volts at controller. (Faulty connections or open circuit in wiring - System inoperative). | Check feed wire (pink) and connectors. Correct as necessary. |
| | Controller faulty. | Replace controller. |
| Brake light comes "on" during a stop, or when brake pedal is depressed firmly, and goes "off" when the brake pedal is released. | Hydraulic fluid leak. | Check for and correct leak in brake system. |
| | Air in brake system. | Check for cause and repair. Bleed brakes, including bleeder screw on modulator. |

FOR THE FOLLOWING CONDITIONS it is assumed that the brake lamp circuit operates normally and there are no hydraulic leaks or air trapped in the brake system:

| | | |
|---|---|---|
| No brake light. System completely inoperative but exercise cycle OK. (Ignition switch "on" or engine running.) | Sensor adjustment incorrect. | Adjust sensor. (NOTE: Wheel bearing adj. must be correct before sensor is adjusted.) |

## Oldsmobile

| CONDITION | POSSIBLE CAUSE | CORRECTION |
|---|---|---|
| | Speed sensor leads shorted to each other (but not shorted to ground). | Disconnect speed sensor connector(s). Check resistance across speed sensor terminals. (Should be 1000-2500 ohms) If out of limits, replace speed sensor. |
| | | Remove connector(s) to controller. Check resistance across terminals AT SPEED SENSOR CONNECTOR. Should be infinite (open). If not, replace harness. |
| | Controller faulty. | Replace controller. |
| No brake light. System completely inoperative and no exercise cycle (ignition switch "on" or engine running.) | Loss of ground connection to controller. | Check black ground wire connection from controller to instrument panel. |
| | Controller connectors not plugged into harnesses. | Plug in harness connectors near controller. |
| | Solenoid valve will not operate. | Disconnect solenoid lead. Remove solenoid from modulator port. |
| | | Momentarily apply 12 volts to solenoid terminals and listen for solenoid core movement (sharp click). If inoperative, replace solenoid. |
| | | Apply 12 volts to solenoid terminals for 2-3 seconds and observe if vacuum leak stops after solenoid "clicks" (with engine running). If vacuum leak does not stop, replace solenoid. |
| No brake light. System completely inoperative and no exercise cycle (ignition switch "on" or engine running.) | Modulator will not cycle when engine is started. | Check for vacuum at modulator. If engine vacuum is not present at modulator check for restricted hose, check valve at connector or for vacuum leaks. If OK replace modulator. |
| | Controller faulty. | Replace controller. |
| Brake light comes on after a 2-5 second delay. System completely inoperative but exercise cycle OK. (Ignition switch "on" or engine running.) | Speed sensor harness or sensor open. | Check speed sensor harness connectors at controller and rear underbody for secure connection. |
| | | Disconnect speed sensor harness at controller and check resistance across terminals E-F and J-K, should be 1000-2500 ohms on both. |
| | | If no resistance was obtained on either, disconnect speed sensor harness at rear underbody and check resistance across terminals (female) L-M and N-P, should be 1000-2500 ohms on both. If so, replace harness from controller to rear underbody connector. |

## Oldsmobile

| CONDITION | POSSIBLE CAUSE | CORRECTION |
|---|---|---|

If resistance was obtained on L-M but none on N-P. Disconnect left sensor connector. If resistance was obtained on N-P but none on L-M. Disconnect right sensor connector.

With sensor disconnected on side with no resistance, check resistance across sensor terminals. If a resistance of 1000-2500 ohms is obtained remove and replace harness from underbody to sensors. If no resistance is obtained, replace sensor.

**Speed sensor harness or sensor grounded.**

Disconnect speed sensor harness at controller and check for continuity between E-G, F-G, J-H and K-H.

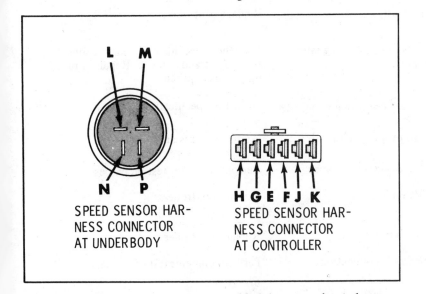

SPEED SENSOR HARNESS CONNECTOR AT UNDERBODY

SPEED SENSOR HARNESS CONNECTOR AT CONTROLLER

If continuity exists, disconnect speed sensor harness at underbody connector and recheck. If continuity still exists, replace speed sensor harness - controller to underbody.

If NO continuity exists, connect one lead to rear axle and the other lead to terminals L, M, N and P (one at a time) at female connector of under body harness.

If continuity exists on terminals L or M, disconnect right sensor connector. If continuity exists on terminal N or P, disconnect left sensor connector.

With right or left sensor disconnected and continuity still exists, replace speed sensor wiring harness - underbody connector to sensors. If no continuity exists, replace sensor.

**Modulator travel switch open.**

Remove connector from modulator travel switch terminal. Check for 0-10 ohm resistance reading from terminal to ground. If out of limits, replace modulator.

**Brake light comes on after a 2-5 second delay. System completely inoperative but exercise cycle OK. (Ignition switch "on" or engine running.)**

**Modulator travel switch connector not making contact with the terminal or open circuit in the lead.**

Check connector at modulator travel switch terminal for security.

Remove modulator travel switch connector from terminal and insert jumper from connector to ground. If system now operates normally, the travel switch is faulty requiring modulator replacement. If system is still inoperative, check continuity of modulator travel switch lead. If open, replace harness.

**Controller faulty.**

Replace controller.

## Oldsmobile

| CONDITION | POSSIBLE CAUSE | CORRECTION |
|---|---|---|
| Brake light comes on after a 2-5 second delay. System complete inoperative and no exercise cycle. (Ignition switch "on" or engine running.) | Solenoid lead(s) open. | Check connector at solenoid valve for security.<br><br>Remove connector and check resistance of solenoid (3-6 ohms). If out of limit, replace solenoid.<br><br>Remove connector(s) to controller. Also disconnect pink feed wire to system harness. Check continuity of terminals C and D (Fig. 5-105) at the harness connector with a jumper temporarily inserted across the solenoid valve connector terminals. If open, replace harness. |
| | Controller faulty. | Replace controller. |
| False releases while car is in motion. | Frayed shield leads causing intermittent short. | Visually check shield leads and connectors for stray strands of wire. Repair or replace harness as required. |
| | Wheel bearing not properly adjusted. | Adjust to specification. |
| | Sensor not properly adjusted. | Adjust as necessary. |
| | Loose electrical connections. | Perform ohmeter test on harness. |
| | Controller faulty. | Replace controller. |
| False releases while car is parked (with engine running or ignition switch "on"). | Controller faulty. | Replace controller. |
| | Loose electrical connections. | Perform ohmeter test on harness. |
| Does not cycle down to 5 mph during maximum braking effort stop. | Insufficient operating vacuum. | Look for severe vacuum leak and correct. |
| | Controller faulty. | Replace controller. |
| Brake light on 2-5 seconds after high brake pressure is applied. | Defective brake combination valve (excessive pressure applied to modulator. | Replace brake combination valve. |

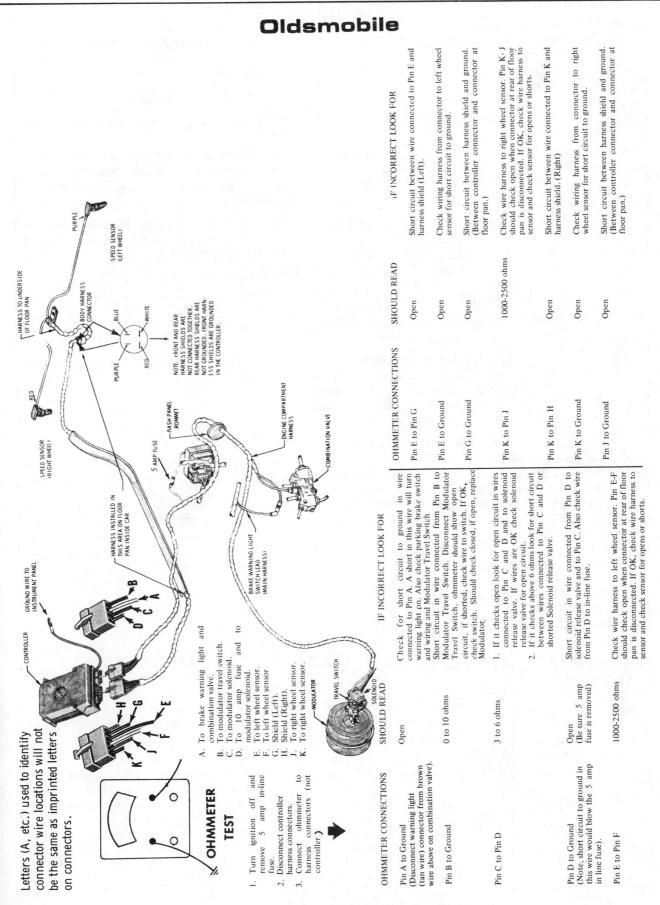

Letters (A, etc.) used to identify connector wire locations will not be the same as imprinted letters on connectors.

## OHMMETER TEST

1. Turn ignition off and remove 5 amp in-line fuse.
2. Disconnect controller harness connectors.
3. Connect ohmmeter to harness connectors (not controller)

A. To brake warning light and combination valve.
B. To modulator travel switch.
C. To modulator solenoid.
D. To 10 amp fuse and to modulator solenoid.
E. To left wheel sensor.
F. To left wheel sensor.
G. Shield (Left).
H. Shield (Right).
J. To right wheel sensor.
K. To right wheel sensor.

| OHMMETER CONNECTIONS | SHOULD READ | IF INCORRECT LOOK FOR |
|---|---|---|
| Pin A to Ground (Disconnect warning light (tan wire) connector from brown wire above on combination valve). | Open | Check for short circuit to ground in wire connected to Pin A. A short in this wire will turn warning light on. Also check parking brake switch and wiring and Modulator Travel Switch. |
| Pin B to Ground | 0 to 10 ohms | Short circuit in wire connected from Pin B to Modulator Travel Switch. Disconnect Modulator Travel Switch, ohmmeter should show open circuit, if shorted, check wire to switch. If OK, check switch. Should check closed, if open, replace Modulator. |
| Pin C to Pin D | 3 to 6 ohms | 1. If it checks open look for open circuit in wires connected to Pin C and D and to solenoid release valve. If wires are OK check solenoid release valve for open circuit. 2. If it checks above 6 ohms look for short circuit between wires connected to Pin C and D or shorted Solenoid release valve. |
| Pin D to Ground (Note, short circuit to ground in this wire would blow the 5 amp in line fuse). | Open (Be sure 5 amp fuse is removed) | Short circuit in wire connected from Pin D to solenoid release valve and to Pin C. Also check wire from Pin D to in-line fuse. |
| Pin E to Pin F | 1000-2500 ohms | Check wire harness to left wheel sensor. Pin E-F should check open when connector at rear of floor pan is disconnected. If OK, check wire harness to sensor and check sensor for opens or shorts. |

| OHMMETER CONNECTIONS | SHOULD READ | IF INCORRECT LOOK FOR |
|---|---|---|
| Pin E to Pin G | Open | Short circuit between wire connected to Pin E and harness shield (Left). |
| Pin E to Ground | Open | Check wiring harness from connector to left wheel sensor for short circuit to ground. |
| Pin G to Ground | Open | Short circuit between harness shield and ground. (Between controller connector and connector at floor pan.) |
| Pin K to Pin J | 1000-2500 ohms | Check wire harness to right wheel sensor. Pin K-J should check open when connector at rear of floor pan is disconnected. If OK, check wire harness to sensor and check sensor for opens or shorts. |
| Pin K to Pin H | Open | Short circuit between wire connected to Pin K and harness shield. (Right) |
| Pin K to Ground | Open | Check wiring harness from connector to right wheel sensor for short circuit to ground. |
| Pin J to Ground | Open | Short circuit between harness shield and ground. (Between controller connector and connector at floor pan.) |

**True-Track Brake Diagnosis**

| CONDITION | POSSIBLE CAUSE | CORRECTIVE ACTION |
|---|---|---|
| No brake light under any condition (check by placing ignition in "START") | Burned out lamp (bulb). | Check for cause. Replace bulb. |
| | Blown 10 amp trans - gage fuse | Check for cause. Replace fuse. |
| | Open electrical leads to brake lamp circuit. | Check for continuity of leads and correct accordingly. |
| Immediate brake light when ignition switch is turned "ON") | Leak in hydraulic system. | Check by removing lead from brake combination valve. If light goes out, a leak in hydraulic system is indicated. |
| | Track Master fuse blown. (Track Master inoperative) | Check harness & connector for cause of blown fuse and correct. Replace fuse. (See remaining causes in this group also) |
| | Shorted solenoid lead to ground-blows Track Master fuse. (Track Master inoperative) | Repair or replace harness. |
| | Shorted solenoid (blows Track Master fuse, Track Master inoperative) | Replace solenoid. |
| | No +12 VDC at Track Master controller. (Faulty connections or open circuit in wiring - Track Master inoperative) Track Master controller faulty. | Check feed wire (pink) and connectors. Correct as necessary. |
| | Track Master controller faulty. | Replace controller. |

FOR THE FOLLOWING CONDITIONS: It is assumed that the brake lamp circuit operates normally and there are no hydraulic leaks or air trapped in the brake system.

| CONDITION | POSSIBLE CAUSE | CORRECTIVE ACTION |
|---|---|---|
| No brake light. Track Master completely inoperative but exercise cycle OK. (Ignition switch "ON" or engine running.) | Transmission sensor seized or not being driven. | Check speedo gear and replace if necessary. Check for cause of seizing and replace. |
| | Eldorado sensor not close enough to teeth or rear hubs. | Check for cause and adjust if necessary. |
| | Both speed sensor leads shorted to each other (but not shorted to ground) | Disconnect speed sensor connectors. |
| | | a. Check resistance across speed sensor terminals. (Should be 1000-2500 ohms). If out of limits, replace speed sensor. (Pack sensor connectors with wheel bearing grease.) b. Remove connectors to controller. Check resistance across terminals at speed sensor connector. Should be infinite (open). If not, repair or replace harness. |
| | Track Master controller faulty. | Replace controller. |

| | POSSIBLE CAUSE | CORRECTIVE ACTION |
|---|---|---|
| No brake light. Track Master completely inoperative and no exercise cycle (ignition switch "ON" or engine running). | Loss of ground connection to Track Master controller. | Check ground lead connection from controller. (Black/white wire) |
| | Controller connector not plugged into controller and modulator harness. | Plug in connector. |
| | Solenoid valve seized in de-energized position. | Disconnect solenoid lead. |
| | | a. Momentarily apply 12 volts to solenoid terminals and listen for solenoid core movement (sharp click). If inoperative, replace solenoid. |
| | | b. Apply 12 volts to solenoid terminals for 2-3 seconds and observe if vacuum leak stops after solenoid "clicks" (with engine running). If vacuum leak does not stop, replace solenoid. |
| | Modulator seized in de-energized position. | Disconnect gray modulator travel switch wire. |
| | | Connect ohmmeter from modulator travel switch to ground. With the engine running, pull solenoid valve out of modulator port and observe ohmmeter. If ohmmeter reflects a change from very low resistance to high resistance as the solenoid valve is removed, the modulator is OK. If not, replace the modulator. |
| | Track Master controller faulty. | Replace controller. |
| Brake light comes on after a 2-5 second delay. Track Master completely inoperative but exercise cycle OK. (Ignition switch "ON" or engine running.) | Speed sensor leads open | Check speed sensor connectors and pack with front wheel bearing grease. Secure connection with clamps. |
| | | Disconnect connectors and check continuity across sensor terminals - should be 1000-2500 ohms. If not, replace sensor(s). |
| | | Remove connectors to controller and check resistance across terminals E & F and K & L at harness connector with the speed sensor connector(s) reconnected (should be 1000-2500 ohms) - if open, replace harness. |
| | Speed sensor lead(s) shorted to ground. | Disconnect speed sensor connectors and check continuity of speed sensor terminals to ground. If any terminal is grounded, replace speed sensor. |
| | | Remove connectors to controller. Check continuity of speed sensor connector terminals to ground. If any terminals are grounded, replace harness. |
| | Modulator travel switch open. | Remove gray wire connector from modulator travel switch terminal. Check for 0-10 ohm resistance reading from terminal to ground. If out of limits, replace modulator. |
| | Modulator travel switch connector not making contact with the terminal or open circuit in the lead. | Check gray wire connector at modulator travel switch terminal for security. |
| | | Remove gray wire modulator travel switch connector from terminal and insert jumper from connector to ground. If system now operates |

## Cadillac

| CONDITION | POSSIBLE CAUSE | CORRECTIVE ACTION |
|---|---|---|
| Brake light comes on after a 2-5 second delay. Track Master completely inoperative but exercise cycle OK. (Ignition switch "ON" or engine running.) (Cont'd.) | Modulator travel switch connector not making contact with the terminal or open circuit in the lead. (Cont'd.)<br><br>Track Master controller faulty. | normally, the travel switch is faulty, requiring modulator replacement. If system is still inoperative, check continuity of modulator travel switch lead. If open, repair or replace harness.<br><br>Replace controller. |
| Brake light comes on after a 2-5 second delay. Track Master completely inoperative and no exercise cycle. (Ignition switch "ON" or engine running.) | Solenoid lead(s) open.<br><br><br><br><br><br><br><br><br><br>Track Master controller faulty. | Check connector at solenoid valve for security.<br><br>Remove connector and check resistance of solenoid (3-6 ohms). If out of limit, replace solenoid. Remove controller and modulator harness connector at controller. Also disconnect pink 12 volt feed wire to harness by removing in-line 4 amp fuse. Check continuity of terminals C & D at the harness connector with a jumper temporarily inserted across the solenoid valve connector terminals. If open, repair or replace harness.<br><br>Replace controller. |
| Pseudo cycling while vehicle is in motion. | Frayed shield leads causing intermittent short.<br><br>Improperly greased sensor connector or missing clamp.<br><br><br>Sensor Damper Deteriorated<br><br>Bad electrical connections.<br><br>Track Master controller faulty. | Visually check shields leads and connectors for stray strands of wire. Repair or replace harness as required.<br><br>Pack connector with front wheel bearing grease and clamp connection.<br><br><br>Replace sensor.<br><br>Clean connector.<br><br>Replace controller. |
| Pseudo cycling while vehicle is parked (with engine running or ignition switch "ON"). | Bad electrical connections.<br><br>Track Master controller faulty. | Clean the connection, pack with front wheel bearing grease and properly clamp connection. |
| Does not cycle down to 5 mph during maximum braking effort stop. | Insufficient operating vacuum.<br><br>Track Master controller faulty. | Look for severe vacuum leak and correct.<br><br>Replace controller. |
| Brake light on 2-5 seconds after high brake pressure is applied. | Defective brake combination valve (excessive pressure applied to modulator). | Replace brake combination valve. |

## General Motors

enough to indicate that the rear wheels are locking up. If the controller determines that the signal is changing at a speed sufficiently rapid to indicate impending lockup, it sends a signal to the solenoid valve. When this valve opens, atmospheric pressure is applied to the diaphragm in the modulator and the hydraulic valve in the modulator blocks the flow of hydraulic fluid to the rear brakes and, at the same time, increases the volume of the rear brake circuit, reducing the pressure. When the wheel speed reaches a steady value, the computer sends another signal to the solenoid which then applies vacuum to the modulator, and brings the valve to a position which allows full hydraulic pressure to reach the rear brakes.

During moderate braking, the unit has no effect. During heavy braking which would normally cause rear

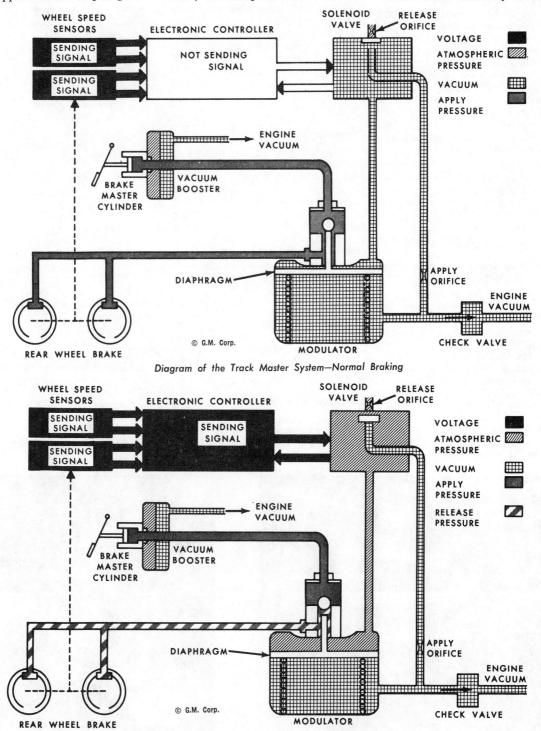

Diagram of the Track Master System—Normal Braking

Diagram of the Track Master System—Release Mode

# General Motors

wheel lockup, the system pumps the rear brakes so as to keep the rear wheels just at the point of normal adhesion to the road and ensure a straight, steady stop.

## General Diagnostic Procedures

The system has several characteristics which should be understood before diagnosis is attempted. Whether or not the brake warning light functions and how soon it comes on after the ignition is switched on, whether or not the system goes through an exercise cycle immediately after ignition switch turn on, and whether or not the system exhibits pseudo cycling are all important factors in tracking down operational problems.

*Immediate Brake Light:* The brake light comes on immediately after the ignition switch is turned to the "on" position. This problem is due to a hydraulic problem or a lack of power to the controller.

*Delayed Brake Light:* The brake light comes on two to five seconds after the ignition switch is turned on. This is a result of a problem existing within the circuitry of the system.

*Exercise Cycle:* When the system is operating properly, the modulator will run through a partial cycle every time the ignition switch is turned on. To measure this characteristic most effectively, run the engine to build up vacuum and connect an ohmmeter connected between the ohmmeter travel switch terminal and ground. Turn the ignition off and then back on. The ohmmeter should indicate that the modulator travel switch has gone from a closed position to an

open position and back again. Lack of an exercise cycle indicates that system problems lie in the lead to the solenoid or in the controller.

*Pseudo Cycling:* The unit should cycle only when the ignition switch is turned on and when the rear wheels are starting to lock up under braking. If the system cycles when only very light pressure, not capable of causing lockup, is applied to the brake pedal, or when no pressure at all is applied, the system is pseudo cycling. Pseudo cycling is generally due to minor system electrical problems or a bad controller.

## Operational Check

Raise the rear of the vehicle so wheels are off the floor. On 1972 and 1973 Cadillacs with rear wheel drive, put the transmission in gear and accelerate until about 40 miles per hour is indicated on the speedometer. Firmly apply the brake while watching the speedometer. The speedometer should gradually approach 0 miles per hour and the cycling of the system should be felt and heard.

On all other vehicles, perform the test on one wheel at a time. Using a wheel spinner, spin the wheel up to a high speed. Remove the drive motor, and have someone apply the brakes firmly while you watch the wheel. It should come *gradually* to a stop.

## Electrical Check

The system power lead and the controller should be disconnected. Measure resistances and compare with the appropriate chart.

## Removal and Installation Procedures

### Wheel Speed Sensor 1973-75 Eldorado

#### Removal

1. Put the car on a hoist.
2. Remove the clamp and connector at the sensor. Remove the screw holding the sensor to the backing plate.
3. Remove the sensor.

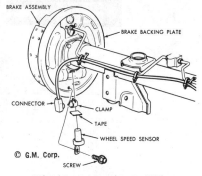

*Wheel Speed Sensor—Cadillac*

#### Installation

*NOTE: Do not remove the pressure sensitive tape supplied on the pick-up end of a replacement sensor.*

1. Place sensor in backing plate, ensuring that the taped end contacts the teeth on the hub.
2. Install the retaining screw and torque to 75 inch pounds.
3. Pack connector with wheel bearing grease, and install the connector and clamp.
4. Lower the car.

*NOTE: If sensor is supplied without tape, step 2 should be preceded*

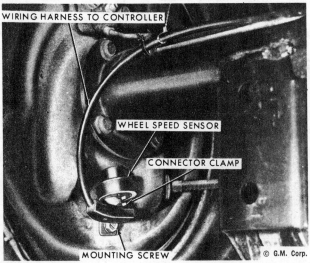

*Wheel Speed Sensor*

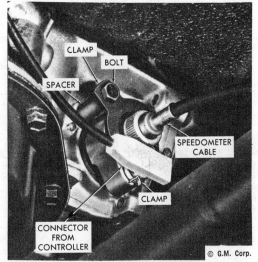

*Transmission Speed Sensor*

# General Motors

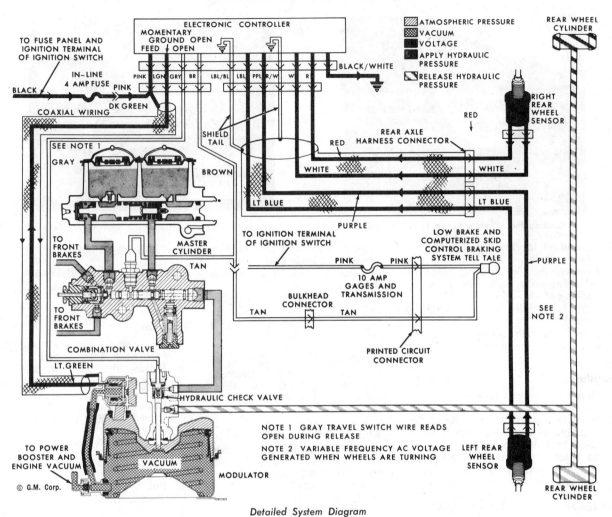

**Detailed System Diagram**

by removal of wheel disc, wheel, and brake drum and insertion of a .010" feeler gauge between the sensor and hub. After performance of step 2, remove the feeler gauge. Then, after performance of step 3, install the brake drum, wheel, and wheel cover.

## 1972 Eldorado and All 1971 Cadillac

### Removal

1. Remove the wheel disc. Remove the screws (3) which secure the cap to the hub assembly and remove the cap.
2. Remove the insulators from the sensor assembly pin and remove the pin.
3. Remove the brake drum. Remove the screws securing the drive cap to the hub, and remove the drive cap.
4. Remove the retaining ring, spindle nut, washer, and outer cone and roller.
5. Pull the hub off the spindle.

6. Disconnect the brake line at the wheel cylinder.
7. Remove the nuts which secure the brake backing plate to the spindle. Remove the backing plate.
8. Screw one backing plate to spindle nut back on just far enough to engage the threads.
9. Using appropriate tools, remove the spindle.
10. Position the clamp that normally secures the rear harness connector on the sensor body. Remove the rear harness connector.
11. Place the spindle on a bench. Using a 1⅝" open end wrench, remove the sensor.

### Installation

1. Put the sensor in place in the spindle, torquing it to 20 foot-lbs.
2. Fill the rear harness connector with lubricant and secure it to the sensor with a clamp.
3. Connect sensor wires, boot, and clamp.

4. Drive the new spindle into the axle.
5. Install a new wheel spindle gasket. Then, install the brake backing plate and secure with four attaching nuts, torquing them to 40 foot-pounds.
6. Connect the brake line to the wheel cylinder, torquing the fitting to 14 foot-pounds.
7. Install the rear hub.
8. Install a new sensor assembly pin and center it in the spindle. Install two insulators onto the pin.
9. Position the cap on the hub assembly so it is aligned with the pin. Tighten the cap screws to 20-inch-pounds.
10. Install the wheel disc.

## 1972-74 Oldsmobile

### Removal

1. Raise the rear of the car on a lift. Remove the wheel, drum, and hub assembly.

## General Motors

*Rotating the Wheel with the Wheel Spinner*

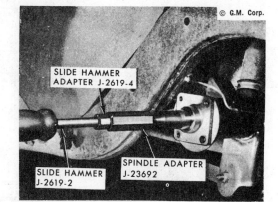

*Removal and Installation of the Rear Wheel Spindle*

2. Disconnect the brake line at the wheel cylinder.
3. Remove the four backing plate attaching bolts, and remove the backing plate.
4. Pull the spindle from the tube assembly.
5. Disconnect the sensor wiring, and unscrew the sensor.

### Installation

1. Screw the sensor into the spindle. Connect the wiring.
2. Start the spindle into the tube assembly and install the four bolts used to hold the backing plate in place. Drive the spindle into the tube while tightening bolts progressively until the spindle is fully seated.
3. Install the backing plate, torquing nuts to 40 foot pounds. Connect the brake line.
4. Put the hub into position over the spindle.
5. Install the outer bearing roller and separator into the hub. Install the outer bearing inner race over the spindle. Install the washer and spindle nut.
6. Install the drum and wheel.
7. To adjust rear wheel bearings, spin the wheel at least three times as fast as the rotation of the nut when checking the torque readings. Tighten the adjusting nut to 25-30 foot pounds.
8. Back the nut off ½ turn. Retighten with the fingers. Back off just until cotter pin can be installed, and install it.
9. Bleed wheel cylinder and add fluid as necessary.

10. Lower the vehicle.

### Transmission Speed Sensor 1972-75 Cadillac With Rear Wheel Drive

#### Removal

1. Disconnect the speedometer cable at the transmission.
2. Release the clamp at the harness connector. Remove the connector.
3. Remove the bolt, retainer and spacer holding the sensor in place.
4. Remove the sensor.

#### Installation

1. Put the sensor in place in the transmission.
2. Install the spacer, retainer and

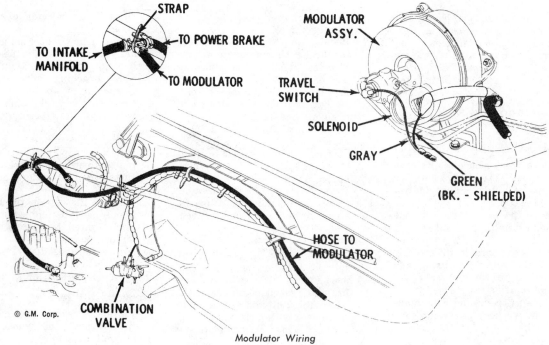

*Modulator Wiring*

# General Motors

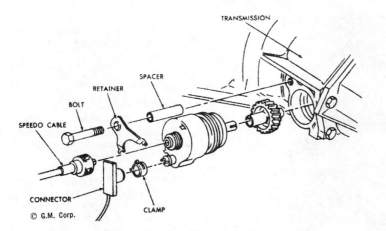

*Transmission Speed Sensor—Cadillac*

bolt securing the sensor in the transmission.

3. Pack the harness connector with front wheel bearing grease and secure it with the clamp.
4. Connect the speedometer cable to the sensor.

## Controller
### 1971-75 Cadillac
#### Removal

1. The controller is located under the instrument panel, to the left of the glove box on 1971-74 models and directly on top of the glove box on 1975 models. Re-

move the wiring harness connector.
2. Remove the securing screws, and remove the controller.

#### Installation

1. Put the controller in place and secure it and the ground wire with the attaching screws.
2. Reinstall the wiring harness connectors.

### 1972-75 Oldsmobile
#### Removal

1. Disconnect the battery cable.
2. Remove the two control bracket to tie bar screws.

3. Disconnect the multiple wiring connectors.
4. Remove the screws attaching control to bracket. Remove the control.

#### Installation

5. Reverse the removal procedure.

## Modulator
### 1971-73 Cadillac
#### Removal

1. Disconnect the positive battery cable.
2. Disconnect both brake lines at the modulator. Disconnect the travel switch and solenoid connectors.
3. Remove the solenoids and check valves. Leave the vacuum hoses attached.
4. Remove the hood hinge located above the modulator.
5. Remove the screws that secure the modulator and remove it.

#### Installation

1. Install the modulator onto the cowl. Secure with three screws.
2. Install the hood hinge.
3. Install the solenoid and check valves.
4. Connect solenoid and travel switch wiring.
5. Install the two brake lines.

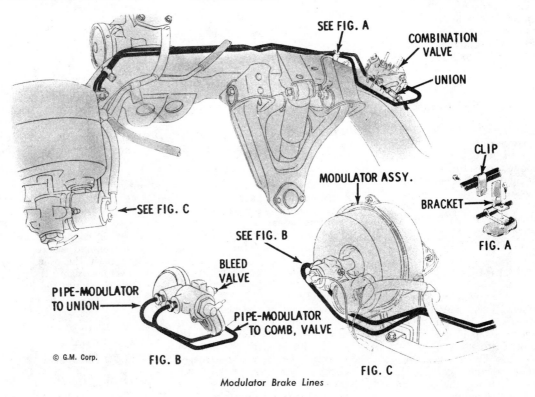

*Modulator Brake Lines*

# General Motors

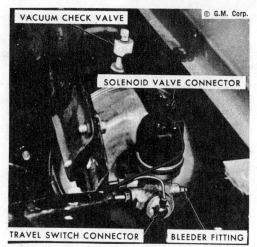

VACUUM CHECK VALVE

© G.M. Corp.

SOLENOID VALVE CONNECTOR

TRAVEL SWITCH CONNECTOR    BLEEDER FITTING

*Modulator Assembly*

6. Bleed brakes thoroughly.
7. Connect battery cable.

## Modulator
### 1974-75 Cadillac

**Removal**

1. Disconnect the negative battery cable.
2. Support the hood and remove the left hand hood hinge.
3. Disconnect the travel switch and the solenoid connectors at the modulator.
4. Remove the vacuum hose at the check valve assembly.
5. Disconnect the two brake lines at the modulator.
6. Remove the modulator retaining screws and remove the modulator.

**Installation**

1. Attach the modulator to the cowl.
2. Connect the solenoid and travel switch connectors.
3. Connect the two brake lines at the modulator assembly.
4. Install the left hand hood hinge.
5. Bleed system.
6. Master cylinder reservoir level should be 1/8" to 3/8" from the top.
7. Connect the negative battery cable.

### 1972-74 Oldsmobile

**Removal**

1. Disconnect battery positive cable.
2. Remove the coolant reservoir.
3. Disconnect solenoid and travel switch connectors.
4. Remove the brake lines from the travel switch and cap the fittings. Remove the vacuum hose at the modulator.

5. Remove the nuts which attach the modulator to the bracket and remove the modulator.

**Installation**

1. Reverse the removal prodecure.
2. Bleed brakes.

## Solenoid
### 1971-75 Cadillac

**Removal**

1. Remove the vacuum hoses.
2. Remove the solenoid connector.
3. Remove the solenoid.

**Installation**

1. Screw the solenoid in place on the modulator.
2. Secure the two vacuum hoses. Install the electrical connector.

## Rear Axle Harness
### 1971-72 Cadillac

**Removal**

1. Raise the rear of the car. Remove the rear hubs.
2. Disconnect the brake line fittings at the wheel cylinders. Remove the brake backing plate securing nuts, and remove the backing plates.
3. Start one backing plate securing nut on one of the studs on either side.
4. Use a slide hammer and appropriate adaptors to remove the spindle.
5. Remove one of the clamps that secures one of the harness connectors and position it on the sensor. Remove the other clamp.
6. Remove the rear axle harness clamp screw, and remove the clamp. Remove the rubber grommet from the axle housing.

7. Remove the body harness from the axle and disconnect the body connectors from the axle harness connectors. Remove the harness from the axle pulling at either end.

**Installation**

1. Locate the harness in the axle.
2. Locate connectors for the axle harness inside the opening in the axle and connect them to the body harness connectors.
3. Push the body and axle connectors into the axle and secure them with the rubber grommet, clamp, and screw.
4. Coat the rear harness connectors with front wheel bearing lubricant and secure the connectors on the sensors with clamps.
5. Drive the spindles back onto the axle with a slide hammer. Install a new spindle gasket on either side.
6. Install the brake backing plates and torque the nuts to 40 foot-pounds.
7. Connect brake line fittings to the wheel cylinders, and tighten to 14 foot-pounds.
8. Install the rear hub and bleed brakes.

### 1973-75 Eldorado

**Removal**

1. Put the car on a hoist. Remove the plastic straps securing the harness to the frame and rear axle.
2. Disconnect the harness connectors.
3. Disconnect the speed sensor connectors from the speed sensors.
4. Remove the harness.

**Installation**

1. Pack the speed sensor connectors with grease. Put the harness into position and install the speed sensor connectors on the speed sensor and secure with clamps.
2. Connect the other harness connectors. Install the plastic straps which secure the harness to the rear axle.

## Body Harness
### 1971-72 Eldorado

**Removal**

1. Disconnect the harness at the

# General Motors

controller. Pull the harness from the firewall.

2. Remove the screw securing the harness assembly at the floor pan. Remove the screw, clamp, and rubber grommet securing the harness to the rear axle.
3. Remove the harness connectors from the rear axle and disconnect them from the axle harness.
4. Cut the plastic straps securing the harness to the brake line, and remove the harness from the frame rail.

## Installation

1. Put the controller connector end of the harness through the firewall and connect it to the controller.
2. Locate the harness along the frame rail and secure it to the brake line with the plastic straps.
3. Connect the body harness to the rear axle and push the connectors into the axle.
4. Install the screw, bracket, and rubber grommet. Install the harness to floor pan attaching screw.

## Controller and Modulator Harness
### 1971-75 Cadillac
#### Removal

1. Disconnect the solenoid and travel switch connectors at the modulator. Disconnect the brown wire at the connector on the left wheelhouse.
2. Remove the upper screw and loosen the lower screw on the grommet retainer on the firewall and remove the split grommet. Push the harness through the cowl.
3. Disconnect the negative battery cable. Open the glove box and remove the two screws securing the top cover to the instrument panel.
4. Remove the four screws which secure the top cover to the instrument panel bezel.
5. Lift the cover slightly and then pull it rearward in order to disengage it from the cowl.
6. Disconnect radio speaker wires. Disconnect twilight sentinel photocell at the left front speaker opening, the clock feed wires

and the lamp assembly by raising the top cover for access. Remove the top cover.

7. Route the harness to the top of the instrument panel area. Disconnect the pink wire that leads to the fuse block.
8. Disconnect the four-way controller connector.
9. Remove the controller and modulator harness.

#### Installation

1. Position the harness on top of the instrument panel and route the pink lead to the controller.
2. Connect the four way controller connector.
3. Connect the single pink wire.
4. Route the harness through the cowl.
5. Connect the solenoid and travel switch connectors at the modulator.
6. Connect the brown wire at the connector on the left wheelhouse.
7. Install the split grommet in the retainer, install the top screw, and tighten the bottom screw.
8. Reinstall the upper instrument panel cover in reverse of steps 4-6 above.

## Buick Max-Trac

### Description

The purpose of the Max-Trac System is to aid the driver in maintaining vehicle directional stability during acceleration. The system accomplishes this by automatically limiting engine power to a value required for maximum acceleration without excessive rear wheel slippage. This system does not prevent brake lock up.

This system consists of a transmission speed sensor, front wheel sensor and speed disc, electronic controller, on-off switch, and electrical harness.

Max-trac begins with a front wheel speed sensor and speed disc which transmits to the controller the speed of the front wheels. There is also a transmission speed sensor which transmits to the controller the speed of the rear wheels. The controller compares the two signals and determines whether the rear wheels are rotating faster than the front (under an accelerating condition). If this is so, it sends a signal to interrupt the ignition circuit, resulting in a power reduction and a corresponding reduction in slippage.

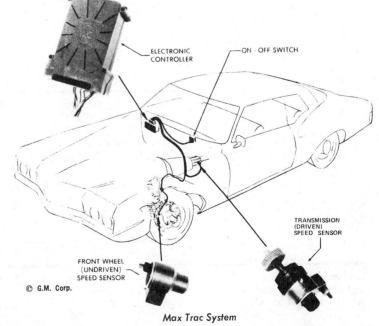

ELECTRONIC CONTROLLER  
ON · OFF SWITCH  
© G.M. Corp.  
FRONT WHEEL (UNDRIVEN) SPEED SENSOR  
TRANSMISSION (DRIVEN) SPEED SENSOR

*Max Trac System*

## Electronic Controller

### Removal

1. Remove the glove box.
2. Remove the controller and mounting bracket attaching

screws from the cowl.
3. Disconnect the wiring harness connectors from the controller pigtails and remove the controller.
4. Remove the controller-to-mounting bracket attaching screws.

# Buick

### DIAGNOSIS CHART

The following chart, showing "Conditions", "Possible Causes", and "Corrections" is offered as a diagnostic tool to aid in effecting rapid repairs in the event of a malfunctioning Max-Trac System. It is recommended that for each symptom, the possible causes be evaluated in the order shown on the attached chart.

| Condition | Possible Cause | Correction |
|---|---|---|
| System inoperative at speeds. | 1. On-off switch set at "Off". | 1. Set switch to "On". |
| | 2. No ground connection to the controller. | 2. Unplug 6 terminal connector at controller. The black wire at the controller connector should be grounded. If not, Connect controller ground wire to ground. |
| | 3. Brake lights dead. | 3. Check fuse and brake lights switch. Replace or repair as necessary. Check brake lights wiring circuit and bulbs. |
| | 4. No signal from transmission speed sensor (faulty harness or an open circuit in the sender). | 4. Unplug 6 terminal connector at controller. Resistance between red and white wires at harness connector should be 1600 to 2400 ohms. If circuit is open, unplug connector at sensor and check resistance across sensor terminals. If open, replace sensor. If 1600 to 2400 ohms, replace the harness. |
| | 5. No signal from front wheel speed sensor (a faulty harness or open circuit in sensor). | 5. Unplug 6 terminal connector at controller. Resistance between light green and white wires in harness connector should be 1250 to 1750 ohms. If circuit is open, unplug connector at sensor and check resistance at sensor terminals. If open, replace sensor. If 1250 to 1750 ohms, replace the harness. |
| | 6. Controller faulty. | 6. Replace the controller. |
| Engine will start but will not run until on-off switch is set at "Off". | 1. No battery (positive) electrical supply to controller. | 1. Unplug 3 terminal connector at controller. With ignition switch "On", battery voltage should be available between the pink wire at the harness connection and ground. If not, repair or replace instrument panel harness. |

## Buick

| Condition | Possible Cause | Correction |
|---|---|---|
| | 2. No connection between controller output and ignition ballast resistor. | 2. Unplug 3 terminal connector at controller. Resistance between pink/black wire at harness connector and positive terminal of coil should be 1.8 ohms. If open, repair or replace harness. |
| | 3. Faulty controller. | 3. Replace the controller. |
| System functions or engine stops during braking. | 1. No B (positive) from brake circuit. | 1. Unplug 3 terminal connector at controller with brakes applied. Battery voltage should be available between white wire and ground. If not, repair or replace instrument panel harness. |
| | 2. Brake lights dead. | 2. Repair car harness. |
| | 3. No connection from controller to brake | 3. Unplug 3 terminal connector at controller. With the brakes applied, battery voltage should be available between white wire and ground. If not, repair or replace the harness. |
| | 4. Malfunctioned controller. | 4. Replace the controller. |
| System functions properly at high speeds but is inoperative at lower vehicle speeds. | 1. Low signal from the front wheel speed sensor (excessive gap between sensor and speed disc). | 1. Check the adjust gap between sensor and speed disc at the sensor mounting. Felt spacer should touch the speed disc. If felt spacer is missing, set gap between end of sensor and speed disc at .050 inches. |
| | 2. Malfunctioned controller. | 2. Replace the controller. |
| System operates when not necessary. | 1. Incorrect speedo gear. | 1. Replace with correct gear. |
| Engine backfires | 1. A.I.R. bypass system not connected. | 1. Connect harness to A.I.R. bypass solenoid. |
| | 2. A.I.R. bypass solenoid not grounded. | 2. Attach solenoid to A.I.R. pump with ground screw. |
| | 3. Front wheel sensor improperly positioned. | 3. Adjust gap between sensor tip and speed disc to .050″. |
| System Functions at Low Speeds Causing Engine Hesitation | 1. Low signal from the front wheel speed sensor (excessive gap between sensor and speed disc). | 1. Check and adjust gap between sensor and speed disc at the sensor mounting. Felt spacer should touch the speed disc. If felt spacer is missing, set gap between end of sensor and speed disc at .050″. |

# General Motors

### Troubleshooting

1. System inoperative at all speeds.
   A. On-off switch set at OFF.
   B. No ground connection to the controller.
   C. Brake lights dead.
   D. No signal from transmission speed sensor (faulty harness or an open circuit in the sender).
   E. No signal from front wheel speed sensor (a faulty harness or open circuit in sensor).
   F. Controller faulty.

2. Engine will start but will not run until on-off switch is set at OFF.
   A. No battery (positive) electrical supply to controller.
   B. No connection between controller output and ignition ballast resistor.
   C. Faulty controller.

3. System functions or engine stops during braking.
   A. No B (positive) from brake circuit.
   B. Brake lights dead.

   C. No connection from controller to brake switch.
   D. Faulty controller.

4. System functions properly at high speeds but is inoperative at lower vehicle speeds.
   A. Low signal from the front wheel speed sensor (excessive gap between sensor and speed disc).
   B. Faulty controller.

5. System functions at low speeds causing engine hesitation.
   A. Low signal from the front wheel speed sensor (excessive gap between sensor and speed disc).

6. System operates when not necessary.
   A. Wrong speedo gear.

7. Engine backfires.
   A. A.I.R. bypass system not connected.
   B. A.I.R. bypass solenoid not grounded.
   C. Front wheel sensor improperly positioned.

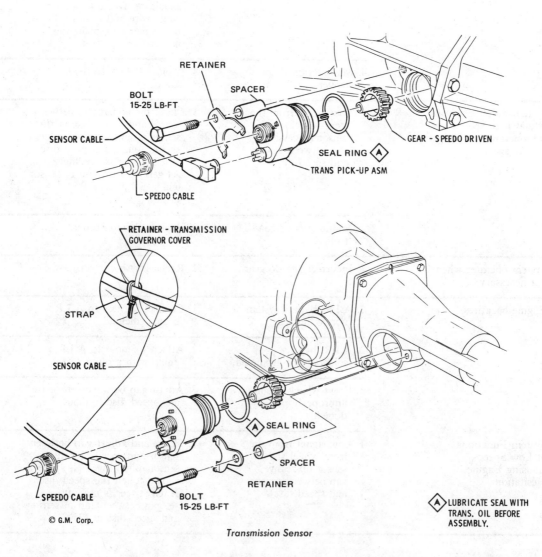

© G.M. Corp.

*Transmission Sensor*

# General Motors

## Installation

1. Assemble the controller and mounting bracket, making sure the controller ground wire is positioned between the controller and bracket and secured with the correct attaching screw and washer.
2. Attach the controller wire connectors to the harness connectors.
3. Attach the controller and mounting bracket assembly to the cowl.
4. Install the glove box.

## On-Off Switch

### Removal

1. Remove the instrument panel cover.
2. Disconnect the on-off switch wiring connector.
3. Remove the on-off switch escutcheon and the on-off switch by removing the two attaching screws.

### Installation

1. Install the on-off switch and escutcheon in the instrument panel with the two attaching screws.

2. Connect the switch wiring connector to the harness connector.
3. Install the instrument panel cover.

## Transmission Speed Sensor

### Removal

1. Disconnect the wire connector from the speed sensor terminal.
2. Disconnect the speedometer cable from the speed sensor.
3. Remove the speed sensor retainer bolt, retainer, and shim sleeve.
4. Pull the speed sensor and driven gear out of the transmission and have a container ready to receive the transmission oil that will drain out.

### Installation

1. Assemble the speedometer drive gear onto the speed sensor and install it, with a new O-ring seal, into the transmission.
2. Install the speed sensor retainer, shim sleeve, and bolt.
3. Connect the speedometer cable to the speed sensor.

4. Attach the harness connector to the speed sensor terminal.
5. Check the transmission fluid level and add as necessary.

## Front Wheel Sensor

### Removal

1. Remove the cable attaching screw from the rotor shield.
2. Disconnect the wire connector from the front wheel sensor.
3. Remove the wheel sensor retaining bolt and sensor.

### Installation

1. Install the wheel speed sensor with the felt tip of the sensor against the speed disc attached to the rotor. If the original wheel speed sensor is reinstalled, an air gap of 0.050 in. must exist between the tip of the sensor and the speed disc.
2. Connect the wire connector to the wheel speed sensor terminal.
3. Attach the cable retaining clamp to the rotor shield.

If any of the major components of this system are found to be defective through diagnosis and checking, they are to be replaced, as they are not repairable.

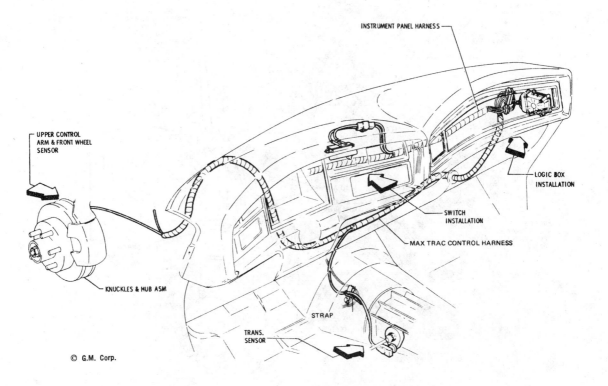

© G.M. Corp.

*Max Trac Component Locations*

# General Motors

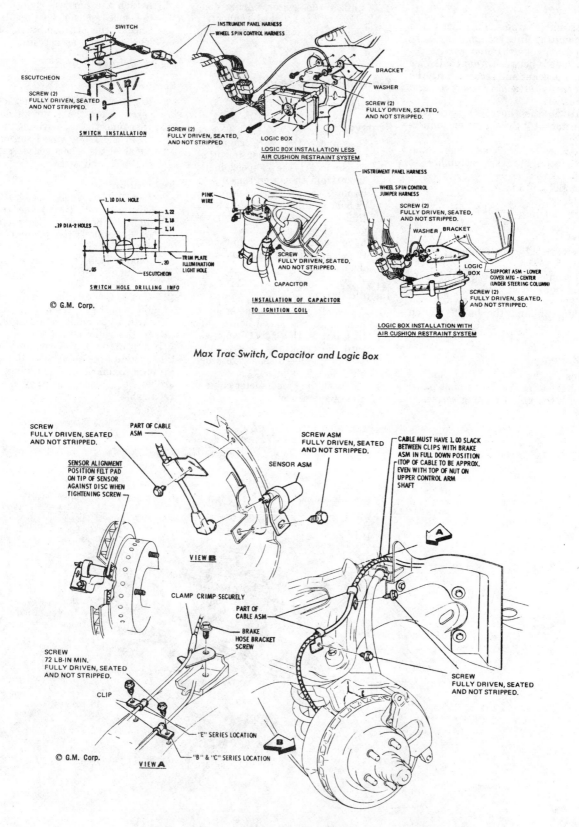

*Max Trac Switch, Capacitor and Logic Box*

*Upper Control Arm and Front Wheel Sensor*

## Chrysler Corporation

### Imperial

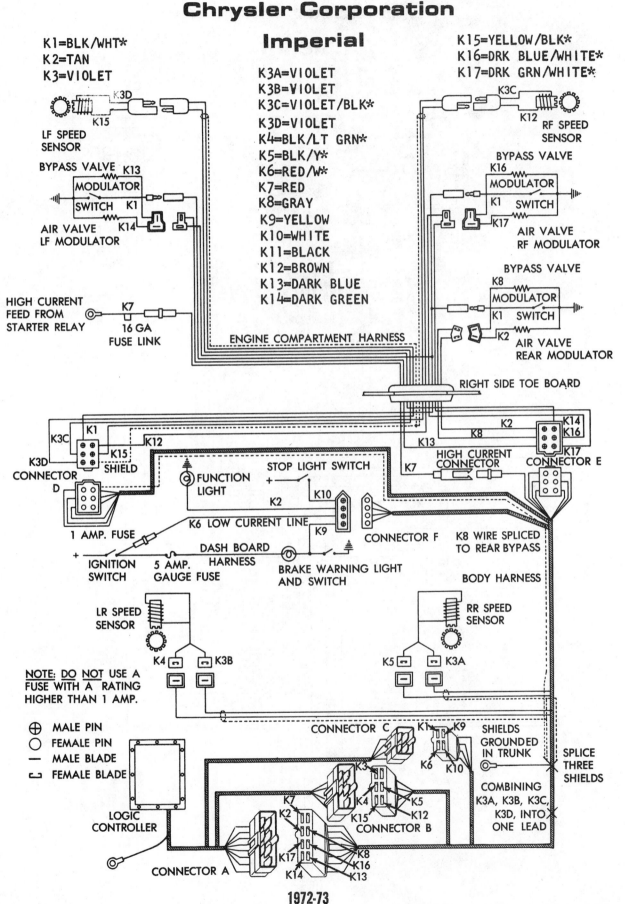

K1=BLK/WHT*
K2=TAN
K3=VIOLET

K3A=VIOLET
K3B=VIOLET
K3C=VIOLET/BLK*
K3D=VIOLET
K4=BLK/LT GRN*
K5=BLK/Y*
K6=RED/W*
K7=RED
K8=GRAY
K9=YELLOW
K10=WHITE
K11=BLACK
K12=BROWN
K13=DARK BLUE
K14=DARK GREEN

K15=YELLOW/BLK*
K16=DRK BLUE/WHITE*
K17=DRK GRN/WHITE*

LF SPEED
SENSOR

RF SPEED
SENSOR

BYPASS VALVE K13
MODULATOR
SWITCH K1
AIR VALVE K14
LF MODULATOR

BYPASS VALVE
K16
MODULATOR
K1 SWITCH
K17
AIR VALVE
RF MODULATOR

BYPASS VALVE
K8
MODULATOR
K1 SWITCH
K2
AIR VALVE
REAR MODULATOR

HIGH CURRENT
FEED FROM
STARTER RELAY
K7
16 GA
FUSE LINK

ENGINE COMPARTMENT HARNESS

RIGHT SIDE TOE BOARD

K3C K1
K3D K15
CONNECTOR SHIELD
D
K12
CONNECTOR
D

1 AMP. FUSE

FUNCTION
LIGHT

STOP LIGHT SWITCH

K2
K6 LOW CURRENT LINE
K9
K10

HIGH CURRENT
CONNECTOR
K7

K14
K16
K17
CONNECTOR E

CONNECTOR F

K8 WIRE SPLICED
TO REAR BYPASS

+
IGNITION
SWITCH
5 AMP.
GAUGE FUSE
DASH BOARD
HARNESS
BRAKE WARNING LIGHT
AND SWITCH

BODY HARNESS

LR SPEED
SENSOR

RR SPEED
SENSOR

NOTE: DO NOT USE A
FUSE WITH A RATING
HIGHER THAN 1 AMP.

K4 K3B

K5 K3A

⊕ MALE PIN
◯ FEMALE PIN
— MALE BLADE
⊏ FEMALE BLADE

LOGIC
CONTROLLER

CONNECTOR C

K1 K9

K6 K10

SHIELDS
GROUNDED
IN TRUNK

SPLICE
THREE
SHIELDS

K3

K7
K2
K4
K15
K5
K12
CONNECTOR B

COMBINING
K3A, K3B, K3C,
K3D, INTO
ONE LEAD

CONNECTOR A
K17
K14
K8
K16
K13

**1972-73**

## Ford Motor Company

## Lincoln

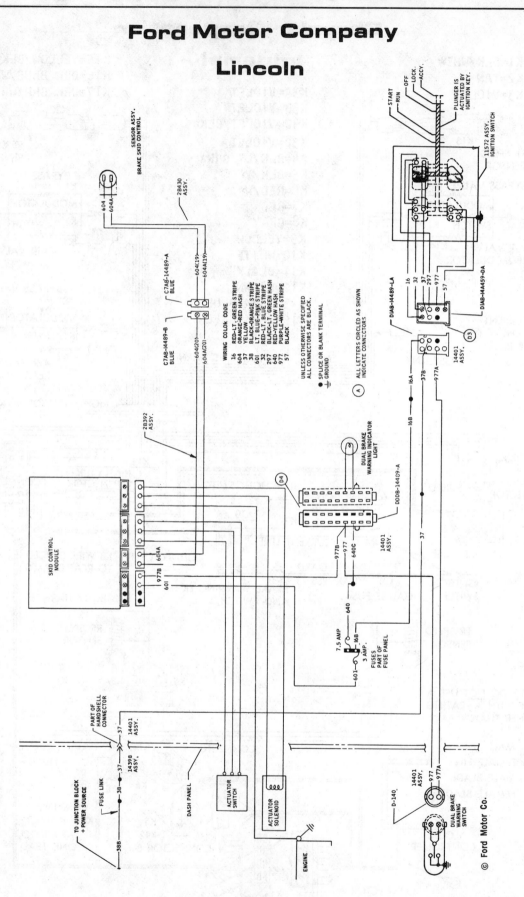

1971

## Lincoln

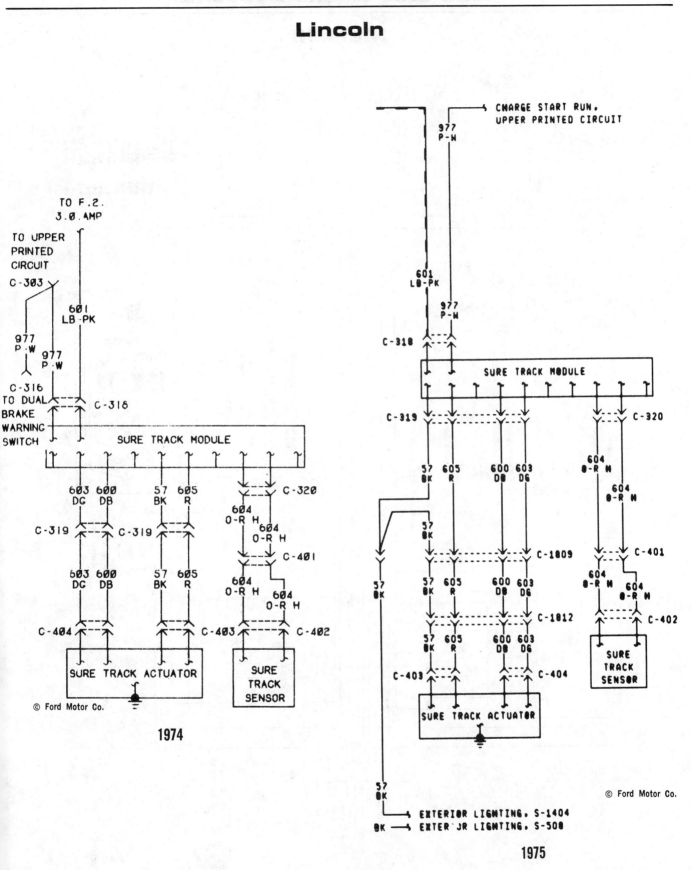

TO F.2.
3.0.AMP

TO UPPER
PRINTED
CIRCUIT

C-303

601
LB·PK

977
P·W

977
P·W

C-316
TO DUAL
BRAKE
WARNING
SWITCH

C-318

SURE TRACK MODULE

603 600        57  605
DG  DB        BK   R

C-319        C-319

604
O-R H
604
O-R H

C-320

C-401

603 600        57  605
DG  DB        BK   R

604
O-R H
604
O-R H

C-404        C-403    C-402

SURE TRACK ACTUATOR

SURE
TRACK
SENSOR

© Ford Motor Co.

1974

CHARGE START RUN.
UPPER PRINTED CIRCUIT

977
P·W

601
LB·PK

977
P·W

C-318

SURE TRACK MODULE

C-319        C-320

57  605        600 603        604
BK   R        DB  DG        O-R H

604
O-R H

57
BK

C-1809    C-401

57  605        600 603        604
BK   R        DB  DG        O-R H

604
O-R H

C-1812    C-402

57
BK

57  605        600 603
BK   R        DB  DG

C-403        C-404

SURE
TRACK
SENSOR

SURE TRACK ACTUATOR

57
BK

57
BK    EXTERIOR LIGHTING. S-1404

BK    EXTERJR LIGHTING. S-508

© Ford Motor Co.

1975

## Mark III

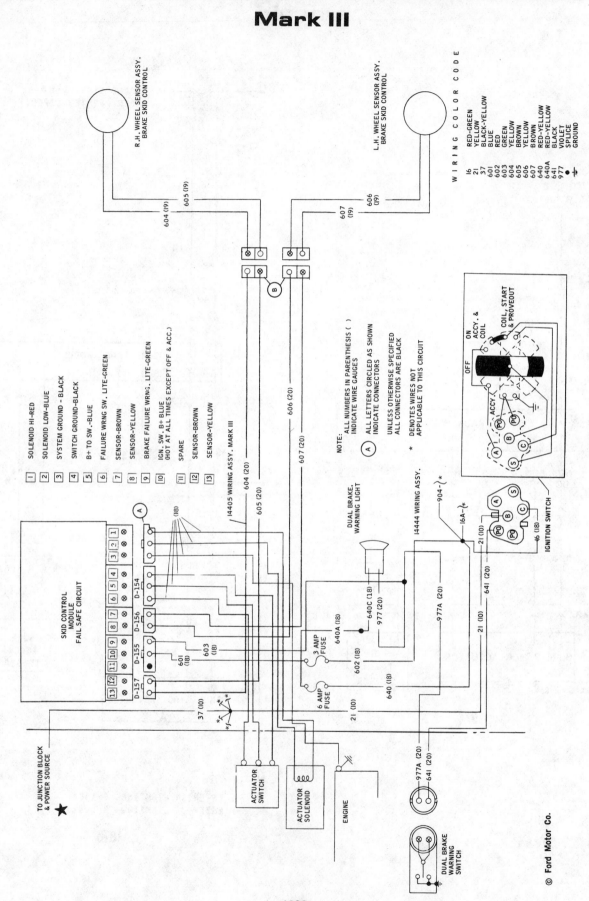

© Ford Motor Co.

1969

## Mark III

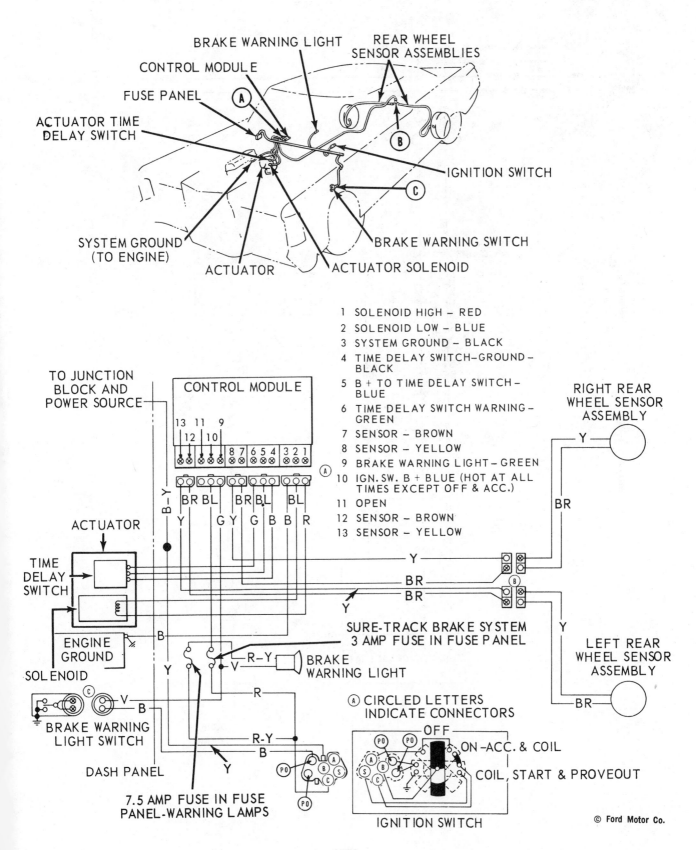

1 SOLENOID HIGH – RED
2 SOLENOID LOW – BLUE
3 SYSTEM GROUND – BLACK
4 TIME DELAY SWITCH–GROUND– BLACK
5 B + TO TIME DELAY SWITCH– BLUE
6 TIME DELAY SWITCH WARNING– GREEN
7 SENSOR – BROWN
8 SENSOR – YELLOW
9 BRAKE WARNING LIGHT– GREEN
10 IGN.SW. B + BLUE (HOT AT ALL TIMES EXCEPT OFF & ACC.)
11 OPEN
12 SENSOR – BROWN
13 SENSOR – YELLOW

**1970**

© Ford Motor Co.

## Mark IV

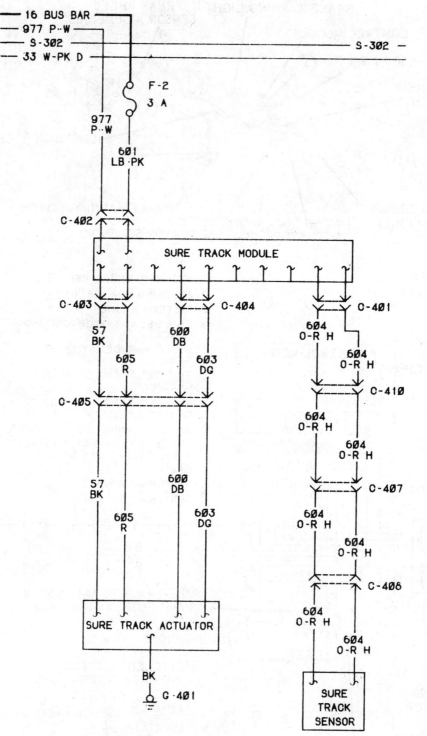

© Ford Motor Co.

1974

## Mark IV

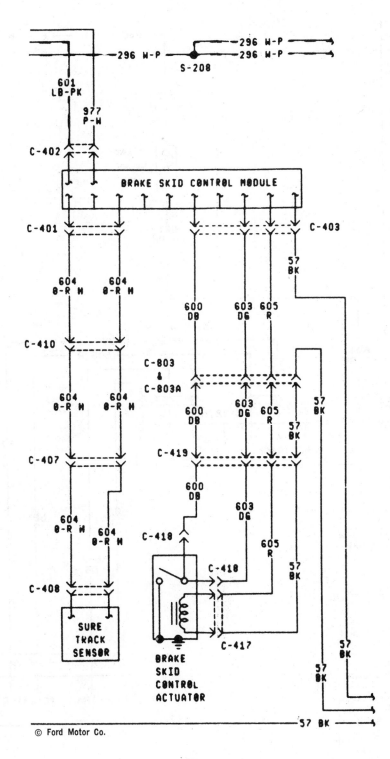

© Ford Motor Co.

1975

## Mercury

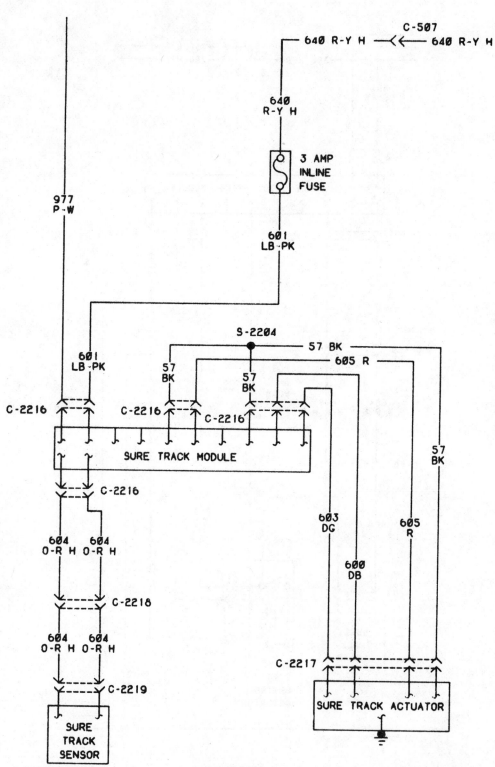

© Ford Motor Co.

1974

## Thunderbird

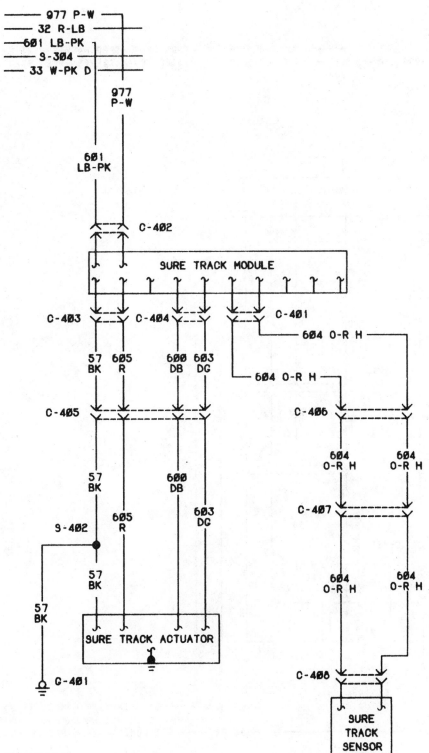

© Ford Motor Co.

1974

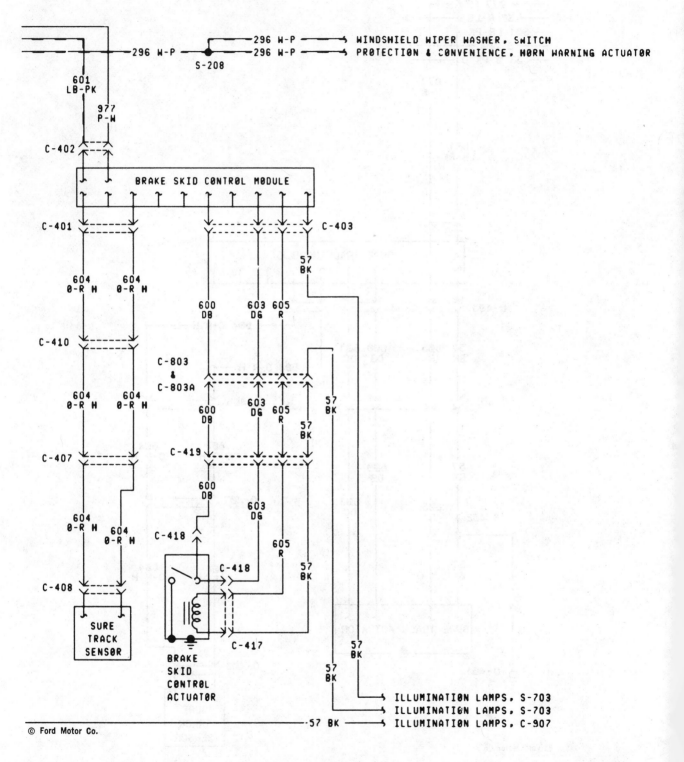

© Ford Motor Co.

1975

# General Motors
## Buick

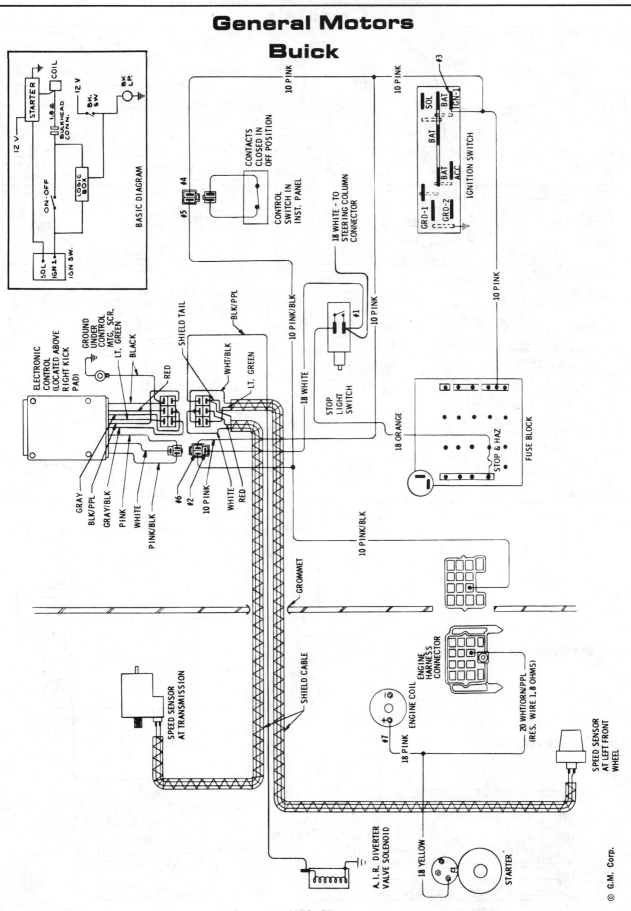

**BASIC DIAGRAM**

CONTACTS CLOSED IN OFF POSITION

CONTROL SWITCH IN INST. PANEL

IGNITION SWITCH

10 PINK

18 WHITE - TO STEERING COLUMN CONNECTOR

ELECTRONIC CONTROL (LOCATED ABOVE RIGHT KICK PAD)

GROUND UNDER CONTROL MTG. SCR. LT. GREEN

BLACK

RED

SHIELD TAIL

WHT/BLK

LT. GREEN

BLK/PPL

10 PINK/BLK

18 WHITE

STOP LIGHT SWITCH

18 ORANGE

STOP & HAZ

FUSE BLOCK

GRAY
BLK/PPL
GRAY/BLK
PINK
WHITE
PINK/BLK
#6
#2
10 PINK
WHITE
RED

10 PINK/BLK

GROMMET

SHIELD CABLE

SPEED SENSOR AT TRANSMISSION

ENGINE COIL

ENGINE HARNESS CONNECTOR

20 WHT/ORN/PPL (RES. WIRE 1.8 OHMS)

#7

18 PINK

SPEED SENSOR AT LEFT FRONT WHEEL

A.I.R. DIVERTER VALVE SOLENOID

18 YELLOW

STARTER

© G.M. Corp.

**1973-75**

# Non Skid Brake Systems
## Cadillac

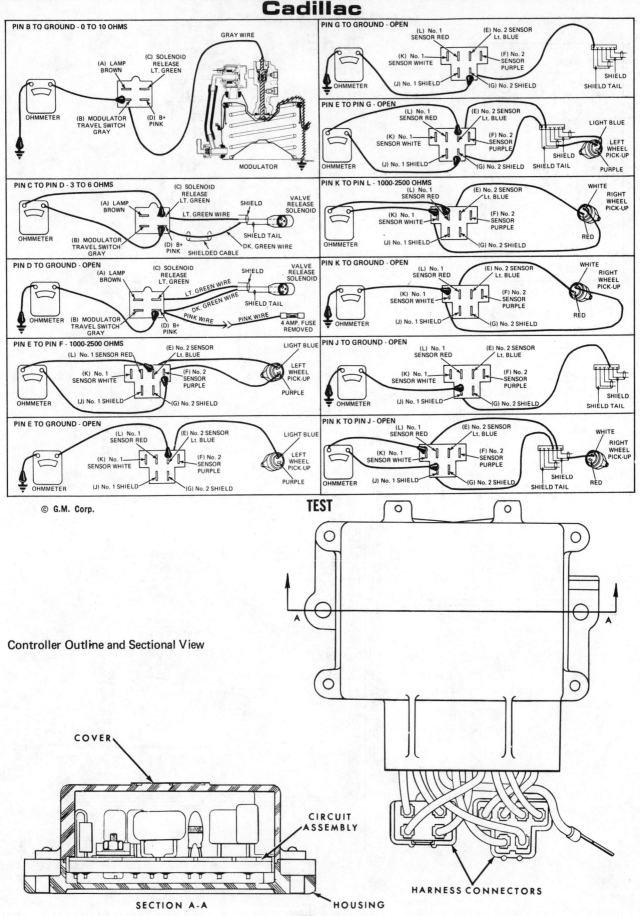

**PIN B TO GROUND - 0 TO 10 OHMS**

GRAY WIRE

(A) LAMP BROWN
(C) SOLENOID RELEASE LT. GREEN
(B) MODULATOR TRAVEL SWITCH GRAY
(D) B+ PINK
OHMMETER
MODULATOR

**PIN G TO GROUND - OPEN**

(L) No. 1 SENSOR RED
(E) No. 2 SENSOR Lt. Blue
(K) No. 1 SENSOR WHITE
(F) No. 2 SENSOR PURPLE
(J) No. 1 SHIELD
(G) No. 2 SHIELD
OHMMETER
SHIELD
SHIELD TAIL

**PIN E TO PIN G - OPEN**

(L) No. 1 SENSOR RED
(E) No. 2 SENSOR Lt. Blue
(K) No. 1 SENSOR WHITE
(F) No. 2 SENSOR PURPLE
(J) No. 1 SHIELD
(G) No. 2 SHIELD
OHMMETER
SHIELD
SHIELD TAIL
LIGHT BLUE
LEFT WHEEL PICK-UP
PURPLE

**PIN C TO PIN D - 3 TO 6 OHMS**

(C) SOLENOID RELEASE LT. GREEN
(A) LAMP BROWN
SHIELD
VALVE RELEASE SOLENOID
LT. GREEN WIRE
(B) MODULATOR TRAVEL SWITCH GRAY
(D) B+ PINK
SHIELDED CABLE
SHIELD TAIL
DK. GREEN WIRE
OHMMETER

**PIN K TO PIN L - 1000-2500 OHMS**

(L) No. 1 SENSOR RED
(E) No. 2 SENSOR Lt. Blue
(K) No. 1 SENSOR WHITE
(F) No. 2 SENSOR PURPLE
(J) No. 1 SHIELD
(G) No. 2 SHIELD
OHMMETER
WHITE
RIGHT WHEEL PICK-UP
RED

**PIN D TO GROUND - OPEN**

(A) LAMP BROWN
(C) SOLENOID RELEASE LT. GREEN
VALVE RELEASE SOLENOID
SHIELD
LT. GREEN WIRE
DK. GREEN WIRE
SHIELD TAIL
(B) MODULATOR TRAVEL SWITCH GRAY
(D) B+ PINK
PINK WIRE
PINK WIRE
4 AMP. FUSE REMOVED
OHMMETER

**PIN K TO GROUND - OPEN**

(L) No. 1 SENSOR RED
(E) No. 2 SENSOR Lt. Blue
(K) No. 1 SENSOR WHITE
(F) No. 2 SENSOR PURPLE
(J) No. 1 SHIELD
(G) No. 2 SHIELD
OHMMETER
WHITE
RIGHT WHEEL PICK-UP
RED

**PIN E TO PIN F - 1000-2500 OHMS**

(L) No. 1 SENSOR RED
(E) No. 2 SENSOR Lt. BLUE
(K) No. 1 SENSOR WHITE
(F) No. 2 SENSOR PURPLE
(J) No. 1 SHIELD
(G) No. 2 SHIELD
OHMMETER
LIGHT BLUE
LEFT WHEEL PICK-UP
PURPLE

**PIN J TO GROUND - OPEN**

(L) No. 1 SENSOR RED
(E) No. 2 SENSOR Lt. Blue
(K) No. 1 SENSOR WHITE
(F) No. 2 SENSOR PURPLE
(J) No. 1 SHIELD
(G) No. 2 SHIELD
OHMMETER
SHIELD
SHIELD TAIL

**PIN E TO GROUND - OPEN**

(L) No. 1 SENSOR RED
(E) No. 2 SENSOR Lt. Blue
(K) No. 1 SENSOR WHITE
(F) No. 2 SENSOR PURPLE
(J) No. 1 SHIELD
(G) No. 2 SHIELD
OHMMETER
LIGHT BLUE
LEFT WHEEL PICK-UP
PURPLE

**PIN K TO PIN J - OPEN**

(L) No. 1 SENSOR RED
(E) No. 2 SENSOR Lt. Blue
(K) No. 1 SENSOR WHITE
(F) No. 2 SENSOR PURPLE
(J) No. 1 SHIELD
(G) No. 2 SHIELD
OHMMETER
WHITE
RIGHT WHEEL PICK-UP
SHIELD
SHIELD TAIL
RED

**TEST**

Controller Outline and Sectional View

A — A

COVER
CIRCUIT ASSEMBLY
HARNESS CONNECTORS
SECTION A-A
HOUSING

**1971**

## Cadillac

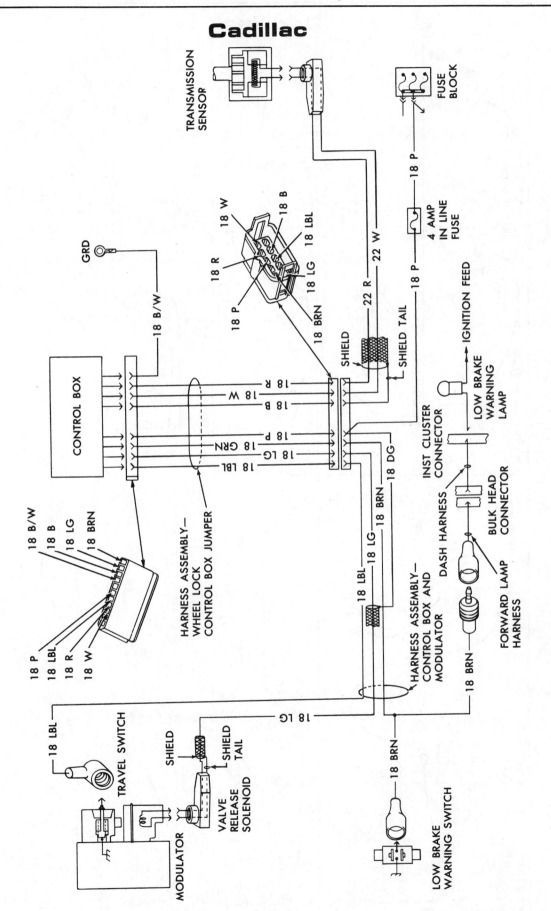

## Cadillac

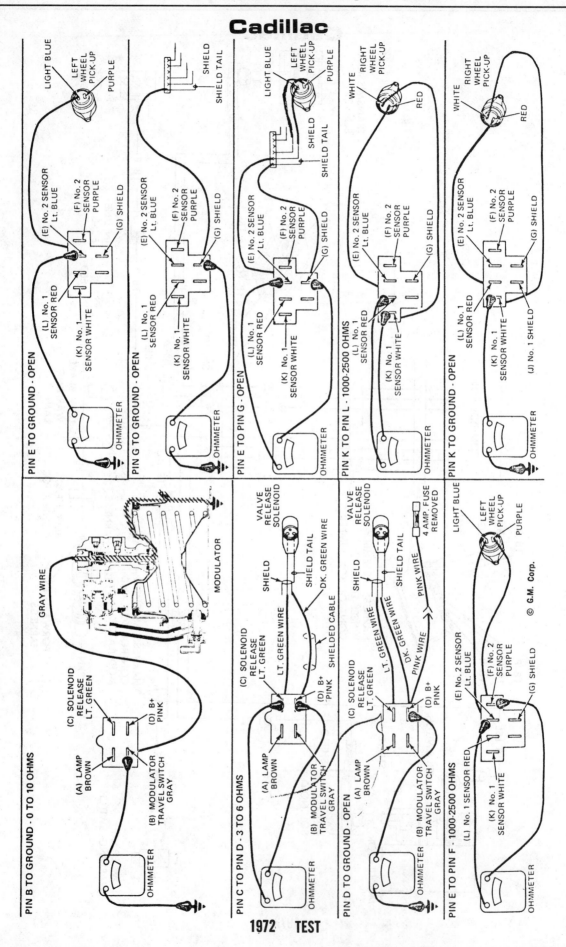

1972 TEST

## Cadillac

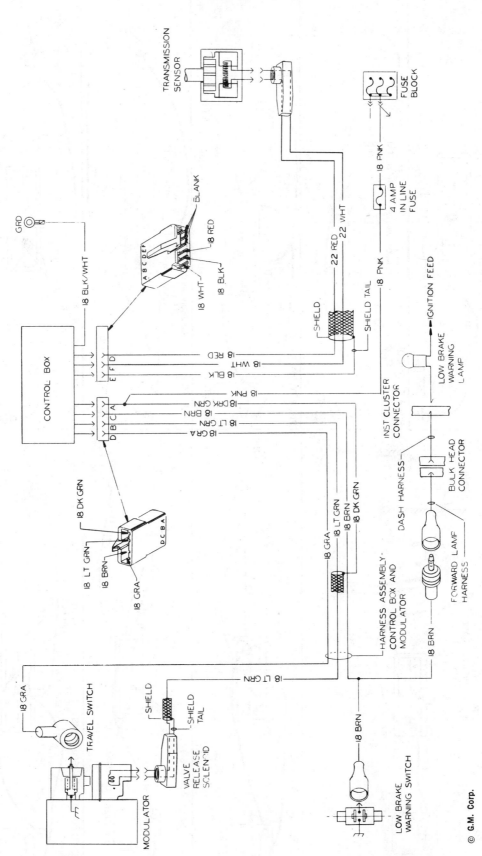

1973

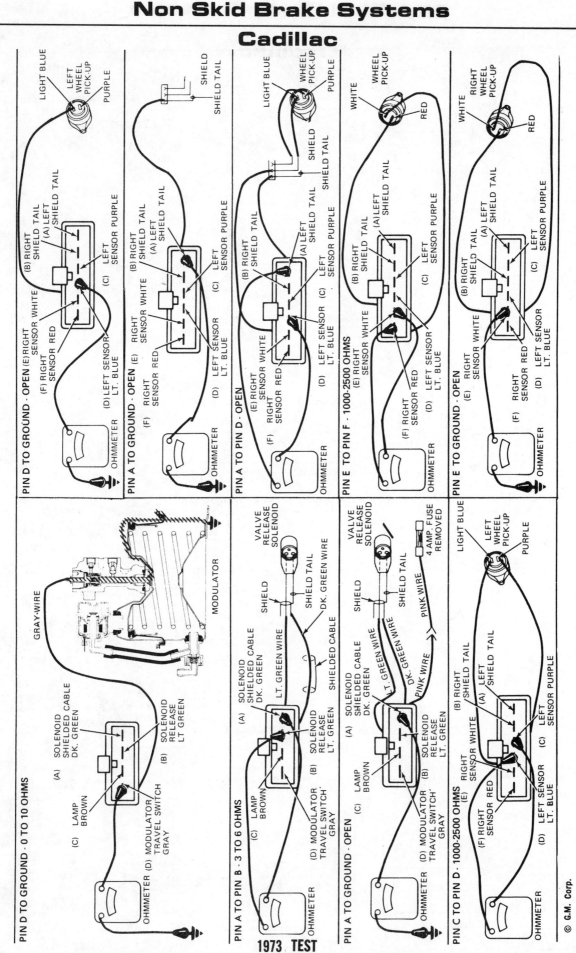

PIN D TO GROUND - OPEN

PIN A TO GROUND - OPEN

PIN A TO PIN D - OPEN

PIN E TO PIN F - 1000-2500 OHMS

PIN E TO GROUND

PIN D TO GROUND - 0 TO 10 OHMS

PIN A TO PIN B - 3 TO 6 OHMS

PIN A TO GROUND - OPEN

PIN C TO PIN D - 1000-2500 OHMS

**1973 TEST**

© G.M. Corp.

## Cadillac Eldorado

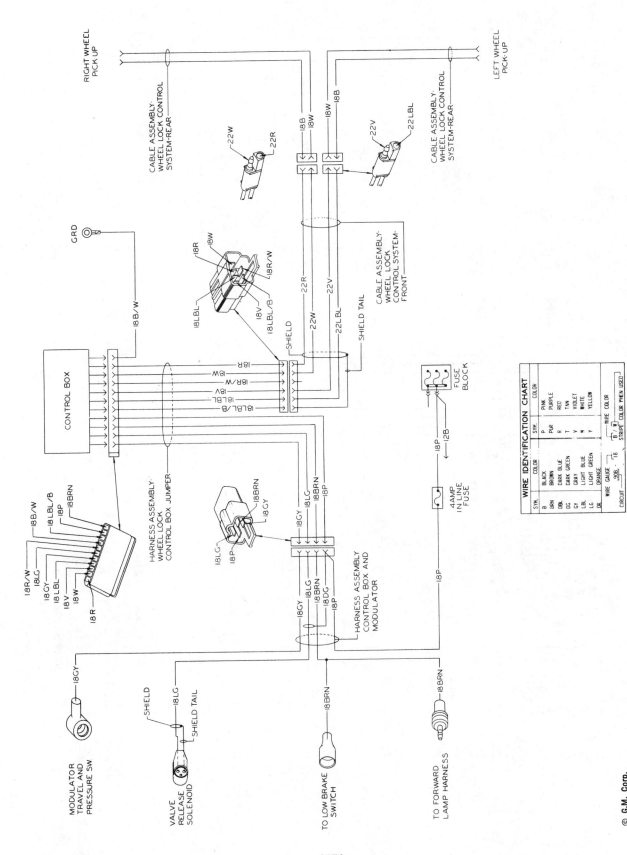

**1971**

## Cadillac Eldorado

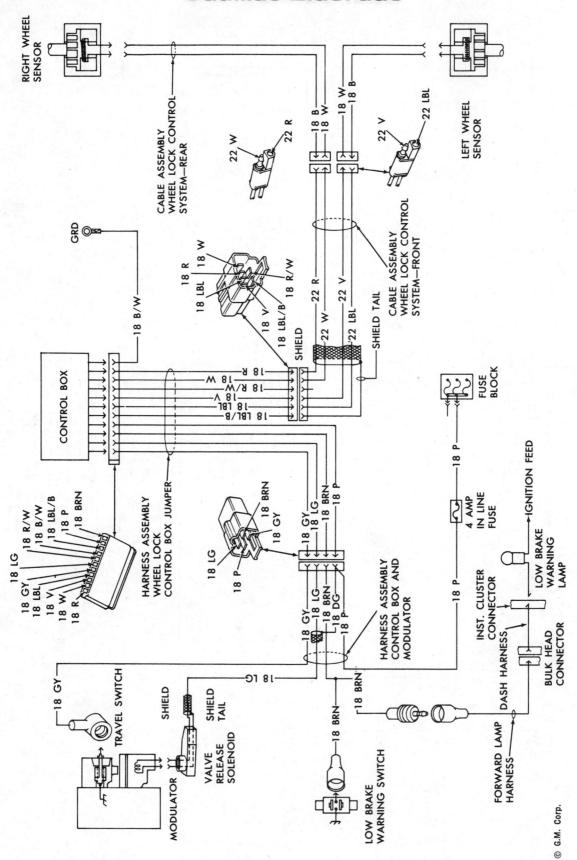

1972

© G.M. Corp.

## Cadillac Eldorado

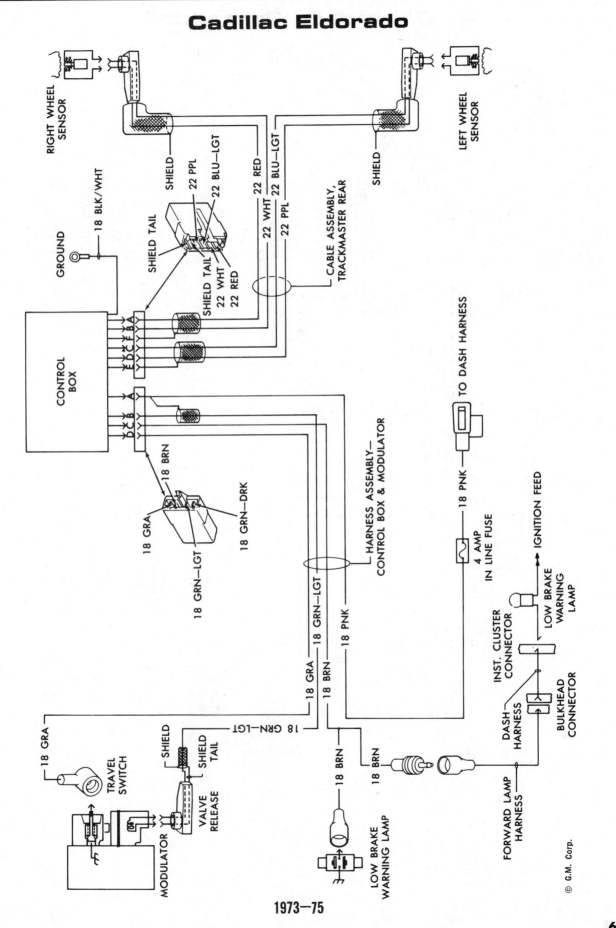

**1973-75**

© G.M. Corp.

## Oldsmobile Toronado

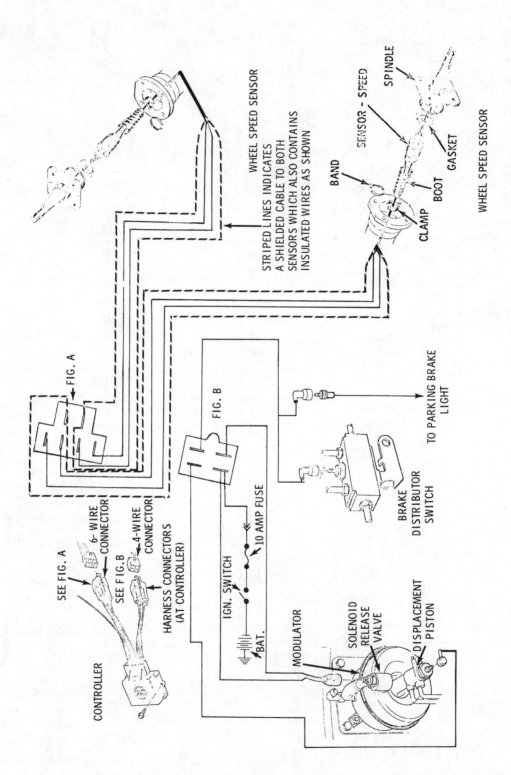

WHEEL SPEED SENSOR

SPINDLE

SENSOR - SPEED

GASKET

BOOT

CLAMP

BAND

WHEEL SPEED SENSOR

STRIPED LINES INDICATES
A SHIELDED CABLE TO BOTH
SENSORS WHICH ALSO CONTAINS
INSULATED WIRES AS SHOWN

FIG. A

FIG. B

TO PARKING BRAKE
LIGHT

BRAKE
DISTRIBUTOR
SWITCH

SEE FIG. A

6- WIRE
CONNECTOR

SEE FIG. B

4-WIRE
CONNECTOR

HARNESS CONNECTORS
(AT CONTROLLER)

IGN. SWITCH

10 AMP FUSE

BAT.

MODULATOR

SOLENOID
RELEASE
VALVE

DISPLACEMENT
PISTON

CONTROLLER

© G.M. Corp.

1971

## Oldsmobile Toronado

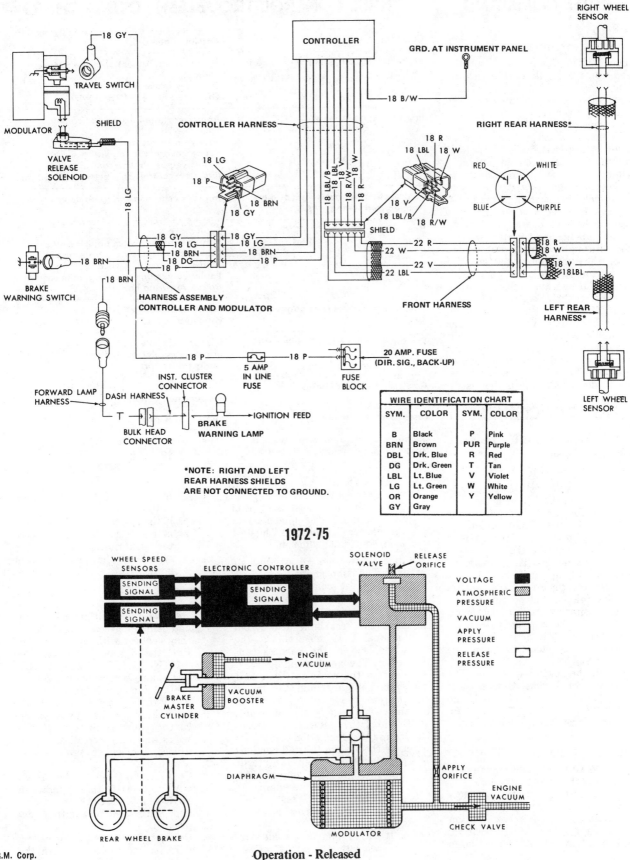

### 1972-75

WIRE IDENTIFICATION CHART

| SYM. | COLOR | SYM. | COLOR |
|------|-------|------|-------|
| B | Black | P | Pink |
| BRN | Brown | PUR | Purple |
| DBL | Drk. Blue | R | Red |
| DG | Drk. Green | T | Tan |
| LBL | Lt. Blue | V | Violet |
| LG | Lt. Green | W | White |
| OR | Orange | Y | Yellow |
| GY | Gray | | |

*NOTE: RIGHT AND LEFT
REAR HARNESS SHIELDS
ARE NOT CONNECTED TO GROUND.

VOLTAGE
ATMOSPHERIC
PRESSURE
VACUUM
APPLY
PRESSURE
RELEASE
PRESSURE

© G.M. Corp.

**Operation - Released**

## American Motors

## CRUISE COMMAND

### 1968-75
### General Description

The Cruise Command Automatic speed control regulates the throttle to maintain any selected vehicle speed between 30 and 85 mph. The speed of the vehicle is interpreted by a speedometer cable driven flyweight which enables the regulator to engage the low speed switch at 30 mph and produce, through solenoid action, a vacuum that is proportional to changes in vehicle speed. The vacuum controls the position of the throttle through a servo consisting of a neoprene bellows operating through a chain linkage. The system is controlled through a slide switch on the flat of the direction signal lever, a push button switch in the end, and a brake pedal operated release switch. The slide switch takes care of "ON" and "OFF" functions, as well as resuming operation after braking has activated the release switch, when it is moved to "RES" position. The push button in the end of the lever causes the system to hold the speed the vehicle is doing when it is depressed.

## TEST PROCEDURES

### Control Switch and Harness Test Procedures
### 1968

Use a 12 volt test lamp for the performance of the following tests.
1. Turn the ignition switch to the accessory position. Connect the test lamp between terminals 2 (brown with a tracer) and 3 (white) on the harness connector. The lamp should light.
2. Push the control all the way in. The light should go out. If not, the switch requires replacement.
3. Connect the test lamp between terminals 2 and 1. The lamp should stay out. Otherwise, the switch is bad.
4. Push the control in slowly. The light should come on when it is first depressed, and should go out when it is fully depressed. Otherwise, the switch is faulty.

### 1969

Use a 12 volt test lamp for the performance of the following tests.
1. Disconnect the multiple connector where it connects with the regulator. Turn the ignition switch to the "ACC." position. Ground one lead of the test lamp

## CRUISE CONTROL TROUBLESHOOTING CHART

| Condition | Possible Cause |
|---|---|
| Brake application does not disengage unit | Improper adjustment of brake release switch<br>Defective brake release switch<br>Grounded Black W/Tracer wire |
| Imprecise speed control | Improper chain linkage adjustment<br>Faulty servo<br>Faulty servo vacuum hose<br>Faulty governor in regulator<br>Defective push button control switch (if system controls only between 60-70 mph) |
| Control effective, but 3 mph or more from desired setting | Improve centering spring adjustment |
| Unit will not engage | Faulty fuse<br>Improper brake switch adjustment<br>Broken drive cable from transmission<br>Inoperative control switch<br>Faulty valve body and magnet in regulator<br>Defective wiring harness |
| Brake release alone re-engages unit | Faulty control switch<br>Faulty valve body and magnet in regulator |
| Throttle does not return to idle position | Improper throttle chain linkage adjustment<br>Improper accelerator linkage adjustment<br>Faulty return spring |
| Accelerator pedal pulsates | Speedometer or drive cable is defective or requires lubrication |
| Fuses blow repeatedly | Ground in wiring |
| Continues acceleration after switch is turned on or pushbutton is depressed | Defective control switch<br>Defective regulator |

to the case of the regulator.
2. Touch the other test lamp lead to terminal 1- the blue lead at the harness connector. The test lamp should not come on.
3. Depress the control switch half way. The lamp should light.
4. Depress the control switch all the way. The lamp should go out.
5. Move the test lamp lead from terminal 1 to terminal 2—the white lead at the harness connector. The lamp should light.
6. Depress the control switch half way. The light should stay on.
7. Depress the control switch all the way. The light should go out.
8. Evaluate the test results according to the information below:
   a. If the system fails all portions of both tests: Repeat all tests, but with the test lamp grounded to a part of the engine. If the system now tests good, ground for the case is defective.
   b. If the system fails some portions, but not all, of either

test: Replace the control switch.
   c. If the system fails all portions of one test: Test the harness for continuity, replace the switch if the harness tests good.

### 1970-74

1. Remove the multiple connector and single green wire where they connect with the regulator. Put the ignition key in the "ACC." position. Using a 12V test lamp, secure one side to a ground known to be good.
2. Turn the system off and check to make sure that there is no current flow from any of the wires under this condition. Otherwise, the switch requires replacement.
3. Connect the lamp to the brown wire, and verify that it lights in "ON" and "RESUME" positions, and with the pushbutton depressed.
4. Connect the lamp to the yellow wire. It should be out with the

# American Motors

switch in "ON" position, but should light in "RESUME" position, and with the pushbutton depressed.

5. Connect the lamp to the green wire. It should light in either switch position, but go out with the pushbutton depressed.

6. Repair or replace any defective wiring in the regulator to control switch harness as in steps 3 and 5.

7. Separate the regulator and control switch harnesses at the steering column, near the ignition switch. Connect the 12V test lamp between red and brown wires. The light should light in "ON" and "RESUME" positions, and be out in the "OFF" position.

8. Connect the test lamp between the red and yellow wires. The light should light only in the "RES" position. If the slide switch fails any of the tests in steps 7 and 8, replace it.

9. Connect the test lamp between the brown and green wires. It should light with the pushbutton in either normal or depressed position.

10. Connect the lamp between the brown and yellow wires. The lamp should be out in the normal position, but light in the depressed position. Replace the pushbutton switch if it fails any of the tests.

## Control Switch Continuity Test 1975

*NOTE: Refer to the slide switch continuity test chart.*

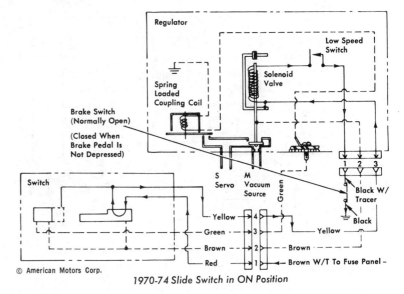

*1970-74 Slide Switch in ON Position*

## Electrical Tests 1975

1. Disconnect both the single and triple connectors at the regulator.

2. Turn the ignition switch to the accessory position.

3. Move the slide switch to the on position.

4. Use a test lamp and ground one test lamp lead and touch the other to the brown wire at the connector. The test lamp should light. If the test lamp does not light, check the fuse automatic speed control relay, engagement switch, and the connection at the power source. Now touch the test lamp wire to the dark green wire at the connector. The test lamp should light, if it does not,

check the engagement switch and connections at the power source, automatic speed control relay and the brake light switch.

5. Push the SET SPEED button all the way in and hold. Ground the one test lamp lead and touch the other lead to each wire connector. The test lamp should light on the brown and yellow wires and should not light on the dark green and light green wire.

6. Release the SET SPEED switch button.

7. Move the slide switch to the RES position and hold it there. Ground one test lamp lead and touch the other lead to each wire in the connector. The test bulb should light on all wires except the light green wire.

*NOTE: If steps one through seven check out then make an independent check of the engagement switch.*

## Engagement Switch Test

1. Disconnect the switch from the wiring harness at the multiple connector in the passenger compartment.

2. Attach a jumper wire from a 12 volt power source to the red lead of the engagement switch.

3. Move the slide switch to the OFF position.

4. Use a test lamp and ground one test lamp lead and touch the other lead in turn, to the brown wire, dark green wire and the yellow wire. The test lamp should not light on any of these wires.

5. Move the slide switch to the ON position and touch a test lamp

*1970-74 Slide Switch in RES Position*

**683**

# American Motors

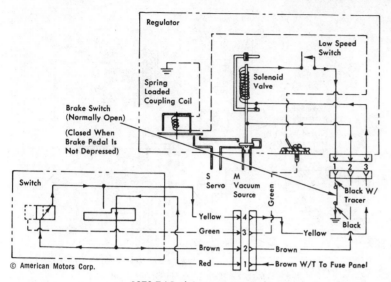

*1970-74 Push Button Depressed*

© American Motors Corp.

to ground and the other lead to the light green wire. The test lamp should not light. Depress the brake pedal 1/4 inch and the test lamp should light. If not, check the fuse, stop light switch, and wire harness to the regulator.

# ADJUSTMENTS

## Vacuum Servo Chain Linkage Adjustment 1968-75

1. Insert the servo chain in the vacuum servo hook in a position that should allow the clevis pin hole to align with the hole in the carburetor throttle lever.
2. Stretch the chain until it is fully extended, and check to make sure the holes align properly. Adjust the chain one ball at a time until the holes align and allow a free pin fit, as necessary.
3. Insert the locking pin, and check to make sure the chain can be deflected very slightly without moving either the carburetor throttle or servo. Readjust as necessary.
4. Bend the servo hook tabs together. Make sure the chain is free in the hook after bending the tabs.

## Centering Spring Adjustment 1968-75

The system should maintain a speed within about 3 mph of the speed selected. Check performance at 60 mph. If the system maintains a speed more than 3 mph above the selected speed, turn the centering spring adjusting screw 1/32 in. toward "S". If speed is more than 3 mph below the selected speed, turn the screw a like amount in the opposite direction. Retest the system and repeat the adjustment, as necessary, up to a total adjustment of 1/4 turn.

lead to the brown wire and then the dark green wire. The test lamp should light on each one. Touch the lead to the yellow wire and the test lamp should not light.

6. Push the SET SPEED all the way in and hold it there, the test lamp should light on the brown and yellow wire and should not light on the green wire.
7. Release the SET SPEED button.
8. Move the slide switch to the RES position and hold it there. Touch the test lamp lead, in turn, to the brown wire, yellow wire and then the green wire and the test lamp should light for each wire.

NOTE: *If steps 1 through 7 do not check out and the engagement switch test, steps 1 through 8 do not check out replace the Cruise Command wiring harness. If steps 1 through .7 check out OK but the engagement switch test does not, replace the engagement switch.*

## Brake Release Switch Test and Adjustment

On 1968 vehicles, disconnect the connector at the control switch, turn the switch to "ACC" position, ground one test lamp lead, and connect the other lead to terminal 2.

On 1969 vehicles, disconnect the connector at the control switch, turn the switch to "ACC" position, ground one test lamp lead, and connect the other lead to terminal C.

On 1970-74 vehicles, disconnect the connector at the regulator, connect one side of a test lamp to a hot lead, and connect the other lead to the black with tracer wire.

On 1968-74 vehicles, the lamp should light when the pedal is released, but go out when it is depressed 1/4 inch for 1968 and 3/8 inch for 1969-74. The switch, located next to the stop light switch, should be adjusted or replaced as necessary.

On 1974 vehicles, disconnect the three wire connectors at the regulator. Connect one lead of a test lamp

## Slide Switch Operation

NOTE: PUSHBUTTON CANNOT BE DEPRESSED WITH SLIDE SWITCH IN RESUME POSITION

| | SLIDE SWITCH OPERATION | | | |
|---|---|---|---|---|
| | SLIDE SWITCH | | | PUSHBUTTON DEPRESSED |
| | OFF | ON | RESUME | SLIDE SWITCH ON |
| RED/BROWN | OPEN | CLOSED | CLOSED | CLOSED |
| RED/GREEN | OPEN | CLOSED | CLOSED | OPEN |
| RED/YELLOW | OPEN | OPEN | CLOSED | CLOSED |

*Cruise Command Schematic*

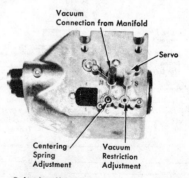

© American Motors Corp.

*1969 Speed Control Regulator Connections & Adjustments*

# American Motors

## Vacuum Restriction Adjustment 1968-69

Screw "R" must not be adjusted. If an attempt has been made to adjust it, turn it clockwise to the stop, and then back it off exactly 1½ turns.

## Control Switch Replacement 1970-75

### Removal

1. Remove the horn button insert and steering wheel. Remove the anti-theft cover, locking plate, and horn contact.
2. Remove the turn signal lever, allowing the handle to hang loose outside the column.
3. Remove the flasher knob, and three hold-down screws and turn signal switch.
4. Remove the trim section from under the column.
5. Disconnect the plastic connector.
6. On tilt columns, remove the wires from the plastic connector and tape two of them back along the harness. Tape a string to the harness. On standard columns, tape a string to the plastic connector.
7. Remove the lever harness assembly from the column.

### Installation

1. Connect the replacement control switch into the connector, and test it as described in the harness testing procedures.
2. Repeat the taping and string tying operation performed during the latter part of step 6 of the removal procedures on the new harness.
3. Feed the harness through the turn signal lever opening and down through the steering column. On tilt column models, the harness must pass through the

hole in the left side of the steering shaft.
4. Replace, in order:
   A. Turn signal switch and flasher knobs.
   B. Cruise command lever.
   C. Horn contact, locking plate, and lock ring cover.
   D. Steering wheel.
   E. Horn button insert.
   F. Steering column trim.

# REGULATOR DISASSEMBLY AND ASSEMBLY

## 1968-69

### Disassembly

1. Remove the cover assembly, and push the air filter out from under the filter cap.
2. Remove the end plate retaining screws, rotate it 180 degrees, and slide it out. Do not tamper with the end plate adapter screw!
3. Remove the governor spring.
4. Remove the actuator pin spring, going in through the end plate assembly hole with needle nose pliers.
5. With a screwdriver, pry upward on the actuator coupling until the pin and magnet assembly can be rotated clockwise. Then, rotate the actuator cup 180 degrees and hook the actuator coupling over the top of the regulator housing.
6. Slide the governor assembly toward the end plate adapter assembly hole until the shaft is free of the bearing, and then remove the governor assembly from the regulator.

© American Motors Corp.

*1969 Actuator Pin Spring*

© American Motors Corp.

*1969 Actuator Coupling*

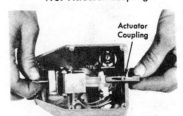

© American Motors Corp.

*1969 Governor Assembly*

7. Remove the three screws holding the valve body and magnet assembly, and remove them from the housing.

### Assembly

1. Put the valve body and magnet assembly into the regulator housing, and install the three screws. The rubber gasket must lie flat against the regulator housing.
2. Insert the long end of the shaft assembly through the adapter hole on the end plate. Make sure

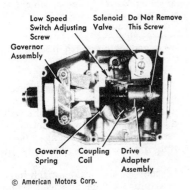

© American Motors Corp.

*1969 Drive Adaptor Assembly*

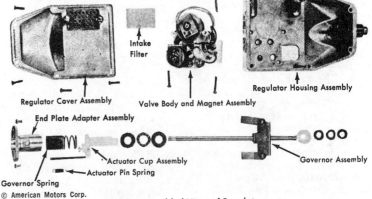

© American Motors Corp.

*1969 Disassembled View of Regulator*

## American Motors

that the actuator coupling is above the edge of the regulator housing assembly.

3. Insert the shaft so as to allow the short end of the governor assembly to be inserted into the bearing, and slide the assembly toward the bearing until it bottoms.

4. Slide the actuator cup down the shaft until it bottoms. Rotate it 180 degrees.

5. Pry the actuator coupling up with a screwdriver and rotate the magnet counterclockwise until the pin engages the slot in the lower actuator coupling.

6. Install the actuator pin spring with needle nose pliers.

7. Install the governor spring over the shaft with the open end toward the actuator cup.

8. Install the end plate adapter assembly into the regulator and ro-

tate it 180 degrees. Secure it with the two screws.

9. Adjust the low speed switch as described below:

   A. Hold the actuator cup in the low speed position (with governor weights inward).
   B. Turn the adjusting screw until the gap between switch points is .020"-.030".
   C. Install the cover assembly.

# Speed Control

## Chrysler Corporation

### General Description

The speed control system generates an electrical signal via speedometer cable driven flyweights, and employs this to operate a vacuum-controlling solenoid. The solenoid then controls the vehicle speed through application of the vacuum to a servo, which is connected to the throttle with a cable.

A control ring on the turn signal lever turns the system on and off, and incorporates a "Resume" position for reactivating the system after use of the brake pedal. The system is made to hold a certain speed above 30 mph by accelerating to the desired speed and depressing the Speed Set button in the end of the control lever.

## TEST PROCEDURES

### Electrical Circuit Testing 1968-69

1. Check the fuse for continuity, and replace if necessary.

2. Disconnect the harness plug at the servo. Connect one lead of a 12V test lamp to the low speed inhibit switch terminal on the servo, and the other end to a 12V positive source.

3. Safely raise the vehicle off the floor so as to permit spinning of the rear wheels. Bring the speed of the rear wheels to about 35 mph. The light should come on between 25 and 33 mph, and go back off at closed throttle at a speed 5 mph lower. Adjust the switch, if necessary.

4. Remove the servo plug and run a jumper from its blue wire lead to a ground. Turn on the ignition and actuate the Speed Set switch. The brake switch should latch on.

## SPEED CONTROL TROUBLESHOOTING CHART

| Condition | Possible Cause |
|---|---|
| System inoperative | Blown fuse<br>Vacuum leak<br>Stop lamp and speed control switch improperly adjusted |
| System does not disengage when brake pedal is depressed | Improper stop lamp and speed control switch adjustment<br>Control cable kinked or faulty<br>Faulty electrical circuit |
| System controls, but at a speed above or below lock-in speed | Speed control cable improperly adjusted<br>Improper control servo lock-in adjustment<br>Vacuum leak |
| Rotation of control ring does not cause system to resume | Faulty electrical circuit |
| System engages without being switched on | Faulty electrical circuit |
| Speedometer noise, needle waver, erratic lock-in performance | Speedometer cable kinked, damaged<br>Faulty cable core<br>Improper cable core lube<br>Loose cable ferrule nut<br>Faulty speedometer head |
| Unit disengages on rough road | Improper stop lamp and speed control switch adjustment |
| Throttle does not fully return to idle speed | Improper speed control cable adjustment<br>Faulty or kinked speed control cable<br>Faulty throttle linkage |
| Control engages at engine start-up or at too low a speed | Faulty low speed inhibit switch in servo<br>Faulty electrical circuit |

5. Depress the brake pedal, and then actuate the Resume speed switch. These actions should cause the brake switch to disengage and then again latch in.

6. If the unit does not function at all, check to ensure that the black lead has 12V supplied to it when the ignition switch is on. Make other repairs, as indicated.

7. If the brake switch does not latch in when actuating the Resume and Speed Set switches, but will do so when the switch actuator arm is lifted to the engaged position, proceed with the tests in the next step.

8. Disconnect the brake switch harness plug, attach one lead from the test light to the red lead in

the harness plug, and attach the other lead to ground. Turn ignition on.

9. Depress the Speed Set button, and actuate the Resume switch. The test lamp should light in both cases.

10. Pull the servo plug and connect a 12V test lamp between the yellow lead and ground. Turn the ignition switch on. The light should light, and then go out when the Speed Set button is depressed. Make repairs to the turn signal switch assembly as indicated by failure of tests in steps 8-10.

## Electrical Circuit Testing 1970-75

Refer to the wiring diagrams in performing the following tests.

1. Check the accessory fuse for continuity, and replace as necessary.
2. Disconnect the four wire connector at the steering column, connect a 12V positive source of voltage to the black wire terminal in the male harness connector, and move the slide switch to the "On" position.
3. Connect a 12V test lamp between the connector yellow wire ground. The lamp should light. Depress the Speed Set button. The lamp should go out.
4. Move the lamp lead to the blue wire of the connector. The lamp should light. Turn the slide switch off. The lamp should go out.
5. Move the test lamp lead to the white wire, and put the slide switch in the "On" position. The light should light both when depressing the Speed Set button, and when moving the slide switch to "Resume" position. Replace switches as necessary.
6. Reconnect the connector loosened in step 2, and disconnect the double connector at stop lamp and speed control switch pigtail. Connect a 12V source to one terminal and a test lamp between the other and ground.
7. Check that the test lamp lights, and then depress the brake pedal more than 1/2 in. and check to see that the light goes out. Adjust or replace the switch, as necessary.
8. Remove the test lamp and reconnect the stop lamp and speed control switch connector. Turn the ignition and slide switches on.

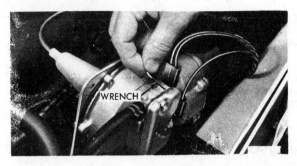

*Lock-In Screw Adjustment*

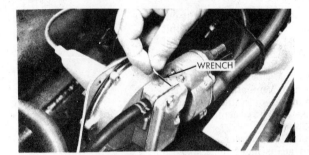

*Lock-In Screw Adjustment*

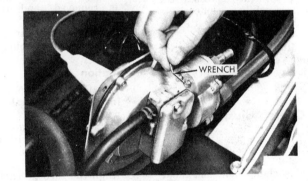

*Cut-In Screw Adjustment*

9. Momentarily disconnect the double connector at the servo terminals, and then reconnect it. This should produce a clicking sound in the servo. Replace the servo if no sound is heard.
10. Connect a test lamp between the black with tracer wire terminal at the servo and ground. Block the front wheels, raise the rear wheels, and bring the rear wheels up to a speed of 35 mph.
11. Turn the slide switch on and depress the Speed set button. The speed should increase slightly and the test lamp should remain on until the brake pedal is depressed. At pedal movement, the test lamp should go out, and the system should disengage. Replace the servo if there are indications of failure in steps 9-11.

# ADJUSTMENTS

## Lock-In Screw Adjustment 1968-75

1. Determine whether or not any of the following could be causing control to be imprecise (more than 3 mph above or below the speed at which the system locks in):
   A. Poor engine performance.
   B. Extreme load (especially trailering).
   C. Improper throttle control cable slack (inspect as described below).
2. If the above three possible causes are ruled out, the lock-in adjusting screw may be turned 1/4 turn for each mph the controlled speed must be changed. Turn

# Chrysler Corporation

the screw clockwise to reduce the controlled speed, counterclockwise to raise it. *Maximum readjustment must not exceed two turns in either direction, or damage to the unit is likely.* If necessary, stake the side of the servo housing near the screw to prevent loss of adjustment.

### Cut-In and Cut-Out Adjustments 1969

1. Test the cut-in and cut-out speeds of the low speed inhibit switch as described in step 3 of "Electrical Circuit Testing 1968-69."
2. Adjust the setscrew clockwise in 1/8 turn increments to lower the cut-in speed, or counterclockwise to raise it. The acceptable range is 25-33 mph.
3. In a similar manner, adjust the cut-out adjustment for a speed 5 mph lower. In this case, a clockwise adjustment increases the road speed, while a counterclockwise adjustment will lower it.

*NOTE: Maximum adjustment of the cut-out and cut-in adjusting screws must not exceed two turns in either direction, or damage is likely.*

### Throttle Cable Adjustment 1969-75

1. Pull the hair pin clip from the carburetor linkage pin, loosen the cable clamp bolt, and make sure that the throttle is in curb idle position with the choke wide open.
2. Insert a 1/16 in. pin between the forward end of the slot in the cable end and the carburetor link-

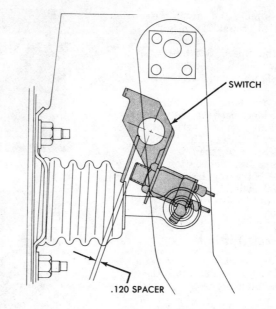

*Stop Lamp & Speed Control Switch*

age pin. Pull the cable toward the dash panel just until all play is removed, and tighten the clamp bolt.
3. Remove the 1/16 in. pin, and replace the hair pin clip.

### Installation

1. Install the servo on the mounting bracket. Install nuts and washers.
2. Install the vacuum hose and carefully secure with the clamp. Connect both drive cables at the servo.
3. Align the throttle cable to servo pin, and install the retaining clip (choke must be in full open position).
4. Install the cable cover and attaching nuts. Connect electrical connectors.

### Throttle Cable Assembly 1969-75

#### Removal

1. Remove the air cleaner. Disconnect the cable at the retaining clamp.
2. Remove the clip ring or hair pin clip and disconnect the cable at the lost motion link.
3. Disconnect the cable at the servo, and remove it.

#### Installation

1. Feed the cable through the master cylinder routing bracket. Connect it at the servo housing and tighten the nuts.
2. Route the cable through the retaining clamp and connect it at the carburetor lost motion link.
3. Adjust the free play as described above, and tighten the clamp nut. Install the clip ring or hair pin clip and air cleaner.

### Brake Switch Adjustment 1969

1. Disconnect the connector at the servo and jumper between the blue wire's terminal of the connector and ground. Turn the key to accessory position, and depress and release the turn signal lever push button.
2. Check the clearance between the actuator arm and brake pedal blade. If it is not .01 in., loosen the switch bracket, reposition the bracket to obtain the clearance, and retighten the mounting nut.

*Servo Throttle Cable Adjustment*

## Chrysler Corporation

3. Recheck the clearance. Remove the jumper and reconnect the servo connector.

### Brake Switch Adjustment 1970-74

1. Loosen the switch bracket, and insert the proper gauge (shown below) between the brake push rod and the switch.
   1974—.120″ P,D,C,Y body cars
   .130″ R,W body cars
   1973—.110″
   1972—.110″
   1971—.130″
   1970—.140″
2. Move the switch assembly toward the push rod until the plunger is fully depressed and the body of the switch contacts the spacer.
3. Tighten the switch bracket bolt and remove the spacer.

### Control Servo Removal and Installation 1968-75

**Removal**

1. Remove the nuts or nuts and washers which hold the cable cover to the servo. Remove the cover. Remove the clip attaching the cable to the servo diaphragm pin.
2. Disconnect both drive cables at at the servo housing. Disconnect the vacuum hose and electrical connectors at the servo housing.
3. Remove the nuts and washers from the mounting bracket, and remove the servo.

# LEVER MOUNTED SPEED CONTROL SWITCH

## Tilt and Telescope Columns 1968-69

**Removal**

1. Disconnect the battery ground. Remove the steering column and turn signal lever access hole cover plates.
2. Remove the wiring harness trough. Cut the speed control switch lead wires at the terminal clips.
3. Pull the wires out through the signal lever access hole.
4. Unscrew the signal lever, and remove it from the turn signal switch.

**Installation**

1. Told the wires close to the turn signal lever shank, and screw the lever into the switch until it is hand tight. Then, use a wrench to screw the lever in four more full turns.
2. *Without turning the lever backwards at any time*, turn it further just until the wiring harness indexes properly with the steering column.
3. Make an appropriate guide wire, and thread one wire at a time through the opening and pull it out through the opening in the column hub. Pull carefully, and ensure that there is enough slack so that chafing will not occur at the hub opening.
4. Install the harness through the

column cover plate. Install the access hole cover plate.
5. Install new terminal clips, and connect each to the proper switch connector. Connect the battery ground.

## Tilt and Telescope Columns 1970-72

**Removal**

1. Disconnect the battery ground. Disconnect the speed control harness connect from the main connector at the steering column.
2. Remove the wires and terminals lever harness connector with a special tool.
3. Tape all the terminals together. Fashion a guide wire long enough to be reached from the bottom of the column tube when inserted into the speed control lever access hole. Then, pull the wires out through the control lever access hole with the guide wire.
4. Unscrew the lever from the turn signal switch.

**Installation**

1. Hold the wires close to the control lever shank, and screw the lever into the switch until it is hand tight.
2. *Do not turn the lever counterclockwise during the following steps.* Tighten the lever four full turns with a wrench, and then continue turning it until the harness indexes with the steering column.
3. Tape the terminals of the new harness, and attach the guide wire hook. Guide the harness through the opening in the steering column hub and down through the hub casting. Pull wires in such a way that there will be no chafing on the hub lever opening.
4. Remove the guide wire, and install each terminal in its proper cavity of the harness connector, checking with the appropriate wiring diagram.
5. Connect the harness connector to the main harness, and connect the battery ground.

## Tilt Columns 1973-75

**Removal**

1. Disconnect the battery ground cable and the speed control connector at the lower end of the column.

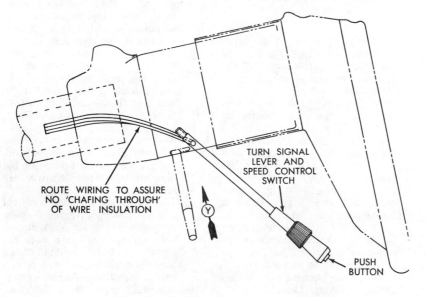

ROUTE WIRING TO ASSURE NO 'CHAFING THROUGH' OF WIRE INSULATION

Y

TURN SIGNAL LEVER AND SPEED CONTROL SWITCH

PUSH BUTTON

*1969 Chrysler & Dodge Turn Signal & Lever Installed*

## Chrysler Corporation

2. Remove the steering wheel. Remove the turn signal switch and lever attaching screw.
3. Remove the steering column cover plate and wiring harness trough. Remove the wires and terminals from the column connector with a special tool.
4. Tape the terminals and pull the lever and wires out of the column.

### Installation

1. Thread the harness through the opening in the column with a guide wire which is long enough to be reached at the bottom of the column before the harness is attached to the upper hook.
2. Install the terminal clips into the switch connector. Connect the switch and harness connectors together. Check the color coding of the wires on the wiring diagram to ensure that are each installed in the proper cavity.
3. Install the harness trough and steering column cover plate.
4. Install the turn signal lever and speed control switch attaching screw.
5. Install the steering wheel and column cover plate. Connect the battery ground.

### Standard Columns
### 1968-75

#### Removal

1. Disconnect the battery ground, and the speed control connector at the lower end of the steering column.
2. Remove the steering wheel. Remove the screw which attaches the signal switch and the lever attaching screw.
3. Remove the steering column cover plate, and support the column while the clamp is removed.
4. Remove the wiring harness trough, and then remove the wires and terminals from the connector with a special tool.
5. Tape the terminals. Turn the direction indicator sideways, pull the lever up, and pull the wires out through the opening between the column and the tube.

#### Installation

1. Make a guide wire that is long enough to permit reaching it at the bottom of the column before the harness is attached to the upper hook. Then, thread the harness through the opening in the column, and pull it through.
2. Install the terminal clips into the

harness connector. Make sure wires are color coded, as shown in the proper illustration.
3. Install the harness trough, and column cover plate and support clamp.
4. Install the signal and speed control switch lever, and its attaching screw.
5. Install the steering wheel, and column cover plate.
6. Connect the battery ground.

### Tilt-A-Scope Columns
### 1968-75

#### Removal

1. Disconnect the negative battery ground. Disconnect the speed control harness connector at the steering column.
2. Remove the wires and terminals from the male connector of the speed control lever harness with a special wiring harness tool.
3. Procure or make a guide wire long enough to be reached at the bottom of the column tube when the harness is withdrawn at the speed control lever access hole. Tape the wire terminals together, and hook them to the end of the guide wire.
4. Rotate the turn signal switch and lever to expose the wires, and pull them out through the control lever access hole.
5. Detach the hook from the terminals. Unscrew the lever completely, keeping the guide wire in place.

#### Installation

*NOTE: Do not turn the lever counterclockwise at any time during installation.*

1. Tape the terminals of the lever harness, and attach the hook of the guide wire to them. Pull the harness through slowly, to eliminate chafing.
2. Hold the lever close to the column with the lever nomenclature in the proper position. Rotate the lever counterclockwise till the harness has made seven loops over it, holding the other end of the harness.
3. Screw the lever into the column until it is hand tight. Using a wrench on the flats, screw the lever three to four turns further in, pulling on the harness on the other end. Index the lettering with the steering wheel.
4. After the harness is pulled through, remove the guide wire. Install each terminal into the

proper cavity in the harness connector, cross checking with the wiring diagram.
5. Connect the speed control harness connector to the main harness, and reconnect the battery ground.

## AUTO PILOT
### General Description

The Auto Pilot drive unit receives a signal for vehicle speed via the speedometer cable, and relates this to the setting on a thumbwheel dial. When the unit is in "On" position via the control switch, a negative pressure is placed on the accelerator linkage via a reversible motor as the dialed speed is reached. When the control switch is moved to "Auto" position, the motor provides full control of vehicle speed. If the brakes are applied, a brake switch eliminates full control until such time as the control switch is returned to "Auto" setting.

## TEST PROCEDURES

### Electrical Circuit Testing

1. Turn the ignition switch to "Acc." position, and turn Auto Pilot control off.
2. Procure a 12V test lamp and connect it between terminal #1 (the red wire) and ground. If the lamp lights, go on to the next step. If the lamp does not light, test for an open in the red wire between the Auto Pilot and ignition circuit.
3. Turn the control switch on, and connect the test lamp between terminal #2 (the black wire) and ground. If the lamp lights, go on to the next step. If not, test for an open circuit between terminal #2 and the ignition circuit.
4. Move the control switch to "Auto". The panel light should come on, and the switch should spring back to "On" position. If either of these conditions fails to occur, make repairs as necessary.
5. Repeat step 3.
6. Test for power between terminal #3 and ground. If there is no power, test for a failure in the blue wire between terminal #3 and the control switch.
7. Test for power between terminal #4 and ground. If there is no power, test for an open circuit between terminal #4 and the Auto pilot brake switch. Check brake switch adjustment if circuit is open there. Adjust so that test light goes out with about $\frac{1}{4}$"-$\frac{1}{2}$" brake pedal movement.

# Chrysler Corporation

## ADJUSTMENTS

### Accelerator Linkage

1. Put the choke in wide open position, and make sure the throttle is in curb idle position. *Do not force the linkage to accomplish this.* Ease the linkage into this position by moving the Auto Pilot exterior arm several times.
2. Loosen the Auto Pilot linkage rod locknut and insert a 1/8″ diameter, two inch long piece of welding rod through the hole in the exterior arm and into the hole in the auto pilot housing.
3. Hold the exterior arm in this position, and tighten the locknut.
4. Remove the 1/8″ rod, actuate the linkage several times, and readjust as necessary.

### Thumbwell Dial Calibration

1. Turn the thumbwheel to the extreme low end of the scale. Operate the car on a level stretch of road, and engage the Auto Pilot.
2. Increase the thumbwheel dial setting *just* to the "3" mark. If the setting passes "3" even slightly, go back and approach the mark from below again.
3. Record the speedometer reading after the system stabilizes with the wheel at "3".
4. Precisely repeat the procedure with the wheel at the "4" mark.
5. Continue the process until the normal driving range has been covered, going both up and down. Avoid overshooting the settings when going down, also.
6. Evaluate the results, and adjust the thumbwheel for the best overall correlation between dial setting and indicated speed as follows:

To lower the speed maintained at a given setting, rotate the thumbwheel to the top end of the range and slip it against spring pressure to change the setting. Do the opposite if the speed maintained by the unit be raised. Then retest the unit, and readjust as necessary.

### Drive Mechanism

#### Removal

1. Disconnect the wiring where it connects at the drive mechanism.
2. Disconnect the speedometer and drive cables at the drive unit. Tape the ferrule nut onto the drive cable.
3. Loosen and then remove the wire clip on the dust shield.

## AUTO PILOT TROUBLESHOOTING CHART

| Condition | Possible Cause |
|---|---|
| No negative Accelerator Pressure | Blown fuse<br>Faulty Electrical Circuit |
| Unit does not provide full control | Insufficient clearance at brake pedal switch<br>Brake pedal does not return fully<br>Faulty electrical circuit |
| Unit does not release when brake pedal is depressed | Brake switch improperly adjusted<br>Brake switch faulty |
| Panel light inoperative | Faulty lamp<br>Blown fuse<br>Faulty electrical circuit |
| Unit disengages and re-engages on rough roads | Insufficient brake switch clearance<br>Faulty electrical connections |
| Speedometer does not register and unit does not operate | Faulty speedometer cable<br>Faulty cable drive pinion in transmission<br>Faulty transmission—Auto Pilot cable<br>Faulty speedometer |
| Fuses blow repeatedly | Short circuit anywhere in system |
| Unit provides full control even when switch is not moved to "Auto" position | Faulty electrical circuit |
| Negative pressure on accelerator at all speeds | Faulty electrical circuit |
| Throttle does not return to idle position | Faulty standard throttle linkage<br>Improper adjustment of Auto Pilot linkage |
| Pulsation in accelerator pedal | Throttle cable needs lubrication<br>Accelerator linkage requires adjustment<br>Speedometer or drive cable kinked |
| Speedometer noisy | Cable requires lubrication<br>Cable kinked<br>Noisy speedometer head |

4. Pull the control cable free from the drive mechanism.
5. Disconnect the accelerator linkage at the exterior arm at the drive unit.
6. Remove the nuts and bolts which attach the drive unit to the mounting brackets, and remove the unit.

### Installation

1. Put the drive mechanism in position on the mounting brackets, and nuts.

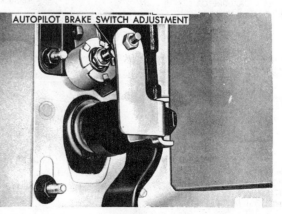

*Auto Pilot Brake Switch*

# Chrysler Corporation

2. Reconnect the drive and speedometer cables.
3. Connect the accelerator linkage, and adjust it.
4. Install the ferrule end of control cable into the dust shield and set the spring wire clip into the slot on the dust shield. Rotate the thumbwheel dial toward the low speed end of the scale until resistance is felt. Increase the pressure enough to cause the cable wire to snap into the governor control rod.
5. Connect the wiring at the drive mechanism.

## Auto Pilot Control

### Removal

1. Disconnect the battery ground. Place tape over the top of the steering column to protect its finish.
2. Remove the steering column trim plate screws, and remove the cover.
3. Loosen the allen screw on the right underside of the steering column as seen from the driver's seat. Remove the gear selector indicator by pushing it forward and rotating it clockwise.
4. Remove the steering column upper clamp nuts. Remove the clamp and allow the column to

*Accelerator Linkage Adjustment*

*Bezel Mounting—Imperial*

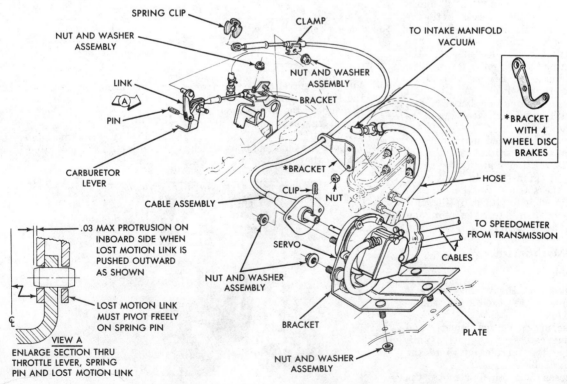

*1970-75 Imperial, Chrysler, Fury, Polara & Monaco Speed Control System*

# Chrysler Corporation

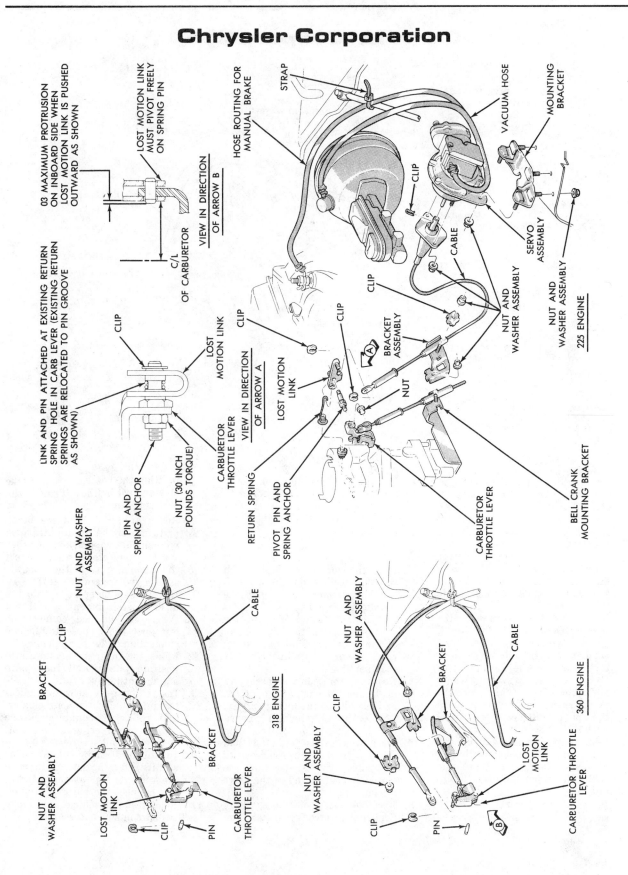

*Servo Throttle Cable Adjustment*

# Chrysler Corporation

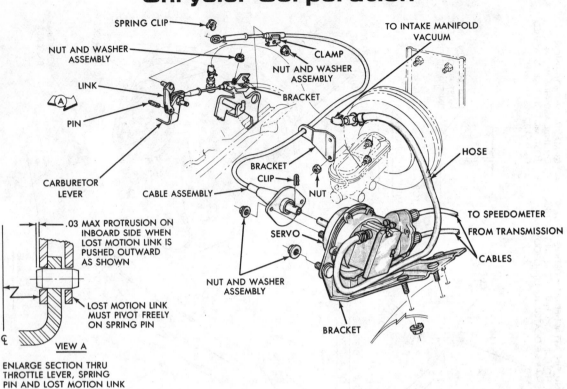

SPRING CLIP

NUT AND WASHER
ASSEMBLY

LINK

PIN

CARBURETOR
LEVER

TO INTAKE MANIFOLD
VACUUM

CLAMP

NUT AND WASHER
ASSEMBLY

BRACKET

BRACKET
CLIP

CABLE ASSEMBLY

NUT

HOSE

SERVO

NUT AND WASHER
ASSEMBLY

TO SPEEDOMETER

FROM TRANSMISSION

CABLES

BRACKET

.03 MAX PROTRUSION ON
INBOARD SIDE WHEN
LOST MOTION LINK IS
PUSHED OUTWARD
AS SHOWN

LOST MOTION LINK
MUST PIVOT FREELY
ON SPRING PIN

VIEW A

ENLARGE SECTION THRU
THROTTLE LEVER, SPRING
PIN AND LOST MOTION LINK

*Lock-In Screw Adjustment*

rest in lowered position. If the car has air conditioning, remove the left spot cooler hose at the T connection under the panel by releasing the alligator clamp.

5. Remove the four upper and four lower bezel screws. Lower screws are located at the lower left bezel corner, either side of the column opening, and inside the ash tray.

6. Raise the lower edge of the bezel. Disconnect the headlight, panel, windshield wiper and washer switch multiple connectors. Remove the vacuum hose from the rear air switch (where applicable) by reaching through the steering column opening in the panel. Remove the bezel with the spot cooler attached.

7. Remove the spring clip on the Auto Pilot dust shield in the engine compartment and pull the cable free from the drive mechanism.

8. Remove the control mounting screws through the cluster bezel

opening in the panel, push the control down under the panel, and withdraw the cable and grommet from the engine compartment.

## Installation

1. Pass the control cable through the bulkhead from the passenger compartment side. Snap the grommet into place.

2. Install the ferrule end of the control cable in the dust shield of the drive mechanism, and secure the spring clip in the slot of the dust shield.

3. Position the control assembly in the instrument panel opening, and install the mounting screws.

4. Rotate the thumbwheel toward the low speed end of the scale until pressure is felt, and then slightly increase pressure until the cable wire snaps into the governor control rod in the drive mechanism.

5. Feed the spot cooler hose, where applicable, into the panel, and

position the bezel in front of the cluster, resting the left side in the panel opening.

6. Reach around behind the bezel, and connect the headlight, panel, windshield wiper and washer switch connectors, and connect the vacuum hose to the rear air switch (where applicable).

7. Install the cluster bezel into the dash. Install mounting screws. Where so equipped, connect the left spot cooler hose to the tee connection under the panel.

8. Raise the steering column into position and install the clamp and mounting nuts.

9. Insert the gear selector indicator into the instrument cluster, and rotate it counterclockwise up into the steering column slot. Tighten the allen screw.

10. Install the steering column cover and its retaining screws. Remove the tape on top of the column, and connect the battery ground.

11. Road test the vehicle, and make adjustments as necessary.

# Ford Motor Company

## FORD MOTOR COMPANY SPEED CONTROL BENDIX SPEED CONTROL SYSTEM

### 1969-75

**General Description**

The speed control system has an OFF-ON switch, a SET-ACCEL switch, and a COAST switch. A speed sensor provides an input (an indication of the actual speed of the vehicle) to an amplifier, which then sends an appropriate signal to the servo assembly. This assembly converts the electronic signal into a controlled vacuum, and then employs this vacuum in a vacuum cylinder to operate the throttle linkage via a chain.

Once the system is turned on, and vehicle speed is between 30 and 80 mph, the SET-ACCEL switch must be depressed in order to activate the system, which will then maintain the speed at which it was activated. To increase the speed, the SET-ACCEL switch may be held in until the desired speed is reached, and then released, or the vehicle may simply be sped up by accelerating, and the system reset by depressing and releasing the SET-ACCEL button. Speed may be reduced either by depressing the COAST button or lightly depressing the brake pedal. Releasing the coast button will cause the system to control at the lowered speed, but if the brake pedal is depressed to slow the vehicle, the SET-ACCEL button must be depressed to reset the system.

## SYSTEM INSPECTION AND TESTS

A visual inspection should precede detailed testing procedures because of the great number of wires, hoses, and linkages which are subject to minor failure which can easily and quickly be detected without special instruments. Check the following:

1. Vacuum hoses for kinks, cracks, or loose connections.
2. Wires for loose or corroded connections, frayed insulation, or internal breakage.
3. Vacuum reserve tanks for leaks or damage.

## COMPONENT LOCATION CHART

|  | Switches | Amp. Assy. | Servo | Sensor | Vacuum Reservoir |
|---|---|---|---|---|---|
| 1969 | Steering Wheel Spokes | Under Dash | Dash Panel | Under Dash | — |
| 1970 | Steering Wheel Spokes | Under Dash | Dash Panel | Under Dash | — |
| 1971 | Steering Wheel Spokes | Under Dash | Dash Panel | Under Dash | — |
| 1972 Ford, Mercury | Steering Wheel Spokes | Under Dash | Dash Panel | Under Dash | — |
| 1972 T-Bird, Cont. | Steering Wheel Spokes | Under Dash | Intake Manifold | Under Dash | — |
| 1973 Ford, Mercury | Steering Wheel Spokes | Under Dash | Dash Panel | Under Dash | Fender Panel— Driver's Side |
| 1973 T-Bird, Cont. | Steering Wheel Spokes | Under Dash | Intake Manifold | Under Dash | Fender Panel— Pass. Side |
| 1974-75 Ford, Mercury | Steering Wheel Spokes | Under Dash | Dash Panel | Under Dash | Fender Panel— Driver's Side |
| 1974-75 T-Bird, Cont. | Steering Wheel Spokes | Under Dash | Intake Manifold | Engine Compartment | Fender Panel— Pass. Side |

## SPEED CONTROL TROUBLESHOOTING CHART

| Condition | Possible Cause |
|---|---|
| System inoperative | Brake switch circuit open<br>Fuse blown<br>Open circuit in wiring harness<br>Disconnected vacuum hose<br>Plugged vacuum hose |
| System surges | Throttle activator chain, or throttle linkage binding<br>Air hoses kinked, or collapsed |
| System does not disengage when brake pedal is depressed | Brake switch defective |
| Steady acceleration or full throttle when system is engaged | Manifold vacuum connected directly to servo<br>Faulty amplifier assembly |

4. Throttle and servo linkage for rough operation or excessive free play (¼ in for the servo chain).
5. Speedometer cables for kinks or loose connections.
6. Blow the horn to check for power to the horn circuit in the steering wheel.

### Control Switch Test 1972-75

1. Disconnect the connector in the wiring between the amplifier and control switches.
2. Depress the "ON" switch, and check for voltage at the lead

## Ford Motor Company

which is light blue with a black hash. This lead comes from the control switches.

3. Connect an ohmmeter between this lead and ground. Depress the "OFF" switch, and check for a resistance of less than 1 ohm.

4. If the resistance is high, check for an improper ground. To do this, connect an ohmmeter between any good body ground and the upper flange of the steering column. The resistance should be less than .5 ohm. Rotate the steering wheel back and forth and up and down, and if a change in resistance is less than 1 ohm, perform the following tests.

5. Connect the ohmmeter between the light blue wire with black hash and a good ground, and depress the speed set switch. The ohmmeter should read about 680 ohms.

6. Depress the coast switch. The resistance reading should change to 120 ohms.

7. If all tests are not passed, replace the switches.

### Speed Sensor Test

1. Disconnect the connector which leads to the speed sensor switch, at the amplifier.

2. Connect an ohmmeter between the dark green with white stripe (1972-75), or green (1969-71) and white wires at the speed sensor end. The resistance should be about 40 ohms. Zero resistance indicates a shorted coil, while infinite resistance indicates an open coil. If resistance is incorrect, replace the coil.

3. If the resistance is approximately correct and the speedometer operates without excessive needle waver, the sensor should be ok. If there is still doubt about its function, substitute a good sensor and test the system.

### Servo Assembly Test

1. Disconnect the ball chain at the carburetor. Disconnect the connector that feeds the servo (the largest one) at the amplifier.

2. Connect an ohmmeter between the orange (with yellow hash mark after 1972) and gray (with black hash mark after 1972) wires of the connector. The resistance should be 85 ohms.

3. Move the one probe from the gray or gray-black wire to the white or white-pink wire. The resistance should still be 85 ohms.

4. Reconnect the ball chain to the throttle linkage.

5. Start the engine. Connect the orange or orange-yellow wire to the positive battery terminal. Jumper the white or white-pink lead to ground.

6. Momentarily touch the gray or gray-black wire to ground. The servo should tighten the bead chain and open the throttle, and then hold it, or slowly release it.

7. Remove the white or white-pink lead ground jumper. The servo should immediately release, and allow the throttle to return to idle.

8. If the servo fails any part of the test, replace it.

### Amplifier Test

1. Procure a voltmeter rated at 5,000 ohms per volt, or higher. Do not use a test lamp!

2. Turn the ignition switch on. Connect the voltmeter to the light blue (1969-71) or light blue with black hash (later models) wire at the amplifier, and to ground. Depress and hold the "On" switch on the steering wheel. The voltmeter should read 12V. If there is no voltage, check the horn relay and control switch.

3. Release the "On" button, and check the voltage. There should still be 12 V. If not, check the amplifier ground, and the circuit breaker or fuse. If these are ok, install a good amplifier and

check for presence of a good "On" circuit, and replace parts as necessary.

4. Depress the "Off" switch on the steering wheel. The voltage reading should drop to zero. If not, check the control switches. If they check out, substitute a known good amplifier and check the "OFF" circuit.

5. Depress the "Set-Accel" button and hold it. The voltage should drop to 10 volts. Rotate the steering wheel back and forth while maintaining all other conditions. The voltage should not vary more than .5 volt. If there is variation, check out the control switches.

6. Depress and hold the "Coast" switch. The voltmeter should read about 6 V.

If all tests are passed, and no deficiencies are uncovered, install an amplifier that is known to be good.

## ADJUSTMENTS

### Linkage Adjustment

1. On vehicles with a solenoid throttle positioner, turn on the ignition switch and open the throttle wide enough to permit extension of the solenoid. Make sure the engine is fully warmed up so that the fast idle will be ineffective.

2. Adjust the bead chain for a minimum of slack *with no effect on the position of the carburetor*

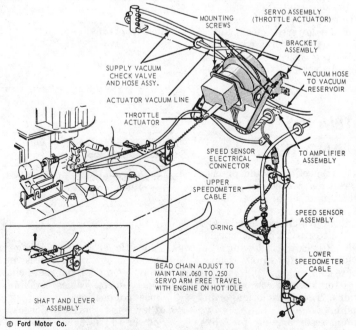

*Adjusting The Bead Chain-Late Model Ford and Mercury*

© Ford Motor Co.

# Ford Motor Company

*lever at idle.* This means .06-.25 in. of play.

# REMOVAL AND INSTALLATION

## Control Switches

### 1971-75 All Models

#### Removal

1. Remove the two retaining screws from the steering wheel foam padding.
2. Lift the padding upward, and disconnect the wiring at the terminals. Remove the pad assembly.
3. Snap the switches out of the plastic retainer.

#### Installation

1. Snap the switches into the plastic retainer, and run the wiring through the center hole.
2. Hook up the wiring at the terminals.
3. Position the pad, and install the two retaining screws.

### 1970 Thunderbird

#### Removal

1. Remove the two retaining screws from the foam pad assembly, and remove it from the steering wheel.
2. Lift the pad off, and disconnect the horn and speed control wires. Remove the pad.
3. Remove the screws attaching the foam pad to the trim pad, and separate the two.
4. Snap the switches out of the plastic retainer.

#### Installation

1. Snap the switches back into the plastic retainer. Run the wiring through the center hole.
2. Position the foam pad back on the trim pad, and install the retaining screws.
3. Attach speed control and horn wiring to the terminals on the steering wheel hub, and install the foam pad assembly back onto the steering wheel.

### 1969-70 Ford and Mercury

#### Removal

1. Pry the switch bezels up with a knife blade. Remove the center trim plate.
2. Remove the two mounting screws, and remove the foam pad from the steering wheel.
3. Remove the three switch-to-steering-wheel attaching screws.
4. Unplug the connector, and remove the switch.

#### Installation

1. Connect the connector, and install the switch and attaching screws.
2. Install the foam pad and attaching screws.
3. Install the center trim plate and switch bezels.

## Ground Brush

### 1970-75 All Models

#### Removal

1. Remove the steering wheel.
2. Snap the brush assembly out of the turn signal switch.

#### Installation

1. Install the brush assembly into the turn signal switch. Reinstall the turn signal switch, if necessary.

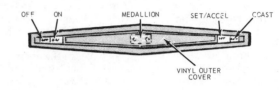

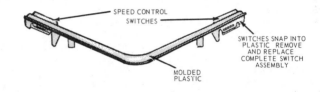

*Replacing Speed Control Switches—1973 models*

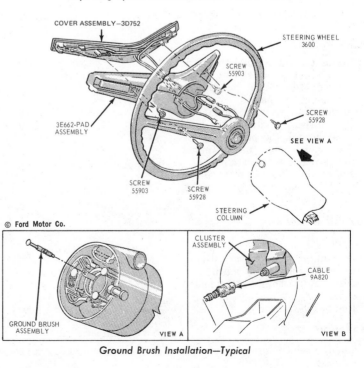

*Ground Brush Installation—Typical*

## Ford Motor Company

### Speed Sensor

#### 1970-75 Exc. 1970 Thunderbird

**Removal**

1. Disconnect the electrical connector leading to the amplifier.
2. Disconnect the upper and lower speedometer cables at the sensor.
3. Remove the mounting nut, and remove the sensor.

**Installation**

1. Put the sensor into position, and install the mounting nut.
2. Install the O-ring seals onto the sensor on 1971-75 Ford and Mercury models.
3. Connect upper and lower speedometer cables.
4. Connect the electrical connector going to the amplifier.

#### 1970 Thunderbird

**Removal**

1. Remove the blue electrical connector leading to the amplifier from the passenger compartment left side under the dash.
2. Disconnect both cables at the sensor in the engine compartment.
3. Remove the four sensor bracket retaining screws.
4. Remove the grommet from the dash panel.
5. Pull the harness and connector through the panel, and then remove the sensor.

**Installation**

1. Mount the sensor into the dash panel with the four screws.
2. Connect the upper and lower speedometer cables.
3. Install the grommet onto the wire harness, and route the harness through the panel into the passenger compartment. Install the grommet in the dash panel.
4. Attach the blue connector to the amplifier connector.
5. Test the system.

#### 1969 All Models

**Removal**

1. Disconnect the sensor wiring under the instrument panel.
2. Disconnect both speedometer cables.
3. Remove the sensor.

**Installation**

1. Put the sensor into position and install mounting bolts.
2. Install each speedometer cable in its former position.
3. Reconnect wiring.

### Servo Assembly (Throttle Actuator)

#### 1969-75 Ford and Mercury
#### 1974-75 Torino, Montego and Cougar (Exc. California)
#### 1970-71 Thunderbird

**Removal**

1. Disconnect the wiring connector where it connects with the amplifier under the instrument panel.
2. Remove the grommet from the dash panel in the engine compartment. Then, pull the harness through the opening.
3. Disconnect the ball chain at the bell crank, and the vacuum hose at the servo.
4. Remove the servo retaining pins, and remove the servo from the mounting bracket.

**Installation**

1. Put the servo in position on the bracket, and install the retaining pins.
2. Connect the vacuum hose.
3. Route the wiring through the dash panel, and then install the grommet.
4. Connect the servo electrical connector to the amplifier.
5. Connect the servo chain to the bellcrank, adjusting it as described in the Adjustments section.

#### 1972-75 Continental, Thunderbird, Mark IV
#### 1974-75 Torino, Montego, Cougar (California)

**Removal**

1. Disconnect the wiring connectors at the servo assembly.
2. Disconnect the servo chain at the bellcrank, and disconnect the vacuum hose at the servo.
3. Remove the servo retaining pins, and remove the servo from the mounting bracket.

**Installation**

1. Put the servo in position, and install the retaining pins.
2. Connect the ball chain, and adjust it as described in Adjustments.
3. Connect the wiring connectors.

### Amplifier Assembly
### 1969 All Models

**Removal and Installation**

1. Disconnect the amplifier wires under the instrument panel.
2. Unplug the connector from the horn relay. Then, remove two amplifier bracket attaching screws and remove the assembly. Transfer the horn relay to the new bracket.
3. Position the amplifier and bracket assembly to the dash. Install the screws. Plug the connector to the horn relay and connect the amplifier wires.

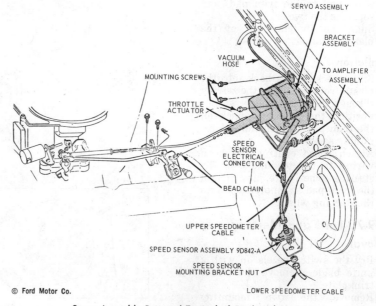

© Ford Motor Co.

*Servo Assembly Removal Typical of Ford and Mercury*

# Ford Motor Company

## 1970-73 All Models

### Removal

1. Disconnect the speed sensor, servo assembly (throttle actuator), horn relay and the amplifier assembly wire harness connectors.
2. Remove the two attaching bolts that fasten the amplifier assembly mounting bracket to the dash panel.
3. Remove the amplifier assembly and mounting bracket from the vehicle.
4. Remove the amplifier assembly from mounting bracket.

### Installation

1. Install the amplifier on the mounting bracket.
2. Attach the amplifier assembly and mounting bracket to the dash panel with the two attaching screws.
3. Connect the speed sensor, servo assembly (throttle actuator), horn relay, and the amplifier assembly wire harness connectors.
4. Test the system for proper operation.

## 1974-75 All Models

### Removal

1. Disconnect the 6 and 8 way connectors at the amplifier.
2. Remove the attaching screws or nuts that fasten the amplifier bracket to the vehicle. On Thunderbird/Mark IV the attaching screws allow removal of the amplifier alone omitting steps 3 and 4 for these models.
3. Remove the amplifier assembly and mounting bracket from the vehicle.
4. Remove the amplifier assembly from the mounting bracket.

### Installation

1. Install the amplifier on the mounting bracket.
2. Attach the amplifier assembly and mounting bracket to the vehicle with the attaching screws or nuts.
3. Connect the 6 and 8 way connectors to the amplifier.
4. Test the system for proper operation.

## Vacuum Reservoir
## 1974-75 Torino, Montego, Cougar

### Removal

1. Under the hood, locate the vacuum line to the vacuum reservoir. Disconnect the line at the vacuum valve and remove the line from the attaching straps along the dash panel.
2. Working inside the left front fender well, remove three screws retaining the plastic splash shield to the fender apron. Remove the shield.
3. Remove the two screw/washer assemblies in the fender apron above the splash shield and three screws attaching the lower rear underside of the fender to the body and sound deadener panel.
4. Remove four screws holding the fender apron to the fender starting at the lower rear edge of the wheel opening and working toward the center.
5. Remove the two nuts holding the vacuum reservoir to the fender apron. Remove the reservoir by spreading the lower rear portion of the fender and fender apron sufficiently to allow clearance for the reservoir and vacuum line assembly. Care should be taken not to damage the vacuum line which must be pulled through from the engine compartment during reservoir removal.

### Installation

1. Install the vacuum reservoir and hose assembly behind the fender apron and thread the vacuum line through the proper opening into the engine compartment.
2. Install the reservoir to the fender apron and securely attach the two retaining nuts.
3. Install and tighten to specification: three lower fender to body screws; four fender to fender apron attaching screws; and two screw/washer assemblies to the fender apron above the splash shield.
4. Install the splash shield and retaining screws. Tighten screws securely.
5. Install the vacuum line through the retaining straps at the dash panel and attach to the vacuum valve.

## 1974-75 Thunderbird and Continental Mark IV

### Removal

1. Under the hood, locate the vacuum hose to the vacuum reservoir. Disconnect the line at the vacuum valve and remove the line from the attaching strap along the upper cowl.
2. Inside the left front fender well, starting at the rear and continuing to the centerline of the wheel opening, remove all the fender apron attaching screws.
3. Remove the two screws attaching the lower rear flange of the fender to the body.
4. Remove the two nuts holding the vacuum reservoir to the fender apron. Remove the reservoir by spreading the lower rear portion of the fender and fender apron sufficiently to allow clearance for the reservoir and vacuum hose assembly to drop down and out from behind the apron.

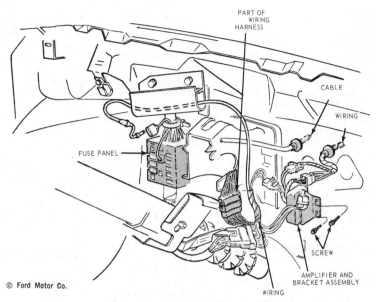

© Ford Motor Co.

*Typical Late Model Amplifier Assembly*

# Ford Motor Company

## Installation

1. Install the vacuum reservoir and hose assembly behind the fender apron and thread the hose through the proper opening into the engine compartment.
2. Install the reservoir to the fender apron and securely attach the two retaining nuts.
3. Install and tighten to specification: two lower rear fender to body attaching screws, and all fender apron attaching screws.
4. Install the vacuum line through the retaining strap at the upper cowl and attach to the vacuum valve.

## PERFECT CIRCLE SPEED CONTROL SYSTEM

### 1969-71 Ford All Models

### Description

The automatic speed control system is a driver operated speed regulating device designed for use on turnpike or other open road driving. It can be used to maintain a constant vehicle speed from 30 to 80 mph on both hilly or level roads. The system does not restrict or affect available engine rpm or sacrifice performance.

The system consists of a speed control regulator assembly, a brake release relay, an ON-OFF switch, a two position turn signal lever (set-speed) switch, a servo assembly, upper and lower speedometer cables, and wires, vacuum hoses, and linkage to connect the components for proper operation.

When the system is in operation, additional speed for passing can be obtained by depressing the accelerator. When the accelerator is released, the vehicle will return to the previously set speed automatically. This override feature allows complete control of vehicle speed without disrupting the memory of the speed control system. When the brakes are applied the memory of the system is cancelled and the speed must be reset.

The vehicle speed may also be controlled by use of the two position set-speed switch on the end of the turn signal lever. Pressing the set-speed switch to the first detent activates the speed control system and increases the vehicle speed as long as the switch is depressed to the first detent. When the switch is released, the vehicle will maintain the new speed. When the set-speed switch is pressed to the coast position (second detent-all the way in), the system is disengaged until the

button is released. The vehicle speed at the time of button release will be maintained providing it is above the minimum speed of 30 mph. The system can be shut off by the ON-OFF switch, located on the lower edge of the instrument panel below the ignition switch.

### Operation

When the ignition switch is ON and the speed control ON-OFF switch is moved to the ON position, electrical power is supplied to the turn signal lever set-speed switch and the speed control regulator assembly. Within the regulator assembly, electrical power is supplied to the vacuum solenoid valve holding circuit, and stops at that point.

Vehicle speed is transmitted to the governor in the regulator assembly with a speedometer cable which is connected to the transmission. As the speed of the vehicle is increased, the governor fly-weights are forced outward by centrifugal force. As the vehicle speed reaches approximately 30 mph, the governor causes the low speed switch point contacts to close. This makes the speed control system ready for operation.

When the vehicle speed reaches approximately 30 mph or faster, the turn signal lever set-speed switch button should then be depressed to the first detent for speed control operation. When the set-speed switch button is depressed to the first detent, the advance solenoid coil is energized. This closes the valve, blocking the atmospheric air port to the regulator assembly. At the same time, the solenoid valve coil is energized and opens the regulator assembly port to the intake manifold. This creates a vacuum in the bellows and increases the throttle opening and vehicle speed. When the solenoid valve coil is energized, the power feed circuit to the coupling coil is also energized but the circuit is not complete until grounded by the advance solenoid valve. The advance solenoid valve must open to complete the coupling coil circuit.

After the desired vehicle speed has been reached, the set-speed switch button should be released. When the button is released, the advance solenoid coil is de-energized and opens the valve, allowing entry of atmospheric air into the regulator assembly. When the valve opens, the ground circuit to the coupling coil is completed and the coil is energized along with the solenoid valve coil. These

two coils remain energized through the holding circuit. When the coupling coil is energized, the governor is locked to the orifice metering valve. The governor, through vehicle speed, allows a metered amount of atmospheric air to equalize vacuum in the bellows and stabilize the set speed.

If the speed is reduced as when climbing a hill, the governor will reduce the orifice opening size. This will restrict the entry of atmospheric air and increase the vacuum drawn from the bellows. This will collapse the bellows and increase the carburetor throttle plate opening and vehicle speed. If the speed is increased, as when descending a hill, the reaction of the governor is the opposite and the orifice size is increased. This allows more atmospheric air to enter the bellows and reduce speed to the speed setting.

When the brake pedal is depressed, the stop light circuit energizes the brake release relay and opens the ground circuit to the solenoid valve coil and the solenoid valve closes the regulator assembly port to the intake manifold. At the same time, the coupling coil is also de-energized and the governor looses control of the orifice metering valve. This releases the carburetor to manual control by the accelerator pedal. The coast position (second detent) of the set-speed switch also de-energizes the solenoid valve coil and the coupling coil (clutch) to reduce speed. When the set-speed switch button is depressed to the coast position, the power feed circuit (holding circuit) is opened and the system reacts the same as when the brake pedal is depressed. When the set-speed switch button is released from the coast position, the switch contacts travel through the speed set position and again energize the speed control system. This automatically sets the speed control system for the speed of the vehicle at the time of release, providing the speed is not less than approximately 30 mph.

## TESTING

### 1969 Mustang and Cougar

### Instrument Panel Switch Test

1. Turn the ignition switch to the accessory position.
2. Pull out on the switch knob. The knob should stay in the out position (on position).

# Ford Motor Company

| TROUBLE | POSSIBLE CAUSES | CORRECTIVE ACTION |
|---|---|---|
| **SWITCH WORKS BUT SYSTEM WILL NOT OPERATE (Cont)** | 6. Vacuum bellows (servo) ruptured.<br>7. Frozen/locked servo, accelerator, or carburetor linkage.<br>8. Speedometer cable (lower) between transmission and speed control regulator sticking or broken.<br>9. Speedometer drive or driven gear broken.<br>10. Ruptured or loose vacuum hose. | 6. Replace bellows (servo).<br>7. Adjust and remove binding conditions in linkage.<br>8. Replace lower speedometer cable.<br>9. Replace speedometer drive or driven gear.<br>10. Replace hoses and/or secure connections as required. |
| **SYSTEM HUNTS (SPEED CONTINUOUSLY CHANGES UP AND DOWN)** | Verify the complaint.<br>1. Ruptured or loose vacuum hose between manifold and speed control regulator bellows.<br>2. Ruptured bellows (servo).<br>3. Speed control regulator not working.<br>4. Sticky accelerator, carburetor or servo linkage.<br>5. Wiring broken or shorted.<br>6. Turn signal lever (set-speed) switch not working. | 1. Replace hoses and/or secure connections as required.<br>2. Replace bellows (servo).<br>3. Replace speed control regulator.<br>4. Adjust and remove binding conditions in linkage.<br>5. Check and repair wiring.<br>6. Replace switch. |
| **SYSTEM OPERATIVE BUT SPEEDOMETER DOES NOT REGISTER** | Verify the complaint.<br>1. Upper speedometer cable between speed control regulator and speedometer stuck or broken.<br>2. Speedometer head not working. | 1. Replace upper speedometer cable.<br>2. Replace speedometer head. |
| **SYSTEM REMAINS ENGAGED WHEN BRAKE IS DEPRESSED** | Verify the complaint.<br>1. Brake stop light switch not working.<br>2. Brake release relay not working.<br>3. Wiring broken or shorted. | 1. Replace switch.<br>2. Replace relay.<br>3. Replace wiring. |
| **INDICATOR LIGHT REMAINS ILLUMINATED AFTER OFF BUTTON IS DEPRESSED** | Verify the complaint.<br>1. OFF switch not working.<br>2. Control relay not working.<br>3. Wiring broken or shorted. | 1. Replace OFF switch.<br>2. Replace relay.<br>3. Repair wiring. |
| **VEHICLE SPEED INCREASES GRADUALLY AFTER INITIAL SET-SPEED** | Verify the complaint.<br>1. Speed control regulator not working.<br>2. Turn signal lever (set-speed) switch not working.<br>3. Wiring broken or shorted. | 1. Replace speed control regulator.<br>2. Replace switch.<br>3. Repair wiring. |

# Ford Motor Company

| TROUBLE | POSSIBLE CAUSE | CORRECTIVE ACTION |
|---|---|---|
| SYSTEM WILL NOT OPERATE WHEN TURNED ON | Verify the complaint.<br>1. Fuse blown.<br>2. ON-OFF switch or control relay not working.<br>3. Wiring broken or shorted. | 1. Replace fuse.<br>2. Replace switch and/or relay.<br>3. Repair wiring. |
| SWITCH WORKS BUT SYSTEM WILL NOT OPERATE | Verify the complaint.<br>1. Wiring broken or shorted.<br>2. Brake release relay not working.<br>3. Brake stop light switch not working.<br>4. Turn signal lever switch (set-speed switch) not working.<br>5. Speed control regulator not working. | 1. Check and repair wiring.<br>2. Replace relay.<br>3. Replace switch.<br>4. Replace switch.<br>5. Replace speed control regulator. |
| SYSTEM INOPERATIVE AND SPEEDOMETER DOES NOT REGISTER | Verify the complaint.<br>1. Speedometer cable (lower) between transmission and speed control regulator sticking or broken.<br>2. Speedometer drive or driven gear broken.<br>3. Speed control regulator not working. | 1. Replace lower speedometer cable.<br>2. Replace speedometer drive or driven gear.<br>3. Replace speed control regulator. |
| SPEED CONTINUES TO INCREASE AFTER TURN SIGNAL LEVER (SET-SPEED) SWITCH IS RELEASED | Verify the complaint.<br>1. Turn signal lever (set-speed) switch not working.<br>2. Speed control regulator not working.<br>3. Wiring broken or shorted. | 1. Replace switch.<br>2. Replace regulator.<br>3. Check wiring. |

3. If the knob does not stay in the out position, check for voltage between the voltage supply connector (green wire) and ground with a test light or voltmeter.
4. If there was voltage at the supply connector, and the knob does not stay in the out position, the switch is bad.

## Turn Signal Lever

### Set-Speed Switch Test

1. Disconnect the set-speed switch connector (three-wire connector at the base of the steering column).
2. With the switch in the normal out position, check for continuity (with ohmmeter of self powered test light) between the connector terminals. There should be continuity between the cen-

*Brake Release Relay*

ter terminal of the connector and the violet wire terminal. There should be no continuity between the two outer terminals.
3. Depress the switch to the first detent, there should be no continuity between the center terminal of the connector and the violet wire terminal. There should be continuity between the two outer terminals.
4. Depress the switch all the way. There should be no continuity between any of the terminals.

### Brake Release Relay Test

1. Disconnect the brake release relay at the quick disconnect. (Mounted on the speed control regulator bracket in the engine compartment).
2. Connect an ohmmeter or self powered test light between the

black-orange wire relay terminal and ground. There should be continuity. If there is no continuity, the relay is bad.
3. Connect the blue-white wire relay terminal to the battery positive terminal by a jumper wire. The relay should click, and there should be no continuity between the black-orange wire terminal and ground. If not, the relay is defective.

### Regulator Assembly Test

1. Check the vacuum hose to the regulator assembly to assure proper connection of the hose at the engine and regulator assembly.
2. Check the wire connectors of the system to be sure that they make good electrical contact.

# Ford Motor Company

3. Road test the vehicle as follows:
   a. Start the engine and pull the on-off switch to the ON position.
   b. Accelerate the vehicle to 35 mph and push the set-speed button to the first detent. The speed control system should control the vehicle speed.
   c. Push the set-speed button all-the-way in. The vehicle should slow down. When the vehicle speed slows to 30 mph, release the set-speed button slowly. The speed control unit should control the speed at about 30 mph.
   d. Depress the brake pedal. The speed control system should be cancelled.
4. The failures of the regulator assembly will generally be the following:
   a. The vehicle continues to accelerate slowly instead of maintaining a constant speed.
   b. Vehicle will not maintain the set speed but will vary slowly around that speed.
   c. The speed control system will not lock in at any speed when all other system components are operating properly.
5. Disconnect the regulator assembly electrical connector, and connect jumper wires from the regulator side of the harness connector to its mating half of the connector.
6. Start the engine and remove the manifold vacuum supply line from the regulator assembly. Check for sufficient vacuum at the regulator assembly. If vacuum is OK, connect the hose to the regulator assembly.
7. Depress the set-speed switch button to the first detent. Check for voltage with a test light between ground and the violet and the white wires. The test light should glow for both voltage checks. If the test light does not glow, check the set-speed and on-off switches.
8. Depress the set-speed switch button all the way (second detent). Check for voltage with a test light between ground and the violet and the white wires. The test light should not glow for either voltage check. If the test light glows, check the set-speed switch in the turn signal lever.
9. Check the black-orange stripe wire for continuity to ground with an ohmmeter or self-powered test light. There should be continuity to ground. If there is no continuity to ground, check the brake release relay.
10. Turn the ignition switch off and disconnect the jumper wires from the regulator assembly connector and the mating half of the connector.
11. Inspect the regulator assembly housing for cracks, loose cover screws, excessive dirt, etc.
12. Any defect makes the regulator assembly faulty and the unit should be replaced. Remove and replace the regulator assembly as required.
13. If the regulator assembly is replaced, check the unit for proper operation by performing the preceeding road test and checks.

## Servo Assembly Test

1. Check the servo assembly for binding linkage and loose vacuum hose. Check the linkage for proper adjustment.
2. Disconnect the servo vacuum hose at the speed-control regulator. Compress the servo bellows, hold a thumb over the end of the vacuum hose. Observe the servo assembly, the bellows should not expand (leak down).
3. If the bellows does leak down, check the bellows hose for leaks, if the hose is OK, the servo assembly has a leak and is defective.

## Brake Stoplight Switch Test

1. Disconnect the stoplight switch connector at the switch.
2. Connect an ohmmeter or self powered test light to the two switch terminals.
3. Depress the brake pedal. The switch should show continuity. If it does not, replace the switch.

# REMOVAL AND INSTALLATION

## On-Off Switch—Mustang and Cougar

### Removal and Installation

1. Disconnect the battery and remove the instrument panel pad.
2. Disconnect the multiple connector from the switch and remove the control knob.
3. Remove the nut and washer and remove the switch from the instrument panel. Discard the switch.
4. Position the new switch to the instrument panel. Install the washer and nut.
5. Fasten the control knob in place and connect the connector to the switch.
6. Install the instrument panel pad and connect the battery.

## Turn Signal Lever

### Set-Speed Switch

#### Removal

1. Disconnect the switch wires at the multiple connector.
2. Remove the wiring trim cover from the steering column.
3. Unscrew and remove the turn signal switch lever from the steering column.

#### Installation

1. Install the turn signal switch lever in the steering column finger tight, then tighten the lever two or more additional turns until the wire from the lever is routed downward in line with the steering column.
2. Install the wiring trim cover over the wires and on the steering column.
3. Connect the wires at the connector.

## Regulator Assembly

### Removal

1. Disconnect the manifold and servo control vacuum hoses from the regulator. Install the protective caps or covers on the vacuum hoses and hose connections of the regulator.
2. Disconnect the speedometer cables from the regulator.
3. Disconnect the wire connectors from the regulator and separate the harness from the regulator and brake release relay.
4. Remove the regulator mounting bracket attaching bolts and remove the regulator and bracket from the vehicle.
5. Remove the regulator from the mounting bracket.

### Installation

1. Attach the regulator to the mounting bracket.
2. Position the regulator and mounting bracket to the vehicle and install the attaching bolts.
3. Connect the wire connectors and harness to the regulator and brake release relay.

## Ford Motor Company

4. Connect the speedometer cables to the regulator.
5. Connect the vacuum hoses to the regulator.

### Brake Release Relay

#### Removal

1. Disconnect the electrical connector plug from the relay.
2. Remove the ground wire retaining screw.
3. Remove the two relay attaching screws and remove the relay.

#### Installation

1. Position the relay to the mounting bracket and install the two attaching screws.
2. Connect the ground wire and connector plug to the relay.

### Servo Assembly

The servo is located under the instrument panel and is bolted to the dash panel. To remove, disconnect the vacuum hose and remove the four servo bracket retaining nuts. Disconnect the throttle cable from the accelerator pedal and remove the servo assembly.

# TESTING

### 1969 Lincoln Continental

A 12 volt test lamp is required for the following tests.

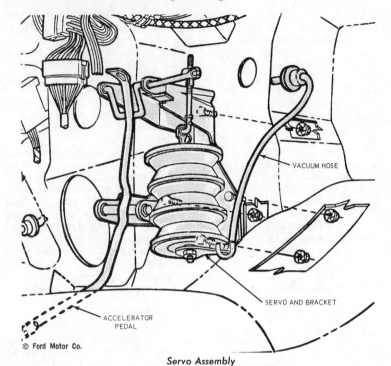

VACUUM HOSE

SERVO AND BRACKET

ACCELERATOR PEDAL

© Ford Motor Co.

*Servo Assembly*

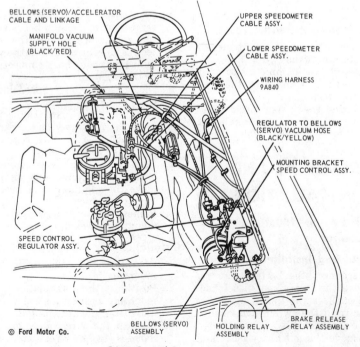

BELLOWS (SERVO)/ACCELERATOR CABLE AND LINKAGE

MANIFOLD VACUUM SUPPLY HOLE (BLACK/RED)

UPPER SPEEDOMETER CABLE ASSY.

LOWER SPEEDOMETER CABLE ASSY.

WIRING HARNESS 9A840

REGULATOR TO BELLOWS (SERVO) VACUUM HOSE (BLACK/YELLOW)

MOUNTING BRACKET SPEED CONTROL ASSY.

SPEED CONTROL REGULATOR ASSY.

© Ford Motor Co.

BELLOWS (SERVO) ASSEMBLY

HOLDING RELAY ASSEMBLY

BRAKE RELEASE RELAY ASSEMBLY

*Cruise Control Component Location*

### Turn Signal Lever
### Set-Speed Switch Test

1. Disconnect the set-speed switch connector (three-wire connector at the base of the steering column.
2. With the switch in the normal out position, check for continuity (with ohmmeter of self powered test light) between the connector terminals. There should be continuity between the center terminal of the connector and the violet wire terminal. There should be no continuity between the two outer terminals.
3. Depress the switch to the first detent, there should be no continuity between the center terminal of the connector and the violet wire terminal. There should be continuity between the two outer terminals.
4. Depress the switch all the way. There should be no continuity between any of the terminals.

### Brake Release Relay Test

1. Disconnect the brake release relay at the quick disconnect. (Mounted on the speed control regulator bracket in the engine compartment.)
2. Connect an ohmmeter or self powered test light between the black-orange wire relay terminal and ground. There should be continuity. If there is no continuity, the relay is defective.
3. Connect the blue-white wire relay terminal to the battery positive terminal by a jumper wire. The relay should click, and there should be no continuity between the black-orange wire terminal and ground. If not, the relay is defective.

# Ford Motor Company

## Speed Control
## Holding Relay Test

Connect the test lamp between ground and the red wire terminal on the holding relay. With the ignition key in the ACC position and the ON button (in the ON-OFF panel) depressed, the test lamp should light.

If the test lamp fails to light and the feed wire to the holding relay is good, the holding relay is at fault and requires replacement.

## Speed Control
## Regulator Assembly Test

1. Check the vacuum hose to the regulator assembly to assure proper connection of the hose at the engine and regulator assembly.
2. Check the wire connectors of the system to be sure that they make good electrical contact.
3. Road test the vehicle as follows:
   a. Start the engine and push the ON button (located in the lower left area of the instrument panel).
   b. Accelerate the vehicle to 35 mph and push the set-speed button to the first detent. The speed control system should control the vehicle speed.
   c. Push the set-speed button all the way in. The vehicle should slow down. When the vehicle speed slows to 30 mph, release the set-speed button slowly. The speed control unit should control the speed at about 30 mph. depress the brake pedal. The speed control system should be cancelled.
4. The failures of the regulator assembly will generally be the following:
   a. The vehicle continues to accelerate slowly instead of maintaining a constant speed.
   b. Vehicle hunts—will not maintain the set speed but will oscillate slowly around that speed.
   c. The speed control system will not lock in at any speed when all other system components are operating properly.
5. Disconnect the regulator assembly electrical connector, and connect jumper wires from the regulator side of the harness connector to its mating half of the connector.
6. Start the engine and remove the manifold vacuum supply line from the regulator assembly. Check for sufficient vacuum at the regulator assembly. If vacuum is OK, connect the hose to the regulator assembly.
7. Depress the set-speed switch button to the first detent. Check for voltage with a test light between ground and the violet and the white wires. The test light should glow for both voltage checks. If the test light does not glow, check the set-speed and on-off switches.
8. Depress the set-speed switch button all-the-way (second detent). Check for voltage with a test light between ground and the violet and the white wires. The test light should not glow for either voltage check. If the test light glows, check the set-speed switch in the turn signal lever.
9. Check the black-orange stripe wire for continuity to ground with an ohmmeter or self powered test light. There should be continuity to ground. If there is no continuity to ground, check the brake release relay.
10. Turn the ignition switch off and disconnect the jumper wires from the regulator assembly connector and the mating half of the connector.
11. Inspect the regulator assembly housing for cracks, loose cover screws, excessive dirt, etc.
12. Any inoperative condition makes the regulator assembly inoperative and the unit should be replaced. Remove and replace the regulator assembly as required.
13. If the regulator assembly is replaced, check the unit for proper operation by performing the preceding road test and checks.

## Servo (Bellows) Assembly Test

1. Check the servo assembly for binding linkage and loose vacuum hose. Check the linkage for proper adjustment.
2. Disconnect the servo vacuum hose at the speed-control regulator. Compress the servo bellows, hold the thumb over the end of the vacuum hose. Observe the servo assembly, the bellows should not expand (leak down).
3. If the bellows does leak down, check the bellows hose for leaks, if the hose is OK, the servo assembly has a leak and should be replaced.

## Brake Stoplight Switch Test

1. Disconnect the stoplight switch connector at the switch.
2. Connect an ohmmeter or self powered test light to the two switch terminals.
3. Depress the brake pedal. The switch should show continuity. If it does not it should be replaced.

# ADJUSTMENTS

## Bellows/Accelerator
## Cable Adjustment

Only one adjustment is required for the speed control system to assure a normal engine idle.

With the carburetor set at hot idle, adjust the Bowden cable to provide $\frac{1}{16}$ inch clearance between the Bowden cable and C washer and the accelerator linkage sleeve.

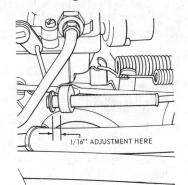

1/16" ADJUSTMENT HERE

*Cable Adjustment*

# REMOVAL AND INSTALLATION

## Bellows (Servo) Assembly

### Removal

1. Remove the cotter pin and carefully separate the cable from the bellows assembly.
2. Disconnect the vacuum hose and install a protection cap or plug in open end.
3. Remove the nut and lock-washer from the stud connecting the bellows to the mounting bracket.
4. Remove the bellows assembly.

### Installation

1. Attach the bellows to the mounting bracket with nut and lock-washer.

# Ford Motor Company

2. Install the cable, insert pin, and secure.
3. Remove the protective cover from the open end of the vacuum hose and attach the hose to the bellows.

## Brake Release Relay and/or Holding Relay

### Removal

1. Remove the plastic protective cover from the mounting bracket.
2. Disconnect wires from the harness at the electrical connector.
3. Remove two self-tapping screws and lift the relay from the mounting plate.

### Installation

1. Secure the relay to its mounting plate with two self-tapping screws.
2. Secure the plastic protective cover to the mounting bracket.
3. Connect the wires to the harness at the electrical connector.

## Speed Control Regulator

### Removal

1. Disconnect the manifold and bellows (servo) vacuum hoses. Install a protective cover or plug in/on the open hose ends and fittings of the speed control regulator.
2. Disconnect the two speedometer cables from the regulator assembly.

3. Remove the electrical connector and separate the wiring harness from the regulator.
4. Remove two bolts securing the unit to the mounting bracket and lift the unit from vehicle.

### Installation

1. Secure the unit to its mounting bracket.
2. Connect the two speedometer cables.
3. Connect electrical wiring harness and secure it to the regulator.
4. Remove the protective cover and/or plugs from the speed control regulator and vacuum hoses. Install hoses to fittings and attach speedometer cables.

## Instrument Panel Actuator (On-Off) Switch

### Removal

1. Remove attaching screws and drop the switch housing from the instrument panel.
2. Remove the screws attaching actuator assembly to the housing.
3. Disconnect the harness connector, (black insulator).
4. Remove the switch and harness assembly.

### Installation

1. Install the screws through holes provided in the actuator into the switch housing assembly.

2. Install the switch housing assembly.
3. Connect the harness connector (black insulator).

## Set-Speed Switch and Turn Signal Lever

### Removal

1. Disconnect the speed control set-speed switch wiring from green connector.
2. Remove the cover from the steering column hub on tilt column vehicles.
3. Remove the wire harness retainer clip from the lower portion of the steering column.
4. Pull the speed control switch wiring up through the steering column.
5. Unscrew the turn signal arm assembly.

### Installation

1. Tape the ends of the three speed control switch wires.
2. Install the turn signal arm assembly into the turn signal switch assembly.
3. Feed the speed control switch wiring into the steering column wiring sleeve and remove the tape from wire terminals.
4. Install the wire harness retainer clip in the lower portion of the steering column.
5. Install the cover on the steering column hub (tilt column).
6. Connect the switch wiring connector.

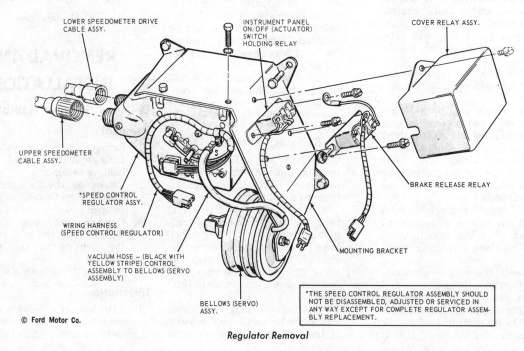

LOWER SPEEDOMETER DRIVE CABLE ASSY.

INSTRUMENT PANEL ON/OFF (ACTUATOR) SWITCH HOLDING RELAY

COVER RELAY ASSY.

UPPER SPEEDOMETER CABLE ASSY.

*SPEED CONTROL REGULATOR ASSY.

WIRING HARNESS (SPEED CONTROL REGULATOR)

VACUUM HOSE – (BLACK WITH YELLOW STRIPE) CONTROL ASSEMBLY TO BELLOWS (SERVO ASSEMBLY)

BELLOWS (SERVO) ASSY.

BRAKE RELEASE RELAY

MOUNTING BRACKET

*THE SPEED CONTROL REGULATOR ASSEMBLY SHOULD NOT BE DISASSEMBLED, ADJUSTED OR SERVICED IN ANY WAY EXCEPT FOR COMPLETE REGULATOR ASSEMBLY REPLACEMENT.

© Ford Motor Co.

*Regulator Removal*

# Ford Motor Company

## TESTING

### 1969 Thunderbird
### Diode Test

Two diodes are used in the speed control system. One diode is located in the wire harness under the instrument panel. The second diode is located in the wire harness under the left front fender.

1. Disconnect the wire connectors.
2. Set the ohmmeter to the 0-100 ohm scale.
3. Short the ohmmeter prods together and adjust the ohmmeter to the SET line.
4. Connect one test prod to each connector terminal and observe the meter reading.
5. Reverse the test prod connections and again observe the meter reading.
6. The readings obtained should be approximately 65 ohms (6.5 on the meter scale) for one test prod hook-up and no meter deflection for the other test prod hook-up. If a low resistance for both hook-ups is obtained, the diode is shorted. If a high resistance is obtained for both hook-ups, the diode is open.

### On-Off Switch Test

Disconnect the switch from the circuit. Connect a self-powered test light across the connector outside terminals. The light should glow with the switch on. Push the switch to the OFF position, the light should go out. Move one end of the test light to the center terminal. The light should not glow. Push the switch to the ON position and the light should glow.

### On-Off Relay Test

To perform an operation test, connect a 12-volt test light to the termi-

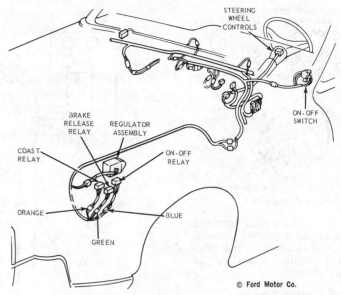

Component Location—Underhood—1969 Thunderbird

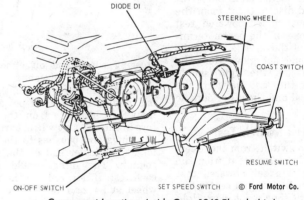

Component Location—Inside Car—1969 Thunderbird

nal in the middle of the connector. Apply a 12-volt supply lead to the other terminal. (Make sure relay is properly grounded.) This should energize the relay coil, close the normally open points and the test light should glow.

### Brake Release Relay Test

Disconnect the relay from the circuit. Connect a self-powered test light across the two female terminals. Since this is a normally closed relay, the light should glow. Apply a 12-

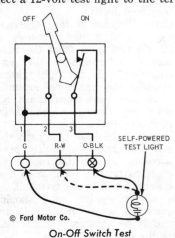

On-Off Switch Test

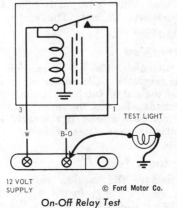

On-Off Relay Test

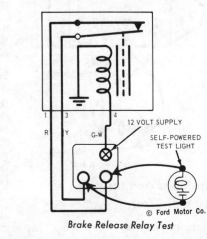

Brake Release Relay Test

# Ford Motor Company

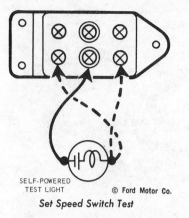

Set Speed Switch Test
SELF-POWERED TEST LIGHT
© Ford Motor Co.

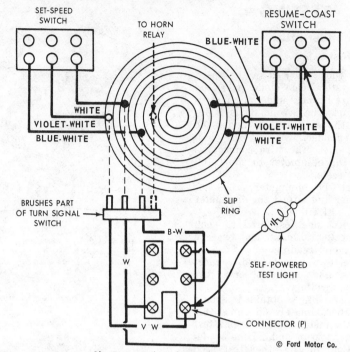

SET-SPEED SWITCH
TO HORN RELAY
RESUME-COAST SWITCH
BLUE-WHITE
WHITE
VIOLET-WHITE
BLUE-WHITE
VIOLET-WHITE
WHITE
BRUSHES PART OF TURN SIGNAL SWITCH
SLIP RING
B-W
W
SELF-POWERED TEST LIGHT
V W
CONNECTOR (P)
© Ford Motor Co.

Slip Rings and Insulator Assembly Test

volt lead to the relay male terminal. (Make sure relay is properly grounded.) This should energize the relay coil, open the contact points and the light should go out.

## Set-Speed Switch Test

Remove the switch from the steering wheel and disconnect it from the circuit. Connect a self-powered test light across one of the center terminals and one of the outside terminals, the light should not glow. Hold the button down and the light should glow. Repeat the test between the center terminal and the other outside terminal.

## Resume-Coast Switch Test

Remove the switch from the steering wheel and disconnect it from the circuit. Connect a self-powered test light between the left and center terminal, the light should not glow. Hold down the resume portion of switch. The light should glow. Move the test light from the left to the right connector, light should not glow. Hold the COAST portion of the switch down, light should glow.

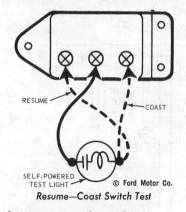

RESUME
COAST
SELF-POWERED TEST LIGHT
© Ford Motor Co.
Resume—Coast Switch Test

## Slip Rings and Insulator Assembly Test

Remove the switches from the steering wheel and disconnect them from the circuit. Disconnect the connector at the lower end of the steering column. Using a self-powered test light for continuity from the connectors in the steering wheel through the slip rings and brushes to the connector at the lower end of the steering column. The light should glow in each test. If not, remove the steering wheel and repair or replace the slip rings or brushes.

## Simulated Road Test

The road test may be simulated by raising the vehicle on a hoist enough to have the rear wheels clear the floor. Remove the vacuum hose from the servo, install a vacuum gauge so that it can be read from the driver's seat.

Start the engine, place the transmission into Drive and raise the speed over 30 mph. The system is now ready to test.

## Servo Test

Disconnect the servo vacuum at the regulator. Collapse the servo and seal the end of the hose. If the servo remains collapsed, the servo and hose do not have a leak. If the servo expands, there is a leak in the servo or hose.

## Vacuum Test

Remove the vacuum source hose at the regulator. Install a vacuum gauge in the hose and start the engine. The reading should be the same as engine vacuum.

Replace the hose on the regulator. Remove the regulator to servo vacuum hose at the regulator.

Simulate the road test. Attach a vacuum hose to the regulator. Install a vacuum gauge in the hose. Increase the speed to 40 mph. Press the set-speed button.

The vacuum reading on the gauge indicates the system is engaged. No reading indicates the system is not engaged.

## Regulator Test

1. Disconnect the regulator from the wiring harness. This isolates the regulator from any other electrical components which may be defective.
2. Check the case of the regulator for a good ground. Connect a 12-volt test light from the battery (+) terminal to the regulator case. If the light glows brightly, the case is well grounded. If the light glows dimly or does not glow, the ground is poor. Repair the ground.
3. With the regulator case properly grounded and the vehicle prepared for a simulated road test, apply battery (+) power to the connector white wire terminal.

The vacuum control valve should open and the gauge should indicate vacuum. If no vacuum is indicated, replace the regulator.

# Ford Motor Company

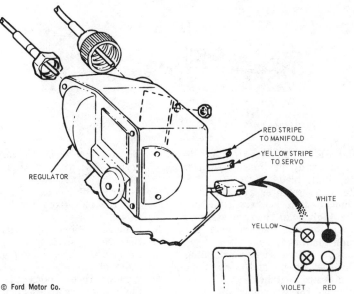

© Ford Motor Co.

*Vacuum Test*

If vacuum was indicated on the gauge, reduce the speed below 20 mph. The inhibit switch should open. The vacuum control valve should close and the gauge should indicate no vacuum.

4. Increase the speed to 35 mph. Apply battery (+) power to the connector white wire terminal. Apply battery (+) power to the connector yellow wire terminal. Remove the power from the white wire terminal. No change should occur in the vacuum reading. If there is any change in the vacuum gauge reading, replace the regulator.

5. Vary the vehicle speed between 30 and 40 mph. Note the vacuum reading. As the speed is increased, the vacuum should drop. As the speed is decreased, the vacuum should increase. If the vacuum does not vary as the speed is increased and decreased, replace the regulator.

6. With the speed held steady at 35 mph. apply battery (+) power to the connector red wire terminal. The vacuum should show an increase. Remove the power from the red wire terminal. Vacuum should drop. If the vacuum does not change, replace the regulator. The regulator that passes these tests is functioning properly.

## ADJUSTMENTS

### Linkage Adjustment

Adjust the servo chain to maintain a ½ to 1 ball link slack with the engine at hot idle.

## REMOVAL AND INSTALLATION

### On-Off Switch

#### Removal

1. Disconnect the battery ground cable.
2. Remove three screws attaching the air control assembly to the lower left side of the instrument panel.
3. Lower the air control assembly. Remove two screws attaching the switch to the bezel, and separate the switch from the bezel.
4. Disconnect the switch at the multiple connector and remove the switch.

#### Installation

1. Connect the switch multiple connector to the wire harness.
2. Position the switch to the air control assembly and install the two attaching screws.
3. Position the air control assembly to the instrument panel and install the two attaching screws.
4. Conr    the ground cable to the batte

### Diode Assembly

1. The diode assembly located on left fender apron may be replaced by disconnecting the old diode and plug the new diode in place. Tape the diode to the wiring loom.
2. When the diode located behind the instrument panel is replaced it is necessary to remove the in-

strument panel pad, radio speaker grille and radio speaker. Access to the diode is then provided through the radio speaker opening in the instrument panel.

### On-Off Relay, Coast Relay, or Brake Release Relay

1. Remove the two relay assembly retaining screws from the relay to be replaced.
2. Disconnect the relay wiring plug connector and remove the relay assembly.
3. Position the new relay and install the two retaining screws.
4. Connect the relay wiring plug connector.

### Regulator Assembly

#### Removal

1. Disconnect the speedometer and transmission cables from the regulator assembly.
2. Disconnect the two large vacuum hoses from the regulator assembly.
3. Remove two screws attaching the control relay and two screws attaching the ON-OFF relay, brake disconnect relay and the retard disconnect relay, and carefully place the relays in such a manner so as to not to damage or shortout the wires.
4. Disconnect the two wire connector plugs from the regulator assembly.
5. Remove two nuts attaching the regulator bracket to fender apron and remove the regulator and bracket assembly from the car after disconnecting the ground wire.
6. Remove three screws attaching the regulator assembly to bracket.
7. Remove two screws attaching the holding relay and air valve to the regulator assembly.

#### Installation

1. Install the holding relay and air valve on the new regulator assembly and attach it with the two screws.
2. Attach the regulator assembly to bracket with the three screws, tighten the screws after installing the ground wire.
3. Install regulator assembly to fender apron and attach it with two nuts.
4. Attach the control relay with two screws.
5. Install ON-OFF relay, brake re-

# Ford Motor Company

tard relay and the brake disconnect relay in the proper location and attach them with two screws.

6. Connect two wire plug connectors and two vacuum hoses to the regulator assembly.

7. Connect the transmission and speedometer cables to regulator assembly.

## Vacuum Servo Assembly

### Removal

1. Remove three screws attaching the servo assembly to the dash panel.

2. Remove the nut attaching the servo assembly to bracket.

3. Remove the adjuster sleeve nut, locking nut and chain assembly from the vacuum servo and remove the vacuum servo.

### Installation

1. Install the bracket on the new servo assembly and attach it with the nut.

2. Install the servo and bracket assembly to dash panel and attach with three screws.

   Install lock nut, adjuster sleeve nut and chain assembly. Adjust chain to maintain ½ to 1 ball slack with engine on hot idle.

## Set-Speed and/or Resume and Coast Switch

### Removal

1. Remove the RESUME-COAST

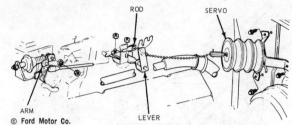

© Ford Motor Co.

*Vacuum Servo Removal*

and SET-SPEED switch bezels by carefully prying up with a thin knife blade.

2. Remove the center trim plate.

3. Remove two screws attaching the high foam pad to steering wheel spokes and remove the high foam pad.

4. Remove three screws attaching the set-speed and/or resume and retard switches.

5. Remove the wire plug connector from the switch and discard the switch.

### Installation

1. Install the wire plug connector on the new switch and attach the switch with three existing screws.

2. Install the high foam and attach it with two existing screws.

3. Install the center trim plate and switch bezels.

## Contact Ring and Insulator Assembly

### Removal

1. Remove the switch bezels from

the steering wheel by carefully prying up with a thin knife blade.

2. Remove the center trim plate and the pad from the steering wheel.

3. Remove the steering wheel from the steering shaft.

4. Remove the horn ring from the index plate.

5. Remove three index plate attaching screws and insulators.

6. Unplug the wires from the SET-SPEED and RESUME and COAST switches.

7. Remove two screws attaching the contact ring and insulator assembly to the steering wheel, and remove the assembly.

### Installation

1. Position the contact ring and insulator assembly to the steering wheel and install the attaching screws. Connect the wires to the speed control switches.

2. Install the index plate, insulator, rubber bushing, and the horn contact cup.

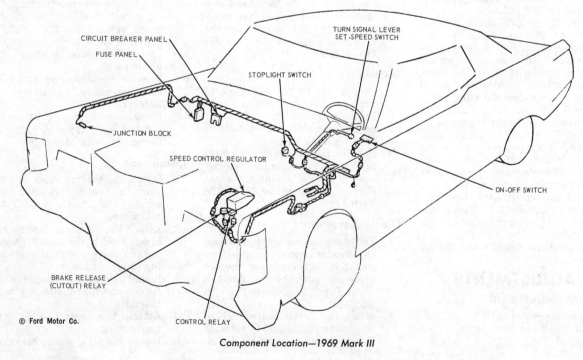

© Ford Motor Co.

*Component Location—1969 Mark III*

# Ford Motor Company

3. Install the steering wheel and pad.
4. Install the center trim plate and switch bezels.

## TESTING

### 1969 Continental Mark III

#### On-Off Switch and Control Relay Test

1. Turn the ignition switch to the accessory position.
2. Move the ON-OFF switch to the ON position. If the speed control indicator light remains ON, the ON-OFF control relay is energizing and it is operating properly.
3. If the indicator light does not stay ON, check for voltage at the control relay red wire. Voltage should be available at the red wire when the ON-OFF switch is actuated and when the ON-OFF switch is released.
4. If voltage is not available at the red wire when the switch is released, check for voltage at the yellow wire. If voltage is available at the yellow wire, replace the control relay.
5. If voltage is available at the red wire, connect a test light between the green and yellow terminals of the ON-OFF switch. If the test light glows, this part of the switch is OK. If the light does not glow, replace the switch.
6. Turn the switch off. The light should go out. If it does not go out, replace the switch.
7. Connect the test light between the green and red terminals of the ON-OFF switch. The test light should not glow. If it does glow, replace the switch. Turn the switch ON. The test light should glow. If it does not glow, replace the switch.

#### Turn Signal Lever Set-Speed Switch Test

1. Disconnect the set-speed switch connector (three-wire connector at the base of the steering column).
2. With the switch in the normal out position, check for continuity (with ohmmeter of self powered test light) between the connector terminals. There should be continuity between the center terminal of the connector and the white wire terminal. There should be no continuity

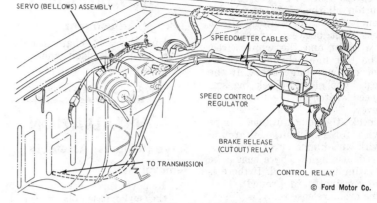

SERVO (BELLOWS) ASSEMBLY

SPEEDOMETER CABLES

SPEED CONTROL REGULATOR

BRAKE RELEASE (CUTOUT) RELAY

TO TRANSMISSION

CONTROL RELAY

© Ford Motor Co.

*Component Location—1969 Mark III*

between the two outer terminals.
3. Depress the switch to the first detent. There should be continuity between the center terminal of the connector and the white wire terminal. There should be continuity between the two outer terminals.
4. Depress the switch all the way. There should be no continuity between any of the terminals.

#### Brake Release Relay Test

1. Disconnect the brake release relay at the quick disconnect. (The relay is mounted on the speed control regulator bracket in the engine compartment).
2. Connect an ohmmeter or self powered test light between the black-orange wire relay terminal and ground. There should be continuity. If there is no continuity, the relay is damaged.
3. Connect the blue-white wire relay terminal to the battery positive terminal with a jumper wire. The relay should click, and there should be no continuity between the black-orange wire terminal and ground. If not, the relay is defective.

#### Regulator Assembly Test

1. Check the vacuum hose to the regulator assembly to assure proper connections of the hose at the engine and regulator assembly.
2. Check the wire connectors of the system to be sure that they make good electrical contact.
3. Road test the vehicle as follows:
   a. Start the engine and move the ON-OFF switch to the ON position.
   b. Accelerate the vehicle to 35 mph and push the set-speed button to the first detent.

The speed control system should control the vehicle speed.
   c. Push the set-speed button all-the-way in. The vehicle should slow down. When the vehicle speed slows to 30 mph, release the set-speed button slowly. The speed control unit should control the speed at about 30 mph.
   d. Depress the brake pedal. The speed control system should be cancelled.
4. The failures of the regulator assembly will generally be the following:
   a. The vehicle continues to accelerate slowly instead of maintaining a constant speed.
   b. Vehicle will not maintain the set speed but will oscillate slowly around that speed.
   c. The speed control system will not lock in at any speed when other system components are functioning.
5. Disconnect the regulator assembly electrical connector, and connect jumper wires from the regulator side of the harness connector to its mating half of the connector.
6. Start the engine and remove the manifold vacuum supply line from the regulator assembly. Check for sufficient vacuum at the regulator assembly. If OK, connect the hose to the regulator assembly.
7. Depress the set-speed switch button to the first detent. Check for voltage with a test light between ground and the violet and the white wires. The test light should glow for both voltage checks. If the test light does not glow, check the set-speed and on-off switches.

# Ford Motor Company

8. Depress the set-speed switch button all the way (second detent). Check for voltage with a test light between ground and the violet and the white wires. The test light should not glow for either voltage check. If the test light glows, check the set-speed switch in the turn signal lever.

9. Check the black-orange stripe wire for continuity of ground with an ohmmeter or self powered test light. There should be continuity to ground. If there is no continuity to ground, check the brake release relay.

10. Turn the ignition switch off and disconnect the jumper wires from the regulator assembly connector and the mating half of the connector.

11. Apply battery voltage to the orange wire terminal of the regulator assembly wire connector. Then check for voltage between ground and the violet wire. The test light should not glow.

12. Inspect the regulator assembly housing for cracks, loose cover screws, excessive dirt, etc.

13. If the regulator assembly is shown inoperative in the preceding tests, if should be replaced.

14. If the regulator assembly is replaced, check the unit for proper operation by performing the preceding road test and checks.

## Servo Assembly Test

1. Check the servo assembly for binding linkage and loose vacuum hose. Check the linkage for proper adjustment.

2. Disconnect the servo vacuum hose at the speed control regulator. Compress the servo bellows, hold a thumb over the end of the vacuum hose. Observe the servo assembly, the bellows should not expand (leak down).

3. If the bellows does leak down, check the bellows hose for leaks, if the hose is OK, the servo assembly has a leak and should be replaced.

## Brake Stoplight Switch Test

1. Disconnect the stoplight switch connector at the switch.

2. Connect an ohmmeter or self powered test light to the two switch terminals.

3. Depress the brake pedal. The switch should show continuity. If it does not, replace the switch.

# ADJUSTMENTS

## Linkage Adjustment

Adjust the servo chain to obtain a 1/2 to 1 ball link slack when the engine is at hot idle.

# REMOVAL AND INSTALLATION

## Servo (Bellows) Assembly

### Removal

1. Remove three screws attaching the servo assembly to the dash panel.

2. Remove the nut attaching the servo assembly to the bracket.

3. Remove the adjuster sleeve nut, locking nut and chain assembly from the vacuum servo and remove the vacuum servo.

### Installation

1. Install the bracket on the new servo assembly and attach it with the nut.

2. Install the servo and bracket assembly to dash panel and attach with three screws.

Install lock nut, adjuster sleeve nut and chain assembly. Adjust chain to maintain 1/2 to 1 ball link slack with engine on hot idle.

## Brake Release and/or Control Relay

### Removal

1. Disconnect the electrical wiring from the harness.

2. Remove the nuts and lockwasher securing the relay to the regulator assembly mounting bracket.

3. Remove the relay.

### Installation

1. Insert the relay studs through the holes provided in the mounting bracket and attach and tighten the lockwashers and nuts.

2. Connect the electrical wiring to the harness at the connector.

## Set-Speed Switch and Turn Signal Lever

### Removal

1. Disconnect the wiring assembly at the wire connector.

2. Connect the pull cord to the signal lever wires.

3. Remove the wire cover from the underside of the steering column (fixed column only).

4. Pull the turn signal lever wires out of the steering column, and disconnect the pull cord from the wires.

5. Unscrew and remove the turn signal lever from the steering column.

### Installation

1. Position the turn signal lever to the steering column and tighten finger tight. Tighten the lever two additional turns until the wires are on the bottom side of the lever.

2. Connect the pull cord to the wires, and thread the wires through the turn signal lever hole and route down the flange and into the turn signal wire trough.

3. Remove the pull cord from the wires, and connect the wires at the connector.

4. Install the wire cover on the lower side of the steering column (fixed column only).

## Regulator Assembly

### Removal

1. Disconnect the wires at the multiple connectors located at the regulator assembly.

2. Disconnect the two vacuum hoses from the regulator assembly.

3. Disconnect the two speedometer cables from the regulator assembly.

4. Remove the nuts retaining the regulator assembly mounting

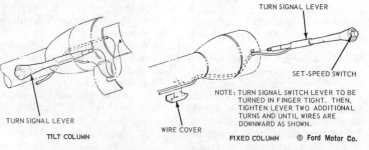

NOTE: TURN SIGNAL SWITCH LEVER TO BE TURNED IN FINGER TIGHT. THEN, TIGHTEN LEVER TWO ADDITIONAL TURNS AND UNTIL WIRES ARE DOWNWARD AS SHOWN.

© Ford Motor Co.

*Set Speed Switch and Turn Signal Lever-Installation.*

# Ford Motor Company

bracket to the left fender apron and remove the assembly.

5. Remove two screws attaching the regulator assembly to the mounting bracket, and separate the bracket from the regulator assembly.

### Installation

1. Position the regulator assembly to the mounting bracket and install the two attaching screws.
2. Position the regulator assembly and the mounting bracket to the left fender apron and install the retaining nuts.
3. Connect the speedometer cables to the regulator assembly.
4. Connect the vacuum hoses to the regulator assembly.
5. Connect the wires to the regulator assembly at the multiple connectors.

### On-Off Switch

1. Remove two screws attaching the switch and retainer to the underside of the cluster hood.
2. Lower the switch and retainer and disconnect the wires at the multiple connector.
3. Connect the switch and indicator light wires at the multiple connector.
4. Position the switch and retainer to the cluster hood, and install the two attaching screws.

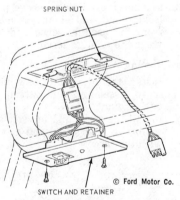

SPRING NUT

SWITCH AND RETAINER

© Ford Motor Co.

*On-Off Switch Removal—1969*

# TESTING

## 1970-71 Lincoln Continental and Mark III

### Visual Inspection

A visual inspection is an important part of the system test. When performing a visual inspection, check all items for abnormal conditions such as frayed wires, loose connections or damaged vacuum hoses. For the speed control system to function properly, it is necessary that the speedometer cable be properly routed and securely attached to the components. All vacuum hoses must be securely attached and routed with no sharp bends or kinks. The servo and throttle linkage should operate freely and smoothly. Electrical connections must be complete and tight. The wiring harness must be properly routed. Check for frayed insulation or evidence of shorts.

Any problems revealed by the visual inspection should be corrected before further tests of the speed control system are made.

### Road Test

Road test the vehicle as follows:
1. Start the engine and move the ON-OFF switch to the ON position.
2. Accelerate the vehicle to 35 mph and push the set-speed button to the first detent. The speed control system should control the vehicle speed.
3. Push the set-speed button all the way in. The vehicle should slow down. When the vehicle speed slows to 30 mph, release the set-speed button. The speed control unit should start to control the speed at about 30 mph.
4. Depress the brake pedal. The speed control system should be cancelled.
   The failures of the regulator assembly will generally be the following:
   a. The vehicle continues to accelerate slowly instead of maintaining a constant speed.
   b. Vehicle will not maintain the set speed but will oscillate slowly around that speed.
   c. The speed control system will not lock in at any speed when all other system components are functioning properly.

### Simulated Road Test

*NOTE: If at any time during the following steps the system should appear to go out of control and overspeed, be prepared to turn the system off at once with the OFF switch or the ignition switch.*

1. Raise the rear wheels clear of the floor.
2. Start the engine
3. Shift the transmission to Drive.
4. Turn on the speed control.
5. Accelerate and hold at 35 mph.
6. Press and release the set speed button. Hold foot pressure very lightly on the accelerator pedal. Normally the speed will continue at 35 mph for a short period of time and then gradually start surging.
7. Press the OFF button. The engine should drop back to idle. Stop the rear wheels with the brakes.
8. Press the ON button, accelerate and hold the speed at 35 mph.
9. Press and hold the set speed button. Slowly remove the foot from the accelerator. The engine speed should gradually increase.
10. When the speed reaches 45 mph, release the set speed button. The surging should start soon.
11. Press the COAST button or the set speed button to the coast position and hold. The engine should idle. Slow the rear wheels to 35 mph with the brakes.
12. Release the COAST button or the set speed button. Speed should set in. Surging should soon start.
13. Press the brake pedal. The system should shut off, the engine should idle and the brakes stop the wheels.

### Regulator Assembly Test

*NOTE: Before making this test, make sure there is engine vacuum at the regulator.*

1. Remove the servo vacuum hose from the regulator.
2. Attach a vacuum gauge to the regulator servo vacuum connector.
3. Disconnect the regulator from the wiring harness.
4. Check the case of the regulator for a good ground. Repair if required. Ground the brake release relay wire terminal.
5. Apply battery power to the terminal of the regulator.
6. With the rear wheels raised, establish vehicle speed of 35 mph. This closes the inhibit switch.
7. Apply power to the set speed circuit terminal(s) of the regulator connector. Vacuum should show on the gauge and increase to approximate manifold pressure. If no vacuum, replace the regulator.
8. Reduce the speed to 20 mph. The vacuum gauge should show no vacuum. If vacuum shows, replace the regulator.

# Ford Motor Company

9. Momentarily apply power to the set speed terminal(s). Increase speed to 40 mph. Vacuum should show on the gauge. Vary the speed between 35 and 45 mph. Vacuum reading on the gauge should vary. As speed increases, the vacuum should go up. If not, replace the regulator.

## On-Off Switch and Control Relay Test

### Mark III

1. Turn the ignition switch to the accessory position.
2. Move the ON-OFF switch to the ON position. If the speed control indicator light remains ON, the ON-OFF control relay is energizing and it is functioning properly.
3. If the indicator light does not stay ON, check for voltage at the control relay red wire. Voltage should be available at the red wire when the ON-OFF switch is actuated and when the ON-OFF switch is released.
4. If voltage is not available at the red wire when the switch is released, check for voltage at the yellow wire. If voltage is available at the yellow wire, replace the control relay.
5. If voltage is available at the red wire, connect a test light between the green and yellow terminals of the ON-OFF switch. If the test light glows, this part of the switch is OK. If the light does not glow, replace the switch.
6. Turn the switch off. The light should go out. If it does not go out, replace the switch.
7. Connect the test light between the green and red terminals of the ON-OFF switch. The test light should not glow. If it does glow, replace the switch. Turn the switch on. The test light should glow. If it does not glow, replace the switch.

## Turn Signal Lever Set-Speed Switch Test

1. Disconnect the set-speed switch connector wire connector at the base of the steering column.
2. With the switch in the out position, check for continuity (with ohmmeter or self powered test light) between the connector terminals. There should be continuity between the red terminal of the connector and the white/orange stripe wire terminal. There should be no continuity between the violet and white (white/orange) or the violet and red wire terminals.
3. Depress the switch to the first detent, there should be continuity between the red terminal of the connector and the violet and white (white/orange) wire terminals. There should also be continuity between the violet and white (white/orange) terminals.
4. Depress the switch all the way. There should be no continuity between any of the terminals.

## Brake Release Relay Test

1. Disconnect the brake release relay at the quick disconnect. (Mounted on the speed control regulator bracket in the engine compartment.)
2. Connect an ohmmeter or self powered test light between the black-orange wire relay terminal and ground. There should be no continuity. If there is continuity, the relay is damaged.
3. Connect the red wire relay terminal to the battery positive terminal and the blue relay terminal wire to ground with jumper wires. The relay should click, and there should be continuity between the black-orange wire terminal and ground. If the relay does not function properly, it should be replaced.

## Speed Control Holding (Control) Relay Test

Connect the test lamp between ground and the red wire terminal on the holding relay. With the ignition key in the ACC position and the ON button (in the ON-OFF panel) depressed, the test lamp should light and remain on when the switch is released.

If the test lamp fails to remain on and the feed wire to holding relay proves good, the holding relay is at fault and requires replacement.

## Servo (Bellows) Assembly Test

1. Check the servo assembly for binding linkage and loose vacuum hose. Check the linkage for proper adjustment.
2. Disconnect the servo vacuum hose at the speed-control regulator. Compress the servo bellows, hold a thumb over the end of the vacuum hose. Observe the servo assembly, the bellows should not expand (leak down).

3. If the bellows does leak down, check the bellows hose for leaks, if the hose is OK, the servo assembly has a leak and should be replaced.

## Brake Stoplight Switch Test

1. Disconnect the stop light switch connector at the switch.
2. Connect an ohmmeter or self powered test light to the two switch terminals.
3. Lightly depress the brake pedal. The switch should show continuity. If it does not it should be replaced.

# ADJUSTMENTS

## Throttle Linkage Adjustment

Adjust the servo chain to obtain a ½ to 1 ball link slack when the engine is at hot idle.

# REMOVAL AND INSTALLATION

## Servo (Bellows) Assembly

### Removal

1. Remove the screws attaching the servo assembly to dash panel.
2. Remove the nut attaching servo assembly to the bracket.
3. Remove the adjuster sleeve nut, locking nut and chain assembly from the vacuum servo and remove the vacuum servo.

### Installation

1. Install the bracket on the new servo assembly and attach it with the nut.
2. Install the servo and bracket assembly to dash panel and attach with the screws.

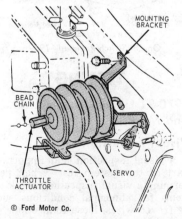

*Servo Assembly—Lincoln Continental*

# Ford Motor Company

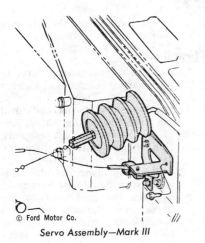

*Servo Assembly—Mark III*

Install lock nut, adjuster sleeve nut and chain assembly. Adjust chain to maintain ½ to 1 ball link slack with engine on hot idle.

## Brake Release Relay and/or Holding Relay

### Removal

1. Disconnect wires from harness at electrical connector.
2. Remove two self-tapping screws and lift relay from mounting plate.
3. Remove the relay.

### Installation

1. Secure the relay to its mounting plate with two self-tapping screws.
2. Connect the wires to the harness at the electrical connector.

## Regulator Assembly

### Removal

1. Disconnect the wires at the multiple connectors located at the regulator assembly.
2. Disconnect the two vacuum hoses from the regulator assembly.

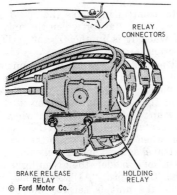

BRAKE RELEASE RELAY    HOLDING RELAY

RELAY CONNECTORS

© Ford Motor Co.

*Brake Release and Holding Relays*

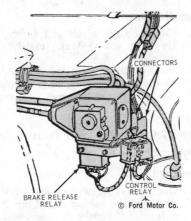

CONNECTORS

BRAKE RELEASE RELAY    CONTROL RELAY

© Ford Motor Co.

*Brake Release and Control Relays*

3. Disconnect the two speedometer cables from the regulator assembly.
4. Remove the nuts retaining the regulator assembly mounting bracket to the left fender apron and remove the assembly. If any spacer washers were used to level the regulator assembly, make sure they are relocated in the same position.
5. Remove two screws attaching the regulator assembly to the mounting bracket, and separate the bracket from the regulator assembly.

### Installation

1. The vehicle must be on a level surface.
2. Position the regulator assembly to the mounting bracket and install the two attaching screws.
3. Position the regulator assembly and the mounting bracket on the left fender apron. Make sure the spacer washers used to level the regulator are properly located.
4. Check the top surface of the regulator assembly for proper leveling. Either add to or reduce the number of spacers or either mounting bracket stud to establish the proper level.
5. Install the bracket retaining nuts.
6. Connect the speedometer cables to the regulator assembly.
7. Connect the vacuum hoses to the regulator assembly.
8. Connect the wires to the regulator assembly at the multiple connector.

## On-Off Switch
### Lincoln Continental

### Removal

1. Remove the three attaching screws and drop the switch retainer from the cluster hood.
2. Disconnect the harness connector.

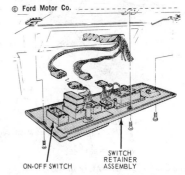

© Ford Motor Co.

ON-OFF SWITCH    SWITCH RETAINER ASSEMBLY

*On-Off Switch—Lincoln Continental—1970-71*

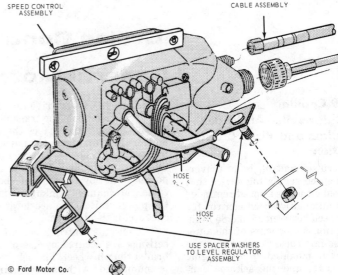

SPEED CONTROL ASSEMBLY    CABLE ASSEMBLY

HOSE    HOSE

USE SPACER WASHERS TO LEVEL REGULATOR ASSEMBLY

© Ford Motor Co.

*Regulator Assembly Installation*

# Ford Motor Company

3. Remove the switch from the retainer assembly.

## Installation

1. Install the switch in the switch retainer assembly.
2. Connect the harness connector.
3. Position the switch retainer assembly to the cluster hood opening.
4. Install the three attaching screws.

## Mark III

### Removal

1. Remove two screws attaching the switch and retainer to the underside of the cluster hood.
2. Lower the switch and retainer and disconnect the wires at the multiple connector.

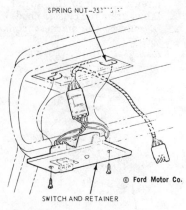

SPRING NUT—35___ __

© Ford Motor Co.

SWITCH AND RETAINER

*On-Off Switch—Mark III—1970-71*

## Installation

1. Connect the switch and indicator light wires at the multiple connector.
2. Position the switch and retainer to the cluster hood, and install the two attaching screws.

## Set-Speed Switch and Turn Signal Lever

### Removal

1. Disconnect the wiring assembly at the wire connector. Make a note of the connector and color code positions.
2. Connect a pull cord to the turn signal lever wires.
3. Remove the wire cover from the underside of the steering column.
4. Pull the turn signal lever wires out of the steering column, and disconnect the pull cord from the wires.
5. Unscrew and remove the turn signal lever from the steering column.

## Installation

1. Position the turn signal lever to the steering column and tighten finger tight. Tighten the lever two additional turns and until the wires are on the bottom side of the lever. For tilt columns, tighten two additional turns and until the wires easily lead around and along the underside of the turn signal wire harness.
2. Connect the pull cord to the wires, and thread the wires through the turn signal lever hole and route down the flange and into the turn signal wire trough.
3. Remove the pull cord from the wires, and insert the wires into the connector. Refer to terminal location color code noted during removal.
4. Install the wire cover on the lower side of the steering column (fixed column only).

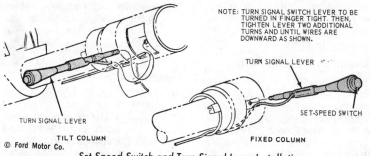

NOTE: TURN SIGNAL SWITCH LEVER TO BE TURNED IN FINGER TIGHT. THEN, TIGHTEN LEVER TWO ADDITIONAL TURNS AND UNTIL WIRES ARE DOWNWARD AS SHOWN.

TURN SIGNAL LEVER

TURN SIGNAL LEVER

SET-SPEED SWITCH

TILT COLUMN

FIXED COLUMN

© Ford Motor Co.

*Set Speed Switch and Turn Signal Lever Installation*

# Cruise Control

# General Motors

## 1968-69 Cadillac
## 1968 Oldsmobile—All Models Exc. Cutlass and Vista Cruiser
## Description

This cruise control is a driver-operated speed regulating device that can be used either as a speed reminder or as an automatic speed control for any car speed between 25 and 85 mph.

The major components of the automatic lock-in Cruise Control are: the power unit, mounted in the engine compartment; and the selector control assembly, located on the left side of the instrument panel.

The power unit is driven by a flexible drive cable from the transmission. The drive cable also drives the speedometer that runs from the power unit to the speedometer. The selector control assembly is connected to the power unit by means of bowden cable. Mechanical linkage connects the power unit to the accelerator and carburetor throttle rod.

The selector control assembly speed settings are secured by use of a calibrated thumb wheel. The selector dial is numbered with speed markings from 30 mph to 80 mph in graduations of 5 mph. An arrow on the selector control indicates the speed on the selector dial for which the unit is set when it is in the ON or AUTO position.

The switch lever turns the unit on and off, and activates the unit for automatic control. The switch lever is in the OFF position when all the way up; in the ON position when in the center; and in the AUTO position when pushed down to the end of its travel against spring tension.

On some models the green light behind the word "AUTO" lights up when the unit is set for automatic control.

# General Motors

## CRUISE CONTROL DIAGNOSIS CHART

| CONDITION | CAUSE | REMEDY |
|---|---|---|
| Speedometer noise. | Cables bent or kinked. | Straighten or replace cables. |
| | Lack of cable lubrication. | Lubricate. |
| | Noisy speedometer head assembly. | Repair. |
| Blowing fuses. | Short or ground in wiring circuit. | Perform electrical checks. |
| | Defective motor. | Check operation of motor. |
| | Locked drive screw. | Check drive screw for binding. |
| No Cruise Control response. | Accelerator linkage broken or disconnected. | Connect or replace linkage and adjust. |
| | Drive cables broken or disconnected. | Connect or replace cables. |
| | Blown fuse. | Perform electrical checks. |
| | Loose connections or broken wires (internal or external). | Perform electrical checks. |
| No Automatic Control when unit is set for automatic lock-in. | Driver riding the brake pedal or driver does not accelerate to selected speed. | Instruct owner. |
| | No current at #2 terminal. | Perform electrical checks. |
| | Improper throttle switch adjustment. | Adjust limit and throttle switch. |
| | Improper Cruise Control switch adjustment. | Adjust Cruise Control switch. |
| Constant pressure on accelerator pedal regardless of dial setting. | Blown fuse. | Perform electrical checks. |
| | No current at #1 terminal. | Perform electrical checks. |
| | Control cable improperly adjusted. | Adjust control cable. |
| | Control cable defective. | Replace selector control cable. |
| | Inoperative motor or locked drive screw. | Check operation of motor and/or drive screw. |
| | Improper limit switch adjustment. | Adjust limit switch and throttle switch. |
| Automatic control engages at selected speed without unit set for automatic lock-in. | Shorted automatic relay switch (red indicator light on instrument panel will be on). | Perform electrical checks. |
| Automatic control remains engaged when brake pedal is depressed. | Improper Cruise Control switch adjustment or defective switch. | Adjust Cruise Control switch. |
| Unit remains operative in the ''OFF'' position. | Limit switch not properly adjusted. | Adjust limit switch and throttle switch. |

# General Motors

## CRUISE CONTROL DIAGNOSIS CHART (Cont'd.)

| CONDITION | CAUSE | REMEDY |
|---|---|---|
| Pulsating accelerator pedal. | Speedometer cable or drive cable kinked or lack of lubrication. | Lubricate or replace cables if necessary. |
| | Improper accelerator linkage adjustment. | Adjust accelerator linkage. |
| | Improper motor feed points adjustment. | Adjust motor feed points. |
| Carburetor does not return to normal idle. | Improper carburetor or accelerator linkage adjustment. | Adjust throttle control rod and accelerator linkage. |
| | Weak or disconnected throttle return spring. | Connect or replace spring. |
| Unit does not control at selected speed. | Improper control cable adjustment. | Adjust control cable. |
| | Improper selector dial adjustment. | Adjust selector dial. |
| | Improper accelerator linkage adjustment. | Adjust accelerator linkage. |
| Unit controls in "ON" position or locks in "AUTO" position at low speed regardless of selected setting. | Control cable not secured to adjustable coupling. | Rotate selector dial to low speed stop to secure. |
| | Cable disengaged at selector control. | Engage cable. |
| Speedometer does not register. | Speedometer drive gear in transmission defective. | Replace gear. |
| | Broken drive cable from transmission to power unit. | Replace driven cable. |
| | Damaged drive gear or nylon gear in power unit. | Replace nylon gear or drive shaft and gear assembly. |
| | Broken speedometer cable. | Replace speedometer cable. |

When the switch is in the OFF position, the unit has no effect at any car speed. Once the switch is moved to the ON position, the unit is on and accelerator back pressure will be felt as a warning at the speed for which the selector dial is set. Moving the switch lever momentarily to the AUTO position activates an automatic relay switch in the power unit and the green light behind the word "AUTO" will light up. This indicates that the unit is set for automatic control. The switch, which is spring loaded, returns to the ON position. Once the unit is set for automatic control, it will lock-in automatically whenever back pressure is felt on the accelerator pedal at the selected speed.

A reversible electric motor in the power unit activates the mechanical linkage between the power unit and the carburetor. Motor feed points for forward and reverse energizing of the motor are closed and opened by a governor. They are under control of a governor spring that is compressed or relaxed to calibrated positions, corresponding to selected speeds. This is done by a bowden cable leading to the selector control.

## Speed Reminder Operation

Push the switch lever to "ON" position, and rotate the selector dial to the desired speed setting, line the speed setting up with the arrow on selector control assembly. The cruise control will now function as a speed reminder by exerting back pressure on the accelerator pedal whenever the speed setting is reached. The unit functions the same way whenever the speed setting is changed.

The cruise control does not interfere with normal acceleration up to the selected speed setting. Further acceleration can be obtained above the set speed by pressing the accelerator pedal past the warning-back-pressure position.

## Speed Control Operation

For automatic speed control, push the switch lever down momentarily to its stop, which is in the AUTO position. The green light behind the word "AUTO" will light up. Rotate the selector dial to the desired speed setting. The unit is now set for automatic control and it will lock-in automatically when back pressure is felt on the accelerator at the selected speed. The car will maintain the selected speed automatically and the driver can remove his foot from the accelerator pedal if desired. The selected speed will be maintained regardless of road terrain, within the limits of engine performance.

When the unit is in automatic control, car speed may be changed by slowly rotating the selector dial upward to increase speed or downward to decrease speed. The car speed can also be increased at any time by pushing the accelerator pedal through the

## General Motors

back pressure. When the accelerator is released, the car will automatically return to the selected speed.

*CAUTION: When using the selector dial to increase the car speed during automatic control, rotate the dial slowly, this will prevent sudden acceleration.*

The automatic control is disengaged when the brake pedal is depressed. It can be re-engaged by accelerating until back pressure is felt. It is not necessary to push the switch lever to AUTO position again to re-engage the automatic control. The AUTO setting may be cancelled by moving the switch lever to the OFF position, without touching the speed setting. This unlocks the unit and cancels the speed reminder and automatic control.

Turning the ignition switch OFF will cancel all cruise control functions by stopping current flow at the ignition switch.

### Preliminary Checks

It is not always necessary to remove and disassemble the power unit when the cruise control is not operating. The following checks should be performed as part of the diagnosis to determine the cause and correct the trouble. This helps eliminate unnecessary work on the power unit.

1. Turn the ignition switch ON. *Do Not start the engine.*
2. Push the switch to the AUTO position. The green light behind the word "AUTO" should light up and stay lit after the lever returns to ON (center position). If the bulb does not light, check the condition of the directional

signal fuse in the fuse panel.
3. Disconnect the connector at the fuse control power unit.
4. Push the switch lever to OFF position.
5. Using a test lamp, ground one lead and touch the other lead to terminal No. 1 (pink with white stripe wire), the lamp should light. If it does not light, the wiring in the selector control assembly, or the assembly itself is defective.
6. Ground one test lamp and touch the other lead to terminal No. 2 (orange wire), and push switch lever to ON (center) position. If the lamp fails to light, check for defective wiring in the selector control assembly.
7. Ground one test lamp lead and touch the other lead to terminal No. 3 (white and black stripe wire). Have someone push the lever to AUTO position and allow the switch to come back to the ON position. The test lamp and "AUTO" light should light up when the switch lever reaches the AUTO position and then go out when the switch lever returns to the ON position. If the test lamp fails to operate as described above, check for defective wiring in the selector control assembly. If the "AUTO" light does not light, check the bulb, feed to bulb, and that a good contact is made at the ON terminal when switch lever is returning from the AUTO to the ON (center) position.
8. Ground one test lamp lead and touch the other lead to terminal No. 4 (pink wire). Have some-

one push the switch lever to the AUTO position and hold the switch lever in the AUTO position. Step on the brake pedal. The test lamp should go out and then come on when the brake pedal is released. If the lamp fails to operate as described above, check for an improperly adjusted cruise control switch or defective wiring in the selector control assembly. Allow the switch lever to return to ON position.
9. Connect wire connector to power unit.
10. Ground one test lamp lead and touch the other lead to terminal No. 3 (white with black stripe wire) at power unit. Have someone push the switch lever to the AUTO position and allow the switch to come back to the ON position. The test lamp should light when the switch lever reaches AUTO position. The test lamp should light when the switch lever reaches AUTO position, and stay lit when the switch lever returns to the ON position. If the test lamp fails to operate as described above, check for loose connections at the relay switch or a defective relay switch.
11. Remove the test lamp and turn the ignition switch off.
12. Remove the three screws securing the power unit cover to the power unit and remove cover.
13. Turn the ignition switch ON and move it to AUTO position to set the unit for automatic control. Do not start the engine.
14. Move the contact arm against the motor feed point on locking arm side of magnet. The magnet assembly should move to the closed throttle position and magnetically pick up the locking arm. Then when the contact arm is released, the magnet should go to the wide open throttle position taking the locking arm with it. If the magnet releases the locking arm at wide open throttle position check the holding switch on back of the magnet assembly.
15. If the magnet fails to pick up the locking arm, check for an improperly adjusted throttle switch, defective wiring in magnet circuit, or a defective magnet coil.
16. Turn the ignition switch OFF and move the switch lever to the OFF position.
17. Install the cover on the power

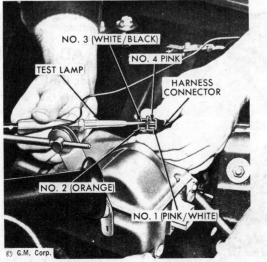

© G.M. Corp.

*Preliminary Electrical Checks*

NO. 3 (WHITE/BLACK)
NO. 4 PINK
TEST LAMP
HARNESS CONNECTOR
NO. 2 (ORANGE)
NO. 1 (PINK/WHITE)

# General Motors

unit and secure in place with the three screws.

18. If the above electrical checks do not correct the trouble, check the following adjustments before removing the power unit:
    a. Selector dial adjustment.
    b. Selector control cable check.
    c. Accelerator linkage adjustment.
    d. Motor feed points adjustment.
    e. Limit switch and throttle switch points adjustment.

## Control Cable Check

1. Release the retainer spring from the dustshield by rotating 90 degrees. Pull the control cable from the dustshield to release it from the adjustable coupling.
2. Rotate the selector dial to the low speed position. Make sure it is positioned against its stop, but do not force beyond the stop.
3. Position the control cable as close to the in-car position as possible, using the No. 3 slot of control cable gauge. The end of the hook should just touch the stop on the gauge and legs of gauge should bottom on the ferrule. If adjustment is more than .005″ off, adjust the control cable.

*NOTE: The control cable must be positioned carefully, otherwise the check will not be accurate as the relationship of the inner cable to the outer cable varies according to the control cable location.*

4. Turn the speed selector to the high speed setting and fit the cable into the dustshield until the ferrule stops against the dustshield. Hold it in this position

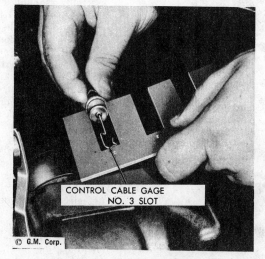

CONTROL CABLE GAGE
NO. 3 SLOT

© G.M. Corp.

*Control Cable Check*

and rotate the retainer spring on the dustshield until it is positioned into the slots.

5. Rotate the selector dial to low speed stop to secure the control cable into the adjustable coupling.

*CAUTION: This stop must be performed or the unit will control in "ON" position or lock-in in "AUTO" position at low speed regardless of the selected setting.*

## Motor Current Test

1. Remove the electric connector at the power unit.
2. Remove the three screws that hold the power unit cover to the housing.
3. Connect the positive lead from an ammeter to the positive terminal of the battery. Connect the negative lead of the tester to the number two terminal on the front of the power unit.
4. Hold the contact arm against the upper feed point and check the reading on the meter. Hold the contact arm against the lower feed point and check the reading. If the reading in either case is more than 5 amps the motor is drawing too much and should be replaced.
5. Remove the test leads and install the cover and electrical connector.

## Motor Operation Check

1. Remove the three screws that hold the power unit cover on and remove the cover.
2. Check the accelerator linkage adjustment.
3. Turn the ignition switch ON but

*Do Not start the engine.*

4. Move the switch lever to the AUTO position to set the unit for automatic control.
5. Move the contact arm so it touches the motor feed point on the locking arm side of the magnet. The motor should rotate the drive screw and move it towards the closed throttle position. The magnet will pick up the locking arm. When the contact arm is released the motor will move the magnet to the wide open throttle position.
6. If the motor does not open or close the throttle through the accelerator linkage, the motor could be binding. Check the alignment of the motor with housing. To check the motor for binding, loosen the motor from the housing without disconnecting the motor leads and disengage the shaft from the drive screw. Push the contact arm against the feed point on wide open throttle side of the magnet assembly to check forward operation. If the motor does not run free, replace the motor. If the motor does run free, current test the motor.
7. The drive screw or the carburetor linkage could also be binding. After making certain the motor runs free, check the drive screw for binding by turning the plastic gear on the motor to check for free rotation. If the drive screw does not rotate freely, it is defective and should be replaced. If the motor and drive screw operate satisfactorily, then adjust the carburetor linkage.
8. Turn the ignition switch OFF, move the switch lever to OFF position, and reinstall the power unit cover.

## ADJUSTMENTS

### Selector Dial

1. Rotate the selector dial up to the high speed position, against its top.
2. Move the switch lever to ON position.
3. Operate the car at a steady speed of 50 mph, as indicated on the speedometer.

*CAUTION: This adjustment must be made on the highway. Do not make these adjustments on a hoist or jackstands.*

4. Rotate the selector dial down until the back pressure is felt on

## General Motors

accelerator pedal, then lock the Cruise Control by momentarily pushing the switch to the AUTO position.

5. With the car at 50 mph, as indicated on the speedometer, the numeral 50 on the selector dial should be lined up with the arrow on the selector control assembly. Observe the reading on the dial, then move switch to OFF position. *Do not rotate selector dial.*

6. If the selector dial agrees with the speedometer, the selector dial is properly adjusted.

7. If the readings do not agree, adjust the selector dial as follows:
   a. With the switch lever in the OFF position, turn the selector dial up (if the dial reads on the low side) or down (if the dial reads on the high side) against its stop. Then, by hand, rotate the dial beyond its stops the necessary amount of travel, as observed in step 5, to correct the selector dial setting. Slipping the wheel will allow the wheel to move past its stop without damage.
   b. Repeat the adjustment procedure until the reading on the selector dial agrees with the reading on the speedometer.

### Control Cable

*NOTE: The control cable is preset at the factory and normally should not require adjustment unless a new cable is installed. This adjustment must be performed off car. First check the control cable and, if necessary, adjust as follows:*

1. Remove the Cruise Control Selector Assembly.
2. Rotate the selector dial to the low speed position until it rests against its stop. Do not force beyond the stop.
3. Position the assembly flat on a work bench and make sure there are no kinks in the cable.
4. Loosen the hex head set screw at the control cable clamp on the selector control just enough so that the outer bowden cable casing may be threaded in and out of the clamp by turning the dustshield.
5. Thread the control cable housing until it is approximately halfway out of the control cable clamp. Position the No. 2 center slot of a control cable gauge so

that the end of the hook touches the stop on the gauge. Hold the hook and gauge assembly until the gauge bottoms on ferrule of control cable. While holding it in this position, tighten the hex head set screw at the control cable clamp.

*NOTE: Threading the outer casing will provide a more accurate adjustment and help retain the inner cable in the retainer.*

6. Install the Cruise Control Selector assembly.

### Linkage

1. Make sure the throttle rod is adjusted properly.
2. Remove the cotter pin that holds the accelerator linkage to the exterior arm, then remove the washer and separate the linkage from the exterior arm of the power unit.
3. Adjust the trunnion so that when it is installed through the exterior arm, the locating hole in the power unit housing and the hole in the exterior arm are aligned. The throttle valves must be in lowest-idle-speed position.

*NOTE: Because of the angle at which the trunnion enters this hole, it is necessary to move the Cruise Control rod when inserting the trunnion. Repeat this operation until the proper alignment is obtained. Be careful not to turn the trunnion on the Cruise Control rod too far forward, or throttle valves will unseat, causing the adjustment to change.*

4. Insert a 1/8 inch drill into the hole of the exterior arm and the power unit housing to check for alignment.
5. Install the washer on the trunnion and secure the trunnion to the exterior arm with a cotter pin.
6. Remove the 1/8 inch drill used to align the holes in the exterior arm and power unit.

### Cruise Control Switch

1. Turn the ignition ON but do not start the engine.
2. Move the selector switch to AUTO position until the green "AUTO" light lights up.

*NOTE: Some vehicles do not have an "AUTO" light. On these models push the switch to the "AUTO" side and then release the switch.*

3. Using a test lamp, ground one test lead and touch the other lead

to terminal #4 (pink harness wire) on the power unit.

4. Loosen the mounting screw that holds the switch to the brake pedal mounting bracket.
5. Adjust the switch so the light lights when the brake is fully released and goes out when the pedal is pressed down about 1/2 inch. Tighten the switch mounting screw.
6. If the switch cannot be adjusted, it is defective and should be replaced.
7. When installing a new switch, repeat step 5.
8. Remove the test lamp and turn the ignition switch and selector switch OFF.

### Motor Feed Points

1. Disconnect the terminal board connector at the power unit housing.
2. Remove the three screws that hold the cover to the housing.
3. Using a 12-volt power source connect the negative lead to the housing.
4. Connect the positive lead to close throttle motor feed point (black wire). The magnet assembly will move to the closed position. Remove the positive lead.
5. Measure the gap between either of the feed points and the center contact arm. This gap should be .070 inch plus or minus .010 inch. Bend either of the feed points to adjust the gap and recheck.

*NOTE: A blackened condition of the feed points does not mean they should be replaced. The points usually do not need replacement unless they are broken.*

6. Touch the positive lead of the power supply to the red wire to open the feed points. This runs the magnet to the wide open throttle position. Remove the positive lead.
7. Insert a 1/2 inch drill through the hole in the exterior arm and the hole in the housing.
8. Spread the governor weights to the limit of their travel.
9. Touch the positive lead of the power supply to the gray wire to move the magnet assembly to the closed throttle position. Remove the lead when the magnet stops moving.
10. If the magnet assembly is less than 1/16 inch from the locking arm, adjust the contact arm by bending the curved tab down slightly. If the assembly is more

# General Motors

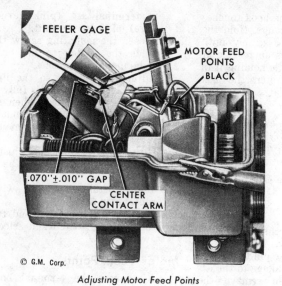

*Adjusting Motor Feed Points*

FEELER GAGE

MOTOR FEED POINTS

BLACK

.070"±.010" GAP

CENTER CONTACT ARM

© G.M. Corp.

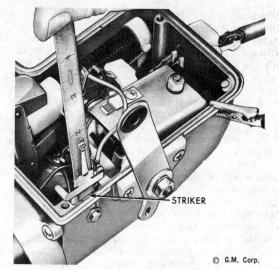

*Limit Switch and Throttle Switch Adjustment*

STRIKER

© G.M. Corp.

than ⅛ inch from the locking arm, bend the tab upward slightly. After each bend, check the magnet assembly to locking arm gap.

11. Remove the power source leads.
12. Remove the ⅛ inch drill from the hole in the exterior arm and the housing.
13. Install the cover on the housing and secure with three screws.
14. Connect the terminal board connector at the housing.

## Limit Switch and Throttle Switch Points

*NOTE: Adjusting the limit switch points also adjusts the throttle switch points.*

1. If working on the car, turn the ignition switch to the ON position, but do not start engine.
2. If working off the car, connect the negative lead from a 12-volt power source to the power unit housing and connect the positive

lead to the No. 1 terminal on the terminal board.

*NOTE: The terminal board is numbered on the inside with respective terminal numbers.*

3. Loosen the screw that holds the striker to housing and move the striker up until the motor stops running. Then slowly move the striker own until the motor just starts running. Move the striker down an additional .020 inch to .030 inch and tighten the screw to perform adjustment.
4. If working on the car, turn the ignition switch off.
5. If working off the car, disconnect the power source leads.

## Power Unit

*NOTE: Whenever the power unit is removed, the car can be driven with the speedometer operating by removing the power unit cables from the speedometer and transmission, and installing a standard speedom-*

eter cable and housing assembly between the transmission and speedometer.

### Removal

1. Disconnect the electrical connector at the power unit.
2. Remove the drive cable and speedometer cable from the power unit.
3. Rotate the retainer spring and slide it back on the control cable. Pull the control cable to remove it from the power unit.
4. Remove the cotter pin from the exterior arm, and separate the Cruise Control rod and washer from the exterior arm.
5. Remove the three screws that hold the power unit mounting bracket to the dust shield and remove the power unit with the bracket attached. Remove two screws securing the bracket to the power unit.

### Installation

1. Attach the power unit to the mounting bracket with two screws. Position the power unit and bracket on the fender dust shield and secure it in place with the three screws.
2. Install the Cruise Control rod and washer on the exterior arm and secure in place with a cotter pin.
3. Rotate the speed selector to the high speed setting.
4. Push the control cable into the dust shield and secure it with the retainer spring.
5. Turn the selector dial to the low speed stop to secure the control cable into the adjustable coupling.

STRIKER ADJUSTING BOLT

© G.M. Corp.

*Limit and Throttle Switch Point Adjustment*

## General Motors

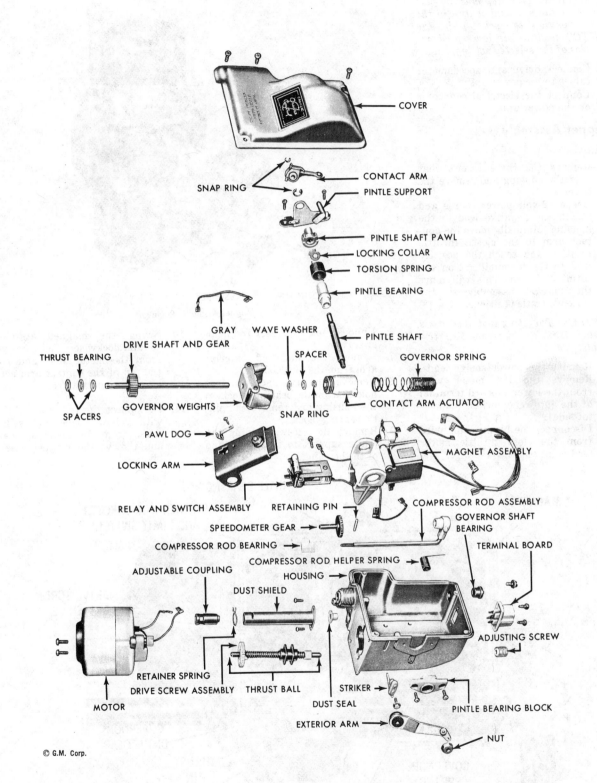

COVER

SNAP RING

CONTACT ARM

PINTLE SUPPORT

PINTLE SHAFT PAWL

LOCKING COLLAR

TORSION SPRING

PINTLE BEARING

GRAY   WAVE WASHER

DRIVE SHAFT AND GEAR

PINTLE SHAFT

SPACER

THRUST BEARING

GOVERNOR SPRING

GOVERNOR WEIGHTS

SNAP RING

CONTACT ARM ACTUATOR

SPACERS

PAWL DOG

MAGNET ASSEMBLY

LOCKING ARM

RELAY AND SWITCH ASSEMBLY

RETAINING PIN

COMPRESSOR ROD ASSEMBLY

GOVERNOR SHAFT BEARING

SPEEDOMETER GEAR

TERMINAL BOARD

COMPRESSOR ROD BEARING

COMPRESSOR ROD HELPER SPRING

ADJUSTABLE COUPLING

HOUSING

DUST SHIELD

ADJUSTING SCREW

RETAINER SPRING

DRIVE SCREW ASSEMBLY   THRUST BALL

STRIKER

MOTOR

DUST SEAL

PINTLE BEARING BLOCK

EXTERIOR ARM

NUT

© G.M. Corp.

*Power Unit*

## General Motors

*CAUTION: This step must be performed or the unit will control in the "ON" position or lock up in the "AUTO" position at low speed regardless of the selected setting.*

6. Connect drive and speedometer cables to the power unit.
7. Connect the electrical connector on the power unit.

### Magnet Assembly

#### Removal

1. Remove the three screws that hold the housing and remove the cover.
2. Use a 12-volt power source and attach the negative lead to the housing. Manually move the contact arm to the closed throttle position and touch the positive lead to the terminal #2 on the terminal board. This will move the magnet assembly to the closed throttle position.

*NOTE: The terminal board is numbered inside by respective terminals.*

3. Remove the power source leads.
4. Remove the red motor wire from the lower inboard terminal of the auto relay switch (capacitor side).
5. Disconnect the black motor wire from the close throttle motor feed point and the free wire.

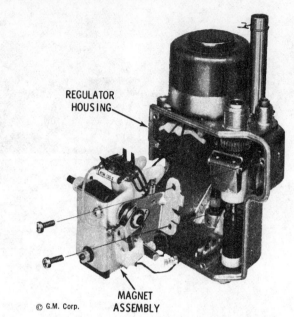

REGULATOR HOUSING

© G.M. Corp.

MAGNET ASSEMBLY

*Magnet Assembly Removal*

6. Unhook the compressor rod helper spring.
7. Remove the nut and exterior arm from the pintle shaft.
8. Remove the two screws that hold the pintle bearing block to the housing and remove the pintle bearing block.
9. Remove the screws holding the pintle support to the other side of the housing.

10. Swing the magnet assembly counterclockwise, as viewed from the motor side, and free the pin of the contact arm actuator from contact arm.

11. Disconnect the red, black, black with yellow stripe and yellow wires from the terminal board and remove the magnet assembly.

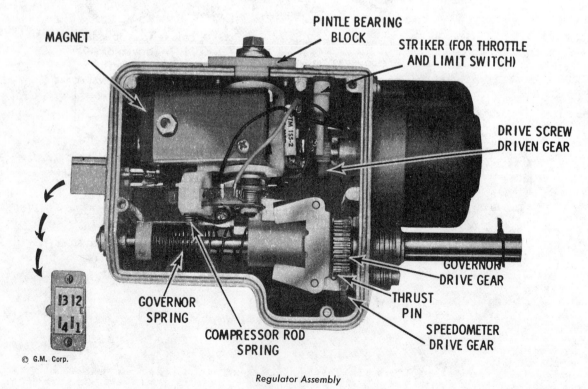

MAGNET

PINTLE BEARING BLOCK

STRIKER (FOR THROTTLE AND LIMIT SWITCH)

DRIVE SCREW DRIVEN GEAR

GOVERNOR DRIVE GEAR

THRUST PIN

SPEEDOMETER DRIVE GEAR

GOVERNOR SPRING

COMPRESSOR ROD SPRING

© G.M. Corp.

*Regulator Assembly*

# General Motors

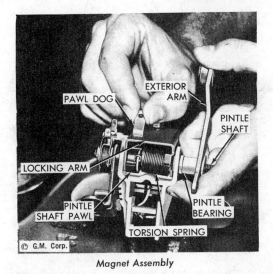

Magnet Assembly

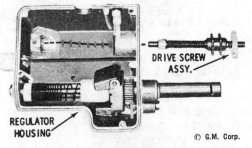

Drive Screw Assembly Removal

## Installation

1. Install the compressor rod helper spring with the shorter end positioned against the tang of the pintle support.
2. Install the magnet assembly into the housing, engaging the pin of the contact arm actuator with the hole in contact arm. Align bracket tangs on bottom of the magnet assembly with grooves in the drive screw nut. The tang on the pintle support must engage the notch in the compressor rod and the long end of compressor rod helper spring should be able to be pulled upward.
3. Install the pintle bearing block and attach with two screws.
4. Install the two screws that hold the pintle support to the housing.
5. Use a pair of needle nose pliers and hook the compressor rod helper spring under the tab on the plastic compressor rod cap.
6. Install the exterior arm on the pintle shaft, so that the hole in the exterior arm can be aligned with the hole in the housing. Secure with nut.
7. Connect the black motor wire on close throttle motor feed point, routing the wire under the black wire at the relay and the gray wire at contact arm.
8. Connect red motor wire on the lower inboard terminal of the auto relay switch (capacitor side).
9. Connect the red, black, black with yellow stripe and yellow wires on terminal board, routing red wire under the helper spring.
10. Perform limit switch and throt-

tle switch points adjustment.
11. Perform motor feed points adjustment.

## Motor
### Removal

1. Remove the three screws that hold the housing cover to the housing and remove the cover.
2. Disconnect the red motor wire from the lower inboard terminal of the auto relay switch (capacitor side).
3. Disconnect the black motor wire from the close throttle motor feed point and free wire.
4. Remove the two screws that secure the motor to the housing and remove the motor.

### Installation

1. Install the motor on the housing and attach with two screws, guiding the red and black wires through the housing. Make certain that the bracket tangs on the bottom of the magnet assembly align with the grooves in the drive screw nut and the drive shaft screw aligns with the hole in the adjusting screw and the hole in the motor.

*NOTE: Be careful not to lose the adjusting screw insert.*

2. Check the drive screw to see if it will turn. If it does not, adjust it as below.
3. Turn the adjusting screw until it is tight. Do not force. Then back off the screw 1/4 turn.

*NOTE: Do not remove the adjusting screw as a normal service pro-*

*cedure. Repeated removal and installation of the adjusting screw will ruin the threads. Remove it only if it has to be replaced. A slight adjustment is all that is needed.*

4. Connect the black motor feed wire on the close throttle motor feed point, routing it under the black wire at the relay and gray wire at the contact arm.
5. Connect the red motor feed wire on the lower inboard terminal of the auto relay switch (capacitor side).
6. Install the cover on the housing and attach with three screws.

## Drive Screw Assembly
### Removal

1. Remove the three screws that hold the cover to the housing and remove cover.
2. Remove the magnet and motor assembly from the housing.
3. Remove the drive screw assembly.

### Installation

1. Lubricate the drive screw assembly sparingly with cam and bearing lubricant and install the drive screw assembly in the housing.

*NOTE: Be careful not to lose the adjusting screw insert.*

2. Turn the adjusting screw until it is tight. Do not force. Then back off the screw 1/4 turn.

*NOTE: Do not remove the adjusting screw as a normal procedure. Repeated removal and installation of adjusting screw will ruin the threads. Remove it only if it has to be replaced. A slight adjustment is all that is needed.*

3. Install the motor and magnet assembly.
4. Install the cover on the housing and attach with three screws.

## General Motors

1968 Cutlass, Vista Cruiser
1969-71 Delta 88, Ninety Eight, Tornado
1972-75 Oldsmobile All Models
1968-75 Pontiac All Models

### Description

The main components of the automatic cruise control are the regulator assembly and the vacuum servo, mounted in the engine compartment, and the engaging switch located in the turn signal lever.

The regulator is driven by a drive cable from the transmission. The speedometer is driven by another drive cable from regulator. The engaging switch electrically controls the vacuum from the intake manifold to the regulator. The governor assembly controls the vacuum to the vacuum servo, which in turn regulates the throttle. A brake release switch is also provided to disengage the unit. At above 30 mph, the Cruise Control maintains the drivers selected speed automatically.

To operate, turn "ON"-"OFF" switch located on the instrument panel to "ON," accelerate the car to the desired speed and push the engage button located on the turn signal lever in and release. The car will maintain the selected speed whether going uphill, downhill or on a level surface. The Cruise Control can be disengaged by depressing the brake pedal or by switching the control switch to "OFF." If the brake pedal is depressed, to re-engage the Cruise Control, again attain desired cruising speed and push engage button in and release.

If a higher cruising speed is desired, accelerate to the new higher speed and depress engage button in and release. The car will now maintain the selected speed until the brake pedal is depressed or the instrument panel control switch is moved to "OFF."

If a lower cruising speed is desired, push the engage button in fully and hold it until desired cruising speed is reached and release engage button.

Brake release switches are provided to disengage the system anytime the brake pedal is depressed. When the pedal is depressed, an electrical switch and vacuum switch are actuated; actuating either of the switches will disengage the Cruise Control system. The vacuum switch opens the regulator to atmosphere disengaging the system.

The car speed can be increased at

| Condition | Apparent Cause | Correction |
|---|---|---|
| 1. Cruise Control does not engage | a. Fuse blown<br>b. Brake switch out of adjustment<br>c. No current to terminal No. 2<br>d. Engaging switch inoperative<br>e. Faulty valve body and magnet assembly<br>f. Faulty low speed switch | a. Replace fuse<br>b. Adjust brake switch<br>c. Repair wire harness<br>d. Replace engaging switch<br>e. Replace valve body and magnet assembly<br>f. Replace low speed switch |
| 2. Cruise Control does not engage when brake is applied | a. Improper brake release switch adjustment<br>b. Defective brake release switch<br>c. Faulty valve body and magnet assembly | a. Adjust brake release switch<br>b. Replace brake release switch<br>c. Replace valve body and magnet assembly |
| 3. Cruise Control re-engages when brake is released | a. Faulty engaging switch<br>b. Terminal No. 1 grounded | a. Replace engaging switch<br>b. Replace or repair wire harness |
| 4. Carburetor does not return to normal idle | a. Faulty Cruise Control linkage cable<br>b. Improper accelerator linkage adjustment<br>c. Weak or disconnected throttle return spring | a. Replace cable<br>b. Adjust accelerator linkage<br>c. Connect or replace spring |
| 5. Pulsating accelerator pedal | a. Speedometer cable or drive cable kinked | a. Replace cables if necessary |
| 6. Cruise Control does not control at selected speed | a. Faulty servo or vacuum hose<br>b. Faulty governor assembly | a. Replace vacuum servo or vacuum hose<br>b. Replace governor assembly |
| 7. Cruise Control controls speed 3 or more MPH above selected speed | a. Improper centering spring adjustment | a. Adjusting centering spring (C) |
| 8. Cruise Control controls speed 1 or more MPH below selected speed | a. Improper centering spring adjustment | a. Adjust centering spring (C) |

anytime by pushing the accelerator. When the pressure on the accelerator pedal is released the car will return to the selected speed.

*NOTE: When Cruise Control is not in operation the I.P. switch should be on the "OFF" position.*

### Operation

The Cruise Control regulator contains the following parts: Flyweight governor, low speed switch, coupling coil, solenoid operated vacuum valve, blade valve, bleed port, reedswitch.

The speedometer drive cable drives the governor. The governor controls the low speed switch and the blade valve. The coupling coil connects the governor to the blade valve when energized. The solenoid operated vacuum valve connects engine vacuum to the servo. The blade valve bleeds off some of the vacuum, according to car speed (governor position), to set the servo, and throttle opening. As the car speeds up, (going down hill) the governor moves the blade valve to bleed off some vacuum and reduce throttle

## General Motors

opening. When the car slows down (climbing a hill), the governor moves the blade valve to cover the bleed port, giving full vacuum to the servo to open the throttle. In this manner the regulator holds a constant car speed.

### Electrical Operation

When the button or the turn signal lever is depressed (above 30 mph), the low speed switch is closed. Current goes through terminal No. 1 at the regulator, through the low speed switch to the coupling coil, and to the solenoid operated valve, and to ground at terminal No. 3. The reed switch, close to the solenoid operated valve, closes due to the magnetic field. With the reed switch closed, and the engagement switch on the turn signal released, current flows through terminal No. 2, through the reed switch, and to the coupling coil, and the solenoid operated valve. The reed switch keeps these two coils energized after the engagement switch is released.

### Preliminary Electrical Checks

It is not always necessary to remove and disassemble the regulator in cases of inoperative Cruise Control. The following checks should be performed as part of the diagnosis to determine the cause and correction of Cruise Control trouble and to eliminate unnecessary service work on the regulator.

1. Disconnect the multiple connector at the regulator.
2. Turn the ignition switch to the run position.
3. Using a test lamp touch one lead to terminal No. 3 and touch the other lead to terminal No. 1. The test lamp should not light. If the test lamp lights, the wiring harness or the engaging switch is defective.
4. Touch one test lamp lead to terminal No. 3 and the other lead to terminal No. 2, the test lamp should light. If the test lamp doesn't light, check the fuse, the brake switch adjustment, and the engaging switch.
5. Touch one test lamp lead to terminal No. 2 and the other lead to terminal No. 1, the lamp should light. If the lamp lights, the engagement switch is defective.

### Vacuum Checks

Check all vacuum hose connections and make sure the hoses are not dried out, cracked or collapsed.

### Brake Release Switch Adjustment—Electric and Vacuum

1. Insert the switch into the tabular clip until the switch body seats on the tabular clip.
2. Pull the brake pedal rearward against the internal pedal stop.

The switches will be moved in the tabular clip providing proper adjustment.

### Engaging Switch Test

1. Turn the ignition switch to the run position.
2. Using a test lamp, touch one test lamp lead to terminal No. 2 and the other to terminal No. 3. The lamp should light.
3. Push the engaging switch button all the way in and the light should go out. If the light does not go out, replace the switch.
4. Touch one test lamp lead to terminal No. 1 and touch the other lead to terminal No. 3. The lamp should not light. If the lamp lights, replace the switch.
5. Push the engaging switch button in slowly. The light should come on when first depressed and go out when the button is fully depressed. If the sequence fails, replace the switch.

### Engagement Switch (Without Air Cushion Restraint System)

The engagement switch cannot be serviced. The complete turn signal lever must be replaced as an assembly.

#### Removal

1. Disconnect the battery ground cable.
2. Remove the steering column lower cover and slide the column

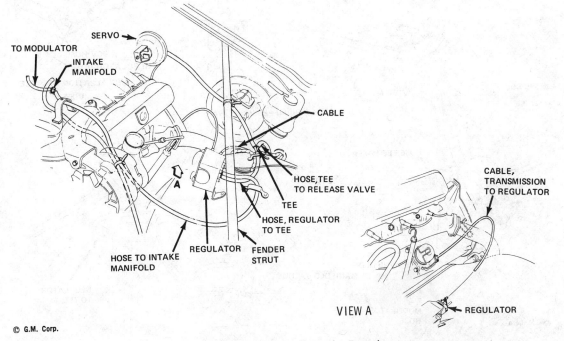

*Vacuum Hose Routing—Toronado—Typical*

© G.M. Corp.

## General Motors

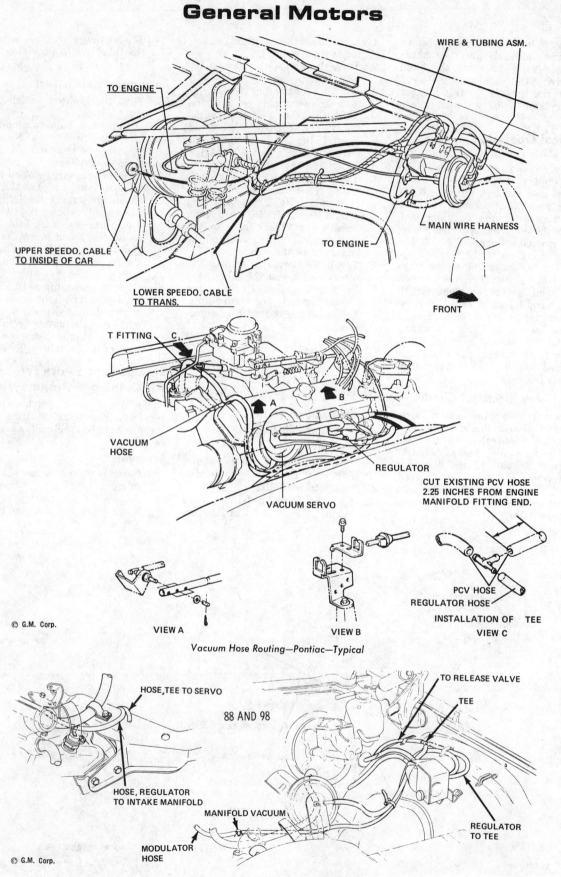

WIRE & TUBING ASM.

TO ENGINE

MAIN WIRE HARNESS

TO ENGINE

UPPER SPEEDO. CABLE
TO INSIDE OF CAR

LOWER SPEEDO. CABLE
TO TRANS.

FRONT

T FITTING

VACUUM
HOSE

VACUUM SERVO

REGULATOR

CUT EXISTING PCV HOSE
2.25 INCHES FROM ENGINE
MANIFOLD FITTING END.

PCV HOSE

REGULATOR HOSE

INSTALLATION OF    TEE
VIEW C

© G.M. Corp.

VIEW A

VIEW B

*Vacuum Hose Routing—Pontiac—Typical*

HOSE, TEE TO SERVO

88 AND 98

TO RELEASE VALVE

TEE

HOSE, REGULATOR
TO INTAKE MANIFOLD

MANIFOLD VACUUM

REGULATOR
TO TEE

MODULATOR
HOSE

© G.M. Corp.

*Vacuum Hose Routing—88, 98—Typical*

## General Motors

harness protector down out of the way.

3. Disconnect the Cruise Control switch harness connector and attach a long piece of piano wire to the switch connector.

4. On Tilt and Telescope steering columns, perform the following:

   a. Before unscrewing the turn signal lever, make a small hook in a thin piece of piano wire.

   b. Insert the wire in the turn signal lever opening.

   c. Using the wire, gently pull the Cruise Control harness out through the opening.

   d. Gently pull the remainder of the harness up through and out of the column.

   e. Disconnect the piano wire from the connector and secure the wire to the column.

*NOTE: The wire must be used so that the Cruise Control harness can be guided through the proper passages during installation.*

   f. Unscrew the turn signal lever, and be sure to pass the Cruise Control harness over the lever each time the turn signal lever makes one complete turn.

   g. Remove the turn signal lever from the car.

5. On standard steering columns, proceed as follows:

   a. Remove the steering wheel.

   b. Remove the three screws securing the lock plate cover assembly to the lock plate and remove the cover assembly.

   c. Work through the lock plate, and remove the screw securing the turn signal lever and remove the lever and harness. Pull the harness up gently so the piano wire can be used to install the new unit.

### Installation

1. Attach the upper end of the piano wire to the switch harness connector and pull the piano wire at the lower end of the column, and feed the harness into the proper location in the column.

2. On Tilt and Telescope steering columns, perform the following:

   a. Gently pull the harness down through the steering column cover part way.

   b. Allow the cruise Control lever to hang free with approximately 16 inches of wire out of the column. Wind the har-

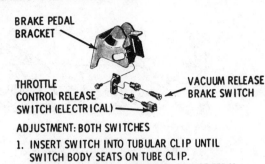

ADJUSTMENT: BOTH SWITCHES

1. INSERT SWITCH INTO TUBULAR CLIP UNTIL SWITCH BODY SEATS ON TUBE CLIP.

2. PULL BRAKE PEDAL REARWARD AGAINST PEDAL STOP. SWITCH WILL BE MOVED IN TUBULAR CLIP PROVIDING THE PROPER ADJUSTMENT.
© G.M. Corp.

*Brake Release Switch Adjustment*

ness counterclockwise around the lever six turns.

   c. Insert the turn signal lever into the opening in the column.

   d. Screw the turn signal lever into position.

   e. If any wire is wound around the lever after the lever has been installed and properly positioned (word "CRUISE" visible from top), pull the wire out of the column and loop it over the lever to remove the excess winding.

   f. After the lever is installed, gently pull the remainder of the harness through the column and into position.

3. On standard steering columns, proceed as follows:

   a. Position the turn signal lever on the turn signal switch. Work through the lock plate

and secure the lever to the switch with one screw. Tighten the screw to 30 inch pounds.

   b. Position the cover assembly on the upper end of the column and install three attaching screws.

   c. Install the steering wheel.

4. Disconnect the piano wire from the switch harness and reconnect the harness.

5. Slide the column harness protector up into position and install the column lower cover.

*NOTE: On Cutlass Salon models the dimmer switch to lever dimension must be aligned. Refer to Turn Signal Lever Dimmer Switch Adjustment.*

6. Connect the battery ground cable.

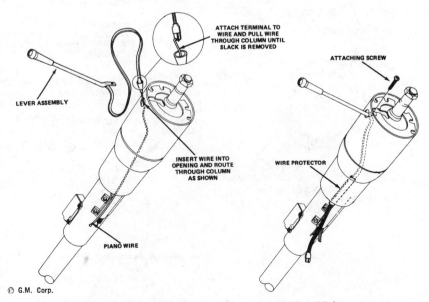

*Cruise Control Lever Installation—Oldsmobile exc. Tilt and Telescopic*

## General Motors

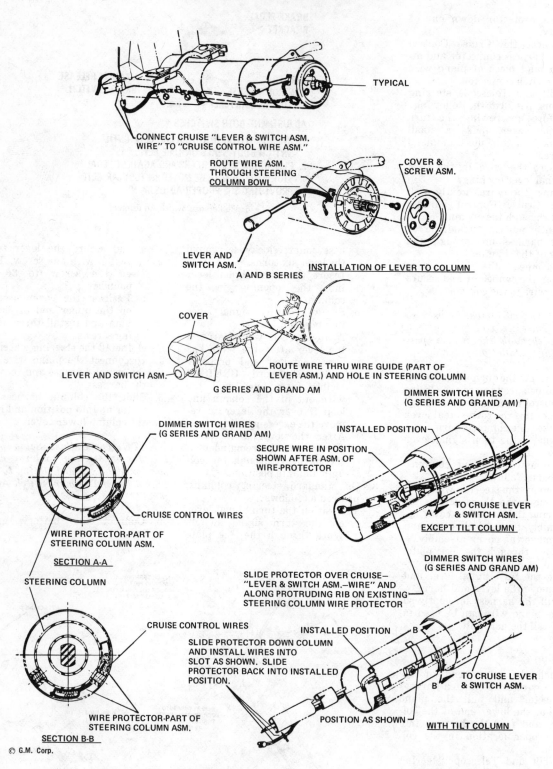

TYPICAL

CONNECT CRUISE "LEVER & SWITCH ASM. WIRE" TO "CRUISE CONTROL WIRE ASM."

ROUTE WIRE ASM. THROUGH STEERING COLUMN BOWL

COVER & SCREW ASM.

LEVER AND SWITCH ASM.

A AND B SERIES

INSTALLATION OF LEVER TO COLUMN

COVER

LEVER AND SWITCH ASM.

ROUTE WIRE THRU WIRE GUIDE (PART OF LEVER ASM.) AND HOLE IN STEERING COLUMN

G SERIES AND GRAND AM

DIMMER SWITCH WIRES (G SERIES AND GRAND AM)

INSTALLED POSITION

SECURE WIRE IN POSITION SHOWN AFTER ASM. OF WIRE-PROTECTOR

TO CRUISE LEVER & SWITCH ASM.

EXCEPT TILT COLUMN

DIMMER SWITCH WIRES (G SERIES AND GRAND AM)

CRUISE CONTROL WIRES

WIRE PROTECTOR-PART OF STEERING COLUMN ASM.

SECTION A-A

STEERING COLUMN

SLIDE PROTECTOR OVER CRUISE— "LEVER & SWITCH ASM.—WIRE" AND ALONG PROTRUDING RIB ON EXISTING STEERING COLUMN WIRE PROTECTOR

DIMMER SWITCH WIRES (G SERIES AND GRAND AM)

CRUISE CONTROL WIRES

INSTALLED POSITION

SLIDE PROTECTOR DOWN COLUMN AND INSTALL WIRES INTO SLOT AS SHOWN. SLIDE PROTECTOR BACK INTO INSTALLED POSITION.

TO CRUISE LEVER & SWITCH ASM.

WIRE PROTECTOR-PART OF STEERING COLUMN ASM.

POSITION AS SHOWN

WITH TILT COLUMN

SECTION B-B

© G.M. Corp.

*Cruise Control Lever Installation—Pontiac*

# General Motors

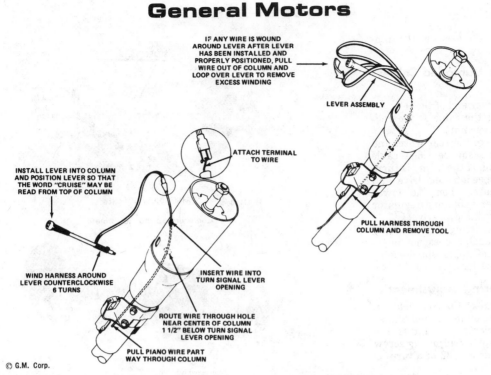

IF ANY WIRE IS WOUND AROUND LEVER AFTER LEVER HAS BEEN INSTALLED AND PROPERLY POSITIONED, PULL WIRE OUT OF COLUMN AND LOOP OVER LEVER TO REMOVE EXCESS WINDING

LEVER ASSEMBLY

ATTACH TERMINAL TO WIRE

INSTALL LEVER INTO COLUMN AND POSITION LEVER SO THAT THE WORD "CRUISE" MAY BE READ FROM TOP OF COLUMN

PULL HARNESS THROUGH COLUMN AND REMOVE TOOL

WIND HARNESS AROUND LEVER COUNTERCLOCKWISE 6 TURNS

INSERT WIRE INTO TURN SIGNAL LEVER OPENING

ROUTE WIRE THROUGH HOLE NEAR CENTER OF COLUMN 1 1/2" BELOW TURN SIGNAL LEVER OPENING

PULL PIANO WIRE PART WAY THROUGH COLUMN

© G.M. Corp.

*Cruise Control Lever Installation—Oldsmobile Tilt and Telescopic*

## Engagement Switch (With Air Cushion Restraint System)

### Removal

1. Turn the ignition switch to the "LOCK" position, disconnect the negative battery cable from the battery and tape the end.

    *NOTE: The first step is important to prevent accidental deployment of the system which could result in personal injury or damage to the system.*

2. The removal of the steering wheel is not necessary.
3. Disconnect the Cruise Control switch harness connector and attach a long piece of piano wire or equivalent to the switch connector.
4. Use a screwdriver with a blade between 1/2 inch and 3/16 inch and insert it between the top of the lever retaining clip.
5. Pull the lever straight out of the column.

### Installation

1. Insert the piano wire into the lever opening and route it thru the column.
2. Attach the piano wire to the connector and pull the wire thru the column until the slack is removed.
3. Push the lever into the retaining clip until it snaps into position.
4. Slide the Cruise Control wire protector over the wire from the lever. Then slide the protector over the rib on the main wire protector until it hits the stop on the main wire protector.
5. Reconnect the negative battery cable.

## Servo Relay Rod Adjustment— All Models

With the slow idle speed correctly adjusted and the carburetor in the slow idle position (engine off), ad-

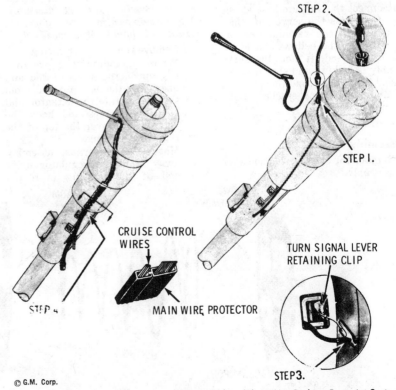

STEP 2.

STEP 1.

CRUISE CONTROL WIRES

TURN SIGNAL LEVER RETAINING CLIP

STEP 4

MAIN WIRE PROTECTOR

STEP 3.

© G.M. Corp.

*Cruise Control Lever Installation—Oldsmobile W/Air Cushion Restraint System*

# General Motors

just the rod at the servo to the minimum slack.

## Checking for Damaged Cables and Gears

1. Raise the rear end of the car.
2. Disconnect the cable at the regulator (larger nut).
3. Slowly rotate the rear wheel and observe the square sided cable drive fitting. If the fitting is turning, the speedometer drive and driven gears, then the lower speedometer cable and regulator are functioning properly.
4. If the drive fitting is turning and the speedometer does not operate then the upper speedometer cable or speedometer is defective.

## Centering Spring Adjustment

1. If the Cruise Control holds a speed, three or more mph higher than the selected speed, turn the centering spring adjusting screw (c), towards S 1/32 of a turn or less.
2. If the Cruise Control holds a speed, three or more mph below the selected speed, turn the centering spring adjustment screw (c) toward F 1/32 of a turn or less.

## Vacuum Servo
### Leak Test

Disconnect the vacuum hose at the servo. Compress the servo and place a thumb over the vacuum tube on the end plate, the bellows should remain compressed, if not, the servo assembly is leaking and should be replaced. Note the condition of the hose and replace any cracked or deteriorated hoses.

## Regulator

### Disassembly

1. Remove the six screws and cover assembly.

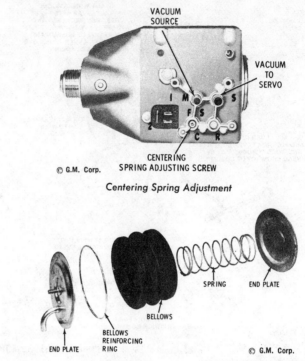

Centering Spring Adjustment

*Servo Assembly—Bellows Type*

2. Remove the two external screws on the bearing support assembly and rotate the assembly 180 degrees and slide it out.

*NOTE: Do not loosen the screw on the bearing support assembly. This screw positions the governor spring and should not be loosened.*

3. Remove the governor spring.
4. While spreading the weights, pry up on the actuator rod and disengage the actuator rod from the pin. Rotate the actuator and rod 180 degrees and hook the actuator rod over the top of the regulator housing.
5. Move the governor assembly away from the regulator drive end of the housing until the

shaft is free of the bearing and remove the governor assembly.
6. Remove the four housing retaining screws then remove the two from the back that hold the valve body and magnet assembly. Remove the assembly from the regulator housing.

## Adjustment on Governor Spring

If the screw is acidentally loosened, it may be adjusted as follows:

Move the collar so it just touches the governor spring and then collapse the spring 1/16 inch. Then tighten the screw. Road test the car to be sure the Cruise Control locks in at 30 mph plus or minus two mph.

If the lock in speed is too low, loosen the screw and move the collar

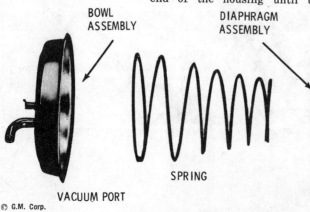

*Servo Assembly—Vacuum Type*

# General Motors

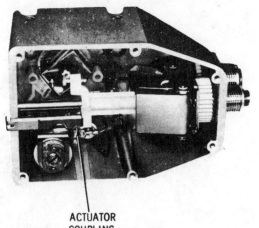

ACTUATOR COUPLING

© G.M. Corp.

*Actuator and Rod Removal*

away from the spring slightly. Road test the car again.

## Regulator

### Assembly

1. Insert the valve body and magnet assembly into the regulator housing and install the four screws, two from the back. Install the drive gear and retaining pin, if removed.

*NOTE: Make sure the foam gasket on the bottom of the valve body and magnet assembly lies flat against the regulator housing. Under no circumstances, should this gasket be glued to the valve body and magnet assembly.*

2. Insert the long end of the governor shaft assembly through the bearing support mounting hole making sure that the actuator rod is above the edge of the regulator housing assembly. Insert the shaft, with weights positioned vertical, far enough to allow the short end of the governor assembly to be inserted into the

bearing. Slide the governor assembly toward the bearing until it bottoms and gears engage.

3. Move the actuator cup down the shaft until it bottoms and rotate 180 degrees. Using a screwdriver, pry the actuator coupling up and rotate the magnet counterclockwise until the pin engages the lower actuator coupling hole.

4. Install the governor spring over the governor shaft with the closed end of the spring toward the actuator cup.

5. Install the bearing support assembly.

6. To remove the air filter from the cover, push the filter out from under the retainer.

*NOTE: Whenever the regulator assembly is disassembled, the low*

RESTRICTOR

IMPORTANT - DO NOT LOOSEN OR REMOVE SCREW (FACTORY ADJ. ONLY)

GOVERNOR SPRING

BEARING SUPPORT ASSEMBLY

© G.M. Corp.

*Bearing Support Assembly*

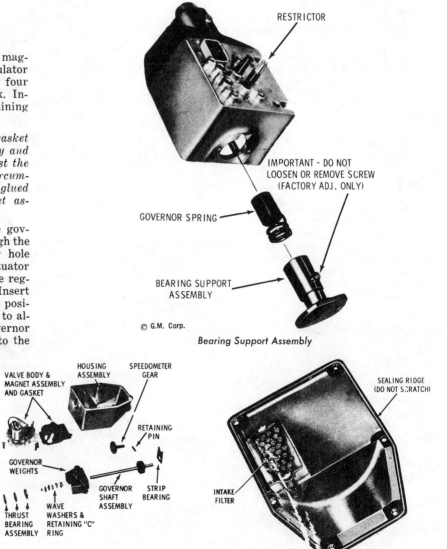

COVER ASSEMBLY AND FILTER

VALVE BODY & MAGNET ASSEMBLY AND GASKET

HOUSING ASSEMBLY

SPEEDOMETER GEAR

RETAINING PIN

BEARING SUPPORT

GOVERNOR WEIGHTS

THRUST BEARING ASSEMBLY

WAVE WASHERS & RETAINING "C" RING

GOVERNOR SHAFT ASSEMBLY

STRIP BEARING

GOVERNOR SPRING

ACTUATOR CUP ASSEMBLY

© G.M. Corp.

*Regulator Assembly—Typical*

SEALING RIDGE (DO NOT SCRATCH)

INTAKE FILTER

© G.M. Corp.

*Intake Filter*

**733**

# General Motors

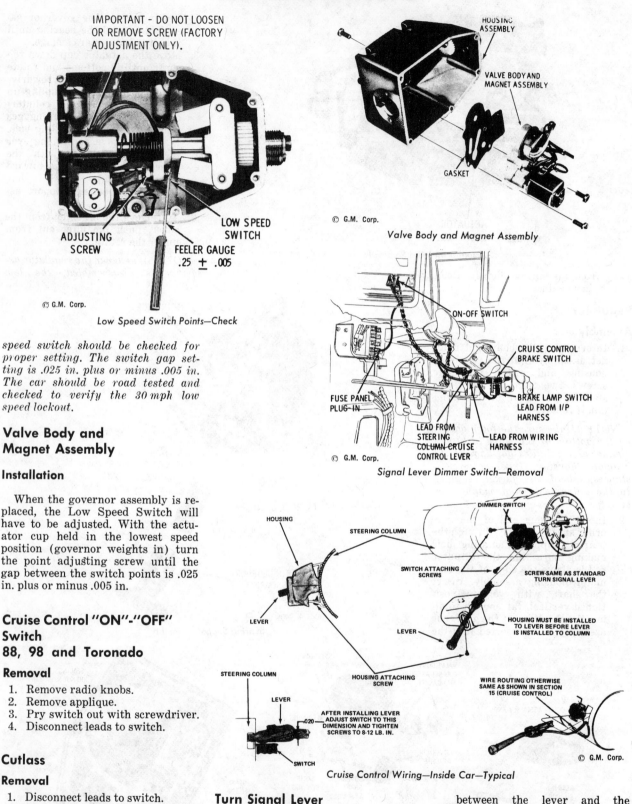

IMPORTANT - DO NOT LOOSEN OR REMOVE SCREW (FACTORY ADJUSTMENT ONLY).

ADJUSTING SCREW

LOW SPEED SWITCH

FEELER GAUGE .25 ± .005

© G.M. Corp.

*Low Speed Switch Points—Check*

HOUSING ASSEMBLY

VALVE BODY AND MAGNET ASSEMBLY

GASKET

© G.M. Corp.

*Valve Body and Magnet Assembly*

ON-OFF SWITCH

CRUISE CONTROL BRAKE SWITCH

FUSE PANEL PLUG-IN

BRAKE LAMP SWITCH LEAD FROM I/P HARNESS

LEAD FROM STEERING COLUMN CRUISE CONTROL LEVER

LEAD FROM WIRING HARNESS

© G.M. Corp.

*Signal Lever Dimmer Switch—Removal*

HOUSING

STEERING COLUMN

DIMMER SWITCH

LEVER

SWITCH ATTACHING SCREWS

SCREW-SAME AS STANDARD TURN SIGNAL LEVER

LEVER

HOUSING MUST BE INSTALLED TO LEVER BEFORE LEVER IS INSTALLED TO COLUMN

STEERING COLUMN

LEVER

HOUSING ATTACHING SCREW

.020

SWITCH

AFTER INSTALLING LEVER ADJUST SWITCH TO THIS DIMENSION AND TIGHTEN SCREWS TO 8-12 LB. IN.

WIRE ROUTING OTHERWISE SAME AS SHOWN IN SECTION 15 (CRUISE CONTROL)

© G.M. Corp.

*Cruise Control Wiring—Inside Car—Typical*

speed switch should be checked for proper setting. The switch gap setting is .025 in. plus or minus .005 in. The car should be road tested and checked to verify the 30 mph low speed lockout.

## Valve Body and Magnet Assembly

### Installation

When the governor assembly is replaced, the Low Speed Switch will have to be adjusted. With the actuator cup held in the lowest speed position (governor weights in) turn the point adjusting screw until the gap between the switch points is .025 in. plus or minus .005 in.

## Cruise Control "ON"-"OFF" Switch
## 88, 98 and Toronado

### Removal

1. Remove radio knobs.
2. Remove applique.
3. Pry switch out with screwdriver.
4. Disconnect leads to switch.

## Cutlass

### Removal

1. Disconnect leads to switch.
2. Remove switch by pushing from behind dash panel.

### Installation

Reverse the removal procedure.

## Turn Signal Lever Dimmer Switch

### Adjustment

1. Loosen the attaching screws.
2. Insert a .020 inch feeler gauge between the lever and the switch.
3. Move the switch back and forth to achieve the .020 inch clearance.
4. Tighten both attaching screws.

# General Motors

**1968-75 Cadillac**
**1969-71 Cutlass**
**1968-75 Buick**
**1968-75 Chevrolet**

## Description

This Cruise Control is a system that uses manifold vacuum to power the throttle servo unit. The servo moves the throttle when a speed adjustment is necessary by receiving a varying amount of controlled vacuum from the transducer unit.

The speedometer cable from the transmission drives the transducer, and a cable from the transducer drives the speedometer. The operation of transducer unit is controlled by an on-off switch on the dash and an engagement switch that is located at the end of the turn signal lever. Two systems for brake release are provided.

An electrical switch is mounted on the brake pedal which disengages the solenoid in the transducer, venting the system vacuum to the atmosphere through the transducer filter. A vacuum dump valve is also mounted on the brake pedal bracket and vents the system vacuum to the atmosphere only if the switch on the transducer valve does not function properly.

## Engagement Switch

The engagement switch, which is, in most cases, in the turn signal lever, and in some is in the dash, has three positions. In the fully released position, the switch allows current to pass through resistance wire to effect a "hold in" magnetic field in the transducer solenoid. There is only enough current to hold the solenoid in place once it has been actuated by the "pull in" circuit. Pushing the button in partially allows current to flow to the transducer solenoid at full voltage by-passing the resistance, which pulls the solenoid in. Depressing the button fully opens the circuit to both the resistance and standard solenoid feed wires and the solenoid becomes de-activated.

During vehicle operation the three switch positions function as follows.

## Switch in Free Position (On-Off Switch "ON")

1. System is not engaged; No function of the system will occur although there is a small amount of current flowing through the solenoid via the resistance wire.
2. System is engaged: The small current flowing through the resistance wire is holding the solenoid in the engaged position.

## Switch Partially Depressed (On-Off Switch "ON")

Full voltage is applied to the solenoid, by-passing the resistor. This sets the transducer to maintain the vehicle speed at the time of transducer engagement.

## Fully Depressed (On-Off Switch "ON")

There is no current flowing to the solenoid and the transducer is inactive. The position is used by the driver when he desires to raise or lower his controlled speed. He may accelerate to the new speed, press the button fully (transducer releases previously set speed) and release the button. Upon releasing the button, current passes through the partially depressed position and the solenoid is "pulled in," then into released position which provides "hold in" current. The driver may also press the button fully with no pressure on the accelerator pedal. In doing this the transducer releases control of the throttle which returns to idle and the car slows. When the bottom is released the solenoid is pulled in and held in respectively and the transducer resumes speed control at the speed of the vehicle during the

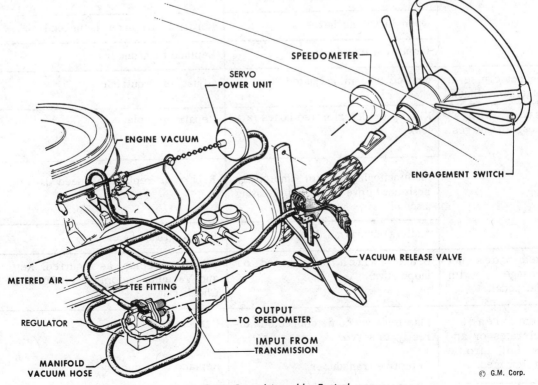

*Cruise Control Assembly—Typical*

© G.M. Corp.

## General Motors

### CRUISE CONTROL DIAGNOSIS CHART

| CONDITION | CAUSE | CORRECTION |
|---|---|---|
| Will not engage - System Inoperative. | On-Off switch "off". | Turn to "on" position. |
| | Brake switch circuit open. | Check connections - adjust or replace switch. Refer to Electrical Check-Out. |
| | Fuse blown. | Replace fuse - if it blows again, check for:<br>1. Incorrect wiring - Refer to Electrical Check-Out.<br>2. Short to ground - Refer to Electrical Check-Out. |
| | Chain from servo to carburetor disconnected. | Connect chain. |
| | Inoperative engagement switch. | Replace as needed - Refer to Electrical Check-Out. |
| | Vacuum leak in servo and/or brake valve and connecting lines. Vacuum hose not connected to vacuum valve. | Vacuum test and repair or replace as needed. Refer to Servo and Vacuum System Check-Out. |
| | Vacuum release valve misadjusted (always open). | Readjust valve. |
| | Crossed hoses at transducer. | Reroute hoses. |
| | Pinched or plugged hose that is connected to the servo. | Free or replace hose. |
| | Open in wiring harness. | Repair or replace as needed. |
| | Inoperative transducer. | Replace transducer. |
| Does not cruise at engagement speed. | Orifice tube misadjusted. | Adjust as required. |
| System hunts, pulses, or surges. | Kinked or deteriorated hoses (air leak). | Repair or replace. |
| | Malfunctioning and/or improperly positioned drive cables and/or casing assemblies. | Repair or replace as needed. |
| | Malfunctioning transducer. | Replace transducer. |
| System does not disengage - with brake pedal. | Brake switch misadjusted or inoperative. | Adjust or replace as required. Refer to Servo and Vacuum System Check Out and Electrical Check Out. |
| System steadily accelerates or applies full throttle when engaged. | Manifold vacuum connected directly to servo. | Reroute hose. |
| | Defective transducer. | Replace transducer. |

### VACUUM CRUISE CONTROL DIAGNOSIS CHART (CONT'D)

| CONDITION | CAUSE | CORRECTION |
|---|---|---|
| Cannot adjust speed downward with engage button. | Defective engagement switch or wiring. | Replace as needed. Refer to Electrical Check Out. |
| Does not engage or engages lower than limits referred to in "Driver Operation" | Defective transducer. | Replace transducer. |
| Slow throttle return to idle after brake is depressed. | Pinched air hose at vacuum release switch. | Free or replace hose. |
| System operates correctly, but constant vacuum bleed when system is disengaged. | Crossed vacuum hoses at transducer. | Reroute hoses. |
| High engine idle speed - independent of carburetor adjustments. Constant air bleed through system. | Tight servo chain. | Loosen chain adjustment. |
| Constant drain on battery. | Power lead connected to "Fused Battery" terminal on fuse block. | Reroute to "Fused IGN" terminal. |
| System can be engaged at idle by depressing switch, but will drop out when switch is released. Solenoid can be heard when switch is depressed when the vehicle is standing still. | Wires reversed at transducer. | Reverse wires - See Fig. 15-31. |
| On light will not turn on even though system cruises satisfactory. | Defective bulb. | Replace. |
| Cruise light will not turn on even though system cruises satisfactory. | Defective bulb or defective ground circuit in transducer. | Replace bulb or replace transducer. |

# General Motors

moment of button release (at vehicle speeds approx. over 24 mph).

## On-Off Switch

This switch is located to the left side of the steering column. The toggle switch completely controls the electrical power to the system. When the switch is in the "OFF" position, the system cannot be engaged. When the switch is in the "ON" position, the "ON" light is lit and the system may be engaged with the switch located in the turn signal lever, at any speed above approximately 24 mph.

## Brake Release Switches

One brake release switch and one vacuum release valve are employed in the system. When the brake pedal is depressed, an electric release switch cuts off the voltage supplied to the engagement switch which cuts off power to the transducer unit. The transducer is then disengaged and requires engagement switch operation to return it to operation. The vacuum release valve operates after the electric release switch whenever the brake pedal is depressed. In case the electrical switch fails to operate, this switch opens a port to atmospheric pressure that dumps the vacuum in the servo unit which returns long as the brake is depressed.

## Servo Unit

The servo unit is a vacuum activated, variable position diaphragm assembly that operates the carburetor throttle when the system is in

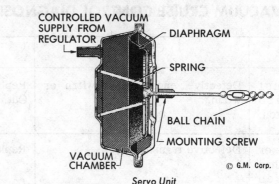

© G.M. Corp.

*Servo Unit*

operation. It is powered by controlled vacuum from the transducer and operates the throttle linkage by a head chain. The servo has a port on the sealed side of the diaphragm housing. When controlled vacuum is applied to this port, atmospheric pressure moves the diaphragm which pulls on the head chain opening the carburetor throttle.

## Transducer

The transducer is located on the cowl near the centerline of the car or is mounted on a bracket on the fender. The transducer has two primary functions which are controlled by the pull-in of the solenoid. First, it is a vacuum switch which, when activated by the driver, supplies vacuum to a "Tee" fitting. Second, it allows the metering valve clutch spring to grasp a rubber clutch which is fixed to the speed cup spindle assembly. A variation in vehicle speed results in a slight rotation of the rubber clutch which in turn moves an air valve

which meters a small variable quantity of air to the system where it blends with vacuum. This provides the servo unit with controlled vacuum that will maintain the selected speed. In operation, at cruise speed, a proper balance of air and vacuum is blended into the system and is imposed upon the servo unit to maintain an "on speed" cruise condition.

An additional function of the transducer is to drive the speedometer. The speedometer cable from the transmission which drives the transducer speed sensing assembly also is directly geared (at a one-to-one ratio) to a second cable connected to the instrument panel speedometer.

The transducer is electrically engaged and disengaged through operation of the engagement switch, on-off switch, and the electric brake release switch. Two others make up the unit: one is the magnetic speed sensing assembly and the other is the solenoid actuated vacuum switch, air bleed and filter, and low limit speed switch assembly.

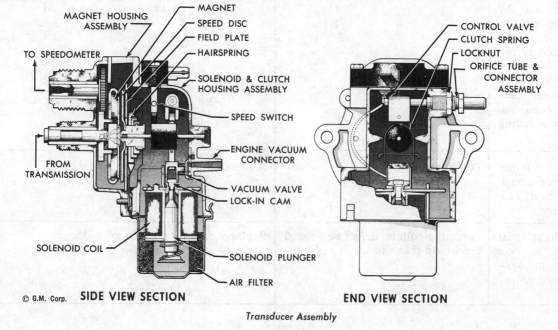

© G.M. Corp.   **SIDE VIEW SECTION**        **END VIEW SECTION**

*Transducer Assembly*

# General Motors

## Magnetic Speed Sensing Assembly

The speed sensing assembly operates in the same way as a speedometer unit, except that instead of rotating a needle through an angle proportional to vehicle speed, it rotates a rubber drum which is clutched to an air bleed valve when the system is in operation.

The assembly is driven by the speedometer cable from the transmission, which rotates a disk shaped ferrite magnet. Facing the magnet is the driven disk which is mounted to the same shaft as the rubber drum. A spiral hairspring is connected to the driven shaft and is calibrated to allow an angular rotation of the rubber drum which is proportional to car speed. If the car doubled its speed, the shaft would rotate to twice its previous angle. The driven disk is sandwiched between the magnet and a field plate. The field plate forms a return path for the magnetic field from the magnetic disk.

## Vacuum Switch, Air Bleed and Filter, and Low Limit Speed Switch

The speed assembly has a rubber drum which extends into the air bleed metering assembly. This rubber drum has a tang extending from its surface. When the car reaches approx. 24 mph, the tang has rotated enough (moved by the driven disk in the magnetic field) to allow a spring loaded electrical contact to close. This contact is in series with the solenoid coil so that below approximately 24 mph, no transducer operation is possible.

Around the rubber drum is a "U" shaped spring clip which is held spread away from the drum by the nose of the solenoid when the solenoid is in the relaxed position. The rubber drum and "U" clip comprise the speed clutch of the transducer. When activated the solenoid nose moves toward the drum and releases the clip ends which are then free to spring inward and clamp itself by friction to the drum. Any change in car speed will rotate the drum and move the "U" clip just as a speedometer moves its needle. The top of the "U" clip is attached to the air bleed valve, which slides on the orifice tube and covers or uncovers air ports in the wall of the tube (the tube inner end is plugged) whenever car speed changes from the speed at which the solenoid was energized. The direction of drum rotation is such that resulting bleed valve operation will cause the servo to decrease engine power if the car exceeds the preset speed and increase engine power if car speed decreases. The air which passes out the orifice tube enters the transducer through the openings in the solenoid housing, passes through the oil wetted polyurethane filter, and then enters the orifice tube ports.

When the solenoid is de-energized, the nose retracts and forces the ends of the "U" clip outward so that the rubber drum is released.

Simultaneously with the clutching and declutching of the "U" clip, the solenoid operates a vacuum valve which slides over two ports in the transducer wall. When the solenoid is de-energized, the slide valve seals the manifold vacuum port and opens the system port to atmospheric pressure inside of the transducer case. When the solenoid is energized, the valve overlaps the two ports and connects manifold vacuum to the control system.

While the system is in operation the following events occur: *below*

1. If the car speed is ~~above~~ 24 mph, the solenoid pull-in circuit cannot function because the rubber drum has not rotated far enough to close the low speed solenoid contact. The solenoid is receiving a small current via 40 ohm resistance wire unless the brake pedal is depressed, engagement switch is fully OFF, ignition switch is OFF, or ON-OFF switch is OFF.

2. If the car speed is above 24 mph, the tang on the rubber drum will have rotated enough to allow the low speed solenoid contact to close. The pull-in circuit is now ready for engagement.

3. If the driver partially depresses the engagement switch full current flows through the solenoid to pull it into operation, releasing the "U" clip which permits the clip's spring tension to grip the rubber drum. Also the solenoid plunger completes the ground for the Cruise light on the drivers control. Simultaneously, the vacuum switch applies manifold vacuum to the system which is blended with air being introduced from the transducer. The balance of air and vacuum is impressed upon the servo to provide initial throttle positioning.

4. If the driver releases the engagement switch, current flows to the solenoid through the 40 ohm wire and since the solenoid is "pulled in," the reduced current flow is sufficient to hold it in position and the cruise light remains On.

5. When the car begins to go up a hill, car speed decreases very slightly and the magnetic force on the driven disk of the speed sensor is decreased thereby reducing the angle of rotation of the rubber drum slightly. Since the "U" clip is gripping the drum, it moves the air bleed valve in that direction which covers more of the air bleed ports. With less air bleeding into the system, a higher vacuum level is achieved at the servo diaphragm, opening the throttle angle to correct for the underspeed condition.

6. When the car begins to go down

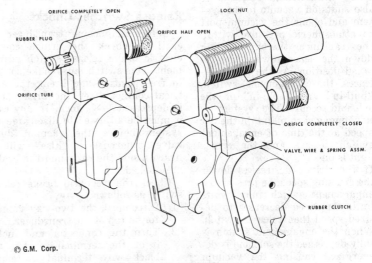

© G.M. Corp.

*Transducer Air Bleed Office Openings*

## General Motors

a hill, car speed increases slightly and the air bleed valve moves in that direction which uncovers the air bleed ports. With more air bleeding into the system, a lower vacuum level is achieved at the servo diaphragm decreasing the throttle angle to correct for the overspeed condition.

7. When the driver accelerates by pressing the accelerator pedal, car speed increases and the system responds by moving the diaphragm to decrease throttle opening. Since a bead chain is used, the chain merely relaxes and has no effect on throttle operation. After the driver releases pressure from the pedal, the throttle will close until car speed decreases to the preset speed. At that point the transducer bleeds less air to the "Tee" fitting which opens the throttle enough to maintain the preset speed and system returns to a stable condition.

8. If the driver desires a higher controlled speed, he presses the accelerator until a new speed is reached, and depresses engagement switch fully and releases the button. The speed sensing assembly tries to turn in a direction that would decrease the throttle opening until the driver fully depresses the engagement switch. Then the current is cut off to the solenoid which retracts; the solenoid cam expands the "U" clip releasing its grip on the rubber drum and removes the ground from the cruise light. The drum and disk assembly then rotates to a new position because of the higher car speed. When the solenoid retracts, it also shuts off vacuum to the system and opens the vacuum port to atmospheric pressure within the transducer thereby bleeding down the servo toward the relaxed position. As the driver releases the engagement switch, "pull-in" and "hold-in" of the solenoid occur. The system is now engaged to maintain the car speed at the time of engagement switch release and the cruise light is on.

9. If the driver desires to lower the cruising speed, he presses the engagement switch fully, waits until car speed decreases to desired speed then releases switch. When the engagement switch is fully depressed the solenoid is de-energized causing the vacuum switch to bleed down the servo

to idle throttle position and the "U" clip of the air bleed valve is released from the rubber drum. The drum and disc assembly is free to rotate to a position which corresponds to vehicle speed as the car slows. When the driver releases the engagement switch, the unit "pulls-in" and "holds-in" in the normal manner. The air bleed valve is clutched to the rubber drum at the car speed corresponding to switch release. Vacuum is again applied to the system and throttle control is assumed by the transducer to maintain the car speed at the time of switch release.

10. If the system is in operation, and the driver applies the brakes, the electric release switch disengages the system first, then the vacuum valve operates. The electric release switch cuts off power to the entire system, the solenoid and cruise light are de-energized, and the vacuum system is vented to atmosphere. The vacuum valve also can vent the system if the brake pedal is depressed far enough. When the driver removes his foot from the brake pedal the electric switch again feeds voltage to the engagement switch and the vacuum brake switch seals the air bleed line. The unit will not re-engage because it receives only a small current through the 40 ohm resistance wire. If vehicle speed is below 24 mph the system may not re-engage since the tang on the rubber drum has opened the low limit switch points in the transducer.

### Release Switches Checks

Before diagnosing transducer operations, check the cruise control electric brake release switch adjustment. This switch must make contact in free position and break the electrical contact when the brake pedal is depressed $1/4$-$5/8$ inch. In any case, it must be adjusted to disengage the system before the vacuum dump valve, otherwise a "hiss" will be heard inside the car when the brakes are applied.

Check the electrical brake release switch as follows:

1. Disconnect the two-way connector on top of the transducer.
2. Turn the connector and install it on the terminal so that the black wire terminal is temporarily connected to the trans-

ducer "Hold" terminal. The other terminal will be empty.

3. With the ignition switch on, move the cruise control switch ON.
4. Engage the switch in the turn signal lever. Push button part way in (about $1/2$ way) and hold. The green jewel next to "CRUISE" should light.
5. Press down the brake pedal $1/4$ inch to $3/8$ inch while holding the lever button depressed. "CRUISE" light should go out. If the light goes out before $1/4$ inch travel or if light did not go on, the electric brake release switch at the brake pedal lever should be readjusted.
6. Turn the ignition switch OFF, and adjust the release switch as required. Adjust the switch by loosening the switch mounting screw, repositioning the switch and tightening the screw.
7. Reinstall the two-way transducer connector on its proper terminals. It is necessary that this step be performed.

As a "back-up" release, in case the electric switch should not operate for any reason, the vacuum brake release valve should disengage the system when the brake pedal is depressed over 1 inch of pedal travel. This does not de-energize the system, the "ON-OFF" switch or ignition switch must be turned off when the car is stopped to disengage the system electrically.

This valve can be checked by:

a. Removing the smaller vacuum hose from the left front of the transducer, and removing the hose to the dump valve from the die-cast "tee."
b. Connect the two hoses together, so that engine vacuum is applied to the dump valve.

With the engine running a "hiss" should be heard when the brake pedal is depressed over 1 inch.

Make sure both hoses are reinstalled properly, when the test is completed.

### Electrical System Check

1. Check the fuse and connector.
2. To check the cruise light circuit:
   a. turn ignition switch and cruise control switch ON.
   b. Connect a jumper lead between the light terminal connector on the transducer and ground.
   c. If the cruise light comes on, transducer replacement is indicated. If cruise light does

## General Motors

not come on, check bulb, cruise light wiring and/or connections.

3. Check the electric brake switch as follows: Unplug the connector at switch. Connect an ohmmeter or self powered test light at two terminals on brake switch. The ohmmeter must indicate infinity when the pedal is depressed from 1/4 inch to 5/8 inch travel and continuity when pedal is released. Replace electric brake switch if needed.

4. Check the engagement switch and connecting wiring as follows: Unplug the engagement switch connector (brown, dark blue, black) at electrical wiring harness connector and perform the following tests.

   a. Text #1—Connect an ohmmeter between the #1 (brown wire) and terminal #2 (dark blue wire). Continuity should be maintained until the switch is depressed all the way in.

   b. Test #2—Connect an ohmmeter between the terminal #1 (brown wire) and terminal #3 (black). No continuity should be shown. When the button is depressed halfway, continuity should be indicated. When the button is depressed all the way down, no continuity should be shown.

   c. Test #3—Connect an ohmmeter between terminal #2 (dark blue wire) and terminal #3 (black). With the button released there should be no continuity. When the button is depressed partially and fully there should be continuity.

5. Disconnect engagement switch wire harness connector from the main harness connector (brown, dark blue, and black wires). Connect an ohmmeter between the dark blue stripe wire in main wire harness and the ground. Make sure the transducer is well grounded to the chassis. The ohmmeter should read between 42 and 49 ohms. If a resistance either above or below the value indicated is shown, then disconnect the connector from the transducer and measure the resistance of the white resistor wire. It should measure 40 ohms ± 2 ohms. If a resistance either above or below the value indicated is shown, the main wiring harness should be replaced.

*NOTE: When disconnecting or reconnecting the main wiring harness connector from the transducer, be careful not to damage the blade connectors or the wiring harness. Disconnecting the connector may be done by prying carefully on the plastic connector with a small bladed screwdriver.*

When measuring the solenoid coil circuit resistance between the hold terminal and ground, the ideal resistance should be between 5 and 6

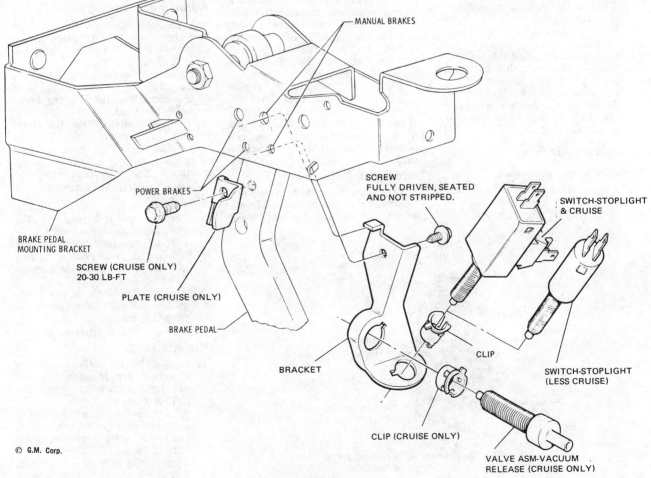

*Brake Release Switch—Typical*

# General Motors

ohms. A reading of less than 4 ohms indicates shorting in the coil circuit. A reading of more than 7 ohms indicates excessive resistance in the coil circuit. Either extremity indicates replacement of the transducer assembly. The black main wiring harness from the switch to the transducer should also be checked for continuity.

## Transducer Assembly

### Removal and Installation

1. Remove the ground cable from the battery.
2. Remove the speedometer cables from the transducer.
3. Remove all the vacuum hoses and wires from the transducer.
4. Remove the bolts that hold the transducer to the bracket and remove the transducer from the car.
5. To install the transducer reverse the removal procedure.

## Servo Assembly

### Removal and Installation

1. Remove the ground cable from the battery.
2. Remove the vacuum line from the servo.
3. Disconnect the chain assembly.
4. Remove the bolts that hold the servo bracket to the car and remove the servo assembly.
5. To install the servo reverse the removal procedure making sure to adjust the chain.

## Transducer Air Filter

### Removal and Installation

1. The air filter should be replaced every 12,000 miles under normal conditions or more frequently if the system is used under severe conditions.
2. Replace the filter by removing the cover from the bottom of the transducer assembly that contains the solenoid and filter. The cover is held on by retaining clips.
3. Remove the old filter and install the new filter in the cover.
4. Position the filter assembly on the transducer assembly and secure in place with the retaining clips.
5. Make sure there is a tight seal between the cover assembly and the transducer.

## Servo and Vacuum Check

To determine the condition of the diaphragm, remove the hose from the servo unit and apply 14 inches of vacuum to the tube opening and hold in for one minute. The vacuum should not leak down more than 5 inches of vacuum in one minute. If leakage is detected, replace the servo. If using the engine as a vacuum source, proceed as follows:

1. Disconnect the servo bead chain and hose and connect the vacuum directly to the servo fitting.
2. Note the position of servo fitting.
3. Start engine—the diaphragm should pull in.
4. Clamp off the engine vacuum supply line and check for leakage.

The cruise release brake switch (vacuum) and connecting hoses can likewise be checked using a vacuum pump.

## Transducer Adjustment

On the transducer there is only one adjustment that can be made. The adjustment is zeroing the set speed with the actual speed of the car. No adjustment should be made until the servo cable is adjusted and all the hoses have been checked.

The adjustment is made with the orifice tube in the transducer.

*NOTE: Make sure to never remove the tube from the transducer because once it has been removed it can not be reinstalled.*

Adjust the transducer as follows:

1. Driving the car on the road, engage the cruise control at 60 mph.
2. If the car cruises above the set speed the orifice tube must be turned in.
3. If the car cruises below the set speed the orifice tube must be turned out.

*NOTE: Each 1/4 turn of the orifice tube changes the speed of the car about 1 mph. Make sure to tighten the lock nut after each adjustment.*

4. If the transducer can not be adjusted it is defective and must be replaced.

## Vacuum Servo Cable Adjustment

Adjust the chain on the servo so that there is very little slack in the chain but that it does not hold the throttle open.

On some models adjust the chain by loosening the jam nut on the back of the servo and turning the servo assembly to adjust.

On most models adjust the chain by removing the chain from the connector and make the chain as tight as possible, leaving a little slack, reinstall the chain in the connector.

## Release Switch Adjustment (Electric)

1. Loosen the lock nut on the switch and move the switch in or out as required to have the plunger of the switch all the way out when the pedal is pressed down 1/4 inch.
2. Tighten the lock nut on the switch and check the switch for proper operation.

## Release Switch Adjustment (Vacuum)

1. Loosen the lock nut on the switch if so equipped. If the switch does not have a lock nut press the switch in or out.
2. Adjust the switch so the switch plunger is all the way out when the brake pedal is pressed down 5/16 of an inch.
3. Tighten the lock, if so equipped, and check the switch for proper operation.

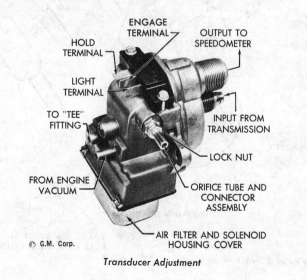

ENGAGE TERMINAL
HOLD TERMINAL
LIGHT TERMINAL
TO "TEE" FITTING
FROM ENGINE VACUUM
OUTPUT TO SPEEDOMETER
INPUT FROM TRANSMISSION
LOCK NUT
ORIFICE TUBE AND CONNECTOR ASSEMBLY
AIR FILTER AND SOLENOID HOUSING COVER

© G.M. Corp.

*Transducer Adjustment*

## American Motors

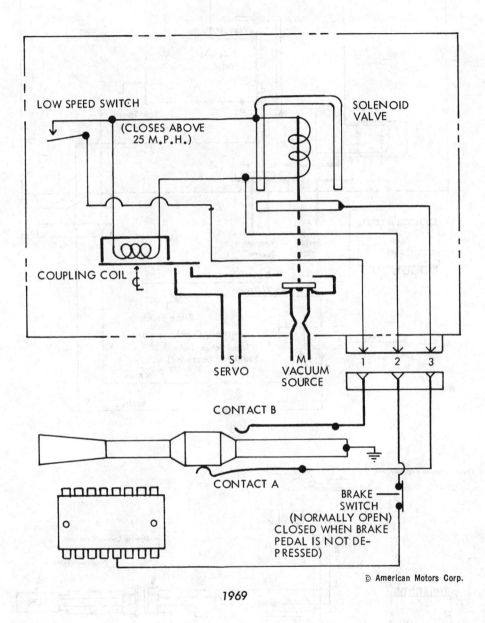

LOW SPEED SWITCH

(CLOSES ABOVE 25 M.P.H.)

SOLENOID VALVE

COUPLING COIL

S SERVO

M VACUUM SOURCE

1   2   3

CONTACT B

CONTACT A

BRAKE SWITCH (NORMALLY OPEN) CLOSED WHEN BRAKE PEDAL IS NOT DE- PRESSED)

© American Motors Corp.

1969

## American Motors

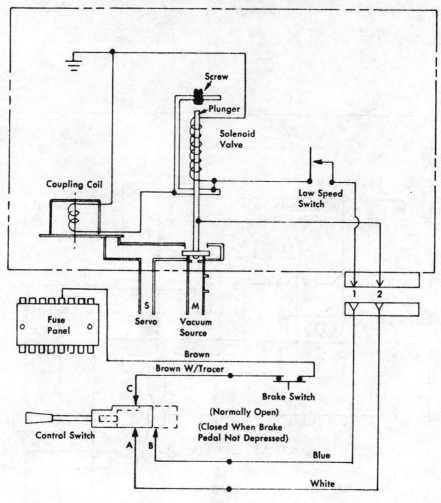

Screw

Plunger

Solenoid
Valve

Coupling Coil

Low Speed
Switch

Fuse
Panel

S
Servo

M
Vacuum
Source

1  2

Brown

Brown W/Tracer

Brake Switch

C

Control Switch

A  B

(Normally Open)

(Closed When Brake
Pedal Not Depressed)

Blue

White

1970

© American Motors Corp.

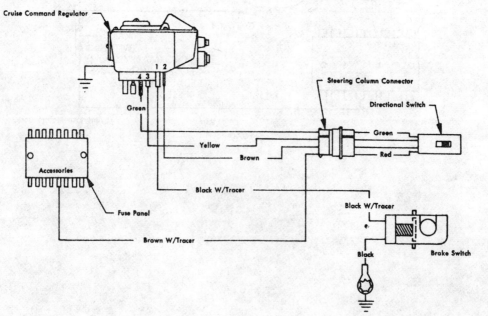

Cruise Command Regulator

1  2
4  3

Green

Steering Column Connector

Directional Switch

Green

Yellow

Brown

Red

Accessories

Black W/Tracer

Fuse Panel

Black W/Tracer

Brown W/Tracer

Black

Brake Switch

1971-73

# Cruise Control Wiring

## American Motors

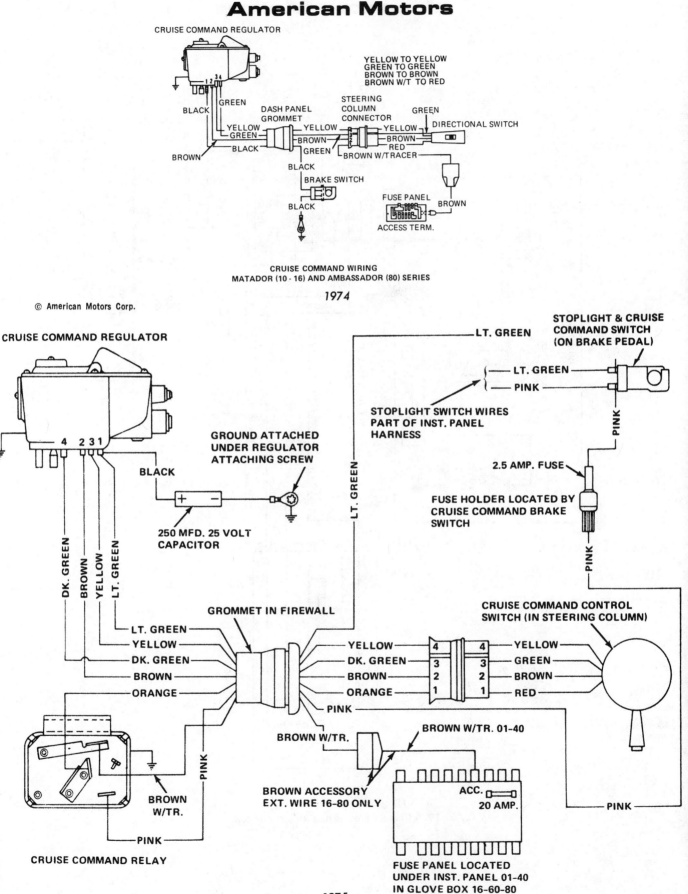

## American Motors

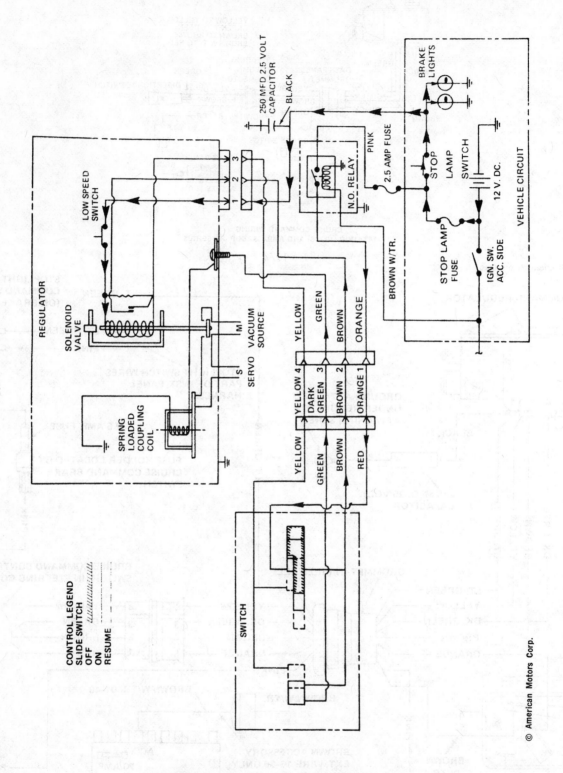

*1975 Current Flow Brake Release Circuit*

© American Motors Corp.

## American Motors

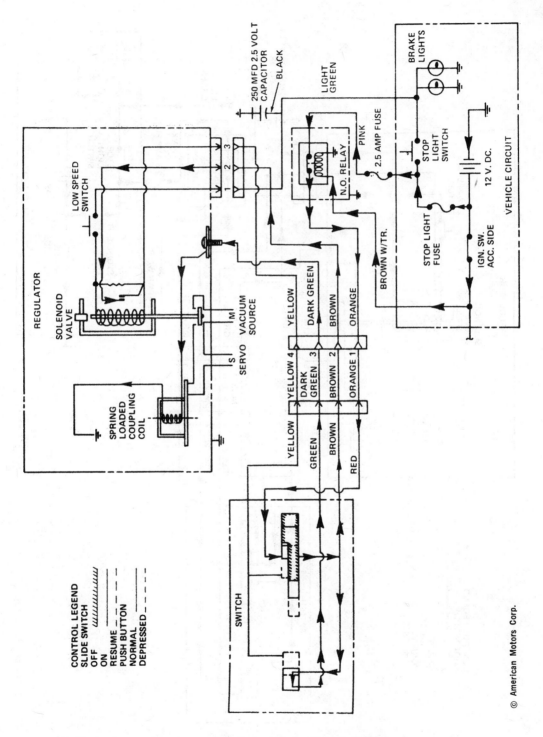

*1975 Current Flow with Slide Switch in ON Position*

© American Motors Corp.

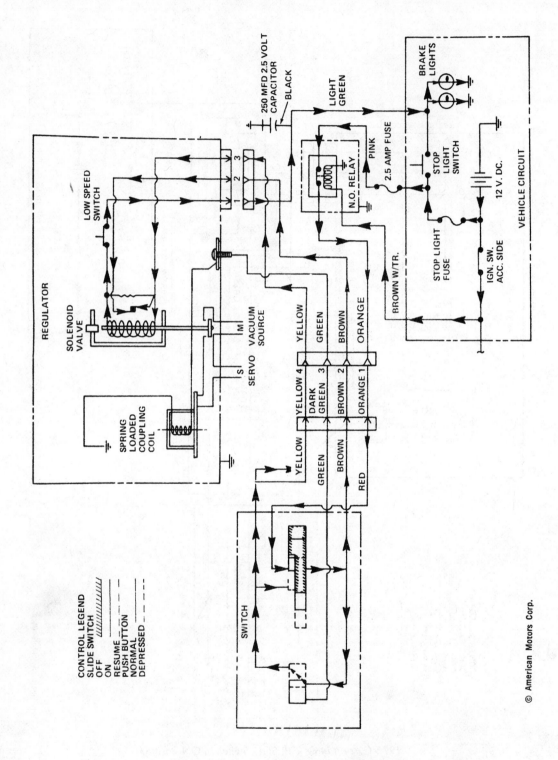

*1975 Current Flow with Push Button Depressed*

© American Motors Corp.

# Cruise Control Wiring

## Chrysler Corporation

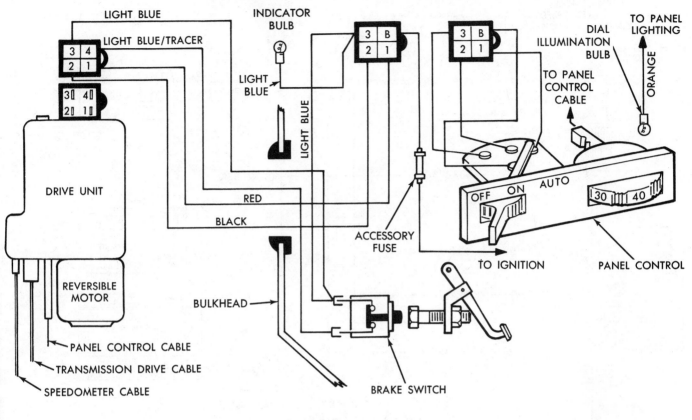

*1968 Auto Pilot Wiring*

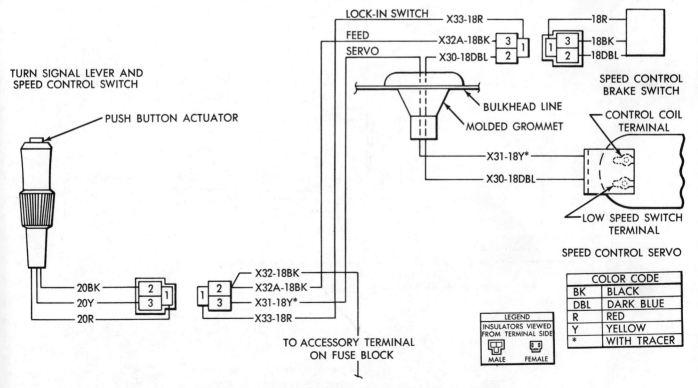

*1968 Belvedere, Satellite, Fury & V.I.P. Speed Control Wiring*

## Chrysler Corporation

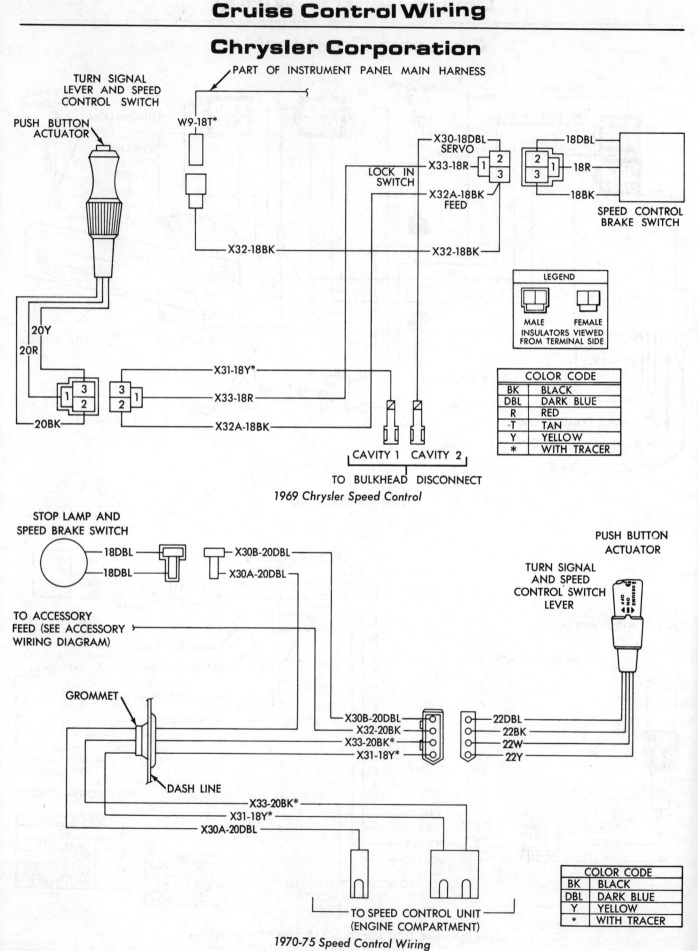

PART OF INSTRUMENT PANEL MAIN HARNESS

TURN SIGNAL LEVER AND SPEED CONTROL SWITCH

PUSH BUTTON ACTUATOR

W9-18T*

X30-18DBL SERVO
X33-18R
LOCK IN SWITCH
X32A-18BK FEED

18DBL
18R
18BK

SPEED CONTROL BRAKE SWITCH

X32-18BK

X32-18BK

LEGEND

MALE       FEMALE
INSULATORS VIEWED
FROM TERMINAL SIDE

20Y
20R

X31-18Y*
X33-18R
X32A-18BK

20BK

| COLOR CODE | |
|---|---|
| BK | BLACK |
| DBL | DARK BLUE |
| R | RED |
| -T | TAN |
| Y | YELLOW |
| * | WITH TRACER |

CAVITY 1   CAVITY 2

TO BULKHEAD DISCONNECT

*1969 Chrysler Speed Control*

STOP LAMP AND SPEED BRAKE SWITCH

18DBL
18DBL

X30B-20DBL
X30A-20DBL

PUSH BUTTON ACTUATOR

TURN SIGNAL AND SPEED CONTROL SWITCH LEVER

TO ACCESSORY FEED (SEE ACCESSORY WIRING DIAGRAM)

GROMMET

X30B-20DBL
X32-20BK
X33-20BK*
X31-18Y*

22DBL
22BK
22W
22Y

DASH LINE

X33-20BK*
X31-18Y*
X30A-20DBL

TO SPEED CONTROL UNIT (ENGINE COMPARTMENT)

*1970-75 Speed Control Wiring*

| COLOR CODE | |
|---|---|
| BK | BLACK |
| DBL | DARK BLUE |
| Y | YELLOW |
| * | WITH TRACER |

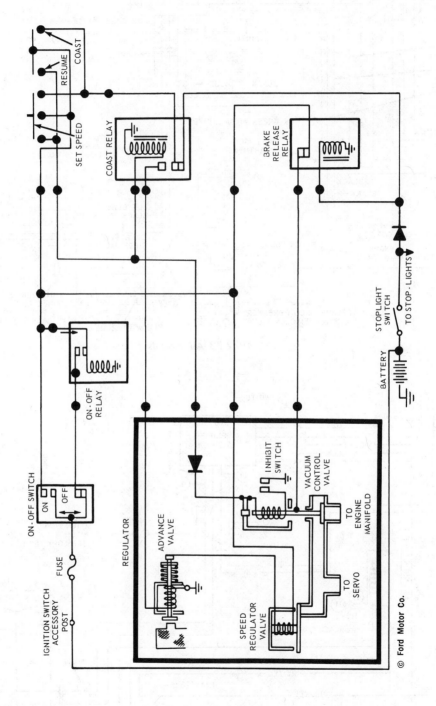

*Perfect Circle Speed Control—1969 Thunderbird Shown (Others Typical)*

## Ford Motor Company

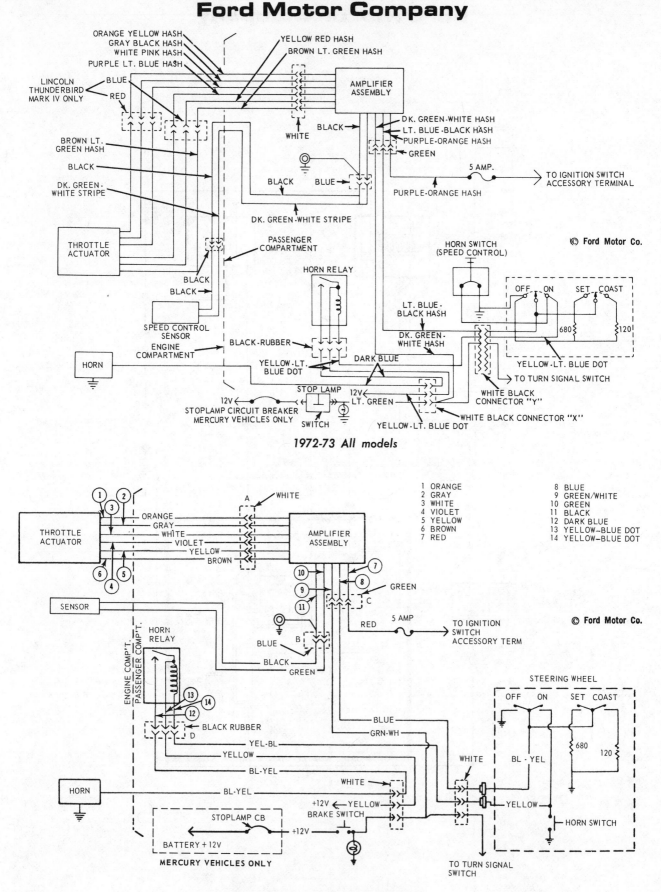

**1972-73 All models**

| | |
|---|---|
| 1 ORANGE | 8 BLUE |
| 2 GRAY | 9 GREEN/WHITE |
| 3 WHITE | 10 GREEN |
| 4 VIOLET | 11 BLACK |
| 5 YELLOW | 12 DARK BLUE |
| 6 BROWN | 13 YELLOW–BLUE DOT |
| 7 RED | 14 YELLOW–BLUE DOT |

**1969-71 Ford, Mercury, Thunderbird**

# Ford Motor Company

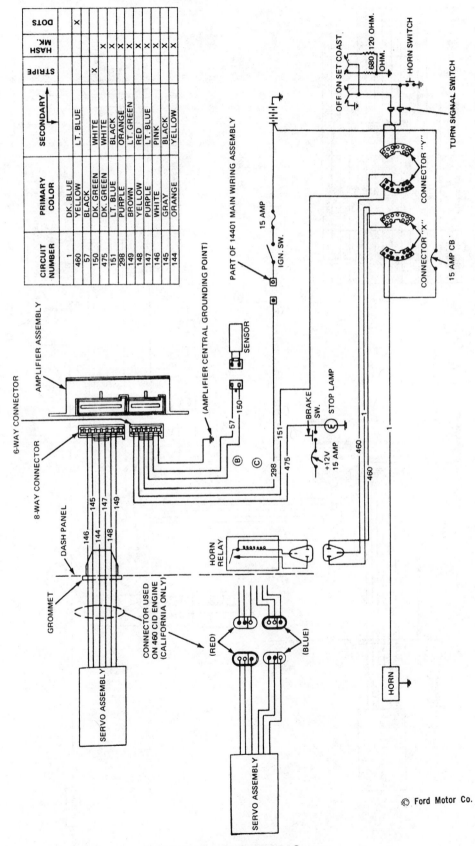

| CIRCUIT NUMBER | PRIMARY COLOR | SECONDARY | STRIPE | HASH MK. | DOTS |
|---|---|---|---|---|---|
| 1 | DK. BLUE | LT. BLUE | | | X |
| 460 | YELLOW | WHITE | X | | |
| 57 | BLACK | WHITE | | | |
| 150 | DK. GREEN | BLACK | | X | |
| 475 | DK. GREEN | ORANGE | | X | |
| 151 | LT. BLUE | LT. GREEN | | X | |
| 298 | PURPLE | RED | | X | |
| 149 | BROWN | LT. BLUE | | X | |
| 148 | YELLOW | PINK | | X | |
| 147 | PURPLE | BLACK | | X | |
| 146 | WHITE | YELLOW | | X | |
| 145 | GRAY | | | X | |
| 144 | ORANGE | | | X | |

*1974-75 Torino, Montego, Cougar*

© Ford Motor Co.

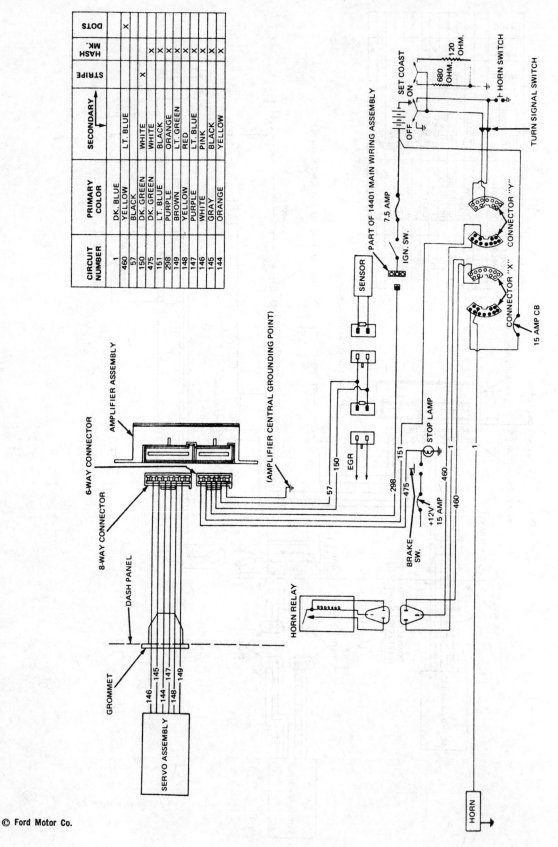

| CIRCUIT NUMBER | PRIMARY COLOR | SECONDARY | STRIPE | HASH MK. | DOTS |
|---|---|---|---|---|---|
| 1 | DK. BLUE | LT. BLUE | | | × |
| 460 | YELLOW | WHITE | × | | |
| 57 | BLACK | WHITE | | × | |
| 150 | DK. GREEN | BLACK | | × | |
| 475 | DK. GREEN | ORANGE | | × | |
| 151 | LT. BLUE | LT. GREEN | | × | |
| 298 | PURPLE | RED | | × | |
| 149 | BROWN | LT. BLUE | | × | |
| 148 | YELLOW | BLACK | | × | |
| 147 | PURPLE | PINK | | × | |
| 146 | WHITE | BLACK | | × | |
| 145 | GRAY | YELLOW | | × | |
| 144 | ORANGE | | | | |

© Ford Motor Co.

*1974-75 Ford, Mercury*

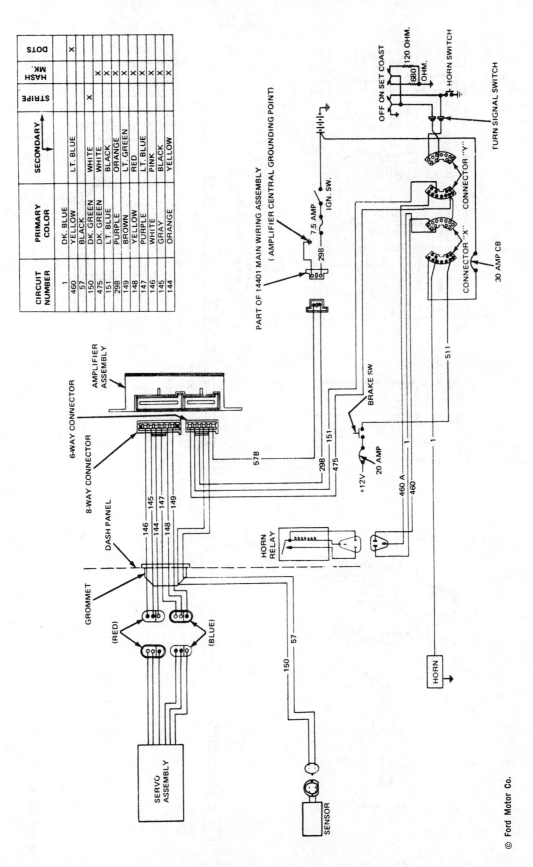

| CIRCUIT NUMBER | PRIMARY COLOR | SECONDARY | STRIPE | HASH MK. | DOTS |
|---|---|---|---|---|---|
| 1 | DK. BLUE | LT. BLUE | | | × |
| 460 | YELLOW | WHITE | × | | |
| 57 | BLACK | WHITE | | × | |
| 150 | DK. GREEN | BLACK | | × | |
| 475 | DK. GREEN | ORANGE | | × | |
| 151 | LT. BLUE | LT. GREEN | | × | |
| 298 | PURPLE | RED | | × | |
| 149 | BROWN | LT. BLUE | | × | |
| 148 | YELLOW | PINK | | × | |
| 147 | PURPLE | BLACK | | × | |
| 146 | WHITE | YELLOW | | × | |
| 145 | GRAY | | | × | |
| 144 | ORANGE | | | × | |

*1974-75 Continental Mark IV, Thunberbird*

© Ford Motor Co.

# Ford Motor Company

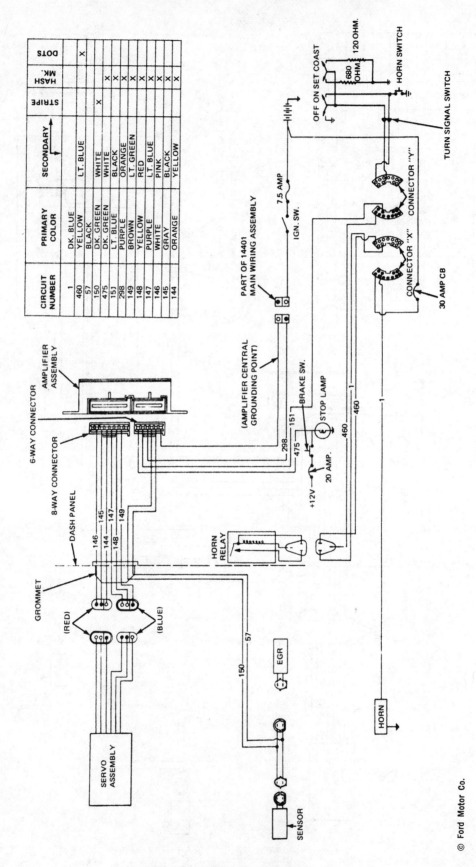

| CIRCUIT NUMBER | PRIMARY COLOR | SECONDARY | STRIPE | HASH MK. | DOTS |
|---|---|---|---|---|---|
| 1 | DK. BLUE | LT. BLUE | | | X |
| 460 | YELLOW | WHITE | | | |
| 57 | BLACK | WHITE | X | | |
| 150 | DK. GREEN | BLACK | | X | |
| 475 | DK. GREEN | ORANGE | | X | |
| 151 | LT. BLUE | LT. GREEN | | X | |
| 298 | PURPLE | RED | | X | |
| 149 | BROWN | LT. BLUE | | X | |
| 148 | YELLOW | PURPLE | | X | |
| 147 | PURPLE | PINK | | X | |
| 146 | WHITE | BLACK | | X | |
| 145 | GRAY | YELLOW | | X | |
| 144 | ORANGE | | | X | |

© Ford Motor Co.

*1974-75 Lincoln Continental*

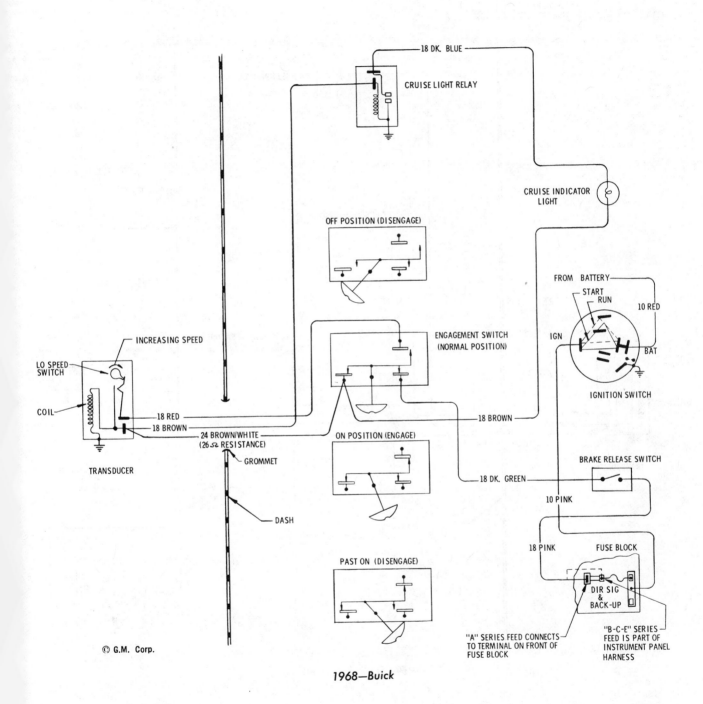

1968—Buick

© G.M. Corp.

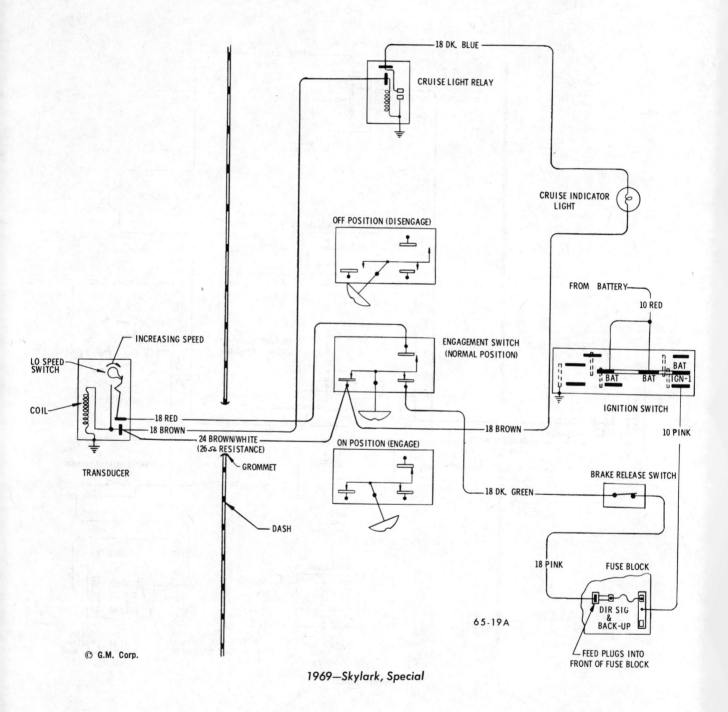

18 DK. BLUE

CRUISE LIGHT RELAY

CRUISE INDICATOR LIGHT

OFF POSITION (DISENGAGE)

FROM BATTERY

10 RED

INCREASING SPEED

LO SPEED SWITCH

ENGAGEMENT SWITCH (NORMAL POSITION)

BAT

BAT    BAT

IGN-1

COIL

18 RED

18 BROWN

24 BROWN/WHITE (26₅₂ RESISTANCE)

18 BROWN

IGNITION SWITCH

10 PINK

GROMMET

ON POSITION (ENGAGE)

TRANSDUCER

BRAKE RELEASE SWITCH

18 DK. GREEN

DASH

18 PINK

FUSE BLOCK

65-19A

DIR SIG & BACK-UP

© G.M. Corp.

FEED PLUGS INTO FRONT OF FUSE BLOCK

*1969—Skylark, Special*

# General Motors

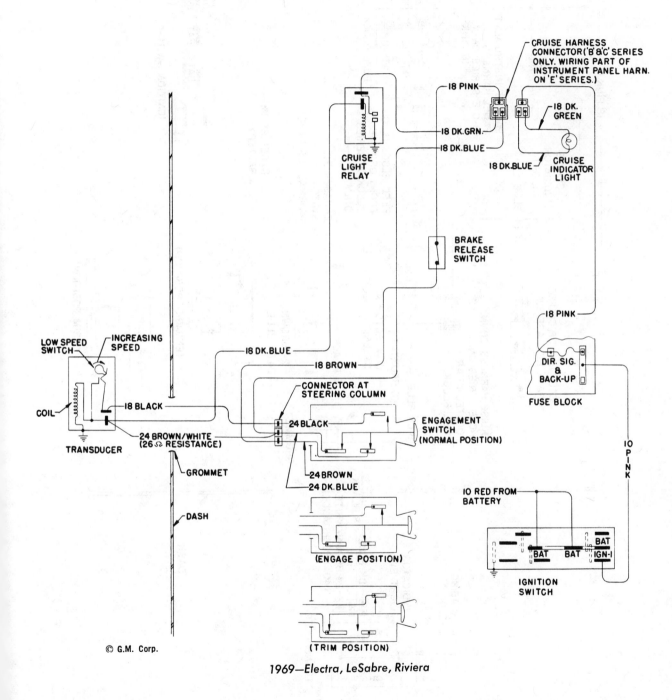

CRUISE HARNESS
CONNECTOR('B'&'C' SERIES
ONLY. WIRING PART OF
INSTRUMENT PANEL HARN.
ON 'E' SERIES.)

18 PINK

18 DK. GREEN

18 DK.GRN.

18 DK.BLUE

18 DK.BLUE

CRUISE INDICATOR LIGHT

CRUISE LIGHT RELAY

BRAKE RELEASE SWITCH

18 PINK

DIR. SIG. & BACK-UP

FUSE BLOCK

LOW SPEED SWITCH

INCREASING SPEED

18 DK.BLUE

18 BROWN

CONNECTOR AT STEERING COLUMN

COIL

18 BLACK

24 BLACK

ENGAGEMENT SWITCH (NORMAL POSITION)

24 BROWN/WHITE (26Ω RESISTANCE)

TRANSDUCER

24 BROWN

24 DK. BLUE

GROMMET

10 PINK

DASH

10 RED FROM BATTERY

(ENGAGE POSITION)

BAT

BAT

BAT

IGN-I

IGNITION SWITCH

(TRIM POSITION)

© G.M. Corp.

*1969—Electra, LeSabre, Riviera*

## General Motors

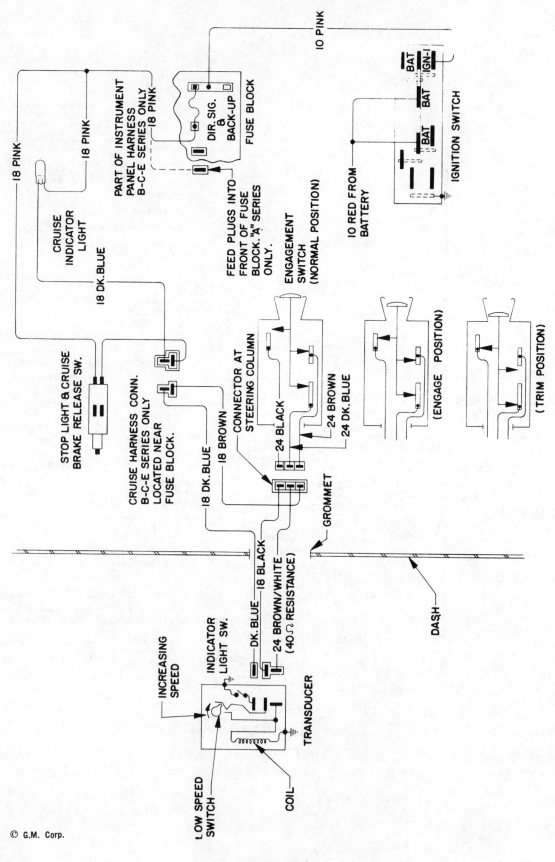

IO PINK

BAT

IGN-I

BAT BAT

IGNITION SWITCH

BAT BAT

DIR. SIG. & BACK-UP

FUSE BLOCK

18 PINK

PART OF INSTRUMENT PANEL HARNESS B-C-E SERIES ONLY

18 PINK

18 PINK

18 PINK

CRUISE INDICATOR LIGHT

18 DK. BLUE

FEED PLUGS INTO FRONT OF FUSE BLOCK. "A" SERIES ONLY.

ENGAGEMENT SWITCH (NORMAL POSITION)

IO RED FROM BATTERY

(ENGAGE POSITION)

(TRIM POSITION)

STOP LIGHT & CRUISE BRAKE RELEASE SW.

24 BLACK

24 BROWN

24 DK. BLUE

CRUISE HARNESS CONN. B-C-E SERIES ONLY LOCATED NEAR FUSE BLOCK.

18 BROWN

CONNECTOR AT STEERING COLUMN

18 DK. BLUE

GROMMET

DK. BLUE

18 BLACK

24 BROWN/WHITE (40Ω RESISTANCE)

DASH

INCREASING SPEED

INDICATOR LIGHT SW.

LOW SPEED SWITCH

TRANSDUCER

COIL

*1970-75 Buick*

## General Motors

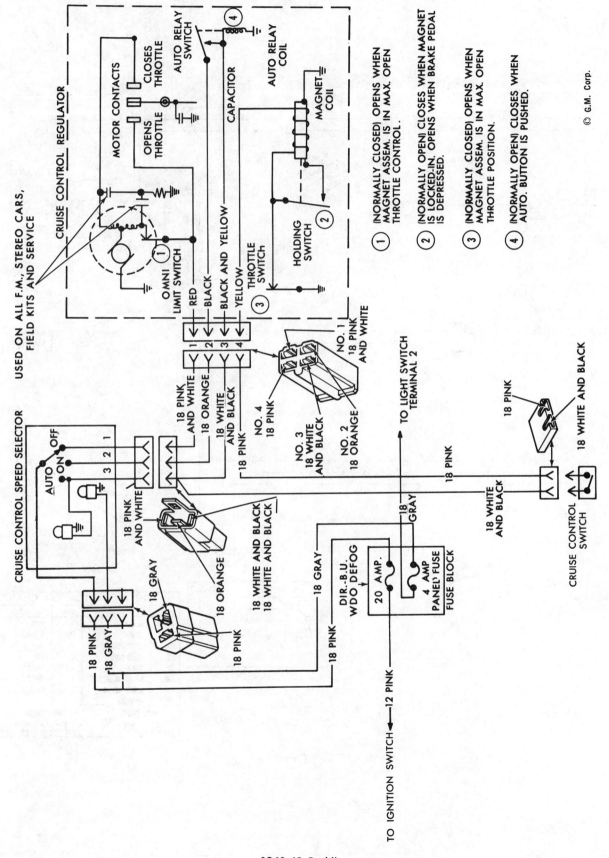

① (NORMALLY CLOSED) OPENS WHEN MAGNET ASSEM. IS IN MAX. OPEN THROTTLE CONTROL.

② (NORMALLY OPEN) CLOSES WHEN MAGNET IS LOCKED-IN. OPENS WHEN BRAKE PEDAL IS DEPRESSED.

③ (NORMALLY CLOSED) OPENS WHEN MAGNET ASSEM. IS IN MAX. OPEN THROTTLE POSITION.

④ (NORMALLY OPEN) CLOSES WHEN AUTO. BUTTON IS PUSHED.

© G.M. Corp.

*1968-69 Cadillac*

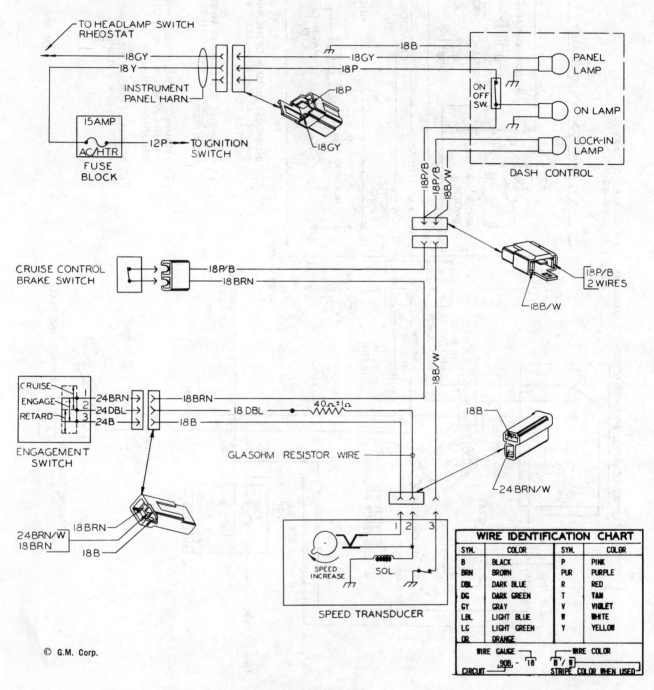

1970-75 Cadillac

# General Motors

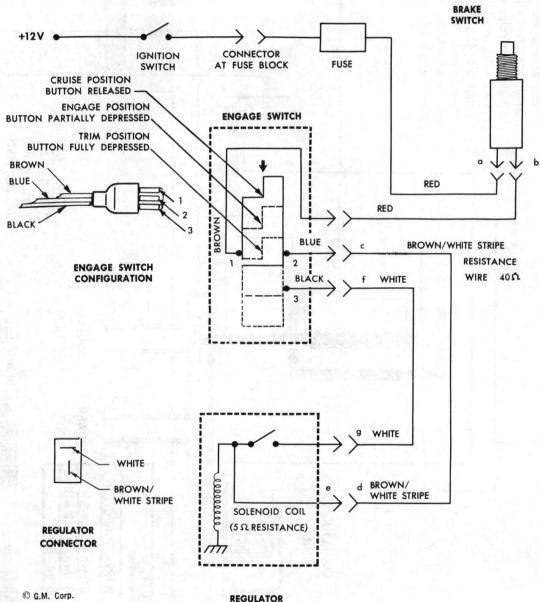

**BRAKE SWITCH**

+12V

**IGNITION SWITCH**

**CONNECTOR AT FUSE BLOCK**

**FUSE**

CRUISE POSITION BUTTON RELEASED

ENGAGE POSITION BUTTON PARTIALLY DEPRESSED

TRIM POSITION BUTTON FULLY DEPRESSED

**ENGAGE SWITCH**

BROWN

BLUE

BLACK

1

2

3

**ENGAGE SWITCH CONFIGURATION**

BROWN

1

2

3

BLUE

BLACK

a

b

RED

RED

c

f

WHITE

BROWN/WHITE STRIPE

RESISTANCE WIRE 40 Ω

WHITE

BROWN/ WHITE STRIPE

**REGULATOR CONNECTOR**

g

e

d

WHITE

BROWN/ WHITE STRIPE

**SOLENOID COIL (5 Ω RESISTANCE)**

© G.M. Corp.

**REGULATOR**

*1968-75 Chevrolet*

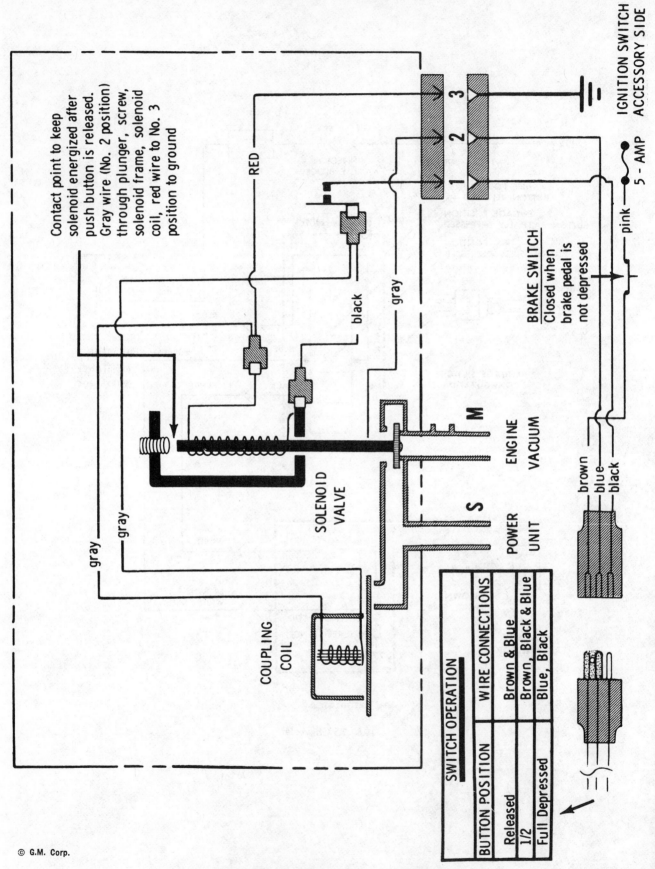

Contact point to keep solenoid energized after push button is released. Gray wire (No. 2 position) through plunger, screw, solenoid frame, solenoid coil, red wire to No. 3 position to ground

IGNITION SWITCH
ACCESSORY SIDE

RED

5 - AMP

pink

BRAKE SWITCH
Closed when brake pedal is not depressed

gray

black

brown
blue
black

ENGINE VACUUM

M

S

POWER UNIT

SOLENOID VALVE

gray

gray

COUPLING COIL

| SWITCH OPERATION | |
|---|---|
| BUTTON POSITION | WIRE CONNECTIONS |
| Released | Brown & Blue |
| 1/2 | Brown, Black & Blue |
| Full Depressed | Blue, Black |

*1968—Cutlass, 1969-71—88, 98, Toronado*

## General Motors

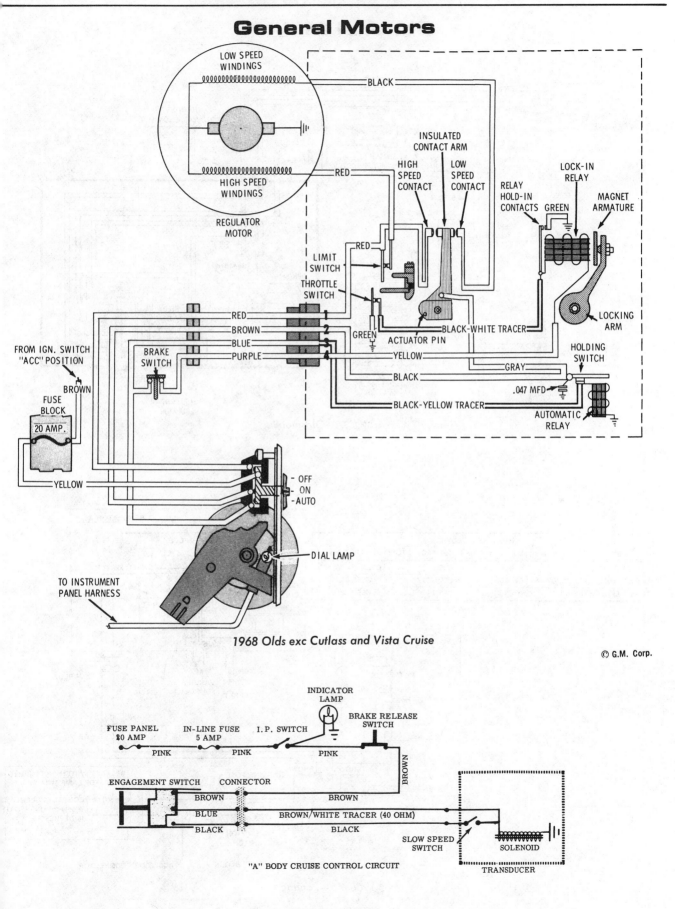

LOW SPEED WINDINGS

HIGH SPEED WINDINGS

REGULATOR MOTOR

BLACK

RED

INSULATED CONTACT ARM

HIGH SPEED CONTACT

LOW SPEED CONTACT

RELAY HOLD-IN CONTACTS

LOCK-IN RELAY

GREEN

MAGNET ARMATURE

RED

LIMIT SWITCH

THROTTLE SWITCH

LOCKING ARM

RED
BROWN
BLUE
PURPLE

1
2
3
4

GREEN

ACTUATOR PIN

BLACK-WHITE TRACER

HOLDING SWITCH

FROM IGN. SWITCH "ACC" POSITION

BRAKE SWITCH

YELLOW

GRAY

BROWN

BLACK

.047 MFD

FUSE BLOCK
20 AMP.

BLACK-YELLOW TRACER

AUTOMATIC RELAY

YELLOW

OFF
ON
AUTO

DIAL LAMP

TO INSTRUMENT PANEL HARNESS

*1968 Olds exc Cutlass and Vista Cruise*

© G.M. Corp.

INDICATOR LAMP

BRAKE RELEASE SWITCH

FUSE PANEL 20 AMP

IN-LINE FUSE 5 AMP

I.P. SWITCH

PINK

PINK

PINK

BROWN

ENGAGEMENT SWITCH

CONNECTOR

BROWN

BLUE

BLACK

BROWN

BROWN/WHITE TRACER (40 OHM)

BLACK

SLOW SPEED SWITCH

SOLENOID

"A" BODY CRUISE CONTROL CIRCUIT

TRANSDUCER

*1969-71 Cutlass*

## General Motors

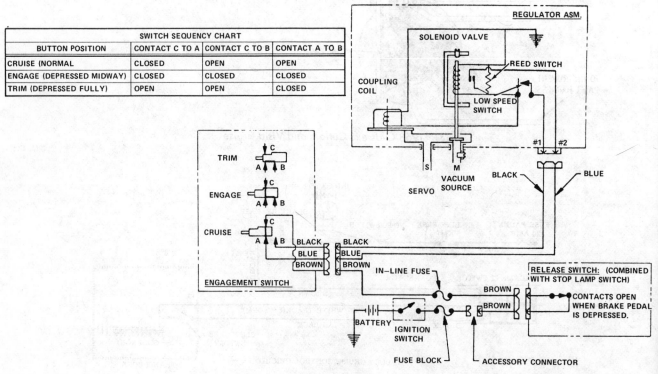

ENGAGEMENT
SWITCH

BLACK    BLUE    COLUMN SWITCH
CONNECTOR

BROWN

HARNESS TO
REGULATOR CONNECTOR

RELEASED POSITION
BLUE AND
BROWN CONNECTED

TAN

BLACK

BLACK

VENT

ENGAGEMENT SWITCH TO
HARNESS CONNECTOR

PARTIALLY DEPRESSED
ALL THREE WIRES
CONNECTED TOGETHER

BROWN

BRAKE
RELEASE
SWITCH

LOW SPEED
SWITCH

FULLY DEPRESSED
BLACK AND BLUE
WIRES
CONNECTED

PINK

GOVERNOR

SOLENOID OPERATED
VACUUM   VALVE

"OFF" - "ON"
SWITCH

REED
SWITCH

COUPLING
COIL

FROM JCT. BLOCK

HEATER   A/C

(IN-LINE)
5 AMP
FUSE

WIPER

BATT.

RADIO

BLADE VALVE

BLEED
PORT

AIR        VACUUM

IGNITION
SWITCH

DIR SIG   BACK UP

PINK

GAUGES   TRANS

MIXING
CHAMBER

CRUISE CONTROL
REGULATOR

1972-75—Oldsmobile

© G.M. Corp.

| | SWITCH SEQUENCE CHART | | |
|---|---|---|---|
| BUTTON POSITION | CONTACT C TO A | CONTACT C TO B | CONTACT A TO B |
| CRUISE (NORMAL) | CLOSED | OPEN | OPEN |
| ENGAGE (DEPRESSED MIDWAY) | CLOSED | CLOSED | CLOSED |
| TRIM (DEPRESSED FULLY) | OPEN | OPEN | CLOSED |

REGULATOR ASM.

SOLENOID VALVE

REED SWITCH

COUPLING
COIL

LOW SPEED
SWITCH

#1    #2

TRIM

C
A   B

ENGAGE

C
A   B

S        M

BLACK        BLUE

CRUISE

C
A    B

SERVO

VACUUM
SOURCE

BLACK    BLACK

RELEASE SWITCH:  (COMBINED
WITH STOP LAMP SWITCH)

BLUE    BLUE

BROWN   BROWN

ENGAGEMENT SWITCH

IN-LINE FUSE

BROWN

BROWN

CONTACTS OPEN
WHEN BRAKE PEDAL
IS DEPRESSED.

BATTERY

IGNITION
SWITCH

FUSE BLOCK

ACCESSORY CONNECTOR

1968-75—Pontiac

# Chrysler Corporation

## 1968-75 Chrysler

### Description

The power operated antenna is telescoping type and is extended and retracted by a coiled nylon cord which is activated by a reversible electric motor.

*NOTE: Before removing the antenna assembly determine whether the problem is with reception or the operation of the antenna.*

### Motor Test

1. Use a 12 volt power source and ground the negative lead to the drive housing.
2. Connect the positive lead to the yellow lead on the motor and test the up operation of the antenna.
2. Connect the positive lead to the brown lead on the motor and test the down operation of the antenna.
4. If the motor will not operate, replace the motor and drive assembly. (See the Trouble Shooting Chart)

## TROUBLESHOOTING CHART

### Power Antenna
### 1968-75 Chrysler

*NOTE: Although the conditions listed below may be related to other parts of the radio system, such as a faulty receiver, the following chart applies to the antenna assembly only.*

| Condition | Possible Cause |
|---|---|
| 1. Weak reception or fading | a. Moisture in tube<br>b. Adjust antenna trimmer<br>c. Clean and tighten connectors<br>d. Check ground |
| 2. Intermittent Reception | a. Defective insulators<br>b. Moisture in tube<br>c. Defective lead in cable |
| 3. Static | a. Upper portion of antenna loose<br>b. Moisture in tube<br>c. Check lead in cable connections |
| 4. Motor operates but antenna will not raise or lower | a. Bent antenna mast<br>b. Improper lubrication<br>c. Excessive dirt |
| 5. Motor does not operate | a. Blown fuse<br>b. Loose electrical connectors<br>c. Defective switch<br>d. Defective motor |

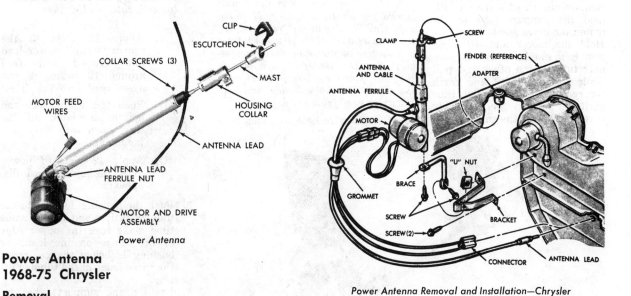

*Power Antenna*

*Power Antenna Removal and Installation—Chrysler*

## Power Antenna
## 1968-75 Chrysler

### Removal

1. Lower the antenna all the way down.
2. Disconnect the negative battery cable.
3. Turn the front wheels all the way to the left and remove the eight right front fender splash shield screws. Pull the shield away from the wheel housing.
4. Disconnect the motor leads at the connector.
5. Remove the antenna lead in cable by unscrewing the nut.
6. Remove the lower antenna bracket mounting screw.
7. On the Imperial models loosen the collar on the antenna mast. On the Chrysler models loosen the collar around the antenna motor.
8. Remove the antenna assembly.

### Installation

1. Position the antenna in the fender and line up the antenna housing collar with the bosses of the escutcheon under the fender and tighten the collar screw.
2. Install the lower antenna bracket mounting screw.
3. Connect the antenna lead to the antenna housing.
4. Connect the motor leads to the connector.
5. Put the fender splash shield back in place and install the retaining screws.
6. Connect the negative battery cable.

# Chrysler Corporation

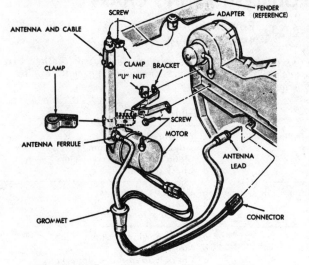

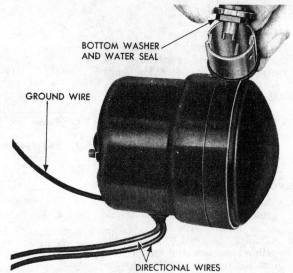

*Power Antenna Removal and Installation—Imperial*

*Removing The Bottom Insulator and Water Seal Washer*

## Power Antenna
## 1968-75 Chrysler

### Disassembly

1. Remove the two screws which hold the lead-in recepticle.
2. Unsolder the pin from the wire.
3. Remove the three screws which hold the support tube to the motor and drive assembly.
4. Hold the motor and drive assembly in one hand and the support tube in the other and pull while applying back and forth rotary motion at the same time until the support tube assembly is removed from the antenna.

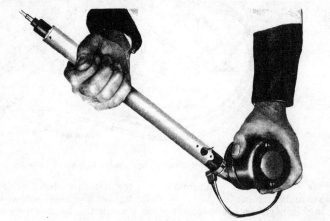

*Removing Support Tube*

5. Hold the motor and drive assembly in one hand and grasp the mast assembly near the bottom with the other. Rock the mast assembly back and forth and pull at the same time and remove the housing from the motor assembly.

6. Apply 12 volts to the (up) power lead and ground, until the entire length of nylon cord has been expelled from the drive. Keep the cord taut to prevent kinking by pulling on the mast.

*NOTE: The motor and drive unit should not be disassembled. If found defective it should be replaced. In order to remove the nylon cord from a defective motor and drive assembly, place the assembly in a vise so that the nylon cord is parallel with the floor. Use both hands and pull the nylon cord from the drive.*

7. Using a wire hook and long nose pliers remove the bottom insulator and water seal washer from the tubular fitting.

### Assembly

1. If the original mast assembly is to be reused, thread the nylon cord through the bottom insula-

tor with the tubular projection down. Then thread the nylon cord through the water seal washers.

*NOTE: A service replacement mast assembly includes the bottom insulator and water seal washer.*

2. (A) Apply 12 volts to the brown "down" power lead and ground and feed around 12 inches of the nylon cord into the drive.

   (B) Push the water seal and bottom insulator all the way down into the tubular fitting.

   (C) Apply 12 volts of power until the nylon cord disappears.

3. Push the housing down onto the tubular fitting and at the same time make sure the upper edge of the flange on the insulator bushing is below the center of the three holes in the tubular fitting.

4. Position the support tube and make sure the hook-up wire is extended through the large hole in the body.

5. Install the three screws which attach the support tube assembly to the motor and drive assembly.

6. Solder the hook up wire to the pin.

7. Assemble the lead in receptacle and replace the two screws.

8. Test the antenna operation by applying 12 volts of power to the yellow and brown antenna leads.

## Chrysler Corporation

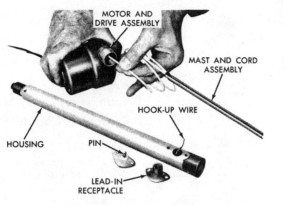

MOTOR AND DRIVE ASSEMBLY

MAST AND CORD ASSEMBLY

HOOK-UP WIRE

HOUSING

PIN

LEAD-IN RECEPTACLE

*Power Antenna—Assembly*

### Antenna Trimmer Adjustment
### 1968-75 Chrysler

The antenna trimmer adjustment must always be made after any repairs have been made to the power antenna or if AM reception is unsatisfactory.

1. Turn the radio on for a few minutes.
2. Move the antenna to a height of 40 inches.
3. Tune the radio to a weak signal somewhere between 1400 and 1600 kc.
4. Increase the radio volume to full volume and set the tone control to maximum treble (fully clockwise) on knob controlled radios or upward on the thumbwheel radios.
5. Remove the right radio control knobs for access to the trimmer control. On thumbwheel radios, the adjuster is located under the instrument panel in the bottom right hand corner of the radio.
6. Adjust the antenna trimmer screw until maximum volume is achieved.

## Ford Motor Company

### Power Antenna
### 1968 Mercury

#### Removal

1. Open the trunk lid and disconnect the antenna leads.
2. Disconnect the antenna cable.
3. Remove the bolt which retains the antenna to the floor pan bracket.
4. Remove the nut retaining the antenna to the fender.
5. Remove the ground strap, spacer and the antenna.

#### Installation

1. When installing a new antenna transfer the lower spacer, ground strap and the upper portion of the lower bracket to the antenna.
2. Position the antenna to the fender and install the spacer and nut.
3. Install the nut that retains the antenna to the floor pan.
4. Connect the cable and leads.
5. Adjust the antenna trimmer if necessary.

### Power Antenna
### 1969 Lincoln Continental

#### Removal

1. Remove the left front fender rear splash shield.
2. Disconnect the antenna cable and the motor wire connector.

3. Remove the collar mount retaining screws, then remove the collar mount.
4. Remove the screws from the motor support bracket.
5. Remove the antenna through the splash shield opening.

#### Installation

1. Position the antenna and loosely install the retaining screws.
2. Tighten the motor support mounting screws; then, tighten the collar retaining screws.
3. Connect the antenna cable and the motor wire connector.
4. Install the splash shield.

### TROUBLESHOOTING CHART

**Power Antenna**
**1968-75 All Models**

| Condition | Possible Cause |
|---|---|
| **1. Motor does not operate** | a. Fuse<br>b. Defective switch or wiring<br>c. Poor ground<br>d. Defective motor |
| **2. Motor operates in only one direction** | a. Defective switch or wiring<br>b. Defective motor |
| **3. Motor runs but rod does not move** | a. Bent or corroded rod<br>b. Defective drive assembly |

### Power Antenna
### 1969-70 Thunderbird
### 1969-71 Continental Mark III
### 1970-75 Lincoln Continental
### 1971-72 Mercury

#### Removal

1. Lower the antenna.
2. Remove the luggage compartment left trim panel.
3. Disconnect the cable from the antenna.
4. Disconnect the motor wires at the connector.
5. Remove the trim nut from the antenna.

# Ford Motor Company

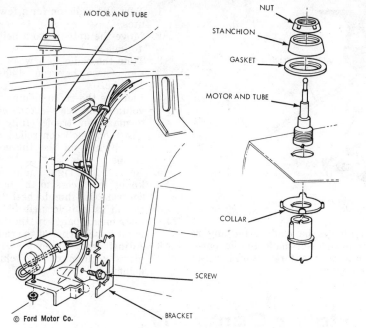

Power Antenna Installation—1971-72—Mercury

5. Tilt the antenna assembly into position slightly inward and rearward then tighten the nuts.
6. Tighten the trim nut.
7. Install the trim panel.

## Power Antenna
## 1972-75 Thunderbird,
## Continental Mark IV

### Removal

1. From under the instrument panel, near the right cowl trim panel, disconnect the antenna lead.
2. Disconnect the motor wires at the connector.
3. Remove the lower bracket attaching screws, located at the fender apron.
4. Remove the trim nut, stanchion, and remove the antenna through the engine compartment.

### Installation

1. Position the antenna and attach the stanchion an dtrim nut, but do not tighten the nut.
2. Install the bracket lower attaching screws but do not tighten the screws.
3. Tighten the top trim nut then tighten the bracket lower attaching screws.
4. Pull the lead through the dash and connect it to the extension cable.
5. Connect the motor wire leads.

6. Remove the nut from the antenna mounting stud located at the bottom of the motor.
7. Loosen the antenna bracket attaching bolt and nuts (screws on some models).
8. Remove the antenna assembly from the car.

### Installation

1. Make sure the quarter panel is clean underneath to assure a good ground.
2. Install the collar on the antenna assembly.
3. Position the antenna to the quarter panel and install the gasket, stanchion, and trim nut. Tighten the nut only finger tight.
4. Install the antenna bracket but do not tighten the nuts.

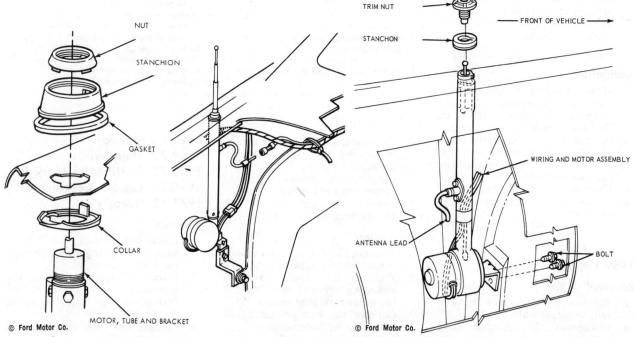

Power Antenna Installation—1971-74—Lincoln Continental

Power Antenna—Installation—1971-74—Thunderbird and Mark III

## Ford Motor Company

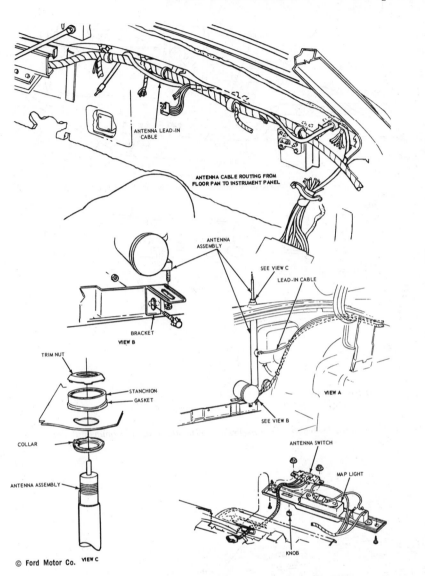

© Ford Motor Co.  VIEW C

*Power Antenna Installation—1970-71—Thunderbird and Continental Mark III*

© Ford Motor Co.
*1974-75—All*

### Antenna Switch
### 1969-71 Thunderbird
### 1969-71 Mark III

#### Removal

1. Remove the two screws which attach the map light to the instrument panel.
2. Remove the switch knob.
3. Remove the two switch attaching nuts and separate the switch from the light.
4. Disconnect the multiple connector and remove the switch.

#### Installation

1. Connect the multiple connector.
2. Position the switch to the map lamp and install the two attaching nuts.
3. Position the map light and install the switch knob and the two attaching screws.

### Antenna Switch
### 1971-72 Mercury

#### Removal

1. Remove the two finish cover retaining screws.
2. Snap the cover away from the retaining clips.
3. Disconnect the switch and remove the finish cover.
4. Release the clips and separate the switch from the cover.

#### Installation

1. Position the switch and connect the switch leads.
2. Push the switch in the retainer and install the two screws.

### Antenna Switch
### 1970-75 Lincoln Continental
### 1972-75 Thunderbird and
### Continental Mark IV

#### Removal

1. Remove the attaching screw.
2. Disconnect the wire at the connector.

#### Installation

1. Reverse the removal procedure.

### Antenna Trimmer Adjustment
### 1968-75 All Models

In some instances a weak signal

**771**

## Ford Motor Company

pick-up may be corrected by adjusting the antenna trimmer. The trimmer is located at the right rear of the radio on most models and on all others the trimmer is located on the front of the radio near the manual tuning control.

1. Make sure the antenna lead-in plug and socket are clean.
2. Extend the antenna to its maximum length.
3. If possible place the car in an open area away from steel buildings.
4. Turn the radio on and leave on for about five minutes in order to reach normal operating temperature.
5. On the Mercury models equipped with an AM radio, remove the selector control knob, disc and fader control (if so equipped), then remove the instrument cluster center and right housings.
6. Tune the radio to a weak station somewhere around 16 on the dial and adjust the volume control so that it can barely be heard.
7. Adjust the antenna trimmer to obtain the maximum signal strength (volume) from the station.

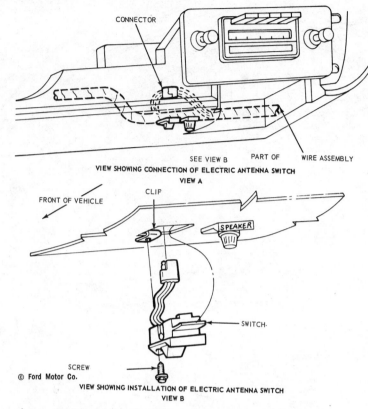

VIEW SHOWING CONNECTION OF ELECTRIC ANTENNA SWITCH
VIEW A

VIEW SHOWING INSTALLATION OF ELECTRIC ANTENNA SWITCH
VIEW B

© Ford Motor Co.

*Antenna Switch Installation—1972-74—Thunderbird and Continental Mark IV*

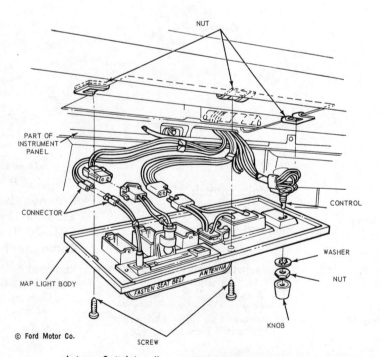

© Ford Motor Co.

*Antenna Switch Installation—1972-74—Lincoln Continental*

# General Motors

## 1968-69 LeSabre, Wildcat and Electra

### Removal

1. Lower the antenna to the full down position.
2. Disconnect the negative battery cable.
3. Disconnect the antenna motor wires at the connector and the lead in cable.
4. Remove the screw or screws which attaches the motor bracket to the trunk floor.
5. Remove the two screws and spacer on some models, which retain the lower mounting bracket to the wheel house flange.
6. Remove the spanner nut, adapter and pad from the top of the antenna and remove the antenna from the vehicle.

### Installation

1. Insert the antenna into position and install the two screws which retain the lower mounting bracket to the wheelhouse flange. Do not tighten.
2. Replace the pad, adapter and tighten the spanner nut.
3. Connect the antenna motor wires at the connector and lead in cable.
4. Connect the negative battery cable.
5. Run the antenna up to the fully extended height and adjust the lower mounting clamp so that the antenna tilts slightly towards the center and rear of the car.
6. Tighten the screws in the lower mounting bracket and install the screw or screws which retains the motor bracket to the trunk floor.
7. Adjust the antenna trimmer adjustment.

## Power Antenna Assembly 1968-69 Riviera

(See illustrations for Removal and Installation)

## Power Antenna Assembly 1969 Skylark, Gransport, Sportwagon

### Removal

1. Lower the antenna to the full down position.
2. Disconnect the negative battery cable.
3. Disconnect the motor wires at the connector and the lead in cable.
4. Remove the screw which attaches the motor bracket to the trunk floor.

# TROUBLESHOOTING CHART

### Power Antenna

*NOTE: Although the conditions listed below may be related to other parts of the radio system, such as a faulty receiver, the following chart applies to the antenna assembly only.*

| Condition | Possible Cause |
|---|---|
| 1. Weak reception or fading | a. Moisture in tube<br>b. Adjust antenna trimmer<br>c. Clean and tighten connectors<br>d. Check ground |
| 2. Intermittent reception | a. Defective insulators<br>b. Moisture in tube<br>c. Defective lead in cable |
| 3. Static | a. Upper portion of antenna loose<br>b. Moisture in tube<br>c. Check lead in cable connections |
| 4. Antenna will not raise or lower | a. Blown fuse<br>b. Loose electrical connectors<br>c. Bent antenna mast<br>d. Improper lubrication<br>e. Defective motor<br>f. Defective switch |

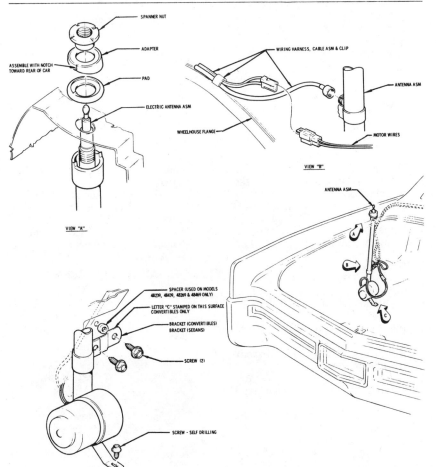

© G.M. Corp.

*Power Antenna Installation—Le Sabre, Wildcat and Electra—1968*

## General Motors

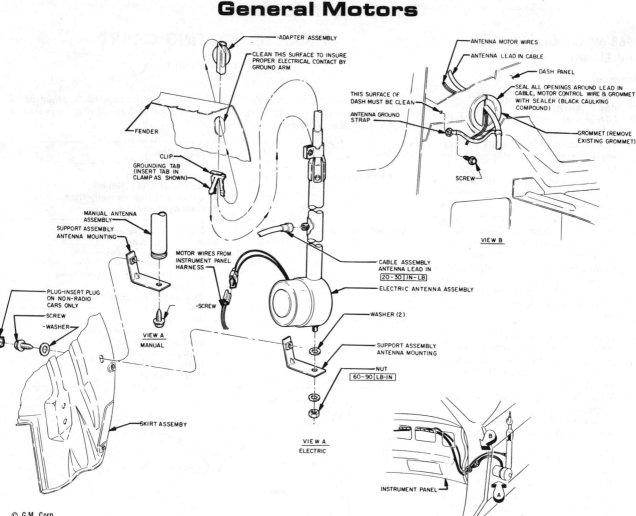

© G.M. Corp.

*Power Antenna—Removal and Installation—Riviera—1968-69*

5. Remove the two screws which attach the antenna clamp to the wheelhouse brace.
6. Remove the spanner nut, adapter and pad from the top of the fender and remove the antenna from the vehicle.

### Installation

1. Assemble the clamping bracket to the antenna, placing the lead in fitting in the notch in the bracket.
2. Insert the antenna assembly into the fender. Loosely tighten the mounting clamp to the rear wheelhouse brace.
3. Place the pad, adapter and spanner nut on the antenna and tighten.
4. Connect the motor wires at the connector and the lead in cable.
5. Tighten the mounting clamp screw to the rear wheelhouse brace.
6. Run the antenna to the full up position and bend the mounting

clamp so that the antenna is vertical.
7. Bend the lower bracket down to the trunk floor and install the screw.
8. Trim the antenna (See Antenna Trimmer Adjustment).

### Power Antenna
### 1968-69 All Models Buick

#### Disassembly

1. Remove the three screws that hold the body and upper insu-

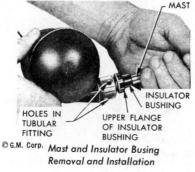

© G.M. Corp. *Mast and Insulator Busing Removal and Installation*

lator assembly to the support tube.
2. While applying a back and forth rotary motion, pull the body upper insulator assembly out of the support tube and partially slide it over the mast until the solder joint is accessible.
3. Unsolder the hookup wire from the mast and remove the body and upper insulator from the mast.
4. Remove the three screws which hold the support tube to the antenna drive.
5. Hold the antenna drive in one hand, the support tube in the other and pull with a rotary motion until the support tube is removed.
6. Hold the antenna drive in one hand and the mast with the other and pull the mast with a rocking motion until the insulator bushing and mast are free from the tubular fitting of the antenna drive.

## General Motors

7. Apply 12 volts to the green wire of the antenna drive until the entire length of nylon cable has been expelled, and remove the mast. Pull the mast to keep the nylon cable taut.

*NOTE: If the antenna drive is inoperative, it will be necessary to remove the nylon cable by hand. Place the unit in a vise so that the normal plane of the nylon cable is parallel with the floor. Using both hands, pull on the 0.30 diameter section of the mast until the cable is completely removed.*

8. Use a wire hook or long nose pliers and remove the bottom insulator and water seal washer from the tubular fitting of the antenna drive.
9. Remove the drive cover.

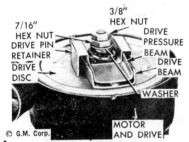

*Antenna Drive Cover—Removed*

10. Hold the 7/16 in. hex nut on the output gear assembly shaft and remove the 3/8 in. hex nut.
11. Remove the 7/16 in. hex nut and washer.
12. Lift the antenna pressure adjuster spring off the shaft.
13. Remove the drive pin retainer.
14. Remove the drive pressure beam.
15. Slide the drive pin from the hole in the shaft and take off the drive beam without loosing the two steel balls at the ends.
16. Remove the two steel balls.
17. Remove the drive disc from the shaft.

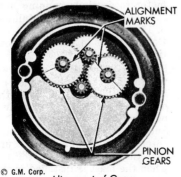

*Alignment of Gears*

*NOTE: Be careful not to bend the drive disc or burr the edges of the channel. It will be necessary to re-align the pinion gear if they have been removed or have fallen out. Realignment is done by positioning the right and left pinion gears so that the mark on each one points at the center of the pinion shaft of the drive gear which receives the motor pinion.*

### Assembly

1. Install the drive disc on the shaft.
2. Replace the two steel balls at the ends of the drive beam and install the drive beam on the shaft. Install the drive pin in the shaft.
3. Install the drive pin retainer.
4. Replace the pressure adjuster spring on the shaft with the largest diameter toward the drive pin retainer.
5. Replace the washer on the output gear assembly shaft and screw in the 7/16 in. hex nut one full turn until it touches the spring.
6. Do not reassemble the 3/8 in. hex nut on the shaft or snap the drive cover in place until step 12 has been completed.
7. Position the water seal washer and bottom insulator in the tubular fitting of the antenna.
8. Thread the nylon cable into the antenna drive. Apply 12 volts of power to the blue power lead to assist the feeding operation. Keep the nylon cable straight to avoid kinking.
9. Push the section of mast and insulator bushing into the tubular fitting. Make sure that the free end of the hook-up wire extends below the lower edge of the body and upper insulator assembly.
10. Solder the free-end of the hook-up wire to the mast section, using rosin flux solder.

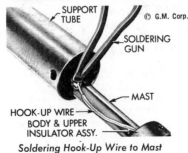

*Soldering Hook-Up Wire to Mast*

11. Position and reassemble the body and upper insulator to the support tube.
12. Perform the antenna adjustment procedure (See Antenna Adjustment)

13. Install the 3/8 in. hex nut and drive cover onto the antenna drive and make sure that the vent hole in the drive cover is at the top when the antenna is installed in the car.
14. Reseal the antenna drive with body sealer and make sure the vent hole in the drive cover and drain hole in the antenna drive are not plugged.

### Power Antenna Adjustment
### 1968 All Models Buick

1. Remove the drive cover and the 3/8 in. hex nut from the antenna drive.
2. Place the antenna drive in a vise so that the center line of the antenna drive is parallel to the bench top.
3. Using 12 volts, adjust the mast tip approximately six inches from the extreme down position.
4. Connect one end of a wire securely to the mast just below the tip and the other end to a 25 lb. capacity spring scale. Secure the spring scale to the bench so that the center line of the scale is in line with that of the mast assembly.
5. Attach a 12 volt power lead to the antenna and drive housing and connect another lead to the blue (down) terminal to work the antenna drive till the point of maximum pull is less than 15 lbs. Turn the 7/16 in. hex nut clockwise a slight amount, and recheck the maximum pull. If the pull is greater than 15 lbs., turn the 7/16 in. hex nut counterclockwise a slight amount and recheck the pull. Repeat until the pull is set at 15 lbs.
6. Hold the 7/16 in. hex nut in position and tighten the 3/8 in. nut against the 7/16 in. hex nut to lock it in place.
7. Disconnect the spring scale and apply power to the green (up) terminal. Run the mast all the way out and allow the motor to continue running until the clutch has made a minimum of fifteen engagements or clicks.
8. Do the same in the down position.
9. Run the antenna up and down for approximately three minutes, then reassemble the spring scale to the mast and recheck for maximum pull. Adjust if necessary.
10. Snap on the front cover onto the antenna drive with the vent hole at the top when the mast is installed in the car.

# General Motors

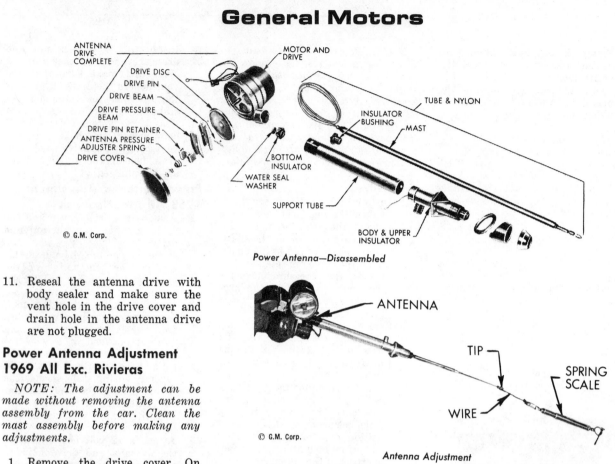

ANTENNA DRIVE COMPLETE

DRIVE DISC
DRIVE PIN
DRIVE BEAM
DRIVE PRESSURE BEAM
DRIVE PIN RETAINER
ANTENNA PRESSURE ADJUSTER SPRING
DRIVE COVER

MOTOR AND DRIVE

TUBE & NYLON

INSULATOR BUSHING
MAST

BOTTOM INSULATOR
WATER SEAL WASHER
SUPPORT TUBE

BODY & UPPER INSULATOR

© G.M. Corp.

*Power Antenna—Disassembled*

ANTENNA
TIP
SPRING SCALE
WIRE

© G.M. Corp.

*Antenna Adjustment*

11. Reseal the antenna drive with body sealer and make sure the vent hole in the drive cover and drain hole in the antenna drive are not plugged.

## Power Antenna Adjustment 1969 All Exc. Rivieras

*NOTE: The adjustment can be made without removing the antenna assembly from the car. Clean the mast assembly before making any adjustments.*

1. Remove the drive cover. On some models it will be necessary to loosen the screws on the support assembly so the motor and drive can be turned to allow the removal of the drive cover.
2. Adjust the mast tip around six inches from the extreme down position.
3. Connect one end of a wire to the mast just below the tip and the other end to a 25 lb. capacity spring scale. Attach the spring scale to a solid overhead object so that the center line of the scale is in line with that of the mast assembly.
4. Engage the motor to the point of maximum pull before the clutch starts to slip. If the maximum pull is less than 15 lbs., turn the self-locking nut clockwise a slight amount, and recheck the maximum pull. If the pull is greater than 15 lbs., turn the self locking nut counterclockwise a slight amount and recheck the pull. Repeat until the pull is set at 15 lbs.
5. Disconnect the spring scale and engage the motor until the mast is at its maximum length and allow the motor to continue running until the clutch has made a minimum of 15 clicks.

6. Do the same in the down position.
7. Run the antenna up and down for about three minutes, then reassemble the spring scale to the mast and recheck for maximum pull. Adjust as necessary.
8. Snap the front cover onto the antenna drive and make sure that the vent hole is at the top.
9. Reposition the motor and drive and tighten the screws on the support assembly.

## Power Antenna Adjustment 1969 Riviera

*NOTE: Clean the mast assembly before making any adjustments.*

1. Remove the antenna assembly from the car.
2. Remove the drive cover and place the antenna drive in a vise so that the center line of the antenna drive is parallel to the bench top.
3. Use 12 volts and adjust the mast tip approximately six inches from the extreme down position.
4. Connect one end of a wire to the mast just below the tip and the other end to a 25 lb. capacity spring scale. Attach the

spring scale to a bench so that the centerline of the scale is in line with that of the mast assembly.
5. Use 12 volts and engage the motor to the point of maximum pull before the clutch starts to slip. If the maximum pull is less than 15 lbs., turn the self locking nut clockwise a slight amount and recheck the maximum pull. If the pull is greater than 15 lbs., turn the self locking nut counterclockwise a slight amount and recheck the pull. Repeat until the pull is set at 15 lbs.
6. Disconnect the spring scale and engage the motor until the mast is fully extended and allow the motor to continue running until the clutch has made a minimum of 15 clicks.
7. Do the same in the down position.
8. Run the antenna up and down for about three minutes, then reassemble the spring scale to the mast and recheck for maximum pull. Adjust as necessary.
9. Snap the front cover onto the antenna drive and make sure that the vent hole is at the top when the mast is installed in the car.

# General Motors

10. Reseal the assembly with body sealer and make sure the vent hole in the drive cover and the drain hole in the antenna are not plugged.
11. Install the antenna assembly.

## 1973-75 Buick

### Description

The antenna is controlled by either one of two switches. One is integral with the radio on and off control which raises the antenna to a pre-set height of approximately twelve inches when the radio is turned on or fully retracts the antenna when the radio is turned off. The other switch is located in the accessory switch panel and is used for raising the antenna higher than the preset height for better reception and lowering when needed for clearance of low overhead objects.

When the switch is activated it operates a reversible electric motor that extends or retracts a cable. The cable is attached to the smallest of three antenna sections. As the cable is extended or retracted the antenna rod is moved upward or downward. Raising or lowering the antenna by hand may damage the operating mechanisms so it is advised that only the control switch be used.

## Power Antenna
### 1973 All Models Buick

#### Removal

1. Remove the right rocker panel moulding
2. Start at the bottom of the fender and to the rear of the tire and remove the five screws which attach the wheel house to the fender.
3. If so equipped, remove the two bottom and one top screws and shims used between the fender and the body.
4. Pull the bottom of the fender out around ten inches and hold out with a block of wood.
5. Remove the special nut, adapter, and trim adapter pad from the top of the fender.
6. Disconnect the antenna lead in cable and unplug the electrical connector.
7. Remove the nut and two washers from the bottom of the antenna assembly and remove the antenna from the car.

#### Installation

1. Place a washer on the bottom antenna stud and position the

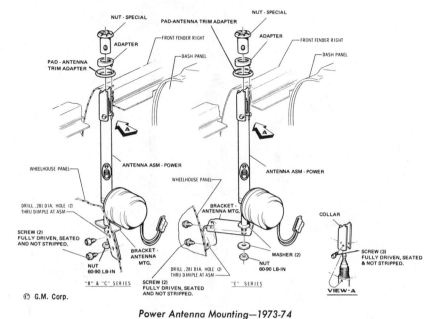

*Power Antenna Mounting—1973-74*

antenna assembly into the lower mounting bracket. Install the washer and nut.
2. Connect the lead in cable and the electrical connector.
3. Install the trim adapter pad, adapter and special nut on top of the fender.
4. Push the fender back in place and install the shims and screws.
5. Install the five screws attaching the wheelhouse to the fender.
6. Install the rocker panel moulding.
7. Adjust the antenna trimmer (See antenna trimmer adjustment).

## Power Antenna
### 1974-75 All Models Buick
#### Removal

1. Disconnect the antenna lead in cable and electrical connector.
2. On top of the fender, remove the special nut, adapter and trim adapter pad.
3. Remove the two antenna mounting bracket to wheel house panel screws.
4. On the Riviera models, remove the bottom mounting bracket nut and washer and remove the assembly from the car. On the Electra and LeSabre models, remove the antenna assembly from underneath the car between the exhaust manifold and frame.

#### Installation

1. Reverse the removal procedure and adjust the antenna trimmer (See antenna trimmer adjustment).

## Antenna Unit
### 1973-75 All Models Buick
#### Disassembly

1. Remove the three screws which attach the clamp at the top of the support tube to the support tube and remove the clamp.
2. Remove the two lead-in receptacle screws and remove the receptacle from the support tube.
3. Unsolder the mast wire from the pin and insulator assembly.

*CAUTION: Be careful not to overheat by slow soldering and melt the insulator.*

4. Remove the three screws which attach the support tube to the drive assembly. Pull the support tube loose with the top insulator attached.
5. Unscrew the tip from the inner telescopic section.
6. Remove the outer mast sections with the insulator bushing attached from the tubular fitting on the drive assembly.
7. The inner mast section with the cable attached can be detached from the drive assembly by applying 12 volts to the black motor wire, while grounding the motor. Pull the remainder for the cable out by hand.

*NOTE: To prevent kinking or bending keep the cable taut.*

8. Insert a small drill through each of the drain holes at the bottom of the tubular fitting and remove the bottom insulator.

# General Motors

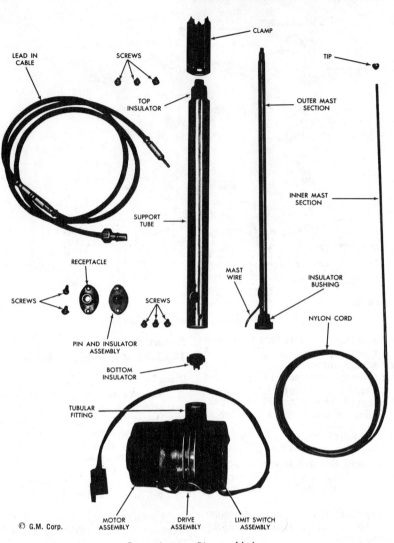

LEAD IN CABLE

SCREWS

CLAMP

TIP

TOP INSULATOR

OUTER MAST SECTION

SUPPORT TUBE

INNER MAST SECTION

RECEPTACLE

MAST WIRE

INSULATOR BUSHING

SCREWS

SCREWS

NYLON CORD

PIN AND INSULATOR ASSEMBLY

BOTTOM INSULATOR

TUBULAR FITTING

© G.M. Corp.

MOTOR ASSEMBLY

DRIVE ASSEMBLY

LIMIT SWITCH ASSEMBLY

*Power Antenna Disassembled*

## Assembly

*NOTE: Before assembling the antenna, check the drain holes in the motor housing below the body tube mounting point to be sure they are not blocked.*

*If the car has been undercoated, make sure that the drain holes have not been plugged.*

*Lubricate the rod with a light coat of oil.*

1. Without forcing, insert the cable into the drive assembly as far as possible.
2. Apply 12 volts to the white motor wire, while grounding the motor, to retract the cable into the drive assembly.

*NOTE: To prevent kinking or bending keep the cable taut.*

3. Insert the bottom insulator into the tubular fitting with the slotted protrusion down and align the slots of the insulator with the ears in the tubular fitting.
4. Place the outer mast section over the inner section and align the slots of the pin and insulator assembly with the ears in the tubular fitting.
5. Install the tip on the inner telescopic section.
6. Place the support tube over the mast assembly, aligning the tang on the tube with the slot in the tubular fitting.
7. Pull the mast wire through the pin and insulator hole and secure the three support tube screws.
8. Insert the mast wire into the pin and insulator assembly and solder, using resin type solder and without overheating.
9. Place the lead-in receptacle over the pin and insulator assembly and install the two screws.
10. Install the support tube clamp and the three retaining screws.

## Antenna Dog Assembly (Antenna Unit off Car) 1973-75 All Models Buick

### Disassembly

1. Clamp the lower mounting base of the antenna in a vise.
2. Remove the automatic switch assembly from the drive housing by removing the spring retaining clip.
3. Use an open end wrench and remove the dog assembly from the shaft by turning it counterclockwise.

### Assembly

1. Loosely install the dog assembly on the shaft by turning clockwise.
2. Using the template provided with the new dog assembly, measure the distance between the top of the longest pin on the dog to the base of the drive housing. Adjust as necessary.
3. Position the automatic switch assembly to the drive housing and install the spring retaining clip.
4. Remove antenna assembly from the vise.

## Antenna Cap and Automatic Switch Assembly 1973-75 All Models Buick (Antenna Unit off Car)

### Disassembly

1. Clamp the lower mounting base of the antenna in a vise.
2. Untape the antenna wiring harness from the support tube.
3. Remove the automatic switch assembly from the drive housing by removing the spring retaining clip.
4. Stagger cut the black and white wires at a midway point between the motor and switch assembly.

### Assembly

1. Solder together the black to black and the white to white switch and motor leads.
2. Tape the solder joints with electrical tape.
3. Position the automatic switch assembly to the drive housing and install the spring retaining clip.
4. Tape the antenna wiring harness to the support tube.

# General Motors

5. Remove the antenna assembly from the vise.

## Antenna Motor and Drive Assembly (Antenna Unit off Car) 1973-75 All Models Buick

### Disassembly

1. Clamp the lower mounting base of the antenna in a vise.
2. Untape the wiring harness from the support tube.
3. Remove the automatic switch assembly from the drive housing by removing the spring retaining clip.
4. Use an open end wrench and remove the dog assembly from the shaft by turning it counterclockwise.
5. Stagger cut the black and white wires at a midway point between the motor and switch assembly.
6. Remove the three screws which secure the support tube to the drive housing and pull the support tube and drive cable completely out of the drive housing.

### Assembly

1. Clamp the new motor and drive unit mounting base in a vise.
2. Using the template provided, measure the distance between the top of the longest pin on the dog to the base of the drive housing. Adjust as necessary.
3. Solder together the black to black and the white to white switch and motor leads.
4. Tape the solder joint with electrical tape.
5. Position the automatic switch assembly to the drive housing and install the spring retaining clips.
6. Apply 12 volts to the black wire in the four way connector while grounding the antenna and run the antenna to the full up position.
7. Put a small amount of lithium grease on the cable and insert the end into the drive housing and push in as far as possible to start the cable.
8. With the antenna grounded apply 12 volts to the white wire in the four way connector and run the antenna all the way down. Guide the cable and mast while retracting.
9. Position the support tube assembly to the drive housing and install the three screws.
10. To adjust the cable for height

run the antenna up until it stops; then down as outlined in steps 6 and 8.

## Antenna Mast and Support Tube (Antenna Unit off Car) 1973-75 All Models Buick

### Disassembly

1. Clamp the lower mounting base of the antenna in a vise.
2. Untape the antenna wiring harness from the support tube.
3. Apply 12 volts to the black wire in the four way connector while grounding the antenna and run the antenna to the full up position.
4. Remove the three screws which secure the support tube assembly to the drive housing and pull the support tube and drive cable completely out of the housing.

*NOTE: If the cable cannot be pulled out by hand remove the antenna dog as previously described.*

### Assembly

1. Put a small amount of grease on the cable and insert the end into the drive housing as far as possible to start the cable.
2. Ground the antenna and apply 12 volts to the white wire in the four way connector and run the antenna all the way down. Guide the antenna and mast while retracting.
3. Position the support tube assembly to the drive housing and install the three screws.
4. To adjust the cable for height, run the antenna up until it stops; then down as outlined in step 3 of disassembly and step 2 of assembly.

## Antenna Trimmer Adjustment 1968-69 and 1973-75 Buick

The antenna trimmer adjustment

must always be made after any repairs have been made to the power antenna or if AM reception is unsatisfactory.

This adjustment applies only to AM radios or the AM portion of AM-FM radios. Trimming for FM reception is automatically accomplished whenever the antenna is raised to 31 inches.

1. Move the antenna to a height of 31 inches.
2. Tune the radio dial to a weak station somewhere around 1400 kc.
3. Remove the right inner and outer knobs.
4. Adjust the trimmer screw until maximum volume is achieved.

*NOTE: When a car is equipped with a rear speaker the speaker control knob must be removed to gain access to the trimmer screw. The speaker knob has three prongs which interconnect three small holes (electrical connecting points) in the receiver. A short jumper wire must be inserted in the center and outside holes to channel the sound to the speaker. It is generally desirable to trim the radio while using the front speaker.*

## 1968-69 Cadillac

### Description

The antenna is controlled by a switch located at the left of the radio dial. The switch activates a reversible electric motor. The motor drives a gear and pulley assembly that extends or retracts a nylon cable. The cable is attached to the smallest of three antenna sections. As the cable is extended or retracted the antenna rod is moved upward or downward.

Raising or lowering the antenna by hand may damage the operating mechanism so it is advised that only the control switch be used.

On AM/FM equipped vehicles the antenna height should be kept at thirty inches for the best reception.

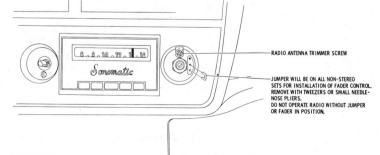

© G.M. Corp.

*Antenna Trimmer and Rear Speaker Jumper Wire*

## General Motors

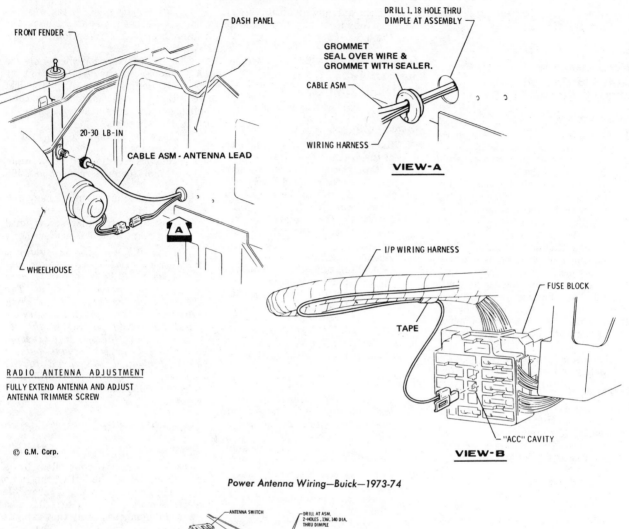

FRONT FENDER

DASH PANEL

DRILL 1. 18 HOLE THRU
DIMPLE AT ASSEMBLY

GROMMET
SEAL OVER WIRE &
GROMMET WITH SEALER.

CABLE ASM

WIRING HARNESS

**VIEW-A**

20-30 LB-IN

CABLE ASM - ANTENNA LEAD

WHEELHOUSE

I/P WIRING HARNESS

FUSE BLOCK

TAPE

"ACC" CAVITY

**VIEW-B**

RADIO ANTENNA ADJUSTMENT

FULLY EXTEND ANTENNA AND ADJUST
ANTENNA TRIMMER SCREW

© G.M. Corp.

*Power Antenna Wiring—Buick—1973-74*

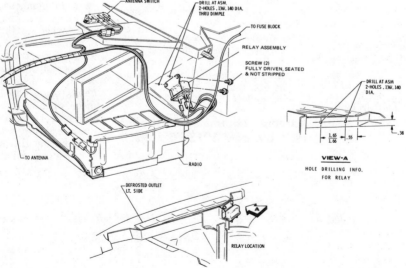

ANTENNA SWITCH

DRILL AT ASM.
2-HOLES .136/.140 DIA.
THRU DIMPLE

TO FUSE BLOCK

RELAY ASSEMBLY

SCREW (2)
FULLY DRIVEN, SEATED
& NOT STRIPPED

DRILL AT ASM
2-HOLES .136/.140
DIA.

TO ANTENNA

RADIO

1.65
1.66

.55

.38

**VIEW-A**

HOLE DRILLING INFO.
FOR RELAY

DEFROSTED OUTLET
LT. SIDE

RELAY LOCATION

*Power Antenna Wiring—Buick—1973-74*

# General Motors

*NOTE: Most antenna problems can be prevented by keeping the antenna rod clean and lightly oiled.*

If moisture is the problem the antenna should be disassembled and thoroughly cleaned. Moisture can be removed from the support tube by using compressed air and pushing a dry cloth through the tube.

## Antenna Assembly
### 1968-69 Cadillac

#### Removal

1. Lower the antenna.
2. Disconnect the negative battery cable.
3. Disconnect the motor wires at the connector and the cable from the antenna.
4. Loosen the clamp screw that holds the antenna to the escutcheon.
5. Remove the screw which holds the antenna and bracket to the right fender dustshield and remove the antenna from the car.
6. The escutcheon may be pushed out through the top of the fender after removing the retaining spring.

#### Installation

1. If removed, install the escutcheon and retaining spring.
2. Position the antenna and make sure the antenna clamp is over the grounding tab of the escutcheon retaining spring.
3. Install the screw that holds the antenna assembly and bracket to the fender dustshield.
4. Connect the cable.
5. Connect the motor wires at the connector.
6. Tighten the screw that clamps the top of the antenna to the escutcheon.
7. Connect the negative battery cable.

## Antenna Unit
### 1968-69 Cadillac

#### Disassembly

1. Remove the three screws which secure the clamp at the top of the support tube and remove the clamp.
2. Remove the two screws which hold the lead-in receptacle to the support tube and remove the receptacle.
3. Unsolder the mast wire from the pin and insulator and remove the wire.

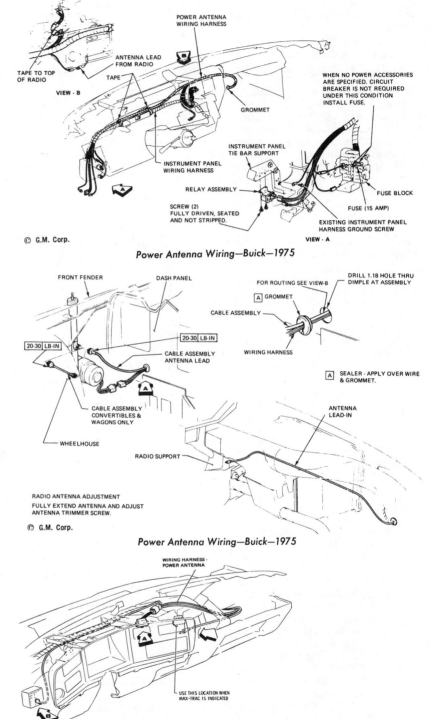

© G.M. Corp.

*Power Antenna Wiring—Buick—1975*

*Power Antenna Wiring—Buick—1975*

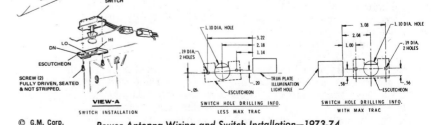

© G.M. Corp.

*Power Antenna Wiring and Switch Installation—1973-74*

# General Motors

*NOTE: Be careful not to overheat by slow soldering and melt the insulator.*

4. Remove the three screws which secure the support tube to the drive assembly. Pull the support tube loose with the top insulator attached.
5. Remove the outer mast section with the insulator bushing attached, from the tubular fitting on the drive assembly.
6. The inner mast section with the cord attached can be detached from the drive assembly by applying 12 volts to the motor wires while grounding the motor.

*NOTE: The cord must be kept taut to prevent kinking or bending.*

7. Remove the bottom insulator from the tubular fitting by inserting a small drill through each of the drain holes at the bottom of the tubular fitting.
8. Unscrew the tip from the inner telescopic section.

## Assembly

*NOTE: Before assembling the antenna, check the drain holes in the motor housing below the body tube mounting point to be sure they are not blocked. If the car has been undercoated, make sure that the drain holes have not been plugged.*

*Lubricate the rod with a light coat of oil.*

1. Install the tip on the inner telescopic section.
2. Insert the bottom insulator in the tubular fitting with the slotted protrusion down, aligning the slots of the insulator with the ears in the tubular fitting.
3. Without forcing, insert the cord through the bottom insulator and into the drive assembly. Then apply 12 volts to the motor wires to retract the cord into the drive assembly. Keep the cord taut to prevent kinking.
4. Place the outer mast section over the inner section aligning the slots of the pin and insulator assembly with the ears in the tubular fitting.
5. Place the support tube over the mast assembly. Align the tang on the tube with the slot provided in the fitting.
6. Pull the mast wire into the pin and insulator assembly and install the three support tube screws.
7. Use only resin type solder and

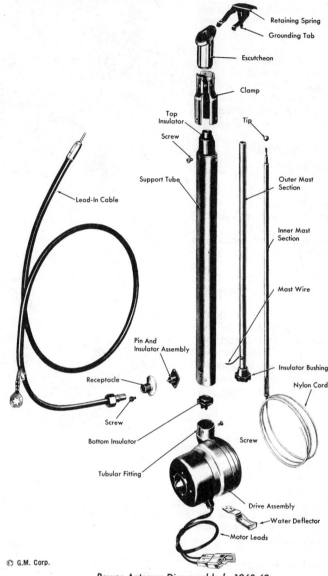

© G.M. Corp.

*Power Antenna Disassembled—1968-69*

solder the wire at the pin and insulator assembly without overheating the insulator.
8. Place the lead in receptacle over the pin and insulator assembly and install the two screws.
9. Position the clamp over the support tube and install the three screws.

## 1973-75 Cadillac

### Description

The antenna is controlled by either one of two switches. One is integral with the radio on and off control which raises the antenna to a pre-set height of approximately twelve inches when the radio is turned on or fully retracts the antenna when the radio is turned off. The other switch is located in the accessory switch panel and is used for raising the antenna higher than the present height for better reception and lowering when needed for clearance of low overhead objects.

When the switch is activated it operates a reversible electric motor that extends or retracts a cable. The cable is attached to the smallest of three antenna sections. As the cable is extended or retracted the antenna rod is moved upward or downward. Raising or lowering the antenna by hand may damage the operating mechanisms so it is advised that only the control switch be used.

# General Motors

## Antenna Trimmer Adjustment
## Cadillac—All

1. Turn the radio on and switch to AM band.
2. Extend the antenna to the full up position.
3. Tune in a weak station around 1400 on the AM dial and turn the volume control to maximum.
4. Remove the right control knob spring and ring and adjust the trimmer screw for maximum volume.

*NOTE: If during the adjustment, the station becomes strong so that change in volume cannot be heard with further screw rotating tune to a weaker station and continue the adjustment.*

## Antenna Unit
## 1973-75 Cadillac

### Removal

1. Lower antenna.
2. Disconnect the negative battery cable.
3. Disconnect the motor wires at the plastic connector.
4. Disconnect the lead-in cable from the support tube.
5. Remove the two screws which secure the upper antenna mounting bracket to the fender.
6. Remove the bolt and washer which secure the antenna to the mounting bracket on the fender and remove the antenna from the car.
7. The escutcheon may be removed by depressing the lock tabs and pushing the escutcheon out through the top of the fender.

### Installation

1. Install the escutcheon.
2. Position the antenna and install the bolt and washer securing the antenna assembly to the fender mounting bracket.
3. Install the two screws which secure the upper antenna mounting bracket to the mounting fender.
4. Connect the lead-in cable to the support tube.
5. Connect the motor wire connector.
6. Connect the negative battery cable.

## Antenna Unit
## 1973 Cadillac

### Disassembly

1. Remove the three screws which

attach the clamp at the top of the support tube to the support tube and remove the clamp.
2. Remove the two lead-in receptacle screws and remove the receptacle from the support tube.
3. Unsolder the mast wire from the pin and insulator assembly.

*CAUTION: Be careful not to overheat by slow soldering and melt the insulator.*

4. Remove the three screws which attach the support tube to the drive assembly. Pull the support tube loose with the top insulator attached.
5. Unscrew the tip from the inner telescopic section.
6. Remove the outer mast sections with the insulator bushing attached from the tubular fitting on the drive assembly.
7. The inner mast section with the cable attached can be detached

from the drive assembly by applying 12 volts to the black motor wire, while grounding the motor. Pull the remainder for the cable out by hand.

*NOTE: To prevent kinking or bending keep the cable taut.*

8. Insert a small drill through each of the drain holes at the bottom of the tubular fitting and remove the bottom insulator.

### Assembly

*NOTE: Before assembling the antenna, check the drain holes in the motor housing below the body tube mounting point to be sure they are not blocked.*

*If the car has been undercoated, make sure that the drain holes have not been plugged.*

*Lubricate the rod with a light coat of oil.*

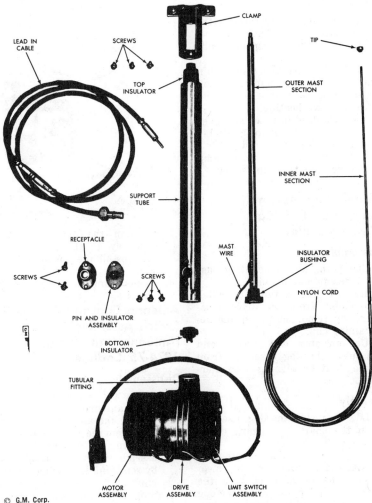

© G.M. Corp.

*Power Antenna Disassembled—1973*

# General Motors

1. Without forcing insert the cable into the drive assembly as far as possible.
2. Apply 12 volts to the white motor wire, while grounding the motor, to retract the cable into the drive assembly.

   *NOTE: To prevent kinking or bending keep the cable taut.*

3. Insert the bottom insulator into the tubular fitting with the slotted protrusion down and align the slots of the insulator with the ears in the tubular fitting.
4. Place the outer mast section over the inner section and align the slots of the pin and insulator assembly with the ears in the tubular fitting.
5. Install the tip on the inner telescopic section.
6. Place the support tube over the mast assembly, aligning the tang on the tube with the slot in the tubular fitting.
7. Pull the mast wire through the pin and insulator hole and secure the three support tube screws.
8. Insert the mast wire into the pin and insulator assembly and solder, using resin type solder and without overheating.
9. Place the lead-in receptacle over the pin and insulator assembly and install the two screws.
10. Install the support tube clamp and the three retaining screws.

## Antenna Dog Assembly (Antenna Unit off Car) 1974-75 Cadillac

### Disassembly

1. Clamp the lower mounting base of the antenna in a vise.
2. Remove the automatic switch assembly from the drive housing by removing the spring retaining clip.
3. Use an open end wrench and remove the dog assembly from the shaft by turning it counter-clockwise.

### Assembly

1. Loosely install the dog assembly on the shaft by turning clockwise.
2. Using the template provided with the new dog assembly, measure the distance between the top of the longest pin on the dog to the base of the drive housing. Adjust as necessary.

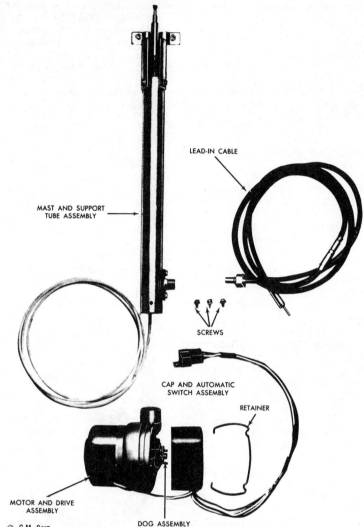

MAST AND SUPPORT TUBE ASSEMBLY

LEAD-IN CABLE

SCREWS

CAP AND AUTOMATIC SWITCH ASSEMBLY

RETAINER

MOTOR AND DRIVE ASSEMBLY

DOG ASSEMBLY

© G.M. Corp.

*Power Antenna Disassembled—1974*

3. Position the automatic switch assembly to the drive housing and install the spring retaining clip.
4. Remove antenna assembly from the vise.

## Antenna Cap and Automatic Switch Assembly (Antenna Unit off Car) 1974-75 Cadillac

### Disassembly

1. Clamp the lower mounting base of the antenna in a vise.
2. Untape the antenna wiring harness from the support tube.
3. Remove the automatic switch assembly from the drive housing by removing the spring retaining clip.
4. Stagger cut the black and white wires at a midway point between the motor and switch assembly.

### Assembly

1. Solder together the black to black and the white to white switch and motor leads.
2. Tape the solder joints with electrical tape.
3. Position the automatic switch assembly to the drive housing and install the spring retaining clip.
4. Tape the antenna wiring harness to the support tube.
5. Remove the antenna assembly from the vise.

## Antenna Motor and Drive Assembly (Antenna Unit off Car) 1974-75 Cadillac

### Disassembly

1. Clamp the lower mounting base of the antenna in a vise.
2. Untape the wiring harness from the support tube.

# General Motors

3. Remove the automatic switch assembly from the drive housing by removing the spring retaining clip.
4. Use an open end wrench and remove the dog assembly from the shaft by turning it counterclockwise.
5. Stagger cut the black and white wires at a midway point between the motor and switch assembly.
6. Remove the three screws which secure the support tube to the drive housing and pull the support tube and drive cable completely out of the drive housing.

### Assembly

1. Clamp the new motor and drive unit mounting base in a vise.

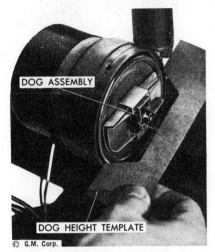

DOG ASSEMBLY

DOG HEIGHT TEMPLATE

© G.M. Corp.

*Measuring Dog Height*

2. Using the template provided, measure the distance between the top of the longest pin in the dog to base of the drive housing. Adjust as necessary.
3. Solder together the black to black and the white to white switch and motor leads.
4. Tape the solder joint with electrical tape.
5. Position the automatic switch assembly to the drive housing and install the spring retaining clips.
6. Apply 12 volts to the black wire in the four way connector while grounding the antenna and run the antenna to the full up position.
7. Put a small amount of lithium grease on the cable and insert the end into the drive housing and push in as far as possible to start the cable.
8. With the antenna grounded apply 12 volts to the white wire in the four way connector and run the antenna all the way

down. Guide the cable and mast while retracting.
9. Position the support tube assembly to the drive housing and install the three screws.
10. To adjust the cable for height run the antenna up until it stops; then down as outlined in steps 6 and 8.

## Antenna Mast and Support Tube (Antenna Unit off Car) 1974-75 Cadillac

### Disassembly

1. Clamp the lower mounting base of the antenna in a vise.
2. Untape the antenna wiring harness from the support tube.
3. Apply 12 volts to the black wire in the four way connector while grounding the antenna and run the antenna to the full up position.
4. Remove the three screws which secure the support tube assembly to the drive housing and pull the support tube and drive cable completely out of the housing.

*NOTE: If the cable cannot be pulled out by hand remove the antenna dog as previously described.*

### Assembly

1. Put a small amount of grease on the cable and insert the end into the drive housing as far as possible to start the cable.
2. Ground the antenna and apply 12 volts to the white wire in the four way connector and run the antenna all the way down. Guide the antenna and mast while retracting.
3. Position the support tube assembly to the drive housing and install the three screws.
4. To adjust the cable for height, run the antenna up until it stops; then down as outlined in step 3 of disassembly and step 2 of assembly.

## Control Switch 1974-75 Cadillac

### Removal

1. Remove the instrument panel pad.
   a. Disconnect the negative battery cable.
   b. Remove the right, left and right center climatic control air outlet grilles by compressing the release tabs and

rotating the grille upward and out.
   c. Reach through the outlet openings and remove the three pad to panel support fasteners.
   d. Remove the screws which hold the pad to panel horizontal support.
   e. Pull the pad outward and disconnect the wiper switch electrical connection.
   f. If necessary, place the transmission shift lever in low range and if equipped with a tilt steering wheel, place the wheel in the lowest position.
   g. Remove the pad.
2. Remove the right hand insert and applique.
   a. Remove the radio knobs, wave washers, control rings and left hex nut.
   b. Reach through the opening in the top of the glove box and remove the attaching screws from the rear of the insert.
3. Push the switch, until it snaps from the housing.
4. Remove the wiring terminals from the switch.

### Installation

1. Connect the wire terminals to the switch.
2. Snap the switch back into the housing.
3. Install the right hand insert and applique and install the screw.
   a. Install the left hex nut, control wings, wave washers and radio knobs.
4. Install the instrument panel pad.
   a. Position the pad to the panel and connect the wiper switch.
   b. Install the screws retaining the pad to the horizontal support.
   c. Reach through the climate control outlet openings and install the three fasteners which hold the pad to the panel support.
5. Install the air outlet grilles.
   a. Position grille and press the release tabs.
   b. Snap the tabs into the retaining holes.
6. Connect negative battery terminal.

## Control Switch 1973 Cadillac

### Removal

1. Pull the accessory switch panel out of the bezel.

## General Motors

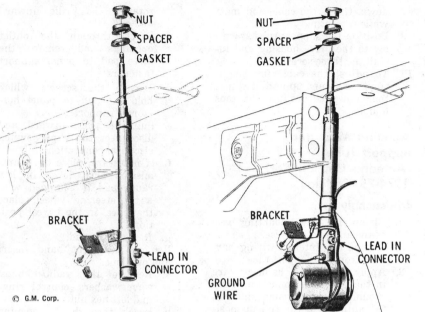

*1968—Oldsmobile Antenna Installation*

2. Disconnect the feed wires from the instrument panel harness.
3. Remove the one switch retaining screw.

### Installation

1. Position the switch in the accessory switch panel and install the retaining screw.
2. Connect the electrical connectors to the instrument panel wiring harness.
3. Install the accessory switch panel into the bezel and pass until secured by the spring catch.

### Switch Test
### 1973-75 Cadillac

1. Pull the accessory switch panel out of the bezel.
2. Disconnect the electrical feed wires from the wiring harness.
3. Using a self-powered test light, touch one lead to the red wire and the other lead to the black wire. When the switch is held in the up position the test light should light.
4. Remove the test light lead from the black wire and touch it to the white wire, the test light should now light when the switch is held in the down position.
5. If the test light fails to light during these tests replace the switch.

### Relay
### 1973-75 Cadillac

**Removal**

1. Pull the carpet away from the front passenger side toe pan.

2. Disconnect the two electrical connectors.
3. Remove the two screws and washers which hold the relay and bracket to the toe pan.

### Installation

1. Position the relay and bracket on the toe pan and install the two retaining screws.
2. Connect the electrical connectors.
3. Put the carpet back in place.

### Antenna Assembly
### 1968-69 F-85, Cutlass

**Removal & Installation**

1. Lower the antenna to the full down position.
2. Disconnect the electrical wires at the connector.
3. Disconnect the ground wire at the support bracket.
4. Disconnect the lead-in cable.
5. Remove the nut spacer and gasket from the top of the antenna.
6. Remove the screw at the lower mounting bracket and remove the antenna ssembly.
7. To install reverse the removal procedure.

### Antenna Assembly
### 1969 88, 98, Toronado

**Removal & Installation**

1. Lower the antenna to the full down position.
2. Disconnect the electrical wires at the connector.

3. Disconnect the ground wire from the body.
4. Disconnect the lead-in cable from the antenna.
5. Loosen the screw at the top retaining clamp and remove clip which notches in the escutcheon under the fender.
6. Remove the escutcheon from the top of the fender.
7. Disconnect the lower mounting bracket screws and remove the antenna assembly.
8. To install reverse the removal procedure.

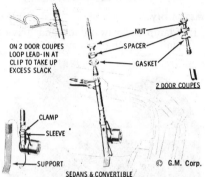

*1969—Power Antenna Installation—F85, Cutlass*

### Antenna Unit
### 1968-69 Oldsmobile
### All Models

**Disassembly**

1. Remove the two screws which attach the clamp at the top of the support tube to the support tube and remove the clamp.
2. Remove the two lead-in receptacle screws and remove the receptacle from the support tube.
3. Unsolder the mast wire from the pin and insulator assembly.

*CAUTION: Be careful not to overheat by slow soldering and melt the insulator.*

4. Remove the three screws which attach the support tube to the drive assembly. Pull the support tube loose with the top insulator attached.
5. Unscrew the tip from the inner telescopic section.
6. Remove the outer mast sections with the insulator bushing attached from the tubular fitting on the drive assembly.
7. The inner mast section with the cable attached can be detached from the drive assembly by applying 12 volts to the black motor wire, while grounding the motor.

# General Motors

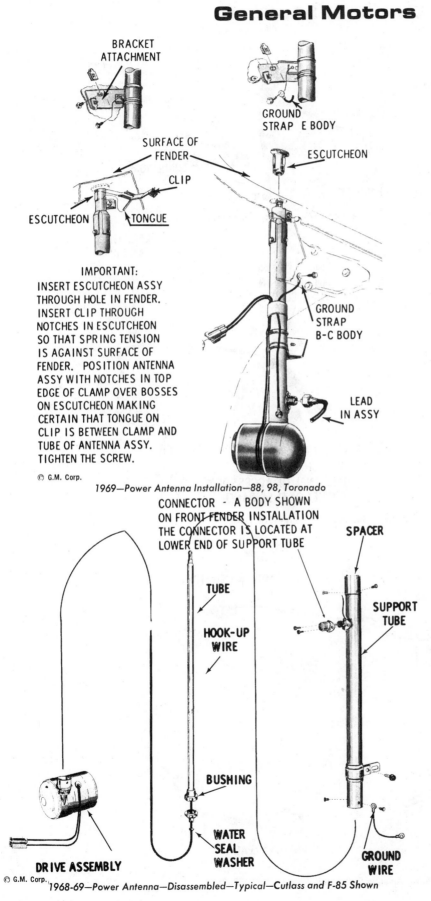

IMPORTANT:
INSERT ESCUTCHEON ASSY
THROUGH HOLE IN FENDER.
INSERT CLIP THROUGH
NOTCHES IN ESCUTCHEON
SO THAT SPRING TENSION
IS AGAINST SURFACE OF
FENDER. POSITION ANTENNA
ASSY WITH NOTCHES IN TOP
EDGE OF CLAMP OVER BOSSES
ON ESCUTCHEON MAKING
CERTAIN THAT TONGUE ON
CLIP IS BETWEEN CLAMP AND
TUBE OF ANTENNA ASSY.
TIGHTEN THE SCREW.

© G.M. Corp.

*1969—Power Antenna Installation—88, 98, Toronado*

CONNECTOR - A BODY SHOWN
ON FRONT FENDER INSTALLATION
THE CONNECTOR IS LOCATED AT
LOWER END OF SUPPORT TUBE

© G.M. Corp.
*1968-69—Power Antenna—Disassembled—Typical—Cutlass and F-85 Shown*

Pull the remainder of the cable out by hand.

*NOTE: To prevent kinking or bending keep the cable taut.*

8. Insert a small drill through each of the drain holes at the bottom of the tubular fitting and remove the bottom insulator.

## Assembly

*NOTE: Before assembling the antenna, check the drain holes in the motor housing below the body tube mounting point to be sure they are not blocked.*

*If the car has been undercoated, make sure that the drain holes have not been plugged.*

*Lubricate the rod with a light coat of oil.*

1. Without forcing insert the cable into the drive assembly as far as possible.
2. Apply 12 volts to the white motor wire, while grounding the motor, to retract the cable into the drive assembly.

*NOTE: To prevent kinking or bending keep the table taut.*

3. Insert the bottom insulator into the tubular fitting with the slotted protrusion down and align the slots of the insulator with the ears in the tubular fitting.
4. Place the outer mast section over the inner section and align the slots of the pin and insulator assembly with the ears in the tubular fitting.
5. Install the tip on the inner telescopic section.
6. Place the support tube over the mast assembly, aligning the tang on the tube with the slot in the tubular fitting.
7. Pull the mast wire through the pin and insulator hole and secure the three support tube screws.
8. Insert the mast wire into the pin and insulator assembly and solder, using resin type solder and without overheating.
9. Place the lead-in receptacle over the pin and insulator assembly and install the two screws.
10. Install the support tube clamp and the two retaining screws.

## Antenna Assembly
## 1973-75 Oldsmobile
## All Models

### Removal & Installation

1. Lower the antenna to the full down position.

# General Motors

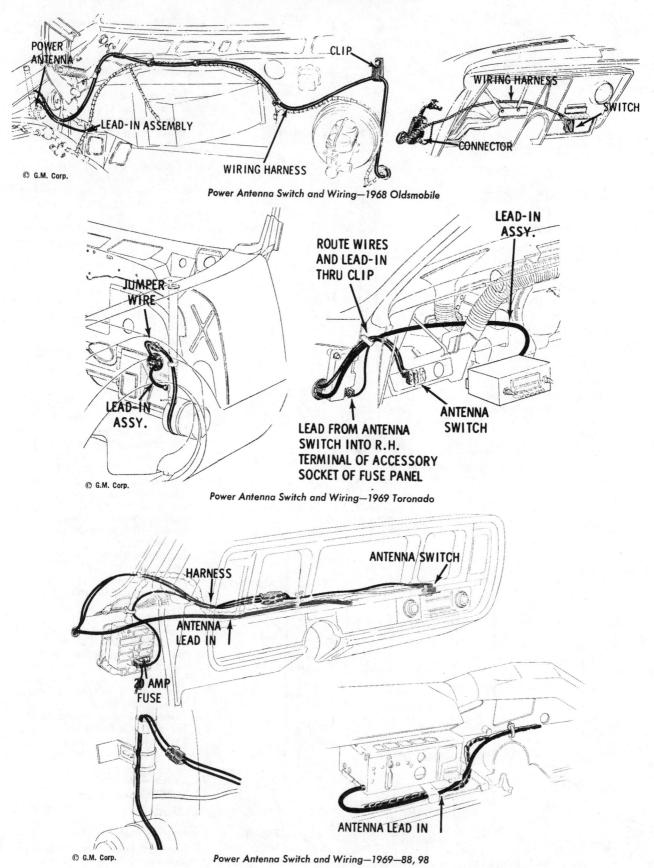

© G.M. Corp.

POWER ANTENNA

LEAD-IN ASSEMBLY

WIRING HARNESS

CLIP

WIRING HARNESS

SWITCH

CONNECTOR

*Power Antenna Switch and Wiring—1968 Oldsmobile*

JUMPER WIRE

LEAD-IN ASSY.

© G.M. Corp.

ROUTE WIRES AND LEAD-IN THRU CLIP

LEAD-IN ASSY.

ANTENNA SWITCH

LEAD FROM ANTENNA SWITCH INTO R.H. TERMINAL OF ACCESSORY SOCKET OF FUSE PANEL

*Power Antenna Switch and Wiring—1969 Toronado*

HARNESS

ANTENNA SWITCH

ANTENNA LEAD IN

20 AMP FUSE

ANTENNA LEAD IN

© G.M. Corp.

*Power Antenna Switch and Wiring—1969—88, 98*

# General Motors

2. Disconnect the electrical wires and the lead in cable.
3. Remove the nut and guide assembly, escutcheon and gasket from the top of the fender.
4. Remove the ground collar retaining screw and remove the collar.
5. Remove the lower mounting support nut and washer and remove the antenna assembly from the car.
6. To install reverse the removal procedure.

## Antenna Trimmer Adjustment 1968-75 Oldsmobile

The antenna trimmer adjustment must always be made after any repairs have been made to the power antenna or if AM reception is unsatisfactory.

This adjustment applies only to AM radios or the AM portion of AM-FM radios. Trimming for FM reception is automatically accomplished whenever the antenna is raised to 31 inches.

1. Move the antenna to a height of 31 inches.
2. Tune the radio dial to a weak station somewhere around 1400 kc.
3. Remove the right inner and outer knobs.
4. Adjust the trimmer screw until maximum volume is achieved.

*NOTE: When a car is equipped with a rear speaker the speaker control knob must be removed to gain access to the trimmer screw. The speaker knob has three prongs which interconnect three small holes (electrical connecting points) in the receiver. A short jumper wire must be inserted in the center and outside holes to channel the sound to the speaker. It is generally desirable to trim the radio while using the front speaker.*

## Power Antenna Assembly 1968-69 Pontiac

### Removal

1. Lower the antenna fully.
2. If necessary remove the spare tire.
3. Disconnect the ground wire, electrical wire at the connector and the lead in cable.
4. Remove the bolt which attaches the lower antenna bracket to the wheel house flange.
5. Remove the horseshoe spring clips which attach the bezel to

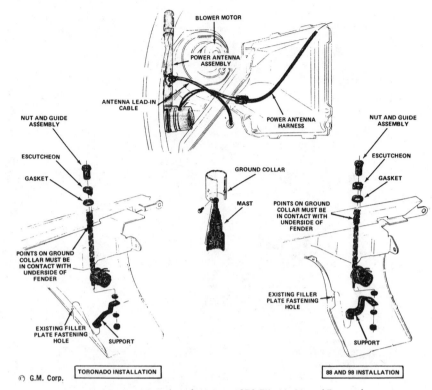

*Power Antenna Switch and Wiring—1973-74—88, 98 and Toronado*

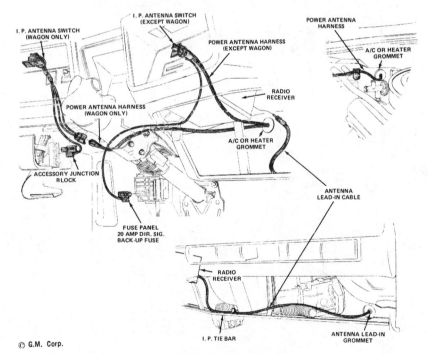

*Power Antenna Wire Routing—1973*

the outer fender panel.
6. Rotate the bezel clockwise to disconnect the bayonet socket and remove it from the mast support tube.
7. Remove the antenna.

### Installation

1. Position the antenna assembly in the car.
2. Install the bezel to the mast support tube turning it counterclockwise.

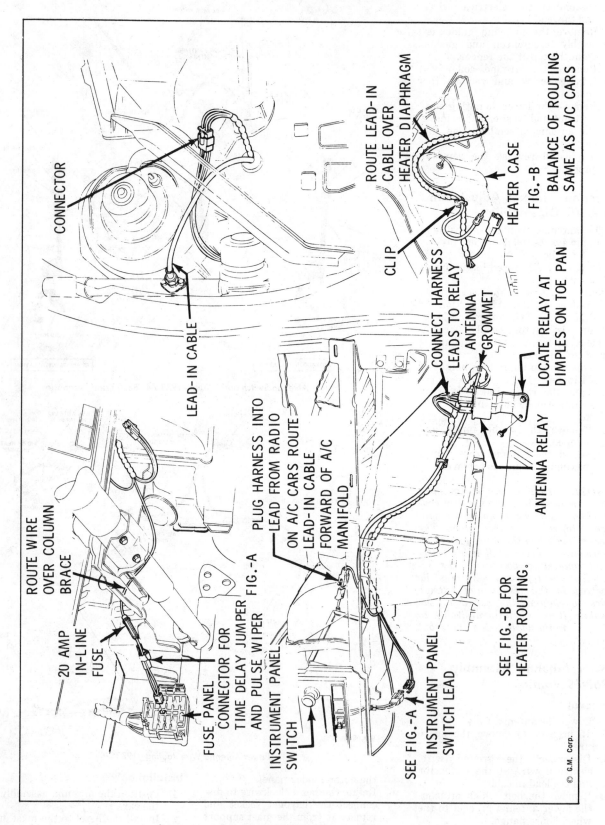

CONNECTOR

LEAD-IN CABLE

ROUTE LEAD-IN CABLE OVER HEATER DIAPHRAGM

HEATER CASE

FIG.-B

BALANCE OF ROUTING SAME AS A/C CARS

CLIP

CONNECT HARNESS LEADS TO RELAY

ANTENNA GROMMET

LOCATE RELAY AT DIMPLES ON TOE PAN

ANTENNA RELAY

ROUTE WIRE OVER COLUMN BRACE

20 AMP IN-LINE FUSE

FUSE PANEL CONNECTOR FOR TIME DELAY JUMPER AND PULSE WIPER FIG.-A

PLUG HARNESS INTO LEAD FROM RADIO

ON A/C CARS ROUTE LEAD-IN CABLE FORWARD OF A/C MANIFOLD

INSTRUMENT PANEL SWITCH

SEE FIG.-A

INSTRUMENT PANEL SWITCH LEAD

SEE FIG.-B FOR HEATER ROUTING.

© G.M. Corp.

*Power Antenna Wire Routing—1974*

# Power Antenna

## General Motors

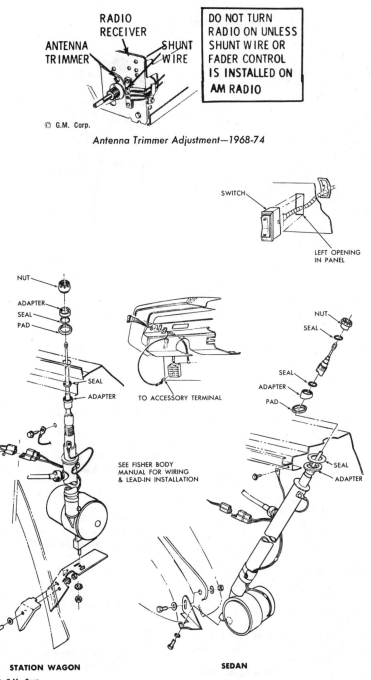

DO NOT TURN RADIO ON UNLESS SHUNT WIRE OR FADER CONTROL IS INSTALLED ON AM RADIO

© G.M. Corp.

*Antenna Trimmer Adjustment—1968-74*

*Power Antenna—Removal and Installation—1968-69—Pontiac*

© G.M. Corp.

3. Install the horseshoe spring clip which retains the bezel to the fender.
4. Install the bolt into the lower bracket and tighten the nut finger tight plus four full turns.
5. Connect the antenna lead-in cable, electrical wire and the ground wire.
6. Adjust the antenna trimmer.

## Power Antenna
### 1968-69 Tempest and Firebird

#### Removal

1. Lower the antenna fully.
2. Remove the bezel nut from on top of the fender.
3. If necessary remove the spare tire.
4. Disconnect the ground wire, elec-

trical wire at the connector and lead-in cable.
5. Remove the bolt which attaches the lower antenna bracket to the wheelhouse frame.
6. Remove the antenna.

#### Installation

1. Reverse the removal procedure.
2. Adjust the antenna trimmer.

## Power Antenna
### 1968-69 Pontiac—All Models

#### Disassembly

1. Remove the three screws that hold the body and upper insulator assembly to the support tube.
2. While applying a back and forth rotary motion, pull the body upper insulator assembly out of the support tube and partially slide it over the mast until the solder joint is accessible.
3. Unsolder the hookup wire from the mast and remove the body and upper insulator from the mast.
4. Remove the three screws which hold the support tube to the antenna drive.
5. Hold the antenna drive in one hand, the support tube in the other and pull with a rotary motion until the support tube is removed.
6. Hold the antenna drive in one hand and the mast with the other and pull the mast with a rocking motion until the insulator bushing and mast are free from the tubular fitting of the antenna drive.
7. Apply 12 volts to the green wire of the antenna drive until the entire length of nylon cable has been expelled, and remove the mast. Pull the mast to keep the nylon cable taut.

*NOTE: If the antenna drive is inoperative, it will be necessary to remove the nylon cable by hand. Place the unit in a vise so that the normal plane of the nylon cable is parallel with the floor. Using both hands, pull on the 0.30 diameter section of the mast until the cable is completely removed.*

8. Use a wire hook or long nose pliers and remove the bottom insulator and water seal washer from the tubular fitting of the antenna drive.
9. Remove the drive cover.
10. Hold the 7/16 in. hex nut on the output gear assembly shaft and remove the 3/8 in. hex nut.

## General Motors

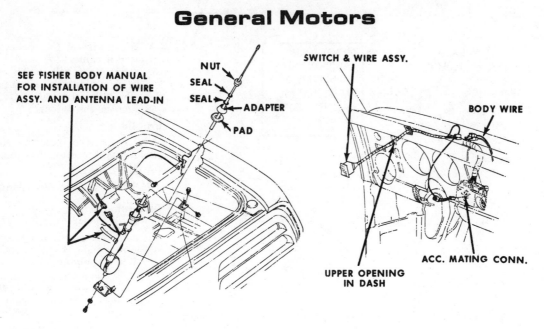

SEE FISHER BODY MANUAL FOR INSTALLATION OF WIRE ASSY. AND ANTENNA LEAD-IN

NUT
SEAL
SEAL
ADAPTER
PAD

SWITCH & WIRE ASSY.

BODY WIRE

ACC. MATING CONN.

UPPER OPENING IN DASH

© G.M. Corp.

*Power Antenna—Removal and Installation—1968-69—Firebird*

11. Remove the 7/16 in. hex nut and washer.
12. Lift the antenna pressure adjuster spring off the shaft.
13. Remove the drive pin retainer.
14. Remove the drive pressure beam.
15. Slide the drive pin from the hole in the shaft and take off the drive beam without loosing the two steel balls at the ends.
16. Remove the two steel balls.
17. Remove the drive disc from the shaft.

*NOTE: Be careful not to bend the drive disc or burr the edges of the channel. It will be necessary to re-align the pinion gear if they have been removed or have fallen out. Re-alignment is done by positioning the right and left pinion gears so that the mark on each one points at the center of the pinion shaft of the drive gear which receives the motor pinion.*

### Assembly

1. Install the drive disc on the shaft.
2. Replace the two steel balls at the ends of the drive beam and install the drive beam on the shaft. Install the drive pin in the shaft.
3. Install the drive pin retainer.
4. Replace the pressure adjuster spring on the shaft with the largest diameter toward the drive pin retainer.
5. Replace the washer on the output gear assembly shaft and

screw in the 7/16 in. hex nut one full turn until it touches the spring.
6. Do not reassemble the 3/8 in. hex nut on the shaft or snap the drive cover in place until step 12 has been completed.
7. Position the water seal washer and bottom insulator in the tubular fitting of the antenna.
8. Thread the nylon cable into the antenna drive. Apply 12 volts of power to the blue power lead to assist the feeding operation. Keep the nylon cable straight to avoid kinking.
9. Push the section of mast and insulator bushing into the tubular fitting. Make sure that the free end of the hook-up wire extends below the lower edge of the body and upper insulator assembly.
10. Solder the free-end of the hook-up wire to the mast section, using rosin flux solder.
11. Position and reassemble the body and upper insulator to the support tube.
12. Perform the antenna adjustment procedure (See Antenna Adjustment)
13. Install the 3/8 in. hex nut and drive cover onto the antenna drive and make sure that the vent hole in the drive cover is at the top when the antenna is installed in the car.
14. Reseal the antenna drive with body sealer and make sure the

vent hole in the drive cover and drain hole in the antenna drive are not plugged.

### Antenna Trimmer Adjustment 1968-69 Pontiac—All Models

The antenna trimmer adjustment must always be made after any repairs have been made to the power antenna or if AM reception is unsatisfactory.

This adjustment applies only to AM radios or the AM portion of AM-FM radios. Trimming for FM reception is automatically accomplished whenever the antenna is raised to 31 inches.

1. Move the antenna to a height of 31 inches.
2. Tune the radio dial to a weak station somewhere around 1400 kc.
3. Remove the right inner and outer knobs.
4. Adjust the trimmer screw until maximum volume is achieved.

*NOTE: When a car is equipped with a rear speaker the speaker control knob must be removed to gain access to the trimmer screw. The speaker knob has three prongs which interconnect three small holes (electrical connecting points) in the receiver. A short jumper wire must be inserted in the center and outside holes to channel the sound to the speaker. It is generally desirable to trim the radio while using the front speaker.*

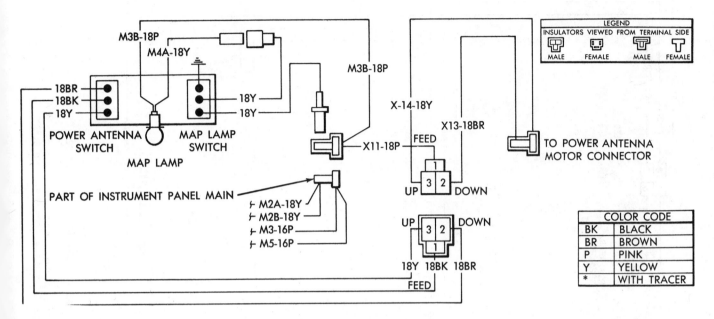

*1968-69—Chrysler, Imperial*

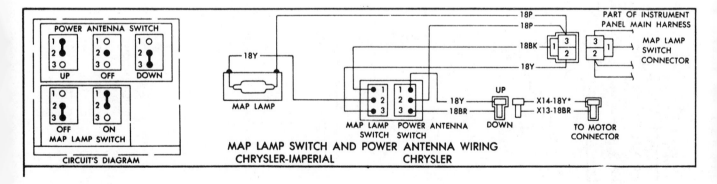

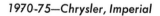

*1970-75—Chrysler, Imperial*

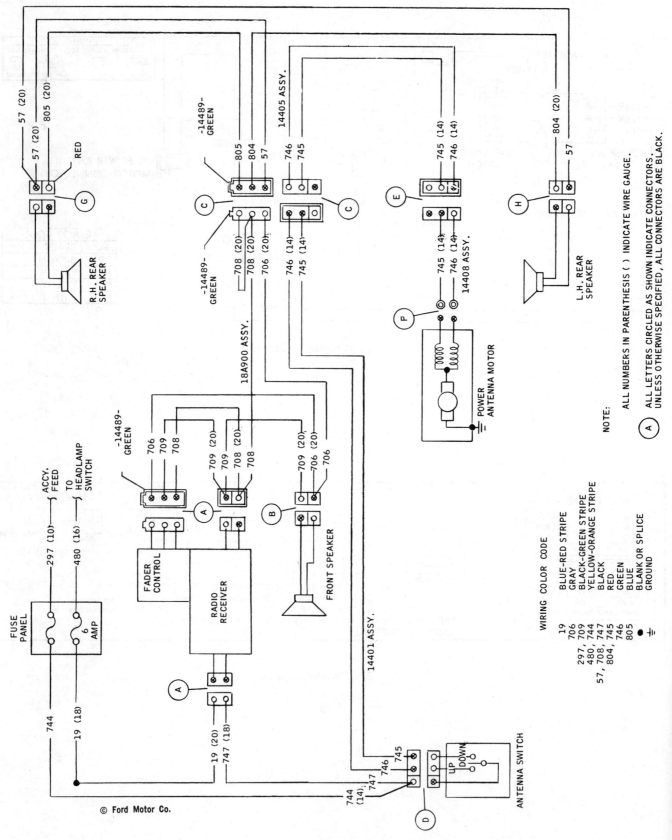

*1968-73—Ford, Typical*

© Ford Motor Co.

# General Motors

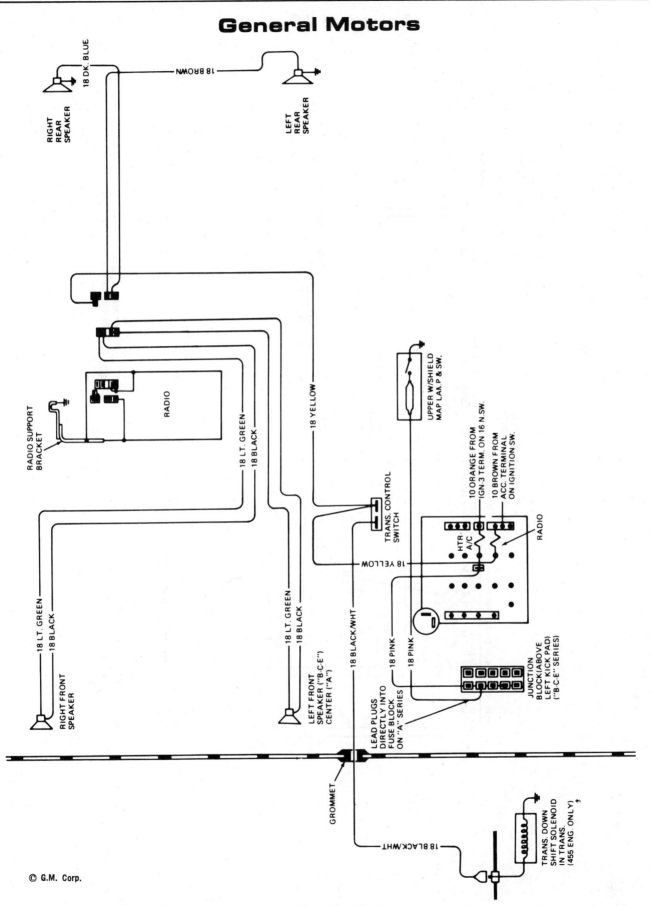

RIGHT REAR SPEAKER

LEFT REAR SPEAKER

18 DK. BLUE

18 BROWN

RADIO SUPPORT BRACKET

RADIO

18 LT. GREEN
18 BLACK

18 YELLOW

18 LT. GREEN
18 BLACK

RIGHT FRONT SPEAKER

18 LT. GREEN
18 BLACK

LEFT FRONT SPEAKER ("B-C-E") CENTER ("A")

18 BLACK/WHT

18 PINK

18 PINK

TRANS. CONTROL SWITCH

18 YELLOW

UPPER W/SHIELD MAP LA. P & SW.

10 ORANGE FROM IGN-3 TERM. ON 16 N. SW.

10 BROWN FROM ACC. TERMINAL ON IGNITION SW.

HTR-A/C

RADIO

JUNCTION BLOCK(ABOVE LEFT KICK PAD) ("B-C-E" SERIES)

LEAD PLUGS DIRECTLY INTO FUSE BLOCK ON "A" SERIES

GROMMET

18 BLACK/WHT

TRANS. DOWN SHIFT SOLENOID IN TRANS. (455 ENG. ONLY)

*1973-74 Buick*

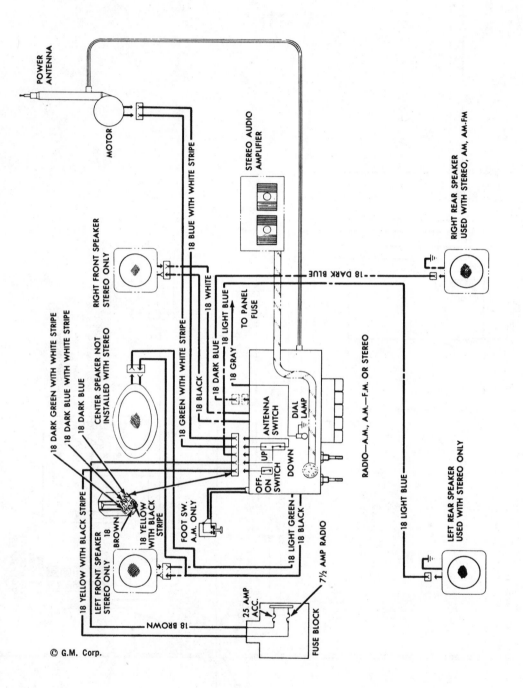

© G.M. Corp.

*1968—Cadillac*

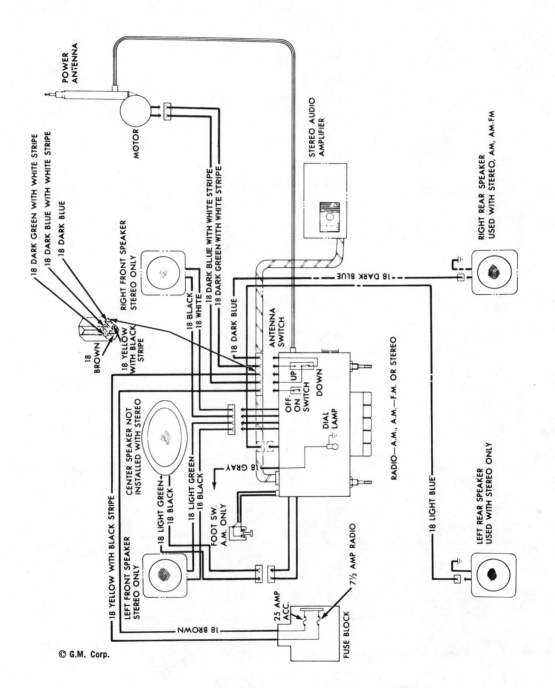

POWER ANTENNA

MOTOR

18 DARK GREEN WITH WHITE STRIPE
18 DARK BLUE WITH WHITE STRIPE
18 DARK BLUE

RIGHT FRONT SPEAKER
STEREO ONLY

18 BROWN

18 YELLOW WITH BLACK STRIPE

18 BLACK
18 WHITE

18 DARK BLUE WITH WHITE STRIPE
18 DARK GREEN WITH WHITE STRIPE

18 DARK BLUE

ANTENNA SWITCH

UP
OFF-ON SWITCH
DOWN

DIAL LAMP

STEREO AUDIO AMPLIFIER

18 DARK BLUE

RIGHT REAR SPEAKER
USED WITH STEREO, AM, AM-FM

CENTER SPEAKER NOT INSTALLED WITH STEREO

18 YELLOW WITH BLACK STRIPE

LEFT FRONT SPEAKER
STEREO ONLY

18 LIGHT GREEN
18 BLACK

18 LIGHT GREEN
18 BLACK

18 GRAY

FOOT SW. AM ONLY

RADIO—A.M., A.M.—F.M. OR STEREO

18 LIGHT BLUE

LEFT REAR SPEAKER
USED WITH STEREO ONLY

25 AMP ACC.

7½ AMP RADIO

18 BROWN

FUSE BLOCK

© G.M. Corp.

*1969—Cadillac*

# Power Antenna Wiring

## General Motors

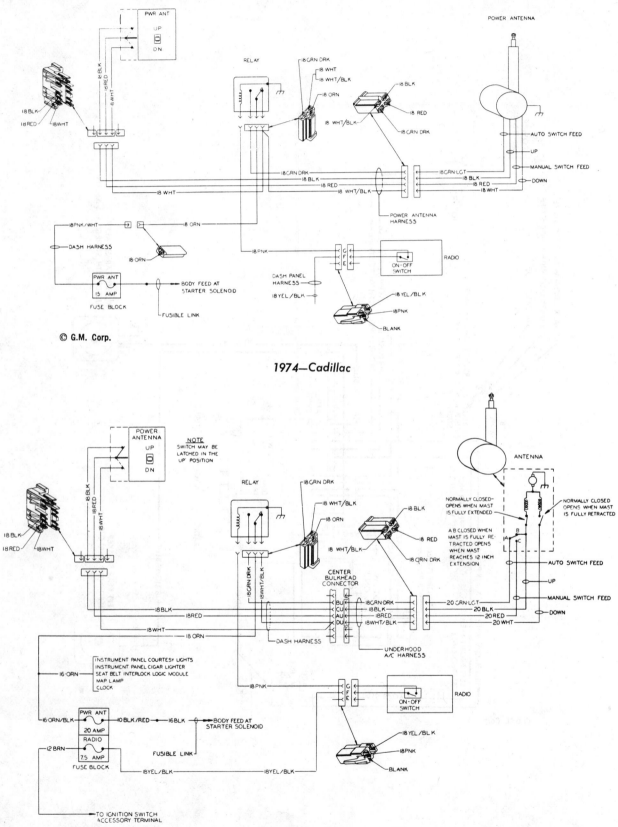

© G.M. Corp.

1974—Cadillac

© G.M. Corp.

1975—Cadillac

# American Motors

## WINDSHIELD WASHERS

There have been several types of washer pumps used. In the earlier models a foot operated pump was used. The pump was mounted on the floor and pressing on the rubber diaphragm assembly forced water out of the pump onto the windshield through the nozzles. This type of pump was available with both vacuum and electric wipers.

Later models used a hand operated pump. There is a control knob on the dash and the water is pumped by pressing in the knob using a pumping motion.

Electric washer pumps are used in the early and late models. They were optional in the early models but are now standard equipment. Electric washer pumps were used only with electric wipers in the early models. The washer is operated by pressing a spring loaded control knob or button to obtain the desired amount of water.

The pump motor for the electric washers is located on top of the water reservoir inside of the engine compartment. The motor is grounded to the body by a wire and is energized by a feed wire from the "W" terminal of the control switch.

## Windshield Washer Hose and Nozzle

On 1974-75 Matador the washer nozzle is attached to the wiper arm so the spray pattern of the water can follow the wiper as it travels over the windshield.

### Removal and Installation

1. To remove the wiper arm raise the blade end of the arm and move the slide latch away from the pivot shaft.

2. Disconnect the washer hose from the connector.
3. On the driver's side disconnect the auxiliary arm from the pivot pin.
4. Remove the wiper arm from the pivot shaft.
5. When working on the spray nozzle refer to the chart.
6. Reverse the removal procedure to install.

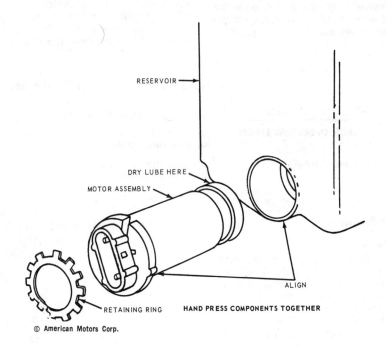

*1973-75 Installing Washer Motor Assembly*

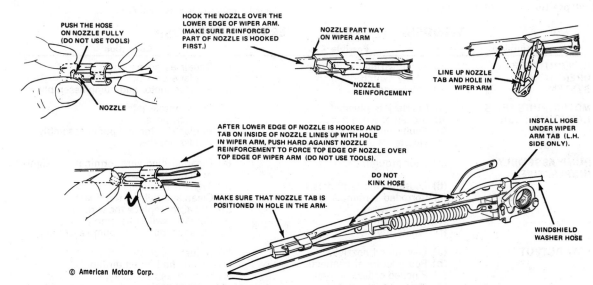

*1974-75 Windshield Washer Hose & Nozzle Removal & Installation*

# Chrysler Corporation

## WINDSHIELD WASHERS

### Foot Operated Windshield Washer Pump

#### 1968-74 Dodge and Plymouth

#### Description

The foot pump is the bellows type and has the reservoir mounted in the engine compartment. The pump has two valves in the back of it to control the flow of water from the reservoir to the pump and from the pump to the nozzles.

2. Install the mounting screws.
3. Remove the clamp from the hose on the reservoir and check the pump for proper operation.

### Electric Pump
#### 1968-75 All Models

#### Description

The pump motor is mounted underneath the reservoir on all models. The motor is a permanently lubricated type and is coupled to a rotor type pump. The washer fluid is gravity feed to the pump from the reservoir and the pump forces the washer fluid up to the nozzles.

The pump motor and the reservoir are serviced as separate units.

### Pump Motor Test

To determine if the pump motor is bad, take a jumper wire and connect one end to the blade terminal of the pump and the other end to the positive side of the battery. If the pump works check the wiring or the switch. If the motor does not work it is defective.

## FOOT PUMP SERVICE DIAGNOSIS

| Condition | Possible Cause | Correction |
|---|---|---|
| HIGH OPERATING EFFORT | (a) Low aimed nozzles.<br>(b) Pinches hoses. | (a) Adjust nozzles.<br>(b) Correct as necessary. |
| LOW OUTPUT | (a) Low aimed nozzles.<br>(b) Leaky hoses.<br>(c) Defective pump. | (a) Adjust nozzles.<br>(b) Correct as necessary.<br>(c) Replace pump. |

### Foot Pump

#### Removal

1. Clamp the hose at the reservoir. This keeps the water in the reservoir from draining into the passenger compartment.
2. Remove the two screws that hold the pump to the floor.
3. Disconnect the hoses from the pump and remove the pump from the vehicle.

#### Installation

1. Attach the hoses to the pump and position the pump in place.

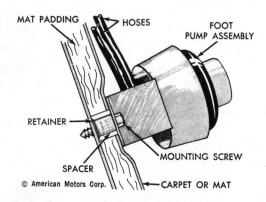

1968-74 Windshield Washer Foot Pump

## WINDSHIELD WASHERS SERVICE DIAGNOSIS

| Condition | Possible Cause | Correction |
|---|---|---|
| INTERMITTENT OPERATION OF SYSTEM | (a) Loose wiring connections.<br>(b) Faulty switch.<br>(c) Faulty motor. | (a) Repair as necessary.<br>(b) Replace switch.<br>(c) Replace motor and pump assembly. |
| MOTOR RUNS DOES NOT PUMP FLUID | (a) Nozzle jets plugged.<br>(b) Broken or loose hose.<br>(c) Faulty pump.<br>(d) Nozzle jet under air intake grille. | (a) Clean nozzle jets.<br>(b) Replace hose.<br>(c) Replace motor and pump assembly.<br>(d) Adjust nozzles. |
| PUMP ASSEMBLY INOPERATIVE | (a) Poor ground.<br><br>(b) Loose wiring terminals.<br>(c) Corroded terminals.<br>(d) Broken wires.<br>(e) Faulty switch.<br>(f) Faulty motor. | (a) Clean ground wire terminal and tighten mounting screw.<br>(b) Tighten terminals.<br>(c) Clean and tighten terminals.<br>(d) Repair or replace the wires.<br>(e) Replace switch assembly.<br>(f) Replace motor and pump assembly. |
| LOW OUTPUT | (a) Low aimed nozzles.<br>(b) Poor electrical connections.<br>(c) Pinched or leaky hoses.<br>(d) Defective motor. | (a) Adjust nozzles.<br>(b) Clean and tighten terminals.<br>(c) Correct as necessary.<br>(d) Replace motor and pump assembly. |

# Chrysler Corporation

## Electric Pump
## All Models 1968-75

### Removal

1. Remove the screws that hold the reservoir to the fender and remove the reservoir. Remove the hose and wires from the reservoir before removing the assembly from the vehicle.

*NOTE: On some models it will be necessary to remove the charcoal canister from the fender in order to remove the reservoir. In other models it may be necessary to move the air conditioner line aside to remove the reservoir.*

2. Empty the reservoir and through the filler opening, use a 7/8 inch deep well socket and remove the ground wire if there is one.

*NOTE: It may be necessary to use a 15/16 inch socket on older models due to the fact that the nylon nut may be expanded from absorbing washer fluid.*

3. Remove the pump from the bottom of the reservoir and throw away the gasket.

### Installation

1. Install a new rubber grommet on the reservoir.

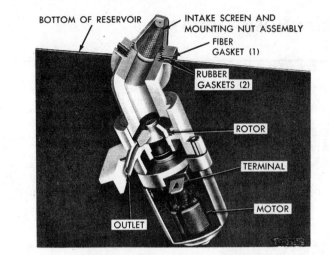

*1968-75 Reservoir & Pump Assembly—Typical*

*NOTE: Any time the pump has been removed the rubber grommet must be replaced.*

2. Install the pump through the reservoir and install the plastic washer under the nut and screen.
3. Tighten the nut securely but *do not* overtighten. It should be tightened to approx. 20 inch lbs.
4. Reconnect the motor ground wire.
5. Install the motor and reservoir assembly in the vehicle and at-

tach to the fender with the attaching screws.

*NOTE: Be sure to replace any other parts that were removed to allow for the removal of the reservoir.*

6. Make sure that the motor ground is installed under one of the mounting screws.
7. Connect the wire to the motor and the hose to the reservoir.
8. Fill the reservoir and check the pump for proper operation.

# Ford Motor Company

# WINDSHIELD WASHERS
# VIBRO-JET
# WINDSHIELD WASHER
# SYSTEM

## 1968 Full Size Ford and Mercury

### Description

This system uses the pendulum action of the left wiper pivot arm to actuate a washer pump located at the left side pivot assembly. The pump is activated by a cam on the pivot arm which synchronizes the spraying of the washer fluid with the sweep of the wiper arms.

The pump is small and delivers high pressure. It is composed of a single, moving piston, with no spring and has a charging and discharging port. The plunger, which is part of the piston, is brought into contact with the pivot arm by vacuum. The vacuum goes through and is con-

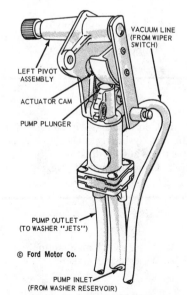

© Ford Motor Co.

*1968 Vibro-Jet Windshield Washer Pump Assembly*

trolled by the wiper control switch. The vacuum causes the piston plung-

er to move up in the pump cylinder thus contacting the cam. Pushing of the wiper switch continuously will keep the plunger riding on the cam which in turn pushes the piston down into the pump cylinder. Vacuum pulls the plunger back to the extended position. The back and forth motion of the piston in conjunction with the valves in the pump base, allows for a continouus stream of washer fluid. This continues as long as the wipers are in operation and the washer switch is in the out position. Releasing the washer portion of the wiper switch stops the vacuum and the plunger will retract from the cam.

There is a vacuum coordinator located near the wiper switch which allows the wipers to cycle when the washers are activated with the wiper switch in the *off* position. If the wiper switch is pushed in momentarily and released, the washers will come on briefly and then shut off. The wipers will continue to operate for another 4 to 8 sweeps. The number of sweeps

## DIAGNOSIS AND TESTING

| | | |
|---|---|---|
| **WASHER INOPERATIVE** (wiper switch in OFF position) **VERIFY THE COMPLAINT** | Wipers Inoperative: 1. Vacuum leak at switch, pump, or coordinator. 2. Vacuum lines pinched or broken. 3. Coordinator defective. 4. Wiper switch defective. 5. Problem in basic wiper system. | Wipers Operate: 1. Low fluid level in reservoir. 2. Restriction in fluid lines or nozzle. 3. Fluid lines broken or split. 4. Pinched or restricted vacuum line to pump. 5. Washer pump defective. |
| **WASHER INOPERATIVE** (wiper switch in ON position) **VERIFY THE COMPLAINT** | Wipers Inoperative: 1. Wiper switch defective. 2. Problem in basic wiper system. | Wipers Operate: 1. Low fluid level in reservoir. 2. Restriction in fluid lines or nozzles. 3. Fluid lines broken or split. 4. Vacuum leak at switch, pump or coordinator. 5. Vacuum lines pinched or broken. 6. Wiper switch defective. 7. Washer pump defective. |
| **WIPERS CYCLE EXCESSIVELY/ WILL NOT CYCLE AFTER WASHER SWITCH IS RELEASED** (wiper switch in OFF position). **VERIFY THE COMPLAINT** | 1. Coordinator Calibration Not Properly Set: a. Turn adjustment screw clockwise to increase number of cycles. b. Turn adjustment screw counterclockwise to decrease number of cycles. | |
| **WASHER/WIPERS WILL NOT SHUT OFF AFTER WASHER SWITCH IS RELEASED** (wiper switch in OFF position) **VERIFY THE COMPLAINT** | Wipers will not shut off. 1. Coordinator is not functioning properly (check Electrical Contacts at Coordinator). 2. Coordinator defective. | Washer and Wipers will not shut off: 1. Check adjustment of coordinator bleed screw. 2. Wiper switch defective. |
| **WASHER WILL NOT SHUT OFF AFTER WASHER SWITCH IS RELEASED** (wiper switch in ON position) **VERIFY THE COMPLAINT** | 1. Wiper switch malfunctioning. 2. Wiper switch defective. | |

# Ford Motor Company

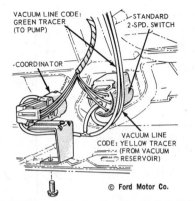

1968 Vibro-Jet Washer Coordinator & Switch

after the release of the switch, can be regulated by the adjusting screw on the coordinator. Clockwise rotation of the screw increases the number of sweeps and counterclockwise rotation will decrease the number of sweeps. There is a small vacuum bleed hole in the side of the piston cylinder which allows for venting of the vacuum as the piston nears the end of its travel. This allows for smooth transition from the wiper sweeping motion to the park position.

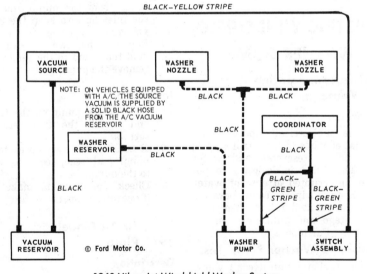

1968 Vibro-Jet Windshield Washer System

## Vibro-Jet Coordinator Test

Use a self powered test light to test for continuity of the coordinator assembly. With the wiper switch in the *on* position, there should be continuity between the top two terminals. With the wiper switch in the *off* position, there should be continuity between the bottom two terminals.

## Vibro-Jet Coordinator

### Removal

1. Disconnect the battery ground.

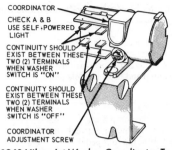

1968 Vibro-Jet Washer Coordinator Test Connections

2. Disconnect the wire connector and vacuum hose from the back of the coordinator which is located under the dash behind the wiper switch.
3. Remove the screws that hold it to the bottom of the dash and remove the coordinator.

### Installation

1. Position the coordinator under the dash and install the retaining screws.
2. Install the wires and the vacuum hose on the back of the coordinator.

3. Reconnect the battery cable and check the operation of the coordinator.

## Pump Assembly

### Removal

1. Remove the wiper blades and arms.
2. Remove the retaining screws from the cowl ventilator and remove the ventilator grille, hood pad and the washer nozzles.
3. Through the cowl opening re-

move the clip that holds the wiper arm to the motor drive arm.
4. Disconnect the vacuum and washer hoses from the plastic connectors on the bottom of the pump assembly and the one on the side.
5. Remove the retaining screws for the pivot assembly and remove the pivot and arms as an assembly.

### Installation

1. Position the pump and pivot assembly through the cowl and install the retaining screws.
2. Install the wiper arms on the motor drive arms and install the retaining clip.
3. Connect the hoses to the pump assembly.
4. Install the washer nozzles and position the cowl top hood pad and grille in place and install the retaining screws.
5. Install the wiper arms and blades.

# FOOT OPERATED WINDSHIELD WASHER SYSTEM

## 1968 Cougar and Mustang

### Description

This system uses a foot operated bellows type pump and an electrical switch that is coordinated with the wiper motor through the wiper switch. Operating the pump is done by pressing and releasing the foot pedal with a pumping motion which in turn ejects a spray of water onto the windshield.

The pump is coordinated with the wipers by a switch that is attached to the pump and is activated when the pump pedal is depressed. Closing the switch completes the circuit which operates the wipers at low speed. then the pump pedal is released it breaks the circuit and the wipers return to the park position.

### Pump Switch Test

Use a self powered test light to test the switch for continuity. Disconnect the wires from the back of the pump and attach one test lead to the terminal on the pump that the red wire goes on and the other test lead to the terminal on the pump that the white

# Ford Motor Company

Foot-Pedal Windshield Washer System Trouble Diagnosis Guide

| WASHER DOES NOT OPERATE WHEN PEDAL IS ACTUATED | Verify the complaint.<br>1. Clogged windshield jets.<br>2. Clogged hoses from fluid bag to pump and to windshield jets. | 3. Possible cracks in pump bellows. |
|---|---|---|
| WASHER OPERATES BUT WIPERS DO NOT | Verify the complaint.<br>1. Defective electrical switch assembly at the foot pedal.<br>2. Open circuit between foot pedal switch and wiper motor.<br>3. Defective windshield wiper switch. | 4. Open circuit between windshield wiper switch and wiper motor.<br>5. Defective wiper motor. |

lead goes to. With the pump pedal in the released position the light should be out. When the pedal is depressed the light should go on. This checks the low speed portion of the switch.

Disconnect the test lead from the red and white wire terminals and connect the leads to the terminals that the black wires go to on the pump. With the pedal in the released position the light should be on. When the pedal is pressed down the light should go out. This checks the park position of the switch.

If the switch fails any of the tests, replace the pump and switch assembly.

## Pump and Switch

### Removal

1. Remove the hose from the reservoir and plug the hole in the reservoir opening.
2. Remove the screws holding the left side cowling panel and remove the panel.

NOTE: Loosen the screws that hold the scuff plate in place to allow for removal of the panel.

3. Remove the four screws that hold the pump assembly to the dash and remove the two hoses and wires from the pump.
4. Remove the pump assembly from the dash.

### Installation

1. Connect the wires and hoses to the pump and position the pump assembly on the dash.
2. Install the four retaining screws on the pump.
3. Install the cowl panel and retaining screws and tighten the scuff plate screws.
4. Reconnect the hose to the reservoir and check the pump and switch for proper operation.

# ELECTRIC WINDSHIELD WASHER PUMP

## 1968 Falcon, Fairlane and Montego

### Description

This is an electrically operated system that consists of a control switch, water pump, reservoir and water lines. The pump is designed to put out an interrupted stream of water only when the wipers are in operation and the wiper switch is pushed in on the Montego and pulled out on the Falcon and Fairlane.

### Windshield Washer Pump Test

If the washer pump doesn't work, disconnect the two wires from the pump and using a test light connect the test leads to the two wires removed from the pump. Turn the wiper switch *on* and operate the washer. If the test light lights the pump motor is defective. If the test light does not light, either the switch is bad or there is an opening in the circuit.

## Washer Pump

### Removal

1. Disconnect the wires from the pump.
2. Remove the inlet and outlet hoses from the pump and plug the inlet hose to keep the reservoir from draining.
3. Remove the two screws that hold the pump to the fender and remove the pump.

### Installation

1. Position the pump on the fender and install the two retaining screws.
2. Reconnect the two hoses to the pump and reconnect the wires to the pump.
3. Check the pump to make sure it operates properly.

## 1969-70 All Models 1971 Pinto

### Description

On all models the pump and motor are located in the bottom of the water reservoir. There is a screen over the top of the reservoir to keep

Electric Windshield Washer Pump Trouble Diagnosis Guide

| INOPERATIVE WINDSHIELD WASHER PUMP | Verify the complaint.<br>1. No fluid in washer reservoir or lines.<br>2. Broken or clogged water lines.<br>3. Open circuit between switch and pump.<br>4. Open circuit between washer pump and wiper motor. | 5. Defective wiper switch.<br>6. Defective washer pump.<br>7. Defective switch on wiper motor.<br>8. Burned, corroded, or damaged switch plate in wiper motor.<br>9. Defective wiper motor.<br>10. Water hose from reservoir to pump routed above reservoir level. |
|---|---|---|

# Ford Motor Company

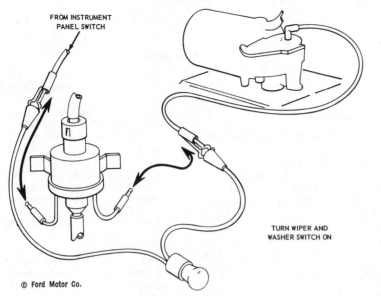

FROM INSTRUMENT
PANEL SWITCH

TURN WIPER AND
WASHER SWITCH ON

© Ford Motor Co.

*1968 Windshield Washer Pump Test*

out dirt. The screen is serviced separately from the washer assembly.

## Washer Pump
## All Models Except Thunderbird, Lincoln Continental and Mark III

### Removal and Installation

1. The reservoir, pump and motor is serviced as one assembly. To remove the assembly disconnect the wires and hose from the reservoir.
2. Remove the retaining screws and remove the assembly from the fender.
3. To install a new reservoir position the assembly on the fender and install the two retaining screws.
4. Connect the wires and hose to the reservoir and check the unit for proper operation.

## Thunderbird, Lincoln Continental and Mark III

### Removal

1. Remove the wire and hose from the reservoir and drain the water from the reservoir.
2. Remove the retaining screws holding the reservoir on the fender and remove the reservoir.
3. With a 15/16 inch deep well socket, work through the top of the reservoir and remove the nut that holds the pump in the reservoir.
4. Remove the nut and screen assembly from the reservoir and remove the pump motor.

### Installation

1. If it is necessary, replace the seal on the pump assembly.
2. Place the pump assembly in the reservoir and fit the rubber seal and plastic washer to the pump from inside the reservoir.
3. To install the screen and nut, use a section of hose fitted around the nut assembly and start the nut on the pump threads. Tighten the nut with the 15/16 inch deep well socket.
4. Position the reservoir assembly on the fender and attach it with the retaining screws.
5. Connect the wires and hose and fill the reservoir and check the washer for proper operation.

## 1971-74 All Models—Except 1971 Pinto

### Description

This system is similar to the earlier ones in that it consists of a reservoir, pump and motor with the pump motor located in the bottom of the reservoir. It differs in the aspect that the pump and motor can be serviced separately from the reservoir.

Use an ammeter and an external power supply to check the motor for current draw. With a jumper wire, connect the negative side of the battery to one side of the motor and on the other side of the motor connect the positive lead from the ammeter. Connect the remaining lead from the ammeter to the positive side of the battery. The current draw from the motor should not exceed four amps. If the draw is over four amps the motor should be replaced. Make sure the motor is pumping fluid when the test is made.

## Washer Pump
## 1971-72 All Models

### Removal

1. Remove the wires and hose from the reservoir.

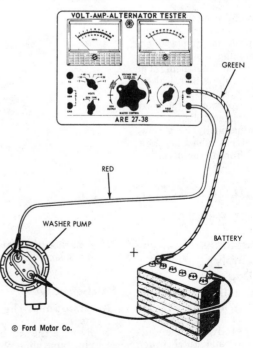

VOLT-AMP-ALTERNATOR TESTER

GREEN

ARE 27-38

RED

WASHER PUMP

BATTERY

© Ford Motor Co.

*1969-75 Washer Pump Current Draw Test*

# Ford Motor Company

2. Remove the screws that hold the reservoir to the fender and remove the assembly.
3. Remove the top from the reservoir and remove the motor and pump assembly from the bottom.

## Installation

1. Install the motor and pump in the bottom of the reservoir and install the top on the reservoir.
2. Position the reservoir assembly on the fender and install the retaining screws.
3. Connect the wires and hose and fill the reservoir and check for proper operation of the pump.

## Water Pump
### 1973-74 All Models

#### Removal

1. Disconnect the wires and hose from the reservoir and remove the attaching screws which hold the reservoir to the fender.
2. Remove the assembly from the

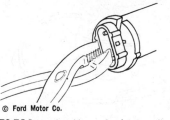

© Ford Motor Co.

*1973-75 Removing Motor, Seal & Impeller*

vehicle and remove the cover and flush out the reservoir.
3. The motor is located on the side of the reservoir with a retaining ring holding it in place. Using a screw driver with a small blade, pry out the retaining ring.
4. Grip one wall around the electrical terminals with a pair of pliers and pull the motor, seal and impeller out of the reservoir. If the impeller and seal come off of the motor when pulling them out, they can be reassembled.
5. Check the reservoir pump cham-

ber to make sure there is no dirt in it.

## Installation

1. Before installing the motor assembly in the reservoir, lubricate the outside of the seal with a dry lubricant. This keeps the seal from sticking to the motor cavity in the reservoir.
2. Align the small projection on the motor end cap with the slot in the reservoir and press the motor assembly in until the seal seats against the bottom of the motor cavity.
3. Use a 1 inch socket and press in the retaining ring against the motor end plate.
4. Reconnect the wires and hose to the reservoir and install the assembly back on the fender. Install the attaching screws.
5. Fill the reservoir with water and check the operation of the pump.

*NOTE: Do not operate the pump unless there is water in the reservoir.*

# General Motors

## ROUND MOTOR AND RECTANGULAR MOTOR WASHER SYSTEMS

### Description

The washer pump used on both the rectangular and round motor wiper system is a positive displacement type pump employing a small piston, spring and valve arrangement. The plastic valve assembly is identical for both except for the programming (Starting and completion of the wash cycle) which is accomplished electrically and mechanically by a relay assembly and ratchet wheel arrangement which is different for both.

## RECTANGULAR MOTOR WASHER SYSTEM

### Washer Disassembly
### Solenoid Assembly
### and Ratchet Dog

1. Remove the ratchet dog retaining screw. While holding the spring loaded solenoid plunger in position, carefully lift the solenoid assembly and ratchet dog off the frame of the pump.

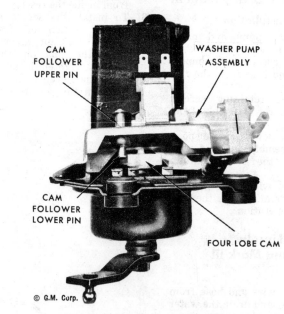

CAM FOLLOWER UPPER PIN

WASHER PUMP ASSEMBLY

CAM FOLLOWER LOWER PIN

FOUR LOBE CAM

© G.M. Corp.

*Four Lobe Cam Drive on Wiper Motor*

2. Separate the ratchet dog from the solenoid mounting plate.

### Ratchet Pawl

1. Disconnect the ratchet pawl spring.
2. Remove the ratchet pawl retaining ring and slide the ratchet pawl off the cam follower shaft.

### Ratchet Wheel

1. Remove the ratchet dog retaining screw. While holding the spring loaded solenoid plunger in position, carefully lift the solenoid assembly and ratchet dog off the frame of the pump.
2. Move the ratchet wheel spring out of the shaft groove and slide the ratchet wheel off its shaft.

# Windshield Washers

## General Motors

### DIAGNOSIS CHART - RECTANGULAR MOTOR WASHER SYSTEM

| CONDITION | APPARENT CAUSE | CORRECTION |
|---|---|---|
| 1. Washer inoperative | A. Inadequate quantity of washer solution | A. Add washer solution |
| | B. Hoses damaged or loose | B. Cut short length to insure air tight connection or replace hose |
| | C. Plugged screen at end of jar cover hose | C. Clean screen |
| | D. Loose electrical connection to washer pump or wiper switch | D. Check electrical connection and repair if necessary |
| | E. Open circuit in feed wire to pump solenoid coil | E. Locate open circuit and repair |
| | F. Wiper switch defective | F. Replace wiper switch |
| | G. Pump solenoid coil defective | G. Replace solenoid |
| | H. Washer nozzles plugged | H. Clean washer nozzles |
| | I. Ratchet wheel tooth missing | I. Replace ratchet wheel |
| | J. Ratchet pawl spring missing | J. Replace ratchet pawl spring |
| | K. Defective pump valve assembly | K. Replace pump valve assembly |
| 2. Washer pumps continuously when wipers are operating | A. Grounded wire from pump solenoid to switch | A. Locate grounded wire and repair |
| | B. Wiper Switch Defective | B. Replace wiper switch |
| | C. Ratchet wheel tooth missing | C. Replace ratchet wheel |
| | D. Ratchet wheel dog broken or not contacting ratchet wheel teeth | D. Replace or repair ratchet wheel dog |
| | E. Lock-out tang broken or bent on piston actuating plate | E. Replace piston actuating plate |

807

## General Motors

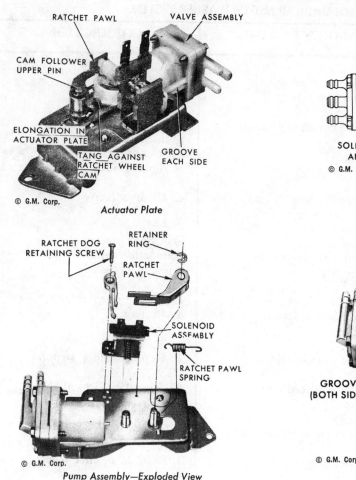

Actuator Plate

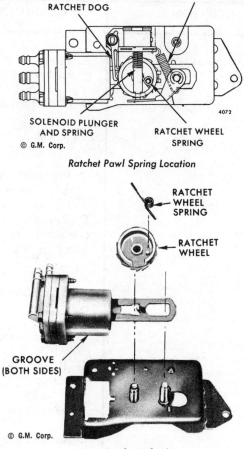

Ratchet Pawl Spring Location

Pump Assembly—Exploded View

Pump Ratchet Wheel

### Pump and Actuator Plate Assembly

1. Remove the ratchet dog retaining screw while holding the spring leaded solenoid plunger in position, carefully lift the solenoid assembly and ratchet dog off the frame of the pump.
2. Separate the ratchet dog from the solenoid mounting plate.
3. Disconnect the ratchet pawl spring.
4. Remove the ratchet pawl retaining ring and slide the ratchet pawl off the cam follower shaft.
5. Move the ratchet wheel spring out of the shaft groove and slide the ratchet wheel off its shaft.
6. Separate the pump and the pump actuator plate from the frame, pull the pump housing in the direction toward the valve end until the grooves in the housing clear the frame.
7. Remove the actuator plate from the ratchet wheel and cam follower shaft.

### Valve Assembly

1. Remove the four screws that attach the valve assembly to the pump housing.

*NOTE: When reassembling the valve assembly, make sure the gasket between the housing and valve plate grooves is installed properly. Also install the triple O-ring properly between the valve body and pipe assembly.*

## ROUND MOTOR
## WASHER SYSTEMS

### Washer Pump Removal

1. Remove the hoses from the pump.
2. Disconnect the wires from the pump relay.
3. Remove the plastic pump cover.
4. Remove the screws which attach the pump frame to the motor

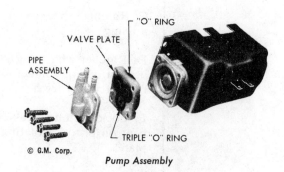

Pump Assembly

# Windshield Washers

## General Motors

### DIAGNOSIS CHART - ROUND MOTOR WASHER SYSTEM

| CONDITION | APPARENT CAUSE | CORRECTION |
|---|---|---|
| 1. Washers inoperative | A. Inadequate quantity of washer solution | A. Add washer solution |
| | B. Hoses damaged or loose | B. Cut short length off end of hose to insure air tight connection or replace hose |
| | C. Plugged screen at end of jar cover hose | C. Clean screen |
| | D. Loose electrical connection to washer pump or wiper switch | D. Check electrical connections and repair if necessary |
| | E. Open circuit in feed wire to ratchet relay coil | E. Locate open circuit and repair |
| | F. Wiper switch defective | F. Replace wiper switch |
| | G. Ratchet relay coil defective | G. Replace ratchet relay |
| | H. Washer nozzles plugged | H. Clean washer nozzles |
| | I. Ratchet wheel tooth missing | I. Replace ratchet wheel |
| | J. Ratchet pawl spring missing | J. Replace ratchet pawl spring |
| | K. Defective pump valve assembly | K. Replace pump valve assembly |
| 2. Washer pumps continously when wipers are operating | A. Grounded wire from ratchet relay to switch | A. Locate grounded wire and repair |
| | B. Wiper switch defective | B. Replace wiper switch |
| | C. Ratchet wheel tooth missing | C. Replace ratchet wheel |
| | D. Ratchet wheel dog broken or not contacting ratchet wheel teeth | D. Replace or repair ratchet wheel dog |
| | E. Lock-out tang broken or bent on piston actuator plate | E. Replace piston actuator plate |

## General Motors

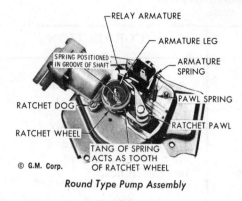

Round Type Pump Assembly

© G.M. Corp.

gear box and remove the pump and frame.

### Washer Pump Disassembly
#### Ratchet Dog

1. Remove the attaching screw and lift the ratchet dog off the mounting plate.

#### Ratchet Pawl and Pawl Spring

1. Disengage the pawl spring from the pawl and slide the pawl off of the cam follower pin.

#### Ratchet Wheel

1. Remove the plastic pump cover.
2. Pry the ratchet spring out of the slot in the shaft, hold the relay armature against the relay coil and slide the ratchet wheel off the shaft.

*NOTE: Be careful not to damage the ratchet dog when reassembling the ratchet wheel.*

#### Four Lobe Cam

1. Remove the push-on retainer and slide the cam off of the shaft.

#### Relay Terminal Board Assembly

1. Remove the four lobe cam.
   a. Remove the push-on retainer and slide the cam off of the shaft.

© G.M. Corp.

Removing Four Lobe Cam

2. Remove the ratchet pawl and pawl spring.
   a. Disengage the pawl spring from the pawl and slide the pawl off the cam follower pin.
3. Remove the relay armature and spring.
4. Chisel off the four bent over tabs which hold the coil mounting bracket to the base. Remove the relay coil and terminal board assembly. When replacing the relay assembly, hold it securely against the base mounting surface and bend the locking tabs over.

*NOTE: When replacing the relay be careful not to damage the coil winding or terminals.*

### Pump Assembly

1. Remove the ratchet wheel.
   a. Remove the plastic pump cover.
   b. Pry the ratchet spring out of the slot in the shaft, hold the relay armature against the relay coil and slide the ratchet wheel off the shaft.

*NOTE: Be careful not to damage the ratchet dog when reassembling the ratchet wheel.*

2. Remove the ratchet dog.
   a. Remove the attaching screw and lift the ratchet dog off the mounting plate.
3. Remove the ratchet pawl and spring.
   a. Disengage the pawl spring from the pawl and slide the pawl off the cam follower pin.
4. The plastic pump housing can be released from the sheet metal base by pulling it in the direction toward the valve end until the grooves in the housing clear the base. Detach the assembly from the cam follower pin.

© G.M. Corp.

Ratchet Wheel—Ramp

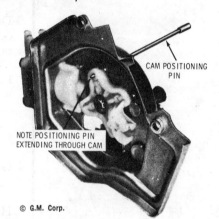

© G.M. Corp.

Cam Alignment Pin Installation

*NOTE: The piston and plastic housing is serviced as a complete assembly.*

### Valve Assembly

1. Remove the four screws that secure the valve assembly to the housing.
2. Save the gasket used between the valve and housing for reassembly.

### Washer Pump
#### Installation

1. Make sure the wiper motor gear is in the park position.
2. Remove the plastic pump cover.
3. Rotate the four lobe cam until the index hole (1/8 in. dia.) in the cam is aligned with the hole in the pump mounting plate. Insert a pin through both of the holes to keep the cam in position.
4. Position the pump on the wiper so that the slot in the four lobe cam fits over the gear drive pin. Secure the pump to the gear housing and remove the locator pin. Connect the wire connector.
5. Turn on the wiper and washer pump to see if the pump is oper-

## General Motors

ating properly. If a loud knocking noise is heard the cam has not engaged the drive pin. If not install the pump cover.

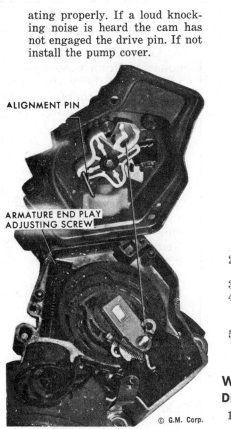

ALIGNMENT PIN

ARMATURE END PLAY ADJUSTING SCREW

© G.M. Corp.

*Installing Washer to Pump*

# PROGRAMMED WASHER SYSTEM

## 1971-73
### Description

The programmed washer system is used in conjunction with the demand wiper system. With the demand wiper system every time the button is depressed to the first detent position the wipers will make one complete wiping stroke and automatically shut off.

When the button is depressed to the second detent position, the washer pump operates through a pumping cycle and stops pumping. The motor continues to operate and provides two additional drying wipes and then automatically shuts off. If the wiper control switch washer button is used to provide a wash cycle it is necessary to move the control switch to the "OFF" position to shut off the wipers after the wash cycle is completed.

## Washer Pump
### Removal

1. Remove the washer hoses from the pump.

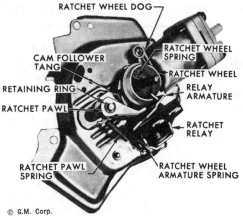

RATCHET WHEEL DOG

CAM FOLLOWER TANG

RETAINING RING

RATCHET PAWL

RATCHET WHEEL SPRING

RATCHET WHEEL

RELAY ARMATURE

RATCHET RELAY

RATCHET PAWL SPRING

RATCHET WHEEL ARMATURE SPRING

© G.M. Corp.

*Washer Pump Assembly*

2. Disconnect the wiring from the pump relay.
3. Remove the plastic pump cover.
4. Disconnect the yellow wire from the holding switch and the green wire from the demand relay.
5. Remove the screws which attach the pump frame to the motor box and remove the pump and frame.

## Washer Pump
### Disassembly

1. Remove the retaining ring and slide the four lobe cam off of the shaft.
2. Remove the screw which retains the holding switch and relay assembly to the pump mounting surface. Separate the relay assembly from the holding switch.

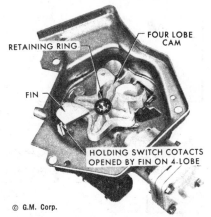

RETAINING RING

FIN

FOUR LOBE CAM

HOLDING SWITCH COTACTS OPENED BY FIN ON 4-LOBE

© G.M. Corp.

*Four Lobe Cam*

3. Remove the retaining screw and lift the ratchet dog off the mounting surface.
4. Remove the ratchet relay armature spring, ratchet pawl spring and remove the ratchet relay armature.
5. Move the leg of the ratchet spring out of the groove in the

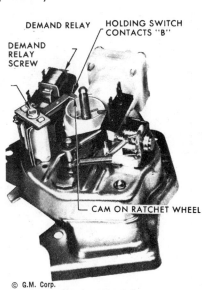

DEMAND RELAY

HOLDING SWITCH CONTACTS "B"

DEMAND RELAY SCREW

CAM ON RATCHET WHEEL

© G.M. Corp.

*Ratchet Wheel Cam*

shaft and slide the ratchet wheel and spring off the shaft.
6. Remove the retaining ring and slide the ratchet pawl off the cam follower pin.
7. Pull the pump housing out until the housing grooves clear the mounting surfaces then lift the pump off the ratchet wheel shaft and cam follower pin.
8. Chisel off the four bent over tabs that secure the coil mounting bracket to the base.
9. Remove the coil and terminal board assembly.

*NOTE: To mount the replacement relay assembly hold the relay against the mounting surface and bend the four tabs over.*

10. Note the position of the valve assembly for reassembly, then remove the four screws that

## General Motors
### DIAGNOSIS CHART- PROGRAMMED WASHER

| CONDITION | APPARENT CAUSE | CORRECTION |
|---|---|---|
| 1. Washer pump pumps continually when wiper motor is "ON". Wiper motor operates normally otherwise. | A. Dark blue wire between washer pump and control switches grounded. | A. Disconnect harness connector from washer pump terminals. If the washer stops pumping, the trouble is in the wiring or wiper control switch.<br><br>If the washer continues to pump, proceed to step C. |
|  | B. Defective wiper control switch. | B. Connect harness to pump and disconnect dark blue wire from wiper control switch. Turn motor "ON".<br><br>If washer pump shuts "OFF", trouble is in wiper control switch.<br><br>If washer keeps pumping, proceed to step C. |
|  | C. Washer pump defective. Washer pump ratchet wheel not being rotated by ratchet pawl. | C. Remove washer pump cover and connect wiring to wiper control switch and pump. Observe if ratchet wheel is rotating while pump is operating.<br><br>If ratchet wheel is not rotating, check for a sheared tooth on ratchet wheel. Check for broken ratchet wheel dog or dog not engaging ratchet wheel teeth. Repair or replace parts as required. |

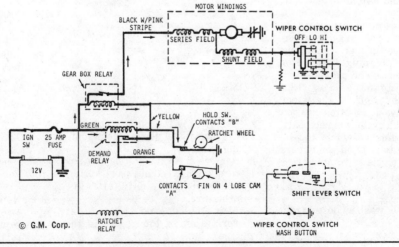

Programmed
Washer
System

© G.M. Corp.

## General Motors

secure the valve ports to the pump housing.

### Assembly

1. Install the pump over the ratchet wheel shaft and cam follower pin with the tang on the pump actuating plate facing up.
2. Align the grooves in the pump housing with the mounting surface, then release the pump housing.
3. Move the leg of the ratchet wheel spring and install the ratchet wheel on the shaft.
4. Move the pump actuating plate tang away and push the ratchet wheel down until the spring locks in the groove of the shaft.
5. Install the ratchet wheel pawl over the pin and install the retaining ring.
6. If removed, install the washer relay coil on the base and bend the tabs to hold the relay coil into position.
7. Install the relay armature.
8. Install the relay armature spring.
9. Install the ratchet pawl spring.
10. Install the ratchet wheel dog and screw.
11. Position the holding switch on the demand relay and install the unit on the pump base by aligning the two plastic guide pins with the holes in the pump mounting plate. Install the retaining screws.
12. Connect the wire connector which is the one nearest to the pump outlets.
13. Position the four lobe cam over the shaft and install the retaining spring.

*NOTE: The wiper motor must be in the "PARK" position to assemble the pump to the wiper motor.*

14. Rotate the four lobe cam so the index hole is aligned with the hole in the pump mounting plates. Insert a .120 inch to .125 inch diameter pin through both holes so the drive slot in the cam will be in the proper position for the drive pin.

*NOTE: Make sure the pump is in the free wheeling position before installing the pin.*

15. Position the pump on the wiper so that the slot in the four lobe cam fits over the gear drive pin.
16. Install the three attaching screws and remove the locator pin which was previously installed.
17. Connect the wiring connectors to

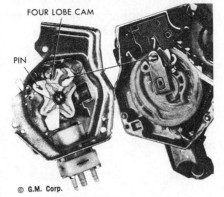

FOUR LOBE CAM

PIN

© G.M. Corp.

*Aligning Pump Assembly to Motor*

the demand relay and install the cover on the washer pump.

## PULSE MOTOR WASHER SYSTEM

### 1974-75
### Description

This washer system is a programmed system which uses a washer pump completely different from the standard pump. The following new components are found on the pulse washer pump. (1) A pulse relay which acts as a switch to provide a ground the wiper motor armature circuit. (2) An override switch is used during the washer pump operation to provide alternate or auxiliary circuits. The switch is actuated by a projection on the rim of the ratchet gear. (3) A holding switch is used in conjunction with the timing device

to control the "Delay" mode of operation. This switch is activated by a fin on the washer pump drive cam. (4) A timing device which consists of a transistor, capacitor, and diode mounted on an insulating board, plus a variable resistor located in the dash switch. (5) A drive cam which drives the pump mechanism and also activates the holding switch.

With the dash switch in the "OFF" position, and the wash button momentarily depressed, a wash cycle will start which consist of eight pumping strokes, four drying wipes, then the blades automatically park. Whenever the dash switch is in the "LO," "MED" or "HIGH" positions and the wash button is depressed the wash cycle will start and pump eight times at the particular speed the wiper switch is positioned, then stop, but the wipers will continue. When the dash switch is in the "DELAY" position and the wash button is depressed, the washers cycle with the wipers in the "LO" speed. At the completion of the wash cycle the wiper motor automatically reverts back to the "DELAY" operation.

### Washer Pump

#### Removal

1. Remove the complete wiper-washer assembly from the vehicle.
2. Remove the plastic tab from terminal six and seven and pull the plastic cover off the mounting pin.
3. Disconnect the yellow lead from terminal 1A, the black lead from

OVER-RIDE SWITCH

TIMING CIRCUIT BOARD

PULSE RELAY

HOLDING SWITCH

© G.M. Corp.

*Pulse Motor Washer Pump*

## General Motors

DIAGNOSIS CHART - PULSE MOTOR WASHER SYSTEM

NOTE: The procedures in this chart cover only that part of the Washer System that is directly related to the pump mechanism and/or delivery of washer solution to the windshield when the motor is operating correctly.

As a preliminary inspection, check the following items:

1) Quantity of washer solution adequate
2) Hoses attached to washer pump, nozzles and jar.
3) Hoses not damaged, kinked or split.
4) Hoses fit tight on washer pump pipes and nozzles. If loose, cut off approximately 1/2 inch and re-attach.
5) Screen at end of hose inside jar not plugged.
6) Nozzles not plugged.

| | CONDITION | DIAGNOSIS PROCEDURE |
|---|---|---|
| 1) | Washer System Inoperative | a) Preliminary Inspection<br>b) Test Numbers 1 and 2 as required |
| 2) | Washer operates whenever wiper motor is operating. | Test No. 3. |
| 3) | Loud "klunking" type noise when pump is operating. (Pump delivers wash solution correctly). | Pump improperly installed on wiper gear box. Gear drive pin not located in drive cam slot. |
| 4) | Wiper shuts off before wash cycle is completed.<br>"With dash switch in OFF position and washer button depressed, wiper starts - blades move out of park position and immediately return to park position and wiper shuts off." | Remove washer pump cover and check the following:<br>a) Over-ride switch contacts are closing.<br>b) Yellow lead is attached to wiper terminal 1A. |
| 5) | When Wiper System is in "Delay" mode of operation, washer pump also operates in "Delay" mode. | Same as Item 4. |

**TEST NO. 1** – WASHER SYSTEM INOPERATIVE

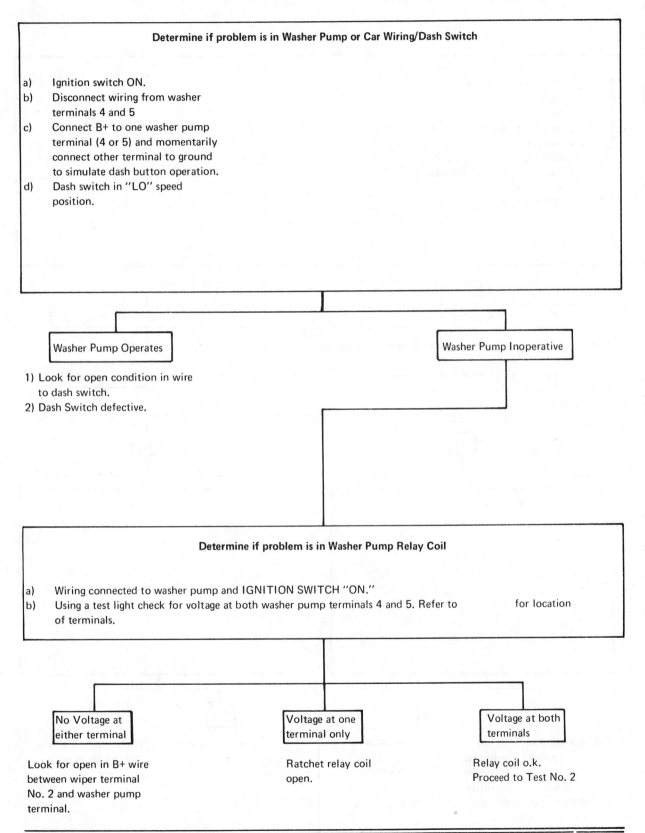

Determine if problem is in Washer Pump or Car Wiring/Dash Switch

a) Ignition switch ON.
b) Disconnect wiring from washer terminals 4 and 5
c) Connect B+ to one washer pump terminal (4 or 5) and momentarily connect other terminal to ground to simulate dash button operation.
d) Dash switch in "LO" speed position.

**Washer Pump Operates**

1) Look for open condition in wire to dash switch.
2) Dash Switch defective.

**Washer Pump Inoperative**

Determine if problem is in Washer Pump Relay Coil

a) Wiring connected to washer pump and IGNITION SWITCH "ON."
b) Using a test light check for voltage at both washer pump terminals 4 and 5. Refer to _____ for location of terminals.

**No Voltage at either terminal**

Look for open in B+ wire between wiper terminal No. 2 and washer pump terminal.

**Voltage at one terminal only**

Ratchet relay coil open.

**Voltage at both terminals**

Relay coil o.k. Proceed to Test No. 2

**TEST NO. 2** – OPERATIONAL CHECK

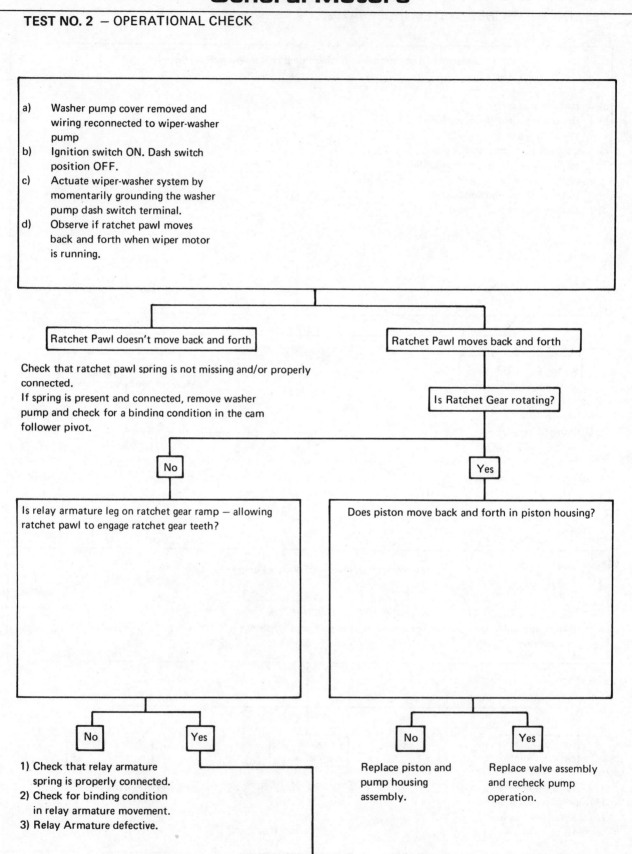

a)   Washer pump cover removed and wiring reconnected to wiper-washer pump

b)   Ignition switch ON. Dash switch position OFF.

c)   Actuate wiper-washer system by momentarily grounding the washer pump dash switch terminal.

d)   Observe if ratchet pawl moves back and forth when wiper motor is running.

Ratchet Pawl doesn't move back and forth

Check that ratchet pawl spring is not missing and/or properly connected.
If spring is present and connected, remove washer pump and check for a binding condition in the cam follower pivot.

Ratchet Pawl moves back and forth

Is Ratchet Gear rotating?

No

Yes

Is relay armature leg on ratchet gear ramp — allowing ratchet pawl to engage ratchet gear teeth?

Does piston move back and forth in piston housing?

No

Yes

1) Check that relay armature spring is properly connected.
2) Check for binding condition in relay armature movement.
3) Relay Armature defective.

No

Yes

Replace piston and pump housing assembly.

Replace valve assembly and recheck pump operation.

## General Motors

### TEST NO. 2 (Cont.)

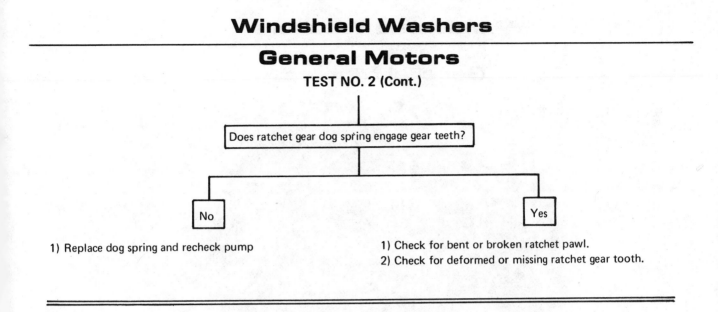

Does ratchet gear dog spring engage gear teeth?

**No**

1) Replace dog spring and recheck pump

**Yes**

1) Check for bent or broken ratchet pawl.
2) Check for deformed or missing ratchet gear tooth.

---

## TEST NO. 3 — WASHER PUMP OPERATES WHENEVER WIPER IS OPERATED.

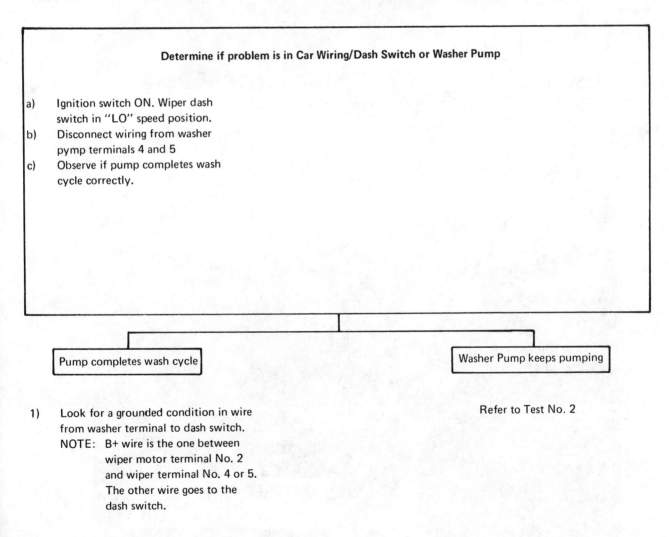

**Determine if problem is in Car Wiring/Dash Switch or Washer Pump**

a) Ignition switch ON. Wiper dash switch in "LO" speed position.
b) Disconnect wiring from washer pymp terminals 4 and 5
c) Observe if pump completes wash cycle correctly.

**Pump completes wash cycle**

**Washer Pump keeps pumping**

1) Look for a grounded condition in wire from washer terminal to dash switch.
   NOTE: B+ wire is the one between wiper motor terminal No. 2 and wiper terminal No. 4 or 5. The other wire goes to the dash switch.

Refer to Test No. 2

## General Motors

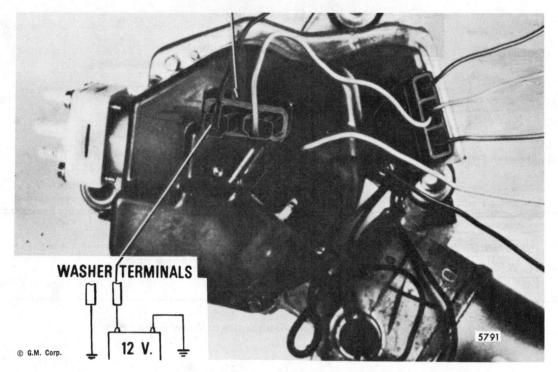

WASHER TERMINALS

© G.M. Corp.    12 V.

5791

*Washer Test 1 and 3, View 1*

RATCHET PAWL
ENGAGING GEAR TEETH

© G.M. Corp.    RELAY ARMATURE LEG ON RATCHET GEAR RAMP

*Washer Test 2, View 1*

## General Motors

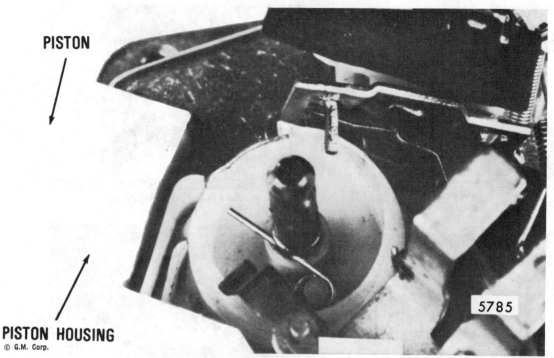

PISTON

PISTON HOUSING
© G.M. Corp.

5785

Washer Test 2, View 2

SMALL SCREWDRIVER

DUST SHIELD

© G.M. Corp.

*Removing Plastic Pump Cover*

YELLOW LEAD TERMINAL 1A

YELLOW

GREEN

BLACK-COTTON BRAID     © G.M. Corp.

*Washer Pump Electrical Lead Location*

the override switch terminal and the green lead from the pulse relay terminal.

4. Remove the three screws that attach the pump to the gear box.

### Installation

*NOTE: The gear box mechanism must be in the park position.*

1. Install a locator pin in the pump mechanism.

2. Position the pump assembly on the gear box and install the three attaching screws.
3. Remove the locator pin.

Fig. PULW-20

4. Route and attach the yellow, black and green leads to the proper terminals.
5. Position the cover on the washer pump mechanism and snap it over the mounting pin.
6. Reinstall the small plastic plate in terminal six and seven opening.
7. Reinstall the wiring and hoses.

### Washer Pump—Disassembly and Assembly
### Valve Assembly

*NOTE: The valve may be replaced with the wiper unit in the car. The pump cover need not be removed.*

1. Note the position of the hose connections at the valve assembly in relation to the pump housing for reassembly then remove four screws that attach the valve assembly to the housing.
2. Remove the seal ring between the housing and valve body and save for reassembly.
3. To install reverse the removal procedure.

## General Motors

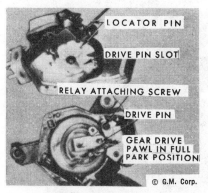

LOCATOR PIN
DRIVE PIN SLOT
RELAY ATTACHING SCREW
DRIVE PIN
GEAR DRIVE PAWL IN FULL PARK POSITION
© G.M. Corp.

*Installing Pump to Motor*

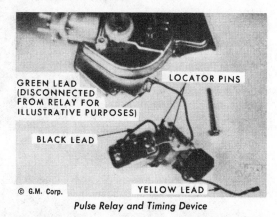

GREEN LEAD (DISCONNECTED FROM RELAY FOR ILLUSTRATIVE PURPOSES)
LOCATOR PINS
BLACK LEAD
© G.M. Corp.
YELLOW LEAD

*Pulse Relay and Timing Device*

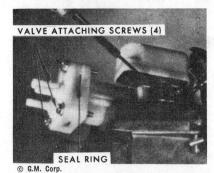

VALVE ATTACHING SCREWS (4)
© G.M. Corp.
SEAL RING

*Valve Assembly*

PUSH-ON RETAINER
RELAY MOUNTING TABS
© G.M. Corp.
*Correct Drive Cam Position*

### Drive Cam

1. Remove the push on retainer and slide the cam off of the shaft.

### Timing Device, Holding Switch and Override Switch Assembly; Pulse Relay Assembly

1. Remove the attaching screw and lift the pulse relay, holding switch, timing device, and override switch assembly off the washer frame surface.
2. Disconnect the green and black leads from the pulse and detach the relay from the locator pins.
3. To reassemble, position the pulse relay on the switch base locator pins, rotate the drive cam counterclockwise to the position

shown in the illustration, then install the screw that retains the complete assembly to the washer pump frame.

4. Connect the black and green leads to the proper pulse relay terminals.

### Ratchet Gear; Dog Spring; Ratchet Pawl; Relay Armature

1. Remove the attaching screw and lift the pulse relay, timing device, holding switch and override switch assembly off the washer frame surface.
2. Remove the dog spring assembly.
3. Remove the ratchet pawl retaining ring, disconnect the pawl spring and slide the pawl off the cam follower shaft.

4. Disconnect the relay armature spring and remove the armature.
5. Release the ratchet gear spring from the groove in the shaft and slide the ratchet gear off the shaft.

*NOTE: If necessary, move the piston actuator plate slightly to permit the ratchet gear ramp to slide by the tang and bottom on the actuator plate.*

### Piston and Pump Housing

1. Remove the attaching screw and lift the pulse relay, timing device, holding switch and override switch assembly off the washer frame surface.
2. Remove the dog spring assembly.
3. Remove the ratchet pawl retaining ring, disconnect the pawl

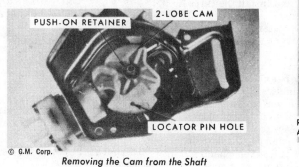

PUSH-ON RETAINER
2-LOBE CAM
LOCATOR PIN HOLE
© G.M. Corp.

*Removing the Cam from the Shaft*

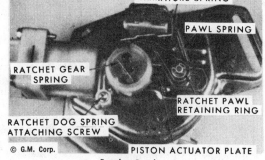

ARMATURE SPRING
PAWL SPRING
RATCHET GEAR SPRING
RATCHET PAWL RETAINING RING
RATCHET DOG SPRING ATTACHING SCREW
© G.M. Corp.
PISTON ACTUATOR PLATE

*Ratchet Pawl*

## General Motors

spring and slide the pawl off the cam follower shaft.

4. Disconnect the relay armature suring and remove the armature.

5. Release the ratchet gear spring from the groove in the shaft and slide the ratchet gear off the shaft.

6. Release the pump housing from the sheet meal base by pulling it toward the valve assembly until the grooves in the plastic pump housing clear the base. Detach the assembly from the cam follower pin.

### Pump Relay and Terminal Board

1. Remove the Drive Cam.
   (a) Remove the push on retainer and slide the cam off the shaft.
2. Remove the timing device, holding switch and override switch assembly, and pulse relay assembly.
   (a) Remove the attaching screw and lift the pulse relay, timing device, holding switch and override switch assembly off the washer frame surface.
   (b) Disconnect the green and black leads from the pulse relay and the relay from the locator pins.
3. Remove the ratchet pawl retaining ring, disconnect the pawl spring and slide the pawl off the cam follower shaft.

4. Disconnect the relay armature spring and remove the armature.

5. Bend or chisel off the four bent over tabs that hold the coil mounting bracket to the base.

## MODIFIED PULSE MOTOR WASHER SYSTEM

### 1975

#### Description

This washer system is a programmed system which uses a washer pump completely different from the standard pump. The following new components are found on the pulse washer pump. (1) A pulse relay which acts as a switch to provide a ground the wiper motor armature circuit. (2) An override switch is used during the washer pump operation to provide alternate or auxiliary circuits. The switch is actuated by a projection on the rim of the ratchet gear. (3) A holding switch is used in conjunction with the timing device to control the "Delay" mode of operation. This switch is activated by a fin on the washer pump drive cam. (4) A timing device which consists of a transistor, capacitor, and diode mounted on an insulating board, plus a variable resistor located in the dash switch. (5) A drive cam which drives the pump mechanism and also activates the holding switch.

With the dash switch in the "OFF" position, and the wash button momentarily depressed, a wash cycle will start which consist of eight pumping strokes, four drying wipes, then the blade automatically park. Whenever the dash switch is in the "LO," "MED" or "HIGH" positions and the wash button is depressed the wash cycle will start and pump eight times at the particular speed the wiper switch is positioned, then stop, but the wipers will continue. When the dash switch is in the "DELAY" position and the wash button is depressed the washers cycle with the wipers in the "LO" speed. At the completion of the wash cycle the wiper motor automatically reverts back to the "DELAY" operation.

### Washer Pump

#### Removal

1. Remove the complete wiper-washer assembly from the vehicle.
2. Remove the plastic tab from terminal six and seven and pull the plastic cover off the mounting pin.
3. Disconnect the green lead from terminal A, the red lead and the black lead with the pink stripes from the pulse relay terminals.
4. Remove the three screws that attach the pump to the gear box.

#### Installation

*NOTE: The gear box mechanism must be in the park position.*

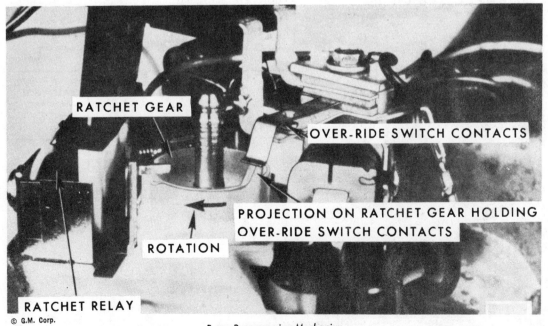

RATCHET GEAR

OVER-RIDE SWITCH CONTACTS

PROJECTION ON RATCHET GEAR HOLDING OVER-RIDE SWITCH CONTACTS

ROTATION

RATCHET RELAY

© G.M. Corp.

*Pump Programming Mechanism*

## General Motors
### MODIFIED PULSE WIPER WASHER SYSTEM
### TROUBLE DIAGNOSIS CHART

### WINDSHIELD WASHER SYSTEM INOPERATIVE
#### (WIPER MOTOR OPERATES CORRECTLY)

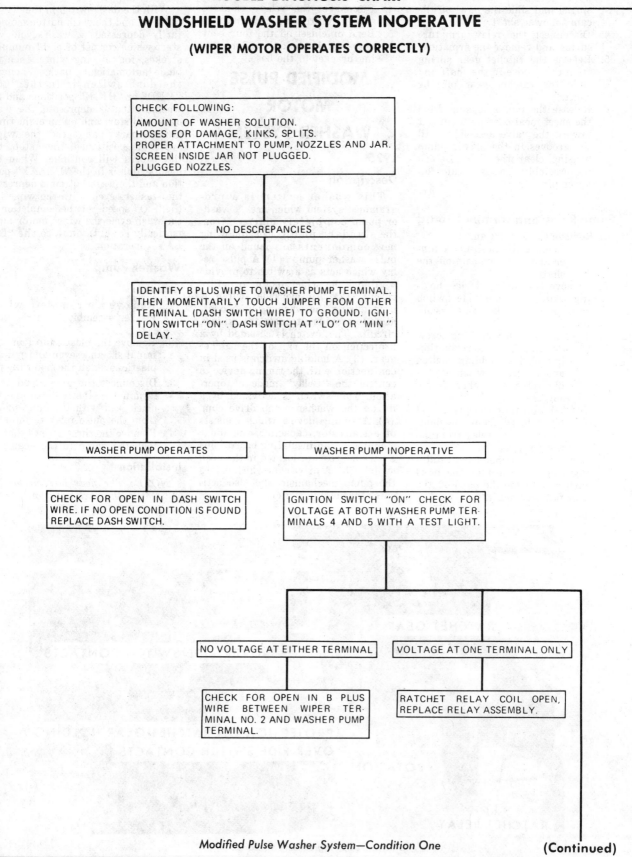

CHECK FOLLOWING:

AMOUNT OF WASHER SOLUTION.
HOSES FOR DAMAGE, KINKS, SPLITS.
PROPER ATTACHMENT TO PUMP, NOZZLES AND JAR.
SCREEN INSIDE JAR NOT PLUGGED.
PLUGGED NOZZLES.

NO DESCREPANCIES

IDENTIFY B PLUS WIRE TO WASHER PUMP TERMINAL. THEN MOMENTARILY TOUCH JUMPER FROM OTHER TERMINAL (DASH SWITCH WIRE) TO GROUND. IGNITION SWITCH "ON". DASH SWITCH AT "LO" OR "MIN" DELAY.

WASHER PUMP OPERATES

CHECK FOR OPEN IN DASH SWITCH WIRE. IF NO OPEN CONDITION IS FOUND REPLACE DASH SWITCH.

WASHER PUMP INOPERATIVE

IGNITION SWITCH "ON" CHECK FOR VOLTAGE AT BOTH WASHER PUMP TERMINALS 4 AND 5 WITH A TEST LIGHT.

NO VOLTAGE AT EITHER TERMINAL

CHECK FOR OPEN IN B PLUS WIRE BETWEEN WIPER TERMINAL NO. 2 AND WASHER PUMP TERMINAL.

VOLTAGE AT ONE TERMINAL ONLY

RATCHET RELAY COIL OPEN, REPLACE RELAY ASSEMBLY.

*Modified Pulse Washer System—Condition One*

(Continued)

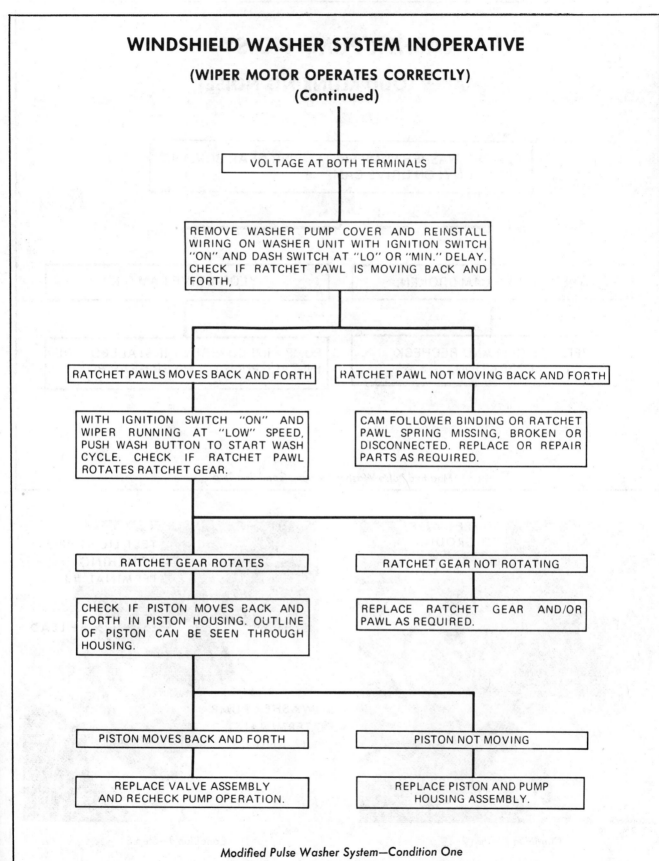

**WINDSHIELD WASHER SYSTEM INOPERATIVE**

**(WIPER MOTOR OPERATES CORRECTLY)**

**(Continued)**

VOLTAGE AT BOTH TERMINALS

REMOVE WASHER PUMP COVER AND REINSTALL WIRING ON WASHER UNIT WITH IGNITION SWITCH "ON" AND DASH SWITCH AT "LO" OR "MIN." DELAY. CHECK IF RATCHET PAWL IS MOVING BACK AND FORTH.

RATCHET PAWLS MOVES BACK AND FORTH

RATCHET PAWL NOT MOVING BACK AND FORTH

WITH IGNITION SWITCH "ON" AND WIPER RUNNING AT "LOW" SPEED, PUSH WASH BUTTON TO START WASH CYCLE. CHECK IF RATCHET PAWL ROTATES RATCHET GEAR.

CAM FOLLOWER BINDING OR RATCHET PAWL SPRING MISSING, BROKEN OR DISCONNECTED. REPLACE OR REPAIR PARTS AS REQUIRED.

RATCHET GEAR ROTATES

RATCHET GEAR NOT ROTATING

CHECK IF PISTON MOVES BACK AND FORTH IN PISTON HOUSING. OUTLINE OF PISTON CAN BE SEEN THROUGH HOUSING.

REPLACE RATCHET GEAR AND/OR PAWL AS REQUIRED.

PISTON MOVES BACK AND FORTH

PISTON NOT MOVING

REPLACE VALVE ASSEMBLY AND RECHECK PUMP OPERATION.

REPLACE PISTON AND PUMP HOUSING ASSEMBLY.

*Modified Pulse Washer System—Condition One*

# WASHER PUMP NOISY

## (MAKES LOUD KLUNKING NOISE)

REMOVE WASHER PUMP FROM WIPER GEAR BOX AND INSPECT NYLON DRIVE CAM.

NYLON DRIVE CAM BROKEN.

NYLON DRIVE CAM O.K.

REPLACE CAM AND RECHECK OPERATION.

PUMP IMPROPERLY INSTALLED. RE-INSTALL PUMP ON WIPER GEAR BOX.

*Modified Pulse Washer System—Condition Two*

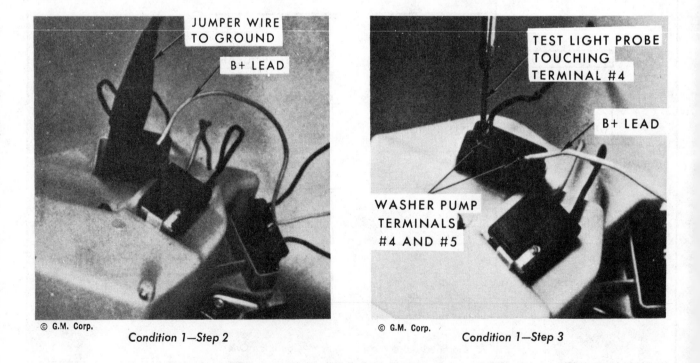

JUMPER WIRE TO GROUND

B+ LEAD

© G.M. Corp.

*Condition 1—Step 2*

TEST LIGHT PROBE TOUCHING TERMINAL #4

B+ LEAD

WASHER PUMP TERMINALS #4 AND #5

© G.M. Corp.

*Condition 1—Step 3*

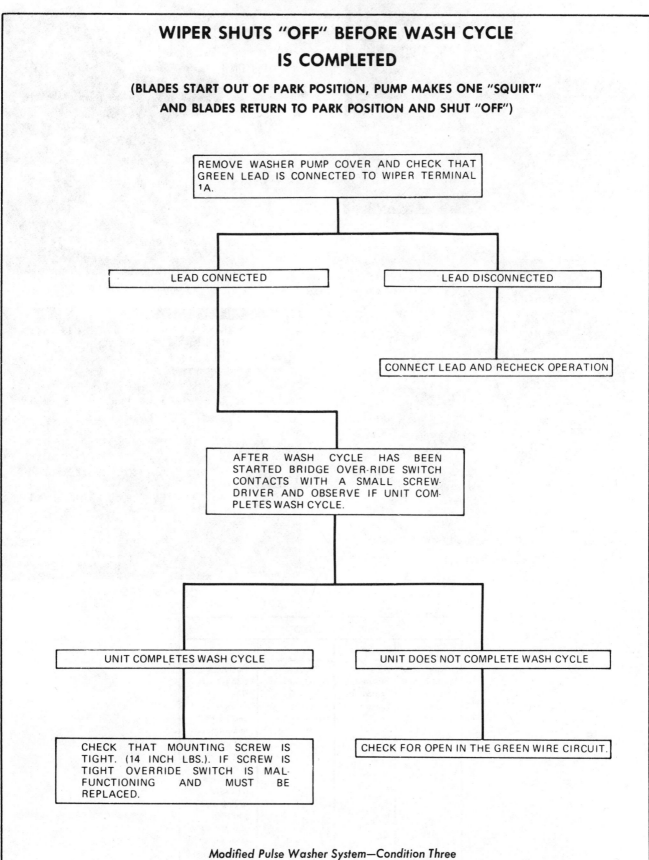

**WIPER SHUTS "OFF" BEFORE WASH CYCLE IS COMPLETED**

(BLADES START OUT OF PARK POSITION, PUMP MAKES ONE "SQUIRT" AND BLADES RETURN TO PARK POSITION AND SHUT "OFF")

REMOVE WASHER PUMP COVER AND CHECK THAT GREEN LEAD IS CONNECTED TO WIPER TERMINAL 1A.

LEAD CONNECTED

LEAD DISCONNECTED

CONNECT LEAD AND RECHECK OPERATION

AFTER WASH CYCLE HAS BEEN STARTED BRIDGE OVER-RIDE SWITCH CONTACTS WITH A SMALL SCREW-DRIVER AND OBSERVE IF UNIT COMPLETES WASH CYCLE.

UNIT COMPLETES WASH CYCLE

UNIT DOES NOT COMPLETE WASH CYCLE

CHECK THAT MOUNTING SCREW IS TIGHT. (14 INCH LBS.). IF SCREW IS TIGHT OVERRIDE SWITCH IS MAL-FUNCTIONING AND MUST BE REPLACED.

CHECK FOR OPEN IN THE GREEN WIRE CIRCUIT.

*Modified Pulse Washer System—Condition Three*

# Windshield Washers

## General Motors

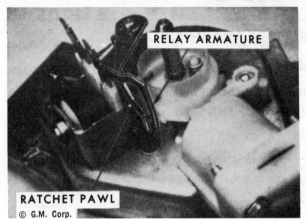

Condition 1—Step 4

Condition 1—Step 6

Condition 3—Step 1

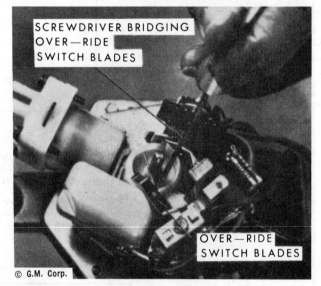

Condition 3—Step 2

| WIPER SWITCH POSITION | | | |
|---|---|---|---|
| **Lo** | **Med** | **Hi** | **Delay** |
| Wiper runs and washes in Lo Speed | Wiper runs and washes in medium Speed | Wiper runs and washes in Hi Speed | Delay operation is over-ridden, wiper runs and and washes in continuous LO speed; completes programmed wash cycle plus four drying wipes and then automatically reverts back to pulse operation. |

## General Motors

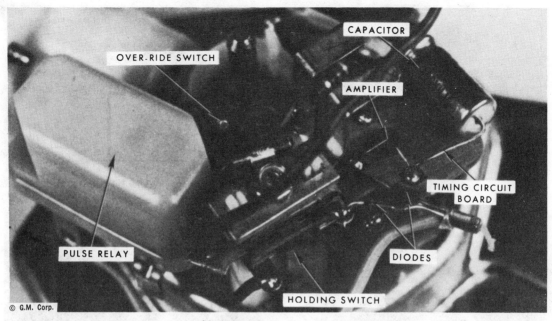

*Modified Pulse Washer Pump Timing Circuit*

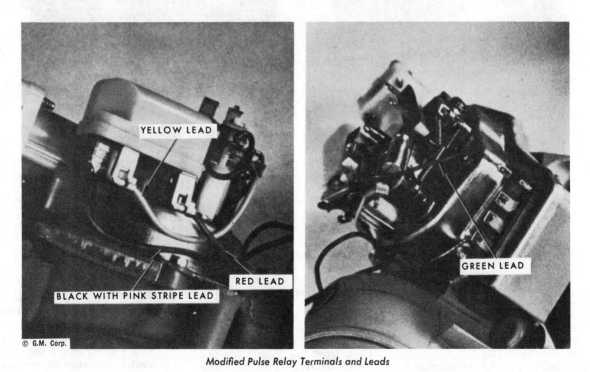

*Modified Pulse Relay Terminals and Leads*

1. Install a locator pin in the pump mechanism.

2. Position the pump assembly on the gear box and install the three attaching screws.

3. Remove the locator pin.
4. Route and attach the red, green, and black with pink stripe leads as shown in the illustration.
5. Position the cover on the washer pump mechanism and snap it over the mounting pin.
6. Reinstall the small plastic plate in terminal six and seven opening.
7. Reinstall the wiring and hoses.

### Washer Pump—Disassembly and Assembly
### Valve Assembly

*NOTE: The valve may be replaced with the wiper unit in the car. The pump cover need not be removed.*

1. Note the position of the hose connections at the valve assembly in relation to the pump housing for

## General Motors

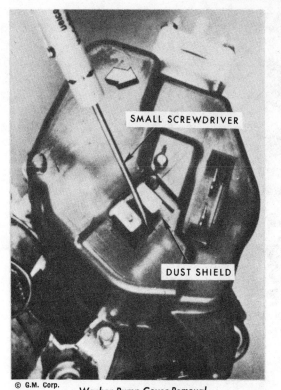

Washer Pump Cover Removal

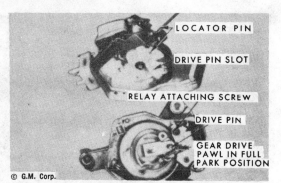

Installing the Washer Pump to the Motor

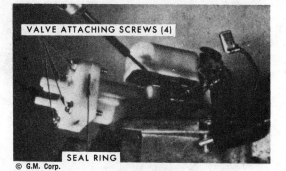

Valve Assembly

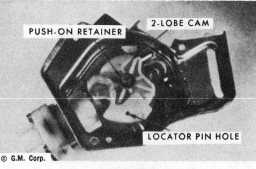

Drive Cam

Ratchet Pawl

reassembly then remove four screws that attach the valve assembly to the housing.

2. Remove the seal ring between the housing and valve body and save for reassembly.

3. To install reverse the removal procedure.

### Drive Cam

1. Remove the push on retainer and slide the cam off on the shaft.

### Timing Device, Holding Switch and Override Switch Assembly; Pulse Relay Assembly

1. Remove the attaching screw and lift the pulse relay, holding switch, timing device, and override switch assembly off the washer frame surface.

2. Disconnect the red and yellow leads from the pulse relay and detach the relay from the locator pins.

3. To reassemble, position the pulse replay on the switch base locator pins, rotate the drive cam counterclockwise to the position shown in the illustration, then install the screw that retains the complete assembly to the washer pump frame.

4. Connect the red and yellow leads to the proper pulse relay terminals.

### Ratchet Gear; Dog Spring; Ratchet Pawl, Relay Armature

1. Remove the attaching screw and lift the pulse relay, timing device, holding switch and override switch assembly off the washer frame surface.

2. Remove the dog spring assembly.

3. Remove the ratchet pawl retaining ring, disconnect the pawl spring and slide the pawl off the cam follower shaft.

4. Disconnect the relay armature spring and remove the armature.

5. Release the ratchet gear spring from the groove in the shaft and slide the ratchet gear off the shaft.

## General Motors

*NOTE: If necessary, move the piston actuator plate slightly to permit the ratchet gear ramp to slide by the tang and bottom on the actuator plate.*

### Piston and Pump Housing

1. Remove the attaching screw and lift the pulse relay, timing device, holding switch and override switch assembly off the washer frame surface.
2. Remove the dog spring assembly.
3. Remove the ratchet pawl retaining ring, disconnect the pawl spring and slide the pawl off the cam follower shaft.
4. Disconnect the relay armature suring and remove the armature.
5. Release the ratchet gear spring from the groove in the shaft and slide the ratchet gear off the shaft.
6. Release the pump housing from the sheet metal base by pulling it toward the valve assembly until the grooves in the plastic pump housing clear the base. Detach the assembly from the cam follower pin.

### Pump Relay and Terminal Board

1. Remove the Drive Cam.
   (a) Remove the push on retainer and slide the cam off the shaft.
2. Remove the timing device, holding switch and override switch assembly, and pulse relay assembly.
   (a) Remove the attaching screw and lift the pulse relay, timing device, holding switch and override switch assembly off the washer frame surface.
   (b) Disconnect the red and yellow leads from the pulse relay and the relay from the locator pins.
3. Remove the ratchet pawl retaining ring, disconnect the pawl spring and slide the pawl off the cam follower shaft.
4. Disconnect the relay armature spring and remove the armature.
5. Bend or chisel off the four bent over tabs that hold the coil mounting bracket to the base.

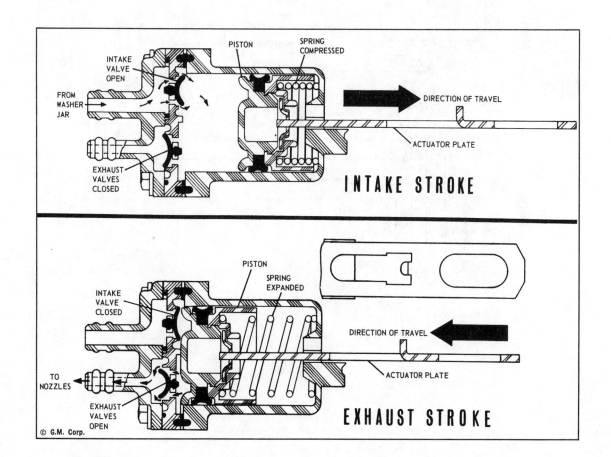

## American Motors

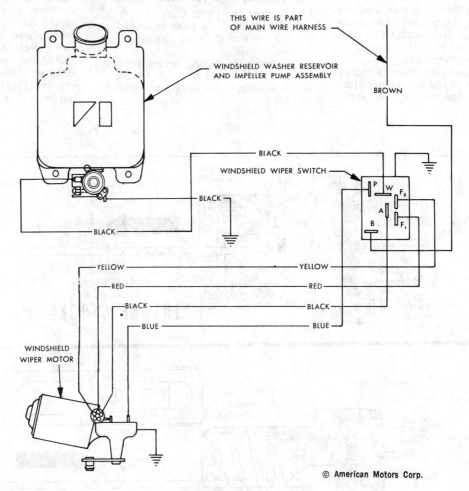

THIS WIRE IS PART
OF MAIN WIRE HARNESS

BROWN

WINDSHIELD WASHER RESERVOIR
AND IMPELLER PUMP ASSEMBLY

BLACK

WINDSHIELD WIPER SWITCH

P   W   F₂
A
B   F₁

BLACK

BLACK

YELLOW            YELLOW
RED               RED
BLACK             BLACK
BLUE              BLUE

WINDSHIELD
WIPER MOTOR

© American Motors Corp.

*1968-72*

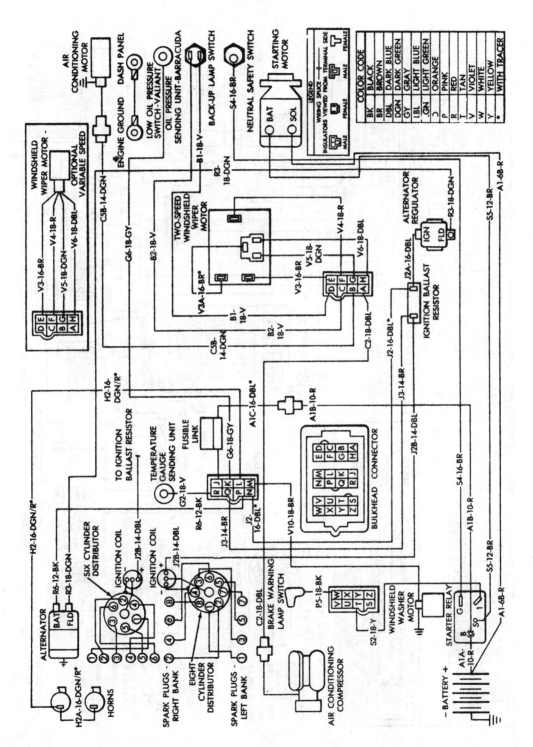

1968-69

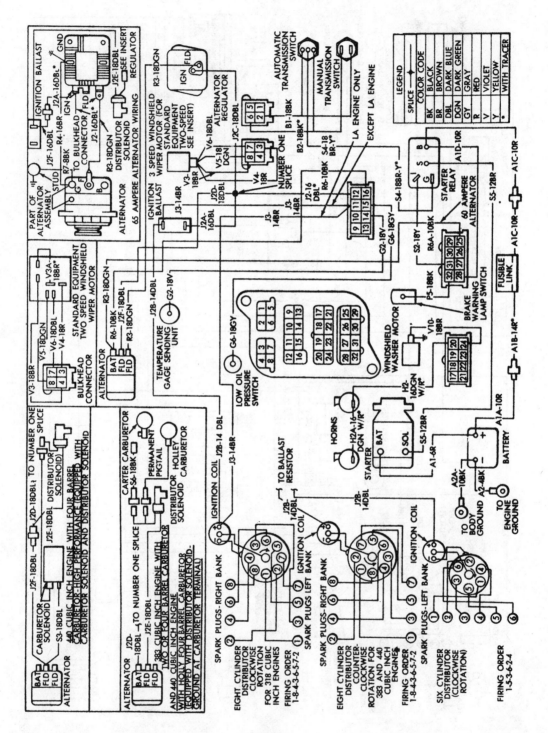

1970-73

## Chrysler Corporation

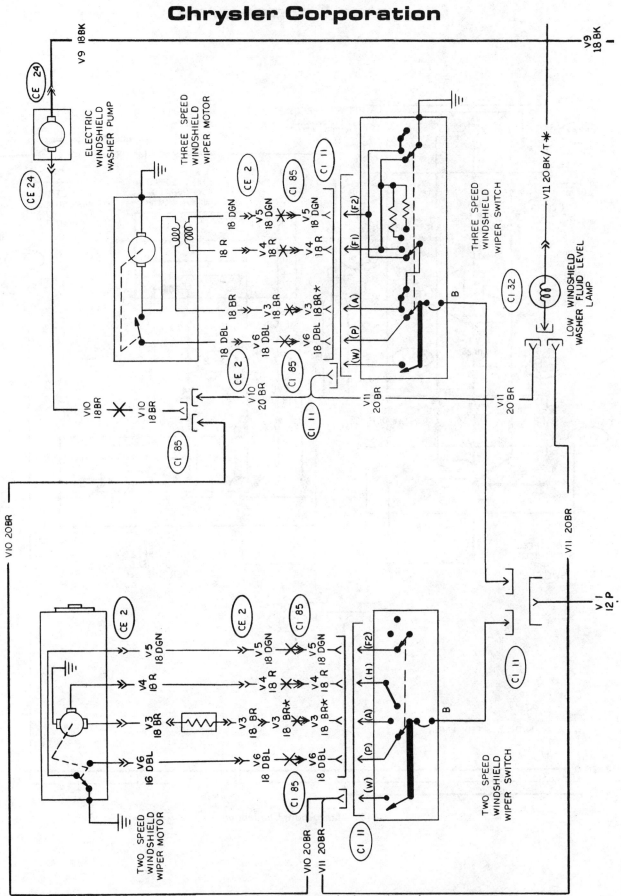

*1974-75—Chrysler, Imperial, Plymouth, Dodge*

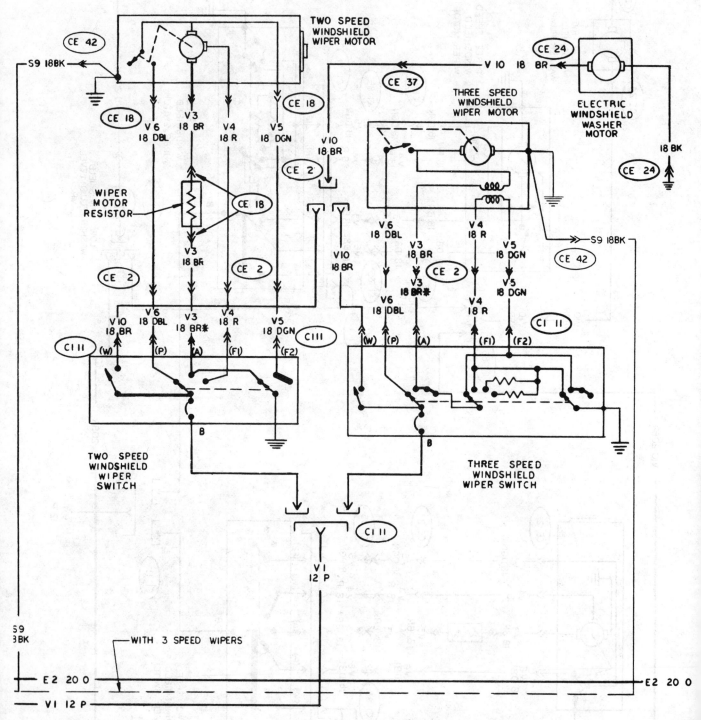

1974-75—Barracuda, Challenger

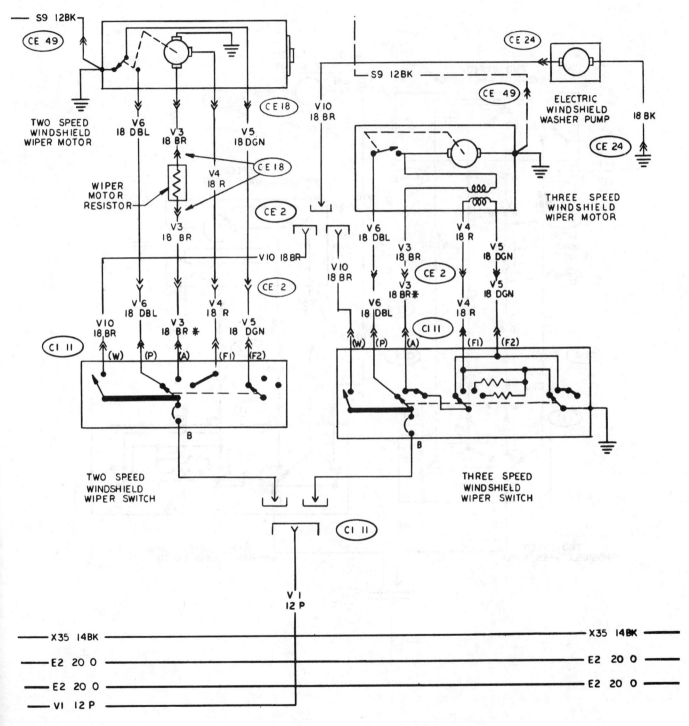

*1974-75—Satellite, Coronet, Charger*

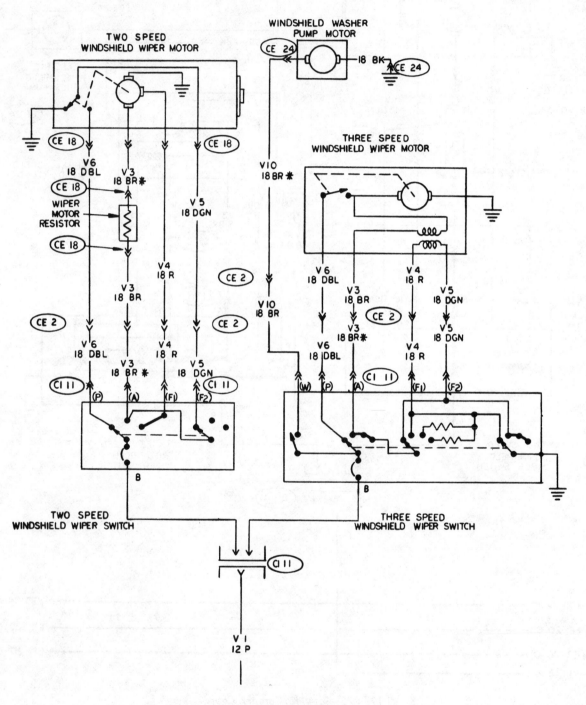

*1974-75—Valiant, Dart*

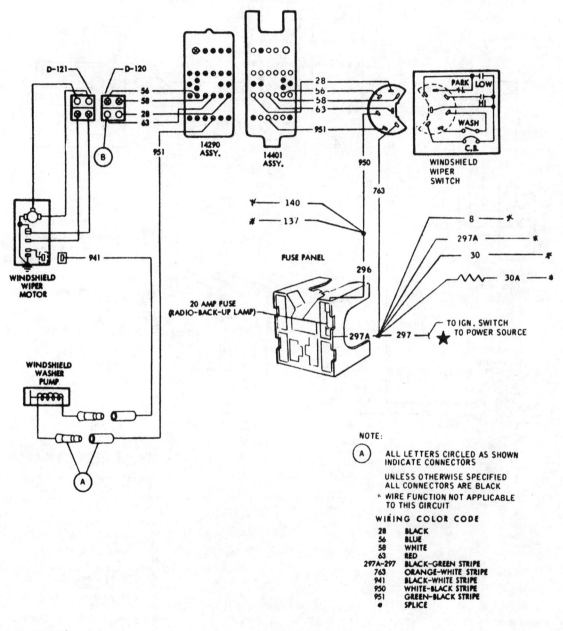

NOTE:

(A) ALL LETTERS CIRCLED AS SHOWN
INDICATE CONNECTORS

UNLESS OTHERWISE SPECIFIED
ALL CONNECTORS ARE BLACK

* WIRE FUNCTION NOT APPLICABLE
TO THIS CIRCUIT

WIRING COLOR CODE

| | |
|---|---|
| 28 | BLACK |
| 56 | BLUE |
| 58 | WHITE |
| 63 | RED |
| 297A-297 | BLACK-GREEN STRIPE |
| 763 | ORANGE-WHITE STRIPE |
| 941 | BLACK-WHITE STRIPE |
| 950 | WHITE-BLACK STRIPE |
| 951 | GREEN-BLACK STRIPE |
| ● | SPLICE |

*1968-69—Falcon*

## Ford Motor Company

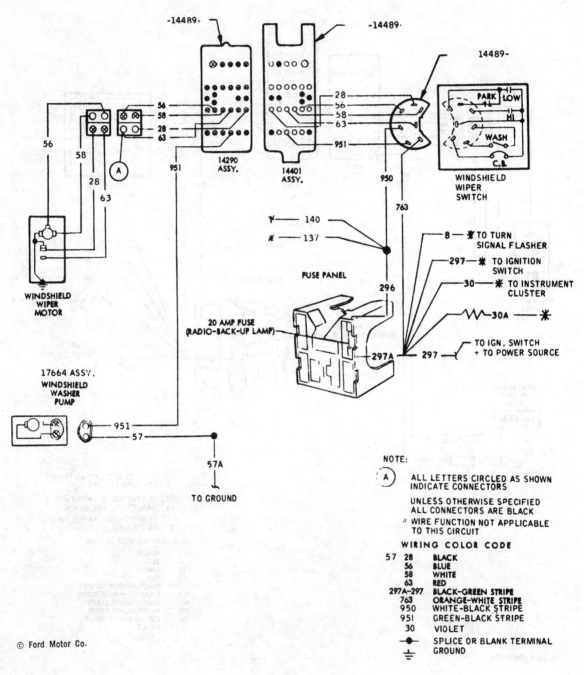

NOTE:

(A) ALL LETTERS CIRCLED AS SHOWN INDICATE CONNECTORS

UNLESS OTHERWISE SPECIFIED ALL CONNECTORS ARE BLACK

✳ WIRE FUNCTION NOT APPLICABLE TO THIS CIRCUIT

**WIRING COLOR CODE**

| 57 | 28 | BLACK |
|----|----|-------|
| | 56 | BLUE |
| | 58 | WHITE |
| | 63 | RED |
| | 297A-297 | BLACK-GREEN STRIPE |
| | 763 | ORANGE-WHITE STRIPE |
| | 950 | WHITE-BLACK STRIPE |
| | 951 | GREEN-BLACK STRIPE |
| | 30 | VIOLET |
| | ● | SPLICE OR BLANK TERMINAL |
| | ⏚ | GROUND |

© Ford Motor Co.

*1970—Falcon*

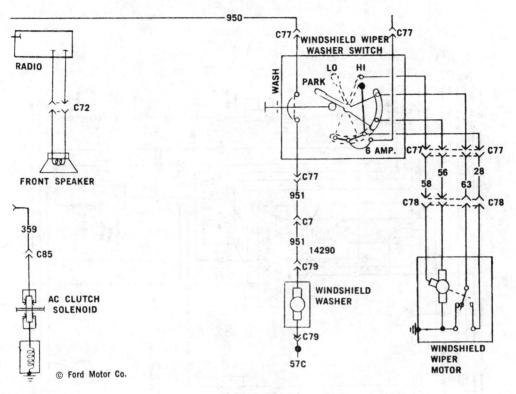

1970—Maverick

© Ford Motor Co.

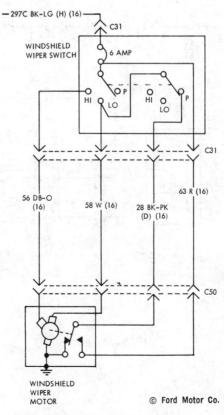

1971-72—Maverick

© Ford Motor Co.

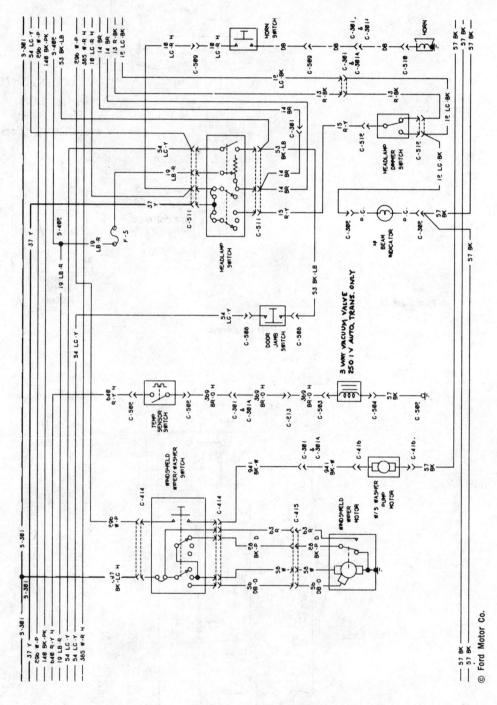

*1973—Maverick*

## Ford Motor Company

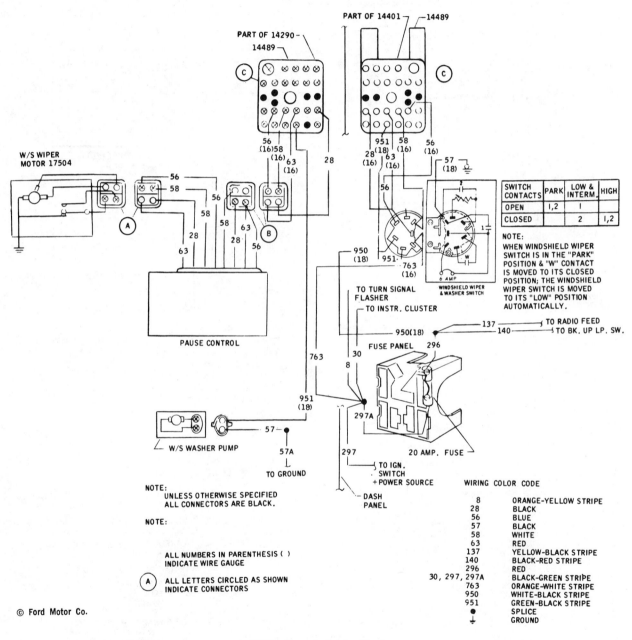

PART OF 14290 —
14489

PART OF 14401 — 14489

W/S WIPER
MOTOR 17504

PAUSE CONTROL

W/S WASHER PUMP

57A

TO GROUND

| SWITCH CONTACTS | PARK | LOW & INTERM. | HIGH |
|---|---|---|---|
| OPEN | 1,2 | 1 | |
| CLOSED | | 2 | 1,2 |

NOTE:
WHEN WINDSHIELD WIPER SWITCH IS IN THE "PARK" POSITION & "W" CONTACT IS MOVED TO ITS CLOSED POSITION; THE WINDSHIELD WIPER SWITCH IS MOVED TO ITS "LOW" POSITION AUTOMATICALLY.

WINDSHIELD WIPER & WASHER SWITCH

6 AMP.

TO TURN SIGNAL FLASHER

TO INSTR. CLUSTER

FUSE PANEL

137 — TO RADIO FEED
140 — TO BK. UP LP. SW.

20 AMP. FUSE

TO IGN. SWITCH
+ POWER SOURCE

DASH PANEL

NOTE:
UNLESS OTHERWISE SPECIFIED ALL CONNECTORS ARE BLACK.

NOTE:

ALL NUMBERS IN PARENTHESIS ( ) INDICATE WIRE GAUGE

(A) ALL LETTERS CIRCLED AS SHOWN INDICATE CONNECTORS

© Ford Motor Co.

WIRING COLOR CODE

| | |
|---|---|
| 8 | ORANGE-YELLOW STRIPE |
| 28 | BLACK |
| 56 | BLUE |
| 57 | BLACK |
| 58 | WHITE |
| 63 | RED |
| 137 | YELLOW-BLACK STRIPE |
| 140 | BLACK-RED STRIPE |
| 296 | RED |
| 30, 297, 297A | BLACK-GREEN STRIPE |
| 763 | ORANGE-WHITE STRIPE |
| 950 | WHITE-BLACK STRIPE |
| 951 | GREEN-BLACK STRIPE |
| ● | SPLICE |
| ⏚ | GROUND |

*1970—Comet—Intermittent*

## Ford Motor Company

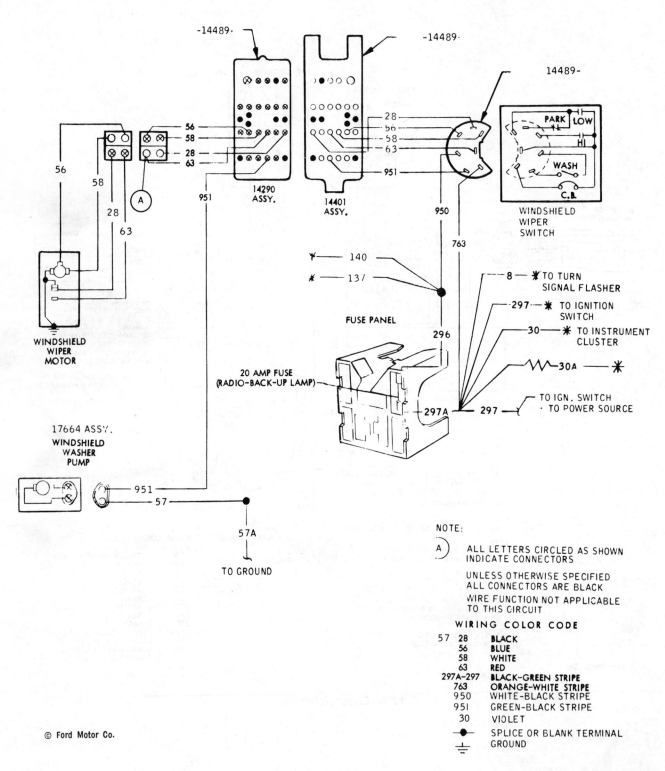

-14489-

-14489·

14489-

| | PARK | LOW |
| HI |
| WASH |
| C.B. |

**WINDSHIELD WIPER SWITCH**

56
58
28
63

56
58
63
951

56
58
28
63

(A)

951

14290 ASSY.

14401 ASSY.

950

763

Y — 140
X — 137

**FUSE PANEL**

296

8 — X TO TURN SIGNAL FLASHER

297 — X TO IGNITION SWITCH

30 — X TO INSTRUMENT CLUSTER

30A — X

**WINDSHIELD WIPER MOTOR**

20 AMP FUSE
(RADIO-BACK-UP LAMP)

297A

297

TO IGN. SWITCH
TO POWER SOURCE

**17664 ASSY.**
**WINDSHIELD WASHER PUMP**

951
57

57A

**TO GROUND**

NOTE:

(A) ALL LETTERS CIRCLED AS SHOWN INDICATE CONNECTORS

UNLESS OTHERWISE SPECIFIED ALL CONNECTORS ARE BLACK

✱ WIRE FUNCTION NOT APPLICABLE TO THIS CIRCUIT

**WIRING COLOR CODE**

| | |
|---|---|
| 57 28 | BLACK |
| 56 | BLUE |
| 58 | WHITE |
| 63 | RED |
| 297A-297 | BLACK-GREEN STRIPE |
| 763 | ORANGE-WHITE STRIPE |
| 950 | WHITE-BLACK STRIPE |
| 951 | GREEN-BLACK STRIPE |
| 30 | VIOLET |
| ● | SPLICE OR BLANK TERMINAL |
| ⏚ | GROUND |

© Ford Motor Co.

*1970—Comet—Two Speed*

# Ford Motor Company

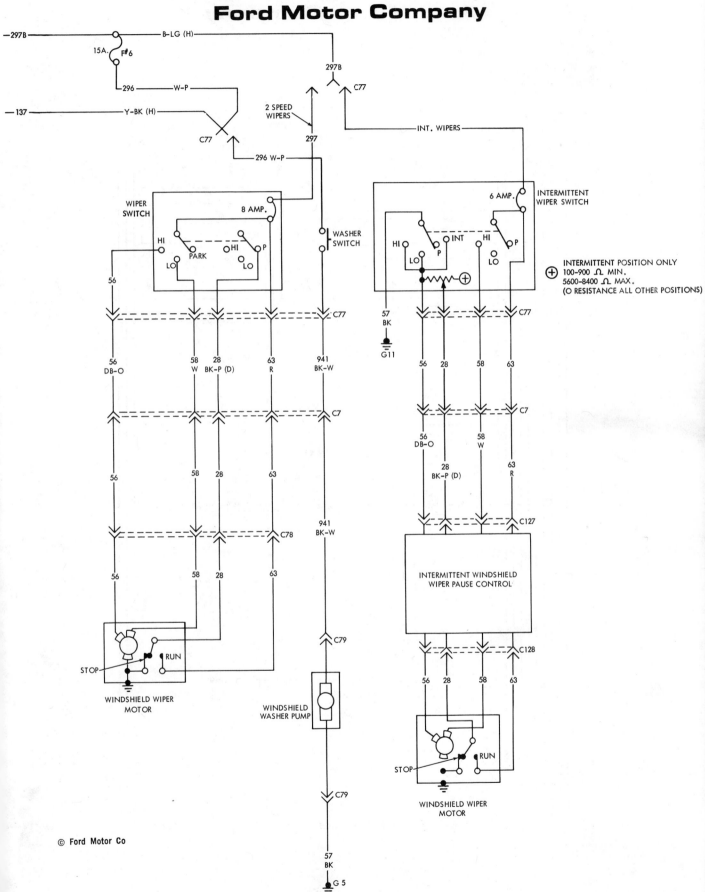

© Ford Motor Co

1971-72—Comet

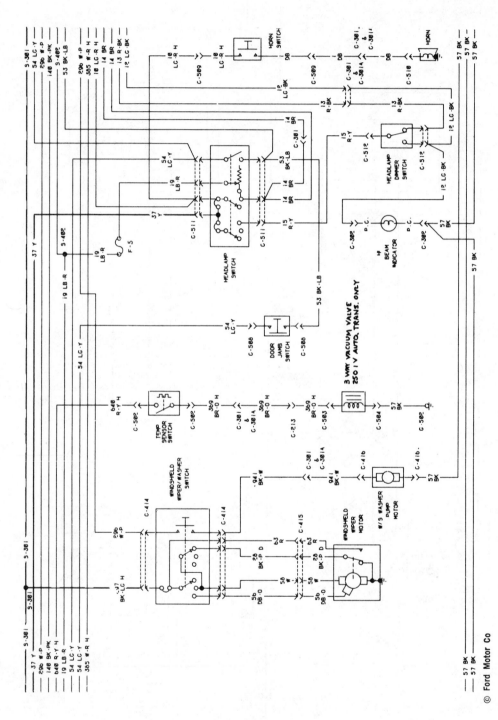

1973—Comet

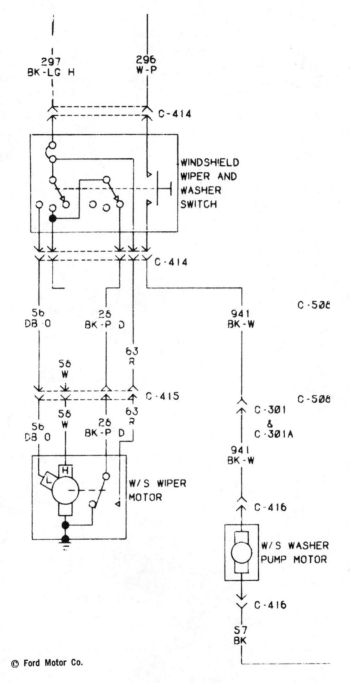

© Ford Motor Co.

*1974-75—Comet*

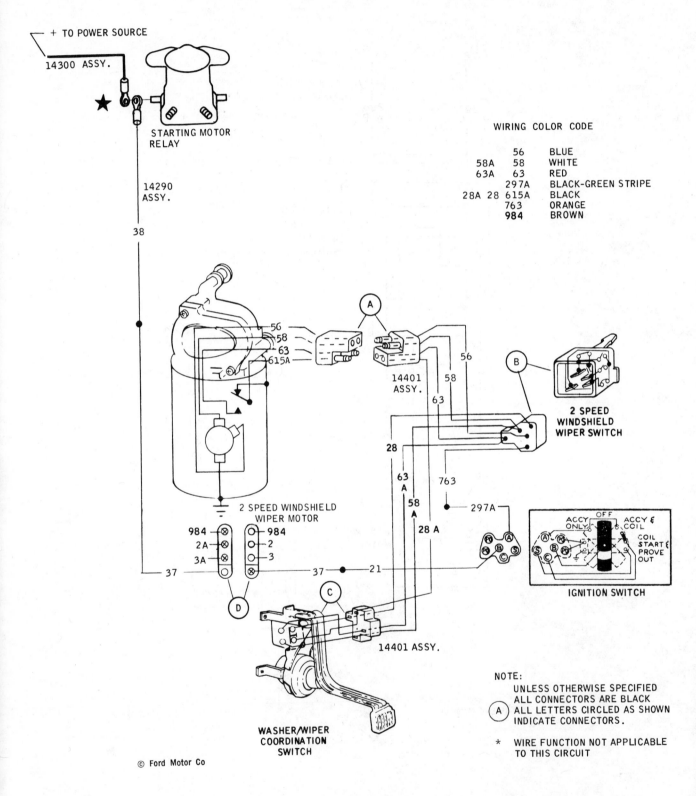

+ TO POWER SOURCE

14300 ASSY.

★

STARTING MOTOR
RELAY

14290
ASSY.

38

WIRING COLOR CODE

| | | |
|---|---|---|
| | 56 | BLUE |
| 58A | 58 | WHITE |
| 63A | 63 | RED |
| | 297A | BLACK-GREEN STRIPE |
| 28A 28 | 615A | BLACK |
| | 763 | ORANGE |
| | 984 | BROWN |

56
58
63
615A

14401
ASSY.

56
58
63

A

B

2 SPEED
WINDSHIELD
WIPER SWITCH

28

63
A

58
A

28 A

763

297A

ACCY.
ONLY
OFF
ACCY &
COIL

COIL
START &
PROVE
OUT

IGNITION SWITCH

2 SPEED WINDSHIELD
WIPER MOTOR

984 — ⊗       ⊗ — 984
2A — ⊗        ⊗ — 2
3A — ⊗        ⊗ — 3

37              37      21

D

C

14401 ASSY.

WASHER/WIPER
COORDINATION
SWITCH

© Ford Motor Co

NOTE:
  UNLESS OTHERWISE SPECIFIED
  ALL CONNECTORS ARE BLACK
Ⓐ ALL LETTERS CIRCLED AS SHOWN
  INDICATE CONNECTORS.

*  WIRE FUNCTION NOT APPLICABLE
   TO THIS CIRCUIT

*1968—Mustang*

# Ford Motor Company

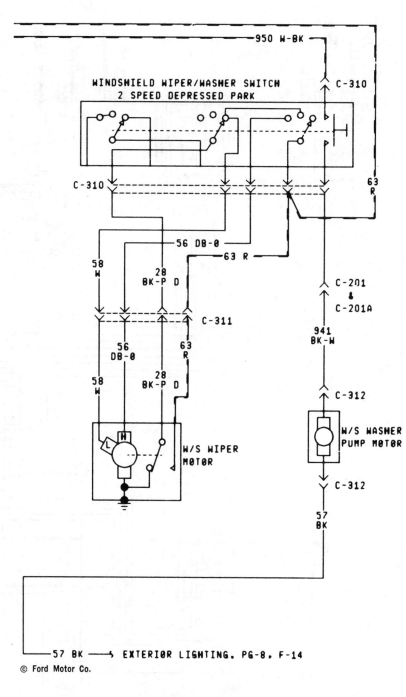

1970—Mustang

## Ford Motor Company

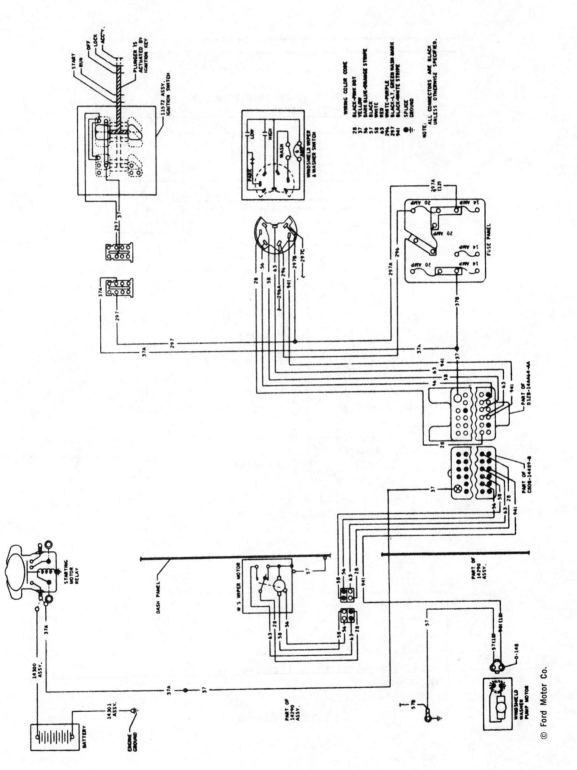

*1971—Mustang—Exc. Intermittent*

# Ford Motor Company

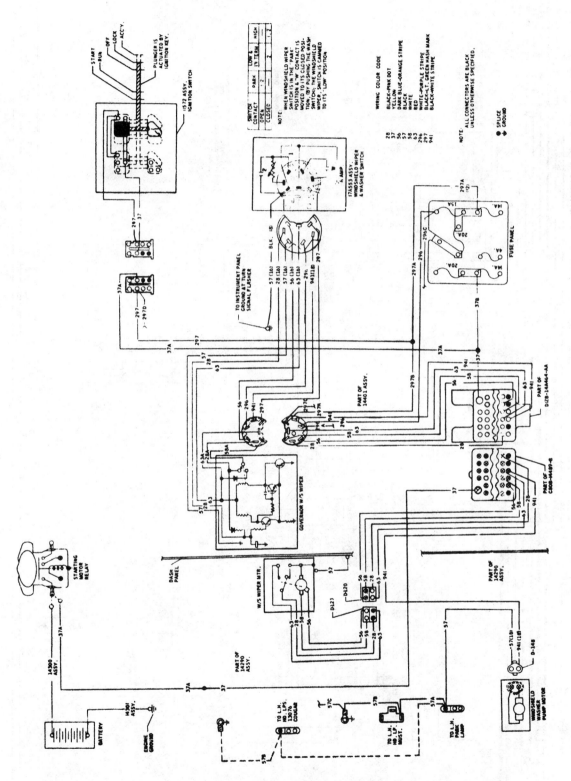

*1971—Mustang—Intermittent*

© Ford Motor Co.

## Ford Motor Company

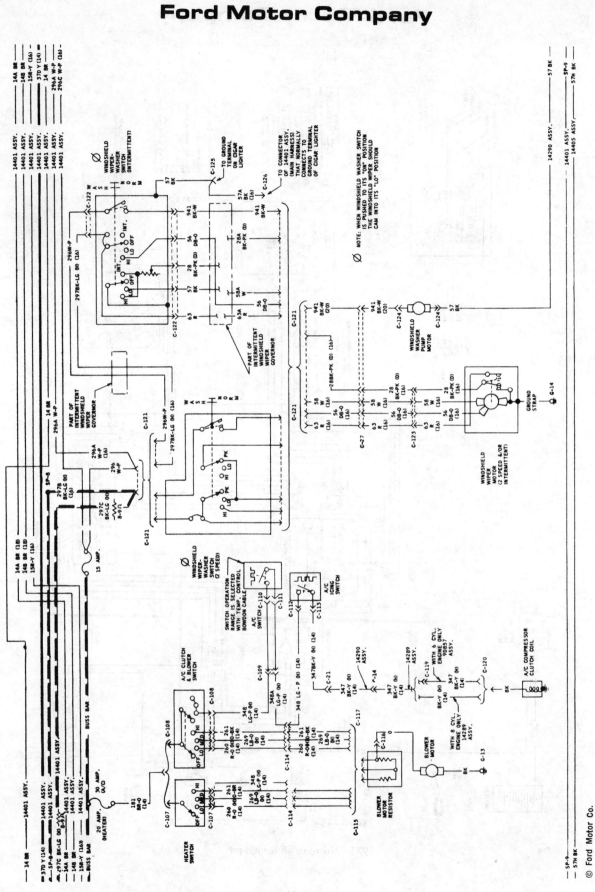

*1972—Mustang*

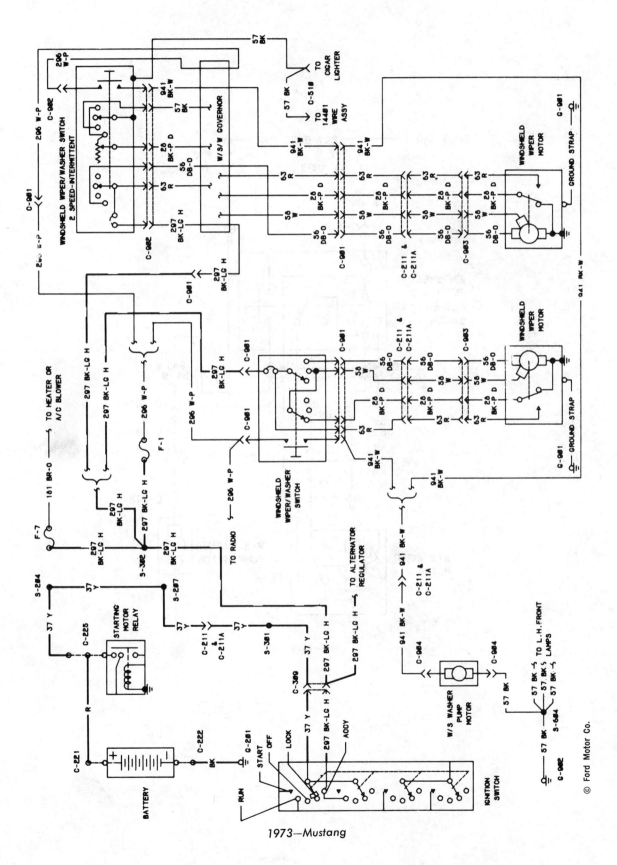

*1973—Mustang*

© Ford Motor Co.

# Ford Motor Company

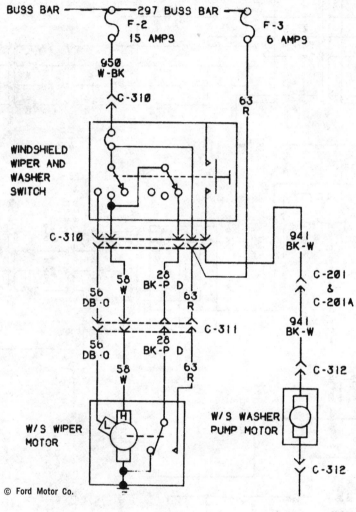

BUSS BAR — 297 BUSS BAR

F-2
15 AMPS

F-3
6 AMPS

950
W-BK

C-310

63
R

WINDSHIELD
WIPER AND
WASHER
SWITCH

C-310

941
BK-W

56
DB·O

58
W

28
BK-P D

63
R

C-201
&
C-201A

941
BK-W

56
DB·O

58
W

28
BK-P D

63
R

C-311

C-312

W/S WIPER
MOTOR

W/S WASHER
PUMP MOTOR

C-312

© Ford Motor Co.

*1974—Mustang*

# Ford Motor Company

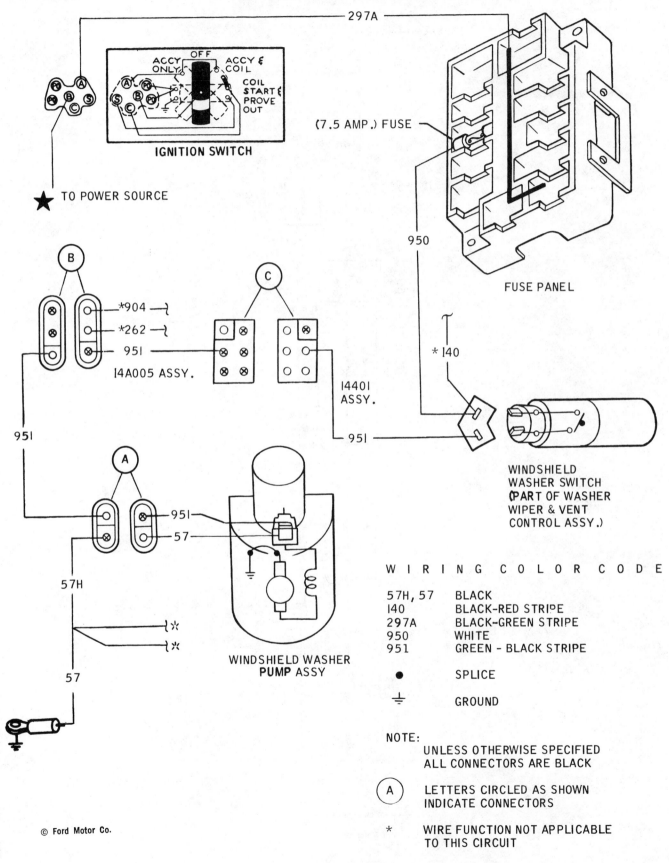

**297A**

ACCY
ONLY

OFF

ACCY &
COIL

COIL
START &
PROVE
OUT

**IGNITION SWITCH**

★ TO POWER SOURCE

(7.5 AMP.) FUSE

950

FUSE PANEL

B

*904
*262
951

14A005 ASSY.

C

14401
ASSY.

951

* 140

951

WINDSHIELD
WASHER SWITCH
(PART OF WASHER
WIPER & VENT
CONTROL ASSY.)

951

A

951
57

57H

WINDSHIELD WASHER
**PUMP** ASSY

57

W I R I N G   C O L O R   C O D E

| | |
|---|---|
| 57H, 57 | BLACK |
| 140 | BLACK-RED STRIPE |
| 297A | BLACK-GREEN STRIPE |
| 950 | WHITE |
| 951 | GREEN - BLACK STRIPE |
| ● | SPLICE |
| ⏚ | GROUND |

NOTE:

UNLESS OTHERWISE SPECIFIED
ALL CONNECTORS ARE BLACK

A   LETTERS CIRCLED AS SHOWN
INDICATE CONNECTORS

*   WIRE FUNCTION NOT APPLICABLE
TO THIS CIRCUIT

© Ford Motor Co.

*1968—Thunderbird*

# Ford Motor Company

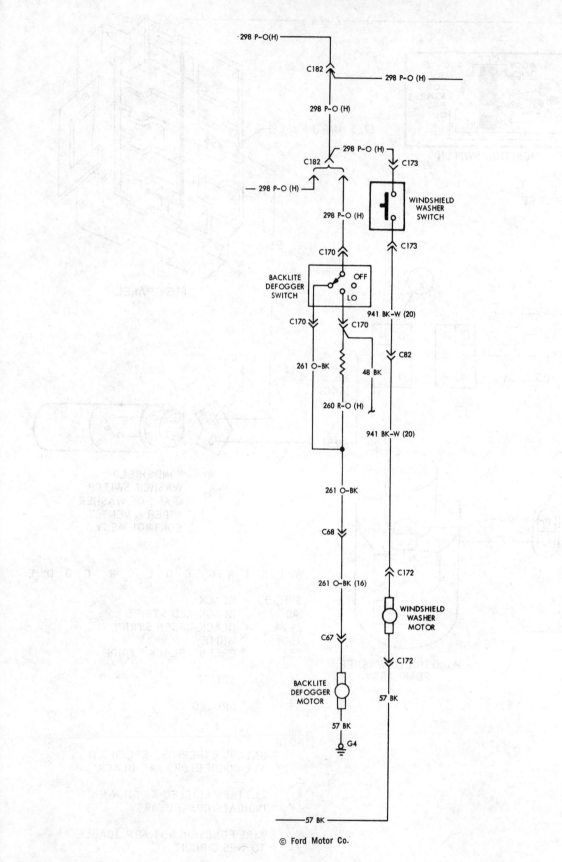

298 P-O(H)

C182

298 P-O (H)

298 P-O (H)

C182    298 P-O (H)    C173

— 298 P-O (H)

WINDSHIELD WASHER SWITCH

298 P-O (H)

C170    C173

BACKLITE DEFOGGER SWITCH    OFF    LO

C170    C170    941 BK-W (20)

261 O-BK    48 BK    C82

260 R-O (H)

941 BK-W (20)

261 O-BK

C68

261 O-BK (16)    C172

WINDSHIELD WASHER MOTOR

C67

BACKLITE DEFOGGER MOTOR    57 BK    C172

57 BK    57 BK

G4

— 57 BK

© Ford Motor Co.

*1971—Thunderbird*

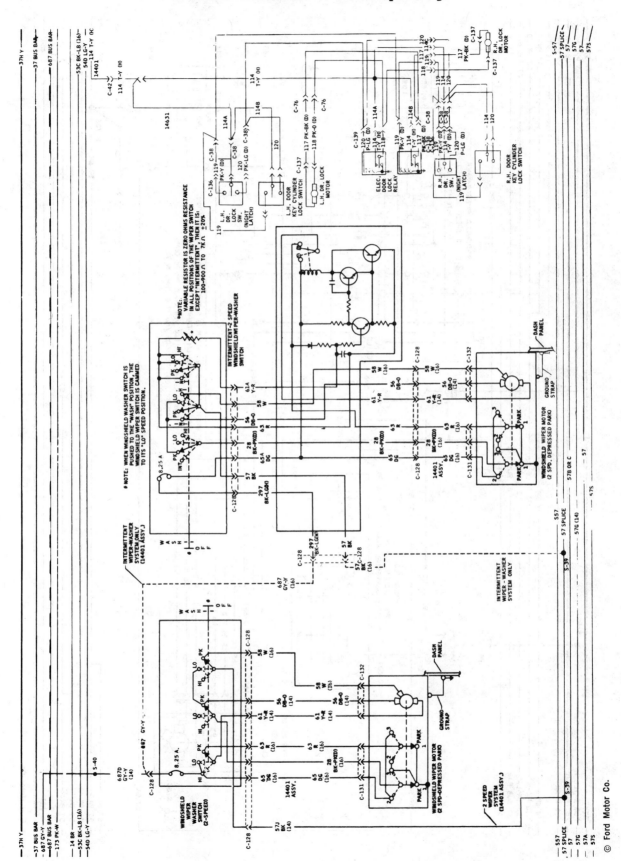

1972—Thunderbird

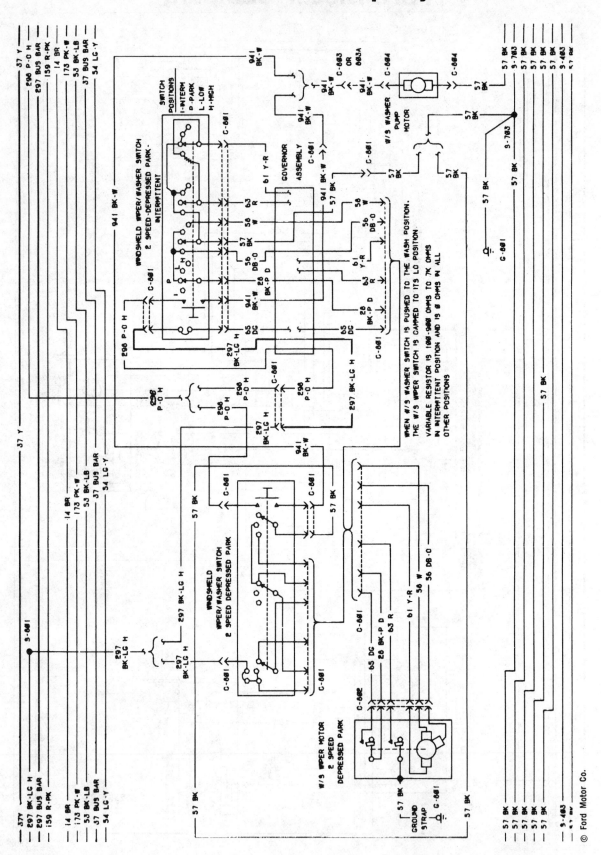

WHEN W/S WASHER SWITCH IS PUSHED TO THE WASH POSITION.
THE W/S WIPER SWITCH IS CAMMED TO ITS LO POSITION
VARIABLE RESISTOR IS 1000-9000 OHMS TO 7K OHMS
IN INTERMITTENT POSITION AND IS 0 OHMS IN ALL
OTHER POSITIONS

© Ford Motor Co.

*1973—Thunderbird*

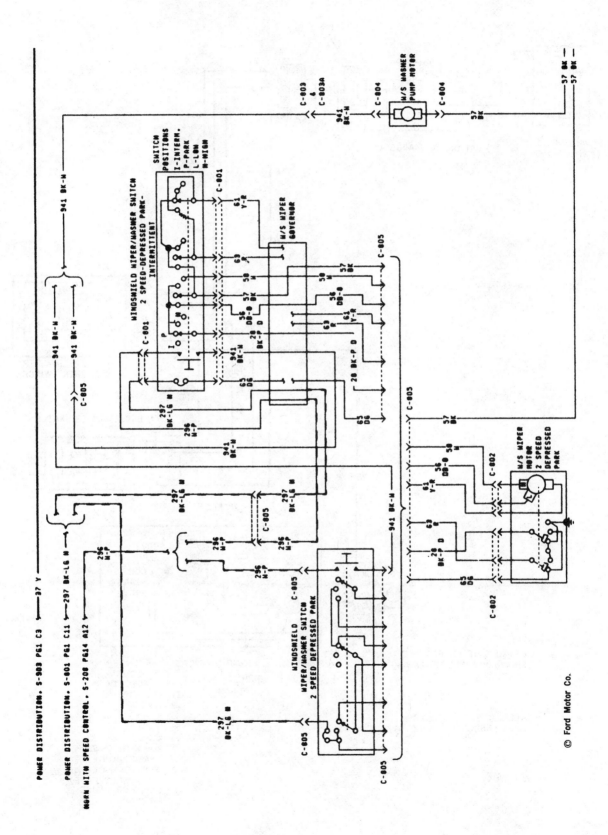

*1974-75—Thunderbird, Mark IV Lincoln*

## Ford Motor Company

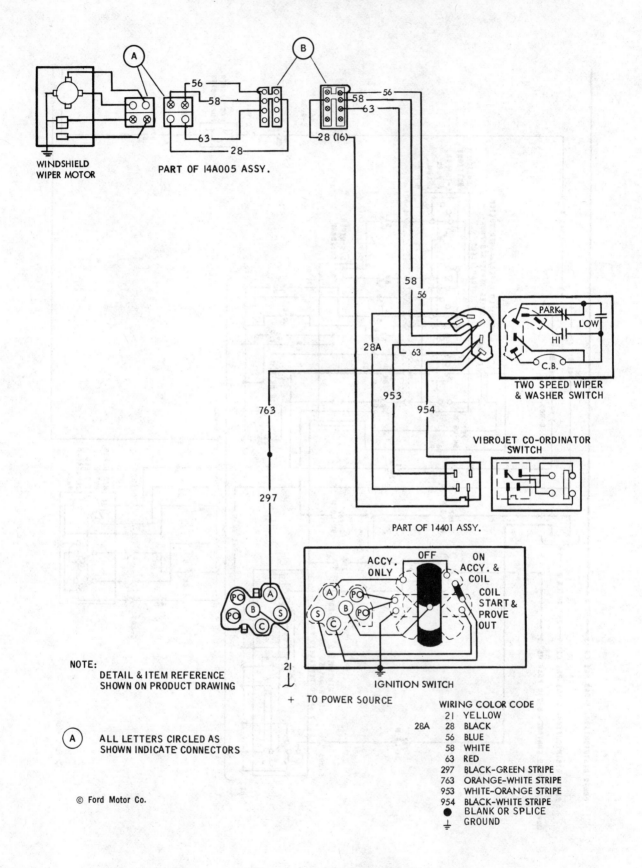

WINDSHIELD
WIPER MOTOR

PART OF 14A005 ASSY.

TWO SPEED WIPER
& WASHER SWITCH

VIBROJET CO-ORDINATOR
SWITCH

PART OF 14401 ASSY.

IGNITION SWITCH

TO POWER SOURCE

NOTE:
DETAIL & ITEM REFERENCE
SHOWN ON PRODUCT DRAWING

(A) ALL LETTERS CIRCLED AS
SHOWN INDICATE CONNECTORS

© Ford Motor Co.

WIRING COLOR CODE
| | | |
|---|---|---|
| | 21 | YELLOW |
| 28A | 28 | BLACK |
| | 56 | BLUE |
| | 58 | WHITE |
| | 63 | RED |
| | 297 | BLACK-GREEN STRIPE |
| | 763 | ORANGE-WHITE STRIPE |
| | 953 | WHITE-ORANGE STRIPE |
| | 954 | BLACK-WHITE STRIPE |
| ● | | BLANK OR SPLICE |
| ⏚ | | GROUND |

*1968—Mercury—Exc. Intermittent*

## Ford Motor Company

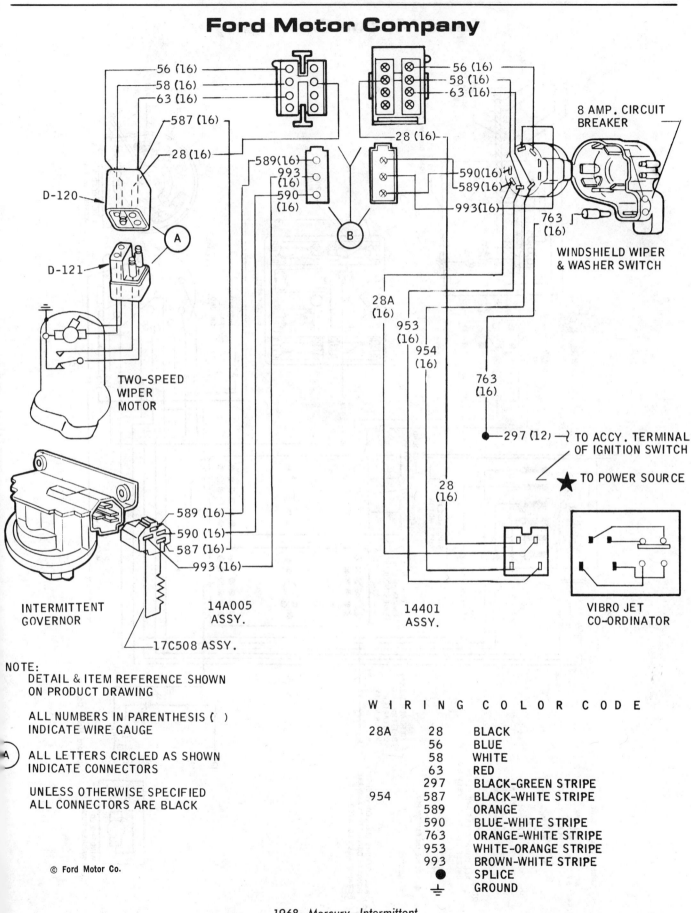

56 (16)
58 (16)
63 (16)
587 (16)
28 (16)

56 (16)
58 (16)
63 (16)

28 (16)

8 AMP. CIRCUIT
BREAKER

D-120

589(16)
993 (16)
590 (16)

590(16)
589(16)
993(16)

A

B

D-121

763 (16)

WINDSHIELD WIPER
& WASHER SWITCH

TWO-SPEED
WIPER
MOTOR

28A (16)

953 (16)

954 (16)

763 (16)

297 (12) — TO ACCY. TERMINAL
OF IGNITION SWITCH

★ TO POWER SOURCE

28 (16)

589 (16)
590 (16)
587 (16)
993 (16)

INTERMITTENT
GOVERNOR

14A005
ASSY.

14401
ASSY.

VIBRO JET
CO-ORDINATOR

17C508 ASSY.

NOTE:
   DETAIL & ITEM REFERENCE SHOWN
   ON PRODUCT DRAWING

   ALL NUMBERS IN PARENTHESIS ( )
   INDICATE WIRE GAUGE

Ⓐ  ALL LETTERS CIRCLED AS SHOWN
   INDICATE CONNECTORS

   UNLESS OTHERWISE SPECIFIED
   ALL CONNECTORS ARE BLACK

© Ford Motor Co.

### W I R I N G   C O L O R   C O D E

| | | |
|---|---|---|
| 28A | 28 | BLACK |
| | 56 | BLUE |
| | 58 | WHITE |
| | 63 | RED |
| | 297 | BLACK-GREEN STRIPE |
| 954 | 587 | BLACK-WHITE STRIPE |
| | 589 | ORANGE |
| | 590 | BLUE-WHITE STRIPE |
| | 763 | ORANGE-WHITE STRIPE |
| | 953 | WHITE-ORANGE STRIPE |
| | 993 | BROWN-WHITE STRIPE |
| | ● | SPLICE |
| | ⏚ | GROUND |

*1968—Mercury—Intermittent*

## Ford Motor Company

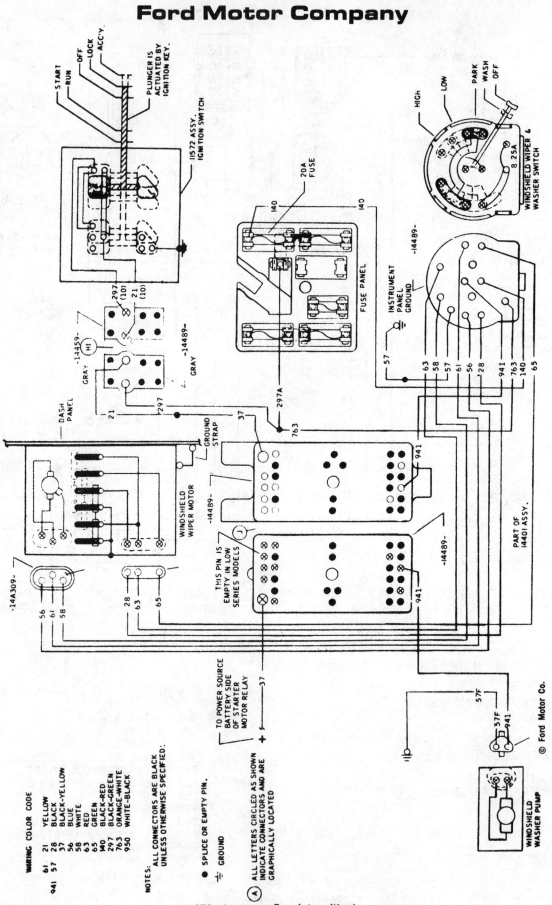

*1970—Mercury—Exc. Intermittent*

# Ford Motor Company

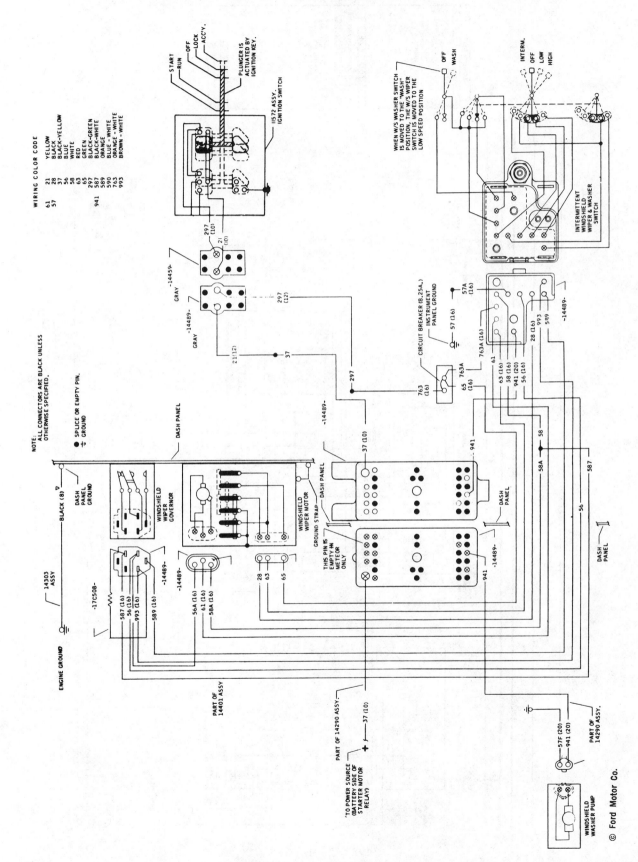

*1970—Mercury—Intermittent*

## Ford Motor Company

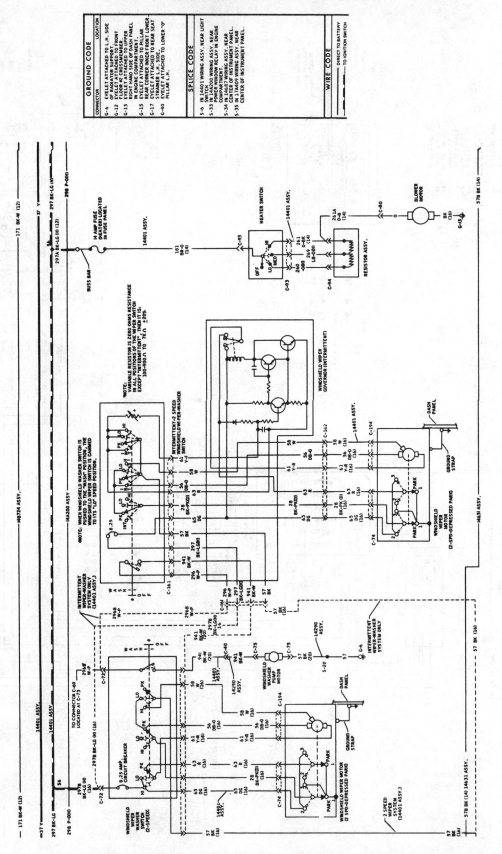

*1971-72—Mercury*

## Ford Motor Company

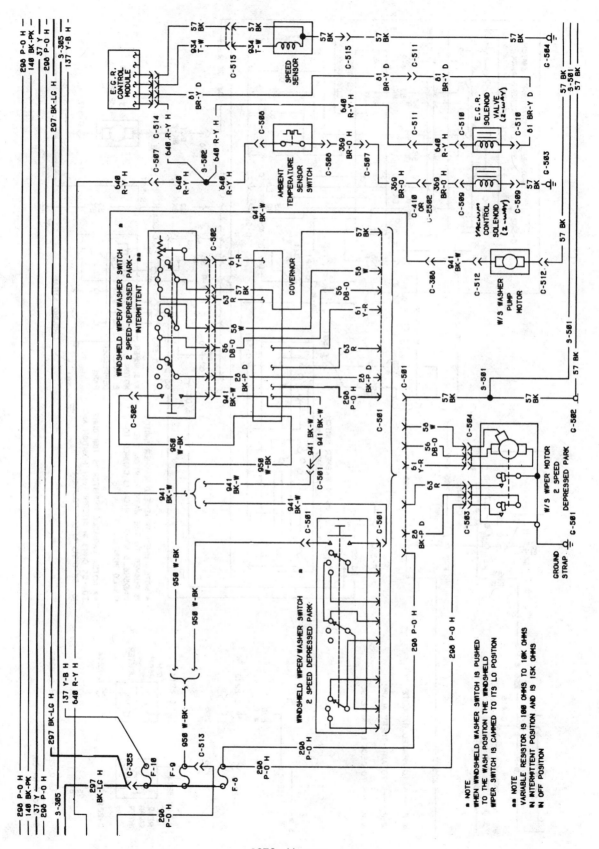

*1973—Mercury*

## Ford Motor Company

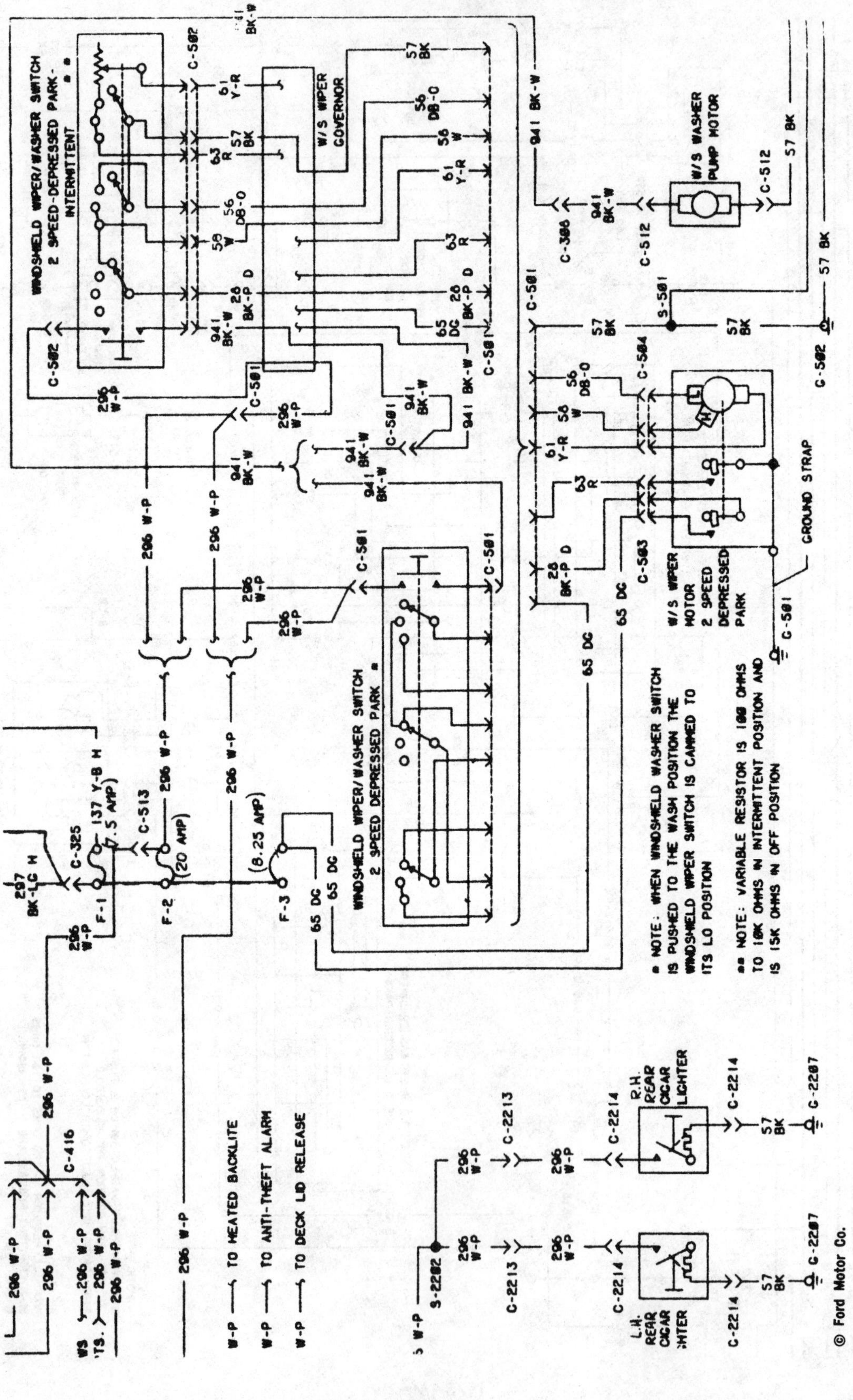

## Ford Motor Company

WASHER
PUMP
MOTOR

951
57A

A
14289
ASSY

14289
ASSY

14A005
ASSY

951

B

951

TO BATTERY
TO POWER SOURCE

STARTING
MOTOR RELAY

FUSE LINK

37

JUNCTION
BLOCK

14289
ASSY

14A005
ASSY

37

C

37A

37B          21

951

951

GREEN          GREEN

D

14A005
ASSY

14A312
ASSY

951

E

950

WINDSHIELD
WIPER/WASHER
SWITCH

FUSE PANEL

297          297A

FUSE
15 AMP

140A          950

ORANGE

F

ORANGE

297

14401
ASSY

14A312
ASSY

★ POWER SOURCE

21 — TO BATTERY TERMINAL OF
IGN. SW.

★ POWER SOURCE

297 — TO BATTERY TERMINAL
OF IGN. SW.

**WIRING COLOR CODE**

| 21 | YELLOW |
|---|---|
| 37 | BLACK-YELLOW STRIPE |
| 57 | BLACK |
| 140 | BLACK-RED STRIPE |
| 297 | BLACK-GREEN STRIPE |
| 950 | WHITE-BLACK STRIPE |
| 951 | GREEN-BLACK STRIPE |

NOTE:

A   ALL LETTERS CIRCLED AS
SHOWN INDICATES CONNECTORS.

● SPLICE OR BLANK TERMINAL

⏚ GROUND

UNLESS OTHERWISE SPECIFIED
ALL CONNECTORS ARE BLACK

© Ford Motor Co.

*1968—Lincoln Continental*

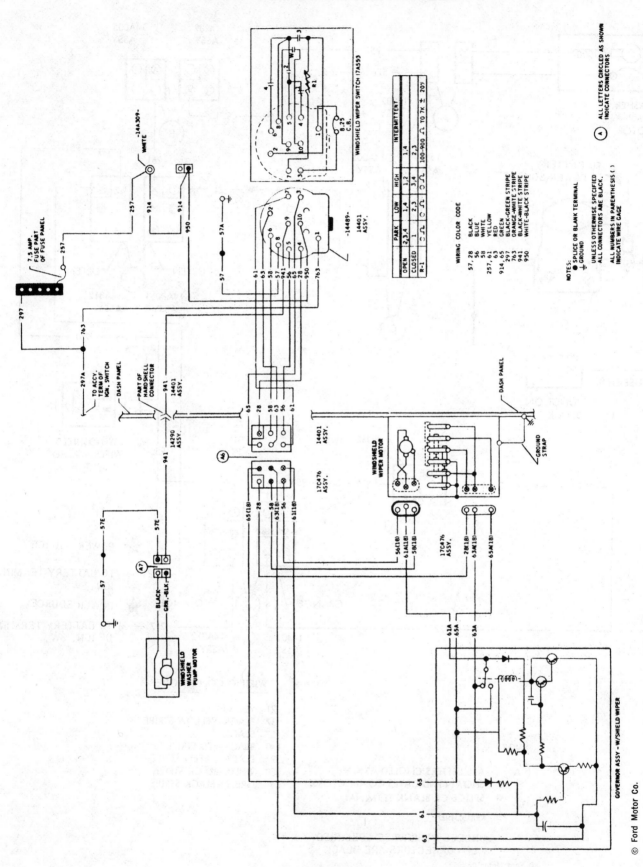

*1970—Lincoln Continental*

## Ford Motor Company

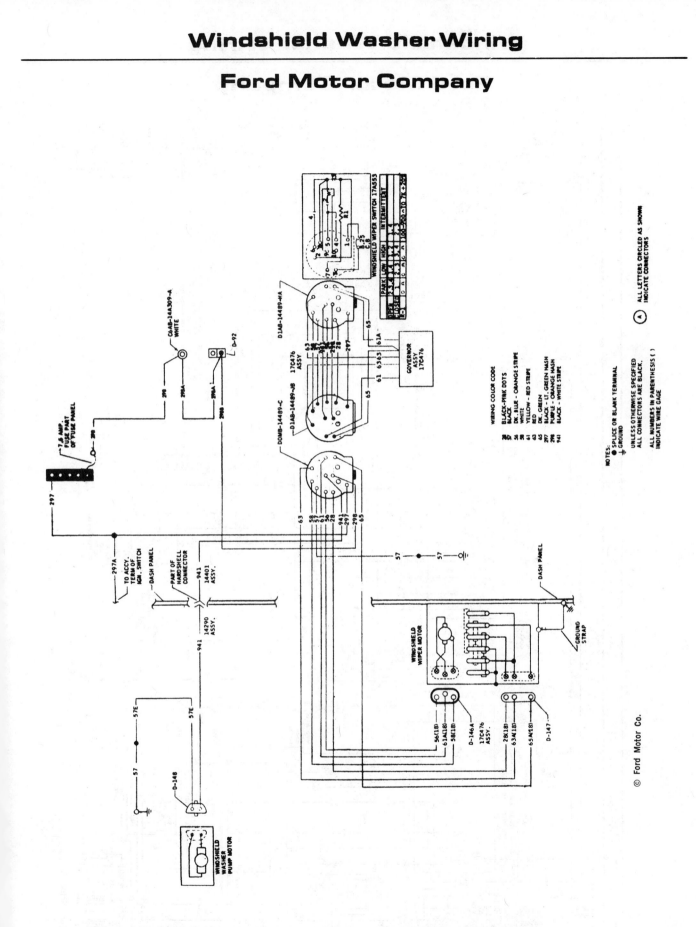

© Ford Motor Co.

*1971—Lincoln Continental*

## Ford Motor Company

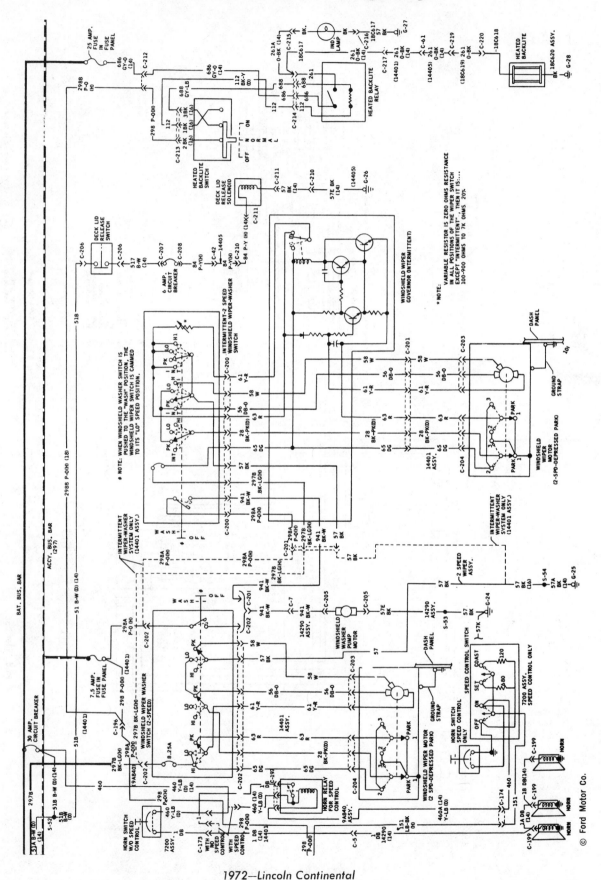

1972—Lincoln Continental

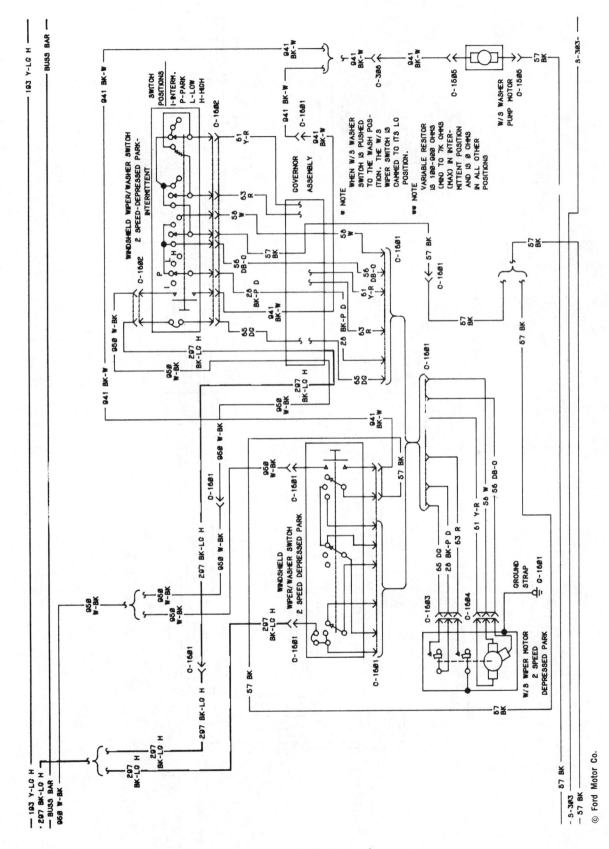

*1973—Lincoln Continental*

# Ford Motor Company

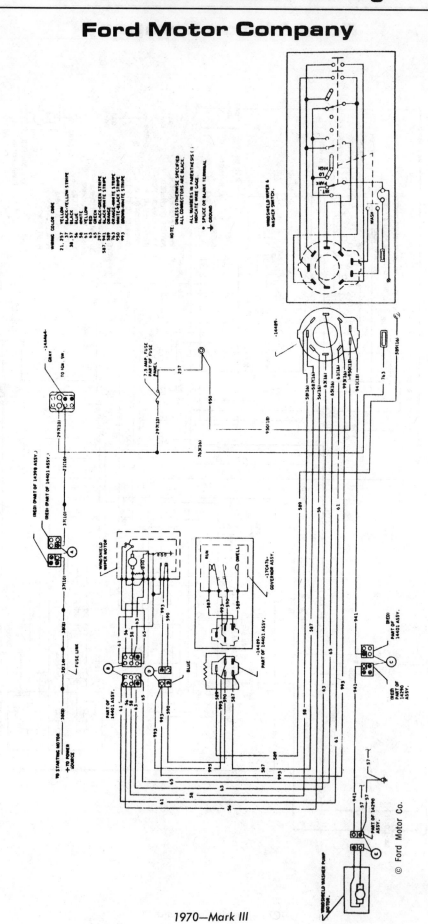

© Ford Motor Co.

*1970—Mark III*

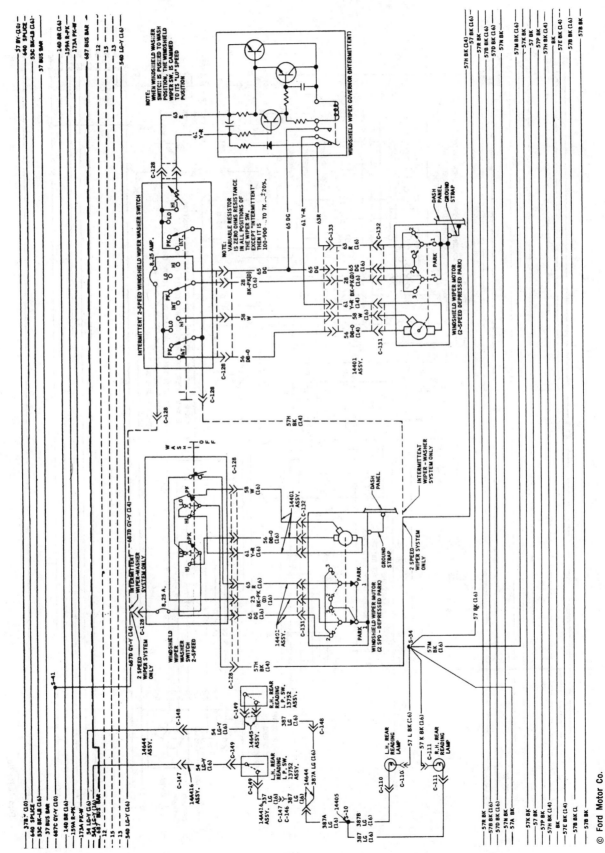

1972—Mark IV

© Ford Motor Co.

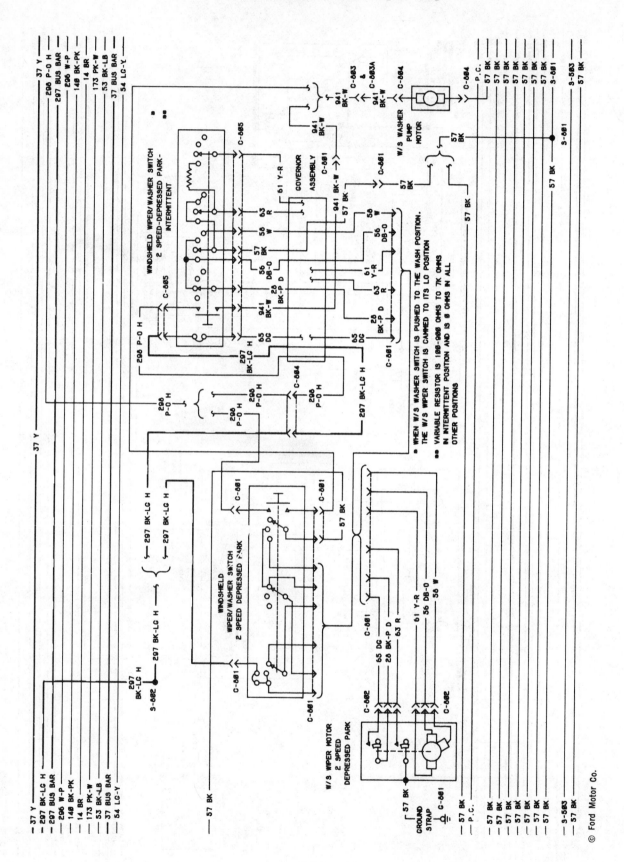

*1973—Mark IV*

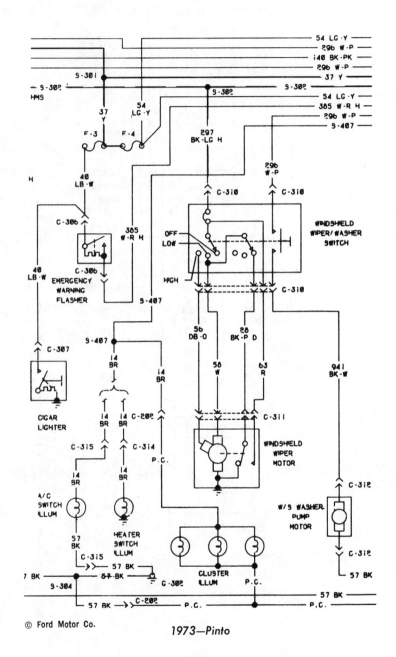

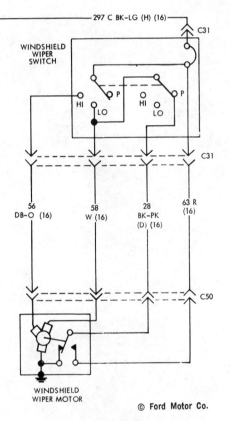

WINDSHIELD
WIPER
SWITCH

297 C BK-LG (H) (16)

C31

HI     P     O   O   P
       O    HI  LO
       LO

C31

56          58         28          63 R
DB-O (16)   W (16)     BK-PK       (16)
                       (D) (16)

C50

WINDSHIELD
WIPER MOTOR

© Ford Motor Co.

*1971-72—Pinto*

54 LG-Y
296 W-P
140 BK-PK
296 W-P
37 Y

S-301

S-302
HMS

S-302          S-302
54 LG-Y
305 W-R H
296 W-P
S-407

37     54
Y      LG-Y

F-3    F-4           297
                     BK-LG H

40                                          296
LB-W                                        W-P

C-306                                C-310        C-310

H                           305
                            W-R H        OFF    WINDSHIELD
40                                       LOW    WIPER/WASHER
LB-W                                            SWITCH

C-306                              HIGH
EMERGENCY
WARNING                                    C-310
FLASHER
              S-407

C-307     S-407
                                    56          28
                14                  DB-O        BK-P D
                BR
                              14
                              BR
                                    58          63
CIGAR               14   14  C-202  W           R
LIGHTER             BR   BR

              C-315    C-314              C-311
                                    WINDSHIELD
              14       14   P.C.    WIPER
              BR       BR           MOTOR
A/C
SWITCH
ILLUM                                                    941
        57             HEATER                            BK-W
        BK             SWITCH                     C-312
        C-315          ILLUM
                                                 W/S WASHER
7 BK         57 BK              G-302   CLUSTER   PUMP
S-304    57 BK   C-202   P.C.          ILLUM     MOTOR
                                                          C-312
                                                 57 BK
                                       P.C.
                                                 57 BK
                                P.C.      P.C.

© Ford Motor Co.        *1973—Pinto*

## Ford Motor Company

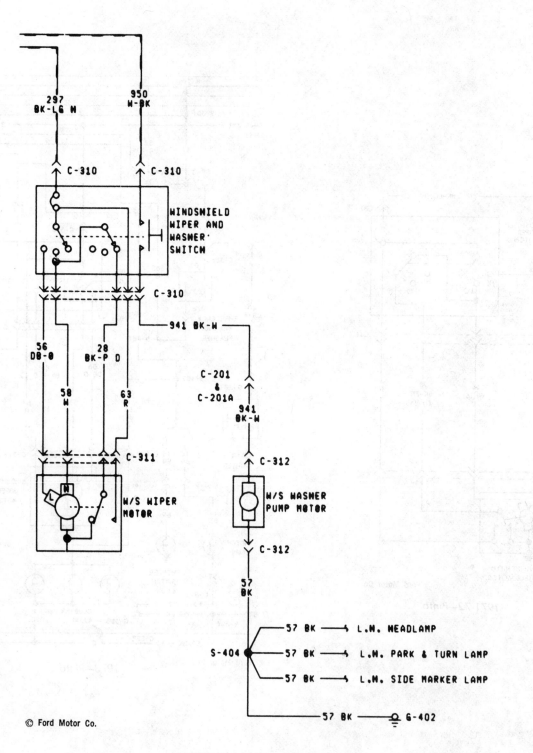

© Ford Motor Co.

*1975—Pinto, Maverick*

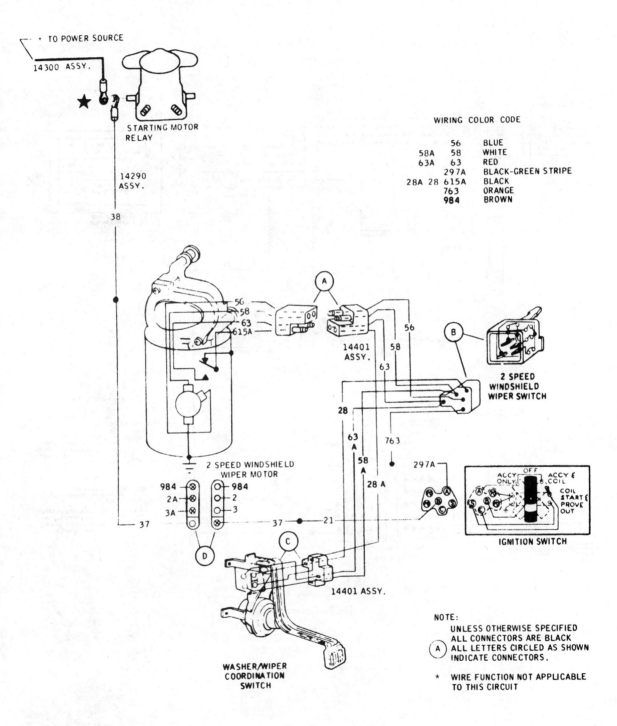

1968—Cougar

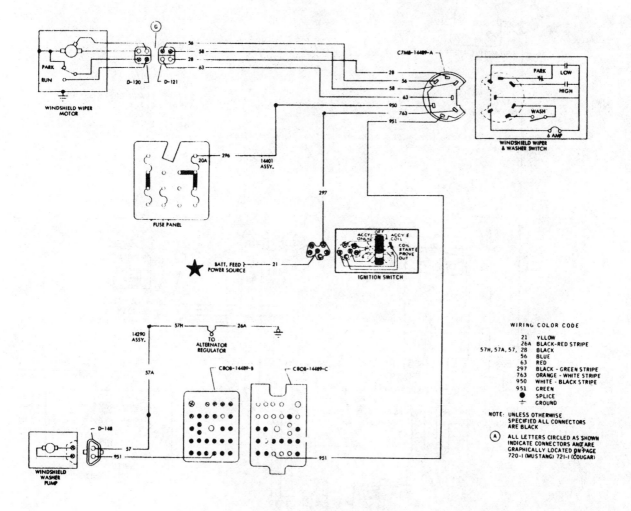

WIRING COLOR CODE

| | |
|---|---|
| 21 | YELLOW |
| 26A | BLACK-RED STRIPE |
| 57H, 57A, 57, 28 | BLACK |
| 56 | BLUE |
| 63 | RED |
| 297 | BLACK - GREEN STRIPE |
| 763 | ORANGE - WHITE STRIPE |
| 950 | WHITE - BLACK STRIPE |
| 951 | GREEN |
| ● | SPLICE |
| ⏚ | GROUND |

NOTE: UNLESS OTHERWISE
SPECIFIED ALL CONNECTORS
ARE BLACK

Ⓐ ALL LETTERS CIRCLED AS SHOWN
INDICATE CONNECTORS AND ARE
GRAPHICALLY LOCATED ON PAGE
720-1 (MUSTANG) 721-1 (COUGAR)

1969—Cougar

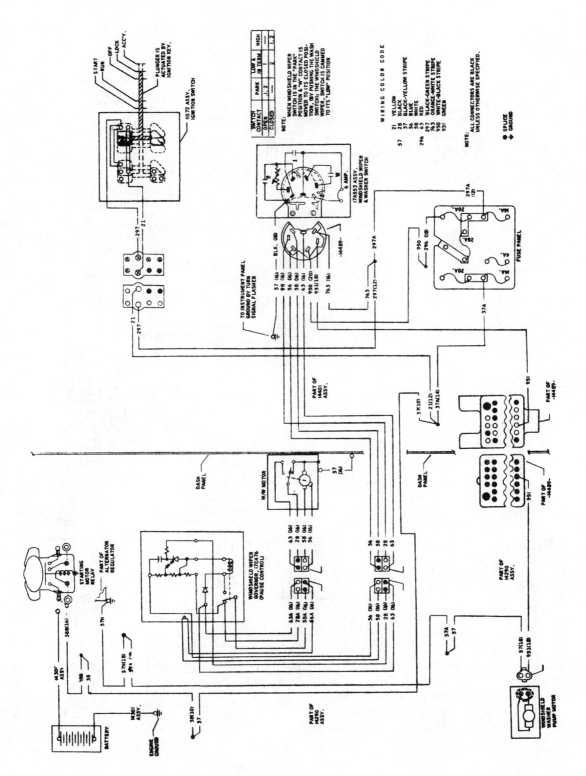

1970—Cougar

## Ford Motor Company

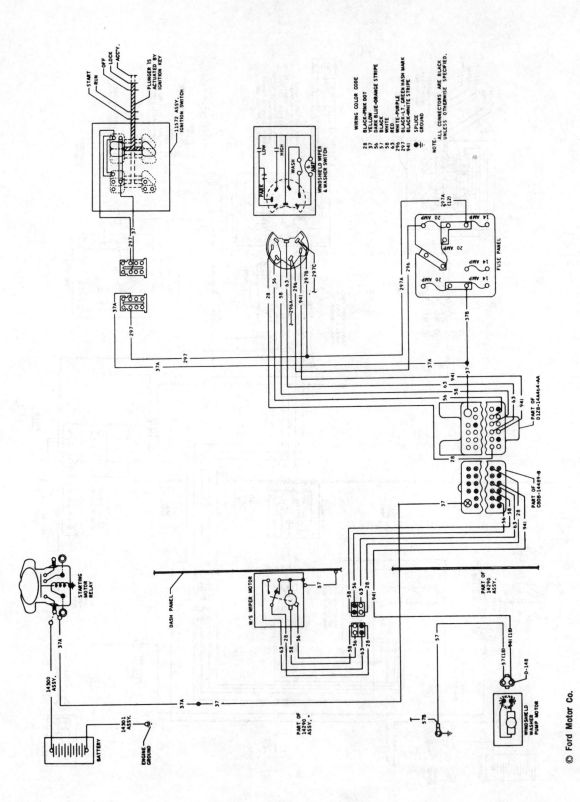

*1971—Cougar—Exc. Intermittent*

## Ford Motor Company

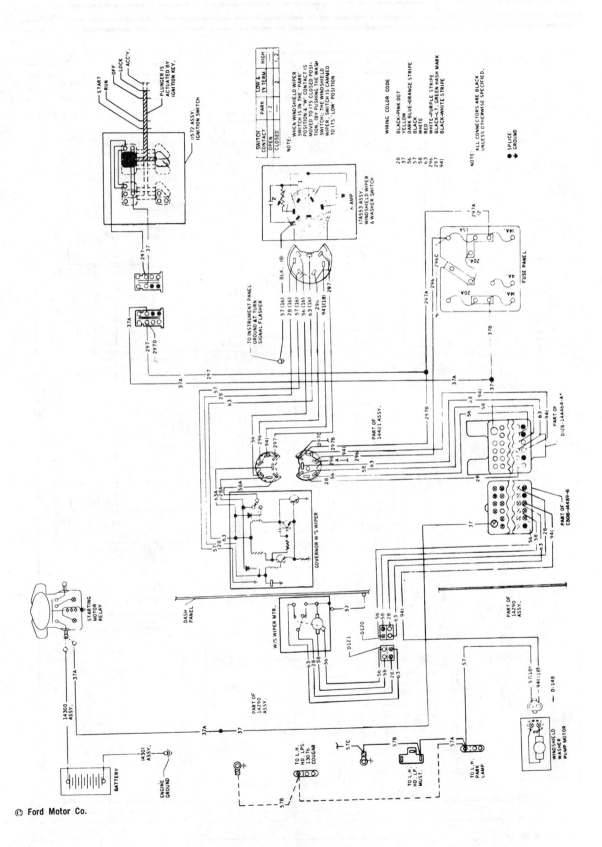

*1971—Cougar—Intermittent*

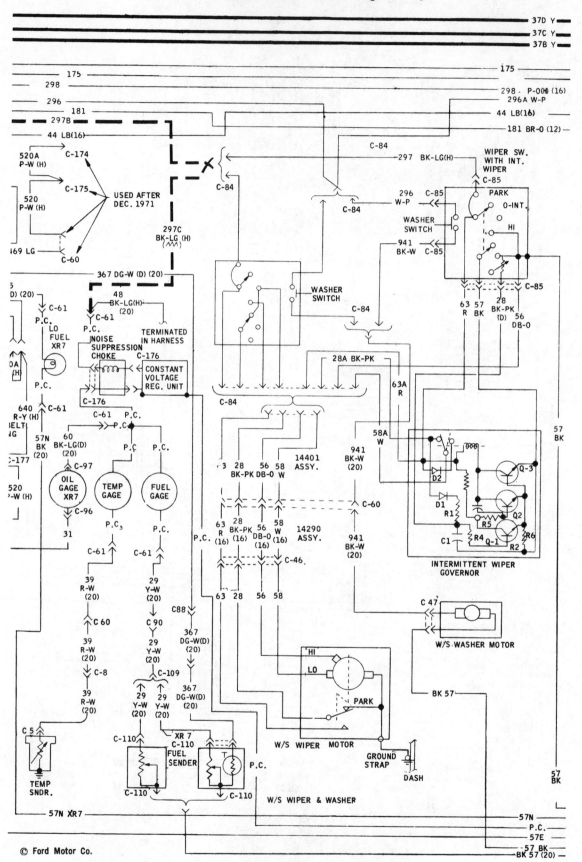

1972—Cougar

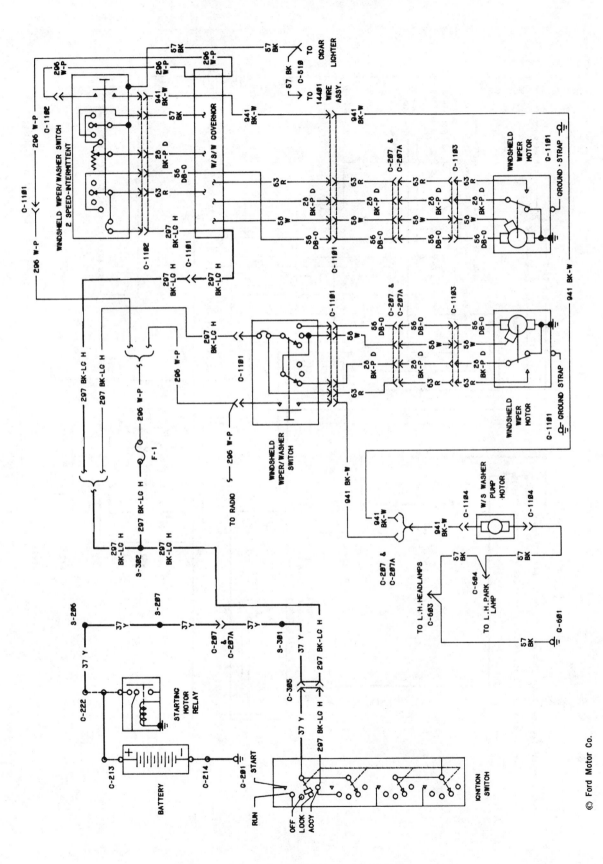

1973—Cougar

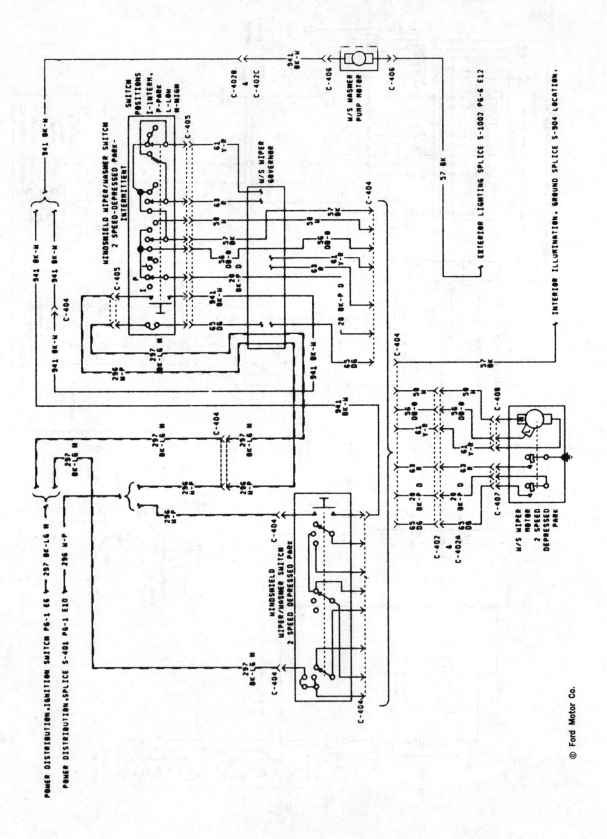

*1974-75—Cougar, Montego, Torino*

# Ford Motor Company

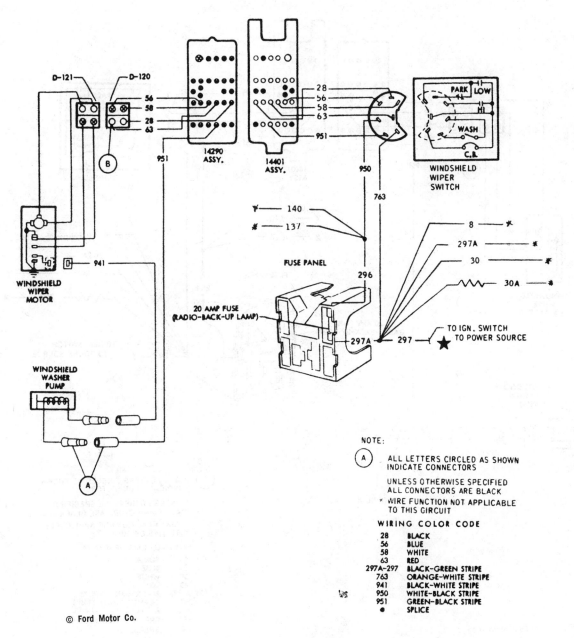

FUSE PANEL

20 AMP FUSE
(RADIO-BACK-UP LAMP)

WINDSHIELD
WIPER
MOTOR

WINDSHIELD
WASHER
PUMP

WINDSHIELD
WIPER
SWITCH

TO IGN. SWITCH
TO POWER SOURCE

NOTE:

(A) ALL LETTERS CIRCLED AS SHOWN
INDICATE CONNECTORS

UNLESS OTHERWISE SPECIFIED
ALL CONNECTORS ARE BLACK

* WIRE FUNCTION NOT APPLICABLE
TO THIS CIRCUIT

WIRING COLOR CODE

| 28 | BLACK |
|---|---|
| 56 | BLUE |
| 58 | WHITE |
| 63 | RED |
| 297A-297 | BLACK-GREEN STRIPE |
| 763 | ORANGE-WHITE STRIPE |
| 941 | BLACK-WHITE STRIPE |
| 950 | WHITE-BLACK STRIPE |
| 951 | GREEN-BLACK STRIPE |
| • | SPLICE |

© Ford Motor Co.

*1968—Fairlane, Torino*

## Ford Motor Company

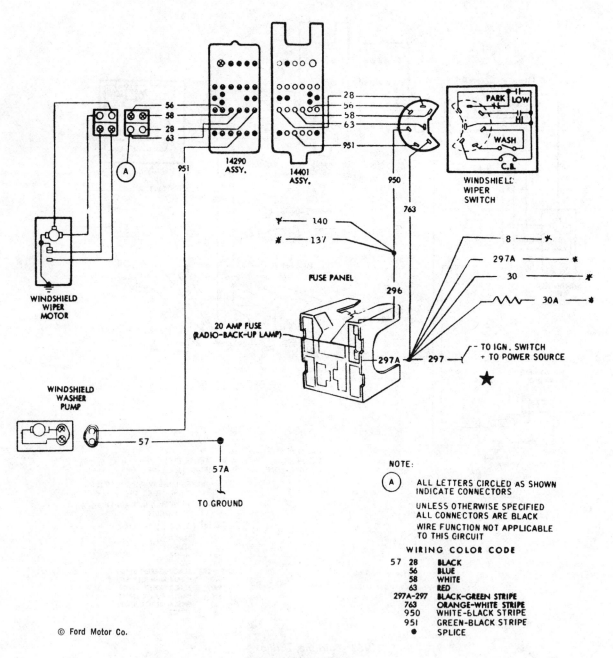

WINDSHIELD
WIPER
MOTOR

56
58
28
63

951

14290
ASSY.

28
56
58
63
951

14401
ASSY.

950

763

WINDSHIELD
WIPER
SWITCH

PARK
LOW
HI
WASH
C.B.

140

137

FUSE PANEL

296

8

297A

30

30A

TO IGN. SWITCH
TO POWER SOURCE

20 AMP FUSE
(RADIO-BACK-UP LAMP)

297A

297

WINDSHIELD
WASHER
PUMP

57

57A

TO GROUND

**NOTE:**

(A) ALL LETTERS CIRCLED AS SHOWN
INDICATE CONNECTORS

UNLESS OTHERWISE SPECIFIED
ALL CONNECTORS ARE BLACK

WIRE FUNCTION NOT APPLICABLE
TO THIS CIRCUIT

**WIRING COLOR CODE**

| | | |
|---|---|---|
| 57 | 28 | BLACK |
| | 56 | BLUE |
| | 58 | WHITE |
| | 63 | RED |
| 297A | -297 | BLACK-GREEN STRIPE |
| | 763 | ORANGE-WHITE STRIPE |
| | 950 | WHITE-BLACK STRIPE |
| | 951 | GREEN-BLACK STRIPE |
| • | | SPLICE |

© Ford Motor Co.

*1969—Fairlane, Torino*

# Ford Motor Company

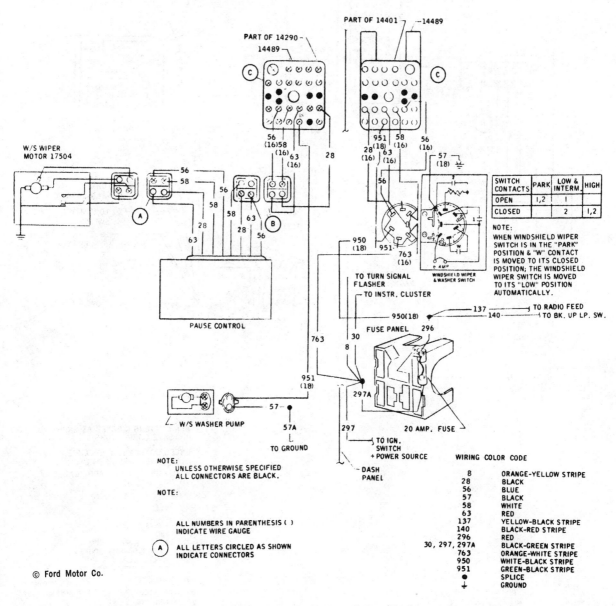

| SWITCH CONTACTS | PARK | LOW & INTERM | HIGH |
|---|---|---|---|
| OPEN | 1,2 | 1 | |
| CLOSED | | 2 | 1,2 |

**NOTE:**
WHEN WINDSHIELD WIPER SWITCH IS IN THE "PARK" POSITION & "W" CONTACT IS MOVED TO ITS CLOSED POSITION; THE WINDSHIELD WIPER SWITCH IS MOVED TO ITS "LOW" POSITION AUTOMATICALLY.

W/S WIPER MOTOR 17504

PART OF 14290 — 14489

PART OF 14401 — 14489

TO TURN SIGNAL FLASHER

TO INSTR. CLUSTER

WINDSHIELD WIPER & WASHER SWITCH

6 AMP

TO RADIO FEED

TO BK. UP LP. SW.

FUSE PANEL

20 AMP. FUSE

TO IGN. SWITCH + POWER SOURCE

DASH PANEL

PAUSE CONTROL

W/S WASHER PUMP

TO GROUND

**NOTE:**
UNLESS OTHERWISE SPECIFIED ALL CONNECTORS ARE BLACK.

**NOTE:**

ALL NUMBERS IN PARENTHESIS ( ) INDICATE WIRE GAUGE

ⒶALL LETTERS CIRCLED AS SHOWN INDICATE CONNECTORS

© Ford Motor Co.

| WIRING COLOR CODE | |
|---|---|
| 8 | ORANGE-YELLOW STRIPE |
| 28 | BLACK |
| 56 | BLUE |
| 57 | BLACK |
| 58 | WHITE |
| 63 | RED |
| 137 | YELLOW-BLACK STRIPE |
| 140 | BLACK-RED STRIPE |
| 296 | RED |
| 30, 297, 297A | BLACK-GREEN STRIPE |
| 763 | ORANGE-WHITE STRIPE |
| 950 | WHITE-BLACK STRIPE |
| 951 | GREEN-BLACK STRIPE |
| ● | SPLICE |
| ⏚ | GROUND |

*1970—Fairlane, Torino—Intermittent*

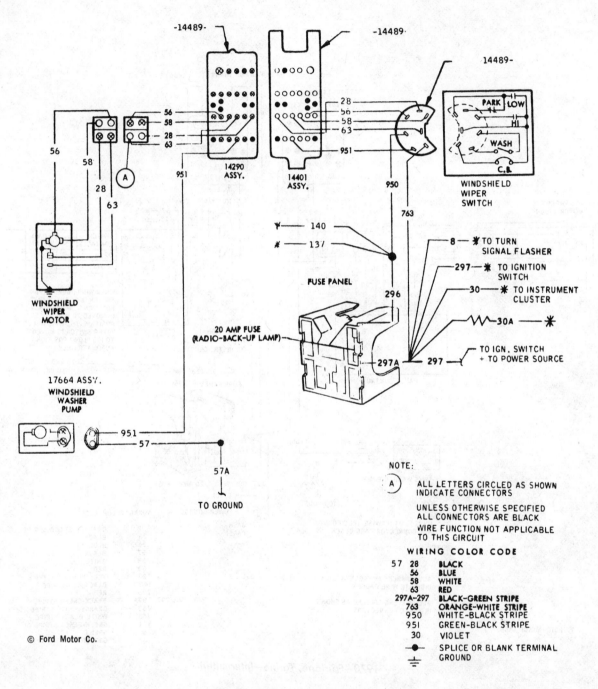

1970—Fairlane, Torino—Two Speed

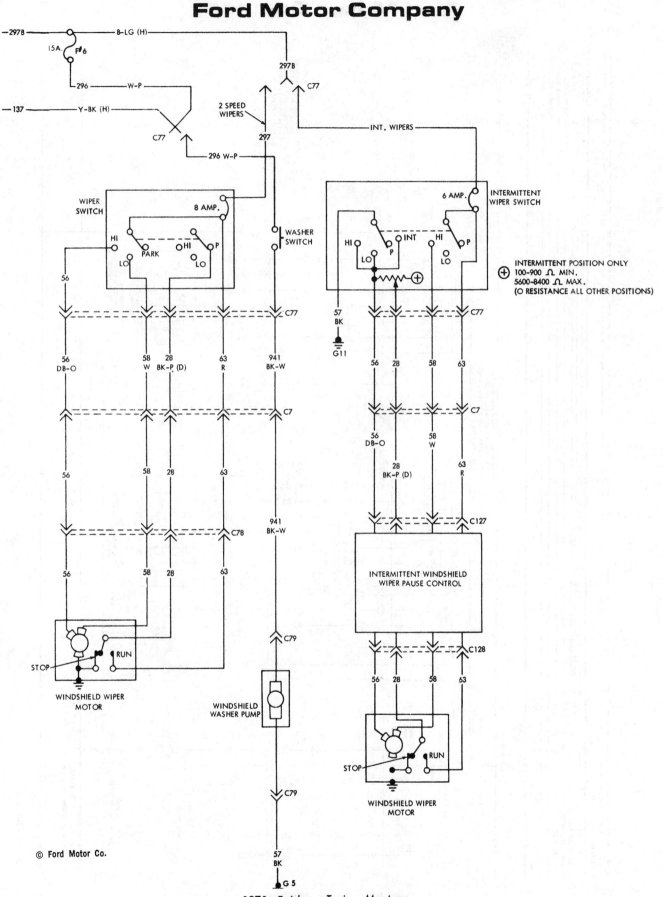

1971—Fairlane, Torino, Montego

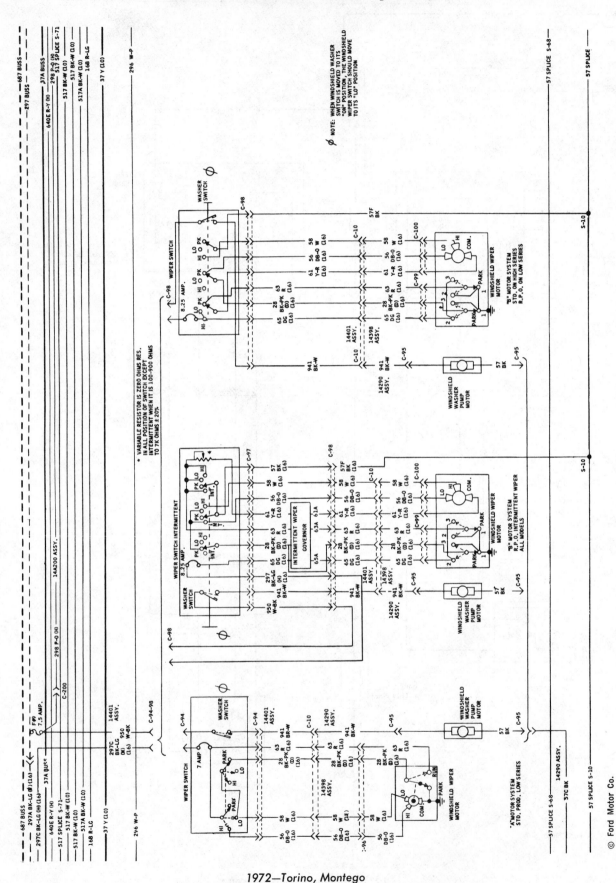

*1972—Torino, Montego*

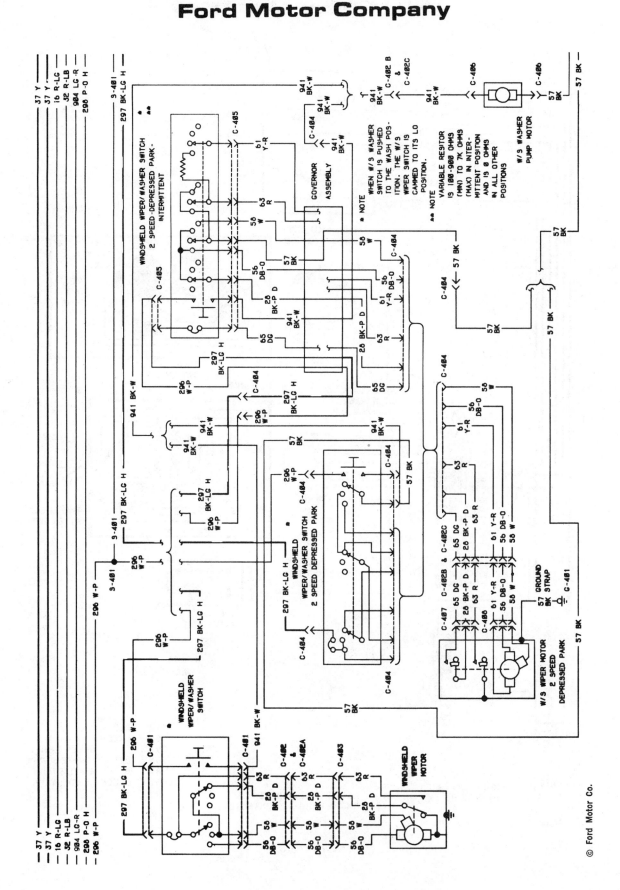

*1973—Torino, Montego*

# Ford Motor Company

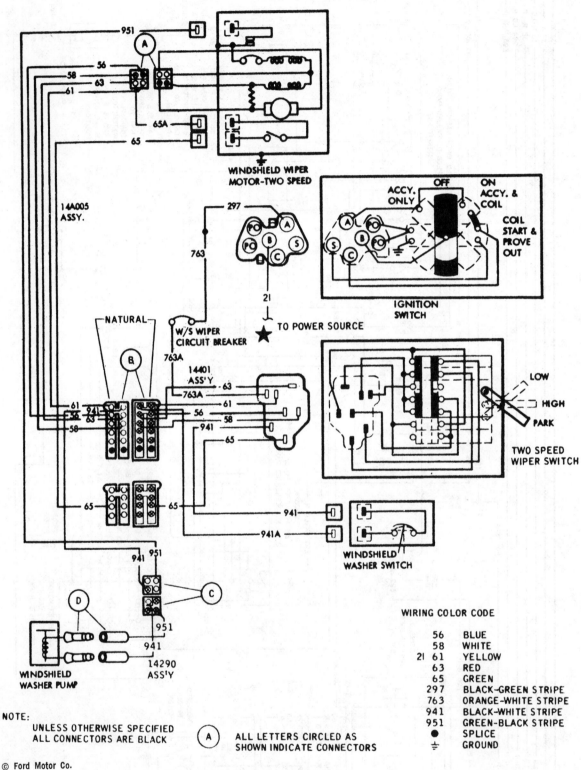

951

A

56
58
63
61

65A

65

WINDSHIELD WIPER
MOTOR-TWO SPEED

14A005
ASS'Y.

297

763

PC
PC

B

A
S
C

21

TO POWER SOURCE

ACCY.
ONLY

OFF

ON
ACCY. &
COIL

A

B

S
C

COIL
START &
PROVE
OUT

IGNITION
SWITCH

NATURAL

W/S WIPER
CIRCUIT BREAKER

B

763A

14401
ASS'Y.

763A
61
63
56
58
941
65

63
61
56
58

LOW

HIGH

PARK

TWO SPEED
WIPER SWITCH

61
941
56
63
58

65

65

941
941A

WINDSHIELD
WASHER SWITCH

941    951

D

C

951

941

14290
ASS'Y.

WINDSHIELD
WASHER PUMP

WIRING COLOR CODE

|  |  |  |
|---|---|---|
| | 56 | BLUE |
| | 58 | WHITE |
| 21 | 61 | YELLOW |
| | 63 | RED |
| | 65 | GREEN |
| | 297 | BLACK-GREEN STRIPE |
| | 763 | ORANGE-WHITE STRIPE |
| | 941 | BLACK-WHITE STRIPE |
| | 951 | GREEN-BLACK STRIPE |
| • | | SPLICE |
| ⏚ | | GROUND |

NOTE:
UNLESS OTHERWISE SPECIFIED
ALL CONNECTORS ARE BLACK

A   ALL LETTERS CIRCLED AS
SHOWN INDICATE CONNECTORS

© Ford Motor Co.

1968—Ford

## Ford Motor Company

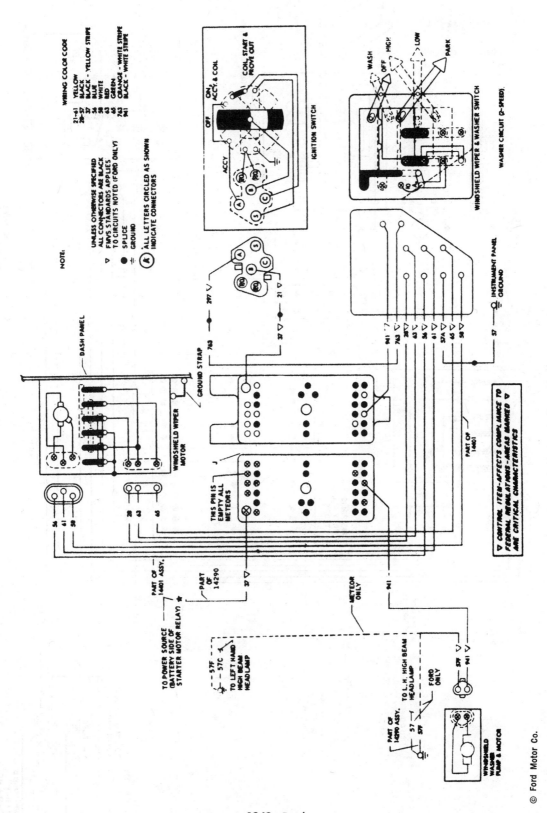

*1969—Ford*

## Ford Motor Company

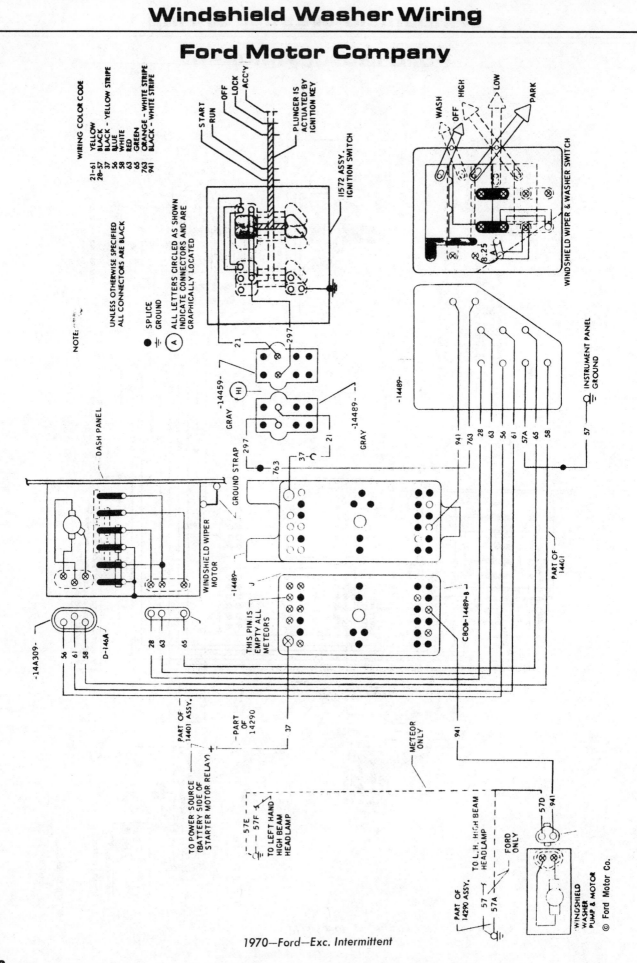

*1970—Ford—Exc. Intermittent*

© Ford Motor Co.

## Ford Motor Company

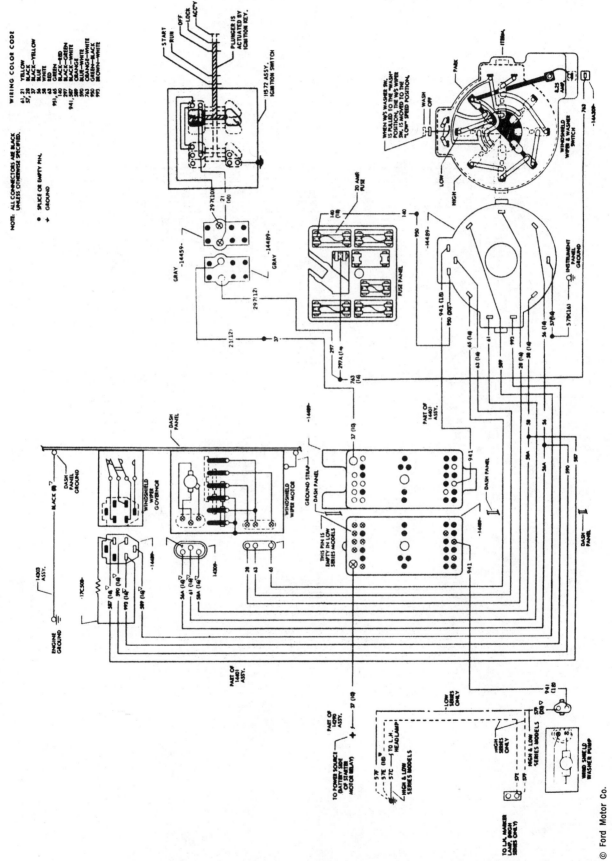

*1970—Ford—Intermittent*

# Windshield Washer Wiring

## Ford Motor Company

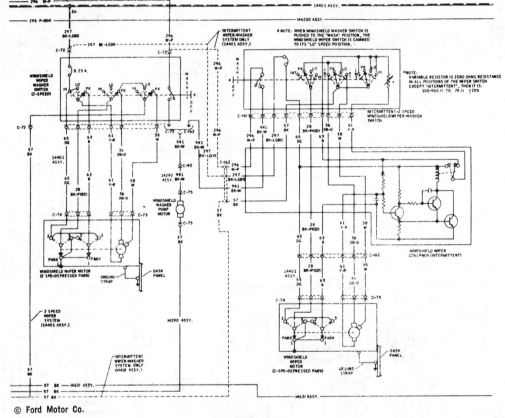

© Ford Motor Co.

1971—Ford

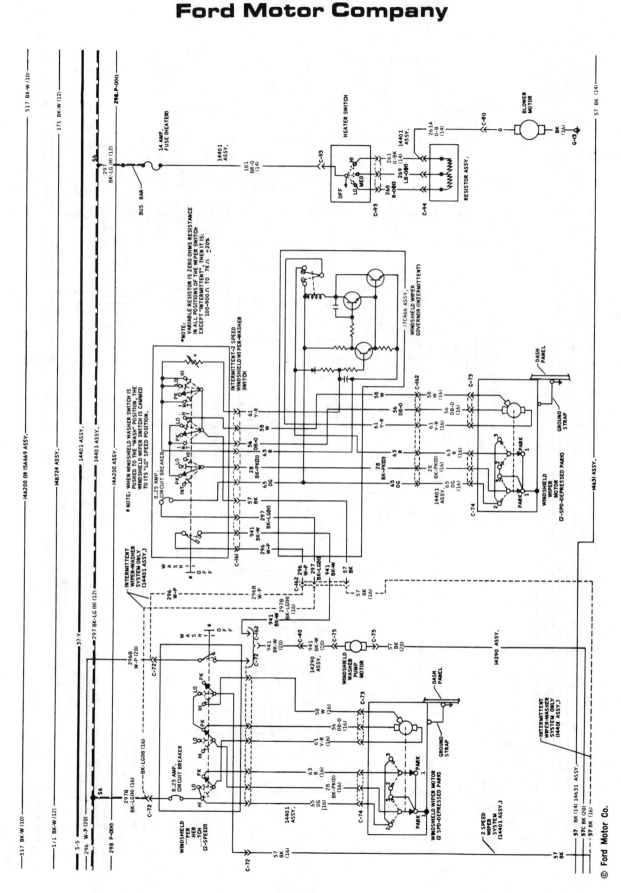

1972—Ford

© Ford Motor Co.

# Ford Motor Company

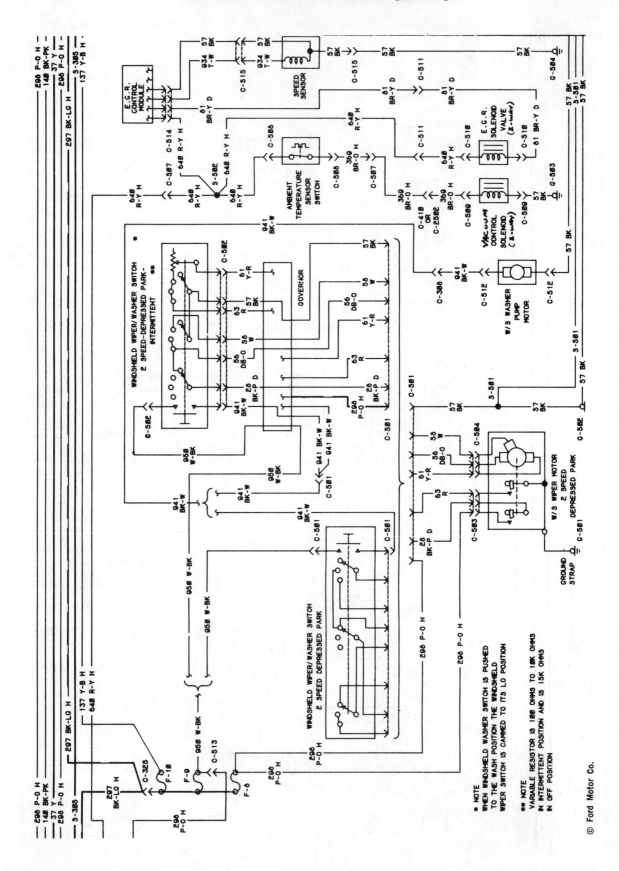

*1973-Ford*

© Ford Motor Co.

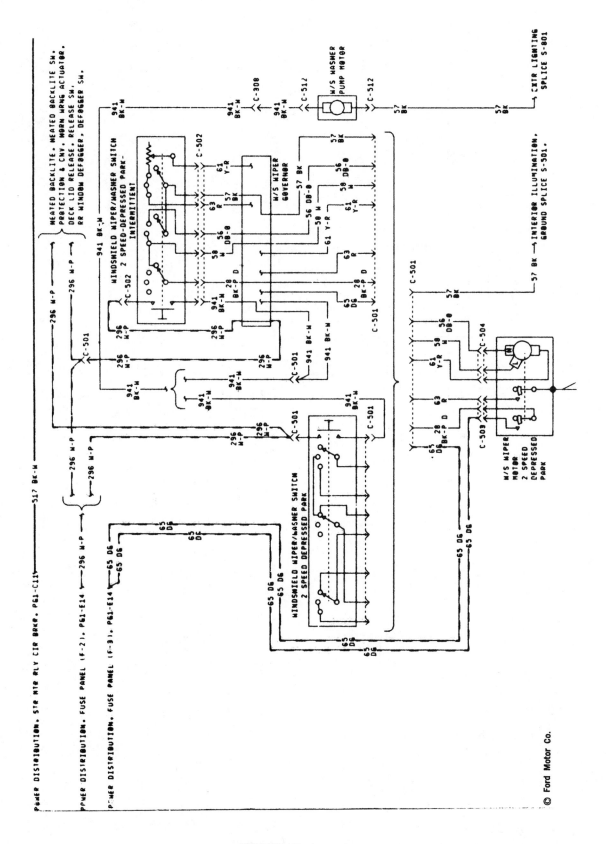

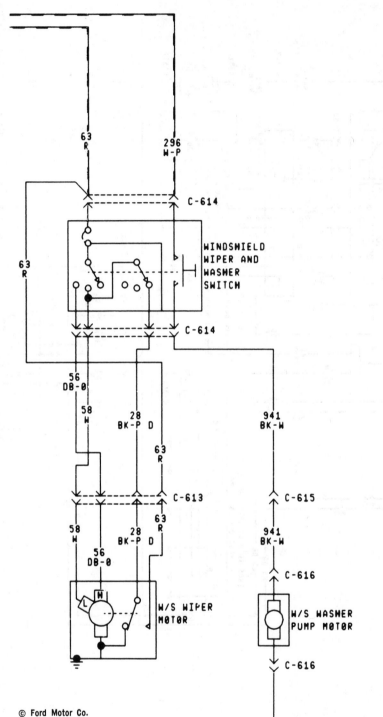

© Ford Motor Co.

*1975—Monarch, Granada*

## General Motors

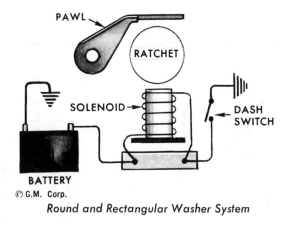

© G.M. Corp.

*Round and Rectangular Washer System*

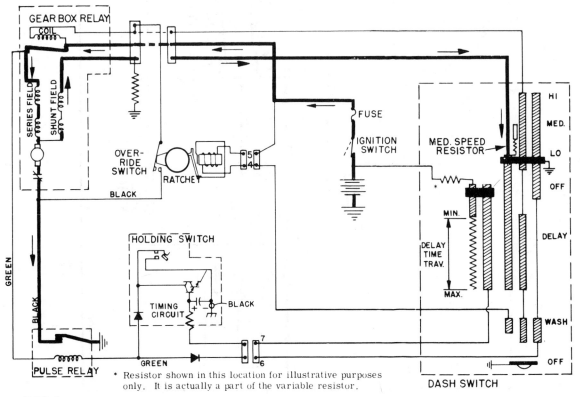

\* Resistor shown in this location for illustrative purposes only. It is actually a part of the variable resistor.

© G.M. Corp.

*Pulse and Modified Pulse Washer System*

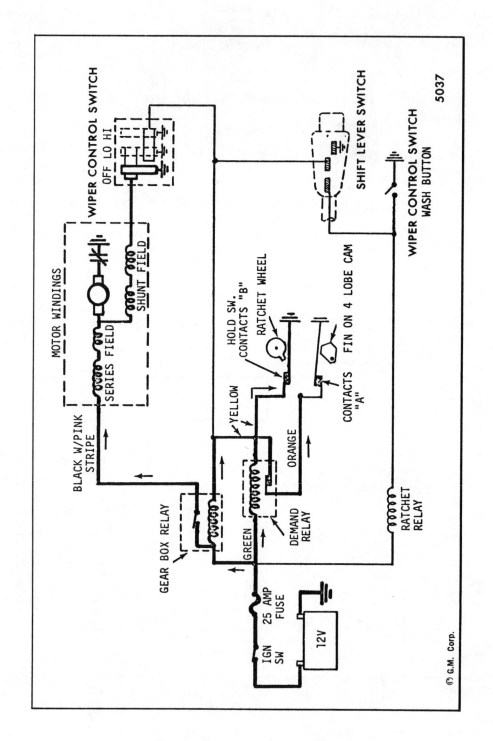

5037

© G.M. Corp.

*Programmed and Demand Washer System*

## General Motors

### AIR CUSHION RESTRAINT SYSTEM (AIR BAGS) GENERAL MOTORS 1974-75 OPERATION AND DIAGNOSIS

*NOTE: Diagnosis of the Air Cushion Restraint System should be done only by a trained serviceman, using only the special analyzer J-24628, and following procedures.*

© G.M. Corp.

*Driver Air Cushion*

### Description

The Air Cushion Restraint System is designed to deploy for front seat occupants when involved in a front end accident of sufficient force, up to 30 degrees off the centerline of the car. The inflatible air cushion assemblies are deployed when an accident has been sensed by the crash sensing mechanisms.

### Driver System

The driver system consists of an air cushion and inflator assembly which is stored in the steering wheel hub beneath the trim cover.

When an accident signal is sensed by the sensing mechanisms a gas producing generator inflates the driver cushion. The trim cover opens at the seams as the system is deployed.

An energy absorbing knee restraint and a telescoping wheel complete the driver protection system.

### Passenger System

The passenger system consists of an inflator, air cushions and trim cover. The system is located low on the instrument panel and to the right of the car and provides restraint for the right and center front passengers. The trim cover opens when the system is deployed.

When a signal is received from the sensing mechanisms, stored gas and gas producing generators inflate the air cushion assembly.

### Sensing Mechanisms

Two devices are used to control the deployment of the driver and passenger systems, a bumper impulse detector and a passenger compartment crash sensor.

These devices detect "low-level" front end impacts equivalent to a 12 to 18 miles per hour barrier crash

early in the accident sequence. When a "low-level" crash signal is received, the driver system is deployed by the gas producing generator. Stored gas in the passenger system inflator assembly is released and one of the two generators is activated to produce "low-level" deployment of the passenger system.

The passenger compartment sensor also detects "high-level" front end impacts equivalent to an 18 mile per hour or greater barrier crash. This activates a second gas producing generator in the passenger system and increases restraint of the system.

### Diagnostic System

The Air Cushion Restraint System has an integral electronic diagnostic system, which monitors the system's electrical circuits. It shows the driver that the system is either operating properly or in need of immediate repair. This is shown by an indicator lamp located on the instrument panel that lights when the ignition switch is first turned "ON."

If the indicator lamp does not light when the ignition switch is first turned "ON," remains lighted after 3 to 9 seconds, or comes on intermit-

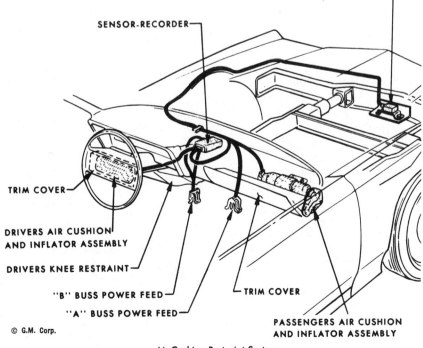

© G.M. Corp.

*Air Cushion Restraint System*

## General Motors

"HIGH LEVEL DEPLOYMENT" (STORED GAS PLUS TWO GAS PRODUCING GENERATORS)

© G.M. Corp.

*High Level Deployment*

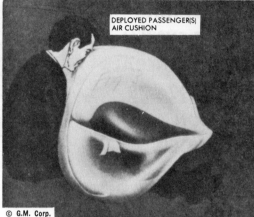

DEPLOYED PASSENGER(S) AIR CUSHION

© G.M. Corp.

*Passenger Air Cushion*

"LOW LEVEL DEPLOYMENT" (STORED GAS PLUS ONE GAS PRODUCING GENERATOR)

© G.M. Corp.

*Low Level Deployment*

tently, the system is in need of immediate service.

If the indicator lamp comes on when the ignition switch is first turned "ON" and goes out after 3 to 9 seconds, the system is operating properly.

## DIAGNOSTIC PROCEDURES

*WARNING: To avoid deployment of system when trouble shooting, do not use electrical test equipment, such as battery powered or A.C. powered volt meter, ohmmeter, etc., or any type of electrical equipment other than specified. Do not use a non-powered probe type tester. Personal injury may result if system is accidently deployed.*

*NOTE: Do not attempt to repair recorder harnesses, bumper impulse detector, drivers module, passengers module or sensor-recorder. All corrections to these components are to be made by replacement only.*

### Description

System Diagnostic Procedures are divided into two categories:

1. Tests to perform when the system indicator lamp does not light ("Never-On") when the ignition switch is turned to any position, except "LOCK."
2. Tests to perform when the system indicator lamp remains 'On Continuously" (brilliant or dim) when the ignition switch is turned to any position, except "LOCK," or comes on intermittently when driving the car.

*NOTE: The indicator lamp is designed to operate properly only after the ignition switch has been left in*

"LOCK" for approximately 150 seconds. This is necessary to allow time for a capacitor discharge within the sensor.

*WARNING: Do not attempt any servicing or disconnecting of system components until negative cable has been disconnected from battery and terminal end of cable taped. This procedure must be followed to prevent accidental deployment of system which could cause personal injury and/or damage to system components. Care must be taken to never strike sensing mechanisms which could cause deployment or improper operation of the system.*

## ANALYZER AND SUBSTITUTE LOADS

Analyzer J-24628 with substitute loads must be used to check the Air Cushion Restraint System to determine if a specific part or the entire system is functioning properly.

*NOTE: Before connecting the analyzer into the system, check all wire harness connectors to make sure the problem is not caused by an improperly engaged connector.*

*WARNING: To avoid deployment of system when trouble shooting do not use electrical test equipment, such as battery powered or A.C. powered voltmeter, ohmmeter, etc., or any type of electrical equipment other than specified. Do not use a non-powered probe type tester. Personal injury may result if system is accidently deployed.*

The analyzer consists of a control panel, a verification test lead and six leads with connectors. The six connectors are labeled P1, P2, J1, J2, J3 and J4 to make easier hook up of the analyzer with the Air Cushion Restraint System. The verification test lead is used to test analyzer lamp bulbs before analyzer use.

The control panel is equipped with six switches, each identified and numbered, two power indicator

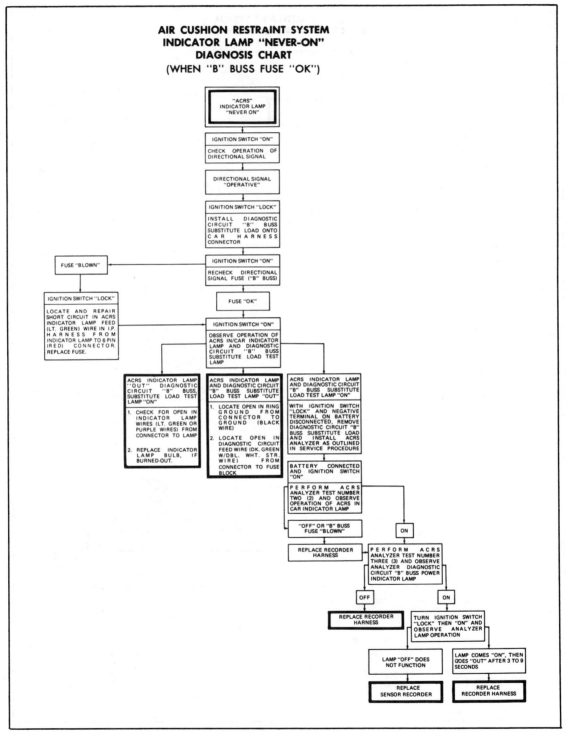

AIR CUSHION RESTRAINT SYSTEM
INDICATOR LAMP "NEVER-ON"
DIAGNOSIS CHART
(WHEN "B" BUSS FUSE "OK")

"ACRS" INDICATOR LAMP "NEVER ON"

IGNITION SWITCH "ON"
CHECK OPERATION OF DIRECTIONAL SIGNAL

DIRECTIONAL SIGNAL "OPERATIVE"

IGNITION SWITCH "LOCK"
INSTALL DIAGNOSTIC CIRCUIT "B" BUSS SUBSTITUTE LOAD ONTO CAR HARNESS CONNECTOR

IGNITION SWITCH "ON"
RECHECK DIRECTIONAL SIGNAL FUSE ("B" BUSS)

FUSE "BLOWN"

IGNITION SWITCH "LOCK"
LOCATE AND REPAIR SHORT CIRCUIT IN ACRS INDICATOR LAMP FEED (LT. GREEN) WIRE IN I.P. HARNESS FROM INDICATOR LAMP TO 6 PIN (RED) CONNECTOR. REPLACE FUSE.

FUSE "OK"

IGNITION SWITCH "ON"
OBSERVE OPERATION OF ACRS IN/CAR INDICATOR LAMP AND DIAGNOSTIC CIRCUIT "B" BUSS SUBSTITUTE LOAD TEST LAMP

ACRS INDICATOR LAMP "OUT" DIAGNOSTIC CIRCUIT "B" BUSS, SUBSTITUTE LOAD TEST LAMP "ON"
1. CHECK FOR OPEN IN INDICATOR LAMP WIRES (LT. GREEN OR PURPLE WIRES) FROM CONNECTOR TO LAMP
2. REPLACE INDICATOR LAMP BULB, IF BURNED-OUT.

ACRS INDICATOR LAMP AND DIAGNOSTIC CIRCUIT "B" BUSS SUBSTITUTE LOAD TEST LAMP "OUT"
1. LOCATE OPEN IN RING GROUND FROM CONNECTOR TO GROUND (BLACK WIRE)
2. LOCATE OPEN IN DIAGNOSTIC CIRCUIT FEED WIRE (DK. GREEN W/DBL. WHT. STR. WIRE) FROM CONNECTOR TO FUSE BLOCK

ACRS INDICATOR LAMP AND DIAGNOSTIC CIRCUIT "B" BUSS SUBSTITUTE LOAD TEST LAMP "ON"
WITH IGNITION SWITCH "LOCK" AND NEGATIVE TERMINAL ON BATTERY DISCONNECTED, REMOVE DIAGNOSTIC CIRCUIT "B" BUSS SUBSTITUTE LOAD AND INSTALL ACRS ANALYZER AS OUTLINED IN SERVICE PROCEDURE

BATTERY CONNECTED AND IGNITION SWITCH "ON"

PERFORM ACRS ANALYZER TEST NUMBER TWO (2) AND OBSERVE OPERATION OF ACRS IN CAR INDICATOR LAMP

"OFF" OR "B" BUSS FUSE "BLOWN"

ON

REPLACE RECORDER HARNESS

PERFORM ACRS ANALYZER TEST NUMBER THREE (3) AND OBSERVE ANALYZER DIAGNOSTIC CIRCUIT "B" BUSS POWER INDICATOR LAMP

OFF

ON

REPLACE RECORDER HARNESS

TURN IGNITION SWITCH "LOCK" THEN "ON" AND OBSERVE ANALYZER LAMP OPERATION

LAMP "OFF" DOES NOT FUNCTION

LAMP COMES "ON", THEN GOES "OUT" AFTER 3 TO 9 SECONDS

REPLACE SENSOR RECORDER

REPLACE RECORDER HARNESS

*Air Cushion Restraint System Indicator Lamp "Never On" ("B" Buss Fuse OK)*

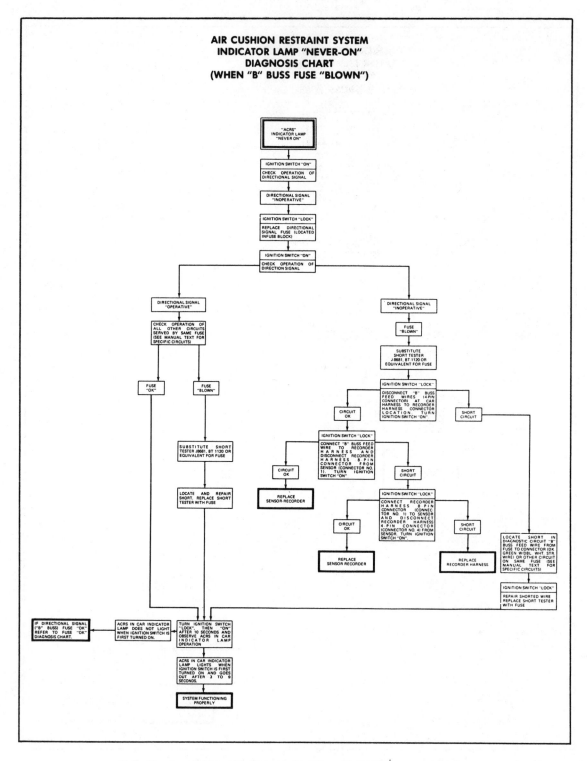

*Air Cushion Restraint System Indicator Lamp "Never On" ("B" Buss Fuse is Blown)*

## General Motors

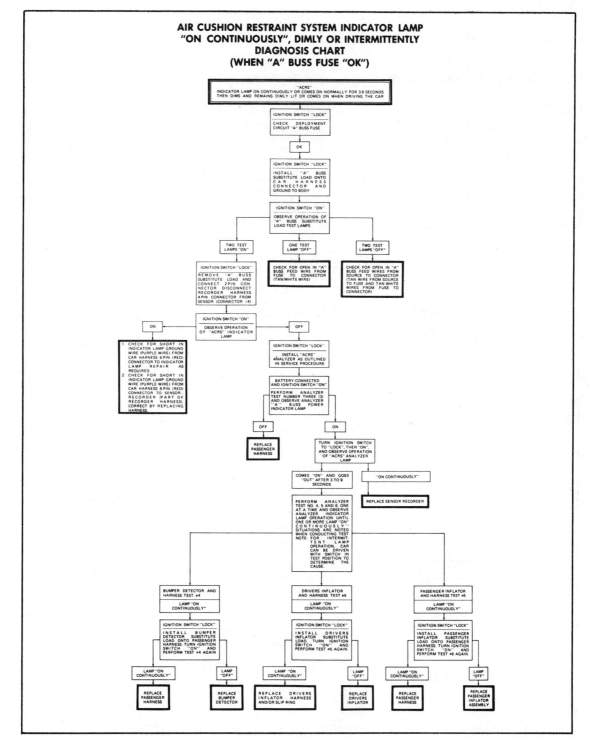

**AIR CUSHION RESTRAINT SYSTEM INDICATOR LAMP "ON CONTINUOUSLY", DIMLY OR INTERMITTENTLY DIAGNOSIS CHART (WHEN "A" BUSS FUSE "OK")**

*Air Cushion Restraint System Indicator Lamp "On Continuously, Brilliant, Dim or Intermittently" ("A" Buss Fuse is OK)*

# Air Cushion Restraint System

## General Motors

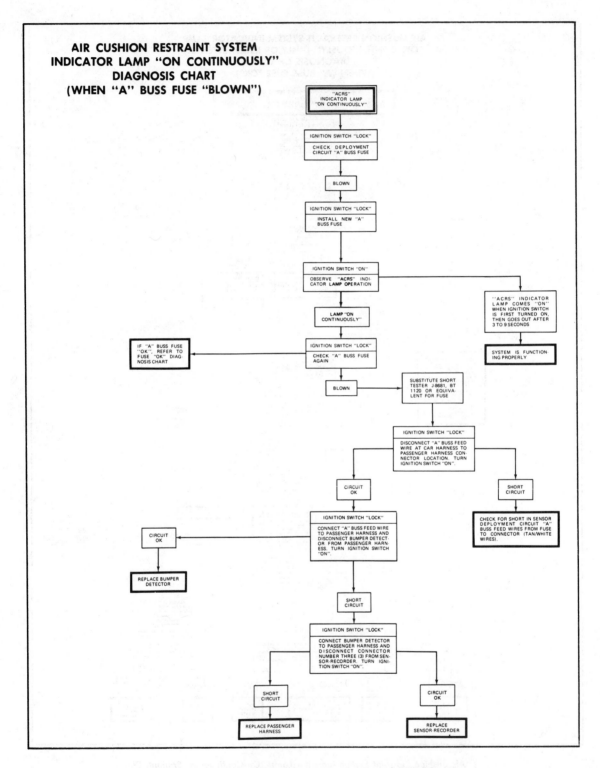

*Air Cushion Restraint System Indicator Lamp "On Continuously" ("A" Buss Fuse is Blown)*

## General Motors

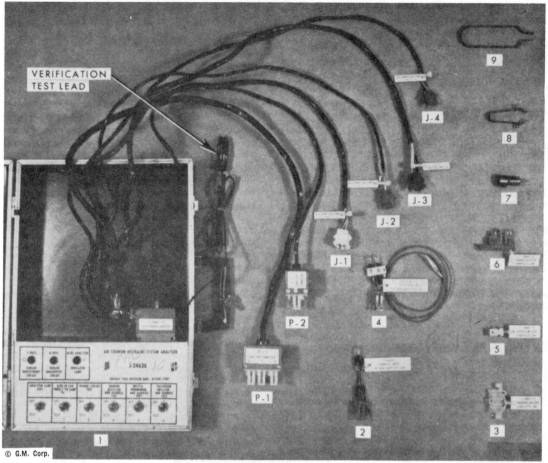

*Air Cushion Restraint System Special Tools*

1. J-24628-Air Cushion Restraint System Analyzer

2. J-24628-11 Diagnostic Circuit ("B" Buss) Substitute Load

3. J-24628-13 Passenger Inflator Substitute Load

4. J-24628-12 Deployment Circuit ("A" Buss) Substitute Load

5. J-24628-15-Driver Module Substitute Load

6. J-24628-14-Bumper Impulse Detector Substitute Load

7. J-24628-2 or BT-7405-Driver Module Removal Tool

8. J-24388 or BT-7402A-Passenger Inflator, Sensor, Bumper Detector and "A" and "B" Buss Connector Extractor

9. J-24628-3-Driver Module Connector Extractor

lamps, and an analyzer indicator lamp. The analyzer lamp simulates operation of the system indicator lamp on the instrument panel. The power indicator lamps are used to indicate if current is present in the deployment and diagnostic circuits in the system.

*NOTE: When the analyzer is hooked up to the system, the in car indicator lamp does not function, only the analyzer lamp which simulates in car operation will light.*

The deployment circuit ("A" buss) is used to supply current to de-

ploy the system. The diagnostic ("B" buss) circuit supplies current to the sensor diagnostics. A failure in the diagnostic circuit will not affect deployment of the system.

The analyzer lamp test (test 1), indicator lamp test (test 2) and power circuit test (test 3) switches are turned in sequence to the test position. Test 1 and 2 determines if the analyzer and in car indicator lamps are operating properly. Test 3 determines if current is present in the diagnostic and deployment circuits.

*NOTE: Test switches 1, 2 and 3*

*are spring loaded and automatically return to the OFF position after the test has been made.*

As test switches 4, 5 and 6 are turned in sequence, the designated system circuit is tested. If the analyzer indicator lamp comes on (remains on continuously or comes on intermittently when driving the car) with the test switch in the test position, a malfunction is present within the circuit being tested. The entire testing procedure for the problem being diagnosed should be followed through since it is possible for a number of

## General Motors

malfunctions to be present in the system. After each test has been completed, test switches 4, 5 and 6 must be returned to the OFF position before proceeding to the next test.

*NOTE: If the analyzer lamp lights momentarily (3 to 9 seconds) when switches 4, 5 and 6 are turned to the test position, this does not indicate a malfunction. The lamp must remain on continuously or intermittently when driving the car to indicate a problem.*

After the testing procedure has been followed to completion and all analyzer switches are in the OFF position, a substitute load can be installed onto the harness connector of the defective circuit. The substitute load simulates a good component in the circuit being tested and when the analyzer switch is turned to the TEST position will isolate the problem as to either the component or the harness.

## DIAGNOSIS WHEN INDICATOR LAMP IS "NEVER ON"

If the restraint system indicator lamp does not light when the ignition switch is first turned ON, check diagnostic circuit "B" buss fuse. The directional signal and Air Cushion Restraint System diagnostic circuit, including indicator lamp, share one fuse located in the fuse panel. This check can be made by turning the ignition switch ON and checking the operation of the directional signal.
1. If the fuse is "blown," proceed to checking procedure "Checking for Short Circuits That Cause Blown "B" Buss Fuse (with Short Tester)."
2. If the fuse is not "blown," proceed to checking procedure "Checking For Open Circuits or Short Circuits That Do Not Blow "B" Buss Fuse (with Analyzer)."

*WARNING: To avoid deployment of system when trouble shooting, do not use electrical test equipment, such as battery powered or A.C. powered voltmeter, ohmmeter, etc., or any type of electrical equipment other than specified. Do not use a non-powered probe type tester. Personal injury may result if system accidently deployed.*

Air Cushion Restraint System Analyzer J-24628 Control Panel

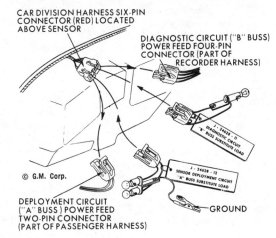

Deployment (A buss) and Diagnostic (B buss) Feed Circuit Substitute Loads

### Checking for Open Circuits or Short Circuits That Do Not Blow "B" Buss Fuse (With Analyzer)

1. With the ignition switch in LOCK and the key removed, use connector extractor J-24388 or BT-7402A and separate the diagnostic "B" buss circuit four pin connector from the car division instrument panel harness six pin connector (red connector located above sensor-recorder).

*NOTE: The deployment circuit is energized when the ignition switch is in any position except LOCK. When diagnosis operations are being performed requiring the ignition switch in LOCK, remove the key to assure that the switch is in LOCK position.*

2. Install diagnostic circuit "B" buss substitute load onto the six pin connector in place of the four pin harness connector. Turn the ignition ON and recheck the directional signal "B" buss fuse.

a. If the fuse is not "blown," proceed to step 3.
b. If the fuse is "blown," turn the ignition switch to LOCK and remove the key. Repair the short circuit in the restraint system indicator lamp harness (light green wire in instrument panel harness from indicator lamp to six pin red connector) to make the indicator lamp and substitute load test lamp light. Replace the fuse and proceed to step 4 to eliminate the possibility of other problems in the system.

3. Turn the ignition switch ON and note operation of the test lamp on the "B" buss substitute load and the restraint system indicator lamp for one of the following conditions.
a. If the system indicator lamp and the substitute load test bulb does not light, check for an open circuit in the ground (black) wire from the six pin connector to the

## General Motors

ground location or the diagnostic circuit "B" buss feed wire (dark green with double white stripe) from the fuse block to the six pin (red) connector. With the ignition switch in LOCK and the key removed, repair or replace the wires to make the substitute load bulb and indicator lamp light.

With the ignition switch in LOCK, remove the substitute load and connect the four pin connector to the instrument panel harness six pin (red) connector. Turn the ignition switch ON and note the restraint system indicator lamp operation. If the lamp comes on when the switch is first turned ON and goes out after 3 to 9 seconds, the system is operating properly. If the lamp does not light, proceed to step 4.

b. If the restraint system indi-

cator lamp does not light and the substitute load test bulb does light, check for an open circuit in the indicator lamp feed or ground wires (light green or purple) from the six pin (red) connector to the indicator lamp bulb. Replace the bulb, or repair or replace the wires as necessary.

With the ignition switch in LOCK, remove the substitute load and connect the four pin connector to the instrument panel harness six pin (red) connector. Turn the ignition switch ON and observe the restraint system indicator lamp operation. If the lamp comes on when the switch is first turned ON and goes out after 3 to 9 seconds, the system is operating properly. If the lamp does not light, proceed to step 4.

c. If the restraint system indicator lamp and the substitute load test lamp lights,

turn the ignition switch to LOCK and remove the substitute load. Connect the four pin connector to the instrument panel harness six pin connector and proceed to step 4.

4. Check the restraint system analyzer lamps by plugging the verification test lead into the cigar lighter and performing analyzer lamp test number 1. If all three analyzer test lamps light, continue with the analyzer hook up. If one or more of the test lamps do not light, replace the defective bulbs or repair the analyzer as required. Remove the verification test lead from the cigar lighter. With the ignition switch in LOCK and the key removed, disconnect and tape the negative terminal of the battery. Then connect the system analyzer.

*WARNING: Do not attempt any servicing or disconnecting of system components until negative cable has*

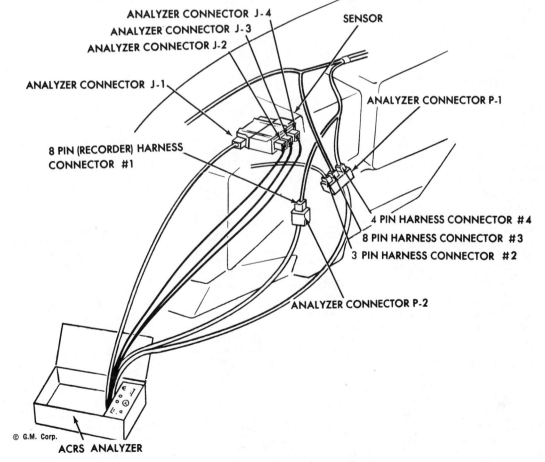

*Air Cushion Restraint System Analyzer Hook-Up*

## General Motors

been disconnected from battery and terminal end of cable taped. This procedure must be followed to prevent accidental deployment of system which could cause personal injury and/or damage to system components. Care must be taken to never strike sensing mechanisms which could cause deployment or improper operation of the system.

*NOTE: Before connecting the analyzer into the system, check all wire harness connectors to make sure the problem is not caused by an improperly engaged connector.*

5. Remove the sensor-recorder attaching screws and lower the sensor-recorder for easier access to the harness connectors.
6. Connect the system analyzer with the system.
   a. Using connector extractor tool J-24388 or BT-7402A, disconnect all harness connectors from the sensor-recorder.
   b. Connect the analyzer eight pin recorder connector J-1 to the side of the sensor-recorder.
   c. Connect the analyzer three pin J-2, eight pin J-3 and four pin J-4 connectors to the sensor fifteen pin connector (located at front of sensor-recorder).
   d. Connect wire harness connectors 2, 3 and 4 to the analyzer fifteen pin connector P-1.
   e. Connect the eight pin recorder harness connector number 1 (white) to the analyzer connector P-2.
7. Install the sensor-recorder with one screw and the ring ground.

*WARNING: Care must be taken to never strike sensing mechanisms in a manner which could cause accidental deployment or improper operation of system, serious injury may result.*

8. Connect the negative terminal to the battery. Turn the ignition switch ON and perform analyzer test 2. Note the operation of the restraint system indicator lamp while performing the test.
   a. If the restraint system in car indicator lamp does not light or blows the directional signal fuse when performing test 2, replace the sensor-recorder harness. Continue to diagnosis b, to eliminate the possibility of other prob-

lems in the system.

*WARNING: Do not attempt any servicing or disconnecting of system components until negative cable has been disconnected from battery and terminal end of cable taped. This procedure must be followed to prevent accidental deployment of system which could cause personal injury and/or damage to system components. Care must be taken to never strike sensing mechanisms which could cause deployment or improper operation of the system.*

   b. If the restraint system in car indicator lamp does light when performing test 2, proceed to test 9.
9. Perform analyzer test 3 and note analyzer "B" buss power circuit lamp.
   a. If "B" buss power circuit lamp does not light, replace the recorder harness.
   b. If "B" buss power circuit lamp does light, proceed to step 10.
10. Turn the ignition switch to LOCK, then to ON, and observe the operation of the analyzer indicator lamp.
   a. If the analyzer indicator lamp does not light, replace the sensor-recorder as described under Instrument Panel Components.
   b. If the analyzer indicator lamp does light, then goes out after 3 to 9 seconds, replace the recorder harness.

*NOTE: If the recorder harness was replaced while performing steps 8 and 9, proceed to step 11.*

11. Turn the ignition switch to LOCK and remove the key. Disconnect the negative cable from the battery and tape the terminal end of the cable. Remove the attaching screw from the ring ground at the sensor-recorder and lower the sensor-recorder.

*WARNING: Do not attempt any servicing or disconnecting of system components until negative cable has been disconnected from battery and terminal end of cable taped. This procedure must be followed to prevent accidental deployment of system which could cause personal injury and/or damage to system components. Care must be taken to never strike sensing mechanisms which could cause deployment or improper operation of the system.*

12. Disconnect the analyzer from the system by using connector extractor tool J-24388 or BT-7402A and connect all previously removed harnesses. Reinstall the sensor-recorder.
13. Connect the negative cable to the battery. Turn the ignition switch ON, and note the operation of the restraint system in car indicator lamp.
   a. If the indicator lamp lights when the ignition switch is first turned ON and goes out after 3 to 9 seconds, the system is operating properly.
   b. If the indicator lamp does not light, continue with the diagnosis.

### Checking for Short Circuits that Cause Blown "B" Buss Fuse (With Short Tester)

1. With the ignition switch in LOCK, replace the directional signal fuse ("B" buss) located in the fuse block.
2. Turn the ignition switch ON and check the operation of the directional signal.
   a. If the directional signal operates proceed to step 3.
   b. If the directional signal does not operate (fuse blown) proceed to step 5.
3. Check the operation of the circuits listed below which are also protected by the directional signal fuse. Recheck the fuse.
   a. Buick—cruise control, back-up lamps and directional signal.
   b. Cadillac—directional signal only.
   c. Oldsmobile — back-up lamps and directional signal.
   If the fuse blows when checking the above circuits, substitute the short tester J-8681 or BT-1120 for the fuse. Locate and repair the short circuit and replace the fuse. Then proceed to step 4.
4. If the directional signal fuse is not blown, turn the ignition switch ON and observe the operation of the restraint system indicator lamp.
   a. If the indicator lamp lights when the ignition switch is first turned ON and goes out after 3 to 9 seconds, the system is operating properly.
   b. If the indicator lamp does not light and the fuse is not blown, refer to checking procedure "Checking For Open

# General Motors

Circuits or Short Circuits That Do Not Blow "B" Buss Fuse (with Analyzer)."

5. Substitute the short tester J-8681 or BT-1120 for the "B" buss fuse. Turn the ignition switch to LOCK and remove the key. Use connector extractor tool J-24388 or BT-7402A and separate the recorder harness four pin diagnostic "B" buss circuit connector from the instrument panel car harness six pin connector (red connector located above sensor-recorder). The short tester indicates a short circuit by producing a clicking noise and/or by a flashing lamp.

*NOTE: The deployment circuit is energized when the ignition switch is in any position except LOCK. When diagnosis operations are being performed requiring the ignition switch in LOCK, remove the key to assure that the switch is in LOCK position.*

6. Turn the ignition switch ON and note the operation of the short tester.
   a. If the short tester indicates a short circuit, repair or replace the "B" buss feed wire (dark green with double white stripe) from the fuse block to the six pin (red) connector or other circuits on the same fuse as listed in step 3. After the short circuit has been corrected, replace the directional signal fuse. Turn the ignition switch to LOCK and remove the key. Connect the recorder harness four pin connector to the instrument panel car harness six pin (red) connector. Perform step 4.
   b. If the short tester does not indicate a short circuit, with the ignition switch in LOCK, disconnect the negative cable from the battery and tape the terminal end of the cable.

*WARNING: Do not attempt any servicing or disconnecting of system components until negative cable has been disconnected from battery and terminal end of cable taped. This procedure must be followed to prevent accidental deployment of system which could cause personal injury and/or damage to system components. Care must be taken to never strike sensing mechanisms which could cause deployment or improper operation of the system.*

7. Connect the recorder harness four pin connector to the instrument panel car harness six pin (red) connector and disconnect the recorder harness eight pin connector from the side of the sensor-recorder (connector 1-white).

*NOTE: To gain access to the eight pin recorder harness connector, the sensor-recorder must be lowered. After the eight pin connector has been disconnected, install the sensor-recorder with one screw and the ring ground.*

*WARNING: Care must be taken to never strike sensing mechanisms in a manner which could cause accidental deployment or improper operation of system, serious injury may result.*

8. Connect the battery, turn the ignition switch ON and note the operation of the short tester.
   a. If the short tester does not indicate a short circuit, replace the sensor-recorder (refer to "Sensor-Recorder Removal and Installation" in the Instrument Panel Components section). Remove the short tester from the fuse block and install a

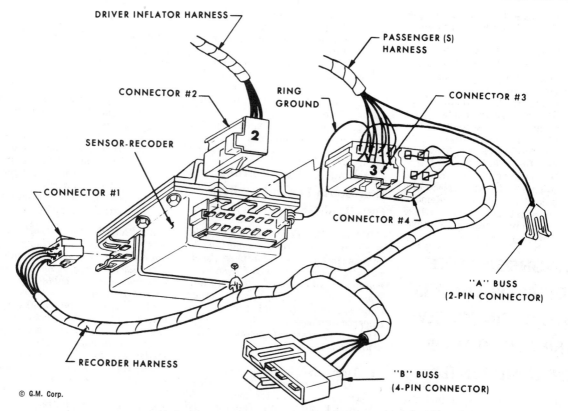

© G.M. Corp.

*Air Cushion Restraint System Sensor—Recorder Installation*

# General Motors

new fuse. Perform step 4.

b. If the short tester indicates a short circuit, with the ignition switch in LOCK, disconnect the negative cable from the battery and tape the terminal end of the cable. Remove the sensor-recorder attaching screw and lower the sensor-recorder. Connect the recorder harness eight pin connector to the sensor-recorder (connector 1) and disconnect the recorder harness four pin connector from the sensor-recorder. (connector 4). Install the sensor-recorder with one screw and the ground ring.

*WARNING: Do not attempt any servicing or disconnecting of system components until negative cable has been disconnected from battery and terminal end of cable taped. This procedure must be followed to prevent accidental deployment of system which could cause personal injury and/or damage to system components. Care must be taken to never strike sensing mechanisms which could cause deployment or improper operation of the system.*

9. Connect the battery. Turn the ignition switch ON and observe the operation of the short tester.

a. If the short tester does not indicate a short circuit, replace the sensor-recorder. (refer to "Sensor-Recorder Removal and Installation" in the Instrument Panel Components section). Remove the short tester from the fuse block and install a new fuse. Perform step 4.

b. If the short tester indicates a short circuit, replace the recorder harness. Remove the short tester from the fuse block and install a new fuse. Perform step 4.

# DIAGNOSIS WHEN INDICATOR LAMP IS "ON CONTINUOUSLY" (BRIGHT, DIM OR INTERMITTENTLY)

If the restraint system indicator lamp remains on continuously, check the deployment circuit power feed

"A" buss fuse (In-line fuse for Cadillac located in a tan wire on right side of steering column near ignition switch. Fuse panel mounted for Buick and Oldsmobile).

*WARNING: To avoid deployment of system when trouble shooting, do not use electrical test equipment, such as battery powered or A.C. powered voltmeter, ohmmeter, etc., or any type of electrical equipment other than specified. Do not use a non-powered probe type tester. Personal injury may result if system is accidently deployed.*

1. If the fuse is not blown, or the replacement fuse does not blow, proceed to checking procedure "Checking For Open Circuits or Short Circuits That Do Not Blow "A" Buss Fuse (with Analyzer)."

2. If the replacement fuse does blow, proceed to checking procedure "Checking For Short Circuits That Cause Blown "A" Buss Fuses (with Short Tester).

*NOTE: If the indicator lamp operates intermittently, check for loose connections at the following locations.*

a. Battery cables to battery.
b. Battery cables to engine block and starter solonoid.
c. Cable connection on junction block.
d. Ignition switch connector.
e. Bulk head connector on dash panel (red feed wire).
f. Loose fuse in "A" buss fuse holder.
g. Improperly engaged restraint system connectors.

## Checking for Short Circuits That Cause Blown "A" Buss Fuse (With Short Tester)

*WARNING: To avoid deployment of system when trouble shooting, do not use electrical test equipment, such as battery powered or A.C. powered voltmeter, ohmmeter, etc., or any type of electrical equipment other than specified. Do not use a non-powered probe type tester. Personal injury may result if system is accidently deployed.*

1. Turn the ignition switch to LOCK and remove the key. Use connector extractor tool J-24388 or BT-7402A and separate the two pin deployment "A" buss

circuit connector from the instrument panel car harness six pin connector (red connector located above sensor-recorder).

*NOTE: The deployment circuit is energized when the ignition switch is in any position except LOCK. When diagnosis operations are being performed requiring the ignition switch in LOCK, remove the key to assure that the switch is in LOCK postion.*

2. Remove the blown fuse and connect the short tester J-8681 or BT-1120, to the input and output side of the fuse clips and wires.

3. Turn the ignition switch ON and observe the operation of the short tester.

a. If the short tester indicates a short circuit, repair or replace the harness from the fuse block to the six pin (red) connector (tan and white wires from fuse to connector).

b. If the short tester does not indicate a short circuit, turn the ignition switch to LOCK and remove the key. Connect the two pin connector to the instrument panel car harness six pin (red) connector.

*NOTE: The short tester J-8681 or BT-1120 indicates a short circuit by producing a clicking noise and/or by a flashing lamp.*

4. Disconnect the negative cable from the battery and tape the terminal end of the cable. Use connector extractor tool J-24388 or BT-7402A and remove the bumper impulse detector connector from the passenger harness. The connector is located in the passenger compartment above the parking brake.

*WARNING: Do not attempt any servicing or disconnecting of system components until negative cable has been disconnected from battery and terminal end of cable taped. This procedure must be followed to prevent accidental deployment of system which could cause personal injury and/or damage to system components. Care must be taken to never strike sensing mechanisms which could cause deployment or improper operation of the system.*

5. Connect the battery. Turn the ignition switch to ON and note

# General Motors

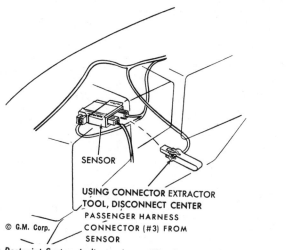

Air Cushion Restraint System Indicator Lamp "On Continuously" Test When "A" Buss Fuse is Blown

the operation of the short tester.
a. If the short tester does not indicate a short circuit, replace the bumper impulse detector as described in the Bumper Section. Proceed to step 8.
b. If the short tester does indicate a short circuit, turn the ignition switch to LOCK and remove the key. Disconnect the negative cable from the battery and tape the terminal end of the cable. Connect the bumper impulse connector to the passenger harness. Observe the warning after step 4. Proceed to step 6.

6. Remove the sensor-recorder attaching screws and lower the sensor-recorder (refer to Instrument Panel Components for sensor-recorder removal). Use connector extractor tool J-24388 or BT-7402A and disconnect the eight pin connector (connector 3) from the sensor. Reinstall the sensor-recorder with one screw and the ring ground.

*WARNING: Care must be taken to never strike sensing mechanisms in a manner which could cause accidental deployment or improper operation of system, serious injury may result.*

7. Connect the negative cable to the battery. Turn the ignition switch ON and note the operation of the short tester.
a. If the short tester does not indicate a short circuit, note the warning after step 4, and replace the sensor-recorder (refer to Instrument Panel

Components section). Proceed to step 8.
b. If the short tester does indicate a short circuit, note the warning after step 4, and replace the passenger restraint system harness (refer to Passenger Module section). Proceed to step 8.

8. Install all removed parts, disconnect the short tester, install a new fuse and check the operation of the restraint system.
a. If the restraint system indicator lamp comes on when the ignition switch is first turned ON and goes out after 3 to 9 seconds, the system is functioning properly.
b. If the restraint system indicator lamp comes on when the ignition switch is first turned ON and remains on continuously and the "A" buss `fuse is not blown. Refer to checking procedure "Checking For Open Circuits or Short Circuits That

Do Not Blow "A" Buss Fuse (with Analyzer).

## Checking for Open Circuits or Short Circuits That Do Not Blow "A" Buss Fuse (With Analyzer)

*WARNING: To avoid deployment of system when trouble shooting, do not use electrical test equipment, such as battery powered or A.C. powered voltmeter, ohmmeter, etc., or any type of electrical equipment other than specified. Do not use a non-powered probe type tester. Personal injury may result if system is accidently deployed.*

1. Turn the ignition switch to LOCK and remove the key. Using connector extractor tool J-24388 or BT-7402A, separate the two pin deployment "A" buss circuit connector from the instrument panel car harness six pin connector (red connector located above the sensor-recorder). Install the deployment circuit substitute load onto the six pin connector and ground to the body. Turn the ignition switch ON and note the operation of the test lamps on the "A" buss substitute load.

*NOTE: The deployment circuit is energized when the ignition switch is in any position except LOCK. When diagnosis operations are being performed requiring the ignition switch in LOCK, remove the key to assure that the switch is in LOCK position.*

a. If neither of the substitute load bulbs light, check for an open circuit in the feed wire from the feed source to the connector (tan wire from source to fuse and tan/white wires from fuse to six pin

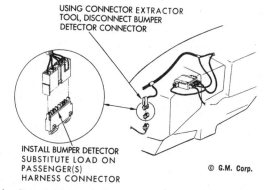

Air Cushion Restraint System Indicator Lamp "On Continuously" Test-Bumper Detector Substitute Load Installation

## General Motors

red connector). Repair or replace wires to make both test bulbs light. With the ignition switch in LOCK, remove the "A" buss substitute load and connect the two pin connector to the six pin (red) connector. Proceed to step 4.

b. If only one substitute load bulb lights, check for an open circuit in the feed wires from the six pin (red) connector to the fuse (tan/white wires). Repair or replace the wires to make both test bulbs light. With the ignition switch in LOCK, remove the "A" buss substitute load and connect the two pin connector to the six pin (red) connector. Proceed to step 4.

c. If both substitute load bulbs light, turn the ignition switch to LOCK and remove the key. Remove the deployment circuit 'A' buss substitute load and connect the two pin connector to the instrument panel car harness six pin (red) connector. Proceed to step 2.

2. With the ignition switch in LOCK and the key removed, disconnect the negative cable from the battery and tape the terminal end of the cable.

*WARNING: Do not attempt any servicing or disconnecting of system components until negative cable has been disconnected from battery and terminal end of cable taped. This procedure must be followed to prevent accidental deployment of system which could cause personal injury and/or damage to system components. Care must be taken to never strike sensing mechanisms which could cause deployment or improper operation of the system.*

3. Remove the sensor-recorder attaching screws and lower the sensor (refer to Instrument Panel Components section for sensor-recorder removal). Using connector extractor tool J-24388 or BT-7402A, disconnect the sensor-recorder harness four pin connector (connector 4) from the sensor-recorder. Reinstall the sensor-recorder with one screw and the ring ground. Connect the battery, turn the ignition switch ON and note the operation of the restraint system lamp. If the lamp does not light, proceed to step 5. If the lamp is

on continuously, check for the following.

a. Short circuit in the restraint system indicator lamp ground wire (purple wire) from the instrument panel car harness six pin (red) connector to the indicator lamp. If shorted, disconnect the battery (note the warning after step 2) and repair or replace the wire. Lower the sensor-recorder and connect the number 4 connector to the sensor-recorder. Install the sensor-recorder attaching bolts, connect the battery and proceed to step 4.

b. Short circuit in the restraint system indicator lamp ground wire (purple) wire from the instrument panel car harness six pin (red) connector to the sensor-recorder (part of recorder harness). If shorted, disconnect the battery (note the warning after step 2) and replace the recorder harness as described in "Recorder Harness Removal and Installation" in the Instrument Panel Components section. Connect the battery and proceed to step 4.

4. Turn the ignition switch ON and note the operation of restraint system indicator lamp.

a. If the indicator lamp lights when the ignition switch is first turned ON and goes out after 3 to 9 seconds, the system is functioning properly.

b. If the indicator lamp comes on and remains on continuously, proceed to step 5.

5. Check the restraint system analyzer (J-24628) lamps by plugging the verification test lead into the cigar lighter and performing analyzer lamp test number 1.

a. If all three analyzer test lamps light, proceed to step 6.

b. If one or more of the test lamps do not light, replace the defective bulbs or repair the analyzer as required. Remove the verification test lead from the cigar lighter.

*NOTE: Before connecting the analyzer into the system, check all wire harness connections to make sure the problem is not caused by an improperly engaged connector.*

6. With the ignition switch in LOCK and the key removed,

disconnect the negative cable from the battery and tape the terminal end of the cable.

*WARNING: Do not attempt any servicing or disconnecting of system components until negative cable has been disconnected from battery and terminal end of cable taped. This procedure must be followed to prevent accidental deployment of system which could cause personal injury and/or damage to system components. Care must be taken to never strike sensing mechanisms which could cause deployment or improper operation of the system.*

7. Remove the sensor-recorder attaching screws and lower the sensor-recorder (as described in the Instrument Panel Components section).

8. Connect the restraint system analyzer J-24628, with the restraint system as follows.

a. Using connector extractor tool J-24388 or BT-7402A, disconnect all harness connectors from the sensor-recorder.

b. Connect the analyzer eight pin recorder connector (J1) to the recorder.

c. Connect the analyzer three pin (J2), eight pin (J3) and four pin (J4) connectors to the sensor fifteen pin connector.

d. Connect the harness connector numbers 2, 3 and 4 to the analyzer fifteen pin connector (P1).

e. Connect the eight pin recorder harness connector number 1 (white) to the analyzer connector (P2).

9. Reinstall the sensor-recorder with one screw and the ring ground.

*WARNING: Care must be taken to never strike sensing mechanisms in a manner which could cause accidental deployment or improper operation of system, serious injury may result.*

10. With the analyzer switch OFF, connect the negative cable to the battery and turn the ignition switch ON.

*NOTE: After the restraint system analyzer has been connected to the system, the entire checking procedure must be followed to the end even though a problem has been detected in the system. This is important due to the possibility of multiple problems.*

# General Motors

11. Perform analyzer test 3 and observe the analyzer "A" buss (deployment circuit) power indicator lamp.
    a. If the "A" buss power indicator lamp lights, proceed to step 12.
    b. If the "A" buss power indicator lamp does not light, replace the passenger harness as outlined in the Passenger Module section. Proceed to step 12.
12. Turn the ignition switch to LOCK, then ON and note the operation of the restraint system analyzer indicator lamp.
    a. If the analyzer indicator lamp comes on when the ignition switch is first on and goes out after 3 to 9 seconds, proceed to step 13.
    b. If the analyzer indicator lamp comes on when the ignition switch is first turned on and remains on continuously, replace the sensor-recorder as outlined in the Instrument Panel Components section. Then proceed to step 13.
13. Perform analyzer test number 4 and note the operation of the analyzer indicator lamp.
    a. If the analyzer indicator lamp does not come on, it indicates that the bumper detector and harness are functioning normally.
    b. If the analyzer indicator lamp comes on and stays on, it indicates a malfunction in the bumper detector and harness circuit. Proceed to step 14.

*NOTE: If the restraint system analyzer indicator lamp lights momentarily (3 to 9 seconds) when switches 4, 5 and 6 are moved to the test position, this does not indicate a problem. The lamp must remain on continuously to show a problem.*

14. Perform driver module and harness test number 5 and note the operation of the analyzer indicator lamp.
    a. If the analyzer indicator lamp does not come on, it indicates that the driver module and harness are functioning properly.
    b. If the analyzer indicator lamp comes on and stays on, it indicates a malfunction in the driver module and harness circut. Proceed to step 15.

15. Perform passenger module and harness test number 6 and note the operation of the analyzer indicator lamp.
    a. If the analyzer indicator lamp does not come on, it indicates that the passenger module and harness are functioning properly.
    b. If the analyzer indicator lamp comes on and stays on, it shows a malfunction in the passenger module and harness circuit.

*NOTE: If a problem is indicated in one or more circuits in steps 13, 14 and 15, refer to checking procedure "Isolation of Components in Circuits Where Problems are Indicated by Analyzer."*

## Isolation of Components in Circuits Where Problems Are Indicated by Analyzer

If one or more problems were detected when performing analyzer tests 4, 5 and 6, all conditions can be isolated and corrected by performing the operations outlined below to each malfunctioning circuit, one circuit at a time.

*NOTE: If the restraint system in car indicator comes on intermittently while driving the car, the vehicle can be road-tested with the analyzer connected to the system. Except for road-testing, the diagnosis and correction procedure is the same as for an indicator lamp "On Continuously."*

When road-testing with the analyzer connected, all sensor-recorder attaching bolts must be installed and properly torqued to assure proper operation of the system.

To isolate and correct the problems indicated by the analyzer, turn the ignition switch to LOCK and remove the key. Disconnect the negative cable from the battery and tape the terminal end of the cable. Select and perform the appropriate circuit test listed below.

*WARNING: Do not attempt any servicing or disconnecting of system components until negative cable has been disconnected from battery and terminal end of cable taped. This procedure must be followed to prevent accidental deployment of system which could cause personal injury and/or damage to system components. Care must be taken to never strike sensing mechanisms which*

*could cause deployment or improper operation of the system.*

1. Bumper Impulse Detector and Harness Circuit Test (Analyzer Test Number 4)—using connector extractor tool J-24388 or BT-7402A, disconnect the harness connector from the bumper impulse detector. Install the bumper impulse detector substitute load onto the harness connector which is located above the parking brake assembly.

*NOTE: The substitute load simulates a good component in the circuit being tested. When the analyzer test switch is turned to the test position, the load will isolate the problem as to either the component or the harness.*

Connect the negative cable to the battery and turn the ignition switch ON. Perform analyzer test number 4 and note the operation of the analyzer indicator lamp.
    a. If the analyzer indicator lamp comes on and stays on, note the above warning and replace the passenger restraint system harness (refer to the Passenger Module section).
    b. If the analyzer indicator lamp does not come on, note the above warning and replace the bumper impulse detector (refer to the Bumper section).

2. Driver Module and Harness Circuit Test (Analyzer Test Number 5)—Refer to the Driver Module section and remove the driver module from the steering wheel. Using connector extractor tool J-24628-3 or BT-7405, disconnect the driver module connector. Install the driver inflator substitute load onto the connector. Connect the negative cable to the battery and turn the ignition switch ON. Perform analyzer test number 5 and note the operation of the analyzer indicator lamp.
    a. If the analyzer indicator lamp comes on and stays on, note the above warning and replace the driver harness (refer to the Driver Module section).

*NOTE: When a problem has been isolated to the driver harness, slip ring resistance should be checked with tester J-24628-4. Replacement*

# General Motors

*of the slip ring could possibly correct the problem without replacing the driver harness.*

   b. If the analyzer indicator lamp does not come on, note the above warning and replace the driver module (refer to Driver Module section).

3. Passenger Module and Harness Circuit Test (Analyzer Test Number 6)—Remove the instrument panel pad on Cadillac and Oldsmobile (refer to the Instrument Panel Components section) and remove the glove box on Buick which will allow access to the harness connector at the passenger inflator.

Use connector extractor tool J-24388 or BT-7402A and disconnect the harness connectors from the passenger inflator. Install the passenger inflator substitute load onto the harness connector.

Connect the negative cable to the battery and turn the ignition switch ON. Perform analyzer test number 6 and note the operation of the analyzer indicator lamp.

   a. If the analyzer indicator lamp comes on and stays on, observe the above warning and replace the passenger restraint system harness (refer to the Passenger Module section).

   b. If the analyzer indicator lamp does not come on, observe the above warning and replace the passenger module (refer to the Passenger Module section).

After all tests have been completed, turn the ignition switch to LOCK and remove the key. Disconnect the negative cable from the battery and tape the terminal end of the cable. Disconnect the analyzer, replace all defective parts and install all previously removed parts. Torque the sensor-recorder attaching bolts to 57 to 87 inch pounds.

Connect the negative cable to the battery. Turn the ignition switch ON and observe the Air Cushion Restraint System Indicator Lamp.

   a. If the restraint system in car indicator lamp lights when the ignition switch is first turned ON and then goes out after 3 to 9 seconds, the

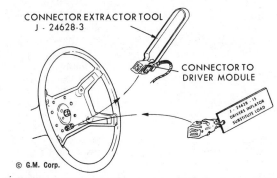

*Air Cushion Restraint System Indicator Lamp "On Continuously" Test-Driver Inflator Substitute Load Installation*

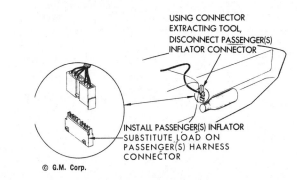

*Air Cushion Restraint System Indicator Lamp "On Continuously" Test—Passenger Inflator Substitute Load Installation*

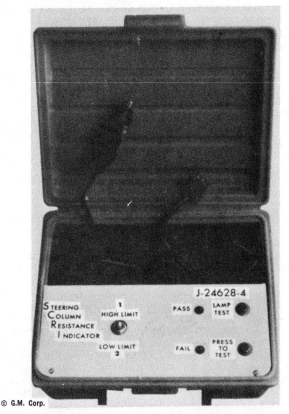

*Air Cushion Restraint System Special Tool—Steering Column Resistance Indicator*

## General Motors

system is functioning properly.

b. If the restraint system indicator lamp stays "On Continuously," continue with the diagnosis.

# INSTRUMENT PANEL COMPONENTS

*NOTE: Whenever the modules are replaced due to cushion deployment, the sensor-recorder must also be replaced. If the modules have deployed due to collision, the bumper detector will have to be replaced along with any damaged harness assemblies in the system. All restraint system components should be replaced if damaged, or carefully inspected, before connecting the negative cable to the battery after module replacement.*

*WARNING: Do not attempt any servicing or disconnecting of system components until negative cable has been disconnected from battery and terminal end of cable taped. This procedure must be followed to prevent accidental deployment of system which could cause personal injury and/or damage to system components. Care must be taken to never strike sensing mechanisms which could cause deployment or improper operation of the system.*

## KNEE RESTRAINT

### 1974-75 Buick

#### Removal and Installation

1. Turn the ignition switch to LOCK, disconnect the negative cable from the battery and tape the cable end.
2. Pry the knee restraint upper mouldings or trim plates from the instrument panel. On 1975 cars first slide the rubber filler ring upward on the column. On 1974 cars equipped with a speed alert speedometer, disconnect the control from the lower edge of the knee restraint.
3. Remove the screws from the upper and lower edges of the knee restraint.
4. Pull the knee restraint rearward to disconnect the lower air conditioner outlet. Lower the assembly to disconnect the courtesy lamp wire connector, brake release cable, ash tray lamp and cigar lighter feed wire. Remove the knee restraint assembly.

5. To install, reverse the removal procedures and torque the screws to 60 inch pounds.

### 1974-75 Cadillac

#### Removal and Installation

1. Turn the ignition switch to LOCK, disconnect the negative cable from the battery and tape the cable end.
2. Remove the glove box as follows.
   a. Remove the screws securing the glove box partition.
   b. Disconnect the glove box light and theft deterrent (1974) and/or trunk release switch.
   c. From top inside of the glove box remove the three attaching screws. Do not remove the two striker screws.
3. Remove the ash tray and tape storage compartment by opening the door on each and removing the screws. Remove the connectors from the lighter and lamps.
4. Remove the screws from the left side and lower edge of the knee restraint.
5. Working through the ash tray and tape storage openings, remove the remaining knee restraint screws.
6. To install, reverse the removal procedures and torque the screws to 75 inch pounds.

### 1974-75 Oldsmobile

#### Removal and Installation

1. Turn the ignition switch to LOCK, disconnect the negative cable from the battery and tape the cable end.
2. Slide the steering column collar up the column so the knee restraint cover can be removed.
3. Remove the screw from the left side of the cover and pull the cover from the retaining clips.
4. Remove the screws from the right and left lower edges of the restraint.
5. Remove the screws from the restraint to restraint brace, and restraint to the tie bar.
6. Remove the screw from the wiring harness ground to the tie bar.
7. Remove the screw from the left courtesy lamp.
8. Disconnect the transmission downshift switch connector.
9. Lower the knee restraint, disconnect the lower left air conditioning hose and parking brake cable at the parking brake. Remove the knee restraint.

10. To install, reverse the removal procedures and torque the screws to 60 inch pounds.

## SENSOR-RECORDER

### 1974-75 Buick

#### Removal

*WARNING: Care must be taken when handling a sensor-recorder to never strike or jar the sensing mechanism in a manner which could cause or result in personal injury or improper operation of the restraint system.*

1. Turn the ignition switch to LOCK, disconnect the negative cable from the battery and tape the cable end.
2. From beneath the instrument panel, disconnect the transmission downshift switch connector.
3. Remove the sensor-recorder attaching screws and lower the assembly. Disconnect the wire connectors using tool J-24388. Remove the sensor-recorder.

*NOTE: The sensor-recorder must be replaced anytime that the Air Cushion Restraint System has been deployed.*

#### Installation

1. Connect the harness connectors to the sensor-recorder.
2. Install the sensor-recorder with the ground wire attached to one of the screws and torque the screws to 57 to 87 inch pounds.
3. Connect the negative battery cable to the battery.
4. Turn the ignition switch to any position but LOCK.
5. Observe the indicator lamp. If operating properly, proceed to step 6, if not, connect the analyzer for diagnosis.
6. Turn the ignition switch to LOCK. Disconnect the negative battery cable and tape the cable end.
7. Connect the transmission downshift switch connector.
8. Connect the negative battery cable to the battery.

### 1974-75 Cadillac

#### Removal

*WARNING: Care must be taken when handling a sensor-recorder to never strike or jar the sensing mechanism in a manner which could cause or result in personal injury or improper operation of the restraint system.*

## General Motors

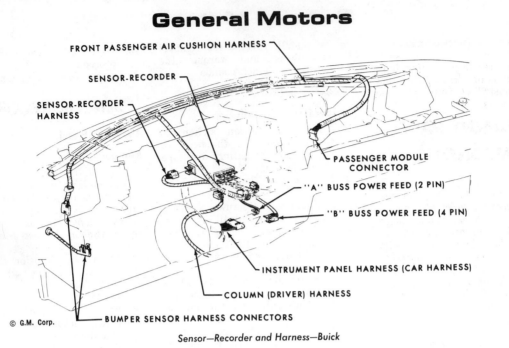

FRONT PASSENGER AIR CUSHION HARNESS

SENSOR-RECORDER

SENSOR-RECORDER HARNESS

PASSENGER MODULE CONNECTOR

"A" BUSS POWER FEED (2 PIN)

"B" BUSS POWER FEED (4 PIN)

INSTRUMENT PANEL HARNESS (CAR HARNESS)

COLUMN (DRIVER) HARNESS

© G.M. Corp.

BUMPER SENSOR HARNESS CONNECTORS

*Sensor—Recorder and Harness—Buick*

1. Turn the ignition switch to LOCK, disconnect the negative cable from the battery and tape the cable end.
2. Remove the knee restraint as previously described.
3. Remove the sensor-recorder attaching screws and lower the assembly. Disconnect the wire connectors using tool J-24388. Remove the sensor-recorder.

*NOTE: The sensor-recorder must be replaced anytime that the Air Cushion Restraint System has been deployed.*

### Installation

1. Connect the harness connectors to the sensor-recorder.
2. Install the sensor-recorder with the ground wire attached to one of the screws and torque the screws to 57 to 87 inch pounds.
3. Connect the negative battery cable to the battery.
4. Turn the ignition switch to any position but LOCK.
5. Observe the indicator lamp. If operating properly, proceed to step 6. If not, connect the analyzer for diagnosis.
6. Turn the ignition switch to LOCK. Disconnect the negative battery cable and tape the cable end.
7. Install the knee restraint and glove box as previously described.
8. Connect the negative battery cable to the battery.

### 1974-75 Oldsmobile

#### Removal

*WARNING: Care must be taken when handling a sensor-recorder to never strike or jar the sensing mechanism in a manner which could cause or result in personal injury or improper operation of the restraint system.*

1. Turn the ignition switch to LOCK, disconnect the negative cable from the battery and tape the cable end.
2. Remove the knee restraint as previously described.
3. If equipped with a convector, remove the convector attaching screws and let the convector hang.
4. Remove the sensor-recorder attaching screws and lower the assembly. Disconnect the wire connectors using tool J-24388. Remove the sensor-recorder.

*NOTE: The sensor-recorder must be replaced anytime that the Air Cushion Restraint System has been deployed.*

#### Installation

1. Connect the harness connectors to the sensor-recorder.
2. Install the sensor-recorder with the ground wire attached to one of the screws and torque the screws to 57 to 87 inch pounds.
3. Connect the negative battery cable to the battery.
4. Turn the ignition switch to any

position but LOCK.
5. Observe the indicator lamp. If operating properly, proceed to step 6. If not, connect the analyzer for diagnosis.
6. Turn the ignition switch to LOCK. Disconnect the negative battery cable and tape the cable end.
7. Connect the transmission downshift switch connector.
8. If equipped with a convector, attach the bracket to the tie bar.
9. Attach the left courtesy lamp.
10. Install the screw in the wiring harness ground to the tie bar.
11. Install the knee restraint as previously described.
12. Install the left hand cover.
13. Slide the collar on the steering column into position.
14. Connect the negative battery cable to the battery.

## SENSOR-RECORDER HARNESS

### 1974-75 All Models

#### Removal and Installation

1. Turn the ignition switch to LOCK, disconnect the negative cable from the battery and tape the cable end.
2. From beneath the instrument panel, disconnect the transmission downshift switch connector.
3. Remove the sensor-recorder attaching screws and lower the assembly.
4. Disconnect the sensor-recorder

# General Motors

harness connectors from the left and rear of the recorder using tool J-24388.

5. Disconnect the recorder harness from the "B" buss power feed connector and remove the harness.

6. To install, reverse the removal procedures making sure the ground wire is secured by one of the attaching screws. Torque the screws to 57-87 inch pounds.

## INSTRUMENT PANEL PAD

### 1974-75 Buick

#### Removal and Installation

1. Turn the ignition switch to LOCK, disconnect the negative cable from the battery and tape the cable end.

2. Remove the retaining screws from the glove box door and the glove box and disconnect the glove box light.

3. Remove the screws from the instrument panel pad.

4. Through the glove box opening, release the right instrument panel cover to cowl clip.

5. Pull the cover rearward and disconnect the air conditioning outlet hoses.

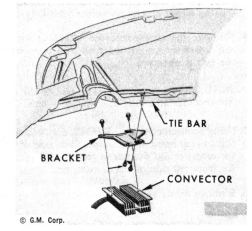

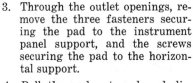

© G.M. Corp.

*Convector Attachment—Oldsmobile*

6. Disconnect the speaker wire.

7. To install, reverse the removal procedures and connect the negative battery cable to the battery.

### 1974-75 Cadillac

#### Removal and Installation

1. Turn the ignition switch to LOCK, disconnect the negative cable from the battery and tape the cable end.

2. Remove the right, right center and left climate control outlet grilles.

3. Through the outlet openings, remove the three fasteners securing the pad to the instrument panel support, and the screws securing the pad to the horizontal support.

4. Pull the pad outward and disconnect the windshield wiper switch electrical connector and bulb.

5. Remove the pad.

6. To install, reverse the removal procedures and connect the negative battery cable to the battery.

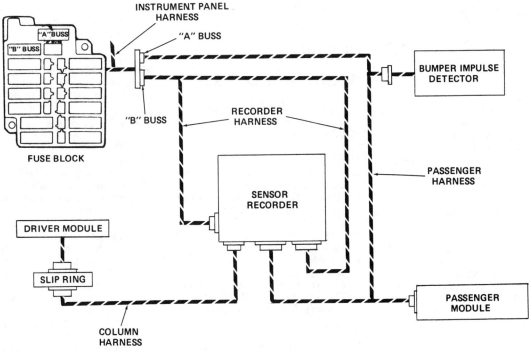

© G.M. Corp.

*Air Cushion Restraint Wiring Harness—Oldsmobile*

## General Motors

### 1974-75 Oldsmobile

**Removal and Installation**

1. Turn the ignition switch to LOCK, disconnect the negative cable from the battery and tape the cable end.
2. Remove the screws from the flood lamps and/or map lamp, disconnect the wiring and remove the lamp assembly.
3. With a wide putty knife, carefully pry the speaker assemblies from the clips, disconnect the wires and remove the speakers.
4. Remove one screw from each speaker cavity in the instrument panel pad.
5. Remove one screw from the left lower outside edge of the instrument panel pad and two screws from the instrument cluster (above speedometer).
6. From inside the glove box, remove one screw from the lower right corner and two screws from the top edge of the glove box.
7. Grip the front center edge of the instrument panel pad and pull to release the clips at the windshield edge of the pad and remove the pad.
8. To install, reverse the removal procedures and connect the negative battery cable to the battery.

## AIR CUSHION RESTRAINT INDICATOR LAMP

### 1974 Buick

**Removal and Installation**

1. Remove the knee restraint upper right trim moulding, instrument cluster lens screws and rotate the lens out of the housing.
2. Disconnect the shift quadrant cable.
3. Remove the speedometer to cluster housing screws, pull the speedometer outward, disconnect the speed alert cable and remove the speedometer.
4. Remove the wedge type restraint system indicator bulb (type 194).
5. To install, reverse the removal procedures.

### 1975 Buick

**Removal and Installation**

1. Remove the instrument panel

trim plates, instrument cluster bezel, lower cluster housing support, cluster lens and filler panel.
2. Remove the speedometer to cluster housing screws and remove the speedometer.
3. Remove the wedge type restraint system indicator bulb (type 194).
4. To install, reverse the removal procedures.

### 1974-75 Cadillac

**Removal and Installation**

1. Remove the instrument panel pad as previously described.
2. Reach under the telltale housing, remove the second socket from the left of the clock and install a new 194 bulb.
3. To install, reverse the removal procedures.

### 1974-75 Oldsmobile

**Removal and Installation**

1. Remove the instrument panel pad as previously described.
2. Disconnect the upper air hose, left of the manifold, and position it out of the way.
3. Reach down behind the instrument cluster on the left side to the bottom lamp socket. Turn the socket one eighth turn counterclockwise and remove the bulb. Replace with a 194 bulb.
4. To install, reverse the removal procedures.

## INSTRUMENT PANEL RIGHT HAND INSERT AND APPLIQUE

### 1974-75 Cadillac

**Removal**

1. Remove the instrument panel pad as previously described.
2. Remove the radio control knobs, wave washers and left hex nut.
3. Disconnect the electrical accessory switch connectors and map light connector.
4. Through the instrument panel pad openings, remove the three screws which secure the insert and applique to the horizontal support. Remove the applique.

**Installation**

1. Position the insert and applique onto the horizontal support and install the attaching screws.
2. Connect the accessory switch

and map light connectors.
3. Install the radio hex nut, control wings, wave washers and knobs.
4. Install the instrument panel as previously described.

## FRONT PASSENGER AIR CUSHION RESTRAINT TRIM COVER ASSEMBLY

### 1974-75 Buick

**Removal and Installation**

1. Remove the knee restraint as previously described.
2. Remove the screw retaining the left end of the passenger side lower trim cover (1974).
3. Remove the screws from the lower air conditioning outlet duct.
4. Remove the screws from the upper edge of the lower trim cover.
5. Pull the top of the lower trim cover outward and rotate downward to release the lower edge from the air bag frame.
6. To install, reverse the removal procedures. Make sure that the lower lip of the trim panel is first hooked over the lower edge of the passenger restraint assembly. Torque the screws to 20 to 30 inch pounds.

*NOTE: Care must be taken that the air cushion is not torn, punctured or damaged or the complete passenger module will have to be replaced.*

### 1974-75 Cadillac

**Removal**

1. Remove the knee restraint as previously described.
2. Remove the air conditioning outlet grilles and instrument panel pad.
3. Remove the radio knob, wave washers and left hex nut.
4. Reach behind the horizontal support and remove the three right hand insert and applique attaching screws.
5. Disconnect the accessory switch harness.
6. Remove the right hand insert and applique.
7. Remove the six screws through the square holes in the horizontal support.
8. Remove the trim screw from the

## General Motors

right side.

9. Remove the trim cover to knee restraint brace screw from the left side.

*NOTE: Care must be taken that the air cushion is not torn, punctured or damaged or the complete passenger module will have to be replaced.*

### Installation

*NOTE: The front lower edge of the right hand trim cover must be hooked onto the air cushion restraint assembly before installation of any attaching screws. The upper edge of the trim cover must be inserted between the reinforcement and horizontal support.*

1. To install, reverse the removal procedures and torque the screws to 20 to 30 inch pounds.

### 1974-75 Oldsmobile

#### Removal

1. Remove the knee restraint as previously described.
2. Remove the glove box door and ash tray.

3. Remove the screw from the left front edge of the trim cover to extension.
4. Remove the screw from the right side of the trim cover to bracket.
5. Remove the screws from the lower front edge of the glove box attaching trim cover.
6. Pull the top edge of the trim cover outward, then lower to unhook from the lower edge of the passenger air cushion restraint assembly.
7. Remove the lower air conditioning outlet assembly from the trim cover.

*NOTE: Care must be taken that the air cushion is not torn, punctured or damaged or the complete passenger module will have to be replaced.*

### Installation

*NOTE: The front lower edge of the right hand trim cover must be hooked onto the air cushion restraint assembly before installation of any attaching screws.*

1. To install, reverse the removal procedures and torque the

screws to 20 to 30 inch pounds.

## BUMPER IMPULSE DETECTOR

*WARNING: On vehicles equipped with the Air Cushion Restraint System do not attempt any adjustment, repair or removal of the front bumper or components until the disconnection procedure is completed. This procedure must be followed to prevent accidental deployment of the system which could cause personal injury and/or damage to system components. Care must be taken to never strike the bumper impulse detector in a manner which could cause deployment or improper operation of the system.*

### 1974-75 All Models

#### Removal

1. Turn the ignition switch to LOCK. Disconnect the negative battery cable and tape the cable end.

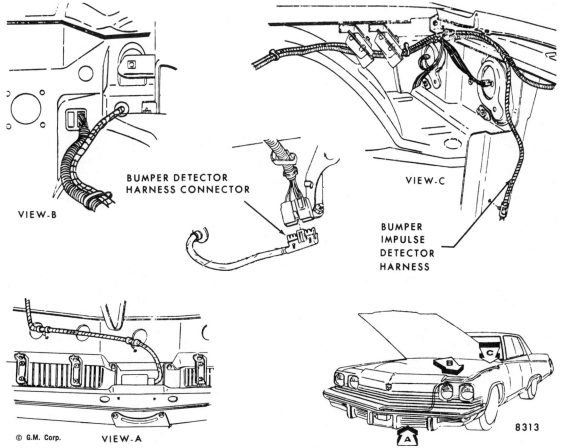

BUMPER DETECTOR HARNESS CONNECTOR

VIEW-B

VIEW-C

BUMPER IMPULSE DETECTOR HARNESS

© G.M. Corp.     VIEW-A

8313

*Bumper Impulse Detector Installation—Buick*

## General Motors

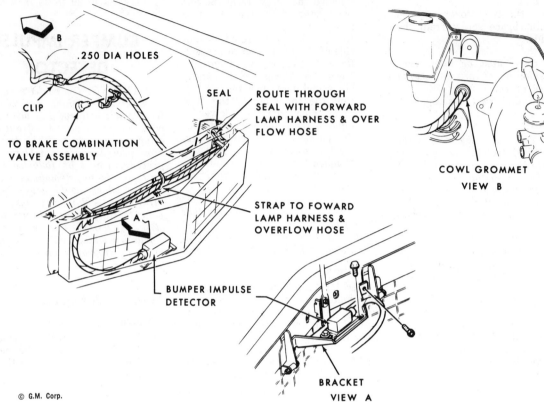

© G.M. Corp.

*Bumper Impulse Detector Mounting—Cadillac*

2. Disconnect the harness connector near the fuse panel using tool J-24388.
3. Remove the grommet from the cowl and feed the harness into the engine compartment.
4. Remove the harness from the engine compartment retainers and feed the harness through or over the radiator support.

5. On 1974-75 cars except the 1974 Riviera, remove the impulse detector attaching bolts and remove the detector from the bumper. On 1974 Riviera, remove the front bumper. Disassemble the bumper enough to gain access to the impulse detector and remove the detector assembly from the bumper.

### Installation

1. To install, reverse the removal procedures and torque the impulse detector bolts to 60 to 90 inch pounds.
2. Turn the ignition switch to any position but LOCK and note the operation of the indicator lamp. If the light is not functioning

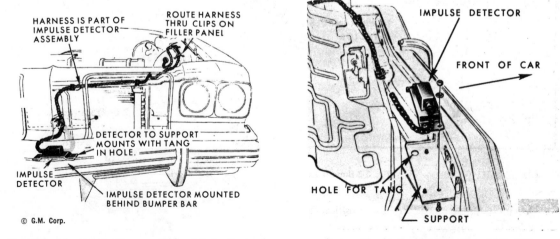

© G.M. Corp.

*Bumper Impulse Detector Harness—Oldsmobile Exc Toronado*

*Bumper Impulse Detector Mounting—Oldsmobile*

## General Motors

properly refer to the Operation and Diagnosis section.

# MINOR BUMPER DAMAGE

### 1974-75 All Models

#### Inspection

When there is minor bumper damage to the front bumper and the restraint system has not been deployed but removal or replacement of the bumper is required, the following procedures must be followed.

1. Turn the ignition switch to LOCK. Disconnect the negative battery cable and tape the cable end.
2. Remove the impulse detector from the bracket.
3. Inspect the impulse detector for any visual damage to the case or mounting. If damaged, replace the assembly.
4. On Cadillac and Oldsmobile, inspect the mounting bracket for rigid attachment to the bumper reinforcement and damage to the bracket. If the attachment is not rigid, replace or retorque the attachment making certain the bolts are torqued as follows:
   a. Cadillac—30 foot pounds.
   b. Oldsmobile except Toronado —25 foot pounds.
   c. Toronado—20 foot pounds.
5. Inspect the wiring harness for chafing, cuts or visible damage. Do not repair the harness. If damaged, replace the harness assembly.
6. If there is no visible damage, tape the bumper impulse detector to the front end sheet metal until all bumper repairs are made.
7. After bumper repairs are completed, remove the tape from the detector and install the detector to the bracket. Connect the negative battery cable to the battery.

# PASSENGER MODULE

*WARNING: The passenger module should always be carried with the inflator and reaction plate between ones body and the cushion. The assembly should be placed on a flat surface with the inflator and reaction plate between the flat surface and the cushion. This is to allow free space for cushion expansion in case*

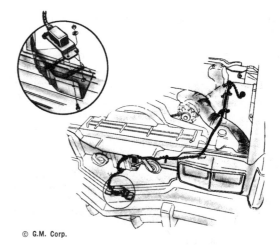

© G.M. Corp.

*Bumper Impulse Detector Harness—Oldsmobile Toronado*

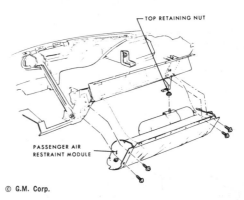

© G.M. Corp.

*Passenger Air Cushion Assembly Installation—Buick*

*of accidental deployment. Otherwise, serious injury may result.*

### 1974-75 Buick

#### Removal

1. Turn the ignition switch to LOCK. Disconnect the negative battery cable from the battery and tape the cable end.
2. Remove the knee restraint and front passenger air cushion trim cover as described in the Instrument Panel Components section.
3. Remove the glove box door and glove box.
4. Disconnect the passenger module harness connector from module using tool J-24388. Loosen the module to top bracket retaining nut.
5. Remove the top screws and side bolts attaching the module assembly to the instrument panel frame.
6. Support the module, remove the top nut and remove the module assembly.

*WARNING: The passenger air*

cushion assembly (non-deployed) should always be carried with the uncovered cushion away from ones body to prevent injury and/or damage in case of accidental deployment.

*NOTE: If the passenger air cushion is to be replaced, refer to the Parts Disposal section.*

#### Installation

1. If the test load was used in the passenger restraint wiring for diagnosis, remove the load from the connector.
2. Position the assembly into place and loosely attach the top nut to the stud through the mounting bracket. Connect the wire connector to the module.
3. Connect the negative battery cable to the battery.
4. Turn the ignition switch to any position but LOCK.
5. Observe the indicator lamp. If operating properly, proceed to step 6, if not, perform a diagnosis test.
6. Turn the ignition switch to

# General Motors

LOCK. Disconnect the negative battery cable and tape the cable end.

7. Install the module attaching screws and bolts finger tight.

8. Torque the top nut 95 to 145 inch pounds, the bolts 15 to 20 foot pounds, and the screws 20 to 30 inch pounds.

9. Install the module trim cover, glove box and door, knee restraint and trim plates.

10. Connect the negative battery cable to the battery.

## 1974-75 Cadillac

### Removal

1. Turn the ignition switch to LOCK. Disconnect the negative cable from the battery and tape the cable end.

2. Remove the front passenger air cushion trim cover as described in the Instrument Panel Components section.

3. Remove the six screws attaching the support and air cushion restraint assembly to the reinforcement.

4. Disconnect the passenger module wiring harness using tool J-24388.

5. Remove the screws from the right and left sides of the cushion restraint assembly.

6. Support the cushion restraint assembly and remove the bolt from behind the instrument panel that attaches the support to the cowl. Remove the passenger restraint assembly.

*WARNING: The passenger air cushion assembly (non-deployed) should always be carried with the uncovered cushion away from ones body to prevent injury and/or damage in case of accidental deployment.*

*NOTE: If the passenger air cushion is to be replaced, refer to the Parts Disposal section.*

### Installation

1. If the test load was used in the passenger restraint wiring for diagnosis, remove the load from the connector.

2. Position the assembly into place and loosely attach the bolt through the support into the cowl. Connect the wiring harness to the module assembly.

3. Connect the negative battery cable to the battery.

4. Turn the ignition switch to any position but LOCK.

5. Observe the indicator lamp. If operating properly, proceed to step 6, if not, perform a diagnosis test.

6. Turn the ignition switch to LOCK. Disconnect the negative cable from the battery and tape the cable end.

7. Reverse the removal procedures to complete installation.

## 1974-75 Oldsmobile

### Removal

1. Turn the ignition switch to LOCK. Disconnect the negative cable from the battery and tape the cable end.

2. Remove the knee restraint and front passenger air cushion trim cover as described in the Instrument Panel Components section.

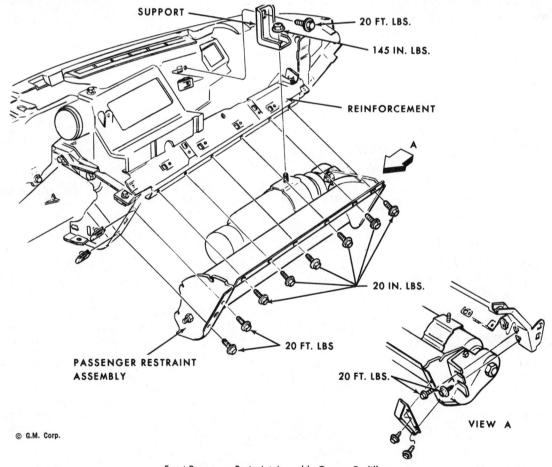

SUPPORT — 20 FT. LBS.

145 IN. LBS.

REINFORCEMENT

A

20 IN. LBS.

PASSENGER RESTRAINT ASSEMBLY

20 FT. LBS

20 FT. LBS.

VIEW A

© G.M. Corp.

*Front Passenger Restraint Assembly Cover—Cadillac*

## General Motors

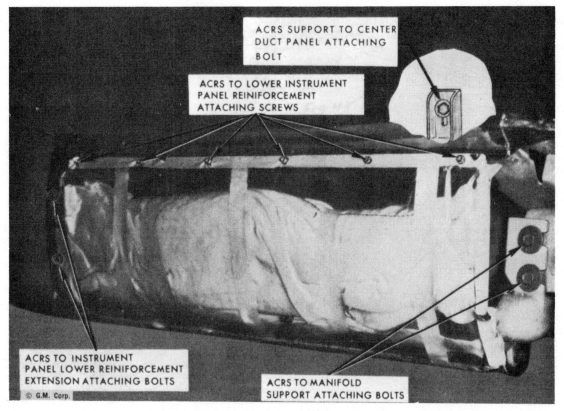

ACRS SUPPORT TO CENTER DUCT PANEL ATTACHING BOLT

ACRS TO LOWER INSTRUMENT PANEL REINIFORCEMENT ATTACHING SCREWS

ACRS TO INSTRUMENT PANEL LOWER REINIFORCEMENT EXTENSION ATTACHING BOLTS

© G.M. Corp.

ACRS TO MANIFOLD SUPPORT ATTACHING BOLTS

*Front Passenger Air Cushion Restraint Assembly—Cadillac*

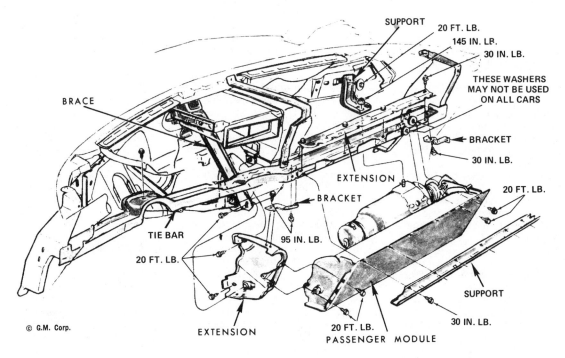

SUPPORT

20 FT. LB.

145 IN. LB.

30 IN. LB.

THESE WASHERS MAY NOT BE USED ON ALL CARS

BRACE

BRACKET

30 IN. LB.

EXTENSION

BRACKET

20 FT. LB.

TIE BAR

95 IN. LB.

20 FT. LB.

SUPPORT

© G.M. Corp.

EXTENSION

20 FT. LB.
PASSENGER MODULE

30 IN. LB.

*Passenger Air Cushion Restraint Attachment—Oldsmobile*

## General Motors

3. Remove the six screws attaching the support and restraint assembly to the tie bar.
4. Remove the instrument panel pad as described in the Instrument Panel Components section.
5. Disconnect the right air conditioning hose at the manifold.
6. Disconnect the passenger module wiring harness using tool J-24388.
7. Remove the screws from the right and left sides of the restraint assembly.

*NOTE: For proper alignment, reinstall the original amount of washers on each bolt between the restraint assembly and the right hand end support.*

8. Support the cushion restraint assembly and remove the bolt from behind the instrument panel that attaches the support to the cowl. Remove the passenger restraint assembly.

*WARNING: The passenger air cushion assembly (non-deployed) should always be carried with the uncovered cushion away from ones body to prevent injury and/or damage in case of accidental deployment.*

*NOTE: If the passenger air cushion is to be replaced, refer to the Parts Disposal section.*

### Installation

1. If the test load was used in the passenger restraint for diagnosis, remove the load from the connector.
2. Position the assembly into place and loosely attach the bolt through the support into the cowl. Connect the wiring harness to the module assembly.
3. Connect the negative battery cable to the battery.
4. Turn the ignition switch to any position but LOCK.
5. Observe the indicator lamp. If operating properly, proceed to step 6, if not, perform a diagnosis test.
6. Turn the ignition switch to LOCK. Disconnect the negative cable from the battery and tape the cable end.
7. Remove analyzer J-24628 from the restraint system and reconnect the restraint connectors to the system.
8. Reverse the removal procedures to complete installation.

# PASSENGER AIR CUSHION RESTRAINT SYSTEM WIRING HARNESS

## 1974-75 Buick

### Removal and Installation

1. Turn the ignition switch to LOCK. Disconnect the negative battery cable from the battery and tape the cable end.
2. Remove the glove box door and glove box. Reach through the opening and disconnect the automatic air conditioning breath sensor and four inch hose from the cover.
3. Release the speed alert cable (1974). Disconnect the ash tray lamp and cigar lighter wires. Remove the knee restraint (refer to the Instrument Panel Components section) and lower the air conditioning manifold (1974).
4. Remove the instrument panel cover (refer to the Instrument Panel Components section).
5. Disconnect the shift quadrant cable. Remove the two steering column to instrument panel mounting nuts and lower the column.
6. Remove the instrument cluster to cowl attaching screws (and radio bracket if stereo equipped).
7. Disconnect the speedometer cable, power antenna cable (1974) and move the assembly rearward.
8. Remove the heater air conditioning upper and lower duct.
9. On 1975, remove the instrument panel frame to cowl center brace.
10. Remove the defroster duct lower center cap screw and straighten the four retainer tabs.
11. Remove the ground strap from the left sensor bracket.
12. With tool J-24388, remove the center connector from the sensor and power feed connector and from the instrument panel harness connector. Disconnect the bumper impulse defector cable from the left side of the fuse block. Remove the connector from the passenger module.
13. Open the cross car conduit and thread both ends of the harness toward the center of the cowl.
14. To install, reverse the removal procedures and torque the steer-

ing column retaining nuts to 20 foot pounds.

## 1974-75 Cadillac

### Removal and Installation

1. Turn the ignition switch to LOCK. Disconnect the negative battery cable from the battery and tape the cable end.
2. Remove the glove box, knee restraint and instrument panel pad (refer to the Instrument Panel Components section).
3. Remove the instrument panel top cover as follows:
   a. Remove the right and left trim screws.
   b. Remove the two studs that hold the top cover to the supports.
   c. Loosen the top nut that secures the top cover to the instrument panel cowl brace (located forward and left of the clock).
   d. Disconnect the radio speaker connector at the radio.
   e. Pull the top cover straight out and lift to disconnect the printed circuit connector, fuel gauge bulb and connector, clock bulb and connector, climate control in-car sensor connector and aspirator hose, twilight sentinal photocell, and map light connector.
4. Remove the sensor-recorder attaching screws and lower the recorder.
5. Using tool J-24388, disconnect the passenger module wiring harness from the sensor-recorder and bumper impulse detector harness.
6. Through the instrument panel pad opening, disconnect the harness from the passenger module.
7. Remove the air conditioning distributor hose. Straighten the tabs on the defroster duct and pull the duct to gain access to the cross bar conduit.
8. Remove the harness from the conduit.
9. To install, reverse the removal procedures.

## 1974-75 Oldsmobile

### Removal

1. Turn the ignition switch to LOCK. Disconnect the negative battery cable from the battery and tape the cable end.
2. Remove the knee restraint (refer to the Instrument Panel Components section).

## General Motors

3. Remove the convector screws and let the convector hang (if so equipped).
4. Remove the flood lamps and/or map lamps.
5. Pry the speaker assemblies from the clips and remove the speakers.
6. Reach through each speaker cavity and remove the instrument panel pad screws.
7. Remove one screw from the left lower outer edge of the instrument panel pad and two screws from the instrument cluster (above the speedometer).
8. Open the glove box door and remove one screw from the lower right corner and two screws from the top edge of the glove box.

9. Grip the front center edge of the instrument panel pad and pull to release the clips at the windshield edge of the pad. Remove the pad.
10. Remove the right and left upper hoses from the outlet ducts and manifold.
11. Remove the screws from the ash tray housing hinge, glove box door, ash tray retainer to glove box door stop and ash tray retainer to glove box.
12. Remove the upper right hand corner trim panel screws.
13. Remove the screw from the upper corners of the right upper trim panel.

14. Remove the three screws from the instrument panel center support.
15. Remove the manifold screw and defroster duct to heater case screw.
16. Straighten the tabs at the top ends of the defroster duct and remove the duct.
17. With tool J-24388, disconnect the passenger harness connectors:
    a. 'A' Buss Power Feed.
    b. Bumper Impulse Detector.
    c. Passenger Module.
    d. Sensor-Recorder.
18. Remove the harness from its protective covering.
19. To install, reverse the removal procedures.

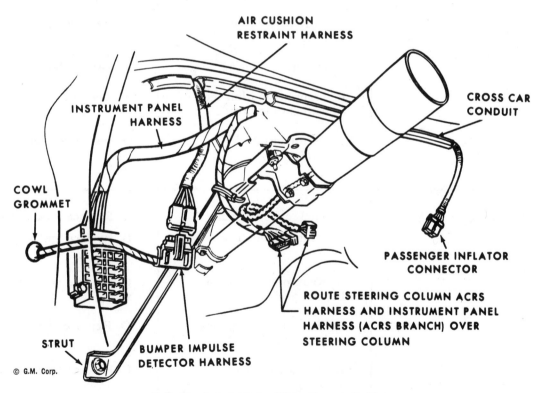

*Air Cushion Restraint System Wiring Harness—Cadillac*

**LOCK SYSTEM**

| CONDITION | POSSIBLE CAUSE | CORRECTION |
|---|---|---|
| 1. Will not unlock | A. Sector stripped | A. Replace sector |
| | B. Lock bolt damaged | B. Replace lock bolt |
| | C. Faulty lock cylinder | C. Replace lock cylinder |
| | D. Damaged housing | D. Replace housing |
| 2. Will not lock | A. Lock bolt spring broken or faulty | A. Replace lock bolt spring |
| | B. Damaged sector tooth | B. Replace sector |
| | C. Faulty lock cylinder | C. Replace lock cylinder |
| | D. Burr on lock bolt or housing | D. Remove burr |
| | E. Damaged housing | E. Replace housing |
| | F. Transmission linkage adjustment incorrect | F. Readjust |
| | G. Sector installed incorrectly | G. Install correctly |
| 3. High effort | A. Lock cylinder faulty | A. Replace lock cylinder |
| | B. Ignition switch faulty | B. Replace ignition switch |
| | C. Rack preload spring broken or deformed | C. Replace rack preload spring |
| | D. Burrs on sector, rack or housing | D. Remove burr |
| | E. Bent sector shaft | E. Replace housing assembly |
| | F. Actuator rod restricted | F. Remove restriction |
| 4. High effort on lock cylinder between "off" and "off-lock" | A. Burr on tang of shift gate | A. Remove burr |
| | B. Distorted rack | B. Replace rack |

## General Motors

**LOCK SYSTEM (Continued)**

| CONDITION | POSSIBLE CAUSE | CORRECTION |
|---|---|---|
| 5. Will stick in "start" | A. Actuator rod deformed<br><br>B. Any high effort condition | A. Straighten or replace<br><br>B. Check items under high effort section |
| 6. Lock bolt hits shaft lock in "off" position and "park" | A. Ignition switch is not set correctly | A. Readjust ignition switch |
| 7. Key can not be removed in "off-lock" | A. Ignition switch is not set correctly<br><br>B. Faulty lock cylinder | A. Readjust<br><br>B. Replace lock cylinder |
| 8. Lock cylinder can be removed without depressing retainer | A. Lock cylinder with faulty retainer<br><br>B. Lock cylinder without retainer<br><br>C. Burr over retainer slot in housing | A. Replace lock cylinder<br><br>B. Replace lock cylinder<br><br>C. Remove burr in housing |

**IGNITION SYSTEM**

| CONDITION | POSSIBLE CAUSE | CORRECTION |
|---|---|---|
| 1. Electrical system will not function | A. Broken fuse in "accessory" circuit<br><br>B. Connector body loose or broken<br><br>C. Faulty wiring<br><br>D. Faulty ignition switch<br><br>E. Air Cushion Restraint System remains on and problems traced to column | A. Replace fuse<br><br>B. Tighten or replace<br><br>C. Repair or replace<br><br>D. Replace ignition switch<br><br>E. Replace slip ring and/or cable. Slip ring serviced as a unit<br><br>NOTE: Problem may be in Air Cushion Restraint System module in steering wheel |

## General Motors

### IGNITION SYSTEM (Continued)

| CONDITION | POSSIBLE CAUSE | CORRECTION |
|---|---|---|
| 2. Switch will not actuate mechanically | A. Faulty ignition switch | A. Replace ignition switch |
| 3. Switch cannot be set correctly | A. Switch actuator rod deformed | A. Repair or replace switch actuator rod |

### COLUMN

| CONDITION | POSSIBLE CAUSE | CORRECTION |
|---|---|---|
| 1. Noise in column | A. Coupling bolts not tightened | A. Tighten pinch bolts to 30 foot pounds Tighten coupling bolts to specified torque. (Parts should be inspected for damage before reassembling. If serrations or threads are damaged, replace parts) |
| | B. Column not correctly aligned | B. Realign column |
| | C. Coupling pulled apart | C. Realign column and replace coupling. Broken intermediate shaft plastic injected joint. If intermediate shaft is damaged, replace - if not, repair joint using repair kit 7810077. |
| | D. Horn contact ring not lubricated | D. Lubricate with Lubriplate |
| | E. Lack of grease on bearings or bearing surface | E. Lubricate |
| | F. Lower shaft bearing tight or frozen | F. Replace bearing. Check shaft and replace if scored |
| | G. Upper shaft bearing tight or frozen | G. Replace housing assembly |

## General Motors

**COLUMN (Continued)**

| CONDITION | POSSIBLE CAUSE | CORRECTION |
|---|---|---|
| | H. Shaft lock plate cover loose | H. Make sure wave washer properly installed so as to put pressure on cover. Tighten three screws to 15 inch pounds CAUTION: Use specified screws |
| | I. Lock plate retaining ring not seated | I. Replace retaining ring Check for proper seating in groove |
| | J. Slip ring noise | J. Some slip ring noise is normal. Do not lubricate or disassemble slip ring assembly to eliminate excessive noise. Replace slip ring assembly |
| 2. One click when in "off-lock" position and the steering wheel is moved | | A. None - normal - lock bolt is seating |
| 3. High steering shaft effort | A. Column assembly mis-aligned in vehicle | A. Align correctly |
| | B. Improperly installed or deformed dust seal | B. Replace dust seal |
| | C. Tight or frozen upper or lower bearings | C. Replace |
| 4. High shift effort | A. Column not aligned correctly in car | A. Realign |
| | B. Lower bowl bearing not aligned correctly | B. Reassemble correctly |
| | C. Improperly installed dust seal | C. Remove and replace |
| | D. Lack of grease on seal or bearing areas | D. Lubicate |

## General Motors

**COLUMN (Continued)**

| CONDITION | POSSIBLE CAUSE | CORRECTION |
|---|---|---|
| 5. Improper transmission shifting | A. Sheared shift tube joint | A. Replace shift tube assembly |
| | B. Improper transmission linkage adjustment | B. Readjust |
| | C. Loose lower shift lever | C. Replace shift tube assembly |
| | D. Improper gate plate | D. Replace with correct part |
| 6. Miscellaneous | A. Shroud loose on shift bowl | A. Bend tabs on shroud over lugs on bowl |
| | B. Housing loose on jacket - will be noticed with ignition in "off-lock" and a torque applied to the steering wheel | B. Tighten four mounting screws (60 inch pounds) |
| 7. Lash in mounted column assembly | A. Instrument panel bracket to instrument panel mounting bolts loose | A. Tighten to 20 foot pounds |
| | B. Broken weld nuts on jacket | B. Replace jacket assembly |
| | C. Instrument panel bracket capsule sheared | C. Replace bracket assembly |
| | D. Instrument panel bracket to jacket mounting bolts loose | D. Tighten to 15 foot pounds |
| | E. Column lower clamp loose | E. Tighten clamp |

**SIGNAL SWITCH DIAGNOSIS**

| CONDITION | POSSIBLE CAUSE | CORRECTION |
|---|---|---|
| 1. Turn signal will not cancel | A. Loose switch mounting screws | A. Tighten to specified torque (25 inch pounds) |
| | B. Switch or anchor bosses broken | B. Replace switch |

932

SIGNAL SWITCH DIAGNOSIS (Continued)

| CONDITION | POSSIBLE CAUSE | CORRECTION |
|---|---|---|
| | C. Broken, missing or out of position detent, return or cancelling spring | C. Reposition or replace springs as required |
| | D. Uneven or incorrect cancelling cam to cancelling spring interference (.120) side | D. Adjust switch position<br><br>1. If interference is correct and switch will not cancel, replace switch<br><br>2. If interference cannot be corrected by switch adjustment, replace cancelling cam |
| 2. Turn signal difficult to operate | A. Actuator rod loose | A. Tighten mounting screw (12 inch pounds) |
| | B. Yoke broken or distorted | B. Replace switch |
| | C. Loose or misplaced springs | C. Reposition or replace springs |
| | D. Foreign parts and/or materials | D. Remove foreign parts and/or materials |
| | E. Switch mounted loosely | E. Tighten mounting screws (25 inch pounds) |
| 3. Turn signal will not indicate lane change | A. Broken lane change pressure pad or spring hanger | A. Replace switch |
| | B. Broken, missing or misplaced lane change spring | B. Replace or reposition as required |
| | C. Jammed base or wires | C. Loosen mounting screws, reposition base or wires and retighten screws (25 inch pounds) |
| 4. Turn signal will not stay in turn position | A. Foreign material or loose parts impeding movement of yoke | A. Remove material and/or parts |

**SIGNAL SWITCH DIAGNOSIS (Continued)**

| CONDITION | POSSIBLE CAUSE | CORRECTION |
|---|---|---|
| | B. Broken or missing detent or cancelling springs | B. Replace spring |
| | C. None of the above | C. Replace switch |
| 5. Hazard switch cannot be turned off | A. Foreign material between hazard support cancelling leg and yoke | A. Remove foreign material<br><br>1. No foreign material impeding function of hazard switch - replace turn signal switch |
| 6. Hazard switch will not stay on or difficult to turn off | A. Loose switch mounting screws | A. Tighten mounting screws (25 inch pounds) |
| | B. Interference with other components | B. Remove interference |
| | C. Foreign material | C. Remove foreign material |
| | D. None of the above | D. Replace switch |
| 7. No turn signal lights | A. Faulty or blown fuse | A. Replace fuse |
| | B. Inoperative turn signal flasher | B. Replace turn signal flasher |
| | C. Loose chassis to column connector | C. Connect securely |
| | D. Disconnect column to chassis connector. Connect new switch to chassis and operate switch by hand<br><br>If vehicle lights now operate normally, signal switch is in-operative | D. Replace signal switch |
| | E. If vehicle lights do not operate check chassis wiring for opens, grounds, etc. | E. Repair chassis wiring as required using manual as guide |

## General Motors

**SIGNAL SWITCH DIAGNOSIS (Continued)**

| CONDITION | POSSIBLE CAUSE | CORRECTION |
|---|---|---|
| 8. Turn indicator lights on, but not flashing | A. Inoperative turn flasher | A. Replace turn flasher<br><br>NOTE: There are two flashers in the system |
| | B. Loose chassis to column connection | B. Connect securely |
| | C. Inoperative turn signal switch | C. Replace turn signal switch |
| | D. To determine if turn signal switch is inoperative, substitute new switch into circuit and operate switch by hand. If the vehicle's lights operate normally, signal switch is inoperative | D. Replace signal switch |
| | E. If the vehicle's lights do not operate, check light sockets for high resistance connections, the chassis wiring for opens, grounds, etc. | E. Repair chassis wiring as required |
| 9. Front or rear turn signal lights not flashing | A. Burned out or damaged turn signal bulb | A. Replace bulb |
| | B. High resistance connection to ground at bulb socket | B. Remove or repair defective connection |
| | C. Loose chassis to column connector | C. Connect securely |
| | D. Disconnect column to chassis connector. Connect new switch into system and operate switch by hand. If turn signal lights are now on and flash, turn signal switch is inoperative | D. Replace turn signal switch |

### SIGNAL SWITCH DIAGNOSIS (Continued)

| CONDITION | POSSIBLE CAUSE | CORRECTION |
|---|---|---|
| | E. If vehicle lights do not operate, check chassis wiring harness to light sockets for opens, grounds, etc. | E. Repair chassis wiring as required |
| 10. Stop light not on when turn indicated | A. Loose column to chassis connection | A. Connect securely |
| | B. Disconnect column to chassis connector. Connect new switch into system without removing old. Operate switch by hand. If brake lights work with switch in the turn posiiton, signal switch is defective | B. Replace signal switch |
| | C. If brake lights do not work check connector to stop light sockets for grounds, opens, etc. | C. Repair connector to stop light circuits |
| 11. Turn indicator panel lights not flashing | A. Burned out bulbs | A. Replace bulbs |
| | B. High resistance to ground at bulb socket | B. Replace socket |
| | C. Opens, grounds in wiring harness from front turn signal bulb socket to indicator lights | C. Locate and repair as required |
| 12. Turn signal lights flash very slowly | A. Inoperative turn signal flasher | A. Replace turn signal flasher |
| | B. System charging voltage low | B. Increase voltage to specified |
| | C. High resistance ground at light sockets | C. Repair high resistance grounds at light sockets |

**SIGNAL SWITCH DIAGNOSIS (Continued)**

| CONDITION | POSSIBLE CAUSE | CORRECTION |
|---|---|---|
| | D. Loose chassis to column connection | D. Connect securely |
| | E. Disconnect column to chassis connector. Connect new switch into system without removing old. Operate switch by hand. If flashing occurs at normal rate, the signal switch is faulty | E. Replace signal switch |
| | F. If the flashing rate is still extremely slow, check chassis wiring harness from the connector to light sockets for grounds, high resistance points, etc. | F. Locate and repair as required |
| 13. Hazard signal lights will not flash - turn signal functions normally | A. Blown fuse | A. Replace fuse |
| | B. Inoperative hazard warning flasher | B. Replace hazard warning flasher |
| | C. Loose chassis to column connection | C. Connect securely |
| | D. Disconnect column to chassis connector. Connect new switch into system without removing old. Depress the hazard warning button and observe the hazard warning lights. If they now work normally, the turn signal switch is faulty | D. Replace the turn signal switch |
| | E. If the lights do not flash, check wiring harness "K" lead (brown) for open between hazard flasher and harmonica connector. If open, fuse block is faulty | E. Replace fuse block |

## General Motors

**KEY BUZZER DIAGNOSIS**

| CONDITION | POSSIBLE CAUSE | CORRECTION |
|---|---|---|
| 1. Buzzer does not sound with key fully inserted in lock cylinder with the driver's door open | A. Faulty buzzer | A. Replace buzzer |
| | B. Bad connection at buzzer | B. Connect securely |
| | C. Power not available to buzzer | C. Check continuity of chassis wiring and repair as required |
| | D. Door jamb switch on driver's side misadjusted or inoperative | D. Readjust or replace - as required |
| | E. Short in chassis wiring | E. Check by separating chassis to column connector. Connect "E" (black) and "F" (black w/pink stripe) female contacts on the chassis side, use a Bent paper clip, if buzzer sounds, continue diagnosis. If not, locate and repair chassis wiring |
| | NOTE 1. If the buzzer fault has not yet been detected, connect a continuity meter (light) to the male "E" and "F" connector contacts   Insert the key the full depth into the lock cylinder. | |
| | If contact is made with the key in, and is not made with it out, the function is normal. Retrace initial diagnostic steps. | |
| | If contact is not established, the fault is in the column. Proceed to Note 2. | |
| | NOTE 2. With the fault isolated in the column, disassemble the upper end of the column until the signal switch mounting screws have been removed. Lift the switch and check the probes of the buzzer switch to insure good contact with the pads on the signal switch. Bend probes, if required, then reseat the signal switch and drive the three screws. Check the function, as in Note 1. | |

**KEY BUZZER DIAGNOSIS (Continued)**

| CONDITION | POSSIBLE CAUSE | CORRECTION |
|---|---|---|
| | F. Short or fault in signal switch wiring | F. Connect male "E" and "F" contacts of connector with jumper Check buzzer switch pads with continuity meter. If contact is made, function is normal. If not, replace signal switch. |
| | NOTE 3. If the fault has not yet been isolated and repaired, connect a continuity meter to the buzzer switch probes Fully insert and remove the key from the lock cylinder. | |
| | If contact is made with the key in, and is broken with it out, the function is normal. Retrace diagnostic steps starting at Note 2. | |
| | If contact is not made, the fault is in the lock cylinder or buzzer switch | |
| | G. Chips, burrs, foreign material preventing actuator tip function CAUTION: Key must be removed or cylinder in "run" position before removing lock cylinder | G. Remove chips, burrs, etc. Reassemble and recheck ref. Note 3. |
| | H. Faulty lock cylinder | H. With the lock cylinder out (observing caution under G), fully insert and remove the key. The actuator should extend and retract smoothly. Total extension of tip should be .050 inches. If not, replace lock cylinder |
| | I. Chips, foreign material affecting buzzer switch operation | I. Remove and clean as required - reassemble and recheck per Note 3. |
| | J. Damaged or broken buzzer switch | J. Replace buzzer switch |
| | K. Switch appears good but will not make buzzer switch function check | K. Connect continuity meter leads to the buzzer switch probes. Press on the actuator pad until the interior points contact If contact is not made, replace buzzer switch |

# Air Cushion Restraint System

## General Motors

**KEY BUZZER DIAGNOSIS (Continued)**

| CONDITION | POSSIBLE CAUSE | CORRECTION |
|---|---|---|
| | L. Buzzer switch contact gap too large<br><br>NOTE 4. Setting the contact gap. Press a .030 inches wire type spark plug gap wire with flat piece of stock on the actuator pad If contact is not made adjust switch until positive contact is made. (Use continuity meter)<br><br>With positive contact at .030 inches, use a .025 inches plug gap wire beneath the flat stock No contact should occur. When the switch will make contact with the .030 inches wire and not with the .025 inches, the buzzer switch is set at the low limit | L. Reset contact gap |
| 2. Buzzer continues to operate with key in the lock cylinder with the driver's door either opened or closed and ceases when key is removed | A. Door jamb switch on driver's side misadjusted or inoperative<br><br>B. Wire from signal switch to door jamb switch shorted<br><br>NOTE 5. This condition indicates the lock cylinder or buzzer switch is at fault. To verify, check for continuity at the "E" and "F" male connector contacts with the key removed from the cylinder If continuity exists, the fault is in the column | A. Adjust or replace as required<br><br>B. If on signal switch side, replace signal switch. If on chassis side, find and repair |

### KEY BUZZER DIAGNOSIS (Continued)

| CONDITION | POSSIBLE CAUSE | CORRECTION |
|---|---|---|
| 3. Buzzer continues to operate with key out, but stops when driver's door is closed | A. Turn lock towards "start" position. buzzer stops in "run" position or when turned past "run" towards "start", the problem is a sticky lock cylinder actuator | A. Replace lock cylinder |
| | B. Chips, foreign material in lock cylinder bore | B. Remove, reassembly and recheck function |
| | C. Sticky lock cylinder actuator tip | C. Replace lock cylinder |
| | D. Damaged or broken buzzer switch | D. Replace buzzer switch |
| | E. Buzzer switch contact gap too close | E. Adjust as specified |

# DRIVER MODULE AND STEERING COLUMN

## Steering Column

*WARNING: On vehicles equipped with the Air Cushion Restraint System, do not attempt any adjustment, repair or removal of the steering column or steering wheel until the disconnection procedure is completed. This procedure must be followed to prevent accidental deployment of the system which could cause personal injury and/or damage to the system components.*

## Disconnect Procedure

Turn the ignition switch to LOCK. Disconnect the negative battery cable from the battery and tape the cable end.

## Trouble Diagnosis Instructions

The diagnosis charts contain information to help locate the cause of steering column malfunction.

# DRIVER MODULE SYSTEM

## Module Maintenance

Periodic maintenance of the module is not required.

## Checking Module

Checking the driver module system with resistance tester J-24628-4 is required after any of the following operations:
1. Driver module removal or replacement.
2. Steering wheel removal.
3. Slip ring removal or replacement.
4. Steering column disassembly.

*NOTE: Battery voltage must be at least 12 volts when checking the system.*

© G.M. Corp.

*Check Column Buzzer Circuit Continuity*

## Module Resistance Tester J-24628-4

### Checking Procedure

1. Turn the ignition switch to LOCK. Disconnect the negative battery cable and tape the cable end.
2. Using tool J-24388, disconnect

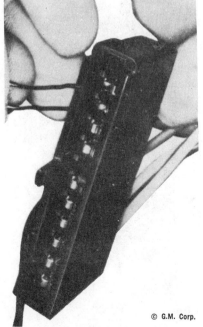

© G.M. Corp.

*Check For Short in Chassis Wiring*

## General Motors

Check Buzzer Switch Pads on Signal Switch

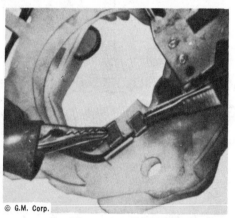

Check Buzzer Switch Continuity

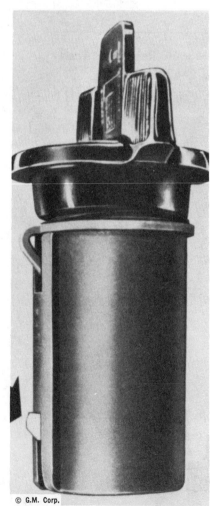

Key In Lock Cylinder—Actuator Extended

Key Out of Lock Cylinder—Actuator Retracted

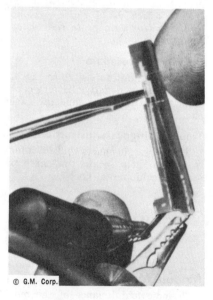

Check Buzzer Switch Continuity

## General Motors

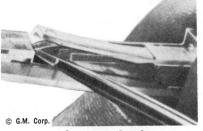

© G.M. Corp.

*Adjust Buzzer Switch*

© G.M. Corp.

*Adjust Buzzer Switch*

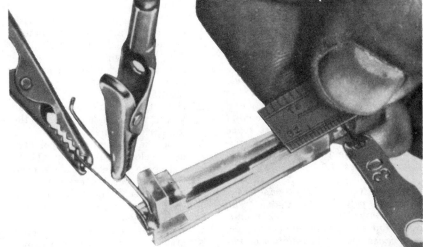

© G.M. Corp.

*Check Contact Gap*

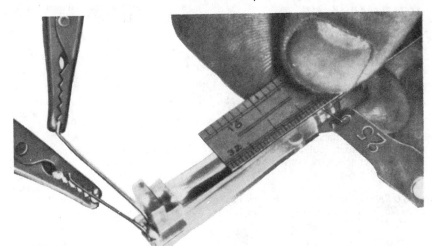

© G.M. Corp.

*Check Contact Gap*

9. Repeat step 8 with the toggle switch in position (2).
10. Perform the following:
    a. If the tester GREEN lamp was ON at all times while performing steps 8 and 9, the driver inflator module system is good. Stop the engine and turn the ignition switch to LOCK. Disconnect the negative cable from the battery and tape the cable end. Remove the adaptor from the cigar lighter. Using tool J-24388, disconnect the resistance tester connector from the driver inflator wiring connector. Connect the driver inflator wiring connector into the sensor-recorder. Connect the negative battery cable to the battery and remove the blocks from the DRIVE wheels.
    b. If the tester RED lamp was on at any time during steps 8 and 9, proceed to step 11 to find which of the following parts are at fault:
       1. Module Assembly
       2. Slip Ring Assembly
       3. Column Harness
11. Turn the ignition switch to LOCK. Disconnect the negative battery cable and tape the cable end.

*WARNING: The driver module should always be carried with the vinyl cover away from ones body and placed on a flat surface with the vinyl*

side up. This is to allow free space for cushion expansion in case of accidental deployment. Otherwise, serious injury may result.

12. Remove the four steering wheel module attaching screws using tool J-24628-2. Raise the module and disconnect the horn wire. Using tool J-24628-3, disconnect the wire connector from the slip ring.
13. Install the driver inflator substitute load J-24628-5 into the slip ring connector.
14. Connect the negative battery cable to the battery.
15. Start the engine and run at slow idle with the selector lever in PARK.
16. Repeat steps 8 and 9.
17. Perform the following:
    a. If the tester GREEN lamp is ON at all times during

steps 8 and 9, the driver module requires replacement (refer to Driver Module Removal and Installation).
    b. If the tester RED lamp is ON at any time during steps 8 and 9, the slip ring should be replaced (refer to Steering Column Slip Ring Removal and Installation) and the system rechecked. If the GREEN LAMP is now ON with the new slip ring, the system is in proper working order. If the RED lamp is still ON, replace the driver module wiring harness (refer to Driver Module Harness Removal and Installation) and install the original slip ring.

*NOTE: Do not attempt to repair the driver module wiring harness, re-*

# General Motors

place it with a new harness.

18. Recheck the system following steps 8 and 9.

## Driver Module

*WARNING: The driver module should always be carried with the vinyl cover away from ones body and placed on a flat surface with the vinyl side up. This is to allow free space for cushion expansion in case of accidental deployment. Otherwise, serious injury may result.*

*WARNING: Do not attempt to repair any part of the module. The module must be replaced as a unit. Soldering wires, changing covers, etc. may cause accidental inflation or impair operation of the module when the vehicle is in an accident.*

## 1974-75 All Models

### Removal

1. Turn the ignition switch to LOCK. Disconnect the negative battery cable from the battery and tape the cable end.
2. Remove the four steering wheel module attaching screws using tool J-24628-2. Raise the module and disconnect the horn wire. Using tool J-24628-3, disconnect the wire connector from the slip ring.

*NOTE: If the driver air cushion module is to be replaced, refer to the Parts Disposal section.*

### Installation

1. Position the steering wheel with the column and wheel alignment marks in the 12:00 o'clock position. This will place the large oval opening for the air cushion connector in the 6:00 o'clock position.
2. Hold the module close to the wheel with the emblem in the lower right corner.
3. Loop the cushion electrical harness clockwise from 11:00 o'clock to the 6:00 o'clock position. Connect the cushion module connector onto the column circuit making sure the connector is fully locked.
4. Install the horn wire connector.
5. Make sure the harness is looped around the guide correctly and install the four module attaching screws, torque the screws to 40 inch pounds.

*NOTE: Do not use substitute screws.*

6. Check the system with tester J-24628-4 (refer to the Module Resistance Tester J-24628-4 section).
7. Connect the negative battery cable to the battery.
8. Turn the ignition switch to any position but LOCK and observe the indicator lamp. If the lamp is not operating properly, reconnect the analyzer for diagnosis.

## Steering Column Slip Ring

## 1974-75 All Models

### Removal

1. Remove the driver module as previously described.
2. Remove the steering wheel using the appropriate tool.
3. Remove the three screws from the retainer and cover and lift the cover and retainer from the column.
4. Insert a screwdriver blade into the three locking tabs and lift the slip ring from the column.

### Installation

*CAUTION: All column fasteners must be replaced with parts of the same parts numbers if replacement becomes necessary. Torque valves must be used as specified to assure proper retention of these parts.*

*NOTE: Do not lubricate or modify the slip ring assembly in any way. The slip ring must be serviced as an assembly.*

1. Align the three slip ring locating tabs with the slots in the bowl and push the slip ring into position. Make sure the tabs are securely positioned.
2. Align the cover over the locating tab, install the screws and torque to 15 inch pounds.
3. Align the steering wheel hub and shaft marks and install the

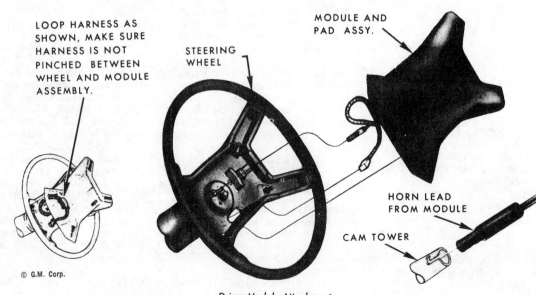

LOOP HARNESS AS SHOWN, MAKE SURE HARNESS IS NOT PINCHED BETWEEN WHEEL AND MODULE ASSEMBLY.

STEERING WHEEL

MODULE AND PAD ASSY.

HORN LEAD FROM MODULE

CAM TOWER

© G.M. Corp.

*Driver Module Attachment*

# General Motors

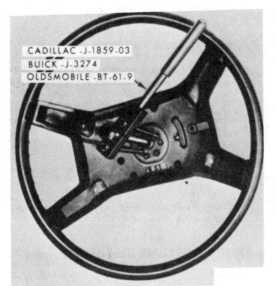

CADILLAC · J-1859·03
BUICK · J-3274
OLDSMOBILE · BT-61·9

DO NOT DISASSEMBLE OR LUBRICATE
THE SLIP RING ASSEMBLY EITHER
ACTION MAY CAUSE ACCIDENTAL INFLATION
OR FAILURE TO INFLATE WHEN NEEDED
RESULTING IN PERSONAL INJURY.

STEERING
WHEEL

COLUMN ASSY.
© G.M. Corp.

ALIGN MARK ON WHEEL WITH MARK
ON SHAFT WHEN INSTALLING WHEEL

*Installing Steering Wheel*

SCREW DRIVER

LOCKING
TAB

SLIP
RING

© G.M. Corp.

ALIGNING SLOT

*Removing Slip Ring*

steering wheel and nut. Torque the nut to 35 foot pounds.

4. Install the driver module (refer to Driver Module Installation procedures).

5. Check the driver module system (refer to Module Resistance Tester J-24628-4).

## Driver Module Harness
## 1974-75 All Models

### Removal

1. Remove the driver module (refer to Driver Module Removal procedures).

2. Remove the steering wheel and slip ring (refer to Steering Column Slip Ring Removal procedures).

*CAUTION: Do not hammer on the end of the steering shaft as this could compress the shaft.*

3. Depress the lock plate downward using tool J-23131 or J-23653 and the steering wheel nut. Pry the retaining ring out of the shaft groove and discard the retaining ring. Remove the nut, tool and lock plate.

*CAUTION: With the ring removed, care should be taken that the shaft does not slide out of the bottom of the column.*

4. Remove the upper bearing preload spring, turn signal cancelling cam and thrust washer from the shaft.

5. Place a screwdriver blade between the turn signal lever and retainer spring. With the screwdriver in place, pull the lever outward to remove.

6. Push the hazard warning switch in and unscrew the knob.

7. Remove the three switch mounting screws and the four bracket mounting screws and remove the bracket. Pull the connector out of the bracket, remove the protector from the jacket and strip the wires from it.

8. Pull the switch straight up, using care not to snag the signal switch wire connector in the housing.

9. Slide the restraint system connector up to disengage it from the housing. Pull the cable

# General Motors

© G.M. Corp.

*Removing or Installing Retaining Ring*

© G.M. Corp.

*Removing or Installing Lock Plate*

© G.M. Corp.

*Cleaning Grounding Surface*

© G.M. Corp.

*Deployed Driver Module*

assembly down through the housing and shift bowl.

## Installation

1. Clean the grounding surface, install the restraint system cable and seat the connector in the housing.
2. Replace the turn signal switch. Feed the connector down through the housing and assemble the wires into the protector. Install the mounting bracket and four screws. Clip the connector into the bracket.
3. Assemble the thrust washer, spring and cancelling cam onto the shaft. Make certain that the turn signal switch is in neutral and the hazard warning plunger is out.
4. Assemble the lock plate on the shaft, depress the parts and install a new retainer ring on the shaft.
5. Install the slip ring making sure that it is seated firmly and plugged into the restraint system cable and the locking tabs are positioned.
6. Install the slip ring cover and retainer. Make sure the cover is over the locating tab, install the screws and torque to 15 inch pounds.
7. Align the steering wheel hub

and steering shaft marks, install the retainer nut and torque the nut to 35 foot pounds.
8. Install the driver module (refer to the Driver Module Installation section).

## PARTS DISPOSAL

*WARNING: Air Cushion Restraining System modules must be deactivated before disposal. Both modules contain explosive materials. In addition, the passenger module contains high pressure gas. Failure to deactivate the modules prior to disposal could result in personal injury.*

*WARNING: The driver module should always be carried with the vinyl cover away from ones body and placed on a flat surface with the vinyl side up. This is to allow free space for cushion expansion in case of accidental deployment. Otherwise, serious injury may result.*

### DISPOSAL PROCEDURE
### (Removed From Vehicle)
### Driver Module (Deployed)

#### 1974-75 All Models

When a deployed driver module has been removed from a vehicle it can be disposed of as with any other scrap material.

### Driver Module (Undeployed)

#### 1974-75 All Models

When an undeployed driver module has been removed from a vehicle, the following disposal procedure will apply:

1. Immediately notify the appropriate local dealer or zone office, a representative will dispose of the module. If it is necessary to remove the module from the vehicle before that time, it should be stored in an Air Cushion Restraint System shipping carton. The carton in which the replacement module is shipped is suitable for storage.
2. No attempt should be made to deploy or dispose of an undeployed driver module by any person other than an authorized representative.
3. When storing the module, the carton should be taped closed and stored on the floor with the proper side up as indicated on the carton.

*WARNING: Do not stack or place objects on the carton. This will allow the cushion to expand in case of accidental deployment. Otherwise, personal injury may result.*

### Passenger Module

#### 1974-75 All Models

Both deployed and undeployed passenger modules must be disposed of in the following manner:

#### Undeployed Module

If a passenger module cannot be immediately disposed of, it must be stored in an Air Cushion Restraint System shipping carton and placed in a secured area until the disposal procedure can be performed. The carton in which the replacement module is shipped is suitable for storage.

When storing the module, the carton should be taped closed and stored

## General Motors

on the floor with the proper side up as indicated on the carton.

*WARNING: Do not stack or place objects on the carton. This will allow the cushion to expand in case of accidental deployment. Otherwise, personal injury may result.*

An undeployed module contains gas under pressure which must be released before disposal of the module is completed. To release the gas pressure the following steps should be taken:

1. Clamp the inflator assembly in a vise (see illustration).
2. Prepare a wooden stop block to be used as a spacer to limit the depth of the drill bit into the drill guide sleeve. Install the stop block over a ¼ in. drill bit and adjust the bit in the drill chuck until the bit extends beyond the stop block as follows:
   a. Eaton or Allied Inflators 2 3/32 in.
   b. Aero-Jet Inflators 1-3/32 in.

*WARNING: Safety glasses or a face shield must be worn by persons in the drilling area during the drilling operation and while the pressure is bleeding down. Metal chips from drilling may cause eye injury.*

3. Insert the drill bit into the drill guide sleeve in the end of the

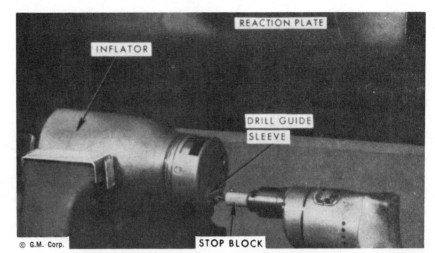

© G.M. Corp.

*Passenger Inflator Disposal (Drilling to Relieve Compressed Gas)*

inflator (see illustrations). Drill until the stop block contacts the end surface of the inflator, or until escaping gas is heard (gas will escape at about the same rate as air from a tire after the valve core has been removed).

4. Remove the drill and leave the assembly in the vise until all of the gas has escaped (12 to 18 minutes).
5. After the gas pressure has escaped, proceed to Deployed Module.

### Deployed Module

The passenger module contains two gas generators for inflating the

module. One or both may have been activated. To assure that both gas generators are deactivated it is necessary to burn the module after the air cushion has been deployed or after the drilling operation as previously described under "Undeployed Module."

*WARNING: Do not dispose of an undeployed module without first releasing the gas pressure. Otherwise, personal injury may result.*

The following steps should be taken to burn the module:

1. Place the module with the cushion side up in a large open top

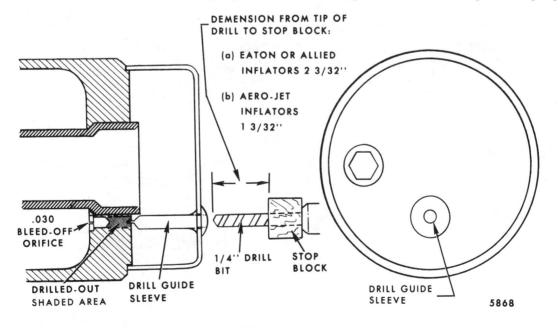

© G.M. Corp.  **SIDE VIEW**                              **END VIEW**

*Passenger Inflator Disposal (Drilling Operation to Relieve Compressed Gas)*

## General Motors

drum (55 gallon drum).

*WARNING: Place the drum in an open area at least 15 to 20 yards from buildings or inflammable material. Burning debris may be thrown from the drum.*

2. Build a wood fire in the drum

which will create enough heat to activate the module. Use a wire mesh across the top of the drum. Module activation can be seen but will not be violent. The fire will make the unit completely inactive.

3. After the module is activated, it

can be disposed of as with any other scrap material.

*NOTE: If deactivation or disposal of the module cannot be performed due to local ordinances, or are impractical, contact the appropriate dealer or zone office for assistance.*

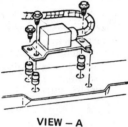

VIEW — A

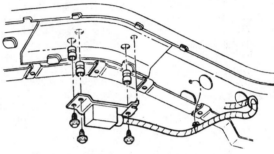

VIEW — B

1974

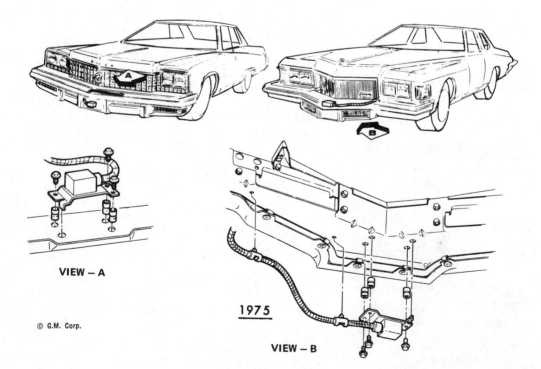

VIEW — A

1975

VIEW — B

© G.M. Corp.

Bumper Impulse Detector Location - Buick Styles

## General Description

Installed in all 1974-75 American made cars is a system whereby passengers in both front seats must first occupy the seat and then fasten the belt system in that order. Only then will the car be able to be started.

### General Motors Corp.

The warning system starts in a sequential manner prior to engine start. Once the engine has been started, the system will operate whenever the seat belts are not occupied at a front seat position and the vehicle is in drive or a forward gear. After the vehicle has been started, the engine may be restarted with the belts unfastened, and the driver's seat occupant in a seated position. The engine may be started with no one in the car by simply reaching in and turning the switch without sitting down. The warning system will be activated when the car is put in a forward gear or drive. The warning can be stopped by cycling the buckle switch. The unit incorporates a bounce feature which prevents inadvertent activation of the system due to bouncing over rough roads or acci-

dental or deliberate moving of the seat position. This is operated through a delay unit connected to the seat sensor which allows a five to ten second delay.

An override feature is also incorporated which allows starting of the vehicle in the event of a system failure.

1. Turn the ignition switch to "ON".
2. Open the hood and depress the release button on the override relay.
3. Start the car normally.

### Chrysler Corp.— American Motors Corp.

These two manufacturers use the same system. Operation of the system is as follows: Sit down and close the door(s). This activates the system and a signal puts the system in the buckle mode. Pull up the torso belt connector from the retractor and insert into the buckle. This completes the cycle and the car can now be started. Once the engine has been started, unbuckling the belts will not affect the engine operation. However,

when the automatic transmission is in drive, or with a manual, the parking brake is released, the seat belt reminder system will be activated. If the engine stalls, the car can be restarted as long as the driver remains seated. In case of system failure, an override switch, located next to the starter solenoid can be used to bypass the system. On this switch, the button must be held down while someone else starts the engine.

### Ford Motor Co.

The system operates as follows: the occupants must first sit down, then extend and/or buckle the lap belts at all occupied front positions. The transmission selector must then be placed in park, for automatics, or neutral, for manuals. After all occupied belts have been buckled, the engine may be started. While the engine is running and the car is in a forward gear, plus neutral on automatics, the belts should be kept buckled. If the car stalls after the initial start, it may be restarted immediately so long as the driver hasn't left his seat.

## Ford Motor Company

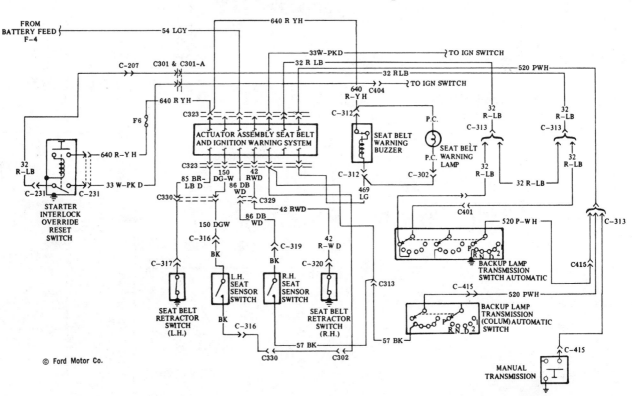

*1974 Ford*

© Ford Motor Co.

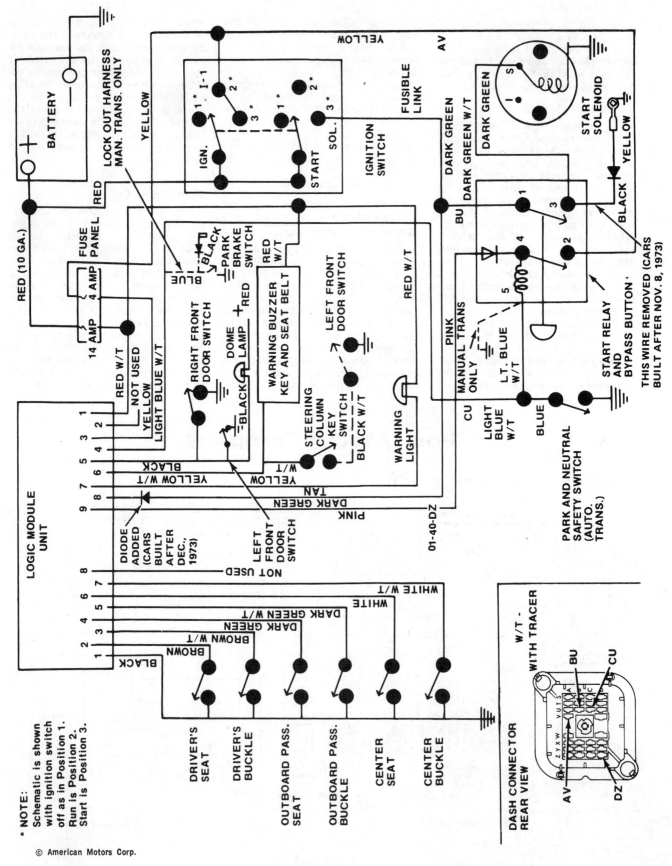

* NOTE:
Schematic is shown
with ignition switch
off as in Position 1.
Run is Position 2.
Start is Position 3.

© American Motors Corp.

*1974-75 American Motors*

## Chrysler

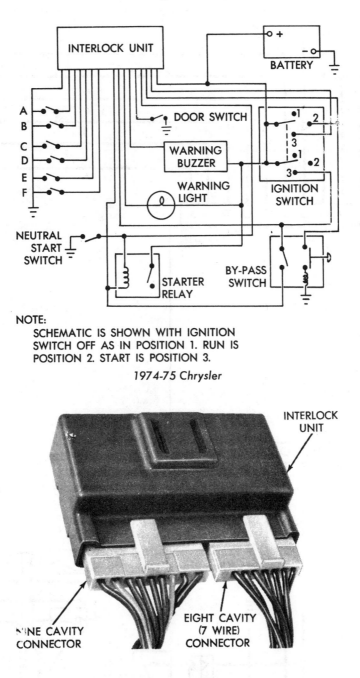

NOTE:
SCHEMATIC IS SHOWN WITH IGNITION
SWITCH OFF AS IN POSITION 1. RUN IS
POSITION 2. START IS POSITION 3.

*1974-75 Chrysler*

## INTERLOCK COMPONENTS LOCATION CHART

| | Buzzer | Buzzer Light Fuse | Interlock Unit | System Fuse | Underhood Switch |
|---|---|---|---|---|---|
| Carline V and L | Left Side of I/P Above Hand Brake | Fuse #7 | Behind Buzzer | Fuse #6 | Left Side on Firewall |
| Carline R and W | Right Side of I/P Near Side Cowl | Fuse #2 | On I/P to Left Of Glove Box | Fuse #1 | Right Side on Firewall |
| Carline B and J | Rear of I/P and Right of Glove Box | Fuse #4 | Left Side of I/P Above A/C Duct | Fuse #1 | Left Fender Shield |
| Carline P,D,C and Y | Left Side of Brake Support Bracket | Fuse #3 | Mounted Above Buzzer | Fuse #5 | Left Hood Hinge |

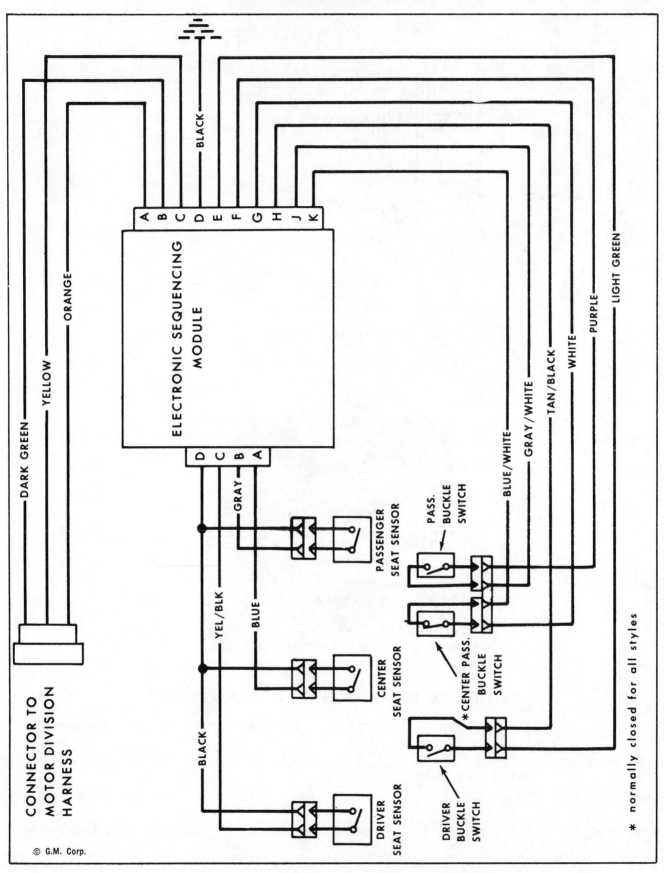

*1974-75 General Motors*

# Turn Signal Flasher and Fuse Box Location Chart

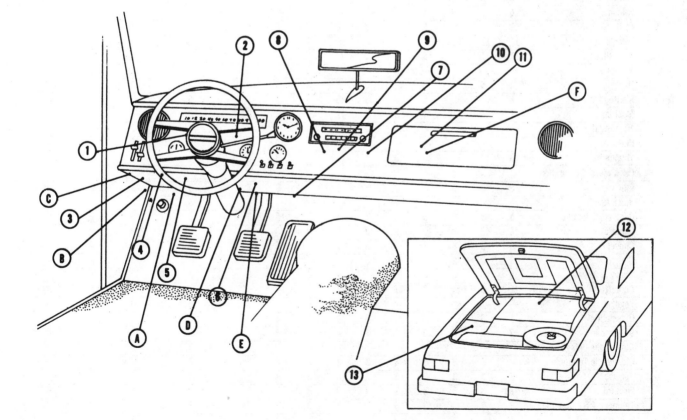

# TURN SIGNAL FLASHER, HAZARD WARNING FLASHER, AND FUSE BLOCK LOCATION

| | 1968 | | 1969 | | 1970 | | 1971 | | 1972 | | 1973 | | 1974 | | Fuse Block Location | 1974 Fuse Block Location |
|---|---|---|---|---|---|---|---|---|---|---|---|---|---|---|---|---|
| | TSF | HWF | TSF | HWF | TSF | HWF | TSF | HWF | TSF | HWF | TSF | HWF | TSF | HWF | | |
| **American Motors** | | | | | | | | | | | | | | | | |
| Ambassador | 2 | 3 | 2 | 3 | 2 | 3 | 2 | 3 | 2 | 3 | 2 | 3 | 2 | 3 | C | F |
| AMX | 2 | 3 | 2 | 3 | 2 | 3 | — | — | — | — | — | — | — | — | C | — |
| Hornet, Gremlin | — | — | — | — | 3 | 3 | 3 | 3 | 3 | 3 | 3 | 3 | 3 | 2 | C | C |
| Javelin | 3 | 3 | 3 | 3 | 3 | 3 | 3 | 3 | 3 | 3 | 3 | 3 | 3 | 3 | C | C |
| Rebel, Matador | 2 | 3 | 2 | 3 | 2 | 3 | 2 | 3 | 2 | 3 | 2 | 3 | 2 | 3 | C | F |
| **Chrysler Corporation** | | | | | | | | | | | | | | | | |
| Barracuda | 8 | 5 | 8 | 5 | 8 | 6 | 8 | 6 | 10 | 6 | 8 | 6 | 6 | 6 | D | G |
| Challenger | 8 | 5 | 8 | 5 | 8 | 6 | 8 | 6 | 10 | 6 | 8 | 6 | 6 | 6 | A | G |
| Chrysler | 8 | 4 | 5 | 4 | 5 | 4 | 5 | 4 | 5 | 5 | 5 | 5 | 5 | 5 | A | A |
| Dart | 8 | 5 | 8 | 5 | 8 | 6 | 8 | 6 | 10 | 6 | 8 | 6 | 8 | 6 | D | D |
| Dodge | 8 | 5, 10 | 4, 8 | 5, 10 | 5 | 6 | 5, 10 | — | 5, 10 | 5 | 8 | 6 | 8 | 6① | A | D② |
| Imperial | 8 | 4 | 13 | 13 | 5 | 4 | 5 | 4 | 5 | 5 | 5 | 6 | 5 | 5 | F | A |
| Plymouth | 8 | 5, 10 | 4, 8 | 4, 6 | 4, 8 | 6 | 5, 10 | — | 5, 10 | 5 | 8 | 6 | 8 | 6① | A | D② |
| Valiant | 8 | 5 | 8 | 5 | 8 | 6 | 8 | 6 | 10 | 6 | 8 | 5 | 8 | 6 | A | D |
| **Ford Motor Company** | | | | | | | | | | | | | | | | |
| Comet | — | — | — | — | — | — | 5 | 5 | 5 | 5 | 5 | 5 | 5 | 5 | E | E |
| Cougar | 13 | 13 | 8 | 10 | 8 | 10 | 11 | 6 | 8 | 10 | 8 | 10 | 3 | 3 | E | C |
| Fairlane, Torino | 6 | 5 | 6 | 5 | 6 | 5 | 5 | 5 | 5 | 5 | 5 | 5 | 3 | 3 | E | C |
| Falcon | 6 | 5 | 6 | 5 | — | — | — | — | — | — | — | — | — | — | E | — |
| Ford | 1 | 2 | 6 | 5 | 11 | 3 | 8 | 3 | 8 | 3 | 8 | 3 | 8 | 3 | E | C |
| Lincoln Continental | 11 | 11 | 11 | 11 | 3 | 3 | 6 | 6 | 3 | 3 | 3 | 3 | 3 | 5 | F | A |
| Mark III, IV | 11 | 11 | 11 | 11 | 11 | 3 | 11 | 3 | 3 | 3 | 3 | 3 | 3 | 3 | F | C |
| Maverick | — | — | — | — | 6 | — | 5 | 5 | 5 | 5 | 5 | 5 | 5 | 5 | E | E |
| Mercury | 4 | 6 | 4 | 6 | 11 | 3 | 8 | 3 | 8 | 3 | 8 | 3 | 8 | 3 | E | C |
| Montego | 6 | 5 | 6 | 5 | 6 | 5 | 5 | 5 | 5 | 5 | 5 | 5 | 3 | 3 | E | C |
| Mustang | 1 | 4 | 1 | 4 | 10 | 8 | 11 | 6 | 8 | 10 | 8 | 10 | — | — | E | — |
| Mustang II | — | — | — | — | — | — | — | — | — | — | — | — | 7 | 7 | — | G |
| Pinto | — | — | — | — | — | — | 10 | 10 | 10 | 10 | 10 | 10 | 10 | 10 | E | E |
| Thunderbird | 13 | 13 | 13 | 13 | 3 | 11 | 11 | 6 | 3 | 3 | 3 | 3 | 3 | 5 | F | C |
| **General Motors Corporation** | | | | | | | | | | | | | | | | |
| Buick | 3 | 3 | 3 | 3 | 3 | 3 | 3 | 3 | 3 | 3 | 3 | 3 | 3 | 3 | B | B |
| Buick Apollo | — | — | — | — | — | — | — | — | — | — | 5 | 3 | 5 | 3 | C | C |
| Cadillac, Eldorado | 5 | 3 | 5 | 5 | 6 | 8 | 15 | 3 | 15 | 3 | 15 | 3 | 6 | 3 | B | B |
| Camaro | 8 | 3 | 8 | 3 | 8 | 3 | 8 | 3 | 8 | 3 | 8 | 3 | 8 | 3 | A | A |
| Chevelle | 8 | 3 | 8 | 3 | 1 | 3 | 7 | 3 | 7 | 3 | 4 | 3 | 4 | 3 | A | A |
| Chevrolet | 8 | 3 | 8 | 3 | 10 | 3 | 7 | 3 | 7 | 3 | 6 | 3 | 6 | 3 | A | A |
| Chevy II, Nova | 8 | 3 | 8 | 3 | 10 | 3 | 7 | 3 | 7 | 3 | 10 | 3 | 10 | 3 | A | A |
| Corvette | 11 | 3 | 11 | 3 | 11 | 3 | 11 | 3 | 11 | 3 | 11 | 3 | 6 | 3 | A | A |
| Vega | — | — | — | — | — | — | 5 | 3 | 5 | 3 | 5 | 3 | 5 | 3 | C | C |
| Oldsmobile | 1 | 3 | 3 | 3 | 1 | 3 | 4 | 3 | 4 | 3 | 4 | 3 | 5 | 3 | C | C |
| Oldsmobile F-85, Cutlass | 3 | 3 | 3 | 3 | 3 | 3 | 4 | 3 | 4 | 3 | 4 | 3 | 5 | 3 | C | C |
| Oldsmobile Omega | — | — | — | — | — | — | — | — | — | — | 5 | 3 | 6 | 3 | C | C |
| Oldsmobile Toronado | 3 | 3 | 3 | 3 | 4 | 3 | 4 | 3 | 4 | 3 | 4 | 3 | 5 | 3 | C | C |
| Pontiac | 3 | 3 | 3 | 3 | 3 | 3 | 3 | 3 | 3 | 3 | 3 | 3 | 3 | 3 | C | C |
| Firebird | 7 | 3 | 3 | 3 | 3 | 3 | 3 | 3 | 3 | 3 | 3 | 3 | 3 | 3 | C | C |
| Tempest, GTO, Grand Am | 3 | 3 | 3 | 3 | 3 | 3 | 3 | 3 | 3 | 3 | 3 | 3 | 3 | 3 | C | C |
| Ventura II | — | — | — | — | — | — | 3 | 3 | 3 | 3 | 3 | 3 | 3 | 3 | C | C |

①—5 on Monaco, Fury
②—A on Monaco, Fury
TSF—Turn Signal Flasher
HWF—Hazard Warning Flasher